A GUIDE TO MANUSCRIPTS RELATING TO AMERICA IN GREAT BRITAIN AND IRELAND

A Revision of the **Guide** Edited in 1961
by B. R. Crick and Miriam Alman

Edited by

John W. Raimo

(*under the general supervision of* Dennis Welland)

Published for the
BRITISH ASSOCIATION FOR AMERICAN STUDIES
by
MECKLER BOOKS
MANSELL PUBLISHING
3 Bloomsbury Place, London WC1A 2QA, England

British Library Cataloguing in Publication Data

A guide to manuscripts relating to America in
Great Britain and Ireland. — Revised ed.
1. United States — Manuscripts
2. United States — Archival resources
— Great Britain 3. United States — Library
resources — Great Britain 4. Manuscripts —
Great Britain
I. Raimo, John W
973 Z6620.U5

ISBN 0-7201-0818-7

Meckler Books
520 Riverside Avenue
P.O. Box 405 Saugatuck Station
Westport, CT 06880
Printed in the United States

Published outside North and South America by
Mansell Publishing
3 Bloomsbury Place
London WC1A 2QA, England

A GUIDE TO MANUSCRIPTS RELATING TO AMERICA IN GREAT BRITAIN AND IRELAND

CONTENTS

Preface xxi
Introduction xxiii
Acknowledgement xxv

ENGLAND 3

AVON
Bath
The American Museum in Britain 5
Bristol
Bristol Archives Office 5
Central Library 7
Port of Bristol Authority 7
Society of Merchant Venturers 7
University of Bristol Library 8

BEDFORD
Bedford
Bedfordshire County Record Office 8
National Graphical Association 9

BERKSHIRE
Reading
Berkshire Record Office 10
University of Reading Library 11
Institute of Agricultural History and Museum of English Rural Life 11

BUCKINGHAMSHIRE
Aylesbury
Buckinghamshire Record Office 11
High Wycombe
Hughenden Manor 13

CAMBRIDGESHIRE
Cambridge
Cambridgeshire County Record Office 13
Letters of Charles Dickens 14
University of Cambridge Library 14
Churchill College 16
Fitzwilliam Museum 16
Magdalene College 16
Trinity College 17
Huntingdon
Cambridgeshire County Record Office 17

CHESHIRE
Bromborough
Fawcett Engineering Ltd. 17
Chester
Cheshire Record Office 18
Chester City Record Office 18
Eccleston
Trustees of the late 2nd Duke of Westminster 19
Warrington
Cheshire Libraries and Museums 19
Wilmslow
Quarry Bank Mill 19

CORNWALL
Falmouth
G.C. Fox & Co. 19
Port Eliot
Earl of St. Germans 19
Truro
Cornwall County Record Office 19
Royal Institution of Cornwall 20

CUMBRIA
Askham Hall
Earl of Lonsdale 21
Carlisle
Cumbria Record Office 21
Stead, McAlpin & Co. Ltd. 21
Frizington
Mrs. M. Holman 22

Kendal
Cumbria Record Office 22
Keswick
Brig. J.W. Kaye 22
Netherby
Sir Fergus Graham 22
Whitehaven
Cumbria County Library 22

DERBYSHIRE
Chatsworth
Duke of Devonshire 23
Chesterfield
Robinson & Sons Ltd. 23
Derby
Derby Central Library 23
Matlock
Derbyshire County Record Office 23
Melbourne Hall
Marquess of Lothian 23

DEVONSHIRE
Exeter
Devon Record Office 24
East Devon Record Office 25
Exeter Central Library 26
Exeter University Library 26
Plymouth
West Devon Record Office 26

DORSET
Dorchester
Dorset Record Office 27
Sherborne Castle
S. Wingfield Digby, Esq. 29

DURHAM
Darlington
Barclays Bank Ltd. 29
Durham County Library — Darlington Branch 29

Durham
Durham County Record Office 29
National Union of Mineworkers (Durham Area) 29
University Library, Durham 29
Department of Palaeography and Diplomatic 29
Ushaw College 30

ESSEX
Chelmsford
Essex Record Office 31
Elmstead
Andrew Chatto, Esq. 33

GLOUCESTERSHIRE
Gloucester
Gloucestershire County Libraries 33
Gloucestershire Records Office 34

HAMPSHIRE
Southampton
Southampton City Record Office 35
Winchester
Hampshire Record Office 36

HEREFORD AND WORCESTER
Hereford
Hereford Herd Book Society 36
Hereford Record Office 36
Stourport-on-Severn
Mr. Edward Nicholas Crane 37
Worcester
Worcester Cathedral Library 37
Hereford and Worcester County Record Office 37

HERTFORD
Gorhambury
Earl of Verulam 37
Hatfield House
Marquess of Salisbury 37
Hertford
Hertfordshire Record Office 39

HUMBERSIDE
Beverley
Humberside County Record Office 42
Hull
Brynmor Jones Library, Hull University 42
City Record Office 43

KENT
Canterbury
Cathedral Library 44
Eridge Park
Marquess of Abergavenny 44
Maidstone
Kent County Archives Office 44

LANCASHIRE
Preston
Lancashire Record Office 46
Whalley
Stonyhurst College 48

LEICESTERSHIRE
Belvoir Castle
Duke of Rutland 48
Leicester
Leicestershire Record Office 48

LINCOLNSHIRE
Grimsthorpe
Earl of Ancaster 49
Lincoln
The Cathedral Library 49
Lincolnshire Archives Office 49

LONDON (GREATER)
Allen & Hanburys Ltd. 50
Anti-Slavery Society 51
Bank of England 51
Barclays Bank Ltd. 52
Trustees of the Bedford Estates 52
Bishopsgate Institute 52

British and Foreign Bible Society 53
British Library 53
Chatto & Windus Ltd. 84
City of London Polytechnic 84
The College of Arms Library 84
The Congregational Memorial Hall Trust Ltd. 84
Corporation of London Records Office 85
Coutts & Co. 86
Custom House Library Services 86
Department of Trade, Companies Registration Office 94
Dr. Williams's Library 94
Faber and Faber Ltd. 96
Robert Fleming & Co., Ltd. 96
Lady Virginia Flemming 96
General Post Office 96
Greater London Record Office, London Section 97
Greater London Record Office, Middlesex Section 97
Guildhall Library 98
The Gunnersbury Park Museum 100
Henry George Foundation *and the*
United Committee for the Taxation of Land Values 100
Historical Manuscripts Commission *and*
National Register of Archives 100
C. Hoare & Co. 105
House of Commons 105
The House of Lords Record Office 106
Huguenot Library 113
Imperial War Museum 113
Inner Temple 114
Institution of Mechanical Engineers 114
Islington Libraries 114
Jonathan Cape Ltd. 114
Lambeth Palace Library 114
Lloyds Bank Ltd. 115
London Library 116
London Missionary Society 116
C. S. Marris, Esq. 116
Marylebone Cricket Club 117
Mercers' Company 117

Methodist Missionary Society 117
Midland Bank Ltd. 117
Moravian Church in Great Britain and Ireland 118
Morgan Grenfell & Co. Ltd. 118
John Murray (Publishers) Ltd. 118
Museum of London 118
National Army Museum 118
National Maritime Museum 119
Public Record Office 122
Rio Tinto-Zinc Corporation Ltd. 145
Royal Artillery Institution 145
Royal Botanic Gardens 145
Royal Commonwealth Society 146
Royal Geographical Society 146
Royal Horticultural Society 147
Royal Institution of Great Britain 147
Royal Society 147
Royal Society of Arts 148
Salvation Army 151
Sion College 151
Society for Promoting Christian Knowledge 152
Society of Friends 152
Society of Jesus 157
Southwark Diocesan Curia 157
Stationers' Hall Registry 157
Times Newspapers Ltd. 157
Trinity House 158
United Reformed Church History Society 158
United Society for the Propagation of the Gospel 158
University of London Library 159
    Imperial College of Science and Technology 162
    London School of Economics 163
    School of Oriental and African Studies 166
    University College 167
Wellcome Institute for the History of Medicine 170
West India Committee 171
City of Westminster, Archives Department 171
Westminster Diocesan Archives 171
Williams & Glyn Bank Ltd. 172

MANCHESTER (GREATER)
Bolton
Bolton Metropolitan Borough Archives 172
Public Library 172
Delph
G.E. Buckley, Esq. 173
Manchester
Co-operative Union Ltd. 173
Manchester University (John Rylands) Library 174
Department of Economic History,
Dr. W.H. Chaloner 178
Public Libraries 178
Oldham
Oldham Local Interest Centre 179
Rochdale
Amalgamated Textile Workers' Union 179
Salford
Salford Central Library 180
Stalybridge
Local Studies Library 180
Stockport
Stockport Central Library 180
Wigan
Wigan Record Office 180

MERSEYSIDE
Liverpool
The Athenaeum 180
Barclays Bank Ltd. 181
Central Libraries 181
Merseyside Chamber of Commerce and Industry 184
Merseyside County Archives 184
University of Liverpool 185
Harold Cohen Library 185
Sydney Jones Library 185

NORFOLK
Alby
Parish Church 185
Arundel Castle
Duke of Norfolk 185

Bawdeswell Hall
R.Q. Gurney 185
Great Ryburgh
Parish Church 186
Heydon
Brigadier H. Long 186
Hindolveston
Parish Church 186
Holkham
Earl of Leicester 186
Norwich
Local Studies Department 187
Norfolk Record Office 187
Saxthorpe
Parish Church 189

NORTHAMPTON
Boughton House
Duke of Buccleuch 189
Northampton
Northamptonshire Record Office 189

NORTHUMBERLAND
Alnwick Castle
Duke of Northumberland 190
Newcastle-upon-Tyne
Northumberland County Record Office 191

NOTTINGHAMSHIRE
Nottingham
Nottingham City Archives Office 191
Nottinghamshire Record Office 191
The University of Nottingham Library 192

OXFORDSHIRE
Blenheim Palace
Duke of Marlborough 193
Oxford
Bodleian Library 193
Rhodes House Library 205
All Souls College 206

Manchester College 208
New College 208
Nuffield College 209
Oxfordshire County Record Office 209
Plunkett Foundation for Co-operative Studies 209
Witney
Charles Early & Marriott (Witney) Ltd. 210

SHROPSHIRE
Gredington
Lord Kenyon 210
Shrewsbury
Corporation of Shrewsbury 211
Salop Record Office 211

SOMERSET
Street
C. &. J. Clark Ltd. 211
Taunton
Somerset Record Office 211
Wellington
Fox Bros. & Co. Ltd. 212

STAFFORDSHIRE
Keele
Keele University Library 212
Stafford
Staffordshire Record Office 213
William Salt Library 216
Stoke-on-Trent
Horace Barks Reference Library 217

SUFFOLK
Bures St. Mary
Lieut. Col. J.F. Todhunter 217
Bury St. Edmunds
Suffolk Record Office 217
Ipswich
Suffolk Record Office 218
Peasenhall
Parish Church 220

SURREY
Guildford
Guildford Muniment Room 220
Kingston-upon-Thames
Central Library 220
Surrey Record Office 220

SUSSEX (EAST)
Brighton
University of Sussex Library 221
Burwash
Parish Church 221
Hastings
Public Museum and Art Gallery 221
Lewes
East Sussex Record Office 221
Sussex Archaeological Society 222

SUSSEX (WEST)
Arundel Castle
Duke of Norfolk, *see* Norfolk
Chichester
West Sussex Record Office 223
Petworth House
John Max, 2nd Baron Egremont 223

TYNE AND WEAR
Gateshead
Gateshead Central Library 223
Newcastle-upon-Tyne
County Archives, Tyne and Wear Department 223
University of Newcastle-upon-Tyne Library 224
South Shields
South Tyneside Libraries 224

WARWICKSHIRE
Coughton Court
Sir Robert George Maxwell Throckmorton 224
Leamington Spa
Rev. Charles E. Surman 224
Rugby
Earl of Denbigh 224

Warwick
Warwick County Record Office 225

WEST MIDLANDS
Birmingham
Archdiocese of Birmingham Archives 225
Public Libraries 225
University of Birmingham, The Main Library 227
Woodbrooke College 227
Coventry
City Record Office 228
University of Warwick Library 228
Hagley Hall
Viscount Cobham 228
Sutton Coldfield
Oscott College 229

WIGHT (ISLE OF)
Bembridge
Ruskin Galleries 229

WILTSHIRE
Devizes
Library of the Wiltshire Archaeological and
Natural History Society 229
Longleat
Marquess of Bath 229
Trowbridge
Wiltshire County Record Office 230
Wilton House
Earl of Pembroke 230

YORKSHIRE (NORTH)
Harrogate
North Yorkshire County Library 230
Leyburn
Lord Bolton 230
Northallerton
C.K.C. Andrew, Esq. 230
North Yorkshire County Record Office 231
Rotherham
Central Library 231

Scarborough
Scarborough Borough Council 231
York
Borthwick Institute of Historical Research 231

YORKSHIRE (SOUTH)
Doncaster
Doncaster Metropolitan Borough Council 232
Sheffield
Sheffield City Library 232
University of Sheffield Library 236

YORKSHIRE (WEST)
Bradford
Central Library 237
Halifax
Belle Vue Library 237
Harewood House
Earl of Harewood 237
Leeds
Brotherton Library, University of Leeds 238
Public Libraries 239

WALES 241

CLWYD
Deeside
Clwyd County Record Office 243

DYFED
Aberystwyth
National Library of Wales 243
Carmarthen
Dyfed Archives 247
Haverfordwest
Dyfed Archives 247

GWENT
Cwmbran
Gwent County Record Office 248

GWYNEDD
Bangor
The University College of North Wales Library 248
Dolgellau
Gwynedd Area Record Office 248
Llangefni
Gwynedd Archives Service 248

POWYS
Brecon
Brecknock Museum Library 249

SOUTH GLAMORGAN
Cardiff
Central Library 249
Department of Trade, Companies Registration Office 249
Glamorgan Record Office 249

SCOTLAND 251

DUMFRIES AND GALLOWAY
Kirkcudbright
Hornel Library 253

FIFE
Kirkcaldy
Museum and Art Gallery 253

GRAMPIAN
Aberdeen
J. &. J. Crombie Ltd. 253
The Diocesan Archive of the Diocese of
Aberdeen and Orkney 253
The University of Aberdeen Library 253

LOTHIAN
Edinburgh
Huntly House Museum 254
National Library of Scotland 254

National Register of Archives (Scotland) 259
Scottish Record Office 272
The University of Edinburgh Library 312

ORKNEY ISLANDS
Kirkwall
Orkney Islands Area Archives 315

STRATHCLYDE
Glasgow
The Mitchell Library 316
Strathclyde Regional Archives 317
University of Glasgow Library 317
Department of Economic History 318
Paisley
Renfrew District Library Service 318

TAYSIDE
Dundee
Alliance Trust Co. Ltd. 318
Northern American Trust Co. Ltd. 318
University Library 318
Perth
Aberdeen-Angus Cattle Society 319
Perth Museum and Art Gallery 319

NORTHERN IRELAND 321

ANTRIM
Belfast
Public Record Office of Northern Ireland 323

ISLE OF MAN 333

Douglas
The Manx Museum 335

CHANNEL ISLANDS 337

Guernsey
Greffe 339
Priaulx Library 339
Jersey
Société Jersiaise 339

REPUBLIC OF IRELAND 341

CARLOW
Bagenalstown
Miss M.B. Bayliss 343

DUBLIN
Dublin
Genealogical Office 343
Irish Manuscripts Commission 343
National Library of Ireland 343
Public Record Office of Ireland 348
Religious Society of Friends in Ireland 349
Royal Irish Academy 350
State Paper Office 350
Trinity College 352
University College, Department of Irish Folklore 353

LONGFORD
Castle Forbes
Earl of Granard 353

TIPPERARY
Knocklofty
Earl of Donoughmore 354

INDEX 355

PREFACE

The original *Guide*, of which the present work is a revision, was issued in 1961. It represented the first major research undertaking of the British Association for American Studies (which had been founded as recently as 1955), and users of the present edition may like to be reminded of how its important and pioneering predecessor came into existence, as well as of the relationship between the two. H. L. Beales, the Director of the original project, gave the definitive account of its compilation in his Preface to the 1961 edition. He spoke of it as "the fruit of two years' work of a research team that began as two people and ended with five working full time." He stressed the value of the team work involved and identified the members as follows:

> Mr. [now Professor] B. R. Crick, who was in general charge of the organization and administration of research and investigation; Mrs. Miriam Alman, who joined the Survey when some of the field work was completed to undertake the formidable task of compiling, checking, and indexing; Mrs. Naomi Connelly, who undertook from Manchester the heavy responsibility of the field work and investigation in the north of England, and then assisted in the editing; Mr. Dennis Porter, now of the Department of Western Manuscripts at the Bodleian Library, who did much field work in the south, including the bulk of the work in the British Museum and the Bodleian Library; Mrs. Anne Daltrop, who did most of the other bibliographical work on printed books and newspapers, but who also worked on manuscripts in London, Cambridge, and the West Country; and right from the beginning of the Survey, Mrs. Anna Hackel was its administrative secretary, with special charge of the vital early stages of circularizing for information. Also Mrs. Eilis Ellis of Dublin worked for the Survey for a month, completing work begun in Dublin by Mr. Crick.

There then followed nearly four pages of acknowledgements to named individuals and institutions, many of whom (or their successors) have again been instrumental in the preparation of this revised edition. Not to reprint the original list here betokens no diminution in our gratitude to those named in it: only on the excellent foundations laid by Bernard Crick and his legion of helpers has it been possible to build the present work at all.

At the outset of the whole enterprise in the 1950's it was wisely thought necessary to begin by surveying "the adequacy of printed resources in British university and other great libraries to support the teaching of American history and literature." This produced two valuable documents. The first is of historic importance: "A Survey of Library Resources in the United Kingdom for the Teaching of American History and Literature in the Universities," in the *Journal of Documentation*, vol. xiv, 1958, pp. 103-18. The second was the "Union List of American Newspapers in Great Britain and Ireland," edited by Bernard Crick and Anne Daltrop, and issued by the British Association for American Studies also in 1958. This was revised in 1974 by Professor D. K. Adams as *American Newspaper Holdings in British and Irish Libraries* and is also available from the Association.

The process of revising the *Guide* may be said to have begun with the publication of the original itself. In his Preface Mr. Beales observed that "the members of the Survey would be the last to deny that much potentially interesting Americana may yet come to light," and the appearance of the *Guide* led at once to the reporting of further material. The original editors produced three lists of addenda which were published in the *Bulletin of the British Association for American Studies* in the 1960's (and are of course incorporated in the present edition). The growth of research in the British Isles into American topics continually brought new items to light, and the desirability of a new edition was thus established. When the imminence of the Bicentennial of American

Independence brought discussion on the possibility of some kind of commemorative activity, there was no doubt in the minds of the members of the committee of the Association as to what form that activity ought to take. Through the energetic endeavours of Dr. Charles Ritcheson, at that time Cultural Attaché at the American Embassy in London, and of the United States–United Kingdom Educational Commission, funds were generously made available to enable the revision of "Crick and Alman" to be undertaken.

As this operation was essentially an up-dating and expansion of the original, it was not necessary to aim at staffing on the scale of the first survey. One full time research worker, Dr. John Raimo, was appointed and it was his enthusiasm, resourcefulness and industry, along with the occasional assistance that he acknowledges below, that produced this edition. In this connection it is again appropriate to quote from H. L. Beales' observations of twenty years ago: "Our greatest debt is to the archivists and custodians of papers, notably the county archivists, too numerous to mention all by name, without whose help and interest this work would have been impossible. Archivists . . . invariably went to great pains in suggesting material and subsequently checking and often expanding our reports." This has been as true of the revision as of the original, and we record unreservedly our gratitude to them all.

We have followed as far as possible the principles on which the original *Guide* was based; the few departures we have made from those principles, and our reasons for so doing, are specified below in Dr. Raimo's Introduction. It has seemed to us that the passage of time has brought so many changes in the whole situation that it would not be helpful here to reproduce Professor Crick's excellent 1959 Introduction, but some of its information has been incorporated in the entries and footnotes to the text of this edition. To that Introduction the attention of the reader is warmly directed for its full and detailed account of the criteria governing the original, as well as for its many valuable comments on archival research in general. Perennially relevant is its advice on "Access to Records":

> *The mention of papers in this volume does not necessarily imply that they are available for inspection.* It must be emphasized that papers in private possession are private property. Most owners are amazingly co-operative considering the inconvenience that permission for a scholarly visitation can put them to; from our experience their continued helpfulness depends upon scholars approaching owners without appearing to assume a right to see papers, explaining to them precisely why their papers may be relevant, asking permission before quoting from the papers in print (even apart from the legal implications), and informing the owners when and where such published work occurs: this last point helps to make private individuals informed custodians of their own records.
>
> A smaller practical adage, which experience has impressed upon us, is the advisability of writing well in advance to the archivist when wanting to inspect papers in almost all local record offices. Record officers will often, when circumstances permit, go to great pains to search out and prepare papers for a wandering scholar when given good warning. They are among the most conscientious and hard-worked of public servants, and among the most helpful—when approached with a proper regard for the difficulties of their high vocation.

Nor can we do better, in defining the aim of this edition, than to repeat the words that Professor Crick italicised in his own Introduction: "*We have striven, in emulation of the best archivists, to put contemporary helpfulness before the chimeras of the complete description and of an absolute consistency.*" We hope that it will prove as useful and as stimulating to research as did its predecessor.

Finally, any reader becoming aware of material that has not been included in this edition is asked to send details to *Guide to Manuscripts*, Department of American Studies, The University of Manchester, Manchester M13 9PL, England, so that lists of addenda may be issued as necessary by the British Association for American Studies.

Dennis Welland
University of Manchester
April, 1979

INTRODUCTION

In 1961 Bernard Crick and Miriam Alman, in the *Guide to Manuscripts Relating to America in Great Britain and Ireland*, defined the scope of their work in these terms:

> This *Guide* seeks to draw attention to the location and to give a brief description of all manuscripts in Great Britain and Ireland relating to the history and literature of the American colonies and the United States which did not fall within the scope of the following volumes published by the Carnegie Institution of Washington, D.C.:[1]
>
> Charles M. Andrews, *Guide to the Materials for American History, to 1783, in the Public Record Office of Great Britain*, 2 vols. (Washington, D.C., 1912, 1914).
>
> Charles M. Andrews and Frances G. Davenport, *Guide to the Manuscript Materials for the History of the United States to 1783, in the British Museum, in Minor London Archives, and in the Libraries of Oxford and Cambridge* (Washington, D.C., 1908).
>
> Charles O. Paullin and Frederic L. Paxson, *Guide to the Materials in London Archives for the History of the United States since 1783* (Washington, D.C., 1914).
>
> "History" and "literature" have both been construed in the widest possible sense to include all materials that could possibly be of significance to political, economic, social, and intellectual history, whether concerning American domestic and international affairs, or direct American influences in the British Isles.
>
> Material *exclusively* West Indian has not been included.[2] However, Canadian material of even marginal relevance to the American colonies or the United States has generally been included down to the British North America Act of 1867.[3]

Since its first appearance, the Crick and Alman *Guide* has come to be regarded as a pioneering reference work, and has encouraged editors of several subsequent manuscript guides to use it as a model.[4] Yet, partly due to the growth in the archival field which their volume helped to stimulate, the British Association for American Studies in the spring of 1976 decided that "Crick and Alman" was in need of comprehensive revision and expansion. During the 1960's local and county record offices grew both in size and in professionalism, and by the mid-1970's virtually every county had a staff of archivists trained in the latest methods of handling and preserving manuscripts. In particular, systematic efforts to provide researchers with suitable handlists and indexes helped to make larger collections more accessible.

Along with this more sophisticated approach of the older record offices and the establishment of new ones, there occurred a development whereby documents formerly in private hands came increasingly into public domain. The county offices took the lead in the gathering and organizing of this material, but university libraries, especially those created in the past twenty years, have also become more active. This movement of documents from the private to the public sphere seems destined to continue in the foreseeable future, although, as this revision will attest, private owners continue to remain conscious of the scholarly significance of manuscripts in their possession.

Apart from an increase in the sheer quantity of American-related material which has become available since 1961, there has been a relative change in the type of documents uncovered. While the original Crick and Alman *Guide* was most strongly represented in the field of political history, the majority of the accessions included here are more frequently related to the fields of economic, social, and immigration history. In part this is due to the diminishing amount of undiscovered manuscripts of political interest. At the same time, the efforts of county archivists have generally been directed towards the accumulation of documents which, with their description of the business activities and migratory habits of local men and women, permit historians to study an aspect of the past which more traditional sources often failed to reveal.

All of these developments have led us to produce a revised *Guide* which, although identical with its predecessor in its definition of scope,[5] has incorporated certain changes in its organization, techniques of data gathering, footnoting, and size. In terms of organization, we have retained the arrangement by counties employed by Crick and Alman, but have made some adjustments to bring this edition into conformity with the new county structures established in the British Isles in 1974. As a result, some entries previously listed under one county are now under another, and several new counties have appeared. Similarly, we have grouped all private papers discovered through the files of the National Register of Archives in London and Edinburgh under those two general categories (*see* pp. 100-5 and pp. 259-72). Although it would have been possible to give the names and addresses of owners of these manuscripts, it was both our opinion and that of the Registers' archivists that the omission of such information was the best means of encouraging scholars to consult the N.R.A. *before* attempting to contact owners. An initial approach to the N.R.A. is helpful even in the case of collections held by public archives and libraries, but it is essential when the documents are in private hands, since the Registers can inform researchers about any restrictions that might govern their use.

Besides these changes in organization, the method by which we have gathered new material has differed substantially from the procedure employed by the workers on the first edition. Whereas the original survey rightly made extensive use of personal visits by field workers, we have, with the exception of the largest entries, relied on correspondence with the appropriate individuals and institutions. At first this tactic was chosen on grounds of necessity, since our research budget did not make major staff expenditures possible. Yet necessity and efficiency soon seemed to work together; early in the project we discovered that the familiarity of archivists and librarians with their own holdings meant that in many cases documents which might have been overlooked by a less knowledgeable researcher were instead brought to our attention. Often, although the handlist to a large collection will contain no specific American references, an informed archivist can direct the researcher to manuscripts within that collection which are relevant to American affairs.

Another editorial point that we considered involved whether documents which are also available on microfilm or microfiche should be so listed. Eventually we decided that, while we would retain from the original *Guide* those notes which referred to the location and/or availability of reproduced material, we would in general not attempt to supplement these references. There were three reasons for this decision. First, the rapidity with which papers are now being microfilmed would make any effort to provide such information hopelessly out of date within a few years. Second, the microfilming of collections is sometimes done selectively; that is, the manuscript collection in a repository may be much larger than those documents which are thought suitable for preservation on microfilm. And finally, there are now other, more current announcements made both by large firms specializing in the reproduction field and by periodical publications such as *Microform Review*[6] in the United States, which seek to keep abreast of the constantly growing list of manuscripts on microfilm and microfiche. The researcher should consult these brochures, periodicals and guides, since they can often save a trip to the archive holding the original papers.

The most obvious change, of course, has involved a substantial increase in the quantity of material now listed. While we are resigned to the fact that some significant items and collections inevitably might have been overlooked in this revision, we believe that we have held our omissions to an acceptable level. We were able to trace about 95 percent of the material listed in the first edition, and although a large percentage of these documents was found to have changed location over the past eighteen years, we have now given, under the names of their current repositories, almost all of the previous manuscripts that were of substantial value. We have also greatly expanded many of the earlier entries and have added over 100 new ones, including new local and county record offices, church archives, university libraries, and private owners. This material is most often relevant to historical studies, though that is by no means always the case; important documents from several recently opened publishers' archives, for example, are described here for the first time. The *Guide* itself is approximately 65 percent longer than its predecessor, and it is our hope that this enlarged version of a valuable reference work will be useful to scholars as "Crick and Alman" proved to be when it first appeared on the academic scene.

John W. Raimo

1. All three of these surveys are available on microfilm from EP Microform Ltd., Bradford Road, East Ardsley, Wakefield, West Yorkshire WF3 2JN, England, and in book form from Kraus Reprint Co., Route 100, Millwood, NY 10546.

There are occasional exceptions to the policy of excluding documents listed in these earlier guides. In the case of a few of the smaller London archives and of H.M. Customs and Excise, we have for the convenience of the researcher compiled complete reports.

2. *See* Herbert C. Bell, David W. Parker, *et al.*, *Guide to British West Indian Archive Materials, in London and in the Islands, for the History of the United States* (Washington, D.C., 1926). *See also* Peter Walne, ed., *A Guide to Manuscript Sources for the History of Latin America and the Caribbean in the British Isles* (London, 1973).

3. Cutting off Canadian material at 1867 does not mean that, for example, Foreign Office and private papers relating to the subsequent Alaska Boundary Question and the Newfoundland Fisheries Disputes have been ignored; they have been included as part of British-American relations.

4. Besides the Walne volume, *see* M. D. Wainwright and Noel Matthews, *A Guide to Western Manuscripts and Documents in the British Isles Relating to South and South East Asia* (London, 1965); Noel Matthews and M. Doreen Wainwright, *A Guide to Manuscripts and Documents in the British Isles Relating to Africa* (London, 1971); and Phyllis Mander-Jones, ed., *Manuscripts in the British Isles Relating to Australia, New Zealand, and the Pacific* (Canberra, 1972).

5. Like the original *Guide*, we have included certain rare or unusual printed materials, while excluding items of strictly genealogical concern.

6. *See also* the annual *Microforms in Print: Author-Title, Subject* and *Supplement* (3 vols.), published by Microform Review Inc., P.O. Box 405, Saugatuck Station, Westport, Conn. 06880, and in Great Britain by Mansell Publishing, 3 Bloomsbury Place, London WC1A 2QA.

ACKNOWLEDGEMENT

Acknowledgements are particularly difficult to make for a work such as this, because it is in the strictest sense the result of the collaboration of hundreds of individuals. The archivists, librarians, and private owners of pertinent material who responded so magnificently to our inquiries deserve first mention, for without their cooperation we could have achieved nothing. The Department of American Studies at the University of Manchester provided a congenial environment during the eighteen months which were spent on the revision, and we would especially like to thank Professor Peter Marshall; by reading the entire manuscript and by offering many useful suggestions, he made our task considerably easier. Thanks are also due to Mrs. Margaret Thomas, whose secretarial assistance was indispensable to the success of our venture; to Dr. Ronald Wells, who assisted on a research trip to Ireland; to Mr. Gregory Palmer, who compiled the entry for the Public Record Office in Kew; and to Mr. David Burnett, who supplied information on a number of archives in the Durham area. The greatly expanded Scottish section of this edition is primarily due to the generous assistance of Dr. John Imrie, Keeper of the Public Record Office in Edinburgh, and Mr. John Bates, the head of the National Register of Archives in Scotland. Professor Esmond Wright and the staff at the Institute of United States Studies at the University of London contributed greatly by offering Dr. Raimo a scholarly base during his research trips to the major London repositories. We are most grateful to Mrs. Rosemary Cleworth, who typed parts of the final manuscript with efficiency and skill, and to Mrs. Nina Smith, who compiled much of the large index which forms a crucial part of such a reference work. John Walsh, the editor-in-chief at Meckler Books, deserves special credit for his careful and intelligent reading of the text, a reading which unearthed some errors and inconsistencies that had not been discovered during the preparation of the typescript. Of course the Crick/Alman Revision Committee, appointed by the British Association for American Studies, consisting of Professor Bernard Crick, Mrs. Miriam Alman, Professor H. G. Nicholas, and Dr. Charlotte Erickson, gave important advice and encouragement at each stage of the project. We are also grateful to the officers and committee members of the Association itself for their help and support. Finally, we would like to express our heartfelt thanks to Mr. John Herrington of the U.S./U.K. Educational Commission and Dr. Charles Ritcheson, the former cultural *attaché* at the United States Embassy in London; together they provided the funding which financed the research for this guide.

John W. Raimo
Dennis Welland
University of Manchester

A GUIDE TO MANUSCRIPTS RELATING TO AMERICA IN GREAT BRITAIN AND IRELAND

ENGLAND

AVON

THE AMERICAN MUSEUM IN BRITAIN, Claverton Manor, Bath BA2 7BD

NODDLE'S ISLAND. Deed of sale. 1667.

Deed of sale, 6 Feb. 1667, of part of Noddle's Island (now East Boston, Mass.).

WOERTENDYCK FAMILY PAPERS. 1714-1875.

A collection, mainly of contemporary copies (but including a few original documents) of wills, inventories, establishment of title, deeds of sale and other papers relating to the Jacobus, Doremus and Woertendyck families of New York and New Jersey.

MANWARING, ASA. Deed. 1756.

Deed of sale dated 1756 concerning sale of property in New London 'in the Colony of Connecticut'.

CURTIS FAMILY PAPERS. 1759-1866.

Deeds of sale, partition of land and other family papers concerning the Curtis family of Cumberland County in the Commonwealth of Massachusetts, which after 1820 became the State of Maine.

MILES COLLECTION. Accounts, receipts, letters, etc. *c.* 1760-1810.

Samuel Miles, of Braintree, Mass., and Lebanon, Conn. His papers include an account book covering the years 1766-94 which includes material relating to his saw mill and lumber sales. They also include papers relating to an ecclesiastical controversy in Wrentham, Mass., in 1793.

RHINELANDER PAPERS. 1771-1844.

Account and receipt books, letters and other papers concerning the privateer *Surprise,* prize ship *Keyserlike Adelair,* brig *Fox,* and Rhinelander's Saratoga and Argyle store, with other papers all ranging in date between 1771 and 1844, saved by the family when the Rhinelander house on Washington Square, New York City was demolished.

CONKEY FAMILY PAPERS OF PELHAM, MASS. Inventories, deeds of sale and account books. 1772-1850.

Relating to the Conkey family, who owned the original tavern now represented in the American Museum by the fireplace lintel with its inscription 'June ye 21st 1776 A.D.', tavern sign and doorway.

CORNELL, PETER. 6 letters. 1778-86.

Flatbush, N.Y., 1778-86, from Cornell to various relatives, on family matters and giving an account of his difficulties with the officers quartered on his farm.

McVICKAR, JOHN. Letter. 1805.

The 7¼-page letter describes McVickar's journey at the age of eighteen from New York to London. (McVickar was later Professor of Moral Philosophy at Columbia.)

FOTHERGILL, ANTHONY. Will. 1810-2.

Nine-page will signed in Philadelphia in September 1810 with codicil dated 1812, includes legacies in Bath and Bristol.

75th REGIMENT OF PENNSYLVANIA VOLUNTEERS, U.S. ARMY. Muster roll.

Muster roll of E Company, giving history of the regiment—pay, deaths, etc.—Battle of Gettysburg information.

'W.R.C.' Letter. 1890-1.

Letter, dated 1890-1, from 7th Cavalry at Fort Riley to Pine Ridge Agency in South Dakota, describing at first hand the action at Wounded Knee.

BRISTOL ARCHIVES OFFICE, Council House, Bristol BS1 5TR

DEPOSITION BOOKS OF BRISTOL. 6 volumes. 1643-87.

These records contain copies of voluntary sworn statements made before the Mayor and one or more of the Aldermen on a wide variety of subjects, including loss of ships, merchandise quarrels, thefts, etc. The first two volumes,[1] 1643-54, contain a number of references to the Virginia trade, tobacco, and one reference to New England. The unpublished volumes[2] seem likely to contain rather more of this type of information.

SERVANTS TO FOREIGN PLANTATIONS.[3] 2 volumes. 1654-79.

In 1654 the City Council of Bristol ordained that, before embarkation, persons bound as servants for overseas were to be articled and enrolled as were the city apprentices. These two volumes contain the fair copies of this system of enrolment. They include the names, with places of origin, of more than 10,000 servants to foreign plantations who sailed from Bristol to Virginia, Maryland, and other parts of the Atlantic coast. Also an entry on the system in Sessions concerns Gloucestershire apprentices bound to serve in Virginia. The City Archives also contain other rough entry books concerned with city apprentices, which note servants bound overseas down to Feb. 1685.

BRISTOL AND FRENCHAY MONTHLY MEETING OF THE SOCIETY OF FRIENDS. Records.[4]

Some of the principal classes of records are:
(*a*) Bristol and Frenchay Monthly Meeting:
(i) Minutes of Men's Monthly meeting, 1667-
(ii) Minutes of Women's Monthly Meeting (merged with the Men's Meeting in the nineteenth century).
(*b*) George Fox and other Friends' letters (MSS. vol. v), 1667-73.

1. Two volumes have been published: *Deposition Books of Bristol*, vol. 1, 1643-7, ed. by H.E. Nott; vol. 2, 1650-4, ed. by H.E. Nott and E. Ralph (Bristol, 1935, 1943) (Bristol Record Society's Publications, vols. vi and xiii).
2. Extracts from these in P. McGrath, ed., *Merchants and Merchandise in Seventeenth Century Bristol* (Bristol, 1955) (Bristol Record Society's Publications, vol. xix).
3. Much of this material has been printed in *Bristol and America*, transcribed by R. Hargreaves-Mawdsley (London, 1929). The original documents contain rather more detail.
4. Extensive use of the material was made by R.S. Mortimer, 'Bristol Quakerism, 1654-1700'. Typescript M.A. thesis, University of Bristol, 1946.

(*c*) Certificates of Removal, 1669-
(*d*) Letters of Discipline, 1671-
While the records were available for examination, only a cursory glance was made at their content. It is to be presumed that they contain scattered Americana similar to that in like classes in the Library of the Society of Friends, London. Some of the Minutes relate to a Friends' committee in Bristol for aiding distressed cotton workers during the Civil War. Vol. v of the collection contains two manuscript diaries of George Fox, which are printed in the *Journal of George Fox,* rev. ed. by John L. Nickalls (Cambridge, 1952).

PENN, WILLIAM (1644-1718). 6 documents. 1681-1713.

These deeds and conveyances were formerly in the archives of the Bristol and Frenchay Monthly Meeting of the Society of Friends. They refer to the lease and sale of land in Pennsylvania, and various agreements between William Penn and others.

VANDERHORST AND DUNCOMBE COLLECTION. *c.* 200 items. 1701-late 19th century.

Consists of deeds, a few letters, and papers (*c.* 200 items) of the Vanderhorst and Duncombe families. Elias Vanderhorst of South Carolina came to England in 1774. He became a merchant in Bristol, and in 1792 he was appointed the first American Consul there. Although most of the documents relate to the affairs of the families in Bristol and South Wales, there is some material concerning slaves and estates in South Carolina and Georgia. There are also official documents relating to Elias Vanderhorst's consulship in Bristol, including a letter of appointment signed by George Washington and Thomas Jefferson.

OPIE PAPERS.[5] 3 letters, few miscellaneous papers. 1704-19.

Three letters, n.d., 5 Nov. 1714, 28 June (?)1719, from John Opie in Virginia to Miss Susannah Opie and Mrs. Eleanor Harte. Also bills and notes of Susannah Opie, 1704-7, concerning the business of her father's estates in Virginia, and the tobacco trade.

JACKSON, ARTHUR. Letters of administration. 12 July 1712.

Administration of the goods of Arthur Jackson of 'Quary Crik, Patomack River, Co. Stafford, Virginia' to Arthur Jackson, his father.

KING, JOHN (d. 1734). Business records. 1716-36(?).

Bristol merchant long engaged in the North American trade. He had interests in the tobacco trade and invested in a Virginia ironworks. The firm of King continued to flourish in Bristol throughout the eighteenth and nineteenth centuries. It is believed that they were prominent in the slave trade. The City Archives also contain various papers and deeds relating to other members of the family, including William Poole King, Samuel King, and Thomas Liston. These contain several references to the Virginia trade and to William Temple of Virginia.

NOBLET RUDDOCK & CO. Bills of lading[6] (1 volume). 1719-21.

General merchants, Bristol. Bills of lading for ships bound to many ports in Europe, Africa, West Indies, and America sent by this firm. The volume has not been examined, but the catalogue references indicate that it might relate to the 'triangular trade'-Bristol, West Africa, North America.

HOBHOUSE PAPERS.[7] Letters. 1723-36.

These are mainly duplicates of those in the Jeffries Collection, volume xiii, in the Bristol Central Library (p. 7).

FELTMAKERS AND HABERDASHERS. Minute-book. 1673-1865.

Contains a copy of the famous 'Hat Act', 1732, which limited the number of apprentices bound to the hat-making trade in the colonies, and forbade the export of hats from the American plantations. The incorporation of this Act into the minute-book might suggest that the Bristol hat-makers regarded the Act of considerable importance, but it seems unlikely that this volume contains other references to the American hat industry.

COGHLAN, JOHN. Articles of agreement. 1781.

An authorization for John Coghlan, a Bristol merchant, to privateer against French, Spanish, Dutch, and American vessels during the War of Independence.

SHARPLES PAPERS. 1794-1852.

Letters and papers of James Sharples (1750?-1811) and his wife Ellen (1769-1849), portrait painters, and their family, of Bath, Bristol, and New York.

PRICHARD, JAMES COWLES. 2 letters. 1837, 1838.

Letters from the American Philosophical Society, Philadelphia, and the Academy of Natural Sciences of Philadelphia to James Cowles Prichard, M.D., informing him of his election as a member of the societies.

ESTLIN PAPERS. Correspondence, notes, etc. 1850's.

Papers of Dr. J.B. Estlin (1785-1855) of Bristol, a prominent anti-slavery supporter. Included are letters from Samuel May, Jr., and others concerning the Boston Anti-Slavery Bazaars. (*See also* Estlin Papers, Dr. Williams's Library, pp. 95-6.)

MARY CARPENTER COLLECTION. Photograph album.

This album was once the property of Mary Carpenter (1807-77), the philanthropist and reformer, who maintained a girls' reformatory school in the Red Lodge, Bristol. The album is of interest only because it contains individual portraits of all the principal American delegates to the International Penal and Prison Congress held in London in 1872, including such figures as G.S. Griffith and Governor Haines of New Jersey. Mary Carpenter also kept a book in which her friends, visiting the Lodge, were asked to write a few verses. This book appears to be of little value except to show that a number of prominent abolitionists and reformers held Mary Carpenter in high regard.

BUTCHER FAMILY. 7 letters. 1876-80.

Seven letters, 1876-80, from W. Butcher and his daughter Marianne to relatives in Bristol. On two visits to relatives living in Brockton, Mass.; travel details; one letter from Washington, D.C.

5. One of these is printed in W.E. Minchinton, ed., *Trade of Bristol in the Eighteenth Century* (Bristol, 1957), p. 140. (Bristol Record Society's Publications, vol. xx).
6. Bills of lading for 1720 printed in ibid., pp. 76-81.
7. See ibid., pp. 74-5, 82-101, 150-1. See also Henry Hobhouse, *Memoirs of the Hobhouse Family* (Taunton, priv. print., 1927).

CENTRAL LIBRARY,
College Green, Bristol BS1 5TL

JEFFRIES COLLECTION.[1] Vol. xiii: letters. *c.* 1722-36. (B 7957)

Consists mainly of about 150 letters written to Isaac Hobhouse,[2] a leading Bristol merchant, and his partners, by ships captains and agents in the West Indies and the American colonies. Of particular importance are the letters describing the trade between West Africa and the Southern colonies, and the relations between New England and the West Indies during 1722-36. These give details of the commodities carried, and the difficulties involved in this trade. This volume also contains one or two letters relating to the colonial shipbuilding industry[3] in Boston and Philadelphia, and to the cost of construction during the 1730's. There is also information on the efforts of British merchants to restrict a 'cheap money' policy in South Carolina and Virginia, and their interest in the Indian trade in deer-skins and hides.

SOUTHWELL PAPERS.[4] (B 11152-61)

Most of this large collection of ten bound volumes of letters and other documents, dating from the late seventeenth century to 1776, relates to the activities of the Southwell family of Kingsweston, near Bristol, who were Bristol merchants. The volumes contain scattered references to the colonial trade, but the relevant material is slight. The volumes covering 1745-76 contain some reference to the tobacco trade with Virginia and Maryland, and a scheme to revise the duty system on American tobacco which was first proposed by the merchants of Liverpool. Other references to the tobacco trade are few and of little value. The volume for 1746-76 also includes a copy of a pamphlet condemning the smuggling prevalent in the American colonies.

DICKINSON, CALEB. Copy-book of letters. 1757-8. (B 19718)

Contains some references to Bristol trade with Virginia and Philadelphia.

For fuller details *see* the Prankard and Dickinson Papers in the Somerset Record Office, Taunton (pp. 211-2.)

BRISTOL PRESENTMENT BOOKS.[5] (B 10750, etc.) (Published by Samuel Worrall from the Custom House records of the port of Bristol, but they are not official Custom House Papers.) Imports: 1770, 1775-80, 1795-6, 1801-18.—Exports: 1773-80, 1790, 1795-6, 1801-18.—Exports and Imports: 1819-20, 1823-4, 1827-8, 1830-44, 1846-1917.

These volumes are composed of weekly or bi-weekly publications listing imports and exports at Bristol. The nineteenth-century series was published every Monday and Thursday, listing every vessel clearing and entering the port of Bristol. Amongst them are vessels trading between Bristol and America. Details of the goods which were exchanged are given.

MERCHANDISE IMPORTED INTO BRISTOL. 1774-88. (B 21259)

This account book lists vessels which entered Bristol from the American colonies and other ports during 1774, and gives the date of arrival and commodities carried. This is most probably derived from the Bristol Presentment Books (q.v.); the volume of imports for 1774 is missing in that series.

SHARPLES, ELLEN (WALLACE) (1769-1849). Diary,[6] 1803-36. (B 19728)

Wife of James Sharples, the artist, who painted portraits of Washington and many other prominent Americans. She was herself an artist of considerable talent. She visited the United States twice. This diary, kept 1803-36, covers the time of her second visit, May 1809 to Feb. 1811, when James Sharples died. She met many prominent figures, and her diary gives a useful picture of life in early nineteenth-century New York. After 1811 the diary contains scarcely any material which is directly relevant to the United States.

EARLY BRISTOL NEWSPAPERS.

There is a published catalogue of the Reference Library collection: *Early Bristol Newspapers: a detailed Catalogue of Bristol Newspapers Published up to and including the year 1800 in the Bristol Reference Library* (Bristol, private circulation, 1956).

PORT OF BRISTOL AUTHORITY,
Port Offices,
St. Andrews Road, Avonmouth, Bristol BS11 9DQ

STATISTICS OF THE PORT OF BRISTOL (printed volumes). 1885- .

The Port of Bristol Authority is responsible for the Bristol City Docks, Portishead Dock, Avonmouth Docks, and West Dock. The printed annual reports of the Port's trade give information about Anglo-American trade, in particular the amount of net register tonnage arriving from and departing for America. Detailed statistics of trade with America are contained in the Authority's archives.

SOCIETY OF MERCHANT VENTURERS,
Merchants' Hall,
The Promenade, Bristol BS8 3NH

(Applications should be made in writing to the Treasurer)

RECORDS OF THE SOCIETY.

Contain material relating to American trade and colonization. A guide to the scope of this material for the seventeenth century is to be found in Patrick McGrath, ed., *Records Relating to the Society of Merchant Venturers of the City of Bristol in the Seventeenth Century* (Bristol, 1952) (Bristol Record Society's Publications, vol. xvii), and in Patrick McGrath, ed., *Merchants and Merchandise in Seventeenth Century Bristol* (Bristol, 1955)

1. See W.E. Minchinton, ed., *Trade of Bristol in the Eighteenth Century* (Bristol, 1957), pp. 82-101, 150-1 (Bristol Record Society's Publications, vol. xx).
2. See W.E. Minchinton, ed., 'The Virginia Letters of Isaac Hobhouse, Merchant of Bristol', *Virginia Magazine of History and Biography*, vol. lxvi (1958), pp. 278-301.
3. See W.E. Minchinton, ed., *Trade of Bristol in the Eighteenth Century*, pp. 93-4.
4. See ibid., pp. 152-3.
5. See ibid., pp. 48-50, 57-71.
6. For copious extracts from the diary see K.M. Knox, *The Sharples* (London, 1931; and New Haven, Conn., 1930).

(Bristol Record Society's Publications, vol. xix). Among the material there is also a manuscript calendar by J. Latimer, *c.* 1897, useful as a summary of the Society's records. Latimer also wrote *The History of the Society of Merchant Venturers of the City of Bristol* (Bristol, 1903), while McGrath has recently written an updated study of the Society's history, entitled *The Merchant Venturers of Bristol* (Bristol, 1975). Both of these histories are of value in examining the sources.

THE LIBRARY, UNIVERSITY OF BRISTOL, Tyndall Avenue, Bristol BS8 1TJ

MARTIN, HENRY (d. 1721). Inspector-General's Ledger of Imports and Exports from Christmas 1715 to Christmas 1716.

Martin was Inspector-General of Imports and Exports. The ledger is a record of English imports and exports, arranged under the names of the countries with which business was done, and classified in a detailed list of commodities. The American colonies are grouped together as follows: Carolina, New England, New York, Pennsylvania, Virginia, and Maryland. The account of colonial exports is arranged under these headings and relates either to London or the outports. Details are given, including the amount and estimated value of both British and foreign merchandise imported and also the relative values of different products in the economy of each group of colonies. Values are totalled and a series of abstracts give the general balance of trade and the particular balance for each group of colonies.

CANER, HENRY (?1700-92). Letter-book. 1728-78.

Anglican clergyman. The letter-book contains draft copies of the letters of Caner, who was taken to the colonies as a child. His father built the first buildings of Yale College, from which the son graduated in 1724. The letters date from his acceptance of the Society for the Propagation of the Gospel mission at Fairfield, Conn., in 1728, and continue through his tenure of the rectorship of King's Chapel, Boston, to his return to England as a Loyalist refugee.

The majority of the letters concern ecclesiastical affairs: reports to the S.P.G., letters to the Archbishop of Canterbury and the Bishop of London, and correspondence with other New England clergymen. There are a number of letters to members of his family, to Barlow Trecothick on financial affairs, and to Governor John Wentworth of New Hampshire.

PINNEY PAPERS.

These deal mainly with the domestic affairs of the Pinney family, and with their West Indian sugar trade and plantations.[1] But in the letter-books there are a few letters to correspondents in the mainland colonies, including a letter,[2] Bristol, 19 Feb. 1785, from Pinney & Tobin to David Ross & Co., Portsmouth, Va., for whom Pinneys acted as commission agents for the sale of sugar, rice, and tobacco, and who supplied corn to Nevis, West Indies. There are also a few letters relating to the mainland amongst the West Indian correspondence in the Pinney Papers, e.g. a letter, 1 June 1775, from John Pinney to Simon Pretor, giving news of a 'skirmish' at Boston.

1. Richard Pares, *A West India Fortune* (London, 1950).
2. W.E. Minchinton, ed., *The Trade of Bristol in the Eighteenth Century* (Bristol, 1957), pp. 129-30 (Bristol Record Society's Publications, vol. xx).

BEDFORD

BEDFORDSHIRE COUNTY RECORD OFFICE[1] County Hall, Bedford MK42 9AP

STUART PAPERS. Pennsylvania papers. *c.* 200 documents, 2 volumes and 2 maps. 1673-1787.

The Stuarts are descended from the Earls of Bute, and are connected by marriage with the descendants of William Penn. Pennsylvania material includes: Maps of 'Neobelgium', *c.* 1673 (printed); and Maryland, 1742. Grants of land by William Penn, 1681-1708 (127 documents). Six miscellaneous deeds, 1692-1786. Legal code, 1704-5; and Charter of Liberties, a 1717 copy of the Charter of 1701 (1 volume). Mortgages on province, 1708-41 (17 documents). Two Acts of Assembly, 1717-8, 1759. Papers on boundary disputes with Maryland, 1732-80; and unlawful settlement in Pennsylvania by men of Connecticut, 1754-74 (14 documents). Depositions as to interference in trade by Virginians, 1774. Minutes of Assembly, 1787 (printed volume). List of American manuscripts, 1674-1737, in this collection, made *c.* 1740.

CARTERET PAPERS. 1 document. 1690.

Release of 1690 includes a copy of the will of Sir George Carteret (d. 1680), who bequeathed plantations in New Jersey.

HOW PAPERS. 1690's-1792.

Quakers in Pennsylvania, 1690's: some letters (HW 85); minutes of meetings, 1756 (HW 93/16); address by Quakers to George Washington, expressing loyalty, and Washington's reply, 1789 (HW93/18); letters relating to land in Pennsylvania claimed by descendants of Thos. Farmborough, 1768-92. (HW 90)

LUCAS MSS. Notes, letters, etc. 1739-86.

(*a*) Political papers, 1739-83, of Thomas Robinson, 2nd Lord Grantham. These papers, of which many are official copies or extracts of manuscripts in the P.R.O., include notes on English and French forts suggested for demolition, n.d. (L29/161); material relating to paper currency in America, 1739-51 (L29/193-5); papers from 'Mr. Blackwell' about attacking Mexico and New Orleans, 1771-2 (L29/200a); notes on conversations with Lord George Germain, 1776, and Major Balfour, 1777, on the American situation (L29/213, 214), etc.
(*b*) Letters to Lord Polwarth from Sir Francis Carr Clerke, 1776, including one written from camp on the eve of Saratoga (L30/12/17); and from N. Balfour, 1777-9, also about the War of Independence. (L30/12/3)
(*c*) Twenty-nine letters, 1778-86, from William Horner and his supporters. Horner was a merchant trading with Liverpool from

1. *Guide to the Bedfordshire Record Office* (Bedford, 1957).

Maryland and Virginia. He had to leave the U.S. and so lost his property there. His letters, requesting help, are addressed to Grantham's brother, Frederick Robinson, M.P. (L30/15/26)

RUGELEY PAPERS. 1740-1849.

Letters relating to settlement in South Carolina (1740-1810); financial concerns; appointment to military and judicial office (1773-95); family and business matters; dispute over inheritance of estate (1812-49) (X 311, covering 1740-1901)

LUCAS PAPERS (Deeds of Manor of Staysmore). 3 documents. 1773-86.

Relate to the disposal of property at Carlton, Beds., by Thomas Palmer, who emigrated and became a merchant in Philadelphia.

ARPIN, EDWARD. Diary (23 pages). 1800-30.

Parish clerk of Felmersham, Beds. Mentions the departure of thirty-nine men, women, and children of the parish for Boston in 1829.

WHITBREAD PAPERS. *c.* 70 letters, 9 printed items. 1810-4.

One file only, inscribed 'American affairs', was available for inspection. It contains letters and printed items addressed to Samuel Whitbread (1764-1815), M.P.

Correspondents include:

Barclay, George. Four letters, 6-12 Feb. 1812, concerned with the capture of an American frigate, the *Dolly,* by the French.

Denham, J.D. Hull, 9 Feb. 1813. Recently in New York, discusses, *inter alia,* distress of British merchants, impressment, British sailors willingly serving in United States ships; character of Madison and Clinton.

Dickins, Asbury. American Consular Office, London, 8 Aug. 1812, sending a copy of a message from his kinsman, Willis Alston, United States congressman for North Carolina, relating to encouragement of Indians by British agents.

Macdonald, Thomas. 1 May 1811, describing the difficulties of his task as First Commissioner for American Claims, and enclosing printed orders of the Board, etc.

Mullett, Thomas. Eighteen letters, London, June 1810-May 1813. Arranges introductions between Whitbread and Americans in London, including William Pinkney; gives advice and encouragement to Whitbread's attacks on government policy towards America, sending him newspapers, letters, and abstracts, which he has received from America, for Whitbread's use in the House of Commons.

White, Campbell P. Belfast, 3 Dec. 1812, sending a document showing the number of American vessels captured by Britain and France.

Wilberforce, W. 29 Feb. 1812, discussing speeches on American affairs.

Witz, T.L. New York, 22 June 1811, opposing proposals for peace with France.

Other correspondents to submit opinions on American disputes, 1812-14, include:

Britannicus, J. Brown, J. Grubb, Jorgen Jorgensen, J.M., Ab. Mann, John Mansfield, Lord Milton, Peter Payne, George Ponsonby, Thos. Potts, William Roscoe, Ralph Stevenson, Thomas Thornely.

Also printed pamphlets and press cuttings relating to American affairs.

CULPIN, EDW. Letters. 1880-4.

Letters of a rover in the U.S.A., 1880 and 1882-4. (X 345/12-13 and 18-25)

PARISH RECORDS.

(*a*) Hockliffe. Overseer's accounts, 1828-38, include an item of £10 for payment of the passage of an emigrant to America in 1833.

(*b*) Oakley. Miscellaneous papers, 1819-44, include accounts of expenses for parishioners who emigrated to America in 1831, with names of emigrants and shippers' receipts.

QUARTER SESSIONS RECORDS.

Include transportation bonds of criminals to America, 1731, 1734.

NATIONAL GRAPHICAL ASSOCIATION, Graphic House, 63-67 Bromham Road, Bedford MK40 2AG

EXECUTIVE COUNCIL MINUTES, 1845- . HALF-YEARLY and ANNUAL REPORTS (printed), 1849- . UNION JOURNALS (printed), 1849- .[1]

The Executive Council Minutes of the Association and its predecessors include some references to the United States, e.g., to the use of American composing machines in the 1890's.

A bound volume labelled 'Typographical Circulars, 1849-59' contains many American references. It consists of the following printed documents: the *Address to the Delegates* of the 1849 Sheffield founding conference of the Provincial Typographical Association; half-yearly reports of this Association, 1849-60; Scottish Typographical Association reports, 1853-7; the *Typographical Societies' Monthly Circular,* 1852-61; and the *Typographical Protection Circular*, 1849-53. The *Address* includes discussion of tramping *vs.* emigration, and a proposed scheme of emigration to 'any of the colonies of Her Majesty, or those of America or elsewhere'. The general functioning of this and later plans is referred to in many of the Provincial Typographical Association half-yearly reports; and letters from branches give the numbers and names of emigrants to the United States (including the Liverpool case in which fares were paid for six 'unfair hands' who were persuaded to emigrate to the United States). Similar material is available in some of the Scottish reports and in the *Typographical Societies' Monthly Circular.* The *Typographical Protection Circular* includes extracts from letters of ex-members giving details of working conditions and wages in America.

A reference of another kind is found in the Bedford branch letter (Provincial Typographical Association eighth report) which notes that at a public dinner the editor of the local newspaper 'with much palaver' proposed the health of Harriet Beecher Stowe; a member of the union, present to report the affair, thereupon 'arose and told the liberal-minded gentleman that. . . he considered him a most exact personification of the Legree of Mrs. Stowe'; a considerable disturbance seems to have ensued.

1. See A.E. Musson, *The Typographical Association* (London, 1954).

BERKSHIRE

BERKSHIRE RECORD OFFICE,[1] Shire Hall, Reading RG1 3EE

DOWNSHIRE PAPERS. 1609-1773.

Largely the papers of William Trumbull (d. 1635), British Minister at Brussels, 1609-25; and his grandson, Sir William Trumbull (1639-1716), M.P., diplomat, and Secretary of State. (*Letters unless otherwise stated.*)

(*a*) 9 Nov. 1609, from John More to William Trumbull, mentions the scattering of Sir Thomas Gates's ships sailing for Virginia.[2]

(*b*) 30 Nov. 1609, from J. Beaulieu to Trumbull, states that all by Gates's vessel have arrived safely, and adds that there is dissension among the settlers 'by reason of their minister being somewhat of a Puritan' and antagonizing the High Church party.[3]

(*c*) 1611-3, to Trumbull, on conditions in Virginia, the lottery, and Spanish opposition to English settlement there. Correspondents include Thomas Albery; Jean Beaulieu; Samuel Calvert; Francis Cottington, agent in Spain; Sir John Digby, Ambassador to Spain; Sir Thomas Edmondes, Ambassador to France; Maurice, Landgrave of Hesse Cassel; John More; John Wither; and John Woodall.

(*d*) Eight letters, 1615-24, to Trumbull, about the Virginia settlement, the attacks upon it by the savages, and its products.

(*e*) Agreement, 9 Apr. 1622, between Sir William Alexander, Sir Robert Mackeleaneane and John Mason of London, and Thomas Hopkins of Rotherhithe, mariner, that the last-named shall take a ship to Virginia or the northern parts of New England in return for a certain sum.

(*f*) Petition, *c.* 1630, of George Rookes, a London merchant, and John Barnabee, a Virginia planter, to trade, and to plant certain commodities and to transport these to His Majesty's dominions. Letter, 30 Sept. 1630, from the Privy Council to the Council and Governor of Virginia, ordering them to allow this. Corn, woad, rapeseed, flax, and hemp are specifically mentioned as allowed to be planted, and tobacco forbidden.

(*g*) Deed of sale, 19 Feb. 1663, of a moiety in Maryland and New England by Henry Alexander, 4th Earl of Stirling, to Lord Berkeley.

(*h*) 12 June 1686, from Don Pedro Ronquillo, Spanish Ambassador in London, to Sir William Trumbull, asking for information about an alleged treaty of commerce between France and the North American colonies.[4]

(*i*) Newsletter, 15 May 1688, to Messrs. Goodman & Martin states, 'A patent is past the seals and a great stock raised for carrying on the copper mines in New England, which are better than those of Denmark or Sweden.'[5]

(*j*) Manuscript newsletter, 1 Aug. 1695, about the arrival of ships from Virginia.

(*k*) 'A short account of the English plantations in America' (endorsed by Sir William Trumbull, *c.* 1695) (volume of 19 pages). Deals with situation, government and trade of Massachusetts Bay, New York, New Hampshire, Virginia, Maryland, New Jersey, Pennsylvania, Delaware, and Carolina.

(*l*) 17 Feb. 1696, from Peter Coode, William Glynn, and Thomas Malby, to Sir William Trumbull, mentions Americans indulging in piracy on the coast of Arabia.[6]

(*m*) Grant of an annuity, 19 Dec. 1696, to Henry Alexander, 5th Earl of Stirling, in return for his relinquishing to the Crown his rights in New York 'and any part thereof in America'.

(*n*) Warminghurst, 4-11 Jan. 1697, from William Penn to Sir William Trumbull, complaining of the usurpation of jurisdiction in the colonies by the Court of Admiralty.[7]

(*o*) 13 June 1709, from John Bartlett to Sir William Trumbull, describing preparations for an expedition against Canada, and the willingness of the New Englanders and Indians to take part.[8]

(*p*) Petition, n.d., of Edward, Lord Cornbury, to be granted a patent of the monopoly of coining pence and groats in the American colonies.

(*q*) 'Present state of the British colonies in America', 1773 (large volume). Contains reports from the governors of some of the colonies, Massachusetts Bay, New Hampshire, Connecticut, New York, New Jersey, Pennsylvania, Virginia, Georgia, and West Florida, in reply to questions put by Lord Dartmouth, Secretary of State for the Colonies. The replies deal with such matters as situation, size, rivers, harbours, constitution, trade, manufactures, smuggling, produce, mines, inhabitants, militia, forts, Indians, revenue, expenses, establishments, and valuation.

HARTLEY RUSSELL PAPERS. 1689-*c.* 1785.

(*a*) Copy of Virginia petition, 20 May 1689, complaining of the 'oppression practiced by the late Governor'.

(*b*) Papers connected with David Hartley, the younger (1732-1813), M.P., and relating especially to peace negotiations with the Americans, 1777-83. These include draft propositions for averting war, and for making peace after the war had broken out; drafts of the preliminaries of peace, 1782; and instructions to the Commissioners. There are a number of unsigned, undated notes by Hartley, one of which argues the American case against Britain (as does a draft speech, for delivery in the House of Commons), and another which describes the benefit to both countries of maintaining the connexion between them. There is also an unaddressed, unsigned copy letter, 11 Aug. 1778, from Hartley to Franklin, about an exchange of prisoners at Calais, and the rejection by Congress of the peace feelers of 1777. (A copy of Congress's resolution of rejection is among the papers.) The subject of American prisoners of war is frequently referred to in these papers. There are several supporting documents on American affairs, mostly copies of letters or of well-known State Papers, some dating back to the Stamp Act controversy.

(*c*) Pamphlets, printed speeches and resolutions about events just before, during, and immediately after the War of Independence, including 'Committee upon the American Trade Bill', 1783, and the 'Case of the American Loyalists', n.d.

BENYON PAPERS. *c.* 1740-1777. (D/EBY)

(*a*) Papers and correspondence on mortgage by Sir James and Sir George Colebrooke to R. Benyon, with statements of contracts by the Colebrookes for supplies for the government in North America, Guadeloupe, etc., 1773-7. (E 63)

(*b*) Statement on the colony of Georgia. n.d. (*c.* 1740). (B 14)

1. *Guide to the Berkshire Record Office* (Reading, 1952).
2. Transcript, H.M.C. Downshire MSS. ii (75), p. 126. (Listed as held by the Marquess of Downshire, Easthampstead Park, Berkshire.) All Virginia material has been microfilmed by the Virginia Colonial Records Project.
3. Transcript, ibid. ii, p. 195.
4. Transcript, ibid. i(i), pp. 181-2.
5. Transcript, ibid., p. 292.
6. Transcript, ibid. i(ii), p. 622.
7. Transcript, ibid., pp. 727-8.
8. Transcript, ibid., p. 877.

LENTHALL PAPERS. Letter. 1749. (D/L1)

A letter among the correspondence of the Carew family of Beddington, Surrey, mentioning a Capt. Washington about to leave for Virginia. 1749. (C1/243)

BELSON PAPERS. 1 document. 1789.

Address, 1789, from the Philadelphia Yearly Meeting of Friends to George Washington, extending good wishes for the success of his administration and his personal happiness, with his reply.[9]

PRESTON PAPERS. Diaries. 1913. (D/EP 8)

Diaries of A.E. Preston of Abingdon and Mrs. Preston giving an account of travel through North America, 1913. (F4(c), 7, 10, 12) (Also two albums of photographs.)

READING AND WITNEY MONTHLY MEETINGS OF THE SOCIETY OF FRIENDS.

The minutes of these Monthly Meetings and their constituent earlier meetings include references to Quaker emigrants from the later part of the seventeenth century.

PARISH RECORDS.

(*a*) Aston Tirrold. Vestry Minutes (1 volume). Resolution of 1852 directs the churchwardens and overseers to borrow £55 for defraying the emigration expenses of poor persons.

(*b*) Moulsford. Register of baptisms and burials, 1772-1812 (1 volume), contains only 19 pages of entries; the rest of the volume consisting of a diary, 1846-1909, kept by successive incumbents and referring to events of local and national interest. The entry for 24 Apr. 1859 mentions two labourers, John Ring and David Horne, as having sailed for New York. A note is added later, 'N.B., they came back at Christmas greatly disgusted.'

(*c*) Reading, St. Mary. Vestry Minutes, 1829-68 (1 volume). Resolution of 1832 that 'the question of advancing money to persons emigrating to America be left to the discretion of the parish officers'.

(*d*) Warfield. Churchwardens' accounts, 1586-1840 (2 volumes). An entry for 1617 'layd out of the churchboxe, for Virginia the XIIth January 5 shills.'.

THE LIBRARY, UNIVERSITY OF READING, Whiteknights, Reading RG6 2AE

MARKHAM NOTE BOOKS. 1750's.

These notebooks were compiled by two members of the Markham family, including William Markham the elder (1686-1771), who in note book six makes a number of poetic references to his American experiences in the 1750's. (MS.1444).[1]

ASTOR PAPERS. 1902-64.

The University Library has among its holdings the papers of Lord and Lady Astor. The voluminous correspondence of Nancy, Viscountess Astor (1879-1964), an American by birth, contains much material of U.S. interest, including general American correspondence, 1902-64 (boxes 248-280), correspondence with American relatives, 1907-46 (box 305), and material on the Christian Science movement, 1915-64 (boxes 281-288). Some information pertaining to America may also be included among the papers of Lady Astor's husband, Waldorf, 2nd Viscount Astor (1879-1952). (MSS.1367/1, 1066/1)

INSTITUTE OF AGRICULTURAL HISTORY AND MUSEUM OF ENGLISH RURAL LIFE, UNIVERSITY OF READING, Whiteknights Park, Reading RG6 2AG

BOARD OF AGRICULTURE. 16 volumes, including 9 minute-books, 2 letter-books, and a register of letters received. *c.* 1789-1810.

Predecessor of the Royal Agricultural Society. Much of the work of the Board of Agriculture (1793-1822) was concerned with county agricultural surveys, but the interest of its members in improved agricultural practices led to a certain amount of correspondence with the United States or about American methods.

The register of letters received, 1793-1819, includes reference to a number of letters of this sort, on such subjects as machinery, gypsum, hemp, peas, and Virginia white thorn. The actual letters, however, are not in the possession of the Institute.

The two letter-books cover the years 1793-1800 and 1810-22, and include copies of some letters from the Board to American correspondents, e.g., to Mr. Jay of New York, in 1796; to Thomas Jefferson in 1789 and 1798; and to Mr. Pinckney and Dr. Logan in 1810.

The minute-books of the Board, covering most of its existence, consist mainly of notes that letters have been received or sent; occasionally there is slightly more information here about the letters listed in the register.

BUCKINGHAMSHIRE

BUCKINGHAMSHIRE RECORD OFFICE, County Hall, Aylesbury HP20 1UA

VERNEY PAPERS. 3 letters. 1676.

(*a*) Two letters from Dr. William Denton to Sir R. Verney. On 12 Oct. 1676 he mentions that 1,000 men are being sent to Virginia 'with a pardon to all but Bacon'. On 19 Oct. 'the drums beat for volunteers for Virginia. Here is much talk of a remonstrance from the city'.[1]

(*b*) 7 Dec. 1676, from John Verney to Sir R. Verney, mentioning Nathaniel Bacon's capture and burning of Jamestown, Va., his taking Sir Thos. Chichely as prisoner, and 'that the Governor Sir Wm. Berkeley was again fled the country'.[2]

TREVOR PAPERS.[3] 5 letters. 1738-40.

Correspondence of Robert Hampden-Trevor, 1st Viscount Hampden and 4th Baron Trevor (1706-83), Minister at The Hague 1739-46.

9. See *Writings of George Washington*, ed. by John C. Fitzpatrick, vol. xxx (Washington, D.C., 1939), p. 416.

1. Sir Clements Markham, *Markham Memorials* (1913).

1. Excerpts, H.M.C. vii, pp. 493-4.
2. Ibid., p. 467.
3. We are grateful to the Earl of Buckinghamshire for permission to make this report.

(*a*) Horatio (or Horace) Walpole to Robert Trevor. Three letters, 31 Mar., 13 June, and 24 Oct. 1738, on American commerce and navigation, and disputes with Spain concerning them; one letter, 3 Oct. 1740, partly about the French in America.[4]
(*b*) M. de Harlé to Robert Trevor, 25 Mar. 1740 (in French). M. de Harlé, a French Protestant who has left France on account of his religion and is living in Holland, states his desire to go to Virginia to examine the possibility of setting up the manufacture of linen and thread, for the production of the raw materials for which the soil of Holland is not suitable.[5]

HOWARD-VYSE DEPOSIT. 1775-7.

This collection includes some letters and reports, 1775 and 1777, sent from Richard Reeve of Boston to Sir George Howard, M.P., all describing the opening months of the War of Independence.
(*a*) Covering note, 16 May 1775, enclosing copy of a letter written by Reeve to one of the Secretaries of the Treasury. This enclosure, 14 May 1775, with additions, 16 May, gives details of the situation in Boston since the 'skirmish which happened on the 19th (April), between H.M. troops and the rebels in the neighbourhood of this town' (Lexington), and the continued threat of attack by the rebels—interception of letter giving details of plan for such attack to be made on 24 Apr.—Situation in Rhode Island and New York—no communication by land with Philadelphia and the Southern colonies. Rebels' plan is for independence—their forces growing steadily and being supplied with provisions by the country people who receive receipts for what they bring 'which are to be paid for by the Province on some future day'.—'It is certain that Great Britain must now subdue the colonies by force of arms, or relinquish her authority over them, for all appearance of accommodation appears to be now at an end.'—Lord Dunmore's threat to declare the Negroes free at Williamsburg, Va. (Enclosed is a printed sheet with resolutions of the Provincial Congress at Watertown, Mass., 5 May 1775, to disobey all orders and proclamations, etc., of General Gage.)
(*b*) Letter, 24 June 1775, compares (very favourably) General Howe with General Gage. Intransigence of people in Northern colonies.

Report, 22 June 1775. Battle of Bunker Hill, 17 June, described in detail. (A list of the officers killed and wounded in this action is enclosed.) Brief reference to delegates from Southern provinces at General Congress who 'are strenuous and very much in earnest for accepting the proposals of Parliament'.
(*c*) Letter, 25 July 1775, sending report on the subject of 'American matters' and the state of the army. Has not seen General Howe for some time, but he is very well 'commanding a corps upon Bunckers Hill'.

Report, 25 July 1775. 'The whole system of American politics is now fully disclosed, the Continental Congress has usurped the sovereign power over the colonies. . . .' In order to subdue the colonists 'it is not supposed that there is any necessity for standing upon punctilios with rebels in arms, might it not therefore be a proper measure to emancipate and arm the Negroes in the Southern colonies and to encourage the warlike Indian nations bordering upon them to ravage and lay waste the country?' Boston now 'blockaded completely by the rebels without'. Rebel bombardment of Roxbury, Mass.; their invasion, in long-boats, of Long Island; and their burning of the lighthouse on one of the Brewster Islands. (Enclosed is a manuscript order of battle of the Army at Boston on 16 July 1775.)
(*d*) Letter, 19 Aug. 1775, enclosing 'further intelligence of the transactions in this country'.

Report, 14 Aug. 1775. Troops' brief attack on rebels, on night of 30 July, near Roxbury, Mass. Loss of some forty marines and carpenters, to the rebels, at the lighthouse which they were repairing. Loss of the armed schooner *Diligence*. Other shipping news, etc. An addition of 16 Aug. 1775 reports the return of the transports from the southward with provisions.
(*e*) Letter, 1 Dec. 1775, enclosing further report of state of affairs. Government's disinclination to regard position in its true light. Four months of winter ahead much to be feared owing to 'want of fuel and provisions'. 'The foe most to be dreaded is the North West wind, which rages at this season of the year and forbids all navigation coming upon this coast.'

Report, 15-26 Nov. 1775. Skirmishes with rebels in Canada. Situation in Rhode Island under the rebels. Building of redoubts to protect Boston against attack when Cambridge Bay is frozen. Shipping news. Scarcity of provisions. Rumour that 'Washington has left the rebel Army but upon what account is not mentioned'. News of the position at Marblehead, Mass., 25 November. Controversy between Commanders-in-Chief and the Board of Customs in Boston as to powers under the Boston Port Act. (Ref. 13/7)
(*f*) Manuscript entitled 'Establishment and disposition of His Majesty's land forces at the close of the year 1777 also general state of the army in America to the same period'. (Ref. 13/9a)
(*g*) Printed items. (Ref. 13/7)

(i) *A circumstantial account of an attack that happened on the 19th April 1775, on His Majesty's troops, by a number of the people of the province of Massachusetts Bay* (Lexington, Mass.).

(ii) Copy of a letter, Hartford, Conn., 28 Apr. 1775, from Jonathan Trumbull, Governor of Connecticut, on behalf of the General Assembly of that colony to General Gage; with a copy of General Gage's reply from Boston, 3 May 1775.

(iii) *Massachusetts Gazette and the Boston Weekly News-Letter*, Thursday, 30 Nov. 1775.

HOBART PAPERS.[6] *c.* 1776-1803.

Papers of Robert Hobart, 1st Baron Hobart, 4th Earl of Buckinghamshire (1760-1816), soldier and statesman; Secretary of State for War and the Colonies in the Addington administration, 1801-4.
(*a*) 'Sketch of the case of Captain Benjamin Roberts', n.d., giving a brief description of his services against the Indians in the Seven Years War and as Superintendent of Indian Affairs among the Six Nations just before the War of Independence.
(*b*) Two certificates, 1798 and 1803, supporting the claims of Captain Daniel Lyman to a consulship in the United States on account of intelligence work by him which led to the interception of French bullion coming from the United States in 1794. (Copies)
(*c*) Three letters, all 1803, from Captain John Murray, who was trying to recover family property in Virginia. There is a long enclosure, the copy of a letter from Ralph Wormeley of Virginia to Murray concerning Jefferson's change of heart from animosity to cordiality towards Britain, which the writer attributes to American fears that, with France once more in possession of Louisiana, free navigation of the Mississippi will disappear.

4. Transcripts, H.M.C. xiv (ix), pp. 15, 18, 24 and 56. (Listed as held by the Earl of Buckinghamshire.)
5. Synopsis, ibid., p. 44.
6. We are grateful to the Earl of Buckinghamshire for permission to make this report.

Should the French treat Monroe 'with hauteur and indignity', says the writer, Monroe has orders to report to London and conclude a treaty.

SHARDELOES PAPERS (AMERSHAM). Letter. 1779.

24 Feb. 1779, from Robert Bourne to William Drake of Shardeloes, about the failure of a 'Rebel descent' upon the Mississippi, the raising of a defence corps by the planters, and the enhancement of land values there.

FREEMANTLE COLLECTION. 1858-62.

Accounts, correspondence, reports, etc., 1858-62, mainly involving munitions supplies to America.

SOMERSET PAPERS. Letters. 1861-6.

(*a*) Fifteen letters from Admiral Sir Alexander Milne (from North American and West Indian Station) to the Duke of Somerset, 1861-3, discussing possible British military action against the Northern States during the American Civil War, and commenting on the progress of the war between the Union and the Confederacy.
(*b*) Correspondence relating to the *Nashville* and *Tuscarora* affair, January 1862. (Confederate ships taking shelter in Southampton waters.)
Including:
(i) Letter from Lt. Pegran, Confederate Navy, to the Duke of Somerset, 27 Jan. 1862, seeking permission to remain in a neutral port.
(ii) Letter from W.G. Romaine to the Duke of Somerset, n.d., giving details of his negotiations with Lt. Pegran of the *Nashville*.
(iii) Letter from Capt. Patey, describing how the *Tuscarora* had requested permission to defer departure on account of weather, but was ordered to proceed without delay.
(*c*) Thirteen letters from Admiral Sir James Hope (from North American and West Indian Station) to the Duke of Somerset, 1864-6, commenting on the final years of the American Civil War, plans in Canada to form a Confederation, and British relations with the U.S.
(*d*) Miscellaneous Correspondence: Nine letters, 1861-5, mostly concerned with naval matters and British-American relations.

HUGHENDEN MANOR (NATIONAL TRUST)
High Wycombe

DISRAELI, BENJAMIN, 1st Earl of Beaconsfield (1804-81). Papers.

Disraeli's papers are preserved in thirty large deed-boxes. Most of the boxes contain papers on a related group of subjects, though some are very miscellaneous; there is no detailed list of the whole, only a very general list of the principal subjects in each box. The collection was too large to locate the Americana in it without a full list in the time available. However the papers were available to Monypenny and Buckle,[1] and the index to volume IV of their work reveals several letters of Disraeli on policy towards America, especially the Civil War and the *Alabama* claims. There are evidently a fairly large group of letters, 1861-5, between Disraeli and other Conservative Party leaders—Beauchamp, Cecil, Derby, Ralph Earle, Edward Bulwer-Lytton, Henry Lennox, Malmesbury, Stanley, and others—which discuss the American Civil War, the question of recognition of the Confederacy, armistice proposals, the Lancashire cotton famine, Canadian defences, Laird and the armoured rams, etc.[2]

CAMBRIDGESHIRE

CAMBRIDGESHIRE COUNTY RECORD OFFICE,
Shire Hall, Cambridge CB3 OAP

COTTENHAM COMMON RIGHTS. 12 documents.[1] 1596-1842. (R50/9/39,45)

Copy of the agreement for the stint, etc., of Cottenham Common, 20 Nov. 1596. Also copy, 1615, by Richard Robinson. Eleven other documents, 1638-1842; copies of the agreement or documents relating to it.

Cunningham states: 'The system [in operation at Cottenham] has interesting analogies with the townships...which were soon to be planted...in New England....The circumstances of the New England settlers gave the opportunity for the reproduction of similar institutions for the regulation of economic affairs. The system in vogue in Massachusetts, at Chelsea in 1638, at Malden in 1678, or at Lexington was closely allied to that which existed at Cottenham in 1596, and the township, in a new atmosphere and in new surroundings came to play an important part in the constitutional and political history of the United States.'[2]

SOCIETY OF FRIENDS. Letters and reports to Huntingdonshire and Cambridgeshire Meetings. 1699-1842.

(*a*) Epistle from the Meeting for Sufferings in London with advice from the Yearly Meeting at Philadelphia on the proper conduct for young men sent over with cargoes, 1699. (R59/25/7/4)
(*b*) Copies of epistles from Women's Yearly Meetings in Philadelphia to Women's Meetings in London (75 items), 1783-1842. (R59/25/8/1-14; R59/26/3/4,6)

HUDDLESTON FAMILY. Correspondence. 1771-93. (488/C2/L15-29)

Seventeen letters from John Lucas, S.J., writing from Queen Tree Patuxent, and St. Inigoe's, Maryland, to Ferdinand Huddleston of Sawston Hall, concerning personal financial matters, English war depredations, life in America, request for garden seed, etc. Also two drafts of Ferdinand's replies, and a note on the life of John Lucas.

1. W.F. Monypenny, *The Life of Benjamin Disraeli, Earl of Beaconsfield*, 6 vols. (vol. 3 by Monypenny and G.D. Buckle; vols. 4-6 by Buckle (London, 1910-20).
2. Many of these are quoted in W.D. Jones, 'The British Conservatives and the American Civil War', *American Historical Review*, vol. lviii, pp. 527-43 (1952-3).

---

1. See W. Cunningham, 'Common Rights at Cottenham and Stretham in Cambridgeshire', in Royal Historical Society, *Camden Miscellany*, vol. xii (London, 1910), pp. 169-296 (3rd series, vol. xviii).
2. Ibid., p. 183.

WESTWOOD, NICHOLAS (Plumber and glazier). Account book. 1776. (252/B3)

Contains memorandum of a fast 'for the suckses of our arms against our friends the Americans'.

MAYNARD FAMILY. Correspondence. 1835-9. (R60/23/1b,1c)

Correspondence (contemporary copies), 1835-9, of the Maynard family, emigrants from England. The letters are mainly from Albany and Troy, N.Y., and personal in content.

CHEVELEY PARISH RECORDS. Vestry minute-book. 1836-1951. (P42/8/1)

Vestry minutes, 1836, include setting up of a fund to assist emigrants; also, there is mention, 1846, of an allotment of £50 to emigrants settling in New Brunswick, providing that the Duke of Rutland (owner of the Cheveley estate) contributes a similar amount.

LITTLE ABINGTON PARISH RECORDS. Vestry minutes. 1837-44. (P2/1/2)

Vestry minutes for 1844 include a proposal to allow the application of James Keath, a pauper, his wife and nine children, for assistance in emigrating to Canada.

CROYDON PARISH RECORDS. Survey of inhabitants. 1843-8. (P53/1/11)

A house-by-house survey of the inhabitants of Croydon by the rector, the Rev. Francis Fulford, recording emigration to Canada and Australia where this took place. Fulford was later the first Bishop of Montreal (1850-60) and Metropolitan Bishop of Canada (1860-68).

OAKINGTON PARISH RECORDS. Draft sermons. 1852-76. (P126/28/5)

Drafts of sermons preached by Rev. George Whitaker in various Canadian communities, principally in Ontario. Whitaker (1811-82) was first Provost of Trinity College, Toronto, from 1852 to 1879, and Archdeacon of York, Toronto, from 1875 to 1879.

RECORDS OF CAMBRIDGE UNION. Papers. 1864. (G/C/AZ35B)

Papers, 1864, concerning the emigration of James Papworth and his family from Cambridge to Canada, including notice of conditions of emigration and correspondence.

THE LETTERS OF CHARLES DICKENS, PILGRIM EDITION, 61 Bateman Street, Cambridge CB2 1LR

DICKENS, CHARLES (1812-70). Letters.

While he was in America in 1842, Dickens wrote a series of journal-letters to his friend, John Forster, which were the basis of *American Notes.*[1] During his lifetime, Forster had them bound, with various pamphlets and newspaper cuttings Dickens had sent him in a volume fitted with a lock. After they had been used for his biography of Dickens they were cut out and destroyed. What is left remains in the John Forster Collection in the Victoria and Albert Museum, South Kensington, London, S.W.7.

Practically all Dickens's extant correspondence with his American friends and acquaintances has remained in American hands. A mere half-dozen of the letters he wrote during his two visits to America, in 1842 and 1867-8, remain in England in private hands, though there are a few more written in England that concern the international copyright controversy. All but one of these have been published. The Editorial Committee of the Pilgrim Edition of the *Letters of Charles Dickens* will publish all his known letters. Three volumes (1820-43) have already been published, and Volume IV (up to 1846) is in the press. They give the locations of manuscripts.

UNIVERSITY LIBRARY, Cambridge

RALEGH, SIR WALTER. The Prerogative of Parliaments, etc. (Dd.3.85)

In this volume of tracts, written in various hands between the sixteenth and eighteenth centuries, there is 'A Discourse concerning a voyage intended for the planting of Christian religion and people in the northwest regions of America in places most apt for ye constitution of our boddies and ye speedy advancement of a state'. (9 leaves.) The 'Discourse' is attributed to Edward Hayes, *c.* 1592.[1]

HUDSON'S BAY COMPANY. 4 documents. 1678-87. (Dd.13.31)

From a volume containing a miscellaneous collection of historical documents. (In French.)

(*a*) No. 5, 1687. Hudson's Bay Company. Memorandum on the claims of the English Crown to the commerce in Hudson Bay, with reply by the French commissioners and a rejoinder by the Company[2] (in parallel columns).

(*b*) No. 5, cont. Abstract of title of the Compagnie de la Baye du Nord du Canada to trade in Hudson Bay with the reply of the Hudson's Bay Company.[3]

(*c*) No. 9. Island of St. Christopher, copy of treaty between English and French representatives, 19 May 1678.

(*d*) No. 11, 1687. Compagnie de la Baye du Nord du Canada: *Mémoire*, a reply to the rejoinder of the Hudson's Bay Company to the French company's reply to the Hudson's Bay Company's memorial.[4]

CHOLMONDELEY (HOUGHTON) MANUSCRIPTS. Sir Robert Walpole's Archive. *c.* 1710-1747. (On deposit)

This collection was deposited in the Library by the Marquess of

1. The fuss and bother that resulted from James Spedding's review of *American Notes,* for the *Edinburgh Review*, can be followed in the Macvey Napier Papers, in the British Library (Add. MSS. 34611-31). Most of this has been published, here and there, in one form or another; but a few snippets have not.

---

1. See D.B. Quinn, 'Edward Hayes, Liverpool Colonial Pioneer', in *Trans. Hist. Soc. of Lancs. and Cheshire*, vol. iii (1959), pp. 25-45.
2. See *Calendar of State Papers: Colonial Series, America and West Indies, 1685-1688, preserved in the Public Record Office* (London, 1899), no. 1258, p. 369, and no. 1324, pp. 388-9.
3. Ibid., no. 1324, p. 389.
4. Ibid., no. 1369, pp. 405-6.

Cholmondeley in Oct. 1951. Some of the papers are duplicates of existing papers in the Public Record Office. A detailed five-volume catalogue of all the letters and papers, together with an index of correspondents, is in the University Library.[5]
American material is found particularly in the following:
(*a*) Trading and colonial papers:

84. Papers relating to the colonies, their settlement, administration, and defence, including schemes for expanding; state of the quit-rents in Virginia, etc., 1710-40 (87 items).

87. Papers relating to the colonization of Georgia under General Oglethorpe and relating to some of his other actions in America; forays into South Carolina, etc., 1738-47 (11 items).

(*b*) Army and Navy papers.

7, items 10 and 11. Correspondence relating to Lt. Washington's complaint to the Board of Ordnance, June 1721.

8. Army estimates, particularly relating to the American expedition, 1741-2.

10. Army expenses. American expeditions, 1711-5, 1740.

13. Lists of ships taken by the enemy, 1688-1713, 1740, including the Quebec expedition.

(*c*) Foreign papers:

26, item 144. Account of negotiations with France about navigation in America, n.d.

(*d*) Treasury, Customs and Excise:

37. Lists of goods imported from Antigua, Barbados, Jamaica, Montserrat, Nevis, St. Christopher, and Virginia. 1715-9 (10 items).

The correspondence, which was not examined, is arranged in chronological order. There are about 3,400 letters in all, many dealing with personal and local affairs. Between 1727 and 1735 subjects covered include diplomatic matters. Throughout the period there are a few letters from the leading politicians of the time.

GEORGIA. 1 volume. 1732-8. (Add. 4269)

Transcripts and notes of official correspondence relating to Georgia, copied by Miss A.E. Seeley for the use of Professor Sir J.R. Seeley, *c.* 1887. They include extracts from Colonial and Foreign Office documents.

WOGAN, LE CHEVALIER DE: PLAN DE LA COMPAGNIE ROYALE AMERICAINE. (Bound volume in French.) 1743. (Add. 6572)

'Projet d'accommodement entre l'Espagne et l'Angleterre... contenant un plan général de commerce entre le vieux et le nouveau monde à l'exclusion de toute contrebande et au profit de tout l'univers.' A plan for an international trading company drawn up under seventy-one articles.

PLUMSTED, ROBERT. Letter-book. 1756-8. (Add. 2798)

Quaker merchant in London. Contains an alphabetical list of addressees and copies of letters to them. Many were merchants in New England. They include a Quaker cousin in Philadelphia with whom he was doing business, and who introduced him to other American merchants, dealing in logwood, furs, and corn, etc., in exchange for guns, anchors, nails, etc.

H.M. FORCES. Volume of returns. 1782. (Add. 4376)

The returns are arranged geographically under stations. The North American station (pp. 22-6) is divided into the commands of General Sir Guy Carleton, 1 June 1782, and General Haldimand (Canada), 1 July 1782. Returns for cavalry and infantry are given separately. The information is written on the blank sheets of printed forms. An abstract of the total forces is given on p. 41.

KEATING, SIR HENRY SINGER (1804-88). Journal. (Add. 3819)

(Typescript made in 1896 by his son, H.S. Keating, M.A., of Trinity College.) Judge. Journal of his travels in Madagascar, Greece, and the United States. Pages 218-340 contain an account of his American journey, July 1830-Jan. 1831. He travelled through New York State into Canada, and back through New England as far south as Philadelphia and Washington. He comments on American habits and customs, modes of travel, religion, including an account of a visit to a Shaker community; the state of American cities, and the military training system at West Point, and such terms as 'Yankees'.[6]

GOOCH, RICHARD. Collectanea. (188 leaves with 15 watercolour sketches at the end, and another copy of Chapter 1.) (Add. 2616)

'America and the Americans', from a collection of six boxes of treatises, published and unpublished extracts, notes, drafts, verses, etc., made 1823-39 by Richard Gooch of St. John's College. Subtitled 'Have at the Americans or: America and the Americans in 1833-4, embellished with 12 engravings, by an emigrant.' It is said to describe the 'manners, customs, habits, climate, fashions, matrimony and courtship, notions of gentility...', etc., of the Americans.

SIMPKINSON, FRANCIS GUILLEMARD (later De Wesselow). Logs and journals. (Add. 7780-2)

Logs and journals of Lieut. F.G. Simpkinson, R.N. While serving on H.M.S. *Sulphur,* surveying in the Pacific, Simpkinson visited Alaska and California in 1837.

ACTON, SIR JOHN EMERICH EDWARD DALBERG, 1st Baron Acton (1834-1902). 5 boxes of notes on America. (Add. 4894-8)

Each item is on a separate numbered slip. They include quotations and extracts from American authors and brief comments on American affairs.

A further accession of Acton's papers in 1973, mainly correspondence, includes letters from American historians, especially in connexion with the *Cambridge Modern History,* and Acton's journal during his visit to America, 1853.

DARWIN, CHARLES ROBERT (1809-82). Papers.

157 volumes or boxes, among which are letters from American scientists, including A. and L. Agassiz, H. Gillman, Asa Gray, J. Torrey, and J. Wyman.[7]

5. See also G.A. Chinnery, *A Handlist of the Cholmondeley (Houghton) MSS: Sir Robert Walpole's Archive* (Cambridge, 1953).
6. See also similar manuscript in the Bodleian Library-MS. Eng. misc. c. 29 (S.C. 32396), but in this the relevant pages are 222-353.
7. There is a printed *Handlist of Darwin Papers at the University Library, Cambridge* (1960). Further papers still uncatalogued, including other letters from Asa Gray, were acquired in 1975.

AMERICAN LECTURESHIP. 1865-6. (Cam. b. 865. 1)

A bound collection made by F.W. Maitland of official documents and various papers circulated as part of the controversy concerning the proposal to establish a Lectureship in the History, Literature, and Institutions of the United States. Henry Yates Thompson was the would-be benefactor; he stipulated that the lecturer should be an American and appointed by Harvard with Cambridge, however, having a right of veto. Charles Kingsley, Professor of Modern History, wrote strongly in support of the proposal. E.H. Perowne bitterly attacked it. Sedley Taylor supported Kingsley but H.R. Baily seconded Perowne and argued that not merely 'Republican' but also 'Socinian' or 'Unitarian' principles would be preached. 'Government, authority, faith, submission, reverence, these are indissolubly bound together, and any shock to one part of the system may be felt throughout the whole.' The Senate defeated the proposal by 110 votes to 82.

CONWAY, SIR WILLIAM MARTIN, Lord Conway of Allington (1856-1937). Letters. 1879-1917. (Add. 7676)

This collection includes several hundred letters between William and Katrina Conway, and Manton and Abigail Marble, 1879-1917. Katrina Conway (née Lambard) was stepdaughter of Manton Marble, editor/owner of the New York *World,* and daughter of Abigail.

HARDINGE PAPERS.

A few letters and papers in volume one of this large collection concern the service of the 1st Baron Hardinge of Penshurst as a Second Secretary at Washington, D.C., 1885-6.[8]

BALDWIN, STANLEY, 1st Earl Baldwin of Bewdley (1867-1947). Political papers.

Four volumes in this large collection deal with Anglo-American relations, 1923-34, particularly the American Debt Settlement.[9]

THE LIBRARY, CHURCHILL COLLEGE, Cambridge

SPRING-RICE, SIR CECIL ARTHUR (1859-1918). Correspondence: 39 manuscript or typescript and 75 photostat letters. 1887-1918.

Diplomat, Ambassador to Washington, 1913-8. Mostly personal correspondence between Sir Cecil Spring-Rice and Mr. and Mrs. Theodore Roosevelt.

FITZWILLIAM MUSEUM, Cambridge CB2 1RB

HENDERSON AUTOGRAPH COLLECTION.

Franklin, Benjamin. Copy of a letter, Passy, 24 July 1782, to a M. Durivall: is sending his grandson to execute legal instrument and collect some papers (or money?). Also a single sheet in French, n.d., anon., of biographical notes on Franklin.

SHARPLES, JAMES (1750?-1811). 2 letters. 1802, 1804. (MSS. 13 and 14—1948)

American portrait painter. Bath, 12 Dec. 1802, to William Strutt of Derby. Discusses his paintings and life in Bath.

London, 2 Mar. 1804, also to Strutt. On painting; also asks for an introduction to General Bentham and talks of his own interest in mechanics.

ASHCOMBE AUTOGRAPH COLLECTION.

Jefferson, Thomas. Letter, Washington, D.C., 19 June 1807, to Caesar A. Rodney. He asks Rodney to send him General Wilkinson's letter of 21 Oct. Rodney has sent the wrong one: 'It was the one which was sowed up in the shoe-soal of the officer, to which my message referred.' He asks Rodney to call on a Mr. John Gordon and possibly a Mr. Graybell; he urges secrecy, and can assure Gordon that his name will not be known out of the Cabinet. It ends: 'I think it material to break down this bull-dog of Federalism (Martin) and to break down the imprudent supporters of Burr by showing to the world that they are his accomplices.'

Madison, James. Note, 1 Jan. 1817, to Isaac Tichenor, requesting his attendance in the Senate Chamber on 4 Mar.

Monroe, James. Memorandum, n.d., on the case of one George W. Irvine as to whether he was a United States citizen or not, having been born in Massachusetts but having resided abroad. Monroe submits the case to the decision of Col. Humphries and Mr. Hichborn in Paris, who annotate the memorandum in Irvine's favour, dated 3 May 1795.

Polk, James K. Short letter, 24 Nov. 1847, to the Secretary of War, William L. Marcy, introducing 'the Hon. Mr. Mitchell, formerly a Member of Congress', from Ohio.

Van Buren, Martin. Letter, 13 Apr. 1820, to John V. Henry, enclosing a letter from the Vice-President, Daniel D. Tompkins.

THE LIBRARY, MAGDALENE COLLEGE, Cambridge, CB3 OAG

BIBLIOTHECA PEPYSIANA.

The following catalogues of the collection have been published: J.R. Tanner, ed., *A Descriptive Catalogue of the Naval MSS. in the Pepysian Library at Magdalene College, Cambridge,* 4 vols. (London, 1903-23) (Publications of the Navy Records Society, vols. xxvi, xxvii, xxxvi, lvii); and *Bibliotheca Pepsyiana. A Descriptive Catalogue of the Library of Samuel Pepys,* 4 vols. (Volumes edited respectively by J.R. Tanner, E. Gordon Duff, M.R. James, and William J. Carlton.) (London, 1914-40).

See also Andrews and Davenport, pp. 424-30.

H.M.C. Pepys MSS. (70) (London, 1911) includes the following: (*a*) Two letters, Madrid, 4 Apr. and 21 June 1565, from Robert Huggins to the Earl of Leicester, mention the anger of the King of Spain at the French taking part of Florida and building a fort

8. There is a printed *Handlist of Hardinge Papers at the University Library,* Cambridge, by N.J. Hancock (1968).

9. See A.E.B. Owen, *Handlist of the Political Papers of Stanley Baldwin* (1973).

there, the latter stating that a Spanish expedition has gone to try to recover it. There is also a letter, Padstow, 20 Sept. 1565, from John Hawkins to the Queen, in which he says, 'I have also discovered the coast of Floryda in those parts where there is thought to be any great wealth.'[1]

(*b*) An undated paper headed 'Expenses in the first plantation of New England', written in a spirit hostile to the Puritan settler, but advocating a policy of conciliation on the part of (?) Charles II rather than force towards them.[2]

(*c*) Among papers taken at the battle of Worcester is one (?1649) from Charles II to the colony of Virginia, mentioning its loyalty to the Royalist cause and giving instructions concerning fortifications and collection of duties.[3]

(*d*) 'A copy of a patent granted by the King of Scots to Sir John Berkely and Sir Willm. Davenett (Davenant) for the office of Treasurer in Virginia',[4] Sept. 1649. (Also in Worcester papers.)

(*e*) Copy of a commission, dated Sept. 1649, appointing 'Davenant to be Treasurer in Virginia in the absence of Sir Jno. Barclay, whom he made Treasurer in the room of Capt. William Clayburne', a parliamentarian.[5] (Among 'Letters brought from Jersey'.)

FERRAR PAPERS.[6] 78 papers. 1617-23.

Papers of the Ferrar family, including those of Nicholas Ferrar and his brother John, active in the affairs of the Virginia Company of London. They include seventy-eight papers—letters from Edwin Sandys and others—relating to the Company, 1617-23.

See also Andrews and Davenport, pp. 429-30.

OTHER RECORDS. Journal. 1676.

'Sir John Berry's Journal of his Proceedings in the Execution of his Majesty's Commission to him & Col. Morison for enquiring into the grievances of his Majesty's Plantation of Virginia, 1676'. (PL 2582)

1. Transcript, H.M.C. Pepys MSS. (70), pp. 54-55, 61, 65-66.
2. Transcript, ibid., pp. 270-1.
3. Ibid., pp. 262-3.
4. Ibid., p. 284.
5. Ibid., p. 302.
6. For an account of these papers see *The Records of the Virginia Company of London*, ed. by Susan M. Kingsbury, vols. iii and iv (Washington, D.C., 1933-5).

THE LIBRARY, TRINITY COLLEGE, Trinity Street, Cambridge CB2 1TQ

LYNDHURST PAPERS. 3 letters. 1792-1859.

A volume of letters, 1792-1864, inscribed 'Used by Sir Theodore Martin K.C.B. in writing the life of Lord Lyndhurst. . .'[1] (John Singleton Copley (1772-1832), Lord Chancellor), includes the following letters: Philadelphia, 12 Dec. 1792, from George Washington to John Singleton Copley, Sen. (1737-1815), the portrait painter, thanking him for his print of the death of the Earl of Chatham;[2] 16 Aug. 1845, from Edward Everett to Lord Lyndhurst; Boston, 4 July 1859, from Josiah Quincy to Lord Lyndhurst.

EVERETT, EDWARD (1794-1865). 38 letters.

(*a*) Thirty letters to William Whewell, Master of Trinity College, Cambridge.

(*b*) Eight letters to Richard Monckton Milnes, 1st Baron Houghton.

HAWTHORNE FAMILY. Letters. 1854-77.

(*a*) Five letters from Nathaniel Hawthorne to Richard Monckton Milnes, 1st Baron Houghton, 1854-61.

(*b*) Six letters, 1868-70, from Sophia Hawthorne to H.A. Bright.

(*c*) Four letters, 1877, from Julian Hawthorne to H.A. Bright.

(*d*) Nine letters from Una Hawthorne to H.A. Bright, [1871-7].

PRINTED MATERIAL.

The Library has a number of seventeenth and eighteenth century tracts and printed pamphlets, some of which relate to America.

1. Sir Theodore Martin, *Life of Lord Lyndhurst* (London, 1883).
2. See *Writings of George Washington*, ed. by John C. Fitzpatrick, vol. xxxii (Washington, D.C., 1939), p. 260.

CAMBRIDGESHIRE COUNTY RECORD OFFICE,[1] Grammar School Walk, Huntingdon PE18 6LF

MANCHESTER COLLECTION[2] (from Kimbolton Castle). 1 document. 1784.

Includes a memorial of Lord Charles Montagu, sometime Governor of South Carolina, to Commissioners for American Claims, for compensation for loss of lands in Carolina and a request for proportionable quantity in Nova Scotia, 1784; and other papers.

1. *Guide to the Huntingdonshire Record Office* (Huntingdon, 1958).
2. There is a copy of the catalogue of this collection in N.R.A. 0902.

CHESHIRE

FAWCETT ENGINEERING LTD., Dock Road, Bromborough, Wirral.

BUSINESS RECORDS.

Marine and general engineers, founded in 1758.[1] The only surviving record is an order book (or engine book) which, from 1815, gives details of engines the firm exported for cane roller mills for Southern sugar plantations, and also the engines of some famous American ships, including the *John Randolph*, the *Royal William*, the *Florida*, and the *Alexandra*.

1. See Horace White, *'Fossets': A Record of Two Centuries of Engineering* (Bromborough, priv. print., 1958).

CHESHIRE RECORD OFFICE
The Castle, Chester CH1 2DN

BAKER WILBRAHAM COLLECTION. 3 letters. 1876-7.

Three letters, 1876-7, from General Sir Richard Wilbraham to Sir William Heathcote, commenting on his travels in America, the 1876 presidential election, and the American church.

WILLIAM SHERWEN MSS. Documents. 1863-72. (DDX 198) (Xerox copies)

These documents relate to the career of Captain Sherwen of New Ferry, who was involved in a long legal dispute after his arrest and imprisonment at Philadelphia in 1862 on suspicion of carrying Confederate agents between U.S. ports and the West Indies. Included among the letters is one from William Seward, stating the U.S. government's reasons for Sherwen's arrest and refusing to allow his claim for damages. There are also extracts from Sherwen's account of his arrest and his imprisonment in Fort Delaware.

FINNEY OF FULSHAW MSS. 1703-64. (DFF)

(*a*) John Finney (*c.* 1671-1728) was the eldest son of Samuel Finney, who served as a member of William Penn's Council in Pennsylvania. The younger Finney accompanied his father in 1701 when Samuel emigrated to America, and stayed there until 1711. John held several positions of note in the colony of Pennsylvania. In 1703 he was appointed High Sheriff of Philadelphia and in 1704 he was chosen captain of a company raised to defend Philadelphia from the attacks of French privateers.

Among his papers are a number of letters from various correspondents concerning his American interests. There are also several documents connected with his position as Sheriff, and a roll of the inhabitants of Philadelphia City and County who enlisted in the company Finney raised as a defence against French privateering.

(*b*) Samuel Finney (d. post 1764) was the eldest child of John Finney. His extravagant tastes led to serious financial difficulties, and in 1738 he left his wife and family, went to America, and never returned to England. Among his papers are about twenty letters (*c.* 1740-64) to and from his son, Samuel Finney III.

CHESTER CITY RECORD OFFICE
Town Hall, Chester CH1 2HJ

MINUTES OF THE CITY ASSEMBLY. 1584-1788.

(*a*) Consideration of a letter from Christopher Carlile to the mayor and citizens, informing them of his proposed voyage to America and asking for contributions to the enterprise. Copy of a reply containing refusal to contribute, as only two persons were willing to advance money. Feb.-April 1584.
(Ref. AB/1 f. 193-194)

(*b*) Consideration of a petition from Elihu Yale asking for remission of the fine imposed upon him at the last Session of the Peace for the city for writing and publishing a scandalous libel against Mrs. Sara Hudson, wife of Gawen Hudson, alderman. Not granted. 7th Jan. 1670.
(Ref. AB/2 f. 165)

(*c*) Elihu Yale and Dudley North, his son in law, were to be offered the freedom of the city and were to be entertained in the Pentice at the city's charge. 7th Aug. 1707.
(Ref. Ab/3 f. 152)

(*d*) Decision that Chester M.P.s present a petition to the House of Commons requesting the regulation of the African slave trade. 15th Feb. 1788.
(Ref. Ab/5 f. 13)

MAYOR'S RECORDS. 1616.

Letter from the Council of the Virginia Company to the mayor, recorder and aldermen of Chester concerning the holding of a lottery in Chester for the benefit of that plantation. 15th June 1616. (Ref. M/L/6/107)

TOWN CLERK'S RECORDS. 1698.

Rough draft of a bond in £500 between the part owners of the ship *Providence of Mostyn* and three Chester merchants relating to the settlement of differences over a voyage to Virginia for tobacco. 30th Sept. 1698.
(Ref. TC/P/LP/15)

QUARTER SESSIONS RECORDS. 1609-1775.

(*a*) Examination before the Mayor of Hugh Catlyn of Kent, who had been hired by Hugh Cornish of Plymouth for a voyage to the 'harbour of grace' in Newfoundland, concerning piracy there. 5th Dec. 1609.
(Ref. Q/E/17)

(*b*) Bonds for the transportation to America of prisoners sentenced at Chester Crownmote and Quarter Sessions court. 1731-75.
(Ref. QRTb/1-16)

(*c*) Contracts for the transportation to America of prisoners sentenced at Chester Crownmote and Quarter Sessions court. 1764-75.
(Ref. QRTc/1-15)

ASSEMBLY RECORDS. 1775.

Loyal address from the mayor, aldermen, sheriffs and common council of Chester to George III. 2 [Nov.] 1775.
(Ref. AF/56)

NON-OFFICIAL COLLECTIONS. 1758-1952.

(*a*) Letter from Joseph Manesty of Liverpool to John Hincks, merchant, of Chester, describing Manesty's trade with planters in Carolina and the West Indies, and his purchase of cotton, rum and ginger. 31st Jan. 1758.
(Ref. D/Hincks/55)

(*b*) MS. list of ships captured by Lord Rodney (1719-92) and Lord Hood (1724-1816) in the War of Independence. [*c.* 1782]
(Ref. D/BC/11r)

(*c*) Letter from Sarah Eddowes in Philadelphia to Catherine Garratt in Chester describing her family's arrival in America and her impression of their new home. 23rd Feb. 1795.
(Ref. G/HS/625)

(*d*) Letter from David Brown at San Francisco to his parents in Chester containing an account of his adventures in the gold rush. [1849].
(Ref. CR31/13)

(*e*) Letter, 1852, from Mrs. Amelia Wilson at San Francisco to David Brown, senior, informing him of his son's death from cholera in America.
(Ref. CR31/15)

(*f*) Scrapbook relating to the Soroptimist Club of Bunning, California. 1950-2.
(Ref. CR104/8)
(*g*) Scrapbook relating to the Soroptimist Club of Old Chester, Pennsylvania. 1952.
(Ref. CR104/9)

TRUSTEES OF THE LATE 2ND DUKE OF WESTMINSTER, Muniment Room, Eaton Estate Office, Eccleston, Chester

WESTMINSTER PAPERS. 1634, 1769.

(*a*) 'A commission for the making laws and orders for the government of English colonies planted in foreign parts. Charles I to William, Archbishop of Canterbury [William Laud], Thomas, Lord Coventry and others. 28th April, 10 Car. I'[1] (4½ pages) [1635].
(*b*) Original grant, 1769, by George III of 12,000 acres of land in East Florida to the Rt. Hon. Richard Lord Grosvenor.

CHESHIRE LIBRARIES AND MUSEUMS, Warrington Divisional Library, Museum Street, Warrington

PRIESTLEY, JOSEPH (1733-1804). Letters.[1] 1794-1802.

Scientist, educator, writer. Most of the sixty-nine letters, 1789-1802, are from Priestley to his brother-in-law, John Wilkinson; a few are from other persons to Wilkinson; a few are from various persons to Priestley—e.g., copies of two well-known letters from Jefferson. The letters from Priestley to Wilkinson written from America, 1794-1802, contain much interesting material, chiefly on life in the Pennsylvania backwoods.

MIFFLIN, ANN. Notebook. 1802-3.

Quaker, Philadelphia. The notebook contains an introductory letter, 8 Dec. 1803, to Pim Nevins, and reports of two visits to the Indians: 'Relation of a Visit made to the Indians [in Massachusetts and New York] in 1802 by K. Kirkbude and Ann Mifflin with other Friends, in the course of their Journey to Upper Canada, with some Observations on their Origin &c.' and 'Account of a Visit to some of the Seneca Nation on Allegany Rivers in the 10th mo. 1803, by John Letchworth, Ann Mifflin, Mary Bell, and Company'. The reports consist mainly of accounts of the speeches made by the visiting Quakers, and the Indian replies to these, together with Ann Mifflin's ideas concerning the Indians as descendants of the ten lost tribes of Israel.

QUARRY BANK MILL, Styal, Wilmslow

GREG FAMILY PAPERS. Two ledgers.

Samuel Greg began spinning at the mill about 1784. The collection of Greg family and business records held there includes two ledgers which contain American material.
(*a*) Ledger giving a description of American lands in the state of New York owned by the Greg family in the 1830's; also includes financial accounts of consignments of goods to the United States between 1798 and 1813.
(*b*) Ledger referring to the use by Samuel Greg of American cotton when other mills were using Brazilian (p.4).

CORNWALL

G.C. FOX & CO., 48 Arwenack Street, Falmouth

UNITED STATES CONSULAR APPOINTMENTS AT FALMOUTH. 8 documents. 1794-1900.

Firm of shipping agents, and United States consular agents 1794-1900. Eight letters of appointment signed by Presidents or Secretaries of State survive. An earlier inspection by the County Archivist mentions 'American Consular Letter-books, 1833-54', but these could not be found (Summer, 1977), although it was not possible to inspect all the records of the firm, scattered around their offices. It seems likely that if a thorough search were possible records of shipments to America would be revealed, possibly of mining machinery.

EARL OF ST. GERMANS, Port Eliot, St. Germans

ELIOT PAPERS. Letter. 1775.

31 May 1775, from Edward Gibbon to the 1st Baron Eliot (1727-1804) on the American rebellion.[1]

OTHER RECORDS. 1740.

Bundle of letters concerning the Hudson's Bay Company, 1740.

CORNWALL COUNTY RECORD OFFICE, County Hall, Truro

EAST CORNWALL WOMEN FRIENDS MONTHLY MEETINGS. Minutes (1 volume). 1762-88. (DD. SF. 58)

The entry under 24 July 1785 records the reading of the epistle from

1. H.M.C. iii, p. 213.

1. Photostat copies are held by the Library of Congress, the Houghton Library of Harvard University, the University of Pennsylvania, and the American Philosophical Society, and there is a typed transcript in the British Library. A brief description of the material was given in Library of Congress *Information Bulletin*, vol. xii, no. 20, 18 May 1953. W.H. Chaloner, 'Dr. Joseph Priestley, John Wilkinson and the French Revolution, 1789-1802', *Transactions of the Royal Historical Society*, 5th series, vol. viii, pp. 21-40, 1958, is based on the letters.

1. H.M.C. i, p. 41. Printed in *The Letters of Edward Gibbon*, ed. by J.E. Norton, vol. ii (London, 1956), pp. 72-3.

the Yearly Meeting of Woman Friends in America; under 23 July 1786 the entry records the visit of one Rebecca Jones, a Friend from America, bringing a certificate from Friends of the Monthly and Quarterly Meetings of Philadelphia.

DAVEY, THOMAS. Letter. 1776.

Pensacola, Fla., 1776, from Davey to his aunt in Cornwall, mentioning the War. (DDX. 161)

ENYS, JOHN. Journals. 1776-88.

John Enys (Ensign 1775, Lt. Col. 1797) served in the 29th (Worcestershire) Regiment of Foot. He sailed to Quebec, helped repulse American troops who had invaded Canada, and took part in the capture of an American squadron on Lake Champlain. His regiment advanced into the interior, where they captured various forts, including Ticonderoga. He returned to England on leave in July 1782.

(*a*) Journal of John Enys.[1] Feb. 1776-July 1783. (1 vol.). (DD. EN. 1799)

(*b*) Journal of John Enys, describing his tour of the U.S.A. Oct. 1787-March 1788. (2 vols.). (DD. EN. 1812-1813)

BLEWETT, HARVEY & VIVIAN & CO. Estimates book. 1834-9. (DD.H. 90/1)

Manufacturers of boilers and pumping engines. The firm, established in the late eighteenth century, still survives. It had worldwide trading connexions, and the book shows a shipment of twelve pumping engines to Virginia in 1835.

The Record Office also holds letter-books for 1809-1903, and most of the records of this firm.

(An advertisement in the *West Briton*, 13 Feb. 1835, inserted by the Union Gold Mines in Virginia asks for engineers and miners for the Virginia gold mines.) (Catalogued.)

BOLITHO BUSINESS RECORDS. List of business and estate records, newspaper cutting-book, letter-books, etc. *c*. 1830-1900.

Cornish fishing, tin, and banking firm.

(*a*) There is a full list of the firm's extensive banking, estate, and trading reports in the Record Office, referring to some 162 volumes. These include vol. 13, 'Foreign ledger, 1841-1853'; and vol. 25, 'Foreign ledger, 1860-1880'; these were not examined. (DD. BL. 13, 25)

(*b*) Cutting-book, 'Facts and scraps', contains miscellaneous clippings from English and American newspapers (some unidentified) on, for example, the state of the American stock market, Dakota tin mining, the McKinley Tariff; it also contains stockholders' reports on, for example, Louisville and Nashville Railroad, all evidently referring to the firm's foreign investments. (DD. BL. 31)

(*c*) A later accession of Bolitho business records, received by the Record Office from the Royal Geological Society, contains further material relating to America, primarily concerning tin exports to the U.S.A. (DD. RG. 49, 51, 55, 59). Several letter-books include a number of copy letters sent to New York. (DD. RG. 71 and 73)

VIVIAN, SIR ARTHUR PENDARVES (1834-1926). Travel diary (50 folios), 1877. (Bosahan MSS.)

Third son of J.H Vivian, a partner in the Hafod copper-smelting works in Swansea; M.P. for West Cornwall 1868-85. The diary concerns his 1877 trip to Canada and the United States. From Canada he travelled from Detroit to Chicago, then via Burlington, Omaha, Cheyenne, and Denver, to Longmont, with hunting in Estes Park and the Black Canyon, etc. This was a holiday trip and he was mainly interested in hunting, but there are some passages on the lumber trade in Canada, railways, and Indians. He wrote a book on the United States, *Wanderings in the Western Land* (London, 1879). His brother, Sir Henry Hussey Vivian, later 1st Baron Swansea, who went with him on the trip, also published *Notes of a Tour in America from August 7th to November 17th, 1877* (London, 1878). (12M/FD/63, DD. PV)

OTHER RECORDS. 1674-1924.

(*a*) Letter from Paschow Morshead to his mother describing visit to Barbados, New England, and Virginia, 1674. (DD. CN. 3478)

(*b*) Bills and receipts regarding provision for His Majesty's troops in Boston, 1775. (DDX. 473/152)

(*c*) Account, 1858, of journey from Plymouth to America. (DDX. 407/47)

(*d*) Journal of voyage to America, 1858. (B/T 530)

(*e*) Letter, 1862, about literature and agriculture in America. (DDX. 53)

(*f*) Letter, 1869, from a Californian miner. (AD. 21, 22)

(*g*) Report, 1883, of the Keston copper mine, Arizona. (DDX. 116/37)

(*h*) References, 1924, to the Bate family in Ohio and Indiana, who emigrated from Camelford. (DD. PP. 250, 251)

ROYAL INSTITUTION OF CORNWALL, County Museum and Art Gallery, Truro

CORNISH EMIGRANTS. Memorial book, etc. 1810-

The large-scale migration of Cornish miners, following the decline of the copper-and then the tin-mining industries, is well known, as is the export of pumping and mining machinery. Although the County Museum was virtually the county archive until recent years, no primary records of these movements could be found. But the present Curator of the Museum, Mr. H.L. Douch, keeps a book in longhand in which he lists and transcribes all references to emigration to be found in the *West Briton*, 1810-56, and the *Royal Cornwall Gazette*, 1801-56, the sailings of emigrant ships, advertisements for skilled miners and engineers from all over the world, including the United States, and also published letters from emigrants and editorial comments and notices of emigration agents' activities. Mr. Douch is glad to show the book to scholars.

The *Mining Journal*, 1835-1909, of which the Redditch Public Library holds a complete file, regularly carried advertisements from the United States for Cornish miners, as did the *Cornubian*, 1830-7, a newspaper of which the museum possesses the only complete file. Various Cornish historical and antiquarian society proceedings in the museum contain occasional references to migration.

1. *The American Journals of Lt. John Enys*, edited by Elizabeth Cometti, were published by the Adirondack Museum and Syracuse University Press in 1976. The Cornwall County Record Office also has the Canadian journals of John Enys, Oct. 1783-1787. (DD. EN. 2073-2074)

CUMBRIA

EARL OF LONSDALE, Askham Hall, Penrith

LONSDALE PAPERS. 1690-1763.

(*a*) 'Memoranda on trade and plantations 1690, September 11th. Affrican Companie. They cannot return in time:—the Plantations ill supplied with Negroes the last year:—they therefore desire convoy:—the castles and plantations will be in danger:—betwixt 30 & 40 ships to be employed, and about 40 men a peece:—they would send before the end of October 16 sail:—12 are the fewest they ought to send in October....'[1]

(*b*) Letter, 16 June 1701, from William Penn to Sir John Lowther, describing the situation and trade of Pennsylvania.[2]

(*c*) Letter, 3 Feb. 1763, from the Earl of Bute to Sir James Lowther, mentioning the French abandonment of Louisiana to the Spaniards.[3]

CUMBRIA RECORD OFFICE, The Castle, Carlisle CA3 8UR

LONSDALE PAPERS. 1672-1843. (D/Lons)

I. Admiralty records.

(*a*) Box 4, Book 7. Estimates of charges of transporting soldiers to New York, 1689-90.

(*b*) Box 5, Book 13. Petitions of merchants trading in Levant and Newfoundland, 1691-3, to Lords of Committee of Trade and Plantations. Also an account of the fishing trade in Newfoundland.

II. Parliamentary papers.

(*a*) Box 4: List of Customs officers in Wales, West Indies, New England, and Canada, *c.* 1770.

(*b*) Sir John Lowther's commonplace book, 1672-94, containing a list of goods exported in the *Resolution* to Maryland, 1685.

(*c*) Sir John Lowther's commonplace book, 1698-1705, including a list of ships at Virginia, 1703, a table of counties in Virginia with numbers of taxable persons and names of representatives at the General Assembly at Williamsburg, 1703, and a list of voyages to Virginia and Maryland made by the ship *Resolution* of Whitehaven, giving names of places where cargo was laden and discharged and names of merchant freighters, 1683-90.

(*d*) Whitehaven estate accounts, 1683-1726, including occasional references to ships being fitted out for Virginia.

(*e*) Whitehaven anchorage accounts, 1699-1702 and 1705-7, giving names of ships sailing from Whitehaven to Virginia and Newfoundland.

(*f*) Miscellaneous accounts: Invoice of cost of goods laden on the *Amity* for Virginia, 1695.

(*g*) Letter-books of John Spedding, 1706-42, contain occasional references to trade with Virginia.

(*h*) Letter and account books of Henry Fleming, a merchant of Norfolk, Virginia, include much information on Anglo-American trade in the 1770's.

(*i*) Bundle of letters about Lady Westmorland's property in Prince Edward Island, Canada, 1843.

BENSON AND MORDAFF RECORDS (Solicitors, Cockermouth). Papers. 1753-78.

(*a*) Account book of the voyages of the brig *Eleanor*, containing accounts for voyages to Virginia in 1763 and 1767. (D/Ben)

(*b*) Book containing trading accounts of J.R. Miller at New York and Philadelphia for a cargo of Messrs. Tate Hodgson & Co., Whitehaven, 1778. (D/Ben)

(*c*) Papers in lawsuit, Hicks *v*. Ellison, include copies of accounts for tobacco in Maryland, 1753-9. (D/Ben 584/4-718/4)

WALTON OF ALSTON FAMILY PAPERS. 1815, 1826

(*a*) Letter from John Railton of Natchez, Mississippi, to Henry Gill of Knaresdale, referring to his cotton business, 1815. (D/Wal)

(*b*) List of families emigrating from Alston to Canada, 1826. (D/Wal)

SENHOUSE OF NETHERHALL MARYPORT RECORDS. Letter. 1765.

Letter from Benjamin Franklin to Humphrey Senhouse about his deafness, 1765. (D/Sen)

CURWEN OF WORKINGTON HALL RECORDS. Deeds. 1733-95.

Deeds of an estate at Winscales and Dean belonging to Robert Shearman of Philadelphia, watchmaker, 1733-95. (D/Cu C.8)

CUMBERLAND QUARTER SESSIONS RECORDS. 1737-70.

Rolls of Petitions to Sessions, especially in the mid-eighteenth century, contain references to transportation of convicted persons to Virginia, especially from 1737 to 1770. (CQF)

CARLISLE PROBATE RECORDS. Wills.

Wills and associated records of persons dying in the U.S. with property in the U.K., e.g. Jonathan Brown, 1784.

VARIOUS DEPOSITS. 1739-1832.

(*a*) Letter-books of Walter Lutwidge of Whitehaven, merchant. The out-letters, 1739-40 and 1746-49, include numerous references to the Virginia tobacco trade. (DX 524)

(*b*) Accounts for the voyages of the brig *Hannah* from Liverpool to Quebec, 1826, 1829. (DX 404)

(*c*) Accounts for a voyage to St. John's and Chalm Bay, B.C., 1832. (DX 404)

STEAD, McALPIN & CO., LTD., Cummersdale Print Works, P.O. Box 1, Carlisle

BUSINESS RECORDS. Firm's order books. *c.* 1890-

Textile printers, machine and hand-block. The firm has carried on a considerable export trade to the United States since the 1890's. Most

1. Transcript, H.M.C. xiii (vii), p. 102.
2. Transcript, ibid., p. 246.
3. Transcript, ibid., p. 132.

of the records kept in London were destroyed during the Second World War, but a large number of order books are still available at the Cummersdale Print Works. For each design, listed by number, these show the date of orders, the amount of cloth ordered, and the names of the customers. Although no addresses are given, many of the customers are known to be American.

MRS. M. HOLMAN, The Dower House Rheda Estate, Frizington

WILSON, W.S. American diary. 1830.

The diary, which begins in the West Indies, mainly concerns Wilson's visit to New York City and his subsequent journey up the Hudson and across to Niagara. On his trip upstate Wilson visited the Shaker village near New Lebanon, N.Y., and he gives description and impressions of the religious and social customs of the community. The diary is interspersed with rather startled comments on American egalitarianism, on availability and method of sale of books, and on the strength of political opinions held.

CUMBRIA RECORD OFFICE (KENDAL), County Offices, Kendal

WALLER, JOHN (naval purser). 2 letters. 1774.

(*a*) Letter, 25 Feb. 1774, from Waller to Abraham Dent, concerning Waller's ship the *Somerset,* bound for Boston, Mass. Refers to the 'troublesome' nature of the inhabitants there. (WDB/63/36)
(*b*) Letter, 8 Apr. 1774, from Waller to Dent, mentioning the government's opinion 'that smaller ships will do the business in America'. (WDB/63/37)

CROSBY RAVENSWORTH MSS. 26 letters. 1855-96. (WDX 204)

(*a*) Six letters, 1855-9, to the Taylor family at Crosby Ravensworth from Edward Taylor in Illinois. Comments on the Panic of 1857, farm prices, and family affairs.
(*b*) Twenty letters, 1868-96, from members of the Davy family in Illinois and Nebraska. Chiefly concern farming and family affairs.

MISCELLANEOUS LETTERS AND DOCUMENTS. 1778-1841.

(*a*) Three letters, 1778-82, from Robert Rauthmell in America to his aunt and uncle in Liverpool, mentioning the War of Independence. (WD/AG)
(*b*) Papers, 1794-7, concerning Thomas Crewdson's purchase of American stock, including receipts, certificate, and six letters dealing with Crewdson's investments. (WD/Cr)
(*c*) Overseers' expenses for the Curwin family's passage to America, 1841. (WD/MG)

BRIG. J.W. KAYE, Millbeck Towers (The Old Carding Mill), Underskiddaw, Keswick

DOVER, YOUNGHUSBAND & CO. Ledger, day-book. 1824-41.

Woolen goods manufacturers, Millbeck Keswick. From the ledger, 1823-56, and the day-book, 1830-41, it appears that the firm shipped blankets and other woolen goods to the United States during the period 1824-39. The ledger gives brief details of charges for particular shipments and payments by the American firms for these; 'loss in sale' is a frequent entry. The day-book contains fuller information about shipments made from 1830 onwards, with contents of and charge for each bale noted separately. The goods, apparently shipped mainly through W.P. Bushby of Liverpool (or Bowe & Bushby, or Bushby, Son, & Foster), went to firms in New Orleans—first Curell, Kilshaw & Co., and later S.T. Hobson; New York—Thos. Dixon & Co., George Mackie & Co., Gabriel Mead & Co., W.B. Bend, and Alex. B. McAlpin; Philadelphia—Wm. Scott, John A. Brown, and Harrison & Watson; and Baltimore—A. Brown & Sons, Campbell & McIlvain, and G.B. Hoffman & Brother.

SIR FERGUS GRAHAM, Netherby, Longtown, Carlisle

GRAHAM PAPERS. 32 letters and papers. 1683 - (late 17th century?).

(*a*) Thirty letters and papers, n.d. but late seventeenth century, relating to Hudson Bay, New England, etc., and disputes with the French.[1]
(*b*) 7 Aug. 1683, from Lord Preston to Secretary Jenkins mentions boundary disputes between Boston and the French, and the French complaints that the English are supplying the Indians with arms.[2]
(*c*) 6 Feb. 1684, mentioning that 'several Scotchmen came... to London under the (pretence) or notion of going to Carolina, and were many of them taken here into custody'.[3]

CUMBRIA COUNTY LIBRARY, Whitehaven Library Lowther Street, Whitehaven CA28 7QZ

BRAGG, JOHN. Diary, etc. (1 volume). 1767-88.

Shoemaker, Whitehaven. The items of American interest in this very mixed volume are as follows:
(*a*) Copies of material from a 'Book of Richard Pike's in Manuscript'. Two letters, 1767 and 1771, from Benjamin Ferriss, Quaker schoolmaster of Wilmington, Pa., to his friend Elizabeth Wilkinson concerning personal affairs.
(*b*) Copies of letters[1] from American relatives of Bragg—John Hadwen and his daughters Elizabeth and Dorcas. Five letters, 1774-88, from Newport, R.I., give news of family members.
(*c*) Diary for 1774-90. Most of the entries for the period 1774-83 relate to the War of Independence. Bragg gives latest news of events leading up to the War and of battles, etc., during the War, with some comment on these; he mentions the arrival of Henry Fleming from Virginia 'with a vessel & crew, passengers &c—all being banished out of that country that durst pretend to be friends to Government' (entry of 6 Sept. 1776); the arrival of a

1. H.M.C. vii, p. 409.
2. Transcript, H.M.C. vii, p. 287. See also p. 392.
3. Transcript, ibid., p. 407.

---

1. Microfilms of these in the Library of Congress, Washington, D.C.

ship from Virginia carrying tobacco intended for France (21 May 1777), and the appearance at Whitehaven during the night of 22 Apr. 1778 of John Paul Jones and his men.

MARTIN, GEORGE. 1 volume.[2] 1779-1800.

Solicitor, London. The volume consists of Martin's copies of claims submitted by him and by his father—Samuel Martin, Whitehaven merchant—for recompense for loss of Virginia property; Edmund Randolph's opinion, 1785, on these claims; and Martin's continuing comments on lack of progress in attaining satisfactory results. The property was originally owned by John Martin, at one time representative of Caroline County in the Virginia Assembly, who died in 1761 leaving his estate to his sons Samuel and Lewis and to their sons; the family's 'attachment to the British government' led the Virginia Assembly to confiscate and sell the considerable property, of which inventories are given in the claims, in 1779.

DERBYSHIRE

DUKE OF DEVONSHIRE, Chatsworth, Bakewell

DEVONSHIRE PAPERS.

Chatsworth contains the extensive papers of the Dukes of Devonshire, the main bulk of which are as yet unlisted (see however, H.M.C. iii, pp. 36-45). These include the personal accounts of the Earls of Devonshire, members of the original Virginia and Somer Islands Companies. These were not available for inspection at the time of compilation, but are normally open to inspection by prior arrangement.

ROBINSON & SONS LTD., Chesterfield S40 2AD

LETTER. 1842.

Letter, 28 January 1842, from the founder of the firm to his wife, describing his journey to New York and his immediate reaction to the city.

DERBY CENTRAL LIBRARY, The Wardwick, Derby

CATTON COLLECTION. Correspondence. 1820's-30's.

This collection consists of over 10,000 documents dating back to the twelfth century, concerning the Horton, Wilmot, and Wilmot-Horton families. Although many of the items are of a purely domestic nature, the majority of the nineteenth-century material is of political importance, containing correspondence relating to Canada and, peripherally, to the United States. (Sir Robert John Wilmot-Horton was Under-Secretary of State for War and the Colonies).

Many of the items in the collection are as yet unlisted, and most of the individual letters are indexed only by correspondent and not by subject. Nevertheless, some of the topics covered can be identified; they include pauperism in and emigration to Canada (1820's-30's), slavery in the U.S.A. (1820's), and the judicial system in Canada (1820's).

DERBYSHIRE COUNTY RECORD OFFICE, County Offices, Matlock DE4 3AG

BERESFORD PAPERS. Lease. 1709. (D158M/T94)

Lease for 1,000 years by William Walker of Quarne (Quarndon) Derbyshire, son and heir of John Walker and wife Mary, daughter of Sir John Zonche late of Virginia, all deceased, to Robert Milward and wife Isabel, another daughter of Sir John Zonche, of his share of Rocksdale Plantation, Virginia, for 40s., and yearly rent of one lb. of tobacco if demanded, 1709.

QUARTER SESSIONS RECORDS.

Papers dealing with the transportation of felons to America, 1720-72.

FITZHERBERT OF TISSINGTON PAPERS. 1771-1850. (D239)

(*a*) Grant of 20,000 acres in Florida to William Fitzherbert, 1771.
(*b*) Correspondence and papers relating to an estate in Ohio, property of William Philip Perin, 1773- *c*. 1800.
(*c*) A few family letters written from Canada to Sir Henry Fitzherbert, *c*. 1835-1850.

DEAVILLE PAPERS. Letters. 1847-54. (D822)

Photocopies of three letters from William and Mary North of Coolspring, U.S.A., to their brothers John Deaville (1779-1857) of New Buildings, Shottle, Derbyshire (farmer), Robert Deaville (1785-1858) of Idridgehay, Derbyshire (butcher), and their sisters, giving family and farming news, 1847-54.[1]

MARQUESS OF LOTHIAN, Melbourne Hall, Derby

COKE PAPERS. 10 letters. 1626-39.

Papers of Sir John Coke (1563-1644), Secretary of State 1625.
(*a*) 20 Jan. 1626, from Sir Robert Heath, Attorney-General, to Sir John Coke on the decayed state of the Virginia tobacco trade.[1]
(*b*) 29 Nov. 1626, 10 Sept., and 17 Nov. 1627, from Captain Christopher Levett to Sir John Coke, sets forth the advantages to the Crown of New England if properly fortified and defended, especially for naval stores and fishing. Seeks a commission to go thither, and 'make that country good against an enemy' at little cost.[2]

2. Microfilm held at Colonial Williamsburg. An article on it appeared in the *Whitehaven News*, 20 Aug. 1953.

1. Originals and other letters from America in the possession of Mr. R.H. Deaville, formerly of New Buildings, Shottle, Derbyshire. Present address unknown.

1. Transcript, H.M.C. xii (i), p. 250.
2. Transcripts, ibid., pp. 287, 321, 331.

(*c*) 16 Jan. 1628, from Lord Baltimore saying that he has no objection to Levett's request as it will not encroach upon his plantation in Newfoundland.[3]
(*d*) 4 Feb. 1632, Massachusetts Bay, from Richard Saltonstall to Emanuel Downing, mentioning the commodities—fish, hemp, flax, pitch, tar, potashes, soapashes, masts, pipestaves, clapboards, and iron—in which New England hopes soon to be able to trade, and asking Downing to encourage men to go over.[4]
(*e*) 12 Dec. 1633, from Emanuel Downing to Sir John Coke, describing the reasons for the settlement of New England and the arguments against the view that 'in time they [New Englanders] will revolt from their allegiance and join in trade with strangers'.[5]
(*f*) 23 Aug. 1634, from Downing to Sir John Coke, concerning trade with New England and suspicion that the Dutch will try to appropriate it.[6]
(*g*) 7 May 1635, Jamestown, Va., from Governor Sir John Harvey to Mr. Kemp, charging him to order the Council 'now gathered together' that their assembly is unlawful and that they must disperse.[7]
(*h*) Extract of a letter, 25 May 1635, from Samuel Mathews 'on the differences between Sir John Harvey (Governor) and the colony of Virginia. The former leaving Jamestown, and the latter appointing Captain John West to act as Governor till his Majesty appoint another.'[8]
(*i*) 11 July 1639, from Sir Francis Wyatt to Coke, announcing that he is ready to sail to take up his appointment as Governor of Virginia; also draft of Coke's answer.[9]

BUCKINGHAMSHIRE PAPERS. 1765-82.[10]

Contain the correspondence of John Hobart, 2nd Earl of Buckinghamshire (1723-93), who was Viceroy of Ireland 1777-80. Many of the letters to him during that period and earlier contain references to the War of Independence, and to the events that led up to it. (*Letters unless otherwise stated.*)
(*a*) North American papers include extracts, 1766-8, relating to the Stamp Act controversy and a representation, 27 Aug. 1765, of the Board of Trade to Council relative to the Virginian Resolutions received in Governor Fauquier's letter of 5 June 1765.[11]
(*b*) Copies of Minutes of the Lords of the Committee of Council for Plantation Affairs, upon considering the state of disorder, confusion, and misgovernment in the province of Massachusetts Bay, 26 June 1770.[12]
(*c*) Paper, entitled 'Commencement of the American Rebellion', in Buckinghamshire's handwriting but unsigned.[13] [1775?]
(*d*) Letters giving general news about the War, 1776-80.[14]
(*e*) Comments on Irish-American trade.[15] [1777?]
(*f*) Letters, 15 and 22 Jan. 1781, and enclosures from Clinton about the threatened mutiny of the Pennsylvanian troops in the American army in 1781.[16]
(*g*) Letter, 21 Jan. 1781, from Peter Holmes, M.P. for the borough of Banagher, King's County, asking Buckinghamshire for a recommendation to a man going to South Carolina to assert his rights to some property there.[17]
(*h*) Letters from Clinton in 1781 and early 1782, the latter group being mainly concerned with Cornwallis's surrender.[18]
(*i*) Three letters from Lord Townshend to the Earl of Buckinghamshire in Feb. 1782, on the Clinton-Cornwallis controversy, and Cornwallis's attempt to have certain letters from him to Clinton brought before the House of Lords. Also 'Notes on the. . . controversy' by Clinton himself; and 'Annotations for Lord Cornwallis's correspondence', containing thirty-three manuscript notes on the controversy.[19]

DEVONSHIRE

DEVON RECORD OFFICE,
Concord House,
South Street, Exeter EX1 1DX

BURROW & CO., CULLOMPTON. Document. 1764. (74B/)

Assignment of shares in Pennsylvania Land Company, 1764. (MT 1984)

SIMCOE PAPERS. 1792-*c.* 1800. (Deposit 1038)

Family and official papers, including some of Lieut. Gen. Sir John Graves Simcoe, first Lieut. Gov. of Upper Canada, 1791-6, referring to Canada and his later command in San Domingo, 1792. Contains copy correspondence relating to two border incidents, Aug. 1794, and a pamphlet, *c.* 1800, by Simcoe, publishing material to refute charges made against him—'I *know,* that under God, I am the instrument that prevented the war between the two countries. . . '

CALMADY HAMLYN MUNIMENTS. 29 letters, 8 accounts. 1778-9. (129M/Transport/D1-5)

Keen (agent), Babb (captain), and others to Hamlyn, owner of the victualling ship *Tuscany;* some dated New York and referring to the French blockade.

ACLAND PAPERS. 1770's-1874. (1148M/)

(*a*) Resolutions relating to disturbances in the North American colonies, presumably 1770's. (9/9)
(*b*) Letters from J. Threlkeld, Georgetown, U.S.A., to Rev. J. Fisher, Kirkoswald, Cumberland, 1799-1817, including comments on the War of 1812. (19/9)
(*c*) Letter and plan of chapel and school-house at Robins Nest, Ill., 1839. (11(i)/13)
(*d*) Letter concerning sects and slavery in America from William Peter, Philadelphia, to Rev. T. Fisher and the 10th Baronet Acland, 1841. (21(ii)7)
(*e*) Bills, papers, and letters relating to the visit of C.T.D. Acland to Canada and the U.S.A., 1874. (6/5-6)

3. Transcript, ibid., p. 337.
4. Transcript, ibid., p. 449.
5. Transcript, H.M.C. xii (ii), pp. 38-9.
6. Transcript, ibid., p. 64.
7. Transcript, ibid., p. 79.
8. Ibid., p. 81.
9. Transcript, ibid., pp. 236-7.
10. Inquiries about the Buckinghamshire Papers should be sent c/o the National Trust, Blickling Hall, Norfolk.
11. H.M.C. Lothian MSS. [62], pp. 260-1.
12. Ibid., p. 289.
13. Ibid., pp. 291-2.
14. Ibid., pp. 295-6, 300-6, 309-12, 315-6, 323-4, 326-7, 342-3, 362, 368-9, 378.
15. Ibid., pp. 306-7.
16. Ibid., pp. 381-4.
17. Ibid., p. 384.
18. Ibid., pp. 387-9, and 396-410 *passim.*
19. Ibid., p. 411.

BULLER PAPERS. Letters. 1815-62.

(*a*) Letter from T.W. Buller, H.M.S. *Bedford*, about the Battle of New Orleans, 1815. (F6/10)

(*b*) Letters from J.W. Buller, all mentioning the Civil War, but written in England, 1861-2. (C/7,29,32)

SIDMOUTH PAPERS.[1] 3 volumes, 6 files. 1822-31. (D. 152)

Henry Unwin Addington (1790-1870), a nephew of the 1st Viscount Sidmouth, was British *Chargé d'Affaires* in Washington 1823-5, and later a British plenipotentiary in negotiations with the United States over the North-East and North-West boundaries with Canada, 1826. American papers included in:

(*a*) Reminiscences, three volumes, 1822-5, include accounts of Congressional debates which Addington attended, the presidential election of 1824; and descriptions of Washington and of trips he made outside Washington; character sketches of leading Americans and of Americans in general.

(*b*) American dispatches and correspondence: 6 files, 1822-31.

(i) Two files, 1823-5, contain copies of his dispatches, chiefly to Canning, and his general correspondence whilst in Washington. Deal with the Monroe Doctrine, the tariff, and the suppression of the slave trade. Include the original of the secret dispatch to Canning of 3 Nov. 1823 about a confidential conversation with John Quincy Adams on the subject of a joint manifesto by Britain and the United States on the revolt in the Spanish colonies as proposed by Canning to Rush in Aug. 1823. Some correspondence with John Quincy Adams and James Buchanan is included.

(ii) Two files entitled 'Negotiations with the U.S.A., 1826-7'. Letters to various members of the government, chiefly to Canning, describing the progress of negotiations with Albert Gallatin on both the North-West and North-East boundaries, and the renewal of the commercial agreements of 1815, including projects for conventions on these subjects. Also private correspondence concerning the negotiations, especially the North-East boundary, with notes on surveys and former treaties and agreements. Files also contain printed correspondence on United States-West Indian trade, the boundary negotiations of 1824, and the 1824 convention with Russia on possessions on the Pacific coast, copies of Anglo-United States peace treaties from 1783, and a compendium of arguments over the interpretation of the Fifth Article of the Treaty of Ghent, 1814 (i.e. on the North-East boundary), with map.

(iii) Two files entitled 'Letters and other papers relating to the North-East boundary, U.S.A., 1828 and 1829': further private correspondence and memoranda on the North-East boundary negotiations by Addington. Includes: 'Statement respecting the differences between Great Britain and the United States of America under the 5th Article of the Treaty of Ghent destined to be submitted to arbitration as provided by the Convention of the 29th September, 1827'; manuscript volume (250 pages), prepared by him for Lord Aberdeen. - 'Skeleton of a project for a second British statement', 1829, manuscript, also by him. - Some papers on the North-East boundary by Sir Howard Douglas, Governor of New Brunswick. - Manuscript copy of the protest by W.P. Preble, American Minister at The Hague, against the award of the Netherlands' arbitrator in the North-East boundary dispute, 1831. - Printed *First statement on the part of Great Britain according to the provisions of the Convention of 29th September 1827 for referring to arbitration the disputed points, under the Fifth Article of the Treaty of Ghent.*—Printed correspondence on the North-East boundary arbitration of 1831.

(iv) Government reports on Canada-U.S.A. boundary dispute, 1820's.

FEWINS, GEORGE. 2 letters.[2] 1850, 1851. (D. 132A/PO 822-3)

'Kanses, Jackson county, State of Missouri', 21 July 1850 and Jan. 1851, from Fewins, a carpenter, to the overseers of the parish of Cheriton Bishop, near Exeter, asking that the parish pay for the transportation of his wife and children to New Orleans, where he emigrated because of poverty in England. In the second letter he curses the overseers for refusing, and states with vulgar emphasis that he will not return to England either to collect his family or to maintain them.

MICHELMORE, LOVEYS & CARTER, TOTNES. Notebook. 1861-2. (867B/)

Reporter's notebook, Civil War, 1861-2. (Z 36)

1. We are grateful to Viscount Sidmouth for permission to make this report.

2. We are grateful to the Chairman of Cheriton Bishop Parish Council for permission to make this report. Photostats in the collection of Letters of Emigrants to America in the British Library of Political and Economic Science, London School of Economics.

EAST DEVON RECORD OFFICE, Castle Street, Exeter

EXETER CITY RECORDS.[1] Letters, papers. 1615-1760.

(*a*) 15 July 1615, from Richard Martyn, thanking the Mayor of Exeter 'for your bountifull returne of ther lottery booke' [on behalf of the Virginia Company], and commenting on 'the coldness and backwardness of other places and persons in returning ther books'.[2]

(*b*) Papers, 1623, relating to New England: comprising a letter from Francis, Lord Russell, to the Deputy-Lieutenants of Exeter, and enclosures - a paper entitled 'Reasons shewinge the benefitt of plantinge in Newe England, 1623', and a copy of the King's letter, 8 Dec. 1623, to the Lords-Lieutenant of Somerset, Devon, and Cornwall. The purpose of all these is to secure further settlers for New England.[3]

(*c*) Various items, 1729-64, concerning criminals transported to America.[4]

(*d*) Guinea, 10 Feb. 1737, from Robert Parker to the Chamber of Exeter, mentioning importance of the Royal African Company's forts to the settlements in America.[5]

(*e*) Resolutions to bestow the freedom of the city upon Cornwallis and Simcoe, and Cornwallis's acceptance, both undated. [1782-3?][6]

COCKINGTON PAPERS. Letter-book.

Fragments of the letter-book of Colonel Thomas Gorges (1618-71), Lieutenant-Governor of New England. Include copy of a letter, 28 Aug. 1641, to the elders of the Church at Boston, and letters describing American conditions.

PALK PAPERS. 2 letters. 1769, 1785.

Letters to Sir Robert Palk, Governor of Madras 1763-7, M.P. 1767-8 and 1774-87, including:

(*a*) Madras, 15 June 1769, from Josias Du Pré, containing the

1. See also a thesis based primarily on the Exeter City Records and the Devon Collection in the East Devon Record Office by E.A.G. Clark, 'The estuarine ports of the Exe and Teign with special reference to the period 1660-1860: a study in historical geography', 3 vols. Typescript Ph.D. thesis, University of London, 1956.

2. Transcript, H.M.C. City of Exeter MSS. [73], p. 99.

3. Transcript, ibid., pp. 166-71.

4. Ibid., pp. 237-8.

5. Transcript, ibid., p. 242.

6. Ibid., p. 252.

sentence: 'Have some mercy, I pray you, upon poor America, or you will repent it by and by.'[7]
(*b*) Madras, 25 Jan. 1785, from George Baker, mentioning the arrival at Pondicherry of the first United States ship there, coming from Philadelphia.[8]

QUICKE PAPERS. 2 letters. 1775, 1776.

(*a*) Letter containing transcript of Gen. Burgoyne's account of the battle of Bunker Hill, 1775. (64/12/29/1/107)
(*b*) Letter concerning the 'present calamity' in Boston, and its effect on trade, 1776. (64/12/29/1/102)

FLOUD PAPERS. 10 letters. 1823-8.

Letters to Margaret ('Peggy') Parrott, servant to the Floud family in Exeter, from her brother John Parrott and her niece Anne, Boston, Mass., describing life in America; also letters from members of the Floud family, with two letters from Margaret Parrott. (68/30/151-60)

KENNAWAY PAPERS. Railway correspondence. 1873-5.

Correspondence and clippings relating to the Atlantic and Great Western Railway, 1873-5. (58/9 Box 53/9)

CHAMPERNOWNE PAPERS. Letters. 1876-7.

Letters from C. Tuttle of Boston, Mass., concerning the Champernowne family, 1876-7. (58/3/6/24)

LETTERS CONCERNING EMIGRANTS FROM DEVON. 3 files containing *c*. 300 letters. 1900-1.

These letters, from persons living in the Empire and the United States, were written in response to a circular published in various newspapers by Sir Roper Lethbridge, the president-elect of the Devonshire Association, asking for information about families of Devonian descent, now settled 'in those lands'.

MISCELLANEOUS COLLECTIONS. 1711-1808.

(*a*) Letter concerning naval and military operations in Nova Scotia, 1711. (49/8/1)
(*b*) Letters, notes and accounts concerning property in St. John's, Newfoundland, 1771-94 and 1804-8. (51/3)

EXETER CENTRAL LIBRARY,
Castle Street, Exeter

HUTCHINSON SKETCHES. Sketchbook. *c*. 1837-8.

Volume two of the sketchbooks of Peter Orlando Hutchinson (1810-97), Devon antiquary, contains sketches - apparently 1837-8 - of American scenes.

EXETER UNIVERSITY LIBRARY,
Prince of Wales Road, Exeter EX4 4PT

GALE/MORANT PAPERS.

'Jamaican estates of E. Morant Gale, 1798-1824'. Four manuscript boxes of papers belonging to two inter-related families with estates in Jamaica. The Gales and the Morants have some importance in the history of the island, and the papers are of particular interest for the light they cast on slavery and the life and work of Jamaican sugar estates. They include, however, other interesting items, e.g. letters about property in America during the War of Independence. (GM 5/1-56)

IRVING, WASHINGTON. Letter. 1830.

One letter, 1830, from Washington Irving to Richard Cattermole of the Royal Society of Literature. (D 5)

MARSHALL COLLECTION. Letter. 1885.

One letter, 9 Oct. 1885, from Eadweard Muybridge (1830-1904), the English-born photographer of motion, most of whose work was done in the U.S.A. (C4)

WEST DEVON RECORD OFFICE,
14 Tavistock Place, Plymouth

PLYMOUTH CITY RECORDS. Collected papers. 1606-1815, n.d.

(*a*) Copy of orders for the government of the colonies of Virginia (1606).[1](W360/89)
(*b*) Copy of letters patent by James I for planting two colonies 'on the coast of Virginia and America' to be called the First Colony and the Second Colony (April 1606).[2] (W360/57)
(*c*) Copy of petition of Captain Robert Robinson touching the needs and condition of Newfoundland, 1609. (W360/91)
(*d*) Letter from the Council of the Virginia Company to the Mayor and Aldermen of Plymouth, inviting them to assist the plantation, 17 Feb. 1609/10.[3] (W359/54)
(*e*) Order for free fishing in New England by the House of Commons, notwithstanding the patent of Sir F. Gorges and his associates, n.d. (W48 fo. 92)
(*f*) Obligations touching the venture of the *Judith* of Stonehouse to Newfoundland, n.d. (W50)
(*g*) Letter from John Lanyon on Newfoundland affairs, n.d. (W360/92)
(*h*) Undated petition of divers merchants trading in Newfoundland, to the Privy Council, n.d. (W360/93)
(*i*) Copy of additional orders for the correction of abuses in the Newfoundland fishing trade, n.d. (W360/59)
(*j*) Copy of letter from John Delbridge to the Mayor of Barnstaple about the Turkish pirates, asserting that 'they will fall upon our fishing shippes both at Newfoundland and Virginea', Feb. 1632/3.[4] (W360/31)
(*k*) Copy of letter of Council to the Mayor of Plymouth for exact observance of the orders for the government of Newfoundland, 4 Dec. 1633. (W360/73)

7. Transcript, H.M.C. Palk MSS. [74], pp. 101-2.
8. Transcript, ibid., p. 363.

1. R.N. Worth, *Calendar of the Plymouth Municipal Records* (Plymouth, 1893), p. 228.
2. Abstract, Worth, op. cit., p. 223. Also H.M.C. ix (i), p. 271 (uu).
3. Abstract, Worth, op. cit., p. 203. Also H.M.C. ix (i), p. 265 (ww).
4. Abstract, Worth, op. cit., p. 219.

(*l*) Copy of laws and ordinances for the government of Newfoundland, 24 Jan. 1633/4. (W360/67)
(*m*) Copies of orders of Council for the Newfoundland fishing trade, Feb. 1633/4. (W360/68-70)
(*n*) Letters patent for the government of Newfoundland, 10 Feb. 1633/4. (W8)
(*o*) Copy of letter patent by Charles I establishing a set of laws and ordinances for Newfoundland, 26 Jan. 1637/8. (W360/71)
(*p*) Letters patent for the remedy of abuses in the Newfoundland fisheries, and for the better government thereof, 27 Jan. 1665/6. (W18)
(*q*) Copy of petition of divers merchants, owners and masters of the towns of Plymouth, Dartmouth, and the Western Ports concerning the fishing trade of Newfoundland. (1665/6). (W19)
(*r*) Deposition taken at Totnes touching Newfoundland and the fisheries, 28 Aug. 1667. (W360/74)
(*s*) Copy of order of Council concerning the conditions and needs of Newfoundland, 15 Dec. 1669. (W360/76)
(*t*) Letter from Secretary of the Council of Trade to the Mayor of Plymouth, touching divers abuses in the trade of Newfoundland, 19 Feb. 1669/70. (W360/75)
(*u*) Recommendation of Committee of Trade and Plantations for the better regulation of the Newfoundland fisheries, Mar. 1670. (W360/82)
(*v*) Letter from William Cotton touching the circular letter from the Lords of the Committee of Trade asking for information concerning the state and needs of the Newfoundland fishing trade, 3 May 1670. (W360/81)
(*w*) Copy of order of Council for observation of orders for the fishing trade in Newfoundland, 10 Mar. 1670/1. (W360/79)
(*x*) Letter from Richard Hooper, Mayor of Barnstaple, to the Mayor of Plymouth regarding answers to the letter of the Committee of Trade and Plantations respecting the Newfoundland fishing trade, 1 Mar. 1674/5. (W360/85)
(*y*) Abstract of papers concerning the Newfoundland fishing trade, 6 Mar. 1674/5. (W360/86)
(*z*) Letter from J. Beckett to the Mayor of Plymouth, informing him, on behalf of Lord Sidmouth, that Mr. Seymour Larpent and Mr. Charles King have been appointed on behalf of the British and American governments to investigate the late unfortunate event at Dartmoor Prison concerning American prisoners, 18 Apr. 1815. Draft reply from town clerk that the prison is not within the borough's jurisdiction, 20 Apr. 1815. (W362/64, 65)[5]

ASTOR PAPERS. 1934-59.

Papers kept by Lord and Lady Astor at their Plymouth home on the Hoe. The collection is restricted.
(*a*) Correspondence concerning American War Relief Trust, 1941-59. (186/19/1)
(*b*) Correspondence concerning the American ambassador's visit, 1934. (186/20/3)
(*c*) Correspondence concerning the visit of the American fleet, 1934. (186/20/4)
(*d*) Correspondence concerning the American Hospitality Committee, 1954-6. (186/20/5)
(*e*) Correspondence concerning American Independence Week, 1943. (186/20/6)
(*f*) Correspondence concerning American wives living in Plymouth, 1949-51. (186/20/7)
(*g*) Correspondence concerning the Anglo-American Relief Fund and societies and nurseries concerned with the evacuation of children under five, 1941-5. (186/21/5)

DORSET

DORSET RECORD OFFICE, County Hall, Dorchester

DORCHESTER BOROUGH RECORDS, 4 documents. 1630-4.

(*a*) Records of Justices of the Peace. Depositions, 23 Nov. 1630, that Thomas Jarvis of Lyme said that 'all the projectors for New England busines are rebells, and that those that are gon over are idolaters, captivated and seperatists.' (B2/8/1)
(*b*) Enrolled indenture, 11 Mar. 1653, of Henry Hobbs to serve Mr. George Cole, now Mayor, as an apprentice for six years in New England. (B2/16/4)
(*c*) Indenture of apprentice William Parker, bound 9 Mar. 1663, to serve Maximilian Gollop, merchant of Dorchester, for nine years from 25 Mar. 1664 in New England. (B2/31/1)
(*d*) From Corporation Minutes, 2 Mar. 1664: 'The steward of the hospitall is desired to disburse unto Mr. Cole the summe of 3 li. for the transportation of John Barber and his family to New England.' (B2/16/15)

SOCIETY OF FRIENDS RECORDS. 1656-1821.

(*a*) 'Account of Ministering Friends from Europe who visited America' (1656-1821), and 'Ministering Friends who went from Pennsylvania and New Jersey to visit England and Ireland' (1693-1821). (N10/V7)
(*b*) Certificate on removal of William Master from Burlington, N.J., 1762, and four letters, 1764. (Certificate is signed by John Woolman, anti-slavery propagandist). (N10/F9)

LYME REGIS BOROUGH ARCHIVES. 1681-1739.

(*a*) Records of the Burridge family of Lyme Regis, merchants and shipping agents:
(i) Certificates regarding seamen on a voyage to Virginia taken into slavery in Algiers, 1681-2. (B7/A4/3)
(ii) Copies of accounts rendered, including many references to trade with America, 1703-31. (B7/N2)
(iii) Memo concerning ship *Friendship*, with cargo of tobacco from Virginia, 1714. (B7/F2)
(iv) '5th Voyage the Elizabeth Capt. John Brett from Potomack River Virginia Imported July 1739'. (B7/N5)
(*b*) Apprenticeship indentures, servants to American colonies, 1683-4, 1689. (B7/M9)

ILCHESTER COLLECTION. Map, deed. 1711, 1775.

Map, 1711, of Hilton Head, Granville County, Carolina (D124); and deed, 1775, of land in New York.

CUTLER-RACKETT-CAILLOUEL PAPERS. 46 letters, documents. 1717-61. (NU)

(*a*) Letters from Dr. John Cutler of Boston, mostly 1755-61, to his nephew and niece, Mr. and Mrs. Thomas Rackett, with some,

5. Abstract, ibid., p. 246. Also H.M.C. x (iv), p. 553 (q).

1744-56, to his sister Abigail Caillouel. Mainly personal, with occasional references to military and naval events during the Seven Years War, and to Indian raids.
(*b*) Two copies of wills of John Cutler of Boston, 1760.
(*c*) Copy of *Boston Gazette and Country Journal*, 24 Sept. 1759.

RYDER COLLECTION. Letter-books. 1746-55.

Letter-books of Henry Fox (War Office), 1746-55, containing occasional references to army establishment in America, transportation, etc. (D86/X3-7)

WELD OF LULWORTH PAPERS. 1760-1889. (D10)

Joseph Weld (1777-1863) of Lulworth Castle had large investments in the Maryland and New York Iron and Coal Co., and a relative, Henry Weld, was an officer at the company's Mount Savage ironworks.
(*a*) Letter from Edward Weld to his son Edward, mentioning that his chaplain (Catholic) is on his way to Philadelphia, 1760. (D10/C40)
(*b*) Letters to and papers of Joseph Weld, 1839-56, concerning Baltimore and Ohio Railroad Co., the Maryland and New York Iron and Coal Co., and the Mount Savage Ironworks, including two letters from his brother James and one from his nephew Henry. (D10/C194)
(*c*) Copy letters, 1846-64, from Henry T. Weld, J.M. Howe, Cary & Co. of New York, etc., to the London Committee of Management of the Mount Savage Ironworks, with annual statement, 1860, table of assets and liabilities to July 1863, and memo of arrangement to sell Mount Savage property, n.d. (D10/C200)
(*d*) Reference to Mount Savage railway in letter of 1851. (D10/C202)
(*e*) Letters, 1852-89, to Joseph, son of Joseph Weld, from Henry Weld, mainly at Mount Savage and Baltimore, with transfer certificate, 1863, for shares in Wenvoe Hematite Iron Ore Co., and statistics, 1842-67, of the Cumberland coal trade. (D10/C288)

These letters relate to the Mount Savage Ironworks, the Mount Savage Railroad, the coal trade, and money matters. On 15 July 1862, there is a reference to a 'Confederate irruption' which 'destroyed the railroad'. In September 1865 Henry Weld describes in detail 'A Month of Wandering in the N.W. of U. States of A'.

RECORDS RELATING TO NEWFOUNDLAND. 1761-1834.

(*a*) Papers of Lester and Garland families, merchants in the Newfoundland trade, including diaries of Benjamin Lester of Poole and Newfoundland, 1761-96; diaries of Isaac Lester of Poole, 1765-78; out-letter books of B. Lester, 1780-4, George Garland, 1794-1826, and G. and J.B. Garland, 1827-34.
(*b*) Letter-book of Messrs. Ledgard, Gosse, and Chancey of Poole, merchants in the Newfoundland trade, 1807-10.
In addition to these manuscripts, the Record Office contains records which include references to individuals apprenticed to Newfoundland in the eighteenth and nineteenth centuries. Also available are settlement examinations of persons who emigrated to Newfoundland.

WHITAKER FAMILY. Testamentary papers. 1771-3. (MN 1031)

Papers relating to legacies, etc. of various members of the Whitaker family, and of Archibald and Elizabeth Allen, all of Maryland.

DAMPIER PAPERS. 1785-6.

Case and opinion on trade debts between Thomas and John Dampier, mentioning John's stay in America, 1785-6. (D128A/L1)

ABBOTT COLLECTION. Correspondence, account books, etc. *c.* 1795-1832. (Part of the Colfox Collection, D43)

Andrew Abbott (1743-1819), London potter. His youngest brother, John, went to New Jersey, and a cousin, Joseph Master, settled in Philadelphia; both were Quakers. The correspondence includes four letters, 1812-6, to Andrew Abbott from Joseph Master, Philadelphia; five letters, 1812-7, to Andrew Abbott from his brother John; three letters, 1818-20, to Andrew's daughter Hannah from John Abbott; one letter, 1832, to Hannah Abbott Colfox from a cousin, William Master, in Philadelphia. These letters contain information on conditions of life in Philadelphia, shipments of china, business associates, etc.

An account book, 1795-6, for the late partnership of John Abbott and James Simpson of Philadelphia, contains references to shipments of merchandise, the dispatch of which Andrew appears to have attended to on his brother's behalf. It is followed by an account of cash taken and goods sold out of stock belonging to the late partnership, 1809.

Included with this collection is a typed manuscript by Mrs. E.M.C. Hulls, 'Some notes on Andrew Abbott and his family by his great granddaughter.'

COLFOX PAPERS. Letter. 1812.

Letter about the American war, from S. and B. Shaw to T.C. Colfox of Bridport, 1812. (D43/C3)

STURGE COLLECTION. Letters. 1814-25.

Copies of letters of John Eliot of Ashmore to other members of the Society of Friends on the Continent and in Philadelphia, Columbia (S.C.?), and Baltimore, 1814-25. (D364/E11-18)

HARRISON PAPERS. 2 letters. 1829, 1833. (D112/3)

New York, 1829 and 1833, from W.H. Harrison, concerning the death of his father Richard Harrison, the oldest member of the New York Bar.

MEATYARD, ROBERT. 2 letters.[1] 1836, 1838.

Written to his mother, Mrs. Mary Meatyard of Twyford, Dorset. The first, Alton, Ill., 22 Mar. 1836, gives an account of his journey to Alton, the price of land, wages of 'mechanics', etc. (NK1). The second, Prasau Creek, Ill., 29 Jan. 1838, is concerned with religious exhortation. (NK2)

WELD OF CHIDEOCK PAPERS. 1839-47.

Letters to Charles Weld from Henry Knight on American Coal and Iron Co., 1839, and from Humphrey Weld about Maryland Coal Loan, 1840. (D16/C21). Also a letter from J.F. Powell to R.S. Palmer, 1847, about the Maryland and New York Iron and Coal Co. (D16/C63)

PARISH RECORDS.

(*a*) Sutton Waldron. Brief received for 'Colleges in America', 1762. (P179/RE2)
(*b*) Corfe Castle. Entries Feb. and Apr. 1802 for relief of distressed American sailors, and entry Sept. 1804 for relief of 'a distressed American'. (P11/OV8)
(*c*) Longburton. 'Colleges of Philadelphia and New York...(for the support of) to be collected from house to house. Charge 12,060.' (P47/IN1)
(*d*) Marnhull. Reference to emigration of paupers, 1827. (P32/VE1)

1. Photostats in the collection of Letters of Emigrants to America in the British Library of Political and Economic Science, London School of Economics.

(*e*) Stalbridge. Reference to emigration of paupers, 1835, 1850. (P208/VE1)
(*f*) Wootton Glanville. Reference to possible emigration of paupers to America, 1845. (P7/OV6)

S. WINGFIELD DIGBY, ESQ., Sherborne Castle, Sherborne

DIGBY PAPERS. 5 letters. 1612, 1755.
(*a*) Four letters, 1612, from Sir J. Digby at Madrid to W. Trumbull, Sir D. Carleton (two), and Sir T. Edmondes, about Spanish displeasure over the English plantation in Virginia and reputed hostile designs against it.[1]
(*b*) 26 Aug. 1755, from John Calcraft to Lord Digby on General Braddock's defeat.[2]

DURHAM

BARCLAYS BANK LTD., Local Head Office, 27/31 High Row, Darlington DL3 7QS

BACKHOUSE COLLECTION. 1774-5.
(*a*) Copy of the will of John Backhouse, dated Philadelphia, March 1st, 1774.
(*b*) Letter from William Backhouse to John Barrow, dated New York, May 4th 1775. Backhouse discusses the interruptions to trade resulting from the unrest in the colonies, and comments on the beginning of violent resistance in New York.

DURHAM COUNTY LIBRARY-DARLINGTON BRANCH, Crowns Street, Darlington DL1 1ND

DARLINGTON SOCIETY OF FRIENDS. Letter. 1863.
Letter from East Mount, Darlington, concerning Quakers in America, 1863. (Unsigned and incomplete)

PEASE, JOHN. 8 letters. 1843-56.
Letters relating to his American journey (including one from Joseph Pease, and two from Friends in Philadelphia), 1843-56. 8 items.

PEASE, JOHN. Transcripts. 1843-7.
Transcripts of material on slavery acquired during a visit to America, 1843-7. 3 items.

DURHAM COUNTY RECORD OFFICE, County Hall, Durham DH1 5UL

MISCELLANEOUS RECORDS. 1842-1914, n.d.
(*a*) Lists of names and addresses of Friends in America, n.d. (D/Ho/F113)
(*b*) Journal of John Pease's religious journey in America, 1843-5. (D/Ho/F116)
(*c*) Letters to John Hodgkin with comments on the Civil War and its aftermath, 1861-71. (D/Ho/C31/83-151)
(*d*) Correspondence, plan and share certificates of the Island Mutual Development Company, Wading River, Long Island, 1913-4. (D/Ho/F68)
(*e*) Letter from Major Woodridge, Richmond, Virginia, *re.* mining affairs, 1842. (NCB I/JB/1663-5)

NATIONAL UNION OF MINEWORKERS (DURHAM AREA), P.O. Box No. 6, Red Hill, Durham

UNION RECORDS (printed).[1] 1877-99.
There are a few references to emigration in the nineteenth-century records of the Durham Miners' Association. A leaflet dated 26 July 1877 announcing the winding-up of a short-lived emigration agency is inserted in the *Minutes and Balance Sheets* volume for July-Dec. 1877. The minutes of the Association also include a report by William Crawford called 'In the Steerage', which is more concerned with conditions on the boat than with experiences in the States.

The Union's *Monthly Circular*, Sept. 1899, consists of an address to the members by John Wilson, M.P., on the subject of working conditions and inadequate union organization of miners in the Pittsburgh-Monongahela River areas of Pennsylvania, based on his recent visit there.

UNIVERSITY LIBRARY Palace Green, Durham DH1 3RN

JOHNSTON, J.F.W. Journal. 1839, 1850-1.
Autograph journal of James Finlay Weir Johnston for 1839 and 1850-1, the latter part concerned chiefly with a visit to North America.
(Johnston was the author of *Report on the agricultural capabilities of the province of New Brunswick* (1850), and *Notes on North America, agricultural, economical, and social* (1851, in two volumes.)

DEPARTMENT OF PALAEOGRAPHY AND DIPLOMATIC, UNIVERSITY OF DURHAM, South Road, Durham

BACKHOUSE PAPERS.[1] Letters, testimonial and poem. 1785-1838.
(*a*) Item 65. Letter, 21 Oct. 1785, from Gustus Nassa and other Negroes to the London 'Meeting for Sufferings' of the Society of Friends, being an address of thanks after reading a book describing the Friends' opposition to slavery and their efforts to abolish it.

1. Transcripts, H.M.C. x (i), pp. 576, 583, 600, and 608.
2. Transcript, H.M.C. viii (i), p. 226.

1. Some of this material was used by Charlotte Erickson, *American Industry and the European Immigrant, 1860-1885* (London and Cambridge, Mass., 1957).

1. Published *List of Backhouse Papers* (1973) may be purchased from the Department of Palaeography and Diplomatic, University of Durham.

Item 272. Copies of two letters, 19 and 27 Sept., n.y., writer and addressee not stated, concerning the condition of slaves in Maryland and the writer's hope that the Friends will work for total abolition of slavery.

(*b*) Item 141. Epistle, 15-17 June 1818, from Yearly Meeting of Women Friends, Rhode Island, to same in London.

(*c*) Items 177-178, 181, 183, 185-187, 190-192, 195, 197, 268-269. Fourteen letters, 1830-[1835], to and from Jonathan Backhouse and his wife, Hannah Chapman Backhouse, during their mission to America on behalf of the Society of Friends and in particular while they were visiting New York, Philadelphia, Rhode Island, Indiana and Salem. Correspondents and recipients of letters include: the children of Jonathan and Hannah Backhouse; Hannah Backhouse's parents, Joseph and Jane Gurney; Jonathan Backhouse's brother, Edward; H[udson] Gurney; J[oseph] Pease; and John Cox. The letters deal mainly with the progress of the Friends' work in America and with family and personal news but they also contain occasional comment on English and European political matters.

(*d*) Item 179. Letter, New York, 29 Oct. 1830, from Martha Hawkhurst to William Hartshorn, criticizing the epistle from the London Yearly Meeting breaking off communication with some American Friends, who are accused of being influenced by 'anti-Christian doctrines'; quotes George Fox and William Penn, and is indignant at the suggestion that Elias Hicks denies Christ.

(*e*) Item 198. Letter, Westhill-in-Baltimore, 3 Nov. 1835, from I.R.S. (?) to Hannah Backhouse, describing Yearly Meeting at Baltimore, the decision to send a certificate of thanks for religious work to Jonathan and Hannah Backhouse, and domestic details about Friends.

(*f*) Item 199. Testimonial, 27 Jan. 1836, formally addressed to Monthly Meeting of Friends at Darlington and Quarterly Meeting at Durham from Monthly Meeting, Philadelphia of work of Jonathan and Hannah Chapman Backhouse as approved ministers. Signed by Chas. Yarnall and Abigail Nicholson, clerks, and sixty-two members of the meeting. Sent to Jonathan Backhouse at Darlington.

(*g*) Item 106. Printed *Copy of a letter addressed by Joseph John Gurney to the grandchildren of his beloved aunt, Jane Gurney*, 25 Dec. 1838. Among other matters this concerns Quaker doctrines and the writer's impressions of America, which he regards 'a noble country' apart from the 'blots' on the American 'escutcheon' of 'Hicksism' and 'slavery'.

(*h*) Item 300. Copy of a poem, 'An Elegy on a Young Lady', written in America by W.A., n.d.

THE EARL GREY PAPERS.[2] Late 18th century-1917.

(*a*) Charles Grey, 1st Earl Grey (1729-1807), general. His papers, now fully catalogued, include copies of some dispatches and letters to and from Sir Guy Carleton and a few other items concerning the War of Independence. Also material concerning American ships seized in the West Indies, 1794.

(*b*) Charles Grey, 2nd Earl Grey (1764-1845), statesman. His correspondence, while Foreign Secretary, 1806-7, includes five letters from the American Minister in London, James Monroe. Also a file (26 items, mainly 1806-7) 'Papers on the United States'.

(*c*) Henry George Grey, Viscount Howick, and afterwards 3rd Earl Grey (1802-94). Papers include three letters from Abbott Lawrence, United States Minister in London, to Grey, 1850.

(*d*) General Charles Grey (1804-70). Two journals covering two visits to the United States, one of these on an official delegacy in connexion with frontier disturbances along the St. Lawrence ('1838. 1st voyage to Canada'), and the other a pleasure trip ('Canada. June 1839. Trip to the United States'). The first contains comment on the excellence of travel facilities in the United States, a report on Grey's interview with President Van Buren, impressions of Washington, D.C. The second is a description of roads, scenery, and city sightseeing through Vermont to Boston, New York, Philadelphia, Baltimore, and Washington.[3]

(*e*) Albert Henry George Grey, 4th Earl Grey (1851-1917). His correspondence while Governor-General of Canada, 1904-1911, includes a great many letters concerning Canadian-American relations. Among the available material (mainly photostats)[4] may be mentioned one box (all photostats), which includes over 200 letters, 1906-8, between Grey and the British Ambassadors in Washington - Sir Mortimer Durand and James Bryce - Theodore Roosevelt, Elihu Root, and others, about the Newfoundland fisheries dispute, Bering Sea fisheries, etc.; and another box (all photostats), containing more than a hundred letters, 1908-10, between Grey and Bryce on the fisheries problems, the boundary waters treaty, possible tariff changes, etc. His papers, still under arrangement, include other American correspondence and business papers.

(*f*) A large collection of pamphlets among the Earl Grey Papers includes items of American interest.

THE LIBRARY, USHAW COLLEGE, Durham

LISBON COLLECTION. 2 letters. 1737.

Two letters from C. Carroll of Annapolis, Maryland, 16 April and 13 August 1737, to Rev. E. Jones, rector of the English College at Lisbon, concerning financial support for his son, the latter through the care of Captain Hughes.

WISEMAN, NICHOLAS (1802-65). Correspondence: 3 letters.[1] 1827, 1837.

Letters from correspondents in the United States to Wiseman while vice-rector and rector of the English College at Rome:

Kenrick, Peter Richard. Philadelphia, 30 July 1837, on particulars of American editions of Wiseman's works, noting that these have revived Kenrick's desire to have Hebrew, at least, taught in American seminaries.

Larkin, John. Baltimore, 12 Feb. 1827, dealing with the study of Hebrew at St. Mary's Seminary, Baltimore; the state and prospects of the Catholic Church and its priesthood in America; the attitude towards the Catholic Church of Protestant bishops and the press; etc. (11 pages).

Maréchal, Ambrose, Archbishop of Baltimore. Baltimore, n.d. but received by Wiseman on 15 Nov. 1827, on the neglect of Oriental studies among Catholics and the pursuit of such studies at the Baltimore seminary.

2. These papers are in the joint custody of the Dean and Chapter of Durham and the University. Published lists of some of these papers may be purchased from the Department of Palaeography and Diplomatic.

3. See W. Ormsby's edition of these journals included in his *Crisis in the Canadas 1838-9* (Toronto, 1964).

4. The originals are held in the Public Archives of Canada, Ottawa.

1. Printed with introduction and notes by John Tracy Ellis, 'Three American Letters from the Wiseman Papers', *Catholic Historical Review*, vol. xliii, pp. 458-72, 1958.

ESSEX

ESSEX RECORD OFFICE,[1]
County Hall, Chelmsford CM1 1LX

ROUND PAPERS. Letters, business and miscellaneous papers. 1585-1776. (*Letters unless otherwise stated.*)

(*a*) Document entitled 'For Mr. Rauleys viage', *c.* 1585. Apparently written by an experienced soldier giving advice to those undertaking Sir Walter Ralegh's project to colonize Virginia.[2] (D/DRh Z1)

(*b*) Thomas Stebbing & Son. Business records. 1743-57. Eighteenth-century linen drapers of Cornhill, London.

(i) Six letters, 1743-4, from Thomas Summersett, master of a packet going to Carolina, to the owners, concerning a voyage to Antigua and South Carolina, with accounts, manifests, and bills of lading. (D/DRc B24)

(ii) Sixteen letters, 1746-65, mostly to Robert Stebbing from John Guerard, of Charleston, S.C., concerning the dry goods trade, with three accounts and three bills of exchange. (D/DRc B26)

(iii) Bills of exchange, 1748-51, drawn in Maryland on London merchants. (D/DRc B27)

(iv) Five letters, 1750-7, from Charles & Alex Stedman, merchants of Philadelphia, concerning the dry goods trade, with six bills of exchange. (D/DRc B29)

(*c*) Perth Amboy, N.J., 14 Nov. 1748, from Governor Belcher of New Jersey to an unknown correspondent, describes the founding of Princeton, and gives a description of the crops raised in New Jersey.[3] (D/DRg 4/65)

(*d*) 5 Apr. 1757, from Thomas Falconer to Charles Gray, mentions that 'Lord Loudon is gone upon an expedition of some consequence, either against Ticonderago or some other fort which opens the way to Crown Point'.[4] (D/DRg 4/5)

(*e*) 30 Nov. 1765, from Falconer to Gray, on the unsatisfactory state of the American colonies. Three further letters, 18 Mar. and 19 Apr. 1766, and 25 May 1767, on American affairs.[5] (D/DRg 4/9-11, 4/17)

(*f*) 10 Feb. 1770, from Falconer to Gray, 'discusses arguments of the Bostonians and their friends', etc.[6] (D/DRg 4/24)

(*g*) 15 Nov. 1775, from Falconer to Gray, says, 'The examination of Pen was of little consequence, but it proves that the Pennsylvanians reject their charter whenever they like and admit it where it is advantagious.' Says 'the sword must decide' the dispute. The Irish may help the Americans. Fears engendered by the Quebec Act. The Glasgow trade will suffer during the suspension of Virginian commerce.[7] (D/DRg 4/31)

(*h*) 13 Apr. 1776, from Falconer to Gray, considers that the root of the rebellion lies in the expulsion of the French from Quebec.[8] (D/DRg 4/32)

ABDY PAPERS. Will. 1642.

Will of Nicholas Abdy, London merchant, includes a bequest of £120 for twenty boys and girls, taken vagrant in the streets of London, to be conveyed to Virginia, New England, or the West Indies. (D/DAy F4)

AUDLEY END PAPERS. Letters and documents. 1673-1779.

(*a*) Eight documents, 1673-1749, chiefly relating to New York, including warrants for delivery and reception of gunpowder there, 1673.[9] Letter, 1675, from the Governor, Sir Edmund Andros, concerning revenue. Petition, *c.* 1680, of the collector of customs for discharge from debt. Copy, *c.* 1725, of a 1711 Act of affirmation for those who cannot take an oath. Letter, 1736, to a Henry Grey on the purchase of land in New York colony, and factories there (11 pages). Report, 1749, on the state of affairs in New York by Governor Clinton, and copies of his letters on finance and Indians. (D/DBy O26-32)

(*b*) Three letters, two in 1700[10] and one in 1702, from William Penn to Lord Grey, Governor of Barbados, congratulating him on his administration. (D/DBy O25)

(*c*) 15 Feb. 1749, from Corbyn Morris to the Earl of Halifax, on the balance of trade with the North American colonies, and on the suppression of their paper currency (7 pages). (D/DBy O53)

(*d*) 12 Apr. 1779, from Rockingham to Sir John Griffin Griffin, stating that many Americans are in favour of returning to their allegiance.[11] (D/DBy C9/28)

GREENWOOD, ROBERT (died *c.* 1814). Commonplace book. *c.* 1710-93. (D/DQ 24)

Quaker of Chelmsford. His commonplace book includes:

(*a*) 'A speech delivered by an Indian Chief in reply to a sermon preach'd...to convert the Indians to the Christian Religion', *c.* 1710.

(*b*) 'Some expressions dropt in Testimony by Willm. Hunt from America about the year 1774'.

(*c*) 'Some remarkable Circumstances attending the pillaging the House of David Sands at North America', *c.* 1780.

(*d*) 'Copy of a Letter of Job Scotts to his Relations in America', 1793.

(*e*) Account of a visit of Indians to Philadelphia, n.d.

SPERLING PAPERS. Ledger, 1719-58; letter, 1795.

Business records of Henry and John Sperling, furriers of London.

(*a*) Numerous ledger entries relate to the Sperlings' dealings with American trappers, and trade with the colonies, under such headings as 'Cargoes to Maryland', 'Voyage to New England', etc. (D/DQ1)

(*b*) 13 July 1795, from W. Jackson of Pennsylvania, commenting on American exports for 1791-5. (D/DSe 5)

KNIGHT PAPERS. Estate and investment accounts. 1720-6. (D/DU 502/1)

Accounts of John Knight of Gosfield Hall include investment of £100 in linen for Carolina, Aug. 1723.

HILL HALL PAPERS. Letter of Privy Seal. 1725. (D/DSh F16/2)

Grant to Sir Chaloner Ogle of proceeds of prizes, with special payment to mariner for overcoming pirates while *en route* to New York in brigantine *Prudence Hannah* of Boston.

1. F.G. Emmison, ed., *Guide to the Essex Record Office,* part ii (Chelmsford, 1948).
2. Printed in A.C. Edwards, ed., *English History from Essex Sources, 1550-1750* (Chelmsford, 1952), pp. 178-9. (This volume includes colonial documents to 1783.)
3. Transcript, H.M.C. xiv (ix), pp. 292-3.
4. Transcript, ibid., p. 295.
5. Extracts, ibid., pp. 297-9, 300-1.
6. Extract, ibid., p. 304.
7. Extract, ibid., pp. 307-8.
8. Extract, ibid., p. 308.
9. Printed in Edwards, op. cit., p. 181.
10. One of these printed in ibid., p. 181.
11. Printed in ibid., p. 200.

DISNEY PAPERS. 3 documents. 1725-1804.

(*a*) Declaration of trust, 1725, from Harvard College to Thomas Hollis of sum of £3,670. 13*s*. 0½*d*. for the salary and support of a Professor of Divinity, which chair Hollis had founded, and for the support of poor scholars. Further declaration, 1730, for the same sum and for a further sum of £1,170 which Hollis had given to found a professorship of Mathematics and Natural and Experimental Philosophy. (D/DDs F8)
(*b*) Probate of will and codicils, 1804, of Thomas Brand Hollis, which includes a bequest to 'the college instituted for the promoting of learning in New England'. (D/DDs F9)

TOWER PAPERS. Letters, documents, etc. (photostats).[12] 1732-8.

Papers of Thomas Tower (d. 1778), a trustee for Georgia in the colony's early days, include:
(*a*) Notes (incomplete) on a palaver with the Indians, n.d. (D/DTw 08/5)
(*b*) Draft charter for Georgia, n.d. (before 1732). (D/DTw 08/1)
(*c*) Copies of a memorial, 1 Dec. 1727, on the importance of a fort on the River Alatamaha, Ga. (D/DTw 08/5)
(*d*) Account, 1732, of a voyage on the *Anne* with James Oglethorpe and settlers for Georgia aboard.[13] (D/DTw 08/2)
(*e*) Letters, both 1738, from Oglethorpe to Sir Robert Walpole[14] and Tower about Georgia. (D/DTw 08/3,6)
(*f*) Oglethorpe's personal account, 1738, of the mutiny at St. Andrew's Fort, Georgia.[15] (D/DTw 08/7)
(*g*) Copy of petition, 1742, from the people of Georgia. (D/DTw 08/4)

PETRE PAPERS. 1733-4, 1854-5.

(*a*) Letters from Darnell family, Maryland, to Catherine, Lady Stourton (widow of 7th Lord Petre), regarding an estate in which she had an interest. 1733-4. (D/DP T329)
(*b*) Journals (2 vols.), 1854-5, of Henry William Clifford; places visited include New York, Montreal, Quebec, Niagara, Detroit, Chicago, Boston, Pittsburgh, Washington, New Orleans, and Havana; comments on slavery. (D/DP Z87)

DU CANE PAPERS. Ledgers. 1734-9. (D/DDc A10-11)

Business ledgers of Peter du Cane of London include accounts of goods shipped to Jacob and John Wendell, Boston.

MILDMAY PAPERS. 2 documents.[16] 1734, *c*. 1750. (D/DM 01/41)

(*a*) Memorial on constitutional development in the American colonies laid before the House of Lords, 1734.
(*b*) Memorandum, *c*. 1750, by William Shirley, Governor of Massachusetts 1741-56, on the economic and strategic value to Britain of the American colonies.

WITHAM MONTHLY MEETING OF THE SOCIETY OF FRIENDS. Certificate.[17] 1751. (D/NF 1/2/13)

Certificate, 19 Aug. 1751, from the East Pennsylvania Monthly Meeting of Friends to the Chelmsford Meeting, certifying the good character of Thomas Wyett, about to journey to England.

RUSSELL PAPERS. 1759-74, 1849-51.

(*a*) Business papers[18] of William and Samuel Braund, merchants of London. William Braund (1695-1774) was a director of the East India Company and of the Sun Fire Office, and a Lloyds underwriter. The journals, arranged under names of merchants with an index in the second volume, record premiums paid, in some cases for insurance on voyages to the North American colonies. 1759-74. (D/DRu B7, 8)
(*b*) Summaries of letters, 1849-51, from Champion Russell; references to Lake Huron, New Orleans, Florida, and Nova Scotia. (D/DRu C4/1,2)

SLAVERY RELEASE. 2 documents.[19] 1760-1. (D/DHt A5)

Document, 9 July 1760, signed by Cornelis C. Wynkoop of New York, providing for the liberation of his slave, Fortin Vrelinghuyson, should the latter go on a cruise on board of H.M. ships then fitting out. Also a certificate, 5 June 1761, by the captain of one of these vessels that this has been done.

RIGBY PAPERS. 1772-82.

Papers relating to the clearing of the public accounts of Richard Rigby, Paymaster-General to H.M. Forces 1768-82. One document is 'a certificate of sums issued to Daniel Wier, Commissary General in North America and to his deputies and assistants' there, 1772-82. Total of £2,071,904. 6*s*. 6*d*. was issued. Includes entries for forage and other supplies to forces fighting in various parts of the colonies during the War of Independence. (D/DHw 048)

TABOR PAPERS. Copies, *c*. 1815, of family correspondence, 1773-88. (D/DU 617)

Letters, 1773-88, from Samuel Tabor of Rotterdam to Rev. William Gordon, including discussion, 1782-3, of the comparison of Dutch and American constitutions in Gordon's proposed *History*. (pp. 23-6, 41-6, 56-61, 78-80)

SMYTH PAPERS. 3 letters. 1781, 1785. (D/DFg Z1)

Correspondence of Sir Robert Smyth (1744-1802), M.P. for Colchester 1780-90, includes:
(*a*) Comments on the Franco-American alliance, Jan. 1781, by Dr. Nathaniel Forster, rector of All Saints, Colchester, and Rev. Charles Onley of Stisted Hall, Essex.
(*b*) Letter, 1785, from John Frederick Sackville, 3rd Duke of Dorset, Ambassador to Paris 1783-9, referring to Adams and Franklin in Paris being 'damned angry' at the British bill to restrain American trade to Newfoundland.

EVANS AND HARVEY-GEORGE FAMILIES' PAPERS. 6 letters and documents. 1793-1808. (D/DU 126/167-72)

Letters and documents from or about John Jee, Jr., who went to the United States in 1793 to escape his creditors in England and apparently died there *c*. 1808. He settled first in Charleston, S.C., and in a letter, 7 Oct. 1794, to his father, describes the unhealthiness of the Charleston climate, the high mortality there, and his intention of going to New York. Thereafter he vanishes and the letters and documents relate to the administration of his estate.

SANFORD AND HUGHES FAMILIES' PAPERS. Letter, journal. 1794, 1796.

(*a*) 1 Sept. 1794, from R.T. Hughes at Pittsgrove, Salem, N.J. to

12. Originals sold to Thomas Gilcrease Institute of American History and Art, P.O. Box 2419, Tulsa, Okla.
13. Extracts printed in Edwards, op. cit., p. 182.
14. Printed in ibid., p. 183.
15. Printed in ibid., pp. 183-4.
16. Printed in ibid., pp. 189-95.
17. See photograph in F.G. Emmison, ed., *Guide to the Essex Record Office*, pt. ii (Chelmsford, 1948), p. 102.
18. See L.S. Sutherland, *A London Merchant, 1695-1774* (London, 1933) which is based on these papers.
19. Printed in *Essex Review*, vol. xlv, pp. 120-1, 1936.

Sheppard Sandford, grocer, South Halstead, Essex. Gives interesting details of fruits grown, price of land, method of farming and quality of soil, timber, shortage of labour because 'every man thinks himself independent'; comments on slave trade, and European war, news of other emigrants, including Mr. Choat from Coggeshall. (D/DU 371/12)

(*b*) Journal, 31 May-9 July 1796 [? kept by R.T. Hughes], of a voyage from America to England. Includes observations on the choice between a French guillotine and an English press-gang and on the writer's reading matter. At end: 'A coppy of a letter to a friend on the present political and agricultural state of America' with a pencilled note, 'Supposed the Revd. Jas. Bass'. (D/DU 371/13)

MAITLAND PAPERS.[20] Will. 1802. (D/DMe F1/5)

Copy of will and codicil of John Shoolbred, an eighteenth-century London merchant, whose son, James, owned a plantation and Negroes in Virginia. The will shows that these Negroes were mortgaged to John as a security for James's debts, and a bond for their value was deposited with Mr. Moodie, British Consul at Charleston, S.C.

WALLACE PAPERS. 1817, 1820. (D/DU 559/22)

Powers of attorney and correspondence (3 papers) relating to the confiscation of the *Rebecca* of Charleston, S.C., by the Vice-Admiralty Court of Sierra Leone.

LLOYD PAPERS. Letter. 1842. (D/DGu C7/4)

Letter (incomplete) from Richard Lloyd, describing visit to Canada and the U.S., 1842.

COPLAND PAPERS. Solicitors' papers. 1859. (D/DDw B4/17)

Power of attorney from Ewen Stabb, merchant and executor of Thomas Snow, shipowner, both of St. John's, Newfoundland, relating to the *Mary of Maldon*.

BULLOCK PAPERS. Letters. 1861-1915. (D/DVv 74)

Letters from Henry Bullock relating to his Georgia plantation, with comments on U.S. politics.

BENSUSAN PAPERS. Letter. 1916. (D/DQ 37/48)

Letter, 3 Dec. 1916, from Frances, Countess of Warwick, to S.L. Bensusan, regarding her proposed articles on 'Why I prefer America'.

PARISH RECORDS.

(*a*) Earls Colne. Document,[21] 14 May 1711, giving the consent of the Colchester Workhouse Corporation to a gardener taking his apprentice to New England. (D/P 209/14/1)

(*b*) Steeple Bumpstead. Overseers' miscellaneous papers, 1811-57. Memorandum of an agreement, 26 Apr. 1832, between the parishioners and certain pauper families that the parish will pay for their emigration to America; and a resolution, 15 May, to borrow £100 for that purpose. (D/P 21/18/5)

(*c*) Writtle. Overseers' accounts include an item for 1631. 'Layd out for parrill [apparel] for two boyes that ware sent to Virgeny', £4. 7*s*. 3*d*.[22] (D/P 50/12/1)

There is more such emigration material, including emigration circulars and poor law union accounts, in other parish records in the Record Office.[23]

QUARTER SESSIONS RECORDS.

Agreement, 1741, by two London merchants to transport certain felons to the colonies and plantations in America and to procure certificates of landing from the governors or chief customs house officers there.[24] (Z/SBb 156/16)

ANDREW CHATTO, ESQ.,
White Barn House, Elmstead, Colchester

MISCELLANEOUS LETTERS. 1870's-1896.

A grandson of the founder of the publishing house of Chatto & Windus, Mr. Chatto owns the following correspondence:

(*a*) A collection of letters from Moncure Daniel Conway and others to John Camden Hotten in connection with the proposed English publication of the uncollected essays of Ralph Waldo Emerson in the early 1870's.[1]

(*b*) Five letters from S.L. Clemens ('Mark Twain') and members of his family in Nov. 1896 to Andrew Chatto, Jr. (son of the publisher) concerning the purchase of bicycles for Clara and Jean Clemens.[2]

GLOUCESTERSHIRE

GLOUCESTERSHIRE COUNTY LIBRARIES,
Divisional Library, Brunswick Road, Gloucester GL1 1HT

SMYTH OF NIBLEY PAPERS. (16524)

John Smyth (1567-1641), antiquarian, steward, and chronicler to the Berkeley family. 'He was chief adventurer in the establishment of a settlement in Virginia and had a good deal to say at meetings of the Virginia Company.'[1] Although the Library contains a collection of nearly 2,000 of his papers, bound in sixteen volumes and described in the published catalogue to the Gloucestershire collection,[2] the papers relating to Virginia were sold separately to the New York Public Library (see their *Bulletin*, vol. i, pp. 186-90, 1897). However, some references to matters relative to Virginia have been found in the volumes of the Gloucestershire collection, mainly in the form of correspondence.

20. See also Fluyder Maitland & Co. business papers (p. 102).
21. See *Essex Parish Records, 1240-1894*, prepared by E.J. Erith, plate ix (Chelmsford, 1950).
22. Printed in Edwards, op. cit., p. 179.
23. See M.D. Wainwright, 'Agencies for the promotion or facilitation of emigration from England to the U.S.A., 1815-61', M.A. thesis, University of London, 1951.
24. Printed in Edwards, op. cit., p. 185.

1. This project is fully described in Dennis Welland, 'John Camden Hotten and Emerson's Uncollected Essays', *The Yearbook of English Studies*, pp. 156-75, 1976, with extensive quotations from the letters.
2. A brief account of this correspondence will be found in Dennis Welland, *Mark Twain and England* (Chatto & Windus, forthcoming).

1. *Commons Debates, 1621*, ed. by Wallace Notestein, Frances Helen Relf, and Hartley Simpson, vol. i (New Haven, Conn., and London, 1935), p. 74 (Yale Historical Publications. MSS. and edited texts, 15).
2. Roland Austin, comp., *Catalogue of the Gloucestershire Collection: Books, Pamphlets and Documents in the Gloucester Public Library Relating to the County, Cities, Towns and Villages of Gloucestershire* (Gloucester, 1928).

WHITEFIELD, GEORGE (1714-70).
Pamphlets. (13918-14073)

George Whitefield, the Methodist preacher and evangelist, was born in Gloucester. The Library has an extensive collection of contemporary printed material by, for, or against Whitefield, several concerning his evangelizing tours of Georgia, Pennsylvania, and New England.

PARISH RECORDS.

Dursley. Copies of printed notices of meeting to be held in Dursley, 28 Mar. 1839, to consent to raising money for emigration purposes. (RF 115. 50 (4-9))

GLOUCESTERSHIRE RECORDS OFFICE,[1] Shire Hall, Gloucester GL1 2TG

GLOUCESTER CORPORATION RECORDS. 1643-59.

(*a*) Two registers of recognizances, 1643-52. Apparently from Bristol Corporation records; not known as yet how they came to be among Gloucester Corporation records. The majority of the bonds relate to ships' cargoes, and give details of ships, tonnage, and shipping routes from Bristol and Ireland to Virginia, Barbados and St. Christopher, Newfoundland, and New England. Both volumes have a personal names index. (GBR 1456/1576; GBR 1457/1577)
(*b*) 'A Booke for Entering of Letters Sent from the Lords of the Councell and Lord Lieutenant, Beginning Anno Domini 1639.' Letter,[2] 27 Mar. 1655, from Henry Lawrence, President of the Council, to the Mayor and Justices of the Peace of Gloucester, on the prohibition of tobacco planting in England in order to benefit Virginia.
(*c*) Apprenticeship register, 1645-59. Apprenticeship bonds of men and women contracting to serve as indentured labour in Barbados and Virginia, 1659-60. (GBR 1458A/1583, pp. 371-8)

GLOUCESTERSHIRE AND WILTSHIRE QUARTERLY MEETING OF THE SOCIETY OF FRIENDS. Records. 1670-1866.

As in all Quaker records, these contain numerous references in the minutes to the affairs of the Friends in America, particularly in Pennsylvania, to the travels of preachers in America and from America, and records of Gloucestershire Quakers who emigrated. The material thus appears to be of the same general character as that of other Meetings elsewhere; it was not examined in detail. (D 1340)

HICKS-BEACH MANUSCRIPTS. Papers. 1869-1939.

Papers of Sir Michael Edward Hicks-Beach, later 1st Earl St. Aldwyn (1837-1916), statesman; and his family. The scattered American material amid a very large collection is:
(*a*) Letters, 1869-70, from Sir Michael while in the United States and Latin America: three to his mother and one to K. Hardy; also a letter of introduction. (2731)
(*b*) Journals, etc., 1869-70, of Sir Michael of a trip to Canada and the United States. (2871)
(*c*) Two printed copies of a lecture on America delivered by Sir Michael on 24 Oct. 1870; also some manuscript notes; and an advertisement of Virginia lands for sale. (3095)
(*d*) Memoranda, 1890's, dealing with, among other matters, the McKinley Tariff and reciprocity between the U.S., Brazil, and Cuba. (21)
(*e*) Correspondence, including some concerning U.S. interests in China, 1896-9. (448)
(*f*) Correspondence with and concerning the American delegation on bimetallism, 1897. (456)
(*g*) Journal, 1905, of a journey by Sir Michael which included America. (2800)
(*h*) Letters, 1934-9, from the 2nd Earl St. Aldwyn to his grandmother, including some from the United States. (2854)

MISCELLANEOUS PAPERS. 1674-*c*. 1890.

(*a*) Correspondence of William Blathwayt as Secretary of Plantations, relating to New Hampshire, Maryland, Virginia, Pennsylvania, New Jersey, and New York, 1674-1705. (D1799/X5)
(*b*) Request to king for governorship of Carolina, *c*. 1725. (D1022/5)
(*c*) Papers relating to Edward Codrington's contract for victualling forces in West Florida, 1764-1812. (D1610/F7-9)
(*d*) Correspondence concerning events in America, 1771-93. (D1571/F654)
(*e*) Correspondence of John Lloyd of South Carolina, 1781-1805. (D1628)
(*f*) Descriptions of Charleston, S.C., by a settler, 1783, 1804. (D303/C1/8,51)
(*g*) Printed credentials, *c*. 1784, of Mrs. Ann Stanley, 'daughter to Wm. Stanley, a very learned and eminent physician in Hampshire'. She, being deaf and dumb, returned to England after her father's death in Philadelphia and claimed to be expert in healing all ailments. (Q/SR)
(*h*) Description of tour including visit to George Washington, 1791-3. (161o/C22)
(*i*) Correspondence and papers, *c*. 1792-1818, of the Rolph family, including Dr. Thomas Rolph, who emigrated to Canada in 1809, and letters from his son John, afterwards Canadian politician and a leader of the 1837 rebellion. (D. 1606)
(*j*) Letter, 1809, from J. Andrews of Albany, N.Y., a recent emigrant from Cheltenham, describing conditions in New York State. (D. 1815)
(*k*) Specification for cloth shearing machine by New York inventor, 1815. (D1347, Acc. 1603)
(*l*) Entries in Uley Baptist Church roll, 1821-61, referring to emigration to America. (D2626 1/1)
(*m*) Advertisement, prospectus, and poster of lands in Upper Canada with detailed map. Covering letter from Canada Company written on back, 1830. (D. 1359)
(*n*) Slimbridge: resolution to borrow money for assisting emigration to North America, 1832. (P298 VE 2/2)
(*o*) Among the Mullings and Ellett Papers (solicitors) is a printed notice of the New York Emigrant Society, on which is written the name of their English agent in Liverpool, Robinson & Bros., merchants; there is also a letter, 1833, written on the back from J. Pilmere of New York to L. Randall of Chedworth, Glos., demanding the sum of £17 apparently belonging to the Emigrant Society. (D. 1388)
(*p*) Papers of J.B.R. Estcourt as member of Commission surveying Canada-U.S.A. boundary, 1834-48, including references to North American life. (D1571/F468-479)
(*q*) Letter, 1835, from William Frederick Hill Rooke to his parents, describing life in America. (D1833/F4/16)

1. *Gloucester Quarter Sessions Archives, 1660-1889, and other Official Records; a Descriptive Catalogue* (Gloucester, 1958).
2. Transcript, H.M.C. xii (ix), p. 510.

(*r*) Letters, 1851-69, from Thomas Phipps in New York and Illinois. (D. 1659)
(*s*) Thirteen letters, 1884-5, from Joseph Biscoe in Florida. (D6/F76)
(*t*) Description of seances at Boston, Mass., *c*. 1890. (D2794/28)

PARISH RECORDS.

(*a*) Chedworth. Receipt and Payment Book of the Overseers, 1836-48. Includes payments for emigration to America. (P77/OVI/5)
(*b*) Dursley. Miscellaneous correspondence of the churchwardens with Somerset House regarding ten applicants for poor-rate assistance for emigration, 1840. (P124a/CW4/4)
(*c*) Frampton. Overseers' Accounts Book, 1687-1788. Entry for 1712: 'paid the widow Ffox when she was goeing to New Yorke, £3'. (P149/OV2/1)

QUARTER SESSIONS RECORDS.

Treasurer's Book, 1726-73, gives disbursements for transportation together with individual bonds of transportation to 'His Majesty's colonyes and plantations in America'. Some sixty documents are included, giving names of convicts, offences, and sentences. Also list of convicts transported, 1750-5. (Q/CBL)

HAMPSHIRE

SOUTHAMPTON CITY RECORD OFFICE, Civic Centre, Southampton SO9 4XL

CORPORATION 3RD REMEMBRANCE BOOK. 1514-1602. (SC2/1/5)

Three short references to the Newfoundland fishing trade in 1549, 1560, and 1589.

CORPORATION ASSEMBLY BOOKS AND JOURNALS. 1602-1835. (SC2/1/6-14)

Occasional references, mainly to trade with North America and Newfoundland fisheries, but including reception of four (named) Iroquois chiefs in 1710, a resolution in 1754 relieving American trade from petty customs, a Loyal Address in October 1775 on the subject of the American rising, and a subscription to relieve distressed soldiers in December 1775.

CORPORATION MINUTE BOOKS. 1835 - present day. (SC2/1/15-)

Occasional references to proposals to encourage American trade, and to visiting U.S. warships (first one in December 1848).

CORPORATION COMMITTEE MINUTE BOOKS. (SC2/3/)

A committee on the Great Exhibition of 1851 proposed the free unloading of American exhibits to encourage the American trade of the port. From 1874 to 1924 the Commerce of the Port Committee contains references to American trade, and to attempts to have Southampton made the main packet station for American mails.

PORT OR PETTY CUSTOMS BOOKS. (SC5/4/1-120)

There are 120 volumes covering 1426-1601, 1637-44, 1723-73. There are references to Newfoundland fish from 1521 to 1601; also to exports, mainly salt, to the American colonies, giving name and place of origin of ship, name of master, date of sailing, name of consignor, and type and quantity of goods, 1723-73.

QUARTER SESSIONS BOOKS OF EXAMINATIONS AND DEPOSITIONS. 1570-1698. (SC9/3/1-14)

References to sailings to or from Virginia, New England and Newfoundland and to trade with them; also references to the Calvert family, Lords Baltimore (1629). The volumes of 1571-9 and 1590-1644 were printed by the Southampton Record Society.

FIRST BOOK OF INSTRUMENTS (REGISTRATION). 1575-86. (SC2/6/5)

Some references to voyages to Newfoundland.

TOWN CLERK'S AND QUARTER SESSIONS PAPERS. 1700-1886.

(*a*) Petition, 19 July 1700, of Gilbert Stokes, an apprentice, to the Mayor and Justices of Southampton, to restrain his master from unlawfully shipping him to Virginia contrary to his indenture. (SC9/4/33.b)
(*b*) Papers (unbound) containing a few bonds and orders for transportation of criminals to the American colonies, 1750-60. (SC9/4/)
(*c*) Draft of Loyal Address to King George II on the taking of Louisbourg, 5 Oct. 1758. (T/C, Box 4)
(*d*) Letter, 7 Dec. 1850, from J. Iselin, of the Southampton Dock Co., to J.R. Stebbing, Secretary to the London and South Western Railway Co., in favour of a 'regularity' of sailing vessels from Southampton to California. (T/C, Box 15/3)
(*e*) Four letters, all Dec. 1850, referring to Southampton's request that the American exhibits for the 1851 Great Exhibition be landed there, the Corporation being willing to pay the railway charges to London. (T/C, Box 15/4)
(*f*) Bundle of letters and some printed material, 1884-6, concerning the attempt of Southampton to have its superiority over Plymouth and Liverpool as a packet station for U.S. mails recognized. (D/Z 5)

PAGE AND MOODY COLLECTION. 1775-1823.

(*a*) Handbills about Loyal Address calling for peace with the colonies, Oct. 1775. (D/PM.4/1/6/1)
(*b*) Affidavits before South Carolina Justice of Peace concerning the marriages of members of the Peyre and Walter families of St. Stephen's Parish, S.C., heirs to property in Southampton, 1797. (D/PM, Box 23)
(*c*) Letter-books and financial accounts of the 103rd Regiment of Foot, largely for 1814-23, including regimental pay lists, lists of prisoners taken by the Americans in the War of 1812 (some of whom later settled in the U.S.), records of deserters to the American side and court-martial proceedings. (D/PM.20)

ST. MARY EXTRA PARISH REGISTER. (PR6/1/1)

This register contains in 1738 the marriages of some twenty couples who were 'bound for Georgia'.

COBB COLLECTION. 1817-23. (D/C6.5 and 6)

Letters and papers of Major General George Stacey Smyth, Governor of New Brunswick, 1817-23; these include the annual report of the Madras Schools in Fredericton for 1823, and information about the difficulty of transport in winter, along with comments on other aspects of life.

HAMPSHIRE RECORD OFFICE, 20 Southgate Street, Winchester SO23 9EF

WRIOTHESLEY DEEDS. 2 documents. 1623.

(*a*) Acquittance, 25 June 1623, to Henry Wriothesley, 3rd Earl of Southampton, as Treasurer of the Virginia Company.
(*b*) Grant, 19 Nov. 1623, by the Virginia Company of twenty shares of land in 'old adventure in Virginia' to the Earl of Southampton in recognition of his services as Treasurer of the Company.

MALMESBURY PAPERS. 6 documents. 1674-85.

(*a*) Letter of appointment, 23 Apr. 1674, by Shaftesbury of Andrew Percival as agent for Carolina. New agreement, 2 June 1680, between Shaftesbury and Percival as to the agency. Sale of stock, etc., 2 May 1685, on St. Giles plantation, Carolina, by the trustees of Shaftesbury to Percival.
(*b*) Three copies of articles of agreement, 6 May 1674, between the Lords Proprietors and Treasurer of Carolina for financing the supply and development of Carolina.

WYNDHAM, HENRY (1709-88). 2 account books. 1725-53.

Merchant of Salisbury and Dinton. The account books contain entries on the trade in tobacco with Virginia.

See also his letters in the Wiltshire Archaeological and Natural History Society, Devizes (p. 229).

OTHER RECORDS. 1664-1859.

(*a*) Appointment of Captain Robert Swanley of London as Deputy Governor of Newfoundland, 1664-5. Incomplete and unattested. (15M50/1646)
(*b*) Acts of Parliament relating to Massachusetts Bay and Quebec, 1741-84. (7M54/272)
(*c*) Lease of plantation in Trinity, Newfoundland, 1745. (11M61/281)
(*d*) Letter from Major Louis Simon Curry from Charlestown, S.C. to his father. Describes his experiences as Quarter Master to Lord Loudoun, 1757. (In French) (4M52/15)
(*e*) Account of Captain Edmond Reilly Cope to Williams and Lyon - cloth, thread, skins, etc. Halifax, N.S., 1792-3. (43M48/2797)
(*f*) Six documents relating to property in Yarmouth, London district of Upper Canada, 1831-47. (27M54/12)
(*g*) There are several entries in parish vestry books and overseers' account books relating to emigration to Canada and the U.S.A. in the 1830's and 1840's.
(*h*) 'Executors of Rev. Samuel Heathcote in A/C with his estate', 1846-50. Includes sale of property in Canada. (27M54/12)
(*i*) Two letters, 1851-3, from Abbott Lawrence of Boston to William Sloan Stanley, discussing free trade and political affairs in general. (10M55/68, 69)
(*j*) The Record Office also has a great deal of correspondence between Lord Malmesbury, Foreign Secretary, and the British Minister in Washington, 1852-9 (ref. 9M73). The permission of the depositor has to be obtained before material from this collection can be produced for students.

HEREFORD AND WORCESTER

HEREFORD HERD BOOK SOCIETY, 3 Offa Street, Hereford HR1 2LL

HEREFORD CATTLE.

Complete records relating to the export of Hereford cattle to the United States from 1817 to the present day.

HEREFORD RECORD OFFICE, The Old Barracks, Harold Street, Hereford HR1 2QX

CRICHTON, A.W. Journal. June-Dec. 1861. (2 vols.)

Crichton sailed from England in H.M.S. *Phoebe,* and voyaged first to Madeira, then to the Bermudas, and reached Halifax at the end of July. He spent several months on a trip throughout much of Canada, visiting Windsor, St. John's, Fredericton, Quebec, Montreal and Toronto. On Nov. 20th he crossed into the United States, and went to Boston, New York, Philadelphia, and Washington.

Along with his comments on visits to several prominent American scientists and botanists, Crichton makes many observations on the military encampments along the Potomac in readiness for the war against the South. In general, however, the journal contains little impression of people met or of atmosphere generally, except in the descriptions of Crichton's hunting trips in Canada. Its major significance lies in the journal's fairly detailed descriptions of landscape, geology, and of buildings and towns. (W7/1)

OTHER MANUSCRIPTS. 1832-1902.

(*a*) Account of the impressions of life and prospects in America, written by an emigrant settler, with a list of his expenditures, during his first few months. This list is headed '1832. Davy Jones and wife aged about 30 years each emigrated to America with £150 in cash and Bank of England Bills...' (copy) (F49/67)
(*b*) Letters to Mary Jay from her cousin Henry Robert Beddoe, written during his employment with the Romanoff Land and Mining Co., Alaska, and after the collapse of the company. Includes some mention of the mining company and life in America. 1898-1902. (J54/316-322)

MR. EDWARD NICHOLAS CRANE,
Oakhampton, Stourport-on-Severn

PENN, WILLIAM (1644-1718). Deed. 1701.

Deed, 25 Aug. 1701, granting land in Philadelphia to Joseph Ranstead. Also a few later notes by others concerning this land.

WORCESTER CATHEDRAL LIBRARY,
8 College Precincts, Worcester WR1 2LG

MUNIMENTS. Letter. 1777. (D.48)

28 Aug. 1777, from W. Digby, Dean of Worcester, says 'It was rumored at Court that Philadelphia was seized by the Quakers for government. Some believed, some not.'[1]

HEREFORD AND WORCESTER COUNTY RECORD OFFICE,
Shirehall, Worcester WR1 1TR

WESTERN QUARTERLY MEETING OF THE SOCIETY OF FRIENDS. Records: bundle of copies of American epistles. 1783-94. (Bulk accession no. 1948, parcel no. 4, class 898.2.)

Copies of annual letters from the Yearly Meeting of Friends or Women Friends held at Philadelphia for Pennsylvania, New Jersey, and the western parts of Maryland and Virginia, to the Yearly Meeting of Friends or Women Friends held in London.

1. H.M.C. xiv (viii), p. 190.

HERTFORD

EARL OF VERULAM,
Gorhambury, St. Albans

See Hertfordshire Record Office: Verulam MSS. (p. 41).

MARQUESS OF SALISBURY,
Hatfield House, Hatfield

CECIL PAPERS. Letters and documents. 1563-1610.

(*a*) 30 June 1563, from the Queen to the Earl of Sussex, 'in favour of Thomas Stuckly, who is about to make a voyage to discover certain lands in the west towards Terra Florida'.[1] (153/147)
(*b*) 22 July 1586, to Lord Burghley mentioning that Drake has 'over-come and spoiled... St. John's in Florida' among other places.[2] (14/77)
(*c*) Before 25 Mar. 1606, from Sir Walter Cope to Salisbury, mentioning that the Lord Chief Justice (Popham) 'is affectionately bent to the plantation of Virginia' in order to provide a place where idle vagrants might be sent.[3] (191/120)
(*d*) Two protests from Plymouth, 10 May 1606: one from Walter Mathewe, the Deputy Mayor, and the other from Sir Ferdinando Gorges, both to Salisbury, complaining about the composition of the Council set up under the Virginia charter.[4] (116/39,40)
(*e*) 19 June 1606, from William Udall to Salisbury, stating that the secular priests and lay Catholics (as opposed to the Jesuits) are about to petition the King to allow 300 Catholic households to settle in Virginia.[5] (192/96)
(*f*) Before Aug. 1607, from William Brewster in Virginia to Dudley Carleton (?), reporting on his arrival in Virginia, and declaring that the 'rocks and mountains' promised 'infinite treasure'.[6] (124/17)
(*g*) Aug. 1607, from Sir Walter Cope to Salisbury. Describes experiences of the Jamestown settlers and reports on the likelihood of discovering gold and pearls in Virginia.[7] (124/18)
(*h*) 1 Dec. 1607, from Sir Ferdinando Gorges to Salisbury, commenting on the reports brought back by a ship from Virginia: 'great news of a fertile country, gallant rivers, stately harbours, and a people tractable'.[8] (123/77)
(*i*) 30 Oct. 1609, from Thomas Holland to Salisbury, reporting on Henry Hudson's explorations in North America, which included a voyage 'into the bay of Chicepeicke'.[9] (128/24)
(*j*) There are numerous other references to the English colony in Virginia in the Cecil MSS. A predominant concern of these correspondents was the problem of Spanish and French resentment of the English settlement, and the possibility that Spain might be preparing a naval expedition to harass the colonists.[10]

PAPERS OF THE 3RD MARQUESS OF SALISBURY.[11]

Papers of Robert Arthur Talbot Gascoyne-Cecil, 3rd Marquess of Salisbury (1830-1903). These are in course of arrangement, but in general it may be said that the major American items will be found in six bound volumes and scattered in small groups throughout the unbound material. A brief description of the contents of the volumes is given below.

The unbound letters, 'Special Correspondence', are alphabetically arranged under writers in several series. The most useful of these is 'Special Correspondence: Main Series', in which the most important name is Julian Pauncefote, 1st Baron Pauncefote; but Americana will also be found for Sir Edward Thornton; Sir George Smyth Baden-Powell; Sir Frederick Stanley, 16th Earl of Derby; Col. George Denison (of Toronto); Goldwin Smith; Lionel Sackville-West, 2nd Baron Sackville; Henry C.K. Petty-Fitzmaurice, 5th Marquess of Lansdowne; Sir James Fergusson;

1. H.M.C. Salisbury (Cecil) MSS i, p. 273.
2. Transcript, ibid., iii, p. 152.
3. Transcript, ibid., xviii, p. 84.
4. Transcript, ibid., pp. 133-4.
5. Transcript, ibid., p. 173.
6. Transcript, ibid., xix, p. 202.
7. Transcript, ibid., pp. 417-9.
8. Transcript, ibid., pp. 353-4.
9. Transcript, ibid., xxi, p. 152.
10. See ibid., xx, especially pp. 53-4, 56, 58, 81, 171, 178 and 194-5. Also see vol. xxi, pp. 60, 87 and 288.
11. We are grateful to the Marquess of Salisbury for permission to make this report. A calendar of the contents of all 140 volumes has been distributed to selected libraries. No photographic reproductions of the papers are allowed.

George Nathaniel Curzon, 1st Marquess Curzon; and William St. J.F. Brodrick, 1st Earl of Midleton, during the periods in which they were Under-Secretaries of State for Foreign Affairs; and George Earle Buckle. In the 'Special Correspondence: Foreign Series' will be found a few letters from Edward John Phelps, Edwards Pierrepont, John Hodges Choate, Charles Richard Williams, Senator Edward Oliver Wolcott, and John Milton Hay; in the main the subjects dealt with are akin to those dealt with in the six bound volumes, a description of which follows:

(*a*) Vol. A/19: 'F.O. (Private Correspondence): United States [Dispatches], 1878-1880.'

(i) Sir E. Thornton to Salisbury. Forty-eight letters and one telegram, 30 Apr. 1878-24 Feb. 1880, on Russian efforts to buy steamers in United States for conversion to cruisers, United States politics (state elections and presidential ambitions), Indian and labour unrest, Fenians, Ontario Boundary Commission, fisheries question, Halifax award, United States relations with Japan, China, Russia, Canada, and Mexico, Chinese immigration, isthmian canal projects, and C.S. Parnell's visit.

(ii) Four American press cuttings.

(iii) J. Welsh to Salisbury, 18 Apr. 1878, on position of three British deserters in 22nd New York Regiment.

(iv) Colonel Stanley (later Lord Derby) to Salisbury, 24 Apr. 1878, on same.

(*b*) Vol. A/21: 'Miscellaneous, 1878-1880.'

(i) Salisbury to Thornton. Three letters, 13 Apr. and 23 Nov. 1878 and 26 Apr. 1880. The first and last are formal; the other deals with the fisheries question.

(*c*) Vol. A/77: 'United States (from) 1887-1890.'

(i) H.G. Edwardes to Barrington. Five letters, 22 Mar.-20 Sept. 1889, on Harrison and Blaine, Bering Sea sealing and seizures of Canadian sealing vessels, and Robert Todd Lincoln.

(ii) M.H. Herbert to Barrington. Five letters, 2 Nov. 1888-8 Feb. 1889, on the 'Murchison letter' affair and its impact on Anglo-American relations and American opinion; Blaine; Samoa.

(iii) Pauncefote to Salisbury (and two to Stanley). Thirty letters and seven telegrams, 3 May 1889-26 Dec. 1890, chiefly about Bering Sea controversy, but also on his reception in Washington, Blaine, extradition, Alaska boundary, International Marine Conference of 1889, Canadian-American relations, international copyright, Samoa. There are also four memos, 1890, by Pauncefote: the first on Haiti, Hawaii, and a merchant shipping convention; the other three (marked 'secret') on movements of American cruisers and the Bering Sea.

(iv) Sackville to Salisbury. Fourteen letters and two telegrams, 30 Jan. 1887-14 Dec. 1888, on fisheries, Blaine's visit to Europe, the Samoan Conference, rejection of the fisheries treaty, the 'Murchison letter' episode. Also a statement by Sackville, 8 Nov. 1888, on this last.

(v) There are also supporting papers on the Bering Sea controversy and a number of American press cuttings sent by Sackville, Herbert, and Pauncefote.

(*d*) Vol. A/78: 'United States (from), 1891-2; United States (to), 1887-92; U.S. Legation, 1887-92; Canada; Fisheries Commission, 1887; Sir G. Baden-Powell, 1891-2.'

(i) 'United States (from), 1891-2': Pauncefote, chiefly to Salisbury, some to Barrington. Thirty letters and four telegrams, 8 Jan. 1891-26 May 1892, on Bering Sea, press attacks on Pauncefote, fisheries, Newfoundland, Tonga, Canadian reciprocity conference, United States relations with Chile, Hawaii, presidential election prospects for 1892, anti-British feeling in the United States. Also included are further correspondence and supporting papers on the Bering Sea controversy and arbitration; a draft maritime convention; and a draft Anglo-American treaty by Pauncefote for recovery of deserters from merchantmen.

(ii) 'United States (to) 1887-92': Similar material.

(iii) 'U.S. Legation, 1887-92': Phelps to Salisbury, 13 Apr. 1887 and 16 Nov. 1888, on the case of Thomas Gallagher and the Sackville incident. Salisbury to Phelps, 16 Apr. 1888, on the Gallagher case; and to Robert Todd Lincoln, 2 Jan. 1892. Henry White to Barrington, 24 May 1888, on Bering Sea.

(iv) 'Canada.' Twenty-six telegrams, 2 July 1888-10 Oct. 1891, between Salisbury and Lord Stanley, Governor-General of Canada, and a letter from Baden-Powell to Stanley; almost entirely about the Bering Sea controversy.

(v) 'Fisheries Commission, 1887': Seven letters, 18 Nov. 1887-16 Feb. 1888, between Joseph Chamberlain and Salisbury, chiefly on the work of the Commission.

(vi) 'Sir G. Baden-Powell, 1891-2': Exclusively concerned with the Bering Sea controversy. Fourteen letters, 5 Aug. 1891-4 May 1892, Baden-Powell to Salisbury; copy, 15 July 1891, of a proclamation by Harrison; minute, 13 Jan. 1892, by Salisbury; copy of a letter, 9 Nov. 1892, from Baden-Powell to Sir John Abbott.

(*e*) Vol. A/139: 'U.S.A. 1895-1898.'

(i) Charles Adams to Salisbury, 23 Oct. 1897, on the Bering Sea conference.

(ii) C.E. Akers. Two letters to Pauncefote, 13 May and 14 Nov. 1896, on Cuba, especially Cuban sugar and the United States and Weyler; and one, 13 May 1896, to Richard Olney on Cuba, especially Spanish bitterness against the United States and absence of atrocities in the islands.

(iii) Count Cassini to Pauncefote. Letter, 15 Nov. 1898, on Nicaraguan canal, etc.

(iv) Lord Gough to Salisbury. Letter, 12 Sept. 1896, repealing 'a message from J. Chamberlain on Major Willoughby's defence'.

(v) Pauncefote to Salisbury. Forty letters and nine telegrams, 25 Oct. 1895-23 Dec. 1898. Bering Sea and, especially, the Venezuela crisis, are the two most important topics; Cuba, the Philippines, McKinley, and the Nicaraguan canal project all enter into the correspondence.

Pauncefote to Olney and Olney to Pauncefote, two copies, both 12 Jan. 1896, on the John Hays Hammond case (in Transvaal). Letter, 27 Mar. 1896, Olney to Pauncefote on the Venezuelan dispute, and copies, 11 and 12 Dec. 1896, Olney to Pauncefote and Pauncefote to Olney, respectively urging and deprecating the appointment of a Venezuelan arbitrator.

Draft by Pauncefote entitled 'Scheme of arbitration for the settlement of the Venezuela Boundary Question'.

Pauncefote to Barrington. Two letters, 31 Jan. and 17 Apr. 1896, both dealing with the Venezuelan dispute; in addition, the former comments on the low standard of the United States Senate, and the latter on the Pacific cable, embassy staff, and the desirability of Pauncefote's absence from the United States during the 1896 presidential campaign.

Pauncefote to Villiers. Letter, 25 July 1897, enclosing one from J.D. Campbell to Pauncefote, 25 July 1897, on the Jubilee.

(vi) R. Tower to Barrington. Two letters, 11 June 1897 and 19 Nov. 1898, the first on American reactions to the Jubilee.

(vii) The volume also contains, besides several press cuttings, a memorandum, Dec. 1895, by H.O. Bax-Ironside on the origin of the President's Venezuela message.

(*f*) Vol. A/140: 'U.S.A. (from) 1899-1900; (to) 1896-1900.'

(i) 'U.S.A. (from) 1899-1900': Farrer Herschell, 1st Baron Herschell, to Salisbury, letter, 25 Nov. 1898, and telegram, 6 Feb. 1899, on the fishery question and the tariff. Pauncefote to

Salisbury, ten letters and eight telegrams, 16 Jan. 1899-6 Nov. 1900, on the Nicaraguan canal, Herschell, 'open door' in China, Canadian-United States relations, the United States and The Hague Peace Conference, Alaska boundary, presidential campaign of 1900, arrangements for Pauncefote's retirement. Pauncefote to Barrington, letter, 31 Oct. 1899, on equal commercial treatment in Samoa of Britain, the United States, and Germany. Tower to Barrington, 29 May 1899, dealing with Canadian-United States negotiations. Also a letter from Barrington to Salisbury, and several minor letters to Barrington.

(ii) 'United States (to) 1896-1900': Salisbury to Pauncefote. Three letters, fourteen telegrams, and three printed drafts, 7 Feb. 1896-27 Mar. 1900, dealing with Venezuela, general arbitration, and the Alaska boundary. Also three letters from Barrington, two from Salisbury to Barrington, and one from Salisbury to Gough on similar topics.

(iii) The concluding section of this volume is entitled 'U.S. Embassy in London'. It contains: Barrington to Salisbury, letter, 6 Apr. 1900, on the Alaska boundary; Barrington to Henry White, letter, 2 Feb. 1899 (and a copy of this) on the Clayton-Bulwer Treaty. E.W.P.' to Crane, St. Louis, Mo., Mar. 1900 on Anglo-American relations, especially as regards the presidential campaign, the anti-canal lobby, the Philippines, etc. Salisbury to Barrington, letter, 28 Feb. 1896, on Venezuela. Six letters, 29 Feb. 1896-25 Jan. 1900, James R. Roosevelt, Henry White, and J.H. Choate to Salisbury or Barrington, on Venezuela, Spanish-American peace negotiations, Nicaraguan canal, and the case of Mrs. Maybrick (an American woman sentenced to imprisonment in Britain for murder). Document, 6 Apr. 1900, entitled 'List of cases in which executive clemency has been requested of other governments by the diplomatic representatives of the United States or Great Britain' (presumably connected with the Maybrick case). Americana will also be found in other volumes, e.g. concerning Samoa in correspondence with Berlin.

HERTFORDSHIRE RECORD OFFICE, County Hall, Hertford SG13 8DE

ASHRIDGE II MANUSCRIPTS. 1753-1833.

Papers of the Egerton family, Dukes of Bridgewater.
(*a*) Abstract of the grants of Maryland, New England, and Pennsylvania, and proceedings in the Maryland-Pennsylvania boundary dispute, 1632-[1753]. (AH 1464)
(*b*) Two letters from T[homas] Dampier, Dean of Durham, to Archdeacon Egerton of Derby, commenting on the military situation in America, 1776. (AH 2264 and 2275)
(*c*) Four letters, 1833, between the solicitors David Lee Willis, Grover, Smith & Grover, and Richard Clarke, concerning the validity of title to land offered to the Earl of Bridgewater's trustees by John Buckmaster, as he wished to emigrate to America. (AH 2435-8)

BAKER MANUSCRIPTS. Letters. 1775-85.

Correspondence of William Baker (1743-1824) of Bayfordbury, Herts., M.P. for several constituencies, including Hertford, at various times between 1768 and 1807.
(*a*) One letter from William Baker to his wife Sophia, 19 Oct. 1775, including his reaction to a report that 'the Provincials' had seized Halifax, N.S. (D/E Bk C13/7)
(*b*) Copies of four letters from William Baker to Edmund Burke, and three original letters from Edmund Burke to William Baker, 22 Aug. 1775-25 Dec. 1777: on Burke's refusal to present the petition of the American Congress, the attitude of the British people towards America, and a scheme for relieving American prisons in Britain. (D/E Bk C13/9-10, C15/1-5)
(*c*) One letter from William Windham to William Baker, 1 Nov. 1777, lamenting the failure of the opposition to rouse the people against the American War, and giving his reaction to the news of the check to Gen. Burgoyne's forces by Gen. Conway. (D/E Bk C15/6)
(*d*) One letter from William Baker to John Penn, Jr., 7 Sept. 1785, on the purchase of Penn's manors by the Assembly and the moral obligations of Britain to the Loyalists. (D/E Bk C21/1)

GILES-PULLER MSS. 1803-90.

Correspondence of Daniel Giles (1760-1831) of Youngsbury, Ware, Herts., M.P. for East Grinstead 1802-9, and St. Albans 1809-12; his nephew Benjamin [Giles] King (1777-1840); Arthur and Charles Giles-Puller (grandsons of Daniel Giles's niece Louisa, wife of Sir Christopher Puller).
(*a*) Seven letters from Benjamin King to his uncle Daniel Giles, 8 July [1803]-11 May [1804], describing a tour of the eastern states of America and of Canada, commenting on American personalities, politics and cultural life, and a visit to the Shaker community of the Green Mountains, Vermont.
(*b*) Two letters from Benjamin King to his mother, Mrs. Mary King, and one to his sister, Louisa King, written during the same period as the above, but less descriptive of his experiences and impressions. (D/EGp C8 [10, 11, 13]
(*c*) One letter from Arthur Giles-Puller to his sister Ellen, 16 Sept. 1874, mostly of a personal nature, with little description of his tour. (D/EGp C17 [28])
(*d*) Two letters from D.M. Salter to Charles Giles-Puller, 2 Apr. and 4 Aug. 1890, describing the scenery and customs of the southern states (written from New Orleans, La., and Ocean Spring, Miss.). (D/EGp C20 [49-50])

HALSEY MANUSCRIPTS. 1770-*c*. 1816.

Papers of the Halsey family of Gaddesden Place, Great Gaddesden, Herts., including papers of the Johnston family of Hilton, Berwick.
(*a*) Letter of attorney and deeds concerning the transfer of copyhold land in Great Gaddesden from Robert Snow, formerly of Hertford, then of Cape Fear, N.C., planter, to Thomas Halsey of Great Gaddesden, Herts., 14 Feb.-3 Aug. 1770. (13485-7, 13493)
(*b*) Appointment of Major-General James Johnston as Governor of the town of Quebec, 8 Nov. 1774. (16008)
(*c*) Appointment, by Sir James Lucas Yeo, of John Frederick Johnston as acting Lieutenant of H.M.S. *Wolfe* on Lake Ontario, 12 July 1813. (16373)
(*d*) Nine letters from John Frederick Johnston to his mother, Mrs. Jane Johnston, 1813-4, written aboard H.M.S. *Woolwich* at sea, and from Kingston [Ontario], describing his first voyage and landing in Quebec, the actions in which he was engaged against the Americans on the Great Lakes; and aboard H.M.S. *Zealous* at sea, off Quebec and at Spithead, describing his second voyage and his return without seeing action. (16292-6, 16307-9)
(*e*) Two letters from C. Cunliffe-Owen [Kingston, Ontario] to Lieut. [John] Frederick Johnston (Montreal), n.d. (incomplete) and 9 May 1814, including an account of naval action against the Americans at Oswego, N.Y. (16378-9)
(*f*) MS. obituary of Lieut. John Frederick Johnston, R.N. (1793-

1816), including an account of his service with Sir James Yeo's expedition to the Great Lakes and his part in the assault on Sackett's Harbour. (16421)

LE HARDY MSS. 1903-39.

Papers of Messrs. Hardy & Page, and Hardy & Reckitt, record agents.

Papers as agents for New Jersey in a case before the United States Supreme Court as to the boundary between New Jersey and Delaware: correspondence, 1903-5, including Judge Howard W. Hayes (Newark, N.J.) and Robert H. McCarter (N.J. Attorney General), and 1931-9, including Duane E. Minard (N.J. Assistant Attorney General); files of notes and transcripts of documents cited; official record of the case, 1930-8. (D/ELh B48-75)

LYTTON (KNEBWORTH) MSS. 1839-69.

Papers of Sir Edward George Earle Lytton Bulwer Lytton, Bart. (1803-73), 1st Baron Lytton 1866, Colonial Secretary 1858-9, novelist.

(*a*) Official papers as Colonial Secretary, including correspondence relating to Canada from the 4th Earl of Carnarvon, George Etienne Cartier, Angela Georgina Burdett Coutts, Sir Edmund Walker Head, Herman Merivale, Richard Clement Moody, Philip Rose, and Edward William Watkin, 1857-69. (D/EK 01)

(*b*) MS. memoranda and correspondence relating to the federation of British provinces in North America, Canadian decimal coinage, the case of George H. Ryland (former Clerk of the Council in Canada), 1839-60. (D/EK 03)

(*c*) MS. and printed papers, 1858-9 and 1869, on the confederation of British Columbia with the Dominion of Canada. (D/EK 05)

(*d*) MS. memoranda and correspondence, 1857-9. (D/EK 06)

(*e*) MS. notes on the Newfoundland fisheries by Sir Edward Bulwer Lytton, 1854-7. (D/EK 07)

(*f*) Letters relating to Canada received at the Colonial Office, 1858-9, with many from prominent English figures, including James Cooper, the 14th Earl of Derby, George Dundas, Sir John Pakington, Lord Stanley, Queen Victoria, Capt. John Washington, and James Wyld. (D/EK 024-027)

(*g*) Letter-books with copies of letters concerning Canada, 1858-9. Correspondents include Prince Albert, the 3rd Earl of Malmesbury, Sir John Pakington, Sir Charles Phipps, William Henry Sykes, Queen Victoria, etc. (D/EK 027A, 028)

(*h*) The general correspondence of Sir Edward Bulwer Lytton, partly in bound volumes and partly in boxes arranged alphabetically by correspondent, is fully indexed by correspondent and not by subject. It is known to contain a substantial amount of material relating to publication in America, particularly concerning the lack of a copyright agreement.[1] Included are letters from William and John Blackwood (D/EK C15, C20, C22), Sir John Fiennes Twisleton Crampton, British Minister at Washington 1852-6 (C11, C16, C17), Charles Dickens (C12), John Forster (C14, C23), Harper & Bros. (C23), and Sampson Low & Co. (C25).

MARTIN LEAKE MSS. Letter. 1901.

One letter from Francis Martin Leake, Vice-Admiral in the Royal Navy, to his mother, Mrs. Isabel Martin Leake, 4 Jan. 1901, written aboard H.M.S. *Bramble* at sea in the China station, and describing a visit to Manila with comment on the conduct of the war in the Philippines by American forces. (87387)

PANSHANGER MSS. 14 letters. 1706-74.

Papers of the Earls Cowper: Sir William Cowper, Bart. (1665-1723), 1st Earl Cowper 1718; George Nassau Clavering-Cowper (1738-89), 3rd Earl Cowper 1764.

(*a*) Seven letters from Joseph Dudley, Governor of Massachusetts, to Lord Cowper, 1706-14, vindicating his administration and urging promotion of emigration from Scotland to Nova Scotia rather than to the West Indies. Also comments on defensive measures against French and Indian attacks and his encouragement of the production of naval stores. (D/EP F144[1-7])

(*b*) One letter from Dr. William Lloyd, Bishop of Worcester, to Lord Cowper, 1 Mar. 1714/5, expressing his high opinion of Col. Dudley and his concern at the appointment of Col. Eliseus Burgess to replace Dudley as Governor. (D/EP F144[8])

(*c*) Two letters from Caleb Heathcote, New York, to Lord Cowper, 3 Feb. and 15 Mar. 1714/5, on the encouragement of trade and industry in the province, and enclosing saw-mill accounts. (D/EP F144 [9-10])

(*d*) Two letters from Congregational and Presbyterian ministers and councillors of New England to Lord Cowper, 1716, requesting his attention to the enclosed statement and expressing loyalty to the Protestant succession. (D/EP F144[11-13])

(*e*) Anonymous letter (with enclosures) by an ejected member of the Council of New York [? Peter Schuyler] to Earl Cowper [1723], complaining of the actions of the Governor [William Burnet], particularly his profiteering from the pay of the forces and the inadequate provision for their welfare. (D/EP F144[14-17])

(*f*) One letter from R.B. Nicholas to Charles Gore, 1774, describing at length his journey from New York to Niagara Falls and up the St. Lawrence River to Montreal and Quebec. (D/EP F[uncatalogued])

RADCLIFFE MSS. 4 letters. 1775-6, n.d. (DE 4323-5)

Papers of the Radcliffe family of Hitchin Priory, Herts., including John Radcliffe (1738-83), M.P. for St. Albans 1768-83.

(*a*) Letter, 19 Aug. 1775, from H. Gardner to John Radcliffe, concerning American politics and the military position of the British forces, enclosing copies of letters from Samuel Adams, Philadelphia, to his wife, n.d., and [James] Warren, 24 July 1775.

(*b*) Letter from Gardner to Radcliffe, 1776, concerning the war in Canada.

SEEBOHM MSS. Correspondence. 18th century-1858.

Correspondence of Benjamin Seebohm (1798-1871), his wife's grandfather William Tuke (1732-1822), and the latter's second wife Esther (1727-94), all of whom were Quakers.

(*a*) Volume containing copies of letters from various Quakers, mostly to William and Esther Tuke, concerning the spiritual progress and personal news of Friends, including several in America. Also an original letter from Rebecca Jones in Philadelphia to Christiana Hustler, Bradford, 1796, including reference to the purchase of a plantation at West Town, about thirty miles from Philadelphia, as a site for a boarding school. Most of the letters in this volume date from the second half of the eighteenth century. (D/ESe C10)

1. See James J. Barnes, 'Edward Lytton Bulwer [sic] and the publishing firm of Harper & Brothers', *American Literature*, vol. 38, no. 1 (March 1966) pp. 35-48, and *Authors, Publishers and Politicians: The Quest for an Anglo-American Copyright, 1815-1854* (London and Columbus, Ohio, 1974).

(*b*) Four letters from Rebecca Jones, Philadelphia, to Christiana Hustler, 1792-1801. (D/ESe C19/1)
(*c*) One letter from Rebecca Jones, Philadelphia, to Elizabeth Wheeler, 1800. (D/ESe C19/2)
(*d*) Two letters from John Adamson to Benjamin Seebohm, 1817, describing his passage to America, American eating and drinking habits, and his tour of the northeastern states. (D/ESe C24/9)
(*e*) Bundle of approximately eighty-five letters from Benjamin Seebohm in America to his wife Esther, 1846-51, almost wholly of a personal and spiritual character. (D/ESe C35/14)
(*f*) One letter from Benjamin Seebohm to Jane Gurney Fox, 1858, referring to the work of Quakers in Indiana. (D/ESe C43)
(*g*) One letter from W.J.A., Burlington (N.J.?), to Benjamin Seebohm, 1852, giving news of Friends. (D/ESe C47)
(*h*) Verses composed by A[nn] A[lexander], a daughter of William Tuke, on encountering a Negro slave in Virginia, 1804. (D/ESe F29)

GORHAMBURY MSS. 1745-66.

Papers of the Grimston family, Viscounts Grimston and Earls of Verulam. (See also the Verulam MSS. below, which form an additional accession to the Gorhambury MSS.).
Bundle of papers (X.K. 16-23b) relating to Françoise Daccarette of Nova Scotia, including:
(*a*) One letter (in French) from Archevesque, chaplain of Cendré, near Cléry-sur-Loire, to his brother in Uiganiche (?), Ile Royale, Terre Neuve, concerning recommendations to French officials in North America for an appointment, 1745.
(*b*) One letter (in French) from Pierre Faribauer at Louisbourg in Nova Scotia, to Mme. Daccarette, 1749, concerning her affairs in Louisbourg.
(*c*) One letter (in French) from Lieut. John Straton, Greenwich, Kent, to [F. Daccarette], 1750, concerning his fears that the colony would be attacked by the French and Indians.
(*d*) Grant of land by Gratian d'Arrigande of Louisbourg to F. Daccarette and Anne Laurence of Halifax, N.S., 1766.

VERULAM MSS. 1769-1848.

Papers of the Grimston family, Viscounts Grimston and Earls of Verulam: James Bucknall Grimston (1747-1809), 3rd Viscount Grimston 1774, M.P. for St. Albans 1783-4 and for Hertfordshire 1784-90.
(*a*) Journal of a tour in Wales and the Midland counties of England, 1769, including passages which comment briefly on the trade of Liverpool and Birmingham with America.[2] (D/EV F19, ff. 220, 236)
(*b*) Three letters to Viscount Grimston from W[illiam] Windham, [Thomas William] Coke, and Lady Forrester, and two draft letters by Viscount Grimston to Thomas de Grey and W[illiam] Windham, 24 Jan.-3 Mar. 1778: concerning county petitions and meetings in Norfolk and Hertford on the American war.[3] (D/EV F25 and F33)
(*c*) Three letters from J. Mervin Nooth, New York, to Viscountess Grimston, 23 Nov. 1779, 18 July 1781, and n.d., on the conduct of the war.[4] (D/EV F25 and F336)
(*d*) One letter from J. Mervin Nooth, Quebec, to Viscount Grimston, 6 Aug. 1795, on the political situation in America, the American attitude to war in Europe, the export of wheat, and drought.[5] (D/EV F27)
(*e*) One letter from Thomas Lashley, Brighton, to Viscount Grimston, 20 Oct. 1793, seeking an appointment with the forces embarking for the West Indies, and enclosing a narrative of his experiences as a Loyalist in trading between the West Indies and America.[6] (D/EV F27)
(*f*) Journal, 1847-8, of a hunting trip in Canada made by Sir Frederick Ulric Graham of Netherby, Bart. (1820-1888). 3 vols. (D/EV F204-6)

THE WASHINGTON FAMILY.

The close connection of the emigrant brothers, John and Lawrence, great-grandfather and great-great-uncle of George Washington, and their sister Mildred with the village of Tring was first discovered by Henry F. Waters, whose 'An Examination of the English Ancestry of George Washington. . . .' appeared first in the *New England Historical and Genealogical Register,* vol. 43 (1889), and later in the same year as a separate pamphlet. Waters' key evidence was the will of Andrew Knowling, proved 29 Jan. 1649/50, in the court of the Archdeacon of Huntingdon, Hitchin Division, and now among the records of the court in the Hertfordshire Record Office. (AHH/75HW6)[7]

QUARTER SESSIONS RECORDS.

Several of the ten volumes of printed calendars of Quarter Sessions Rolls and Books, 1589-1843, contain references to persons being sentenced to transportation, but except during the period 1755-75, the destination is not usually stated to be America. (Hertford County Records, vol. 8, Sessions Books 1752-99)

ARCHDEACONRY RECORDS.

The records of the Archdeaconry of St. Albans and the Hitchin Division of the Archdeaconry of Huntingdon contain a few documents relating to collections which were ordered to be taken throughout the Church of England for the establishment of churches and schools in Virginia.[8]
(*a*) Thomas Edwardes, Official of the Bishop of London, to the Official of Dr. John Bull, Archdeacon of St. Albans, 25 June 1616, giving instructions for making collections. (ASA 5/4[219])
(*b*) James Rolfe, Official of the Archdeacon of St. Albans, to his apparitor, John Grynsell, 4 July 1616, including instructions for summoning clergy and churchwardens. (ASA 5/4[220])
(*c*) List of clergy and churchwardens in the Archdeaconry of St. Albans, convened on 29 July 1616. (ASA 5/4[221])
(*d*) Records of amount collected, in Archdeaconry of St. Albans Act Book, 10 Oct. 1616. (ASA7/26, ff. 27v, 28v)
(*e*) Rough notes referring to collections for Virginia, in Archdeaconry of Huntingdon (Hitchin Division) Act Book, 26 Feb. and 12 Mar. 1616/7. (AHH 5/8, ff. 18r, 23r)
(*f*) Visitation process issued by James Rolfe, Official of the Archdeacon of Huntingdon in the Hitchin Division, 27 Sept.

1. Woburn MSS., H.M.C. 250.
2. Transcript, H.M.C. Verulam MSS. [64], pp. 271, 274.
3. Transcripts, ibid., pp. 125-7.
4. Transcripts, ibid., pp. 127-8, 129-30, 183.
5. Transcript, ibid., pp. 157-8.
6. Transcript, ibid., pp. 151-2.
7. A good discussion of this and other relevant documents is in Peter Walne, 'The English Ancestry of George Washington: Some New Evidence', *New England Historical and Genealogical Register,* vol. 129 (April 1975), pp. 106-32.
8. See Peter Walne, 'The Collections for Henrico College 1616-1618', *Virginia Magazine of History and Biography,* vol. 80, no. 3 (July 1972), pp. 259-66.

1617, for a visitation of Baldock on 7 Oct. 1617 to inquire into (*inter alia*) the collections for Virginia. (AHH 8/1)

PARISH RECORDS.

Registers and other records have been deposited by most parishes in the county. There appear to be few records specifically concerning emigration to North America, but the following have been noticed:

(*a*) Ashwell: One bundle of papers concerning the emigration of nine Ashwell men to Canada, 1836. (D/P7 19/2)

(*b*) Bishop's Stortford: One bundle of correspondence, notes, extracts, and pedigrees compiled by the local historian John Laybank Glasscock, and the draft of a paper entitled 'Stortford Emigrants to New England, 1630-1640', 1892-1928. (D/P21 29/36)

QUAKER RECORDS.

The only papers directly relating to America are MSS. and lithographed copies of epistles to Yearly Meetings of Women Friends held in London from Yearly Meetings of Women Friends held in Philadelphia (1789, 1790, 1815, 1822, 1842), Rhode Island (1816, 1843), New York (1817), and North Carolina (1845). (Q134/1-10)

MISCELLANEOUS DEPOSITS. 1695-1891.

(*a*) Admission in the manor of Cheshunt of William Hart to one-fourth part of a messuage in Cheshunt on the surrender of John Saffin and his wife Rebecca, of New Bristol, New England, made at Boston on 9 Oct. 1694 to Sir William Phips, Governor of Massachusetts, 1 Oct. 1695. (44039)

(*b*) Mortgage (unexecuted) by Nicholas Cole Spencer and William Spencer, executors of Nicholas Spencer, late of Nominy, Westmoreland County, Va., to Thomas Starke of London, merchant. Lands in King Capscoe, Nominy, Popes Creek, and elsewhere in Virginia, including the moiety of a 5,000 acre plantation held jointly with Capt. Lawrence Washington, 11 Dec. 1702. (27085)

(*c*) Assignment of possessions of John Beale of Hertford, maltster, a bankrupt, 15 Mar. 1716/7, including 1,000 acres of land in Pennsylvania. (39443)

(*d*) Agreement between Thomas Matthew of London and John Matthew of Rickmansworth, Herts., 1732, for payment of an annuity in exchange for various properties, including the moiety of a plantation at Kerry Point, Northumberland County, Va. (44523)

(*e*) Bond of Thomas Cumming of New York, merchant, and Claud Nisbet of London, merchant, to James House of St. James's, Clerkenwell, 1752, for quiet possession of a piece of ground in Queen St., New York. (73825)

(*f*) Contract between the Lords Commissioners of H.M. Treasury and John Stewart of London, merchant, 1757, for transporting malefactors from the county jails of Hertford, Buckingham, Essex, Kent, and Sussex, to America. (19789)

(*g*) One letter to William Lee (Colworth House, Sharnbrook, Beds.), 1777, endorsed by recipient with news of the victory of the British forces over 'the Rebels' at Stanton Hill, Philadelphia. (68871)

(*h*) Copy of will (5 Sept. 1803) and probate (4 Dec. 1805) of Alexander Ellice, formerly of Mark Lane, London, late of Bath, including lands in 'the Island of St. Johns or Prince Edward' and (unspecified) lands in the U.S.A. (D/EAS 3376)

(*i*) Cuttings of eleven newspaper reports on the American Civil War, written by [James Edwin Cussans] from New York, 25 May-28 Sept. 1861, and published in the *Morning Chronicle*, 10 June-12 Oct. 1861 (with MS. notes by the author). (D/EX164 Z4)

(*j*) Three letters from John T. Underwood (of Underwood's Inks, New York) to Walter Justice, London, 13 Jan.-21 Dec. 1891, reporting on the progress of his business despite the loss of custom from the Remington Typewriter Co., and his successful introduction of the manufacture of typewriter ribbons in America, assisted by the McKinley Tariff. (D/Z24 B7)

HUMBERSIDE

HUMBERSIDE COUNTY RECORD OFFICE, County Hall, Beverley

GRIMSTON PAPERS. Correspondence. 1777-1820.

Correspondence which includes references to the War of Independence, quails, cranberries and other goods, and emigration. 1777-9, 1795, 1810, 1820. (DDGR 42/27, 28 and 29; DDGR 43/15, 30 and 40)

MAXWELL-CONSTABLE OF EVERINGHAM. Letters. 1858-1902.

(*a*) Letters to M.F. Maxwell-Constable, including some from America, 1858-1902.

(*b*) Letter from Thomas Constable about his son Walter's emigration to America, *c*. 1872.

BRYNMOR JONES LIBRARY, HULL UNIVERSITY, Hull HU6 7RX

CHICHESTER-CONSTABLE OF BURTON CONSTABLE. Will and assignment. 1659, 1704.

(*a*) Copy will of Sir Thomas Danby of Thorp Perrow. Bequest of (*inter alia*) plantations in Virginia. Reference to son Christopher and wife returning to Virginia to plant and reside there, 11th Nov. 1659. (DDCC/134/13)

(*b*) Assignment by John Freame of Wapping, shipwright, to Robert, Viscount Dunbar, of two of J.F.'s ten shares (out of 250) of all wrecks in America, for three years, 29th Aug. 1704. (DDCC/135/53)

HOTHAM COLLECTION. 1771-1815.

(*a*) Thompson, Sir Charles Hotham (1739-92). *c*. 100 letters from America. 1771-9. (DDHO 4/16-21)

Adjutant-General to the Forces in the Seven Years War. Some hundred letters in his correspondence are from persons serving with the British forces in America and others, referring to American affairs.

(*b*) Hotham, William, 1st Baron Hotham (1736-1813). 23 letters. 1776-80.

Admiral. Commodore on North American Station during War of Independence.

(i) 29 Apr. 1776-13 July 1780 from Lord Howe. Eighteen from New York, Philadelphia, or H.M.S. *Eagle*, off America, four from London, dealing with the movement of ships, the state of anchorages, etc., off the American coast; with a few references to rebel activities ashore. (DDHO 5/1)

(ii) 9 Nov. 1776, from General Howe, Camp at Dobbs Ferry, N.Y., asking if the artillery ships can be got up more quickly, as the stores in them are needed. (DDHO 5/2)

(*c*) Copy of a loyal motion passed by the Beverley Corporation relating to the War of Independence. (DDHO 4/272)

(*d*) Hotham, Vice-Admiral Sir Henry (1777-1833). Letters, 5 letter-books, orders, two journals, miscellaneous documents. 1811-15.

Captain of the Fleet on the North American Station during the earlier stages of the War of 1812.

(i) Standing Orders on North American Station, July 1811-July 1814; Halifax, N.S., Port Orders, Oct. 1813; 'Public Orders of the Commander-in-Chief' of the North American Station, Apr.-Nov. 1814; 'Public Orders issued by Commodore Hotham', Aug. 1814-Mar. 1815. (DDHO 7/45-48)

(ii) Copy of a report, 15 Nov. 1812, of Captain James Stirling, *Brazen* sloop, on Florida. (DDHO 7/99)

(iii) About 350 letters, Mar. 1813-May 1815, to Sir Henry while First Captain and second-in-command of the fleet on the North American Station, relating, *inter alia*, to the war with America; Sir Henry's orders and instructions; safe-conducts and passports for neutrals and others; United States Navy; the coastline blockade; and the neutrality of the island of Nantucket, Mass. (DDHO 7/2)

(iv) Five letter-books (four are partly order books), Apr. 1813-July 1814. Letters, all from Bermuda, are mainly about routine naval matters, but include references to American weakness, prisoner of war exchanges, employment of refugee American Negroes in the West Indies, impressed seamen claiming to be American citizens, etc. (DDHO 7/30-34)

(v) Book of 'remarks', 1813, suggesting ways and means of attacks on America in the prosecution of a war. (DDHO 7/99)

(vi) Proceedings of a court martial, 28-31 May 1813, of the captain and crew of the *Macedonia*, captured by American ships. (DDHO 7/97)

(vii) Proceedings, 7 June 1813, of a court martial of the captain and crew of British ship *Peacock* captured by U.S.S. *Hornet*. (DDHO 7/98)

(viii) Twelve documents, 1814-5, giving information about the American forces in the area of the North American Station. (DDHO 7/70)

(ix) Four documents of secret instructions, 1814-5, from the Admiralty in the event of the American fleet putting to sea. (DDHO 7/71)

(x) Twenty-nine letters, July 1814-Apr. 1815, being instructions from Admiral Sir Alexander Cochrane, Commander-in-Chief of the North American and West Indian Station. (DDHO 7/4)

(xi) Journals, two volumes (the second unbound), Apr.-Dec. 1814. Chiefly records of ships arriving and departing, but mentions also the shipping of American prisoners to Halifax, N.S., and the blockade. (DDHO 7/52-53)

(xii) Twelve letters, Oct.-Nov. 1814, 'delivered to me by Captain Hayes the senior officer off New London [Conn.] on the 14th Dec. 1814, being a correspondence held between Colonel Barclay (later British Consul General for the Eastern States of America) and the Commanding Officer on it, in my absence, respecting his leaving the United States, and from the Dutch and Swedish Ministers on other subjects'. (DDHO 7/5)

PENNINGTON OF WARTER. Memorandum. 1779.

Memorandum on cost of American War, 1779. (DDWA/13/69)

THOMAS PERRONET THOMPSON. Plan. 1808.

Plan for forming a Black Corps in Sierra Leone from slaves from American vessels, 1808. (DTH/1/35)

SIR CHARLES CHICHESTER. Letters and diaries, 1822-45.

(*a*) Copies of letters to Gen. Putnam of U.S. Army, 1838. (DDCH/43)

(*b*) Diaries of Sir Charles - travels in U.S., comments on the people, War of Independence, Anglo-American affairs, 1822-3, 1838-40, 1844-5. (DDCH/70, 71, 76, 77, 81, 82)

(*c*) Diary of Lady Chichester, [Buffalo], 1844. (DDCH/88)

BAINES OF BELL HALL. 4 letters. 1852.

Four letters from Henry Baines describing his voyage to America (New York, Philadelphia, Baltimore, Washington, Niagara), 1852. (DDBH/26/8)

LLOYD GREAME OF SEWERBY. Letters and journal. 1864, 1866.

(*a*) Four letters from Yarburgh George Lloyd, describing his travels (New York, Philadelphia, Niagara), 1866. (DDLG/46/16)

(*b*) Journal of Yarburgh George Lloyd of his travels in the U.S., 1864. (DDLG/48/19)

ROBERT ARTHUR TAYLOR, M.P. Diary. 1928.

Diary of a visit to America, 1928. (DX/112/1)

WINIFRED HORRABIN. Journal. 1949.

Journal of a visit to America, 1949. (DWH/1/43)

CITY RECORD OFFICE, Guildhall, Kingston-upon-Hull HU1 2AA

ROSE DOWNS AND THOMPSON LTD. Manufacturers of food processing machinery. Order books and letters. 1875-1943.

(*a*) Order books, 1875-1943, containing orders from the U.S.A. (DBR 751-831)

(*b*) Eighteen letters from William Downs in the U.S.A., 1883-93. (DBR 1555-8, 2052-6)

(*c*) Four letters from A.B. Lowther of Chicago, 1876-7. (DBR 2072, 2074)

OTHER RECORDS. *c*. 1750-1876.

(*a*) Accounts of the ship *Neptune* on a voyage to New York, 1815-8. (DBX 1/3)

(*b*) Water bailiff's accounts for dues levied on shipping, including shipping to or from American ports, *c*. 1750-1876. (WB)

(*c*) Quarter sessions records containing orders for the transportation of felons to America, and less frequently, receipts for felons from the Virginia authorities, *c*. 1750-70. (CQB 24-29)

(*d*) Correspondence concerning the protection of the town and coastal and Baltic shipping during the War of Independence generally, and specifically during the events surrounding the engagement between the ships of John Paul Jones and H.M.S. *Serapis* off Flamborough Head, 1778-82. (BRL/1386, 1391)

KENT

CATHEDRAL LIBRARY, Canterbury

MAXTED PAPERS. Diary, letters, 1832-70.

(*a*) A diary kept by William Bullock Maxted; describes a voyage to New York in 1832, detailed descriptions of the city, then of journey up the Great Western Canal; buys a 292 acre farm near Syracuse, takes part in a cricket match; returns to England in 1834.

(*b*) Some papers of Frederick Maxted, *c.* 1870, while a cowboy in Colorado.

MARQUESS OF ABERGAVENNY, Eridge Park, Tunbridge Wells, Kent

ABERGAVENNY PAPERS. Letters. 1774-84.

(*a*) 19 Nov. 1774, from Lord North to John Robinson, '...The state of America is neither better nor worse than when you were in London....'[1]

(*b*) 14 June 1775, Boston, from General Burgoyne to Lord North, proposing that he be relieved from military responsibilities and be allowed to travel through New York and Pennsylvania in the cause of conciliation, prior to a return home.[2]

(*c*) Three letters, 1775, concerning the rebellion: July, from A. Wedderburn to Lord North, criticizing the conduct of the war. 31 July, Lord North to General Burgoyne, promising reinforcements and expressing optimism about the war. 8 Nov., from Captain Pearson, commander of the *Speedwell*, to Mr. Stephens, recounting 'his proceedings with regard to the *Patriote*, a snow of Altona, supposed to be laden with arms and saddles for the rebels in America'.[3]

(*d*) Letters listed for 1777: 17 May, 'Declaration by Count Floridablanca to Mr. [Arthur] Lee as to the intentions of the King of Spain relative to the United States of America.' 18 May, 'Reply of Mr. Arthur Lee to [the above]'. 17 July, John Robinson to P. Stephens 'concerning the ship *Richard Penn* starting for America' (copy). July, Extracts from a letter from a spy (?) at Paris concerning the relations between England, France, and America. 7 Aug., 'Memorial delivered to France and Spain by the three commissioners of America' (copy). 25 Aug., William Eden to Lord North on the French attitude, and on ships for America. 18 and 19 Dec., letters from the three American Commissioners to Samuel Adams (copy). 19 Dec., Arthur Lee to the Secret Committee at Congress (copy.)[4]

(*e*) 6 June 1777, from New York, Sir William Howe to John Robinson in which he says that the war will not be terminated during that campaign but that he hopes to 'strike deep towards concluding it in the next.'[5]

(*f*) 'Memorial, presented to the States of Holland by B. Franklin and A. Lee, Plenipotentiaries for the United States of America' (copy) [1778].[6]

(*g*) 11 Jan. 1778, from John Robinson to Lord North concerning, *inter alia*, 'the policy to be adopted towards America'.[7]

(*h*) 15 Jan. 1778, from 'the three American Commissioners to Captain Paul Jones of the *Amphitrite*'[8]

(*i*) 18 Jan. 1778, Minute of Lord Amherst's opinion that it would not be possible to reduce the colonies without an extra 30,000 men and that, therefore, future operations must be principally naval.[9]

(*j*) 14 Feb. 1778, from 'the three American Commissioners to the Secret Committee at Congress'. Also 'secret intelligence from France' mentioning Lord North's plan of reconciliation.[10]

(*k*) New York, 19 and 20 July 1778, from William Eden to Lord North describing the French blockade of New York.[11]

(*l*) 1 Jan. 1779, Downing Street, from William Eden to Lord North: 'Lord Carlisle and I cannot make any claim to a continuance of the emoluments annexed to the American commission. As to the great object we have been quite unsuccessful. Yet our commission had its uses. We have been the means of transmitting above a million sterling of British property to this country and into mercantile circulation. By accepting that temporary situation, I quitted a profitable office in England.'[12]

(*m*) 6 Jan. 1784, from John Robinson to Lord North, sending him, *inter alia*, a packet of papers relative to 'transactions with[the] American Army...5 October 1781'.[13]

KENT COUNTY ARCHIVES OFFICE,[1] County Hall, Maidstone ME14 1XQ

SIDNEY PAPERS. 2 letters. 1609. (U1475 C8/811, 813)

18 and 23 June 1609, from Sir William Browne to Viscount Lisle, mention the possibility of a Lieutenant Saunders joining the second expedition to Virginia under De La Warr.[2]

SANDWICH BOROUGH RECORDS. 1611-1773.

(*a*) Letter, 1611, from Sir Edwin Sandys and twelve others, seeking financial backing for the Virginia Company, with copy of registered list of adventurers and list and numbers of tradesmen to be sent out with Sir Thomas Gates[3] and letter, 1612, containing order to subscribe £25.[4] (Sa/ZB 2/64-68)

(*b*) Returns of persons taking passage from Sandwich to America, 1635-7[5] (Sa/AC7)

(*c*) Contracts, bonds, etc., for transportation of convicts to the American colonies, including two certificates of landing, 1721-73. (Sa/JQb 145)

1. H.M.C. x (vi), p. 7.
2. Transcript, ibid., p. 8.
3. Extracts, ibid., pp. 9, 12.
4. Ibid., pp. 16-17, 19.
5. Ibid., p. 16.
6. Ibid., p. 21.
7. Ibid., p. 19.
8. Ibid.
9. Ibid.
10. Ibid., p. 20.
11. Ibid., p. 22.
12. Ibid., pp. 23-24.
13. Ibid., p. 65.

---

1. *Guide to the Kent County Archives Office* (Maidstone, 1958). The office also published a supplement to its *Guide* in 1971.
2. H.M.C. De L'Isle and Dudley (Penshurst) MSS. iv [77], pp. 130, 132.
3. Printed in Alexander Brown, *Genesis of the United States*, vol. i (London, 1890), pp. 461-70.
4. Printed in ibid., vol. ii, p. 555.
5. Transcribed (not fully) in William Boys, *Collections for a History of Sandwich*..., 2 vols. (Canterbury, priv. print. 1792, repr. 1842), pp. 750-2. Transcribed and edited, Eben Putnam, 'Two early passenger lists, 1635-7', in *New England Historical and Genealogical Register*, vol. lxxv, pp. 217-26, 1921.

TUFTON PAPERS. Volume and 13 estate documents. 1613-67. (U455 E21)

Papers relating to the holding of Sir Nicholas Tufton in Virginia with later questons for opinion of counsel, 1613-*c.* 1667.[6]

LENNARD, SIR SAMUEL (*c.* 1553-1618). Will. 1618. (U312 T17/2)

References to money 'adventures' in Virginia and Newfoundland.

POLHILL-DRABBLE PAPERS. 8 documents. 1629-*c.* 1800. (U1007 037, Z12/1-3)

(*a*) Copy of Letters Patent to Sir Robert Heath to establish the colony of Carolina, 1629. (U1007 037)
(*b*) 'History of the American War, 1779-81', by Charles Polhill, *c.* 1785. (U1007 Z12/2)
(*c*) 'American Anecdotes', by Charles Polhill, *c.* 1785-8. (U1007 Z12/1)
(*d*) Papers and designs for monument to George Washington, *c.* 1800. 5 docs. (U1007 Z12/3)

SACKVILLE PAPERS.

The De La Warr and Cranfield Papers are part of the Sackville collection from Knole. Some of these were reported on in H.M.C. iv (i) pp. 276-317, and H.M.C. vii, pp. 249-60. These papers are now in the Kent County Archives Office, and include material relating to Virginia, as listed on pp. 705-10 of the H.M.C. list.

FILMER PAPERS. 21 documents. 1653-83. (U120 C8-9)

Include letters from Henry Filmer, who emigrated to Mulberry Island in Virginia in 1653, to relatives in Kent; and discharge signed by the parish officers of Mulberry Island for legacy left by Filmer to provide communion plate for the parish church there.

WYKEHAM-MARTIN PAPERS. Family papers and correspondence: 206 documents. 1672-1820. (U23, C1, 2, 5, 6, 18, 23, 24, 27)

Correspondence of the Culpeper, Fairfax, and Martin families, referring particularly to the family estates in Virginia, the difficulties inherent in owning American property after the War of Independence, and the claims for compensation for loss of land. Contain also many letters from Bryan Martin (1731-98), who settled permanently in America.

CRIPPS PAPERS. 1 document. 1684. (U17/271)

Conveyance of a part of a share in the province of East Jersey, 1684.

SMITH-MASTERS PAPERS. 1 volume. 1691-1704. (U1127 A32)

Ledger of merchant trading with New England, etc.

KENNETT, MARGARET. 2 letters. 1725. (U352 C1)

Written to her father, Dr. Thomas Brett, giving detailed description of conditions in Charleston, S.C.

AMHERST MANUSCRIPTS.

Sir Jeffrey, 1st Baron Amherst, was the son of Jeffrey Amherst of Riverhead (1677-1750). His successful army career culminated with the capture of Montreal in 1760 and Amherst's knighthood. In 1776 he received a barony, and this was extended to the barony of Amherst of Montreal in 1788, with remainder to his nephew. The papers listed below are mainly correspondence and official in character, and an attempt has been made to separate the papers of Sir Jeffrey from those of the rest of his family.

I. Sir Jeffrey, 1st Lord Amherst.
(*a*) Personal and correspondence: A very large collection of letters, 1740-83, from a variety of correspondents, including American soldiers and politicians and others.
(*b*) Official: This very considerable collection includes papers of his military career in America, with copies of much of Amherst's 'out' correspondence and dispatches, as well as the 'in' papers.
(i) The American campaign.
Journals, 1758-63; military orders, 1758-63; accounts, etc., 1758-64; dispatches in both directions: William Pitt, 1757-62, Admiral Boscawen, 1758, Lord Ligonier, 1758-63, Lord Barrington, 1758-61, Charles Townshend, 1761-3, Lord Egremont, 1761-3, Welbore Ellis, 1763-4; papers regarding capitulation of Louisbourg, 1758, including correspondence with Brig. Gen. Wolfe and regarding Gen. James Abercromby's campaign; copies of letters regarding Indian affairs, 1764, including copy of treaty with chiefs of Ottawa and Chippewa nations, showing their picture signs in lieu of autographs; journal of Major Robert Rogers from Montreal to Detroit, 1761; journal of Major John Montresor to relieve Detroit during the Pontiac Rebellion, 1763; grant to Jeffrey Amherst of freedom of New York, 1760; correspondence with and documents taken from the Marquis de Vaudreuil, French Governor of Canada, 1755-60, including descriptions of 'La Louisiane' and dispositions of French troops; reports on state of Canada and the government of Quebec, proposals for settling Nova Scotia, *c.* 1760-6; detailed study of Western Canada and the route to the Mississippi, by C. de Lotbinière, 1764; papers regarding the government of Quebec and the Jesuit estate there, 1764-1804.
(ii) The American War of Independence.
Cabinet papers and correspondence with Lord North, 1778-82; papers and dispatches regarding the war in America, 1775-8; letters from General Gage, 1770-5; from General James Robertson, 1771-82; and from various correspondents in America, 1770-84; American newspapers and proclamation, 1774-5.

II. Other records, not Sir Jeffrey's.
(*a*) Accounts: farm and estate accounts, statements, etc., for Montreal estate, 1734-1923.
(*b*) Official: Lt. Gen. William Amherst: journals, 1758; papers for the Newfoundland campaign, July 1762 to Jan. 1763 (very full account of this brief campaign).
(*c*) Miscellaneous: MS. account of taking of Louisbourg, Quebec, and Montreal, and of the War of Independence by Ensign James Miller. Entitled 'Memoirs of an Invalid', and offered to Lord Amherst in 1792.

DEAL BOROUGH RECORDS. 1749-86. (De JP1)

Memorandum of bond to serve four years in H.M. plantations in America, 1752.

PRATT PAPERS. Letters and official papers. 1769-90. (U840 C173, 0136, L5)

(*a*) Copy Cabinet minute on removal of duties and related papers, 1769. 5 docs. (U840 0136)
(*b*) Copy inhibition under Act prohibiting trade with the American colonies. (U840 L5)
(*c*) Letters, 1775-90, from Sir Charles Pratt, 1st Earl Camden, to Robert Stewart, Earl and Marquess of Londonderry. Includes comments on the War of Independence, etc. 105 docs. (U840 C173)

6. See F. Hull, ed., 'The Tufton Manuscripts and the Virginia Connection', *Virginia Magazine of History and Biography*, vol. lxv, pp. 313-27, 1957.

TWISDEN FAMILY PAPERS. 2 notebooks. 1776-84.

(*a*) References in a notebook covering 1776-84, to Sir William Twisden going to America with James Gambier, 1777. (U49 F4/2)
(*b*) Notebook, by an unidentified writer, includes four pages on the War of Independence, *c*. 1780. (U49 F3)

COLLET MANUSCRIPTS (St. Clerc Estate).

This collection consists principally of the business and personal correspondence of Sir Mark Wilks Collet, bart. (1816-1905), especially for the period 1830-52; and also of documents relating to the St. Clerc estate, Ightham, which he purchased in 1878. Sir Mark's business career was especially concerned with the financial and banking aspects of the American cotton market. He worked in Liverpool, 1832-63, and visited the United States on a number of occasions. He was partner in the firm of Brown, Shipley and Co., merchant bankers, from 1851, and moved to London in 1863. He became a director of the Bank of England in 1866 and Governor 1887-9.
(*a*) Correspondence: Several thousand letters to, and copy letters from, Mark Wilks Collet, 1830-87; principal correspondents are Henry Patry & Co., Thomas Wilson & Co., and Purton Parker & Co., all of Liverpool, and Brown, Shipley & Co. Topics include import of cotton and other goods from the U.S. and the West Indies; investment in U.S. stocks; letters from New York and the cotton states, 1840-50; from Philadelphia, with account of social conditions and slave laws, 1783-92, and from Illinois, 1824.
(*b*) Accounts: Mark Wilks Collet: investment accounts with Brown Bros. of New York.
(*c*) Business: Mark Wilks Collet: papers concerning railway companies in Oregon and the Glenwood Hot Springs Co., U.S.A., 1838-94; accounts and memoranda of Anglo-American trade, 1846-50.

GAMBIER PAPERS. 15 documents, 1785-1817. (U194 F34)

Papers concerning compensation for land in Florida.

MACKESON, JOHN. Correspondence. 1807-14. (U47/34 C1 and U511 C8)

Includes references to his experiences in the West Indies and to the war with the United States, 1812-4.

GARRETT PAPERS. 21 estate documents. 1830-51. (U888 E4)

Concerning land in Ohio.

NORMAN PAPERS. 5 letters. 1831-42. (U310 C187)

Letters from Myer Myers in Norfolk and Richmond, Va., including comments on American financial practices.

MARTIN, GEORGE F. (d. 1852). 23 letters. 1834-52. (U442 F/10/2)

Letters from or relating to George F. Martin, who emigrated to Rochester, N.Y., in 1834, and died of cholera in 1852. (There are some later letters from his widow, *c*. 1869.) Martin refers to the immigration of Irish paupers to the United States, railroad building in New York in 1837, the 'infamous' war with Mexico, etc. There are also letters of advice to his relatives who emigrated to New York in 1850-1.

HOLWORTHY PAPERS. 13 documents. 1844-1930. (U929 F9, F35)

(*a*) Letters from W.T. Holworthy from New York and New Orleans, 1844-8. 12 docs. (U929 F9)
(*b*) Diary of a journey to the U.S.A., 1929-30. (U929 F35)

WOODGATE PAPERS. 7 letters. 1868-95. (U1050 C25)

Letters from Harvey Woodgate from Long Beach, Washington Territory, where he was successively a school teacher, lumber merchant, and a dealer in fancy fowls and plants.

PARISH RECORDS.

(*a*) Headcorn (P181/18/27), Marden (P244/12/185), and Staplehurst (P347/18/11). Correspondence regarding emigration of paupers to America and Canada from these parishes. The emigration papers of the parish overseers include notices from ship owners on their terms for transporting the emigrants, applications from the overseers for permission to borrow money against the parish rate to finance emigration, approval of this by the Poor Law Commissioners, lists of emigrants, etc.
(*b*) Bearsted (P18/8/1); Boxley (P40/8/1); Brasted (P42/8/5); Brenchley (P45/8/2); Brenzett (P46/8/1); Burmarsh (P53/11/3); Charing (P78/8/7; 18/127); Speldhurst (P344/28/54). These parish records may also contain significant information on emigration to America.

QUARTER SESSIONS RECORDS.

(*a*) Occasional bonds for transportation occur after the Act of 4 Geo. I (1717). (Q/SB)
(*b*) Certificates concerning apprentices sent to Pennsylvania or Maryland. 1 bundle. 1719. (Q/SB 1719)

LANCASHIRE

LANCASHIRE RECORD OFFICE,[1] Bow Lane, Preston PR1 8ND

BARCROFT PAPERS.[2] (Part of the Parker of Alkincoats and Browsholme Muniments.) 10 letters and 5 papers. 1682-1783. (DDB 61, 74)

Eight letters are from America to relatives in or near Colne, Lancs.: three, 1752-7, from William Barcroft in Virginia refer to payment of an annuity due to him; one, 1 Mar. 1723, from Ambrose Barcroft of Solebury, Pa., gives details of management of his estates; and four, 1752-80, from Ambrose Barcroft, Solebury and Philadelphia, concern financial and family affairs. In addition there are: a letter, 1737, to William Barcroft in Virginia; a letter, 1682, from Ireland to Lancashire, concerning the emigration of Thomas Barcroft to help divide the land in Pennsylvania; and papers concerning the exchange of Lieut. Barcroft of the British Army for Lieut. Allen of the Virginia Line, and his passage home, 1781-3.

1. R. Sharpe France, *Guide to the Lancashire Record Office* (Preston, 1948). A revised *Guide* was published in 1962.
2. Microfilms made by the Virginia Colonial Records Project.

KENYON MUNIMENTS. 2 letters. 1683-4. (DDK e/9)

Both letters are from Roger Kenyon to his father, Roger Kenyon, in Peel, near Manchester. The first, 'Road Island', 30 May 1683, explains how Kenyon has been sold to Mr. Coddington, the Governor's brother, as a three years' servant, and appeals for money to obtain his discharge. [DDKe 9/92 (107)]. The second, 'Marshfeild', Mass., Nov. 1684, written on Kenyon's arrival again in America after a period in England, discusses family affairs, including the impending birth of his son. [DDKe 9/50 (87)].

CLARKE, OGLETHORPE ACCUMULATION. Letter. 1752. (DDO 11/57)

On board the *Elizabeth* in Rappahannock River, Va., by Thomas Harrison to his wife in Lancashire, describing slaving voyage from Gambia.

HART JACKSON ACCUMULATION. 2 deeds. 1753, 1765. (DDHj: acc. 1372)

Sale for £64 of a plantation of 150 acres in Bartie Co., North Carolina, by David Sinclar of that place to James Stockdale of Liverpool, 3 Dec. 1753; agreement to prevent survivorship of a joint tenancy in an estate of 646 acres adjoining Albemarle Sound, North Carolina, between James Stockdale, Ellin Sandys, and others, 8 Oct. 1765.

CROMBLEHOLME ACCUMULATION. 11 letters. 1760-6. (DDCm)

William and Henry Rigby, Philadelphia, to their Lancashire relatives, referring to disturbed international affairs and trouble with the Indians.

GARNETT MUNIMENTS. Papers. 1774-1890. (DDQ)

Deeds and papers concerning land in Virginia.

HOUGHTON MUNIMENTS. 22 letters.[3] 1778-1846. (DDHt 12; DDHo 419)

These letters, written from various places in Pennsylvania, Virginia, Ohio, and New York, are addressed to members of the Morris family in Lancashire. They include details of the voyages, information concerning the weaving trade and the work and wages of blacksmiths, prices of food, etc. These muniments also contain one letter, dated 8 Jan. 1778, from D. Houghton to Mrs. Houghton, Lambeth, referring to the American War of Independence.

GRUNDY FAMILY PAPERS. Letter. 1782. (DDX 207/32)

New York, 14 Dec. 1782, from Messrs. Parson & Prior to Messrs. Cooke, Relph & Barnardeston, London, including a large textile order and referring to transport conditions and the need for convoys.

WOODCOCK ACCUMULATION. 3 documents. 1782-3. (DDWo)

Certificate of sale by public vendue of 228 kegs of split peas from the schooner *Polly* from Charlestown, with sale account and certificate of survey by the wardens of the port of New York, 7 Oct. 1782, 20 May 1783.

BADGERY ACCUMULATION. 236 letters. 1817-70. (DDBd 52)

Letters relating to the interests of the Hargreaves family of Lancashire in Ware County, Ga.

BIRKET(T) FAMILY PAPERS. 14 letters.[4] 1833-59. (DP/265-278)

The letters are written from Peoria and Mount Pleasant, Ill., to relatives in Lancashire. Most are from John Birket. Besides news of relatives in Vermont and Illinois, they include discussion of the religious and financial problems involved in the attempt to provide a Protestant Episcopal Church and school in Mount Pleasant.

DOCTON ACCUMULATION. Letter. 1839. (DDX 116/10)

New York, 5 June 1839, from John Barrow to his uncle in Lancashire concerning Quaker affairs in America and criticizing Thomas Shillitoe's recently published journal.

CLIFTON MUNIMENTS. 2 letters. 1842. (DD Cl 1192)

Myerscough House, 22 Mar. 1842, from John Cunliffe, includes extensive discussion of the effects of United States and British import duties on cheese, in the light of the difference in quality between the cheeses of the two countries.

Knowsley, 28 Feb. 1842, from Thomas Statter, refers to the shipment of pigs to Kentucky and Tennessee.

WALMSLEY ACCUMULATON. 2 letters. 1846, 1851. (DDX 140/9, 10)

New Jersey, 1846, describing conditions of work and land prices in several states; Wisconsin, 1851, giving advice and comment on the journey from Liverpool.

BULLER FAMILY PAPERS. Letter. 1850. (DDX 362)

New York, 19 June 1850, from Agnes Hardman to her brother in Lancashire, referring to flourishing trade and the coming Fourth of July celebrations.

BOND FAMILY PAPERS. 29 letters. 1870-99. (DDX 719)

The letters are written from Milford, Conn.; Grafton, W. Va.; Bunker Hill, Kans.; and Richmond Hill, Ind. Most are from Kate (Catherine) Bond to her brother, sister, and uncle. The family appears to have emigrated from Aughton or Sefton, Lancs.; the letters include farming and social information with family news.

W. & J. FOSTER RECORDS. Papers. 1896-7. (DDX 438/9-11)

Letter, 10 June 1896, from Isaac W. Lamb, Perry, Mich., to James Foster, with an essay by Foster and an offprint from the *Knitters' Circular and Monthly Record*, 1897, concerning invention and development of the parallel bed knitting machine.

PARISH RECORDS.

Include emigrant material, for example, the minute-book of the Select Vestry of Barnacre contains the resolution, 21 Mar. 1833, that a meeting be held 'for taking into consideration of a family going into America'.

QUARTER SESSIONS RECORDS.

Among the petitions (QSP) are at least four referring to America; there may be others.

(*a*) 1666. (284/5): Relief for a man who has returned after thirty years in the plantations in America.

3. Photostats in the collection of Letters of Emigrants to America in the British Library of Political and Economic Science, London School of Economics.

4. Loc. cit.

(*b*) 1676. (444/25): Relief for the wife of a man 'who is gone into Virginia'.
(*c*) 1686. (625/2): List of servants to go to America.[5]
(*d*) 1708. (968/13): The proposed sending of Robert Gregory as a slave to Virginia.

LANCASHIRE COTTON TRADE.
Because of the influence of American cotton on the life of Lancashire's weavers, many of the Record Office's holdings pertaining to nineteenth-century Lancashire also have some relevance for U.S. history.

STONYHURST COLLEGE, Whalley, Blackburn

PAPERS OF THE COLLEGE. 3 documents. 1737-95.
(*a*) Two conveyances of land in Maryland by the Rev. George Thorold of 'Anairundle' co., Md., 1737, and the Rev. James Charles Thompson, 1795.[1]
(*b*) Disposition of estates in Maryland by the Rev. Richard Molyneux, 8 Mar. 1758.[2]

LEICESTERSHIRE

DUKE OF RUTLAND, Belvoir Castle, Grantham

RUTLAND PAPERS. Letters. 1611-1780.
(*a*) 10 Mar. 1611, from Bruz to Rutland says: 'Sir Thomas Dale is departed to Virginia with three hundred men, and the Cumpanye hath spent therein ayght thowsand pownes. They should have sent with them at lest twise as many wemen to have mad a good and spedye plantatione.'[1]
(*b*) 12 Oct. and 7 Dec. 1676, from Lady Chaworth to her brother Lord Roos, mention Bacon's rebellion.[2]
(*c*) Various letters, 1763-5, touching upon such matters as operations against the Indians, a description of West Florida, and the Sons of Liberty.[3]
(*d*) 20 Dec. 1766, from Gage at New York, to the Marquess of Granby, concerning the transport of troops. Also makes a number of complaints [no detail of complaints given].[4]
(*e*) Two letters to the Marquess of Granby: the first, 16 Jan. 1768, from Samuel Martin, recommending his brother for the position of Quartermaster-General in North America; the second, 7 Feb. 1768, from Colonel Charles Hotham, applying for his regiment to be sent to America.[5]
(*f*) 9 June 1769, from Lieutenant-Colonel Edward Maxwell to the Marquess of Granby, 'as to the prosecution arising out of a conflict of jurisdiction between a court martial and the civil government of the province in the southern district of America'.[6]
(*g*) Report on West Florida and part of French Louisiana, by John Thomas to General Williamson, 28 Nov. 1769 (11 pages).[7]
(*h*) A description of the Battle of Bunker Hill. 25 June 1775.[8]
(*i*) 28 June, 2 Sept., 26 Nov., 26 Dec. 1776, from Edmund Stevens to the Marquess of Granby, describing the fighting on Long Island, divisions on the American side, the capture of General Lee.[9]
(*j*) Various letters to the Marquess of Granby, with some mention of American affairs.
(i) Aug.-1777, from Lord Robert Manners - French naval movements. 30 Aug. and 9 Oct. 1777, from Edmund Stevens - troop movements and skirmishes in America.
(ii) 6 and 28 Nov. 1777, from the Marquess of Rockingham - the first mentions the precarious situaton of Burgoyne's army and the second 'not a word of news as yet from America through the ministerial channels'.[10]
(*k*) Philadelphia, 13 Dec. 1777, from E. Stevens to Marquess of Granby, referring to the disaster to Burgoyne, says that only a reinforcement of not less than 25,000 to 30,000 men could reduce the country, but even then he doubts if it could be done.[11]
(*l*) '1778 [*c*. April]. List of prices of various articles as they were formerly and a few months ago in Pennsylvania, showing in several instances a tenfold increase.'[12]
(*m*) Long letter, compiled at various dates between 19 July and 14 August 1780, from Lord Robert Manners, with the fleet off Rhode Island, to the Duke of Rutland. Gives a very optimistic picture of the overall British position in the war, which he expects to end in an American capitulation within a year. Gives also a description of the French fleet at anchor off Rhode Island and French fortifications ashore.[13]
(*n*) 20 Sept. 1780, from Lord Robert Manners, at sea, to the Duke of Rutland, mentions that Cornwallis 'has gained a very complete victory at South Carolina'.[14]
(*o*) 27 Sept., 4 and 31 Oct. 1780, from Lord Robert Manners, at sea, to the Duke of Rutland, mainly describing the superiority of the French fleet, the poor condition of the English, and the dangerous situation of Cornwallis's army. Also mention the defection of Benedict Arnold from the American side.[15]

LEICESTERSHIRE RECORD OFFICE, The New Walk, Leicester LE1 7JB

VIRGINIA COMPANY. 3 letters. 1618.
Letters between the Virginia Company and the Mayor and Aldermen of Leicester concerning local arrangements for the Virginia lottery.

5. *Genealogists' Magazine*, vol. xii, p. 234, 1956.

1. H.M.C. x (iv), p. 197.
2. Ibid., p. 191.

1. Transcript, H.M.C. xii (iv), p. 429.
2. Transcripts, H.M.C. xii (v), pp. 30, 32.
3. Transcripts, H.M.C. Rutland (Belvoir) iv [24], pp. 231-5.
4. Synopsis, H.M.C. xii (v), p. 289.
5. Ibid., pp. 300-1.
6. Ibid., p. 311.
7. Ibid., p. 312.
8. H.M.C. xiv (i), pp. 2-3.
9. Transcripts, ibid., pp. 5-8. Also letter, 29 Dec. 1776, of Thomas Thoroton to his mother, p. 8.
10. Transcripts, ibid., pp. 9-10.
11. Ibid., p. 12.
12. Ibid., p. 13.
13. Transcript, ibid., pp. 31-4.
14. Transcript, ibid., p. 36.
15. Transcripts, ibid., pp. 37-9.

NEW ENGLAND. Grant. 1620.[1]

Grant of New England by James I to a council established at Plymouth, 1620. (DG7/Col. 2)

VIRGINIA. Papers. 1674-1701.

(*a*) Protest by inhabitants of Virginia against royal grant of colony to Earl of Arlington and Lord Culpeper, 1674; Orders in Council relating to same, 1676. (DG7/Col.3)
(*b*) List of ships entered and cleared in Rappahannock District, Virginia, 1694-6.
(*c*) Invoice of tobacco shipped to Bristol, 1697. (DG7/Col. 5,6)
(*d*) Instructions to William Selwyn, Governor, and Order in Council on same, 1701.

WASHINGTON, GEORGE. 4 letters. 1786-91.

From George Washington to Mrs. Catharine Macaulay Graham:
(*a*) Mount Vernon, 10 Jan. 1786, congratulating her on safe travelling in very bad weather.[2]
(*b*) Mount Vernon, 16 Nov. 1787, referring to a Mr. Pine's historical paintings, and Washington's own difficulties in framing and forming the Federal Convention.[3]
(*c*) New York, 9 Jan. 1790, thanking her for her congratulations on the Presidency; he reflects for three pages on the responsibilities and difficulties of his position and the effects of the situation in America on the new government, the increase in commerce and manufactures, etc., and the constitutional effects he thinks it may have in France.[4]
(*d*) Philadelphia, 10 Feb. 1791, acknowledging receipt of a treatise on education and excusing himself from writing at length because of pressure of public business.[5]
(One surviving envelope is addressed to Mrs. Macaulay Graham at 'Bracknal' (Bracknell), Berkshire, England.)

POOR LAW RECORDS.

Lutterworth Union Minute-book, 1838-40. Minute for 24 Apr. 1838 records the reading of a letter from the Poor Law Commissioners about the emigration of paupers to the United States.

QUARTER SESSIONS RECORDS.

Forty-nine bonds, 1721-83, and nine orders, 1720-83, for the transportation of criminals, chiefly to Virginia and Maryland.

OTHER LETTERS. *c.* 1810-1863.

(*a*) Letters addressed to Sir Henry Halford I and Sir Henry Halford II.
(i) Rebecca Blodgett at New York, concerning American politics, threats to Britain, etc., *c.* 1810-4. (DG24/825/8)
(ii) Charles R. Vaughan (British Minister to the U.S., 1825-35) at Paris: discussion of French relations with Britain and the U.S.A.; forecast of future trouble from an industrialized U.S., 1836. (DG24/835/40)
(iii) Daniel Webster at Washington: account of voyage to America, American financial situation, etc., 1840. (DG24/866/12)
(iv) Marquis Wellesley at Marble Hill, Twickenham, Middlesex: includes a reference to the American Confederacy, 1863.
(*b*) Letter from John Leech at Charleston, S.C., to his aunt in Liverpool (?): news of Charleston, comparison of England and America, etc., 1816. (Misc. 397)
(*c*) Letter from Earl of Dalhousie at Quebec to Hon. S. Canning, requesting information from Canning's successor on Congressional business relating to northern or western frontiers, 1823. (DE 1274/1, f.53b)
(*d*) Letter, 1849, from G.L. Marchet, describing conditions in Newfoundland.

1. 'DG7' references in the Leicestershire Record Office indicate items which are part of the Finch MSS. There are also other references under New York, New England, etc. in vols. 1 and 2 and especially vol. 4 of the printed H.M.C. Calendar of the Finch Papers.
2. See *Writings of George Washington*, ed. by John C. Fitzpatrick, vol. xxviii (Washington, D.C., 1938), pp. 370-1.
3. Ibid., vol. xxix, pp. 316-7.
4. Ibid., vol. xxx, pp. 495-8 (1939).
5. Ibid., vol. xxxi, pp. 213-4 (1939).

LINCOLNSHIRE

EARL OF ANCASTER, Grimsthorpe, Bourne

ANCASTER PAPERS. Letter. 1585.

London, 15 Nov. 1585, from 'Jhohn Stubbe' to Lord Willoughby in Denmark, mentions the Virginia voyage of Sir Richard Grenville, and encloses a letter (not printed) concerning it.[1]

1. H.M.C. Ancaster MSS. [66], pp. 16-7.

THE LIBRARY, THE CATHEDRAL, Lincoln

The Cathedral Library is rich in seventeenth-century manuscripts, pamphlets, and broadsheets, as well as early printed books. There is, for instance, a rare copy of Captain John Smith's *The Seaman's Grammar*...(London, 1627); and of more especial relevance:
(*a*) A broadsheet (bound in 'Various Treatises', numbers 5-27): *Proportion of Provisions Needfull for Such as Intend to Plant Themselves in New England, for One Whole Year.* Printed at London for Fulke Clifton, 1630.[1]
(*b*) A photostat of the broadsheet, *The Capitall Lawes of New-England, as They Stand Now in Force in the Common-Wealth, by the Court. In the Years 1641. 1642.* This was the first known codification. The original is now in the library of the Harvard Law School.
(*c*) MS. diary of Benjamin Ingham, Wesleyan minister, who went to Georgia in 1736 to preach to the settlers.

1. See A.M. Cook, *Lincolnshire Links with the U.S.A.* (Lincoln, priv. print., 1956), p. 59.

LINCOLNSHIRE ARCHIVES OFFICE, The Castle, Lincoln LN1 3AB

PRESTON FAMILY PAPERS. 1637. (Preston 4/1/1-2)

Grant of part of Nova Scotia and of a baronetcy to George Preston in consideration of his zeal in promoting the plantation of the region. 1637.

MASSINGBERD OF GUNBY MSS. 1698-1711.

Five account books of Thomas Meux, citizen and mercer of London, merchant in Narva and London, who also traded with the West Indies and the mainland of North America (New England, Virginia), 1698-1711. (Massingberd of Gunby (M.G.) 7/1-5)

MASSINGBERD AND MASSINGBERD-MUNDY DEPOSITS. Letters. 1699-1714.

From Elizabeth and Edward Hyrne from Charleston, S.C., to Elizabeth's brother Burrell Massingberd of South Ormsby, Lincs., about trade with South Carolina and the purchase of a plantation between the Bath and Cooper Rivers. (Mass. 21; M.M. 2/1)

ANCASTER DEPOSIT. Correspondence, etc. (*c.* 100 items). 1716-36.

Papers regarding bequests under will of William Heathcote to children of his brother, Col. Caleb Heathcote of New York, including letters of James De Lancey, who became Chief Justice and Lieutenant Governor of New York. (Anc. 11/B/1-5)

MONSON FAMILY PAPERS. Letters, documents, etc., *c.* 1737-1833.

(*a*) Papers of John Monson, 1st Baron Monson (1693-1748), Commissioner for Plantations, 1737, and of Charles Monson, Deputy Paymaster-General. (Monson 13, *passim*)
(*b*) Hampton, Va., 1740, from William Blakney [or Blakeney] to Henry Pelham on the condition of troops there, their payment, and embarkation for Jamaica. (Monson 25/2/49)
(*c*) Correspondence[1] of the 1st and 2nd Barons Monson: including letters from Thomas Pownall, Governor of New Jersey, addressed to John Monson, 2nd Baron Monson (1727-74), which gives an account of the colonies but more especially New Jersey, 1754-6. (Monson 25/1/44-48)
(*d*) Bargaintown, N.J., 29 July 1833, from Louisa Canfield to Mrs. Sarah Stone, Italy Hill, Yates County, N.Y., containing mainly family news. (Monson 25/3/19)

ASWARBY MUNIMENTS (Whichcote Family Papers). *c.* 80 letters, papers and accounts. 1742-73.

(*a*) Nathaniel Tregagle, a Cornishman, married a daughter of Sir Paul Whichcote. Papers relating to his affairs in Carolina. Seventy-six estate accounts, bills, and letters concerned with the administration of an estate and the business as importer of Nathaniel Tregagle of Georgetown and Charleston, S.C., 1742-64. Various letters, papers and accounts marked 'South Carolina', 1759-62, including an alphabetical list of debts due to Tregagle, Georgetown, S.C., 1760. Copy of Tregagle's will, 4 June 1760, which provides for the manumission of his two Negro slaves, Cubah and Quashebald, with the interest of £100 for their clothing. (Asw 1/23, 10/67)
(*b*) Letters, Charleston, S.C., 1742-84, from A. Johnston and George Appleby. Some refer to war against Indians. (Asw 1/23, *passim*)
(*c*) Letter, 1761, from George Appleby to T. Whichcote, describing the war and the difficulties of war-time trade in South Carolina. (Asw 10/67/9)
(*d*) Bill of exchange drawn by Alexander Rose of South Carolina on Messrs. Berwicke & Co. of London, 1763. (Asw 10/43/20)
(*e*) Letter, 1773, from William and Mary College, Virginia, on death of Josiah Johnson and copy of his will. (Asw 10/48/6-7)

AMCOTTS DEPOSIT. 1 document. 1779. (Amc 4/6/1)

Deed of partnership, 1779, between Robert Weston Cracroft and his brother Francis, and Robert Bourne, planter, of Katesbourne, W. Fla., to share the profits of planting and the buying and selling of Negroes.

LANGTON MSS. 6 letters. 1818-32.

Six letters about the administration of the Langton family's estate on Prince Edward Island, 1818-32. (Langton 6/2)

HOLLAND DEPOSIT (Bertie Family Papers). Correspondence. *c.* 1835-60. (H.D. 66/3)

Edward Codwise, an American, married the heiress and succeeded to part of the property at Long Sutton. His correspondence with his lawyer, *c.* 1835-60, contains many references to his stage career in England and America.

FANE OF FULBECK DEPOSIT. Journals, diaries, etc. 1838-90.

(*a*) Two journals, 1838-40, of Mrs. Thomas Chaplin, Canada and U.S. (Fane 6/12/2-3)
(*b*) Journal, 1851-2, kept by Col. Francis Fane of a tour in Canada and the U.S.; diaries, 1851-3, covering this tour; report, 1890, of his visit to Canada as member of a tenant farmer delegation. (Fane 6/8/2; 6/8/1/4-5; 6/8/3-4)

BOSTON BOROUGH RECORDS. Pishey Thompson diary. 1842-44.

Thompson, the historian of Boston, Lincs., went to the U.S.A. in 1819. He was for many years a bookseller and publisher in Washington, D.C. This diary covers a stay in England in 1842-3, followed by his return to Washington. Among subjects covered are his attempts to persuade the U.S. government to employ him to set up a Bureau of Statistics.[2] (Boston Borough Records 19/13)

BRACE DEPOSIT. Diary. 1875.(Brace 22)

Ship's master's diary, 1875, Hull to New York.

PEAKE, SNOW, AND JEUDWINE DEPOSIT. 1 bundle. 1877-1919.

Executorship of Miss E.J. Haynes of Manhattan Island. (P.S.J. 7/15)

MISCELLANEOUS DEPOSIT. Notebook. 1873-87. (Misc. Dep. 17/18)

Small notebook relating to financing Algernon L.H. Short on his going to Ridgeway, Warren County, N.C.

1. Photostats of these items have been sent to the Library of Congress, Washington, D.C., at the request of Lord Monson.
2. These records are not at the L.A.O., but are in the custody of the Boston District Council, Municipal Buildings, West Street, Boston.

LONDON, GREATER

ALLEN & HANBURYS LTD., Bethnal Green, London, E.2

BUSINESS RECORDS.[1] 1777-1885.

Manufacturing chemists and makers of surgical instruments. The firm, founded in 1715 by Sylvanus Bevan and continued by Joseph

1. These were used by D. Chapman-Huston and E.C. Cripps for *Through a City Archway: the Story of Allen and Hanburys, 1715-1954* (London, 1954) which includes a chapter on the firm's early trade with America based on research by Whitfield J. Bell, Jr.

Gurney Bevan, William Allen, and others, carried on a considerable trade with New York, Philadelphia, and other American cities both before and after the War of Independence. The records held which contain material relating to this trade are as follows:
(*a*) Letter-books. Eleven volumes, 1774-1849, containing the originals written by the various partners (the letters actually sent to customers were copies of these); also a volume of duplicates for 1865-85. Of the volumes examined, the earliest, 1775-8, includes a number of 1777 letters to Donald McLean, William Brownjohn, and William Stewart of New York, about orders and shipping problems; letters to the United States in the 1795-1806 volume mainly concern debts owed the firm; the 1826-49 volume includes much correspondence, 1845-7, with Hull and Bowne of New York, and the volume for 1865-85, letters, 1885, to W.H. Scheiffelin & Co. of New York about the market for their pills in Britain.
(*b*) Ledgers. Ten ledgers covering, with a few gaps, 1777-1866. Most include the accounts of firms in various American cities; these are particularly frequent in the earlier volumes.
(*c*) Order and 'waste books'. Twenty order books containing orders for 1777, 1801-4, and 1855-78; eight 'waste books', containing the same information in a different form, are available for 1773, 1776-8, and 1851-71.

MISCELLANEOUS RECORDS.
In addition to the business archives described above, the following material is held by the firm:
(*a*) Pennsylvania Hospital. Photostats of records in the minutes of the Managers' Committee of the Pennsylvania Hospital, and typed transcripts of these. Included are invoices of drugs bought from the Bevans in 1752; letters to Silvanus Bevan and Thomas Hyam, the London agents for the hospital, from Benjamin Franklin and other managers; etc.
(*b*) William Allen (1770-1843). Correspondence.

(i) Envelope labelled 'William Allen's Letters' includes a copy of a letter, Philadelphia, 4 Mar. 1796, from Joseph Bunghurst to William Cowper, expressing best wishes from Bunghurst and other Philadelphia admirers of the poet. On the copy is written 'N.B. The copy was given to me on the—April 1830 by Eliza Fothergill. Edinburgh. John McCoy.'

(ii) Volume labelled 'Letters of William Allen' includes a letter to Allen from W. Dillwyn, Dec. 1810, containing an extract about Paul Cuffe from a letter from John James and Alexander Wilson of Pennsylvania. It also includes letters to Allen from J.W. Griscom, New York, 1812; Nathan Hunt, Springfield, N.C., 1812; Stephen Pretter, Burlington, N.J., 1843; and Benjamin Silliman, New Haven, Conn., 1815.

(iii) Volume labelled 'African Correspondence' contains copies of correspondence, 1811-9, among Allen, Thomas Clarkson, John Kizell, Henry Warren, Captain Paul Cuffe (American Negro seaman), and others, about the affairs of the African Institution of London and the Friendly Society of Freetown, Sierra Leone. Cuffe's letters concern the attitudes of American Negroes towards emigration to Sierra Leone, news of embarkation for Freetown, etc.

(iv) Folder labelled 'William Allen Letters' includes a letter, New Bedford, Mass., 12 July 1811, from W. Sawyer Wall to Allen, with news of friends and comment on the American political scene.

(v) Volume labelled 'William Allen - letters, notes, diaries, etc.' includes a typed transcript of a letter, 4 June 1812, from Allen to John Griscom, New York, about scientific instruments.
(*c*) Parcel marked 'Old orders on A & H' includes a document, 22 Nov. 1803, giving John Murray the younger, of New York, power of attorney to act for Joseph Gurney Bevan in collecting debts; and a letter, London, 7 June 1819, from Josiah Forster (to Allen?) on the Quaker Yearly Meeting he has recently attended - his brother's 'concern to visit Friends in America', information about Friends' activities, mainly relations with Negroes, in various states, etc.

ANTI-SLAVERY SOCIETY,
60 Weymouth Street, London W1N 4DX

SLAVERY AND THE ANTI-SLAVERY MOVEMENT. Printed books, journals, and pamphlets (*c.* 1,200 volumes). 1823- .

The Anti-Slavery Committee was founded in 1823. The Aborigines Protection Society (1837) and the British and Foreign Anti-Slavery Society (1839) amalgamated in 1909 to form the Anti-Slavery and Aborigines Protection Society. (The 'working' title was recently changed to 'Anti-Slavery Society'.)
Journals in the collection include: *Anti-Slavery Magazine* (Derby), 1824; *Anti-Slavery Reporter* (New York), 1825-1950 (1836-40 not published); *Anti-Slavery Record* (New York, for American Anti-Slavery Society), 1835-7; *Anti-Slavery Examiner* (American Anti-Slavery Society), vol. i, nos. 2-8, 1836; *Publications of the British and Foreign Anti-Slavery Society,* two volumes, *c.* 1840, and *Annual Reports,* two volumes, 1840-52; *Proceedings of Anti-Slavery Conventions,* London, 1840, 1843, and Paris, 1867; *Aborigines Friend and Colonial Intelligencer* (name varies), 1847-1909 (with Annual Reports of the Aborigines Protection Society).

See also Anti-Slavery Papers in Rhodes House Library, Oxford (pp. 205-6).

BANK OF ENGLAND,
Threadneedle Street, London EC2R 8AH

The Archives of the Bank are not primarily an historical archive, but are a working archive for the daily business of the Bank itself. However, permission to inspect records of an earlier date than a hundred years ago may be granted on occasion for specific scholarly purposes. For records of a later date access is granted only in exceptional circumstances. Applications should be made to the Secretary of the Bank, and the applicant should be sponsored by the academic body concerned in the research.

Sir John Clapham's history, *The Bank of England*, 2 vols. (Cambridge, 1944), made use of all available types of records in the Bank, and so its footnotes and index furnish an easily accessible guide to the Bank's principal records. There are five main series of records, in any or all of which important transactions may figure:

(i) The General Court of Proprietors - Minute Books (G.C.B.).
(ii) Court of Directors - Minute Books (C.B.).
(iii) Committee of Treasury Minute Books (C.T.).
(iv) Letter Books (L.B.).
(v) General Ledgers (G.L.).
(vi) Drawing Office Ledgers (D.O.).

In addition, certain other collections in the Bank, such as the Dobrée MSS., contain relevant material. The main records are kept chronologically; there is a General Index to the two series of Court Books and to the Committee of Treasury Books. The most important incidents relating to American affairs - leaving aside routine business entirely - appear from Clapham to be:
1836. To help straighten out its affairs on the expiring of its charter, the Bank of the United States was arranging a loan in London. (See the Governor's memorandum for the Chancellor of the Exchequer of Aug. 1836 in the 'Minutes of Correspondence with H.M. Government, 3'.)

1836. The Committee of Treasury Books (C.T.) for this year continually refer to the affairs of the seven English or Anglo-American firms who were most involved in the over-extension of finance for American trade and American loans: Baring, Brown, Lizardi, Morrison, and the notorious 'three W's', Wilson, Wiggin, and Wildes (e.g. C.T. 22, 27 July 1836; and the entry for 26 October shows Baring's American specialist, Joshua Bates, advising the committee, and also Lizardi's supplying information about billdrawing at New Orleans). In June 1836 Nicholas Biddle of the Bank of the United States asked for an account and open credit with the Bank of England (C.T. 8 June 1836).

1837. Further entries in the Court Books (C.B.) about the affairs of the 'three W's' in relation to the failure of American credit (see, especially, C.B. Ib., 13 April, 3 and 30 May, 8 and 22 June; the entry for 13 April is a memorial from 200 Liverpool businessmen and merchants referring to the intense distress that the American panic was causing to the cotton trade).

The Directors sent an agent, John W. Cowell, to America to inquire into debts due from firms in the United States to them, as backers and creditors of English houses. He was to contact the President of the Bank of the United States, then doing business as the United States Bank of Pennsylvania (see C.B. 14 Sept.).

1838. Biddle's request for credit was turned down (C.B. Ib., 15 Feb.), and Biddle complains that the Bank of England would not receive his funds (C.B. Ib., 15 Feb.). Further exchanges in this controversy - C.B. Ib., 22 Feb. and Kb., 19 Apr. But in March of that year the Bank decided to let the American market have gold (C.B. Ib., 15, 22, and 29 Mar.).

1857. The world-wide panic of 1857 started similarly in the American market, and is reflected in the Bank's records for that year. (See especially C.B. Ec., report to the Chancellor of the Exchequer of 1 December 1857. Also the Diary and Letters of Bonamy Dobrée, the Deputy Governor, touch on these matters; see the Dobrée MSS.).

1881. The American silver question and the international bimetallic controversy led to the American Minister, James Russell Lowell, sounding out the views of the British Treasury, and so in official and more private letters the Governor of the Bank explains to the Chancellor the history and practice of the Bank's silver buying (see especially C.B. Dd., 30 June, and L.B. 19, 30 June).

BARCLAYS BANK LTD., Head Office, 54 Lombard Street, London EC3P 3AH

BANK RECORDS.

Records have been found relating to American investments in the 1870's by the London and Provincial Bank, some in United States stock but mostly in railways, and to similar investments by the London and South Western Bank. The railways concerned are the New York Central; Atlantic and Great Western; Erie, Philadelphia and Reading; and the Grand Trunk.

These two banks amalgamated in 1917 as the London Provincial and South Western Bank, which in turn amalgamated with Barclays Bank Ltd. in 1918.

TRUSTEES OF THE BEDFORD ESTATES, Bedford Office, London WC1B 5BL

BEDFORD PAPERS. 1593-1763.

(*a*) 'An abstract of the lawes of Newe England', n.d. [Imperfect].[1]

(*b*) 'A discourse upon our forraigne plantations...and the grounds of erecting a West India company', n.d.[2]

(*c*) 'Travills, adventures, and observations of Captaine John Smith, in Europe, Asia, Africa, and America, 1593-1629, etc.'[3]

(*d*) Letter, 6 Feb. 1734, from Thomas E___, of W___, includes 'considerations relating to the present condition of the colonies'.[4]

(*e*) 'Some observations on the right of the Crown of Great Britain to the North west continent of America, with copies of Mons. Geraldine's letter, 1736, to the trustees of Georgia, and the answer of the Indian nations in Georgia in alliance with Great Britain (in Mr. Martyn's of Apr. 7, 1748)'.[5]

(*f*) 'Peace of 1763. Vol. 1 (March 1761-August 1762).[Copied by Mr. Wiffen?] Peace of Paris. (March 1761-June 1763.) (Copies.) 2 vols.'[6]

1. Woburn MSS., H.M.C. 250.
2. Ibid., H.M.C. 264.
3. Ibid., H.M.C. 259.
4. Ibid., H.M.C. 207.
5. Ibid., H.M.C. 208.
6. Ibid., H.M.C. 80 and 81.

BISHOPSGATE INSTITUTE, 230 Bishopsgate, London EC2M 4QH

GEORGE HOWELL COLLECTION.

George Howell (1833-1910), bricklayer; secretary of the London Trades Council 1861-2, and of the Reform League 1864-7; Liberal M.P. 1885-95.[1]

(*a*) Library of *c.* 20,000 volumes of books and pamphlets on economics, the early history of trade unionism, and the labour movement. It includes many early works on emigration generally, slavery, the American labour movement, etc. There are several pamphlets on the *Alabama* dispute, American agriculture and land systems, and Anglo-American trade. Constitutions and rules of trade unions often contain union regulations about emigration of members and assistance from union funds, e.g., *Constitution and Rules of the National Agricultural Labourers Union,* 1874.

(*b*) Eight volumes of manuscripts, being several drafts for 'Notes on the Life of a Toiler', Howell's unpublished autobiography. Includes accounts of the working-class movement's reactions to the Civil War. Incorporate a series of letters, 1870-5, and a review of the years 1876-9, sent to a friend in America.

(*c*) Diaries, about thirty volumes, *c.* 1864-1910.

(*d*) Thirteen letter-books of George Howell and the Reform League, 1865-84; and of letters to Howell. The first four letter-books are concerned with the Reform League; the later ones include Howell's personal letters. There are references to American institutions[2] and to the *Alabama* dispute, 1872. The letters to Howell are indexed under the sender's name, the letters for each year being in a separate envelope; they include a series of letters from Goldwin Smith at Cornell describing American opinion, Republicanism, British emigrants in the United States, etc.

(*e*) Minute-book of the First International Workingmen's Association, 1866-9. Scrapbook of cuttings and notes made by George Howell on the Association's meetings. List of members, 1865-70.

1. For Howell's biography, see F.M. Leventhal, *Respectable Radical* (London, 1971).
2. See Henry Pelling, *America and the British Left: from Bright to Bevan* (London, 1956), p. 24.

The minute-book includes many entries of American interest. The minutes of a meeting on 4 Dec. 1866 contain a report of a statement by Orsini on his return from a visit to the United States that Wendell Phillips, Charles Sumner, and Horace Greeley had joined the Association. The Annual Report, 1866-7, of the American secretary of the General Council of the International Workingmen's Association contains references to the Report of the National Labour Congress of working-class delegates of the United States, efforts to open up correspondence between workingmen's assocations in the old and new world, the progress of the eight-hour movement, cheaper postage between the United States and Europe, efforts to finance the emigration of Lyons silk weavers to America, etc. At a council meeting held on 9 July 1867 a letter was read from Mr. Sylvis, president of the United States Iron Molders' Union, offering to organize voluntary contributions from members for London tailors on strike, and describing the establishment of co-operative foundries. On 23 July 1867, 'Citizen Marx has received letters from New York announcing the affiliation of the Communist Club...[to the I.W.A.]'. There are reports of the exchange of newspapers, letters from corresponding secretaries of American unions, resolutions to the working men of America, etc.

HOLYOAKE COLLECTION.

George Jacob Holyoake (1817-1906), co-operator and secularist.[3] The collection consists of 359 books and 424 pamphlets dealing with the early co-operative movement and manuscript diaries for 1848-1905. Holyoake visited America in 1879 and 1882,[4] and the diaries give brief entries during the 1882 period. Pamphlets include several on American topics by Holyoake.[5]

See also Holyoake's correspondence in the Library of the Co-operative Union Ltd., Manchester (p. 173).

BRITISH AND FOREIGN BIBLE SOCIETY,
Bible House, 146 Queen Victoria Street, London EC4V 4BX

The British and Foreign Bible Society was founded in 1804 as a non-denominational and predominantly Evangelical organization, which confined itself exclusively to the translation, publication and distribution of the Bible in any and every language. It encouraged the formation of similar Bible Societies which operated either as independent societies, or as auxiliaries to the Society in London. Auxiliary Societies, founded in Canada from 1810 onwards, sent money to London and were supplied with Bibles for distribution. Bible Societies in the U.S.A. (beginning with Philadelphia in 1808) usually received an initial donation from the BFBS, but were autonomous and did their own printing.

The Society's material consists largely of correspondence with other Bible Societies in Canada and the U.S.A. about the dispatch of money and Bibles, and news of printing and distribution. There may also be correspondence with individuals who, for instance, asked for Bibles to distribute in their locality. The BFBS also encouraged and at times sponsored the translation of the Bible into Indian languages and there is probably correspondence on this also.

The correspondence is filed in 'incoming' and 'outgoing' series, each being further divided into a 'Home' and a 'Foreign' series. Thus letters from America are principally in the FC Inwards series, although in the very early years some are found in HC Inwards. Both Inwards series cover 1804-56 only: all the incoming correspondence from 1857-1900 is, unfortunately, lost. The letters are indexed by name of the writer, and for the period to 1856 there are one or more letters from a hundred or so individuals in the U.S.A. and from perhaps two hundred in Canada.

BRITISH LIBRARY,[1]
London WC1B 3DG

The following summary of manuscripts is simply a continuation of Andrews and Davenport, pp. 1-169, and Paullin and Paxson, pp. 494-555. Andrews and Davenport carried their work on the pre-1783 manuscripts down to Additional Manuscript (Add.MS.) 37067 (that is, for all accessions up to 1905); Additional Charter (Add. Ch.) 43062 (to the end of 1895); and Egerton Manuscript (Eg. MS.) 2860 (to the end of 1895). Paullin and Paxson later worked over the same ground for their post-1783 materials and brought their list down to Add. MS. 37951 (to the end of 1909) and Eg. MS. 2860 (to the end of 1905) - with no additions to Add. Chs. They also brought Andrews and Davenport's work on the pre-1783 materials down to the same dates.

Therefore the following list summarizes the Americana collected by the Library during 1910-76 for Add. MSS.; 1906-76 for Eg. MSS.; and 1896-1975 for Add. Chs.

The entries were compiled with the aid of the following lists: *Catalogue of Additions to the Manuscripts in the British Museum*, which in 1976 extended only to the end of 1945 (i.e., to Add. MS. 46172, Eg. MS. 3319 and Add. Ch. 71756); and the *Catalogue of the Gladstone Papers* (1953), which covers Add. MSS. 44086-835. For accessions since 1945 - to the end of 1976 for Add. MSS. and Eg. MSS., and to the end of 1975 for Add. Chs. - there are 'rough registers' of accessions, made up of handwritten or typescript entries and giving usually short descriptions of manuscripts, though in some cases (fortunately most of the important collections) cuttings from the *British Museum Quarterly* give a fuller description.[2] Additionally, several very large collections, such as the Dilke and Stanmore MSS., are described in separate lists.

It is relatively simple to locate particular subjects for the period covered by the printed and indexed *Catalogue of Additions*. But for the period thereafter, it being thought impracticable (indeed almost impossible) to search all the papers since 1945, the hunt for Americana was much more empirical - for the short titles of the scrapbooks often give no clue at all, particularly in the large collections. We examined scores of volumes, on a remote likelihood of their containing Americana, which, in fact, contained nothing relevant. It is likely that we will have missed some items; but it is unlikely that we have missed any large or important body of Americana. Some of the collections here listed are, of course, so well known that, as in the Public Record Office, we have not normally attempted to note the names of published works that we have relied on, or which illuminate particular sections of these papers; but we have checked that accessions since 1945 which are mentioned in recent scholarly monographs have been included below.

3. See Joseph McCabe, *Life and Letters of George Jacob Holyoake*, 2 vols. (London, 1908).
4. See his *Travels in Search of a Settler's Guide-Book of America and Canada* (London, 1884).
5. See C.W.F. Goss, *A Descriptive Bibliography of George Jacob Holyoake* (London, 1908).

1. Virginia material microfilmed by the Virginia Colonial Records Project.
2. The 'rough registers' for 1961-5, 1966-70, and 1971-5 have been published by the List and Index Society.

ADDITIONAL MANUSCRIPTS

38144. PAPERS RELATING TO NEGOTIATIONS BETWEEN JAMES II AND THE POPE.

Papers relating to negotiations between James II and the Pope, 1689-90, in which James (ff. *2b*, *3b*) says that his Catholicism has caused the Revolution, also 'Unica turbarum contra nos excitatorum origo est, quod Catholicam fidem complexi simus et candem in tria regna, et late sparsas per Americam subditorum nostrorum colonias reducare statuissemus'. (The sole source of the disturbances stirred up against us is that we have adopted the Catholic faith, the same faith in three nations, and that we have decided to withdraw the widely scattered colonies of our subjects in America.)

38161. NOTES OF SPEECHES AND DEBATES IN PARLIAMENT, taken by Philip Yorke, 1st Earl of Hardwicke, his son Philip, the 2nd Earl, and others.

f. 141. Questions for the Judges on an Act of Pardon passed by the Massachusetts Assembly, temp. George III.

38190-489. LIVERPOOL PAPERS.[3]

The papers of Charles Jenkinson, 1st Earl of Liverpool (1727-1808), and of Robert Jenkinson, the 2nd Earl (1770-1808).

38193. ff. 65, 184. Two letters from George Canning to Lord Liverpool. In the first, Lisbon, 14 Jan. 1815, Canning gives his opinion of the American peace; he is cool, but concedes that Liverpool has done what is 'wise and necessary'. In the second, Storrs, 30 Aug. 1823, he encloses a letter to him from the American Minister, Richard Rush, from London, 27 Aug. 1823, which states that the United States would look with disfavour upon any attempt by European powers to interfere in South America, suggests that Britain should recognize the independence of the former Spanish colonies, and implies that the United States is willing to consider any suggestions for joint action with Britain about South America.

38197

f. 1. Correspondence of G. Clarke, Deputy Auditor, concerning the revenues of New York, 1718. (Copies.)

38202

f. 342. Refusal by the Assembly of Massachusetts of the offered alternative to the Stamp duty, 1764.

38207

f. 285. Minute of Governors of King's College at New York, 1773. (Copy.)

38221

f. 334. Letter, 1787, of American merchants to (?) the 1st Earl of Liverpool.

38223

f. 222. Abstract of a letter on Spanish interests in North America, 1788.

38225

f. 162. (*See also* 38394, f. 65*b*.) Reports on memorials from the inhabitants of Vermont, 17 Apr. 1790. (Copy.) Concerns the wishes of the inhabitants of Vermont to 'negociate a commercial and friendly intercourse' with 'His Majesty's Dominions'. The report is by S. Cottrell, on behalf of the Lords of Trade, to W.W. Grenville.

f. 315. Copy of a letter, 9 Nov. 1790, from 'an eminent merchant of Philadelphia to his friend in New York', on the industries and commerce of the United States.

38229

f. 340. Project of an Anglo-United States treaty, 1794. This outline of a proposed treaty is unsigned but endorsed 'In Mr. Jay's Aug. 6th 1794'. It is presumably Jay's original draft of what developed into Jay's Treaty.

38252

ff. 3-8, 32, 34, 353, 355. (*See also* 38253, ff. 74, 92, 217; 38256, ff. 176-81, 205; 38257, f. 359; 38267, f. 142; 38271, ff. 16, 18; 38272, f. 343; 38274, f. 246; 38379, ff. 26, 80, 287.) Papers relating to claims of British subjects lately residing in the United States, 1813, 1814, 1818.

38259

ff. 43-58, 91-103, 118, 178. (*See also* 38362, f. 195; 38363, ff. 12, 149; 38365, ff. 153-78.) Papers relating to the War of 1812 and the negotiations for peace, 1812-4. Includes correspondence from Castlereagh and Goulburn.

f. 218. Passengers of the *Jenny* from Rhode Island, 1814.

38284

ff. 232, 238. Correspondence of American Loyalists with the 2nd Earl of Liverpool, 1820.

38303

f. 12. Headed 'Observations on American affairs, 16th September, 1812' - unsigned - urges adoption of a 'lenient' mode of warfare against the Americans; followed by a paper headed 'Extract of a letter dated New York, 27th September, 1818' - unsigned and unaddressed - on the obscurity of the American objectives in the War.

f. 140. Chronological 'precis of the operations in North America from July 1812 to January 1813'.

38329

f. 12. Grant of parts of Maine and New York by Charles II to his brother James, 1674. (Copy.)

f. 17. Headed 'Copy of the 8th article of instructions given by James Duke of York and Albany. . . to Major Andros, Governor of New York, 1st July 1674'. Concerns the 'publick payments and impositions and the course of justice for determining all differences amongst the inhabitants'.

38330

f. 91. Treasury warrant to William Burnet, Governor of New York, 1722, regarding refusal by the Treasurer of the province to render an account to H.M. Auditor-General. Orders the Governor to ensure that the Treasurer do so. (Copy.)

3. N.S. Jucker, *The Jenkinson Papers* (London, 1949), is a useful introduction to this very important collection.

38334

ff. 68, 250. (*See also* 38332, f. 227.) Returns of troops furnished by the several provinces, in eleven colonies, excluding Delaware and Georgia. 1760-2.

f. 134. 'Charges for carrying on the Indian Service. . . in North America', by **E. Atkins**, Superintendent for Indian Affairs 1756-60. (Incomplete.)

f. 223. State of the present branches of the Customs in North America, with hints for their improvement (after 25 Dec. 1762).

f. 229. Note on the quit-rents of New York, 1762.

f. 273. Lists of Customs officers (twelve officers, including those at St. Augustine, Fla., and Mobile, Ala.), 1762-3.

38335

ff. 1, 14-36, 68-77. (*See also* 38334, f. 297.) Reflections on the settlement and government of British North America, 1763. Regards the colonies as raw material producers. It is in Britain's interest to keep their population down. Their benefits to Britain include the use of British shipping to transport their raw materials and the consumption of British manufactures by the colonies.

ff. 37, 90. Lists of officers in North America absent from duty, 1763.

ff. 40, 82, 148-53, 237, 241. (*See also* 38201, f. 33; 38337, ff. 50, 60; 38373, ff. 80-84*b*, 111*b*-122.) Papers relating to quit-rents in Virginia, 1761-3.

ff. 81, 95*b*-98, 240. Accounts of Virginia tobacco duty, 1763.

f. 87. Drawbacks on foreign goods re-exported from England to North America, 1761.

ff. 103, 144, 154, 327-31. (*See also* 38339, f. 250.) Reports, treasury minutes, etc., on the customs revenue from British North America, 1763.

f. 209*b*. Number of ships annually cleared from American colonies, 1760-2. Shows number going to or coming from British and foreign ports and total tonnage.

f. 233. Report of the Lords of Trade on the colonization of Florida, 1763. (Copy.)

f. 243. Estimate of tea, sugar, and molasses illegally imported into British North America, (?) 1764.

38336

f. 155. Account of Spanish Florida by Dr. Campbell, *c.* 1763.

38337

f. 1. Abstract of a Bill for encouraging the trade of British North America, (?) 1763.

f. 60. Quit-rents of the several provinces, Virginia, the Carolinas, Georgia, and New York, 1764.

ff. 162-73*b*. Extracts from report on whale fishing, fur trade, and bounty on hemp in the American colonies, 1764.

f. 234. Note on the trade of North America, especially imports of Carolinian rice, 1764.

f. 245. Report of seizures of uncustomed and prohibited goods at Philadelphia, Boston, Quebec, and in Virginia, 1763-4.

f. 314. Auditor-General's report on the Quit-Rent Act of New York, 1764.

38338

f. 39. Address, 1764, from the Assembly of New York, to the Lieutenant-Governor, Cadwallader Colden. (Copy.) Expressing loyalty but stating circumspectly that it will be taxed only with its own consent, and asking Colden to point out to the Ministry 'the many mischiefs arising from the Act commonly called the Sugar Act'.

38339

ff. 131, 182-9, 306. Notes on the right to tax the colonies, *c.* 1765.

f. 180. Change of military establishment in American colonies, 1750, 1765.

f. 235. Agreement of West Indian and North American merchants, 1766.

f.302. Decrease of British exports to North America since the repeal of the Stamp Act, 1766.

38340

ff. 163-5. Estimates of military expenses in British North America, 1767.

f. 192. Petition, *c.* 1767, of London merchants trading with North America, representing that their trade has been seriously affected by the Townshend Duties and praying for relief by Parliament.

ff. 201-378*b*, *passim*. Papers relating to the collection of Customs in British North America, 1767-71. Includes legal opinion of Jonathan Sewall, Attorney-General of Massachusetts, 1768.

38341

ff. 29, 69, 163, 329. Papers relating to the collection of Customs in British North America, 1767-71.

ff. 104, 135. Proposals for amending the taxation of the North American colonies, *c.* 1769.

f. 125. Ships entering outwards from London for British North America, 1765-70.

f. 324. Quantities of wheat exported from British North America, 1768-72.

38342

f. 32. Protest of Massachusetts against the claims of Parliament to authority over the colony, 1773.

f. 34. Paper on the state of unrest in Massachusetts, *c.* 1773.

f. 39. Paper on the Virginia tobacco trade (after 1773), giving a brief history of the trade during the eighteenth century.

f. 82. Note on the rate of exchange in New England, (?) 1774.

f. 153. Paper on grants of land in North America, *c.* 1775-6.

f. 157. Paper urging the creation of a special fund for the American colonies. (n.d., but seems likely to be late 1760's.) The document does not make clear the purpose of the proposed fund, but the author's argument is that there should be set up an orderly system of colonial government to prevent the colonies combining and becoming 'untractable' as they are already doing by misapplying Locke's writings.

ff. 161-221, 281. Letters and papers relative to the rebellion of the American colonies, 1774-7, including various declarations and petitions of the colonists, proposals of parliamentary bills affecting America, etc.

38343

ff. 1-22*b*. (*See also* 38342, f. 302.) Account of what the Treasury has done in freighting provision ships for America, with lists of ships, etc., 1775-7.

ff. 117-219*b*. Papers relating to the War of Independence, 1777, 1778.

38344

ff. 103-24. Plan for a permanent union between Great Britain and her American colonies, 1779, sent by Joseph Galloway, an American Loyalist of Philadelphia, to Charles Jenkinson.

38345

f. 59. Articles 4-6 of the treaty of peace between Great Britain and the United States, 1783.

f. 173. (*See also* 38346, f. 27.) General orders for intercourse with the United States, 1784-5.

f. 177. Observations on the trade between the West Indies and the United States, *c*. 1784.

38346

f. 18. Narrative respecting trade between Jamaica and the United States, 1785.

f. 39. Remarks by Committee of Loyalists of New York on proposed bill for their relief, 1785.

f. 54. King's Advocate's opinion as to granting registration to ships built in the United States, 1785.

f. 67. American ships arrived in the port of London, 1783-5.

f. 87. Paper on the increased price of produce in the United States, 1785.

ff. 279*b*, 281*b*. Imports from the United States duty free, or subject to especially low duty, 1786.

38347

f. 104. Proceedings of the Supreme Court of Pennsylvania, 1786.

38348

ff. 65-68*b*. (*See also* 38375, ff. 132, 136; 38376, f. 103.) Papers relating to debts due from the United States to British subjects, etc., 1785-9.

f. 116*b*. Statement of duties imposed on British ships and goods by the United States, *c*. 1788.

38349

ff. 203, 358-62. Papers relative to British trade with the United States, 1789.

f. 332. Petition of merchants banished from the United States, to the House of Commons, 1789.

38350

f. 97. State of shipping in the United States, 1789.

f. 202. Note on industries in the United States, *c*. 1790.

f. 215. Statistics of whale oil industry in the United States, 1790.

f. 246. Report of Committee of Council of Trade on commerce with the United States, 1791. (Proof with corrections. Imperfect.)

38352

f. 290. Corn exported by the United States, 1790-3.

f. 381. Objections to admitting American ships to West Indian ports, *c*. 1793.

38353

f. 301. Order in Council for regulating trade with the United States, 1795. (Draft.)

38354

ff. 38-55. 'Project of heads of proposals to be made to Mr. Jay.' 1794.

38356

ff. 1-4. Commercial treaty between United States and Prussia, 1800. (Extract.)

ff. 101-4. Paper concerning West Florida, 1801.

ff. 278-82. Papers concerning American relations with Britain, *c*. 1807.

38357

f. 31. Paper concerning Napoleon's intentions regarding Florida, 1801.

38363

ff. 155-60*b*. Memorials to the British government on the American-Canadian frontier, claiming protection for the Indians, 1783, 1794, 1813.

ff. 184-98. (*See also* 38358, f. 139.) Papers relative to the Commission for American Claims, 1813. Stipulating the duties required of the commissioners in deciding which citizens had a right to claim a share of money to be paid by the United States under the treaties of 1783 and 1794.

f. 200. Memorial of American Loyalists pressing for compensation under the decisions of the above Commissions, 1813. (Copy.)

38374

f. 107. Reflections on the rebellious state of New York, 1775.

38375

f. 136. Memorial of Duncan Campbell, Chairman of the Committee of Merchants of London, Bristol, Liverpool, Whitehaven, and Glasgow, trading to Virginia, Maryland, and North Carolina, 'previous to the year 1776', to the Foreign Secretary, complaining of inability to recover debts.

38376

f. 77*b*. Numbers and tonnage, etc., of ships clearing from Massachusetts Bay, 1787-8.

f. 112. Report on trade with the American colonies (and later with the United States) before and after the War of Independence, 1789.

38387

f. 53. 'Account of all foreign goods exported to the British colonies in America, particularly wines and calicoes', 1762-4, by John Tankyns, Assistant Inspector-General of Customs, 12 June 1765.

38389-93

passim. Minutes of the Committee of Council on Trade relative to intercourse with the United States, 1786-92; e.g. 38389, ff. 63*b*, 68*b*: references to rice exported from South Carolina; and ff. 64, 68*b*: trade with Georgia, 1786.

38396

'Five representations made by the Board of Trade [to the King] on the fishery and trade of Newfoundland.' Dated 19 Dec. 1718, with heads of a bill of 24 Dec.; 29 Apr. 1765; 27 Mar. 1766; 17 Mar. 1786; 10 May 1790.

38416

f. 63. Act of the Commonwealth of Massachusetts to prevent the slave trade, 1788. (Printed.)

38465

Letters and papers of William Draper, Treasurer of Greenwich Hospital, 1704 - *c.* 1718, with additions. One addition, f. 210, is an 'Account of the number of seamen employed in the merchants' service at the several ports in America, 1763-1772' (dated Receiver's Office for Greenwich Hospital on Tower Hill, 21 Jan. 1778).

See also LIVERPOOL PAPERS SUPPLEMENT, 38564-81.

38510. MISCELLANEOUS PAPERS.

f. 101. Report on descent and property of the Todd family of Caroline County and Dorchester County, Md., with a pedigree from Michael Todd 'about 1693'. (Typewritten.)

f. 126. 'An account of the coast [of America] from Cape Mendosino [on the coast of California] to the Port of Acapulco [on the west coast of Mexico] by Rev. Father Fry [i.e. Fray] [*sic*] Anthony de la Conception, a Carmelite, second cosmographer in the fleet dispatched by... the County of Monterey... Viceking of New Spain in... 1602.' (Translation.)

38564-81. LIVERPOOL PAPERS SUPPLEMENT.

38568

f. 46. Lisbon, 9 Dec. 1814, Canning to Liverpool, asking to be kept informed of the progress of the American war, and stating that opinion in Portugal leans 'towards the Yankees'.

38577

f. 1. Grievances of the several provinces of North America, 1769.

f. 39. Papers on the War of 1812 and the negotiations for peace, 31 Aug. 1814.

38650. MISCELLANEOUS PAPERS.

ff. 1-34. Letters relating to North America. 1775, 1780.

f. 1. 7 Aug. 1775 from New York, William Tryon, Governor of New York, to the Earl of Dartmouth, urging a change of policy towards the American colonies. (Copy.)

f. 3. 5 or 6 Dec. 1775, Major-General Richard Montgomery to General Sir Guy Carleton at Quebec, calling upon him to surrender the city.

f. 5. Copies of letters,[4] Richmond, Va., 27 July-13 Sept. 1780, of Thomas Jefferson as Governor of Virginia, mainly referring to military operations. The manuscript (apparently an incomplete letter-book) was found by Benedict Arnold on his capture of the town in 1781.

f. 56. Report, San Ildefonso, Spain, 16 Aug. 1796, of Michel-Ange Bernard Mangowit, late French Consul at Charleston, S.C., to the French Foreign Minister, on the attitude of the United States towards France. (*In French.*)

38712. PAPERS OF EDWARD SOUTHWELL AND OTHERS.

f. 116. Minutes, 1707, of Council at Portsmouth, N.H., concerning a deficiency in the rendering of the accounts of the revenue and expenditure of the province to the Council for Trade and Plantations.

38734-70. HUSKISSON PAPERS.

Papers of William Huskisson (1770-1830), statesman.

38744

ff. 167-9. Extracts and notes concerning trade with the United States, 1823.

f. 251. Instructions, 27 June 1823, from John Quincy Adams to Richard Rush, the United States Minister in London. (Copy.)

38745

ff. 219-23. Letter, 8 Mar. 1824, from Lord Grenville to Charles W.W. Wynn concerning trade with the United States. (Copy)

ff. 286-93. (*See also* 38746, ff. 1, 7-9.) Letters, etc. relating to the United States-Canadian frontier, 1824.

38746

ff. 67, 71, 73. American bill for constituting Oregon a territory, 1824. (3 copies.)

ff. 265-8. Paper on commercial intercourse of the United States with England and Russia, 1825.

38747

ff. 217-46. Papers relating to proceedings in Congress on commercial regulations, 1826.

38748

f. 3. Letter relating to British trade with the United States, 1826.

f. 10. Act of the General Assembly of Rhode Island to regulate process against banks, etc., 1826. (Copy.)

ff. 214-24. Papers on reciprocity in the carrying trade between British and American vessels, 1826, 1827.

38756

f. 255. Letter on the dependence of the British cotton trade upon the United States, 1828.

38763

f. 93*b*. Table of regulations of trade between the British colonies and the United States, *c.* 1824.

ff. 103*b*-8. Statistics of United States trade and shipping, 1824-5. (Printed.)

38766

f. 208. Comparison of the British and American navies, 1826.

f. 251. Papers relating to America, 1805 and 1822-8. Relate to negotiations on the North-East boundary and of the regulation of the trade of the United States with the British West Indies. Also papers on Spanish America and Canada.

38823. HOBY, SIR EDWARD (1560-1617). Commonplace book.

Includes:

f. 1. Instructions for a voyage of discovery to North America, beginning imperfectly at f. 4 with instructions for geographical

4. For printed sources of these letters see *Catalogue of Additions to the Manuscripts in the British Museum, 1911-15, sub.* 38650 (London, 1925). Also *The Papers of Thomas Jefferson*, ed. by J.P. Boyd and others, vol. iii (Princeton, N.J., 1951), pp. 508-646, *passim.*

and scientific observation, followed by 'Instructions for the master' and 'Instructions to be observed by Thomas Bavin', 1582.

f. 5*b*. 'How the Crowne of England hath most right to all the mayne land and islands alongst the costes of America from the Cape of Florida to 58 degrees northwardes.' n.d.

f. 7. Things known to be in the countries about the river of Norumbega[5] (late sixteenth century).

38835. TALLACK, WILLIAM (1831-1908). Autograph letters to him. Secretary of the Howard Association.

ff. 18, 20. Spiegel Grove, Fremont, Ohio, 25 Jan. 1890, and 21 Oct. 1891, from Rutherford B. Hayes.

f. 23. London, 19 Sept. 1884, from James Russell Lowell. Chiefly about meeting or articles on prison reform.

38861. PRIVY COUNCIL MEMORANDA, 1540-1718.

20. Petition of [Peter] Sonmans in a dispute with [Joseph] Ormston concerning lands in East New Jersey, *c*. 1718.

38898-913. HAZLITT PAPERS.

Letters of William Hazlitt, the younger, and his son William Carew Hazlitt (1834-1913).

38906

f. 89. Boston, 11 Apr. 1890, from Francis H. Lincoln to W.C. Hazlitt, on an early Hazlitt working in New England as a portrait painter.

f. 91. Hartford, Conn., 23 Apr. 1890, from Henry Barnard to W.C. Hazlitt, on school textbooks.

38912

f. 13. Boston, 8 June 1908, from Charles Francis Adams, president of the Massachusetts Historical Society, to W.C. Hazlitt, about a manuscript describing New England, 1783-7, said to have been written by Hazlitt's great-aunt, Margaret.

38931-39164. LAYARD PAPERS.

Private and official papers of Sir Austen Henry Layard (1817-94), M.P., Under-Secretary of State for Foreign Affairs 1852 and 1861-6, and first Commissioner of Works 1868-9; and thereafter Minister at Madrid and Constantinople respectively.

Layard was Under-Secretary under Russell, 1861-5, and Clarendon, 1865-6, and as in both cases his superior sat in the House of Lords, he was Government spokesman on foreign policy in the Commons. Thus the papers contain many items relating to the American Civil War, the *Alabama* claims, etc. Major items are as follows. (*Letters unless otherwise stated.*)

38951-62. Correspondence of Layard with Edmund Hammond, who was Permanent Under-Secretary for Foreign Affairs 1854-73.

38951-4. Letters, 1861-75, of Hammond to Layard.

Chiefly of interest as containing the comments of a pro-Southern Englishman on the Civil War. The almost total disappearance of references to America in the period 1864-5 is significant in view of Hammond's opinions.

38951

f. 2. 29 Nov. 1861, mentions *Trent* incident.

ff. 20, 22. 22 Feb. 1862 (2 letters) discuss the Northern blockade.

f. 52. 21 Apr. 1862, says that Adams has sent one of his periodical 'blustering' communications about 'our countenancing the South', and 'Seward shows his teeth about British designs in Mexico'.

f. 70. 12 June 1862, comments on a complaint from Liverpool merchants that British ships are being stopped by Northern vessels in British West Indian waters. Hammond has no sympathy for them as they are carrying contraband. He mentions General Butler's proceedings in New Orleans and their adverse effect on British feeling. (*See also* f. 74, letter, 15 June 1862.)

f. 93. 10 July 1862, mentions blockade running.

f. 95. 14 July 1862, mentions serious Northern position before Richmond; also blockade running.

f. 100. 18 July 1862, states 'Federals have had a most complete licking'. The South has almost completely established its claim to recognition, but British should not interfere until 'the Northern cause is more thoroughly degraded'. If Britain wants to 'pick a quarrel' it can find reason in 'Butler's proceedings at New Orleans'.

f. 114. 28 July 1862, discusses the finding of funds for a mission to the Confederacy 'which before many months elapse, we must be prepared to accredit'. Says also 'the Federal cause is fast going to the dogs'.

f. 130. 17 Aug. 1862, more comments on the very bad position of the Federals, and the overlarge demands of the United States government for troops. Hammond thinks that Lincoln is acting deliberately in this in order to make the North demand peace. (*See also* f. 134, letter, 24 Aug. 1862.)

f. 137. 28 Aug. 1862, mentions the recoaling of Southern ships in British ports.

f. 143. 9 Sept. 1862, notes the Southern threat to Washington.

f. 150. 18 Sept. 1862, comments on the bad state of the North; and adds that nearly 4 million bales of cotton are available in the South if means could be found to export it.

f. 160. 6 Oct. 1862, minimizes the importance of Antietam, and thinks that emancipation will do little good.

f. 164. 12 October 1862, states that he does not think that recognition of the South will be necessary, as things are 'working to an early end without it'. Again criticizes the preliminary Emancipation Proclamation.

f. 170. 17 Oct. 1862, thinks that mid-term elections may well cause a 'civil war within civil war'.

f. 174. 18 Oct. 1862, refers to lack of action, except at Corinth, Miss., and threatened retaliation by the South for the Emancipation Proclamation.

f. 182. 24 Oct. 1862, says the next two months will be critical for the North. He has told Lord Lyons, who is returning to the United States, that he will be lucky if he does not arrive in a blood-stained city (i.e. New York at election time). Mentions Gladstone's Newcastle speech.

f. 186. 27 Oct. 1862, states that the idea of recognizing the South has been given up because 'of its inexpediency'.

f. 212. 25 Nov. 1862, states that the *Nashville* must not be allowed to arm herself at Southampton, and mentions her activities in the Channel.

f. 215. 26 Nov. 1862, also on the *Nashville*.

f. 220. 7 Dec. 1862, on the activities of British consuls in the South. Adams has alleged that one of them (Bunch?) has communicated with the Confederates in diplomatic matters.

f. 241. n.d. encloses note, 16 Jan. 1863, from Consul Archibald at New York about the growth of a peace party in the North, especially in New Jersey, which he thinks, will bring about an armistice by April.

5. Name applied by sixteenth- and seventeenth-century map makers to undefined region along east coast of North America north of Florida.

38952

f. 16. 8 Apr. 1863, on the seizure of the *Alexandra*.

f. 39. 27 June 1863, mentions Lee's invasions of Maryland and Pennsylvania.

f. 50. 13 July 1863, thinks only the capture of New York and Philadelphia will bring the war to a speedy close.

f. 63. 26 July 1863. After Gettysburg, still thinks there is a good chance of Northern disintegration. (*See also* f. 65, letter, 29 July 1863.)

f. 70. 1 Aug. 1863, expresses first doubts of ultimate Southern success,but says the South has a 'set-off' in the New York riot and the reported removal of Meade. This, if true, he says, proves that Lincoln does not want any competitor for the presidency.

f. 82. 13 Aug. 1863. The Confederates are recovering. The French Mexican scheme will worry the North, but there is no reason why Britain should oppose it.

f. 95. 22 Sept. 1863. The iron-clad issue has been finally disposed of (but contrast f. 99, letter 26 Sept. 1863).

f. 100. 3 Oct. 1863. Smashing defeat of Federals [at Chattanooga, Tenn.]. The Confederates have an abundance of everything and are preparing for a great efort. The iron-clads are obviously Confederate and must be held.

f. 108. 17 Oct. 1863. A great disaster is facing the North in Tennessee. The Southern cause is 'looking up'.

f. 111. 2 Nov. 1863. The difficulties experienced by the government over the *Alexandra*.

f. 153. 1 June 1864, on the *Florida*.

f. 159. 21 June 1864, on a proposed commercial convention with the United States, projected as long ago as 1854 (the Reciprocity Treaty of that year). (*See also* f. 164, letter, 24 June 1864.)

f. 193. 27 Aug. 1864, on McClellan's candidacy for the presidency; the capture of the *Georgia*.

f. 197. 6 Sept. 1864, still says 'a renewal of the Union' is 'out of the question'.

38953

f. 3. 21 Sept. 1864, thinks McClellan's candidacy will cause a 'crash' in the Northern camp.

f. 33. 19 Nov. 1864. American denunciation of the Anglo-American agreement concerning armed vessels on the Lakes, and Northern 'impudence' in pressing for withdrawal of British recognition of Southern belligerency.

38954

f. 1. 19 Nov. 1865, mentions Fenianism in the United States.

f. 127. 21 Oct. 1871, mentions good relations with the United States. Does not have a high opinion of the *Alabama* arbitrators.

f. 138. 2 Feb. 1872. The storm raised in Britain by the United States pressing the indirect claims. The Cuban insurrection.

f. 142. 4 Mar. 1872. American surprise at outburst of British feeling over the indirect claims.

f. 148. 20 June 1872, thinks the British view on indirect claims will prevail at Geneva. The proceedings there had better remain secret.

f. 154. 13 Dec. 1872, on the United States, Spain, and Cuba.

f. 163. 22 Feb. 1873, on Daniel Sickles, United States Minister at Madrid.

f. 169. Extract from a letter from Thornton, 11 Mar. 1873, which says that Grant's administration does not 'care a straw' for Cuba.

f. 171. 12 Mar. 1873, on the scramble of American lawyers to recover large sums for British clients from the Mixed Commission on Claims.

f. 184. 22 Apr. 1873, extract from a letter from Thornton, on the unscrupulous financial activities of Sickles.

f. 223. 16 Nov. 1874, mentions the Democratic success in 1874 elections.

38987-96. General correspondence, 1861-9.

38987

f. 184. Memorandum, 8 Sept. 1861, headed 'Convention with the United States'. States that there is little chance of the United States accepting the convention (? on maritime rights).

f. 198. 10 Sept. 1861, Montreal, from W.F. Williams to Layard, on impending anarchy in the United States and anti-British sentiment there.

f. 218. Memorandum, 20 Sept. 1861, on Southern plan to withhold cotton from Britain, and Northern suspicions of British intentions in Mexico.

f. 271. Memorandum, 27 Sept. 1861, on 'right of search'.

f. 301. Memorandum, 20 Oct. 1861, on recognition of Confederacy. Likely that South will win independence, in which case it will be a valuable market for British manufactured goods, but the war thus far has been too indecisive to make recognition feasible.

f. 343. Memorandum, 16 Nov. 1861, from Hammond to Layard on the Northern blockade.

f. 355. Memorandum, 24 Nov. 1861, discussing question as to whether Britain could detain the *Nashville*.

f. 373. Memorandum, 27 Nov. 1861, on the *Trent* incident.

f. 392. 5 Dec. 1861, from the Rev. Dr. John Waddington to Layard deprecating any British sympathy for the South, and possible war with the North.

f. 410. Memorandum, 17 Dec. 1861, on possible understanding with the South.

f. 424. Memorandum (n.d. but Dec. 1861), on request from Delane, the editor of *The Times*, for information regarding Russell's avoidance of the term 'United States' to Mason and Slidell, the Southern Commissioners. Apparently from Layard to Russell, with reply written at the end by Russell.

38988

f. 9. 7 Jan. 1862, United States Legation, Vienna, from J.L. Motley to Layard, on the folly of war between Britain and the United States, which no one in the United States desires.

f. 190. 11 July 1862, Montreal, from W. Williams to Layard, on McClellan's defeat in the Peninsula, Va.

f. 216. Memorandum, 29 July 1862, on the *Alabama*. States that the vessel slipped out to sea just before the arrival of the law officer's opinion that it should be detained.

f. 220. Note, 30 July 1862, from Russell to Layard. A 'pity' the *Alabama* escaped.

f. 386. 27 Nov. 1862, Vienna, from J.L. Motley to Layard, on Confederate raiders and blockade runners.

f. 390. 28 Nov. 1862, from the Rev. Dr. John Waddington to Layard. Hopes that the British government will give no aid to the slavery cause.

38989

f. 18. 12 Jan. 1863, Montreal, from W. Williams to Layard, on Burnside's defeat. Says the South hates Britain as much as does the North.

f. 48. 7 Feb. 1863, Norwich, from W. Elwin to Layard, on French proposal of mediation between North and South. (*See also* f. 178, n.d. [? June 1863].)

ff. 264-341 *passim*. Memoranda and notes, 19 Aug.-9 Sept. 1863, addressed to Layard on the question of the iron-clad rams fitting out at Liverpool, and the arguments for and against their detention. Chiefly from Russell and Sir Roundell Palmer. Also one from Layard to William Stuart, Secretary of the Legation in Washington.

f. 333. Note, 7 Sept. 1863, from Palmerston to Layard on British subjects allegedly employed on the *Alabama*.

38990

f. 6. A peace plan to end the Civil War (n.d. but 1863).

ff. 62-69. A series of undated cryptic notes on the Civil War (? on recognition of the Confederacy).

38991

f. 128. Request, n.d. (presumably to Layard), by Russell, for the exact dates of law officer's opinion on detention of the *Alabama*, and of Layard's telegram to Liverpool ordering detention.

f. 129. Unsigned memorandum, 14 Mar. 1865, presumably by Layard, in reply, giving dates and circumstances. Blame for delay is put upon Charles Francis Adams.

f. 159. Memorandum, n.d. (25 Apr. 1865), unsigned (? by Russell), on the assassination of Lincoln.

f. 336. Note, 7 Aug. 1865, from Russell, on Seward's hostility to Britain.

f. 388. 19 Aug. 1865, London, from Russell to Layard. United States will not press demand for *Alabama* compensation to the point of war, and Russell thinks that the question may well 'drop out of sight.'

f. 392. 22 Aug. 1865, from Layard to Russell, on delay in completing the draft on the *Alabama* to be given to Adams. (The printed version of this draft, dated Aug. 1865, is in 39157, f. 79.)

38997-39011. Correspondence of Layard while British Minister at Madrid Oct. 1869 - Mar. 1877. Contains the following relevant to the United States-Spanish tensions over Cuba, the *Virginius*, etc.

39001

f. 403. Two notes. (? 4 Apr. 1872), from Daniel Sickles to Layard, the first on 'rascals [? Spanish] bleeding us', the second on the Geneva Arbitration.

39003

ff. 329-33. Two notes. 15 Oct. 1873, from Sickles to Layard, on the Cuban customs regulations. Further note, 25 Oct. 1873, on United States-Spanish friction over Cuba - especially on the slaves there.

39005

f. 222. 19 Mar. 1874, Washington, D.C., from Sir Edward Thornton to A.G. Dunlop, British Consul General in Havana, says United States government and 'the sensible part of the population have no wish whatever to acquire Cuba', but if affairs like that of the *Virginius* continue to occur, it will be difficult to suppress public clamour.

39007

f. 246. 14 Jan. 1875, Washington, D.C., from Thornton to Dunlop, similar in tone to 39005, f. 222 (above) - Spain should not provoke the United States.

39101-20. Semi-official correspondence with British Ministers and Consuls, 1861-6.

39101

f. 66. Draft letter, Liverpool, 15 Sept. 1861, from T.M. Mackay to Layard, on the seriousness of the American conflict for Europe, especially the threat of the cessation of cotton supplies.

f. 104. 19 Sept. 1861, Liverpool, from Mackay to Layard, on effects of stoppage of cotton.

f. 237. 7 Nov. 1861, from Mackay to Layard, hopes Napoleon III will take initiative in recognizing the Confederacy.

f. 248. 8 Nov. 1861, London, from Mackay to Layard. Thinks a war with the United States would be popular with the commercial classes.

39102

ff. 15, 26. 4 and 6 Dec. 1861, Liverpool, from Mackay to Layard. Preparations for transfer of 'Yankee' ships to nominal ownership of Englishmen in view of impending Anglo-United States war.

f. 30. 9 Dec. 1861, Liverpool, from Mackay to Layard. War threat receding. Britain's right to demand end of Northern blockade.

f. 33. 10 Dec. 1861, from Sir J. Harding to Layard, on precedents in *Trent* incident.

f. 161. 14 Jan. 1862, New York (misdated, should be 1863) from Sir James Caird to Layard: Northern determination, American relief for Lancashire; advises against foreign interference in Civil War.

39103

f. 284. Copies of two anonymous letters. One, London, 30 July 1862, from an American living in voluntary exile in England, thanks (?) Layard for his efforts on behalf of 'humanity' and 'justice' in America. The other, St. Louis, Mo., 31 July 1862, tells of conditions in the border states (Union ill treatment of anyone suspected of Confederate sympathies, etc.) and prays for British intervention to end the War.

39104

f. 225. 27 Dec. 1862, Washington, D.C., from a British officer stationed at Montreal (signature illegible) to Layard. His opinions of the Federal Army formed on a visit to the Army of the Potomac before Fredericksburg. Potentially excellent soldiers, but dirty, undisciplined, ill equipped, etc.

39105

f. 183. 25 Mar. 1863, Western Circuit, Taunton, from Sir Robert Collier to Layard, giving his opinions of the legal aspects of the detention or non-detention of the *Alabama*.

39106

f. 117. Letter and memorial, Paris, 25 and 21 May respectively, from Alex. Barclay to Layard, on advisability of British recognition of eight of the Southern States as a separate nation (i.e. Virginia, North and South Carolina, Georgia, Florida, Alabama, Mississippi, and Tennessee). This arrangement, the writer thinks, would be accepted by both American belligerents and by France.

f. 172. 5 June 1863, Paris, from Barclay to Layard, on same subject as f. 117 above, with views of Southern representatives in Paris (they expect no help from Britain or France).

f. 334. Memorandum, *c.* 10 July 1863, about the visit of the pro-Confederate M.P.s, Roebuck and Lindsay, to Napoleon III, and his attitude on recognition of the independence of the South.

39107

f. 225. 18 Sept. 1863, Washington, D.C., from William Stuart, Secretary of the Legation at Washington, to Layard, on communications with the State Department on the rams. Fears that Seward may have sent 'blustering instructions' to Adams had he not communicated news of the rams' detention immediately upon receipt.

39108

f. 183. Note on the jurisdiction of American consuls in Great Britain, 1864.

39109

f. 9. 2 Mar. 1864, Liverpool, from William Rathbone, Liverpool shipowner, to Layard, on the implications of the rams incident for international law.

f. 277. 'Mem: as to case of *Tuscaloosa*' (? by Layard). On question of prize at sea *re* Confederate raiders (with printed letters). (? 23 Apr. 1864.)

39110

f. 99. 20 May 1864, Liverpool, from William Rathbone to Layard, that it would be in Britain's interest to forbid the use of her ports to all Confederate vessels which may previously have caused a breach of her neutrality, e.g. by fitting out in British ports.

f. 308. June 1864, New York, from John Gilmary Shea to (?) Layard, on the military situation, and prospects for the 1864 presidential election. Maintains that Lincoln's chances are very strong.

39111

f. 36. 9 July 1864, New York, from John G. Shea to (?) Layard, on the confused and divided state of the Democratic Party; unrest in New York City; Irish immigration into the United States; the military situation.

f. 66. 13 July 1864, New York, from Shea to (?) Layard, that Democrats seem to be working for a revolution to force the North to sue for peace.

f. 264. 9 Sept. 1864, Montreal, from W. Williams to Layard, mentions Sherman's capture of Atlanta, Ga.

39112

f. 218. 28 Nov. 1864, Washington, D.C., from J. Hume Burnley, British *Chargé* at Washington, to Layard, on a conversation with Seward on the capture of the *Florida*, with a postscript on the sinking of that vessel.

f. 245. 1 Dec. 1864, Washington, D.C., from Burnley to Layard, on Seward, and 'the matter of the exequaturs'; also the *Florida* incident.

39113

f. 66. 20 Jan. 1865, Montreal, from W. Williams to Layard, thinks the Civil War may last another year; wants Southern independence *and* emancipation of slaves.

39114

f. 189. 25 Mar. 1865, London, from James Whitbread to Layard, on a report that certain emigrants sent out by the Discharged Prisoners Aid Society have been arrested in New York.

f. 290. 4 Apr. 1865, Washington D.C., from J. Hume Burnley to Layard, on an article in the *North American Review*, vol. lxxxii, pp. 478-512, 1856, on the Monroe Doctrine, unsigned, and a discussion on it.

ff. 392 and 432. 17 and 25 Apr. 1865, London, from William Tasker Smith, British Consul at Savannah, Ga., to Layard, asking for transfer to Richmond, Va.

See also 42711.

39168. MISCELLANEOUS PAPERS.

f. 95, 'O Star of France', poem by Walt Whitman. The printed text, first published in 1872, differs considerably from the present draft. (Holograph.)

f. 128. Letter, 1 Feb. [1774] from William Fraser, Under Secretary of State, to the Earl of Holderness, on the Massachusetts petition praying the King to remove Governor Hutchinson and Lieutenant Governor Oliver. Presented by Franklin to 'the Council' and rejected.

39190. MACKENZIE PAPERS, vol. iv.

ff. 204-11. Include letters, Boston, 10 and 28 Dec. 1774, 16 Feb. 1775, of Major John Pitcairn of the Marines (killed at Bunker Hill, 1775) to Lieutenant-Colonel John Mackenzie of the Marines, recounting his difficulties in America.

39245. WODEHOUSE PAPERS.

f. 20. Letter, 22 Feb. 1615, from the Privy Council to the Deputy Lieutenants of Suffolk, promoting a lottery for benefit of Virginia.[6]

39255. MISCELLANEOUS PAPERS.

f. 26. Appointment of Jacob Mark, of Maryland, as United States Consul at Cork, 16 Dec. 1817; signed by James Monroe, President, and John Quincy Adams, Secretary of State; with paper seal. Engraved.

39304-16. BERKELEY PAPERS.

Papers of George Berkeley (1685-1753), Bishop of Cloyne, and his family. Berkeley lived in America from Jan. 1729 until the autumn of 1731. The papers include:

39306

ff. 140*b*-63. Notes for sermons preached at Newport, R.I., 1729-31.[7]

39311

ff. 12-13. Letter, London, 23 June 1729, from Martin Benson to Berkeley about ideas in England as to what Berkeley and his wife are doing in Rhode Island.[8]

ff. 17-20. Letter, 1730, from Reverend Samuel Johnson of Stratford, Conn., on Berkeley's philosophical theories.

ff. 158-9. Copy of a letter, London, 4 May 1764, from Sir Alexander Cuming, chief of the Cherokees, to the Earl of Bute, asking for alleviation of his poverty. (Enclosed is a letter from Cuming to George Berkeley, son of Bishop Berkeley, 8 May 1764.)

6. H.M.C. xiii(iv), p. 437.
7. Printed in *The Works of George Berkeley, D.D.*, ed. by A.C. Fraser, vol. iv (Oxford, 1871), pp. 634-9.
8. Printed ibid., pp. 170-2.

39316

ff. 31-33. Indentures of sale of two slaves to Berkeley, 7 Oct. 1730, with confirmation, 17 Oct. 1731, by Governor Joseph Jenckes of Rhode Island.

39561. C. G. LELAND COLLECTION, vol. x.

ff. 71-79. 'The cattle-range idiom' for a projected dictionary of Americanisms. List of words with meanings, apparently compiled in the late 1880's.

39577. AUTOGRAPH LETTERS.

f. 57. 20 July 1869, London, from J.L. Motley to J.A. Froude, declining an invitation and referring to his historical studies.

f. 64. 4 June 1898, from Bret Harte to Miss Froude, declining an invitation.

39855. CUMING, SIR ALEXANDER (1690?-1775). Autobiographical notes. 1 volume (42 folios).

Cuming went to South Carolina in Dec. 1729 and drew up a scheme for the reform of its currency system. In Mar. 1730 he crossed the Cherokee Mountains, and was received by the Cherokees as their law giver. He returned to England taking with him seven chiefs of the Cherokees. On 18 June 1730 he presented them to George II, who received their submission.

39869. MISCELLANEOUS PAPERS ON NAVAL MATTERS.

'Abstract of the general printed Sailing and Fighting Instructions and Vice-Admiral Arbuthnot's Additional Signals, 1779...for the North American Station.' Arbuthnot was commander of the Station 1779-81.

f. 45. 'General observations on the coast of South Carolina': an account of bays, shoals, islands, etc., from Winyah Bay, S.C., to Tybee Island, Ga.

f. 49*b*. 'General observations on the weather on the coast of South Carolina.'

f. 50. Short accounts of 'Fishing ground'; Nantucket Island; George's Bank;...a shoal in Delaware Bay on which the *Santa Magritta* struck, 11 Dec. 1781.

39908. AUTOGRAPH LETTERS OF ALL THE PRESIDENTS OF THE UNITED STATES FROM WASHINGTON TO WILSON.

Up to and including Hayes, the letters are inlaid in a printed book, *The Presidents of America*, by H.W. Smith and John Fiske (Boston and New York, 1879).

The only letters of more than calligraphic interest are:

(*a*) 30 Nov. 1812, Headquarters (?), Franklinton, La., from William Henry Harrison to his father-in-law John C. Symmes of Cincinnati, Ohio, about provisioning the army in the North-West.

(*b*) 17 June 1817, Quincy, Mass., from John Adams to James Madison, on universal suffrage and on tyranny in Europe.

(*c*) 3 Mar. 1840, Washington, D.C., from John Quincy Adams to Nathaniel F. Williams of Baltimore, sending him two copies of the *National Intelligencer* containing Adams's two letters of 1839 to the petitioners 'who had entrusted me their petitions, memorials or remonstrances to the House of Representatives ...during the preceding session of Congress', which session, he says, proved unsatisfactory 'to both the great parties to the slavery, abolition, and petition controversies.'

(*d*) 26 Mar. 1840, Nashville, Tenn., from James K. Polk to Samuel H. Loughlin, on the coming Democratic Convention in Baltimore.

(*e*) 2 Mar. 1843, Springfield, Ill., from Abraham Lincoln to Richard Symmes Thomas, Jr., about a rumour that Lincoln did not wish to be a candidate for Congress; a Bill forming electoral districts in Illinois. Suggests that Thomas become a delegate for his county to the district Congressional convention. Reports a Whig meeting, and has hopes that the Whigs will soon control the State of Illinois.[9]

(*f*) 27 Jan. 1845, Washington, D.C., John Tyler to his daughter, mentions his pleasure at the passage through the House of the joint resolution for annexing Texas, and hopes that it will pass the Senate.

(*g*) 13 Dec. 1851, Washington, D.C., from Andrew Johnson to A.O.P. Nicholson, on prospects for the 1852 Democratic Convention.

(*h*) 30 Apr. 1883, New York, from U.S. Grant to General Adam Badeau, on defensive potentialities of Havana. He thinks it would be easy for a first-class power, and especially the United States, to capture it in a war.

39954. OWEN, SIR RICHARD (1804-92).

Superintendent of the Natural History Department of the British Museum 1856-83. Non-scientific correspondence; letters to Owen with some draft replies by him, *c*. 1838-89. Of American interest is his correspondence with James Russell Lowell, f. 636, and J.L. Motley, f. 493.

40108-22. HONE PAPERS.

40122

ff. 47, 50. Correspondence of French and Spanish diplomats on the independence of the American colonies, consisting of English translations. Two brief notes, 10 Mar. 1778 and 27 May 1779. Although the above is the catalogue description, an endorsement on one of the manuscripts says that they are 'draft letters to King George III'. The first is slight; the second more important, relating to Spain's attitude to the conflict in America.

40177-80. GRENVILLE, GEORGE NUGENT-TEMPLE-, 1st Marquis of Buckingham (1753-1813).

Letter-books while he was Lord-Lieutenant of Ireland 1782-3 and 1787-9.

40177

Volume I, 1782-3. Two letters to Lord North. The first, 19 May 1783, states that Grenville is enclosing a copy of a memorial of Messrs. Mitchell and Anderson, Dublin merchants, concerning the export of wines to 'Charlestown in America', to be submitted to H.M. Commissioners of Revenue. The subject of the memorial, he says, affects the whole commercial intercourse 'between this kingdom and America'. With the second letter, 30 May 1783, he sends the Commissioners' report to North, and in both letters he says that, as the law now stands in Ireland, all trade with America is precluded on any other footing than that of a foreign nation.

9. See *Collected Works of Abraham Lincoln*, ed. by R.P. Basler, vol. i (New Brunswick, N.J., 1953), p. 309.

40181-617. PEEL PAPERS.

Papers of Sir Robert Peel (1788-1850), statesman. (*Letters unless otherwise stated.*)

40192

ff. 176-8. Numbers of Irish emigrants to America, 1813-16.

40312

f. 81. 14 Dec. 1829, London, from Peel to Aberdeen, in which he doubts the wisdom of allowing American students unrestricted access to the State Papers, as their study may exacerbate anti-British feeling in America. (Copy.)

f. 83. 31 Dec. 1829, London, from Peel to Aberdeen, asking for statistics of British trade with the United States. (Copy.)

f. 114. 27 July 1830, Foreign Office, from Aberdeen to Peel, and Peel's reply, Whitehall, 28 July 1830. (Copies.) On a note from Mr. McLane, the American Minister, concerning Anglo-United States trade.

f. 294. 14 Feb. 1838, Argyll House, from Aberdeen to Peel, on the North-East boundary question as it stood in 1830, and the arbitral award of the King of the Netherlands in 1831.

40333

f. 32. Remarks by J.D. Hume on duties upon United States goods, 1828. (Copy.)

40365

f. 12. *Education for the Ministry in the American Episcopal Church,* 1824. (Printed.)

40455

Correspondence, 1845-6 *passim*, between Aberdeen and Peel on Oregon, Mexico, California, and tariffs.

40464

f. 335. Memorandum on trade with the United States, by Lord Ashburton, 1843.

40467

f. 302. Statement of wheat exported from the United States to Britain through Canada, 1842.

40468

ff. 209-13. Stanley to Peel, 5 Sept. 1845, and Peel to Stanley, 7 Sept. 1845, on Canadian-American relations and defence of the Great Lakes.

40469

f. 278. Memoranda concerning the trade and resources of the United States, 1841, 1842. Contain some statistics, e.g. the number of persons employed in manufacturing and agriculture; investments in woolen and cotton manufactures, etc. Describes high and low tariff groups; production of wheat, etc.; prospects of British trade with Illinois, etc. via the Mississippi (endorsed 'from General Duff Green').

f. 282. London, 6 Oct. 1842, from General Green to J. Macgregor, on American high-tariff agitation.

40492

f. 306. 22 Oct. 1841, from Ashburton to Peel, on Daniel Webster and the British Minister, Henry Fox.

40497

f. 382. Headed 'England and America No. 1.' Treatise, with statistics of Anglo-United States trade, 1835-40, on the United States tariff, especially as it affects Britain, with several comments on the American production of corn.

40500

ff. 239-44. 20 Jan. 1842, from Lord Ashburton to Peel, written just before Ashburton's departure for the United States, where he was to negotiate the Webster-Ashburton Treaty, enclosing a paper headed 'The case of the *Creole*', concerning American ships carrying slaves from Virginia to Louisiana putting into British West Indian ports because of bad weather, etc. or slave revolt on board.

There are no letters from Ashburton while in the United States.

40511

ff. 114-33. Letters and papers from James Buchanan, Consul at New York, consisting of a printed pamphlet by Buchanan (published anonymously), *War with England* (New York, 1838), on averting war over Canadian border incidents; two letters, June 1842, from Buchanan to Peel and Edward Drummond on his retirement and on emigration to Canada; a printed pamphlet by Buchanan on this latter subject, *Letter to. . . Sir Charles Bagot* (New York, 1842); and an 1842 clipping from the Quebec *Gazette* of a letter of Buchanan's on emigration.

40516

ff. 115-17. 28 Sept. 1842, from Peel congratulating Ashburton on the success of the mission, and one of Ashburton's thanks in reply.

40517

ff. 1-10: 13, 16, and 22 Oct. 1842; and 40492, f. 250: 18 Oct. 1842 [a misplaced letter]. There is some correspondence on the subject of a suitable honour to be awarded to Ashburton in recognition of his services in the United States.

40523

f. 99. New York, 3 Nov. 1842, from J. Horsley Palmer, Governor of the Bank of England, to Walter Forward, United States Secretary of the Treasury, relating to United States currency, etc., and the possible measures to improve American banking and currency systems in the absence of a Bank of the United States.

40526

f. 432. Washington, D.C., 29 Mar. 1843, from Daniel Webster, then Secretary of State, to Edward Everett, Minister to Britain, on a possible commercial treaty between Britain and the United States, and Webster's views on the tariff.

40562

ff. 292, 293. Memoranda on prices of Louisiana sugar, 1845.

40563

f. 394. Memorandum relative to the Oregon boundary question, 1845.

40574

ff. 380-5*b*. Two letters from Edward Everett to Peel. The first, Boston, 29 Sept. 1845, on his voyage home at the termination of his service as Minister to Britain, the good grain harvest and poor potato crop of the United States in 1845. The second letter, Boston, 28 Nov. 1845, again mentions crops, recession of the threat of a Mexican war, and his assumption of the presidency of Harvard. Peel's reply, Drayton Manor, 16 Oct. 1845, mentions the bad state of the potato crop, especially in Ireland.

There is a great deal of correspondence between Everett and Peel, 1837-48, and especially during Everett's term as Minister 1841-5, but most of them are no more than slight notes. (*See* 40423, 40504, 40518, 40520, 40524, 40528, 40531, 40532, 40534, 40540, 40547, 40554, 40556, 40557, 40559, 40562, 40565, 40566, 40569, 40571, 40597, 40600.)

f. 448. Report on the United States harvest, 1845, with remarks on potato disease.

f. 448*b*. *Prices current of grain, flour, and meal in the United States, 1845.* (Printed.)

40576

f. 87. Copy of a dispatch, Washington, D.C., 13 Sept. 1845, from Sir Richard Pakenham, British Minister to the United States 1843-7, to Aberdeen, in which he gives the opinions of the American Secretary of the Treasury as to the probable influence of the elections of 1844 on the tariff. Secretary Walker believes that the new House will have a low tariff majority, but local issues will, as always, complicate the voting. Walker also believes the present tariff to be detrimental to revenue.

40581

ff. 425-31. Official correspondence of the United States with Britain relative to the slave trade, 1843. (Printed.)

ff. 432, 434. Everett's dispatches, both undated, to Webster and H.S. Legaré, on slave trade.

40588

ff. 70-71. Copy of a letter, 19 Jan. 1846, from F.C. Matthiesson, Charleston, S.C., to Thomas Bazley, Manchester, concerning tariffs and Anglo-American relations; forwarded to Peel by Edward Tootal.

ff. 161-8. Three letters, 1846, from Robert Owen to Peel, concerning the Oregon question.

40590

f. 338. 28 Apr. 1846, from Everett to Peel, mentions Oregon question.

40602

f. 28. Letter relative to gold diggings in California, 1849. (Printed.)

40611

ff. 117-50. Papers relative to the North-West boundary negotiations, 1824-6. (Printed.)

40612

f. 117*b*. 'A statistical account of the population, product, etc. of the United States of America for the year 1840 distinguishing each state.' Gives for each state: number of senators; number of representatives in this, and 'the next' Congress; population in 1820 and 1840; area; capital invested in manufactures of wool and cotton; production in 1840 of wheat, oats, Indian corn, meat cattle, swine, cotton, and tobacco; number of persons employed in trades and agriculture. (Apparently sent to Peel by Gladstone in 1842.)

40690. MISCELLANEOUS PAPERS. (*Letters.*)

f. 21. Middlebrook, 5 Apr. 1779, from George Washington to George Clinton, Governor of New York, concerning the movement of troops from Minisinck, N.Y.[10]

f. 23. West Point, N.Y., 10 Oct. 1779, from Washington to Clinton, concerning preparations for an expedition against New York.[11]

f. 27. Philadelphia, 18 Jan. 1781, from Major-General Baron von Steuben, offering an appointment as aide-de-camp to Major Benjamin Walker.

ff. 87-110. To, and relating to, Dr. J.G. Cogswell, Superintendent of the Astor Library, New York, largely written during his visits to Europe to purchase books for the Library, 1825-58. Among the writers are W.H. Prescott, Washington Irving, and Edward Everett. Mostly slight personal notes, also some enclosing books or about forthcoming publications of reviews.

40760. FRANCIS PAPERS, vol. v.

Letters and papers of, and relating to, the Rev. Philip Francis (1708?-73) and his son, Sir Philip Francis (1740-1818).

ff. 220-70. Correspondence,[12] 9 Nov. 1755-5 Sept. 1756, of Major-General William Shirley, Governor of Massachusetts Bay, with Henry Fox, William Wildman Barrington, Major-General Sir William Johnson, Horatio Sharpe, Governor of Maryland; Major-General James Abercromby, Commander-in-Chief, North America 1758, and John Campbell, 4th Earl of Loudoun. (All copies.)

41064. QUIETUS TO 'JAMES (EDWARD) OGLETHORPE, ESQ., General and Commander-in-Chief of His Majesty's Forces in South Carolina and Georgia in America upon his account thereof between the 22nd of September 1738 and Michaelmas 1743'.

Official certified copy from the record in the Roll of Foreign Accounts of 32 Geo. III at the Pipe Office. Oglethorpe's bills were disputed by the Treasury and the account was not settled until 25 Feb. 1792, more than four years after his death. Vellum roll, 1792.

41178. MISCELLANEOUS LETTERS AND PAPERS.

D.f. 19. Brief letter, London, 26 Sept. 1870, from Jefferson Davis to George Bryan Jennings, of personal interest only.

E.f. 26. Letter, 16 May 1854, from Nathaniel Hawthorne, as United States Consul at Liverpool, to James Buchanan, United States Minister in London, protesting against the levying of British income tax on his consular fees. There is also a letter, 19 May 1854, from Lord Clarendon, as Foreign Secretary, to James Wilson, Financial Secretary to the Treasury, requesting that immediate attention be paid to Hawthorne's claim.

10. See *Writings of George Washington*, ed. by John C. Fitzpatrick, vol. xiv (Washington, D.C., 1936), pp. 337-8.

11. Ibid., vol. xvi, pp. 452-3.

12. Most of these letters are printed in *Correspondence of William Shirley*, ed. C.H. Lincoln, 2 vols. (New York, 1912).

41206-52. CAMPBELL-BANNERMAN PAPERS.

Letters of Sir Henry Campbell-Bannerman (1836-1908), Prime Minister 1905-8.

41211

f. 284. New York, 7 Oct. 1904, frrom James Bryce to Campbell-Bannerman, says that Roosevelt is expected to win the 1904 election.

ff. 359, 369. 26 Dec. 1906, 17 Jan. 1907, 8 Apr. 1908, from Bryce to Campbell-Bannerman, on the appointment of Bryce as British Ambassador to the United States, and a letter (copy) 28 Dec. 1906, from Campbell-Bannerman to Bryce. In the letter of Apr. 1908 Bryce regrets that Campbell-Bannerman has had to resign.

41295. MISCELLANEOUS PAPERS.

f. 20. Certificate by John Wesley to Richard Whatcoat and Thomas Vasey of their appointment as Elders for the work of the ministry in America, 2 Sept. 1784.

41340. MISCELLANEOUS PAPERS.

f. 125. Letter, 10 Feb. 1913, from Henry James to Miss E. Lea, giving his opinion (which is unfavourable) of 'Ouida' (Marie Louise de la Ramée).

41346-41475. MARTIN PAPERS.

Papers of the Martin family, planters of Antigua, 1714-1878, including many late eighteenth- and nineteenth-century naval papers (but not the War of 1812).

41352

'Letter-book of Josiah Martin, the elder, originally of Antigua, but after 9 July 1739 of "Rockhall" Far Rockaway, Long Island, North America', 19 Mar. 1729-8 Dec. 1740. Also some accounts.

41361

Correspondence, 21 Dec. 1752-19 Nov. 1785, of Josiah Martin (nephew of Josiah, the elder; see 41352), Governor of North Carolina 1771-6, mainly with his brother, Samuel Martin, Jr. The letters are chiefly concerned with Josiah's financial difficulties, from which Samuel had often to rescue his brother. Samuel's influence obtains for Josiah the governorship of North Carolina, but Josiah continues to plead for money and further offices. The letters, mostly written in the 1770's, also touch on the defection of New York from the other colonies and their reproaches of it - especially recriminations between Boston and New York; sale of patents by the governor of New York; boundary disputes between New York and Connecticut; riots in North Carolina under his predecessor Tryon; the revenues of the various colonies; his flight to a warship in Cape Fear River, N.C., in 1775; his return to Long Island; and the expedition of General Clinton to invade South Carolina, which army Josiah accompanied.

41409

Volume of letters containing correspondence relating to the Navy of the U.S.A., 1858.

41567. MISCELLANEOUS PAPERS.

ff. 212-47*b*. Sixteen letters, 3 Apr. 1861-31 Mar. 1863, from George Henry Herbert, of Newcastle-upon-Tyne, while serving with the Northern Army in the Civil War, to his relatives in England. Herbert served first in Virginia under General Butler and took part in the attack upon Fort Hatteras. While later stationed at Roanoke Island he gives a very favourable picture of Union prospects in the early part of 1862. Subsequently there are descriptions of the evacuation of Fredericksburg, the preliminaries to the battle of Antietam, and the battle of South Mountain. He describes in much detail the 'thrashing' taken by the Federals at the battle of Fredericksburg. Early in 1863 his attitude is one of disillusionment: 'instead of fighting for a principle, we are fighting for a set of scheming politicians, army contractors and would-be Generals'.

41760. GREVILLE LETTERS.

Twenty letters, London (and one from Paris), 15 June 1855-10 June 1856, from Charles Cavendish Fulke Greville (1794-1865), the diarist, to Sir Charles Ash Windham serving in the Crimea. Deal, *inter alia*, with differences with America, chiefly the activities of British recruiting agents in the United States, which in the spring of 1856 seemed likely to threaten war.

42083-8. GRENVILLE PAPERS.

Some 500 original letters of the Grenville family, 1767-77, chiefly of Richard Temple Grenville, afterwards Grenville-Temple, Earl Temple (1711-99), but also of his brother George (1712-70), including the latter's political diary.

This correspondence of the author of the Stamp Act and his brother contains many glancing references to the American question amid letters predominately on other topics. Only the specifically American items are noted below since the diary and most of the correspondence have been published in *The Grenville Papers*, ed. W.J. Smith, 4 vols. (London, 1852-3). (*Letters unless otherwise stated.*)

42083

The political diary of George Grenville, 1761-8. It contains only a few brief references to parliamentary debates on American affairs, 1765-7.

42084-7

28 Feb. 1767, from the Earl of Suffolk to George Grenville on the Duke of Bedford's motion in the House of Lords for all correspondence of the several governors in America.

17 July 1768, from George Grenville to Mr. Pownall, on the possibility of seating American members in the House of Commons; also the general situation in America.

15 Oct. 1768, from Commodore Hood to George Grenville on the extension of his American command, and his probable dispositions in view of the threatening state of affairs in America; also the landing of Gage's troops at Boston.

27 Oct. 1768, from Mr. Whately to George Grenville, on prospects of revolution at Boston (*see also* same to same, 28 Oct. 1768).

1 Nov. 1768, from Mr. Knox to George Grenville, says 'the revolt of New England is now unquestionable'.

7 Nov. 1768, from John Temple, a Commissioner of Customs at Boston, to George Grenville, on his disagreeable position.

15 Dec. 1768, from Knox to George Grenville, on negotiations with the colonies over the Townshend Duties.

3 Jan. 1769, from Whately to George Grenville, on the spread of disaffection to Virginia and South Carolina.

15 Apr. 1769, from Hood to George Grenville, on the former's forbearance in order not to exacerbate American feeling.

5 Aug. 1769, from Whately to George Grenville, on a report that the troops are retiring from Boston.

2 Sept. 1769, from Hood to Earl Temple, on the worsening situation at Boston over the duties.

19 Sept. 1769, from Knox to George Grenville, mentions the duties.

22 Sept. 1769, from Whately to George Grenville, on a report by ex-Governor Bernard on the situation in Massachusetts.

3 Dec. 1769, from Whately to George Grenville, on a plan for an American parliament; also on American non-importation.

24 Sept. 1777, from Lord Chatham to Temple, in which he says, whatever the result of the conflict with the colonists, 'poor England will have fallen upon her own sword'.

See also Add. MSS. 57804-37 (p. 79).

42242-56. SIR WILLIAM ASHLEY PAPERS.

Official papers of William James Ashley (d. 1927), Professor of Commerce at the University of Birmingham, relating to his public work during and after the First World War.

42249

ff. 342-52. Report of statement, etc., by Herbert Hoover before the Consumer's Council, 1918. (Typewritten.)

42257-496. STEVENS TRANSCRIPTS.

Benjamin Franklin Stevens (1833-1902), an American bookman and antiquarian, devoted many years to collecting transcripts of papers and letters relating to American history between 1744 and 1784. The transcripts, which amount to somewhere between 45,000 and 50,000 leaves, are taken from various sources, including the British Library, the Public Record Office, French and Dutch archives; but the greater portion are from private collections, particularly the Lansdowne[13] and Carleton[14] Papers. However, these papers in the British Library are only some of the raw materials for the various series of transcripts now housed in the Library of Congress. There is a very incomplete index which accompanied the deposit.

42535-54. PIGGOTT PAPERS.

Historical collections relating to the international law of blockade, etc. compiled by Sir Francis Taylor Piggott (d. 1925), author of numerous books and articles on international law, includes material for a study of 'The Relations between the Belligerents and the United States' during the Napoleonic Wars (42547); also contains collections illustrating the policy of the U.S. on questions of international maritime law, mostly during the period 1778-1821. (42552-3)

42559. CAPT. THOMAS NAIRNE ACCOUNTS.

Accounts by Capt. Thomas Nairne, agent of the Board of Indian Commissioners of South Carolina, of the customs and institutions of the Chickasaw, Ochese, Talapoosa, and other Indian tribes, written in the form of letters, 1708. (Copies.)

42568. PAPERS RELATING TO THE MEXICAN PROVINCE OF YUCATAN. 1764-1877. (In Spanish.)

Papers and correspondence of the Captains-General of Yucatan, 1797-1818. The greater part (ff. 16-102) concerns the occupation, in May 1818, of the Spanish fort of Pensacola in Florida by Major-General Andrew Jackson, including copies and translations of letters exchanged between Jackson and the Spanish commander of the fort, Colonel José Masot.

42575-85. SHERBORN AUTOGRAPHS

Original letters and papers, mainly of the nineteenth and twentieth centuries, selected from the collection of Charles Davies Sherborn, D.Sc. (d. 1942), which was formed largely in connection with his work at the British Museum (Natural History). Included are a number of letters from American philosophers, scientists, and naturalists, among them E.D. Cope, the editor of *The American Naturalist* (42585, ff. 42, 45, 49); R.W. Emerson (42575, f. 251); J.D. Dana, the naturalist (42579, ff. 223-4); and Henry Edwards, the entomologist (42579, f. 273).

42592-3. BROCKMAN PAPERS.

Miscellaneous parliamentary and political papers, mainly of William Brockman (d. 1742), in whose hand many are written. Includes papers relating to the reversal of Jacob Leisler's attainder, 1695. (42593, ff. 61-72)

42711. MISCELLANEOUS PAPERS.

P. Eighteen letters, unbound, 1845-57, from Sir Austen Henry Layard to Miner K. Kellogg, the American artist and art critic. Mainly about archaeology and art in general, but there is a little about American art.

There are seven letters, 1845-57, in the LAYARD PAPERS-Add. MSS. 38976, ff. 222, 373; 38977, f. 355; 38983, f. 75.

42772-846. ROSE PAPERS.

Correspondence and papers, official and private, of George Rose, the statesman and friend of William Pitt, together with the papers of his son, Sir George Henry Rose, the diplomat, and of his grandson, Field-Marshall Hugh Henry Rose, Baron Strathnairn.

42774

f. 104. Letter from Rufus King, U.S. Minister to Great Britain, to George Rose, 1798.

ff. 231-3*b*. Correspondence, 1807, of James Monroe as envoy to England, with G. Rose.

43039-358. ABERDEEN PAPERS.

George Hamilton Gordon, 4th Earl of Aberdeen (1784-1860), statesman. While Foreign Secretary 1841-6, he negotiated the Oregon Treaty of 1846.

There may be other smaller items of Americana amid this large collection, but the principal American papers appear to be:

43060

ff. 288, 309. Papers relating to the Canadian boundary question, 1842.

43062, 43243

Papers and correspondence relating to the Maine and Oregon boundary questions. (43062, ff. 36-43; 43243, f. 85) Also correspondence between Aberdeen and George Jones, the American actor and author, 1844 (43243, ff. 325-30*b*, 339); and a letter, 1842, from Charles Power, merchant at Galveston, Texas, to Sir R. Peel (43062, f. 78).

43121

Letter-book containing abstracts or copies of the official dispatches to the British Minister in the United States, Charles Vaughan, June 1828-Nov. 1829 (32 pages). Mentions Mexican affairs; the Canadian

13. Now in the William L. Clements Library, Ann Arbor, Mich.
14. Now in the Public Record Office, Kew.

boundary islands - their division between the United States and Britain under the Treaty of Ghent; the North-Eastern boundary arbitration under the convention of 1827; detention at Key West, Fla., of slaves taken from a Spanish vessel by a British ship.

43122

As 43121 above, from Vaughan, May-June 1828 (13 pages). Appointment of American arbitrators on North-Eastern boundary; the Tariff of 1828; opposition in Congress to wishes of John Quincy Adams; slowness of Britain in handing over boundary islands allotted to the United States by the Treaty of Ghent.

43123

Diplomatic correspondence and papers relating to the United States, 1841-6, arranged as follows:

f. 1. Correspondence, described as mainly 'private', of Aberdeen as Foreign Secretary, with Ashburton, chiefly concerning the latter's special mission to the United States as negotiator of the Webster-Ashburton Treaty.

f. 212. Similar correspondence with Henry Stephen Fox, Nov. 1841-Nov. 1843, and Richard Pakenham, Oct. 1843-July 1846, successive British Ministers to the United States. The correspondence with Pakenham relates to the settlement of the Oregon question.

f. 312. Correspondence, Apr. 1842-Aug. 1845, with William Peter, Thomas Colley Grattan, and William Ogilby, British Consuls at Philadelphia, Boston, and Charleston, S.C., respectively.

f. 370. Correspondence, Oct. 1841-Oct. 1846, with Andrew Stevenson, Edward Everett, and Louis McLane, successively American Ministers to Britain.

43126

Correspondence of Aberdeen with:

f. 31. Captain Charles Elliot, British *Chargé d'Affaires* in Texas, Sept. 1842-May 1846.

f. 88. William Kennedy, British Consul at Galveston, Tex., Sept. 1841-July 1844.

f. 113. General James Hamilton and General G.W. Terrell, successively Plenipotentiaries in London for the Republic of Texas, Oct. 1841-Sept. 1842, and June 1845.

43154

Letter-book containing abstracts or copies of the official dispatches which were sent by Aberdeen to the successive British Ministers to the United States, Fox and Pakenham, Sept. 1841-May 1846. The subject most frequently touched upon is that of the division of Oregon, over which relations can be seen worsening after the accession of Polk to the presidency; and the Disputed Territory Fund. Other subjects represented are the McLeod trial; the investigation by British warships of suspected slavers flying the American flag; the Ashburton mission and Webster-Ashburton treaty; the *Creole* case (in which slaves bound for New Orleans took control of the ship transporting them and sailed it to Nassau); attacks by American citizens on British vessels on the Great Lakes; Texas, and especially slavery there.

43155

Letter-book containing abstracts or copies of the official dispatches which were sent to Aberdeen by the successive British Ministers to the United States, Aug. 1841-June 1846. In addition to the topics dealt with in 43154, including considerably more about the McLeod trial and Texas, there are remarks about Tyler's break with his Cabinet and party in Congress; various messages, Bills, etc., for which several letters are covers; joint Anglo-American naval action for the suppression of the slave trade - the wholeheartedness of the United States in this is suspect; the occupation of Monterey, Calif., by American naval forces under the impression that war with Mexico had broken out; Hawaii.

43236-7

Official correspondence, etc., of Lord Aberdeen relating to Canada, 1834-5. (43236, ff. 261-420, *passim*; 43237, ff. 3, 8, 13, 22-33)

43240

ff. 128-30. Correspondence, 1842-3, of Robert Howe Gould, American author, with Lord Aberdeen.

43245-6

Correspondence, 1846, of Robert Barnwell Rhett of Washington, D.C., with Lord Aberdeen. (43245, f. 362; 43246, f. 79)

43246-9, 43255

Correspondence of Edward Everett, American author and diplomat, with Lord Aberdeen, mid-nineteenth century. (43246, ff. 312, 328; 43247, ff. 3, 64; 43248, ff. 238, 269; 43249, ff. 272, 343; 43255, f. 215)

43249-50

Correspondence, 1853, of Franklin Pierce with Aberdeen. (43249, f. 307; 43250, f. 168)

43254

ff. 260, 266. Letters, 1854, from James Buchanan, U.S. Envoy in London, to Lord Aberdeen.

43356

Confidential memoranda and papers printed during Aberdeen's tenure of the office of Foreign Secretary for Cabinet use, dealing with the United States, i.e. North-West boundary and Canadian fisheries.

43357

Similar to 43356, concerning the slave trade.

43377. MISCELLANEOUS PAPERS.

H. Slight note, 26 Oct. 1904, from Theodore Roosevelt to Edmund Lauterbach.

43383-92. JOHN BRIGHT PAPERS.

John Bright (1811-89), radical leader, M.P. for Durham, Manchester, and Birmingham 1843-85. Two volumes of his correspondence consist of letters from the United States and from American representatives in Europe, nearly all from supporters of the Federal cause during the Civil War, expressing their gratitude for Bright's advocacy of the Northern cause in opposition to the general trend of British opinion, and discussing the progress of the war. Other volumes contain occasional references to American affairs.

43390

ff. 1-49. Thirteen letters, 1861-8, from John Bigelow, first from France and then from America. He discusses, *inter alia*, French attitudes and policies to the Civil War; Gladstone's unfriendly attitude to the North (sending Bright a list of subscribers to the Confederate Cotton Loan in England for him to verify if Gladstone's name properly belonged there), the building of Confederate ships in England; and sends copies of letters concerning the Southern Independence Association in Britain.

ff. 50-122. Seventeen letters, 1853-87, from Edward L. Pierce, ranging through topical political events, particularly Massachusetts' politics and the problem of ex-slaves. Also much on Charles Sumner, of whom Pierce wrote a biography.

ff. 123-286. Sixty-four letters, 1861-8, from Sumner; also enclosures of letters to Sumner by various people, including William H. Seward. They discuss, *inter alia*, Sumner's irritation with Britain's attitude during the Civil War; the *Trent* incident; emancipation (Lincoln holds back because of the border states); removal of McClellan; criticism of Seward; disputes in Lincoln's Cabinet over naval policy; British building of ships for the Confederacy (Sumner appears prepared to have the North go to war with Britain); case of Alfred Ruberg, a Birmingham youth imprisoned for 'piracy' against the North and later pardoned by Lincoln at Bright's request; Sumner's and Lincoln's plans for reconstruction of conquered Confederate states; the presidential campaign of 1864; *Alabama* claims; confiscation and break-up of large plantations; Lord Lyons and strained Anglo-American relations; armed vessels on the Lakes; possible effect of death of Lincoln on national affairs; his (Sumner's) belief that Andrew Johnson is in agreement with Sumner's policy on reconstruction, and his later 'immense disappointment' in Johnson; American finances after the war; rumours of an American expedition against the French in Mexico; the 'folly' of Johnson's plans for reconstruction; the struggle between President and Congress over reconstruction in 1866; the Philadelphia 'Union' Convention of 1866; Sumner's opinion, 1868, that Johnson 'is as bad as J.D. [Jefferson Davis]'; the currency question in 1868.

43391

The whole volume consists of miscellaneous letters, 12 Jan. 1853-14 Oct. 1887, to Bright from Americans. The correspondents include Charles Francis Adams, Henry Adams, George Bancroft, Salmon P. Chase, Schuyler Colfax, Neal Dow, Dorman B. Eaton, William M. Evarts, Cyrus W. Field, Horace Greeley, Reverdy Johnson, Hugh McCulloch, John Lothrop Motley, Charles Eliot Norton, George Peabody, G.P. Putnam, William H. Seward, Governor James Smith of Rhode Island, Lewis Tappan, Amasa Walker, John Greenleaf Whittier.

Most of the letters are for the Civil War years and express gratitude to Bright for his advocacy of the Northern cause, and communicate views on the progress of the struggle.

43392

Contains miscellaneous memoranda, notes for speeches, etc., by Bright, including:

f. 131. An extract 'from a letter of Jefferson's - March 1810', on the characters of the sovereigns reigning while he was in Europe.

f. 159. Notes, n.d., on the size of the United States and of various states, and a comparison in size with European nations.

f. 170. *Considerations on the Military Position of Great Britain with respect to the United States*, 28 May 1869. (Printed.) A review of the defence potentialities of Canada, against any possible American attack.

43510-644. RIPON PAPERS.

The papers of George Frederick Samuel Robinson, 2nd Earl and 1st Marquess of Ripon (1827-1909), who, as Earl de Grey, was chairman of the Joint High Commission on the *Alabama* and other claims, which drew up the Treaty of Washington, 1871.

Letters mentioning the claims are found scattered throughout the non-Indian portion of the Papers; the most important of these groups are noted below. In addition, the Papers include letters from Thomas Hughes (*see* 43548-9).

43510

Contains two draft memos, 29 May 1872, by Ripon to the Queen on matters arising from the Treaty of Washington. There are also some letters, 1871, to Ripon from Julia Dent Grant, wife of U.S. Grant, and one letter, 1871, from President Grant to Ripon.

43514

ff. 78, 81, 102, 104. Correspondence with Gladstone, 1870-8. Contains four letters, 3 Apr.-28 Nov. 1871, on the dismissal of Sumner from the chairmanship of the Senate Foreign Relations Committee; Macdonald and the Canadian fisheries; and claims of British holders of Confederate bonds.

43519

ff. 110-212, *passim*. Correspondence, 27 Feb. 1871-12 Mar. 1873, with Sir Stafford Northcote (with an enclosure from Lord Lisgar to Northcote, 6 May 1871, on Sir John Macdonald), on the Treaty of Washington, the claims, the Geneva Arbitration, Fenians, etc.

43528

ff. 1-88. Correspondence, 7 Feb. 1871-4 Dec. 1872, with Lord Tenterden. Mostly from Tenterden to Ripon, a few written while they were both serving on the Joint High Commission at Washington in 1871, but most subsequent to their return. On rules laid down in the Treaty of Washington, the indirect claims, and the Geneva Arbitration.

43542

f. 17. Letter, 22 Sept. 1902, from James Bryce to Ripon, on Andrew Carnegie's method of making benefactions.

43548-9

Correspondence, 1857-88, of Lord and Lady Ripon with Thomas Hughes, including a letter from Hughes, 14 Nov. 1870, concerning his meeting in Boston with Julian Harney, the Chartist, and a number in 1880-1 concerning his Rugby, Tenn., venture.

43621-40. General correspondence of Ripon, 1849-1909.

43622

A few letters, Apr. 1863-Feb. 1871, concerning de Grey's arrival in America, chiefly of the welcome he received, but also including one from Thornton, the British Minister, on meeting the President, and a long one from Edward Armstrong of New York on the *Alabama* claims, in which he says that the replacement of wood by iron is the chief cause of the American shipping decline.

43623

Letters, Mar.-May 1871, almost all from Americans; mainly slight notes including some from Bayard, Edmunds, Fish, Schurz, and Sumner. Numerous begging letters and invitations to attend Masonic functions; also letters from Mrs. Jane P. Thurston, who claims to own the state of Maine. Chiefly important for several letters from Sir John Macdonald on the Canadian viewpoint in the Washington negotiations, and a few from people setting forth their reactions to the Treaty.

43624

Letters, June 1871-Apr. 1872, including letters from Macdonald on Canadian indignation over the Treaty of Washington; correspondence with Fish and Bernard; and references to the indirect claims.

43625

Letters, May 1872-Dec. 1875, including correspondence with

Bernard, Rush, Cyrus W. Field, Thornton, etc.; copies of letters to Bayard; letters on the Johnson-Clarendon Convention, the British case at Geneva, the indirect claims controversy, the Clayton-Bulwer Treaty, the proceedings at Geneva; several letters of congratulation at the dropping by the United States of the indirect claims; also a letter of 'Washington gossip', Dec. 1872, from Henry Stafford Northcote, including an explanation of how Horace Greeley received the Liberal Republican nomination in 1872.

43647-78. COBDEN PAPERS.

Richard Cobden (1804-65), statesman.
There may be more odd items of Americana in this large collection, but the principal items appear to be those listed below.

43652

f. 138. Letter to Cobden, 1864, from J.S. Morgan, American banker.

43652, 43671

Letters, 1864-5, to R. Cobden from Benjamin Moran, secretary to the U.S. legation in London. (43652, ff. 199, 207; 43671, ff. 131-3, 176, 187-90, 198, 220-3*b*)

43659

Letters from Cobden to the Rev. Henry Richard:

f. 83. London, 12 July 1861, on the blockade of the South and its effect on cotton supplies.

f. 86. Midhurst, 17 Aug. 1861, commenting that the Federal Government is more accommodating since Bull Run, and mentioning Northern taxes.

ff. 102, 131. Midhurst, 17 Oct. and 7 Dec. 1861, on the blockade.

ff. 126, 138, 140, 142. Midhurst, 3 and 18 Dec. 1861 and 10 Jan. 1862, on the *Trent* incident.

43664

f. 1. Letter to Joseph Parkes, 1845, from Charles Sumner.

43669

f. 30. Letter, 1856, from George Bancroft, American historian, to Richard Cobden.

43670-1

Letters, 1860's, from John Bigelow, U.S. Minister in Paris, to Richard Cobden. (43670, f. 182; 43671, ff. 76, 98) Also letters, 1863-4, from W.M. Evarts, U.S. statesman, to Cobden. (43671, ff. 67, 74, 78, 112-8*b*)

43671

ff. 58-63*b*. Letters, 1863, from Henry Adams, American historian, to Cobden.

43676

ff. 79-104. Typed copies of letters, 28 May 1861-5 Jan. 1862, from Richard Cobden to John Slagg, mainly on the Northern blockade, the cotton famine, and the *Trent* incident.

ff. 115-58, *passim*. Typed copies of letters, 9 May 1862-12 Feb. 1865, from Cobden to Slagg, chiefly on cotton, and on European sympathy for the Confederacy. Also, f. 139, a letter from H. Sanford to Cobden which says that the North lacks 'grim earnestness' and has not really felt the war yet, but will not terminate the conflict until the whole South submits.

ff. 159-260. Typed copies of letters, Mar. 1848-Mar. 1865, from Cobden to Charles Sumner, on 'peace campaigns'; Brooks's attack on Sumner; recession (Cobden regrets that the North did not let the South go in peace, but admits obstacles to this course); the capture of Mason and Slidell; cotton; maritime disputes and precedents (especially of right of search, and blockade); confusion of British opinion over the Civil War; American tariffs; the necessity of lifting the Northern blockade, which is bringing misery to Europe and turning people against the North; desirability of Northern recognition of the South as a belligerent; strained Anglo-American relations after the *Trent* incident; British sympathy with emancipation; building of Confederate ships in Britain; Sumner's denunciation of Britain and France in 1863; the arming of Negroes; the character of Lincoln; the Thirteenth Amendment. There are a few slight American references in the letters of Cobden to E. Alexander, Jr., which comprise the rest of the volume.

43677

ff. 78-84. Typed copies of letters, from Cobden to Henry Catt. In the first, 16 Dec. 1861, Cobden regrets that he cannot attend a meeting of Brighton working men called to deplore the possibility of war with the United States, and argues in favour of arbitration. In the second, 18 Dec. 1861, he advises the working men to send a memorial in favour of arbitration to Palmerston.

43678

A few letters from Americans about Cobden, written after his death.

See also 43807-8.

43688. MISCELLANEOUS LETTERS.

U. 29 Dec. 1890, Oliver Wendell Holmes, Sen. to F.D. Flory, of London.

Y. Papers described as 'a collection of American literary autographs'. There are eight in all, but only five of the letters appear to be from American literary figures - all poets. They are: Fitz-Greene Halleck, New York, 29 Dec. 1826, to J.W. Olcott, a slight note on financial matters. Paul H. Hayne, Augusta, Ga., n.d., to an unknown correspondent, about a cheque. Charles Fenno Hoffman to R.W. Griswold, no place, n.d., about Sir Walter Scott. Sidney Lanier, Macon, Ga., 21 Aug. 1867, to his publishers. Henry Timrod, Orangeburg, S.C., 10 Apr. 1856, to Oscar Keeler, enclosing a stanza.

43722. STURGE PAPERS.

Joseph Sturge (1793-1859), Quaker philanthropist and abolitionist.

Two letters from Richard Cobden to Sturge:

f. 122. 7 June 1856, on Anglo-American differences, war fears, and the evil influence of *The Times* on Anglo-American relations.

f. 320. 3 July 1859, comparing American banking and railroad management with British.

43742. MONCK, SIR CHARLES STANLEY, 4th Viscount and 1st Baron Monck (1819-94).

Governor General of Canada 1861-8.

Letters, 1867-8, from Lord Monck and others to the 3rd Duke of Buckingham and Chandos, mainly on a reported threat of an invasion of Canada by Fenians from the United States. (*See also* 41860.)

43807-8. COBDEN, RICHARD (1804-65). Diaries in America,[15] 1835 and 1859.

43841. ACCOUNT BOOK OF THE CAPTAIN OF THE *MONGOVO GEORGE*, a Liverpool schooner, while engaged in the slave trade, 1785-7.

Entries, June 1785-Jan. 1786, detail various purchases of slaves on the west coast of Africa; and, reversing the volume, the subsequent sales in America, Oct. 1786-Apr. 1787. Also included is a copy of instructions left with a mercantile house in New Orleans, authorizing the firm to collect moneys due the slaver in America and to remit them to William Denison, a Liverpool merchant.

43846. TRISTAN DA CUNHA RECORDS.

A collection of documents, 1817-21, relating to the annexation and colonization of this island due to its having been used as a raiding base by United States cruisers during the War of 1812. The documents are printed and described by D.M. Gane in 'The Early Records of Tristan da Cunha; the discovery in New London', *United Empire*, vol. xxiv, pp. 589-98, 651-8, 709-13, 1933.

43873. MISCELLANEOUS LEGAL PAPERS AND DOCUMENTS.

f. 2. Bond relating to the transportation of felons to Maryland or Virginia, 1740.

43874-967. DILKE PAPERS.[16]

Correspondence, literary MSS., and other papers of Sir Charles Wentworth Dilke (1843-1911), British politician.

43909-22

General Correspondence. The Dilke Papers include amongst its general correspondence numerous letters from Americans to Dilke. Included are the publisher F.H. Holland (43914, f. 302); Robert Underwood Johnson, the American poet, 1906 (43919, f. 75); James Russell Lowell, American author and diplomat, 1880-2 (43911, ff. 108, 151, 178, 196-7, 250, 272, 274; 43912, f. 100); W.H. Rideing, editor of the *North American Review*, 1889-90 (43914, ff. 153, 203*b*. 248); Joaquin Miller, American author, 1873 [to N. MacColl] (43909, f. 365); Eugene Schuyler, American diplomat, 1887 (43914, f. 33); John Wentworth, American congressman, 1874 (43910, f. 1); and Brigham Young, the Mormon leader, 1872 (43909, f. 300).

43975-89. FURTHER RECORDS OF THE CHISWICK PRESS, the printing establishment controlled successively by Charles Whittingham I (the uncle) and Charles Whittingham II (the nephew).

43985

ff. 23-36. Letters, etc., relating to Joaquin Miller's 'Songs of the Sierras', etc. 1892-1906.

44085. MISCELLANEOUS PAPERS.

C. Letter, 1794, written from America by Samuel Hart, an English settler in New Jersey. Deals with land and crops, and describes outbreak of yellow fever.

44086-835. GLADSTONE PAPERS.

The papers of William Ewart Gladstone (1809-98) comprise some 750 volumes, the largest collection of any Prime Minister found in the British Library. The following list relies almost entirely on the special and separately printed *Catalogue of the Gladstone Papers* (London, 1953); and the following is by no means complete, for Gladstone had numerous minor American correspondents - but most of these can be readily located in the admirable index to the *Catalogue*. (*Letters unless otherwise stated.*)

44133-4. Correspondence with Clarendon.

44133

ff. 194-229, *passim*. 28 Feb., 22 and 26 Mar., 15 and 20 May 1860, from Clarendon to Gladstone on Reverdy Johnson and the *Alabama* claims convention.

44134

ff. 64-166, *passim*, ff. 201-5. 15 and 23 Oct., 24 and 27 Nov., 4 and 24 Dec. 1869; 18 and 23 Jan., 17 Mar., 15 and 18 May 1870, Clarendon to Gladstone on the claims, negotiations over which were at a standstill after the Senate's rejection of the Johnson-Clarendon Convention.

44136

ff. 146-75, *passim*, ff. 248-74, *passim*. Correspondence with Cobden. Ten letters, six from Cobden to Gladstone, 11 Dec. 1861-20 Feb. 1865, and four from Gladstone to Cobden, 13 Dec. 1861-22 Feb. 1865. Include a long letter from Cobden pleading with Gladstone to use his influence against war with the United States over the *Trent* incident. Also letters on emancipation in the border states; the Northern blockade; the proposed Atlantic cable; a comparison of the British and American navies; the defence of Canada and armaments on the Great Lakes.

44168

Correspondence with Granville.[17]

ff. 36, 62, 114-7, 229, 246-80, *passim*. Twelve letters, 27 Jan. 1871-30 June 1872, mostly from Gladstone to Granville, but including letters from Granville to Gladstone; Granville to Northcote; Sir Alexander Cockburn, British arbitrator at the Geneva Convention, 1872, to Granville; and Robert Schenck, United States Minister in London, to Granville. Chiefly on appointments to the Washington Commission; the Treaty of Washington; the indirect claims; and the Geneva Arbitration.

44183

Correspondence with Edmund Hammond, permanent Under-Secretary for Foreign Affairs 1854-73.

ff. 438, 472. Two letters from Hammond to Gladstone. The first, 26 Mar. 1869, on a draft to be sent to Thornton, presumably on the Claims Convention, altered at Bright's suggestion, and on American activities off Cuba. The second, 3 Sept. 1872, on the Geneva award.

15. *The American Diaries of Richard Cobden*, ed. by Elizabeth H. Cawley, with an introduction (Princeton, N.J., 1952).
16. These papers have now been catalogued.
17. Printed in *The Political Correspondence of Mr. Gladstone and Lord Granville, 1868-1876*, ed. by Agatha Ramm, 2 vols. (London, 1952).

44217

Correspondence with Sir Stafford Henry Northcote, Conservative leader in the House of Commons, and member of the Washington Commission.

ff. 115-37. Four letters (and one enclosure from Lord Lisgar to Northcote), Washington, D.C., 17 Mar.-21 Apr. 1871, from Northcote to Gladstone. Deal with the San Juan question; Canadian fisheries and reciprocity; the committee system of Congress; the *Alabama* claims; the danger to a settlement arising from the adjournment of the Senate between April and May.

44249

f. 49. Newark, N.J., 16 Apr. 1868, from James Roosevelt Bayley, Roman Catholic Bishop of Newark, to Cardinal Manning, on American attitudes on the Irish question and its effect on Anglo-American relations.

44272

Correspondence with Palmerston. Two letters, 9 Jan. and 24 Sept. 1862, from Palmerston to Gladstone; two letters, 25 Sept. 1862 and 8 Oct. 1863, from Gladstone to Palmerston, deal with the *Trent* incident. Palmerston suggests and Gladstone agrees that the time has come to offer mediation in conjunction with France and Russia, and that, should the North refuse and the South accept, Britain should recognize Southern independence; in his 1863 letter Gladstone says that the Queen 'did not appear to lean toward over-reconciliation of the Federal government' in the rams issue.

44285

Correspondence, 1887-97, with William Henry Rideing, editor of the *North American Review*.

44286

Correspondence with Earl de Grey, later 2nd Earl and 1st Marquess of Ripon, Chairman of the Joint High Commission.

ff. 110-4. Letter, 21 Mar. 1871, from de Grey to Gladstone, on the work of the Commission, especially on the *Alabama* claims and San Juan boundary; also on the Grant-Sumner quarrels. (Copy in RIPON PAPERS, 43514, f. 73, q.v.)

44292

Correspondence with Lord John Russell, 1st Earl Russell (1792-1878).

ff. 43-56, *passim*, 84-7, 162-81, *passim*. Eight letters, 30 Oct. 1861-17 Sept. 1865, from Russell to Gladstone; and two letters, 2 and 6 Sept. 1865, from Gladstone to Russell. On cotton; the *Trent* incident; Sumner's accusations that Britain had encouraged the South to take up arms; Gladstone's Newcastle speech, 'Jefferson Davis and other leaders of the South . . . have made a nation' - for which Russell mildly rebukes him; recognition of the South, American claims for depredations of Confederate cruisers and Britain's refusal to go to arbitration in 1865.

44303

f. 190. Ithaca, N.Y., 14 May 1871, from Goldwin Smith to Gladstone, on the good effect of the Treaty of Washington on American public opinion.

44352-526. Gladstone's general correspondence, 1826-98.
Scattered American references include the following:

44400

f. 192. [New York], 8 Apr. 1863, from William Adams, American clergyman, to Cyrus W. Field, on the war aims of the North and British misunderstanding of them.

44412

f. 274. (*See also* 44442, f. 117.) London, 7 May 1867, from Charles Francis Adams, American Minister to Britain, to Gladstone, introducing John Sherman.

44420

f. 180. Copy of a letter, 1869, to the Duke of Argyll from J.L. Motley, referring to and refuting some accusation that he had called Gladstone a liar in a dispute which had accidentally reached the American press.

44427

f. 232. Also 44428, ff. 90, 96, 182, 211, 213, 276, 290; 44439, f. 23. (*See also* 44766, f. 201.) Letters, 1870-3, from J.L. Motley to Gladstone. Mostly slight notes, with some mention of possible mediation in the Civil War reparation disputes of American interests, and of Fenian prisoners in England.

44428

ff. 282, 284. Official memoranda, 1870, on the *Trent* case from Lord Tenterden to Gladstone, showing how the draft of the Cabinet's proposed dispatch to Lord Lyons, then British Minister at Washington, was in 1861 altered by the Prince Consort.

44433-50

44433, ff. 235, 264; 44434, ff. 1, 82; 44435, f. 49; 44437, ff. 43, 148; 44438, f. 305; 44442, ff. 33, 324; 44445, ff. 194, 213; 44447, f. 319; 44448, f. 88, 231; 44449, ff. 3, 11; and 44450, f. 194. Correspondence, 1872-6, between General Robert Schenck, United States Minister to Britain, and Gladstone. One or two letters are personal notes or letters of introduction; some of the earlier letters contain references to the indirect claims. The main interest of the correspondence lies, however, in 44437, f. 148, 44442, f. 324, and the letters in 44445-9; these deal with Gladstone's attempts to obtain from Hamilton Fish, through Schenck, a statement that the use made of his allegedly anti-Northern sentiments during the Civil War in the American case at the Geneva Arbitration did not imply that the United States considered him unfriendly towards it. Schenck finally obtained from Fish a letter in which the Secretary of State says that he believes that Gladstone had no 'consciousness of hostility' towards the North but was simply reflecting the general feeling of middle and upper class Britain at the time.

44452

f. 35. New Britain, Conn., 6 Oct. 1876, from Elihu Burritt, American philanthropist, to Gladstone, on the teaching of Sanskrit.

44490-525

Scattered through these volumes is correspondence with Andrew Carnegie, 27 Apr. 1885-8 June 1897. Fourteen letters and a telegram from Carnegie to Gladstone; five letters from Gladstone to Carnegie. Mostly personal notes, e.g., on Gladstone's health, Carnegie's hopes that Gladstone will write an autobiography, etc. Other subjects dealt with are the possibility of a general arbitration treaty between the United States and Britain, which Carnegie expects to see signed when Gladstone and James G. Blaine are in office at the same time; a contribution by Carnegie to Liberal Party funds; the presentation to Lord Acton of his library during his lifetime, which Carnegie financed; the inevitability, according to Carnegie, of Canada's joining the United States; the Venezuela dispute of 1895; an appeal by Gladstone to Carnegie to help the Bodleian Library, and Carnegie's refusal.

44524
f. 23. Memorandum by A. and E. Howland on religious persecution in New England, 1684.

44527-51. Letter-books. Copies of Gladstone's letters written while he was holding various offices under the Crown, 1835-94. There are few letters of American significance; even the letter-books for the Civil War period (chiefly 44531-4) appear to contain very little of importance. Major items include:

44536
30 Mar. 1869, to Clarendon, on an 'outrageous' proposal of Reverdy Johnson - presumably on the claims - and the way in which the 'indefensible' frontier of Canada forces Britain into a submissiveness to the United States. 11 May 1869, to the Duke of Argyll, on Motley and Sumner. 12 May 1869, to Clarendon on Motley.

44537
23 and 25 Oct., 22 Nov. 1869, to Clarendon, on Fish's dispatch to Motley on the *Alabama* claims.

44538
24 and 25 Dec. 1869, 20 and 24 Jan., 18 Mar. 1870, to Clarendon on the *Alabama* claims and the San Juan boundary; highly critical of Sumner; but has hopes of Fish. 28 June 1870 on the same subjects, to Sir John Young.

44539
9 Jan. 1871, to Granville, on possibility of arbitration of claims; composition of Washington Commission, and progress of negotiations. 3 and 4 Apr. 1871, to Earl de Grey at Washington, on the Commission. 30 Mar. and 3 Apr. 1871, to Sir Stafford Northcote, also on the Commission.

44540
12, 13, 14, 17, and 21 Apr.; 1, 2, 3, 11 May 1871; to Granville on the wording of the preamble of the Treaty of Washington - especially on the word 'rebellion'; San Juan boundary; fisheries; importance of British Commission's leaving Washington before the Senate meets; Fenian raids into Canada.

44563-635. Gladstone's official papers, including memoranda prepared for the use of the Cabinet, 1834-95. (Mostly printed.) The following contain material concerning the Civil War:

44593, ff. 47, 55, 83, 84, 86, 99, 104.
44594, ff. 26, 36, 44, 115.
44595, ff. 66, 72, 77, 82, 84, 86, 94.
44597, f. 32.
44599, f. 97.

(*See also* 44511, f. 23; 44752, ff. 51, 305, 342; 44754, f. 120.)

Examples of the type of material contained in this group are:

44593
Instructions to Lord Lyons respecting hostilities in the U.S., 1861. (Printed.)

Judicial Decision on the blockade of U.S. Ports by Judge Dunlop, 1861. (Printed.)

Various printed memoranda on the *Trent* incident, 1861, especially as regards precedents.

44595
Present Conditions of Affairs in the U.S., by Russell, 13 Oct. 1862. (Printed.)

Report of a Chicago meeting held on 20 Sept. 1862 to discuss the first Emancipation Proclamation. (Printed.)

Various memoranda, Oct.-Nov. 1862, by Sir George Cornewall Lewis, Gladstone, and Russell, arising from Russell's memorandum of 13 Oct. 1862, cited above, chiefly on recognition of the Confederacy. (Printed.)

Report on travels in the West, by H. Percy Anderson, 1862. (Printed.)

44601-20
The following contain material on the *Alabama* claims and the Treaty of Washington: 44601, f. 17; 44603, ff. 71, 83; 44610, f. 45; 44617, f. 8; 44618, ff. 51, 86, 113; 44619, ff. 29, 62, 88, 98, 126; and 44620, ff. 48, 94. (*See also* 44107, f. 322; 44760, f. 194; and 44761, f. 181.)

Examples of the type of material contained in this group are: 44617, *Memorandum Explanatory of some of the Articles of the Treaty of Washington,* by Lord Tenterden, 1871. (Printed.) 44618, Various memoranda on the meaning of certain parts of the Treaty of Washington, especially on the claims. (Partly printed.) 44619, Various memoranda on the indirect claims, and the Geneva Award, 1872. (Mostly printed.)

Miscellaneous subjects are dealt with in the following: 44616, f. 149. Manuscript memorandum on the Southern states, 1871. Discusses whether or not they 'rebelled'. 44617, f. 169. *The Case of the Confederate Cotton Bondholders.* An 18-page printed pamphlet, 1871, giving the opinions of the Lord Chancellor, Attorney-General, and others.

44625
f. 110. Manuscript memorandum entitled 'Extracts from Cushing's *Manual*', on cloture in the United States, 1880.

44633
ff. 36, 45, 59. (*See also* 44497, f. 367; and 44768, f. 14.) Papers on the American attitude to the Irish question, 1884-6. Include a clipping from the *Daily News*, 1886, entitled 'American sympathy with Home Rule'; an extract from a letter, 11 June 1886, from E. L. Godkin to James Bryce; and a list of public bodies in the United States which had sent communications on Home Rule, 1886.

44636-48. Cabinet minutes.
Minutes by Gladstone of Cabinet meetings which he attended as Chancellor of the Exchequer and as Prime Minister, 1853-94. Included are also notes and minutes made by other members of the Cabinet.

These were available only with the written permission of the

Cabinet Office, and were not examined.[18] It was, however, known that 44638-40, covering 1870-2, contain minutes on the *Alabama* claims and the Treaty of Washington; and 44636 probably contains material on the Civil War.

44649-80. Notes and memoranda for speeches, etc.

44654
f. 201. (*See also* 44746, f. 26.) Memoranda, 1856, concerning opposition to recruitment in the United States for the British army. 44746 appears to contain three drafts of a motion on this subject.

44681-714. Gladstone's literary works (original manuscripts).

44690
f. 55. Address on the cotton famine and distress in Lancashire and Cheshire, delivered at Chester, 27 Dec. 1862.

44701
f. 251. 'The Future of the English-Speaking Races', published in the American *Youth's Companion*, Nov. 1888.

44702
f. 296. A review of Mrs. S.D. Smedes' *Memorials of a Southern Planter* (Baltimore, 1887),[19] published in the *Nineteenth Century*, Dec. 1889.

44703
f. 296. Corrected proof sheets, followed, f. 305, by manuscript additions of an article in the *Nineteenth Century,* Nov. 1890, entitled, 'Mr. Carnegie's Gospel of Wealth' (published in London, 1890).

44734
ff. 1, 260; and 44735, f. 2. (*See also* 44575, f. 71, printed.) Memoranda on commercial relations with the United States. For example, claim of United States for repayment of duties on rough rice, 13 Jan. 1844; and the commercial aspects of the Treaty of Ghent.

44752
Memoranda (manuscript), 1862-3, on public opinion in the United States, effect of foreign opinion on the United States; possible British intervention to end the Civil War; possible joint action with France and Russia to the same end; recognition of the Confederacy; the United States public debt; the Foreign Enlistment Act, the iron-clad rams, and British neutrality.

44773
f. 96. Memorandum entitled 'For fair play all round', on tariffs, 1889. Argues against American protectionism.

44790
f. 131. Autobiographical memorandum, 'Some of my errors', 1894. One of the subjects treated is his attitude towards the Civil War.

44791
f. 29. In 'Recorded errors', 1896, again mentions his attitude towards the Civil War.

f. 131. 'First period of leadership, 1865-75 and to 1880', 1897. The section headed 'First Cabinet, 1868-74' contains remarks on the claims question.

44793
f. 158. Notes by Gladstone on *Letters* of 'Massachusettensis', n.d. 'Massachusettensis' was Daniel Leonard, who published his *Letters to the Inhabitants of the Province of Massachusetts Bay* in 1775.

44889-90. MISCELLANEOUS PAPERS.
Manuscript of Nathaniel Hawthorne's *The Marble Faun*, which was published in 1860, first under that title and then as *Transformation.* Also letters from Hawthorne to H.A. Bright, 1860, and Smith, Elder and Co., 1860.

44914. MISCELLANEOUS PAPERS.
Chart and record of a voyage to America in the S.S. *Oceanic*, by Charles Kingsley, 1874.

44992-45022. RUSSELL OF BIRMINGHAM PAPERS.[20]
William Russell (1740-1818) and his son, Thomas Pougher Russell (1775-1851), of Birmingham, were friends of Joseph Priestley, and exporters to the United States. They migrated to the United States in 1795 and lived there until 1800.
A full list of contents of the papers is given in 45022. They include seven letters from Priestley - one written from Philadelphia; and a letter, 28 Sept. 1798, from George Washington on agricultural matters.[21] Also:

Bundle xviii, item 11. George Russell's accounts with Thomas Russell, 1803-12. Gives the latter's expenses as George Russell's American agent.

Bundle xx, item 9. Duplicate copy of an Act of the Maryland Assembly in favour of William Russell, Annapolis, Md., 3 Nov. 1793.

Accounts xiv. Labelled '1812-18. Waste Book June 1812.' William Russell's French farming accounts and other miscellaneous accounts in France, England, and America, 20 June 1812-Jan. 1818. Entered by William Russell until Dec. 1817; continued by Thomas Russell.

Accounts xxii. Labelled 'Waste Book 1813-21'. Thomas Russell's yearly accounts of his own business ventures in France, England and America, 6 Nov. 1813-5 Nov. 1821.

Accounts xxiii. Labelled 'Journal 1813-23'. Thomas Russell's yearly journals of accounts in France, England and America, 6 Nov. 1813-1 Nov. 1823. Duplicates material in Accounts xxii up to 1821.

See also Russell Diaries, Birmingham Public Libraries (p.226).[22]

18. This restriction has now been lifted.
19. Published in London in 1889 as *A Southern Planter.*
20. See S.H. Jeyes, *The Russells of Birmingham in the French Revolution and in America, 1791-1814* (London, 1911).
21. See *Writings of George Washington*, ed. by John C. Fitzpatrick, vol. xxxvi (Washington, D.C., 1941), pp. 469-70.
22. Other Russell Papers, mostly those relating to their American sojourn, are owned by the Pennsylvania Historical Association.

45102. MISCELLANEOUS LETTERS AND PAPERS.

C. Letter from William Sydney Porter, *al.* 'O. Henry', American short story writer, to Robert Underwood Johnson, associate editor of *The Century*, relating to a contribution, probably 'The Missing Child', 9 Mar. 1904.

S. (4). Letter from William Gilmore Simms, American author, to the Rev. Rufus Wilmot Griswold, American journalist, while the latter was on a visit to Charleston, S.C., regarding publications, 10 Feb. 1846.

45186-7. LETTERS TO EDWARD WHEELER SCRIPTURE.

Scripture was Professor of Experimental Phonetics in the University of Vienna, and the letters, from English, American, and German poets and other writers, are mainly in reply to a questionnaire on poetic method that he had circulated among them. American correspondents in 45186 include John Gould Fletcher, n.d. (ff. 25-6) and J.R. Jeffers, American poet, 1927 (f. 31).

45227-64. POSITIVIST PAPERS.

Letters from Positivists and others, addressed to Mr. and Mrs. R. Congreve, 1863-1900.

45240

f. 5. Letter from Benjamin W. Austin, Dallas, Texas, 1891.

f. 79. Letter from Jennie Cunningham Croly, New York, 1878.

f. 200. Letter from Gerald McCarthy, Raleigh, N.C., 1893.

45241

f. 165. Letter from Emory McClintock of New Jersey, 1898.

45284-9. MAHATMA PAPERS OF ALFRED PERCY SINNETT.

Correspondence and papers in connection with the Theosophical movement, 1880-90.

Includes letters to Mme. H.P. Blavatsky from J.W. Bouton, a New York publisher, 1886 (45289B, f. 212), and Elliott Coues, American naturalist (45288, f. 273).

45290-7. ARCHER CORRESPONDENCE.

Correspondence and papers of William Archer (1856-1924), literary and drama critic.

45291

f. 2. Letter to Archer from Annie Payson Call, American author, 1889.

f. 126. Letter to Archer from C.W. Eliot, 1914.

45292

f. 229. Letter to Archer from Bronson Howard, American playwright, 1891.

f. 231. Letter to Archer from William Dean Howells, 1890.

45293

ff. 137*b*-211. Numerous letters to Archer from J.B. Matthews, American author, 1883-1923.

f. 330. Letter to Archer from W.L. Phelps, Professor of American Literature at Yale, 1907.

45295

f. 34. Letter from Theodore Roosevelt to Archer, 1910.

Also includes a letter from J.N. Ireland, American author, to J.B. Matthews, 1888 (45293, f. 153).

45338-53. CORRESPONDENCE AND PAPERS OF WILLIAM MORRIS.

Besides the papers of Morris (1834-96), poet and artist, there are some items in the collection which relate to members of his family.

45345

Letters to Morris from J.R. Lowell, 1882 (ff. 48, 52), and from John Swinton, American journalist [before 1887] (f. 140).

45346

ff. 94, 107. Letters to Miss May Morris from Charlotte Perkins Gilman, American author, 1896-1935. (One letter in 45348, f. 32)

f. 152. Letter, 1899, to Miss Morris from Stevens & Brown, American booksellers.

f. 162. Letter, 1902, from Stevens & Brown to E. Walker.

45347

f. 189. Letter from Joseph Pennell, American artist and author, to B.H. Newdigate, 1922.

45348

f. 12. Letter, 1927, from Harold Peirce of Philadelphia, to Miss Morris.

45498. MISCELLANEOUS LETTERS AND PAPERS.

E. Letter from Herman Melville, American author, to an unknown correspondent, regretting his inability to keep an appointment, 27 Nov. 1857.

S. Letter from William Dean Howells, American author, to Major George H. Putnam, publisher, concerning a book for review, 7 Feb. 1915.

45538-64. HALL GRIFFIN PAPERS.

Collections of William Hall Griffin (d. 1907) for his *Life of Robert Browning*.

Includes a letter from M.D. Conway, American author, to Griffin, 1893 (45563, f. 30).

45578-663. BLECHYNDEN PAPERS.

Includes journal of Richard Humphrys, of the 28th Regiment, describing campaigns in Canada and the West Indies, and mentioning the capture of Louisbourg in 1758 and Quebec in 1759 (45662).

45669-79. NOTEBOOKS, ETC. OF JOHN HALL.

Hall (*c.* 1631-1709) was a physician and Dissenter from Bradford in Yorkshire.

45675

ff. 378-388*b*. Notes of sermons preached by Thomas Shepherd, later a Congregational minister in New England.

45728-30. AUCKLAND PAPERS.

Papers of William Eden, 1st Baron Auckland (1744-1814), who was one of the Peace Commissioners sent to America in 1778.

45728

ff. 99-100. Letter, Madrid, 26 Feb. 1789, from Eden to Lord Sheffield, on a reported Russian settlement on the California coast.

There are also AUCKLAND PAPERS in 46490-1.

45734-41. PALGRAVE PAPERS.

Manuscripts from the library of Francis Turner Palgrave (d. 1897), compiler of the *Golden Treasury*.

45741

f. 98. Letter to Palgrave from O.W. Holmes, 1886.

f. 137. Letter to Palgrave from J.R. Lowell, 1883.

45744-5. LETTERS TO MAUDE DOMINICA MARY PETRE.

Biographer of Father George Tyrell. From various correspondents, chiefly on religious matters and more particularly on the Modernist movement in the Catholic church.

45745

ff. 197, 199. Letters, 1922, to Miss Petre from Fr. Arnold Weyman, rector of St. Anthony's, Detroit, Mich.

45750-849. NIGHTINGALE PAPERS, SECOND SERIES.

A selection from the correspondence, literary manuscripts, and other papers of Florence Nightingale (d. 1910).

45796-815. General correspondence, 1853-1910, n.d.

Includes letters to Florence Nightingale from John Eaton, U.S. Commissioner of Education, 1879 (45805, f. 200); T.M. Jackson of Boston, 1868 (45800, ff. 245, 246*b*, 252*b*, 253); Mary T. Leiter, wife of L.Z. Leiter, American merchant, 1895 (45813, ff. 114-9); Mrs. L.W. Quintard, of St. Luke's Hospital, N.Y., 1899 (45815, ff. 95, 97); Linda A. Richard, American nurse, 1877 (45804, ff. 208, 228, 230, 235, 251, 253, 259); H.G. Taylor, president of N.J. Training School for Nurses, 1893 (45811, f. 281; 45812, ff. 31, 37); Alice O. Tippet, of the American Guild of St. Barnabas for Trained Nurses, 1895 (45813, f. 94); Anna A. Warder of the Women's Centennial Committee for Ohio, 1875-6 (45804, ff. 117-20, 148); and Abby D. Williams of New York, 1897 (45814, f. 181).

45918. MISCELLANEOUS AUTOGRAPH LETTERS.

ff. 4, 5, 9. Letters from P.T. Barnum, American showman, to T.D. Spain, 1882-90.

f. 83. Letter, 1893, from M.D. Conway to ?.

ff. 167-8. Letters, 1881 and 188[7?], from C.S. Leland, American author, to Miss A. Smith and T.D. Spain.

f. 223. Letter from George Peabody, American philanthropist, to J. Mitchell, 1867.

45926-7. SHERBORN BEQUEST.

Miscellaneous autographs, including a letter to D.W. Morrow from Calvin Coolidge, 1926 (45926, f. 25); letter, 1896, to Mrs. [Conover?] from W.D. Howells (45926, f. 95); letter, 1921, to D.W. Morrow from Gen J.J. Pershing, American Commander-in-Chief (45927, f. 62); and letter to J.J. Morrow from W.H. Taft, 1909 (45927, f. 126).

45928. KEPPEL PAPERS.

Papers of, or collected by, Gen. Sir George Keppel and Gen. Sir William Keppel. The material is connected with the discharge of their respective offices and appointments in Cuba, Jersey and Guernsey.

ff. 170-81. Affidavits, etc., relating to the seizure of Jersey vessels in Newfoundland waters, 1768-9. (English and French.)

45985-46118. HERBERT GLADSTONE PAPERS.

Correspondence, official and private, of Herbert John Gladstone, Viscount Gladstone (1854-1930).

46048-86. General correspondence, 1880-1930.

Includes letters to Lord Gladstone from Raymond H. Arnot, American lawyer, 1921 (46084, ff. 294, 309); Joseph Choate, U.S. Ambassador to London, 1903 (46061, f. 37); S.H. Emmens, American industrialist, 1892-8 (46053, f. 243; 46054, ff. 19, 24-45, 48, 61; 46057, f. 6); Rev. H.M. Field, American author, 1887 (46052, f. 244); Burton J. Hendrick, American author, 1927, 1929 (46086, ff. 208, 210); H.A.S. Kennedy, U.S. journalist, 1928 (46086, f. 87); Paul Knaplund, American historian, 1923-8 (46085, ff. 108, 126; 46086, ff. 22, 32, 103); F.A. Ogg, American historian, 1927 (48086, f. 33); Thomas O'Reilly, American physician, 1891-2 (46053, ff. 155-163*b*, 226*b*); Charles S. Osborne of Michigan, 1913 (46074, f. 287); Whitelaw Reid, U.S. Ambassador to London, 1907, 1909 (46064, f. 267; 46067, f. 210); and W.H. Rideing, 1894 (46055, f. 175).

Gladstone's papers also include correspondence of Frank D. Butler of Philadelphia with Sir G. Parker, 1914 (46079, ff. 288-90), and of Paul Knaplund with H.N. Gladstone, 1923, 1926 (46045, f. 289; 46085, ff. 273-7).

46125-8. MURCHISON PAPERS.

Miscellaneous letters from persons of note, English and foreign, addressed to Sir Roderick Impey Murchison (1792-1871), geologist.

American correspondents include Edward Everett, U.S. Minister in London, 1845-54 (46126, ff. 100-8); Henry Grinnell, New York, 1852 (46126, f. 338); J.R. Ingersoll, U.S. Minister in London, 1852 (46126, f. 452); J.K. Kane, American jurist, 1857 (46127, f. 1); Sidney Kopman, Secretary of the Kane Monument Association of New York, 1858 (46127, f. 40); Jared Sparks, American historian, 1858 (46128, f. 96); and Andrew Stevenson, U.S. Minister in London, 1838 (46128, f. 141).

46196. ROLLO PAPERS.

Letter 'C. Townshend', from the War Office to Lord Rollo in America, 25 Feb. 1762, informing him that he has been breveted colonel by the King.[23]

46490-1. AUCKLAND PAPERS.

Papers of William Eden, 1st Baron Auckland (1744-1814).

Two letters from Lord North to Eden. The first, 18 Sept. 1775, praises General Gage, Governor Tryon of New York, and Gover-

23. H.M.C. iii, p. 407.

nor Campbell of South Carolina for their actions in America, and details the troops to be sent there. The second, 1777, refers to Eden's appointment to the Peace Commission under Lord Carlisle. Also a letter, 30 Mar. 1778, from Eden to North, giving the conditions on which he is prepared to go to America with the Commission.

Fifteen letters, 1777-8 and undated, from Alexander Wedderburn to Eden (one incomplete, but apparently from Wedderburn); and seven, 1778, from Eden, unaddressed but presumably to Wedderburn. The earlier letters contain general comments on American affairs, e.g. the procrastination of the Howes, the apparent policy of wearing down the rebels rather than defeating them, the Franco-American treaty, the possibilities of peace. Then two letters on the composition of the Peace Commission, and another in which Wedderburn reports a rumour that North is of the opinion that American independence must be granted. Most of the others are written by Eden while in America, in which he describes the evacuation of Philadelphia, which he thinks needless and which convinces him that the government did not intend to give the Peace Commission a fair chance - he complains bitterly of this 'shameful treatment' and (?) Wedderburn writes answering his complaints; the blockade of New York - to where the Commission moved - by d'Estaing; the American evacuation of Rhode Island; the 'race' between the fleets of Howe and d'Estaing for Boston, which the French won; General Howe's pessimism on American affairs, and his poor strategy; Eden's belief that some exertion on Britain's part would speedily end the rebellion as the Americans are already, Sept. 1778, feeling that they have neither 'a grievance [nor] a just object'; the failure of the Peace Commission. In another letter, n.d., Wedderburn introduces to Eden someone who has a plan for 'an accommodation with the Americans'.

Nine letters and papers, 1777, sent by Hugh Elliot in Berlin to the Earl of Suffolk. These, which are marked 'most secret', etc., and are partly in code (?), concern the connexions of France and Spain with the Americans. Some are transcripts of intercepted communications from A. Lee. (Three are in French.)

Three letters, 1777-9, two from Berlin and one from London, from Elliot to Eden. On the 'close correspondence' between Prussia and the Americans, and various naval actions in 1779 - one against John Paul Jones. Elliot suggests that Britain should grant independence to her American colonies, and then force the independence of all French and Spanish American colonies.

46840. MISCELLANEOUS PAPERS.

Diary of the siege of Quebec by an American force, written by J. Danford, a member of the garrison, 10 Nov. 1775-6 May 1776.

46920-47213. EGMONT PAPERS.

Papers of the Perceval family, principally collected by Sir John Perceval, Viscount Perceval and 1st Earl of Egmont (1683-1748).

47032

Letter-book, 1727-30, including copies of correspondence, 1729-30, mainly between George Berkeley and Perceval, concerning the former's Rhode Island visit to purchase land in order to supply a proposed college in Bermuda.[24] Berkeley's letters include description of Newport, R.I., and his activities there.

47053

Papers, 1764, concerning Nova Scotia estates.

47054

Papers, late eighteenth century, concerning estates in Nova Scotia, Florida, and elsewhere.

47060-71

Diaries, 1730-47, of Viscount Perceval (from 1733, 1st Earl of Egmont).[25] These contain much information about the early days of the colony of Georgia. (Perceval was the first president of the trustees of the colony.)

47287. LIEVEN PAPERS, vol. lii.

Papers of Prince Christopher Lieven (1774-1839), while Russian Minister to Britain, include American letters, 1818-27.

Bundles 3 and 4. Two letters to Lieven from Pierre de Poletica, the Russian Minister to the United States, and two draft replies, Nov. 1819-Mar. 1822 (in French). The first letter from Poletica at Washington, D.C., mentions a packet to be sent to Count Nesselrode, and says that he (Poletica) has been comparing information from Madrid with John Quincy Adams. The second letter is personal, and the draft replies illegible.

Bundles 7 and 8. Three slight notes, London, 1818-24, from Richard Rush, the American Minister, to Lieven.

Bundle 10. Four slight notes, 1826-7, from Albert Gallatin to Lieven. Also a letter, 1 Apr. 1833, from Aaron Vail, United States *Chargé d'Affaires* in London, about a commercial treaty (presumably between the United States and Russia) about to be signed by the President. (All in French.)

47559-601. CHARLES JAMES FOX PAPERS.

Charles James Fox (1749-1806), statesman. His papers include:

47561-3

Scattered references to the peace negotiations with the Americans in Paris, 1782-3. The letters are chiefly to Fox from the Duke of Manchester and are concerned mainly with the French and Spanish aspects of the negotiations. The most important letters from the American standpoint are nine, 10 May-9 July 1782, to Fox from Thomas Grenville in Paris; also copy letter, London, 10 June 1782, Fox to Grenville (47562, ff. 1-34). These letters illustrate the British wish to detach America from France in the negotiations, which Grenville thinks will be difficult in view of Franklin's attitude. 47563 contains an undated and unsigned memorandum on the American-Spanish commercial convention of 1802.

48212. MISCELLANEOUS PAPERS.

B. Long letter, 29 Oct. 1866, from William V. Walton of 'Hooyelles parish', La., to his brother in England, describing his experiences as a Confederate soldier. The letter is, as he says, 'an account of the War as seen and experienced by myself' while serving with the 2nd Louisiana Infantry. He describes the Peninsula campaign, and especially 'Stonewall' Jackson's part therein, and the battles of Malvern Hill, Cedar Mountain, Fredericksburg, Chancellorsville, Winchester, and Gettysburg. The South, he

24. Extracts, H.M.C. vii, pp. 242-4. The correspondence has been printed in Benjamin Rand, *Berkeley and Percival* (Cambridge and New York, 1914), pp. 237-68.

25. Published in three volumes in H.M.C. Egmont MSS. [63].

says, lost because it had insufficient manpower and no navy. He also includes remarks on the injustice of reconstruction, high prices, poor crops, and the incompetence of the Negroes.

48417-589. PALMERSTON PAPERS.

The papers of Henry John Temple, 3rd Viscount Palmerston (1784-1865), run to some 180 volumes and are not yet fully indexed. This list should, therefore, be regarded as illustrative rather than exhaustive. There are no papers later than 1850 in the collection, but see report (pp. 103-5) on the papers held at the H.M.C.

The Foreign Office letter-books (140 volumes) include:

48495

'To North America', 1835-41. Copies of dispatches to Ministers Vaughan and Fox, and to *Chargé* Bankhead. Chief topics dealt with are Britain's offer of mediation in American-French dispute over French blockade of Mexican ports; Canadian fisheries; the selling into slavery of a coloured British subject in Florida; Canadian boundary; armed incursions into Canada by American citizens; and the *Caroline* incident.

48547

'To and from U.S.A.', 1846-9. Copies of dispatches, chiefly from, but also to, Ministers Pakenham and Crampton. Major matters dealt with are the Oregon question; the Mexican War - especially as regards blockade and possible British mediation; arrests of Negroes on board British ships calling at Charleston, S.C., and New Orleans, La.; United States tariff; Buchanan, whom Pakenham thinks neither 'honest [nor] sincere'; Canadian boundary, especially as regards the Strait of Juan de Fuca; the Wilmot Proviso; the United States militia; Central America, especially the Mosquito Coast; postal rates between Britain and the United States; disputes between the administration and Generals Taylor and Scott; the peace treaty with Mexico; rumours of Britain's desire for California; establishment of American relations with the Papacy; the slavery issue in Congress; the isthmian canal; rescues and attempted rescues of Irish insurgents by Irish-American mobs; the presidential election of 1848; Canadian reciprocity and fisheries; measures to prevent filibustering against Cuba.

48548

'To and from U.S.A.', 1849-50. To and from the Minister, Sir Henry Bulwer. Major topics dealt with are commerce between the United States and Canada; killing of cattle in the Falkland Islands by American seamen; the Clayton-Bulwer Treaty; United States disputes with Portugal over the destruction of an American privateer, the *General Armstrong*; the threatening situation over Cuba; hostilities between Haiti and the Dominican Republic; clashes along the Juan de Fuca Strait and Puget Sound; slavery debates in Congress; the Compromise of 1850; Anglo-United States friction in Central America; filibustering; Cuba and Nicaragua; the characters of Taylor and Fillmore.

There is also a F.O. letter-book, 'From America', 1830-4, in a later accession of Palmerston Papers. See 49963-4, p.78.

49063. MISCELLANEOUS PAPERS.

Collection of autographs (no letters) of Presidents of the United States and their wives, from General Washington to General Eisenhower.

49173-95. SPENCER PERCEVAL PAPERS.

Spencer Perceval (1762-1812) became Chancellor of the Exchequer in 1807 and was Prime Minister from 1809 until his death. The twenty-three bundles of unbound correspondence and papers include:

49177

Correspondence with James Stephen. Various letters from Stephen, 1807-10, contain comment on the Orders in Council, which Perceval originated and drafted. A memorandum, *'Coup d'Oeuil* on an American War', Dec. 1807, is a discussion by Stephen of American politics and an attack on the United States for its pro-French policies.

49178

Papers relating to the Orders in Council: notes, statistics, etc.

49179

Papers relating to the message of the President of the United States: printed *Documents accompanying the Message of the President...to the two Houses of Congress...*(Washington, D.C., 1810), about the Berlin Decrees, Orders in Council, right of search, etc. Chiefly composed of letters from William Pinkney and Secretary of State R. Smith.

49289-353. W.S. GILBERT PAPERS.

49334

ff. 1-153. Letters and seating returns sent to W.S. Gilbert relating to the production of 'Engaged' in the U.S.A. and Canada, 19 Feb.-11 June 1879.

49340

Notebook recording theatre takings and expenses of the production of 'H.M.S. Pinafore' and 'The Pirates of Penzance' in the U.S.A., 1 Dec. 1879-20 Mar. 1880, with a summary of profits from the latter.

49683-962. BALFOUR PAPERS

Papers of Arthur James Balfour, 1st Earl Balfour. Cabinet, Committee of Imperial Defence and Foreign Affairs.

49740

Correspondence, 1915-7, with Sir Cecil Spring-Rice, Ambassador to the U.S.A. Topics include relations with America during the early years of the First World War, reaction of the U.S. to the 'Irish question', and events leading to America's entry into the war on the side of the Allies. Also much attention to American domestic politics.

49741

Correspondence with Sir W. Wiseman and Lord Reading in the U.S., 1917-9. Again, chiefly concerned with the war and U.S. participation. Also much material on Wilson's 'Fourteen Points' policy and his advocacy of a League of Nations.

49742

Correspondence with U.S. diplomats, statesmen, etc. 1888-1930. Correspondence on a wide variety of subjects. Includes letters from Robert Lansing, American Secretary of State under Wilson, Joseph Choate, U.S. Ambassador to Great Britain from 1899 to

1905, Henry Cabot Lodge, U.S. senator, Nicholas Murray Butler, president of Columbia University and head of the Carnegie Endowment, and Andrew Carnegie, American financier and philanthropist.

49963-9. PALMERSTON PAPERS. (Additional to 48417-589.)

49963-4

'From America', 1830-4. Major topics dealt with are the North-east boundary dispute between Great Britain and the U.S.; rumours of American collaboration with Russian plans for privateering; the Congressional elections of 1830; questions involving British sailors on the high seas; commerce and the Tariff of 1828; American politics; the tariff debates of the early 1830's; and the nullification controversy with South Carolina.

50078-114. HUTTON PAPERS.

Correspondence and papers of Lieut.-Gen. Sir Edward Thomas Henry Hutton, organizer of the Mounted Infantry, General Officer commanding the Canadian militia (1898) and the military forces of the Commonwealth of Australia.

50078

ff. 139-43, 146. Correspondence with Theodore Roosevelt, 1899-1901. Mostly courtesy notes.

50508-743. BERNARD SHAW PAPERS.

50543

Correspondence of Shaw with Richard Mansfield, American actor and producer, 1895-8. Concerns the performance in America of Shaw's works.

50549

Letters to Shaw and other correspondents from Upton Sinclair and his wife, Mary, 1911-42. Topics include American socialists and the First World War, literary matters, etc.

51020. MISCELLANEOUS PAPERS.

A. Letter of Francis Scott Key, author of the words of 'The Star-Spangled Banner', to Clatworthy Birnie, 6 May 1816.

51071-204. CECIL OF CHELWOOD PAPERS.

51144

Correspondence of Lord Edgar Algernon Robert Cecil, Viscount Cecil of Chelwood, with Nicholas Murray Butler of the Carnegie Endowment, 1925-45, and with Thomas W. Lamont, the American financier, and his wife, 1923-41. Subjects discussed include the international business community, international politics, world peace, etc.

52623-773. COCKERELL PAPERS.

Correspondence of Sir Sydney Carlyle Cockerell (1867-1962), Director of the Fitzwilliam Museum at Cambridge. Includes, among other prominent Americans, J. Pierpont Morgan (1927).

52916-23. SCHIFF PAPERS.

52923

Three letters, 1947-8, to Mrs. Sydney Schiff, wife of the writer ('Stephen Hudson'), from Thornton Wilder, regarding her request that Wilder call the public's attention to her husband's work.

53817-54155. WENTWORTH BEQUEST.

Family papers, relating mainly to Wilfrid Scawen Blunt, author and politician (1840-1922), and Lady Anne Blunt.

54143-4

Correspondence with Col. Spencer Borden of Fall River, Mass., 1876-1916, and with Randolph Huntingdon of Long Island, N.Y., 1884-1902, concerning horse breeding.

54510-64. NAPIER PAPERS.

Correspondence and papers of Lieut.-Gen. Sir Charles James Napier (1782-1853), G.C.B., Governor of Sind.

54510

Correspondence and papers relating to American Prize Money, 1816-9, n.d.

54786-56035. MACMILLAN ARCHIVE.

The following items only represent some of the most significant letters from American authors in this very large collection. Other MSS. of American interest are to be found throughout the archive, especially in the letter-books from Macmillan Co. of New York, 1891-1940. (55283-315)

54931

Over 130 letters from Henry James, mostly discussing the arrangements for the publication of his works in England, but with other comments on a wide variety of subjects, 1878-1914, n.d.

54956-7

About 200 letters, 1901-30, from Edith Wharton to Macmillan. Almost all about publishing questions and the American editions of her works.

54967

About twenty letters from Julian Hawthorne about publishing matters, with some mention of personal affairs, 1876-95. Also numerous letters, 1897-1907, n.d., from Gertrude Atherton, written from various European countries and the U.S. Although these almost exclusively concern publishing matters, there are occasional references to proposed and completed work, including *American Wives*. There is also an appraisal of Edith Wharton: 'I don't think she is an absorbingly interesting writer, but she has brains and I like the way she says things.' (2 Dec., n.d.)

Besides these Hawthorne and Atherton letters, this volume includes over forty letters, 1909-14, from Walter McClintock, mostly in Pittsburgh, Pa. McClintock discusses his work on American Indians, *The Old North Trail*, and his lectures on the subject.

56106-225. FLEMING PAPERS.

Correspondence, notebooks and papers of Sir Alexander Fleming (d. 1955), the discoverer of penicillin.

56109

Correspondence with American doctors E.G. Gill, 1949-50, Hugh Payne, 1949-54, and M. Bryner, 1953-4.

56110-1

Correspondence with Americans and Canadians, 1943-55.

56196

Notes on Fleming's visit to Oklahoma, June-July 1949.

56575-57264. SOCIETY OF AUTHORS ARCHIVE.

56964-6

Correspondence with Train and Bayne, 1913-6, B.H. Stern, 1909-19, and Paul Turner, 1919-25, U.S. legal representatives of the Society.

56988(3)

Papers relating to U.S.A. copyright, 1906-23, n.d.

57263

Letters to B.H. Stern, U.S. legal representative, 1918-20.

57486. MISCELLANEOUS PAPERS.

J. Two letters from J. Edgar Hoover, Director of the F.B.I., to Major Thomas Coulson of the Franklin Institute in Pennsylvania, 25 June 1936 and 29 June 1939. (Typewritten and signed.)

57562-635. LONDON BOOKBINDERS' PAPERS.

57626

Letters of T.W. Faulkner of New York, 1844-7, largely to John Jaffray. Mostly about the fight for higher pay for English bookbinders led by Faulkner in the 1790's, with occasional references to his later experiences after emigrating to America.

57734-68. HAROLD MONRO AND POETRY BOOKSHOP PAPERS.

Papers of and relating to Alida Monro (d. 1969), wife of Harold E. Monro, poet and bookseller.

57753

Diary of a visit to the U.S.A., n.d.

57804-37. GRENVILLE PAPERS.

57835

Political notes, mainly by Lord Temple, concerning a variety of subjects, including the Americas, 1758-1776(?), n.d.

See also Add. MSS. 42083-8 (pp. 65-6).

57927-8. WESTON PAPERS.

These papers were being bound at the time of our survey (Spring, 1977), and could only be consulted briefly. However, this inspection revealed the following items of American interest:

57928

ff. 23-4. Letter, 17 Jan. 1765, from Edward Sedgwick to Edward Weston, announcing Gen. Gage's success in forcing the (?)Shawnee and Delaware tribes 'to accept Peace on his own Terms'.

ff. 41-2. Letter, 5 Feb. 1765, Sedgwick to Weston, referring to French attempts to invite Acadians to settle in French territory. (*See also* ff. 47-8 and ff. 53-4.)

ff. 49-50. Letter, 14 Feb. 1765, Sedgwick to Weston, commenting on the recalcitrance of colonial assemblies.

ff. 180-1. Letter, 24 Dec. 1765, Sedgwick to Weston, asserting 'the Right of the British Legislature to tax the Colonies'.

ff. 203-4, 205, 218-9, 220-1, 224-5, 284-5, 297-8, 304-5. These letters, 1767-70, are all from Sedgwick to Weston, and concern disaffection in the American colonies, including the introduction of non-importation measures.

ff. 246-7. Letter, 12 Aug. 1768, from Sir James Porter to Edward Weston, including the comment 'I think whatever measures government may adopt with the Americans; they will succeed without any great difficulty it is at Boston but two or three degenerate wretches who occasion the bustle and when it comes to the push I dare say they will fear the rod.'

There are also some letters in Add. MS. 57927, mostly dated 1764, which discuss events affecting Canada and Newfoundland.[26]

58079. MISCELLANEOUS PAPERS.

W. Two letters of John Singer Sargent to Mrs. Rita Jacomb-Hood, 1 Jan. 1915, n.d.

X. Letter of Henry James to Mrs. Rita Jacomb-Hood, 25 or 26 Nov. 1915.

58283-367. MITCHELL PAPERS.

Parliamentary papers, trade returns, etc. from the papers of Sir Andrew Mitchell of Thainston, M.P.

Time did not permit a complete examination of this large collection, which is in any case unlikely to contain a great deal of American material. However, the S.R.O's *List of American Documents* (Edinburgh, 1976) has noted that Mitchell's parliamentary papers do contain several accounts regarding trade in linen and tobacco between Scotland and America in the 1730's and 1740's, while his miscellaneous letters include several dating from the 1750's which comment on Gen. Braddock's defeat in North America.

58447-770. MARIE STOPES PAPERS.

Correspondence and papers of Marie Charlotte Carmichael Stopes (1880-1958), co-founder with her husband, Humphrey Verdon Roe, of the Mother's Clinic for Constructive Birth Control, London, and president of the Society for Constructive Birth Control and Racial Progress.

58585

Volume of correspondence with the U.S. reformer Mrs. Mary Ware Dennett, 1919-40.

58586

Volume of correspondence with the American advocate of birth control Mrs. Margaret Sanger, 1915-50, n.d.

58587-8

Two volumes of correspondence with America, 1916-54, n.d.

58855-59494. DROPMORE PAPERS.

Correspondence of William Wyndham Grenville, Baron Grenville (1759-1834), statesman.

26. The Weston Papers have also been the subject of a report by the Historical Manuscripts Commission: see H.M.C. x(i).

These papers were purchased by the British Library from the executors of G.G. Fortescue, Boconnoc, Lostwithiel, Cornwall, in Mar. 1970, and incorporated in Dec. 1975. Since they have not yet been fully listed, the following information has been taken from the H.M.C. report on the collection. In the Add. MS. series, the major American groupings are 59049-50, special correspondence, including letters, 1794-1803, John Jay and Rufus King; 59083-92, which consist of précis books and papers of Lord Grenville concerning America, 1789-1809, chiefly while he served as Foreign Secretary; and 59230-41, which contain correspondence and papers relating to British North America, 1764-1817.

(*a*) Dublin Castle, 22 Jan. 1783, from Earl Temple, Lord-Lieutenant of Ireland, to W.W. Grenville, mentions evacuation of Charleston, S.C., and Loyalists leaving America.[27]

(*b*) Various letters, Dublin Castle, Feb. and Mar. 1783, from Lord Temple to W.W. Grenville, which mention trade with and emigration to America.[28]

(*c*) Stowe, 8 Dec. 1786, from the Marquis of Buckingham to W.W. Grenville, includes the following comment: 'I have received a very large packet from Mr. Temple (now Sir John Temple) with a long detail of American misery, discontent and anarchy; and seemingly with a strong inclination of putting his finger into every one of these thirteen pies. . . .'[29]

(*d*) 19 Jan. 1790, from W.W. Grenville to the Lord Chancellor, Thurlow, in which he compares claims of settlers on 'Mosquito Shore' with those of East Florida.[30]

(*e*) Cabinet minute, 30 Apr. 1790, regarding British vessels captured at Nootka Sound, recommending that satisfaction be demanded of Madrid, and that a squadron be fitted out to prevent further outrages.[31]

(*f*) Hollwood, 23 June 1791, from W. Pitt to Grenville, concerning the slave trade and the part of American ships therein.[32]

(*g*) London, 20 July 1791, from P. Colquhoun to Grenville, enclosing an extract from a letter from Colonel William Stephens Smith, 'late Secretary of Legation at the Court of London from the U.S.A.', now in Philadelphia. Smith had apparently been combatting 'false impressions', circulated by those hostile to the resumption of normal commercial relations.[33]

(*h*) 5 and 8 Aug. 1791, from P. Colquhoun to Grenville on American trade, and especially the prospect of enlarging British markets.[34]

(*i*) 24 Sept. 1791, from P. Colquhoun to Grenville, stating that he has used his influence with Robert Morris to counteract erroneous and unfriendly information emanating from Britain, and enclosing extracts from letters received from Morris.[35]

(*j*) 15 Nov. 1791, from P. Colquhoun to Grenville, enclosing letters from Robert Morris: Aug. 27, on the need for a capable British Minister, and John Brown Cutting; 12 Oct., on 'the credit and even opulence of the United States', and its indifference to a commercial treaty with Great Britain.[36]

(*k*) Four dispatches, 1791-3, from Philadelphia, from George Hammond, first British Minister to the United States 1791-5, to Grenville. He considers that Washington's offering the London appointment to anyone will give him [Hammond] sufficient reason to present his credentials. Mentions anti-British tactics of Jeffersonians. That of 2 Feb. 1792 mentions difficulties arising regarding the North West frontier. That of 12 Oct. 1793 on the epidemic in Philadelphia.[37]

(*l*) 5 Jan. 1792, from Henry Dundas to Grenville, recommending Colquhoun (whose Glasgow mercantile house had just failed) for an American consulship, and Grenville's reply, 6 Jan., regretting his inability to do so.[38]

(*m*) The Hague, 9 Nov. 1792, Lord Auckland to Grenville, suggests that American wheat, which is cheap, be imported into Britain to avert scarcity.[39]

(*n*) 15 Aug. 1793, from Grenville to Henry Dundas, on [presumably French] 'prisoners taken aboard an American ship still detained at Liverpool'.[40]

(*o*) Foreign Office Journal of J.B. Burges. Entry for 28 Dec. 1793 makes mention of a call by Pinckney to protest against 'the new instruction to commanders of ships of war and privateers', which would shut American trade out of French islands, as the Act of Navigation already shut it out from the British.[41]

(*p*) Leghorn, 1794, from Francis Drake to Lord Grenville, enclosing three bulletins, 10 and 27 Feb. and 11 Mar. 1794, from Paris, concerning the American Minister [Gouverneur Morris]; and bulletin, 26-31 May 1794, on England and the United States (bulletins in French).[42]

(*q*) 22 June 1794, from Lord Auckland to Grenville, enclosing an extract from a letter to 'Mr. Elliot, heretofore Lieutenant-Governor of New York' on the character of Jay.[43]

(*r*) July 1794, from Pitt to Grenville, about a meeting held with a group of American merchants to discuss the American debts.[44]

(*s*) 6 Aug. 1794, from Buckingham to Grenville, on impressment of American seamen and the importance of the western posts, particularly Detroit.[45]

(*t*) Copy, 9 Dec. 1794, from Grenville, recalling George Hammond.[46]

(*u*) H.M.C. Fortescue (Dropmore) MSS. iii[30]. Contains many letters of importance concerning Anglo-American relations during Grenville's term as Foreign Secretary 1796-1801, including a 'precis [dated Sept.-Oct. 1794] of correspondence relating to alleged breaches of the treaty of peace. . .', pp. 520-8.

16 Aug. and 24 Oct. 1794, touching on Anglo-United States friction regarding Indians and debts respectively, p. 530.

9 Nov. 1794, from Grenville to Portland on the Prize Courts in the West Indies, and their effect on Anglo-American relations, p. 533.

From Jay, 1794-5, pp. 34, 38, 516, 528, 534.

To Jay, 1794-5; from Grenville, pp. 68, 517; from Randolph, p. 529.

28 June 1795, describing Gouverneur Morris's view of the Jay Treaty, pp. 87-9.

7 Oct. 1795, from Grenville to Dundas enclosing article proposed by Jay on American trade to the East Indies, pp. 136-7.

27. Transcript, H.M.C. xiii(iii) (Fortescue (Dropmore) MSS. i[30]), p. 184.
28. Transcripts, ibid., pp. 190-1, 193, 195, 200.
29. Transcript, ibid., pp. 275-6.
30. Transcript, ibid., p. 559.
31. Transcript, ibid., p. 579.
32. Transcript, H.M.C. xiv(v) (Fortescue (Dropmore) MSS. ii[30]), p. 104.
33. Transcript, ibid., pp. 145-6.
34. Transcripts, ibid., pp. 157-8, 160.
35. Transcript, ibid., p. 197.
36. Transcript, ibid., p. 228.
37. Transcripts, ibid., pp. 223, 229, 254, 443-4.
38. Transcript, ibid., p. 249.
39. Transcript, ibid., p. 329.
40. Transcript, ibid., p. 414. Dundas's reply is on p. 416.
41. Transcript, ibid., pp. 488-9.
42. Transcripts, ibid., pp. 526, 541, 579.
43. Transcript, ibid., p. 578.
44. Transcript, ibid., p. 607.
45. Transcript, ibid., pp. 610-1.
46. Transcript, ibid., p. 651.

8 Sept. 1796, from P. Bond in Philadelphia to Grenville on good effects of the Jay Treaty, pp. 243-4.

25 Aug. 1797, from Rufus King to Grenville, concerning the expulsion of Senator Blount for a 'project' detrimental to the United States; and reply from Grenville, 30 Aug., pp. 360-1.

(*v*) H.M.C. Fortescue (Dropmore) MSS. iv[30].

July and Aug. 1798, between Rufus King and Grenville on the United States' quarrel with France, pp. 269, 272-3, 288; and United States intercourse with Santo Domingo, 1799, p. 437.

13 Sept. 1798, and reply, 18 Sept., from Grenville to Cornwallis on American government's wish to buy small arms in England, pp. 314, 317.

(*w*) H.M.C. Fortescue (Dropmore) MSS. vi[30].

Letters, 1800, from Rufus King and Dundas to Grenville on commissioners appointed to consider claims of British merchants upon United States, pp. 202-3, 370.

Two of Jan. 1800, from Dundas to Grenville, on American trade, pp. 107, 112.

28 Feb. 1800, from Grenville to Liston, British Minister to the United States, deploring situation in United States ('system of the American Government seems. . . to be tottering') and granting him provisional leave of absence, p. 146.

24 and 29 Oct. 1800, from Thomas Macdonald to Grenville; the first dealing with American opinion of Britain, especially as represented by American newspapers; and the second with Secretary of State Marshall, pp. 358-60, 365-6.

12 Feb. 1801, from Rufus King, on probable policy of new United States administration, pp. 444-5.

(*x*) H.M.C. Fortescue (Dropmore) MSS. viii[30]. This volume contains a large number of letters, 1806, some from Grenville, but most to him from Auckland, and also Holland, concerning chiefly questions of trade with the United States, American trade with the West Indies, and the abortive Anglo-American treaty of Dec. 1806. The impressment of American seamen, and the dispute over 'continuous voyage' are also touched upon. The main references are: pp. 36, 47, 54, 58, 63, 85, 87, 102, 112, 138, 140-1, 263, 265, 285, 290, 293, 296-8, 302, 310, 357, 406, 410-1, 429, 441-2, 446, 458-9, 472, 484-5, 489, 491.

(*y*) H.M.C. Fortescue (Dropmore) MSS. ix[30]. This volume contains a number of letters, 1807-9, chiefly by Auckland to Grenville, criticizing the Orders in Council and prophesying war with the United States because of them. There is also one letter, p. 141, touching upon the *Chesapeake* incident. The main references are: pp. 143, 146-7, 151, 158, 164, 177-9, 182, 193, 198-9, 200-1, 206, 277, 279, 302, 438-9.

(*z*) H.M.C. Fortescue (Dropmore) MSS. x[30]. Several letters, mostly from Auckland to Grenville, touching on the War of 1812, written mainly in that year, 1813, and 1814. The major references are: pp. 88, 125, 194, 223, 286, 290, 292-3, 322, 394-5.

59541-97. SIR EVELYN WRENCH PAPERS.

Correspondence and diaries of Sir John Evelyn Leslie Wrench (1882-1966), founder of the Over-Seas Club, 1910, and of the English-Speaking Union of the Commonwealth, 1918.

59563

Diary: Canada and the United States, 1906, in the form of typewritten copies of letters from Wrench to his parents.

59584-5

Diary of honeymoon tour, 1937-8, including description of a trip from San Francisco to Washington to Miami.

59595-7

United States, 1947-50, in the form of typewritten copies of letters from Wrench.

Wrench's correspondence, arranged chronologically, also contains some items of American interest (Add. MSS. 59541-7).

EGERTON MANUSCRIPTS

2952. MISCELLANEOUS PAPERS.

A. Letters of Samuel Langhorne Clemens ('Mark Twain') to the publishing firm of Chatto & Windus.

f. 1. Hartford, Conn., 7 Oct. 1881, referring to the publication of *The Prince and the Pauper*.

f. 3. Hartford, Conn., 1 Sept. 1883, writing of his new book, *Adventures of Huckleberry Finn*, as a 'rattling good one'.

f. 6. Elmira, N.Y., 17 Sept. 1888, referring to *A Connecticut Yankee in King Arthur's Court*.

f. 7. 27 Jan. 1892, giving instructions as to the publication of 'six newspaper letters', which he had been writing from Europe.

2972. LE MARCHANT, SIR JOHN GASPARD (1803-74). Correspondence.

Soldier and administrator. Lieutenant-Governor of Nova Scotia 1852-7, connected with the raising in the United States and elsewhere in North America of a foreign legion for service in the Crimean War, 1855-6, etc. Some of the letters are addressed to his secretary, Lewis M. Wilkins. The writers include John F.T. Crampton, British Minister to the United States, whose first two letters, 1853-4, refer to the fishery and reciprocity questions; Joseph Howe, Nova Scotia statesman; Lieutenant John W. Preston; C. H. Stanley, British Consul in New York; and others.

At the beginning of the volumes, f.1, is an opinion (? given in 1842) on the American Neutrality Act of 20 Apr. 1818; and at the end, f. 414, is the *New York Herald*, European edition, 25 Sept. 1855.

2978. HEATH AND VERNEY PAPERS, vol. I.

5. f. 10. 'A comparison. . .between the contract made by the companies for Virginia and Summer Islands, in the year 1622, and the contract lately made by some undertakers who were the chief breakers [*sic*] of the former.' An analysis of a new contract for the exploitation of the tobacco plantations in Virginia and Somers Islands, drawn up apparently soon after the revocation of the charter of the Virginia Company in 1624.

3090-7. EDWARDS PAPERS.

Further correspondence and papers of Frederick George Edwards, F.R.A.M. (1853-1909), editor of the *Musical Times* 1897-1909. Miscellaneous letters, chiefly of musicians or on musical matters, including letters to Edwards from E.A. MacDowell, American composer, 1903 (3096, f. 25) and H.W. Parker, American musician, 1902 (3095, ff. 246, 251).

3247-8. ERNEST RHYS PAPERS.

Original letters from British and American literary men, artists, etc., nearly all addressed to Ernest Rhys, editor of Everyman's Library. American correspondents include J.R. Lowell, 1886, 1888 (3247, ff. 56, 57); Ezra Pound, American poet, 1932, n.d. (3247, ff. 75, 76, 78, 79, 80-83); and Walt Whitman (postcards), 1886-9 (3248, ff. 81-88). There is also a postcard from Whitman to P. Doyle [1873?] (3248, f. 89).

3301-6. PERCY PITT PAPERS.

Correspondence of Percy Pitt (d. 1932), musical director at Covent Garden 1902 and the British Broadcasting Co., 1922. American correspondents include L.R. Lewis, Fletcher Professor of Music at Tufts College, Mass., 1926, 1929 (3305, ff. 72, 73); H.A. Parker, American composer, 1902 (3305, f. 204); S.S. Sanford, American pianist, 1908 (3306, ff. 130, 132); and H.W. Savage, operatic manager at New York, early twentieth century (3306, f. 59*b*).

3324-3508. LEEDS PAPERS.

Correspondence and papers of the family of Osborne, Dukes of Leeds, including the papers of Robert D'Arcy, 4th Earl of Holderness.

These 185 volumes, acquired in 1947, supplement Add. MSS. 28040-95.[47] They were formerly at Hornby Castle, where they were the subject of a report by the Historical Manuscripts Commission, which clearly, however, did not cover all the deposited collection.

The papers are not yet listed, so it was not practicable to examine them; the entries below refer to the H.M.C. report. (*Letters unless otherwise stated.*)

(*a*) 1675, from Sir William Berkeley, Governor of Virginia, against a patent granted to Lord Culpeper [Colepeper].[48]

(*b*) Eight articles by Edward Randolph against the government of Boston: 'that the Bostoners have no right either to land or government in any part of New England, but are usurpers', etc.[49] n.d. [*c.* 1676].

(*c*) 1676, from Edward Randolph, Boston, giving an account of trade, army, etc.[50]

(*d*) Copy of a writ, 1676, issued by Governor Berkeley for the electing of a new Assembly; with notes of memorials on the condition of Virginia.[51]

(*e*) 27 Mar. 1677, from the Commissioners of Virginia forwarding petitions, etc.[52]

(*f*) Extract from a memorial by the dissenters in New England presented to the King by Increase Mather, Samuel Newel, and Elizabeth Hutchinson, and read before him in July 1688.[53]

(*g*) 28 Feb. 1690, from the Earl of Effingham about his commission and departure for Virginia.[54]

(*h*) Narrative of hostilities committed by the French on the Ohio in 1754, with papers relative to the negotiations in 1755 relating to these.[55]

(*i*) 27 July 1759, from Captain Peter D'Arcy, giving an account of the capture of the French fort at Ticonderoga.[56]

(*j*) Short notes, 26, 27, and 28 May 1785, from John Adams to Lord Carmarthen on his arrival in England as first American Minister.[57]

(*k*) 16 Dec. 1785, Pitt to the Marquis of Carmarthen (Francis Osborne, later 5th Duke of Leeds), concerning a memorial from Adams of which Pitt says 'the demand seems itself fairly founded upon the treaty', but that the English also have claims which must go hand in hand, particularly 'satisfaction respecting the debts due from America to our merchants'.[58]

ADDITIONAL CHARTERS

59151

Sale by the trustees for the Free Society of Traders in Pennsylvania to Jeremiah Langham of Bucks. county, of 2,000 acres of unlocated land in Pennsylvania, 15 Feb. 1725. Signatures and seals of vendors.

66210

Extracts from the records of the court of New Haven, Conn., relating to James Davids, *al.* John Dixwell (d. 1690), of Folkestone, Kent. Copy attested by Gurdon Saltonstall, Governor of the colony, 1710. Signed.

67378

Letters patent of William III and Mary, extending the powers and privileges of the 'Governor and Company of Copper Miners in England' to New England, 19 Oct. 1691.

71106

Settlement of Richard Penn (son of William Penn) of a claim for maintenance against his son, John, 1756.

LOANS

29. PORTLAND PAPERS.

The collection mainly contains late sixteenth- to early eighteenth-century papers of various members of the Harley family, including those of Sir Robert Harley (1579-1656), his sons Sir Edward Harley (1624-1700) and Sir Robert Harley (1626-73), and his grandson, Robert Harley, 1st Earl of Oxford (1661-1724). There are over 300 volumes, thirty-nine of which contain papers arranged chronologically in two series, 1582-1724 and 1625-1708.

Much of the collection was, before its transfer to the British Library, the subject of reports by the Historical Manuscripts Commission in H.M.C. xiv (ii) and xv (iv), and in the ten volumes of the Portland MSS. [29]. As the collection has not been listed, it was not practicable to check the relevant material listed by the H.M.C. However, the following, drawn from the H.M.C. reports, are almost certainly still in the collection. (*Letters unless otherwise stated.*)

(*a*) 28 May 1608, from Lord Eure to Sir Robert Harley, says that the Virginia ship is returned, and Captain Newport has brought over Captain Wingfield.[59]

(*b*) 3 Nov. 1662, from Sir Robert Harley to Sir Edward Harley, describing plans for a settlement 'in the West Indies, on that part which adjoynes to Virginia next to Florida. . . Sir George Cartwright is engaged in the thing'.[60]

(*c*) 7 Aug. 1691, from Sir Thomas Clarges to Robert Harley, says, 'I cannot but be troubled for our plantations in America, for if the ships which were going there with provisions are taken, with their convoy, I know not how they or the ships we have there can subsist.[61]

47. See Paullin and Paxson, pp. 546-7.
48. H.M.C. xi(vii), p. 10.
49. Ibid., p. 38.
50. Ibid., p. 11.
51. Ibid., p. 14.
52. Ibid., p. 19.
53. Ibid., p. 31.
54. Ibid., p. 32.
55. Ibid., p. 45.
56. Ibid.
57. Ibid., p. 55.
58. Ibid., p. 54.
59. H.M.C. xiv(ii), (Portland MSS. iii[29]), p. 5.
60. Transcript, ibid., p. 268.
61. Transcript, ibid., p. 471.

(*d*) 18 Aug. 1694, to Robert Harley from an unknown correspondent, 'the Queen has signed a revocation of that part of Colonel Fletcher's commission relating to Pennsylvania, as also a warrant to restore William Penn to that colony, who intends to go there about a month hence'.[62]
(*e*) 12 Oct. 1697, from W. Snowe to Robert Harley, 'The news from Virginia is that Admiral Nevill and Mees, Captain Lilcot, Holmes, Belwood, Dyer, Studley and Fisher are dead, and all the Dutch captains but one, with 1,500 seamen [of Nevill's squadron]'.[63]
(*f*) 30 Jan. 1699, from William Penn to Robert Harley, pleading for fair treatment for the colonists.[64]
(*g*) Boston, 5 and 7 Mar. 1700, from the Earl of Bellomont to various people, mainly about piracy and Captain Kidd.[65]
(*h*) Two letters from William Penn to Robert Harley, the first dated 27 Aug. 1701, the second undated but apparently in the same year. The first sets forth the advantages of proprietary governments; the second is an account of the trade of the colonies.[66]
(*i*) The case of Sir Matthew Dudley and others concerning their petition for the incorporation of a company to import naval stores from North America. 1704.[67]
(*j*) ?1704, from Sir Henry Ashurst to (?) Robert Harley, recommending that Major General Waite Winthrop be appointed Lieutenant-Governor until a Governor is sent over.[68]
(*k*) 9 Feb. and 3 Mar. 1704, from William Penn to Robert Harley on affairs in the colonies.[69]
(*l*) Report, 31 May 1705, from the Board of Trade on a petition from merchants of Virginia and Maryland, against the projected establishment by certain merchants of a monopoly of the tobacco trade with Muscovy.[70]
(*m*) 30 Dec. 1710, from P. Schuyler to an unknown correspondent concerning missions to the Indians.[71]
(*n*) 10 May 1711, from Thomas Coutts to Dr. Arbuthnot, 'concerning a proposal he had made for advancing the revenue upon tobacco which he thinks will bear testing by the Commissioners of the Customs and the merchants trading to Virginia'.[72]
(*o*) July 1711, from Daniel Defoe to the Earl of Oxford, says that the advantages of planting settlements in America have been made obvious by the success of New England, New York, etc., which are both strong and healthy.[73]
(*p*) New Haven, Conn., 10 Sept. 1711, from Gurdon Saltonstall to the Earl of Oxford, describing the raising of troops in the northern colonies for an expedition against Canada.[74]
(*q*) Two letters, New York, 1712, from Caleb Heathcote to the Earl of Oxford. The first, 21 June, is on the abuses and mismanagements in relation to the men-of-war stationed for securing the American coasts and trade, and the supply of naval stores; the second, 8 July, complains that the great danger in America, both to Church and State, lies in the Charter governments, and goes on to give a description of the sad state of the Church of England in America, particularly in Connecticut.[75]
(*r*) 20 June 1713, from Thomas Coram to the Earl of Oxford, supporting the plea of some disbanded officers to be allowed to settle in Acadia.[76]

57. BATHURST PAPERS.

Correspondence, 1777-1826, of Henry, 3rd Earl Bathurst (1762-1834), Secretary for War and the Colonies 1812-27.

The following list has also been compiled from the H.M.C. report of the papers. When consulting the MSS. themselves, special reference should be made to vols. 1-23 (correspondence, 1621-1904, mainly political and official), and vol. 56 ('private' letters from various correspondents in North America, 1824). (*Letters unless otherwise stated.*)
(*a*) 9 Dec. 1777, from Bathurst to Lord..., criticizing the handling of the rebellion, and advocating peace.[77]
(*b*) 13 Aug. 1807, from Vice-Admiral Geo. Berkeley to [?] Bathurst, on warlike preparations and anti-British sentiment in the United States.[78]
(*c*) 24 and 25 Mar., 15 Apr. 1809, from George Canning to Bathurst, on the American embargo and non-intercourse.[79]
(*d*) Bathurst's proposals for modifying the Orders in Council of November 1807, with comments thereon by other Cabinet members. Apr. 12 [1809].[80]
(*e*) 2 Feb., and 10 and 29 Aug. 1810, one from the Earl of Malmesbury and two from George Rose, on Orders in Council.[81]
(*f*) 3 Apr. 1812, from George Rose to Melville, alludes to fur trade between Canada and the United States.[82]
(*g*) 25 May 1812, from Major-General Isaac Brock to the Earl of Liverpool on Canadian preparations to resist United States invasion.[83]
(*h*) 15 Sept. 1812, from Thomas Tackle to Bathurst offering information respecting the policy of the United States to the Indians.[84]
(*i*) Number of additional letters, 1814, from the Earl of Liverpool, concerning the Conference and Treaty of Ghent.[85]
(*j*) Three accounts, 1814, of the Battle of Plattsburg, including opinions of Sir James Yeo and Sir Frederick Philipse Robinson.[86]
(*k*) 4 Oct. 1814, from Castlereagh to Bathurst, in which he deprecates 'spoiling America by acts signally unjust to our own subjects'.[87]
(*l*) Paris, 4 Nov. 1814, from the Duke of Wellington to Bathurst offering to take command in America the following year, if required.[88]
(*m*) 15 Dec. 1814, from Henry Goulburn to Bathurst, about disputes with the American delegates at Ghent over the fishery issue. (A note is added to the effect that this is one of a collection of letters 'from Goulburn to Bathurst written during the negotiations at Ghent; but all except the above are to be found in the *Supplementary Dispatches of the Duke of Wellington*, and are therefore not given here'.)[89]

62. Ibid., p. 553.
63. Ibid., p. 590.
64. Transcript, ibid., pp. 601-2.
65. Transcripts, H.M.C. Portland MSS. viii[29], pp. 69-77.
66. Transcripts, H.M.C. xv(iv), (Portland MSS. iv[29]), pp. 19-21, 30-2.
67. Transcript, H.M.C. Portland MSS. viii[29], pp. 164-5.
68. H.M.C. Portland MSS. x[29], p. 62.
69. Transcripts, H.M.C. xv(iv), (Portland MSS. iv[29]), pp. 79-81.
70. See further ibid., pp. 191-2.
71. Transcript, ibid., p. 649.
72. Ibid., p. 686.
73. H.M.C. Portland MSS. v[29], p. 67.
74. Transcript, ibid., p. 89.
75. Transcript, ibid., pp. 186-91 and 199-200.
76. Transcript, ibid., p. 297.
77. Transcript, H.M.C. Bathurst MSS. [76], pp. 16-7.
78. Transcript, ibid., pp. 63-5.
79. Transcript, ibid., pp. 86-7, 89-90.
80. Transcript, ibid., pp. 87-9.
81. Transcripts, ibid., pp. 139-40, 144, 146.
82. Transcript, ibid., pp. 170-2.
83. Transcript, ibid., pp. 174-5.
84. Ibid., p. 212.
85. Ibid., pp. 285-8, 294, 302, 319, 320, 324, 370-1.
86. Transcripts, ibid., pp. 285, 286, 290-4.
87. Transcript, ibid., pp. 295-6.
88. Transcript, ibid., p. 303.
89. Transcript, ibid., p. 316.

(*n*) Quebec, 21 Aug. 1818, from the Duke of Richmond to Bathurst, mentions Canadian border incident, 1818.[90]
(*o*) 6 Aug. 1820, from Bathurst to Viscount Castlereagh, mentions the United States' wish to buy Santo Domingo from Spain.[91]
(*p*) 1 Oct. 1821, from Henry Goulburn to [Earl Bathurst]; and one, 22 Dec. 1821, from Liverpool to Bathurst; comments on United States-West Indies trade in 1821.[92]
(*q*) 28 Apr. 1824, from Sir Howard Douglas to Bathurst, giving 'reasons against allowing the Americans free navigation of the St. Lawrence'.[93]
(*r*) Synopsis of letter, 23 July 1824, from Stratford Canning to William Huskisson, on delay in handing over islands in the St. Lawrence to the United States.[94]
(*s*) 7 Nov. 1825, from Wellington to Bathurst, mentions 'the report of the commissioners sent to North America' and also complains of the 'insolence' of the South American states in inviting the North Americans to the congress at Panama and not inviting Britain.[95]
(*t*) 27 Apr. 1826, from Lord Carbery to Bathurst, on emigration from Ireland to the United States.[96]

CHATTO & WINDUS LTD., PUBLISHERS, 40-42 William IV Street, London WC2N 4DF

CORRESPONDENCE WITH AMERICAN AUTHORS.

The firm's letter-books go back to 1855 when it was founded by, and under the name of, John Camden Hotten. Hotten and his successor Andrew Chatto were prominent in the publishing of American authors and, in addition to the firm's correspondence with them, a quantity of letters from some of them also survives. Among these are the following:
(*a*) Conway, Moncure Daniel. Conway began publishing with the firm when it was owned by Hotten. He negotiated the publication with them of *The Adventures of Tom Sawyer*, acted as Mark Twain's agent for some years, and introduced other American authors to them. He also published a number of original works with them, and they have retained a number of miscellaneous letters from him.
(*b*) James, Henry. Two letters, 1879, concerning the publication of *Confidence*.
(*c*) Clemens, Samuel L. ('Mark Twain'). Forty-five letters and communications, Mar. 1880-22 Nov. 1902.[1]

See also the entry for Andrew Chatto, Esq. (p. 33).

CITY OF LONDON POLYTECHNIC, Calcutta House Precinct, Old Castle Street, London E1 7NT

AMERICAN WOMEN SUFFRAGISTS. Letters: volume III, part B: 'Emancipation of women: United States of America, 1876-1948', and other letters, 1865-97, from a general autograph collection.

These letters show that there has been a continual, detailed, and lively exchange of help and information between American and British women's suffrage movements. Of particular interest are letters from:

Catt, Carrie Chapman, president of the International Woman Suffrage Alliance and of the National American Woman's Suffrage Association;

Gilman, Charlotte Perkins, publisher of the *Forerunner*, author and lecturer, who made a lecture tour of England in 1913;

Marion, Kitty, suffragist and birth-control pioneer, mainly to Alice Park concerning, *inter alia*, the politics of the American birth-control movement and reminiscences about the early days of the women's suffrage movement;

Park, Alice, whose letters contain much comment on women's suffrage campaigns in various states, notably New York and California, and also allude to financial help of American women in keeping the British movement alive during the First World War.

PAMPHLETS AND NEWSPAPER CUTTINGS.

This collection includes obituary notices, and contains many relating to the American suffrage and other women's movements. The pamphlets include two bound volumes of American Suffrage Tracts 1845-64, containing the *Proceedings of the Woman's Rights Convention* held at Syracuse, N.Y., 8-10 Sept. 1852; an *Address adopted by the Woman's Rights Convention* held at West Chester, Pa., 2-3 June 1852; Woman's Rights Tracts 1-10 including Samuel J. May, *Rights and Condition of Women*, 1845; *Speeches of Wendell Phillips Esq. and of Abby Kelley Foster*, 1851; Paulina Wright Davis, *Education of Females*, 1851; Anon., *Enfranchisement of Women*, 1850; Mrs. Oakes Smith, *Sanctity of Marriage*, 1851; Mrs. Nichols, *Responsibilities of Women*, 1851; speech of Mrs. M.J. Gage at the Woman's Rights Convention, Syracuse, N.Y., Sept. 1852; *Letter from Angelina Grimké Weld*, 1852; *Letters from Mrs. Elizabeth C. Stanton*. There are many later pamphlets and tracts published by various American woman's suffrage organizations.

THE LIBRARY, COLLEGE OF ARMS, London EC4V 4BT

Considerable genealogical material is held here. The Library is private and may be used only by special application.

THE CONGREGATIONAL MEMORIAL HALL TRUST LTD., Memorial Hall, 2 Fleet Lane, Farrington Street, London

SPRAGUE PAPERS. Sermons and letters. 1683-1863.

Dr. William Buell Sprague (1795-1876), clergyman, biographer, and collector of manuscripts and pamphlets, of Massachusetts and New York; author of 150 books, including *Annals of the American Pulpit*, 9 vols. (New York, 1857-69).

90. Ibid., p. 454.
91. Transcript, ibid., p. 485.
92. Transcripts, ibid., pp. 518, 525.
93. Synopsis, ibid., pp. 568-9.
94. Ibid., p. 572.
95. Transcript, ibid., pp. 591-2.
96. Ibid., pp. 601-2.

1. These letters are quoted and fully discussed in Dennis Welland, *Mark Twain and England* (Chatto & Windus, forthcoming) which also deals with the other material listed.

His papers include sermons, 1683-1797, by American divines; and about 190 autographs and autograph letters of American divines, missionaries, and statesmen, 1704-1863 (MS. 11 C1). For these, see Andrews & Davenport, pp. 347-9. In addition Sprague's papers include:

Letters from Sprague to Joshua Wilson, London. About a hundred letters, 1828-55, with four letters from Wilson to Sprague, 1834, 1836, and 1861. Most of Sprague's letters concern books and periodicals which he is sending to Wilson, or which the latter has sent to him. There is also some discussion of Sprague's autograph collections and of American, political and religious affairs. (MS. 11 C14)

GREY, ZACHARY (1688-1766). Correspondence: 4 letters. 1725-35. (MS. 11 C3)

Rector of Houghton-Conquest, Bedfordshire.

Boston, 10 Dec. 1725, from John Checkley, describing his attempts to convert certain Indian tribes from Roman Catholicism to Anglicanism.

Boston, 7 May 1726, 18 May 1727, and 5 June 1735, from Timothy Cutler, the first two on the progress of the Church of England in New England and the third on heresies rampant there.

WHITEFIELD, GEORGE (1714-70). Correspondence: 5 letters, 1745-54. (MS. 11 C9)

Methodist preacher. Whitefield made preaching tours of the American colonies in 1738-9, 1740-1, 1744-8, 1751-2, 1754-5, 1763-5, and 1769-70. He was appointed minister of Savannah, Ga., in 1739, and founded an orphanage there in 1740.

15 Jan., 3 June 1745, and 30 Oct. 1754, from James Davenport in New Jersey, the first two describing the state of religion in his area as 'dead', and the third, to Mrs. Whitefield, telling of her husband's evangelistic activities in New Jersey.

Charleston, S.C., 25 Jan. and 4 May 1752, are from John Edwards; the first is personal, the second deals with the religious situation in Charleston.

PALMER, CHARLES RAY. Letter. 1898.

New Haven, Conn., 31 Mar. 1898, from Charles Ray Palmer, son of Dr. Ray Palmer, the author and hymn writer, to Rev. J. Griffiths of Gainsborough, Lincs. Comments on the apparent imminence of war over Cuba and the silver party's support for it.

MISCELLANEOUS LETTERS AND PAPERS.

The letters are mainly personal in nature, written by Americans or from America; also an appeal to the American churches on behalf of evangelistic work in Paris by Horatius Bonar, the hymn writer (MS. 11 C53); and a remonstrance from the English Congregational churches to the churches in South Carolina, on John Brown's death sentence for assisting a slave to escape, 1844 (Z2g30H). Included are:

(*a*) Letter, Philadelphia, 2 May 1847, from Albert Barnes, the American Bible commentator. (MS. 11 C53)

(*b*) Several letters from the Rev. J. Waddington concerning appeals for funds, some to the United States, for the building of the Pilgrim Fathers' Church, Southwark, in the 1850's. Waddington visited the United States in 1859, but made no comments on his visit. (MS. 11 C53)

(*c*) Letter, 12 Sept. 1896, from Thomas F. Bayard, United States Ambassador in London, to the Rev. J. Griffiths of Gainsborough, Lincs., introducing Senator George F. Hoar; and an undated note by Senator Hoar. (MS. 11 C53)

CORPORATION OF LONDON RECORDS OFFICE,[1] P.O. Box 270, Guildhall, London EC2P 2EJ

The Corporation's records, listed in Andrews and Davenport, pp. 280-3, as part of the Guildhall collection, are vast; but the following classes appear to contain the most significant American items:

JOURNAL OF THE COMMON COUNCIL.[2]

(*a*) Fourteen miscellaneous petitions, motions, addresses, 1618-1762, dealing with such matters as transportation to Virginia, the tobacco trade, and military successes, e.g., Cape Breton, 1758, and Belle Isle, 1761. *See* Andrews and Davenport, pp. 280-1.

(*b*) A number of letters, petitions, addresses, remonstrances, etc., 1775-83, to and from the Mayor and Corporation during the War of Independence. *See* Andrews and Davenport, pp. 281-2.

COMMON HALL BOOKS.

Include addresses to the King, 1775, concerning the War of Independence. *See* Andrews and Davenport, pp. 282-3.

MAYOR'S COURT.

(*a*) Files of original Bills *temp.* Edward III (but mainly *temp.* Elizabeth)-1733. (317 files.) May contain items concerning American trade and transportation to America. Unindexed, but a manuscript list giving the chronological limits of each box is available in the Office.

(*b*) Depositions in the Mayor's Court. There are fifty-five boxes, 1640-*c.* 1835, containing material variously known as 'depositions', 'affidavits', 'certificates', 'affirmations' (when by Quakers), etc. Many of these deal with overseas trade and some may have reference to America. Unindexed, but a manuscript list giving the chronological limits of each box is available in the Office.

QUARTER SESSIONS RECORDS.

(*a*) Servants' indentures (3 boxes), 1718-40, with a few items for 1749-59. Memoranda or certificates of agreement to serve a stipulated number of years - three to seven, but usually four - in America or the West Indies. These certificates, of which there are nearly 3,000, give the age and native town of the contracting person, and are signed or marked by him; they state also to which colony he is bound, and sometimes a particular wage is laid down.

(*b*) Register of servants' indentures (1 volume), 1718-32. Names of those persons voluntarily binding themselves to go to the colonies and plantations in America. (A comparison of the register with the memoranda discloses more names in the former

1. Philip E. Jones and Raymond Smith, *A Guide to the Records in the Corporation of London Records Office and the Guildhall Library Muniment Room* (London, 1951).

2. Microfilm copies of the Journals from 1618 are held by the following U.S. institutions: 1618-94, University of California Research Library; 1618-94, Princeton University Library; 1618-94, University of Rochester Library, Rochester, New York; 1618-26, 1673-94, Memorial Library, University of Wisconsin; 1638-43, Henry E. Huntingdon Library, California; 1640-66, Lockwood Library, State University of New York at Buffalo; 1687-1702, The University Libraries, University of Iowa.

than appear on memoranda; in a very few cases there are memoranda with no corresponding entries in the register.)[3]

(c) Bonds for transportation of felons. Single items, 1667-70, 1680, 1698, 1715-35. Bonds, with two sureties, given to the justices of the peace by mariners and others that they would transport to America felons thus sentenced, or pardoned on condition of transportation. Also eighteen bonds, 1746-73, for Southwark Quarter Sessions.

(d) Certificates of landing at American ports (44 items), 1718-36. Certificates of the naval officers of the American ports, chiefly in Maryland and Virginia, where felons were landed, giving their names and numbers landed, the names of the ships carrying them and of the ships' commanders, and, usually, the names of those who had died during the voyage.[4]

(e) The principal series of Sessions books and files for the City of London, 1662-1785, will include sentences of transportation upon conviction and references to the trials of persons of American interest, e.g. William Penn, August 1670. There are indexes to persons named in the indictments from 1714. Similar records exist for Southwark Quarter Sessions from 1666. (Unindexed.)

MISCELLANEOUS PAPERS.

(a) A few miscellaneous items relating to the sending of children and vagrants to Virginia, 1618-9. *See* Andrews and Davenport, p. 283.

(b) Manuscripts relating to French Protestant refugees, some settling in America, *c.* 1680-1710. *See* Andrews and Davenport, p. 283, for some which were formerly in the Guildhall Library.

(c) Notes on freedoms and entertainments connected with America, 1853-1945. (Misc. MSS. 23.33); invitation and menu cards, 1910-71.

COUTTS & CO., 440 Strand, London WC2R OQS

RUSSELL PAPERS.[1] *c.* 200 letters. 1767-1806 (mainly 1773-5).

The collection consists mainly of letters addressed to James Russell, a merchant, of 2 Hylords Court, Crutched Friars. Mrs. Ann Russell, for whose executors the papers are now held, is assumed to be his widow. (Although there are two accounts with Coutts & Co. in the name of James Russell, neither can be definitely identified with James Russell of 2 Hylords Court.)

Most of the correspondence and papers are from agents and firms in Maryland and Virginia, and the letters concern cargoes of tobacco, with occasional mention of other freight such as wheat; and various other matters, such as the collection of debts and requests for manufactured goods to be sent from England. Some also contain comments on the political situation, full of loyalty to the King and criticism of his ministers. A few are dated from the West Indies and from Europe, mostly from ports in England, Scotland, France, and the Netherlands.

Of particular interest are the names of two later Governors of Maryland: Thomas Sim Lee and George Plater; also of Richard Henry Lee and of Thomas Pownall, the Governor of Massachusetts and writer on colonial affairs. The correspondents also include members of the Fendell, Galloway, Jenifer, Johns, and Warfield families of Maryland, and the Washington family of Virginia.

There are also some bonds and legal papers relating to New York; their connexion with Russell's correspondence is not obvious. Among them are four bonds, 1775-6, to the Loyalist, the Rev. Charles Inglis, then assistant to the rector of Trinity Church, New York, and from 1787 first Bishop of Nova Scotia. Further details as to names of correspondents are in N.R.A. 5612.

LIBRARY SERVICES, MUSEUM AND RECORDS UNIT, CUSTOM HOUSE, Room MO4E, Lower Thames Street, London EC3R 6EE

Since this report incorporates, not merely extends, the work of Andrews, vol. ii, pp. 111-30, and since the records are singularly complex, an extended introduction has been thought useful.

INTRODUCTION

At Michaelmas 1671 the English customs collections in general were finally taken out of farm, although certain of the minor farms were not finally wound up until some years later. A board of commissioners was vested by royal letter patent[1] with full power and authority to manage, levy, and collect the duties in England and Wales.

The customs of Scotland were not taken out of farm until the Union, but in 1707 a board of commissioners was set up in Scotland, likewise by royal letter patent. An Act of 1723[2] provided that English and Scottish customs might be placed under the management of a single commission for 'the whole United Kingdom' (of Great Britain); the current patents were therefore cancelled, and a single commission was set up accordingly.[3] In 1742, however, the existing joint patent was cancelled by royal warrant,[4] and separate boards were again appointed in respect of England and Scotland.[5] This arrangement continued until 1823 when an Act[6] was passed to consolidate the customs boards and the excise boards of England and Scotland and the revenue board for Ireland, into two boards only, one of customs and one of excise, both for the whole of the United Kingdom.

Although an Act of 1872[7] authorized the English commissioners to control the collection of duty upon enumerated goods shipped in the plantations but not brought to England, the authority was never apparently explicitly stated (either in the statutes or in any of the early patents) for the English Board of Customs to control the plantation customs generally. Nevertheless, special collectors of customs were appointed in America and the West Indies, and such officials were directly under the control of the commissioners in England until 1767, when a board of American commissioners

3. A microfilm of the indentures, 1718-59, and of the register is held by the Virginia Colonial Records Project, Virginia State Library. Also see J. and M. Kaminkow, *A List of Emigrants from England to America, 1718-1759* (Baltimore, 1964), and Michael Ghirelli, *A List of Emigrants from England to America, 1682-1692* (Baltimore, 1968).
4. Microfilmed by the Virginia Colonial Records Project.

1. Microfilmed by the Virginia Colonial Records Project.

1. Pat. roll: 23 Car. II, p. 2, no. 1, mem. 35, *dorsa* (27 Sept. 1671).
2. 9 Geo. I, cap. 21.
3. Pat. roll: 9 Geo. I, p. 2, no. 12 (27 June 1723).
4. Royal sign manual, 25 Aug. 1742.
5. Pat. roll: 15 Geo. II, p. 5, nos. 3 and 4 (9 Sept. 1742).
6. 4 Geo. IV, cap. 23.
7. 25 Car. II, cap. 7.

was created with headquarters at Boston.[8] The collectors of Bridgetown (Barbados), Roseau (Dominica), Grenville Bay (Grenada), Kingston and Montego Bay (Jamaica), Sandy Point (St. Christopher), and the ports of Montserrat and other Leeward Islands remained subject to the old board, but those of Accomac, Bermuda, Boston, Beaufort, Brunswick, Chester and Patapsco, Charleston, Halifax, Upper and Lower James River, Mobile, Nantucket, New York, New Haven, Newfoundland, New London, Potomac, Philadelphia, Patuxent, Pensacola, Piscataqua, Plymouth, Pocomoke, Rhode Island, Rappahannock, Sunbury, Salem and Marblehead, Savannah, Salem and Cohenzie (Cohansey), and York River were transferred to the establishment books of the board in America.

In England the outports were divided, for purposes of administrative convenience,[9] into 'the Northern ports', which were those from the Thames 'north-about' to Barmouth on the river Mawddach in West Wales; and 'the Western ports', which were those from the Thames 'south-about' to the river Mawddach.

In the head office, the principal officials in the two 'departments' were 'the Northern clerk', and 'the Western clerk'. When the English commission first assumed responsibility for plantation affairs, the plantation ports were laid to 'the Western department' which became 'Western and plantations', and the clerk the 'Western and plantation clerk'.[10] Later a separate 'plantation clerk' was appointed, and he in time was conceded an 'assistant plantation clerk'. In certain other departments or branches separate officials were appointed in respect of the plantation business - for example, the 'solicitor of debts standing out in the plantation receipts'. The 'surveyor of the Acts of Navigation' was not specifically a plantation official, as the navigation laws (or Acts of Trade) had to be enforced in relation to Europe, Africa, and Asia also.

After 1767 (when the separate board of American commissioners was set up at Boston)[11] the particular staff in the London Custom House dealing with plantation affairs could be reduced, for example, by the discontinuance of such offices as the 'assistant plantation clerk', and the 'assistant to the husband of the four-and-a-half-per-cent'.[12]

The board of commissioners in England was legally concerned with the enforcement of the Acts of Trade and with the collection of the plantation duty imposed by the Act of 1762.[13] This duty was established not so much as a source of revenue as to prevent direct trade with the continent of Europe; the collections therefore in the earlier years, particularly from Virginia and Maryland, where the large rivers and the great distances rendered the work of the collectors difficult, were very meagre, the whole produce of the imposition being little more than sufficient to defray the officers' salaries and the incidental charges for boat hire.[14] After 1696, with the increased number of collectors and the improved condition of the service, the amount became larger and the net returns sufficient to constitute an item in the commissioners' states of the revenue.[15]

The English Commissioners of Customs had no real power of appointment to ports in the plantations, but they were able to control the personnel of the establishment through their right to nominate and approve. They approved of the minor officials selected by the surveyors general there, but in all cases the actual appointment lay in the hands of the Treasury.

Appointments were either 'on the establishment' or 'by incident'. Of the 'established officers', some of the principal officials of the ancient ports of England and some of the plantations held by patent; others held by commission out of the Treasury, and others (by the end of the colonial period, by much the major part) by warrant to the Commissioners of Customs to issue their deputation to the persons named. The 'incident officers' were normally appointed by the Commissioners of Custom. Executive deputies to titular patentees were variously appointed, usually by nomination of the patentee or the Treasury, or upon recommendation to the commissioners, and (latterly at least) always subject to the satisfaction of the commissioners as to competence and so forth.

Officials on the plantation establishment received their authority, pay, leave of absence, instructions, and power to hire boats and boatmen, by means of Treasury warrants. From 1767 to 16 Oct. 1783 this method of procedure was changed by the creation of the American board. During those years, some of the incidental officers, but not those on the establishment, were appointed by the board in England, others by the surveyors general in the colonies, with the approval of the American board, and still others by the American board itself.[16] The commissioners in England not only drew up special instructions for the colonial officials, but also wrote the general instructions to the governors, so far as these instructions concerned the part which the governors were to play in upholding the collectors and surveyors in the performance of their duties. The same was true of all colonial laws that affected trade. Such laws were sent by the Board of Trade to the customs commissioners for approval and ratification.

Before Pitt's consolidation of the customs duties and his constitution of the consolidated fund in 1787,[17] the system of assessing, collecting, and accounting the customs duties was necessarily a very complex matter. The legislature's practice of appropriating the *net* yield of particular enactments to specific purposes led inevitably to great complexity in accounting, for the same goods were usually chargeable under a number of heads, each one of which being required by law to be assessed and accounted separately. That the gross yield of certain of the plantation ports or English outports was occasionally hardly enough to bear the costs of administration is, however, of no particular significance, for certain of the enactments were not intended to be revenue producing, and certain of the regulations were frankly cautionary and preventive.

In London there have been a number of Custom Houses, all of them on more or less the same site. The fact that three of them were almost completely destroyed by fire - in 1660, 1715, and again in 1814 - is not without effect on the surviving records.

8. Pat. roll: 7 Geo. III, p. 5, no. 11 (8 Sept. 1767). See also Edward Channing, 'The American Board of Commissioners for the Customs', *Proceedings of the Massachusetts Historical Society*, vol. xliii, pp. 477-90, 1909-10; and D.M. Clark, 'The American Board of Customs, 1767-1783', *American Historical Review*, vol. xlv, pp. 777-806, 1939-40.
9. E.E. Hoon, *The Organization of the English Customs System, 1696-1786* (New York, 1938), p. 69.
10. When Dr. Hoon said (ibid., p. 194) that 'the western ports were concerned primarily with the plantation . . . trade', she could not have meant the 'Western' ports in this technical sense, for such important plantation ports as Liverpool, Lancaster, and Whitehaven were 'Northern ports' in this classification.
11. Pat. roll: Geo. III, p. 5, no. 11 (8 Sept. 1767).
12. British Library Add. MSS. 8133 C.
13. 25 Car. II, cap. 7.
14. Blathwayt's Journal, Library of Congress transcript, i. 354.
15. For references see T38/346-7 in Andrews, vol. ii, p. 217.
16. See Customs 34-151-153 (p. 90).
17. 27 Geo. III, cap. 13.

Various bundles and volumes containing Custom House accounts may now be found in the Public Record Office, among the Colonial Office Papers, the Treasury Papers,[18] and the series described below (composed of original Custom House documents) the greater part of which appear to have been earlier deposited in the Treasury. Some 565 volumes were transferred thence to the Custom House in 1835, and of these 438 were removed to the Rolls House in 1848 and the remainder in 1851. Many volumes were brought directly from the Treasury Chambers in 1846, 1847, and 1853. A number of volumes were returned to the Custom House in 1853 and 1854.

The bundles in the Treasury series that contain customs accounts will be found in Treasury, classes 38 and 64,[19] to which the searcher may be referred; those of the Board of Trade series may be found among the Colonial Office Papers, class 390: 6-11, already described, but of which a supplementary account is given here, together with a brief entry of a few volumes now in the modern Board of Trade series.

I. PUBLIC RECORD OFFICE

(*a*) BOARD OF TRADE SERIES.

Custom House Accounts: C.O. 390/6-11

6. 1677-1731. Custom House Accounts: an entry book of the Board of Trade, containing tables of exports and imports, arranged under the name of colony or subject: Newfoundland (fishery and inhabitants), Jamaica (goods), Barbados (goods), Leeward Islands (goods), Virginia (goods exported and shipping), Maryland (goods exported), Italy, Spain, Portugal ('State of the trade'), East India (goods and ships), Coinage, Naval stores (from all countries, including the plantations, 1701-23). Also a 'Scheme of the fishery of Newfoundland', 1720, 1722-7, 1729-31, by Capt. Percy. Also tables of goods imported and exported, Jamaica, 1718-22.

7. 1670-1729.

8. 1712-7.

9. 1725-71.

A Board of Trade volume, containing the original reports sent from the Custom House at the request of the board in the years 1760-72. There would seem to be some duplicating of information in the lists. Early returns are of hemp and rice imported, 1752-62; hats exported, 1735-8, 1750-3, 1759-62; beaver skins, imported and exported, 1735-8, 1750-3, 1759-62; beaver wool, exported, 1735-8, 1750-3, 1759-63; beaver skins, imported, 1749-63.

Miscellanea. First Committee. Papers. BT6/80-81 and 83-88.

80. 1783-4. America: commercial intercourse (correspondence).

81. 1783-6. America: commercial intercourse (minutes, etc.).

83. 1784. America and West Indies: commercial intercourse (minutes, etc.).

84. 1784-5. America and West Indies: commercial intercourse (correspondence).

85. 1784-6. American intercourse with Great Britain.

86. 1783-4. American intercourse with Great Britain (Custom House accounts).

87. 1783-5. American intercourse with Newfoundland and Nova Scotia.

88. 1804-7. America and West Indies: commercial intercourse.

(*b*) CUSTOMS SERIES: INSPECTOR-GENERAL'S ACCOUNTS.

In England the collection of primary material for the express purpose of the compilation of statistics of foreign trade was commenced by the Inspector-General of Imports and Exports[20] in 1696. The new office was charged to produce 'a true account of the importacions and exportacions of all commodities into and out of this Kingdom, and to and from what places the same are exported and imported'.

Customs 2 (10 volumes). 1696-1702. Accounts of imports and exports, specifying the trade from London and the outports, to and from the English plantations.

Customs 3 (80 volumes). 1697-1780. Ledgers of imports and exports showing: I, Importations, and II, Exportations, through (*a*) London and (*b*) the outports, of (i) foreign goods and (ii) English goods, all separately (and additionally) distinguished.

Customs 4 (94 volumes). 1792-1899. Ledgers of imports - under countries.

Customs 5 (162 volumes). 1811-99. Ledgers of imports - under commodities.

Customs 6 (22 volumes). 1832-53. Ledgers of imports into colonies - under countries.

Customs 8 (140 volumes). 1812-99. Ledgers of exports of British merchandise - under countries.

Customs 10 (97 volumes). 1809-99. Ledgers of exports of foreign and colonial merchandise - under countries.

Customs 16 (1 volume). 1768-73. Ledger of imports and exports: America. Valuable and informative annual analytical accounts of the vessels (with their description, tonnages, and voyages) entered and cleared the several ports of North America, the shipment of goods in the British and foreign West Indies, general overseas, and coastwise trades; all based upon returns rendered by the American Board of Customs at Boston.

Customs 17 (30 volumes). 1772-1808. States of navigation. Statistical tables showing *inter alia* the number, tonnage, and voyages of British and foreign ships entering and clearing at British ports, from or to overseas places; with detailed accounts, in quantities and values, of merchandise shipped, including that to and from British and foreign America, distinguishing England from Scotland.

(*c*) ESTABLISHMENT REGISTERS.

Quarterly salary-books, in respect of Lady Day, Midsummer, Michaelmas, and Christmas quarters (1 volume per quarter), of the English customs establishment.

Customs 18 (607 volumes). 1675-1813. Two volumes in particular, no. 310 for Midsummer 1767, and no. 312 for Christmas 1767, include an 'Establishment of the Officers of His Majesty's Customs in the Plantations', the latter to the date of the establishment of the American Board (8 Sept. 1767). In the Customs Library (*See* Customs 34-151-153, p. 90) is another volume showing the American establishment just prior to that date.

18. Though no Customs In-books have survived, many of the letters received by the Board can be traced through the Treasury Out-Letter Books: (Customs) (T11) from 1667. See Andrews, vol. ii, p. 209.
19. T38/339-66; T64/137-54 and 238-57.
20. See G.N. Clark, 'The Inspectors-General of Imports and Exports', in *Guide to English Commercial Statistics, 1696-1782* (London, 1938) (Royal Historical Society Guides and Handbooks, no.1).

(*d*) EXCHEQUER PORT-BOOKS.[21]

These are the most important source for the study of English maritime trade, both overseas and coastwise, in the sixteenth and seventeenth centuries. After 1696 interest transfers to the records of the Inspector-General of Imports and Exports (see p. 88). The port-books, however, were not intended to be either commercial records or statistical returns; they were part of the financial records of the customs administration.[22] They are vellum books of varying size and thickness, usually about 11 inches by 15 inches, returned into the Exchequer by the principal officers at the various head-ports and 'creeks' in response to an order of 1564. The series (of 1,464 bundles) contains altogether between 14,000 and 15,000 books. They vary greatly in physical condition, some being well-preserved, others little injured, but a few hardly legible. Although some of the books from certain of the creeks are in English from the commencement, the entries until the end of the sixteenth century are generally in Latin - but in a Latin Dr. N.J. Williams calls 'a patois known rarely outside the custom house'. About half the surviving books relate to the overseas trade, and half to the coastwise trade. The great value of the books for colonial history lies in the record they contain of the nature and distribution of colonial staple products and of goods exported from the English outports to America. This record is not confined to the direct trade between Great Britain and America, but includes also a very large body of material showing the reshipment and re-exportation of colonial staples to other parts of Great Britain and Ireland and to the Continent, and the transportation of such commodities inland as well as by water. For the British coastwise trade the books are indispensable, and of this traffic American staples formed an important part. Furthermore, in these books are hundreds of names of vessels, either plantation- or English-built or taken as prize, that were concerned in the trade and passenger traffic between England and America, and these books date back to the beginning of that history.[23]

A good idea of the character of the information contained in this class of record can be obtained from the introduction and text of R.W.K. Hinton's *The Port Books of Boston: 1601-1640* (Lincoln, 1956) (Lincoln Record Society, vol. 50) and E.A. Lewis's *Welsh Port Books: 1550-1603* (London, 1927). For a good critical study and demonstration of their value as historical sources *see* N.J. Williams's papers, 'Francis Shaxton and the Elizabethan Port-Books', in the *English Historical Review*, vol. lxvi, pp. 387-95, 1951; and 'The London Port Books' in *Transactions of the London and Middlesex Archaeological Society*, vol. xviii, pp. 13-26, 1955.

1-160. London. 1565-1697.

161-84. Berwick. 1606-1784.

185-302. Newcastle upon Tyne. 1579-1798.

303-86. Hull, including Scarborough and Grimsby, 1565-1644, 1654-1787.

387-424. Boston (Lincs.) 1565-1773.

425-70. Lynn. 1565-1794.

471-586. Great Yarmouth, with Blakeney, Dunwich, Walberswick, Southwold, Aldborough, and Woodbridge. 1565-1780.

587-637. Ipswich, including Colchester and Malden, 1565-1736.

638-736. Sandwich and Deal, with Rochester, Milton, Faversham, and Dover. 1565-1756.

737-813. Chichester, with Folkestone, Hythe, Romney, Rye, Winchelsea, Hastings, Pevensey, Matching (Meeching, now Newhaven), Lewes, New Shoreham, Arundel, and Littlehampton. 1565-1731.

814-63. Southampton and Portsmouth. 1565-1731.

864-924. Poole, including Lyme and Weymouth. 1565-1759.

925-1009. Exeter, with Dartmouth, Barnstaple, Bideford, and Ilfracombe. 1565-1788.

1010-80. Plymouth, with Looe, Fowey, Penryn, Truro, Helston, Mount's Bay, St. Ives, and Padstow. 1565-1758.

1081-1127. Bridgwater and Minehead. 1566-1776.

1128-1240. Bristol. 1565-1788.

1241-69. Gloucester. 1581-1776.

1270-97. Cardiff, including Chepstow, Neath, and Swansea.

1298-1322. Milford, including Bury, Carmarthen, and Cardigan. 1565-1784.

1323-1447. Chester, including Beaumaris, Conway, Caernarvon, Liverpool, and Lancaster, 1565-1789.

1448-61. Carlisle, with Whitehaven. 1611-1743.

1462-4. Uncertain ports.

II. AT CUSTOM HOUSE, LONDON[24]

(*a*) Board's Minutes and Letter-books (English, later Great Britain, later United Kingdom).

Customs 29-1-15 (14 volumes). Digest of Board's Minutes, 1696-1869.

Originally compiled for Sir William Musgrave, Commissioner 1763-86, and continued thereafter; the only complete chronological record of the Board's administration throughout the period.[25]

Board's Minutes.

Customs 42-1-8. Receiver-General's Minutes, 1716-84.

Customs 28-1-335. General Business Minutes, 1734-1813; Board's Minutes, 1814-85.

The above minute-books record the board's general business, including, for example, the incidents during the Civil War, 1861-5. There are also references to plantation trade generally, especially tobacco from Virginia and Maryland, rum from New England, and coffee from the West Indies; registry of plantation-built ships, prizes and privateers.

Board's letter-books.

Customs 31-2-270. Western letter-books, 1787-1909.

Copies of out-letters to the various ports, from London 'south-about' to Cardigan.

Customs 31-271-495. Northern letter-books, 1812-1910.

Copies of out-letters to the various English ports, from London 'north-about' to Aberystwyth.

21. For an informative introduction see G.N. Clark, 'Note on the Port Books', in op. cit.

22. N.J. Williams, 'The London Port-Books', in *Transactions of the London and Middlesex Archaeological Society*, vol. xviii, pp. 13-26, 1955.

23. For a note on the port-book entries of the *Mayflower* see R.G. Marsden's memorandum, *First Report of the Royal Commission on Public Records*, vol. i, part ii, p. 49 (Cd. 6395/1912). There is also a port book exclusively concerned with tobacco, which has been printed in N.J. Williams, 'England's Tobacco Trade in the Reign of Charles I', *Virginia Magazine of History and Biography*, vol. lxv, pp. 403-49, 1957.

24. It is to be noted that these records may be deposited with the Public Record Office at Kew in 1978; this has yet to be decided.

25. E.E. Hoon, *The Organization of the English Customs System, 1696-1786* (New York, 1938), p. 293.

Customs 30-195-224. Treasury letter-books, 1814-82.
Copies of out-letters from Board of Customs to Treasury.
There are also other letter-books, etc. in other series.

(*b*) Opinions of Counsel. England. Customs 41-1-30. Copies of legal opinions, 1701-1854.
Occasional informative discussion regarding application and interpretation of laws of trade, the nationality of vessels built in America between 1776 and 1783 ('in some of the provinces in America at the time when they were in actual Rebellion'), and the precise legal status of particular vessels and seamen in immediate post-1783 period.
(*c*) Plantation Records.

Customs 34-151-153. American colonies: Customs establishment. 1767-76. General establishment of all officers employed in the service of His Majesty's Customs in America, 1767-76, including notes on the source of emolument, whether 'established' or 'incidental', and if the latter, whether appointed by the board in England, the board in America, or the Surveyor General confirmed by the board in America. Includes quarterly salary accounts of the Boston headquarters establishment and of the ports from Newfoundland to Bermuda.

Customs 34-79. 1767-75. Plantation ledger.
Showing yields, incidences, and balances under various headings in the different collections (including the collectors' names). (James River, lower part, James River, upper part, York River, Rappahannock, South Potomac, North Potomac, etc.)

III. OUTPORT RECORDS (ENGLAND AND WALES) AT CUSTOM HOUSE, LONDON[26]

The following notes on the material in the main English and Welsh records are intended only to indicate in general terms the nature of their contents. Although most of the notes relate to pre-1783 records, the later volumes of letter-books are important also; for example, for the War of 1812 and for the trade of the United States as late as the period of the Civil War. There are occasional references to trade during the 'Prohibitory Acts' (16 Geo. III, cap. 5 and 17 Geo. III, cap. 7), and to the departure of 'artificers' contrary to the provisions of the Acts of 1718, 1749, and 1785. There are in the Records Unit, Custom House, London, sets of typewritten transcripts of the various letter-books, both inwards and outwards, selected from each of the main outports. There is also a bound volume of papers relating to the *Alabama* incident in 1862. A list of these outport records can be obtained from the Librarian, H.M. Customs and Excise, to whom all applications for access to the papers should be addressed.[27]

Dover (Customs 54)[28]	No. of volumes
Board to Collector, from 1746	20
Collector to Board, from 1784	88
Other letter-books, etc., from 1792	7
Other records, from 1693	9

Of little American significance, except for the clandestine trade in tobacco, mostly in contravention of the Acts of Trade.

Portsmouth (Customs 58)[29]	No. of volumes
Board to Collector, from 1726	140
Collector to Board, from 1748	151
Other letter-books, order-books, etc., from 1810	15
Other records, from 1689	8

Few direct references to American affairs: return of stamps from Nova Scotia on repeal of Stamp Act; passage of continental emigrants from Rotterdam (via Portsmouth for quarantine) for Philadelphia, 1774; arrival of Parker's fleet from South Carolina after Americans' attack on Charleston harbour, with casualty list, 1776; taking of the American privateer, *Rising States*, 1777; discharge of cargo of American prize *Thomas Koulikan*, loaded with guns, shot, drugs, 'and many other things for the use of the Americans', 1778; shipment of 'considerable sums of money for the service of His Majesty's Forces in America', 1778; HMS *Ranger* from South Carolina at Spithead; details of naval vessels under Sir Peter Parker to land troops at Sullivan Island; reports of Americans assisting the enemy.

Southampton (Customs 62)	No. of volumes
Board to Collector, from 1756	128
Collector to Board, from 1714	126
Other letter-books, order-books, etc., from 1814	16
Other records, from 1728	18

Little of direct American interest, but much information about clandestine trade in American tobacco from Channel Islands, in contravention of the Acts of Trade; also a reference to an Act of Assembly 'lately passed in Virginia'.

Cowes (Customs 61)	No. of volumes
Board to Collector, from 1703	79
Collector to Board, from 1749	60
Other letter-books, order-books, etc., from 1703	27
Other records, from 1810	7

Little of American interest, but much referring to contraband, and some reference to privateers, quarantine, etc., and to the clandestine trade in American tobacco from the Channel Islands in contravention of the Acts of Trade.

Poole (Customs 60)	No. of volumes
Board to Collector, from 1760	6
Collector to Board, from 1820	16
Other letter-books, order-books, etc., from 1758	28
Other records, from 1793	4

26. Scottish outport records are at the Scottish Record Office, Edinburgh.
27. It is to be noted that these records may be deposited with the Public Record Office at Kew in 1978; this has yet to be decided.
28. In this and in the following outports, the sum of the volumes given for each category ('Board to Collector', etc.) is *not* the same as the number of volumes concerning that port now on deposit in the Library. During the transfer of the volumes from the outports to the Library, some outports were found to possess slightly more or slightly fewer volumes than originally had been reported. At the same time, of course, later records are continually being added for many of the ports. Nevertheless, the *proportional distribution* of volumes is still substantially correct, and these figures have been retained as an indication of the relative size of each category for each port.
29. For an excellent discussion of Portsmouth's customs records, see E.A. Carson, 'The customs records of Portsmouth', *Journal of the Society of Archivists*, vol. 5, pp. 429-36, 1977.

The earlier records were lost in a fire at the Custom House in 1813, but those surviving are very informative about the affairs of Newfoundland and the whale fisheries.

Weymouth (Customs 59)	No. of volumes
Board to Collector, from 1694	117
Collector to Board, from 1716	103
Other letter-books, order-books, etc., from 1812	37
Other records, from 1801	6

A remarkably complete body of port records.

Exeter (Customs 64)	No. of volumes
Board to Collector, from 1676	121
Collector to Board, from 1743	50
Other letter-books, order-books, etc., from 1822	20
Other records, from 1738	12

Much information about the affairs of Newfoundland, the whale and other fisheries of Greenland and Newfoundland, and some references to mid-eighteenth century trade (e.g. in rice, deer-skins, etc., with Carolina), and the later activities of the American privateers.

Dartmouth (Customs 65)	No. of volumes
Board to Collector, from 1675	112
Collector to Board, from 1775	38
Other letter-books, order books, etc., from 1800	4
Other records, from 1687	14

References (in 1775) to the guard to be placed upon all ports to prevent the shipment of 'any goods, especially gunpowder or other military stores' being 'clandestinely put on board' any vessel bound for North America, to the proclamation of 22 Apr. 1779, relating to the trade of New York, and Newport in Rhode Island, etc.

Plymouth (Customs 66)	No. of volumes
Board to Collector, from 1775	229
Collector to Board, from 1799	4
Other letter-books, order-books, etc., from 1818	16
Other records, from 1835	5

Of special interest for the War of 1812, particularly with regard to contraband and prize of war, the seizure or retention of American vessels on suspicion, the infringement of the Acts of Trade (in the unshipment of tobacco in the Channel Islands), etc.

Falmouth (Customs 67)	No. of volumes
Board to Collector, from 1780	134
Collector to Board, from 1867	5
Other letter-books, order-books, etc., from 1853	15
Other records, from 1817	25

Mostly about the packet service, with little of American interest.

Penzance (Customs 68)	No. of volumes
Board to Collector, from 1722	119
Collector to Board, from 1738	35
Other letter-books, order-books, etc., from 1849	6
Other records, from 1777	4

Much information about the French wars, and illicit trade generally.

Bristol (including Barnstaple and other creeks) (Customs 70)	No. of volumes
Board to Collector, from 1717	90
Collector to Board, from 1727	56
Other letter-books, order-books, etc., from 1816	71
Other records, from 1760	23

The greater part of the earlier records of the port of Bristol itself (as distinct from its creeks) were lost in the burning down of the Custom House during the Reform Bill riots of 1831. However, the remaining records contain occasional references to America, e.g. concerning the effect of the blockade of American tobacco ports on Bristol trade.

The earlier Barnstaple records, from 1727, refer to the American tobacco and Newfoundland trades, including returns of the names of vessels, and quantities of tobacco in hogsheads, from Virginia and Maryland (separately) in each of the years 1722-32; other references to later trade with America, and privateers generally, and the shipment, in 1776, of grain as stores to the army.

Cardiff (Customs 72)	No. of volumes
Board to Collector, from 1689	93
Collector to Board, from 1746	23
Other letter-books, order-books, etc., from 1813	7
Other records, from 1704	32

Of little or no direct American relevance except as regards the activities of 'wreckers' plundering cargoes of tobacco, cotton, sugar, coffee, ginger, and other plantation produce.

Swansea (Customs 73)	No. of volumes
Board to Collector, from 1709	155
Collector to Board, from 1730	43
Other letter-books, order-books, etc., from 1806	17
Other records, from 1711	23

Only occasional references to American affairs, as when the *Gloucester Lass* left Swansea 'for Boston in New England with eighty chalder coals' duty-paid, but foundered in the bay, 1755; or when the brigantine *Sally* (a prize 'taken from the Americans') from Boston with cargo and ten passengers, bound for London, was forced into Swansea 1776; or the ship *James and Peggy*, a transport of Leith, from New York in ballast for London, arrived in Swansea, 1777.

Caernarvon (including its creeks) (Customs 77)	No. of volumes
Board to Collector, from 1714	103
Collector to Board, from 1757	53
Other letter-books, order-books, etc., from 1806	23
Other records, from 1817	13

Many references to illicit trade with Isle of Man (before 1765) in American and East Indian produce, contrary to Acts of Trade.

Liverpool (Customs 80)

For the text of the port letter-books, to and from the Board, etc., see *Customs Letter Books of the Port of Liverpool, 1711-1813*, ed. by R.C. Jarvis (Manchester, 1954) (Chetham Society Publications, third series, vol. vi). There is much information about colonial and plantation trade and shipping generally, the whale fisheries, tobacco, trade practices, the slave trade, the privateers, the Prohibitory Acts, and so forth, transatlantic ship-ownership and shipbuilding.

Heysham (Lancaster) (Customs 81)	No. of volumes
Letter-books, order-books, etc., from 1715	6
Other records, from 1689	1

Many references to the eighteenth-century colonial and plantation trade and shipping.

Whitehaven (Customs 82)	No. of volumes
Board to Collector, from 1703	19
Collector to Board, from 1730	32
Other letter-books, order-books, etc., from 1779	42
Other records, from 1771	13

Many references to plantation and colonial trade and shipping, particularly the tobacco and lumber trades and shipbuilding. Occasional brief references to American affairs, e.g. to 'prisoners from North America' ('tall lusty young men' but 'very ragged and shabby') taken in the Ohio Expedition in 1755, to affairs generally during the War of Independence, e.g. to the detailed operation of the Prohibitory Act, the seizure of American vessels in 1778, the return of General Burgoyne's ships, 13 May 1778, to Paul Jones' attack on the port, and so forth.

Newcastle-upon-Tyne (Customs 84)	No. of volumes
Board to Collector, from 1706	27
Collector to Board, from 1724	120
Other letter-books, order-books, etc., from 1725	164
Other records, from 1764	19

Principally the coal trade, including vessels bound for New York in 1777 with coal; some references to the whale fisheries and the privateers (mostly French); and to the tobacco trade from Virginia and Maryland as early as 1727.

Sunderland (Customs 85)	No. of volumes
Board to Collector, from 1740	103
Collector to Board, from 1732	65
Other letter-books, and order-books, from 1810	4
Other records, from 1832	3

Relating principally to the coal trade, but some references to the whale fishery and the privateers, principally French; and, for example, a report of the harbour, light, buoyage, and clearance dues payable by American vessels in 1789.

Stockton-on-Tees (Customs 89)	No. of volumes
Board to Collector, from 1675	71
Collector to Board, from 1736	35
Other letter-books, order-books, etc., from 1838	6
Other records, from 1748	7

References to the plantations and whale fisheries from the beginning of this series.

Whitby (Customs 90)	No. of volumes
Board to Collector, from 1816	42
Collector to Board, from 1721	10
Other letter-books, order-books, etc., from 1715	16
Other records, from 1808	4

Many and detailed references to the Greenland whale fishery.

Hull (Customs 92)	No. of volumes
Board to Collector, from 1799	118
Collector to Board, from 1843	24
Other letter-books, order-books, etc., from 1733	213
Other records, from 1756	18

References to plantation and colonial trade (e.g. Virginia tobacco trade), to the late eighteenth-century privateers, and details of the doings of Paul Jones on the eve of the *Serapis* action. Also: 1777, rebels in North America commissioning vessels in France to take ships of His Majesty's subjects; 1793, yellow fever raging in Philadelphia- report of an American vessel gone there with English sailors in the crew, contrary to law.

Boston (Customs 95)	No. of volumes
Board to Collector, from 1732	99
Collector to Board, from 1766	14
Other letter-books, order-books, etc., from 1862	1
Other records, from 1815	8

Have been said to be possibly of genealogical interest to American families originating in this part of Britain.

King's Lynn (Customs 96)	No. of volumes
Board to Collector, from 1700	124
Other letter-books, order-books, etc. from 1728	25
Other records, from 1817	4

Many references to smuggling and to lights, lighthouses, and light dues, but little of plantation, colonial, or American interest-notwithstanding that George Vancouver's father, and his brother and biographer, were once in charge here.

Great Yarmouth (Customs 97)	No. of volumes
Board to Collector, from 1662	114
Collector to Board, from 1702	110
Other letter-books, order-books, etc., from 1731	99
Other records, from 1777	8

Of importance in the continental and fishing trades in the eighteenth and nineteenth centuries, particularly with regard to wreck salvage, etc. - but little of plantation, colonial, or American interest. A reference, however, to American privateers in the North Sea in 1777.

Harwich (Customs 99)	No. of volumes
Board to Collector, from 1699	129
Collector to Board, from 1713	89
Other letter-books, order-books, etc., from 1794	28
Other records, from 1699	10

Of importance in the continental trade of the late eighteenth and early nineteenth centuries, particularly the packet service and refugee immigrants, but only very occasionally anything of plantation, colonial, or American interest. There is, however, a reference, for example, 30 Nov. 1775 - the brig *Despatch* of New York, from Malaga to Hamburg with wine, to the shipment from Hamburg to New York of 'arms and ammunition for the use of the American rebels'.

Maldon (Customs 101)

1732: reference to act for encouraging the growth of coffee in the plantations in America.

IV. SHIPS' REGISTERS (ENGLAND, SCOTLAND AND WALES)

The statutory registers of British merchant ships date mostly from 1786, the date of the first Act of General Registry, but occasionally commence earlier (e.g. Liverpool and Campbeltown) and occasionally later (e.g. Bristol, Dartmouth, and Plymouth). After the American War of Independence, many American ships were still trying to claim the privileges of British ownership, and in order to tie up any loopholes an Act was passed (26 Geo. III, cap. 60) requiring the re-registry of every foreign-going British merchant vessel then afloat. The records therefore contain many registries of plantation-built vessels, and in the later period references to American vessels captained by British privateers and British vessels lost to American privateers.

The registers are retained at the port of registry, and a list is shown below.[30] Requests to use the ships' registers should first be made to the Librarian, H.M. Customs and Excise, Museum and Records Unit, Custom House, Lower Thames Street, London.

Port	*Date*
Aberystwyth	1824 to date
Aldeburgh (Ipswich)	1824-45
Arundel (Littlehampton)	1824-55
Barnstaple	1824 to date
Barrow	1868 to date
Beaumaris (Holyhead)	1786 to date
Berwick	1824 to date
Bideford (Bristol)	1786-1831
Bideford (Appledore)	1831 to date
Blyth	1897 to date
Boston	1827 to date
Bridgwater (Bristol)	1786-1841
Bridgwater	1841 to date
Bristol	1824 to date
Brixham	1864 to date
Cardiff	1838 to date
Cardigan (Fishguard)	1824 to date
Caernarvon	1840 to date
Carlisle (Silloth)	1786-1886
Carmarthen (Llanelly)	1839-49
Chepstow (Gloucester)	1786-1881
Chester (Connah's Quay)	1836 to date
Chichester (Littlehampton)	1837-52
Colchester	1786 to date
Cowes	1786 to date
Dartmouth	1824 to date
Dover	1824 to date
Deal (Dover)	1829-78
Exeter	1786 to date
Falmouth	1842 to date
Faversham (Whitstable)	1824 to date
Fleetwood	1897 to date
Folkestone	1855 to date
Fowey	1786 to date
Gloucester	1824 to date
Goole	1828 to date
Grimsby	1824 to date
Hartlepool	1845 to date[31]
Hartlepool West	1860-1967
Harwich	1824 to date
Hull	1804 to date
Ilfracombe (Barnstaple)	1824-37
Ipswich	1824 to date
King's Lynn	1836 to date
Lancaster (Heysham)	1786 to date
Littlehampton	1855 to date
Liverpool[32]	1786 to date
Llanelly	1824 to date
London Port	1786 to date
Lowestoft	1852 to date
Lyme Regis (Exeter)	1786-1880
Maldon	1786 to date
Manchester (Salford)	1894 to date
Maryport (Silloth)	1838 to date
Middlesborough	1861 to date
Milford	1827 to date
Newcastle	1786 to date
Newhaven	1856 to date
Newport	1824 to date
Padstow	1824 to date
Penzance	1786 to date
Plymouth	1824 to date
Poole	1855 to date
Portsmouth	1824 to date
Port Talbot	1917 to date
Preston	1786 to date
Pwllheli (Caernarvon)	1840-51

30. The following list is also given in Edward Carson, *The Ancient and Rightful Customs: A History of the English Customs Service* (London, 1972), pp. 285-6.
31. From 1 Apr. 1967 Hartlepool and West Hartlepool were merged. The Hartlepool register was to be used for all future registrations, while the West Hartlepool register was to die out.
32. Some earlier 'wool' registers are held at Liverpool.

Ramsgate	1850 to date
Rochester	1824 to date
Runcorn	1862 to date
Rye (Dover)	1855-94
Rye	1893 to date
St. Ives	1786 to date
Salcombe	1863 to date
Sandwich (Ramsgate)	1786-1849
Scarborough	1786 to date
Scilly	1786 to date
Shields, North	1848 to date
Shields, South	1859 to date
Shoreham	1821 to date
Southampton	1855 to date
Stockton	1838 to date
Sunderland	1786 to date
Swansea	1824 to date
Teignmouth	1853 to date
Truro	1824 to date
Wells & Cley (King's Lynn)	1832-59
Weymouth	1786 to date
Whitby	1786 to date
Whitehaven	1786 to date
Wisbech (King's Lynn)	1836-54
Woodbridge (Ipswich)	1786-1880
Workington	1839 to date
Yarmouth	1886 to date

DEPARTMENT OF TRADE, COMPANIES REGISTRATION OFFICE
(*a*) Companies House, 55-71 City Road, London EC1Y 1BB
(*b*) Companies House, Crown Way, Maindy, Cardiff

Since 1856 a file has been begun here for each company at the time of its registration, containing memoranda and articles of association, details of financial structure, members and directors and, since 1968, copies of annual accounts. When companies are dissolved, their files are retained for a further twenty years, after which those files of public companies, of large private companies and a selection of the remainder are passed to the Public Record Office. The main contents of the files of all companies in existence in 1973, and all created since, are being microfilmed, and once this has been completed, early copies of any company's files in microfiche form may be obtained by personal application or by post from either of the above addresses.

DR. WILLIAMS'S LIBRARY, 14 Gordon Square, London WC1H OAG

The Library is primarily theological, but contains many historical and other works. The following is additional to the material listed in Andrews & Davenport, pp. 343-6 (which are mainly the papers of the Rev. Richard Baxter (1615-91):

JOLLIE PAPERS. 3 letters. 1681-8. (12.78)

Dedham, Mass., 29 Apr. 1681 and 2 Nov. 1682, from W. Adams, of religious interest.

Watertown, New England, 26 Sept. 1688, from John Bailey to Henry Bailey, giving some details of Indian attacks on the settlers; and of attempts to convert the Indians to Christianity which, he feels, is effort wasted.

WODROW-KENRICK CORRESPONDENCE. 1750-1810. (24.157)

Correspondence between James Wodrow (1730-1810), minister of Stevenston, Ayrshire, and Samuel Kenrick (1728-1811) of Bewdley, covering the years 1750-61, 1768-71, 1774-1810. This long correspondence has many references to American affairs and English attitudes towards them, particularly during the periods of the American and French Revolutions.

RIX PAPERS.

This collection, for the most part collected and arranged and indexed by Samuel Wilton Rix of Beccles, Suffolk, is principally concerned with the families of Rix, Parker, and Wilton. It includes correspondence of Joseph Parker of Newington (1714-93), amanuensis to Dr. Isaac Watts; his son, Joseph Parker of Mattingham (1744-1834); and the latter's brother-in-law, Dr. Samuel Wilton (1744-78). There are items of interest in the correspondence of the younger Joseph Parker and of Samuel Wilton, including letters from William Gordon (1728-1807) from America, documents relating to missionary work in Massachusetts, copies of petitions for the grant of Deer Island and Fox Island, 1772. Letters from Gordon are also transcribed in a MS. entitled 'Some account of the Nonconformist Churches at Hail Weston and St. Neots. . .Huntingdon', compiled by Joseph Rix (1803-78), a brother of the above S.W. Rix.

MAYHEW, JONATHAN (1720-66). Memoir. 1766. (24.71)

Brief memoir of Jonathan Mayhew by Harrison Gray, Treasurer of Massachusetts, dated Boston, 25 Nov. 1766.

HENRY CRABB ROBINSON CORRESPONDENCE. 1767-1855.

Henry Crabb Robinson (1775-1867) had few American correspondents. There are letters to him from William Buell Sprague during the years 1832-47, to whom he supplied many autographs.
The following items were given to Robinson by Sprague:
(*a*) Woolman, John. Verses on the death of his sister Elizabeth.
(*b*) Franklin, Benjamin. Letter to Ezra Stiles from London, 28 Aug. 1767, with notes by Stiles on the verso.
(*c*) Jay, John. Letter, 2 Dec. 1812, to Horatio Gates Spafford, Bedford.
(*d*) Channing, W.E. Letter, 31 Oct. 1819, to Benjamin Abbot, Boston.
(*e*) Webster, Daniel. Letter. 7 Sept. 1822, to George Bliss, Boston.
(*f*) Clinton, De Witt. Letter, 23 Mar. 1826, to Horatio Gates Spafford, n.p.

There are many letters to Robinson from James Cook Richmond, an Episcopalian minister whom he met on the Continent. Richmond was an unstable character, and a great embarrassment to Robinson. (The letters cover the years 1830-55.) There is also a single letter from Eliza Julia Flower (with a note from her husband George) from Albion, Ill., 27 Dec. 1834. The letter is mostly of a personal nature, describing their life, family, etc.

LINDSEY, THEOPHILUS (1723-1808). 8 letters. 1788-94. (24.86)

Letters to Lindsey from the United States, chiefly concerning Unitarianism, with three of merely personal interest.
(*a*) Four letters, all from Boston, from James Freeman, first Unitarian minister of King's Chapel, Boston, and a founder of the Massachusetts Historical Society:

(i) 29 Mar. 1788, referring to the adoption of the Constitution and matters connected with this.

(ii) 15 Oct. 1788, commenting adversely on the American bishops.

(iii) 16 June 1793, touching on religious liberty in the United States.

(iv) 13 June 1794, dealing with Unitarianism in America.

(*b*) Letter, 1789, from J. Smith of Cambridge, Mass., remarks that the new government enjoys the confidence of all the people, and will clear the national debt.

PRIESTLEY LETTERS. Volume of correspondence, letters. 1794-1832. (12.13)

(*a*) Volume of correspondence from Joseph Priestley, while resident at Northumberland, Pa., from 1794 until his death in 1804. Letters, 1794-1803, to Theophilus Lindsey and Thomas Belsham, dealing chiefly with Priestley's religious activities and writings, but containing incidental references to American politics, including the respective strengths of the Federalists and anti-Federalists, and the violence of American party feeling. There are some references to Washington and John Adams. The passage of Jay's Treaty occasions a remark on the conduct of business in Congress. There are some sidelights on the Alien and Sedition Laws, under which Priestley considered himself in danger as a friend of France, a view which appears to be supported by a letter from Jefferson, 18 Jan. 1800,[1] part of which is transcribed in the correspondence, regretting the 'persecution' to which Priestley has been subjected; and also asking Priestley's advice on the foundation of a university in Virginia. There is praise for Jefferson's administration; and a brief comparison of the American and English forms of government, to the advantage of the American. In 1803 Priestley expresses the opinion that events are moving in the direction of Negro emancipation, and mentions the Southerners' fears of slave insurrections. The Louisiana Purchase is mentioned, and the view expressed that even if Britain had occupied Louisiana, the increasing population of the United States 'would in time have burst thro' that feeble barrier'.

(*b*) Letter, Philadelphia, 17 Aug. 1832, from James Taylor to the Rev. Hugh Hutton, extra-illustrator of the *Life and Correspondence of Joseph Priestley* (London, 1832), includes comments on the consequences of the re-election of Jackson. (12.79-80)

COKE, THOMAS (1747-1814). Letter. 1800. [24.180(15)]

Written from Philadelphia, 21 Apr. 1800, to Alexander Knox. Has lately arrived. General Conference of the Methodists next month. Health of Francis Asbury. 'Political disputes run very high indeed ....I have considerable fears that the Democratic party gains strength.'

KENRICK PAPERS. 4 letters. 1810-23. (24.107)

Letters to Thomas Belsham (1750-1829), Unitarian minister, from correspondents in the United States.

(*a*) Boston, 14 July 1810, from W. Buckminster, mentions the rejection of the Erskine agreement, says that neither Britain nor the United States really wishes to compose the differences between them.

(*b*) Boston, 11 Dec. 1813, from Samuel Cary, on the increase of Roman Catholicism in the United States, and the growth of intolerance.

(*c*) Boston, 25 June 1816, from Rev. Francis Parkman, on Unitarianism.

(*d*) Baltimore, 20 June 1823, from Jared Sparks, the editor and historian, comments on Jefferson's opinion of Christianity. Contains quotations from a letter from Jefferson to Sparks ('over two years ago') in which Jefferson adheres to the principle of first-century Christianity without the erroneous accretions of later centuries.

HEYWOOD, ROBERT (1786-1868). Travel diary.[2] 1834. (28.158)

Heywood left England for America on 1 May and returned on 11 Oct. 1834. He travelled from New York via Philadelphia, Baltimore, Washington, D.C., through Kentucky, by steamer to Cincinnati, thence to Columbus, Ohio, Wheeling, W. Va., Pittsburgh, Pa., Buffalo, N.Y., and Niagara, into Canada, and back via Ticonderoga, N.Y., Albany, N.Y., Boston and Newport, R.I., to New York. The diary is of some interest to the social historian but does not deal with political or economic matters.

ESTLIN PAPERS. 1840-84. (24.120-7)

Mary Estlin was the daughter of Dr. J.B. Estlin (1785-1855), a prominent opthalmic surgeon of Bristol, a Unitarian reformer, and anti-slavery supporter. She was a member of the Bristol and Clifton Auxiliary Ladies Anti-Slavery Society and maintained an extensive correspondence with abolitionists in the United States, which she visited in 1868; after the Civil War she transferred her energies to the women's rights campaign.

The most important items are:

(*a*) Minute-book, 1840-61, of the Bristol and Clifton Auxiliary Ladies Anti-Slavery Society. References to slavery in the United States, the raising of funds to assist fugitive slaves, and the American Anti-Slavery Society.

(*b*) Part of a letter, n.d., from Parker Pillsbury, American reformer travelling in Ireland, on the evils of slavery and the reluctance of the clergy and politicians to fight it.

(*c*) Letters, 1844-51, of anti-slavery interest, to Dr. Estlin from James Martineau; Mr. Donaldson of Cincinnati, mentioning also Oberlin College and Negro education; Dr. S.G. Howe of Boston; Joshua Coffin of Newbury, Mass.; W.E. Whiting (letter to unnamed person - Estlin? - 1847); Dr. Joseph Sargent in 1850, deploring the visit of George Thompson, British abolitionist; and Frederick Frothingham of Cambridge, Mass.

(*d*) Letters, 1851-84, to Mary Estlin.

(i) 1851-83, from Mrs. M.W. Chapman of Massachusetts, dealing with certain political events of the day, as they affect the abolitionist cause. (Also copies of some letters from Mrs. Chapman to others.)

(ii) 1852-84, chiefly to Mary Estlin from Sarah Pugh. References to anti-slavery; the transfer of abolitionists' energies after 1865 to the women's rights movement; moral education and anti-vice campaigns; and, in a letter of 1879, the exodus of Negroes from the deep South to the West.

(iii) 1853-4, from Mary Grew and Abby Kimber, referring to the anti-slavery movement.

(iv) *c.* 1854-81, about William Lloyd Garrison from Oliver Johnson, Abby Kimber, Sarah Pugh, and Maria Weston Chapman. (There is also the copy of a letter on Garrison by the Rev. Samuel Alfred Steinthal to an unknown person.)

(v) Oberlin, Ohio, 1862, from the Rev. John Keep, describing Oberlin College.

(vi) Roxbury, Mass., 1863-9, from William Lloyd Garrison, mainly personal, with comments on political events of the period.

1. Printed in *The Writings of Thomas Jefferson*, ed. by P.L. Ford, vol. vii (London and New York, 1897), pp. 406-10.

2. Privately printed (limited edition of 100 copies), *A Journey to America in 1834* (Cambridge 1919).

(vii) New York, 1863, from Mattie Griffith, giving an eyewitness account of the New York Draft Riots.

(viii) New York, 1869 and 1872, from Oliver Johnson, editor and reformer, on the Grant administration.

(ix) Boston, 1869, from Anne Waterston, rejoicing over Grant's election, and including references to J.L. Motley.

(x) 1877-81, from Frank J. Garrison, including references to his father, the women's suffrage movement, and Chinese immigration.

(*e*) Letters, 1852-69, from Mrs. Harriet Beecher Stowe [also to Mrs. E.L. Follen, Joseph Sturge (copy), and Miss Wigham (copy)] include acknowledgements of donations from England for her scheme to establish a school for Negro children in Mandarin, Fla.

(*f*) Letters, 1858, from Samuel May, Jr., the anti-slavery advocate, to various people, including copy of one to R.D. Webb on the American Anti-Slavery Society and the *Advocate*.

(*g*) Letters from Mary Estlin, while in America in 1868, to Rebecca Moore. References to William Lloyd Garrison, Gerrit Smith, and other anti-slavery leaders whom she visited; the division of the anti-slavery movement, now concentrating on the betterment of the Negroes' conditions, between those advocating better education and those wishing to ensure intelligent use of the suffrage; an account of an address by Anna Dickinson criticizing the Republican Party; an account of schools in New York; and reports brought back by teachers returning from the South.

(*h*) Letters, 1868-9, and poems by Dr. Ann Preston (1813-72), one of the first graduates of the Female Medical College of Pennsylvania and later its Dean and Trustee.

ADAM, WILLIAM. Sermons. (24.156)

Adam went to India as a Baptist missionary, but was converted to Unitarianism in 1821 under the influence of Rammohun Roy. His career was peripatetic. He preached at Toronto (1845-6) and Chicago (1846-9). Of the forty-eight MS. sermons in this collection, most are noted as having been preached in Chicago.

FABER & FABER LTD., PUBLISHERS, 3 Queen Square, London WC1N 3AU

ARCHIVES.

The firm has correspondence, sometimes extensive, with twentieth-century authors published by them, notably T.S. Eliot, Robert Lowell, Sylvia Plath, and other Americans. Access to these papers cannot be guaranteed, since scholarly work is currently in progress on many of them. Inquiries should be directed to the Chairman.

ROBERT FLEMING & CO., LTD., 8 Crosby Square, London EC3A 6AN

BUSINESS RECORDS. 1 volume. 1901-9.

Bankers. The firm holds a volume which includes simply a list of American railroads in whose financing Robert Fleming assisted, 1901-9. Among the major investments, ranging from 1 to 3 million dollars, were those in the Atchison Railroad, Bangor & Aroostook, Carolina Clinchfield, Chicago Great Western Railway Syndicate, Kansas City, Fort Scott; Kansas City Street Railway, Pennsylvania Railroad and Union Pacific (these two through Kuhn, Loeb & Co.), Western Pacific, and the Wisconsin Central.

LADY VIRGINIA FLEMMING, G 3, Burton Lodge, Portinscale Road, London, S.W. 15

COIT, STANTON (1857-1944). Memoir.

Typescript (44 pp.) of 'Ventures on the Highway of Truth', unpublished memoir by Stanton Coit, ethicist and socialist, describing his adoption of the Humanist Code of ethics while an undergraduate at Amherst College in Massachusetts. Coit disseminated interest in the ethical movement in Great Britain from 1887, and eventually founded the Ethical Church, Bayswater; he twice stood unsuccessfully as Labour candidate for Wakefield. Since it was written when Coit was in his 80's, the memoir is not as polished or organized as many of his other writings.

GENERAL POST OFFICE, St. Martin's le Grand, London EC1A 1HQ

TREASURY LETTER-BOOKS. 831 volumes. 1686-1931. (Volumes to 1859 are indexed individually, after that cumulatively; volumes from 1891 are mainly in typescript.)

Copies of letters passing between the Postmasters-General and the Lords Commissioners of the Treasury. After 1783 the letter-books cease to be of interest for the internal history of American mails, but contain much scattered material relating to such matters as contracts, e.g. with Cunard, for, and costs of, packets to carry mails across the Atlantic, frequency of such services, postal rates, illegal conveyance of letters, and the forwarding of letters for America from the Continent.

See further, Andrews & Davenport, pp. 273-5, which deal with the first ten volumes to 1783; Paullin & Paxson, pp. 476-8, for volumes to 1859.

PACKET REPORT BOOKS. 6 volumes. 1807-37. (Index for each volume.)

Supplement the Packet Minute Books below.

PACKET MINUTE BOOKS. 228 volumes. 1811-1920.[1] (Index for each volume, 1811-63; cumulative index for 1864-1920.)

Indexed under 'United States' will be found all the important material relating to transatlantic mail services for the period covered, such as dates of sailings, irregularities of dispatch, surcharges due, establishment of a direct mail route to California via Panama, etc. See Paullin & Paxson, p. 479, which describes the volumes for 1811-59.

AMERICAN LETTER-BOOKS.[2] 40 volumes. 1849-1920. (Each volume contains an index.)

Copies of letters sent from the General Post Office to both British American and United States post offices on all aspects of postal communication between the hemispheres. See Andrews & Davenport, p. 276, for separate American letter-book, for 1773-83, not in the main series.

1. Two catalogues of the Packet Minute Books, 1811-1900 and 1901-20, have been prepared.

2. In this and several other series, volumes survive only at five-yearly intervals. The intervening volumes were pulped for salvage during the Second World War.

For other series, containing slight references to American business, see Andrews & Davenport, pp. 275-6, and Paullin & Paxson, pp. 478-80.

GREATER LONDON RECORD OFFICE, LONDON SECTION,
Room B.21, The County Hall, London SE1 7PB

There is no large body of American material deposited in the London section of the Greater London Record Office, though records are constantly being added. There are the usual types of parish records arranged alphabetically under metropolitan boroughs. A brief examination of estate records showed scattered references to colonial Americans involved in land transactions. Included among the records of the Board of Guardians (taken over by the Council in 1930) are registers of children sent to Canada, etc., in the late nineteenth and early twentieth centuries. Among the office's own papers are:

MINUTES OF PROCEEDINGS. *c.* 100 volumes. 1889-to date.

Bound indexes to Council Minutes cover 1889-1937. A brief survey showed that the kinds of material contained in the Minutes include accounts of visits by Council officials to America, e.g. 1904, Chairman of Highways Committee appointed Council's representative at opening ceremony of New York Tramway Subway; 1905, report on American tramways by above to be published. Exchange visits by teachers, e.g. 1907, visit of inquiry to educational institutions, reports submitted by teachers; 1908, visits of teachers from United States, free admission to Council's classes for teachers; 1917, gift of copies of President Wilson's New Declaration of Freedom received from British-American Peace Centenary Committee; 1925, report of visit of Council's architect to America.

PERSONAL PAPERS.

American Loyalist Claims Commission—rough report books, etc., *c.* 1780-3, among the Records of the Foundling Hospital, (A/FH/-)

GREATER LONDON RECORD OFFICE, MIDDLESEX SECTION,
1 Queen Anne's Gate Buildings, Dartmouth Street, London SW1H 9BS

Only a short general note on these records appears in Andrews & Davenport, p. 284, under Westminster Guildhall or Session House, where they were.

More detail has been included to show the kind of minor information that can be found in most County Archives which possess the records of the Courts of Quarter Sessions and large estate collections. Such minor information has not been generally noted elsewhere.

QUARTER SESSION RECORDS.

In the first half of the seventeenth century offenders sentenced to death were sometimes reprieved on condition that they left England for the colonies. Such sentences were recorded in the Sessions Rolls or Registers. An early example of such a case is that of Stephen Rogers in 1617, sentenced to be hanged for manslaughter but 'reprieved for Virginia' because the plantation needed carpenters. Again, in July 1663, twenty-three persons gained the King's pardon on condition that they left England in two months for the colonies. A number of such cases are recorded in the published calendars to the Middlesex Sessions records.[1]

Other classes of official records which contain reference to America are:

TRANSPORTATION BONDS. 1682-1837.

These give the names of ships and ships' owners, the names of the felons transported therein, and the colony to which they were destined.

INDENTURES. *c.* 1,000. 1683-4.

These are indentures of persons willing to serve in the plantation of America in accordance with the Order of the Privy Council of 1682. They give name and place of origin of the apprentice, the name of the master to whom he is bound and his trade, the colony in which he is to serve, and the period of the apprenticeship. This class has been much used in the past by American historians and genealogists.

MIDDLESEX SESSIONS PAPERS. 1689- (Listed up to 1751 but there is no index yet.)

For example, petition of Robert Nevell *v.* Captain Dodson of the *Robert Samuel* for abuse *en route* for Maryland. R. Nevell obtained a warrant against Captain Dobson on arrival in Cecil County and brought him before a Justice of the Peace there. Several men had to stay in Maryland because of abuses from Captain Dobson. (MSP Aug. 1697, petition 24)

DEPOSITED FAMILY AND ESTATE PAPERS.

(*a*) Papers, 1724-9, concerning the lease of 10,000 acres of land in Pennsylvania by William Aubrey, merchant, of London, and his wife Letitia (one of the daughters of William Penn) to John Knight of Westminster. (Acc. 262/St. 57/47-57)
(*b*) Statement of property of the West New Jersey Society, 1775. (Acc. 617/270)
(*c*) Certificate of registration issued to John J. Austen, a white alien intending to live in Pennsylvania, 1800. (Acc. 751/1)
(*d*) Various certificates and affidavits, 1800-37, proving marriages or deaths of members of families in America. (Acc. 69/1815-28)
(*e*) Documents mainly concerning legacies to be paid to Ann Torbek and her daughters of Frederick County, Maryland, 1804-19. (Acc. 1057/65-6, 72-3)
(*f*) Letters from an emigrant farmer, James Martin, living in Delaware and Ohio, 1821-37. (Acc. 1063/130-150)
(*g*) Five bills of exchange, 1827-9, payable to William B. Wood, signed Juliana Simpson. (Acc. 69/1829-33)
(*h*) Memorandum of release, Duke of Buckingham and Chandos to Thomas Grenville, for money paid as compensation for loss of Florida estates to Spain, 22 Feb. 1834. (Acc. 262/St. 57/63-67)
(*i*) Letters from Thomas Read, emigrant, describing his attempts to make a living in New York City and State, 1834-83. (Acc. 1093/159-189)

1. J.C. Jeaffrison, ed., *Middlesex County Records, Old Series (Extracts), 1549-1687,* 4 vols. (London, 1886-92), and W. Le Hardy, ed., *Middlesex County Records, New Series, 1612-1618,* 4 vols. (London, 1935-41).

(*j*) Letters of administration of the goods of Mrs. Juliana Wood, wife of William Burke Wood of Philadelphia (intestate), 7 July 1837. Administration to Charlotte Howis, widow, and attorney of William Burke Wood, in the Prerogatory Court of Canterbury. (Acc. 69, no. 1742)
(*k*) Hicks family letters, including a number from the U.S.A. describing life there, 1830's-40's. (Acc. 538 [2] 3837)
(*l*) Five letters, 24 July 1849-4 Mar. 1850, from Henry Howick of Bridgeport, Conn., about the Howick family of Sussex, England. (Acc. 333/8/12)
(*m*) Downton Family Papers. Letter, affidavit. 1850, 1851. (Acc. 333/21/1)

(i) Letter, 8 Nov. 1850, from William Downton to F.I. Kent, solicitor, about his father, mother, and brother (John Downton). Written on the back of a printed announcement (1 Jan. 1850) from Robert Low & Son, of the Strand, London, that Mr. Jules Hauel, manufacturing perfumer, Chestnut Street, Philadelphia, had been restrained by a United States Circuit Court decree from making and selling an imitation of Low's Brown Windsor Soap.

(ii) Affidavit by Jackson Sparrow of Covington Ky., residing in 'St. Geo. Hanover Square, Middlesex, England', concerning James Downton of Hampton, Middlesex, deceased (Jackson Sparrow's father-in-law), and John Downton, who emigrated to the United States in 1831 and died unmarried in 1841 in the town of Jackson near New Orleans. 6 Aug. 1851.

(*n*) Correspondence concerning help to be given to novelist G.P.R. James, British Consul in Norfolk, Virginia, 1853. (Acc. 976/222)
(*o*) Journal of Samuel Lloyd Howard of journey to America, describing visits to Boston, New York, Philadelphia, Baltimore, etc., 1854. (Acc. 1017/1618)
(*p*) Letter, 2 May 1855, from Henry Butts, Goshen, Cincinnati, Ohio, to his mother in Devonshire. Mentions legacy, weather, health, family matters, etc. 'We have some notion of getting our Daguereotypes taken. . . . ' (Acc. 319)
(*q*) Bicknell Family Papers of Maplewood, South Orange, N.J. Death certificate, 11 Oct. 1874. Letters of administration, 19 Oct. 1880. Inland revenue account with next of kin, 3 Dec. 1880. (Acc. 361/2-4)
(*r*) Letters, Apr.-Dec. 1886, as to raising £1,000 from trust funds to buy a farm in America. (Acc. 351/102-14)
(*s*) Rickards Family Papers. 1887-98. (Acc. 448)

Mortgage bonds, share certificates, and minor papers, 1887-98, relating to lands in Kansas, Missouri, and Colorado, including some relating to the South West Kansas Land and Irrigation Company and the Syndicate Lands and Irrigating Corporation, Colorado.

(*t*) Letters, 1893-4, from Henry Rankin written on paper headed 'Waterbury Watch (Sales) Co. Ltd., 7 Snow Hill, London E.C. Factory, Waterbury, Conn. U.S.A.'. (Acc. 333/39/7)
(*u*) Letter from R.B. Briggs in San Jose, California, describing the effects of the recent earthquake, 1906. (Acc. 538[2]4886A)

SESSIONS PAPERS OF THE SESSIONS GAOL OF DELIVERY AT NEWGATE (MIDDLESEX PRISONERS) HELD AT THE OLD BAILEY. 1755-96. (Fully listed but not yet indexed.)

For example, information per William Platt re ship *Philippa* bound for Georgia and East Florida, 1775, with arms, etc., consigned to individuals there. On 7 July 1775 met by an armed schooner off Tybee Bar, Ga.; forced to stop and give arms to champions of American liberty in Savannah, Ga., by order of 'The Provincial Congress of the province of Georgia', which then ruled the province, leaving the Governor powerless. Lively account of conditions in Georgia in summer, 1775. (Old Bailey S.P./1777/4*a* & 4*b*)

Also, information before the Coroner concerning the death in duels of:
(*a*) Lloyd Delany, 1782. The cause of the duel was a newspaper attack on his brother, Daniel Delany, 'Secretary of Maryland'. (OBSP 1782 Jy/23)
(*b*) Lt. Col. Frederick Thomas, 1783. Thomas and his protagonist, Col. Cosmo Gordon, were serving in America in 1780 and the duel followed various difficulties between them which arose there. (OBSP 1783 Sept./63-66, including letters exchanged between Thomas and Gordon.)

MISCELLANEOUS LETTERS. 3 letters. 1822-5.

Letters (in French) from Madame de Coigny to Lady Jersey, wife of the 5th Earl.
11 Sept. 1822. Mentions return of Lafayette to France covered with glory earned in America fighting for liberty (with transcript). (Acc. 510/615)
18 Apr. [1824?]. Asking for the new novel by 'the American Walter Scott of the day', James Fenimore Cooper. (Acc. 510/630)
3 Nov. 1825. Comments on Lord Wellesley's second marriage to an American. (Acc. 510/664)

MIDDLESEX TONTINE. 1826-32.

George Manners, H.M. Consul in Massachusetts, and his wife Charlotte, living in Boston: sworn statements, 1826, 1829, 1832, as to survival of nominees, Middlesex Tontine.

GUILDHALL LIBRARY,[1]
Aldermanbury, London EC2P 2EJ

NEW ENGLAND COMPANY.[2] Papers: miscellaneous collection of charters, books of account, minute-books, journals, ledgers, general correspondence, etc. (Most of the records are incomplete, or contain large gaps.) 1649-

Originally created by Ordinance in 1649 as the Society for the Propagation of the Gospel in New England, and chartered by Charles II, 7 Feb. 1662, as the 'Company for Propagation of the Gospell in New England and the parts adjacent in America'. The New England Company, as it is usually known, is the oldest Protestant missionary society still in existence. Its funds were spent largely on salaries of missionaries to the Indians, among whom were John Eliot, Thomas and Experience Mayhew, and John Cotton.

The Company functioned continuously until the War of Independence, but at the beginning of the War it discontinued its payments to New England, and after the War its funds were diverted to Canada.[3] Thus, although the company's records are still in progress, only those relating to the colonial period are of value in the study of American history. These are as follows:

1. Philip E. Jones and Raymond Smith, *A Guide to the Records in the Corporation of London Records Office and the Guildhall Library Muniment Room* (London, 1951).
2. See William Kellaway, 'The Archives of the New England Company', *Archives*, vol. ii, pp. 175-82, 1954, and his *New England Company, 1649-1776* (London, 1961).
3. William Kellaway, 'The Archives of the New England Company', *Archives*, vol. ii, p. 176.

(*a*) Treasurers' individual and sundry accounts, 1649-1728 (1 file). An account of moneys received and disbursed, 1649-55 (double sheet). Treasurers' general accounts, 1659-84 (incomplete, 4 ternions). Treasurers' general and estate account books, 1660-1764 (3 volumes). Treasurers' ledgers: volume 1, 1726-65; volume 2, 1764-1801. Treasurers' journals: volume 1, 1764-1801.

(*b*) Loose court minutes with some committee minutes, 1655-1816, with lacunae 1729-43, 1808-15 in one box. General court and committee minute-books: volume 1, 1770-1816, and index volume, 1770-1830. Also a photostat of the court minute-book, 1655-85, now in the Library of the Massachusetts Historical Society.

(*c*) Original correspondence[4] relating to affairs in New England, 1657-1714, one large folio; this is an artificial collection made *c.* 1896. Each letter has a printed transcript mounted opposite the original. Includes several letters from John Eliot, the Hon. Robert Boyle, a principal benefactor of the Company, and the Commissioners of the United Colonies; one letter from the President and Fellows of Harvard College; and one from a group of sixteen Indians of Natick, Mass., to Eliot. Also the journals of Experience Mayhew relating to missions to the Indians, 1713 and 1714.

(*d*) General correspondence, 1668-1818. Principally in-letters, with some draft out-letters (1 box). Letter-book, 1762-72, chiefly copies of out-letters.

(*e*) Correspondence[5] from Boston, mainly by the Commissioners to the Company in London, relating principally to Indian affairs, 1677-1761 (2 files).

(*f*) Official copy minutes of the Commissioners for Indian Affairs at Boston, 1699-1784 (1 file). (Increase and Cotton Mather were commissioners.) Accounts of Indian stock, i.e. receipts and disbursements of the Company's Commissioners at Boston, 1657-1731 (2 files).

In addition to the above the collection contains:

(*g*) Charter of incorporation by Charles II, and a contemporary office copy of the same, 7 Feb. 1662.

(*h*) Several series of muniments of title for the Company's properties, dating from 1543 onwards; the only American deeds are those for Martha's Vineyard, Mass., 1671-1730. A transcript, made in 1910, of a volume (among the Rawlinson MSS. C934 in the Bodleian Library[6]) of papers relating to the proceedings of the Company, 1649-56.

ROBERT HOOKE PAPERS. Essay (87 pages). 1666.

Entitled 'American pirates'. Chiefly concerned with the West Indies, and only incidentally with the mainland. This is part of a translation of Exquemelin's *De Americaensche Zee-Rovers*.

GUILD RECORDS.

The records of seventy-one of the City livery companies, including the Fishmongers, Grocers, Haberdashers, Ironmongers, and Vintners of the twelve 'great' companies. Items relating to Virginia appear for the seventeenth century.

DISSENTING CONGREGATIONS IN THE CITY.

Records of Baptists, Congregationalists, Protestant Dissenters, French Protestants, Independents, Scottish Presbyterians, some late seventeenth century but mostly eighteenth century. Minute-books, lists of members, etc., might yield details about members emigrating to America.

DAVISON, NEWMAN & CO. Business records. 1753-1897.

Grocers and importers of West Indian produce, founded in 1650; carried on business at the Sign of the Three Sugar Loaves and Crown, Gracechurch Lane. The firm was taken over by the West Indian Produce Association in 1911. Its dealings with the mainland colonies, and later the United States, were incidental, but the collection contains papers relating to its agents in Boston, and in Charleston, S.C. The firm's current account with its Boston agent, Henry Lloyd, for 1772-3, is framed, because one item mentions Francis Rotch, the master of the *Dartmouth*, one of the ships involved in the Boston Tea Party. A file of seventy to eighty letters and copies, 1791-1816, from John Ward, the Charleston agent, consists mainly of enclosures with bills, but there is some discussion of current news, e.g., on 4 Jan. 1794 Ward refers to the recovery of British debts, and the adverse effect of the French Revolution on American commerce.

LLOYD'S OF LONDON. Loss and casualty books. 1774-1969.

Loss and casualty books, listing movements and losses of vessels underwritten by Lloyd's members, with names of masters, and details of cargo and type of ship, 1774-1969. Includes many American vessels and voyages.

MORRISON, CRYDER & CO. Correspondence and papers. 1832-51.

London-American and general merchants of 9 Broad Street Buildings, later Morrison, Sons & Co., of the same address and of 62 Moorgate.

Correspondence, accounts, legal and insurance papers, etc., 1832-51. Includes letter to Daniel Webster (1782-1852), American statesman, and letters from George Peabody (1795-1869), American financier and philanthropist, concerning American stock, 1837-46; also papers relating to the American economic crisis of 1837, and to American finance and trade, 1841-2.

THE LONDON ASSURANCE. Risks book. 1854.

Risks book covering, *inter alia*, voyages to and from the U.S.A., Newfoundland, British America, Havana, Mexico, West Indies, etc., giving name of vessel, voyage made, type of cargo, value, and premium. 1854.

PEABODY MEMORIAL COMMITTEE. Minute-book. 1866-70.

Minutes of meetings of the Committee held to consider the erection of the statue of George Peabody in London.

GUARDIAN ASSURANCE CO. LTD. Report books. 1866-94.

Report books relating to existing and potential business in the U.S.A., describing, *inter alia*, topography, development, building methods and materials, local regulation, fire records, fire prevention facilities, trade, population, present liabilities, etc., of various cities and localities. 1866-94.

4. This correspondence has been printed in John W. Ford, ed., *Some Correspondence between the Governor and Treasurers of the New England Company in London and the Commissioners of the United Colonies in America* (London, 1897).

5. 'The correspondents include such distinguished colonial figures as Adam Winthrop and Samuel Sewall, and their letters often shed an interesting light, not only on the work of the missionaries and the Company's affairs, but also upon colonial society', Kellaway op. cit., p. 179.

6. See Andrews and Davenport, pp. 405-6.

COUNCIL OF THE CORPORATION OF FOREIGN BONDHOLDERS. Minutes and correspondence. 1868-1912.

Established 1873, primarily to protect the interests of holders of sterling bonds publicly issued in the U.K. on behalf of overseas governments, states, and municipalities. Records include committee minutes for Alabama, 1873-80; Louisiana, 1874-9; and Virginia, 1872-91. There are also correspondence books for Alabama, 1872-1912; Arkansas, 1871-3; Florida, 1870-1909; Georgia, 1871-3; Indiana, 1868-74; Louisiana, 1873-1912; North and South Carolina, 1873-1912; Tennessee, 1873-4; and Virginia, 1872-93.

LONDON STOCK EXCHANGE. Minutes and papers. 1888.

General Purposes Committee: minutes and papers for subcommittee on dealings in American railroad shares, 1888.

SCOTT, CAPTAIN BUCHANAN. Letters. 1888-90.

Copy out-letters to officers of the International Co. of Mexico (registered in U.S.A.), 1888-9, and Mexican Land and Colonisation Co. Ltd. (registered in U.K.), 1889-90, relating to Capt. Scott's services as general manager based at Ensenada, Calif., in the development, settlement, and commercial exploration of Southern California by farming, salt, sulphur, iron ore and gold mining, and improving communications.

GENERAL.

In the nineteenth and early twentieth century the City of London was a major centre of international commercial activity, much of it linked with America. The Library holds many records of this activity, some of which are listed above; however, much material cannot be itemized in the scope of this *Guide*, since it is not archivally distinct but incorporated and scattered in substantial general series of records, e.g. minute-books, accounts, share registers, letter-books. In this category may be included the records of insurance companies (several of which were active in the American market); stockbrokers (several of which dealt in American stocks and shares or on behalf of American clients); bankers; etc., and also of organizations which regulated or promoted commercial activity, e.g. the London Stock Exchange and the Association of British Chambers of Commerce. Full catalogues of these records are available in the Library.

THE MUSEUM, GUNNERSBURY PARK, London, W.3

COLLINSON, ADMIRAL SIR RICHARD (1811-83). Letter. 1837.

Collinson served from 1828 on ships employed on survey work mainly on the South American coast. A letter, 20 Nov. 1837, written to his father from H.M.S. *Sulphur*, San Francisco, says, 'This is the country for emigration...Bullocks are killed for their hide and tallow...deer in thousands...Geese and ducks in myriads, corn in abundance. It only wants one million of inhabitants instead of 20,000 to make it the nation of the Pacific Ocean. At present the inhabitants consist of uneducated Spaniards without the slightest energy, Kentucky backwoodsmen and Englishmen of very doubtful character who would just as soon make 500 per cent as any Jew in the United Kingdom.'

HENRY GEORGE FOUNDATION, AND THE UNITED COMMITTEE FOR THE TAXATION OF LAND VALUES LTD., 177 Vauxhall Bridge Road, London, S.W.1

PRINTED RECORDS.[1]

These propagate the doctrines of Henry George (1839-97), American economic and political reformer. No manuscript materials appear to be available; however, the printed records include the volumes of the *Single Tax*, monthly organ of the Scottish Land Restoration Union, vols. i-vii, 1894-1901, continued as *Land Values*, monthly organ of the Movement for the Taxation of Land Values, vols. viii-xix, 1902-19, continued as *Land and Liberty*, monthly organ of the United Committee for the Taxation of Land Values, vol. xx, 1919-(in progress). These journals, which form a continuous series, contain much information about the progress of Henry George's ideas and include contributions from American sympathizers.

1. This material was used by Elwood P. Lawrence, *Henry George in the British Isles* (East Lansing, Mich., 1957).

HISTORICAL MANUSCRIPTS COMMISSION AND NATIONAL REGISTER OF ARCHIVES, Quality House, Quality Court, Chancery Lane, London WC2A 1HP

The Historical Manuscripts Commission has published, since 1870, some 230 printed reports on manuscript collections in Great Britain, mostly of the eighteenth century or earlier.[1] Scholars wishing to consult the original documents, many of which have changed location, should apply to the Secretary, Historical Manuscripts Commission, Quality House, Quality Court, Chancery Lane, London WC2A 1HP

The Commission also maintains the National Register of Archives, which consisted (in 1975) of some 19,000 unpublished reports on collections of papers. These reports vary greatly in scope and format, according to their origin. Some are outline lists which summarize the contents of the bundles or files of papers in a collection without identifying individual items. Others offer full descriptive lists, identifying documents individually, with some indication of the contents of each. These indexes and reports may be inspected on application to the Secretary, Historical Manuscripts Commission, who welcomes serious scholars and can often direct them to the sources they seek.[2]

The following items represent some of the American material included in the (mostly privately-owned) collections which have

1. The most detailed account of those reports published before 1957 was given in E.L.C. Mullins, *Texts and Calendars: An Analytical Guide to Serial Publications*, Royal Historical Society Guides and Handbooks No. 7 (1958), pp. 61-90. Index volumes of personal names and places in reports and calendars issued down to 1957 have been published in a separate *Guide to the Reports of the Royal Commission on Historical Manuscripts* (7 vols., 1914-74).

2. Since 1957 the Commission has issued yearly a list of *Accessions to Repositories*. It also advises individual owners and custodians of primary historical research material about the proper preservation of manuscripts; likewise, the Commission offers, upon request, advice on means of transferring documents to an appropriate alternative home.

been surveyed by the National Register of Archives. They are of course only a small fraction of the documents of American interest which have been inspected by the Register's workers, since much of the N.R.A.-listed material has appeared elsewhere in our *Guide* under the name of the appropriate owner. Indeed, there are likely to be listings of Americana among the Register's files which do not appear anywhere in this *Guide*, simply because the number and length of the Register's lists made it impossible for us to scrutinize them in any exhaustive manner. The items given below, then, should only be seen as illustrative of the information which may still be found.

The number following the name of the collection is the reference number of the survey. The location of the documents themselves is given in the appropriate survey, but it must be emphasized that to view such material, when it is in private hands, application should always be made through the Secretary, *never* directly to the owners.

SHIRLEY, GENERAL WILLIAM (1694-1771). 2 dispatches (copies). 1756. (0010)

On the arrival of British troops in America, 1756.

BARHAM PAPERS.[3] Miscellaneous naval papers. 1773-93. (0315)

Charles Middleton, 1st Baron Barham (1726-1813), admiral, was Comptroller of the Navy 1778-90, and First Lord of the Admiralty in 1805.

(*a*) Letters, 1780-2, concerning the West Indian and American Stations from Parker, Rodney, Graves, Prescott, Spry, Rowley, Hunt, Hood, and Thompson.

(*b*) Nineteen miscellaneous papers, 1773-93, on the War of Independence (one signed by Hood).

(*c*) Books A and B, 1779-83, 290 letters, drafts, lists, and notes on victualling and convoys for America and Gibraltar (including victuals for the Army) with twenty-six letters and drafts by Sir Charles Middleton.

HAMMOND PAPERS. Miscellaneous family papers. 1792-1877. (0566)

George Hammond (1763-1853), diplomat, first British Minister to the United States; married in 1793 to Margaret Allen of Philadelphia. American material includes:

(*a*) Certificate of membership of George Hammond to the 'Society of the Sons of St. George', Philadelphia, 25 Jan. 1792.

(*b*) Lord Grenville to George Hammond - appointment of Hammond as Minister to Washington, and his initial instructions, 24 May 1792.

(*c*) Letter, 1 Jan. 1793, from Hammond to Grenville on his marriage in Philadelphia; 5 Feb. 1793, from Phineas Bond to William Hammond on George Hammond's marriage.

(*d*) Edward, Duke of Kent, to George Hammond on strengthening armed forces in Nova Scotia, 27 Apr. 1796.

(*e*) 'Original [Biographical] Sketches, nos. 6 and 7.' June 1809. Addressed from Philadelphia to Mrs. George Hammond. No. 6 is chiefly on Thomas Paine; No. 7 on Mrs. [James] Madison.

(*f*) George Hammond to ? Hamilton, declining to be Commissioner to make peace with America, 30 Apr. 1814.

(*g*) Wills of William Hammond, 1832; Anthony Merry, 1835 (codicil); George Hammond (copy), 1877.

JOHNSON PAPERS. 1784-1885, n.d. (0616)

(*a*) Sir William Johnson (1715-74) and Sir John Johnson (1742-1830). Scrapbook, 1784-1885. Sir William and his son Sir John both held office as Superintendent of Indian Affairs in North America. Sir John commanded the Queen's Own American Regiment - 'Johnson's Greens' - during the War of Independence. The scrapbook contains letters, copies of letters, and notes on family history.

(*b*) 'Narrative of Lady Johnson.' Bound volume, n.d. Relates her adventures during the War of Independence.

(*c*) Johnson Family History. Notebook, n.d. Copied by Mrs. A.E.O. Chevallier from a collection of old letters made by her father, Vice-Admiral John Ormsby Johnson, and including notes by Sir John Johnson. Refers to North America.

HARROWBY PAPERS.[4] (1561)

The collection of 105 volumes contains some American items.

(*a*) Volume IX: General Correspondence, 1803-9.

Nos. 83-86. Lord Bathurst to Lord Harrowby, 30 July 1808, giving, *inter alia*, a detailed account of the causes of the quarrel with the United States over the right of search.

(*b*) Volume XI: General Correspondence, 1803-9.

Nos. 55-56. George III to Lord Harrowby, 2 Oct. 1804, on Spain, America, Russia, France.

(*c*) Volume XI: General Correspondence, 1803-9.

Nos. 120-1. Lord Melville to Lord Harrowby, 17 Sept. 1804: 'The power of France has laid hold of the rulers of America.'

(*d*) Volume XII: General Correspondence, 1803-9.

Nos. 39-40. William Pitt to Lord Harrowby, 18 Sept. 1804. No likelihood of a rupture between Spain and America.

Nos. 173-8. Earl of Warwick to Lord Harrowby, 27 June 1804. Covering two letters to the writer from Charles Vancouver: the first, 23 June 1804, concerns Vancouver's position in Kentucky, his knowledge of the United States, his acquaintance with Mme. Jerome Bonaparte, his fears of French designs in the United States, an offer of his services to the British government; the second, 18 July 1804, is on his secret mission to Holland.

Nos. 223-4. James Wormeley to Lord Harrowby, 27 Nov. 1804. Prospect of war with Spain, due to the latter's regret at loss of Louisiana, and fears for South American colonies; offering his services in Virginia.

(*e*) Volume XXXII.

pp. 1-10. Lord Bathurst, President of the Board of Trade, presumably to William R. Hamilton, Under Secretary for Foreign Affairs, 28 July 1811. Discusses the United States opposition to the British Orders in Council and the American refusal to let British men-of-war use their ports. It ends, 'I think some advantage might be derived from thus making an unpopular measure of their own government (the Non-Intercourse Act) the ground upon which a rupture takes place, if this question is so to end?' (Copy.)

(*f*) Volume XXXV: Miscellaneous Papers.

pp. 175-206. Report on Newfoundland, by John Reeves, Chief Justice, 1791.

pp. 207-64. Report on Newfoundland fisheries, 1792, 1795.

(*g*) Volume XCIV: Third series: Letters and Papers of Rt. Hon. Richard Ryder, Home Secretary 1809-12.

ff. 5-16. Memoranda on responsibility for government of the

3. Some of these have been published in *Letters and Papers of Charles, Lord Barham, Admiral of the Red Squadron 1758-1813*....3 vols. (London, 1907-11) (Publications of the Navy Records Society, vols. xxxii, xxxviii, xxxix).

4. See Bradford Perkins, 'George Canning, Great Britain and the United States', *American Historical Review*, vol. lxiii, pp. 1-22, 1957.

plantations; the first being an extract from a representation of the Board of Trade, 1721.

ff. 215-16. William Pinkney to R. Ryder, 4 Jan. 1810.

ff. 219-20. R. Ryder to William Pinkney, 4 Jan. 1810.

FLUDYER MAITLAND & CO. Business papers. 1790-1801. (3640)

(*a*) Valuation of lands in Luzerne County, Pa.; Alexandria, Va.; and Skin Bottom, Va.; note of lands about a hundred miles from Philadelphia, n.d.

(*b*) Letter, 2 June 1790, from Miers Fisher of Philadelphia to the firm of Fludyer Maitland & Co. of London, enclosing draft of declaration by John Maitland of London, merchant (trading with George Bridges Brudenell as the above firm), as to the indebtedness to him of William and Luke Morris, merchants, late of Philadelphia.

(*c*) Accounts of John Coles and John Maitland, 22 May 1801. References to Pennsylvania; Alexandria, Va.; and Skin Bottom, Va.

(*d*) Remarks of John Coles on the state of American property and investments. 2 June 1801.

There is also material relating to New Brunswick fisheries.

ANDRÉ, JOHN (1751-80). Envelope containing printed poem and letter. 1781. (4101)

(*a*) Printed poem. *Monody on Major André*, by Anna Seward, 1781.

(*b*) Letter, 1 Oct. 1780, from André to General Washington asking to be shot not hanged. (Copy?)

COKE MANUSCRIPTS. Diaries. 1832, 1866. (4221)

(*a*) Diaries and sketches written during a journey to the United States and Canada in 1832 by Edward Thomas Coke. These diaries evidently form the basis of a book published in 1833, *A Subaltern's Furlough*, by E.T. Coke, Lieutenant of the 45th Regiment (New York and London, 1833).

(*b*) Diary of S.T. Coke from 1 Jan. 1866 to Dec. 1866 during military duty at Montreal.

WEST, JAMES (1704?-72). Letters from correspondents in America. 1750's. (4349)

One bundle of letters and papers relating to Major General Braddock's expedition to North America.

HAYWARD, JACOB SCOTT. Diary. 1839-60. (4595)

Diary of Jacob Scott Hayward, 1839-60, chiefly on social matters, including information on two years spent in the United States from 1842 to 1844.

SEATON PAPERS. 1828-67. (5288)

Sir John Colborne, 1st Baron Seaton (1778-1863), was Governor-General and Commander-in-Chief of Canada during the Canadian rebellion of 1838. The collection includes his private letters, official papers, memoranda, speeches, and reports concerning Canada.

SANDWICH PAPERS.[5] Volume of treaties; letters. 1739-78. (5472)

John Montagu, 4th Earl of Sandwich (1718-92), First Lord of the Admiralty 1763-5 and 1771-82. The packet of letters contains copies of letters concerning the attack on St. Lucia and other West Indian islands, 1778. The collection of treaties contains some papers relating to boundaries of Florida, Carolina, etc., 1739.

PRATT, JOHN. 14 letters. 1779-1805. (5972)

John Pratt served in the 4th (American) Pioneer Regiment during the War of Independence and during subsequent Indian wars. The letters are military orders or discuss military operations.

BAGOT PAPERS. 1814-40. (6234)

In this large collection of family papers the papers of Sir Charles Bagot (1781-1843), Minister to the United States 1815-20, Governor-General of Canada 1841-3, contain American material.

(*a*) One volume 'Negotiations at Ghent', 1814, concerning North America, Canada, West Florida, etc.

(*b*) From two boxes containing bound volumes entitled 'Letters and Papers of Sir Charles Bagot, G.C.B.': Series II, vols. 1-7, 1815-9.[6]

Volume 1: Official, to Secretary of State for Foreign Affairs.

Volume 2: Official and private, to Secretary of State for Foreign Affairs.

Volume 3: Official, from Secretary of State for Foreign Affairs.

Volumes 4 and 5: Correspondence with Secretary of State of United States.

Volume 6: Canada, 1816-9.

Volume 7: Consuls - Appendix.

(*c*) Letters from various correspondents, not all of them addressed to Bagot, regarding public affairs, Russia, U.S.A., etc., received probably in Russia, 1820-2.

(*d*) Two documents concerning Canada, dated 1819 and 1840, the first with regard to a banknote forgery.

(*e*) Birth certificates and some private correspondence in America.

TARLETON PAPERS. Correspondence. 1776-84. (7189)

Thirty-one letters, 1776-84, from Gen. Sir Banastre Tarleton (1754-1833) to his mother and brother John, some of which mention the American campaign.

See also Tarleton Papers, Central Libraries, Liverpool (p. 181).

ASTLEY PAPERS. Account. 1772-83. (7293)

Brief chronological account of the adventures of Eli Heywood during the years 1772 to 1783. He left England in the *Industry*, a ship commanded by Capt. Lowe, which was bound for Richmond, Va. Heywood was eventually taken prisoner during the American War of Independence.

BERNARD FAMILY PAPERS. (7343)

Includes several of Sir Francis Bernard (1712-79), Governor of New Jersey 1758-60, and of Massachusetts 1760-71.

(*a*) Official - England. 1789-91.

Files of correspondence, 1789-91, from various correspondents and about a number of subjects, including the Province of Quebec. (OE/4/1-14)

(*b*) Official - Ireland. 1782-4.

Correspondence, 1782-4: Scrope Bernard-Morland and Walter Logan, an American pensioner. (OI/13/1-7(b))

5. Some published in *The Private Papers of John, Earl of Sandwich, First Lord of the Admiralty 1771-1782*, ed. by E.R. Barnes and J.H. Owen. 4 vols. (London, 1932-8) (Publications of the Navy Records Society, lxix, lxxi, lxxv, lxxxviii).

6. See Bradford Perkins, 'George Canning, Great Britain and the United States', *American Historical Review*, vol. lxiii, pp. 1-22, 1957.

(*c*) Personal papers - appointments. 1738-1899.

(i) Commissions, passports, etc. 1738-1899, including Francis Bernard's commission as Governor-in-Chief of the Provinces of New Jersey and Massachusetts Bay. (PFF/1-22(b))

(ii) Orders, 27 May 1761, issued to Francis Bernard, Esq., Captain-General and Governor of the Province of Massachusetts Bay, New England, relating to the trade and navigation laws of Great Britain and her colonies in America. (J/152(a))

(*d*) Personal papers - correspondence. 1773.
Richard Morland, 1773, to his brother from New York. (P343/1)

(*e*) Charities. 1789-1858.
Correspondence, 1789-1858, with various charities, including a college in Nova Scotia. (PFH/1/1-32)

(*f*) Miscellaneous. n.d.
Extract, n.d., from journal of a march from Quebec to settlements in New England. (M/78)

LADY HUNTINGDON'S AMERICAN PAPERS. (12352)

I. Students' Papers. 1770-1780's.

(*a*) About twenty letters, 1770-4, from various correspondents in America to Selina, Countess of Huntingdon (1707-91), mostly about religious matters. Writers include Phillis Wheatley and Anthony Benezet. This group also contains miscellaneous documents and printed matter. (A3/1)

(*b*) Lists and inventories, 1770-80, of Negroes, lands, etc., at Bethesda, [Ga.] (A3/2)

(*c*) About twenty letters and documents, 1772-9, from various correspondents, mostly to the Countess of Huntingdon. These include an account of rice plantations and a note concerning a boundary dispute in Susquehannah. (A3/3)

(*d*) Sixteen letters, 1772-3, from various correspondents in Georgia to the Countess of Huntingdon. (A3/4)

(*e*) Twenty-four letters, 1770-3, from correspondents in Georgia, New York, etc., to the Countess of Huntingdon. (A3/5)

(*f*) About twenty letters, 1773-5, from correspondents in America, mostly to the Countess of Huntingdon. (A3/6)

(*g*) Numerous letters and papers from America, 1779-83, largely to the Countess of Huntingdon. Includes Bethesda accounts (1779-82), bonds for and lists of Negroes at Bethesda, and information on the cultivation of rice at Bethesda (1778-80). Many letters from Henry Laurens to the Countess. (A3/7-10)

(*h*) Many letters and papers, 1780's, from Americans to the Countess of Huntingdon, with some copies of return correspondence from her. Several letters from George Washington (1783 and 1785). (A3/11-12)

II. Piercy's Letters. 1773-84.

(*a*) About forty letters, 1773-7, almost all from William Piercy in America to the Countess of Huntingdon. Also some copies of return correspondence from the Countess to Piercy. (A4/1-3)

(*b*) Various letters and documents (some copies), 1774-83, relating to America. Includes letter, 25 Feb. 1781, from Sir James Wright in Savannah, Ga., to Lord George Germain. (A4/4)

(*c*) Various letters and documents, 1771-84, many pertaining to America and to slavery in Bethesda. (A4/5-7)

Lady Huntingdon's American Papers also contain references to her Connexion's American activities in the letters of Robert Keen and others, 1770-8, and in the American account books for 1772-9. (A1 and A2)

NEW COLLEGE ARCHIVES. (13042)

New College, London, was a divinity school of the University of London, intended primarily for the training of men and women for the Congregational ministry. It was closed in 1977, and the bulk of its contents transferred to Dr. Williams' Library, London.

I. Main Series.

(*a*) Packet labelled 'Papers relating to the Legacy of the Rev. Andrew Bennett (or Bennet) of Barbadoes. . . including several long and curious letters from the Testator'. Contains a few letters from Bennett to Joseph Stonard, 1801-2, discussing the advisability of investments in America and commenting on developments in transport and agriculture in the U.S. (278/1, 2). Also contains various other items relating to America and American trade in the early nineteenth century.

(*b*) Letter, New York, 21 Mar. 1831, from Rev. John Hill to Thomas Wilson. Describes his experiences in the U.S. (299/2)

II. Literary Manuscripts.

(*a*) Several letters, 1748-50, from Aaron Burr, Newark, N.J., to Dr. Philip Doddridge. (L1/4/154-7)

(*b*) Letter, 8 Mar. 1830, from Rev. W.B. Sprague, Albany, N.Y., to Rev. Thomas Lewis of Islington, describing his new charge. (L52/5/21)

(*c*) Four letters, 1833-4, concerning the delegation to the Presbyterian and Congregational churches of the U.S.A. (L52/5/47-8, 53, 57)

(*d*) Letter, 29 Aug. 1840, from the New York General Congregational Association to the Congregational Union of England and Wales. Welcomes the idea of close relationships, and expresses its desire for the abolition of slavery. (L52/5/127)

(*e*) Letter, 22 July 1817, from Edward Busk. Commentary on Mr. Bromley's opinions on support for the North American Indian Institution. (L53/1/38)

(*f*) 'Extract from Mr. Davis's Letter to Mr. Forset [or Fawcet]'; two copies in different hands of letter reporting missionary work in Virginia, n.d. (L61/3)

(*g*) 'An Extract from Mr. Davis's Letter' and 'An Extract from Mr. Tods' Letter'; missionary reports, n.d. (L61/4)

(*h*) Letter, 13 Nov. 1739, from John Brainerd to Dr. Philip Doddridge, from Bethel [the Indian town], N.J. (L1/4/124)

PALMERSTON PAPERS.

The papers of Henry John Temple, 3rd Viscount Palmerston (1784-1865) have been indexed and listed by the Royal Commission on Historical Manuscripts, and they remain at present on the Commission's premises. Students may read the papers in the Commission's search room (Quality House, Quality Court, Chancery Lane, London WC2A 1HP). Special permission is not required, but readers are asked to order the material they require twenty-four hours in advance. The Trustees do not normally grant permission for microfilming or photocopying. A typescript list (N.R.A. report 12889) is available in the search room, and may also be consulted in certain national libraries and repositories.

Some of the papers listed below are, of course, copies of, or copied in, papers in the Public Record Office and elsewhere, but certainly there are a large number of papers both unique and important.[7]

I. North American Boundary Questions. 1837-59.

(*a*) Letter from Henry Stephen Fox, concerning the north-east boundary of the U.S.A., 1837. (GC/FO/166)

7. Some of these papers were used by Sir Charles Kingsley Webster in his *Foreign Policy of Palmerston, 1830-1841: Britain, the Liberal Movement and the Eastern Question*, 2 vols. (London, 1951).

(*b*) Letter to Dr. James McHenry, 1839, returning Mr. Trevor's letter on prospects of a peaceful settlement to the boundary question. (GC/MA/35)
(*c*) Letter from Sir William Molesworth, 1839, M.P. for Leeds, giving notice of questions he intends to put on American boundary question. (GC/MO/2)
(*d*) James Harvey, from New York, to William Brown, of Brown, Shipley & Co., Liverpool: on the North American boundary question and the danger of delay in settlement. 1 Apr. 1840. (MM/US/4)
(*e*) Copy of memorandum of state of North American boundary question: instructions of Lord Palmerston to take copy and send original to Lord Melbourne. 4 May 1840. (MM/US/5)
(*f*) Four letters, 1843, to and from A.B. Ashburton, who negotiated for the English in the boundary controversy. (GC/AS/2-5)
(*g*) Letter, 1844, from William Anson, engaged in tracing the New England boundary line in accordance with the Treaty of Washington. (GC/AN/22)
(*h*) Extract of letter, 14 May 1846, from Boston giving character of American statesmen and regarding the boundary question. (MM/US/7)
(*i*) Note of Lord Palmerston, 12 Feb. 1849, asking for copy of question and answer to Parliament in 1842 or 1843 concerning some papers on the American boundary question presented to Congress. Reply of F.O. clerk enclosing copy of a question and answer concerning the Boundary Commission's report. (MM/US/8)
(*j*) Letter, 16 July 1859, from the Duke of Newcastle, concerning an American claim and including supporting correspondence. (GN/NE/76-79)

II. Defence of Canada and the American Civil War. 1861-5.
(*a*) Letter from the Duke of Newcastle, 30 Aug. 1861, against the sending of more troops to Canada. (GC/NE/98)
(*b*) Letter, 30 Nov. 1861, from Sir James Fergusson concerning the line of march for British reinforcements between Halifax, N.S., and Rivière du Loup, Quebec. (GC/FE/19)
(*c*) Memorandum from Lord Monck, Governor-General of Canada, to Sir George Lewis: defence of Canada in the event of an American invasion. 22 Aug. 1862. (MM/CA/1)
(*d*) Secret print of memorandum by W.E. Gladstone, 25 Oct. 1862, for use of the Cabinet, on the war in America. (MM/US/20)
(*e*) Letter, 30 Dec. 1862, from Sir George Cornewall Lewis, concerning the defence of Canada, with an enclosure on the cost of permanent works, including purchase of land, recommended by the Defence Commissioners for Canada. (GC/LE/167)
(*f*) Confidential report (printed), 12 July 1864, on the defence of Canada, from the commission under the general guidance of Sir John Fox Burgoyne. Initialled 'W.E.G.' (William Ewart Gladstone). (MM/CA/2)
(*g*) Memorandum by the defence committee on the report by Lieutenant-Colonel Jervois on the defence of Canada, 1864. Received 17 May 1865. (MM/CA/3)

III. The American Civil War: Diplomatic Correspondence and Personal Observations. 1861-4.
(*a*) Minute of Evelyn Ashley to Lord Palmerston, 23 Oct. 1861, enclosing printed copy of speech by W. Porcher Miles, of South Carolina, in which secession from the Union is mentioned. (MM/US/14)
(*b*) Lord Derby, enclosing Sir James Fergusson's account of his visit to the Union and Confederate armies, Nov. 1861. (19 pages.) (GC/DE/69-70)
(*c*) Part of a letter, 1 Dec. 1861, from Sir Charles Wood on war preparation against America. (CAB/A/146)
(*d*) 13 and 15 Oct. 1862. Printed Foreign Office memoranda by Russell urging compulsory mediation. Also printed memorandum, 17 Oct., by Sir George Cornewall Lewis, opposing these, and Russell's answer to Lewis in a further memorandum of 24 Oct. (MM/US/16-19)
(*e*) Palmerston to John Arthur Roebuck, M.P., urging him to adjourn the debate on his motion demanding recognition of the Confederacy. 9 July 1863. (GC/RO/5)
(*f*) Foreign Office paper, 25 Jan. 1864, relating to the *Chesapeake* affair. (MM/US/21)
(*g*) Memorandum, 1864, concerning a question by Roebuck in the House of Commons on alleged Union recruitment in Ireland. (MM/US/22)

IV. General Diplomatic Correspondence. 1832-65.
(*a*) U.S.A., 1832-41: Thirty-three letters, mainly between Palmerston and Andrew Stevenson, U.S. Minister in London, 1836-41, but some from Aaron Vail, U.S. *Chargé* in London, to Palmerston. Also three from Martin Van Buren, two slight notes while in England, but a long letter from Washington, D.C., 3 Mar. 1836, on relations between America and France.
(*b*) Sixteen letters and draft dispatches to and from Charles Bankhead, *chargé d'affaires* in U.S.A., 1835-6. (GC/BA/241-256)
(*c*) Memorandum on the stages of the dispute between America and France on the settlement of American claims, with annexure. 11 Dec. 1835. (MM/US/1)
(*d*) Anonymous letter, 28 Mar. 1836, to Lord Palmerston: enclosing cutting from a letter from the U.S. approving of Lord Palmerston's conduct in mediating in the French dispute. (MM/US/2)
(*e*) Anonymous letter, 16 Oct. 1836, from New York to Lord Melbourne concerning the conduct of the Resident British Consul at New York in the cause of Francis Wyse *v.* James Buchanan, and enclosing a printed pamphlet on the subject. (MM/US/3)
(*f*) Several letters, 1830's, to and from Sir Charles Richard Vaughan on the French and American quarrel and English steps to mediate between them. (GC/VA)
(*g*) Letter from Major J. Richardson, 1837, suggesting plans for the improvement of the government of Canada. (GC/RI/6)
(*h*) Letter from Thomas Morgan, 1837, proposing means for preparing to meet and counter the aggression of America and Russia. (GC/MO/148)
(*i*) Three letters, 1838, from Henry Francis Roper-Curzon, 14th Baron Teynham, on American affairs. (GC/TE/374-376)
(*j*) John W. Cowell, an agent in the U.S. of the Bank of England, from Philadelphia, to Timothy Abraham Curtis, Governor of the Bank, transmitting the plan below. 24 Mar. 1839. (GC/CU/6)
(*k*) Letter, 22 Apr. 1839, from Curtis, enclosing 'a Plan' drawn up by Cowell, 24 Mar. 1839, 'for hostile operations against the United States in the event of war with them'. (GC/CU/7-8)
(*l*) Letter from John Abel Smith enclosing a further memorandum on the same subject as that of 24 Mar. 1839, sent to him by Cowell, who had just returned from the United States.
Smith said that the memorandum had been sent to the Horse Guards by Col. William Napier, who had also submitted a plan of his own, but that the Duke of Wellington had preferred Cowell's. The plan turned upon political and economic means of 'liberating' the South from dependence on the North. Signed and dated, 5 Mar. 1841. (GC/SM/15)
(*m*) Twenty-five letters to and from Gen. James Hamilton to Palmerston, 1840-1, mainly relating to Texas. (GC/HA/174-198)
(*n*) Letter, 1840, from Major C.F. Head, discussing possible improvements in British North American provinces. (GC/HE/1)
(*o*) Letter, 1846, fromWilliam Peter, discussing the state of opinion

in the United States. (GC/PE/112)
(*p*) Letters, including one from A. O'Reilly, 1850, about the U.S.A. and Cuba. (GC/NO/324-365)
(*q*) Memorandum, 1850, from Lord John Russell, concerning an overture to France and the U.S.A. on the slave trade. (GC/RU/)
(*r*) Memorandum by Lord Palmerston on a draft from Lord Clarendon to Mr. Crampton about American destruction of Grey Town. 10 Sept. 1854. (MM/US/11)
(*s*) F.O. memorandum on motion of Mr. Monckton Milnes for protection of American merchant seamen on the high seas. 1 Aug. 1859. (MM/US/12)
(*t*) One letter, 1863, from Edward Yates, offering information on the state of affairs in the U.S.A. (GC/YA/1)
(*u*) Comparison of the navies of Great Britain, France, and the United States. Jan. 1865. (ND/D/30)

V. Miscellaneous. 1841-64.
(*a*) Memorandum as to the laws which exist in the Southern states of the United States with respect to free persons of colour. 4 Mar. 1841. (MM/US/6)
(*b*) Letter from Samuel Paull, 1852, on the increase of prices resulting from discoveries of gold in California and Australia. (GC/PA/191)
(*c*) Letter from William Mountford, 1854, noting that voting by ballot in the U.S.A. is not secret. (GC/MO/174)
(*d*) Letter, 1859, from Evelyn Ashley in South Carolina, to the Earl of Shaftesbury, concerning slavery. (SHA/PC/7)
(*e*) Five letters from the Duke of Newcastle, 1860, describing the Prince of Wales' visit to Canada and the U.S.A. (GC/NE/80-84)
(*f*) Extract of a fulsome letter, 1860, from Charles Sumner about a visit to the Speaker of the House of Commons. (GC/SU/84)
(*g*) Letter, 31 Aug. 1860, from J.P. Coppinger, Adjutant of the 9th Regiment, New York City Guard, requesting permission to visit England in uniform. (GC/CO/38)
(*h*) Diaries of Henry John Temple, 3rd Viscount Palmerston, 1806-64; include very occasional references to America and American affairs, e.g., a note of a striking speech made in 1860 by Mr. Gregory, M.P. for Galway, who spoke on the 'ruinous effects of Democracy in America'. (D20)

C. HOARE & CO., 37 Fleet Street, London EC4P 4DQ

BRAY, DR. THOMAS (1656-1730). Accounts: 1 notebook. 1700-04.
Clergyman. The notebook contains various accounts, mainly 'benefactions, missions, and libraries' for Maryland. Part I contains Bray's accounts for 1700 and 1701, with the report of the committee of the Society for the Propagation of the Gospel which examined these; Part II brings the accounts up to Lady Day, 1704; Part III relates to libraries 'rais'd or augmented' both abroad and at home.

MISCELLANEOUS HOLDINGS. 1775-93.
(*a*) Two papers, written in Boston, 14 June 1775. One certifies on behalf of the Governor, Thomas Gage, that Peter Oliver is Chief Justice of Massachusetts Bay; and the other is a power of attorney given to Hoare's by William Burch, one of the Massachusetts Bay Commissioners of the Customs.
(*b*) 'Suffering Clergy'; three letters, 1776 and 1777. The Bank acted as the agent for a fund collected in England to aid the 'suffering clergy' in America, and three letters reporting to the Bank the drawing of £50 from this fund are held. These are from W. Serjeant, Boston; William Clark, Boston ('Missionary for the Venble. Society etc. in Stoughton & Dedham, New England'); and John Tyler, Norwich in New England.
(*c*) Three papers relating to the purchase of $5,000 in United States loan stock by William Rawson & Co. of London, 5 Feb. 1793, through George Morewood of New York.

BANK'S LEDGER. 1789-1895.
The ledger entries give details of investment by Hoare's Bank in the following American concerns:
American Debentures, opened 18 Nov. 1789;
St. Paul-Minneapolis Railway, opened 1891, closed 11 Aug. 1896;
United States Brewery Co., opened 1892;
Pennsylvania Railway Co., opened 4 Jan. 1892, closed 13 July 1895;
New York Central Railway, opened 4 Jan. 1892, closed 11 July 1895;
Chicago, Milwaukee, and St. Paul Railway, opened 14 Jan. 1892, closed 13 July 1893;
Illinois Central Railway, opened 17 Feb. 1892, closed 14 Mar. 1892;
United States Government 4 per cent., opened 3 Apr., closed 10 Apr. 1895.

THE LIBRARY, HOUSE OF COMMONS, Westminster, London SW1A OAA

As will appear under the entry for the House of Lords Record Office, that other place is the main repository of Parliamentary Records.[1] But there are two series peculiar to the House of Commons. It must be borne in mind that the Library of the House of Commons is a private one intended solely for the use of Members of Parliament; yet despite its private nature and its primary duty to assist Members, the Library has been willing on occasion to help *bona fide* students to use material which does not exist in any other accessible source. The two series are:

UNPRINTED PAPERS. 1851-to date.
The vast majority of these consist of Statutory Instruments which are later published; the unpublished material is simply that which government departments have thought to be of so little public interest as not to be worth publishing. All these papers are indexed, of course, in the printed *Journals* of the House (see introduction to House of Lords Record Office, below) and thus their titles can be traced. But it appears that students only very rarely find any need to consult the unpublished items. Students wishing to do so, however, should apply to the Speaker through the Librarian.

DEPOSITED PAPERS.
These papers are deposited by Ministers in the Library for the information of Members, usually in connexion with a parliamentary question. Since they are occasionally deposited subject to the condition that they are not to be published, the Library invariably refers outside inquirers to the issuing department. The existence of such papers can be established through the *Official Report of Parliamentary Debates, House of Commons* (Hansard).

1. The Library of the House of Commons was, of course, destroyed in the fire of 1834.

THE RECORD OFFICE, HOUSE OF LORDS, Westminster, London SW1A OPW

The House of Lords Record Office in the Victoria Tower at Westminster is (as is plainly not widely realized) the general archive of Parliament. The Commons (see above) possess no Record Office of their own. Apart from two sets of records which have been deposited in the Commons Library, practically all original parliamentary papers of post-1497 date that have been kept by or restored to the parliamentary record officers have come to rest in the vertiginous confines of the Victoria Tower.

All intending researchers are asked to write to the Clerk of the Records at least two days before their first visit, explaining the nature of their research and, if possible, the specific documents they wish to consult. No special passes or introductions are required.

The materials are immense in both mass and variety; but they can be approached through five main guides within the House of Lords Records Office.[1]

1. *General Index to the Journals of the House of Lords,* 1509-to date, taken together with the *General Index to the Commons' Journals,* 1547-to date. These make a complete guide to the formal history of parliamentary transactions. A parliamentary journal, however, is a highly artificial composition, made up from the records and minutes of the clerks some time after the frequently crowded, informal, and even nocturnal events; it does not lie, but it may not always tell the whole truth. There are two sets of papers that stand between the transactions of the Lords and the final record, and which may sometimes be instructively compared with the latter. These are the Manuscript Minutes, and the Clerks' Assistants sheets. The Minutes have been printed since 1825.

2. *Indexes to the Lords' and Commons' Journals.* That is, the index at the back of each sessional volume,[2] which have been found to be somewhat easier to use, and perhaps more reliable, than the *General Index* series.

3. *Indexes to Accounts and Papers, Reports of Commissioners, Estimates, etc.,* 1801 onwards. A great deal of historical source material coming before Parliament is contained in the two printed series of accounts of numerous transactions delivered to either House. Reports known to have been submitted in this form, or to have subsequently been ordered to be printed, may sometimes be more easily found through the *Index to Accounts and Papers* than in the other indexes mentioned, though strictly speaking everything mentioned in the *Accounts* indexes for the Lords and Commons must be duplicated in one of the others.

4. 'House of Lords Papers.' Manuscript List in the H.L.R.O. Search Room. This list (which continues in brief form the printed Calendars, 1497-1718, mentioned in footnote one.) is planned to include all papers laid before the House of Lords and now preserved in the Victoria Tower. It has by diligent perseverance been brought down to 1913 and inches its way forward every day.

5. *Guide to the Records of Parliament,* by M.F. Bond (1971). The *Guide* contains the following sections: (i) Records of the House of Lords; (ii) Records of the House of Commons; (iii) Records of the Lord Great Chamberlain; (iv) Records of the Clerk of the Crown; (v) Other Records of Palace of Westminster (Statute Law Committee; Scottish Commissions, 1803-56; Sir John George Shaw-LeFevre Papers; Exchequer Chief Usher Papers); (vi) Historical Collections of the House of Lords Record Office, of the House of Lords Library, and of the House of Commons Library. Printed as well as manuscript records are described.

It will be useful to note the differences between the parliamentary transactions as recorded by the *Journals* and the extant documents as recorded in the Manuscript List. There have been many transactions of which no account has got into the archives. Some of the papers seem to have missed their way at the beginning; others have strayed; but some, fortunately, have been brought back, as in the case of the important Braye Manuscripts, acquired 1952-62, from Lord Braye. Students should go to the *Journals* to find out what happened in Parliament and then to the Manuscript List to find out whether the relevant documents have been preserved. It may be added that while the index entries are self-explanatory, those in the Manuscript List are very brief, and will be of most use to those who already know fairly well what kind of detail they are looking for and in what categories it will fall.

Records pertaining to American history before 1718 are calendared in the volumes noted;[3] those before 1783 are listed in Andrews & Davenport, pp. 189-272; the succeeding period to 1903 is covered by Paullin & Paxson, pp. 326-60. In the present survey, the work of Andrews & Davenport *has been taken as read*, but that of Paullin & Paxson has been *supplemented* by two further lists:

(*a*) A fuller guide just for 1787 to 1902 has been provided through a search of the Manuscript List referred to above, which did not exist in Paullin & Paxson's day. This, of course, is a *supplement* to their list and *not* a replacement.

(*b*) The list of references has been brought down from 1904 to 1953 by use of the indexes to the sessional *Lords' Journals.*

The example of Paullin & Paxson has been followed in omitting references to slavery and the slave trade. Many of these references, which are numerous throughout the period, refer to the United States; many do not. Students of those subjects will want to treat them in their entirety, which would not have been practical here. Trade returns are also omitted for similar reasons (these are normally found in the first quarter of each year). The texts of treaties have also been excluded, as these have been published in the Treaty Series since 1892. Further equipment for the study of the parliamentary records is provided by several pamphlets issued gratis by the House of Lords Record Office:

The Journals, Minutes and Committee Books of the House of Lords (London, 1957). (Records Office Memorandum No. 13.)

Select List of Classes of Records in the House of Lords Record Office (revised edition, 1973).

P. and G. Ford, *A Guide to Parliamentary Papers* (Irish University Press, 3rd ed., 1972), may also be referred to, though it does not concern itself with manuscript records.

The sessional *Lords' Journals* are hereafter referred to as L.J.

Additions to Paullin & Paxson, pp. 329-60, from 'House of Lords Papers' Manuscript List, 1787-1902.

1787, Apr. 2. American Debts Bill. (L.J. 37, p. 644)

1789, July 20. Tobacco Duty Bill: petition against, of several manufacturers of tobacco. (L.J. 38, p. 505)

1789, July 23. Tobacco Duty Bill: petition against, Corporation of London (rejected) Evidence (printed and manuscript). (L.J. 38, p. 509)

1789, July 31. Tobacco: accounts of imports and exports, etc. (L.J. 38, p. 514)

1790, May 5. Tobacco Duty Bill: petition against, of manufacturers of tobacco in the Port of London. (L.J. 38, p. 618)

1790, May 5. Trade with North West coast of America and Southern Whale Fishery: motion for state of. (L.J. 38, p. 622)

1790, May 7. Tobacco and snuff: accounts re. (L.J. 38, pp. 625-7)

1790, May 10. Southern Whale Fishery: state of. (L.J. 38, p. 626)

1. Documents to 1693 were calendared by the H.M.C. (see full list of their reports in Andrews & Davenport, p. 189). Material to 1718 calendared in *Manuscripts of the House of Lords* (New Series), vols. i-xii, 1693/5-1718 (London, 1900-76).
2. Only from 1820 for the *Lords' Journals.*
3. See footnote 1, above.

1790, May 14-28. Tobacco Duty Bill: evidence taken at Bar, with printed copy. (L.J. 38, p. 633)

1790, May 21. Tobacco, account of, delivered for home trade. (L.J. 38, p. 647)

1790, May 31. Tobacco: accounts re.; three accounts (L.J. 38, p. 657)

1790, Dec. 23. Whale fisheries and Northern lighthouses: two accounts (L.J. 39, p. 33)

1792, Feb. 29. Whale fisheries: accounts. (L.J. 30, p. 291)

1793, Jan. 7. Whale fisheries and Northern lighthouses: two accounts. (L.J. 39, p. 512)

1794, Mar. 24. Whale fisheries and Northern lighthouses: two accounts. (L.J. 40, p. 86)

1794, May 26. Differences between the United States and Indian tribes, motion for address for instructions to Lord Dorchester *re* (negatived). (L.J. 40, p. 215)

1795, Feb. 19. Whale fisheries and Northern lighthouses: two accounts. (L.J. 40, p. 308)

1796, May 14. Cotton wool imported: account delivered. (L.J. 40, p. 745)

1796, Oct. 19. Explanatory article to American Treaty. (L.J. 41, p. 24)

1797, Mar. 16. Whale fisheries and Northern lighthouses: accounts *re*. (L.J. 41, p. 130)

1799, May 27. West India Islands: motion for accounts of imports and exports, etc. Secret committee, report from. Annexed, printed. (L.J. 42, pp. 222-4)

1799, June 21, Vessels which entered and cleared West India Islands: account. (L.J. 42, p. 279)

1799, July 1-4. London Port Bill. Petitions, in support, of planters, merchants, and ship owners in West Indian trade; against, of London sugar refiners; and of ship owners trading from London (L.J. 42, pp. 302-13)

1800, Feb. 25. Whale fisheries and Northern lighthouses: accounts. (L.J. 42, p. 380)

1800, July 10. Foreign wheat imported into Port of London: account (L.J. 42, p. 620)

1801, Dec. 4. Whale fisheries: accounts. (L.J. 43, p. 423)

1803, Feb. 10. Convention with America. (L.J. 44, p. 53)

1807, June 29. American commerce: Order in Council *re*. (L.J. 46, p. 218)

1807, June 30. American commerce: motions for accounts respecting, etc., four motions. (L.J. 46, p. 224)

1807, July 18. American trade with Ireland, papers: five returns with a covering letter. ~~(L.J. 46, p. 269)~~ No LJ Ref.

1808, Feb. 4. Message from President of United States to Congress: motion for address for. Declaration of H.M. plenipotentiaries to America: motion for address for (negatived). (L.J. 46, p. 427)

1808, Feb. 15. Neutral vessels brought in under Orders of Council, motion for account of; Orders of Council: motion for a committee to consider. (L.J. 46, p. 436)

1808, Feb. 18. Message of President of the United States to Congress, etc; and communications with America *re*. French decree, three motions *re*. (L.J. 46, pp. 442-3)

1808, Feb. 26. Neutral vessels brought in under Orders of Council, etc.: two motions for. (L.J. 46, p. 454)

1808, Mar. 7. Answer to Mr. Madison's note: motion for address for (negatived). (L.J. 46, p. 471)

1808, Mar. 8. Orders of Council *re* neutral commerce: motion on (negatived). (L.J. 46, p. 473)

1808, Mar. 10. Vessels entered and cleared Port of London: account of. (L.J. 46, p. 477)

1808, Mar. 17. Orders in Council: motion for committee on (negatived); Orders in Council: petition against, from merchants of Kingston-upon-Hull. (L.J. 46, p. 494)

1808, Mar. 18. Orders in Council: petition against, of merchants and manufacturers of Manchester; annexed, motion for petitioners to be heard by Counsel (negatived). (L.J. 46, p. 504)

1808, Mar. 22. Orders in Council: motion to refer to a Committee of Whole (withdrawn). (L.J. 46, p. 506)

1808, Mar. 23. Orders in Council: motion for them to be referred to Committee of Whole, with petitions. Motion for amendment to this. (L.J. 46, p. 508)

1808, Mar. 24. Orders in Council: motion for address for. (L.J. 46, p. 510)

1808, Mar. 28. Orders in Council: message to Commons for evidence (L.J. 46, pp. 516-7)

1808, Mar. 29. Orders in Council: motions *re*, five motions (negatived). (L.J. 46, pp. 523-4)

1808, Mar. 31. Orders in Council: copies of six orders. (L.J. 46, p. 527)

1808, May 5. Orders in Council: evidence of Commons on. (L.J. 46, p. 595)

1809, Jan. 23. Orders in Council: motion for address for correspondence with the United States respecting. (L.J. 47, p. 15)

1809, Feb. 10. America: two motions for addresses for papers *re*. (L.J. 46, p. 37)

1809, Feb. 17. America: motion for address *re* (negatived). (L.J. 47, p. 50)

1809, Feb. 23. Letter from Canning to Pinkney and answer: motion for address for. (L.J. 47, p. 58)

1809, Apr. 17. America: motions *re* (negatived). (L.J. 47, p. 148)

1809, Apr. 26. America: motions for address for papers *re* (negatived). (L.J. 47, p. 180)

1809, May 3. America: motion for address *re* (negatived). (L.J. 47, p. 221)

1810, Feb. 1. America: list of papers *re*, ten papers. (L.J. 47, p. 434)

1810, Feb. 5. America: two motions for papers *re*. (L.J. 47, p. 435)

1810, After Feb. 16. Ireland: account of vessels and men and boys employed in them that entered and cleared ports of Ireland in three years ended 5 Jan. 1810, etc. (No L.J. ref.)

1810, May 25. Trade and navigation commercial licenses: motions for accounts respecting. (L.J. 47, pp. 699-700)

1810, June 5. British and foreign ships in Commission and in ordinary, returns of: schedule and four returns. (L.J. 47, pp. 730-1)

1811, Mar. 28. Dollars: papers *re*. (L.J. 48, p. 158)

1811, Mar. 29. Dollars: paper *re* circulation of bank dollar tokens. (L.J. 48, p. 162)

1812, Jan. 9. Naval timber, etc.: accounts *re*, four accounts. (L.J. 48, p. 516)

1812, Feb. 24. Orders of Council: *re* specie and grain, eight orders. (L.J. 48, p. 596)

1812, Feb. 25. Vessels and tonnage, etc.: motion for account *re*. (L.J. 48, p. 598)

1812, Feb. 28. Message from Commons for attendance of Lord Grenville at committee *re* American claims. (L.J. 48, p. 609)

1812, Mar. 5. Message from Commons for Earl of Liverpool to attend committee *re* American claims. (L.J. 48, p. 620)

1812, Mar. 5. Revenue, trade and navigation, etc. (Ireland) accounts *re*: list and three accounts, one missing. (L.J. 48, p. 621)

1812, Mar. 23. British and foreign manufactures: motion for statement *re*. (L.J. 48, p. 662)

1812, Apr. 10. Imports and exports, grain and spirits (Ireland), motion for accounts *re*. (L.J. 48, p. 697)

1812, Apr. 13. Cottons, etc.: statement *re*. (L.J. 48, p. 700)

1812, Apr. 24. Orders in Council: declaration of Prince Regent re. (L.J. 48, p. 761)

1812, May 5. Same entry. (L.J. 48, p. 810)

1812, May 14. Imports and exports between Great Britain and the United States: account of, motion for. (L.J. 48, p. 838)

1812, June 12. Committee on petitions against Orders in Council: papers laid before. (L.J. 48, p. 894)

1813, Feb. 18. America: motion for address re. (L.J. 49, p. 95)

1813, Mar. 31. British naval force on American stations: motion for statement of the. (L.J. 49, p. 245)

1813, Apr. 7. American coast, motion for, account of ships on the. (L.J. 49, p. 281)

1813, Apr. 12. Troops in America - ships taken by the Americans, etc.: motion for six papers re. (L.J. 49, p. 294)

1813, May 1. Court martial of officers and crew of the *Java*: motion for address for proceedings of the. (L.J. 49, p. 337)

1813, May 14. War with America: motion for a committee re (negatived). (L.J. 49, p. 391)

1813, June 23. Cotton Trade (Ireland) Bill (printed with manuscript amendment). (L.J. 49, p. 528)

1814, Apr. 4. Ships of war built in private yards, and oak timber. (L.J. 49, pp. 774-5)

1814, Nov. 15. War in America: motion for five papers re. (L.J. 50, p. 13)

1814, Dec. 1. American War: papers, list and five papers. (L.J. 50, pp. 34-5)

1815, Feb. 9. American War: motions for papers re. (L.J. 50, pp. 49-50)

1815, Feb. 15. Frigates *Prompte* and *Psyche*: motion for letter re. (L.J. 50, p. 50)

1815, Feb. 20. American War: papers re. (L.J. 50, p. 54)

1815, Apr. 5. Duties on foreign articles imported: account of. (L.J. 50, p. 124)

1815, Apr. 13. Negotiations for peace with America; motion for address re (negatived). (L.J. 50, p. 146)

1815, Apr. 17. America: motion for address respecting peace with. (L.J. 50, p. 151)

1815, May 2. North American Station: order for returns of ships for the. (L.J. 50, p. 193)

1816, June 10. Stamped dollars: minute of Court of Directors of Bank of England. (L.J. 50, p. 682)

1819, Apr. 26. Cotton goods and yarn exported 1785-1818: account of. (L.J. 52, p. 305)

1819, June 10. Canadian trade accounts. (L.J. 52, p. 678)

1820, June 6. Select committee on foreign trade: evidence. (L.J. 53, p. 110)

1820, July 7. Report on foreign trade. (L.J. 53, p. 266)

1820, July 13. Timber, etc.: Baltic and American trade accounts. (L.J. 53, p. 294)

1821, Feb. 16. Foreign trade accounts. (L.J. 54, p. 46)

1821, Feb. 21. Select committee on foreign trade appointed. (L.J. 54, p. 57)

1821, Feb. 26. Report from House of Commons on foreign trade. (L. J. 54, p. 67)

1821, Apr. 11. Exports to Denmark and North America: accounts delivered. (L.J. 54, p. 188)

1821, Apr. 11. Report from Commission on foreign trade. (L.J. 54, p. 188)

1821, May 9. Timber duties: petition from New Brunswick. (L.J. 54, p. 394)

1821, July 11. Foreign trade: minutes of evidence, one box. (L.J. 54, p. 582)

1822, May 6. Grain and flour imported, etc.: accounts. (L.J. 55, p. 151)

1822, May 14. Grain and flour imported, etc.: accounts bundle. (L.J. 55, p. 179)

1822, May 17. Foreign grain and flour imported: account of. (L.J. 55, p. 200)

1822, May 24. Grain and flour imported and warehoused in Ireland. (L.J. 55, p. 200)

1822, June 19. West Indian and American Trade Bill. (L.J. 55, p. 253)

1824, Feb. 23. Exports to North American colonies: accounts ordered. (L.J. 56, p. 42)

1824, May 14. Exports to South and North America: accounts. (L.J. 56, p. 227)

1824, June 21. Emigration from Ireland: reports ordered re. (L.J. 56, p. 450)

1825, Apr. 13. Vessels moored in Port of London: account of. (L.J. 57, p. 535)

1825, May 4. Accounts of ships entered into Port of London and account re transit trade, delivered. (L.J. 57, p. 746)

1825, May 11. Vessels laden with grain: account delivered. (L.J. 57, p. 784)

1825, May 13. Vessels entered London Docks and Commercial Dock: account of. (L.J. 57, p. 803)

1825, June 3. Memorials from Canadian legislature on corn laws, delivered. (L.J. 57, p. 977)

1825, June 28. Corn, grain and flour, ships and vessels: accounts delivered, six papers. (L.J. 57, p. 1181)

1825, June 30. North American corn and grain imported. (L.J. 57, p. 1201)

1826, Apr. 12. Imports and exports, Scotland and Ireland: accounts ordered re. (L.J. 58, p. 179)

1826, Apr. 25. Exports from Ireland. (L.J. 58, p. 241)

1826, May 9. American Steam Navigation Bill. (L.J. 58, p. 309)

1826, May 11. Foreign grain in warehouse. (L.J. 58, p. 323)

1826, Nov. 29. Export and import of grain in foreign countries: address re. (L.J. 59, p. 27)

1826, Dec. 1. Price of wheat, foreign oats, etc., admitted for home consumption, etc.: accounts delivered. (L.J. 59, p. 29)

1826, Dec. 7. Emigration petitions re Glasgow Emigration Society, Govan, Camachie Emigration Society, Paisley Emigrant Society. (L.J. 59, p. 36)

1826, Dec. 8. Report of House of Commons on emigration, communicated. (L.J. 59, p. 38)

1826, Dec. 12. Foreign grain admitted for home consumption: account of. (L.J. 59, p. 40)

1827, Feb. 9. Foreign and British vessels importing corn and flour; foreign exchanges and gold and silver coinage: accounts re ordered. (L.J. 59, p. 56)

1827, Feb. 15. Foreign corn: account re ordered, six papers. (L.J. 59. p. 76)

1827, Feb. 20. Foreign grain: accounts ordered, three papers. (L.J. 59, p. 88)

1827, Feb. 26. Foreign and colonial corn and flour imported: six papers. (L.J. 59, p. 102)

1827, Feb. 27. Foreign corn: further accounts re delivered. (L.J. 59, p. 115)

1827, Mar. 2. Ships entered ports of London and Liverpool. (L.J. 59, p. 124)

1827, Mar. 2. Foreign grain. (L.J. 59, pp. 124-5)

1827, Mar. 5. Timber and corn imported from America,

vessels entered and cleared: accounts delivered. (L.J. 59, p. 133)

1827, Mar. 8. Import of foreign grain: select committee appointed, two papers. (L.J. 59, p. 145)

1827, Mar. 9. Wool imported and re-exported and woollen manufactures exported: accounts ordered. (L.J. 59, p. 151)

1827, Mar. 12. Grain: regulations of foreign countries re export and import. (L.J. 59, p. 154)

1827, Mar. 12. Foreign and British corn: nine papers. (L.J. 59, p. 155)

1827, Mar. 19. Foreign oats, etc., imported; woollen manufactures exported; sheep exported: papers delivered. (L.J. 59, p. 174)

1827, Mar. 22. Foreign and British wool and woolen manufactures: four papers. (L.J. 59, p. 183)

1827, Apr. 10. Foreign wool and grain: accounts re. (L.J. 59, p. 248)

1827, May 7. Foreign grain: further papers re. (L.J. 59, p. 278)

1827, June 1. Message to House of Commons for second report on emigration. (L.J. 59, p. 375)

1828, Feb. 1. Wool imported; cotton, linen and woollen goods, leather goods and unwrought leather exported: accounts ordered. (L.J. 60, p. 16)

1828, Feb. 21. Wool, etc., exported: account of ordered. (L.J. 60, p. 58)

1828, Mar. 5. Second report of House of Commons on emigration communicated. (L.J. 60, p. 97)

1828, Apr. 1. Duties on foreign corn account; foreign grain re-exported; importation of foreign oats. (L.J. 60, p. 153)

1828, Apr. 1. Wool, etc., exported: account re. (L.J. 60, p. 155)

1828, May 13. Foreign wool imported into London. (L.J. 60, p. 442)

1829, May 8. Grain and wool imported; British manufactures exported: accounts delivered. (L.J. 61, p. 442)

1829, June 1. Coals, etc., exported: account of delivered. (L.J. 61, p. 529)

1830, Apr. 26. Flour imported into Liverpool, navigation: accounts rendered. (L.J. 62, p. 218)

1830, May 6. Foreign wheat, barley, and oats admitted for home consumption; accounts. (L.J. 62, p. 333)

1830, May 11. Foreign trade with China: account delivered. (L.J. 62, p. 366)

1830, June 14. British articles exported in American vessels to China and the East Indies: statement ordered. (L.J. 62, p. 720)

1830, June 16. Return by British consuls of grain prices: address for. (L.J. 62, p. 726)

1830, June 29. Return by British consuls on foreign grain. (L.J. 62, p. 787)

1830, July 12. Commercial intercourse at Canton, correspondence. (L.J. 62, p. 866)

1831, Feb. 8. Commercial intercourse at Canton, correspondence re, delivered. (L.J. 63, p. 211)

1831, Mar. 9. Tobacco imported and exported: papers delivered. (L.J. 63, p. 305)

1832, Jan. 19. Emigration: returns of people emigrating from the United Kingdom to North America, etc. (L.J. 64, p. 23)

1832, Aug. 9. Emigration reports, address. (L.J. 64, p. 439)

1832, Aug. 15. Exports and imports from Haiti; annexed, price of sugar after revolution in Santo Domingo. (L.J. 64, p. 464)

1833, Apr. 30. Foreign wheat: account delivered. (L.J. 65, p. 224)

1833, May 1. Grain imported from America: account of. (L.J. 65, p. 227)

1833, May 8. Foreign wheat: accounts respecting. (L.J. 65, p. 262)

1833, Aug. 7. Foreign affairs, secret service and embassies: accounts re delivered, five papers. (L.J. 65, p. 554)

1835, Aug. 21. North American Association Bill amendments. (L.J. 67, p. 602)

1836, Mar. 15. Accounts delivered, referred to Agriculture Committee: prices of wheat at Mark Lane 1815-35, foreign grain; grain imported from Ireland and America, etc. (L.J. 68, p. 68)

1836, Mar. 30. Foreign grain imported into American colonies, etc.: account of, delivered and referred to Committee on agriculture. (L.J. 68, p. 101)

1837, Mar. 22. Foreign grain, etc.: account of. (L.J. 69, p. 151)

1837, June 2. Emigration: address for papers. (L.J. 69, p. 364)

1838, Mar. 9. Exports and imports, North American provinces. (L.J. 70, p. 150)

1838, May 22. Emigration: address for papers. (L.J. 70, p. 354)

1838, July 9. Lower Canada: papers re delivered. (L.J. 70, p. 524)

1838, Aug. 2. Affairs of Canada. (L.J. 70, p. 661)

1839, Feb. 25. Return of grain imported. (L.J. 71, p. 66)

1839, Mar. 11. Indians in America: address for papers re. (L.J. 71, p. 104)

1839, Mar. 19. Ships off coast of Mexico: return re delivered. (L.J. 71, p. 147)

1839, July 26. Returns of wheat, flour, etc., delivered. (L.J. 71, p. 537)

1839, Aug. 15. (*a*) Return of sugar from foreign states; (*b*) report of Board of Customs to Board of Trade re sugar. (L.J. 71, p. 608)

1840, Feb. 24. Land and emigration commissioners. (L.J. 72, p. 64)

1840, May 14. Emigration to Canada: papers delivered. (L.J. 72, p. 297)

1840, May 19. Wheat and flour, importation of: account. (L.J. 72, p. 316)

1841, Jan. 29. Lower Canada: papers re delivered. (L.J. 73, p. 13)

1841, Feb. 23. Seminary of Montreal: address for dispatch re. (L.J. 73, p. 49)

1841, Mar. 11. St. Sulpice (Canada): papers re ordered. (L.J. 73, p. 86)

1841, Mar. 11. St. Sulpice (Canada): returns delivered. (L.J. 73, p. 86)

1841, Mar. 11. St. Sulpice (Canada): motion for address re. (L.J. 73, p. 92)

1841, June 15. Wheat: returns delivered. Imported, 1838-40. (L.J. 73, p. 516)

1841, Aug. 27. Ordinances, Lower Canada. (L.J. 73, p. 584)

1842, June 23. North American Colonial Association of Ireland Bill. (L.J. 74, p. 360)

1842, June 27. North American Colonial Association (Ireland). (L.J. 74, p. 370)

1843, Mar. 2. Newfoundland: supplementary commission to governor. Annexed: copy of edict passed by legislature of Canada. (L.J. 75, p. 68)

1843, Mar. 31. Boundary of British North America: address for papers. (L.J. 75, p. 122)

1843, Apr. 7. Treaty of Washington resolution. (L.J. 75, p. 141)

1843, June 26. Apprehension of Offenders (America) Bill. (L.J. 75, p. 452)

1844, Apr. 1. Church in Canada: papers re delivered. (L.J. 76, p. 114)

1846, Feb. 2. United States tariff: address for. (L.J. 78, p. 25)

1846, Feb. 19. Canada: wheat account. (L.J. 78, p. 76)

1846, Mar. 17. Oregon: address for papers re. (L.J. 78, p. 153)

1846, June 4. Canada: copy of petition. (L.J. 78, p. 514)

1846, June 4. Canada: copy of dispatches. (L.J. 78, p. 514)

1847, Feb. 16. Fires at St. John's, Newfoundland and Quebec: papers re ordered. (L.J. 79, p. 46)

1847, Feb. 18. Destitute poor (Ireland), etc.: relief of, from Nova Scotia. (L.J. 79, p. 48)

1847, Apr. 30. Australian and British North American colonies: account of exports and imports ordered. (L.J. 79, p. 173)

1847, Apr. 30. Newfoundland: papers re delivered. Subscriptions raised for relief of the destitute poor in Ireland. (L.J. 79, p. 174)

1847, May 18. Exports and imports from Australia and British North American colonies: accounts re. (L.J. 79, p. 227)

1847, June 22. British American Land Co.: bill, especially reported. (L.J. 79, p. 492)

1848, July 7. Canada Union Act Amendment Bill: Act. (L.J. 80, p. 520)

1849, Apr. 19. St. John's, Newfoundland. Rebuilding Bill. (L.J. 81, p. 136)

1849, June 28. Canada Indemnity Bill: address for papers re. (L.J. 81, p. 369)

1849, July 16. Education in Canada: papers re delivered. (L.J. 81, p. 439)

1851, May 16. Canada, etc., Railroad Co.: address for papers re. (L.J. 83, p. 189)

1851, June 26. European and American Printing Telegraph Co., etc. Bill reported from Standing Order Committee. (L.J. 83, p. 291)

1851, June 26. Emigrant ship *Washington*: address for papers re. (L.J. 83, p. 291)

1851, July 7. European and American Printing Telegraph Co., etc. Bill: instruction to committee on. (L.J. 83, p. 332)

1851, July 28. European and American Printing Telegraph Co., etc.: bill amendments. (L.J. 83, p. 438)

1851, Aug. 1. Canada and New Brunswick Boundary Bill Amendment. (L.J. 83, p. 481)

1852, Feb. 12. Canada: Act to make provision for the management of the temporalities of the United Church, etc. (L.J. 84, p. 20)

1852, Feb. 16. Canada guaranteed loan. (L.J. 84, p. 24)

1852, Feb. 19. Canada: Act to provide for the establishment of a church society of the United Church of England. (L.J. 84, p. 28)

1853, Feb. 15. Clergy reserves (Canada): papers re. (L.J. 85, p. 71)

1853, Feb. 22. Canadian clergy reserves: message from House of Commons. (L.J. 85, p. 101)

1853, Mar. 15. Clergy reserves, Canada: address for papers. (L.J. 85, p. 129)

1853, Apr. 8. Canada clergy reserves. (L.J. 85, p. 156)

1853, Apr. 18. Clergy reserves (Canada) Bill. Petitions against. (L.J. 85, p. 175)

1853, Apr. 25. Clergy Reserves (Canada) Bill. (L.J. 85, p. 191)

1854, June 16. Canada: papers re delivered. (L.J. 86, p. 251)

1855, Jan. 25. Clergy reserves, etc. (Canada): dispatch from the Governor-General. (L.J. 87, p. 21)

1855, Mar. 19. New Brunswick: papers re delivered. (L.J. 87, p. 64)

1855, May 25. Church in Canada: address for paper re. (L.J. 87, p. 175)

1855, June 11. Canada: copy of an address presented to Her Majesty praying for the removal of disadvantages to which the Church in Canada is subject. (L.J. 87, p. 198)

1856, May 20. Canada Company Bill: report from the Standing Order Committee. (L.J. 88, p. 176)

1856, May 27. Military establishment (Canada): address for papers re. (L.J. 88, p. 199)

1857, July 7. New Brunswick and Canada Railway and Land Co. Bill: summons for witness. (L.J. 89, p. 185)

1857, July 7. Atlantic Telegraph Co. Bill: the Queen's consent signified. (L.J. 89, p. 186)

1857, July 13. New Brunswick and Canada Land Co. Bill: report from Standing Order Committee. (L.J. 89, p. 218)

1857, July 20. Correspondence on the subject of colonial Church affairs in the diocese of the colonies of Canada and Victoria. (L.J. 89, p. 248)

1857, July 31. New Brunswick and Canada Railway and Land Co. Bill: the Queen's consent signified. (L.J. 89, p. 315)

1857, Aug. 17. Hudson's Bay Co.: report from the House of Commons Select Committee. (L.J. 89, p. 370)

1858, Apr. 16. Prince Edward Island Loan. Paper on the subject of affording the imperial guarantee to a loan. (L.J. 90, p. 111)

1858, Apr. 23. Telegraph to America: address for papers re. (L.J. 90, p. 125)

1858, June 11. Atlantic Telegraph Co. Bill: report from Standing Order Committee. (L.J. 90, p. 235)

1858, July 26. Atlantic Telegraph Co. Bill: amended copy of bill. (L.J. 90, p. 467)

1859, July 19. North-Western Territories (British America) Bill: printed copy of the bill, amendments written within. (L.J. 91, p. 371)

1859, July 28. The British and Canadian Telegraph Co. Bill: report from the Standing Order Committee. (L.J. 91, p. 410)

1860, Mar. 13. British Columbia: proclamation having the force of law issued by the Governor of British Columbia. (L.J. 92, p. 144)

1860, May 3. British Columbia: proclamation having the force of law issued by the Governor of British Columbia. (L.J. 92, p. 280)

1860, May 22. New Brunswick and Canada Railway and Land Co. (Ltd.) *v.* Conybeare *et al.*: petition and appeal of the New Brunswick and Canada Railway and Land Co. (Ltd.) and the answers of J.C. Conybeare and other respondents. Order of Service. (L.J. 92, p. 351)

1860, May 24. New Brunswick and Canada Railway and Land Co. (Ltd.): appeal. (L.J. 92, p. 357)

1860, July 2. New Brunswick and Canada Railway and Land Co. (Ltd.) *v.* Conybeare *et al.*: petition of the appellants for leave for time to deliver in cases. (L.J. 92, p. 478)

1860, July 30. New Brunswick and Canada Railway and Land Co. (Ltd.) *v.* Conybeare: appeal. (L.J. 92, p. 630)

1860, Aug. 2. New Brunswick and Canada Railway and Land Co. (Ltd.) *v.* Conybeare. (L.J. 92, p. 644)

1861, Feb. 14. New Brunswick and Canada Railway and Land Co. (Ltd.) *v.* Conybeare: appeal. (L.J. 93, p. 22)

1861, June 7. British Columbia: proclamations. (L.J. 93, p. 365)

1861, June 14. Copies of correspondence between the Treasury, the Post Office, and the Atlantic Mail Steam Navigation Co. (L.J. 93, p. 396)

1861, July 1. Royal Atlantic Steam Navigation Co. (L.J. 93, p. 444)

1862, Feb. 7. Papers concerning the arrest of Shaver, a Canadian subject, by order of Mr. Seward. (L.J. 94, p. 10)

1862, Feb. 25. New Brunswick and Canadian Railway and Land Co. *v.* Conybeare. (L.J. 94, p. 32)

1862, Mar. 10. Blockade of ports of the Confederate States of America. (L.J. 94, p. 67)

1862, May 15. American mails. (L.J. 94, p. 213)

1862, July 4. Hudson's Bay Company. (L.J. 94, p. 382)

1862, Aug. 4. Papers concerning the Confederate States of America. (L.J. 94, p. 561)

1863, May 18. United States Prize Courts. (L.J. 95, p. 272)

1863, June 15. American blockade. (L.J. 95, p. 363)

1863, July 2. Hudson's Bay Company. (L.J. 95, p. 446)

1863, July 3. British Columbia Boundaries Bill. (L.J. 95, p. 452)

1864, Feb. 16. United States: address for papers re. (L.J. 96, p. 34)

1864, Apr. 5. North America: address for papers. (L.J. 96, p. 103)

1865, Mar. 17. Explorations (North America): papers re. Maps, sections, and index to illustrate Capt. Palliser's journals of his explorations between Lake Superior and the Pacific Ocean, laid before Parliament, 19th May 1863. (L.J. 97, p. 81)

1865, May 1. Assassination of President of United States of America: motion for address to H.M. by the Earl Russell, to convey abhorrence of the crime, and their sympathy with the government and people of the U.S. (L.J. 97, p. 175)

1865, May 4. Assassination of President of the United States: the Queen's answer to address, re. (L.J. 97, p. 196)

1865, May 4. New Brunswick and Canada Railway and Land Co. Bill: report from the Committee of Selection. (L.J. 97, p. 199)

1865, May 8. New Brunswick and Canada Railway and Land Co. Bill: report from the Select Committee on. (L.J. 97, p. 212)

1865. June 19. Canada: papers relating to conferences, etc. (L.J. 97, p. 418)

1867, Feb. 12. British North America Bill. (L.J. 99, p. 23)

1867, Feb. 22. British North America Bill. (L.J. 99, p. 41)

1867, Feb. 26. British North America Bill. (L.J. 99, p. 48)

1867, Mar. 7. Atlantic Telegraph Co. Bill. (L.J. 99, p. 58)

1868, July 31. United States: resolution re a volume presented to the House. (L.J. 100, p. 495)

1870, May 13. Request for returns of the number of emigrants from Irish ports in February, March, and April 1870. (L.J. 102, p. 234)

1870, June 13. Return of number of emigrants who have left Irish ports in February, March, and April 1869 and 1870. (L.J. 102, p. 289)

1870, July 22. Motion by Lord Carnarvon respecting joint action by British troops and Canadian volunteers against the Fenian attacks on Canada. (L.J. 102, p. 454)

1870, July 25. Copy of dispatch from the Earl of Granville concerning the Fenian raids. (L.J. 102, p. 458)

1871, May 19. Papers concerning Irish emigrants. (L.J. 103, p. 286)

1872, July 5. Treaty of Washington Bill read. (L.J. 104, p. 504)

1879, Apr. 21. Returns of American meat. (L.J. 111, p. 130)

1885, Feb. 27. Direct United States Cable Co., Ltd.: petition and appeal - draft judgment. (L.J. 117, p. 72)

1888, Mar. 12. United States and South American Investment Trust Co. Copy of special resolution. (L.J. 120, p. 66)

1888, Apr. 13. New York Life Insurance Co. *v.* Styles: petition and appeal. (L.J. 120, p. 100)

1890, Nov. 27. Anglo-American Brush Electric Light Corporation Ltd. *v.* King, Brown and Co. Ltd.: petition of appeal. (L.J. 123, p. 10)

1891, Jan. 22. Anglo-American Brush Electric Light Corporation appeal. (L.J. 123, p. 33)

1902, July 31. Kodak Ltd. *v.* General Commissioners of Taxes. (L.J. 134, p. 331)

Additions to Paullin & Paxson, 1904-53.

Treaties and conventions have been omitted since they have been published since 1892 in the Treaty Series.

1904, Feb. 2. Correspondence on Alaska Boundary; map to accompany same. (L.J. 136, p. 12)

1906, Dec. 6. Correspondence on Newfoundland fisheries. (L.J. 138, p. 448)

1907, Mar. 18. Probation system: memorandum on probation system as at present in force in the United States. (L.J. 139, p. 63)

1908, Jan. 29. Notes exchanged with American Ambassador on Newfoundland fisheries. (L.J. 140, p. 10)

1911, Apr. 4. Cost of living in American towns. Report on inquiry by Board of Trade into working-class rents, housing and retail prices, together with rates of wages in certain occupations in principal industrial towns of the United States; with introductory memorandum and comparison of conditions in the United States and the United Kingdom. (L.J. 143, p. 120)

1913, Apr. 24. Proposed new customs tariff. New United States Tariff Bill with comparisons of proposed and existing rates of duty. (L.J. 145, p. 73)

1914, July 16. Notes exchanged between H.M. Ambassador at Washington and the United States Government on the subject of oil properties and mining rights in Mexico. (L.J. 146, p. 311)

1917, Apr. 18. United States: Entry into Albania. Resolution of appreciation on entry of the United States into war, 'in joining Allied powers'. (L.J. 149, p. 85)

1919, Oct. 29. American Aviation Mission Report. (L.J. 151, p. 415)

1921, Apr. 7. Correspondence on alleged delay by British authorities of telegrams to and from the United States. (L.J. 153, p. 99)

1923, July 12. Dispatch from H.M. Ambassador at Washington enclosing memorandum on effects of prohibition in United States. (L.J. 155, p. 216)

1923, Nov. 13. Dispatch from H.M. Ambassador at Washington reporting conditions on Ellis Island immigration station. (L.J. 155, p. 291)

1924, July 23. Correspondence between the governments of the U.K. and U.S. concerning the appointment of an Irish plenipotentiary at Washington. (L.J. 156, p. 306)

1926, May 4. Correspondence between the governments of the U.K. and U.S. concerning the prevention of liquor smuggling. (L.J. 158, p. 118)

1926, Oct. 25. Correspondence between the U.K. and U.S. concerning the reduction of passport fees. (L.J. 158, p. 296)

1928, May 21. Correspondence with the U.S. Ambassador in London concerning U.S. proposals for the renunciation of war. (L.J. 160, pp. 143, 232)

1932, Nov. 15, 29, 30; Dec. 8, 13. Exchange of notes between the U.K. and U.S. concerning British war debt. (L.J. 164, p. 343; L.J. 165, pp. 14, 15, 22, 24)

1933, June 14, Nov. 7. Papers relating to British war debt. (L.J. 165, pp. 204, 327)

1934, June 5, 26, Dec. 11. Papers relating to British war debt. (L.J. 166, pp. 213, 258; L.J. 167, p. 20)

1935, June 17, Dec. 10. Papers relating to British war debt. (L.J. 167, p. 218; L.J. 168, p. 30)

1936, June 11. Papers relating to British war debt. (L.J. 168, p. 229)

1936, Dec. 10. Papers relating to British war debt. (L.J. 169, p. 55)

1937, June 14. Papers relating to British war debt. (L.J. 169, p. 259)

1937, Oct. 21. Correspondence re U.S. rights in Palestine. (L.J. 169, p. 392)

1937, Dec. 9. Papers relating to British war debt. (L.J. 170, p. 40)

1938, June 14. Papers relating to British war debt. (L.J. 170, p. 252)

1938, Dec. 12. Exchange of letters between the U.K. and Canada concerning the Anglo-American Trade Agreement. (L.J. 171, p. 38)

1938, Dec. 15. Papers relating to British war debt. (L.J. 171, p. 46)

1939, March 22. Papers relating to British war debt. (L.J. 171, p. 214)

1940, Jan. 22. Correspondence between U.K. concerning censorship of mails. (L.J. 172, p. 33)

1941, July 1. Exchange of notes between Argentina, Australia, Canada, U.K., and U.S. on wheat discussion at Washington. (L.J. 174, p. 144)

1948, June 29. Notes on most favoured nation treatment for West Germany, to be exchanged between U.K. and U.S. (L.J. 180, p. 339)

1950, July 11. Exchange of notes between U.S. and U.K. re financial issues arising out of the Bizonal Fusion Agreement. (L.J. 182, p. 161)

1952, July 10. Exchange of notes between U.S. and U.K. re relief from taxation for U.S. expenditures in the U.K. (L.J. 184, p. 139)

1953, Feb. 25. Aid to U.K. expenditure under the Mutual Security Act. (L.J. 185, p. 82)

1953, Mar. 20. Proposed arrangements for Marshall Aid scholarship scheme. (L.J. 185, p. 193)

HISTORICAL COLLECTIONS

AMERICAN PAPERS (RUSSELL, EDWARDS, ETC.). 1732-1836.

This collection consists of:

(*a*) Brief for counsel appearing before the Privy Council relating to grants made by proprietors of Carolina in South Carolina in support of the confirmation of a Quit Rent Act, *c*. 1732.

(*b*) Deeds, letters of attorney, etc., relating to affairs and property of Thomas Pruson, Northampton, Va.; William Walter of Williamstown, Va.; *et al.*, 1745-78 (seventeen documents).

(*c*) The Edwards partnership papers, including articles of co-partnership between John Edwards of Charleston, S.C., and Charles Goodwin and Walter Thomas of the city of Chester, 1755, and similar articles between J.E., C.G., James Fisher, and James Ballantine, all merchants of Charleston, 1772; file of letters and accounts of the partnership; bill in equity concerning partnership in the Circuit Court of South Carolina, 1755-94 (thirty-seven documents).

(*d*) Two packets of papers relating to the affairs of James Russell, ironmaster, of Nottingham, Md., including letters, lists of bonds, current accounts, certificates and valuations of confiscations, 1764-1804 (eighty-five documents).

(*e*) Lee Family Papers, including declaration of trust as to 10,400 acres in Mason, Kanawha, and Fayette Counties, in the states of Virginia and Kentucky, the property of John Lee, LL.D., of Hartwell House, Co. Bucks., 1778-1836 (fifty-two documents).[4]

BEAVERBROOK MSS.

The deposit in 1975 of the greater part of the Beaverbrook Library into the House of Lords Record Office has brought some important Americana into the public sphere.

(*a*) Beaverbrook Papers. 1903-64.

The Beaverbrook Papers contain much material on American, Canadian, and Russian relations during and after the Second World War, including papers relating to the North American Supplies Council; post-war civil aviation; Anglo-American talks on oil in July and Aug. 1944; the questions of Lend-Lease, the currency situation, and other economic problems; and various visits to the U.S.A. made by Lord Beaverbrook, Sir Winston Churchill, and Harold Balfour. There is also some correspondence with a number of prominent Americans including Joseph Kennedy and his children, President F.D. Roosevelt, Averell Harriman, Harry Hopkins, and Harry Luce (editor of *Time* and *Life* magazines), covering the period 1932-64.

(*b*) Blumenfeld Papers. 1891-1948.

Ralph David Blumenfeld, born in the U.S. in 1864, owned a newspaper business in Watertown, Wisconsin. In 1894 he arrived in London, and by 1904 he had become editor of Beaverbrook's *Daily Express*. His personal correspondence reflects his American background, friends, and acquaintances.

(*c*) Hannon Papers. 1874-1963.

Sir Patrick Joseph Henry Hannon, born in Ireland in 1874, had a varied career in industry, agriculture, and politics. His parliamentary papers (he served as M.P. for Moseley, Birmingham) include information on the British-American parliamentary group, 1941-9.

(*d*) Lloyd George Papers.

The Lloyd George Papers contain much material on Anglo-American relations, particularly during and just after the First World War. Topics include munitions supplies from the U.S. and Canada; the question of U.S. entry into the war; American influence in France, India, and other countries; the post-war peace conferences and the Washington Conference of 1921; inter-allied debts and reparations; the League of Nations and the Irish question in the U.S.A. There is a fair amount of official and semi-official correspondence with the embassies, the American government, and British representatives in the U.S.A., and correspondence concerning a number of government missions to the American continent. There are also a few American papers

4. List available in H.L.R.O.

after 1922, including correspondence relating to Lloyd George's visit to the U.S.A. in 1923.

(*e*) Strachey Papers. 1885-1927.

John St. Loe Strachey was both editor and proprietor of the *Spectator* from 1898 to 1925, two years before his death. Among his political papers is some correspondence on the strengthening of Anglo-American ties in the early twentieth century. Some of his correspondents and the topics covered were Nicholas Murray Butler of Columbia University (Anglo-American relations and the spread of socialism in the West), Woodrow Wilson (the League of Nations), and James Beck, the American Solicitor-General (literary matters). His political (general) papers include three boxes on America, 1899-1927, consisting of correspondence with President Theodore Roosevelt and with American journalists, notably F.C. Warrin (editor of the *Atlantic Monthly*) on American and British politics. (boxes 25-7)[5]

SAMUEL PAPERS.[6]

Administrator and politician. The papers of Herbert, First Viscount Samuel (1870-1963) were deposited in the Record Office in 1963. They include a few items of American interest, e.g. a journal in letter form, Aug.-Oct. 1913, describing Samuel's visit to the U.S. and Canada as Postmaster-General (A/42); there is also an account of his trip to the U.S. and Canada in 1933, with notes on a conversation with President Franklin D. Roosevelt (A/96).

STANSGATE MSS.[7]

The papers of William Wedgwood Benn, First Viscount Stansgate (1877-1960) were placed in the House of Lords Record Office by his widow, the Dowager Viscountess Stansgate, and his eldest son, the Rt. Hon. Anthony Wedgwood Benn M.P., in May 1973. The papers now constitute Historical Collection 141.

Among the collection's International Papers are some relating to North America (ST 196), and dating from the 1940's and 1950's. Most of this is printed or typed material covering various aspects of Anglo-American relations and American politics. The papers on South African affairs contain some items, 1957-8, including a letter to Stansgate from the American Committee on Africa signed by Eleanor Roosevelt, Rev. James A. Pike, and Rev. Martin Luther King, inviting him to join them and other world leaders as sponsors in a Declaration of Conscience (ST/230/17).

The General Personal and Family Papers of Stansgate contain miscellaneous items (correspondence, diaries, itineraries, notes, etc.) concerning his overseas visits from 1903 to 1956, including one paid to the U.S.A. in 1933 (ST/289).

HUGUENOT LIBRARY, UNIVERSITY COLLEGE,
Gower Street, London WC1E 6BT

Applications for permission to use the library must be made to the Hon. Librarian, Huguenot Society of London, University College.

This library was formed from the library of the Huguenot Society of London and from the library and archives of the French Hospital, formerly at Hackney, now at Rochester, Kent. It contains material on the early Huguenot settlements in the United States, and a few privately printed histories of the Huguenot families in America. Pamphlet material of general Huguenot interest is particularly strong for the seventeenth century.

There are the following papers:

AUFRÈRE PAPERS.[1] 1683-1758.

A collection of personal papers of the Rev. Israel Antoine Aufrère (1667-1758), minister of the French Reformed Church, exiled in London, together with some letters of the Rev. Claude Groteste de la Mothe, minister of the Savoy Church, London. The letters give some information about refugee French congregations in America, and the activities of the Society for the Propagation of the Gospel in Foreign Parts.

LAFAYETTE, MARQUIS DE (1757-1834). Letter. 1828.

Letter, dated La Grange, 17 Sept. 1828, to 'M. Duponceau à Philadelphie', introducing M. Capoulade of Bordeaux.

See also the publications of the Huguenot Society of London: *Proceedings*, vol. i, 1885/6-in progress; and *Quarto Publications*, vol. i, 1887-in progress.

DEPARTMENT OF LIBRARIES AND ARCHIVES, IMPERIAL WAR MUSEUM,
Lambeth Road, London SE1 6HZ

The documents at the Imperial War Museum consist mainly of the private papers of individuals who have served in the British armed forces during the two World Wars. Some of these acted as liaison officers with American forces or had some American connections. There is available for reference a subject catalogue and a catalogue of names. The following individual collections are listed in the catalogue as containing American material.

I. 1st World War.

(*a*) Foster Hall
(*b*) Rawlinson Collection (Fourth Army Papers)
(*c*) Stanford Papers
(*d*) J.F. Sharp
(*e*) C.H. Dixon
(*f*) M.W. Peters

II. 2nd World War.

(*a*) E.R. Meade-Waldo
(*b*) R.S. Raymond
(*c*) G.E. Dale. Includes diary of American D-Day landings, April-July 1944.
(*d*) Capt. A.V.S. Yates. Contains correspondence with Reginald E. Gillmore, an American employee of Sperry Gyroscope. The letters cover the years 1939 to 1945.
(*e*) Wing Commander N. Tangye. Includes diary, July-Oct. 1944, as R.A.F. liaison officer to the Commanding General, U.S. Strategic Air Forces in Europe.

5. For further information on the Beaverbrook holdings in the House of Lords Record Office, see Katharine V. Wheeler, *A Guide to the Political Papers, 1874-1970, deposited by the First Beaverbrook Foundation* (Record Office Memorandum No. 54, 1975).
6. See H.S. Cobb, *The Political Papers of Herbert, First Viscount Samuel* (Record Office Memorandum No. 35, second edition, 1974).
7. See *Handlist of the Papers of William Wedgwood Benn, M.P. First Viscount Stansgate*, compiled by S.K. Ellison (Record Office Memorandum No. 56, 1976).

1. See Winifred Turner, ed., *The Aufrère Papers, Calendar and Selections* (London, Huguenot Society, priv. print., 1940) (Huguenot Society, Quarto Series, vol. xl).

(*f*) J.C. Wedgwood, Baron of Barlaston. Contains various letters and accounts of America's role and influence in both World Wars.

THE LIBRARY, INNER TEMPLE, London, EC4Y 7DA

MASERES MANUSCRIPTS. Document[1] (77 pages). 1758.

'Instructions for Georgia. 1758.' Includes copies of various documents as follows: Extract of Sir William Gooch's answer to the queries of the Board of Trade, in 1749; instruction to Henry Ellis, Captain General and Governor of Georgia in 1758; orders and instructions to Ellis 'in pursuance of several laws relating to the trade and navigation of. . . Great Britain, and our colonies and plantations in America', July 1758; and a list of ships which have entered ports in Georgia 'with the particular quantity and quality of the loading of each vessel'. (I.T. Misc. MS. 29)

OTHER MANUSCRIPTS.[2] 1634-1762.

(*a*) 'A Commission for making laws and orders for government of English colonies, planted in foreign parts, to William, Archbishop of Canterbury, *et al.*', 28 April 1634, followed by a 'Proclamation for the restraint of transportation of H.M.'s subjects to the new plantation in the parts of America but upon special licence', 30 April 1637. (I.T. Petyt MS. 538/51, item 7)
(*b*) 'Letter from Law Officers of the Crown to Secretary of State in reply to. . . the petition of seven persons, natives of France, but now resident in the Province of Lower Canada in America, praying for Letters of Denization under the Great Seal of Britain, together with affidavits made before the Chief Justices of that Province and of the District of Montreal', n.d. (I.T. Mitford MS. 58, pp. 132-4)
(*c*) 'State of Quebec in 1762'. Includes report from James Murray, Governor of Quebec to Rt. Hon. the Earl of Egremont, 5 June 1762, divided into the following heads:

(i) Return of H.M.'s forces in his Government of Quebec and dependencies thereof.
(ii) State of the fortifications.
(iii) State of the Government under the French administration.
(iv) Its revenues and expenses.
(v) Church government.
(vi) Indian natives residing within the Government.
(vii) Nature of the soil and its produce.
(viii) Population.
(ix) Trade.
(x) Character of the people.

Also given are a number of documents and letters, dealing primarily with currency, trade and commerce. (I.T. Misc. MS. 28)

INSTITUTION OF MECHANICAL ENGINEERS, 1 Birdcage Walk, London SW1H 9JJ

TAWS, LEWIS. Letter.[1] 1851.

19 May 1851, from Lewis Taws, of J.P. Morris & Co., Philadelphia, to James Nasmyth, engineer at Patricroft, Lancs., concerning the prospective visit to Manchester of George Scott, who 'is well acquainted with our operations, having built for him a number of machines for the manufacture of bricks, the best machines I have yet seen for that purpose'.

ISLINGTON LIBRARIES, 2 Fieldway Crescent, London N5 1PF

PRICE, HENRY EDWARD (1824-1908?). Scrapbook (1 volume).

Price, an inmate of the workhouse at Warminster, Wilts., was sent to America, under the Poor Law emigration scheme, in May 1842, and returned to England in 1848. From 1850 he was a cabinet-maker in Islington.

The scrapbook, which was apparently compiled a considerable time after the events, describes the cargo and passengers on the ship, his employment as a varnisher and polisher, and as a cabinet-maker in New York, Staten Island, and Oswego. Touches on the coming of the telegraph to New York, Phineas Barnum, mesmerism, and racial segregation (e.g., in trams). Two letters from a friend in Buffalo, N.Y., 1847-8, are included.

ISLINGTON LITERARY AND SCIENTIFIC SOCIETY. 3 papers (1 printed).

Include papers read to the Society on 'The Life of Washington', by Thomas Gale, and 'Was America known to the ancient world?', by Thomas Calvert Girtin (d. 1874). Also a printed notice sent to the Society's members advertising a dramatic reading from *Uncle Tom's Cabin* on 6 Oct. 1856 by Mrs. Mary E. Webb, 'a coloured native of Philadelphie'.

JONATHAN CAPE LTD., 30 Bedford Square, London, W.C.1

ARCHIVES.

As a firm Jonathan Cape has published the works of a number of American authors since the early 1920's. The company's archive, though decimated through the 1930's and 1940's when much correspondence was destroyed, probably still contains many items from American men of letters, including writers of the stature of Ernest Hemingway and Sinclair Lewis. Further information about other American authors published by the house of Cape can be found in Michael S. Howard, *Jonathan Cape, Publisher* (London, 1971).

LAMBETH PALACE LIBRARY, London SE1 7JU

The extensive papers of the Bishops of London, who were virtually the diocesan heads of the Episcopal Church in America

1. H.M.C. xi (vii), p. 304.
2. These documents are described in greater detail in Dr. J. Conway Davies (ed.), *The Catalogue of Manuscripts in the Library of the Honourable Society of the Inner Temple*, 3 vols. (Oxford, 1972).

1. Photocopy in the James Nasmyth Collection, Public Library, Eccles, Lancs.

during the colonial period, were at one time divided between Lambeth Palace and Fulham Palace - and thus were separately described by Andrews & Davenport, pp. 286-301 and 302-329.[1] The slightest glance at their list shows the great importance of this archive for almost every aspect of colonial history - few things were not, or could not be made, relevant to the affairs of the Church. However, it is clear that not all the papers can have been available to Miss Davenport. Large sections of the papers, mainly unlisted, were in 1957 found to be in considerable disorder, having undergone much accidental and random rearrangement.

Since then, however, much work has been done to restore order to these papers, and a number of useful catalogues, calendars, and indexes have been compiled to guide the researcher through this voluminous material.

(*a*) Archbishops' Papers. Papers of the Archbishops of Canterbury from the time of Archbishop Longley.

These include correspondence with American bishops, particularly over Lambeth Conferences, visits, and the jurisdiction of the Protestant Episcopal Church abroad. A forty-year ruling applies to all these papers.

See:

J.E. Sayers and E.G.W. Bill, *Calendar of the Papers of Charles Thomas Longley, Archbishop of Canterbury, 1862-1868, in Lambeth Palace Library* (London, 1976).

Index to the Letters and Papers of Edward White Benson, Archbishop of Canterbury, 1882-1896, in Lambeth Palace Library (to be published by Mansell shortly).

Melanie Barber, *Index to the Letters and Papers of Frederick Temple, Archbishop of Canterbury, 1896-1902, in Lambeth Palace Library* (London, 1975).

For other Archbishops, see lists and letter registers available in the Library.

(*b*) Eighteenth-Century Archbishops' Papers.

The Papers of Archbishop Moore include a bundle of correspondence with the Secretary of S.P.G., some of which relates to the American colonies.

(*c*) Papers of the Bishops of London: Fulham Papers.

See:

W.W. Manross, *The Fulham Papers in the Lambeth Palace Library. American and Colonial Section. Calendars and Indexes* (Oxford, 1965).

The 'London Series' of the Fulham Papers also include some relevant materials, e.g.:

(i) Letter on the conduct of marriages in the colonies, 1729. (FP 141)

(ii) Appointment of Governor of Rhode Island, 1651. (Copy.) (FP 314(4))

(iii) Alphabetical list, 1723-48, of clergy ordained and licensed by the Bishops of London for the diocese and the colonies. (FP 521)

(iv) Complaints, 1759, 1764, of the clergy in Virginia against Acts of the Assembly. (FP 550)

(v) Case Papers: John Camm, minister of Yorkhampton *v*. Charles Hansford and William Moss, collectors of the parish levies, 1765. (FP 550)

(vi) Papers, 1721, 1763, on William and Mary College. (FP 550)

(*d*) Lambeth Conference Papers, 1867-present.

(*e*) S.P.G. Papers.

See:

W.W. Manross, *S.P.G. Papers in the Lambeth Palace Library. Calendar and Indexes* (Oxford, 1974).

(*f*) Manuscripts.

See:

Henry J. Todd, *A Catalogue of the Archepiscopal Manuscripts in the Library at Lambeth Palace* (London, 1812; reprint London, 1965). Notably MSS. 1123 and 1124 on the American colonies and the S.P.G.

E.G.W. Bill, *A Catalogue of Manuscripts in Lambeth Palace Library* (Oxford, 1972). Notably correspondence with American bishops and report on Poor Law administration, 1872.

E.G.W. Bill, *A Catalogue of Manuscripts in Lambeth Palace Library. MSS. 1907-2340* (Oxford, 1976).

A list of more recent accessions is available, including MSS. on the American episcopacy and jurisdiction of the Bishops of London, lists of clergy licensed to officiate in America (eighteenth century), and Archbishop Davidson's visit to America. (MSS. 2576, 2589, 2607)

(*g*) Christian Faith Society Papers. (originally Boyle's Charity).

The Society originated in a bequest of Robert Boyle in 1691 for the advancement of religion amongst infidels, and includes material on the American colonies, 1691-1794. List in Reading Room.

LLOYDS BANK LTD., Head Office, 71 Lombard Street, London EC3P 3BS

BANK RECORDS.

The fullest use of the Bank's records was made by R.S. Sayers, *Lloyds Bank in the History of English Banking* (Oxford, 1957).[1] From this, it appears that there was not any major involvement of Lloyds in American financial affairs, but there are occasional references to the United States in the records, as follows (the page numbers refer to Professor Sayers's book):

p. 131. Lloyds asked Hanbury, Taylor, Lloyd & Bowman for advice on which of the American stocks was considered to be the safest and what price should be paid for it, 1839. (Taylor & Lloyds: letter, 14 Sept. 1839.)

p. 183. Lloyds found that stock exchange securities deposited by stockbrokers were mostly American stocks which had taken a bad fall, and so asked for additional cover, 1841. (Taylor & Lloyds: letter, 1 Nov. 1841.)

p. 184. Securities deposited, 1884, by Mills, Cave, Baillie & Co., Bristol, with Barnetts, Hoares, Hanbury & Lloyd, proved to be worthless certificates substituted by one of the stockbrokers, who had abstracted the true documents in order to cover his unsuccessful speculation in North American railway stocks. (Barnetts, Hoares: letters, Mar. 1884.)

1. Footnote references to material in the Bank's records have been omitted from Professor Sayers's book, but are available as a supplement, *Reference Notes*, at the Bank itself, the British Library, the British Library of Political and Economic Science, London School of Economics, the Marshall Library of Economics, Cambridge, the Bodleian Library, Oxford, the Library of the Institute of Bankers, London, and Birmingham Public Libraries. For permission to use the records, application should be made to the Secretary of the Bank.

p. 186. Hanbury, Taylor, Lloyd & Bowman went into American bonds as early as 1817. (Taylor & Lloyds: ledger, 1817.)

p. 187. After Francis Lloyd's visit to America, 'the bank was in 1827 persuaded by Rathbones of Liverpool to sell, in America, some of their United States Government bonds and to invest the proceeds in raw cotton'. (Taylor & Lloyds: letters, 11 Aug., 26 and 28 Sept., and 30 Oct. 1827, and 19 July 1828.)

p. 187. Gloucestershire Banking Co. thought of buying United States Government bonds, 1838. (Gloucestershire Banking Co.: minutes, 1 June and 6 July 1838.)

p. 188. Bucks & Oxon Bank held American bonds, 1869. (Bucks. & Oxon Union Bank Ltd.: balance sheet, 31 Dec. 1869.)

There may also be relevant material in the Liverpool Union Bank board minute-books, which contain information about cotton brokers (p. 93); and in Twining & Co. security registers (kept at Lloyds' Law Courts Branch), concerning investment in North America (p. 107).

LONDON LIBRARY, 14 St. James's Square, London SW1Y 4LG

PREVOST, AUGUSTINE (1723-86). Journal (50 leaves).[1] 1774.

Major-General Prevost was apparently Governor *pro tem.* of Pennsylvania awaiting the arrival of someone whom he repeatedly calls 'His Lordship'. The journal, Apr.-Sept. 1774, contains details of travel through Pennsylvania, Maryland, and Virginia, and of negotiations in conjunction with George Croghan, the Indian agent and trader, with the Shawnee Indians.

READE, CHARLES (1814-84). Papers, clippings.[2] *c.* 1860-84.

Author. Reade suffered from 'pirating' in America, and his papers include his manuscript, 'The Rights and Wrongs of Authors', on the absence of international copyright. They also include numerous clippings of reviews, etc., of his work from American sources, and material on libel action, 1868-9, against an American magazine, in which an American jury awarded him six cents damages.

ASHBEE, CHARLES ROBERT (1863-1942). Memoirs, 1884-1938, with letters (6 volumes). (Carbon typescript)[3].

Architect, designer, and town planner; founder of the Guild of Handicraft; civic adviser to the Palestine Administration 1918-22; author of numerous books on the arts, and also of *The American League to Enforce Peace* (London, 1917).

Ashbee visited the United States seven times, travelling through all the Northern and Western states, and the Memoirs contain full descriptions of these visits and provide a picture of America as seen through the eyes of an artist. The first visit, in 1896, was to lecture on the arts. The second lecture tour, in 1900, was made on behalf of the National Trust, and Ashbee met many American leaders. The third visit, in 1908, was for his Guild of Handicraft, an artistic colony in Gloucestershire, lately saved from dissolution by the American millionaire Joseph Fels. The fourth, fifth and sixth visits - two in 1915 and one in 1916 - were made as representative of the 'Bryce Group', first to encourage Americans to join the Group in an organization to guarantee peace after the war, and later to assist in the formation of the American League to Enforce Peace. The account of these visits is relevant to an understanding of the attitude of neutral America. Ashbee interviewed Bryan and Roosevelt; also Brandeis, Frankfurter, and other eminent jurists; and many German-Americans. On the seventh and final visit, in 1923, he lectured on the Arab-Zionist question and also the arts.

1. The diary and related letters and documents have been published in Nicholas B. Wainwright, 'Turmoil at Pittsburgh: Diary of Augustine Prevost, 1774', *Pennsylvania Magazine of History and Biography*, LXXXV (1961), pp. 111-62.

2. The collection is described by E.G. Sutcliffe, 'Charles Reade's Notebooks', in *Studies in Philology*, vol. xxvii, pp. 64-109, 1930.

3. Copies also in King's College Library, Cambridge (original typescript), and the Library of Congress, Washington, D.C.

LONDON MISSIONARY SOCIETY, 11 Carteret Street, London SW1H 9DL

UNITED STATES CORRESPONDENCE. 104 letters (1 box). 1799-1840.

Ninety-three letters from the United States, five copies of letters from London, and six from other parts of the world, to America or concerning Americans. The period mainly represented is 1807-11. Concerned with matters of mutual interest, which include the question of the dispatch of American missionaries under the auspices of the Society. There are requests for literature, applications for appointments, and letters of reference. A few early letters refer to work with the Indians and frontiersmen (e.g. in Kentucky); a few contain comments on the state of religion in America, and there is an occasional reference to the political situation, e.g. non-intercourse and the War of 1812.

MORRISON, ROBERT (1782-1834). Journal. 1807.

Missionary in China. Entry for 1807 contains brief comments on his visits to New York and Philadelphia *en route* from Britain to China, and the gift to him by Oliver Wolcott of a passage to China.[1]

1. These manuscripts and the Society's Library and Archives up to 1940 are on permanent loan to the School of Oriental and African Studies, University of London, Malet Street, London WC1E 7HP.

C.S. MARRIS, ESQ., 9 Douglas House, Maida Avenue, London W2 1TQ

CROWTHER FAMILY. Business and private papers: *c.* 100 letters; some miscellaneous papers.[1] 1769-1825.

Woollen manufacturers and merchants, Gomersal, Churwell, and Leeds, Yorkshire. The correspondence relates both to family and to business affairs.

The earliest item of American interest appears to be a letter, 30 Aug. 1769, from Buchanan Hastie & Co., Glasgow, to George Crowther & Co., concerning a bill remitted from Virginia for payment in Whitehaven; the latest, a letter, 8 and 9 Oct. 1825, from David Crowther, Liverpool, to George Crowther & Co., including comment on the probable demand for woollen goods in the New York market. The two major blocks of relevant material, however, consist of correspondence relating to the American journeys, 1772-5, of Benjamin Crowther, and to the stay in the United States, 1811-24, of his nephew, David Crowther.

1. See H. Heaton, 'Yorkshire Cloth Traders in the United States, 1770-1840', *The Thoresby Miscellany*, vol. xi, pp. 225-7, 1945. (Thoresby Society Publications, vol. xxxvii).

(*a*) The first of these two includes letters from Burntisland, Scotland, and Boston, written by George Parker of Glasgow and Wilmington, N.C., as whose apprentice Benjamin Crowther went to America; and letters written by Crowther from Burntisland, from New Brunswick, and from Boston. The letters are addressed to George Crowther or to Crowther & Porrit; they deal with Parker's shipbuilding and merchanting affairs, Crowther's impressions of Boston, etc.
(*b*) The second group consists mainly of letters written from New York by David Crowther:

(i) Letters to his brothers George and Thomas, 1819-24, usually concern business matters - demand for various types of woolens; news of other Yorkshire merchants; trade with Havana ('we endeavour to keep our Havana business as much a *secret* as possible and pray you do the same'); suggested revision of their partnership agreement in order to lessen cost of United States customs duties.

(ii) Letters to his sister, Mrs. Ann Barrett, 1811-5, to her son George, 1817-24, and to her daughter Mary, 1817-24, concern family affairs, political and religious conditions and customs, etc.

(iii) There is also some correspondence relating to the death and settlement of the affairs of George Crumbleholme, the Charleston, S.C., agent of the Crowthers, 1820; a printed letter, Philadelphia, 1 Mar. 1818, *To the Merchants of Great Britain Trading to the United States of America* (4 pages), by John Cook; and a copy of a document, 9 Feb. 1824, giving David Crowther power of attorney to dispose of the South Carolina Bank shares held by Sarah Nussey of Batley, Yorks.

See also Crowther Family letters in the Brotherton Library, University of Leeds. (p. 239).

MARYLEBONE CRICKET CLUB, Lord's Ground, London NW8 8QN

RECORDS.

The Marylebone Cricket Club has amongst its records miscellaneous papers relating to cricket in the U.S.A., notably the English tour of 1872.

MERCERS' COMPANY, Mercers' Hall, Ironmonger Lane, London, E.C.2

RECORDS.

The Acts of Court of the Mercers' Company, which began in 1453, contain such things as orders made for the investment of money in the early seventeenth-century Virginia ventures; and in the nineteenth century the Company was making grants to assist emigrants from its Irish estates. There may be more American material in the other records of the Company.

METHODIST MISSIONARY SOCIETY,[1] 25 Marylebone Road, London NW1 5JR

'LETTERS OF SPECIAL INTEREST.' 1736, 1788.

(*a*) Letter from Georgia, 5 Feb. 1736, from Charles Wesley to Mrs. Sally Kirkham Chapone, chiefly about his spiritual condition.[2]
(*b*) Letter, Bath, Va., 15 Aug. 1788, from Francis Asbury, first Bishop of the Methodist Episcopal Church, to 'my dear Winscom', describing his circuit ('a thousand miles'), mentioning that he has just opened a school, and expatiating on the need for cordial Anglo-American relations.

COKE PAPERS. Certificate; letter. 1784, 1806.

(*a*) Certificate, 2 Sept. 1784, signed by John Wesley, appointing Thomas Coke superintendent of Methodist work in America.
(*b*) Letter from New York, 7 May 1806, from Francis Asbury to Thomas Coke, describing his extensive travels through Eastern America, and mentioning the work beyond the Mississippi. Asbury says, 'in Delaware the millenium is certainly begun. They can live without slavery or liquid fire', and 'American sinners are the greatest sinners upon earth'.

LETTERS. 1802-31.

Chiefly concerned with the progress of Methodism in America.
(*a*) Twenty-four letters from New York, Virginia, Georgia, South Carolina, Maryland, Washington, D.C., Pennsylvania, and Rhode Island (none from a well-known figure), 1802-6, 1815-7 (included in a box marked 'Canada, 1802-1818'). Deal chiefly with spiritual experiences, the number of conversions, mentioning also mission work among Negroes, and camp meetings.
(*b*) Seven letters from New York, 1827-8, 1830-1 (included in box marked 'Home, 1825-1831'), from the headquarters of the Missionary Society of the Methodist Episcopal Church, New York, to the Wesleyan Methodist Missionary Society in London. Chiefly business matters and copy resolutions. Mention missions in South America and Liberia.

ORDINATION CERTIFICATES.

Joshua Marsden to the office of Elder in the Methodist Episcopal Church of America, signed by Francis Asbury, 1 June 1802; and to the office of Deacon in the same, signed by Richard Whatcoat, Associate Bishop, 2 June 1802.

1. See Rosemary Keen, *A Survey of the Archives of Selected Missionary Societies* (London, 1968).
2. Printed in Frank Baker, *Charles Wesley as Revealed by his Letters* (London, 1948), pp. 21-3. (Wesley Historical Society Lectures No. 14).

MIDLAND BANK LTD., Poultry, London EC2P 2BX

The bank holds an extensive collection of banking and other business records. Nineteenth-century sources include records of about fifty joint-stock banks which were amalgamated by the Midland Bank before 1918. Several constituent banks in Lancashire had close links with the cotton trade (for example, Leyland and Bullins, 1807-1901, Preston Banking Company, 1844-94, and North and South Wales Bank, 1836-1908).[1]

The main classes of nineteenth-century records are minute-books of directors' and shareholders' meetings, balance sheets, general ledgers, with some letter-books and memoranda. The minute-books of constituent banks contain a number of references to American affairs, notably the finding of gold in California and

1. See W.F. Crick and J.E. Wadsworth, *A Hundred Years of Joint Stock Banking* (London, 1936), for a history of the Midland Bank.

the disruption of trade during the Civil War and the Spanish-American War. Other relevant records include:
(*a*) North and South Wales Bank, memoranda book, 1851-1907. Includes correspondence about investment in, *inter alia,* United States 4 per cent funded stocks (1880), and advances to cotton brokers (1895).
(*b*) Leyland, Bullins & Co., Liverpool, 'ledger no. 14', 1887-94. Entries include accounts of firms in Galveston, Houston, New Orleans, New York, Philadelphia and Savannah, Ga., as well as accounts of an 'adventure in cotton' from Augusta, Ga., and one from Galveston, and an 'adventure in seedcake' from New Orleans. Many of the accounts appear to have been transferred from Lemonius & Co., Liverpool, liquidated in 1887.

In the twentieth century the Midland Bank was the first British clearing bank to open a Foreign Exchange Department, and the Bank holds records relating to American exchange transactions from 1905 onwards. Early foreign business and financial agreements in the First World War are documented in correspondence and statistical records.

Detailed catalogues of the Bank's records are complete or in progress. Requests to consult the records should be supported by a university or other centre of research, and should be addressed to the Archivist, Midland Bank.[2]

MORAVIAN CHURCH IN GREAT BRITAIN AND IRELAND, 5 Muswell Hill, London

ARCHIVES.
The British headquarters of the Church in Fetter Lane, London, was destroyed by enemy action in 1941.[1] The surviving papers are in process of being listed and reassembled.

The records now available in London consist of bound volumes, and of packets of unbound papers, as follows:
(*a*) Bound volumes of minutes (some in German), extracts from or translation of minutes, miscellaneous collections of material concerning bishops, etc.; eighteenth and nineteenth centuries. There is likely to be relevant material scattered throughout these, since, from the time of the 1735 settlement of Moravians in Georgia, the Church was very active in missionary work in America, especially among the Indians and the Eskimoes. The eighteenth-century translation of the 'Headquarters Diary' for 1747, for example, includes, for 12 June, references to correspondence with Lord Baltimore about land in Maryland and to plans for settlements in Pennsylvania and Georgia.
(*b*) Two packets contain contemporary extracts from 1745 and 1747 'prayer day' proceedings in London. Included is material concerning missionary work among the Indians and other activities of the Brethren in America, mainly in Pennsylvania, in the form of letters (including one from George Whitefield, 4 Mar. 1745), reports, and journals.

MORGAN GRENFELL & CO. LTD., 23 Great Winchester Street, London EC2P 2AX

The firm of Morgan Grenfell, merchant bankers, is willing to make its older records available to senior research students, subject to approval of any proposed published use. However, a list of queries concerning the role of George Peabody and Junius Morgan in the flotation of various American issues in the London market, or of investments in American railroad stock, revealed that almost all their papers had been repatriated to New York, as has Junius Morgan's business correspondence with J.P. Morgan.

Inquiries should be addressed to the Administration Director.

JOHN MURRAY (PUBLISHERS) LTD., 50 Albemarle Street, London W1X 4BD

INTERNATIONAL COPYRIGHT. 1842, 1852.
The firm's files of the following authors contain letters on the subject of international copyright.
(*a*) Charles Dickens. A letter (printed), 7 July 1842, concerns attitudes in the United States towards international copyright legislation; letters of 2 Aug. 1842 and 18 May 1852 are also on international copyright.
(*b*) Edward Bulwer Lytton. A letter (copy), 14 June 1852, from Sir John Crampton, the British Minister in Washington, to Lytton, says that things in America are at the most favourable stage for the passage of international copyright legislation. Another letter, 19 June 1852, from Crampton to Lytton, states that 'the public feeling is very much changed on the subject since Mr. Dickens was here', and discusses the relationship of federal and state jurisdiction and action in the matter. There is also a letter, 9 July 1852, from Lytton, concerning subscriptions to a fund for the copyright cause, and an undated memorandum headed 'Mem. Am. Copyright', listing contributions to the fund.
(*c*) Philip Henry Stanhope, Viscount Mahon (later 5th Earl Stanhope). Seven letters, Mar.-May 1842, on the wording of the Copyright Bill and its passage through Parliament.

MUSEUM OF LONDON, London Wall, London EC2Y 5HN

SUFFRAGETTE FELLOWSHIP COLLECTION.
A collection of papers donated by the Suffragette Fellowship. Included is a file on the international women's suffrage movement which contains correspondence, *c.* 1921, with Alice Paul, Chairman of the National Woman's Party in the United States, and the typewritten autobiography of Kitty Marion describing the part she played in the birth-control movement in the United States.

NATIONAL ARMY MUSEUM, Royal Hospital Road, London SW3 4HT

TOWNSHEND PAPERS. 1755-60. (6806/41)
(*a*) MS. 'French Account of Genl. Braddocks Defeat near Fort Du Queens, July 1755.' (In English.)

2. A valuable guide to British insurance records in general is H.A.L. Cockerell and Edwin Green, *The British Insurance Business, 1547-1970* (London, 1976). Although the published results of this survey are primarily concerned with U.K. insurance business, there are a number of general overseas references.

1. The existence of relevant records at the Fetter Lane headquarters was noted in the preface to Andrews & Davenport, p. vi.

(*b*) MS. volume of General Orders by Lord Townshend, Quebec, 21 Sept. 1759 to 27 May 1760.
(*c*) Four leather bound notebooks, MS. 'Journal of the Campaign against Quebec', by Lord Townshend.
(*d*) MS. instructions for officers commanding battalions in Canada, signed by Montcalm. (In French.)
(*e*) MS. letters, notes, journals, etc. relating to the Quebec campaign.

SEVEN YEARS WAR - OTHER DOCUMENTS. 1732-62.
(*a*) MS. notebook (inscribed on front Lieut. Hamilton), written *c.* 1760. Includes orders given by Major-Genl. Wolfe in America: Halifax, April 30th 1759. (6707/11)
(*b*) MS. book dealing with the organization and distribution of the British Army, 1732. Includes detailed distribution of British troops in North America. (6807/217)
(*c*) MS. Journal of Lieut. D.A. Gordon, 40th Regiment, covering the period May 18th to July 25th, 1758, and describing the siege of Louisbourg. (The Journal is a copy written by his son, William Augustus Gordon.) (6807/131)
(*d*) Two MS. books of the orders of Major Genl. James Wolfe. (These are later transcripts of orders issued by Wolfe at various times during his military career.)
Vol. 50: includes orders and regulations of Major General Wolfe, Commander-in-Chief of a Body of Troops employed up the River St. Lawrence, North America, 4th May to 9th Sept. 1759.
Vol. 51: Orders given by Major General Wolfe in America, 1759. (6807/50-51)
(*e*) 'A Report of the Particulars relating to the Fortifying of this place (Halifax) made according to Instructions from the Honourable Board of His Majesty's Ordnance, dated 23rd May 1758, and by Order of his Excellency Major-General Amherst, dated 14th Sept. 1766.' Halifax, Nova Scotia, 29th May 1761, by P. Mackillar, Sub-Director and Major of Engineers. (6807/129)
(*f*) Various documents relating to the surrender of St. John's, Newfoundland to the French, 27th June 1762; and its restitution, 18th Sept. 1762. (6807/430)
(*g*) MS. letter to Brig. Gen. George Townshend, London, from Guy Carleton, 3rd Jan. 1761, saying that he is not aware of the attacks being made on the General in regard to the late campaign in Canada. (6510/100)

AMERICAN WAR OF INDEPENDENCE. 1775-83.
(*a*) Extracts from various standing orders, mid-18th cent., and letters of Maj. Genl. Francis Laye, R.A., to his father, while serving in America, 1775-81. (6807/154)
(*b*) Two letters, 18th and 19th Sept. 1777, from the Americans Brig. Genl. Warner and Col. J. Brown to Brig. Henry Watson Powell at Ticonderoga, demanding his surrender, with Powell's reply. Also includes a note by Powell's ADC, Lt. Thomas Bonnor, 15th Foot. (6807/429)
(*c*) Account of the services of George Dawson in the American War of Independence. (6603/60)
(*d*) 14th Regiment orderly book: detachment of Regiment at Halifax, Nova Scotia, 1776. (5904/175)
(*e*) MS. book 'Proceedings of a General Court-Martial held at Brunswick in the State of New Jersey by order of his Excellency Gen. Washington, Commander-in-Chief of the Army of the United States of America, for the Trial of Maj. Gen. Lee, July 4th 1778...(6807/99)
(*f*) Letter of Gen. Guy Carleton to Brig. Gen. Fox, expressing appreciation of his services, Nov. 24th 1783. (6807/451)

VERE HODGE MSS. (6510/146 (2))
(*a*) Letter from Mr. Pownall relating to His Majesty's woods in America.
(*b*) Representation of the state of the colonies in 1754. Plan for the union of the Northern colonies.

COOTE PAPERS. (6912/14)
The Coote Papers include the order books of Lt. Gen. Sir Eyre Coote (1762-1823), including those for North America, 1776-82. (14 vols.)

NATIONAL MARITIME MUSEUM, Romney Road, Greenwich, London SE10 9NF

The manuscript material in the National Maritime Museum has been brought together from a variety of sources, including public and semi-public records, private papers and collections of documents made by persons interested in particular aspects of naval history. The following is a summary of American material found in official Admiralty records, including the collection of ships' plans and drawings; personal papers and library collections; Lloyd's Register; and ships' logs. It is by no means exhaustive, as the collection is very large and is still growing.

ADMIRALTY RECORDS
(*a*) Orders from Admiralty to Navy Board, 1688-1715; Navy Board Replies 1738-1831. 1,492 volumes.
A great deal of American material would be found in these records. Some information on such topics as the supply of timber and naval stores, shipbuilding practice, and charting of the North American coast has been extracted by the Custodian of Manuscripts for specific purposes, such as exhibitions held at the Museum. The following are examples:
(i) Naval Stores, 1696-1784.
Admiralty to Navy Board. 31 Dec. 1696, instructions for agents to investigate the supply of naval stores in New England. (ADM/A/1837)
Admiralty to Navy Board. 17 Dec. 1701, trial to be made of turpentine imported from New England, with a report on it from the officers at Deptford Yard. (ADM/A/1887)
Admiralty to Navy Board. 3 Jan. 1728, opinion asked for on Thomas Coram's petition concerning his work in promoting supply of naval stores in America, and settlement of shipwrights, etc., in New England. Draft reply. (ADM/A/2159)
Navy Board to Admiralty. 26 Apr. 1748, contract with Messrs. Hennikers for masts from New England, forwarded for the grant of a royal licence. (ADM/B/138)
Navy Board to Admiralty. 30 Oct. 1772, report on Mr. Duer of New York's plan for obtaining masts from New York and the proposal from shipbuilders of New York for building a frigate for His Majesty's service, the latter again not recommended. (ADM/B/187)
Navy Board to Admiralty. 17 Apr. 1777, details of bounties paid on import of naval stores from America. Copy of reply sent to Treasury. (ADM/B/194)
Navy Board to Commissioner Duncan at Halifax. 1 May 1784, asking for report on naval stores available in his neighbourhood. Commissioner Duncan's reply (letter-book copy). (HAL/F/2)
(ii) Timber, 1700-73.
Admiralty to Navy Board, 13 Dec. 1700, letter and papers from Lord Bellomont, Governor of New England, on timber supplies. Has

sent specimens to England, sets out advantages of using American timber. Asks for a report on his proposals. (ADM/A/1878)

Admiralty to Navy Board, 1 Apr. 1740, letters and report from David Dunbar, Surveyor of Woods in America, forwarded for opinion. Concerned with supply of masts for His Majesty's Navy. (ADM/A/2282)

Navy Board to Admiralty, 19 Apr. and 17 Oct. 1771, report on information about American timber received from Roger Fisher of Liverpool, author of pamphlet *Heart of Oak, the British Bulwark* (London, 1763; 2nd edition 1771). Praises American live oak and pitch pine. (ADM/B/185)

Navy Board to Admiralty, 30 Apr. 1773, report on undesirability of building ships in North America. Messrs. Begbie & Manson, shipbuilders, of Hobeau, S.C., have offered to build a 32-gun ship with live oak and pine timber and desire employment in refitting navy ships. Navy Board gives unfavourable opinion of American materials and workmanship. (ADM/B/187)

(iii) Charting the North American Coast, 1720-37.

Capt. J. Gascoigne was employed by the Admiralty on a survey of the North American coast. The log of his ship *Aldborough* kept during this period records details about coastline, harbours, surveying practice, etc. (ADM/L/A/79) (ADM/A/2161)

(iv) Shipbuilding practice, 1747.

Navy Board to Admiralty, 4 Mar. 1747, report on building 44-gun ship in New England. Builder - Col. Meserve. Also report on repairing of the *Bien Aimé* by Benjamin Hollowell of Boston. (ADM/B/138)

(*b*) Correspondence between the Commissioners for taking care of sick and hurt seamen and the Admiralty relating to the American prisoners of war. 2 volumes; some loose papers. 1777-83. (ADM/M/404, 405)

The arrangements for the care of prisoners of war were at this time the responsibility of the Commissioners appointed for taking care of sick and wounded seamen. There are letters in these volumes on the arrangements for setting up and staffing a prison at Plymouth; petitions from prisoners requesting permission to serve on British ships, and pardons for prisoners 'on condition of their entering and continuing to serve us in our Royal Navy'. From autumn 1778 negotiations were under way for the exchange of prisoners. Authorizations from the Lords Commissioners of the Admiralty to Commissioners for taking care of sick and hurt seamen and for exchanging prisoners include names and ranks and ships on which the prisoners had served; a letter, 25 July 1778, from David Hartley, concerns a report from Benjamin Franklin on English prisoners held at Brest; a letter from Passy, 1 Jan. 1779, from Franklin signifies agreement for arrangements for exchanging prisoners. (Hartley and Franklin were principal agents appointed to arrange exchanges of prisoners.)

(*c*) Emigration of American Loyalists, 1783-5. From the volume of Treasury Transport letters, Jan. 1783-Dec. 1789. (ADM/O.T./1)

These transport orders sent from the Lords Commissioners of the Treasury to the Admiralty include detailed orders for moving American Loyalist families to other British colonies, for example, Bahamas and Nova Scotia.

(*d*) The Museum holds the Admiralty collections of ships' plans of ships built for or purchased by the Royal Navy, 1700-1900. A list has been compiled of the plans of American-built ships which the Royal Navy captured or purchased and also of ships of the Royal Navy captured by the Americans. There are thirty-eight names in these two lists.

PERSONAL PAPERS

KEPPEL, ADMIRAL THE HON. AUGUSTUS (1725-86). Coast of North America: order books. 1754-5. (46.MS.9580)

Appointed Commander-in-Chief, North American Station 1754. The order books contain copies of instructions sent out by Keppel; included are instructions for sending a small party of seaman up the Potomac to join General Braddock's troops and assist them in crossing rivers and building vessels on the Great Lakes, Mar. 1755. and for the examination of all ships passing through Hampton Roads, Va., May 1755.

HOOD, ADMIRAL VISCOUNT (1724-1816). Log books, 1760-95; letter and order books, 1767-95; letters received, 504 letters, 1771-1815. (50.MS.0096)

Samuel, 1st Viscount Hood, Commander-in-Chief North America 1767-70. Sent to join Graves in New York 1781-2. Letters include a memorandum in Hood's writing on the events of 5 Sept. 1781, dated Coast of Virginia, 6 Sept. 1781.[1]

GRAVES, ADMIRAL THOMAS (1725-1802). Log books, 1779-82; loose papers; drafts of letters to the Admiralty, 1764-82; private papers, 1782-95. (MS.9365)

Later 1st Baron Graves. Served with Vice Admiral Byron's squadron in North America 1778, and on the North American Station 1781-82. Orders of sailing, instructions, rendezvous, etc., are to be found in the papers 1781-82.

CORNWALLIS, ADMIRAL SIR WILLIAM (1744-1819). Letters received; journals; order and letter-books. 1770-9.

(*a*) Letters received[2] (35.MS.0105). These are mainly letters addressed to Sir William Cornwallis, a naval captain during the War of Independence, and a brother of Lord Cornwallis. The letters thus touch upon both military and naval aspects of the War, although not to any important extent.

(*b*) Orders received while commanding the *Isis* on the North American Station 1777, with some draft replies. This book is one of the sixty-one volumes of Cornwallis Papers known as the Cornwallis West Collection. (MS. 9575)

STARKE, LIEUTENANT JOHN: 'The case of Lieutenant John Starke of H.M. Navy', together with a short sketch of the operations of the war in Canada in which he was employed during the years 1775-1777 (34 pages). (49.MS. 129)

Starke's service was in the defence of Quebec, on the St. Lawrence River and on Lake Champlain. His memorial was written to show to Lord Sandwich, to gain employment.

COLLIER, ADMIRAL SIR GEORGE (1738-95). Journal, papers. 1776-9.

(*a*) Personal journal of the war in America, 1776. (35.MS.0085) Sir George sailed for America in the *Rainbow* in 1776, carrying reinforcements of Hessian troops. Soon after arrival he was sent by Lord Howe to Halifax, N.S., where he took command as senior officer. The notebook contains jottings of incidents and remarks which he used for letters he sent back to England. It shows a clear change of confidence in the American situation between August and September 1776.

(*b*) 'A Detail of Some Particular Services Performed in America during the Years 1776-1779 by Commodore Sir George Collier, Commander-in-Chief on the American Station.' Compiled from journals

1. Printed in *Letters Written by Sir Samuel Hood...in 1781-2-3* (London, 1895) (Navy Records Society Publications, vol. iii). See also *Letters to the Ministry from Governor Bernard, General Gage and Commodore Hood* (London and Boston, 1769).

2. This collection was formerly the property of Major R.F. Wykeham-Martin and is reported in H.M.C. Various Collections vi [55], pp. 297-434.

and original papers by G.S. Rainier (Collier's secretary) (174 pages). (MS. 9612) A note at the end suggests that this narrative was intended for publication. The text was carefully written and corrected in several places.

KEITH, ADMIRAL VISCOUNT (1746-1823). Letters. 1776-82.

Letters, 1776-82, sent and received while in command of *Perseus* and *Warwick* off the coast of North America, including information on the reduction of Charlestown.

LEWIS, CAPTAIN THOMAS (1742-95). Letters and papers. 1778-82.

Letters, 1779-82; papers relating to the Carlisle Peace Commission, 1778.

WARREN, ADMIRAL SIR JOHN BORLASE (1753-1822). Correspondence with Lord Melville during the War of 1812: 34 letters. 1812-4. (MS. 9622)

Admiral Warren commanded the North American Station 1812-4. These private letters to Lord Melville include accounts of the progress of the sea war, of the effects of the blockade on American trade, of the treatment of British merchants and prisoners of war, etc. Warren encloses newspaper cuttings from American newspapers with his own marginal comments, and many intercepted American letters containing comments on the war.

HULBERT, GEORGE REDMOND (1774-1825). Letter-books, account books, and letters received. 1813-23. (MS. 56/040)

Naval agent and Admiral's secretary. Served with Admiral Warren 1808, 1810-4. Hulbert acted as agent for several prizes. There is information about the procedure followed in the collection and distribution of prize money, etc.

CODRINGTON, ADMIRAL SIR EDWARD (1770-1851). Personal papers referring to Codrington's service while commanding H.M.S. *Tonnant* in American waters, 1814-5, including official letters and order books. (MS. 9278)

Served on the American Station 1814-5. Included are a bundle of private letters[3] describing the destruction of Washington, the taking of Alexandria, the failure at Baltimore, the New Orleans expedition of 1815. There are plans and orders for the New Orleans expedition and for landing troops.

BOWKER, COMMODORE JOHN (b. 1770). Letter- and order book. 1818

Letter- and order book, Feb.-May 1818, of Commodore John Bowker on the Newfoundland Station.

MILNE, ADMIRAL SIR ALEXANDER (1806-96). Papers. 1860-64. (49. MS. 117)

The Milne Papers, while including some papers of other members of the family, cover in detail the career of Sir Alexander Milne, Commander-in-Chief, North American and West Indian Station 1860-4; First Naval Lord 1866-8, 1872-6; member of the Committee appointed to deal with the claims arising from the *Alabama* dispute. Records for the time when he was commanding the North American and West Indian Station are very full. There are also papers collected together by Milne whilst at the Admiralty, which include memoranda on naval policy. American material includes:

(*a*) Nine volumes of letter-books containing copies of Milne's letters to the Admiralty, 14 Jan. 1860-5 Apr. 1864. Fully indexed.

(*b*) Three volumes of letter-books containing copies of Milne's letters to ambassadors, governors, consuls, etc., 13 Mar. 1860-10 Apr. 1864. There are letters to British ambassadors, consuls and commanders of United States forces on the seizure of British ships by American cruisers, and on questions of contraband, etc., memoranda on policy to be followed by British ships in blockaded ports and when involved in incidents arising from the Civil War; and letters asking British Consuls for confidential information on shore defences of ports and harbours within their consular jurisdiction.

(*c*) Several parcels of letters received by Milne, 1860-4, include a selection of Admiralty letters marked by Milne 'Very important letters on the American Command'. These include *c*. 100 letters, confidential reports, etc., on the seizure of ships, the right of search, *Trent* case, Newfoundland fisheries, etc., and also several of Milne's own memoranda: Memorandum relative to the North American and West Indian Station for the information of his successor, deals with the defence of Canada, the Canadian canal system, the reception of British ships in American ports, etc. (115 pages). Memorandum relative to the Civil War in America, containing detailed notes on the effects of the war on the Station and discussion of various cases including the *Alabama* and matters arising from blockade-running, etc. (72 pages). Précis of papers relating to the Civil War in America (67 pages).

(*d*) Dispatch box containing about fifty letters, 1861-2, 1864, from Lord Lyons, British Minister in Washington, dealing with the interests of British citizens, prize-court captures, American opinion on war events and war news, etc; seven letters from William Stewart about the *Alabama* and the *Blanche*; many letters from the Duke of Somerset, First Lord of the Admiralty, with some draft replies by Milne, including a bundle inscribed by Milne 'most important letters from Duke of Somerset in case of war with the United States, 1861-1862'. About fifty letters, Jan. 1860-Apr. 1863 (these were returned to Milne after Grey's death) from Milne to Sir Frederick Grey; several pressed copybooks of private out-letters, 1860-2.

(*e*) Papers collected together by Milne during his period at the Admiralty include many memoranda on naval policy, among which are:

(i) Folder on the 'Newfoundland Fisheries, 1840'. Including Milne's own printed report and various letters and notes on the Newfoundland and Nova Scotia fisheries.

(ii) Folder on 'Naval Policy in North America, 1861-1866'. Mostly printed reports dealing with the defence of Canada in the event of war with the United States; but including a manuscript list of vessels suitable for the protection of the North American lakes, 1865.

(iii) Folder on the '*Alabama* case, 1863-1872'. Including a bundle of about fifty letters from Lord Lyons in Washington, 1863, and many letters addressed to Milne as a member of the *Alabama* claims committee, 1872. There are manuscript notes of the proceedings of the committee and several printed reports.

LLOYD'S REGISTER OF BRITISH AND FOREIGN SHIPPING.

Surveyors' reports and plans of ships, from American ports: Baltimore, 1 report, 1890; New York, 1 report, 1898; Philadelphia, 2 boxes, 1880-1901; Portland, Ore., part of one box, 1898-9; San Francisco, part of one box, 1877-1900. (Printed forms filled in in manuscript.)

The reports occasionally have ships' plans and correspondence as enclosures.

3. See *A Memoir of the Life of Admiral Sir Edward Codrington with Selections from his public and private correspondence*, edited by his daughter Lady Bourchier, 2 volumes (London, 1873).

SHIPS' LOGS.

A large collection of the logs of both merchant and warships. While the logs kept by officers of ships of the Royal Navy were preserved by the Admiralty, there was no central repository for the records of merchant ships until the middle of the nineteenth century. In consequence the latter are a haphazard collection, but the former provide a continuous record from the late seventeenth to the early nineteenth century. The following are examples of logs with American interest:

(*a*) Personal journals. 'Journal from Bristol towards South Carolina in the ship *Lloyd*. Jan.-Oct. 1768'. One volume covering two voyages. An illustrated journal kept by the master, Nicholas Pocock, marine artist. There is some description of trade with South Carolina in rice, turpentine, skins, etc. The ship was owned by Richard Champion. (MS. 56/051)

(*b*) An official Admiralty log. 'A Journal of the proceedings of His Majesty's Ship *Eagle* by Captain Henry Duncan commander. 1776-1780.' One volume (ADM/L/E/11). The ship was ordered to New York and anchored off Chester in the Delaware River. In Nov. 1777 the log records fighting between the rebels on Mud Island and royal troops, and describes the supplying of the army with provisions, etc.

(*c*) 'Journal of a voyage in the *Isaac Hicks*, merchant ship (Captain Dickenson) from Liverpool to New York, kept by a passenger.' Feb.-Apr. 1829 (8 pages). An account of an eighty-six day crossing. (50.MS.0165)

PUBLIC RECORD OFFICE,
Ruskin Avenue, Kew, Richmond

The Public Record Office is the official custodian of most of the separate archives of the various departments of the British government and of the central courts of law. Its holdings have been described in the guides by Andrews & Davenport, Andrews, and Paullin & Paxson, which include elaborate notes on the administrative history of the departments concerned and also general descriptions of lists, indexes, and other aids to finding material; *this information is not repeated here*.

Since these earlier guides were published, several changes have taken place at the P.R.O. The Public Records Act of 1967 opened most of the public records to inspection thirty years after the 1st of January of the year in which they were created. There are certain exceptions to this rule; some records are available without restriction of date, and others remain closed for longer periods. Whole classes affected are noted in a list displayed at the P.R.O., and in other cases the time limit is given in the class lists.

The records are divided between two depositories - at Chancery Lane and at Kew. Those at Chancery Lane are mainly legal documents, most of which are described in Volume I of the *Guide*, and census returns; departmental records are housed at Kew. Of the documents listed here, the following classes are kept at Chancery Lane:

Admiralty, High Court of
Bankruptcy, Court of
Chancery
Exchequer
Gifts and Deposits (Certain classes only)
Privy Council Office
Treasury Solicitor

The remainder of the groups surveyed are only available at Kew.

The *Guide* is in three volumes:

Guide to the Contents of the Public Record Office, vol.I: Legal Records, etc. (London, 1963); vol. II: State Papers and Departmental Records (London, 1963); vol. III: Documents Transferred, 1960-1966 (London, 1968). The latter covers transfers of records to the end of 1966. A new guide is in preparation; meanwhile a typescript Supplement, giving details of more recent accessions, is available in the searchrooms of the P.R.O.

The Public Record Office has also published a series of handbooks; those relevant here are listed with the record groups to which they refer. The *Guide* and handbooks should always be consulted before attempting to use the records. Also useful are Hilary Jenkinson, *Guide to the Public Records: Introductory* (London, 1949), V.H. Galbraith, *An Introduction to the Use of the Public Records* (London, corrected edition, 1952), and *The British Public Record Office: History, Description, Record Groups, Finding Aids, and Materials for American History with Special Reference to Virginia* (Richmond, Va., Virginia State Library, 1960).

Every class of records has a class list, usually descriptive, and many have subject indexes as well. This report has been compiled from these lists, but there are of course a great many, and it has been impossible to explore them completely for references to the United States. This report should not therefore be regarded as exhaustive. Legal records have not been surveyed except for the High Court of Admiralty, the Court of Bankruptcy, and the Court of Chancery; and Customs and Excise Records have been treated in a separate report.

As records are released each year under the thirty-year rule, not only are existing classes added to, but new classes, or even groups, become available. For example, records of the Air Ministry, Ministry of Aviation, Cabinet Office, Prime Minister's Office, and United Kingdom Atomic Energy Authority have all become available since the first edition of this guide appeared. An annual summary of records *transferred* to the P.R.O. is published as an appendix to the *Annual Report of the Keeper of Public Records on the Work of the Public Record Office* (Deputy Keeper before 1959), and from the thirty-year rule the date of their *release* can be predicted.

It should be noted when using the earlier guides that, since these were prepared, changes have been made in the classification, numbering, etc., of some records, and also that certain material described as being in other depositories has been transferred to the Public Record Office; no attempt has been made here to survey these changes in detail.

Finally, applications for reader's tickets can be made in person or by post. Application must be supported by a recommendation from someone of recognized position to whom the applicant is known personally, or from a recognized institution, e.g. High Commission's Office, embassy, university, etc.

The collections are arranged by their P.R.O. codes, as follows:

AB.	United Kingdom Atomic Energy Authority
ADM.	Admiralty
AIR.	Air Ministry
A.O.	Exchequer and Audit
AVIA.	Ministry of Aviation
B.	Court of Bankruptcy
B.T.	Board of Trade
C.	Court of Chancery
CAB.	Cabinet Office
C.O.	Colonial Office
E.	Exchequer
F.O.	Foreign Office
G.F.M.	Captured Enemy Documents
H.C.A.	High Court of Admiralty
H.O.	Home Office
IND.	Copyright Office
M.A.F.	Ministry of Agriculture and Fisheries
M.H.	Ministry of Health
M.T.	Ministry of Transport
P.C.	Privy Council

PREM. Prime Minister's Office
P.R.O. Public Record Office: Gifts and Deposits
T. Treasury
T.S. Treasury Solicitor
W.O. War Office

UNITED KINGDOM ATOMIC ENERGY AUTHORITY

Lists, etc.: 'United Kingdom Atomic Energy Authority: Class List' (typescript).

AB. 1. CORRESPONDENCE AND PAPERS. 1939-51.

Contains a number of items, on U.S., U.K., and Canadian scientific cooperation.

ADMIRALTY

Lists, etc.: P.R.O. *Lists and Indexes No. XVIII: List of Admiralty Records* (1963), with additions and corrections.
P.R.O. *Lists and Indexes, Supplementary Series No. VI: List of Admiralty Records to 1913* (1966), 2 vols.
'List of Admiral's Journals' (typescript and duplicated).
'Admiralty: Ships' Logs', 3 vols. (manuscript).
'Admiralty: Ships' Logs to 1946', 15 vols. (duplicated).
'Admiralty Station Records' (typescript).

ADM. 1/5691-19128. ADMIRALTY AND SECRETARIAT: PAPERS. 1858-1945.

Included are reports of courts martial, letters from admirals, captains, government departments, etc.; indexes and digests are available in ADM. 12. Examination of ADM. 1/5871 (1864) showed it to include correspondence about American ships in the Rio Grande, eighty-seven pages on the Civil War in a memorandum by Sir A. Milne on transferring the command of the North American and West Indian Station to Sir J. Hope, etc.

ADM. 7. SECRETARY'S DEPARTMENT: MISCELLANEA.

7/624. Lakes and rivers of Canada: defences. 1861-2.
7/625. Captain Warden's report on Canada. 1845-6.
7/626. United States defences: seaboard, lakes, and Canadian frontier, 1845.

ADM. 13. SUPPLEMENTARY.

13/1-63. Out-letters.[1] 1814-69.

Registers to these are available, for 1860-8, in ADM. 13/66-67. Examination of ADM. 13/66, the register for 1860-3, showed it to contain, under 'United States', thirteen pages of lists of letters, on the subjects of the blockade, the slave trade, etc.

13/184/9. *Standing Orders for the Squadron Employed on the North American and West Indian Station* (Halifax, N.S., 1862), with inserted manuscript notes.

ADM. 50. ADMIRALS' JOURNALS.

Journals for the North American and West Indian Station for 1854-85 are in ADM. 50/300-7; those for 1885-1909 are in ADM. 50/349-53.

ADM. 53. SHIPS' LOGS.

There may be some scattered material in these volumes, which are open without restriction as to date.

ADM. 110-13. VICTUALLING DEPARTMENT.

Out-letters, minutes, accounts, and registers all provide details for provisioning the eighteenth-century fleet on the American Station, giving prices and contractors' names, etc.

ADM. 116/1-5459. SECRETARY'S DEPARTMENT: CASES 1852-1945.

These are reports on every aspect of naval policy: reports from stations, international conferences, naval intelligence, etc. A number of American items are listed in the subject index.

ADM. 121. STATION RECORDS: MEDITERRANEAN.

121/64. Correspondence, American Civil War, 1861-5.

ADM. 123. STATION RECORDS: AFRICA.

123/164. American activities, 1857-60.
123/166. American and Portuguese activities, 1857-64.
123/167. French and American activities, 1860-3.

ADM. 125. STATION RECORDS: CHINA.

Correspondence on naval operations covering much of the Pacific, Japan, and ports in North Russia.

125/143. The Spanish-American War and the rebellion in the Philippines, 1898-1900.

ADM. 128/1-153. STATION RECORDS: NORTH AMERICA AND WEST INDIES. 1810-1913.

Correspondence, reports, memoranda, treaties, conventions, etc., relating to the Western Atlantic seaboard. Includes seven volumes of correspondence arising from the American Civil War. There are partial indexes in IND. 24314 and 24315.

ADM. 137/1-3955. HISTORICAL SECTION: 1914-8. WAR HISTORIES. 1900-23.

This class consists of documents assembled for writing the official history of the First World War. Many American items are listed, including a large number of telegrams.

ADM. 199/1-2363. WAR HISTORY: 1939-45; CASES AND PAPERS.

This list contains many items on American operations, Anglo-American and Allied cooperation, military assistance, convoys, merchant shipping, etc. Included are:

199/453. Lethbridge Joint Services Mission to the U.S.A.: recommendations, reports, etc., 1943-6.
199/460, 461. U.S. actions in the Pacific: reports by U.S. officers, 1942-4.
199/691. Anglo-American cooperation: report of the Bailey Committee and a history of U.S. naval bases in the U.K. War in the Far East: reports.

AIR MINISTRY

AIR. 40. DIRECTORATE OF INTELLIGENCE AND OTHER INTELLIGENCE PAPERS.

40/349-1133. Reports, etc., on U.S. bombing operations, 1942-5.

1. The Library of Congress holds photostats of part of volume 13/4: instructions to Rear-Admiral Sir Houston Stewart, Commander-in-Chief North American and West Indian Station, 3 Feb. 1857 and 7 Feb. 1860.

AIR. 42. COMBINED OPERATIONAL PLANNING COMMITTEE. 1943-5.

This committee coordinated bombing raids by the R.A.F. and the U.S.A.A.F.

AIR. 45. R.A.F. DELEGATION, WASHINGTON, D.C., 1942-5.

AIR. 46. AIR MISSIONS.

Several items concerning the U.S. and air training in Canada, 1939-46.

AIR. 48. UNITED STATES STRATEGIC BOMBING SURVEY, 1945-7.

Reports of bombing in Germany and occupied territories, and also of the effects of the atomic bomb on Hiroshima and Nagasaki.

EXCHEQUER AND AUDIT

Lists, etc.: P.R.O. *Lists and Indexes No. XLVI: List of the Records of...the Exchequer and Audit Department* (1921), with additions and corrections.

A.O. 2. ACCOUNTS DECLARED AND PASSED, IN BOOKS.

A.O. 2/1, 7, 12, 18, 20, 24, 30, 32 include accounts, 1828-36, of T. Crafer, paymaster of pensions to Loyalists. The class also includes the accounts of governors, agents, commissariats, etc., in New Brunswick, Upper Canada, etc.

A.O. 3. ACCOUNTS VARIOUS.

3/276. Compensation to Loyalists and other refugees. 1788-1837.

A.O. 16. MISCELLANEA.

16/44. Exemplification of 1775-7 accounts of Lord Dunmore, Governor of Virginia. 1801.

MINISTRY OF AVIATION

AVIA. 38. NORTH AMERICAN SUPPLIES. 1939-47.

Papers concerning the purchase of aircraft, components, materials, and fuel in the United States by British government departments.

COURT OF BANKRUPTCY

Lists, etc.: 'Court of Bankruptcy: Class List' (typescript and duplicated).

B.3. COMMISSIONS: FILES. 1759-1911. (Mainly 1790-1842.)

B. 4. COMMISSIONS: DOCKET BOOKS (REGISTERS). 1710-1849.

The registers contain summary particulars relating to the issue of commissions and renewed commissions of bankruptcy - see, e.g., W.E. Minchinton, ed., *The Trade of Bristol in the Eighteenth Century* (Bristol, 1957) (Bristol Record Society's Publications, vol. xx), which gives on pp. 184-9 a list of the bankruptcies of Bristol merchants, 1711-70, taken from B. 4/1-20; a few of the merchants and their creditors are noted as being resident in Virginia or elsewhere in America. The files relating to some of the cases listed in the register have survived, and the names of the bankrupt firms involved are given in the class list for B. 3.

B. 9. SELECTION FROM THE FILES OF PROCEEDINGS UNDER THE BANKRUPTCY ACTS, 1832-1902.

Several Americans are listed.

B. 10. PROCEEDINGS UNDER THE JOINT STOCK COMPANY ACTS, 1858-60.

10/23-29. Europe and American Steam Shipping Co., Ltd., 1858-9.
10/88. St. John's United Copper and Lead Mining Co., Newfoundland, Ltd., 1861.

BOARD OF TRADE

Lists, etc.: 'Board of Trade Records: 1846-1885' (duplicated) contains much more detailed descriptions of some of the records available for that period in B.T. 1 and a few other classes.
'Board of Trade: B.T. 31', 6 vols. (typescript).
P.R.O. *Lists and Indexes, Supplementary Series No. XI: List of Board of Trade Records to 1913* (1964).

B.T. 1/358-560. IN-LETTERS AND FILES, GENERAL, 1840-63.

The following, based on the duplicated list, shows the type of subjects covered in this class; further items may be found by use of B.T. 4/13-40, containing registers and indexes for 1840-64.
1/467/2205. American tariff for Mexican ports. 1847.
1/468/322. Postage on letters to the United States. 1848.
1/470/2506. Vancouver Island: grant to Hudson's Bay Co. 1848.
1/472/1298. Application from W.A. Adair, an American citizen, to send his brig *Eureka* through the St. Lawrence to the Atlantic. 1849.
1/473/2261. Prince Edward Island: relaxation of the treaty between the United States and Britain regulating the fisheries. 1849.
1/477/1395. United States: engaging of seamen. 1850.
1/478/1952. Statement of Vancouver Island Steam Sawing Mill & Agricultural Co. 1850.
1/479/2448. Adoption of one of the harbours of Ireland as a port of embarkation for America. 1850.
1/479/2767. Atlantic-Pacific ship canal convention: copy of convention between Britain and the United States relative to the establishment of a ship canal between the Atlantic and Pacific in Nicaragua; and copy of the dispatch from Sir Henry Bulwer.
1/479/2870. Letter from Norfolk, Va., Consulate concerning an outrage by a British ship's captain on a New Brunswick Negro seaman. 1850.
1/480/3299. Jamaica: duty on American vessels with coals. 1850.
1/485/1572. Granting of subsidy to promote steamship service between Nassau and America. 1851.
1/498/2161. London, Liverpool & North American Screw Steam Ship Co.: statistics of ships cleared to New York from London and Liverpool, and protest against charter of Mr. Cunard. 1852.
1/500/26. Consideration of charter of London, Liverpool & North American Screw Steam Ship Co. 1852.
1/502/338. Bavaria: emigrants to America. 1853.
1/515/1468. Vancouver Island and the United States. 1854.
1/532/2166. Sandwich Islands: effect of treaty with the United States on trade with the United Kingdom and Vancouver. 1855.
1/545/1726. Electric telegraph: claim of Mr. Morse for use of his invention. 1857.
1/545/2049. United States-Peruvian treaty concerning whalers in Peruvian ports. 1857.
1/547/709. London & Virginia Gold and Copper Mining Co.: registration as a foreign company. 1858.
1/557/771. Opening of port of New Orleans and effect on cotton trade. 1862.

1/560/1076. Illegal imprisonment: appointment of assessors to assist law officers to decide case against United States. 1863.

1/560/1423. Telegraph line through Asiatic Russia to connect European and American systems. 1863.

B.T. 2/4-5, 11-14. IN-LETTERS, FOREIGN OFFICE. 1838-45.

No detail is given about these in the available list. Examination of one volume (B.T. 2/13: 1841-4) showed it to be unindexed and to contain mainly covering letters from the Foreign Office together with copies of dispatches from Consuls in the United States and elsewhere.

B.T. 3/29-64. OUT-LETTERS, GENERAL. 1840-63.

The available list gives only the destination of the letters in each volume - e.g. Colonial Office, Customs, Miscellaneous Offices and Individuals. One volume (B.T. 3/33: 1844-7) of this last type examined showed only a few routine letters concerning American tariffs, and concerning trade in the Columbia River area.

B.T. 5. GENERAL: MINUTES. 1839-1952.

These are only rough drafts; the minute-books have either not been kept or are still in the Department.

B.T. 6. MISCELLANEA.

6/34. Canada: extracts from reports by J.W. Duscomb, 'the Commissioner appointed to inquire into the state of the Customs establishments on the Lower Canada Inland Frontier'. 1844.

6/80-81, 83-88. See report on H.M. Customs and Excise (p.88).

6/151-2. Lists of machinery, permission for the exportation of which was considered by the Board, including date, name of applicant, description of machinery, place to which exportation is desired (including the United States and specific American ports), and decision taken. 1825-43.

6/274-8. Miscellaneous papers. 1838-46.

There are likely to be scattered references to the United States among these. Examination of B.T. 6/278 showed, for example, that it included a letter from English ironmasters dated 2 July 1844, complaining of the high American duty on English iron.

6/290. Coasting trade: notes of action taken by other countries to remove restrictions.

The volume includes copies of reports from Crampton of conversations with the American Secretary of State, Marcy, on this matter, 1854.

B.T. 11. COMMERCIAL DEPARTMENT: CORRESPONDENCE AND PAPERS. 1866-1950.

There is an index of subjects and countries. A large number of items are listed under 'United States', mostly concerned with Anglo-American trade and with Lend-Lease.

B.T. 12/1-160. COMMERCIAL DEPARTMENT: OUT-LETTERS. 1864-1921.

There are probably scattered references to the United States among these volumes, all of which are indexed. The volume for 1871 (B.T. 12/8), for example, contains copies of letters to the Colonial Office about Canadian tariff policies and consequent trade relations with the United States, as well as answers to various routine inquiries about American tariffs. Indexes to the out-letters from 1897 are available in B.T. 36.

B.T. 15/1-398. FINANCE DEPARTMENT: CORRESPONDENCE AND PAPERS. 1865-1966.

There are a few minor items here, e.g.;

15/9/5449. Charleston, S.C., Consul: payment of legal expenses incurred in resisting extortionate claims by crew of British vessel. 1873.

B.T. 26/1-1476. STATISTICAL DEPARTMENT: PASSENGER LISTS INWARDS. 1878-88, 1890-1960.

B.T. 27/1-1922. STATISTICAL DEPARTMENT: PASSENGER LISTS OUTWARDS. 1890-1960.

B.T. 28. MINISTRY OF PRODUCTION. 1941-6.

Includes the correspondence and papers of the Anglo-American Coordinating Committee (Supply).

B.T. 31. COMPANIES REGISTRATION OFFICE: FILES OF DISSOLVED COMPANIES.[2] 1856-1953.

Each file contains the memorandum and articles of association of the company, with names, addresses, and occupations of its shareholders, and a few papers relating to its voluntary winding-up. A good many firms with American interests are included, e.g. the list of companies registered in 1873 includes such firms as Direct United States Cable Co. Ltd., Chicago Silver Mining Co. Ltd., Anglo-Californian Bank Ltd., and Central City (Colorado) Mining Co. Ltd. Alphabetical index available for 1933-48.

B.T. 32/1-15. REGISTER OF PASSENGER LISTS RECEIVED. 1906-51.

B.T. 35/1-28. COMMERCIAL DEPARTMENT: INDEXES AND REGISTERS OF CORRESPONDENCE. 1897-1918.

The correspondence to which these relate has not been transferred to the Public Record Office, but a considerable number of references to the United States appear in the registers.

B.T. 37. BANKRUPTCY DEPARTMENT: CORRESPONDENCE AND PAPERS.

37/18. Extradition treaty with the U.S. 1907.

B.T. 41. FILES OF JOINT STOCK COMPANIES REGISTERED UNDER THE 1844 AND 1856 ACTS.

Includes several firms with American interests, e.g.:

41/19-20. Anglo-Californian Gold Mining and Dredging Co.

41/709. United States Land Company.

B.T. 55. RECORDS OF DEPARTMENTAL COMMITTEES.

Contains several reports on U.S. industry, e.g.:

55/5/7. Memorandum on Cotton Industry in the U.S. 1929.

55/41/11. Combinations in the Iron and Steel Industries of the U.S. 1917.

B.T. 58. COMPANIES DEPARTMENT: CORRESPONDENCE AND PAPERS. 1858-1964.

Includes correspondence with a great many American companies.

2. The Bancroft Library holds microfilms for selected documents relating to Western history.

B.T. 59. DEPARTMENT OF OVERSEAS TRADE: OVERSEAS TRADE DEVELOPMENT COUNCIL.

Contains reports of several market investigations in the U.S. 1930-39.

B.T. 60. DEPARTMENT OF OVERSEAS TRADE: CORRESPONDENCE AND PAPERS. 1918-46.

The Department of Overseas Trade was established in 1918 to control commercial representation abroad and the formation of overseas commercial policy. It was merged with the Board of Trade in 1946. This class and B.T. 61, the establishment files, contain several items concerning commercial representation in the U.S., and Anglo-American trade.

B.T. 64. INDUSTRIES AND MANUFACTURES DEPARTMENT: CORRESPONDENCE AND PAPERS. 1918-50.

A number of items concerning American industry and Anglo-American trade are listed in the subject index. Out-letters from 1918-21 are in B.T. 85.

B.T. 87. MINISTRY OF PRODUCTION: MINISTERS' PRIVATE OFFICE PAPERS.

Several American items, 1942-5, e.g.:
Visits of Minister to U.S.; supply of steel from U.S.

B.T. 88 POST WAR COMMODITY POLICY AND RELIEF DEPARTMENT. 1940-3.

88/4-7. Negotiations with U.S. 1940-2.

COURT OF CHANCERY

C. 66. CHANCERY ENROLLMENTS: PATENT ROLLS.

Andrews, vol. i, Appendix A, pp. 268-73, traced the passage of a Patent through the seals to its final issue and enrollment. Of the various series of enrollments, the Patent Rolls, which include grants to discover colonies, charters of trading companies, appointments of colonial officials, and instructions to governors, are the most important.

C. 103-16. MASTERS' EXHIBITS.

Lists, etc.: 'Lists of Chancery Masters' Exhibits' (photostat).
In suits before the various Masters of the Court of Chancery, papers put forward as exhibits sometimes remained with the Court. They are listed under the names of the plaintiff, the defendant, and the places concerned. The following are only the obviously relevant papers where America is mentioned in the list; numerous mentions of merchants' papers in London, Bristol, and the West Indies would probably repay a detailed search.

104/13-14. Isaac *v.* Defriez. Invoices, receipts, journals, and freight books relating to the shipping business of Nathan Simson in New York and London. Some in Hebrew. 1700-26.

105/19. Love *v.* Cohen. Commercial correspondence and price lists. Jamaica and Philadelphia. 1784-8.

105/39. Grants of land under the colonial great seal, plans, and valuations. East Florida. 1767-83.

110/163. Fleming *v.* Lynde. Mercantile correspondence and accounts. North America and West Indies. 1753-68.

110/168. Holway (? Holman) *v.* Hynman. Letters relating to the Holman family. United States. 1785-1800.

110/186. Williams *v.* Wallaby. Letters of marque, accounts, and correspondence concerning the ship *Oliver.* London and North America. 1758-67.

CABINET OFFICE

Lists, etc.: *List of Cabinet Papers, 1880-1914* (P.R.O. Handbook No. 4, 1964).
List of Cabinet Papers, 1915 and 1916 (P.R.O. Handbook No. 9, 1966).
The Records of the Cabinet Office to 1922 (P.R.O. Handbook No. 11, 1966).
S.S. Wilson, *The Cabinet Office to 1945* (P.R.O. Handbook No. 17, 1975).
List of Papers of the Committee of Imperial Defence to 1914 (P.R.O. Handbook No. 6, 1964).
The Second World War: A Guide to Documents in the Public Record Office (P.R.O. Handbook No. 15, 1972).

Class lists and indexes are noted under each class.

CAB. 1. MISCELLANEOUS RECORDS.

1/11. file 40. U.S. pro-German policy, 1915.
1/15. files 5, 33. Arms purchase in the U.S., 1916.
1/18. file 46. Proposed reorganization of trade with the U.S., 1916.
1/21. file 11. Dependence on U.S. for munitions, 1916.
1/23. file 20. Benefit to merchant shipping if the U.S. entered the war, 1917.
1/25. files 5, 12. Anglo-American relations, 1917; file 25: shipping required for upkeep of an American army in France, 1917.
1/26. files 5, 6, 15. Irish and Catholic questions in the U.S.; attitude of the U.S. government to the Paris Resolutions, 1918.
1/27. file 15. Export restrictions in America.
1/28. file 22. Views of America on the peace treaty and U.S. internal affairs.

CAB. 21. REGISTERED FILES.

This class consists of the working papers of the Cabinet Office since its establishment in 1916, as distinct from the printed memoranda and the Cabinet conclusions or minutes. It contains a considerable number of items on Anglo-American relations and international conferences. The list is roughly chronological, and there is a subject index to the file code numbers.

CAB. 23. CABINET MINUTES. 1916-39.

A record of Cabinet proceedings was not kept until 1916. Reports of the proceedings were given by the Prime Minister to the Monarch, and are in the Royal Archives at Windsor. The P.R.O. has copies of these (see CAB. 41 below). The official minutes or conclusions made after 1916 are not a complete record of the proceedings, but summarize the pros and cons of the argument and give the decision reached. Photocopies of Cabinet minutes are on open access in the P.R.O., and there is an index to conclusions. Several items are listed under 'United States' in each volume of the index, but it is obviously incomplete. It would be necessary to consult the minutes on the dates when a particular matter of American interest might have been discussed.

CAB. 24. CABINET MEMORANDA. 1915-39.

These are papers circulated to Cabinet Ministers beginning with the Committee of Imperial Defence before the Cabinet Office was set up. There is an index in twenty-one volumes, which includes numerous references to American material.

CAB. 25. SUPREME WAR COUNCIL. 1917-9.

The most important problems of cooperation between the Allies were dealt with after November 1917 by the Supreme War Council. U.S. participation commenced with the second of its eight sessions. This class contains the files of the permanent Military Representatives at Versailles.

CAB. 27. CABINET COMMITTEES: GENERAL SERIES. 1915-39.

There are undoubtedly a number of American items in the files of several Cabinet committees, e.g.:
27/622-627. Foreign policy: minutes and memoranda, 1936-9.
27/548. British war debt to the U.S.A., 1933.
Titles of Cabinet committees are given in S.S. Wilson, op. cit., Annex II, Parts 1-3, pp. 181-239.

CAB. 28. ALLIED WAR CONFERENCES: PAPERS. 1915-20.

Minutes of the Supreme War Council and of other miscellaneous conferences. Each volume contains a subject index.

CAB. 29. INTERNATIONAL CONFERENCES. 1916-39.

Contains the British records of the Paris Peace Conference: Minutes and memoranda of the War Cabinet in Paris, minutes and memoranda of the British Empire delegation, minutes of the Council of Four and the Council of Ten. Also the proceedings and papers of the London Reparations Conference, 1924; Hague Conference, 1929-30; London Naval Conferences, 1930 and 1935-6; and the London Conference, 1931.

CAB. 30. WASHINGTON CONFERENCES: PAPERS. 1921-2.

CAB. 31. GENOA CONFERENCE: PAPERS. 1922.

CAB. 37. CABINET PAPERS. 1880-1916.

This class consists of papers which Cabinet Ministers had printed for circulation to their colleagues before the establishment of the Cabinet Office. It has been assembled from various departmental and private collections, and is incomplete. There are many American items. (Listed in P.R.O. Handbooks Nos. 4 and 9.)

CAB. 38. COMMITTEE OF IMPERIAL DEFENCE: MEMORANDA AND MINUTES, 1888-1914.

Photocopies of papers of the Cabinet Defence Committee, after 1902 the Committee of Imperial Defence, assembled from various other classes. There are a few items listed in which the United States is mentioned, and there may be others containing American interests. A list is published in P.R.O. Handbook No. 6.

CAB. 41. COPIES OF CABINET LETTERS IN THE ROYAL ARCHIVES. 1868-1916.

These are copies of letters from Prime Ministers to the Monarch after each Cabinet meeting. They contain many items of American interest, and can be used in conjunction with the memoranda in CAB. 37.

CAB. 45. HISTORICAL SECTIONS. OFFICIAL WAR HISTORIES: CORRESPONDENCE AND PAPERS.

Papers used in the compilation of the official war histories, mainly of the First World War.
45/176. President Wilson's note on German peace proposals, 1916.
45/223. American account of Turkish forces at Gallipoli.
45/267. Account from the correspondence of W.J. Bryan of the sinking of the *Lusitania* and the *Falabia*.

CAB. 65. WAR CABINET: MINUTES. 1939-45.

Photocopies on open access.

CAB. 66. WAR CABINET: MEMORANDA. W.P. AND C.P. SERIES.

Photocopies on open access.

CAB. 67. WAR CABINET: MEMORANDA. W.P.(G) SERIES.

Photocopies on open access.

CAB. 68. WAR CABINET: MEMORANDA. W.P.(R) SERIES.

Photocopies on open access.

CAB. 78. WAR CABINET: AD HOC COMMITTEES. 1941-7.

78/1. Misc. 10. Method of conducting discussions with the American delegation, 1941.
78/14. Anglo-American discussions under Article VII, 1943.
78/23. Gen. 39. Proposed Anglo-American supply clearing house for N.W. Europe, 1944.
78/24-25. Lend-Lease and Mutual Aid in stage two, 1944.
78/32. Combined Supply Review in Washington, 1945.

CAB. 85. WAR CABINET: ANGLO-FRENCH COMMITTEES.

85/59-80. Mainly Anglo-French purchases in the U.S.A., 1939-40.

CAB. 87. WAR CABINET: COMMITTEES ON RECONSTRUCTION.

87/60. Post-war economic problems and Anglo-American cooperation, 1941-2.
87/87-88. Civil air transport: British-U.S. informal discussions.

CAB. 88/1-108. WAR CABINET: COMBINED CHIEFS OF STAFF COMMITTEES AND SUB-COMMITTEES. 1942-7.

CAB. 92. WAR CABINET: COMMITTEES ON SUPPLY, PRODUCTION, PRIORITY, AND MANPOWER.

92/27-38. North American supply committee, 1940-6.
92/49-52. British missions in Washington, 1942.
92/115. Minister of Production's mission to Washington, 1942.
92/117. Committee on disclosure to U.S.A. of secret information relating to supply matters.

CAB. 98. WAR CABINET: MISCELLANEOUS COMMITTEES.

98/6. U.S. bases, 1940-1.
98/17. Ministerial committee on U.S. bases, 1941.
98/46. US.-British planning, 1942.

CAB. 99. WAR CABINET: COMMONWEALTH AND INTERNATIONAL CONFERENCES.

99/5-39. Mainly reports and proceedings of conferences between British and American chiefs of staff, 1941-5, on mutual aid and U.S. assistance.

CAB. 103. HISTORICAL SECTION: REGISTERED FILES. 1915-50.

103/70. Correspondence with U.S. Navy Department, 1918-24.
103/96. Correspondence: questions at issue between Great Britain and the U.S., 1914-5.
103/127. Records: Allied armies, Italy, 1944.
103/141. Conference of historians: Washington, 1948.

CAB. 105. WAR CABINET: TELEGRAMS. 1941-6.

These are listed in categories such as 'From the British Supply Council, Washington, to the War Cabinet Office, London', then within covering dates and by telegram numbers. There are several thousand, and they appear to be mainly transatlantic.

CAB. 106. HISTORICAL SECTION: FILES (ARCHIVIST AND LIBRARIAN SERIES).

Papers assembled for the preparation of the official war histories. There are reports on the operations of the U.S. Army, and of the build-up of American troops in Europe.

CAB. 108. CENTRAL STATISTICAL OFFICE: MINUTES AND MEMORANDA.

108/40-42. Supply of statistics to the U.S. administration, 1941-5.
108/43-44. Statistics relating to the war effort of the United States, 1941-2.
108/45. U.S. munitions record. 1942-3.
108/46-53. Anglo-American munitions production, 1942-5.
108/85. Non-food consumption in the U.K., U.S.A., and Canada, 1944-5.
108/89. Losses at sea of U.S. and Canadian shipments to Britain, 1941-2.

CAB. 109. LONDON MUNITIONS ASSIGNMENT BOARD: SECRETARY'S FILES.

This committee and its equivalent in Washington organized the pooling and reassignment of the entire U.S./U.K. munitions production, 1942-5.

CAB. 110. JOINT AMERICAN SECRETARIAT: SECRETARY'S FILES. 1942-5.

Mostly concerned with supply. Includes the papers of the North American Supply Committee.

CAB. 111. ALLIED SUPPLIES EXECUTIVE.

Papers concerning Anglo-American aid to Russia, 1941-6; also to the Middle East, East Europe, and China.

CAB. 115. CENTRAL OFFICE FOR NORTH AMERICAN SUPPLIES.

Papers of the various committees and missions concerned with supplies from the U.S. and Canada to Britain and the other Allies, 1941-4, including Lend-Lease.

CAB. 122. BRITISH JOINT STAFF MISSION: WASHINGTON OFFICE FILES. 1941-7.

Concerned with political and military aspects of combined operations, preparations for international conferences, surrender arrangements, post-war policy, repatriation of prisoners, etc.

CAB. 127. PAPERS OF MINISTERS AND SENIOR OFFICIALS DEPOSITED IN THE CABINET OFFICE.

Those of Lord Ismay, Sir Stafford Cripps, Lord Beaverbrook, and Lord Bridges contain American items.

CAB. 128. CABINET MINUTES FROM 1945.

Photocopies on open access at the P.R.O. Subject index available.

CAB. 129. CABINET MEMORANDA FROM 1945.

Photocopies on open access at the P.R.O.

CAB. 130. AD-HOC COMMITTEES: GEN. AND MISC. SERIES.

130/6, 7. Keynes mission to Washington, 1945-6.
130/8. Anglo-American discussions on atomic energy, 1945.

CAB. 133. INTERNATIONAL CONFERENCES FROM 1945.

133/82. Conference between the Foreign Secretaries of the U.K., U.S.A., and U.S.S.R.: Moscow, 1945.

COLONIAL OFFICE

Lists, etc.: 'List of Colonial Office Records to 1947', 13 vols. (typescript).
'List of Colonial Office Records: Supplementary List', 2 vols. (typescript).
'List of Colonial Office Registers: 1886-1902' (duplicated).
'Colonial Office: Indexes to Correspondence: 1815-1870' (duplicated).
R.B. Pugh, *The Records of the Colonial and Dominions Offices* (P.R.O. Handbook No. 3, 1964).
List of Colonial Office Confidential Print to 1916 (P.R.O. Handbook No. 8, 1965).
Calendar of State Papers, Colonial Series: America and West Indies. 1574-1738 (London, 1860-1969).
K.G. Davies (ed.), *Documents of the American Revolution, 1770-1783* (Shannon, Ireland, 1972-) (In progress.).

Most of the Colonial Office papers are arranged by colony, with classes for each colony of in-letters, out-letters, Acts, sessional papers, etc. Material can, for example, be found for Canada in C.O. 42, for British Columbia in C.O. 60, and for Vancouver Island in C.O. 305. There are also classes for 'Colonies (General)' which include Canadian and other material. In addition, relevant items are to be found in the following classes:

C.O. 80. CONFIDENTIAL PRINTS: NORTH AMERICA. 1871-91.

Included is relevant material concerning fisheries, reciprocity, extradition, etc.

C.O. 81. CONFIDENTIAL PRINTS: AUSTRALIA.

81/9/133. Fiji: land claims of American citizens: correspondence. 1885-92.

C.O. 84. CONFIDENTIAL PRINTS: WEST INDIES.

84/4/53. Reciprocity negotiations with the United States: memoranda. 1885.
84/4/68. United States demand for reciprocity: correspondence. 1890-1.

C.O. 386. EMIGRATION: LAND AND EMIGRATION COMMISSION.

386/81-86. Letters to the Colonial Office: North America. 1840-76.

C.O. 537. SUPPLEMENTARY.

537/137-44. British North America. 1834-60.
537/139. Upper Canada: dispatch, etc., about the destruction of the United States steamship *Caroline*. 1838.
537/140-3. Canada: confidential dispatches, private letters, etc., from and to Sir Charles Bagot, Governor-General 1841-3, and Sir C.T. Metcalfe, Governor-General 1843-5 (some are copies or drafts).

C.O. 700. COLONIAL OFFICE MAPS.

American maps in this class are listed in P.A. Penfold (ed.), *Maps and Plans in the Public Record Office*, vol. 2, *America and West Indies* (1974).

EXCHEQUER: KING'S (OR QUEEN'S) REMEMBRANCER

Lists, etc.: 'Exchequer K.R. Class List' (manuscript and typescript).

E. 154. INVENTORIES OF GOODS AND CHATTEL.

154/4/17/. Invoice of goods shipped in the *Sivilla Merchant*, bound for Virginia, *c.* 1640.

E. 157. LICENSES TO PASS BEYOND THE SEAS.

Included are a number of registers, 1624-77, containing the names and, in some cases, other information, about passengers for Holland, New England, Virginia, and Maryland; the only ports of embarkation noted in the class list are the ports of London and Gravesend. Most of the material has been printed; see, *inter alia*, J.C. Hotten, ed., *The original lists of ...{persons emigrating} to the American Plantations, 1600-1700* (London, 1874), and C.B. Jewson, *Transcript of Three Registers of Passengers from Great Yarmouth to Holland and New England, 1637-1639* (Norfolk, 1954) (Norfolk Record Society, vol. xxv).

E. 190. PORT BOOKS. See report on H.M. Customs and Excise (pp. 89).

EXCHEQUER: LORD TREASURER'S REMEMBRANCER

E. 371. ORIGINALIA ROLLS.

These rolls, from the medieval period, contain enrolments of charters, grants and patents, etc., and pleadings and proceedings relative to tenures and estates until 1851; among them are to be found some colonial charters, etc.[3]

EXCHEQUER OF RECEIPT

E. 407. MISCELLANEA.

407/15. Contract for victualling the garrisons of Placentia and Annapolis Royal. 1720.
407/82. Petitions under the hand of the Bishop of London for the payment to clerks in holy orders taking up appointments in America of the bounty of £25. 1743-70.

FOREIGN OFFICE

Lists etc.: P.R.O. *Lists and Indexes No LII: List of Foreign Office Records to 1878* (1963), with additions and corrections.
P.R.O. *Lists and Indexes, Supplementary No. XIII: Vols. 1-22. Foreign Office Records, 1879-1945* (1964-74).
The Records of the Foreign Office, 1782-1939 (P.R.O. Handbook No. 13, 1969).

F.O. 2. GENERAL CORRESPONDENCE: AFRICA.

2/318-24, 484, 485, 621, 622. Consular and other reports, drafts, etc., from America. 1900-2.
2/686. Boer agents in the United States. Outrage on British ship *Mechanician* at New Orleans. Libel action against Consul A.C. Vansittart. 1901-2.

F.O. 5/755-2625. GENERAL CORRESPONDENCE: AMERICA, UNITED STATES OF. 1861-1905.

This very extensive class, the most important of the F.O. series, consists of the original dispatches, reports, etc., to the Foreign Office from British Ministers (from 1893, Ambassadors), Consuls, *Chargés d'Affaires*, and other agents of the government in the United States; of correspondence with American Ministers (from 1893, Ambassadors) and other agents in Britain; of miscellaneous correspondence from individuals; and of drafts or copies of letters sent by the Foreign Office.[4] See F.O. 84 for such correspondence concerning the slave trade. See also F.O. 115 for the archives of the British Legation and Consulates in the United States.

Dispatches and other communications from Ministers, etc., may be found for particular years by use of the lists noted above, and so are not itemized here. In 1890, for example, the list shows, for the Washington and London Legations:

5/2079. Sir J. Pauncefote [British Minister]. Diplomatic drafts.
5/2080. Sir J. Pauncefote. Diplomatic dispatches, 1-100.
5/2081. Sir J. Pauncefote and Mr. [Henry G.] Edwardes [Secretary of the Legation]. Diplomatic dispatches, 101-71.
5/2082. Sir J. Pauncefote. Diplomatic telegrams and paraphrases.
5/2083. Sir J. Pauncefote. Consular and treaty.
5/2084. Sir J. Pauncefote. Commercial. Drafts.
5/2085-9. Sir J. Pauncefote. Commercial. Dispatches, vol. 1-5.
5/2093-4. Domestic. Mr. [Robert T.] Lincoln [American Minister] and Mr. Henry White [*Chargé d'Affaires*]. Diplomatic, vols. 1-2.
5/2095. Domestic. Mr. Lincoln, Mr. White, and Mr. Robert S. McCormick [Second Secretary of Legation]. Consular, commercial and treaty.
5/2096-2102. Various. Diplomatic, consular, commercial, treaty.

Similar headings are to be found for the other years of the period, through 1903, during which the British Ministers were Lord Lyons, 1861-4; Sir Frederick Bruce, 1865-7; Mr. (later Sir) Edward Thornton, 1868-81; Lionel Sackville-West, 1881-8; Sir J. Pauncefote, 1889-1902; Sir M. Herbert, 1902-3; and Sir M. Durand, 1903; and the American Ministers to London were George Mifflin Dallas, 1861; Charles F. Adams, 1861-8; Reverdy Johnson, 1868-9; J.L. Motley, 1869-70; Robert C. Schenck, 1871-6; Edwards Pierrepont, 1876-7; John Welsh, 1877-9; James Russell Lowell, 1880-5; Edward John Phelps, 1885-9; Robert T. Lincoln, 1889-93; Thomas F. Bayard, 1893-7; John Hay, 1897-8; Joseph H. Choate, 1899-1902.

3. See Edward Jones, *Index to Records called the Originalia and Memoranda on the Lord Treasurer's Remembrancer's Side of the Exchequer...*, 2 vols. (London, 1793-5), for the period from Henry VIII to the reign of Anne, a copy of which is in the Record Office.
4. The Library of Congress holds photostats or microfilms of many of these volumes.

Consular and/or vice-consular reports are available annually from 1861 to 1902 for the following cities: Baltimore, Boston, Charleston, S.C., Galveston, Tex., New Orleans, New York, Philadelphia, San Francisco. In addition, there are such reports for other cities as follows: Buffalo, N.Y., 1861-71; Chicago, 1861-2, 1867-9, 1884, 1886-1902; Mobile, Ala., 1861-87, 1895, 1898, 1900; Pensacola, Fla., 1876-9, 1881, 1884, 1886-7, 1889, 1892, 1894, 1897-8, 1900-2; Portland, Me., 1861-85, 1898, 1899; Portland, Ore., 1873, 1882, 1894-1902; St. Louis, Mo., 1863-6; Savannah, Ga., 1861-3, 1865-6, 1868-86, 1888, 1900. For 1899-1902 there are annual reports from Havana, Honolulu, Manila, Puerto Rico, and Santiago de Cuba. There are also occasional reports throughout the period from other cities.

The volumes of such reports show a great diversity of subject matter and form. In a volume for 1862 (F.O. 5/846), for example, the section for the Portland, Me., consulate includes: drafts of letters from the Foreign Office to the Consul; letters from the Consul about transit of British troops through Portland to Canada; property in Maine of a British subject, etc.; printed material sent to the Foreign Office by the Consul, such as pamphlets containing speeches of the Governor of Maine, printed annual reports of the State Superintendent of Schools and of the Maine Bank Commissioners, etc. The section of the volume containing consular reports from Richmond Va., includes the statement of Mr. Zacharie, a New Orleans merchant, on being forcibly taken from a British schooner while *en route* from Havana to Matamoros, Mexico; and letters from the Consul about the Confederate Sequestration Act, the encounter between the Confederate *Virginia* and the Federal *Cumberland*, military movements, reactions in the South to the Emancipation Proclamation, etc. Clearly some of these files would furnish interesting and important material for the history of American politics and opinion generally, as well as commercial intelligence.

In addition, F.O. 5 contains a large body of material relating to specific subjects, as follows:[5]

Alaska:

5/1638. Cession of Alaska by Russia to the United States. 1835-68.

5/1639/1640, 1971, 1972, 2133, 2287, 2383, 2384, 2415-7, 2479, 2510. Alaska boundary: correspondence, vols. 1-13. 1872-7, 1886-1902.

Civil War Claims:

5/1236-95. Claims arising out of the Civil War, vols. 1-60. 1861-71.

5/1296-1312. Conferences at Washington, D.C.: correspondence, archives, etc. 1870-1.

5/1390-1409, 1554, 1555. Geneva Arbitration, vols. 1-22. 1871-3.

5/1410-6. Geneva Arbitration: log books, vols. 1-7. 1872.

5/1417-26. Geneva Arbitration: archives, vols. 1-10. 1871-2.

5/1570. Treaty of Washington: three rules. 1871-6.

5/1602-29. Claims Commission: drafts, dispatches, reports, etc. 1871-7.

Extradition:

5/1673-8, 2042, 2104. Extradition treaty: negotiations, vols. 1-8. 1870-90.

5/1708-16, 1749, 1781, 1864, 1865, 1896, 1973. Extradition: correspondence, vols. 1-15. 1875-86.

5/2478. Supplementary extradition treaty. 1893-1901.

5/2516. Extradition: trial for offence other than that for which extradition was granted. 1893-1902.

Fenians:

5/1125. Claim of Mr. Burns for damage done by Fenians. 1866-67.

5/1334-51, 1427, 1535, 1556, 1599, 1706, 1707, 1745, 1746, 1776-80, 1816-20, 1860-3, 1928-32, 1975, 2044, 2359. Fenian Brotherhood, vols. 1-48. 1864-97.

Many of these reports contain shrewd and detailed evaluations of the role of 'Ireland-in-exile' in American politics.

5/2348. Dynamiters. 1896-7.

Fisheries:

5/1093. Fishery Commission, vol. 2. 1860-6.

5/1458-65. Canadian fisheries, vols. 1-8. 1867-73.

5/1557-69, 1630, 1631, 1671, 1672, 1782, 1897-9, 1933, 1934, 1965-70, 2009-13, 2045-9, 2072, 2103, 2132, 2169-71, 2207, 2278. North American fisheries, vols. 1-47. 1873-95.

5/1632-7. Halifax Commission: miscellaneous papers. 1875-7.

5/1748. Halifax fisheries. 1878-80.

5/1821-7. Fortune Bay, Newfoundland, and fisheries dispute, vols. 1-7. 1875-82.

5/1974, 2014, 2015, 2050, 2051, 2073-7, 2105-12, 2134-45, 2173-83, 2211-8, 2251-60, 2279-86, 2308-15, 2349-56, 2385-7, 2418, 2453, 2512. Seizure of fishing vessels in Bering Sea, vols. 1-89. 1886-1902.

5/2184, 2208-10. Seizure of fishing vessels in Bering Sea: drafts and dispatches. 1892-3.

5/2219-30. Bering Sea arbitration: archives, vols. 1-11, 13. 1891-3. (For volumes 12 and 14-6 *see* F.O. 97/542-5.)

5/2231, 2358. Bering Sea: miscellaneous. 1893, 1897.

5/2250. American claim concerning fishing schooner seized by Newfoundland authorities. 1891-4.

5/2277. North Pacific seal fishery: Order in Council, 1893; Bering Sea award: Order in Council, 1895. 1893, 1895.

5/2318. Professor Thompson's report on Bering Sea seals. 1896.

5/2622, 2623. Newfoundland fisheries, vols. 1-2. 1902-5.

North-West Boundary and Hudson's Bay Company:

5/809-16, 1466-77, 1505, 1506, 1532, 1666-70. North-West boundary and island of San Juan: correspondence, etc., vols. 1-29. 1846-78.

5/1352-5. Hudson's Bay Company, vols. 4-7. 1859-71.

Ships:

There are a large number of entries in F.O. 5 relating to cases of particular ships, including F.O. 5/1000-3, Case of the ironclads built at Birkenhead, 1863-4; F.O. 5/1235, Case of the *Peterhoff* - trade between neutral ports, 1863-71; F.O. 5/1317, Case of the *Georgia* at Liverpool, 1864-71; F.O. 5/1318-32, *Alabama*, vols. 1-15, 1862-71; F.O. 5/2514, Seizure of the American fishing vessel *Frederick Jerring Jr.* - jurisdiction in territorial waters, 1896-1902.

In addition, F.O. 5 contains the following miscellaneous material:

5/934. Case of free Negro emigration. 1862-3.

5/937. Proceedings of American cruisers at St. Thomas. 1863.

5/996, 1045. Case of Mr. J. O'Neill. 1864-5.

5/1004. Case of Captain Sherwin. 1862-4.

5/1006, 1007. Trade with Bahamas. 1862-4.

5/1008. Confederate ships sold to British subjects. 1863-4.

5/1046. Case of Mr. J. Hardcastle. 1863-5.

5/1047. Seizure of cotton at Savannah, Ga. 1865.

5/1053. Confederate enlistments. 1863-5.

5/1056-8. St. Albans, Vt., raids. 1864-5.

5/1089-92. Commercial negotiations and reciprocity treaty. 1858-66.

5/1099. Gunboats on Canadian lakes. 1864-6.

5/1101. Case of Burley's extradition. 1865-6.

5. Much of this material on Alaska, Civil War claims, extradition, Fenians, fisheries, North-West boundary and Hudson's Bay Company, and ships are in the Library of Congress in either microfilm or photostat form.

5/1124. Case of imprisonment of Mr. Shaver. 1862-7.
5/1149-53. Blockade runners: imprisonment of British subjects. 1863-8.
5/1155. Case of William Ross and Colonel Grenfell. 1861-8.
5/1181. Matamoros, Mexico, seizures. 1863-9.
5/1231. Case of Mr. Purvis. 1864-71.
5/1233. Case of Mrs. Molyneux. 1865-71.
5/1356-7. Naturalization.
5/1453-5. Emigration.
5/1456-7. Mr. Stewart's cotton claim. 1866-73.
5/1534, 2005, 2006, 2146. Copyright. 1852-75, 1880-7, 1889-91.
5/1571. British legation house at Washington, D.C. 1857-76.
5/1572. Abduction of John Blair. 1876.
5/1600, 1601. Consular convention between Britain and the United States. 1869-77.
5/1641. Claims against Major David, late Vice-Consul at Pensacola, Fla. 1876-7.
5/1643. Correspondence concerning the Philadelphia Exhibition. 1873-7.
5/1717. Louisiana quarantine. National Board of Health. 1879.
5/1747. Transit trade, Canada and the United States. 1874-80.
5/1866. Bankruptcy of A. Collie. Claim of Mr. Young, trustee, on the American government. 1882-3.
5/1900. Alleged kidnapping of Alfred Sheldon. 1884.
5/1963, 1964. Murder of J.H. Tunstall in New Mexico. 1878-86.
5/2007. Sovereignty over Pedro Cays, Jamaica; and the case of the *Nathalie*. 1884-7.
5/2008. Pre-emption, homestead, and exemption laws. 1886-7.
5/2016. Regulations for liquor traffic. 1887.
5/2041. Merchant shipping conventions. 1882-8.
5/2043. Report on status of aliens and foreign companies in the United States. 1886-8.
5/2078. International Marine Conference at Washington. 1889.
5/2172. Merchant seamen: Deserters Convention. 1889-92.
5/2232. Registration of trade marks in Great Britain: complaints of American citizens. 1892-3.
5/2316. Arbitration: American addresses to the Queen. 1896.
5/2317. Navigation of the Great Lakes (collisions). 1895-6.
5/2357. Claims of American citizens to lands in Fiji. 1879-97.
5/2419. Robert Francis: property in Cuba. 1880-99.
5/2420, 2452, 2480, 2511. Crimping in American ports. 1898-1902.
5/2421-4, 2482. Joint Commission for the settlement of questions pending between the United States and Canada. 1898-1901.
5/2454. Immigration and exclusion of Chinese. 1881-1900.
5/2483. Bankruptcy declaration. 1899-1901.
5/2513. St. Louis, Mo., Exhibition, 1904. 1901-2.
5/2515, 2517. War between the United States and Spain: ships' claims and mediation proposals. 1898-1902.
5/2518. Claim of Cayuga Indians against New York State. 1897-1902.
5/2519. Transit of Canadian prisoners through American territory. 1901-2.
5/2520. Pan-American conferences. 1900-2.
5/2613-5. Philippine claims. 1898-1905.
5/2616-9. Cuban claims. 1898-1905.
5/2620. Illegal detention of Mr. Kenneth Harper at Honolulu. 1903-5.
5/2621. Cay Sal: question of sovereignty. 1898-1905.
5/2624. Case of the Rio Grande Irrigation and Land Company. 1904-5.
5/2625. American claims (including Standard Oil Company) against Great Britain. 1884-1905.

F.O. 50. GENERAL CORRESPONDENCE: MEXICO.[6]

50/189, 203, 214. Consular reports from California. 1845-7.

F.O. 55. GENERAL CORRESPONDENCE: COLOMBIA.

55/248, 249, 250, 271, 281, 282, 290, 291, 299, 320, 336, 346, 356, 360, 365, 385, 386, 392, 398, 399, 405, 406, 420, 432. Panama and Nicaragua Ship Canals (Clayton-Bulwer Treaty, etc.), vols. 1-24.[7] 1868-1905.

F.O. 58. GENERAL CORRESPONDENCE: PACIFIC ISLANDS.

58/241, 279, 288, 304, 309, 319. Designs of the United States on Hawaii, vols. 1-6. 1886-98.

F.O. 64. GENERAL CORRESPONDENCE: PRUSSIA.

64/1516, 1517. German telegraph cables to America. 1898-1900.

F.O. 72. GENERAL CORRESPONDENCE: SPAIN.

72/1266, 1267. Aid to Cuban insurgents: case of American vessel *Mary Lowell* seized in British waters. 1869-70.
72/1307. Cuban insurrection: mediation of Britain and the United States. 1870-1.
72/2091-7, 2159. War between the United States and Spain: observance of neutrality.[8] 1898-1901.
72/2143. Fees levied by H.M.'s consular officers in Spain while in charge of American interests. 1898-1900.

F.O. 83. GENERAL CORRESPONDENCE: GREAT BRITAIN AND GENERAL.

Information, etc., from the United States is noted as being included in the following:
83/179, 187, 390. Consular service. 1856-9, 1871-2.
83/295. Technical and industrial education. 1867-8.
83/333, 336, 379. Industrial classes. 1869-72.
83/340. Land tenure. 1869.
83/376. Inventions and patents. 1872.
83/396. British trade. 1872.
83/480. Conventual and monastic institutions. 1874-5.
83/720. Homicidal crime. 1880.
83/762. Interchange of documents. 1880-1.
83/1046. Port tonnage and light dues. 1885-8.
83/1571. Sixtieth anniversary of the accession of Queen Victoria. 1896-7.

6. Microfilms of F.O. 50/1-531 are in the Bancroft Library, University of California, Berkeley.
7. Parts of F.O. 55/392, 405, and 406 are printed in C.S. Campbell, Jr., *Anglo-American Understanding, 1898-1903* (Baltimore, 1957).
8. Letters from F.O. 72/2097 are printed in G.P. Gooch and H. Temperley, eds., *British Documents on the Origins of the War*, vol. i (London, 1927), pp. 105-7.

83/2077. Bishops' licenses, etc. 1868-1902.
83/2168. Arbitration treaties. 1904-5.
83/2204-26. Law Officers' reports. 1781-1876.[9]
Also included in this class are:
83/1888, 1889, 2166. Washington and Rome Postal Congresses. 1897, 1906.

F.O. 84. GENERAL CORRESPONDENCE: SLAVE TRADE.

There is ministerial and consular correspondence from the United States for the period 1861-92. Also the following material:
84/1436. Fugitive Slaves Commission (1814-26): compensation paid by British government for slaves removed from America in 1814.
84/1700. United States: Machada claims correspondence. 1879-84.

F.O. 93. PROTOCOLS OF TREATIES.

93/8/17-216. Papers concerning various American treaties. 1842-1946.

F.O. 94. RATIFICATIONS OF TREATIES.

Various items between F.O. 94/341 and 1547 are for American treaties, 1842-1946.

F.O. 95. MISCELLANEA: SERIES I.

95/684. Correspondence between British sovereigns and American presidents, about appointments, deaths, etc. 1817-34.

F.O. 96. MISCELLANEA: SERIES II.

96/143-6. Accounts of expenses of North American Boundary Commission. 1843-6.
96/200. Anglo-American arbitration memorial. 1896.

F.O. 97. GENERAL CORRESPONDENCE: SUPPLEMENT.

97/34-35. Consular correspondence, Cincinnati, 1852-6.
97/37-47. Depredations of American ships in the Guano islands; law officers' reports on Civil War claims, etc. 1859-68.
97/431. Slave trade (including draft of American slave trade treaty). 1862.
97/439-40. Geneva arbitration: archives. 1872.
97/465-70. Fisheries: Halifax Commission: affidavits, etc. 1850-77.
97/471. Consular convention between the United States and Great Britain. 1878-82.
97/472-5. Fenian Brotherhood: press incitements. 1881-5.
97/476. North American fisheries. 1870-87.
97/541. Falkland Island fisheries. 1883-92.
97/542-5. Bering Sea arbitration. 1820-93.
97/546. New Zealand land claims of William Webster, an American citizen. 1887-94.
97/606. America: imprisonment of Joseph Weir. 1897-1904.

F.O. 99. GENERAL CORRESPONDENCE: MOROCCO: SERIES II.

99/159. Case of Mr. Scott, a British subject in American employ, refusing to acknowledge jurisdiction of H.M.'s Consul. 1871-3.

F.O. 115. EMBASSY AND CONSULAR ARCHIVES: AMERICA, UNITED STATES OF: CORRESPONDENCE.

115/238-1284. Correspondence with the Foreign Office, United States government, Consuls, etc.[10] 1861-1903.
Registers are available in F.O. 117 for these.

F.O. 128. EMBASSY AND CONSULAR ARCHIVES: BRAZIL: CORRESPONDENCE.

128/199. Foreign naval commanders (United States, France, Italy, and Portugal) and rebel Brazilian naval commanders. 1893-4.

F.O. 162. EMBASSY AND CONSULAR ARCHIVES: CHILE: PUNTA ARENAS: CORRESPONDENCE.

162/2. Papers concerning the claim of the Falkland Islands Co. against Richard T. Green, owner of the American schooner *Enola C.* (Copies). 1899.

F.O. 185. EMBASSY AND CONSULAR ARCHIVES: SPAIN: CORRESPONDENCE.

185/687. Commercial negotiations between Spain and the United States. 1887.

F.O. 198. EMBASSY AND CONSULAR ARCHIVES: TURKEY: MISCELLANEA.

198/21. American Civil War. 1862-8.

F.O. 275. EMBASSY AND CONSULAR ARCHIVES: AMERICA, UNITED STATES OF: MANILA.

275/1. Philippine Islands: cessation of Spanish rule upon seizure by the United States. 1898.

F.O. 281. EMBASSY AND CONSULAR ARCHIVES: AMERICA, UNITED STATES OF: NEW YORK: CORRESPONDENCE.

281/1-45. Correspondence with Washington Legation, Foreign Office, etc. 1816-1911.
Registers to these for 1847-1911 are at F.O. 283.

F.O. 282. EMBASSY AND CONSULAR ARCHIVES: AMERICA, UNITED STATES OF: NEW YORK: LETTER-BOOKS.

282/1-36. Copies of letters to the Foreign Office, Board of Trade, Washington Legation, etc. 1842-94.

F.O. 284. EMBASSY AND CONSULAR ARCHIVES: AMERICA, UNITED STATES OF: NEW YORK: SHIPPING.

284/1A. Register of British vessels entering Philadelphia. 1787-9.
284/1B-11. Movements of British ships: registers. 1858-81.

F.O. 285. EMBASSY AND CONSULAR ARCHIVES: AMERICA, UNITED STATES OF: NEW YORK: MISCELLANEA.

285/1. Correspondence (mainly slave trade, etc., from the Foreign Office) and papers. 1834-42.

9. The Library of Congress holds photostats of these. Abstracts are printed in A.D. McNair, ed., *International Law Opinions*, 3 vols. (Cambridge, 1956). Extracts from or transcripts of F.O. 83/2204-10 are printed in A.D. McNair, *Law of Treaties: British Practice and Opinions* (Oxford and New York, 1938).

10. Photostats of many of the volumes to 1877 (F.O. 115/617) are in the Library of Congress. The Bancroft Library has microfilmed the volumes relating to the American West.

285/2. Subject index to Foreign Office dispatches, etc. 1871-8.
285/3-4. Extradition cases. 1893-1901.

F.O. 301. ARCHIVES OF COMMISSIONS: AMERICA: FISHERIES.

301/1-9. Correspondence, minutes, etc. 1873-6, 1887-8.

F.O. 302. ARCHIVES OF COMMISSIONS: AMERICA: NORTHWEST BOUNDARY.

302/1-29. Correspondence, accounts, etc. 1872-6.

F.O. 305. ARCHIVES OF COMMISSIONS: BRITISH AND AMERICAN CLAIMS, 1871.

305/1-98. Papers relating to particular claims; correspondence, awards, printed papers, etc. [Names of claimants are in *Lists and Indexes* No. LII.] 1871-5.

F.O. 312. ARCHIVES OF COMMISSIONS: SLAVE TRADE: CAPE TOWN.

312/23, 26, 29, 40. British and American letter-books, minute-books, accounts, etc. 1862-70.

F.O. 315. ARCHIVES OF COMMISSIONS: SLAVE TRADE: SIERRA LEONE.

315/16. Minute-books: American. 1862-8.

F.O. 317. ARCHIVES OF COMMISSIONS: MISCELLANEOUS.

317/2. Register of correspondence of the commission at Washington. 1871.
317/4, 5. Bering Sea Commission: register of correspondence and notes of evidence. 1891-2.

F.O. 331. EMBASSY AND CONSULAR ARCHIVES: AMERICA, UNITED STATES OF: HONOLULU.

331/1-55, 59. Correspondence with the Foreign Office, Hawaiian authorities, etc. 1824-94.

F.O. 333. EMBASSY AND CONSULAR ARCHIVES: AMERICA, UNITED STATES OF: MISCELLANEA.

333/1. List of archives. 1791-1856.
333/2, 5, 6. Registers of correspondence: E. Seymour Bell, British commercial agent in Chicago and New York. 1900-8.
333/3, 4, 7-9. Foreign Office annual reports - confidential prints. 1906-13.

F.O. 360. HOWARD DE WALDEN PAPERS.

Included in F.O. 360/4 is a copy of a private letter, 6 July 1826, from George Canning, Secretary of State, to C.R. Vaughan, Minister to the United States, about the Northwest coast of America.

F.O. 362. GRANVILLE PAPERS.

The papers of Granville George Leveson-Gower, 2nd Earl Granville (1815-91) include:
362/1. America, drafts. 1870-4.
(*See also* P.R.O. 30/29, pp. 139-40)

F.O. 363. TENTERDEN PAPERS.

The collection consists of five volumes of private papers of Charles Stuart Aubrey Abbott, 3rd Baron Tenterden (1834-82) while Under-Secretary of State for Foreign Affairs. Included are:
363/1. Francis Ford. About twenty letters from Halifax, N.S., and Newfoundland about United States and Canadian fisheries. 1876-7.
363/3. F.R. Plunkett: three letters from the British Legation in Washington about the American political scene and American attitudes towards Russia, Germany, Mexico, etc., 1877. H.C. Rothery: about thirty letters, mainly from New York, about fisheries, the case of the *Virginius,* etc. 1873-4.
363/4. Sir Edward Thornton. About seventy letters from Washington, D.C., on Canadian-American relations, American politics, American relations with Spain, etc. 1874-9.
363/5. R. Bourke. Letter to Lord Derby on the Halifax Fisheries Commission and the Treaty of Washington, and Tenterden's notes on this. 1876.

F.O. 366. CHIEF CLERK'S DEPARTMENT: CORRESPONDENCE.

366/210-14. Accounts: extraordinaries, United States. 1825-66.
366/300. Accounts: Washington Mixed Claims Commission. 1871-4.
366/570. Correspondence (papers): Washington High Commission, Geneva Arbitration, San Juan boundary. 1871-5.
366/725. Messengers: Washington, etc. 1867-88.

GENERAL CORRESPONDENCE AFTER 1906.

The Foreign Office changed its filing system after 1906, and instead of being kept in classes corresponding to countries, the files were arranged in classes corresponding to eleven departments: *Africa, New Series* (F.O. 367); *Commercial* (F.O. 368); *Communications* (F.O. 850); *Consular* (F.O. 369); *Contraband* (F.O. 382); *Dominions Information* (F.O. 627); *Library* (F.O. 370); *News* (F.O. 395); *Political* (F.O. 371); *Prisoners of War and Aliens* (F.O. 383); and *Treaty* (F.O. 372). The class lists up to 1938, which have been printed, contain only the file numbers arranged by year and by country or subject. After 1938 the title of each file is given. An annual index compiled while the documents were at the Foreign Office is available in the P.R.O., and is the only way to locate documents before 1938. It is primarily a subject index, and entries under 'United States' are not exhaustive. The index gives the numbers of the individual papers (preceded by a letter), a file number, and an index number, which for the United States is 45. The appropriate section of the class list for the year is then consulted, e.g. United States, the file and paper numbers located in the right hand column, and the P.R.O. reference number read off the left hand column. The index is on cards from 1906 to 1919 (in the case of a few departments until 1920) and printed from 1920. There are notes on its use inside each volume.

The most useful class for American scholars is F.O. 371, *Political,* in which the F.O. 5 series is more or less continued. But there is also a considerable quantity of American material in the *Commercial, Contraband, Consular, News,* and *Treaty* classes, and of lesser importance in the *Library* and *Communications* classes. It would not be useful or practical to attempt to summarize this extensive archive. Guidance to it can be obtained from P.R.O. Handbooks Nos. 13 and 15, and from Sir Llewellyn Woodward, *British Foreign Policy in the Second World War* (London, 1970-). It is essential to consult P.R.O. Handbook No. 13: *The Records of the Foreign Office 1782-1939* (London, 1969) before using Foreign Office records.

F.O. 374. PEACE CONFERENCE OF 1919-20. ACTS OF THE CONFERENCE. PUBLISHED 1922-35.

Reports and other official proceedings of the Peace Conference and of its several commissions and committees.

F.O. 414. CONFIDENTIAL PRINT: NORTH AMERICA, 1711-1941.

United States and Canada.

F.O. 461. CONFIDENTIAL PRINT: AMERICA, 1942-1956.

United States, Canada, and South and Central America.

F.O. 519. COWLEY PAPERS.

519/203. Semi-official and private correspondence of Henry Richard Charles Wellesley, 1st Earl Cowley (1804-84), British Ambassador at Paris, including letters from Sir John Crampton from Washington, D.C. (11 Dec. 1855 concerning *New York Herald* articles thought to be written from the Paris Embassy) and from Spain (15 Sept. and 13 Nov. 1861, commenting on probable United States role in Cuba and Mexico).

F.O. 550. EMBASSY AND CONSULAR ARCHIVES: AMERICA, UNITED STATES OF: SAVANNAH, GA.

550/1. Register of inward and outward correspondence. 1880-9. (The archives themselves are missing.)

F.O. 581. EMBASSY AND CONSULAR ARCHIVES: AMERICA, UNITED STATES OF: NEW ORLEANS.

Registers of correspondence. 1850-1938.

F.O. 598, 599. EMBASSY AND CONSULAR ARCHIVES: AMERICA, UNITED STATES OF: WASHINGTON, D.C.

Correspondence and registers of correspondence. 1922-9.

F.O. 600. EMBASSY AND CONSULAR ARCHIVES: AMERICA, UNITED STATES OF: SAN FRANCISCO.

Registers of correspondence. 1906-41. The correspondence has been destroyed.

F.O. 608. PEACE CONFERENCE OF 1919-20.

Correspondence. 1919-20. There is an index with the class list.

F.O. 610-14. PASSPORT OFFICE RECORDS.

Volumes simply listing applications for passports and giving names of recommenders and destinations; these might be relevant to tracing the movements of specific individuals to the United States. 1795-1948.

F.O. 620. EMBASSY AND CONSULAR ARCHIVES: AMERICA, UNITED STATES OF: BOSTON.

Correspondence. 1914-40. Open after fifty years.

F.O. 621. EMBASSY AND CONSULAR ARCHIVES: AMERICA, UNITED STATES OF: BOSTON.

621/1-5. Registers of correspondence. 1903-14. (The correspondence itself is believed to have been destroyed.)

F.O. 660. WAR OF 1939-1945. MINISTERS RESIDENT.

660/1-11. Political liaison officer with the U.S. forces in Great Britain and North Africa, 1942-3.

F.O. 700. EMBASSY AND CONSULAR ARCHIVES.

700/1-3. Atlanta. Register of correspondence. 1924-9.
700/4. El Paso. Register of correspondence. 1914-6.
700/5. Key West. Declarations of loyalty and nationality. 1880-98.
700/6. Miami. Register of correspondence. 1918-25, 1931-6.
700/7. Port Arthur. Register of correspondence. 1924-9.
700/8-9. Providence. Registers of births, 1902-30. Register of deaths, 1930.
700/10-19. Detroit. Register of correspondence. 1924-6.
700/20-21. Tacoma. Register of deaths, 1892-1907. Register of births, 1896-1921.
700/22-23. Aberdeen. Register of deaths, 1914. Register of births, 1916.
700/24-25. Dallas. Register of deaths, 1951. Register of births, 1951-4.
700/26-27. El Paso. Register of deaths, 1914-26. Register of births, 1916-30.
700/28-29. Seattle. Broadcasts. 1944.
700/30. Atlanta. Validity of marriage contract. 1944.
700/31-35. Cincinnati. Register of births, 1929, 1943-8, 1951-8. Register of deaths, 1947, 1950-5.
700/36-43. Cleveland. Register of births and deaths, 1914-30, 1944-64.
700/44-53. Detroit. Registers of births and deaths. 1910-69.
700/54-60. Kansas City. Registers of births and deaths. 1904-61.
700/61. Omaha. Register of births. 1906.
700/62-63. Pittsburgh. Registers of births. 1954-6.
700/71-74. St. Paul. Registers of births and deaths. 1943-66.

F.O. 701. EMBASSY AND CONSULAR ARCHIVES: AMERICA, UNITED STATES OF: GALVESTON.

Correspondence, letter-books, and registers of correspondence. 1900-34.

F.O. 702. EMBASSY AND CONSULAR ARCHIVES: AMERICA, UNITED STATES OF: HOUSTON.

Registers of correspondence. 1909-32.

F.O. 703. EMBASSY AND CONSULAR ARCHIVES: AMERICA, UNITED STATES OF: BALTIMORE.

Letter-books and registers. 1821-35, 1867-1938.

F.O. 706. EMBASSY AND CONSULAR ARCHIVES: AMERICA, UNITED STATES OF: BOSTON.

Registers of births and deaths. 1871-1930.

F.O. 707. EMBASSY AND CONSULAR ARCHIVES: AMERICA, UNITED STATES OF: PORTLAND (OREGON).

Registers of births and deaths. 1880-1929.

F.O. 708. EMBASSY AND CONSULAR ARCHIVES: AMERICA, UNITED STATES OF: PROVIDENCE.

Registers of correspondence. 1902-30.

F.O. 739. EMBASSY AND CONSULAR ARCHIVES: AMERICA, UNITED STATES OF: ST. LOUIS.

Registers of correspondence. 1908-37.

F.O. 740. EMBASSY AND CONSULAR ARCHIVES: AMERICA, UNITED STATES OF: LOS ANGELES.

Correspondence. 1927-35.

F.O. 794. PRIVATE OFFICE: 'INDIVIDUAL' FILES.

794/5. Sir Thomas Aubrey Spring-Rice: transfer from Washington Embassy to Foreign Office. 1917.
794/17. Sir Ronald Lindsay: correspondence as Ambassador to Washington, 1933-9.
794/18. Lord Lothian: appointment as Ambassador to Washington and sudden death. 1938-40.

F.O. 800. PRIVATE COLLECTIONS: MINISTERS AND OFFICIALS: VARIOUS.

800/81-86. Sir Edward Grey: United States. 1905-16.
800/144. Marquess of Lansdowne: United States. 1900-5.
800/151. Lord Curzon: United States. 1919-23.
800/181. Sir Francis Bertie: United States. 1905-18.
800/196. Viscount Cecil: United States. 1915-7.
800/208-9, 211. Earl of Balfour: United States. 1917-22.
800/219. Ramsay MacDonald: United States. 1923-4.
800/223. Marquess of Reading: Oil to U.S. 1918-9.
800/232. Sir Henry Bulwer, envoy to Washington: Correspondence. 1848-51.
800/241-2. Sir C.A. Spring-Rice: Misc. correspondence. 1903-18.
800/392, 397-8, 404. Miscellaneous, U.S. 1934-43.
800/424. Stanley Baldwin: United States. 1940-1.

F.O. 837. MINISTRY OF ECONOMIC WARFARE.

837/1063-1118. War trade, contraband control, etc.: United States. 1939-45.
837/1213-7. Relief programmes: Anglo-U.S. relief policy. 1940-4.
There are a number of other American items, e.g.:
837/1129. U.S.S.R.: imports from U.S.A. 1940-1.

F.O. 845. WAR OF 1914-1918. RESTRICTION OF ENEMY SUPPLIES.

845/10. Agreement between the British, French, and Italian governments with the War Trade Board of the U.S.A. and the Dutch government regarding Dutch agricultural exports.

F.O. 862. EMBASSY AND CONSULAR ARCHIVES: AMERICA, UNITED STATES OF: CHICAGO.

Correspondence. 1936-7.

F.O. 879. EMBASSY AND CONSULAR ARCHIVES: AMERICA, UNITED STATES OF: PHILADELPHIA.

Correspondence. 1936-41.

F.O. 885. EMBASSY AND CONSULAR ARCHIVES: AMERICA, UNITED STATES OF: PENSACOLA.

Registers of births and deaths. 1880-1905.

F.O. 892. WAR OF 1939-1945. BRITISH MISSION TO THE FRENCH NATIONAL COMMITTEE.

Contains several items concerning U.S.-French relations.

F.O. 893. PEACE CONFERENCE OF 1919-20. CONFERENCE OF AMBASSADORS, PARIS, 1920-30.

Minutes.

F.O. 897. MIXED ARBITRAL TRIBUNALS: ANGLO-AMERICAN PECUNIARY CLAIMS.

Claims to the Permanent Court of Arbitration at The Hague under the Arbitral Convention of 1908. 1911-23.

F.O. 898. WAR OF 1939-1945. POLITICAL WARFARE EXECUTIVE. 1938-46.

Concerned with propaganda, mainly in Europe, but also in North Africa and the Far East. Some American items, e.g.:
898/103-9. British missions in the U.S. 1941-4.

F.O. 902. WAR OF 1914-1918. RECORDS OF TEMPORARY DEPARTMENTS.

'Weekly Bulletins of Trade Information', War Trade Intelligence Department, 1915-9. Ministry of Blockade: Minutes of committee, 1917; Finance section, 1916-9.

F.O. 921. MINISTER OF STATE: CAIRO.

921/22. U.S. representation. 1942.
921/39. Anglo-American relations in the Middle East. 1942.
921/94. Liaison with U.S. 1943.
921/110-1. U.S. troops in Cairo. 1943.
921/119. U.S. oil interests in the Middle East. 1943.
921/174. U.S. policy in Persia. 1944.
921/192. U.S. policy in Saudi Arabia. 1944.
921/229-33. Policy in the Middle East and press censorship. 1944.
There is undoubtedly American material in other files, e.g. those on Lend-Lease.

F.O. 922. WAR OF 1939-1945. MIDDLE EAST SUPPLY CENTRE. 1938-45.

The centre organized civil imports into the Middle East from 1938 to 1945. After America entered the war, the centre became Anglo-American.

F.O. 924. CULTURAL RELATIONS.

924/37. Distributing 'Britain Today' in the U.S. 1944.
924/52. Anglo-American school in Guatemala.
924/107. U.S. cultural cooperation programme. 1938-43.

F.O. 925. FOREIGN OFFICE MAPS.

Contains a large number of North American maps, many of them showing boundaries. They are also listed in P.A. Penfold (ed.), *Maps and Plans in the Public Record Office*. Vol. 2, *America and West Indies* (1974).

F.O. 951. EMBASSY AND CONSULAR ARCHIVES: INDEXES OF CORRESPONDENCE. 1916-29.

CAPTURED ENEMY DOCUMENTS

Lists, etc.: 'German Foreign Ministry: Class List', 3 vols. (photostat).

G.F.M. 1-23. COPIES OF GERMAN FOREIGN MINISTRY RECORDS. 1863-1944. (Also some other German official holdings.)

Large sections of these German records were captured by the Allies in 1945 and later removed to Britain for safe keeping during the Berlin blockade. The originals have now been returned to the custody of the Federal Republic of Germany.

All the main political files were examined and films were made of the documents considered to be of historical interest, while the archives were in Allied custody. Those of 1920-44, together with certain major topics in the preceding period, were filmed chiefly by the American, British, and French governments, while the filming of the remainder was sponsored by other governments, universities, and research institutes. Copies (paper prints or microfilms) of all the films made are held by, or are in course of transfer to, the Public Record Office. G.F.M. 10, for example, contains the bulk of the German-American diplomatic papers centring on the Bismarck era, and was filmed by the University of California, so that copies are to be found there too.

A Catalogue of Files and Microfilms of the German Foreign Ministry Archives, 1867-1920 (New York, 1959), sponsored by the Committee for the Study of War Documents of the American Historical Association, contains full details of film references and a topical index.

For the period after 1920 catalogues of the filmed files of the various German departments will also be available in the Record Office. During the period 1920-36 the Ministry was organized on the basis of regional departments, of which Department III handled political and economic relations with America. After the reorganization in 1936, political and economic relations were handled by Division IX of the Political Department (Pol IX) and Division VIII of the Economic Policy Department respectively. Other important collections containing material on America are those of the Foreign Minister; the State Secretary; the German Embassy in Washington; the Reich Chancellery; Department IIIB, 1920-36, and Political Division M.C., 1936-41, dealing with mixed claims; and the papers of Ritter, Wiehl, and Clodius, of the Economic Section of the Foreign Ministry.

For the period 1933-41, *Documents on German Foreign Policy*, Series C (1933-6) and Series D (1937-41) (London, H.M.S.O., and Washington, D.C., G.P.O., 1950-66) include the principal documents on German relations with America. Each volume contains an appendix listing the files used, together with their film reference numbers.

HIGH COURT OF ADMIRALTY

Lists, etc.: 'High Court of Admiralty: Class List', 2 vols. (typescript).
'High Court of Admiralty: Descriptive List of Means of Reference' (duplicated).

H.C.A. 30/899-1000. INSTANCE AND PRIZE COURTS: MISCELLANEA. 1772-1948.

30/978. American embargo ledger, 1812.
30/979. American embargo journal, 1812.
30/980. American embargo bill book, 1812-3.
30/981. American embargo: list of ships detained, 1812-3.

H.C.A. 35/1-89. SLAVE TRADE: GOVERNMENT REPORTS. 1821-91.

Examination of H.C.A. 35/78 (1860-3) showed it to include copies of letters and reports to the Treasury from H.C. Rothery, Admiralty Registrar, about the New York slave ship *Tavernier*, and the proposed British and American regulations for the suppression of the slave trade.

H.C.A. 36. SLAVE TRADE: ADDITIONAL PAPERS.

Parliamentary papers and printed copies of treaties; some correspondence, drafts, etc. Much of the material relates to the 1876 Royal Commission on fugitive slaves.

H.C.A. 50. ADMIRALTY MUNIMENT BOOKS.

Entry books containing copies of commissions, letters patent, and warrants relating to the establishment of vice-admiralty courts in the colonies, and the appointment of judges and officials thereto.

HOME OFFICE

Lists, etc.: 'Home Office and Signet Office, 1838-1900' (typescript).
'Home Office Registered Papers (H.O. 45) Subject Index, 1841-1855' (photostat).
'Home Office Domestic: Registered Papers (Old Series) Subject Index, 1856-1871' (typescript).
'Home Office Registered Papers (H.O. 45), 1871-1878' (typescript).
'Home Office Registered Papers (H.O. 45), 1879-1900' (typescript).
'Home Office Registered Papers (H.O. 45), to 1909' (typescript).
'Home Office Registered Papers (H.O. 45), to 1919' (typescript).
Index to Registered Papers (H.O. 45), 1920' (typescript).
'Index to Registered Files (H.O. 45) 1921-1922' (typescript).
'Home Office Class List, H.O. 45 (Subject Index), to 1947' (typescript, 2 vols.).

H.O. 5. ALIENS' ENTRY BOOKS.

These are noted by Paullin and Paxson, p. 226, as containing occasional references to American aliens.

H.O. 45. REGISTERED PAPERS.[11]

The subject indexes listed above show relevant material under such headings as 'disturbances', 'emigration', 'extradition', 'foreign', 'Ireland (Fenians)', 'ships', and 'war'. Included are, for example, the following:

45/6877. Disaffected Irish in the United States and Canada. 1859.
45/7232. Extradition: case of American fugitive slave Anderson in Canada. 1861-2.
45/7261. Civil War. General papers, mainly concerning recruiting in England, and the fitting out of ships in England. 1861-6.
45/7523 and 7523A. Distress and riots in cotton districts of Lancashire and Cheshire. 1863.
45/7799. Fenian movement. Chiefly concerning designs of Fenians in the United States and shipment of arms to Ireland. 1865-70.
45/9294/8148. Arming of Confederate ships in the Channel Islands, 1863. Correspondence with the Foreign Office about the *Alabama* claims, 1871-2.

11. This class is open after thirty years, and the subject indexes are regularly updated.

45/9422/59279. Address from the Irish people to the American President. 1876-7.
45/9584/87022. Mormon emigration to the United States: steps to warn emigrants of American law on polygamy. 1879-85.
45/9635/A29278. State-aided emigration of Irish pauper families, and their return to the United Kingdom by the United States government. 1883-5.
45/9660/A42380F. Dispatch from H.M. Consul at Chicago reporting trial of anarchists. 1886.
45/9832/B9588. Emigration of Mormons to the United States. 1890-1.
45/9986/X69316 and X69316A. Spanish-American War: British declaration of neutrality; detention of American destroyer. 1898-9.

H.O. 134/1-27. ENTRY BOOKS: EXTRADITION. 1873-98.

Examination of H.O. 134/1 showed it to include copies of letters to the Foreign Office about the Extradition Treaty between Britain and the United States, warrants to police and magistrates for the apprehension of American citizens, etc. These records are closed for 100 years.

H.O. 168. EXEQUATURS AND RECOGNITIONS.

Out-letter books. 1899-1921.

COPYRIGHT OFFICE

IND. 6012-38. FOREIGN REGISTERS.

A series of registers lists the names of foreign products, inventions, compositions, etc., made copyright in Great Britain. 1847-1912.

MINISTRY OF AGRICULTURE AND FISHERIES

M.A.F. 7/3. MISCELLANEOUS AGRICULTURAL STATISTICS. 1730-1883.

Included are, e.g., statistics of number and estimated weight of cattle, sheep, and swine imported from the United States in 1883.

M.A.F. 97. BRITISH FOOD MISSION, WASHINGTON. 1941-50.

Contains items concerning U.S. agriculture, Lend-Lease, and post-war aid.

MINISTRY OF HEALTH

Lists, etc.: 'Ministry of Health: Class List' (typescript).
'Ministry of Health: Poor Law Union Papers (M.H. 12)', 2 vols. (typescript).

M.H. 1-4. POOR LAW COMMISSIONERS FOR ENGLAND AND WALES: MINUTE-BOOKS, 1834-47.

M.H. 12. POOR LAW UNION PAPERS. 1834-1900.

Material about parish-assisted emigration under the new Poor Law of 1834 is to be found in these classes. For example, M.H. 12/8156, containing the papers of the Aylsham Poor Law Union, Norfolk, for 1834-7, includes lists of persons emigrating, with occupations and destinations (mainly Upper Canada, but in at least one case New York), letters from the Poor Law Commissioners in London, letters from individual parishes within the Union about the financing of emigration, etc.

M.H. 13. GENERAL BOARD OF HEALTH AND LOCAL GOVERNMENT ACT OFFICE: CORRESPONDENCE.

Included in M.H. 13/252 is correspondence, 1853-4, between the General Board of Health and the Colonial Land and Emigration Commissioners, with letters (originals, drafts, and copies) about the outbreak of cholera on the American emigrant ship *Silas Greenman*, and concerning the general problem of mortality on emigrant ships leaving Liverpool.

M.H. 19. POOR LAW COMMISSIONS, POOR LAW BOARD, AND LOCAL GOVERNMENT BOARD: GOVERNMENT OFFICES CORRESPONDENCE AND PAPERS.

19/22. Emigration Commissioners. 1836-76.

Among the correspondence about emigration to Canada and the extracts from reports from Mr. Buchanan (the emigration agent in Quebec) are a few scattered references to the United States.

MINISTRY OF TRANSPORT

Lists, etc.: 'List of the Records of the Ministry of Transport' (typescript).
'Ministry of Transport (Marine Department), List of Records 1856 to 1937: Indexes to Ships and Places' (typescript).

M.T. 9. BOARD OF TRADE MARINE DEPARTMENT. 1856-1952.

After 1850, Acts for the inspection and survey of passenger steamers gave the Board of Trade certain executive duties specially connected with merchant shipping. The Marine Department was created as a separate department of the Board of Trade in 1850, and now forms part of the Ministry of Transport. The class list for the years 1886-90 illustrates the kind of material available.
9/283. Emigrants. Carriage of passengers in vessels previously used in carrying cattle. 1886.
9/285. American legislation relating to the advance of seamen's wages, allotments, owners' liability, etc. 1886.
9/294. Engagement and discharge of crews. Engagement at New York and other United States ports of seamen in British ships bound for China. 1886.
9/303. Dietary scale of emigrant ships. 1887.
9/324. Transit of Buffalo Bill's Wild West Show to the United States, and status of attendants, etc. 1888.
9/328. Extensive crimping at San Francisco. 1888.
9/381. Riotous conduct, larceny, and receiving by American cattlemen on board S.S. *Chicago*. 1890.
The index of places for this class from 1856 to 1937 has five pages of entries for the United States. There is a subject index to records after 1903.

PRIVY COUNCIL

Lists, etc.: 'P.C. 1: Unbound Papers', 4 vols. (typescript).
'Parliament and Council: List of Records' (typescript).

P.C. 1. UNBOUND PAPERS.

The following (petitions, drafts, reports, etc.) is the relevant material apparently additional to that seen by Andrews & Davenport, pp. 170-87, and by Paullin and Paxson, pp. 292-325, except that the papers in P.C. 1/46-57 have been excluded since they were covered by James Munro in his *Acts of the Privy Council - Colonial Series: Vol. VI. The Unbound Papers* (London, 1912).

The available list for this class contains much more detail for the colonial than for the later period, and this fact is necessarily reflected in the following:

1/14. Petitions concerning Pennsylvania, Newfoundland, etc. 1712.

1/15. Draft proclamation about possible invasion of Britain. 1779.

1/18. Order removing prohibition on importation of corn from the United States. 1789.

1/19. Reports on American legislation on duties. 1791.

1/20. Act for regulating trade with the United States. 1793.

1/21. Quarantine papers, including some for Pennsylvania; letter with copy of order re warehoused American rice; petitions about payment of bills drawn in North America. 1794.

1/34. Emigration to America. 1796.

1/35. Emigration. 1796.

1/37. Export of gunpowder and saltpetre to New York, 1796; emigration, 1797.

1/38. Trade with the United States. 1797.

1/39. Emigration. 1797.

1/40. Appeals in cases of seizure of American vessels. 1797.

1/41. Emigration; provisions for Newfoundland; alleged capture of American ship *Mentor* after peace preliminaries (twelve papers); removal of property from East and West Florida to Great Britain. 1798.

1/42. Removal of British property from East and West Florida to the Bahamas. 1798.

1/43. Licence to import cotton in American ships, 1798; American-cargoed prize ship, 1799; Jesuit estates in Canada, 1799.

1/44. Entry of American ships. 1799.

1/45. East Florida Vice-Admiralty Court: concerning the *Fame*. 1799.

1/58-60. A large group of Board of Trade and other reports, petitions, representations, etc., concerning the various colonies, on such subjects as boundaries, relations with Indians, appointments of governors and other officials, repeal of laws, land grants, etc. P.C. 1/58 covers the period, 1701-61, with a few earlier items about Massachusetts Bay; P.C. 1/59, 1762-9; P.C. 1/60 (where relevant items are considerably fewer), 1769-78.

1/61. Papers concerning Jesuit estates, 1769-91; papers concerning Prince Edward Island, chiefly complaints against Governor Patterson, 1783-5; papers concerning New Brunswick, Cape Breton, Nova Scotia, Quebec, Newfoundland - land grants, etc., 1784-5; papers concerning East Florida, 1785; West Indian trade with the United States, 1785-6.

1/62. Papers concerning Prince Edward Island, 1786-91; West Indian trade with the United States, 1787-90; slave trade, 1788.

1/63-66. Miscellaneous papers about trade with the United States, appointments of officials for Canada, etc., 1791-9. P.C. 63 includes an account of Capt. Meares's voyage on the Northwest coast of America, and P.C. 1/65 includes a memorial from T. Hasyard, an American Loyalist.

1/1924. Patent rights in Canada of the American inventor [Morse] of the electro-magnetic telegraph. 1846-7.

1/3130-53. Material similar to that in P.C. 1/58-60. 1706-82.

1/3161-3. Papers concerning Nova Scotia. 1767-84.

1/3164-7. Papers concerning Prince Edward Island. 1763-86.

1/3182-4. Papers concerning Newfoundland. 1708-76.

1/3474-4467. Roughly chronological series, 1800-44. Relevant headings among the brief summaries of bundle contents given in the available list include:

1/3477. American grain crop. 1800.
1/3583. Fever at New York. 1803.
1/3646. Fever at Charleston, S.C. 1805.
1/3730, 4060, 4146. Emigration. 1806-18.
1/4025. Importation of flax seed from America. 1813.
1/4109-11. Booty taken at Chesapeake, Ocracock [Ocracoke] Bay, and Georgia. 1816-21.
1/4182, 4203. Hudson's Bay Co.: settlers. 1820-1.
1/4210. Public health in America. 1821.

There are also many headings referring to trade with the United States or American shipping.

P.C. 4/1-17. MINUTES. 1670-1928.

For discussion of these, and comparison of them with the Registers (covered by Paullin & Paxson), see R.B. Pugh, 'Privy Council Minutes Newly Transferred to the Public Record Office', *Bulletin of the Institute of Historical Research*, vol. xxii, pp. 11-21, 1949.

P.C. 5/14-16. PLANTATION BOOKS. 1784-1806.

There are likely to be references to the United States scattered throughout these; the volume inspected (P.C. 5/16) consisted of copies of instructions to the governors of West Indian islands, Newfoundland, etc., occasionally relating to trade or fishing arrangements with the United States.

P.C. 6/9. MISCELLANEOUS BOOKS: WAR MATTERS.

The volume, which consists of a list of communications received and brief minutes relating to these, contains a section labelled 'North American (United States) Civil War'. The letters noted as having been received mainly concern the shipment of gunpowder and lead to various parts of the world, those from firms generally being requests for permission for particular shipments, and those from government departments being queries on such matters as the sending of munitions to the United States from the Continent.

P.C. 7/1-54. LETTER-BOOKS: ENTRY BOOKS OF OUT-LETTERS. 1825-99.

7/10. War matters, etc. 1859-77.

This volume includes copies of answers to the types of communications noted as being received in P.C. 6/9.

Most other volumes in P.C. 7 are noted in the available list as being on 'General Matters'; indexes are, however, to be found in the individual volumes.

PRIME MINISTER'S OFFICE

PREM. 1. CORRESPONDENCE AND PAPERS TO 1940.

1/60. Proposed appointment of a Canadian military attaché in Washington, D.C. 1928.

1/74. American naval memorial. 1929.

1/99. Anglo-American arbitration treaty and agreement on maritime belligerent rights.

1/117. Reparations: revision following Hoover moratorium. 1931-32.

1/229. Exchange with Lord Tweedsmuir on Anglo-American cooperation. 1937.

1/259. President F.D. Roosevelt's plan for a lasting peace; U.S. attitude towards recognition of Italy. 1938.

1/261. Anglo-American relations. 1937-8.

1/291. Anglo-American trade agreement. 1937-8.

1/366. Letter of support and further correspondence from President F.D. Roosevelt. 1939.

1/367. Message from President F.D. Roosevelt. 1938-9.
1/433. Proposed visit of T.U.C. leaders to the U.S. 1940.

PREM. 3. 'OPERATIONAL' PAPERS. 1940-5.

These are the papers of the office of the Prime Minister in his capacity as Minister of Defence from the War Cabinet Office. Specific American matters are listed on pp. 110-20 of the class list, but further American material, such as U.S. relations with other countries, can be found under other subject headings in the index. This class, together with PREM. 4, has sometimes been cited as the Churchill Papers.

PREM. 4. 'CONFIDENTIAL' PAPERS. 1939-46.

These papers deal mainly with civil and political matters, and were kept at No. 10 Downing St. Specific American items are 21/1 to 27/10, but there is further Americana under other subject headings.

PREM. 8. CORRESPONDENCE AND PAPERS FROM 1945.

8/6. Abolition of Munitions Assignment Board, Washington, D.C. 1945.
8/10. Investigation of the combined bombing offensive. 1945.
8/16. Discussion with President Truman and Mr. Byrnes on civil aviation. 1945.
8/28. Questions at Yalta about Allied occupation of Korea. 1945.
8/32. Message from S.E.A.C. to Gen. MacArthur. 1945.
8/35. Discussion on Lend-Lease. Lord Keynes' proposals for U.S. assistance. 1945.
8/89. President Truman's memo on Palestine, with correspondence. 1945.
8/110. Anglo/U.S./Netherlands agreement for the supply of thorium. 1945.
8/114. Memorandum by British group of scientists at Berkeley urging international control of atomic energy. 1945.
8/117. U.S./U.K./Canadian cooperation on atomic energy. 1945.
8/120. Future of British Joint Staff mission in Washington, D.C. 1945.

PUBLIC RECORD OFFICE: GIFTS AND DEPOSITS

Lists, etc.: Most of the following are described in 'P.R.O. 30 Class List', 2 vols. (typescript); where separate lists are available, this is noted.

P.R.O. 30/6. CARNARVON PAPERS.[12]

Henry Howard Molyneux Herbert, 4th Earl of Carnarvon (1831-90), was Under-Secretary for the Colonies 1858-9, and Colonial Secretary 1866-7 and 1874-8. His papers include:
30/6/26-31. Correspondence: Canadian government, etc. 1874-8.
30/6/71. Confidential Prints (Cabinet and various departments): fugitive slaves, etc. 1833-77.

P.R.O. 30/9. COLCHESTER PAPERS.

The collection includes the papers of Charles Abbot, 2nd Baron Colchester (1798-1867). Among these are:
30/9/1/4. Correspondence with William Sandom about Canadian affairs. 1839-42.
30/9/6/1/13. Correspondence, memoranda, etc., about American military activities on the Canadian border. 1841-6.

P.R.O. 30/11. CORNWALLIS PAPERS.[13]

Bundles 60-283 have been deposited since Andrews' report on the collection; of these, bundles 60-110 contain Americana, as follows:
30/11/60-71. Letters to Cornwallis from Lord George Germain, Sir Henry Clinton, Lt.-Col. Alured Clarke, Lt.-Col. Balfour, Francis Rawdon (later successively Baron Rawdon and Marquis of Hastings), and others. 1778-81.
30/11/72-94. Letters from Cornwallis to Clinton, Germain, Balfour, and others; correspondence with American commanders about prisoners, etc. 1780-4.
30/11/95-100. Correspondence of Clinton with Maj.-Gen. Phillips, Maj.-Gen. Leslie, George Washington, etc.; miscellaneous letters. 1777-81.
30/11/101-5. Miscellaneous papers: Cornwallis's proclamations and warrants concerning the Carolinas, intelligence reports, intercepted letters, etc. 1778-81.
30/11/106-10. Miscellaneous items: papers of Gen. William Davidson; and material concerning South Carolina (currency depreciation, dispatches from Balfour at Charleston, copy of the accounts of John Cruden, Commissioner of Sequestered Estates, etc.). 1780-2.

P.R.O. 30/22. RUSSELL PAPERS.[14]

The papers of Lord John Russell, 1st Earl Russell (1792-1878), who was Foreign Secretary during the Civil War, include, in addition to the following, correspondence and papers (chronologically arranged, 1804-78) and correspondence with the Cabinet (1859-65); there is likely to be additional American material among such classes.
30/22/34-38. United States: Correspondence - Legation in Washington. 1859-65.
30/22/39. United States: Correspondence - Legation in London and miscellaneous. 1859-65.
30/22/96. United States: Correspondence (drafts) - Legation in Washington (including two 1859 letters from Lord Lyons). 1859-62.
30/22/97. United States: Correspondence (drafts) - Legation in Washington, 1863-5, and Legation in London and miscellaneous, 1859-65.

P.R.O. 30/26. MISCELLANEOUS.

30/26/58/3. Exchequer. (?) [American Loyalist Claims Commission]. Warrant for payment, No. 3247. Archibald Hamilton. 18 Mar. 1789.

P.R.O. 30/29. GRANVILLE PAPERS.[15]

This collection of the papers of various members of the Granville family includes the following of Granville George Leveson-Gower, 2nd Earl Granville (1815-91), Colonial Secretary 1868-70, and Foreign Secretary 1870-4 and 1880-5:
30/29/67. Correspondence with Sir Roundell Palmer and Lord Westbury about the *Alabama* claims arbitration. 1871-2.

12. A class list is available.
13. Microfilms of these are in the Library of Congress.
14. Some of the relevant correspondence has been published in *The Later Correspondence of Lord John Russell, 1840-1878*, ed. by G.P. Gooch (London, 1925).
15. A class list is available.

30/29/80. Correspondence: United States: British Legation in Washington. 1870-4.
30/29/81. Correspondence: United States: Legation in London, etc. 1871-4.
30/29/106. Correspondence with Lord Tenterden, mainly about the United States. 1871-4.
30/29/142. Correspondence: Cabinet. Including letters from Earl Spencer, Lord-Lieutenant of Ireland, enclosing copy of the *United Irishman* of New York, 10 June 1882.
30/29/154. Correspondence: United States. 1880-5.[16]
30/29/196. Correspondence (drafts): United States, etc. 1880-5.
30/29/215. Letter-book: in- and out-letters, précis, drafts, etc. United States, etc. 1851-2.
30/29/221-38. Confidential Prints (Foreign Office). United States.
  30/29/221-34. Papers connected with the Geneva Arbitration Tribunal of 1871.
  30/29/235-6. German arbitration: North-West boundary. 1842-72.
  30/29/237. North American fisheries. 1803-73.
  30/29/238. Miscellaneous. 1783-1872.
30/29/271. Confidential Prints (Foreign Office). United States: Newfoundland fisheries. 1879-82.
30/29/272. Confidential Prints (Foreign Office). United States: Miscellaneous. 1880-4.

There may also be relevant material in the classes containing the 2nd Earl's Cabinet and other correspondence from 1839 onwards.

See also F.O. 362 (p. 133).

P.R.O. 30/32. LEEDS PAPERS.

The fifty-six volumes of this collection mainly contain the papers of Sir Thomas Osborne, successively 1st Earl of Danby, Marquis of Carmarthen, and 1st Duke of Leeds (1631-1712), while Lord High Treasurer 1673-9. Included are Treasury minutes, warrants and orders, customs quarter bills, etc. There is likely to be some Americana among these; for the basic series of Treasury records which they supplement see Andrews, vol. ii, pp. 136-265.

P.R.O. 30/36. STUART PAPERS.

The papers of William Stuart, *Chargé d'Affaires* and Secretary of the Legation in Washington 1861-3, include the following:
30/36/1-2. United States: dispatches to the Secretary of State, and entry book to these. 1862.
30/36/10. United States out-letters: entry book; etc. 1858-71.

P.R.O. 30/39. DOCUMENTS OF UNKNOWN OWNERSHIP.

30/39/1. Surgeon Richard Hope. Fifteen letters to relatives in England from Quebec, Boston, New York, and the *British King* off Staten Island. 1770-82. Hope was Surgeon of the 52nd Regiment of Foot 1756-76, when he was transferred to the staff of the hospitals for the forces in North America. With the letter of 20 Aug. 1775 is a copy of the *Massachusetts Gazette and Boston Weekly News-Letter* for 17 Aug. 1775.

P.R.O. 30/42. NICHOLL PAPERS.

Sir John Nicholl (1759-1838) was King's Advocate General 1798-1809, and these papers consist mainly of his rough drafts and notes for reports and opinions on the matters referred to him by the Privy Council and the Home and Foreign Secretaries. Included are:
30/42/3/10, and 4/8, 4/11, 5/1, 7/8, 10/1, 12/3. Drafts of reports to the Privy Council concerning trade with America, including licenses for importing from Florida and exporting to New Orleans and elsewhere. 1799-1806.
30/42/17/2, and 18/7, 20/5, 21/5. Drafts of reports to the Home Secretary, as follows:
  30/42/17/2. American ships clearing for India. 1799.
  30/42/18/7. Blockade of Cadiz and American trade to Spain. 1800.
  30/42/20/5. Maritime matters affecting British ships in United States ports: twenty-five papers (copies of documents showing relations between Anthony Merry and James Madison). 1804.
  30/42/21/5. Licence to import flour-milling machinery from the United States into Cadiz; and violation of neutral waters of the United States. 1806.
30/42/22/3, and 22/7, 22/10, 23/3, 24/4, 24/7, 25/11, 26/5, 26/8, 28/1, 28/10, 29/4, 29/5, 29/11-14, 29/17, 33/4-7, 34/3. Drafts of reports to the Foreign Secretary about America. 1799-1808 (The originals of some of these may be found among the Law Officers' Reports in F.O. 83/2204-5.)

P.R.O. 30/46. EYRE PAPERS.

The collection includes the papers (P.R.O. 30/46/9-20) of Maj.-Gen. Sir William Eyre (1805-59) while in command of the forces in Canada 1856-9; some of these concern the Red River Settlement, Fort Garry, etc.

P.R.O. 30/47. EGREMONT PAPERS.[17]

The diplomatic and political papers of Sir Charles Wyndham, 2nd Earl of Egremont (1710-63), who was Secretary of State for the Southern Department 1761-3 include:
30/47/14/1. Virginia: memorial of Armistead Churchill, and other papers. 1761-3.
30/47/14/2. South Carolina and Georgia: journals of expeditions; surveys; appointments of officers. 1703-63.
30/47/14/3. Florida: report on the expedition against St. Augustine, 1739-40; and notes on the settlement of the colony by the British, 1763.
30/47/14/4. Louisiana: survey of the coast and the Mississippi River. 1757-8.
30/47/14/5. New Spain: projects of attacks on various Spanish settlements.
30/47/14/6. America, general: papers concerning appointments; proposals of Henry Ellis for attacks on various enemy possessions; etc. 1760-3.
30/47/15-16. Canada: various. 1759-63.
30/47/22/1. Board of Trade: report on trade with colonies and plantations in America. 1733-4.
30/47/22/2. Board of Trade: letters and reports about the government of Canada and of Florida. 1763.
30/47/24. Board of Trade: military: details of disposition of forces, North America, 1763.
30/47/25. Board of Trade: postal. Letters concerning packet boats to North America and West Indies. 1763.
30/47/27-29. Semi-official and private correspondence. 1749-63. (These include a number of letters of congratulation on the war, 1760-2, and letters asking for appointments in America.)

16. See P. Knaplund and C.M. Clewes, ed., 'Private Letters from the British Embassy in Washington to the Foreign Secretary, Lord Granville, 1880-1885'. *Annual Report of the American Historical Association*, 1941, vol. i, pp. 73-189.

17. The Library of Congress holds microfilms of P.R.O. 30/47/14 and 30/47/22. The Illinois Historical Survey, University of Illinois, holds photostats of P.R.O. 30/47/11, twenty letters, 1761-3, from the Comte de Viry, Sardinian Ambassador to London, about negotiations for peace with France.

P.R.O. 30/48. CARDWELL PAPERS.

Papers of Edward Cardwell, Viscount Cardwell (1813-86), who was Secretary for the Colonies 1864-6 and Secretary of War 1868-74. Included is correspondence, 1864-6, on Canadian Confederation (30/48/6/39 and 40); there may be some relevant material in other parts of the Colonial Office and War Office correspondence and memoranda.

P.R.O. 30/50. NEVILLE AND ALDWORTH PAPERS.

Among these are the papers of Richard Neville Aldworth (assumed name of Neville in 1762) (1717-93) as Under-Secretary of State 1748-51, including:
30/50/39. Miscellaneous colonial correspondence, 1748-51. Letters from Hugh Davidson in Halifax, N.S., about relations with the Indians and with New England merchants: notes about correspondence with Governor Belcher of New Jersey; a letter from Corbyn Morris suggesting regulations for currency in the American colonies; etc.
30/50/43. Relation of negotiations for a convention with Spain. Included are notes, copies of letters, etc., relating to Spanish plans for attacking South Carolina, and other matters relating to 'Spanish depredations' in America, 1737-46.

There may also be some relevant material in his papers as Secretary to the Embassy in Paris 1762-3, during the period of negotiating a peace treaty for the Seven Years War.

P.R.O. 30/55. CARLETON PAPERS.[18]

Records of British Army Headquarters in America, 1775-83. The 107 volumes contain the official notes at British Headquarters in America of General Thomas Gage, Sir William Howe, Sir Henry Clinton, and Sir Guy Carleton, as successive commanders-in-chief in America.

P.R.O. 30/67. MIDLETON PAPERS.

St. John Brodrick, 1st Earl of Midleton, held various offices between 1886 and 1905, and was involved in Irish affairs until 1922. His papers include correspondence with Wade Chance, described as an American correspondent, 1920-33.

P.R.O. 30/68. ANDERSON PAPERS.

Papers of Sir Allan Garrett Anderson (1877-1952), a civil servant concerned with food supplies and trade between 1916 and 1926.
30/68/9. War Cabinet minutes on transport in the U.S. 1917.
30/68/10-12. Balfour mission to the U.S., on which Anderson was Wheat Commission representative. 1917.

P.R.O. 30/69. RAMSAY MacDONALD PAPERS.

Includes diaries and notebooks, correspondence, official papers, manuscripts of writings, speeches, and press cuttings. There is probably a great deal of American material in the correspondence. Some indication is given in:
30/69/4/3. Index to 'Anglo-American Relations' file, 1929-35.
30/69/4/4. Index to 'P.M.'s visit to U.S.A.' file, 1929.
30/69/4/5. Index to 'P.M.'s visit to Canada' file, 1929.
30/69/6/87-99. Visit to U.S.A. and Canada: correspondence and papers, 1929.
There is a separate list to this class.

P.R.O. 30/70. HOARE (PITT) MSS.

These papers must have originally formed part of the family papers of the Earl of Chatham and William Pitt, described in Andrews, vol ii, pp. 351-65, but they have come to the P.R.O. in a separate and more recent gift. They include correspondence of John, 2nd Earl of Chatham, who was aide-de-camp to Gen. Guy Carleton in Quebec 1774-5. It contains several items concerning America and Canada, e.g.:
30/70/194. Letter from Benedict Arnold asking for promotion to Major-General. 6 Aug. 1795.

TREASURY

Lists, etc.: 'T. 1: Treasury Board Papers, 1557-1920'. 3 vols. (typescript).
'Treasury Out-Letters (T. 5-28, 97, 101): 1838-1902' (photostat).
P.R.O. *Lists and Indexes, Supplementary Series No. XII: List of Treasury Records 1838-1938* (1970).
'Treasury Board Papers, Class List T1/319 to 388, 429-436 (1746-1758, 1764). Descriptive List with index' (typescript).
'Subject Index to Treasury Long Papers T1' (photocopy).
'Treasury Files for 1939 in the P.R.O.' (duplicated).
'Treasury Board Papers T1/12200-T1/12625, September 1918-June 1920. Descriptive list of documents of interest to social scientists and historians', prepared by Brenda Swann and Maureen Turnbull (duplicated).

Some of these calendars have been published by the List and Index Society.

T.1/3237-12626. IN-LETTERS: TREASURY BOARD PAPERS.[19] 1838-1920.

These can be used by means of the indexes to be found in T. 2, T. 3, and T. 108. Examination of T. 108/4, the subject register for 1866-70, showed only a few very minor items of relevance.

T. 5-28. OUT-LETTERS.

These classes contain copies of letters to various government departments. Examination of T. 11/113 Out-letters: Customs, 1860-3, showed that relevant matter - e.g. concerning British ships leaving Charleston, S.C. - was mainly in the form of letters transmitting Foreign Office material. Examination of T. 12/2 Out-letters: Foreign Office, 1860-3 showed letters about the Liverpool fitting-out of gunboats for the Confederacy, the duty-free entry of breadstuffs from the United States for Lancashire, etc.; again these are mainly covering letters for documents forwarded.

T. 29/397-619. MINUTES. 1838-70.

There may be scattered relevant material among these.

18. These were formerly in the Royal Institution, see H.M.C. *Report on American Manuscripts in the Royal Institution of Great Britain* [59], 4 vols. (London, 1904-9). They were acquired by an American owner in 1929, were rearranged and rebound by the New York Public Library for Colonial Williamsburg, who presented them to H.M. Queen Elizabeth II in 1957. There are copies of these documents in the British Library - Stevens Transcripts, Add. MSS. 42257-496.
19. The Library of Congress has a transcript of T. 1/5083/18349: Expenses of Lord Ashburton's mission, 12 Sept. 1845.

T. 39. ACCOUNTS: TREASURY CHEST.

There may be relevant material in T. 39/9-14, which contain accounts for Canada, 1846-71. Included in T. 39/24 are accounts for Fort Garry, 1846-9, and for New York, 1855-6.

T. 160. IN-LETTERS AND FILES: FINANCE.

T. 161. IN-LETTERS AND FILES: SUPPLY.

T. 163. IN-LETTERS AND FILES: GENERAL.

After 1920 the Treasury Board Papers T. 1 were continued in four divisions, of which only the three above are likely to contain American material. There are subject indexes to each class, and although there are very few entries under 'United States', there may be American items under other subjects. These papers are available after thirty years.

T. 170. PRIVATE OFFICE PAPERS AND PRIVATE COLLECTIONS: BRADBURY PAPERS.

Sir John Bradbury was Financial Adviser and Joint Permanent Secretary to the Treasury.
170/62. American exchange. 1915.
170/63. American loan, telegrams. 1915.
170/95. Interdepartmental committee to consider dependence of British Empire on United States of America. 1916.
170/99. American securities. 1916.
170/107. American commitments. 1916.
170/109. American securities, correspondence. 1916-7.
170/111. Dollar claims against France. 1917.
170/124. American sterling balances. 1918.
170/130. Report of the American Dollar Securities Committee. 1919.
170/134. British government transactions in America. 1915-22.

T. 172. PRIVATE OFFICE PAPERS AND PRIVATE COLLECTIONS: CHANCELLOR OF THE EXCHEQUER'S OFFICE: MISCELLANEOUS PAPERS.

172/3. Proposals on currency made by the Special Envoys from the U.S. (*See* 170/953.)
172/143. Minutes of resumed conference of bankers to discuss the financial position of the U.S. 1914.
172/358. Trade and Britain's relationship with the U.S. 1916.
172/360. American financial proposals. 1916.
172/416-8B. American resources; dollar securities. 1916-7.
172/422-60. Mainly concerned with the financial situation in America. 1917-20.
There are several other American items scattered throughout the class.

TREASURY SOLICITOR

Lists, etc.: 'Treasury Solicitor: Class List' (typescript).

T.S. 12. WEST NEW JERSEY SOCIETY.

Correspondence, minutes, accounts, deeds, maps, and plans, 1675-1921. Also manuscript and printed volumes of Joseph Paine's history of the Society, 1895. The Society was formed about 1691 as a company for the purchase of land in West and East New Jersey, Pennsylvania, New England, and elsewhere.

T.S. 13. QUEEN'S PROCTOR: PRIZE AND PRIZE BOUNTY DECREES AND AFFIDAVITS. 1939-54.

Many of the ships listed appear to be American.

T.S. 23. MISCELLANEA.

23/24. *Narrative of facts relative to American affairs*, 1768. (Printed.)
23/31. Correspondence and papers concerning the assignment of proceeds from the capture of American ships before the declaration of war. The case of the *Acteon*, William and Rufus King.

T.S. 27. REGISTERED FILES: TREASURY AND MISCELLANEOUS SERIES.

27/1. North American fisheries: arbitration before The Hague Convention. 1909-11.
27/7. Request by U.S. Embassy for instances in which claims may be enforced against H.M. Government and municipal corporations. 1910.
27/70. Proposed loan by H.M. Government to the British American Nickel Corporation. 1919.
27/78. Loan to be raised in U.S.A. 1919.

WAR OFFICE

Lists, etc.: P.R.O. *Lists and Indexes No. LIII: Alphabetical Guide to War Office and Other Military Records* (1931).
P.R.O. *Lists and Indexes No. XXVIII: War Office* (1963)
P.R.O. *Lists and Indexes, Supplementary Series No. VIII: List of War Office Records. Vol. 1. Continuing No. XXVIII.* (1968)
'Amherst Papers (W.O. 34) Calendar', 6 vols. (typescript).
'W.O. Ordnance: Index to In-Letters' (typescript).
The Second World War, a Guide to Documents in the Public Record Office: P.R.O. Handbook No. 15 (1972).

W.O. 6. OUT-LETTERS: SECRETARY OF STATE.

6/133. Arming of militia and inspection of field officers for militia in British possessions in North America. 1808.
6/154. Disclaimer by the United States as to giving orders for hostilities in British possessions in North America. 1814.

W.O. 28. HEADQUARTERS RECORDS.

28/303-17. Canada. 1811-7.

W.O. 32. REGISTERED PAPERS, GENERAL SERIES.

32/136. Cuba: military attaché's report on Spanish-American War. 1898.
32/209. Geneva Convention: Red Cross Convention - maritime warfare, Spain and the United States. 1898.
32/257. Canada: mobilization report, Esquimalt. 1900.
32/273. Canada: garrison of Halifax, N.S. 1904.
32/275. Canada: various reports and proposals concerning defences. 1897-1904.
32/317. Canada: enrolment of pensioners for service at Fort Garry. 1848.
32/420. North America: general considerations by the Honours and Distinctions Committee of the Indian Wars, 1763-4. 1910.

32/500. Canada: provision of armament and garrisons for defence of Esquimalt. 1891.
32/910. America: terms of emigration of British German Legion. 1856.
32/1027. President Roosevelt's objections to formation of depots for horse purchasing. 1904.
32/1034. Bermuda: proposed route via New York for military details. 1911.
32/1082. Sanction for payment of pension in the United States. 1901.
32/1117. United States: inquiry as to position of cables in Australia and New Zealand. 1913.
32/2490. Visits to England in 1896 and 1903 by the Ancient and Honorable Artillery Company of Massachusetts.
32/3605. Report on industrial mobilization in the U.S. 1928-9.
32/3606. 'Explosives in America'. 1929.
32/3607. 'Chemical warfare in America'. 1929.
32/3608. American military activities in the Caribbean. 1929.
32/4125. Report on West Point. 1936.
32/8335. German Foreign Legion: terms of emigration to the U.S. 1856.
32/9464. Military mission to the U.S. 1940-1.
32/9586. Recruitment of Poles in U.S. and Canada. 1941-2.
32/9590. Leased bases: American order of battle. 1941-4.
32/9620. Relations between British Military Mission and North American Supply Council. 1941.
32/9621. Reciprocal loans to U.S.: arrangements. 1941-2.
32/9622. North American Bureau. 1941-2.
32/9623. American citizens killed while serving in British forces. 1941-3.
32/10266. American troops in the U.K.: hospitality. 1942.
32/10267. Anglo-American Relations Committee. 1942-3.
32/10268. Anglo-American relations: policy. 1943-4.
32/10544. U.S. awards to British soldiers. 1942-4.
Further American items can be located under other subject headings in the class list.

W.O. 33. REPORTS AND MISCELLANEOUS PAPERS.

This class consists of printed reports, memoranda, reports of select committees and commissions of enquiry, operations and intelligence summaries from 1853 to 1945. There is a separate class list, but since items are usually described by subject it is difficult to locate American material. Apart from the items listed here, the Americana seems to be concerned with the U.S./Canadian border in the late nineteenth and early twentieth centuries, and with Anglo-American or American operations in both world wars.
33/10. Unsatisfactory contract for supply of rifles by American firm. 1861.
33/11. Defence of British possessions in North America: report of Commissioner and memorandum by Sir John Burgoyne. 1862.
33/12. Peace, etc., suggestions concerning the Civil War. 1862.
33/14. Report on American military affairs. 1864.
33/15. Report on defences and British naval stations in North Atlantic. 1865.
33/20. Military position of Britain with respect to the United States. 1869.
33/21-22. Correspondence, instructions, and reports on the Red River expedition and settlement. 1870-1.
33/26. Report on American submarine mining establishment. 1874.
33/45. Army estimates: notes on procedures in parliaments of various countries, including the United States. 1886.
33/47. Fortifications and armaments of Halifax, N.S. 1887.
33/49. Tour through the United States and notes on principal government establishments, etc., there by Major G.S. Clarke, R.E. 1888.
33/55. Report on military aspects, etc., of frontier with the United States, 1893; and defence works at Esquimalt, 1895.
33/56. United States: land forces. 1896.

W.O. 34/1-260. AMHERST PAPERS.[20] 1712-84.

The collection consists mainly of the official correspondence of Jeffrey Amherst, Baron Amherst (1717-97). Most of the material relates to his period in charge of the British forces in America, 1758-63 (correspondence with governors of the various colonies, with French officials in North America, etc.), and to his later role as Commander-in-Chief and adviser on the American war, 1778-82 (letters from Germain, Lord North, Cornwallis, etc.). See the six-volume calendar for details.

See also the Amherst MSS. in the Kent County Archives Office (p. 45).

W.O. 36/1-4. AMERICAN REBELLION: ENTRY BOOKS. 1773-99.

These are the documents described in the report on the War Office Library given on p. 188 of Andrews & Davenport.

W.O. 40. SELECT UNNUMBERED PAPERS.

40/1. Capt. Preston and eight others prosecuted on charge of causing a riot, Boston, 1770. Destruction of tea in Boston Harbour by the Sons of Liberty: report by O.C. troops, 1773. Report of Gen. Carleton on the condition of affairs at Quebec, 1776. Garrisons of Chambly and St. Johns not blamed for surrendering, 1777.
40/2. German recruits for service in America: reports by Maj.-Gen. Fawcett, 1780. Exchange of prisoners of war: lists of officers, 1781.
40/5. Charleston, S.C.: application for the return of bells of St. Michael's, taken by the English. 1783.
40/6. Newfoundland: a corps of volunteers raised for the defence of Fort Townsend. 1793.
40/10. British half-pay officers in America allowed to enter into the service of the United States. 1798.
40/12. America: troops under Lord Amherst not given prize money. 1799.
40/27. Ferdinand Smyth Stuart: statement of his services, losses in America, etc. 1807.
40/32. Instructions from Lt.-Col. Bruyeres, R.E., to Lieut. Gangreben for the defence of Fort Niagara and the frontier. 1814.

W.O. 44. ORDNANCE: IN-LETTERS.

In addition to the items listed below, this class also includes in-letters from various parts of Canada up to 1855.

20. The Library of Congress holds microfilms of nearly all of these.

44/239. American frigate *Chesapeake* purchased and registered in the Royal Navy list. 1815.
44/502. Mr. Howe, United States: plan for drowning magazines in case of fire. 1852.
44/504. Improvement in the navigation of the St. Lawrence. 1834.
44/506. Lieut.-Col. Kearney, United States Army, permitted to ascertain positions of points on the British shores of Lake Erie and the Northern Lakes for a hydrographical survey, 1845. Settlement in 1846 of the boundary between the United States, Canada, and New Brunswick, as established by the treaty of 1842.
44/532. Warrant for distribution of prize money for capture on Lake Huron in 1814 of the American vessels *Tigress* and *Scorpion*. 1818.
44/539. Dr. Alexander Jones, United States: invention of breech-loading carbine. 1842.
44/540. Surrender of Detroit and Michilimackinac reported to the Board of Ordnance by Maj.-Gen. Glasgow, R.A. 1813.
44/541. Employment of engineers on the boundary survey between the United States and Canada. 1844.
44/622. J. Christopher, United States: process for improving the quality of iron for ordnance. 1855.
44/623. W. Baynton, United States: method of making castings for ordnance. 1855.

W.O. 71. JUDGE ADVOCATE GENERAL'S RECORDS: COURTS MARTIAL: PROCEEDINGS.[21]

This class contains proceedings and papers for 1668-1850. Included are, e.g.:
71/19, 126. Trial and acquittal of Lieut.-Gen. James E. Oglethorpe. 1746.
71/61. Trial of Col. the Hon. Cosmo Gordon for neglect of duty at Springfield, North America. 1782.

W.O. 72. JUDGE ADVOCATE GENERAL'S RECORDS: CORRESPONDENCE RELATIVE TO COURTS MARTIAL.

Included is, e.g.:
72/103. Inquiry into failure of Albany expedition of Lieut.-Gen. John Burgoyne. 1778.

W.O. 80. MISCELLANEA: MURRAY PAPERS.

Sir George Murray (1772-1846) was Governor of the Canadas in 1814, Colonial Secretary 1828-30, and later Master-General of the Ordnance. His papers include:
80/4. Original correspondence, including correspondence with Sir James Kempt, Governor-General of Canada 1828-30, and a letter of 18 Dec. 1844 to Edward Everett acknowledging receipt of maps and surveys.
80/11. Miscellaneous papers on the defence of Canada. 1815-9, 1839-46.

W.O. 81. JUDGE ADVOCATE GENERAL'S RECORDS: CORRESPONDENCE: LETTER-BOOKS.

There are 125 volumes, covering the period 1715-1880; most contain an index. Included are the following:
81/8, 9. Court martial of Maj.-Gen. Lord Charles Hay, North America. 1759.
81/13. Lieut.-Gen. John Burgoyne: failure of Albany expedition. 1778.
81/64. Transportation to Bermuda from America of soldiers under sentence. 1824.
81/111. Possession of passenger's ticket for New York not proof of desertion. 1864.

W.O. 95. WAR DIARIES. 1914-22.

These contain the daily records of events, reports on operations, intelligence summaries, etc., from all British and Colonial units in all theatres of war during the First World War, and of the armies of occupation, 1919-22. It includes the operations of the Canadian contingents and (Part IX) Allied intervention in Russia.

W.O. 106. DIRECTORATES OF MILITARY OPERATIONS AND INTELLIGENCE.

106/17. Correspondence and papers concerning the withdrawal of international troops from North China, including papers about the March 1906 meeting of representatives of the United States, Britain, and other countries to arrange withdrawal.
106/25. China: revolution and civil war: analysis of disturbances-alleged headquarters of reformers' group in England and America, 1903; attack on American mission at Peking, 1905; protection of American interests - troop reinforcements for Manila, 1906.
106/40. Defence and operational plans.

Included is a section on North America, 1896-1910: e.g. defence of the Canadian frontier, Feb. 1897; conditions of a war between the British Empire and the United States, Jan. 1908; etc.

This class also contains a great deal of material in the sections covering the First World War and its aftermath, and the Second World War. For the First World War, see especially:
106/464-543. American Expeditionary Force in Europe. 1917-21.
106/982-1333. Allied intervention in Russia. 1918-20.

The Second World War is covered by:
106/1595-5127. American material can be found throughout.

W.O. 107. QUARTERMASTER GENERAL: PAPERS.

107/6. Canada expedition: troop movements, etc. 1861-2.
107/9. Red River expedition: journal, etc. 1870.

W.O. 108. SOUTH AFRICAN WAR: PAPERS.

108/81. Miscellanea: purchase of ordnance from Germany, Austria, France, North and South America. 1899-1900.

W.O. 165-179. WAR OF 1939-1945: WAR DIARIES.

Those which are most likely to contain American material are:
W.O. 169. Middle East Forces.
W.O. 170. Central Mediterranean Forces.
W.O. 172. South East Asia Command and Allied Land Forces, South East Asia.
W.O. 175. British North African Forces.
W.O. 176. Various smaller theatres.
W.O. 178. Military Missions.
W.O. 179. Dominion Forces.

These classes are closed for 100 years, except to those who are prepared to sign an undertaking not to disclose information of a personal nature.

21. The Library of Congress holds photostats from W.O. 71/131: Proceedings of court martial held at Loyal Hannon, 26 Oct. 1758.

W.O. 197-205. WAR OF 1939-1945: MILITARY HEADQUARTERS PAPERS.

Those which appear to contain American material are:
W.O. 199. Home Forces.
W.O. 201. Middle East Forces.
W.O. 202. Military Missions.
W.O. 203. Far East.
W.O. 204. Allied Forces.
W.O. 205. 21st Army Group. This was the British Army group set up to plan the invasion of Europe. It contains many items on the American and Canadian parts of that operation.

W.O. 208. WAR OF 1939-1945: DIRECTORATE OF MILITARY INTELLIGENCE.

Contains several U.S. intelligence reports on other countries.

W.O. 215. PAPERS OF LORD ALEXANDER OF TUNIS. 1942-51.

Includes telegrams to and from Combined Chiefs of Staff, Washington, D.C.; items on Canadian forces; and items on operations in the Mediterranean theatre.

W.O. 216. CHIEF OF THE IMPERIAL GENERAL STAFF: PAPERS. 1935-46.

Deals with military operations throughout the world. There are several American items.

RIO TINTO-ZINC CORPORATION LTD., 6 St. James's Square, London SW1Y 4LD

FINANCIAL AND ORGANIZATIONAL PAPERS. 1925 - 56.

(*a*) Financial, commercial and operational papers - and some photographs of Wilmington Plant - of the Pyrites Company, Inc. (PYCOINC), 1925-55.

(*b*) Financial and organizational papers of Weiss Geophysical Corporation of Canada & the U.S.A. (later known as the Barbican Corporations of Canada & the U.S.A.), 1952-6.

THE LIBRARY, ROYAL ARTILLERY INSTITUTION, Woolwich, London SE18 4JJ

'A JOURNAL CONTAINING THE MANNER, METHOD AND EXECUTION OF THE DEMOLITION OF THE FORTIFICATIONS OF LOUISBOURG.' 1 volume. 1760. (MS. 6)

Daily journal, June-Nov. 1760, of the demolition. Mainly reports of the numbers and ranks of carpenters, miners, and others employed, and the work accomplished.

HOWE, SIR WILLIAM, 5th Viscount Howe (1729-1814). 1 volume. 1777-8. (MS. 58)

General orders, 27 Sept. 1777-21 Feb. 1778, of the Army in North America under General Howe. The volume contains orders concerning deserters from the American Army, marching orders, etc.

PATTISON, JAMES (1724-1805?). 5 volumes. 1777-81.

Pattison served with the British Army in North America during the War of Independence, and was commander in New York 1779-80.

(*a*) 'Brigade orders, Royal Artillery, from September 28 1777 till February 21 1778 by Brigadier General James Pattison.' Similar to the Howe volume above. (MS. 57)

(*b*) 'Warrants. Bills of Lading. Record of Commissions. Day Book. This volume contains warrants by Pattison, 1777-80; bills of lading concerning supplies for the artillery, 1779; record of commissions, 1779-80; and a day book for Pattison's New York command, 1779-80. It also contains 'Orders and regulations of the Superintendent General of the police of the city of New York and its dependencies authorized by Major General Jones', 1778-9. (MS. 11)

(*c*) Letter-books containing copies of letters sent by Pattison, 1777-81.

(i) Letters, Philadelphia and New York, 1777-8, to the Board of Ordnance, Viscount Townshend, Samuel Cleaveland, and others, mainly about deserters from the American Army, rumours of strife in Congress, etc. (MS. 7)

(ii) Letters, mainly from New York, 10 Jan. 1779-11 Jan. 1781, to Amherst, Clinton, Germain, Lt.-Col. Innes, Townshend, and others, concerning the progress of the war.[1] (MS. 9)

(iii) Letters, New York, 10 July 1779-18 August 1780, to a large number of correspondents, mainly about Pattison's administration of New York. (MS. 9)

'BOOK OF RETURNS ETC. FOR THE CORPS OF ARTILLERY IN CANADA COMMENCING THE 1ST JULY 1778.' 2 volumes. 1778-83.[2] (MS. 19)

One volume contains orders, monthly returns of forces, etc.; and copies of letters, Quebec and elsewhere, 1778-83, from Forbes Macbean to Pattison, Townshend, and others, concerning defences, supplies, etc. The other volume lists ordnance and ordnance stores at the various posts in Canada in 1778 and 1783.

THE LIBRARY, ROYAL BOTANIC GARDENS, Kew, Richmond TW9 3AB

HOOKER CORRESPONDENCE. 1823-65.

The library holds an extensive collection of letters on botanical matters written to Sir William Jackson Hooker (1785-1865), Director of the Gardens, together with two index volumes to these. Volumes lxi-lxv are devoted to letters from American correspondents or from America, 1832-65, while volume xliv includes some earlier relevant letters.

Among Hooker's many correspondents in the United States the following are represented by fifteen or more letters each: Daniel C. Eaton, George Engelmann, Jno. Evans, Asa Gray, Benjamin D. Greene, Thomas P. James, Thomas Nuttall, Charles W. Short, and John Torrey. There are also twenty-four letters from Thomas Drummond, written from the United States, 1831-5, while on a plant-collecting trip; and letters from the Northwest from David Douglas, 1825-30, and from D. Lyall of the North American Boundary Commission, 1859-61.

GRAY, ASA (1810-88). Letters (2 volumes). 1839-88.

Botanist; Professor of Natural History at Harvard University. Two volumes, labelled 'Kew Correspondence: Asa Gray', consist of letters

1. Microfilm held by the Library of Congress, Washington, D.C.
2. Microfilm held by the Library of Congress, Washington, D.C.

from Gray to the British botanists George Bentham and Sir Joseph Hooker.

MISCELLANEOUS LETTERS. 1865-1914.

Among the bound volumes of letters to Kew - mainly to the director of the time - are volumes as follows (an alphabetical index to the writers of the letters is given at the beginning of each volume or section):

'United States Letters. North. 1865-1900': three volumes of letters from correspondents in the Northern states.

'United States Letters. South and West. 1865-1900': (1 volume).

'Supplementary Foreign Letters. 1865-1900': one volume, including a considerable number of letters from America or Americans, including some from D. Lyall of the North American Boundary Commission to Joseph Hooker, 1858-61.

'United States Letters. 1901-1914. Nat. Museum, Harvard, Dept. of Agric.': one volume, containing letters from the Smithsonian Institution, the Botanical Garden of Harvard University, and the Bureau of Plant Industry of the United States Department of Agriculture.

'United States Letters. 1901-1914. Britton, Missouri B.G., Sargent, S. United States, etc.': one volume, containing letters from the New York Botanical Garden - mainly from Elizabeth G. Britton; from the Missouri Botanical Garden in St. Louis; from the Arnold Arboretum at Harvard University - mainly from C.S. Sargent; and miscellaneous letters from the Southern and Western states.

'Brit. N. America, S. United States, and Bermuda Letters. 1901-1914': this volume includes letters from the Northern (not the Southern) states.

HILL, ARTHUR W. (1875-1941). Diary (1 volume). 1926.

Botanist; Director of the Gardens. The diary of his trip to the United States in 1926 consists of brief comments on plants seen, people met, etc., in his journey across to California and back by way of Canada.

REGISTERED FILES. 1911-49.

The library is a statutory place of deposit under the Public Record Acts and therefore retains its own official files instead of transferring them to the Public Record Office. The standard thirty-year rule applies for access. A selection of titles of files which relate to the U.S.A. which have been permanently preserved is as follows: New York Botanical Gardens (1929-49); U.S. Dept. of Agriculture, Bureau of Plant Industry (1929-48); Harvard University, Gray Herbarium and Arnold Arboretum (1929-48); Washington National Museum (1911-48); St. Louis Botanical Garden (1930-6); Chicago, Field Museum of Natural History (1928-36); University of California, Berkeley (1929-46); also additional files and letters from named individuals.

ROYAL COMMONWEALTH SOCIETY, Northumberland Avenue, London WC2N 5BJ

NORTH WEST COMPANY. Miscellaneous papers.[1] 1697-1904.

The North West Company, a group of fur traders operating from Montreal, was the major rival of the Hudson's Bay Company until the two merged in 1821. The following manuscripts deal with such subjects as navigability of rivers, customs and attitudes of various Indian tribes, adequacy of beaver supply, etc.

(*a*) Joseph de la Penja: Grants of sovereignty in Labrador. Two legal documents on parchment, granting and confirming 'seigneurial and territorial rights, high, middling and low justice' over land in Labrador from 54° to 60° N, to Joseph de La Penja, citizen of Rotterdam. 1697, 1768.

(*b*) Duncan M'Gillivray: 'Journal'[2] kept during 1794-5 at Fort George on the North Saskatchewan River (94 pages).

(*c*) William M'Gillivray (?): 'Some account of the trade carried on by the North West Company'[3] (early 19th cent.) (58 pages).

(*d*) David Thompson:

(i) 'Narrative of the expedition to the Kootenai and Flat Bow Indian countries, on the sources of the Columbia River, Pacific Ocean', 1807[4] (27 pages).

(ii) 'Remarks on the countries westward of the Rocky Mountains', 1813 (4 pages).

(*e*) Willard Ferdinand Wentzel, 'An account of Mackenzie's River', 1821 (7 pages).

(*f*) Alfred Roche (1819-76): 'Notes on Hudson Bay Territory', 1857.

(*g*) Letter to Archibald Ross from President Theodore Roosevelt, 1904, giving his views on U.S. responsibility to the Filipinos.

ROYAL GEOGRAPHICAL SOCIETY, Kensington Gore, London SW7 2AR

CORRESPONDENCE FILES. 1830-1920.

Large numbers of letters from corresponding American societies or individuals, but for the most part simply requests for, or acknowledgements of, the periodical publications of the Society or covering dispatch of American publications.

(*a*) 22 June 1850, from John Charles Frémont, acknowledging receipt of the Society's medal.

(*b*) Twenty-four letters, 1852-63, from American Ministers in London - mostly from George Mifflin Dallas. Mainly letters of thanks for books, invitations, etc.

(*c*) Washington D.C., 17 Apr. 1852, from Henry R. Schoolcraft to Sir Roderick I. Murchison, about the career of General William Clarke, the American explorer, who had just died.

(*d*) Eight letters, 1855-8, from the American Geographical and Statistical Society asking for advice or concerning papers read before the respective societies.

(*e*) Long letter, 12 Dec. 1874, from Henry Nichols of New York, asking for an appointment to the Society's next expedition to the North Pole, and suggesting that the only way to reach the Pole is by balloon.

(*f*) Seven letters, 1878, from T.W. Goad, about papers on his explorations in New Mexico.

(*g*) Two letters, Oct. 1880, from the *New York Herald* asking the Society's opinion on the probable safety or otherwise of Lieutenant Schwatka's American Arctic expedition in the *Jeannette*, of which there has been no news for some time.

1. Listed in *Subject Catalogue of the Library of the Royal Empire Society*, vol. iii (London, 1932). Hudson's Bay Company, London, has a microfilm of the collection.

2. Photostats held by the Public Archives of Canada. Also published as *The Journal of Duncan M'Gillivray*, ed. by A.S. Morton (Toronto, 1929).

3. Photostats held by the Public Archives of Canada. The 'Account' was printed in the *Report* of the Public Archives of Canada for 1928. According to A.S. Morton, *A History of the Canadian West to 1870-71* (London 1939), p. 936 the manuscript was 'revised by William M'Gillivray to suit the occasion and published as *On the Origin and Progress of the North West Company* (London, 1811)'.

4. Photostats held by the Public Archives of Canada. Published under the title 'The Discovery of the Source of the Columbia River' in the *Quarterly of the Oregon Historical Society*, vol. xxvi, pp. 23-49, 1925.

(*h*) Twenty-seven letters, 1892-1910, from Robert E. Peary, concerning his Arctic expeditions, lectures, and articles for the Royal Geographical Society.

(*i*) Sixty-two letters, 1903-19, from Professor W.M. Davis, many of which refer to the American Geographical Society's transcontinental excursion of 1912, others to his work on coral reefs, etc.

(*j*) Fourteen letters, 1908-20, from Isaiah Bowman, chiefly written on behalf of the American Geographical Society.

(*k*) Seven letters, 1914-5, from Theodore Roosevelt, concerning arrangements for his lecture to the Royal Geographical Society.

In addition to these letters, the Society possesses an important collection of memoirs and travel journals compiled by individuals exploring Canada and the western United States in the nineteenth and twentieth centuries. Mrs. Christine Kelly, the Society's archivist, is now in the process of publishing in the *Journal* of the Society a handlist to these records.

ROYAL HORTICULTURAL SOCIETY, Vincent Square, London SW1P 2PE

DOUGLAS, DAVID (1798-1834). 2 journals and a summary of one of these.[1] 1823-7.

Botanist and traveller. The journals kept by Douglas during two trips to North America as collector for the Royal Horticultural Society are held in the Society's library. The first of these relates to a trip to the United States in 1823, and the second (together with Douglas's own summary of it) to a period spent in Washington, Oregon, etc., 1824-7. The journals consist of daily accounts of plants, birds, etc., seen; and of transport and other difficulties.

1. These were published with some additional material as *Journal kept by David Douglas during his Travels in North America, 1823-1827* (London, 1914).

ROYAL INSTITUTION OF GREAT BRITAIN, 21 Albemarle Street, London W1X 4BS

RUMFORD LETTERS. 31 letters. 1798-1807.

Sir Benjamin Thompson, later Count von Rumford (1753-1814), the American-born scientist and adventurer, founded the Royal Institution in 1799. The letters are mostly written during absences from London. All except five are addressed to William Savage, clerk of the Royal Institution, who looked after Rumford's affairs in his absence. They all deal with either personal or routine matters.

ROYAL SOCIETY,[1] 6 Carlton House Terrace, London SW1Y 5AG

This list is supplementary to Andrews & Davenport, pp. 355-68, their introductory paragraphs being particularly useful.

LETTERS AND PAPERS COLLECTION.

The manuscript catalogue of the Letters and Papers include entries up to 1806; subsequent entries will be found in the general card catalogue. Papers which have been printed in the *Philosophical Transactions* can be easily traced through its indexes.

Letters and papers of American interest, 1781-1897:

(*a*) There are a number of letters from and papers by Sir Benjamin Thompson, Count von Rumford, who was born in America, but these do not appear to have any specific bearing on America. 1781-1812.

(*b*) Letter, Passy, 30 Aug. 1783, from Benjamin Franklin to Sir Joseph Banks, president of the Royal Society, on the first hydrogen balloon[2] (5 pages with 2 postscripts).

(*c*) Letter, Passy, 8 Oct. 1783, from Franklin to Sir Joseph Banks, on a hot air balloon[3] (2 pages).

(*d*) Paper entitled 'Of the earthy substance found near Niagara Falls and vulgarly called "spray",' by Robert McCausland. Nov. or Dec. 1784 (10 pages).

(*e*) Paper entitled 'Of the nature and customs of the Indians of North America', by Robert McCausland. Read 16 Feb. 1786[4] (9 pages).

(*f*) Paper entitled 'Halos and Parhelia of the sun seen in 1771 in North America' by Alexander Baxter. Read 7 Dec. 1786[5] (5 pages including 1 page of figures).

(*g*) Paper entitled 'Observations and conjectures on the state, motion and phenomena of heat in the earth' by Samuel Williams, Professor of Mathematics at Harvard University. 1790 (4 pages).

(*h*) Paper entitled 'Analysis of a mineral from North America containing metal hitherto unknown', by Charles Hatchett. Read 26 Nov. 1801[6] (20 pages).

(*i*) Letters, 1868-97, from the following American scientists were traced through the general card catalogue; in most cases they were simply letters of thanks for election to the Royal Society, or for award of one of its medals; or concern the distribution of publications: Alexander Agassiz, James Dwight Dana, Josiah Willard Gibbs, Benjamin Apthorp Gould, Asa Gray, Samuel Pierpont Langley, Simon Newcomb, Hubert Anson Newton, Benjamin Peirce, and Henry Augustus Rowland.

BOYLE, HON. ROBERT (1627-91). 8 letters. 1670-88.

Natural philosopher and chemist. A founder of the Royal Society and a governor of the New England Company.

(*a*) Volume ii contains seven letters, Roxbury, Mass., 30 Sept. 1670-7 July 1688, from John Eliot, the missionary to the Indians, dealing with the 'religious walking and wayes of the praying Indians' and the translation of the Scriptures into their language.

(*b*) Volume v contains a letter, 13 Aug. 1676, from Katherine, Viscountess Ranelagh, Boyle's sister, to Eliot, giving him sympathy and moral counsel.

CATESBY, MARK (1679?-1749). 22 letters, 1722-5. ('Dr. Sherard's Phil. Letters', nos. 163-84.)

Naturalist. The twenty-two letters, 1722-5, from Catesby to William Sherard, are from America - mainly Charleston, S.C. - where Catesby was on a plant-collecting trip.

BLAGDEN, SIR CHARLES (1748-1820). 21 letters. 1779-1817.

Physician. Served in that capacity with the British Army in the War of Independence. In this large collection of twenty-three box files of letters and papers, there are nineteen letters from American correspondents, and two copies of letters from Blagden to Americans,

1. Virginia material microfilmed by the Virginia Colonial Records Project.
2. Printed, with the first postscript, in *Proceedings of the American Antiquarian Society*, vol. xviii, pp. 260-3, 1906-7.
3. Printed, ibid., pp. 263-5.
4. Printed in *Philosophical Transactions*, vol. lxxvi, pp. 229-35, 1786.
5. Printed in ibid., vol. lxxvii, pp. 44-6, 1787.
6. Printed in ibid., vol. cxii, pp. 49-66, 1802.

1779-1817. Most are brief notes, letters of introduction or of admission to learned societies, but some letters are from brother officers in America, written to Blagden after his return to England in 1780, describing the military and naval situation in that year, and later the peace negotiations of 1783 and the exodus of Loyalists to Nova Scotia.

There are two letters from Robert Walsh: the first: Philadelphia, 26 June 1810, sets out Walsh's views on American politics, which, he thinks, are conducted by 'contemptible men' - although he excepts Madison from this description, he thinks that even he labours under unreasoning anti-British prejudice. The second, Baltimore, 4 Apr. 1817, gives a glowing account of American progress and prosperity, with some description of Monroe and John Quincy Adams. Other correspondents include John Adams, John André, George Clark, Rufus King, Archibald Lee, D. Paine, R. Patterson, E. Pearson, and F. Smyth.

HERSCHEL, SIR JOHN FREDERICK WILLIAM (1792-1871). American correspondence: 62 letters (59 to him and 3 copies or drafts from him). 1829-71.

Astronomer. A few items deal only with the exchange of publications; the other topics almost all concern astronomical matters, except a comment on a proposed biography of James Grahame, author of a *History of the United States* (London, 1836). The correspondents are: Cleveland Abbe, George Bancroft, George Phillips Bond, Nathaniel Bowditch and his executors, Alvan Clark, John William Draper, Edward Everett, Asa Gray, Edward C. Herrick, Elias Loomis, Peter Lesley, Matthew Fontaine Maury, Benjamin Peirce, Eliza Susan Quincy, Josiah Quincy, William C. Redfield, J.D. Runkle, Charles W. Tuttle, Samuel Tyler, Daniel Vaughan, and Robert Winthrop.

SABINE, GENERAL SIR EDWARD (1788-1883). 45 letters from American correspondents; and 5 papers on American subjects by Sabine. 1832-64.

Army officer. Served in the War of 1812 in the Niagara campaign. Astronomer, geophysicist, and President of the Royal Society 1861-71.

The letters deal with the following subjects: the work of the United States Coast Survey and the establishment of observation stations in Maine, Florida, and Washington State; solar spots and magnetic disturbances; eclipses; a newly found species of American pine tree; the climate, topography and flora of Upper California; magnetic and meteorological observations; Matthew F. Maury, with some criticisms of his scientific work, and his 'desertion to the rebels' in 1861; Chicago and its growth; the foundation and work of the Smithsonian Institution; the feasibility of a Pacific railroad in 1853; American weather; the Civil War. The correspondents are: Alexander Dallas Bache, George Phillips Bond, David Douglas, an Englishman sent to California by the Royal Horticultural Society, William H. Emory, James Melville Gilliss, J.D. Graham, Joseph Henry, Peter Lesley, and M.A. Renwick.

The five papers are:

(i) 'Observations taken on the Western Coast of N. America, by the late Mr. David Douglas, with a Report on his Papers by Major Edward Sabine, R.A.' 1837 (8 folios). Chiefly an account of Douglas's botanical and geographical activities in California, etc.

(ii) 'Report on Mr. David Douglas's Papers...by Major Edward Sabine, R.A.' 1837 (10 folios). Geographical observations on the Columbia River and its tributaries, and in California, with several tables giving latitudes and longitudes.

(iii) 'A Memorandum on various "points" - a relic from Sabine's active service on the United States-Canada frontier.' n.d. A list of frontier posts, or possible frontier posts, with locational data, etc.

(iv) 'American birds.' Includes species from Canada and Greenland (list of 31 folios). n.d.

(v) 'Lists of American and British birds', with explanatory notes (9 folios). n.d.

METEOROLOGICAL ARCHIVES.

Include observations made at Gardiner, Me., in 1839; Boston in 1725-6; Cincinnati in 1840; Hudson, Ohio, 1839; Burlington, Vt., 1839.

MANUSCRIPTS (GENERAL) SERIES.

Include astronomical observations made at the United States Naval Observatory, Washington, D.C., by Lieut. J.M. Gilliss. 1840-1.

ROYAL SOCIETY OF ARTS,[1]
John Adam Street, London WC2N 6EZ

The Royal Society of Arts was founded in 1754 as the Society for the Encouragement of Arts, Manufactures, and Commerce.[2] Among its major early objectives was the development in the American colonies of potash and pearl-ash manufacture, mulberry tree growing and silk manufacture, etc.; premiums were awarded for such activities or for importing such goods into England.[3]

GUARD BOOKS. 1754-70.

The communications considered by the Society to be most important at the time of their receipt were preserved in fourteen guard books. Subject and author card indexes to these have been completed, those for volumes 1-11 being based on a contemporary chronological index. The correspondence, etc., from or about America is as follows:

An Englishman. 7 Nov. 1758. Growth of tea in America.

Anon. n.d. Reasons for producing opium in Georgia.

Anon. n.d. Culture of spices, tea, and silk in the colonies.

Anon. n.d. An account of the expenses of the filature in Georgia in 1757.

Anthill, Edward. New Brunswick, N.J., 9 May and 28 Aug. 1766, concerning vineyards; and 28 Feb. 1769 and n.d., concerning his agricultural improvements.[4]

Appleton, N. Boston, 31 Mar. and 28 July 1766. Silk-worms and silk.

Baker, H. 17 Feb. 1762. Matapany tea sent by Dr. Brooke of Maryland.

Barnes, H. Boston, 4 Jan. 1766. Sarsaparilla from Massachusetts.

Bernard, Francis. Boston, 13 Aug. 1763, recommending Mr. Willard, a maker of potash; and 28 Aug. 1767, two letters concerning potash produced by William Frobisher.

Blodget, Samuel. Boston, 20 Jan. 1766. Pearl-ash.

Bridgen, Edward. London, 23 Oct. 1765, urging premium for importing hemp from America.

1. Virginia material microfilmed by the Virginia Colonial Records Project.

2. See D. Hudson and K.W. Luckhurst, *The Royal Society of Arts, 1754-1954* (London, 1954), and D.G.C. Allan, 'The Origin and Growth of the Society's Archives, 1754-1847', *Journal of the Royal Society of Arts*, vol. cvi, pp. 623-9, 1958.

3. B. Hindle, *The Pursuit of Science in Revolutionary America, 1735-1789* (Chapel Hill, 1956).

4. R.P. McCormick, 'The Society, the Grape and New Jersey (i-ii)', SIS[H]A xxii, *Journal of the Royal Society of Arts*, vol. cx, pp. 119, 265, 1962.

Broadfield, E. Philadelphia, 10 Dec. 1763, sending sturgeon.

Bull, William. Charleston, S.C., 6 Aug. 1765, certifying that Jean Louis Gibert has produced thirty-five pounds of silk; and 20 Jan. 1770, concerning vines planted in South Carolina by Christopher Sherb. *See also* Garth.

C., F.C. n.d. Bees and wool in Virginia.

Caiger, E. Charleston, S.C., 15 Sept. 1766. Silk in Georgia.

Campbell, Archibald, 3rd Duke of Argyll. n.d. Two letters concerning the New England five-leaved pine.

Carter, Charles. Virginia. Seven letters, two of 1762 and five undated, on a variety of subjects.[5]

Clap, Thomas (and Jared Eliot). New Haven, Conn., 2 June 1760. Silk in Connecticut.

Colden, Cadwallader. New York, 6 Feb. 1761. Winter food for cattle.

Collinson, Peter. 10 Nov. 1763. Provincial garden in West Florida.

Committee for Promoting Arts, Williamsburg, Va., 14 Feb. and 16 Nov. 1759. Minutes.

Crevet, John. Philadelphia, n.d. Papers concerning rewards for encouraging industry in Pennsylvania.

Cushing, Thomas. Boston, 6 Sept. 1766, requesting advice about potash manufacture; and copy of a letter, July 1767, acknowledging receipt of pamphlets on this.

Daux, J.A. London, 1760, concerning a sawmill for clearing lands in America.

Delemare, J., and others. London, 29 Mar. 1755. Certificate concerning the quality of some Georgia silk.

Dick, Charles. Virginia, 22 June 1762 and n.d., on pearl-ash, and an undated letter on the 'polite arts'.

Duane, James, and others. New York, 30 Mar. 1765. Foundation in New York of a society for encouraging arts.[6]

Eliot, Jared. Seven letters, Killingworth, Conn., 1761 and 1762, mainly on black iron sand. Also an undated extract from his essays on field husbandry in America, and an extract from a letter, 26 Mar. 1760, on grapes and wine-making. *See also* Clap and Ruggles.

Ellis, Henry. Georgia, 27 June 1758. Silk, olives, madder.

Ellis, John. Georgia. 16 Dec. 1761. Rhubarb.

Ellis, John and Henry. Georgia, n.d. List of plants for manufacturers that would grow in Georgia, Carolina, and the Bahamas.

English, J. South Carolina, 15 Nov. 1760, on premiums offered for the colonies.

Evans, Lewis. Philadelphia. 1 Nov. 1754, on settling plantations in America.

Fauquier, Francis. Williamsburg, Va. An undated letter concerning Zant grapes and, with others, a certificate, 6 Aug. 1763, concerning William Carter's vineyards.

Fearon, Benson. 9 Oct. 1764, certifying that he has received two planks, which have been laid at Mill Creek on the James River, Virginia (as part of the Society's tests concerning destruction of ships' bottoms by worms).

Ferguson, James. Belfast, 7 May 1767. American potash.

Franklin, Benjamin. Five letters, 1755-66: 14 May 1755, on the establishment of a society in America;[7] 15 June 1756 (copy of letter of 27 Nov. 1755), concerning membership in the Society of Arts;[8] 12 Aug. 1763 concerning Mr. Willard's methods of potash production; 2 Sept. 1764, noting the sending of sturgeon; 29 Oct. 1766 enclosing a letter from William Alexander ('Earl of Stirling'); New Jersey, 31 July 1765, about Aaron Miller's compass.[9]

Frobisher, William. Boston, 21 and 25 Aug. 1767 and 13 May 1768, on potash.

Gale, Benjamin. Five letters, Killingworth, Conn., 1763-8, on black grass, his drill plough, and other subjects.

Garden, Alexander. Letters, extracts, and copies, South Carolina, 1757-60 and undated, on various subjects.[10]

Garth, Charles. Three letters, 1770, concerning Christopher Sherb's vine-planting (one includes an extract from a letter of William Bull on this subject).

Gibert, Jean Louis. Silk Hope, S.C., n.d. His production of cocoons.

Gilpin, F. Philadelphia, 16 May 1769. A letter to Franklin about windmills for pumping in mines or ships.

Goddard, James Stanley. n.d. American isinglass.

Habersham, James, and J. Otolonghe. Georgia, 20 May 1756. Premiums for silk in Georgia.

Harrison, G. 18 June 1766. Black grass and sand from Dr. Benjamin Gale.

Harvey, Joel. Connecticut, 20 Aug. 1764. A description of a corn-threshing machine.

Homes, William. London, 16 Jan. 1764, proposing various premiums for America.

Hyam, Thomas. London, 12 Sept. 1760. Import of hemp from Philadelphia.

Ingersoll, Jared. London, 24 Dec. 1760, on the cultivation of maize in North America (8 pages); and 13 Mar. 1765, concerning Joel Harvey's threshing machine.

Johnston, James. Berkeley County, S.C., 22 Oct. 1770. Christopher Sherb's vine-planting.

Leadly, John. London, 1765, certificate of sale of New York potash, and a 1766 affidavit of the quality of pearl-ash imported by Sir W. Baker.

Lewis, William. 27 Jan. 1767, concerning American potash, and an undated paper containing experiments on Virginia saltpetre.

Livingston, Philip, and Peter Remsen. New York, 3 May 1765. Establishment of a potash works.

Ludwell, Philip. Virginia, 21 Apr. 1760. Articles to be produced in America.

Maine, David. London, 26 Mar. 1760. Seeds for Carolina and Georgia.

Mascarene, J. Cambridge, Mass., 10 Feb. 1766. Potash.

Mason, A. n.d. Proposing to write a description of North America.

Mayhew, Jonathan. Boston, 20 Jan. 1766, concerning pearl-ash, and an extract from another 1766 letter.

Moffat, Thomas. Newport R.I., 26 Jan. and 26 June 1761. New England climate.

More, Samuel. 16 July 1763. Rough draft of experiments on Virginia saltpetre.

Neave, Messrs. E. London, 7 Nov. 1760. New England potash.

Neilson, James, and William Oake. New Jersey, 28 Aug. 1765. Certificate concerning Edward Anthill's vineyards.

5. See R.H. Hilldrup, 'A Campaign to Promote the Prosperity of Colonial Virginia', *Virginia Magazine of History and Biography*, vol. lxvii, pp. 410-28, 1959.

6. Extracts printed in K.W. Luckhurst, 'The Society's Early Days: New Light from its Correspondence', *Journal of the Royal Society of Arts*, vol. cii, pp. 292-313, 1954.

7. Copy. Original presented to American Philosophical Society.

8. Printed in Luckhurst, op. cit., pp. 297-9.

9. Printed in Leonard W. Labaree (ed.), *The Papers of Benjamin Franklin*, vol. 6 (New Haven and London, 1963).

10. Edmund Berkeley and Dorothy Smith, *Dr. Alexander Garden of Charles Town* (Chapel Hill, 1969); Dr. J.I. Waring, 'Correspondence between Alexander Garden, M.D., and the Royal Society of Arts', *South Carolina Historical and Genealogical Magazine*, vol. lxiv, pp. 16-86, 1963.

Otolonghe, Joseph. Georgia, 3 May 1756, on silk. *See also* Habersham and Otolonghe.

Pattison, Nat. and others. London, 18 Dec. 1765. Certificate of the quality of J.L. Gibert's South Carolina silk.

Perrie, J. London, 21 Mar. 1766. New England sarsaparilla.

Peters, M. Dublin, 24 Aug. 1766. Ohio grass seed.

'Phylopatria'. 10 Apr. 1760. Import of hemp, iron, etc., from America.

Pinckney, Thomas. 1 Apr. 1755. Mulberry trees in Carolina and Georgia.

Pringle, Robert. South Carolina, 24 Aug. 1759. South Carolina logwood.[11]

Quincy, Edward. Boston, 17 Oct. 1766, certificate concerning pearl-ash made by Samuel Blodget; 30 June 1765 on various matters; and an undated certificate concerning pearl-ash.

Remsen, Peter. *See* Livingston and Remsen.

Ruggles, Thomas. n.d. A method for marking sheep, originally sent from Jared Eliot to Mr. Collinson.

Rutherford, William. New York, 29 Mar. 1766, on trade with the colonies.

Rutherford, William, and William Smith. n.d. Articles to be encouraged in the colonies.

Schuyler, Philip. New York, 24 Jan. 1765. Letter to P. Skeene concerning the erection of a hemp mill.

Selden, Cary. Virginia, 27 Aug. 1765. A certificate of John Bennet, pilot, that two planks delivered to him have been sunk in Mill Creek, Virginia, and then taken to London (part of the Society's tests concerning destruction of ships' bottoms by worms).

Shakespear, John. 30 Nov. 1765. Letter sent with some American hemp.

Shipley, William. 15 July 1755. The importance of vines, hemp, etc., to South Carolina and to England.

Shubrick, Thomas. London, 4 Feb. 1765. The possibilities for use in making red dye of a root from the Indian country in America.

Skeene, P. New York, 14 Feb. 1765. Indian dye and potash.

Smith, William. *See* Rutherford and Smith.

Stoker, V., and others. n.d. Certificate that silk imported by J.L. Gibert is of his own growth.

Tryon, William. North Carolina. Extract from letter, July 1767, to Edward Bridgen, concerning Mr. Stansfield's sawmill.

Wentworth, John. New Hampshire, 20 July 1767. Extract from a letter acknowledging receipt of pamphlets on potash.

Whitworth, Sir Charles. 31 July and 24 Aug. 1755, concerning letters from Alexander Garden.

Willis, Thomas. n.d. Experiments on American isinglass.

Woodin, Thomas. South Carolina, 28 Oct. 1766, on various matters, and a copy of a letter of the same date on lucerne.

Woodmason, Charles. Carolina, 23 May 1763, on various matters.

Wright, Jermyn and Charles. Georgia, 27 Oct. 1766, concerning vineyards, and 30 May 1768, concerning balsam found in Georgia.

Young, Henry. Georgia, 23 Dec. 1766, on leek taw or Chinese vetch introduced into Georgia by S. Bowen.

There are also in the guard books some Customs' and other documents relating to the importation of silk, hemp, etc., from America; a 1765 list (printed) of premiums offered in New York province; and undated descriptions of the timber sent to North America by the Society.

LOOSE ARCHIVES. 1755-1840.

Baker, Benjamin ('an American refugee'). Letter, received 12 Apr. 1779, describing his geometrical instruments.

Box, George. London, ?1759. Draft of a letter to Alexander Garden thanking him for observations on the soil and climate of Carolina.

Bromwich & Co. London, 15 Mar. 1775. Letter concerning a 'Carolina stain'.

Cheffins, Richard. London, 5 Mar. 1806, about his 'American borers'.

Clarke, Isaac W. 11 Sept. 1808, on hemp in Canada.

Colpitts, Thomas. Liverpool, 24 May 1797. Brown cotton in North Carolina.

Davies, Lieut.-Col. London, 6 Feb. 1792. Northwest Passage.

Dossie, Robert. 1767. Manuscript of his 'Observations on the Pot-Ash brought from America...to which is subjoined Processes for Making Pot-Ash and Barilla, in North America'. Published in London, 1767, and related papers and minutes.

Fawkener, W. (of the Privy Council). London, 22 Feb. 1791, concerning new methods of manufacturing potash and pearl-ash in Quebec, enclosing copies of letters, from Motz, Macdonald, and Nooth (q.v.)

Flindall, Murray. Bay of Quinte, Upper Canada, 23 May 1823. Letter and drawings concerning his axe and drill, with remarks on life in Canada.

Fraser, John. London, 17 Nov. 1788, on an 'extraordinary grass' which Thomas Walter of South Carolina has discovered; and 30 Nov. 1789 presenting a book on the new American grasses.

Glenny, James. Quebec, 1791. Copies of memorials to the King and to the Privy Council on his new method of producing potash, and a copy of an account of this method.

Habersham, James. Savannah, Ga., 20 May 1756. Mulberry trees in Georgia.

Habersham, James, and Joseph Otolonghe. Savannah, Ga., 23 Oct. 1758, reporting payment for cocoons.

Hampton, Samuel. Philadelphia, 23 Jan. 1790. His standards of invariable weights and measures.

Lane and Booth. London, 15 and 30 Jan. 1765, on potash.

Lawrence, Robert. Washington, D.C., 28 Nov. 1840, concerning the laws and constitution of the National Institute for the Promotion of Science.

Long, Borden. Longueuil, Upper Canada, 10 Apr. 1808, concerning his perpetual motion machine (with an introductory letter from I.W. Clarke).

Macdonald, Arthur. Quebec, 8 Jan. 1791, copy of a report to the King on James Glenny's new method of producing potash, and a copy of a letter of 24 Nov. 1790 to H. Motz concerning potash.

Mease, James. Philadelphia, 2 Apr. 1801, concerning the possibility of introducing British machinery into the United States, with observations on scientific education there.

Motz, Henry. Copy of a letter of 24 Nov. 1790 to Scrope Bernard [-Morland] about potash.

Nooth, J. Mervin. Copy of a letter of 24 Nov. 1790 to Sir Joseph Banks about potash.

Otolonghe, Joseph. Savannah, Ga., 20 and 24 May 1756, about mulberry trees in Georgia, and 1759, listing persons receiving premiums for cocoons. *See also* Habersham and Otolonghe.

Paine, Thomas. Rotherham, Yorks., 25 May 1789, to Sir George Leonard Staunton about single-arch bridges (enclosed in a letter from Paine, 30 Apr. 1790).

Percy, Sir Hugh, 2nd Duke of Northumberland. 9 Mar. 1802, about Canadian hemp.

Pettibone, Daniel. Philadelphia, 24 May 1810. His improvements in domestic heating.

11. Walter B. Edgar, 'A Letter from South Carolina (i-iii)', SIS[H]A cv-cvii, *Journal of the Royal Society of Arts*, vol. cxxii, pp. 95, 171, 231, 1974.

Rose, Lewis. Savannah, Ga., 1 Sept. 1792. New species of cinchona.

Solly, R.M. London, 20 May 1823, presenting a pot of American grasses.

Stewart, James. London, 23 Aug. 1774, on 'American productions'.

Tatham, Col. William. Letters, London, 1801-2, mainly on Canadian hemp.[12]

Walter, John. London. Letter, received 1 Dec. 1784, concerning his new method of printing, mentioning encouragement from Franklin.

Walter, Thomas. Santee, S.C., 24 Dec. 1787. Two copies of his pamphlet on American grass.

Watson, John. 3 June 1755. Receipt for £18 to be used for rewarding the planting of white mulberry trees in Georgia.

West, Benjamin. London, 1 and 16 Nov. 1796, concerning his portrait of Samuel More.

In addition to the above, there are a large number of certificates relating to the export from America and import into England of potash[13] and sturgeon; letters on behalf of various American bodies acknowledging receipt of the Society's *Transactions*; letters from the Society to Alexander Garden about cork trees sent to Carolina, 6 Feb. 1760, and to Thomas Hyam about his hemp imports, 6 Oct. 1760; and a petition sent during the 1750's to the parish of St. Peters, Purisburgh, S.C., about the encouragement of the cultivation of silk.

TRANSACTIONS.

(*a*) Dr. Templeman's Transactions.

Peter Templeman (1711-69), who became the secretary of the Society in 1760, compiled an 'Historical Register of the Transactions of the Society....' in two volumes, covering 1754-8. This contains extracts from letters received, reports of matters discussed, lists of members, etc. An author and subject card index, combined with that for the Society's later manuscript transactions, is available. There is some material of American relevance similar to that listed above.

(*b*) Manuscript Transactions.

The early transactions of the Society, 1770/1-1783/4, are in manuscript form. The card index to these shows a small amount of American material, again similar to the above.

MINUTES.

There are manuscript minutes of the Society from 1754, and minutes for standing committees (including 'Colonies and Trade') from 1758. The minutes throw light on the Society's attitude towards the correspondence received by it, and include discussion of premiums to be offered.

LETTERS RECEIVED.

The four volumes contain contemporary copies of, or copies of extracts from, some of the letters received by the Society, 1767-78. These letters have not yet been compared with those in the guard books and the loose archives, but there may be some among them whose originals are not in either of these two groups.

LETTERS SENT.

Four volumes contain contemporary copies of letters sent by the Society, 1770-1850.

LITERARY SECRETARY, THE SALVATION ARMY, International Headquarters 101 Queen Victoria Street, London E.C.4

Most of the Salvation Army records were destroyed during the Second World War by enemy action.

BOOTH, EVANGELINE (1865-1950). 5 typewritten letters. 1904-05.

New York, Dec. 1904-Apr. 1905: four to General William Booth and one to Bramwell Booth, dealing with the Salvation Army's farm colonies in Colorado, California, and Ohio, which were established in 1898. They refer to the mission of Rider Haggard, who was sent out by the British government to inspect the colonies in 1905, and whose report was issued as a blue book by the Colonial Office in the same year.

Printed material on these colonies is available in the volumes of *All the World* for 1902, 1904, and 1905, which may be consulted in the Library.

SION COLLEGE,[1] Victoria Embankment, London, EC4Y ODN

RECORDS OF THE PROVINCIAL ASSEMBLY OF LONDON. 1 volume. 1647-60. (ARC/L40. 2/E17)

(*a*) Entry for 27 Dec. 1649 (page 102 verso), 'Ordered that papers concerning New England be committed to ye care of ye grand Committee'.

(*b*) Entry for 21 Jan. 1650 (page 103 recto), 'R[esolved] that it shall be referred to the Grand Comittee to consider whether there shall be a letter drawn up for the promoting the businesse of New England, and that the report be given in in writing to the Province.' (Doubtless arising from the Ordinance of 1649 for the establishment of the Society for the Propagation of the Gospel in New England.)

(*c*) The entry in the minutes for 19 Mar. 1659 accepts a proposal, that came from the New England Company, to print the Bible 'in the Indian language' - what became the 'Massachusetts Bible'. 'Dr. Reignolds bee desired to call the Ministers of the citty together for the carrying on of this grand affaire.'

CUTLER, TIMOTHY (1684-1765). Letter (5 pages).[2] 1739. (72H. 22)

Cutler was rector of Yale 1719-22, and later an Episcopal clergyman in Boston. The letter, 28 May 1739, is to someone unnamed, but addressed as 'My Lord' (probably Edmund Gibson, Bishop of London), and contains a highly critical account of the effects of the doctrines of Jonathan Edwards. He gives examples of reported fanaticism, but thinks that the revival will have no lasting effects.

PAMPHLET COLLECTION.

The Library contains a large collection of pamphlets - catalogued under 'Americana', 1641-1878 (but mostly eighteenth century). This includes pamphlets by Increase Mather, R. Baylie (a friend of Roger Williams), Jonathan Edwards, John Adams, and Thomas Clarkson. There are also printed letters of George Whitefield, accounts of

12. See D.G.C. Allan, 'Colonel William Tatham, an Anglo-American Member of the Society, 1801-4', ibid., vol. cviii, pp. 229-33, 1960.

13. L. Gittins, 'Premiums for Vegetable Alkali - The Society and the Supply of Potash, Barilla and Kelp, 1758-1827', SIS[H]A xxx, ibid., vol. cxi, p. 577, 1963.

1. Virginia material microfilmed by the Virginia Colonial Records Project.

2. Bound with a volume of pamphlets, but is marked as a manuscript in the pamphlet catalogue under 'Americana'. This letter has been edited by Douglas C. Stenerson, 'An Anglican Critique of the Early Phase of the Great Awakening in New England: A Letter by Timothy Cutler', *William and Mary Quarterly*, Third Series, vol. xxx, pp. 475-88, 1973.

actions in the French wars of the seventeenth and eighteenth centuries, reports of missions to Indians, and pamphlets on emigration, the tobacco trade, expeditions north of California in 1790, and the War of Independence.

SOCIETY FOR PROMOTING CHRISTIAN KNOWLEDGE,[1] Holy Trinity Church, Marylebone Road, London, N.W.1

Almost all the relevant documents relate to the colonial period and have been briefly described in Andrews & Davenport, p. 331. The actual missionary work in the colonies took place only from 1698 to 1701, when this work was taken over by the Society for the Propagation of the Gospel in Foreign Parts (see pp. 158-9); after 1701 the Society's main work in America was the dispatch of books and pamphlets. The relevant material is not extensive. It can readily be traced through the card index. Additional material includes the following:

NEWMAN LETTERS.[2] New England letters (5 volumes), 1721-43; miscellaneous letters (9 volumes), 1735-43.

These are copies of letters sent by Henry Newman (1670-1743), Secretary of the S.P.C.K. 1708-43. (The archives also contain typed transcripts.)

SALZBURG EMIGRATION PAPERS. 8 volumes and some loose letters. 1731-71.

Accounts and correspondence relating to the settlement of German Protestant exiles in Georgia from 1731 onwards.[3]

EMIGRATION COMMITTEE MINUTES, 1882- (in progress). (7 volumes to 1936.) LADIES EMIGRATION COMMITTEE MINUTES, 1879-1921 (2 volumes).

There are scattered references in the Society's minutes and annual reports of the first half of the nineteenth century to occasional help given to emigrants, mostly concerned with counselling emigrants at Plymouth and Liverpool, but in 1868 the Society's Liverpool chaplain began to make the round trips across the Atlantic to care for the spiritual needs of emigrants; in 1882 the Emigration Committee was created to supervise this work.[4]

LIBRARY OF THE SOCIETY OF FRIENDS, Friends House, Euston Road, London NW1 2BJ

The Religious Society of Friends (Quakers) developed as a significant body in the 1650's, and from this time kept considerable records. By 1654 the first Friends had arrived in America, and the transatlantic community remained a living one (see Frederick B. Tolles, *The Atlantic Community of the Early Friends,* 1952; Thomas E. Drake, *Patterns of Influence in Anglo-American Quakerism,* 1958). The Library contains the official records of the Society of Friends in Great Britain and an extensive collection of other manuscript material from the mid-seventeenth century to the present.

Friends in Great Britain were, as later explained, organized into London Yearly Meeting, the Half-Year's Meeting in Ireland being technically subordinate to it, though growing into increasing independence. By the end of the seventeenth century Yearly Meetings had been established on the American continent for New England (1661), Maryland, afterwards Baltimore (1672), Philadelphia (1681), New York (1696) and North Carolina (1698). From the early nineteenth century Friends took part in the increasing westward migration, resulting in the establishment of further Yearly Meetings in the middle and far west - Ohio (1813), Indiana (1821), Western, or West Indiana (1858), Iowa (1863), Kansas (1872), Wilmington, or Southwest Ohio (1892), Oregon (1893), California (1895), Nebraska (1908). Moreover, the scene was made more complex by separations in Philadelphia in 1827 and Baltimore, Indiana, New York and Ohio the following year: British Friends recognized the 'orthodox' or evangelical group, the 'Hicksite' Yearly Meetings maintaining an isolated existence (see Edwin B. Bronner, *'The Other Branch': London Yearly Meeting and the Hicksites, 1827-1912,* 1975). New England Yearly Meeting in 1845, Ohio (orthodox) in 1855 and other Yearly Meetings at a later date suffered separations of 'conservative' Friends which, again, London Yearly Meeting declined to recognize. An understanding of these separations is therefore essential to an appreciation of the significance of official records of the period.

Friends House Library has, besides a card catalogue, numerous typescript indexes, some of which may be mentioned here and others in the more detailed entries which follow. Since 1959 it has been building up, jointly with the Quaker Collection at Haverford College, Pa., a typescript 'Dictionary of Quaker Biography'. This by 1976 contained entries for some 15,000 Friends, mainly British and American. The Digest Registers, made in 1840 and 1857, transcribe material up to 1837 from the individual registers of births, marriages, and burials maintained by local meetings until that year and then surrendered to government: a surname index is in preparation and the registers are of assistance in identifying little-known Friends.

Much material has been printed or described in the *Journal of the Friends Historical Society* (1903, in progress) or the *Bulletin of Friends Historical Society of Philadelphia* (1906, in progress; from 1924, *Bulletin of Friends Historical Association:* from 1962, *Quaker History*). A typescript index to *JFHS* is available in Friends House Library.

Material in the Library is arranged as follows:

- Great Britain: central archives
- Great Britain: local archives
- Other major MS collections with items relating to America
- Quaker journals with American detail
- Miscellaneous correspondence and documents relating to America

GREAT BRITAIN: CENTRAL ARCHIVES

The final governing body of the Society of Friends in Great Britain is London Yearly Meeting (1668). Subordinate to it were quarterly meetings (initially one for each county, but later for a group of neighbouring counties); subordinate to them were monthly meetings (which were and are the primary meetings for church affairs) which usually comprised a number of neighbouring meetings for worship, or particular meetings.

Quakers, though having no appointed, paid, or separated ministry, early recognized that some of their number had a greater gift in the vocal ministry than others: these were referred to as 'Publick Friends' or, later, as recorded or acknowledged ministers. The practice of recording was discontinued by London Yearly Meeting in

1. Virginia material microfilmed by the Virginia Colonial Records Project.
2. Leonard W. Cowie, *Henry Newman: an American in London, 1708-43* (London and New York, 1956), has made full use of all these papers and contains an excellent bibliography showing other archives possessing Newman papers.
3. See George Fenwick Jones (ed.), *Henry Newman's Salzburger Letterbooks* (Athens, Ga., 1966).
4. See also W.O.B. Allen and E. McClure, *Two Hundred Years: the History of the Society for Promoting Christian Knowledge, 1698-1898* (London, 1898), pp. 402-21. Contains extracts from reports by the Plymouth and Liverpool chaplains.

1924. The Atlantic community of Quakerdom was sustained by the journeys of recorded ministers who were 'liberated for service' by their monthly and quarterly meetings and by Yearly Meeting or, from the mid- eighteenth century, the Yearly Meeting of Ministers and Elders.

Important also are two bodies, initially held weekly and national in scope, though until the late eighteenth century predominantly composed of London Friends. The Second Day Morning Meeting (1673) was a gathering of ministering Friends, later with elders, responsible for approving publications for the press and for liberating ministering Friends for service in the intervals of Yearly Meeting. Meeting for Sufferings (1676), though at first concerned with the relief of Friends' sufferings and with attempts to redress them, quickly became in effect an executive committee of Yearly Meeting, very wide in its range of concerns.

Yearly Meeting maintained a panel of 'correspondents' both with the quarterly meetings in Great Britain and with Yearly Meetings in America: those correspondents formed the basic membership of Meeting for Sufferings. The records of Yearly Meeting, Yearly Meeting of Ministers and Elders, Morning Meeting, and Meeting for Sufferings, while far from exclusively Anglo-American in scope, are nevertheless essential for any Quaker studies relating to America.

(*a*) Yearly Meeting

(i) *Minutes* (27 vols., 1672-1865; vols. 28-39, 1866-1936; in print 1857 to date) contain considerable references to American Yearly Meetings and to concerns (e.g. anti-slavery) arising from their epistles. They contain also transcripts of the accounts of a number of British Friends visiting America up to the mid-eighteenth century, including those of Aaron Atkinson (1665?-1740) in 1698-9 (vol. 2, pp. 312-4), Josiah Langdale (d. 1723) in 1705 (vol. 3, pp. 199-200), William Baldwin (1677?-1720) in 1709 (vol. 4, pp. 211-8), Thomas Chalkley (1675-1741) in 1707-11 (vol. 4, pp. 65-73, 294-6), Josiah Langdale and Thomas Thompson (1673-1727) in 1715-7 (vol. 5, pp. 254-8), Benjamin Holme (1682/3-1749) in 1717 (vol. 5, pp. 446-64), Henry Frankland (d. 1739) in 1730-2 (vol. 7, pp. 340-4), Samuel Hopwood (1674-1760) in 1741-4 (vol. 9, pp. 341-2), Edmund Peckover (1695/6-1767) in 1742-4 (vol. 9, pp. 322-9). There is a microfilm of minutes to 1865. Typescript index at Friends House Library covering 1672-1856; printed index 1857-1906; typescripts at Friends House 1907 onwards.

(ii) *Epistles received* (11 vols., 1683-1916) contains a transcript of the letters, mainly pastoral and exhortatory, but with important detail and information on shared concerns, from the American Yearly Meetings. Microfilm 1683-1897 available. A typescript checklist of vols. 1-5 (to 1801) is available at Friends House Library, with an index of signatories to epistles.

(iii) *Epistles sent* (12 vols., 1683-1949) contains a transcript of the responses from London to the American epistles. From 1923 there are brief accompanying letters to the Yearly Meeting's General Epistle. Microfilms 1683-1916 available.

(iv) *Great Book of Sufferings* records under the names of individuals any imprisonments, distraints or other persecutions of Friends: volume 2 (1650-80) includes New England entries. No other American entries appear in the series.

(v) *Women's Yearly Meeting* minutes (1784-1907) are mainly formal, but other documents include epistles from 1753 from various Women's Yearly Meetings in America.

(vi) *Testimonies concerning ministers deceased* (7 vols., 1728-1872) contains the monthly and quarterly meetings memorials presented to Yearly Meeting. Testimonies are, in the main, printed in *Yearly Meeting proceedings*, and always so printed from 1783. A typescript index is at Friends House Library; the 'Dictionary of Quaker Biography' (*see above*) contains entries for all those for whom testimonies were prepared.

(*b*) Yearly Meeting of Ministers and Elders

Minutes (9 vols., 1857-1906) contain records of the liberation of British Friends for service in America and 'returning minutes' for American ministering Friends travelling in Europe. In some cases reports on travels are included. A typescript index (with one to minutes of the Morning Meeting, *see below*) is at Friends House Library, which also maintains an index, 'Quaker Transatlantic Journeys', listing chronologically from the seventeenth century British Friends liberated for service in America and *vice versa*.

(*c*) Second Day Morning Meeting

(i) Minutes (10 vols., 1673-1901) contain records of liberation and of returning minutes issued in the intervals of Yearly Meeting. In 1901 the Morning Meeting was laid down and its functions transferred to Meeting for Sufferings. A typescript index (with that to the minutes of the Yearly Meeting of Ministers and Elders, *see above*) is at Friends House Library. Microfilm of minutes 1673-1725 available.

(ii) *Book of ministering Friends* (22 vols., 1682-1793) records the attendance of ministers at the various London first-day and weekday meetings for worship and is therefore of value in tracing the movements of American Quaker ministers in England.

(*d*) Meeting for Sufferings

(i) *Minutes* (46 vols., 1676-1857; vol. 47 ff. 1857 to date) contains records of a detailed correspondence between British and American Friends though, in general, not the letters themselves. Typescript index to vols. 15-46 (1700-1857) available in Friends House Library. Microfilm 1676-1860 available.

(ii) Letters to and from Philadelphia (2 vols., 1757-1857): transcripts of the official correspondence between the London Meeting for Sufferings and Philadelphia Meeting for Sufferings covering many matters of general import (e.g. the slave trade) as well as more domestic matters. Microfilm available.

(iii) *Casual correspondence* (1 vol., 1785-1881) contains copies of various letters and epistles, other than those in *Epistles sent* and *Epistles received*, some of which were sent to or from meetings in America. Several of these refer to the slavery question, e.g. two of 1834, one touching on the respective powers of the federal and state governments in the matter, and one on colonization in Liberia (pp. 204-11).

(iv) *Book of cases* (4 vols., 1661-1918), while comprising mainly legal reports, precedents and opinions affecting British Friends, contains also reference to various colonial cases.

GREAT BRITAIN: LOCAL ARCHIVES

Local archives comprise in the main the records of the quarterly meetings (which may be compared to a diocese), monthly meetings (compared to a rural deanery) and preparative meetings (compared to a parish). As stated above, the monthly meeting is the primary meeting for church affairs. At each level there are likely to be minutes of (a) a men's meeting, (b) a women's meeting and (c) from the mid-eighteenth century, a meeting of ministers and elders. There are also likely to be books of sufferings and disownments and other membership and financial records. The men's minutes are the principal series. The minutes of ministers and elders, though often appearing slight and formal, often record the presence of ministering Friends from America where the corresponding men's minutes do not.

From the mid-eighteenth century monthly meeting minutes tend to be more thorough in recording certificates for the transfer of membership of Friends emigrating to America. Until that time, although such certificates were drawn up and taken to America (the originals often being available there: see, for instance, Albert Cook Myers, *Quaker Arrivals at Philadelphia, 1682-1750, being a list of certificates of removal received at Philadelphia Monthly Meeting of Friends*, 1902), it is unusual to find any reference in monthly meeting minute-books to authorization for such certificates.

(*a*) London

The records of London and Middlesex Quarterly Meeting, the Six Weeks Meeting (which in earlier days had wider functions than its later specialization on finance and property), the Women's Two Weeks and Box Meetings, and the several monthly meetings (for most of the period to 1850: Devonshire House; Gracechurch Street; Peel; Westminster; Ratcliff; Southwark) and preparative meetings (insignificant until about 1900) are in the custody of Friends House Library. The records of Gracechurch Street MM were largely destroyed in a fire in 1821. A typescript index to the minutes of Quarterly Meeting, 1690-1867, and Six Weeks Meeting, 1671-1868, is available at Friends House Library. The most satisfactory guide to the records of London Quakerism is still William Beck and T. Frederick Ball, *The London Friends' Meetings,* 1869. Most London monthly meetings retained files of correspondence received, some of which bear on American matters: these are cited as Southwark MSS. (6 vols., 1667-1777), Westminster MSS. (2 vols.), etc. Typescript inventories are available in Friends House Library in most cases. The Box Meeting MSS. (Epistles, 1676-*c.* 1750) contain (a) an epistle, probably from George Fox 'To our friends in New Jersie', n.d., and (b) thirteen manuscripts from women's meetings in Virginia, Maryland, Rhode Island, New Jersey and Pennsylvania, 1676-1751, and also a few from London to Pennsylvania.

(*b*) Country

Most local Quaker records (outside London and Middlesex QM) are deposited in county or municipal record offices; some are in strong rooms or safes in Friends Meeting Houses. Friends House Library in its typescript 'Meeting records' notes the whereabouts of records and provides an administrative guide to the history of the quarterly and monthly meetings. Minute-books in print include *Minute book of the monthly meeting...for the Upperside of Buckinghamshire, 1669-1690*, ed. B.S. Snell, 1937; *The first minute book of the Gainsborough Monthly Meeting...1669-1719*, ed. H.W. Brace, 3 vols., 1948-51; *Minute book of the men's meeting...in Bristol, 1667-1686*, ed. Russell Mortimer, 1971.

OTHER MAJOR MS COLLECTIONS WITH ITEMS RELATING TO AMERICA. (*Arranged chronologically.*)

(*a*) A.R.B. (Abram Rawlinson Barclay) Manuscripts. 2 volumes (also 2 volumes of transcripts). 1654-88.

Collection of 250 letters, 1654-88, of early Friends, containing a number of items concerning America - e.g. an account of a journey 'by land and water' from Virginia to New England in 1658 (ARB/13); and a letter, 1686, from John Archdale in North Carolina to George Fox, describing the country. (ARB/68)

(*b*) Spence Manuscripts.[1] 3 volumes. 17th century.

Volumes 1 and 2 comprise the manuscripts of the 'Journal' of George Fox (1624-91) and volume 3 consists of numerous letters to and from the Fell family. Volume 1 of Fox's 'Journal' contains letters from his friends describing travels in America.

(*c*) Gibson Manuscripts. 10 volumes and portfolios. 1660-1861.

Certain original letters, drawings, news cuttings, etc., collected by Thomas Thompson of Liverpool. Include many letters from Friends in America, and also a grangerized copy of the printed journal of Thomas Story of Philadelphia, to William Penn; and correspondence between Story and James Logan of Philadelphia.[2] Also a letter, 1 Dec. 1674, from Penn to George Fox.

(*d*) W.C. Braithwaite Manuscripts. 1661-end of 18th century.

Contain the transcripts of the documents examined by William Charles Braithwaite, historian of the Quaker movement. Include items relating to early Quakerism in America, and also his draft of a chapter on 'Work in America', which was not printed in his *Beginnings of Quakerism* (London, 1912) in order to avoid overlapping with Rufus M. Jones and others, *The Quakers in the American Colonies* (London, 1911).

(*e*) Reynolds Manuscripts. 1 volume. 1663-early 18th century. Contains the correspondence of the Reynolds family, Anglo-American merchants in London and Philadelphia. Mainly of religious interest. Late eighteenth- or early nineteenth-century copies of documents, 1663-1779, compiled by Richard Reynolds (1735-1816) of Coalbrookdale and Bristol.

(*f*) Barclay of Bury Hill Manuscripts. Correspondence, minutes, etc. 1664-1855. (Temp. MSS 285)

(i) Minute-book of the Lords proprietors of New Jersey from 1664 to 1683. This volume also includes a number of official documents.

(ii) About fifteen letters from John Hunt and others relating to the proceedings under Robert Barclay of Urie's claim to a portion of East New Jersey, in right of David Barclay, 1760-86. (Boxes II, III, nos. 175-191, 193)

(iii) Correspondence of Robert and Charles Barclay of Bury Hill, Dorking, relating to their American estates, 1794-1855.

Robert Barclay (1751-1830) was born in Philadelphia but was brought up in England. In 1793 he and other Friends instructed Phineas Bond of Philadelphia to purchase land on their behalf in America, and transactions were completed in 1794 for the acquisition of land in Northumberland and Luzerne Counties, Pennsylvania. Later, before Robert's death, the administration of the estates passed to his eldest son Charles (who had left the Society of Friends).

The letter-book in the Library contains letters and other documents, 1794-1813, to Robert Barclay from Phineas Bond, and manuscripts, 1816-8, to Barclay from Thomas Cadwallader, who succeeded Bond as agent. There are also letters and documents, 1820-36, to Charles Barclay from Cadwallader and others, 1835-55, to Charles from Samuel Rhoads, Jr., who succeeded Cadwallader.

(*g*) Southwark Manuscripts. 6 volumes. 1667-1777.

Contains letters and other data relating to the history of London Friends; some of the material bears upon American matters.

(*h*) Penn Manuscripts. 2 albums. 1682-1779.

Miscellaneous assortment of originals, transcripts, facsimiles, engravings, and newspaper clippings. There are also many other manuscripts relating to Penn in the Library and catalogued under his name. See Andrews and Davenport, pp. 351-4.

(*i*) Swarthmore Manuscripts.[3] *c.* 1,400 original documents. 17th century.

Illustrate seventeenth-century Quakerism. Include many letters to Margaret Fell from Friends both at home and overseas. There are also transcripts of later date.

(*j*) Thompson Family Papers. Manuscripts (5 volumes). 18th century. Contain the correspondence of the Thompson family, Anglo-American merchants of Philadelphia in the eighteenth century.

(*k*) Crosfield Manuscripts. Letters. 1754-8.

This collection includes approximately thirty-five letters, 1754-8, from Samuel Fothergill (1715-72) to members of his family. The letters are sent from various places in America, including Philadelphia, South Carolina, and Virginia. There are also a few letters from other American correspondents, including William Logan, John Pemberton, Mary Pemberton, Israel Pemberton, and Anthony Benezet.

1. See Appendix B. W.C. Braithwaite, *Beginnings of Quakerism* (London, 1912).
2. Printed in the *Bulletin of the Friends' Historical Association*, vol. xv, 1926, supplement.
3. See Braithwaite, op. cit., Appendix B.

(*l*) Dimsdale Manuscripts. List, letters. (Temp. MSS., boxes 68, 69)

(i) MS. list of the Public Friends from America who attended the Yearly Meeting of London, anno 1785. (Folder 4/33)

(ii) The Dimsdale MSS. also include scattered letters from America from the late eighteenth and early nineteenth centuries. Almost all of these concern personal and family matters.

(*m*) Gurney Manuscripts. 1772-1850.

Mainly letters written to Joseph John Gurney (1788-1847) while on his famous ministry in America for the English Society of Friends to refute the teachings of the Hicksites, 1836-40. The principal correspondents are Anna Gurney, Amelia Opie, Elizabeth Fry, and the Buxton family—also a few letters from William Wilberforce, Joseph Sturge, and J.G. Whittier. There are also many from J.J. Gurney describing the course of his ministry, American life and topography, slavery, etc. A few other family papers relating to America, mainly of an earlier period, are included.

(*n*) Wilkinson Manuscripts. Letters. 1789-1812. (Temp. MSS. 128)

(i) Eleven letters, 1789-93, from John Pemberton in Philadelphia to Thomas Wilkinson (1751-1836), dealing with various matters, but particularly with the slave trade, which Pemberton had gone to Philadelphia to oppose. (Wilkinson MSS. 4/18-21, 23-29)

(ii) Five letters, 1795-8, from James Pemberton in Philadelphia to Thomas Wilkinson, mostly about family and Friend affairs, although there is mention of an epidemic in Philadelphia in 1797. (Wilkinson MSS. 4/31, 33-36)

(iii) Statement by Joseph Holt and ? Fisher, dated Philadelphia, 13 Sept. 1796, about Henry Moss, a black man who 'turned white'. (Wilkinson MSS. 4/32)

(iv) Four letters, 1790-1812, from Thomas Stewardson in Philadelphia to Thomas Wilkinson, chiefly about American attitudes towards Indians, blacks, and the slave trade. (Wilkinson MSS. 22/8, 14, 33-34)

(v) There are also a few other references to America in the Wilkinson MSS., primarily concerning the slave trade and the divisions among Friends resulting from the Hicksite controversy in the 1820's.

(*o*) Anna Braithwaite Manuscripts. Letters. 19th century.

Anna Braithwaite (1788-1859), daughter of the banker Charles Lloyd of Birmingham, was a prominent Friend and a recorded minister. She made three visits to America (1823-4, 1825-6, and 1827-8) and, as a visiting Friend, was closely involved in the tensions which led up to the Hicksite separation of 1827-8 and in its aftermath. Many of the ninety-eight letters in the collection refer to America, and those of Isaac Stephenson to Anna Braithwaite, written from 1823 to 1825, refer specifically to the problems resulting from the Hicksite affair.

(*p*) Stacey Manuscripts. Letters. 1827-46. (Temp. MSS. 130)

(i) MS. letter from Yearly Meeting of Women Friends in Philadelphia to Yearly Meeting of Women Friends in London, 1827. (Folder 10/12)

(ii) MS. letter from Yearly Meeting of Women Friends in London to Yearly Meeting of Women Friends in North Carolina, 1842. (Folder 10/13)

(iii) Three letters, 1844-6, to George Stacey from various American correspondents. Subjects discussed include a smallpox outbreak and the threat of war between England and America. (Folder 2, 31-33)

(*q*) Pritchard Manuscripts. Henry Newman Letter-Book: Correspondence, etc. 1830-68.

(i) Eighteen letters, 1830-5, to Henry Newman (*c.* 1775-1835) from American correspondents, many written to him while he was visiting the U.S. from 1833 to 1834. Newman's correspondents discuss a number of issues, including prison reform in the U.S., outbreaks of cholera, and American slavery. (64/3/5-22)

(ii) A detailed account of the settlement and population of twenty-five sections of land in Edwards County, Ill., from the spring of 1817, when the first settlers arrived, to 31 Dec. 1832. ($76/3^B$)

(iii) Letter, 1833, to George Newman from his brother Henry in Illinois, giving a very detailed account of his journey and visits to people and places in the U.S. (78/8)

(iv) Eleven letters, 1856-68, to Henry Newman (1818-1908) and his wife, from E.H. Bonsell, Philadelphia, and Charles Bonsell, Cincinnati. Subjects discussed include American slavery and the Civil War, Lincoln's assassination, and journeys to Pittsburgh and Cincinnati. (Folder no. 4)

(v) Letter, 1858, to Newman from Samuel H. Colton, Worcester, Mass., about safe investment in the U.S. (52/4)

(vi) Letter to Henry Newman from his cousin John Barrow in New York, 1863, discussing Americans relations in general. (8/9)

(vii) A long unsigned, undated account of pioneers in the U.S. (76/2)

(viii) There are also a number of other letters to and from America, mostly concerning the personal affairs of the Newman family.

(*r*) Elihu Burritt (1810-79). Letters to Anna Mary Southall. 1853-5.

Burritt's letters to Southall, about twelve of which deal with America, cover a wide variety of subjects. He comments on American political developments in the 1850's (especially in its relation to the slave issue), schemes for compensated emancipation of the slaves, and his hopes to form 'Olive Leaf Societies' in the United States.

QUAKER JOURNALS WITH AMERICAN DETAIL. (*Arranged chronologically.*)

(*a*) Mary Weston (1712-66). Travel journal.[4] (A transcript made from the original by her son-in-law, John Eliot), 1735-52. (138 folio pages.)

Toured the colonies preaching to Quaker Meetings, 1750-2. The journals mainly describe her preachings and spiritual experiences; they contain a list of Meetings visited in New Jersey, Maryland, Pennsylvania, Virginia, and the Carolinas; also maps of her tours; a few family letters; and some verses in her honour by Thomas Merryworthy.

(*b*) Rachel Wilson[5] (1720-75). Journal of a visit to America (copies, both manuscript and typescript; original in private possession). 1768-9.

Visited American Meetings, chiefly in Pennsylvania, Virginia, and the Jerseys. The journal is of almost exclusively religious interest.

(*c*) Elizabeth Robson[6] (1771-1843). Travel diaries, letters, and family papers: 26 volumes. 1813-43.

Preacher. Wife of Liverpool linen merchant, himself a Quaker Elder. Travelled extensively and was twice in America, 1824-8 and 1838-42, visiting probably every Meeting of the Friends. Diaries mostly describe these Meetings, contain much of the 'Hicksite' controversy, and also on mission meetings with soldiers, sailors, miners, Indians, and Negroes; a list of Meetings visited in Philadelphia in 1828; and some general description of American life. The diaries for the first trip, 1824-8, are originals, but for the second, 1838-42, are transcripts made by her son, Henry Robson, shortly after her death as part of a nine-volume manuscript 'Memoir'.

4. See also 'Mary Weston's Journal', *J.F.H.S.*, vol. iv, p. 130, 1907.

5. See John Somervell, *Isaac and Rachel Wilson, Quakers of Kendal, 1714-1785* (London, 1924).

6. See also 'Elizabeth Robson', *J.F.H.S.*, vol. xiv, pp. 75-8, 1917.

(*d*) Richard Smith (1784-1824).[7] Journals: 7 volumes. 1817-24.
Small trader and Quaker missionary. Went to the United States in 1817, settled for a short while at Smithfield, Ohio, and then journeyed back to the coast on foot. The journals are very detailed, both personal and social, reflecting an odd and observant mind. Fascinating account of Indian settlements in Ohio and Isaac Hervey's mission at Wapakoneta, Ohio. While at Smithfield he joined the Friends; he returned to England in 1820, and in 1823 he offered himself for service with the Friends' 'Committee on African Instruction', obviously from seeing the plight of the American coloured peoples. He died of fever in Birkow in Gambia in 1824.

Also a memorial to Smith by the Staffordshire Monthly Meeting; and eighteen manuscripts connected with him, including a few of his letters from America to his father and brother.

(*e*) Joseph Metford. Travel account. 1839.
'Transatlantic Travels': an account of a visit to America in 1839 by Joseph Metford (1776-1863). (MS. vol. 226 - xerox copy of typescript)

(*f*) Joseph Crosfield (1821-79). Letters written during American journeys, 1845 and 1865-6: 2 volumes of typewritten copies (originals held by the Crosfield family).
During his first journey in 1845 Crosfield travelled chiefly in Ohio, Indiana, Illinois, Kentucky, Virginia, and North Carolina, visiting prisons, asylums, schools, and institutions for coloured people. The letters contain a certain amount of material of topographical and sociological interest.

The second journey, in 1865-6, was mainly in the South, especially in Tennessee and North Carolina, and the letters contain some observations on the Civil War and its aftermath.

(*g*) Robert Lindsey (1801-63) and Sarah Lindsey (1805-76). American travel journals:[8] 5 volumes, 1846-51; 7 volumes, 1857-61.
On the first visit, 1846-51, Robert Lindsey was accompanied by Benjamin Seebohm. Their journey was confined largely to the Eastern and Middle-Western states. Sarah, his wife, accompanied him on the second visit, and wrote six volumes of the journals. In 1857-61 they visited also California and Oregon. The interest is chiefly religious, but descriptions of the country, and observations on slavery, are included.

(*h*) John Candler (1787-1869). Journal of a visit to the West Indies and the United States: 1 volume. 1850.
Quaker minister. Visited the United States with his wife in 1850 after a tour of the West Indies, and his account of America occupies about a quarter of his journal. He visited New York, Long Island, Philadelphia, Baltimore, and Washington, D.C., and then travelled through Ohio and Indiana. The journal contains some description of the cities and country visited and of agriculture in the Middle West; some observations on the Compromise of 1850, the Senate debate on which Candler attended while in Washington. Here he also interviewed Zachary Taylor on the slavery question.

(*i*) Priscilla Green (1802-77). Letters from America: 1 volume. 1856-8.
Quaker minister. Worked in the United States, 1856-8. The letters are mainly of religious interest, but touch on the slavery issue.

(*j*) Norman Penney. Diaries. 1911, 1913.
The American diaries of Norman Penney, 1911, 1913. 2 vols. (MS. vols. 179, 180)

MISCELLANEOUS CORRESPONDENCE AND DOCUMENTS RELATING TO AMERICA

(*a*) Miscellaneous correspondence and papers. 1666-1947.
Originals and/or copies of unofficial Quaker correspondence and papers during the last three centuries. Important from the standpoint of American studies are:

(i) Copies of letters, 1766-76, from Dr. John Fothergill to William Logan and James Pemberton before and during the War of Independence.[9]

(ii) Copy of a letter, 31 Mar. 1776, from David Barclay to Benjamin Franklin.[10]

A few examples of other relevant items:

(iii) Accounts of Quaker travellers, e.g. Elizabeth Hooten in 1666, (Port 3/80) Susanna Wright in 1714 (Port 14/88) and Joseph Gill in 1734 (Port 2/43).

(iv) Substance of an occasional conversation at Israel Pemberton's between Sarrogada, an Indian chief, and several other Indians and Israel Pemberton and several other Friends, 19 Apr. 1756. (Box 10/31)

(v) Quaker address to the Governor of Pennsylvania in 1756 against war with the Indians.

(vi) Letter from Robert Proud to his mother, Ann Proud, Philadelphia, 12 Aug. 1766. (Temp MSS. 35/3/6)

(vii) Letter from Robert Proud to his brother, Thomas, Philadelphia, 12 Oct. 1768. (Temp MSS. 35/3/7)

(viii) Letter from Anthony Benezet to Zachariah Cockfield, Philadelphia, 19 Oct. 1771. (Box 4)

(ix) Letter, 18 Jan. 1773, from Patrick Henry to Anthony Benezet, admits the evils of slavery but says that he personally cannot do without slaves. (Port 17/28)

(x) T.E. Latchworth collection of MSS., including Philadelphia Monthly Meeting memorial to Anthony Benezet, 1783. (Box 97/1)

(xi) Ann Mifflin: remarks on a visit made to the Indians, 1802. (Box 65/6)

(xii) Catherine L. Braithwaite Collection: Miscellaneous papers and letters to and from Josiah Forster, 1820-68, including some on Indian and Freedmen's affairs in the U.S. (Box 16/10)

(xiii) Friends Association for Abolishing the State Regulation of Vice; Letter of introduction (draft?) to Friends in North America, on behalf of James Paterson Gladstone and Henry Joseph Wilson, n.d. (Box 23/5)

(xiv) Biographical notes on the Thompsons of Liverpool, owners from 1817 to 1830 of the Black Ball Line, the first regular passenger and mail service between Liverpool and New York.

(xv) Letter, 1834, from North Carolina Friends, on the raising of funds to buy slaves and send them to the free states.

(xvi) Epistles, minutes and other papers (some copies) relating to difficulties among Friends in America, including queries sent by the New York Yearly Meeting and answers to them, 1834. (Box 7/9)

(xvii) Catherine L. Braithwaite Collection: Correspondence regarding Indian Affairs Committee (America), 1845-6. (Box 10a/14)

(xviii) Letters from slave holders in the United States, 1854. (Box 11/8)

(xix) Caroline Cadbury: describing a visit to J.G. Whittier, 1881. (Box 4a/12)

(xx) There are other scattered letters and journals of American interest among the Library's miscellaneous papers. Most of these are primarily of religious interest.

(*b*) Thomas Broadbank (1752-1808). Miscellaneous documents. 1720, 1801.
Some correspondence, 1801, relative to the shares of Thomas Broad-

7. See also J.D. Crosfield, 'Richard Smith and his Journal', *J.F.H.S.*, vol. xiii, pp. 49-58, 89-98, 129-41, 1916; and vol. xiv, pp. 15-25, 59-69, 108-21, 161-7, 1917.
8. Extracts from the journals have been printed in the *Travels of Robert and Sarah Lindsey* (London, 1886).
9. Originals in the Library of the Historical Society of Pennsylvania.
10. Original in the possession of the American Philosophical Society.

bank in the Pennsylvania Land Company; and some share transfers, signed Thomas Story and dated 1720.

(*c*) Lewis Tappan (1788-1873). Letter. 1840.

Abolitionist. Letter, 25 Mar. 1840, deals with Prussian immigrants to the United States bound for Milwaukee, and refers also to the evils of slavery.

(*d*) John Greenleaf Whittier (1807-92). 6 letters and manuscript poems. 1842-91.

American poet and abolitionist. Letters deal with slavery and slave trade, capital punishment, pacifism, and his ancestry. The poems are 'Unity' and 'Abolition rhymes'.

(*e*) Elihu Burritt (1810-79). 2 letters (photostat copies; originals in private possession). 1861-2.

Both letters are to Henry Richard. The first, 26 May 1861, is concerned chiefly with dissension among American pacifists caused by the Civil War. The second, 27 Oct. 1862, gives a more general account of the war itself, Northern opinion, and the Emancipation Proclamation.

(*f*) William Jones (1826-99) and Katherine Jones (1850-1929). Letters (unbound). 1889.

Written during a world tour, 1889-90, in the cause of promoting arbitration of international disputes. The letters from the United States, 1889, include references to the Pan-American Congress, and an account of their interview with President Harrison.

DEPARTMENT OF HISTORIOGRAPHY AND ARCHIVES, ENGLISH PROVINCE OF THE SOCIETY OF JESUS, 114 Mount Street, London W1Y 6AH

SOCIETY OF JESUS. Correspondence. 18th-19th centuries.

The London archives of the Society of Jesus contain an important amount of eighteenth- and nineteenth-century correspondence to and from various American outposts of the Society. Although time did not permit a complete search of the archives, the following MS. volumes are known to include American-related material:

(*a*) English Province Correspondence, 1746-1854.
(*b*) Arch. Prov. Angl. S.J., vol. 12, 1754-1829.
(*c*) Stone, Sewell, Connell Correspondence.
(*d*) Arch. Prov. Angl. S.J., vol. 7, miscellany: 1771-1820.
(*e*) Foreign Correspondence, 1776-1859.
(*f*) Bishops and Cardinals, 1753-1853.
(*g*) Letters, etc., 1805-18.
(*h*) Strickland Letters, 1786-1811.
(*i*) Fr. Thorpe's Letters, 1787-90.
(*j*) Maryland - Letters of Jesuits and of Bishops, 1773-1815.

There are also a number of loose letters in the archives dealing with such topics as Jesuit missions in the United States. See especially:

(*a*) Maryland: 1729-1815, 1871, 1903, 1921. (BN/3/1)
(*b*) Miscellaneous: 1727-1927. (BN/3/2)
(*c*) Missouri: 1823-34, 1868, 1871, 1887. (BN/3/3)

SOUTHWARK DIOCESAN CURIA, Archbishop's House, St. George's Road, London SE1 6HX

ARCHIVES.

Stonor, Monsignor Christopher (d. 1795). From 1748 to 1790 Stonor was agent in Rome for the affairs of the English Catholics. For information about the American material in the volume (MS. 37) of his copies of documents, 1759-90, held in the Diocesan Archives *see* Andrews & Davenport, pp. 340-1, in the report on the Westminster Archdiocesan Archives.

STATIONERS' HALL REGISTRY, Stationers' Hall Court, London E.C.4.

The Records of the Stationers' Company contain a few references to the Virginia lottery and other minor connexions with Virginia. The records are printed in *The Records of the Court of the Stationers' Company, 1602-40*, edited by William Jackson (London, 1957).

TIMES NEWSPAPERS LTD., New Printing House Square, Gray's Inn Road, London WC1X 8EZ

ARCHIVES.

The fact that *The Times* has been for so long a newspaper of national record means that Anglo-American relations permeate large sections of the accumulated papers and memoranda in this archive, and it is difficult to be too specific. Frequently such widely disparate sources as *The Times* correspondents in, say, Tokyo and Paris, would dwell in their editorial briefing letters on the influence of the United States on the territories which they covered. It is, however, possible to suggest that material of interest to American scholars might be found in the groups of records listed below.

Access to the archive's records is governed by the normal thirty-year rule, except in the case of papers requiring direct clearance by the Editor. A summary contents-guide to the archive appears in Chris Cook's *Sources in British Political History, 1900-1951*: vol. 1, *A Guide to the Archives of Selected Organizations and Societies* (Macmillan, 1975). There is also a note in *Business Archives*, in the Jan. 1976 issue.

It *must* be stressed that this is not a clippings library, and for material which has appeared in the paper reference should be made to the printed *Index*, available in most large libraries which keep *The Times* on microfilm. Reference should also be made to the five-volume official *History of the Times, 1935-1952*.

The archivist is constantly searching for new material of interest, such as university dissertations and broadcast transcripts, and a collection of some 2,000 books and pamphlets directly bearing on the paper and its staff is also kept in the archives.

A. Proprietor's papers.
(*a*) Walter Papers (1780's -).
(*b*) Northcliffe Papers (1889 - , including War Mission to the U.S.A. in 1916).
B. Editor's papers.
(*a*) Delane Papers (1841-77).
(*b*) Dawson Papers (Editor of *The Times*, 1912-9 and 1922-41).
(*c*) Steed Papers (Foreign Editor, 1914-9; Editor, 1919-22).
(*d*) Barrington-Ward Papers (1941-8).
C. Editorial diaries, 1857-to date. Particularly useful in identifying the writers of news articles.
D. Managerial letter-books (out-letters), 1847-1910.
E. Foreign Editor's letter-books, 1891-1910.
F. New York/Washington/Philadelphia correspondents (also other

cities in the U.S.A., a record of which is kept in the archives). 1840's to date. After about 1847 it may reasonably be assumed that no one held office for any considerable time without leaving some record of his existence in either the Manager's or Foreign Department letter-books, but these do not often show the dates of appointment, resignation, or transfer. This means that for many correspondents the archive has only a name and a city, for others only fragmentary records, but in the cases of William Howard Russell, George Smalley, Francis Lawley, Robert Percival Porter, Sir Arthur Willert, Sir Willmott Lewis, and their successors, there are fairly substantial collections.

G. U.S.A. boxes.

Include:

(*a*) Confidential memoranda, 1952-70.

(*b*) New York and Washington Office correspondence relating to news services; election coverage; special numbers on the U.S.A.; marketing campaigns; syndications; telegraph communication; relations with U.S. newspapers, A-Z; *Stars and Stripes; Homage to the War Dead; American Air Force Daily;* etc.

TRINITY HOUSE, Tower Hill, London EC3N 4DH

EARLY TRANSACTIONS AND MINUTE-BOOKS.

These records were saved although the rest of the library was completely destroyed by enemy action in 1940. They are described in Andrews & Davenport, pp. 277-9, and in H.M.C. viii (i), pp. 235-62.

UNITED REFORMED CHURCH HISTORY SOCIETY, 86 Tavistock Place, London WC1H 9RT

THE ARCHIVES, *and* W.B. SHAW LIBRARY.

The Library, formerly in the care of the Presbyterian Historical Society, contains some early printed works on American Presbyterianism, including biographies and histories of American churches. It also contains the *Journal of the Presbyterian Historical Society*, Philadelphia, and other volumes of reports, minutes and proceedings of the American Presbyterian Churches.

There is in the Archives available for reference a certain amount of manuscript material, including minutes and baptismal registers of many English Presbyterian congregations from the eighteenth century onwards. Anyone wishing to consult the books or documents should write to the Librarian of the Society.

UNITED SOCIETY FOR THE PROPAGATION OF THE GOSPEL,[1] 15 Tufton Street, London SW1P 3QQ

The U.S.P.G. was formed in 1965 by the amalgamation of the Universities' Mission to Central Africa with the Society for the Propagation of the Gospel in Foreign Parts.

The S.P.G. was founded in 1701, and the American colonies were its chief field of missionary activity until the War of Independence.

(Arrangement of 'A' to 'X' MSS. is alphabetical, *not* chronological.)

'A' MSS. Letters received (contemporary copies): 27 volumes.[2] 1702-36 (with a few earlier documents).[3]

Letters from missionaries, would-be missionaries, potential supporters of the Society, those requiring its assistance (e.g., in books or cash), civil equipment; personal and civil affairs (the latter mainly from Governors and Lieutenant-Governors); work among Indians and Negroes, especially the education of Indian children; the cruelties of slavery; the building of churches; crops (e.g., tobacco in Virginia); etc. There are also offers of legacies, letters of complaint, requests for ministers, letters of introduction, etc. Include some letters of, or about, Francis Nicholson, who was Governor or Lieutenant-Governor of five colonies.

See also Andrews & Davenport, p. 332.

'B' MSS. Letters received (including the originals of some of the 'A' MSS. and a number of miscellaneous documents): 43 volumes, bound under colonies,[4] 1701-1800.

Covered by the description of the 'A' MSS. above. The later letters include references to difficulties encountered by the Society's missionaries during and after the War of Independence. Vol. 5 contains papers relating to Thomas Thomlinson's attempts at running a school at New Bern, N.C., 1763-71. *See* further details in Andrews & Davenport, pp. 332-3.

'C' MSS. Miscellaneous unbound manuscripts relating to the American colonies: 15 boxes. 1635-1811.

Include much correspondence, mostly pre-Revolution, from and to missionaries: early deeds to lands in America, 1691-1767; treatises on the state of the church in various colonies; certificates, testimonials, petitions from Indians and others; lists of subscribers to local churches; papers relating to charity schools; accounts, bills of exchange, receipts, and grants of salaries. The contents of the boxes cover: New York and New Jersey, 1707-91; Connecticut, 1635-1796; Pennsylvania, 1703-84; Massachusetts, 1712-1812; Maine, New Hampshire, Vermont, 1755-1811; Southern Colonies, 1712-84; Rhode Island, 1658-1800; Virginia and Pennsylvania deeds, 1691-1767.

'D' MSS. Letters received: United States, 1852-9 and 1871-4, and America, 1875-7 and 1880-1930: 56 volumes.

These volumes contain miscellaneous letters concerned with such topics as co-operation in missionary work between the Church of England and the Protestant Episcopal Church in America; common days of prayer; the West Indian bishoprics; letters of introduction; and requests for historical information.

'G' MSS. Letters sent (copies): United States: 2 volumes. 1851-1928. (Also include a few letters from the United States.)

Deal with such matters as donations to the Society from the United States; visits of American prelates to Britain; requests for information by historians of individual churches and organizers of centenary and other celebrations; sale of the Society's property in the United States; etc.

1. Virginia material microfilmed by the Virginia Colonial Records Project.
2. The Library of Congress, Washington, D.C., has both transcripts and microfilms of vols. 1-26.
3. Some of the originals of the 'A' MSS. are at Lambeth Palace - see William W. Manross, *S.P.G. Papers in the Lambeth Palace Library* (Oxford, 1974). See also 'B' MSS. below.
4. The Library of Congress has both transcripts and microfilms of these volumes.

'X' MSS.

Nos. 141-53: Letters sent (copies): 13 volumes. 1773-1833. Mostly to the Society's missionaries. The first two volumes, 1773-8 and 1778-84 (nos. 141 and 142), are devoted almost exclusively to America and deal particularly with the affairs of the English church in the rebel colonies. The succeeding volumes deal to a lesser extent with United States affairs - mainly with adjustments made by individual missionaries after the War of Independence.
No. 167: Letters (typescripts) relating to S.P.G. property in Vermont, New Hampshire, Connecticut, New Jersey, and Pennsylvania: 1 file. 1855-1907. Contains also a calendar of the manuscripts relating to the properties scattered throughout 'D' MSS. and 'G' MSS.
No. 171: Photostat of will, 1727, of Governor Francis Nicholson, bequeathing most of his property, especially in New England, Pennsylvania, and Virginia, to the Society, of which he was a member.
No. 234: Edmund Hobhouse (1817-1904). Five letters, 3 Oct.-12 Nov. 1853, to his parents, written while visiting the United States with an S.P.G. delegation. Hobhouse attended a Protestant Episcopal convention in New York, and then travelled to Philadelphia, Baltimore, through up-state Maryland, Washington, D.C., Norfolk, Va., Wilmington, N.C., Charleston, S.C., and Savannah, Ga., visiting Protestant Episcopal bishops, clergymen, churches, and other institutions. Letters contain numerous observations on slavery.

ANNUAL REPORTS OF THE SOCIETY (printed), 1704-
ANNUAL ANNIVERSARY SERMONS, 1702- .

The Reports of the Society contain lists of the names of the missionaries in America up to the War of Independence, extracts from their letters, and other material relating to the state of the church in the colonies.

JOURNALS AND MINUTES OF THE SOCIETY AND ITS COMMITTEES.[5]

1701- . (With abstracts of letters received.)

(*a*) Journal. Since 1701 the S.P.G. has kept a Journal, that is, a record of the minutes of the meetings of the Society as a whole. The early volumes often record the discussions and resolutions concerning such matters as the appointment of missionaries to work in the plantations, their work there and payment to them. The later volumes contain occasional references to American bishops, S.P.G. property in America, etc. For much of the period there are two copies of the Journal, as follows:

(i) Rough copy, 1714-1833: 107 volumes.

(ii) Fair copy, 1701-1833; changes to rough copy, 1833-1932: 62 volumes from 1701 to 1932. (Another fair copy of 1701-17 is bound in two large folio volumes.)

Appendixes to the fair copy contain copies of important documents.

(*b*) Minutes of the meetings of the Standing (i.e. executive) Committee of the S.P.G., 1702- . Sometimes two copies exist, as with the Journal of the Society:

(i) Rough copy, 1714-1819: 64 volumes.

(ii) Fair copy, 1702-58: volumes 1-8. Changes to rough copy, 1833-1938: 3 unnumbered volumes, 1833-8, and volumes 21-76, 1839-1938.

ACCOUNTS AND ACCOUNT BOOKS. 1701- .

Include entries of payments to missionaries, many of whom worked in the American colonies before the War of Independence.

See Andrews & Davenport, p. 333.

FULHAM PAPERS: Letters from abroad to the Bishop of London. Letter. 1820.

Volume 1 of the four volumes contains a letter, Charleston, S.C., 22 June 1820, from Frederick Dalcho, giving an account of the progress of the Protestant Episcopal Church in the United States since its foundation in 1789.

MANUSCRIPTS OF DR. BRAY'S ASSOCIATES.

Those of American interest cover the period before the War of Independence.

See Andrews & Davenport, pp. 334-5, for a full description.

CANADIAN MATERIAL.

The U.S.P.G. archives also include a good deal of Canadian material; many of these manuscripts after 1780 concern Loyalist refugees from the United States.

PRINTED MATERIAL IN THE LIBRARY.

Large collection of (mainly) sermons dating chiefly from the latter half of the nineteenth century, delivered in America or by American ministers, especially of the Protestant Episcopal Church, visiting Britain. Also annual reports of American churches and mission boards, reports of conferences, etc.

UNIVERSITY OF LONDON LIBRARY, Senate House, Malet Street, London WC1E 7HU

Printed *Catalogue of the Manuscripts and Autograph Letters in the University {of London} Library* (London, 1921), together with the *Supplement, 1921-1930* (London, 1930); also a typescript catalogue 'Additions to the manuscripts and autograph letters received in the University of London Library since 1930', is available in the Library.

PRIVY COUNCIL PAPERS. 2 papers. 1609. (MS. 20)

The papers in this volume, covering *c.* 1600-25 (where dated), are apparently transcripts in contemporary handwriting. They include the following:
No. 15. 'The coppie of a comission made by Duke Montmorancye Lo: of Dampvill and Admirall of France unto the Lo: Raverdiere for createinge of him Vice Admirall, and freeinge of his shippes and provisions made for his voyage unto Guyana and other parts of Affrica and America in the yeare of o^r Lord 1609.' (ff. 159v.-161v.)
No. 16. 'The coppie of a comission made by the Lord of Raverdiere by vertue of the K[ing] of Frances letters unto Robert le Brette Lo: Dubose, constituteinge the said Lord Dubose his Lieftennant in the countries of Guyana and other parts of America in A° 1609.' (ff. 162-3v.)

H.M. CUSTOMS REVENUES. 1 volume. 1679-1760. (MS. 46)

The gross and net produce of all the branches of the revenue under the management of the Commissioners of H.M. Customs. It includes tables of sums yielded, e.g. from enumerated duties from the

5. The Library of Congress has prints or photostats of vols. 1-24 of the fair copy of the Journal, and microfilm of vols. 23-54 and App. B. of this; microfilms of vols. 1-8 of the fair copy of the Minutes of the Standing Committee and of vols. 28-49 of the rough copy of these.

American plantations, 1704-11, and there are other American references. A pencil note on one of the end-papers says that this volume was specially drawn up by the officers of the Crown for the private use of successive Chancellors of the Exchequer.

HUDSON'S BAY COMPANY. 1 volume. *c.* 1801. (MS. 147)

Bound volume of extracts from documents originally written 1684-1719. This is stamped with the Company's coat of arms. The documents are petitions, proclamations, reports of court decisions, etc., relating to the Company; for example, a petition to the King against interlopers, 1688; abstract of the rights of the Crown of England to Hudson Bay in 1699.

DARIEN COMPANY. 1 volume. 1696-1707. (MS. 63)

Papers and transcripts (13 items) relating to the Darien Company, 1696-1707.

VALUE OF TRADE OF GREAT BRITAIN AND IRELAND. 1 volume of statistical tables. 1698-1765. (MS. 126)

The table giving the value of exports and imports to Great Britain compared with the excess of each country. From 1747 to 1762 gives separate figures for each colony under the general heading of 'Plantations'. There are various other entries for the plantation. The manuscript has bookplates of John Baker Holroyd, 1st Earl Sheffield.

COMMITTEE OF PRIVY COUNCIL FOR TRADE AND PLANTATIONS. Report, 1703 (1 volume). Minutes, 1823-7 (5 volumes).

(*a*) MS. 78. Volume entitled 'Report from the Commissioners of Trade and Plantations, 16 December 1703', presented to the House of Lords. As well as details about the trade of each colony, the report contains information on defence measures taken to protect the subjects and the trade of the American colonies during the war against France and Spain. There is also a copy of 'Proposals to the Lords Commissioners for Trade and Plantations about the surrender of my province of Pennsylvania', drawn up by William Penn.
(*b*) Minutes (5 volumes). (MS. 159.) These volumes consist mainly of brief statements from, *inter alia*, British consuls in the United States that report that letters relating to trade with that country have been received; in a few cases there is included also the Committee's minute or letter dealing with the issue raised - e.g. a discussion, 5 Mar. 1824, of American duties on rolled and hammered iron, containing the suggestion that the British should threaten as a reprisal to treat American cotton as a manufactured product for tariff purposes.

BIRCHFIELD, MAURICE. Papers and documents. 1709-27. (MS. 750)

Papers and documents (12 items) relating to Birchfield's work as Surveyor-General of the Customs of the Northern Survey and of the Southern District of America.

GEE, JOSHUA (d. 1730). Memorials relating to the trade of the plantations. *c.* 1720. (MS. 99)

From a bound volume of papers covering various features of mercantilist policy. In a note on a fly-leaf in the handwriting of George Chalmers, Scottish antiquarian, Joshua Gee is described as a London Quaker merchant, frequently consulted by the government on matters of trade, manufacture, and the colonies, who wrote tracts and *The Trade and Navigation of Great Britain considered* (London, 1729). The papers were, he says, preserved in the archives of the Board of Trade, but never printed.
(*a*) 'Memorial from Mr. Joshua Gee relating to the trade of the plantations, particularly with respect to iron, copper, hemp, flax, boards, timber, and to the enumerated commodities which are now restrained to be first imported into Great Britain', 1721.
(*b*) 'Memorial to the Honourable the Lords Commissioners for Trade and Plantations.' The answer of Joshua Gee to the Board of Trade on the subjects proposed to him by the Board respecting the trade, raw produce, and manufactures of the Colonies and about producing naval stores in the Colonies. (In a letter of the Board, 20 Feb. 1728.)

ANGLO-AMERICAN TRADE. 2 folios. 1739-61. (MS. 749)

Account of the imports to England from the North American colonies, and of exports from England to North America, from 25 Dec. 1739 to 25 Dec. 1761.

ROYAL AFRICAN COMPANY. Petition. 1742. (MS. 109)

A petition to the King in Council for a Charter to enable the Company 'to fit out one or more ship or ships of force for the attacking surprising taking or destroying the ships goods settlements factories or lands of the Spaniards or any other of your Majesty's enemies in America'. Dated 'African House March ye 26th 1742'.

POSTLETHWAYT, MALACHY. Paper. 1746. (MS. 493)

Unpublished autograph manuscript, 1746, 'Considerations on a future treaty of navigation & commerce with Spain; with regard particularly to the freedom and security of the British trade in *America*, and an *Assiento* for supplying the Spanish Indies with negroes.'

GLEN, JAMES (1701-77). 'Answers...to the queries from the ...Lords Commissioners for Trade and Plantations'. *c.* 1749 (1 volume). (MS. 114)

Governor of South Carolina 1743-56. A detailed description of the climate, soil, administration, trade, Indian tribes, etc., of South Carolina, with some statistical tables of exports and imports, etc.

POST, CHRISTIAN F. 2 authorizations. 1759. (MS. 503)

Copies of two authorizations, 1759, given to Post by William Denny, Lieutenant-Governor and Commander-in-Chief, Pennsylvania, 'to preach the gospel amongst any of the Indian nations in alliance with his Majesty.'

CANADA. 1 folio. 1762. (MS. 392)

Account of duty paid on spirits imported at Quebec between 26 May and 31 Aug. 1762.

PORTEUS LIBRARY.

The library collected by Beilby Porteus (1731-1809), Bishop of London 1787-1809, contains over 150 uncatalogued volumes of pamphlets. They contain an extensive section on the War of Independence, and another on the West Indian slave trade. Thirty-eight volumes of pamphlets are specifically entitled 'Slave Trade', and range in date 1772-1807. It is probable that a considerable number of works in both these categories are also in the Goldsmiths' Library.

HOLROYD, JOHN BAKER, 1st Earl Sheffield (1735-1821). (MS. 139)

A French translation of Lord Sheffield's *Observations on the Commerce of the American States*, 1784.

ABSTRACT OF SHIPS REGISTERED IN THE BRITISH DOMINIONS, 1788-93 (6 volumes). (MS. 230)

Section 5 of each volume contains an examination taken at the committee of the Council for Trade and Plantations with the opinions of insurers and underwriters on the shipping and manner of navigation of Britain compared with that of the nations of Europe and the United States. A comparison is made of premium rates, etc.

IRVING, THOMAS. 'State of the navigation revenues and commerce of Great Britain.' 1790 (1 volume). (MS. 140)

A report made to Pitt by Thomas Irving, 12 Dec. 1791. It includes the number of United States ships from each state entering and clearing British ports; a report on the condition of British trade with the American states; a comparison of British and foreign shipping entering and clearing the ports of the American states.

SHEDDEN PAPERS. 1794-1823. (MS. 622)

Correspondence and papers (16 items) of Robert Shedden & Sons, merchants of London, and of William Shedden of New York. The letters are mostly from London to Shedden's New York representative.

STONINGTON, CONNECTICUT. 1 folio. 1799. (MS. 466)

Bill of lading for the schooner *Pearl* bound for Demerara.

ATTWOOD-HADLEY PAPERS. 1812. (MS. 642/2)

Letters to Thomas Attwood from Samuel Whitbread. One letter, dated 20 July 1812, remarks on Whitbread's attitude to North America.

NEWFOUNDLAND. 8 folios. 1814. (MS. 637)

(*a*) Memorandum presented by 'the committee of merchants trading from London...with the island of Newfoundland' to the Prime Minister, Lord Liverpool, with a covering letter dated 11 Jan. 1814. (Copy.)

(*b*) Memorandum presented by 'the merchants engaged in the [fishing] trade from Poole [Dorset] to the island of Newfoundland' to the Lords of the Treasury. (Copy.)

PHILADELPHIA AND NEW YORK. Invoices. 1833-79. (MS. 675)

Collection of 240 invoices addressed to 107 companies and individuals in Philadelphia, Pa., and to two in New York, from eighty-nine British manufacturers. Goods involved were mostly textiles, textile machinery, pottery, cutlery, and tools.[1]

MANTON MARBLE COLLECTION.[2] 190 file boxes of newspaper clippings and pamphlets and 26 boxes of scrapbooks. Mainly 1860-90.

Manton Marble (1835-1917), editor and owner of the Democratic New York *World*, 1862-76; part author of Tilden's platform of 1876 and also of the Democratic platform in 1884; sent abroad by President Cleveland in 1885 to sound European governments on bimetallism. The collection consists of his own library of press clippings. Boxes 1-26 are 'biographies' of persons, notably Tilden; 27-51 are 'political series'; 52-187 are 'special collections'. The 'special collections' contain what must be a unique coverage of the silver controversy and also of the Election Commission over the disputed presidential election of 1876. The collection would be invaluable for any life of Tilden, work on bimetallism, or the Democratic Party after the Civil War, especially in New York. He appears to have clipped every important comment or story on these topics.

BOOTH PAPERS. Correspondence. *c.* 1860-1916. (MS. 797)

Contains correspondence of Charles Booth relating to his travels on business in North America.[3]

AUTOGRAPH LETTER COLLECTION.

(*a*) Letter of Jean Pellerin, *c.* 1699, to ?, urging the English to support the Scottish colony at Darien. (A.L. 97)

(*b*) Letter, 2 Sept. 1785, from Sir Samuel Romilly to John Baynes, a fellow member of Gray's Inn, including comment on John Adams and his daughter. (A.L. 237)

(*c*) Letter of Richard Smith, 9 Dec. 1794, to Seth Barton of Baltimore, concerning insurance for the *London Packet* and its cargo on its voyage to Baltimore. (A.L. 387)

(*d*) Letters of John Gale Jones, 25 and 28 Apr. 1828, probably to George Agar Ellis, concerning subscriptions to his pamphlet *An Oration on the late General Washington* (London, 1825). (A.L. 290/1-2)

(*e*) P.E. Du Ponceau. Philadelphia. 19 Nov. 1831, to J. Vaughan, Esq., asking him to send the enclosed [a copy of *An historical review of the ...Silk Culture, Manufacture and Trade in Europe and America, &c.* (Philadelphia, 1831), in which the letter is inserted] 'to your excellent nephew'. (A.L. 47)

(*f*) Letter, 1 Jan. 1848, from David Irving to John Ramsay MacCulloch, commenting on the laws of succession in France and North America and their influence on the constitutions of these countries. (A.L. 187/16)

(*g*) Letter, 11 Aug. 1849, from Thomas H. Webb in Camden, Me., to Joseph Hume about postal reform and a 'people's library'. (A.L. 234)

(*h*) Thomas Babington Macaulay, 1st Baron Macaulay. London, 14 Oct. 1853, to Augustus de Morgan, thanking him for some papers, 'I am afraid that I shall not live to write the history of the American war. Indeed heaven knows when I shall have done with King William.' (A.L. 75)

(*i*) Letters from Henry George Grey, 3rd Earl Grey, 16 and 22 June 1855, to John Lewis Ricardo, commenting on the Free Trade Agreement between Canada and the West Indies. (A.L. 184/1-2)

(*j*) Henry James. London, 1886-98, to 'Lady Blanche'. (A.L. 147)

(*k*) Henry George. New York, 16 Sept. 1891, to Swan Sonnenschein & Co., relating to the publication of his *The Condition of Labor: an open Letter to Pope Leo XIII* (New York, 1891). (A.L. 51)

GOLDSMITHS' LIBRARY OF ECONOMIC LITERATURE. Printed material, pamphlets and broadsides.

The Goldsmiths' Library, presented to the University of London by the Goldsmiths' Company in 1903, is a valuable collection of more than 60,000 books and pamphlets of the sixteenth to nineteenth centuries, in English and other languages, covering a wide range of economic, historical, and social topics. It is naturally particularly strong in English material on trade and finance. Besides works of particular interest for American studies, such as a large number of

1. Handlist available in the Palaeography Room, University of London Library.

2. This collection was part of a bequest made to the Institute of Historical Research in 1921 by Marble's step-daughter, Lady (Martin) Conway. A typescript catalogue in two volumes is in the Library, giving the general content of each box and a detailed inventory listing each clipping up to Box 101. There is also a chronological card index to the boxes 27-51, 'political series'.

3. See T.D. Rogers and H.M. Young, 'A Handlist of the personal correspondence of Charles Booth and Mary Catherine Booth', 1973, reproduced by the Historical Manuscripts Commission.

pamphlets on the causes of the War of Independence and the War of 1812, the Library's collection of early works on trade and on emigration is relevant, and it possesses also a collection of works on slavery. For the period after 1800, this collection is of approximately 400 volumes, among which there are forty-nine volumes of bound pamphlets. There are approximately thirty bound volumes of pamphlets on bimetallism, 1876-1904.

The Ludlow Collection of nineteenth-century trade union pamphlets contains material relevant to trade union assistance to emigrants. Broadsides in the Library are listed in a *Catalogue of the Collections of Proclamations and Broadsides in the University Library* (London, 1930), and include several on trade and economic affairs in the plantations.

OTHER MANUSCRIPTS:

(*a*) Professor W.P.M. Kennedy: Two judgements 'in the matter of a reference as to the meaning of the word "persons" in Section 24 of the British North America Act, 1867'. ff. 38. (Typescript.) (I.H.R. MS. 471)

(*b*) Anonymous work presented by Professor Crane on 'Origins of a merchant class in Rhode Island during the eighteenth century'. 19--?. ff. 23. (Typescript.) (I.H.R. MS. 497)

(*c*) Sir Charles Firth: notes on colonial records, access to them, etc. ff. 70. (I.H.R. MS. 576-581)

COLLEGE ARCHIVES, IMPERIAL COLLEGE OF SCIENCE AND TECHNOLOGY, Sherfield Building, London SW7 2AZ

RAMSAY PAPERS.

Sir Andrew Crombie Ramsay (1841-91).

The Ramsay Papers are in the process of being listed. They include two field notebooks describing Ramsay's visit to the U.S. and Canada in 1857. There are also geological notes and sketches of the Hudson River, etc.

HUXLEY PAPERS.

The papers of Thomas Henry Huxley (1825-95) are listed in W.R. Dawson, *The Huxley Papers, a Descriptive Catalogue of the Correspondence, Manuscripts and Miscellaneous Papers*...(London, 1946). Huxley kept in touch with many of the American publicists of the new scientific movements associated with himself and Darwin, as well as receiving numerous random letters from American admirers (or vilifiers), an astonishingly large number of which are preserved. Most of the letters are to Huxley; there are comparatively few from him. The main American correspondents are:

Agassiz, A. Twenty-nine letters, 1874-95, exchange of scientific news and schemes for the promotion of science.

Fiske, John. Eleven letters, 1873-93.

Gilman, Daniel Coit. Four letters, all of 1876, and concerned with Huxley's address at Johns Hopkins University in that year.

Lowell, James Russell. Fourteen letters, 1880-7, one being about the Copyright Treaty, together with a draft of Huxley's reply.

Yeomans, Edward Livingston. Four letters, 1864-71, about the sale of scientific books, particularly Huxley's, in America.

There is also a small notebook that is a diary kept by Huxley on his American tour of 1876.

Since 1961 there have been further additions to the collection of Huxley material. These include Huxley's scientific papers, which were listed in 1968, and his family correspondence, which has only been partly listed. There are a number of letters from Eliza Scott, Huxley's sister, who settled in the U.S. and lived in Montgomery, Ala., and Nashville, Tenn. There are a few letters exchanged between Huxley and his wife during their visit to the States in 1876. And finally, there are the following letters among Huxley's scientific papers:

Brooks, William Keith (1848-1908). Three letters, including one enquiry about Brooks' paper on Crustacean embryology, 1880, and one dealing with research on the lower Macrura, 1881.

Coues, Elliott. One letter on medical service in the U.S. Army, 1883.

PLAYFAIR PAPERS.

Lyon Playfair, 1st Baron Playfair of St. Andrews (1818-98) was Professor of Chemistry at the Royal School of Mines, one of the constituent colleges of Imperial College, from 1851-3. He had a distinguished career in both science and politics. His third wife was Edith Russell, an American from Boston, Mass. There are some references to travels in America in his domestic correspondence and in the following letters:

Agassiz, Elizabeth (1822-1907). One letter on her husband's biography, 1886.

Buckle, George Earle (1854-1935). Two letters, 1896, on the Venezuela dispute and on the Monroe Doctrine.

Chatard, Francis Silas (1834-1918). Letter, 1895, on state of opinion in America about the Venezuela dispute.

Holmes, Oliver Wendell (1809-94). Three letters, copies of speeches, etc., 1879-83.

James, Henry (1843-1916). Three letters, 1898, including letters of sympathy to Lady Playfair.

Lowell, James Russell (1819-91). Two letters, 1883, including one on his election as Rector of Edinburgh University.

THOMPSON PAPERS.

Silvanus Phillips Thompson (1851-1916).

Bell, Alexander Graham (1847-1922). Six letters, 1879-80, on experiments with telephone, photophone, etc.

Carhart, Henry Smith (1844-1920). Two letters, on work in hand and on Röntgen photography.

Channing, William Francis (1820-1901). One letter, 1883, review of book on Phillip Reis and the Bell Telephone monopoly.

Martin, Thomas Commerford (1856-1924). Two letters, on copyright of a book by Thompson, 1906, and on his review of the *Life of Kelvin*, 1910.

Nipher, Francis Eugene (1847-1927). Two letters, sending a book for review, 1895, and research on the Holtz machine, 1908.

Thomson, Elihu (1853-1957). Five letters, 1893-1916, social correspondence, research on alternocurrent motors, etc.

UNWIN PAPERS.

William Cawthorne Unwin (1838-1933).

Adams, Edward Dean (d. 1931). Twenty-eight letters and papers: Correspondence on electric system for Niagara Falls; Adams's book on 'Niagara Power', etc. Memorandum by Unwin on the Niagara scheme; two letters from Unwin to Adams. Papers range from 1890 to 1929.

Cooper, Theodore (1839-1919). One letter, 1888, on American principles of bridge building.

Rowland, Henry Augustus (1848-1901). One letter, 1893, asking Unwin to support his claim against the Cataract Company.

Sellers, Coleman (1827-1907). Three letters, 1892-3, on progress of works at Niagara, personal enquiries.

The Unwin Papers also include a scrapbook of material relating to the Cataract Construction Co. and Niagara Falls, 1894-1905.

ARMSTRONG PAPERS.

Henry Edward Armstrong (1848-1937) and Edward Frankland Armstrong (1878-1945).

Acheson, Edward Goodrich (1856-1931). One letter, discussing the work of Professor Mabery, etc., 1912.

Hendrick, Ellwood (1861-1930). Two letters, on work of women in the Eastman Laboratory, 1922, and on a scheme for an institute of osmics, 1928.

Ickes, Harold L. (1874-1952). One letter, 1940, on the international situation.

Mallett, John William (1832-1912). One letter, 1892, about his paper on the determination of atomic weights.

HUMPHREY PAPERS.

Herbert Alfred Humphrey (1868-1951).
Preliminary report, 1927, on a visit to power plants in the U.S.

BRITISH LIBRARY OF POLITICAL AND ECONOMIC SCIENCE, London School of Economics, Houghton Street, London WC2A 2AE

BRAY, JOHN FRANCIS (1809-97).

Social reformer. Bray, born in the United States, went to England with his father in 1822; he returned to America in 1842. The Library holds the following material by or about Bray:[1]

(*a*) Bray Collection. 4 volumes. 1823-1943. (R(SR)203, Col. Misc. 72+)

One of these volumes contains the typescript (carbon copy) account by Miss Agnes Inglis, Ann Arbor, Mich., 13 June 1943, of her visits in 1937 and later to Bray's daughter-in-law, Mrs. Anna Bray, in Pontiac, Mich., and of the manuscripts and other material relating to Bray found there. It is these letters and papers of which the Library now has photostats or originals.

The remaining three volumes contain notes by Miss Inglis; photostats or original clippings by or about Bray from the *Leeds Times* and from various American labour and socialist periodicals; a manuscript notebook used by Bray for French lessons (he visited Paris in 1842) and as a scrapbook for news-cuttings on astronomy and other scientific subjects; and photostats of letters from and to Bray. Included is the photostat of a letter from Bray to his mother, 1823; and the photostats of letters to Bray from his brother, Charles Frederick Bray, Boston, 1835-42, from Elihu Finnie, Leeds, 1883 and 1894, and from Karl Reuben, Pittsburgh, Pa., 1893, 1895, and 1896.

(*b*) Original manuscripts of articles and books by Bray:

'A voyage from Utopia to several unknown regions of the world by Yarbfj translated from the American', 1842.[2] (R(SR)1047)

'Common sense for farmers' (incomplete), *c.* 1870. (R(SR)198)

'Machine-made Christians', *c.* 1870. (R(SR)201)

'The wage workers' declaration of independence', *c.* 1870. (R(SR)199)

'A new declaration of independence'. *c.* 1875. (R(SR)200)

'The God of the Jews and the God of the universe; (and Matter for thought)', *c.* 1880. (R(SR)202)

'Brief sketch of the life of John F. Bray', 1890-1. (R(SR)208)

The Library also has Bray's own copy of his *Labour's Wrongs and Labour's Remedy* (Leeds, 1839), with manuscript notes. (R(SR)122)

WEBB TRADE UNION COLLECTION. (Collection E)

The collection consists of manuscript and printed material collected for use in the Webb's *History of Trade Unionism* (London, 1894), *Industrial Democracy* (London, 1897), etc. It contains manuscript notes and letters and printed trade union reports, rules, etc; a list is available. The collection is in five parts: Section A. Chiefly manuscript material; Section B. Non-serial printed matter; Section C. Rules; Section D. Printed reports and other periodical material; Section E. Miscellaneous additional material.

The main American relevance of the collection is the material about trade union sponsored emigration to the United States.[3] In Section A the volumes of notes on various unions and industries include some reference to emigration, mainly copies from printed matter - see, e.g., volume XI for the Amalgamated Society of Carpenters Emigration Fund, and volume XVI for the Amalgamated Society of Engineers Emigration Fund; Section A also includes, in volume XLVII, seven pages of notes, 1913-4, on women in trade unions in the United States. The large collection of rules and journals in Sections C and D contain, for some unions, information on the subject of emigration, including, in C. 86, the manuscript rules, n.d., of the Potters' Emigration Society, London District Committee.

FARRER COLLECTION ON BANKING AND CURRENCY. 1864-98. (Coll. S.R. (SR) 1018)

Sir Thomas Henry Farrer, 1st Baron Farrer (1819-99), was an active opponent of bimetallism and one of the founders in 1895 of the Gold Standard Defence Association. The collection consists of eleven volumes of manuscript and printed letters and papers, and of news-cuttings. These mainly concern Indian currency, but an examination of the typescript calendar showed the following relevant material (*Letters unless otherwise stated*):

Volume I, items 1-2. 28 Sept. and 9 Oct. 1897, Charles Francis Adams to Farrer, giving an opinion on the importance of a statement of British policy on the Indian currency question.

Volume I, item 55. 8 Jan. 1897, E.L. Godkin to Farrer, concerning the visit to England of Senator Edward Oliver Wolcott, a bimetallist.

Volume III, item 55. 4 May 1894, Cecil [Spring-Rice?] to Stephen [Spring-Rice?], on American monetary policy and the free coinage of silver. (Typescript.)

Volume III, item 108. 13 Nov. 1898, Horace White to Lord Farrer, on financial conditions in the United States and India.

Volume VI, item 3. Horace White, *Answers to Questions of the Gold and Silver Commission*, 29 Sept. 1887. (Printed.)

Volume VI, items 6-7. [Sir David Miller Barbour], *Course of Trade between England and the United States*, Aug. 1887; and *Alteration of the Relative Scale of Prices in England and the United States*, Sept. 1887. (Printed.)

Volume VI, item 29. 21 Sept. 1887, David Ames Wells to Farrer, concerning the monetary conditions of California. (Printed.)

Volume VIII, item 56. Statistics of English and American national banks, the data for the latter covering 1864-93. *c.* 1894.

HUGHES, THOMAS (1822-96). Microfilm. 1880-93. (Acc. N.=M655a)

A microfilm presented by the Tennessee State Archives in 1959 of letters, newspapers, and pamphlets relating to Thomas Hughes and the foundation and management of the attempted colony of Rugby, Tenn. (Not catalogued.)

1. Much of this material has been used by M.F. Lloyd-Prichard for the introduction to Bray's *A Voyage from Utopia* (London, 1957). See also H.J. Carr, 'John Francis Bray', *Economica*, n.s. vol. vii, pp. 397-415, 1940; and M.F. Joliffe, 'John Francis Bray', *International Review of Social History*, vol. iv, pp. 1-36, 1939.

2. Published in London, 1957.

3. This material has been used by W.S. Shepperson, *British Emigration to North America* (Oxford, 1957), and by C. Erickson, *American Industry and the European Immigrant, 1860-1885* (London and Cambridge, Mass., 1957).

PASSFIELD PAPERS. 1873-1938.

The papers of Sidney Webb, 1st Baron Passfield (1859-1947), and his wife, Beatrice (Potter) Webb (1858-1943).

I. Diaries.

Fifty-eight manuscript notebooks (each with two typescript copies) contain Beatrice Webb's diaries for 1873-1943.[4]

Volume 1 includes a precocious account of her first visit to the United States, Sept.-Dec. 1873. Her account is mainly topographical although while in Chicago she visited public schools; and in Salt Lake City she showed interest in Mormonism.

Volumes 17 and 18 are wholly concerned with the visit of Mr. and Mrs. Webb to the United States, 29 Mar-10 July 1898; and volume 19, pp. 1-10 (of the typescript copy) with their stay in the recently annexed Hawaii, 13-20 July 1898. The Webbs ranged from New York to San Francisco. They made a special point of visiting universities and colleges. Among those they met, and in most cases interviewed, were Charles Francis Adams, Jane Addams, Governor Altgeld of Illinois, Senator Bailey, D.R. Dewey, President Eliot of Harvard, Worthington C. Ford, E.L. Godkin, Professor Jenks, Robert Lincoln, Henry Cabot Lodge, Seth Low, Josiah Quincy, Thomas B. Reed, Theodore Roosevelt, Albert Shaw, Morse Stephens, Von Holst, Mayor Van Wyck of New York, Lester Ward, Woodrow Wilson, Governor Wolcott of Massachusetts, and Carroll D. Wright. While in Washington, D.C., they attended sessions of both the House and the Senate, and observed the war fever over Cuba. They interviewed Reed and Wilson on the workings of American national government; stayed at Hull House in Chicago; and probed deeply into Mormon beliefs and practices in Salt Lake City, Utah. But their chief concern was the study of American municipal government, and for their reports and views of this topic the diary is invaluable. They devoted much time to observing the operations of Tammany Hall in New York.

Volume 18, pp. 58-70, is an essay entitled 'Superficial notes on American characteristics'.

II. Letters.

(*a*) Postcard from New York, 17 Sept. 1888, and a letter from Boston, 13 Oct. 1888, to Graham Wallas, written by Sidney Webb during his brief visit to the United States. The letter describes the Massachusetts Institute of Technology and Harvard University, and gives a detailed account of the wages of workers in the *Atlantic Monthly* printing works. Webb is of the opinion that Cleveland will carry all the doubtful states in the presidential election.

(*b*) Seven letters written during the Webbs' visit to the United States in 1898. Four from Beatrice Webb to Lady Kate Courtney and one to Mary Playne cover much the same ground as the diary entries. A letter, 26 Apr., from Sidney Webb to George Bernard Shaw, discusses the visits to Washington, D.C., and to various universities, and describes the American machinery of central government as 'infantile'; another, of 5 June, describes Chicago as 'viler than tongue can tell and hopeless as the Inferno'.

(*c*) Two letters to Beatrice Webb and one to Sidney Webb by Sir Charles Philips Trevelyan while both they and he were in the United States in 1898. He touches on the corruption of Pittsburgh, Pa., city government and the attitudes to organization, etc., of the steelworkers; the filthiness of Chicago; war fever; the progress of the campaign for municipal ownership of utilities in the West. He met and describes Altgeld and William Jennings Bryan.

(*d*) Typescript copy of a six-page letter, *c.* Mar. 1924, from Beatrice Webb to a Miss Thomas on the differences in Britain and the United States on the questions of the regulation of women's labour and equal pay.

(*e*) Typewritten letter, Knoxville, Tenn., 14 Feb. 1938, from Herman Finer to Beatrice Webb, describing his work as director of an 'Administrative Study of the Tennessee Valley Authority'.

(*f*) Letter, Cardiff, 17 Sept. 1938, from Selig Perlman to Beatrice Webb, on American 'industrial government', especially in the coal industry.

VII. Articles and books.

Beatrice Webb, 'Round the English-speaking world', 1930's. A draft chapter in typescript for inclusion in *Our Partnership* but omitted by the editors (see their Preface, p.v). Written in the mid-1930's, it is simply a more polished version of the diary. The first 102 pages (with footnotes, which are not, of course, in the diary) relate to the American part of the journey.

HARRISON, FREDERIC (1831-1923). English writer and positivist philosopher. Correspondence. 1888-1915.

(*a*) Two letters, 1900, 1910, from Raymond H. Arnot in America, president of the Frederic Harrison Club, discussing positivism and praising Harrison's works on the subject. (1/1)

(*b*) Letter, 1901, from Eugene Cary in Chicago, discussing Theodore Roosevelt: 'Certainly, his favorite adjective - "strenuous" - applies to him in an especial degree. He has high ideals of official duty and of the office of government....Of one thing we may be sure: that while he holds the office *he will be President*.' (1/26)

(*c*) Two letters, 1901 and n.d., from Charles A. Codman in New York, praising Harrison's work and discussing Comte and positivist thought. Also some comment on New York politics at the turn of the century. (1/28)

(*d*) Two letters, 1888 and n.d., from Edward King, describing the impact of positivist ideas on America and introducing a young man who would like to meet Harrison. (1/45)

(*e*) Five letters from Charles Eliot Norton, 1877-1901, discussing a variety of subjects, including American politics: 'The descent from Washington to McKinley is as from Gabriel to Lucifer, and to-day McKinley is the more "popular" of the two....Roosevelt is a better man, but he has not equally the art & craft by which popularity is to be gained.' Also two letters, 1912, from Norton's daughter Sara, with some comments on America. (1/95)

(*f*) Six typewritten letters, 1901-12, from Theodore Roosevelt, mostly courtesy notes, but containing occasional comments of interest, e.g., 'I have always said that what we needed for women was equality of consideration, but recognition of the fact that there was complete difference of function. The family is the unit in the State. It is more important than the State, because it is on the family that the State rests; and in the family the woman is and ought to be supreme.' (1/100)

(*g*) Fifteen letters from Katrina (Mrs. Spencer) Trask, *c.* 1905-15, almost exclusively of a personal nature, with some effusive praise of Harrison's writings. (1/110)

Other American correspondents include Charles F. Adams, W.C. Bamburgh, Joseph H. Choate, E.B. Culling, Francis W. Halsey, David Hutcheson, Henry James, George Philips, and Ruth Putnam. These letters are mostly concerned with personal matters, or consist of acknowledgements and expressions of thanks. The letters of Ethelberta Harrison, Frederic's wife, contain occasional letters from a few Americans, including Henry James.

4. See *My Apprenticeship* [to 1892] (London, 1926); *Our Partnership* [1892-1911], ed. by Barbara Drake and Margaret Cole (London, 1948); *Beatrice Webb's Diaries, 1912-1924*, ed. by Margaret Cole (London, 1952); and *Beatrice Webb's Diaries, 1924-1932*, ed. by Margaret Cole (London, 1956).

MOREL, EDMUND DENE (1873-1924). Papers.[5]

Political reformer; founder of the Union of Democratic Control. (This organization is said to have had some initial success in the United States, and it is likely that a thorough search of the very large collection of Morel's papers would yield some letters from Americans on its general work.)

Morel visited America in the last quarter of 1904 to arouse support for an investigation into Belgian misrule in the Congo Free State. Specifically, he addressed the Universal Peace Conference in Boston, October 1904, and interviewed Theodore Roosevelt and his Secretary of State, John Hay, on the topic. A file in the collection, 'Congo Reform Association: America', contains correspondence and papers (64 manuscript and 104 typed letters, and 8 printed papers), 1904-11. Most of the correspondence arises either directly from the visit, or from the associations established as a result of it. The letters, many to and from prominent journalists and publicists, show vividly how Morel built up in a very short time an effective lobby. A student of American attitudes towards imperialism would find this collection useful, particularly:

(*a*) A series of wide-ranging and thoughtful letters from Robert E. Park, the sociologist, as secretary of the Massachusetts Commission for International Justice.

(*b*) A series from Thomas S. Barbour of the American Baptist Missionary Union.

(*c*) Two long letters from Senator J.T. Morgan of Alabama, 29 June and 6 Oct. 1904, both dealing candidly with the American Negro problem and speculating on the possibility of encouraging the emigration of educated American Negroes to help administer a reformed Congo Free State.

(*d*) 'Report of the Honorary Secretary of the Congo Reform Association on his visit to the United States', written by Morel for his British committee some time early in 1905, and containing an account of his short interview with Theodore Roosevelt, and of a longer and more informative one with John Hay.

SULZER, WILLIAM. Papers: 1 volume. 1916-20.

Sulzer, Democratic governor of New York 1913, was a Tammany Brave who turned honest in office, and so was impeached. But these papers, an isolated bound volume whose origin cannot be traced, relate only to investments - oil in Oklahoma, gold in Alaska, etc. (Coll. Misc. 396)

WEBSTER, SIR CHARLES KINGSLEY (1886-1961). Historian and internationalist. Papers. 1925-52.

Webster was a prominent British historian who began his academic career in 1914 as professor of modern history at the University of Liverpool. By the 1920's he had become a specialist in international affairs, and was appointed Wilson Professor of International Politics at the University College of Wales, Aberystwyth, in 1923. From 1928 to 1932 he taught at Harvard University, and although he returned to England in 1932 to teach at the London School of Economics, his professional experience and interests enabled him to serve in several American-related jobs during the Second World War. From 1939 to 1941 he was the head of the American section of the Royal Institute of International Affairs, and from 1941 to 1942 he was in New York as Director of the British Library of Information. After the war he attended the Dunbarton Oaks Conference in 1944 as a Foreign Office advisor; he was also a delegate to the U.N. Conference on International Organization at San Francisco in 1945. Webster again visited the United States in 1952 as a researcher at Princeton's Institute for Advanced Study.[6]

I. Section 1: Correspondence, 1925-42.

(*a*) Letters concerning Webster's visit to America in 1925. (1/8)

(*b*) Correspondence on Anglo-American relations and items dealing with Webster's Harvard professorship, 1926-9. (1/9)

(*c*) Discussions of U.S. politics and several offers of a permanent appointment at Harvard as professor of American history, 1930-4. (1/11-13)

(*d*) Comments on American opinion of the war, 1939-40. (1/17, 19-20)

(*e*) Information on Webster's visit to the U.S.A. from 31 Mar. to 15 May 1941, and his appointment as Director of the British Library of Information in New York. (1/21)

(*f*) Semi-official correspondence received and answered when Webster was Director of the British Library of Information, Aug.-July 1942. (1/22)

Americans figuring in Webster's correspondence include William E. Borah, J.B. Conant, J.K. Fairbank, Alger Hiss, J. Franklin Jameson, William L. Langer, Kenneth B. Murdock, Robert Oppenheimer, Arthur Schlesinger, and Adlai Stevenson.

II. Section 8: Papers, 1941.

Papers relating to Webster's visit to the U.S.A. in 1941, containing background memoranda, his report to the Minister of Information, and material arising from the visit, Apr.-July 1941. (8/13)

III. Section 20: Papers, 1952.

Papers on Webster's visit to the U.S.A. in 1952 to spend the first term of the academic year at the Institute for Advanced Study at Princeton, including correspondence on administrative arrangements, etc. Also correspondence on a lecture delivered at the Air War College and work in U.S. libraries. (20/1)

The Webster Papers also include much information on his teaching at Harvard, some miscellaneous correspondence with Charles P. Howard on Anglo-American relations, 1930, and numerous references to U.S. participation in the creation of the United Nations.

BEVERIDGE, WILLIAM HENRY, 1st Baron (1879-1963). British economist. Papers. 1928-61.

I. Visits Abroad (XI): Correspondence and diaries, 1928-61.

(*a*) Correspondence about conference of economists held at Dartmouth College, 1928. (23 JII 1b)

(*b*) Correspondence about visit to Rockefeller Foundation in New York and Huntington Library in California, 1930. (26 JII 1b)

(*c*) Correspondence about visit to see aspects of the American recovery programme, 1933-4. (27 JII 1a, c)

(*d*) Diary of visit to America, 20 Oct. - 28 Nov. 1933. (29 JII 1a, c)

(*e*) Correspondence about visit to North America to promote the Beveridge Plan, his comprehensive social security system, 1943-4. (31 JII 1d, e, h)

(*f*) Correspondence from Americans about the Plan, 1943. (34 JII 1d. f)

(*g*) Diary of a visit to the U.S.A., 2 May - 15 July 1943. (36 JII 1d)

(*h*) Correspondence about visit to the U.S.A., 1954. (855 II 2a)

(*i*) Diary of a visit to the U.S.A., 31 May - 27 June 1961. (91 A1. 100)

II. Addresses on America, 1933-4.

(*a*) Five volumes, entitled 'Situation in the U.S.A., 1933', containing newspaper cuttings, speeches and notes for speeches, and other correspondence, regarding Beveridge's addresses in America, 1933-4. (Col. Misc. 8, 1-5)

5. See Robert Wuliger, 'The idea of economic imperialism with special reference to the life and works of E.D. Morel', Ph.D. thesis, University of London, 1953.

6. An American view of Webster, written during his lifetime and giving some evaluation of his work, is John Edwin Fagg's 'Sir Charles Webster', in S.W. Halperin (ed.), *Some Twentieth-Century Historians* (Chicago, 1961).

(*b*) Two volumes entitled 'Addresses on America', consisting of MS. notes and typewritten speeches discussing America's 'New Deal' programme for economic recovery. (Col. Misc. 8, 6-7)
III. General and Personal Correspondence.
Among Beveridge's general and personal correspondence are letters from numerous Americans, including Dwight D. Eisenhower, Felix Frankfurter, Robert Frost, Oscar Hammerstein, John D. and David Rockefeller, and Franklin Roosevelt.
IV. Miscellaneous.
The Beveridge Papers also contain numerous pamphlets, memoranda, lectures, etc., concerning his work to promote the Beveridge Plan in America.

DALTON, HUGH (1887-1962). British economist and politician. Papers. 1939-50.

(*a*) Sir John Simon to Dalton on Sir John Pratt's letter to *The Times* concerning the U.S.A. and Manchuria, 13 Jan. 1939. (5/2)
(*b*) Dalton to John Snyder, U.S. Treasury Secretary, on financial arrangements for Germany, 25 Nov. 1946. (9/2)
(*c*) Two letters from Harold Laski to Dalton, 1947, discussing, among other matters, England's financial relations with the U.S.A. (9/3)
(*d*) Dalton to R.F. Harrod concerning his speech on the American loan, 27 Oct. 1947. (9/3)
(*e*) Copy letter of Dalton to Clement Attlee regarding Truman's statement on the atomic bomb, 30 Nov. 1950. (9/9)
The Dalton Papers include, of course, some references to America in documents dealing primarily with other issues, but these do not seem of sufficient significance to require individual listing.

LETTERS OF EMIGRANTS TO AMERICA.

Six archive boxes of original emigrant letters and photostat and typewritten copies of letters are deposited in the Library. Although they mostly date from the first half of the nineteenth century, there are some from both the eighteenth and the latter half of the nineteenth century. The letters commonly contain information about the Atlantic crossing, comparative prices, land values, the state of crops, wages and industry, advice to prospective immigrants, and family news. The following letters in the collection are originals:
(*a*) Letter, 1767, from James Murray in New York to Rev. Baptiste Boyd in Co. Tyrone, Ireland. Gives an optimistic description of the country and of the opportunities to make money in America.
(*b*) *c*. 150 letters from the Fridge and Murdock families of Philadelphia, later Baltimore, to relatives living in Elgin and Forres, Scotland. Alexander Fridge emigrated to Philadelphia in 1785 and later set up a dry goods business in Baltimore. The letters contain much information about life, politics, and trade in Philadelphia and Baltimore; and American investments made on behalf of Scottish relatives.
(*c*) Letter, 1786, from John Wilson, Philadelphia, to Jonathan Dixon, Cockermouth, Cumberland. Trade and politics.
(*d*) Fifteen letters, 1816-30, from T.L. Ogden, New York, to Mr. or Miss Lawrence, c/o Forde & Co., Liverpool. Stockbroker and land agent. The letters are about American investments made on behalf of the Misses Lawrence. Ogden was also interested in settling land on an estate in the St. Lawrence area, and during the 1820's his letters tell of improvements to the land, the type of settlers required, and answer queries raised by prospective immigrants.
(*e*) Three letters, 15 Jan. - 14 Nov. 1817, from Samuel Williams, broker, of London, to Forde, Liverpool, about the purchase of Louisiana stock.
(*f*) Two letters to Mr. Poulton, Sr., Hounslow, Middlesex. One, 10 Mar. 1834, from his son George Poulton, Troy, N.Y., a schoolteacher. The other, 26 May 1834, from his daughter-in-law Mary Poulton, Lockport, N.Y. Recent immigrants. Misfortunes.
(*g*) Nine letters from Alexander McKenzie to James and John McKenzie in Scotland, 1840-7. Primarily concern McKenzie's finances and his farming activities in Canada. Also three letters from John Baird to James McKenzie, 1848-51.
(*h*) John Norman, Harlem, N.Y., 30 Jan. 1848, to John Philpot, Walpole, Suffolk. Also a letter, 10 May 1854, from Mary Smith, Harlem, to Mr. Self, Woodbridge, Suffolk, about the death of John Norman.
(*i*) Two letters, 15 May and 19 Sept. 1850, from John Yates, Hall Town, Va., to Messrs. W.E. Bleaymire, Penrith. Property owner. Claims to English estates.
(*j*) One letter, 1850, from Thomas Rutter, an emigrant living in Buffalo, N.Y. Discusses his voyage across the Atlantic and his trip to Buffalo via Albany.
(*k*) Letter, 1851, from 'E', in Jail Hospital, Chester, Pa., to Rev. Bleaymire, Penrith, Cumberland. Needing money.
(*l*) Twenty-eight letters, 1853-66, from Titus Crawshaw in the U.S. to his father, William Crawshaw of Huddersfield, Yorks. The letters are written from various places in the States, including New Jersey, Pennsylvania and Virginia. Those dating from the 1850's mostly consist of comments on Crawshaw's difficulties in finding work and complaints about the 'stagnation of trade'. After the outbreak of the Civil War Crawshaw was drafted into the Union Army, and writes about his wartime activities until 1862, when he is discharged due to ill health. The last few letters continue Crawshaw's pre-war lament over his failure to find wealth in America.
(*m*) Four letters, 1857-73, from Ch. Aglionby, Charles Town, Va., to Messrs. Bleaymire, Penrith. Farmer. Property in England and losses during the Civil War.
(*n*) Four letters, 1864-80, from Ann and Alfred Jones, Missouri, to C.R. Wace, solicitor, Shropshire. Farmers. Mostly about property in England.
(*o*) John Wiles, Camp of the 152nd Regiment, New York State Volunteers, Army of the Potomac, near Stevensburg, Va. Letter, 20 Jan. 1864, describing army life and conditions in the Southern states.
(*p*) Letter, 1870, from Robert Savery, Phoenix, Arizona, to Richard Scarlett [in London?]. Farming and irrigating government land.
(*q*) Three letters, 1888, from J.W. Jendwine, Bowman's Bluff, N.C., to Mr. Wace, solicitor, Shropshire. Gentleman farmer. Farming conditions, information about borrowing money in U.S.; tries to borrow money to start a general store.

SCHOOL OF ORIENTAL AND AFRICAN STUDIES, University of London, Malet Street, London WC1E 7HP

PAPERS OF SIR WILLIAM MACKINNON. Private correspondence. 1865-93.

(*a*) Letters (six files) from George Augustus Thomson of the Florida Land and Colonization Company, Ltd., to Sir William Mackinnon, 1865-93.
(*b*) Letters (eight files) from Gerald Waller, agent of the Florida Land and Colonization Company, Ltd., to Mackinnon, 1877-84.
(*c*) Letters (one file) from Collis P. Huntingdon, the American railway magnate, to Mackinnon, 1887-91.
(*d*) Letters (one file) from Captain J.M. Lachlan, general manager, U.S. and Brazil Steamship Company, to Mackinnon, 1888-91.

PAPERS OF SIR HENRY MORTIMER DURAND (1850-1924). 1870-1907.

British Ambassador to Washington, 1904-6.

(*a*) Fifteen diaries, 1870-1907, including comment on his years in Washington.

(*b*) Foreign Office papers: letters, telegrams, and dispatches, 1901-6.

(*c*) Speeches, 1904-7, mainly in the U.S.

(*d*) Miscellaneous correspondence, press cuttings, photographs, etc., relating to Durand's Washington appointment.

THE LIBRARY, UNIVERSITY COLLEGE, Gower Street, London WC1E 6BT

BENTHAM, JEREMY (1748-1832). Manuscripts.

Bentham's papers came to University College through John Bowring, his executor - see a *Catalogue of the Manuscripts of Jeremy Bentham in the Library of University College, London*, compiled by A. Taylor Milne (London, 1937). The Americana is here listed under boxes and folders and is, indeed, listed rather than surveyed, since the labyrinthian character of the papers almost defeats summary. (*Letters unless otherwise stated.*)

Box 9, folder 3. Epping, 5 Oct. 1818, from Governor William Plumer of New Hampshire to Bentham, stating that he has communicated Bentham's papers to the legislature which has referred them to a committee.

Box 10, folder 26. 25 Jan. 1830, from Bentham to Southwood Smith, concerning a revised and augmented version of Edward Livingston's penal code for Louisiana[1] (copy sent by Livingston to Bentham, 10 Aug. 1829). Livingston has asked Bentham to prepare an article on his code for the *Jurist* and Bentham passes the request on to Smith.

Box 12, folder 2. Correspondence, 1817. Five letters from W. Vaughan and two from J. Adams Smith to Bentham; letters from Bentham to John Quincy Adams (two), Francis Place, and Vaughan. Vaughan and Bentham were interchanging books and papers, Vaughan furnishing Bentham with information about the United States. John Adams Smith, nephew of John Quincy Adams, was on terms of friendship with Bentham and sent him information, pamphlets, and papers from the United States. Bentham requests John Quincy Adams to forward copies of his codification circulars to various people in America, including the President, Vice-President, Secretary of the Treasury, Professor Cooper of Philadelphia and governors of twenty states; a draft letter from Bentham to Adams asks for information about legal and religious matters.

Box 12, folder 3. Correspondence, 1817-8. Letters to Bentham from Henry M. Francis, Francis Place, Richard Rush, and J. Adams Smith (two); letters from Bentham to Francis (one copy, one draft) and to Smith. Mostly concerned with the circulation in the United States of Bentham's codification proposals. Letter, J.H. Hoe to Smith, asking as to receipt of packet of letters in the United States. Portion of *Niles' Register* (already in Bentham's possession), 9 May 1818. Letter concerning actions of General Jackson, unaddressed, unsigned, undated.

Box 12, folder 4. Correspondence, 1821. Four (one copy) letters from Richard Rush to Bentham, and three from Bentham to Rush; mostly making appointments to meet, but a few have information about the United States. Two letters from J. Adams Smith to Bentham concerning the exchange of pamphlets and tracts. Draft of a letter, 5 Aug. 1821, from Bentham to the editor of the *National Calendar* of the United States, requesting an index to the calendar (not sent).

Box 12, folder 6. Correspondence, 1822. Letter from Bentham to Rush; two letters from Rush and three from J. Adams Smith to Bentham. Concern exchange of pamphlets, introductions, invitations, etc.

Box 12, folder 9. Correspondence, 1823. Three letters to Bentham from Rush and two from Bentham to Rush: deal with the arrangement of a meeting for Bentham to give Rush some news (about Spain?). Letter, Philadelphia, 27 Aug. 1823, from Charles Jared Ingersoll to Bentham; account of recent happenings in the United States said to be (but not) enclosed.

Box 12, folder 10. 29 May 1823, from Bentham to Smith, inviting the American Consul, Hunter, to dine with him; and Smith's reply, 30 May.

Box 12, folder 12. 4 Dec. 1823, from Bentham to Rush, requesting a second copy of the New York constitution and assistance in transmitting a paper to 'your secretary of secretaries' (Copy). Rush, in replies of 5 and 8 December, promises to help.

Box 12, folder 13. Five letters to Bentham from Rush and three from Bentham to Rush, Jan. and Feb. 1824. Rush is about to open negotiations with the British government 'of great scope and more than common interest'. Bentham has lent Rush a copy of a letter from 'Col. L.S.' (Stanhope), and wants to borrow American books.

Box 12, folder 16. 18 June 1824, from Henry M. Francis to Bentham, introducing a Mr. Phillips, an officer of the American Army, and asking that Bentham explain the chrestomathic plan of education to him 'for the benefit of my countrymen'.

Box 17, folder 4. Extracts from Lord Sheffield's *Observation of the Commerce of the American States* (London, 1783). In Bentham's hand, with page references; five sheets. These extracts form part of the outlines of the different projects begun by Bentham on the *Manual of Political Economy*, *c.* 1790-1800.

Box 21, folder 4. 1811-9.

(*a*) Draft of a letter, first sheet of postscript dated 9 Aug. 1811 and second sheet 1 Oct. 1811, from Bentham to President Madison discussing constitutional amendment and asking for various books and law reports.

(*b*) Information in Bentham's hand from Aaron Burr about legal codification; entered under places from which Burr wrote and containing notes on when to write to him, through whom, and under what alias, Oct. 1811.

(*c*) June 1817, from Bentham to John Quincy Adams on the law of libel, religious freedom, and the Unitarian and Trinitarian controversy in the United States. Adams answers in the margins of the same letter.

(*d*) Form of a letter of credence compared: from the United States President, and from George III. 1819.

Box 21, folder 5. 'Tabular Digest of the Constitution of the Anglo-American United States', June and Nov. 1818 (*c.* 60 pages). The manuscript, most of it in a copyist's hand, is largely from a work by Dr. William L. Smith of South Carolina, *Comparative View of the Constitutions of the Several States* (Philadelphia, 1796).

Box 21, folder 6. Parliamentary Reform Bill, United States election table notes (*c.* 15 pages). Bentham's comments, Oct. and Nov. 1818, on American constitutions, modes of voting, etc.

Box 21, folder 7. Collectanea. United States passport. *National Gazette*, 9 Nov. 1820. Governor's message, Pennsylvania, 1816. *National Intelligencer*, 15 May 1817. Letter of Secretary of Treasury transmitting estimate of appropriations, 1817. Printed testimony in

1. *A System of Penal Law for the State of Louisiana* (Philadelphia, [1833]).

the case of an ejectment pending for the recovery of Dr. William Oxley's estate in the city of Philadelphia, 1821, 1823, 1827 (17 items, none in Bentham's hand); these give information about politics and morals in the United States.

Box 23, folder 1. United States Constitutional Code: Bicameral system, anti-senatica. This is a marginal outline only. (7 sheets) Nov. 1829.

Box 24, folder 15. Tripoli. Bentham to John Quincy Adams, 10-23 Jan. 1823. Fourteen sheets in Bentham's hand, beginning 'The Barbary powers are a constant plague to you. I am not without hopes of seeing you rid of it'. Support of United States wanted in attempt to reform the government of Tripoli. (There is codification material on the backs of several sheets.)

Box 24, folder 16. Tripoli. Hassuna D'Ghies, Ambassador from the Sovereign of Tripoli at the Court of St. James, to John Quincy Adams, Secretary of State. Jan. and Feb. 1823. Ostensibly written by D'Ghies, but written for him by Bentham, this is a request to the United States to back the reform party in Tripoli. Bentham's manuscript is written on the back of cancelled codification offer manuscript. (58 pages copy and outline, 65 pages Bentham's manuscript.)

Box 44, folder 2. Rudiments of the United States Constitutional Code: marginal notes in Bentham's hand. 15-17 Mar. 1823 (3 sheets).

Box 44, folder 3.[2] United States Constitutional Code: An attack on the second chamber. Also codification material on back of sheets. 17 Mar. 1823 - 12 Feb. 1825.

Box 44, folder 4. United States Constitutional Code. Attack on second chamber, etc. In hands of various copyists; copied 1822-30.

Box 44, folder 5. United States Constitutional Code. Appendix in folder inscribed '1830 June 7, U.S. Antisenatica'. With further copy of manuscripts concerning second chamber. *c.* 1823-4. About twenty-five sheets, in copyist's hand.

Box 64, folder 2. Penal code: Neal's extracts. Apr.-Aug. 1826 (*c.* 120 sheets). These are brief digests in copyist's hand apparently intended by John Neal, Bentham's secretary, to serve as a guide to penal law in the United States.

Box 158, folder 4. United States codification offer, 1811: Bentham to the people of the United States and to the President. Letter, 1817, Bentham to Madison (35 sheets). Marginal outlines in copyist's hand, with a few insertions in Bentham's hand.

Box 169, folder 19. *c.* 1781 from Bentham possibly to Benjamin Franklin. Draft of a letter, probably not sent, about future codification.

OGDEN MANUSCRIPTS COLLECTION. Letters. 1808-78.

(*a*) Two letters from Aaron Burr to Jeremy Bentham: 22 Aug. 1808, 'It has been my misfortune to attract the attention of Lord Hawkesbury' (2nd Earl of Liverpool); is sending articles to Bentham which may assist in the cross-examination. 21-28 Dec. 1808, describing his travels in Oxford and Birmingham, and the people he has met *en route*. (MS. Ogden 66)

(*b*) John Bright. 826 letters, 1847-78, to his second wife, Margaret Elizabeth Leatham. Bright often refers to American affairs, particularly immediately before and during the Civil War, but only in a commonplace manner. (MS. Ogden 65) (Calendared.)

(*c*) Harriet Martineau. Eleven letters addressed to William Tait, publisher of *Tait's Edinburgh Magazine*, are inserted in a copy of the first edition of Harriet Martineau's *Autobiography, with Memorials by Maria Weston Chapman*, 3 vols. (London, 1877). Letter, 16 July 1837, deals with the reception of her book, *Society in America* (London, 1837), and comments on the work still to be done in the cause of abolition in America. (MS. Ogden 101)

BROUGHAM, HENRY PETER, 1st Baron Brougham and Vaux (1778-1868). Correspondence. 1809-65.

Statesman. A collection of *c.* 60,000 letters to, and a great many from, Lord Brougham. The letters reflect Brougham's extremely wide range of interests and activities, particularly in the causes of law reform, abolition of the slave trade and slavery, and education, as well as international affairs. Although he had some American correspondents and there are a number of letters dealing with American legal matters, the greatest number of letters with American interest to emerge are between Brougham and British correspondents. These include people with whom he corresponded over a period of years and who discussed all political affairs, including American and British abolitionists and opponents of the slave trade. An index to the letters under the name of the sender has been compiled; an inspection of this index reveals as of especial interest:

(*a*) American correspondents. Edward Everett, 21 letters, 1838-61. James A. Hamilton, lawyer and politician, two letters, 1842. Thomas Jefferson, copy of a letter, 25 Apr. 1824, to Rush. A. Stevenson, two letters, 1838-9. Charles Sumner, 16 letters, 1838-59. Lewis Tappan, three letters, 1839, 1843. B.B. Thatcher, author and lawyer, three letters, 1838.

(*b*) Letters on American legal matters. John Bell, Manchester, 3 Aug. 1830. John Christophers, 2 May 1851. Robert Dodge, 15 June 1847. Thomas Falconer, county court judge and legal author, six letters, 1842-54. David Graham, American lawyer and author, two letters, 1850. Henry Hiort, 27 Feb. 1839. Henry Knill, three letters, 1837-9. John Charles Laycock, n.d., but endorsed 1847. John Livingston, 1 Feb. 1851. R. Shelton Mackenzie, author and journalist, three letters, 1842-50. William Pentland, 6 Aug. 1850. Silas Moore Stilwell, American lawyer and financial writer, three letters, 1842, 1847.

(*c*) Some British correspondents discussing American affairs:

Baring, Alexander, 1st Baron Ashburton. A number of letters, 1842-7, including: 24 Sept. 1842, on the treaty he has negotiated with the United States; 6 Sept. 1843, on relations with the United States; 26 Sept. 1843, on Lord Palmerston's 'flippant opinions of America', his estimate of Thomas Jefferson; 27 Jan. 1844, American policy in Oregon and Texas.

Cassell, John, publisher and popular educator. Three letters: 25 Nov. 1859, leaving for America, the social science movement; January, endorsed 1860, on conditions in the United States; 2 Nov. 1860, on the success of his visit to the United States.

Copley, John Singleton, Baron Lyndhurst, Lord Chancellor. Many letters, 1828-63, including 20 Aug. endorsed '1852, the Yankee question settled'; n.d. [1852], the 'American affair'; n.d. [1858], right of search; 30 Sept. endorsed 1859, American policy; 12 Nov. endorsed 1859, relations with the United States, a contemporary account of Lord Chatham's speech on the American situation; n.d., endorsed 1861, the American situation; 18 Aug. 1862, Americans offended with Lord Brougham; 2 Sept. endorsed 1862, Northerners confident that the South will accept the abolition of slavery; 8 Oct. 1862, Lincoln and the Southern slaves; 24 Oct. endorsed 1862, Civil War; 18 Aug. endorsed 1863, bitterness of American feeling towards Britain; n.d. [1863], settlement of Northerners in South prolonging the Civil War; n.d. endorsed 1863, victory of Vicksburg great blow to South.

2. Part of this material was published in C.W. Everett, ed., *Anti-Senatica. An Attack on the American Senate, sent by Jeremy Bentham to Andrew Jackson* (Northampton, Mass., 1926) (Smith College Studies in History, vol. xi, no. 4).

Gladstone, William Ewart. Six letters: 31 July 1843, Slave Trade Suppression Bill; 27 Dec. 1861, the American constitution and rupture between Northern and Southern states; 15 Jan. 1862, Seward's dispatch and the attitude of British law officers to his doctrine; 9 Sept. 1862, the American Civil War and sympathy drawn towards the South; 20 Feb. 1863, Lord Brougham's views on the anti-slavery policy of Lincoln; 12 Sept. 1864, hopes success at Atlanta, Ga., will not encourage the Federal cause too much.

Hall, Basil (1788-1844), naval captain and author. Letter, 31 Oct. 1828, on his visit to New York, American mechanics' institutes, Carvells of New York, best agent for the publications of the Society for the Diffusion of Useful Knowledge.

Law, Edward, 1st Earl of Ellenborough. Many letters, 1831-65, including: 9 Dec. 1845 and Dec. 1861 on France and America; 21 Jan. 1863 on Lincoln's Proclamation, 'one of the most wicked acts in history'.

Martineau, Harriet. Four letters. Three, 1836, on American copyright, and one, 21 Nov. 1858, on the American Anti-Slavery Society.[3]

Parkes, Joseph. Many letters, 1834-65, particularly on the Civil War.

There are also letters from Lord Brougham, 1 Aug. 1812 to T. Thornely on the War of 1812, and 30 Sept. 1842 to Lord Grey on the American offer on the Boundary Question in 1833.

(*d*) Letters about slavery and the slave trade with particular reference to America. (Many of these are taken from series of letters covering a period of years.) Sir Thomas Fowell Buxton, 12 letters, 1827-44. Louis Alexis Chamerovzow, secretary of the British and Foreign Anti-Slavery Society, many letters, 1855-66. Thomas Clarkson, several letters, 1838-43. Thomas Denman, 1st Baron Denman, many letters, 1838-51, including several on the African Squadron. George Hamilton Gordon, 4th Earl of Aberdeen, letters, 1841-58. Hunter Gordon, 1843-4. Joseph Sturge, 1837-59. William Wilberforce, 1809-31. Zachary Macaulay, 1811-34.

There are letters from various anti-slavery societies to Brougham, mainly 1830-40, which, though largely concerned with the West Indies, also contain American references; there are also four letters, 1859-62, from the Young Men's Anti-Slavery Society.

(*e*) Letters containing miscellaneous information about America. Antonio de Anina to Professor Manvers, 20 Apr. 1857, about life in Memphis, Tenn. Thomas Dodds, 18 July endorsed 1835, United States newspapers; comparative prices. Henry Jones, 6 Feb. endorsed 1838, the poems of Phillis Wheatley. G. Joy, 19 Apr. 1848, Orders in Council and the United States. J. Larish, 19 Oct. 1812, news from Philadelphia of impending attack on Canada. James Lock, 23 May 1822, Russia, America, and England. George McHenry, 27 Aug. 1861, sending a copy of a speech by Jas. A. Bayard. Thomas Martin, 1 Aug. 1812, England and America.John G. Parker, 25 Aug. 1842, sad case of Americans transported to New South Wales.

(*f*) Emigration.

Although Brougham was interested in emigration and corresponded with various emigration societies, there are few direct references to emigration to America. Letters from James Mill, 5 Feb. 1831, from John Bright, 5 July 1842, and from Alexander Mundell, 26 Feb. 1831, make general observations on emigration.

SOCIETY FOR THE DIFFUSION OF USEFUL KNOWLEDGE. Papers. (Handlist and index available.)

Adult education society, founded by Lord Brougham and patronized by leading Whigs and Radicals.

The Society's papers throughout throw considerable light on Anglo-American publishing problems, the relative cost of production and the copyright controversy. There is correspondence relating to the republication in the United States of various of the Society's series (Carvell's of New York published the 'Library of Entertaining Knowledge'). A letter, 30 Mar. 1833, from Condy Raquet, a leading citizen of Philadelphia, perhaps demonstrates the success of the Society's publications in Philadelphia; a letter, New York, 25 July 1841 from Professor George Tucker of the University of Virginia to George Long concerns the law of copyright and Tucker's plan for two novels, one designed 'to lessen the prejudice between North and South'. Minutes of 17 Jan. 1833 show James Mill expressing concern at English ignorance of American affairs and moving a resolution in favour of a 'free interchange' of 'literary productions' between the two countries; apparently a deputation then visited the American Minister in London. Committee minutes of 1831 give information about assistance to various American societies, and letters from Alonzo Potter to T. Coates, 20 July [1837] and 25 May 1841 concern the American Society for the Diffusion of Useful Knowledge.

HUTH, FREDERICK, & CO. LTD. Business records.[4]

Merchant bankers, London; dissolved in 1936. The Library's collection of the firm's records consists of 274 volumes,[5] 1812-1904. Huth's world-wide dealings included some with the United States, particularly, it appears, in cotton and in state bonds.

(*a*) Letter-books. Letters from the London office were written in English, Spanish, or German, and of the 179 volumes of copies of letters sent from there, sixty-six are 'English letters', 1827-51. Most of the letters to the United States are, of course, in this group, but there are apparently also some in the volumes of 'German letters' and 'Spanish letters'. Each volume contains an index, and from these it appears that there was correspondence with firms in New York; New Bedford, Mass.; Philadelphia; Baltimore; Richmond, Va.; Mobile, Ala.; New Orleans; Tallahassee, Fla.; and other American cities. Subjects dealt with include the financing of cotton shipments, credit arrangements in Europe for the firms, purchase and sale of American securities. Unfortunately, a large proportion of the copies are so faded as to be illegible.

(*b*) Letters. A volume of letters, Jan.-June 1839, to the London firm from Frederick Huth & Co., Liverpool, contains references to flour, cotton, corn, and rice from the United States, and discussion of American agencies and the ways in which other firms - Barings, Browns, etc. - handle American business.

There is also relevant material in the ledgers, the volumes listing bills payable and receivable, etc.

PARKES, JOSEPH (1796-1865). Papers. 1829-65. (Handlist available.)

Politician and Birmingham solicitor.

(*a*) Letter, 3 May 1829, from Parkes to Sutton Sharpe about proposed article in the *Jurist* on the jurisprudence of Louisiana.

(*b*) Typed copies of letters from Parkes to E.J. Stanley, later 2nd Baron Stanley of Alderney, and replies from Stanley. The letters are mostly about elections and internal Whig politics, but there are occasional American references, e.g. 30 Sept. 1841, from Parkes, 'A Boston steamer will be in Liverpool today or tomorrow. It will

3. See R.K. Webb, *Harriet Martineau, a Radical Victorian* (London, 1960).

4. The letters from Huth's agents and partners in or about the United States used by R.C. McGrane, *Foreign Bondholders and American State Debts* (New York, 1935) do not appear to be in this collection.

5. Including thirteen Glyn, Mills and Co.'s cash books.

probably bring the first day's trial of McLeod and the President's decision on the second edition of the Bank Bill.'

(*c*) One loose letter, Staples Inn, 9 Feb. 1853, from Parkes to Richard Cobden, describes how in 1830 - to aid the Real Property Commission - Parkes had acquainted himself with United States law and legal practice and had published a volume on inheritance, registration, etc., of land in the United States. Proposes to send a copy of this to Cobden.

(*d*) One letter, Rochdale, 9 Dec. 1861, from Bright to Parkes, concerns a speech of his about war with the United States: 'I conclude war is intended here, from the preparations being made and the excitement purposely created....Our ruling class may over-reach themselves.'

(*e*) There are other scattered letters of American interest in the collection, including letters to Parkes from Richard Henry Dana, Jr. (1856) and Charles Francis Adams (1861).

There are also letters of condolence to Mrs. Parkes from C.F. Adams and Charles Sumner.

ROUTLEDGE AND KEGAN PAUL LTD. Papers. 1853-

Accounts, stock books, agreements, etc., of George Routledge & Co., 1853-1902; Kegan Paul, Trench, Trübner & Henry S. King, 1858-1912; post-war publishing records of Routledge & Kegan Paul Ltd.

This collection of over 250 items has recently been acquired by the Library, and the correspondence has not yet been unpacked or indexed. However, a preliminary investigation by the librarian indicates that there are at least a few items of American interest, e.g. the Routledge contracts for H.W. Longfellow's *Aftermath* and *New England Tragedies*.

CHADWICK, SIR EDWIN (1800-90). Papers. (Handlist and index available.)

Sanitary and administrative reformer.

This large collection includes an important range of information about subjects such as cholera, education, the franchise, public health, roads, and sanitation in the U.S.A. Chadwick was in frequent touch with American individuals and organizations interested in the problems of public health and education, and was exchanging pamphlets and statistical information with them. The dates of the letters range from 1843 to 1889, though most are during the 1870's and 1880's. Chadwick received letters from such notable educators, and civil and sanitary engineers, as John Billings, J. Eaton, Charles Emery, Rudolph Hering, Mayor Hewitt of New York, Edward Jarvis, and George Waring; and from Boards of Health, Bureaux of Education, the American Social Science Association, the *Sanitarian* (a monthly magazine devoted to the preservation of health, mental, and physical culture), etc. Chadwick was also engaged in compiling comparative vital statistics between America and Britain, based on information supplied to him by local correspondents in the United States.

GALTON, SIR FRANCIS (1822-1911). Papers and correspondence. Late 19th and early 20th centuries. (Handlist and index available.)

Sir Francis Galton was a prominent British scientist who devoted his life to travel and to the study of a succession of virtually unexplored fields. Among his interests were the weather, physical and mental characteristics of men and animals, the influence of heredity, especially in twins, and fingerprints and personal identification.

In the main section of his voluminous correspondence are letters to Galton from a number of prominent Americans, including Henry Adams (1892) and Oliver Wendell Holmes (1880). There are also letters and commendations from several American societies, such as the American Association for the Advancement of Physical Science and the American Breeders' Association. Galton's notebooks reflect his interest in American horsebreeding. There are two exercise books for 1897 containing his notes on American trotting horses, and a card index for the same year giving the names of fifteen American horse breeders.

FLEMING, SIR (JOHN) AMBROSE (1849-1945). Correspondence and papers. 1884, 1908. (MSS. Add. 122)

British scientist and inventor of the rectifying valve.

(*a*) Experimental notebook: MS. report on the Edison Electric Light Station in New York, *c*. Sept. 1884.

(*b*) Bundle labelled 'important papers relative to the Valve Action in the U.S.A.' containing copies of correspondence dated 1908 submitted in action between the Marconi Company of America and the de Forest Radio Co.; copies of correspondence and reports relating to other actions defending Fleming's patents in the U.S.A.

WELLCOME INSTITUTE FOR THE HISTORY OF MEDICINE, 183 Euston Road, London NW1 2BP

AUTOGRAPH COLLECTION.

The collection contains about 100,000 items, arranged in folders alphabetically by name of author; no list is yet available. It is probable that the collection includes more relevant material than noted below.

Barton, Benjamin Smith. Philadelphia, 1 Nov. 1791, to Count de la Cépède about oviparous quadrupeds and serpents. Philadelphia, 2 Sept. 1799 to Messrs. Robinson, London booksellers. 19 Mar. 1810, to Dr. John C. Lettsom about the possibility of joining the Royal Society. London, 1 Mar. 1811, to Dr. Lettsom about the copper-plate of the Pennsylvania Hospital diploma.

Holmes, Oliver Wendell, Sr. Five letters, 1872-92, including two to Dr. John Milner Fothergill in London.

Morse, Samuel F.B. United States Telegraph Office, Washington, D.C., 14 May 1846, to M. Arago, Secrétaire Perpetuel de l'Académie des Sciences.

Peabody, George. Salem, Mass., 25 Feb. 1867, to Edward Haslewood about Mississippi Bonds.

Priestley, Joseph. Eight letters, 1777-94, including one of 6 Apr. 1794 to Thomas Cooper about their proposed settlement in the United States and Cooper's religious beliefs.

Rush, Benjamin. Philadelphia, 30 Nov. 1794, to Dr. James Currie of Liverpool, about yellow fever in Philadelphia, the insurrection in western Pennsylvania, etc.

Smith, Nathan. Hanover, N.H., 27 May 1808, to Dr. John C. Lettsom, introducing Lyman Spalding.

Spalding, *see* Waterhouse.

Washington, George. A list of medicines and household commodities to be sent from England, dated 20 Sept. 1759.[1]

Waterhouse, Benjamin. Cambridge, Mass., 6 Sept. 1800 to Lyman Spalding, Portsmouth, N.H., and Spalding's answer of 10

1. *Writings of George Washington*, ed. by John C. Fitzpatrick, vol. ii (Washington, D.C., 1931), pp. 330-6. Letter from Mount Vernon of that date to Robert Cary & Co. includes the list as 'Invoice of sundries to be sent...for use of George Washington'.

Sept.[2] Also a letter from Waterhouse, 14 Apr. 1801,[3] to an unknown correspondent, comparing Jefferson and John Adams and containing discussion of other political and scientific affairs.

WEST INDIA COMMITTEE, 18 Grosvenor Street, London W1X 0HP

MINUTES. 1769-1816.

There is scattered material in these minutes relating to the supply of lumber and provisions from America, the effects of the War of Independence on West Indian trade, etc. See the description of 'West India Committee, Minutes, West India Merchants' in H.C. Bell, D.W. Parker, and others, *Guide to British West Indian Archive Materials, in London and in the Islands, for the History of the United States* (Washington, D.C., 1926), pp. 318-9.

CITY OF WESTMINSTER, ARCHIVES DEPARTMENT, Victoria Library, 160 Buckingham Palace Road, London SW1W 9UD

WESTMINSTER CITY COUNCIL ARCHIVES.

Among these extensive archives only one reference to America could be traced: 'Warrant of the Trustees incorporated to encourage the development of the colony of Georgia, America, appointing the minister, churchwardens and gentlemen of the parish of St. Margaret to gather money for the said purpose.' 1733.

WESTMINSTER DIOCESAN ARCHIVES, Archbishop's House, Ambrosden Avenue, London SW1P 1QJ

ARCHIVES IN THE KEEPING OF THE ARCHBISHOP OF WESTMINSTER.

(*a*) Section A: Main Series. This section of the archives consists of seventy-six volumes and boxes containing a very miscellaneous group of manuscripts (and some printed matter), mainly in chronological order, covering 1509-1850. A general index is available through 1700 (vol. 37), and later volumes through 1808 (vol. 53) have individual indexes. Andrews & Davenport, pp. 339-40, list some of the available material to 1791; one of these items - a letter from General Retz to Charles Shireburn, 23 May 1744 - could not be found at the time of the present search. Other relevant material - mostly letters (unless otherwise stated) to the London bishops - is as follows:

Vol. 20, no. 59. Advices on the present state of English Catholics...and in the Dominions. *c.* 1626.

Vol. 31, no. 208. Suppression of the Jesuits: names of the Jesuits in Maryland and Pennsylvania, enclosed in a letter of submission by Thomas Sanders. 1773.

Vol. 40, nos. 173-4. Printed papers: *The Defence of John Ury* and *New Lightmen*, Philadelphia, *c.* 1781.

Vol. 42, nos. 39, 45, 53, 54, 70. Bishop James Talbot: correspondence concerning North America. 1783-5.

Vol. 42, no. 108. *Act of Incorporation of Roman Catholics in Philadelphia.* 13 Sept. 1788. (Printed.)

Vol. 46, nos. 169, 200. 20 Mar. and 19 May 1796, granting faculties in the 'American Islands' to the Capuchins.

Vol. 49. Correspondence, 8 July and 8 Oct. 1798, of Rev. Leonard Neale of Philadelphia concerning the marriage of Bird-Quin.

Vol. 54. 17 Nov. 1811, from the Vicars Apostolic to John Carroll and the American Bishops concerning the troubles with Bishop Milner.

Vol. 55. 25 Feb., 2 Mar., 4 May, and 15 June 1812, from Carroll, Bishop Thomas Smith, etc., on the above.

Vol. 57. 9 Sept. 1815, from John Conolly, Bishop of New York.

Vol. 60. 2 May 1819, from Ambrose Maréchal, Archbishop of Baltimore.

Vol. 63. 10 Nov. 1822, giving Rev. Francis P. Kenrick's report of the distress of the Bishop of Bardstown, Ky. (B.J. Flaget) about the collection being made in England for his church.

Vol. 64. 1 Oct. 1823, from Henry Conwell, Bishop of New York.

Vol. 65. 14 Jan. 1824, concerning the presence in Liverpool of the 'unhappy Hogan' (William Hogan, the leader of the Philadelphia schism); and a letter, 11 Oct. 1824, giving information about another leader of the schism, Thadeus O'Malley.

Vol. 66. 1 Jan. 1825, from Henry Conwell from Philadelphia. Letter, 12 Apr. 1825, from Edward Fenwick, Bishop of Cincinnati, Ohio, giving information about the new cathedral there and about Ohio in general.

Vol. 66. A document in Latin concerning Thadeus O'Malley, 25 July 1825. A letter, 23 Dec. 1825, from Ambrose Maréchal concerning Catholic affairs in Washington, D.C., and in Philadelphia (in French).

Vol. 67. 19 Mar. 1826, from Henry Conwell.

Vol. 68. 29 Jan. 1827, from Henry Conwell. Letter, 11 July 1827, from Joseph Rosati, Bishop of Tenagra, from Missouri. Letter, 29 May 1827(?), from John Dubois, Bishop of New York.

Vol. 69. 8 Mar. 1829, from T.J. Donaghue, Pastor of St. Joseph's Church, Philadelphia, urging that Rev. W.V. Harold not be sent to Cincinnati, Ohio; the letter is written on the back of a printed leaflet consisting of a letter, 2 July 1828, about the matter from Harold to Henry Clay, Secretary of State. A Rome notary public's statement about Henry Conwell (in Italian), 18 Mar. 1829.

Vol. 70. 28 Oct. 1831, from James Whitfield, Archbishop of Baltimore, commenting on the number of Protestants attending Catholic schools.

Vol. 71. 10 Apr. 1832, from James Whitfield concerning provision of schools and churches. Copy of a letter, 3 Sept. 1831, from Rome to Henry Conwell (in Latin), but enclosed in a letter of 8 Nov. 1832.

Vol. 73. A document, 20 June 1846, showing Nicholas Wiseman's election as an honorary member of the American Ethnological Society, and a letter, 26 June 1846, concerning this from J.R. Bartlett, the Society's corresponding secretary.

(*b*) Section B: Miscellaneous Archives.

The papers of 1812-47 contain documents concerning the United States and Canada, since the Bishop in London was used both to forward correspondence and money between America and Rome, and to mediate between Canadian bishops and the government. Bishop Gradwell, when rector of the English College, Rome, from 1818 to 1828, acted as agent for many American Bishops, and on his return to London brought back some of his correspondence and his diary.

2. Facsimiles of these letters appear in E.A. Underwood, 'Edward Jenner, Benjamin Waterhouse, and the introduction of vaccination into the United States', *Nature*, vol. clxiii, p. 826, 1949.

3. Part of this letter printed in Underwood, op. cit., p. 827.

The papers of Cardinal Wiseman (1847-65) contain little of these matters, but there are personal letters to a few bishops. There are no papers of American interest amongst the few documents of Cardinal Manning's period, and his successor, Cardinal Vaughan (1892-1903), destroyed most of his correspondence, though there remains a diary of his travels in the United States (1864 and 1872).

Papers for the twentieth century are available under the thirty-year rule, but there is little of American interest, except during the Second World War. As later years become available there will be more material.

Visits to use documents in the Westminster Diocesan Archives are by appointment only.

WILLIAMS & GLYN BANK LTD., 20 Birchin Lane, London EC3P 3DP

TRANSFER OF SHARES. Printed document. 1692.

Relates to the transfer of shares in West Jersey, 4 Apr. 1692.

ROBSON, ROBERT (b. 1754). Letters and documents. 1800-5.

Robson, a notary public, occupied 67 Lombard Street before Glyn, Mills & Co. acquired it in 1821. The papers he left there contain a number of letters from LeRoy, Bayard and M'Evers of New York; Thomas M'Euen & Co. of Philadelphia; the United States Register's Office; and the Bank of the United States. They deal with investment, the transfer of shares, lawsuits concerning debts between British and American nationals, administration of estates, current exchange rates and quotations, the bankruptcy of an American company which had British creditors, and the collection of dividends in the United States for British investors. There are also statements of Robson's account with the Bank of the United States; and correspondence about the renewal of share certificates lost at sea in 1803 with the packet *Lady Hobart*. In a letter, 22 Sept. 1800, LeRoy, Bayard & M'Evers assure Robson that British fears that funds will fall, should Jefferson be elected, are groundless as Jefferson will attempt no major changes in the government, will not involve the United States in war with Britain, and will be economical.

GOLD STANDARD DEFENCE ASSOCIATION. Papers. 1895-1901.

It seems highly likely that these papers (account books, letter-books, letters, lists of subscribers, pamphlets, etc., in a large tin box; as yet unsorted and uncatalogued) contain correspondence relevant to the silver controversy in the United States in the 1890's. A very cursory examination revealed two letters from Professor F.W. Taussig in 1897, a copy letter to the Director of the United States Mint, and a pamphlet on bimetallism in America.

CURRIE, BERTRAM WODEHOUSE (1827-96). Memoirs, 2 volumes (privately printed). 1901.

Currie, a partner in the bank of Currie & Co., which amalgamated with Glyn's in 1864, travelled extensively in America in 1850. He was one of the British delegates to the International Monetary Conference in Brussels, in 1892, called at the request of the United States government to discuss the possibility of international bimetallism. Currie opposed bimetallism, and in 1895 he founded the Gold Standard Defence Association. Volume 1 includes the letters written by him while in the United States, 27 Apr.-26 Nov. 1850; also papers connected with the Brussels Conference. Volume 2 is his journal for 26 Apr.-12 Aug. 1850.

MANCHESTER, GREATER

BOLTON METROPOLITAN BOROUGH ARCHIVES, Arts Department, Le Mans Crescent, Bolton

HEYWOOD CORRESPONDENCE. 1812-6.

Correspondence of Messrs. John Heywood & Son of Bolton, counterpane manufacturers, including letters of John Fray, Montego Bay, Jamaica, to Robert Heywood, Bolton - references to naval War of 1812, British attack on New Orleans, effects of war with U.S.A. on West Indian trade, social conditions of new emigrants to U.S.A., 1812-6. (ZHE)

BRAMWELL CORRESPONDENCE. 1840.

Correspondence of Thomas Bramwell of Bolton, including letter from William Parker, emigrant to Kiercuck, Iowa Territory, describing social conditions, prices of commodities, emigrant route via Liverpool, New Orleans, and St. Louis, 1840. (ZZ/7)

PUBLIC LIBRARY, Civic Centre, Bolton

WHITMAN COLLECTION.[1] Letters; diary (5 volumes); lectures, etc. 1880-1953.

The Bolton group of Walt Whitman admirers, known as the Eagle Street College or the Bolton Whitman Fellowship, had many contacts with Whitman.

Most letters from him were given to the Library of Congress in 1924, but there remain in the library collection one letter, 1885, and two postcards, 1884 and 1885, to Bessie and Isabella Ford; the draft of a letter, 1889, to Thomas B. Harned;[2] and an extract, probably in Whitman's own hand, from a letter he sent in July 1891 to R.M. Bucke. The collection includes several hundred letters, 1880-1921, from Whitman's literary executors, H.L. Traubel, R.M. Bucke, and T.B. Harned to J.W. Wallace, as well as letters to Wallace with a Whitman interest from Robert Blatchford, John Burroughs, Edward Carpenter, Keir Hardie, Ramsay MacDonald, and others; it also includes the correspondence, 1891-1953, of Anne Montgomerie Traubel with Wallace and with Mrs. M. Whiteside.

There are a number of manuscripts of talks given on Whitman by Wallace and the manuscript diary of his visit to Whitman in 1891. There is also an extensive group of books and periodicals containing the works of Whitman and biography and criticism.

See also the Walt Whitman material in the John Rylands University Library, Manchester (p. 177).

1. See H. Hamer, *A Catalogue of Works by and Relating to Walt Whitman in the Reference Library, Bolton* (Bolton, 1955).
2. There is some doubt as to whether this letter is in Whitman's own handwriting.

G.E. BUCKLEY, ESQ. Brookfield, Delph, Oldham

BUCKLEY FAMILY. Papers. 1805-69.

John Buckley, of Broadhead, Saddleworth, Yorkshire, was a woollen manufacturer whose sons Henry and Hugh were merchants in New York and in Lisbon. The family traded with America throughout the nineteenth century. The papers of American interest in the small collection are:

I. Business correspondence. 1805-22.

(*a*) Three letters, 1805-6, to Henry Buckley, New York, from Richard Milne, Philadelphia, discussing trade in Savannah, Ga., and the state of the cotton market in England.

(*b*) Two letters, 1806, from American firms to Henry Buckley, giving prices of rice and cotton.

(*c*) Two letters, 1806-7, to Henry Buckley from his father, John Buckley. Refers to goods being manufactured by their firm and being sent to America.

(*d*) Letter, 1807, to Henry Buckley from James Green, Liverpool. Comments that 'our political relations with America are understood to be in a very favourable state'.

(*e*) Letter, 1817, from John Buckley & Sons, Saddleworth, to Messrs. John McAdam, Liverpool, regarding the insurance of goods bound for Charleston, S.C.

(*f*) Letter from Hugh Buckley to his father, John, 1821. Refers to the family firm's trade in America.

(*g*) Letter, 1821, to Hugh Buckley from H. Scholfield & Co., Liverpool. Discusses American trade in some detail, including the sale of wool and flour.

(*h*) Two letters, 1821, to Hugh Buckley from his brother, Abraham. Mentions American trade, in particular the shipping of cashmeres to New York for auction.

(*i*) Letter to John Buckley from Hugh Buckley, 1822. Gives prices of Portuguese wool bought for the American market.

II. Minute-book. 1830-69.

The Buckley Papers also include a minute-book of the early schools in Saddleworth. Under the date 25 June 1840 appears an entry which refers to a 'subscription raised amongst certain parties resident in New York & Philadelphia for the benefit of Saddleworth Sunday Schools'. There follows a resolution to extend the committee's 'warmest thanks' to the American donors.

CO-OPERATIVE UNION LTD., Holyoake House, Hanover Street, Manchester M60 OAS

OWEN, ROBERT (1771-1858). Correspondence and papers. 1825-56.

Socialist and philanthropist. Owen visited the United States four times between 1824 and 1828; on the first of these trips he founded New Harmony, Ind. In 1828 he went to help the colonization of land in Texas to be granted by the Mexican government. He lived in the United States, 1844-7, and most of his children settled there, notably Robert Dale Owen, United States congressman and diplomat.

The correspondence and papers consist mainly of letters to Owen, 1822-58. Previously organized in bundles, the material is now numbered from 1 to 2,964 and kept in folders by the hundred, in roughly chronological order. There are good typescript chronological and name catalogues.

Among the numerous individual letters and papers of American interest the following groups stand out:

(*a*) New Harmony. Conditions, purchase, paraphernalia of Owen's visit (hotel bills, letters of introduction, notes for advice); the first letter is dated 16 Dec. 1825 and the last (a French reference to New Harmony) 10 July 1848.

(*b*) Mexico and Texas. 1828-50. Concern Owen's projected Texas scheme, 1828-30; Texas annexation and possible British intervention in Mexico, 1844-6; and requests for advice about emigration to Texas.

(*c*) Emigration. Besides the overlap with (*a*) and (*b*) above, there are one or two interesting individual letters, e.g. a scheme of emigration by Robert Gouger, 19 Mar. 1830; and letters, 1847, from W.S. Peters, founder of a colony in Texas, urging Owen to go there and to take many Scots.

(*d*) Robert Owen in America, 1844-7. Parting wishes to Owen, 1844 (items 1327-37). A section called 'Robert Owen in the U.S.A.' (items 1340-1534) includes requests to speak (e.g. from 'Committee of Socialists at Cincinnati', 31 Oct. 1844); letters of introduction; talk of books; Owen's contacts with Congress; the Oregon question.

(*e*) Oregon question, 1846. Among the correspondence on this subject is item 1456, 'Confidential correspondence between Robert Owen and Earl of Aberdeen and Sir Robert Peel on new state of affairs between the British nation and the United States'. This comprises three letters from Peel to Owen, three from Owen to Peel, two from Aberdeen to Owen, and one from Robert Dale Owen to his father, all Apr. or May 1846. Peel is very cool to Owen; Aberdeen more friendly. Owen's letter from his son is the most interesting: 'Webster's manifesto... on the Oregon question' was enclosed. 'You will see how pointed he is in regard to the utter impossibility of a line South of 49.... If the British ministry are not now persuaded how things actually stand, "neither would they be persuaded though one rose from the dead".' In addition there are two foolscap sheets: Last American Proposition, 12 July 1845, and Last British Proposition, 26 Aug. 1844.

(*f*) Spiritualism, 1855-6. Owen was converted to spiritualism by an American medium in 1854, so odd letters touch this pursuit, e.g., item 2393 from the American spiritualist Hume, and 2555 and 2541 from Colonel E. Brand.

(*g*) Robert Dale Owen. Letters, 1830-48, touching, *inter alia*, upon national education in the United States, the Panic of 1837, Cuba, and the Wilmot Proviso.

HOLYOAKE, GEORGE JACOB (1817-1906). Correspondence.[1] 1835-1906.

Co-operator and secularist. Twelve packets of letters to and from Holyoake are numbered 1-4415 and are preserved in folders in chronological order. The typescript index to these letters was completed in 1967.

Among the letters are several from Americans, particularly during the period of Holyoake's two visits to the United States in 1879 (items 2538-2563) and 1882 (items 2761-2793). Included are letters from R.G. Ingersoll, George William Curtis, E.L. Godkin, W. Ledue, Josiah Quincy, Rutherford B. Hayes, and to General E.E. Barnum. There is also one from Rosamund Dale Owen, mainly in defence of her father, Robert Dale Owen.

See also the Holyoake Collection in the Bishopsgate Institute, London (p. 53).

1. See Joseph McCabe, *Life and Letters of George Jacob Holyoake*, 2 vols. (London, 1908).

MISSISSIPPI VALLEY TRADING CO. Papers.[2] 1875-8.

Many leaders of the English Co-operative Union were connected with this project. The collection includes articles of association and alterations thereto; contemporary press cuttings on the project; correspondence between Dr. Worrall, manager, American Co-operative Union, and Edward Vansittart Neale, and other letters; pamphlets on direct trade between Mississippi Valley and Great Britain; a tract on the order of the Patrons of Husbandry. There are also extracts of a report of Lieutenant A. Gillmore, Corps of Engineers, on transportation from St. Mary's River on the Atlantic through Okefinokee, Ga., to the Gulf of Mexico. There are also references to the project in the reports of the Co-operative Union Congress and *Co-operative News*. The principal item in this collection is the Company's letter-book, containing duplicates of out-letters, mostly from E.V. Neale or Joseph Smith, Apr. 1875-Aug. 1878.

JOHN RYLANDS UNIVERSITY LIBRARY, Deansgate,[1] Manchester

AUTOGRAPH COLLECTIONS. Letters and manuscript notes. 1658-1874.

Includes the following (unless otherwise stated, merely letter of politesse):

Audubon, J.J. 12 Dec. 1827, to an unknown correspondent. After giving a brief autobiographical sketch, Audubon asks for the support of 'the learned & wealthy'.

Bryant, George. n.d., to Dr. Raffles. Manuscript of a poem beginning 'While thee I seek protecting powers.'

Bryant, W.C. [Oct. 1848], to Mr. Gourlie.

Cobbett, William. Ross, Herefordshire, 4 June 1830, to Thomas Smith, Liverpool, making arrangements to have a copy of the *Register* published as a pamphlet in New York as quickly as possible. 'It is the *finest blow* that the Borough-villains have got for years.'

Cooper, James Fenimore. Paris, 3 Aug. 1831, to J.D. Hammond.

Emerson, R.W. 18 Apr. 1850, to Walter Langdon, thanking him for his gift of a book.

Franklin, Benjamin. New York, 2 July 1756, to George Whitefield.[2] 'I sometimes wish, that you and I were jointly employ'd by the Crown, to settle a colony on the Ohio'; plans for this utopia.

Irving, Washington. New York, 17 Dec. 1833, to James M. Wayne, Washington, D.C., asking Wayne to present the views of the bearer.

Lincoln, Abraham. Washington, D.C., 4 Dec. 1861, to Mrs. A. Van B. Nash.

Longfellow, Henry Wadsworth. Cambridge, Mass., 9 Jan. 1850, to an unknown correspondent.

——. Cambridge, Mass., 9 Feb. 1854, to T. Hitchcock.

Mather, Cotton. Manuscript sermon (8 pages), 1701. Manuscript notes (8 pages), 26 May 1702.

Mather, Increase. Manuscript notes (4 pages), 31 July 1658 and 23 June 1668. Manuscript (2 pages), July 1688.

Mather, Richard. Manuscript notes (1 page), n.d.

Motley, J.L. 1 May 1870, to Mr. Neilson.

Penn, John. Philadelphia, 3 Sept. 1768, asking his correspondent to arrange accommodation for him along his route to Fort Stanwix for the 'Congress of the Indians'.

Penn, Thomas, London, 6 June 1769, to Sir William Johnson, informing the latter that his 'grant' has come through.

Penn, William. Philadelphia, 3 Feb. 1684, to Dr. Ralph Tretwell, mainly concerning the navigability of the Schuylkill River and the fertility of the land bordering it.

Rogers, William. Philadelphia, 27 Feb. 1796. He has not yet seen the 'historic defence' written by his correspondent in London; when it arrives he will try to prevent its republication in Philadelphia.

Thacher, Peter. Two letters to Thomas Prince: Middleborough, Mass., 4 Jan. 1722, on family affairs, and 28 Aug. 1722 asking Prince to use his influence with 'his Excellency' so that Thacher may get back his servant Jonathan Wood.

Washington, George. Philadelphia, 9 Sept. 1787, to his nephew George Augustine Washington. State of the crops, question of railing for fences, and other farm and household affairs.

Webster, Daniel. Washington, D.C., 18 July 1823, to Jeremiah Nelson, Newburyport, Mass. Discussion of cases being heard before 'the Commissioners'.

Whistler, James A.M. Oct. 1874, to an unknown correspondent.

Whitefield, George. Savannah, Ga., 18 Jan. 1747, to James Habersham, Charleston, S.C.

Willis, Nathaniel Parker. Morristown, N.J., 5 Apr. 1842, to Theodore Ledyard Cuyler.

MORAVIAN COLLECTIONS. Diaries, minute-books, letters, notes.

Much of the Library's extensive collection of material dealing with the Moravian Church relates to America. Among the manuscripts are, for example, the following:

(*a*) Headquarters' diary, 1747-64 (eighteenth-century translation from the original German). (Eng. MSS. 945-50)

Relevant entries include those of 19 Jan. 1763, an account of the building up of new settlements in Carolina, 1753-61; and 5 Oct. 1763, text of a letter fom Brother Nathanael in New York on missionary activities, the Indian wars, etc.

(*b*) Moravian Church in America (Eng. MS. 1080). Historical and bibliographical notes and papers relating to John Jacob Fries, minister at Bethabara, N.C., including a copy of his diary, 27 Apr.-31 July 1754; Benjamin Mortimer (teacher at Nazareth Hall, Pa., 1791-8; missionary among the Indians, 1798-1812; appointed pastor of First Moravian Church, New York, 1812); and the Mortimer family.

MAYHEW, JONATHAN (1720-66). 3 letters. 1751-61.

Clergyman; early champion of Unitarianism and political liberty in New England. The letters were written from Boston to Dr. George Benson in London. The first, 6 Dec. 1751, deals with the sad state of Harvard College finances, and thanks Benson for his advice concerning tolerance towards 'those of different sentiments in religion'. The second, 7 Jan. 1754, is a discussion of John Taylor's *Scripture Doctrine of Atonement*. The third, 28 Aug. 1761, includes adverse comment on the (flourishing) state of 'bigottry and enthusiasm' in New England.

BAKER, HENRY (1698-1774). Correspondence. 1753-68.

Naturalist and scientist. Twenty-one letters to Baker, twelve from Alexander Garden in South Carolina and nine from Richard Brooke in

2. These papers were used by Clifton K. Yearley, *Britons in American Labor: a History of the the Influence of the United Kingdom Immigrants on American Labor, 1820-1914* (Baltimore, 1957) (Johns Hopkins University Studies in History and Political Science, series 75, no. 1).

1. Virginia material microfilmed by the Virginia Colonial Records Project.
2. Printed in *Evangelical Magazine* (London, 1803), pp. 50-1, and in *The Papers of Benjamin Franklin*, ed. by Leonard W. Labaree, vol. 6 (New Haven and London, 1963), pp. 468-9.

Maryland, discussing the natural history of the areas and reporting on 'scientific curiosities' which had come to their attention. There is also an extract of a letter from Garden to 'Mr. Shipley' dealing with scientific matters.[3]

SLAVE TRADE DOCUMENT. (1 folio). 1756-73. (Eng. MS. 517)

One of the three sheets in this collection is a list of ships engaged in the slave trade during the years 1749-87, showing 'where slaved', 'where sold', numbers who died, net sales. Four of the cargoes are noted as having been sold in Carolina, and one in Maryland.

HULTON, HENRY (*c.* 1731-91). 16 letters (copies). 1769-76.

Government official. Hulton's correspondence with Robert Nicholson, a Liverpool merchant, includes fifteen letters, 1769-76, written by Hulton from in or near Boston, where he had gone as Revenue Commissioner, and one from Halifax, N.S., May 1776, before his embarkation for England.

Copies are also held by Manchester College, Oxford, and fuller details are given in that report (p. 208).

WALSH, JOHN (1725?-95). Letter. 1772. (Eng. MS. 724)

Scientist, secretary to Clive. Included in the diary of his visit to France is a copy of a letter, Paris, 21 June 1772, to Benjamin Franklin. It includes his plans for experimenting on torpedo fish, and discussion of French electrical experimentation.[4]

BAGSHAWE OF FORD HALL MUNIMENTS. Letters. 1776-9. (B3/13/110-5)

Six letters (imperfect) to and from John, later Sir John, Caldwell. Caldwell's letters to his parents comment on his life as a British soldier during the Revolutionary War. Topics discussed include rumours of American troop movements and an opportunity for Caldwell to purchase a lieutenancy. His father's reply points to the difficulty of raising the money needed to buy the commission and to pay his son's other debts. A letter from his uncle informs the absent Caldwell of the death of his mother.

FRANKLIN, BENJAMIN. Letter (copy). 1787. (Eng. MS. 1110)

A volume containing copies of letters to members of the Wedgwood family from various correspondents includes a letter, 15 May 1787, from Franklin to Josiah Wedgwood thanking him for the present of a cameo depicting a slave. (The letter Wedgwood sent with the cameo is printed in vol. ii, p. 566 of E. Meteyard's *Life of Josiah Wedgwood* (London, 1865).)

MICKLETHWAITE, JOHN. Letters and business papers. 1790-1818. (Eng. MS. 1138)

Merchant of Leeds and Ardsley, Yorkshire. The items of American interest are:

(*a*) Printed broker's circular, 179(?): *An Account of the Nature and Prices of American Stocks,* D.De Berdt & Co., London.

(*b*) Three letters, 7 Aug., 8 Aug., and 8 Aug./10 Sept. 1805, to Micklethwaite from C. Comegys in Baltimore, concerning Micklethwaite's property in Delaware, etc.

(*c*) Philadelphia, 29 Dec. 1818, from John Young to Micklethwaite, asking whether during his visit to the United States he can perform any commissions for Micklethwaite in relation to the latter's property there.

(*d*) Two letters, 1794, and two legal documents, 1790, 1794, from John Ellis, merchant, of New York, concerning the estate of his sister, Mary Ellis of Barnsley and Liverpool. These came into Micklethwaite's possession because he was, with John Benson of Liverpool, an executor of this estate.

OWENS, OWEN & JOHN. Business records. 1806-52. (On deposit.)

Manufacturers and merchants, Manchester. The firm exported cotton and woollen goods, umbrellas, hatters' trimmings, and skins; the United States was one of its principal markets. The firm also imported raw cotton and some flour from the United States.

Five letter-books cover 1821-52, and contain copies of letters to Philadelphia, 1821-6, to Thomas Owen, and to New York, successively from 1821 to George Wragg & Co., William Barraclough, Oakeys & Robinson, and John Robinson. Five sales-books, 1819-46, contain invoices of shipments to the two cities. Incoming letters, 1839-45, include letters from New York and New Orleans. Ledgers contain a few references to the firm's early trade with the United States, 1806-18.

McCONNEL & KENNEDY. Business records.[5] 1807-35. (On deposit.)

Fine cotton-spinning firm, Manchester. The records of this firm (thirty-one boxes containing letters, receipts, etc.; *c.* fifty volumes of letter-books, ledgers, etc.) include, from 1807 onwards, correspondence with agents in Savannah, Ga., and/or Charleston, S.C. Letters from the agents are available until 1826: during the first few years of the correspondence these include discussion of the changing political relations between Britain and the United States and the effects of these on raw cotton exports; later letters - of which there are, for example, over 100 in 1825 - appear to be confined to discussion of the state of the cotton crop, invoices of shipments, etc. Letters include some from A.L. Molyneux, Savannah; J. Speakman & Co., Savannah; Thomas H. Hindley, New York and Charleston (these are the early ones about political developments); J. & W. Longsdon, Charleston. There are copies of letters from the firm to the agents through 1835.

NICHOLSON PAPERS. Correspondence: including 60 business letters. 1817-26. (Eng. MSS. 1041-5)

The family correspondence of the Nicholsons includes some letters referring to America - e.g., two (nos. 498, 503) in 1817 concern the departure for America of Robert Dent.

There are in addition about sixty business letters from the United States agents of the Liverpool merchant firm (mainly linen) of James & Thomas Nicholson. These were written 1822-6; most of them are from Wood Gibson in New York, with a few each from Sam Mordecai, Petersburg, Va.; J.S. and G. Hobson, Philadelphia; Beckett and Davies, Charleston, S.C.; Francis Thompson, New York; and Peter Remson & Co., New York. The letters report progress, or lack of it, in selling the goods, mainly linens, shipped by the Liverpool firm, and include information about prices, demand, etc.

3. The Baker correspondence has been used in Edmund Berkeley and Dorothy Smith Berkeley, *Dr. Alexander Garden of Charleston* (Chapel Hill, 1969).

4. Printed in *The Papers of Benjamin Franklin*, ed. by William B. Willcox, vol. 19 (New Haven and London, 1975), pp. 189-90.

5. See G.W. Daniels, 'The Early Records of a Great Manchester Cotton-Spinning Firm', *Economic Journal*, vol. xxv, pp. 175-88, 1915; and his 'American Cotton Trade with Liverpool under the Embargo and Non-Intercourse Acts', *American Historical Review*, vol. xxi, pp. 276-87, 1916. Also Roland Smith, 'Manchester as a Centre for the Manufacture and Merchanting of Cotton Goods, 1820-1830', *Birmingham University Historical Journal*, vol. iv, pp. 47-65, 1953.

IRVING, WASHINGTON (1783-1859). Letter. n.d.

London, n.d., apparently to William Godwin. Irving acknowledges receipt of 'your manuscript' which he will forward to America, having already told his New York agent that it will be arriving.

RAWSON COLLECTION.[6] Minute-book; 2 boxes letters, notes, drafts of speeches, etc. 1825-67. (Eng. MSS. 741-3)

This collection of anti-slavery material consists of the minute-book of the Sheffield Female Anti-Slavery Society, 1825-33; and letters and other papers concerning various aspects of the anti-slavery movement, particularly as connected with the Sheffield group. Included are two letters from Neal Dow; a copy of a letter, 7 Dec. 1859, from Frederick Douglass, giving his views on the Harpers Ferry incident and the use of force in general; a private circular from the Birmingham and Midland Freedmen's Aid Association giving particulars of four Americans who will be addressing them: George Cabot Ward, Robert J. Parvin, Phillips Brooks, Sella Martin, etc.

GASKELL COLLECTION. 13 letters. 1828-56. (Eng. MS. 730-4)

(*a*) The two volumes of letters to E.C. and W. Gaskell include the following:

Palfrey, John G. London, 21 June 1856, to Mrs. Gaskell, promising to send her some books on the Salem witchcraft trials when he returns to the United States.

Stowe, Harriet Beecher. Boston, 24 May 1856,[7] to Mrs. Gaskell, introducing her friends, Mr. and Mrs. Webb. Mrs. Webb, the daughter of a fugitive slave, gives dramatic readings.

(*b*) The three volumes of miscellaneous letters include the following (trivia unless otherwise described):

Bryant, W.C. London, 22 June 1845, to Mr. Fox.

Buchanan, James. United States Legation, London, 29 Dec. 1855, to Nathaniel Hawthorne, requesting Hawthorne to look into the case of H.N. Johnson, who has been kept in prison five months in Liverpool waiting to be sent to New York for trial.

Channing, W.E. Boston, 29 Nov. 1828, to Rev. James Yates.

Emerson, R.W. Manchester, 2 Mar. [1848], to [Mr. Shuttleworth].

Furness, W.H. Philadelphia, 8 Oct. 1854, to H. Bright.

Hawthorne, N. Liverpool, 23 Jan. [1855], to Mr. Bright.

——. Liverpool, 2 Nov. [1855], to H.A. Bright.

Longfellow, H.W. 14 Nov.--, to Mr. Chapman.

Sedgwick, Catharine M. New York, 17 Apr. 1853, to Mr. Bright.

Stowe, Harriet Beecher, to Lady Atherton, n.d.

Webster, Daniel. Boston, 14 May 1833, to Mathew Carey, discusses doctrine of nullification.

GORDON, JOHN (1807-80). 15 American letters. 1831-99.

Unitarian minister.

Bartol, C.A. Glasgow, 30 Sept. 1854, and Edinburgh, 13 Oct. 1854, to John Gordon, Edinburgh.

Channing, William Henry. 5 Apr. 1859, to John Gordon.

Choate, Joseph H. London, 16 Oct. 1899, to Samuel A. Steinthal, London.

Clarke, James Freeman. Boston, 24 Nov. 1860, to J.R. Beard, Manchester.

Rodgers, A. Robertson. New York, 28 Sept. 1831, to George Kenrick, London.

Thomas, Abel C. Nine letters, 1852-77, to John Gordon. Six from London and one from Philadelphia, 1852-3, relate to his preaching engagements, people he has met in England, etc.; the letter of 15 Feb. 1853 asks 'What do you think of a Unitarian preacher [Mr. Solly of Carter Lane Chapel, London] who declined to invite me into his pulpit because I am not as ultra as *he* is on the subject of Negro slavery?' Two letters, Tacony, Pa., 1876 and 1877, give details of his life since the trip to England: 'The war of the rebellion took vital hold of my thots, and I am neither sorry nor ashamed of anything I said or did in that regard.' etc.

AMERICAN LETTERS. Envelope containing 18 letters. 1834-1907.

Allen, Joseph H. London, 27 Aug. 1855, to John Gordon, Edinburgh.

Bellows, Henry W. New York, 5 Nov. 1856 and 19 Mar. 1867, and London, 13 June 1868, to J.R. Beard.

——. 20 June 1868, to James C. Street, Newcastle.

Channing, William Henry. Huntingdon, 19 June 1884, to James C. Street. In answer to a question from Street concerning William Ellery Channing's death-bed attitude towards Unitarianism, Channing states that 'every word and act of his proved conclusively that he remained *serenely happy in his Unitarian faith* to the end'.

Collyer, Robert. Chicago, 23 Mar. 1874, to James C. Street.

——. New York, 20 Sept. 1887, to Thomas Read Elliot.

Conway, Moncure D. Hammersmith, 9 Apr. 1879, to James C. Street.

Dewey, Orville. New York, 22 Apr. 1845, to J.R. Beard.

Douglass, Frederick. Anacostia, D.C., 23 May 1894, to Samuel A. Steinthal, informing Steinthal of the prospective visit to England of Ida B. Wells, and containing a plea for strong English protests against the continuing oppression of Negroes in the United States.

Dow, Neal. Portland, Me., 7 Dec. 1857, to Samuel A. Steinthal.

Gannett, William C. Rochester, N.Y., 27 Mar. 1894, to Christopher J. Street, Manchester.

Hale, Edward Everett. Boston, 22 Nov. 1907, to Christopher J. Street, Bolton.

Hosmer, Frederick L. Chicago, 12 Oct. 1893, to Christopher J. Street, Manchester.

——. Berkeley, Calif., 21 Dec. 1903, to Samuel A. Steinthal.

Howe, Julia Ward. Boston, 19 Feb. 1871, to James C. Street, presenting the purposes and activities of the Woman's International Peace Association, with the hope that a world congress can be held in London if support is forthcoming from such people as Street in England.

Tuckerman, Joseph. Stapleton Grove, near Bristol, 9 Jan. 1834, to J.R. Beard, Manchester.

STILLMAN CORRESPONDENCE. 14 letters. *c.* 1860-early 1900's. (Eng. MSS. 1267, 1281)

Seven letters, *c.* 1860-85, from John Ruskin to W.J. Stillman (1828-1901), the American Pre-Raphaelite; two letters, 1892 and 1898, from Stillman, and five letters, early 1900's, from his wife Marie, to Charles Fairfax Murray.

THOMPSON, GEORGE (1804-78). 24 letters. 1864-5.

The Library has a collection of letters, letter-books, diaries, and printed works of and concerning George Thompson, the English anti-slavery advocate. In the course of his activities Thompson visited America, and this is reflected in his correspondence, which includes twenty-four letters from America, 1864-5.

6. See N.B. Lewis, 'The Abolitionist Movement in Sheffield, 1823-1833', *Bulletin of the John Rylands Library*, vol. xviii, pp. 377-92, 1934.

7. This letter was printed in full in R.D. Waller, ed., 'Letters Addressed to Mrs. Gaskell by Celebrated Contemporaries', *Bulletin of the John Rylands Library*, vol. xix, pp. 164-5, 1935.

ANTI-SLAVERY COLLECTION. Pamphlets, society reports, periodicals, etc. 19th century. (R 107337)

There are materials relating to the United States in 19 of the 25 boxes in this collection: 10 of these contain anti-slavery pamphlets, 5 contain society reports, 3 contain periodicals (among them a few numbers of anti-slavery journals), and 1 contains leaflets and posters. Some of the pamphlets were published in the United States, but most in England and Scotland; they range from exhortations to the Christian women of the United States, to protests against the building of the *Alabama*, and include speeches by Garrison, first-hand accounts of what it is like to be a slave, political maps of the United States. The annual reports of anti-slavery societies consist of those American societies as well as of the Birmingham and Midland Freedmen's Aid Association and other British groups.

STANLEY CORRESPONDENCE. 17 letters. 1871-3. (Eng. MS. 1094)

Fifteen letters were written by Mrs. Sarah Anne Ellis Dorsey (1829-79), author, mainly from Louisiana, to Edward Lyulph Stanley. One letter was written to Mrs. Dorsey by 'J.M.S.' (J.M. Sandidge?) and one by Thomas P. Farrar. The letters 'offer a glimpse at first-hand of life in a Southern State in the years after the American Civil War ... and they reveal something of the nature of Anglo-American relations during the nineteenth century'.[8]

LANCASHIRE INDEPENDENT COLLEGE MSS. 5 unbound volumes. 19th century. (On deposit.)

This collection consists of hundreds of letters to and from Independent clergymen throughout Great Britain. Although most of the missionary work mentioned is in areas other than North America, there are occasional letters from and references to proselytizing in Canada and the United States. American correspondents include Rev. Axel Wetter, Albany, N.Y., n.d.; Rev. Edward Taylor, Binghamton, N.Y., 1872; and Rev. John W. Baynes, Hudson, Mich., 1874 and 1876.

HERFORD, BROOKE (1830-1903). Sermons (1 volume and 10 separate manuscripts); article. 1876-91.

Unitarian minister. The bound volume contains six manuscript sermons on 'Preaching and pastoral care', originally given at Harvard Divinity School in 1891, and notes for a talk on 'The Ministry', given at Harvard in 1890. Ten sermons in individual envelopes are marked as having been first preached at Arlington Street Church, Boston, 1887-91. The Library also holds a manuscript, 'Account of a visit to the Mammoth Cave of Kentucky, U.S.A. in April 1876' (4 pages).

WHITMAN, WALT (1819-92).

(*a*) Miscellaneous letters and papers, 1880-1948, of Charles F. Sixsmith of Anderton, Lancs., respecting his Whitman interests. Included is a group marked 'Summer in Canada 1880', among which are thirty-nine letters to Whitman from various correspondents. (Eng. MS. 1170)

(*b*) Miscellaneous letters and papers respecting Whitman's friend J.W. Wallace, and the Bolton Whitman Fellowship. Included are copies and drafts of fifty-three letters, 1887-91, from Wallace to Whitman, six items concerning Mr. and Mrs. Horace L. Traubel, and a typescript 'Diary of Visits to Walt Whitman, etc., in 1891 by J.W. Wallace' (135 pages). (Eng. MS. 1186)

(*c*) Correspondence, 1891-1918, of Horace L. Traubel. (Of the 178 letters, 117 were written in 1892.) (Eng. MS. 1172)

(*d*) The Department of Printed Books holds over 250 books and articles by and about Whitman, a collection of over 150 newspaper and other cuttings relating to Whitmaniana and to members of the Bolton Whitman Fellowship, and an incomplete set of the *Conservator*, edited in Philadelphia by Traubel.

See also the Whitman Collection in the Bolton Public Library (p. 172).

FREEMAN, E.A. (1823-92). 12 letters. 1882-5.

British historian. The Freeman Papers include twelve letters (mostly typewritten), 1882-5, to Freeman from Herbert B. Adams at Johns Hopkins University, Baltimore, and in Amherst, Mass. Although these are largely related to academic affairs and scholarly work, there are some comments on political developments, e.g. 24 Feb. 1882: 'Baltimore, as well as Philadelphia, is awakening from the torpor of the Boss regime.' Also, 5 Sept. 1884, a letter discussing the presidential campaign of that year, with appraisals of James G. Blaine, Roscoe Conkling, Grover Cleveland, etc. A letter for 12 Jan. 1885 reports that 'all the young College men of America are greatly delighted at the success of our candidate for the presidential chair. Cleveland is a sturdy, stiff-backed, honest man. He believes in Civil Service Reform and in Tariff Reform, the two greatest issues in American Politics.'

BURGESS, WALTER H. (1867-1943). Notebooks, loose notes, correspondence (4 boxes).

Unitarian minister; historian. Burgess wrote extensively about the Pilgrim Fathers, and his papers include manuscript notes for a life of William Brewster, correspondence with American descendants of John Robinson, etc.

TOUT, THOMAS FREDERICK (1855-1929). Letters. 20th century.

British historian. The papers of T.F. Tout contain occasional items of American interest. These include an itinerary, Feb.-July 1928, of a trip Tout paid to America, with references to lectures arranged at Columbia, Vassar, Bryn Mawr, Western Reserve, Harvard, etc. There are also small groups of letters from some American academics and historians, notably James F. Willard of the University of Colorado (early 1920's) and Nellie Nelson of Mt. Holyoke College, Mass. (1927-8). These, and several letters from other scholars in America, are almost exclusively on personal or academic affairs.

NEILSON, FRANCIS (1867-1961). Correspondence.

Francis Neilson was a prominent advocate of the principles of Henry George, the American tax reformer. Born in England, Neilson lived in the United States for almost fifty years until his death in 1961.

(*a*) Letters, 1939-61, to and from Will Lissner. Topics discussed include their opposition to America's entry into the Second World War, their distrust of American censorship during the war, and their belief in Georgite economic principles.

(*b*) Correspondence files, alphabetically arranged, of letters to Neilson, containing much material of American interest.

STEVENS, WALLACE (1879-1955). Correspondence. 1941-51, 1963.

(*a*) 106 letters of Wallace Stevens, American author and literary critic, all addressed to the director or manager of the Cummington Press and dealing chiefly with the publication of *Notes toward a Supreme Fiction, Esthétique du Mal, Three Academic Pieces,* and a private

8. See Marcus F. Cunliffe, 'Notes on the Dorsey-Stanley Correspondence (1871-1873)', *Bulletin of the John Rylands Library*, vol. xxxvi, pp. 360-85, 1954.

work concerning the Stevens' family portraits. Together with carbon copies of eighty - five letters addressed to Stevens by the director or manager of the Cummington Press.
(*b*) Correspondence concerning the Stevens Papers, mainly 1963.

METHODIST ARCHIVES.

The archives of the Methodist Church, formerly in the possession of the Methodist Archives and Research Centre, London, are to be transferred to the John Rylands University Library by the end of the summer, 1977. While there are a few items of American interest in the collection (e.g. Charles Wesley's poems on the American War of Independence),[9] the archives do not appear to contain a large or significant body of Americana. Enquiries should be addressed to Mr. D.W. Riley at the John Rylands University Library, who will be responsible for organizing the material.

MODERN POETRY COLLECTION.

Since about 1970 the Library has received from the editor of *Critical Quarterly* manuscripts of all poems published in that journal, together with corrected proofs and associated correspondence. American poets represented in the collection include Louis Simpson, William Stafford, and others.

GUARDIAN ARCHIVES.

The archives of the *Guardian* (formerly the *Manchester Guardian*) are, unlike the documents described above, at present housed on the University site and not in the Deansgate building. The records include forty-eight boxes ('Guardian staff files') consisting of about 45,000 letters and other documents to and from over 6,600 correspondents. Most of these manuscripts, which date primarily from the 1930's through the 1950's, concern the operation of the newspaper as a business and have little direct connection with American affairs. There are, however, 772 letters, 1945-56, to and from Alastair Cooke when he served as a correspondent for the *Guardian* in America. There are also scattered letters to and from American newspapers such as the New York *Herald Tribune,* the New York *Times*, the Baltimore *Sun,* and the Raleigh (N.C.) *Times,* as well as occasional correspondence to and from prominent Americans, e.g. Eleanor Roosevelt. A typescript list of names is available in the Library.

DR. W.H. CHALONER, Department of Economic History, University of Manchester, Manchester M13 9PL

CREIGHTON, ROBERT. Letter-book and diary. 1856-7.

Letter-book and draft diary of Robert Creighton, textile merchant of Philadelphia, 1856-7, kept during a buying trip to Europe. Creighton's diary gives a good deal of information about the U.S. export trade in textiles (linen and cotton) in the 1850's.[1]

PUBLIC LIBRARIES, St. Peter's Square, Manchester M2 5PD

JEFFERSON, THOMAS. Notes on the State of Virginia (printed). 1782.

Jefferson had 200 copies of this book privately printed in 1782 for his friends. Opposite the title page is the author's presentation inscription to Dr. McMahon, '... unwilling to expose them [the notes] to the public eye he begs the favor of Dr. McMahon to put them into the hands of no person on whose care & fidelity he cannot rely to guard them against publication'.

PETER STUBS LTD. *and* STUBS, WOOD & CO. Business records.[1] 1796-1827. (On deposit.)

File, pin, etc., manufacturers of Warrington, Lancs. The records of this firm (forty-four boxes containing letters; a number of parcels containing loose, unsorted papers; miscellaneous letter-books, account books, etc.) include letters from Sheffield, Birmingham, etc., from 1796 onwards referring to goods ordered from Peter Stubs for the American trade. Correspondence with agents in New York began at some time prior to 1821, and continues until 1827, the last year for which letters are available. The letters include some from each of the following: John Sharp, Jr., Philadelphia; Wright, Taylor & Co., New York; T. Sherman, New York.

MANCHESTER CHAMBER OF COMMERCE. Proceedings and minutes.

This body was once known as the Manchester Association of Importers and Exporters. The Library holds 178 volumes, 1821- 1964. There are references to trade with the United States scattered throughout the volumes.[2]

AUTOGRAPH COLLECTIONS. Letters and notes. 1841-95.

Include the following, mainly trivia:

Bispham, David S. Leeds, 1 Oct. 1895, to Max Mayer. (Mayer Collection.)

Burritt, Elihu. Draft of an article, 'The loss of capital by war', n.d. (Withers Collection.)

Gaskell, E.C. Manchester, *c.* 1852, to Mrs. Schwabe, giving her impressions of Harriet Beecher Stowe. (Gaskell Collection.)

Holmes, Oliver Wendell. Boston, 3 May 1888, to Stanley Withers. (Withers Collection.)

Lardner, Dionysius. New York, 14 Dec. 1841, to Samuel Butler, actor, at the Tremont Theatre, Boston. (Swain Collection.)

Lowell, James Russell. Cambridge, Mass., 16 Feb. 1890, to Stanley Withers. (Withers Collection.)

Sargent, John Singer. London, n.d., to Charles Hallé. (Withers Collection.)

ALEXANDER IRELAND COLLECTION. Newspaper and periodical clippings; letters (5 boxes). 1846-88.

The collection, on Ralph Waldo Emerson, consists mainly of clippings from British and American newspapers and periodicals: reviews of books about Emerson, reports of his lectures, evaluations of his writings, obituaries. It also includes a few letters:

9. See Donald S. Baker, 'Charles Wesley and the American War of Independence', *Proceedings of the Wesley Historical Society*, vol. xxxiv, pp. 159-64, 1964, and vol. xl, pp. 125-34 and 165-182, 1976. Also see Donald S. Baker, 'Charles Wesley and the American Loyalists', *Proceedings of the Wesley Historical Society*, vol. xxxv, pp. 5-9, 1965.

1. See 'A Philadelphia Textile Merchant's Trip to Europe on the Eve of the Civil War: Robert Creighton, 1856-7', in *Trade and Transport: Essays in Honour of T.S. Willan*, ed. W.H. Chaloner and B.M. Ratcliffe. (Scheduled to have been published by Manchester University Press in 1977.)

1. See T.S. Ashton, *An Eighteenth Century Industrialist: Peter Stubs of Warrington, 1756-1806* (Manchester, 1939). Exports of 'P.S. files' to the United States in 1796 and 1797 are mentioned on p. 59.
2. See, *inter alia*, A. Redford, *Manchester Merchants and Foreign Trade*, vol. ii, 1850-1939 (Manchester, 1956).

Anon. Eulogy of Emerson, n.d., addressed to 'Christopher North' [John Wilson]. (12 pages.)

Carr, T. 28 Apr. 1888, to Alexander Ireland, including copy of a letter to Carr from George Crawley concerning his acquaintance with Emerson.

Emerson, Annie L. Concord, Mass., 28 May 1882, to Mrs. Conway, giving an account of Emerson's last illness. (Copy.)

Harris, W.T. Concord, Mass., 1 May 1882, to James H. Stirling. A tribute to Emerson. (Copy.)

Lytton, Edward Robert Bulwer, 1st Earl of Lytton. Carlsbad, Austria, 18 July 1882 (to Ireland?), comparing Emerson and Whitman. (Copy.)

THE NATIONAL (FORMERLY LANCASHIRE) PUBLIC SCHOOL ASSOCIATION. Letters. 1847-54.

The Association was formed in 1847 for the purpose of promoting the establishment of a general system of secular education in Lancashire, to be financed by local rates and controlled by local boards elected by the ratepayers. Among the Association's papers are many letters referring to the application of the Lancashire 'plan' in America, especially in New England, 1847-54.

ST. PAUL'S LITERARY AND EDUCATIONAL SOCIETY. MS. magazines, letters. 1850's-1962.

The Library has a collection of MS. copies of 'Odds and Ends', the (unpublished) magazine of St. Paul's Literary and Educational Society. The Society was founded in Oct. 1843 as Bennett St. Sunday School Mutual Improvement Class, and the magazine was issued from 1855 to 1962. Articles, some by eminent men of the time, deal with such subjects as the American Civil War, the American West, and American cities in the nineteenth and early twentieth centuries. Also included are several letters from America (Boston, New York) in the 1850's. (M38/4/2/1-106)

SMITH, JOHN BENJAMIN (1794-1879). 3 letters. 1866.

M.P. for Stockport, Cheshire, 1852-74. The sixteen-volume collection of his correspondence includes three letters on the *Alabama* case and Anglo-American relations, two from Smith to Lord Stanley, and one from Stanley to Smith.

WOMEN'S SUFFRAGE COLLECTION.

This 'Women's Suffrage Collection' is in fact two separate collections, donated to the Library in 1922 by Miss Margaret Ashton, formerly (1906-15) chairman of the Manchester Society for Women's Suffrage, and Mrs. Millicent Garrett Fawcett, LL.D., former president of the National Union of Women's Suffrage Societies. Although most of the material pertains exclusively to women's suffrage and women's rights in the United Kingdom, there are frequent references to America, especially for the years 1889-1916. There are also comments on American attitudes towards the First World War in letters from Mrs. Carrie Chapman Catt, president of the International Woman Suffrage Alliance.

CHORLTON UNION (POOR LAW GUARDIANS). 'Register of children emigrated to Canada.' 1906-22.

Contains details - name, under whose auspices emigrated, etc. - of some emigrants to the United States: of children in 1906, 1909, and 1920, and of families in 1921 and 1922.

SIMON PAPERS.

Notebooks, diaries, etc. of E.D. Simon, Lord Simon of Wythenshawe (1879-1960), including material relating to education and broadcasting in the U.S. and his visits there in 1942 and 1948.

MISCELLANEOUS LETTERS. 1815-91.

(*a*) Letter from William Scales of Glasgow, solicitor, to Job Wragg of Manchester, 17 Mar. 1815, about proceedings against Wragg to recover a debt, proceedings held up by the war between the two countries. (Misc/201)

(*b*) Letters of Richard and Frederick Cobden about trading in muslins with America. (M87/2/1/10, 11)

(*c*) Two letters from Edward Hardy of America to Frederick Cobden in Manchester, advising caution in dealing with the American market, and describing his farm in Lockport, N.Y. (M87/2/1/28, 29)

(*d*) John Bright, the English reformer, to Miss Arden, 16 May 1865, referring to the assassination of Abraham Lincoln. (Misc/16/9)

(*e*) Eight letters from Thomas Holt of Cheetham, designer for calico printers and Unitarian lay preacher, to relatives in America, Jane, Rowena, and Jessie. 1883-91. (Misc/390)

(*f*) Ashton Papers. Two letters from Elizabeth Gair Greene to Elizabeth Ashton, one from Boston and one from New York. Elizabeth Ashton was the mother of Elizabeth Marion Ashton, wife of James Bryce, who in 1906 became British Ambassador to the U.S. Also twenty-six letters from Margaret Ashton to her mother, Elizabeth Ashton, while visiting relatives in America, Aug. 1884-Jan. 1885. She gives her impressions of New York, Boston, Yellowstone Park, Salt Lake City, American policemen, education and food, etc.

OTHER DOCUMENTS. 18th century-1910.

(*a*) The autobiography of William Stout of Lancaster (1665-1752), Quaker grocer and ironmonger, contains references to trade with America. (MS. 923.8S8)

(*b*) 'Some Remarks Made on Board the Ship "Robert Burton" Whilst sailing from Liverpool to the United States of America. To which is added a few observations relative to the manners & customs of the People of New Jersey.' By Joseph Hurst, 1848-9.

(*c*) 'The American War of Independence' - two typed accounts of the American War of Independence, including the activities of the 1st Brigade, the Manchester Regiment, in the campaign. 1910.

OLDHAM LOCAL INTEREST CENTRE, Greaves Street, Oldham

ANNUAL REPORTS (printed). 1871-

Annual expenditure of the Oldham Operative Cotton Spinners and its branches, as given in these reports, 1871 onwards, included for some years - e.g., 1872-4, 1876-8, 1900 - money 'paid to members for emigrating'.

AMALGAMATED TEXTILE WORKERS' UNION, Textile Union Centre, 5 Caton Street, Rochdale OL16 1QJ

NORTHERN COUNTIES AMALGAMATED WEAVERS' ASSOCIATION. Minutes of General Council Meetings (printed). 1888.

There are references in the minutes of 1 and 22 Sept. 1888 to the payment of union funds to finance the emigration of a group of weavers, with their children, from Lower Heys Mill, Macclesfield, Cheshire, then on strike, via Castle Garden, N.Y., and the attempt of their employer to prevent their being allowed to land in the United States.

SALFORD CENTRAL LIBRARY, Peel Park, Salford M5 4WU

AMERICAN LETTERS. 3 letters. 1772-82.

(*a*) Franklin, Benjamin. London, 22 Aug. 1772, to John Bartram, Philadelphia, on horticultural matters.
(*b*) von Linnaeus, Carl. 24 June ?, to John Bartram, praising him for his horticultural knowledge.
(*c*) Washington, George. 26 Oct. 1782, thanking Captain Pray for a gift of oysters.

LOCAL STUDIES LIBRARY, Stalybridge, Tameside

HURST MILLS. Testimonial. 1862.

Testimonial, Dec. 1862, presented to John Whittaker ('Respected Master') by the workpeople of Hurst Mills, near Ashton-under-Lyne, 'for his generous conduct towards them during the period of the Cotton Famine, caused by the War in America'. The bulk of the fifty-two page manuscript consists of the signatures of the workpeople.

STOCKPORT CENTRAL LIBRARY, Wellington Road South, Stockport SK1 3RS

CHRISTY COLLECTION. Business records. 18th-20th century.

(*a*) Business correspondence and documents concerning beaver purchases from New York, 1823.
(*b*) W. Barlier's (?) notes on his American visit, 10 Aug.-23 Sept. 1859.
(*c*) Christy & Co. to C.M. Keller, New York, 1864, about a patent for a hydraulic press.
(*d*) Memoranda, diaries, and notes of visits to America by Stephen Christy, H. Barlier, W. Wild, etc., 1874-1928.
(*e*) Letter, 1882, to R.D. Greenlees from H.W. Beadie & Co. of Washington, D.C., concerning the law of trade marks.
(*f*) U.S.A., 1882-3: Correspondence with Beatty and Kennedy concerning piracy cases.
(*g*) Bundle of correspondence from Edmunds Johnson to the Trademarks Protection Society about the registration of Lincoln Bennett's trade mark in the U.S.A. [1886-8?]
(*h*) Correspondence, 1896, concerning the deposit of bonds of the Baltimore and Ohio Railroad Co. loan of 1885, and of the New York, Pennsylvania, & Ohio Railroad Co.
(*i*) Correspondence, 1950's, regarding exports to America, including correspondence with Bernard L. Salesky of the Hat Corporation of America about the possible manufacture of American hats under licence.

The Christy Collection contains other printed and manuscript documents of American interest, including catalogues, acts, bond issues, magazines, directories, patents and correspondence about patents, etc., many of which refer to the fur trade from the eighteenth to the twentieth century.

WIGAN RECORD OFFICE, Leigh Town Hall, Wigan

FOLLIOTT, GEORGE. Diary (1 volume), 1765-6. (Part of Edward Hall MS. Diary Collection.)

General merchant, New York. The diary was kept during a visit to England, spent mainly in London. While in London Folliott frequented the Exchange, the New York Coffeehouse, and the Antwerp Club. He discussed American affairs, particularly the question of a molasses tax, with Lord Rockingham. He visited the Victualling Office to arrange contracts for the supply in London of hogs and oxen, and in New York of beer, bread, pork, etc.; he discussed with Mr. Evory a contract for supplying warships at New York. His expenditure on laundry, travel, etc., is noted in some detail, and extensive lists of books bought and sent to New York are included.

COAL MINING PAPERS. 1838-94.

Chesterfield, Virginia, U.S.A.— Coal mining papers, 1838-94. (D/D Sc.B)

MERSEYSIDE

THE LIBRARY, THE ATHENAEUM, Church Alley, Liverpool L1 3DD

GLADSTONE COLLECTION. Bill of exchange book, 1784-1805; notebook, 1829.

(*a*) Bill of exchange book, 1784-1805. A large number of these bills were drawn in the United States, particularly in Philadelphia (these mainly by Robert Morris). The business is probably that of Corrie & Co., originally corn merchants of Liverpool, which John Gladstone (1764-1851) joined in 1786; the firm was subsequently known as Corrie, Gladstone & Bradshaw, and later as Gladstone & Co.[1]
(*b*) R.G. (?Robertson Gladstone) (1805-75), 'Journal of a voyage to, and residence in, the colony of Demerara, with a continuation of the same tour through the West India Islands & North (U.S. & British) America, & thence to Liverpool, commencing 12th October 1828, ending August 1829' (notebook of 85 pages). The section dealing with the author's visit to New York, Philadelphia, Albany, Buffalo, etc., consists largely of an impersonal record of such facts as layout of streets, number of theatres, major exports of the ports visited. A list of 'acquaintances formed' is included.

LIVERPOOL REGISTER OF SHIPPING (printed). 2 volumes (156, 10 pages). 1835, 1838.

These registers were compiled, because of a feeling that Lloyd's paid insufficient attention to local matters, by 'a committee of shipowners, merchants, and underwriters'. A large number of ships on the American run are included.

1. See Thomas Ellison, *The Cotton Trade of Great Britain including a History of the Liverpool Cotton Market and of the Liverpool Cotton Brokers' Association* (London, 1886).

LIVERPOOL ATLANTIC CATTLE TRADE, 1887-90 (printed) (90 pages). 1890.

This book, marked 'private and confidential: not for publication', is the 'Statement and Evidence of the Liverpool Steamship Owners' Association and Messrs. F. Leyland & Co.' about conditions on board the ships, sanitary precautions, etc.

PAMPHLET COLLECTION.

At least sixteen of the pamphlets, published 1769-83, concern political or military relationships between Britain and America; nineteenth- and twentieth-century pamphlets of American interest in the collection concern free trade, the Civil War, and other subjects.

BARCLAYS BANK LTD., Head Office, 4 Water Street, Liverpool L69 2EX

MARTINS BANK LTD. Bank records.[1] 1786-1903.

After an extensive search of the records of Arthur Heywood, Sons & Co. (absorbed 1893), the Liverpool Commercial Banking Company (absorbed 1889), the Bank of Liverpool (original name of Martins Bank), and various Liverpool offices of Martins Bank, officers of the Bank found the following material:

(*a*) Arthur Heywood, Sons & Co. (established 1773).

(i) Arthur Heywood's private ledger, containing a balancing of the accounts of the copartnership as of 4 Jan. 1786. Three of the entries refer to money due from the United States, the debtors being Andrew Brunner of Philadelphia, Reade & Bogardus of New York, and Donaldson & Stotts of Virginia; the first two are noted as unlikely to pay.

(ii) Two ledgers, covering the years 1791-7 and 1801-12. A quick search showed relevant references only in the account of Richard Heywood and James Currie, which includes entries of sums paid for American stock in 1791 and 1792, and for proceeds of sale of such stock in 1793.

(iii) Four signature-books - 1836, 1842, 1847, and one undated. The books contain specimen signatures of customers with addresses. The only American address noted was that of David Acheson of Washington, Pa., in the 1836 volume.

(*b*) Bank of Liverpool (established 1831).

Minutes of Directors' Meetings, 1831- . The first seven volumes, covering 1831-1903, contain various references to dealings with the United States, among which are the following: copies of letters sent to the Western Bank of Philadelphia and the Union Bank of Louisiana, 21 May 1833; a resolution that the Bank have no dealings in the bonds of Slave States, 26 Mar. 1839; purchase of Indiana Stock and other affairs of the North American Trust & Banking Co., 27 Oct. and 3 Nov. 1840, 9 July 1844, 11 July 1854; discussion concerning the propriety of continuing the account of the Bank of Charleston, 26 July 1844 and 8 July 1845; notes on the Bank's purchase and sale of United States Funded Loans, 1875-82; report of the failure of Martin, Wise & Fitzhugh, cotton merchants of Liverpool and Paris, Tex., 23 Mar. 1897.

CENTRAL LIBRARIES, William Brown Street, Liverpool L3 8EW

LIVERPOOL TOWN BOOKS.[1] (352 COUI)

These records, which are in the process of being published, contain occasional references to America - e.g. in Feb. 1733, concerning a grant to settle prisoners in Georgia; in Sept. 1779, concerning defence measures to be taken against possible attack by John Paul Jones.

NORRIS PAPERS.[2] Letters. 1693-1708. (920 NOR)

The letters to Richard Norris (1670-1731), merchant, Mayor of Liverpool, M.P., include some dealing with Virginia, from merchants or agents in London, Dublin, and elsewhere (not America). They note the arrival of the Virginia fleet, and include comment on tobacco crop prospects, tobacco prices, customs costs, the Virginia embargo, salt exports; many of these are from Thomas Johnson, who later was a customs officer in Virginia.

WHITLOCK, JOHN. Papers. 1751-92. (MD 3)

Correspondence, 1751-92, relating to the winding up of the affairs of John Whitlock of Manchester, sometime trader in Philadelphia. Although most of these documents concern the settling of Whitlock's estate, there are occasional references to his business in Philadelphia. Whitlock went to America in 1751 and, in partnership with John Green, began trading. They experienced some financial difficulties, however, and left a complicated legal tangle after their deaths.

TARLETON PAPERS.[3] Letters, deeds, and business accounts. 1754-80.

(*a*) John Tarleton, Sr. (1719-73), merchant, Liverpool. Included are his annual profit and loss accounts for most years from 1749 and those of Messrs. Tarleton & Backhouse, 1786-1810, also incomplete. The Tarleton business, both in John's lifetime and that of his sons, was very varied, including slave trading, privateering, West Indian estate owning, cotton importing, sugar refining, etc. Mention is made in the accounts of 13 June 1754 of money due to him 'by voyage to Philadelphia'; of 26 Apr. 1758 of money due 'brig *John* of Philadelphia' and of money owed 'to Henry Harrison of Philadelphia'; in 1761 there is a reference to 'lead unsold at New York', and in 1776 to 'brig *Fanny* to Pensacola' Fla.; there may well have been later trade with America, since, e.g. accounts with Nicholas Waterhouse, the Liverpool broker, appear in 1810.

(*b*) Sir Banastre Tarleton (1754-1833), one of the four sons of the above; officer in the British Army during the War of Independence. Two letters written in 1780 to 'my dear brother', one[4] from Winnsboro, S.C., and the other from Camp Camden, S.C. (copy), the latter giving an account of the battle at Camden on 16 Aug. 1780.

CASE AND SOUTHWORTH. Sales ledger. 1754-5. (380 MD, 33-36)

Merchants' and shipbrokers, Kingston, Jamaica. The sales ledger

1. Virginia material microfilmed by the Virginia Colonial Records Project. Since the first edition of the *Guide*, Martins Bank has merged with Barclays Bank Ltd.

---

1. See J.A. Twemlow, ed., *Liverpool Town Books, 1550-1862*; vol. i, 1550-71; vol. ii, 1571-1603 (Liverpool, 1918-35). Also see George Chandler, *Liverpool Under James I* (Liverpool, 1960), and *Liverpool Under Charles I* (Liverpool, 1965), which contain transcripts of the Liverpool Town Books for 1603-49.

2. Some of the letters are printed in T. Heywood, ed., *The Norris Papers* (Manchester, 1846) (Cheetham Society Publications, vol.ix).

3. See W.R. Serjeant, 'The Tarleton Papers: a Merchant's Accounts', *Liverpool Libraries, Museums and Arts Committee Bulletin*, vol. vi, pp. 28-31, 1956.

4. W.R. Serjeant, op. cit., includes a reproduction of this letter on p. 28.

includes a few references to cargoes - flour, staves, decanters - from Philadelphia. The collection also includes two account books for the period.

PARKER FAMILY PAPERS.[5] *c.* 600 items: almanac, notebook, 216 bundles (mainly letters). 1760-95. (920 PAR)

James Parker (1729-1815), merchant, and his family. Parker went to America as a young man, and became a merchant in Norfolk, Va. He fought as a captain in the British Army during the War of Independence. About two-thirds of the items in the collection relate to his career in Virginia or during the War, or to that of his son Patrick in Norfolk after the War. They include much family correspondence, including letters written by Parker, while a prisoner-of-war, to his wife and 150 letters, from Patrick - mostly from Norfolk - between 1785 and 1795; Parker's diary of the War in the form of letters; and miscellaneous papers concerning prize money accounts. Also in the collection are 'copies of Franklin documents, three Williamsburg imprints (a Purdie & Dixon interleaved almanac of 1771, an annotated copy of the Virginia Association of 1771, and a printed letter of Edmund Randolph dated 1774, indicating that he has assumed Mr. Jefferson's law practice in the General Court), a letter of Robert Morris [*re* the Boston Tea Party], . . . a letter of William Aitchison's, November 14, 1774, describing the proceedings in Williamsburg after the York River tea party'.[6]

SAMWELL, DAVID (1751-98).[7] 3 letters. 1774-95. (920 GRE 2/17)

Surgeon, London and on ships. Most of the fifty-six letters in the collection are from Samwell to Matthew Gregson, upholsterer and antiquarian, of Liverpool. A few of these contain comment on Anglo-American relations, 1774, 1775; and on Thomas Paine, 1795.

CURRIE, JAMES (1756-1805). 'Journal of a Voyage from Nixonton No. Carolina to the Island of Saint Martin's.'[8] 1775-6. (Currie Papers, 920 CUR)

Physician. This journal, kept during the voyage in 1776, includes a balancing of the good and bad experiences of his five years' stay in America. At the end of the notebook Currie has copied from the original manuscript a letter 'which I wrote in Mar. 1775, & which appeared in Pinkney's [*sic*] Gazette [*Virginia Gazette*] of 24th of that month'. This letter, sent anonymously, is a defence of the Scots merchants in Virginia against attacks which had been made on them; Currie notes that the letter as he here transcribes it includes some sentences 'which were thought too severe' by Pinckney and so omitted in the publication of the letter.

HOLT AND GREGSON PAPERS. 1778-early 19th century. (920 HOL)

This is a collection of nineteen volumes of manuscript and printed material for a history of Liverpool, made by John Holt during the latter part of the eighteenth century and by Matthew Gregson until about 1830. Volume 10 includes statements of monthly imports of cotton from various countries into London and Liverpool in 1792; it also includes a section on docks, shipping, and commerce; and list of the ships, statistics, and documents connected with the slave trade. Volume 19 includes a compilation by Gregson of all vessels that were taken by Liverpool privateers between 28 July 1778 and 13 Apr. 1779; a number of the ships taken are listed as having come from American ports. There may be other relevant material in the papers.

HORNBY LIBRARY AUTOGRAPH LETTERS. 1782-1857.

Of no intrinsic interest, merely letters of *politesse* from the following:

Barnum, P.T. Bridgeport, 9 Nov. 1848, to J. Nimms.
Cooper, James Fenimore. Paris, 15 Aug. 1827, to an unknown correspondent.
Franklin, Benjamin. Passy, 9 Apr. 1782, to F. Nogarei.
Hawthorne, Nathaniel. Liverpool, 10 Aug. 1857, to H.A. Bright.
Irving, Washington. New York, 21 Mar. 1835, to Robert Southey, introducing the Rev. Francis L. Hawks of New York.

SPARLING & BOLDEN. Letter-book. 1788-99. (MD 219)

John Sparling and William Bolden, Liverpool merchants. Most of the letter copies are to merchants in Virginia, mainly to John Lawrence & Co. Business affairs dealt with relate to export from Liverpool of nails, twine, salt, linens, and import of tar, turpentine, tobacco; many of the letters refer to attempts to settle debts contracted before the War of Independence. There is also some discussion of other matters, such as French privateering, and yellow fever epidemics and fires in Norfolk, Va.

ROSCOE PAPERS. Correspondence; some manuscript notes, pamphlets, etc. 1794-1831. (920 RDS)

William Roscoe (1753-1831), historian, poet, reformer, M.P., of Liverpool. His great interest in prison reform is the major topic of his large American correspondence, but many letters concern current Anglo-American political affairs, and some his commercial interests. (A typescript calendar, arranged alphabetically, is available.)

(*a*) Correspondence on American prison management and reform, 1816-31.

Letters from Alden Bradford, Gamaliel Bradford, C.A. Busby, John F. Champlin, Thomas P. Cope, Caleb Cresson, Louis Dwight, Thomas Eddy, William Eustis, John Griscom, S.M. Hopkins, Edward Livingston, William Maxwell, James Mease, Josiah Quincy, William Tudor, Gulian C. Verplanck, and Chauncey Whittelsey. There are also drafts or copies of letters from Roscoe, or, in a few cases, letters written on his behalf, to most of these correspondents, as well as to Elizabeth Fry, General Lafayette, and T.I. Wharton.

In addition, the collection includes printed pamphlets and reports, 1795-1826, on American prisons.

(*b*) Correspondence on other American topics, 1794-1830.

Bradbury, John. Most of the correspondence, 1806-11, concerning his plant collecting trip has been published.[9]

Brougham, Henry Peter (later Baron Brougham and Vaux). 1812-13. At least fourteen of the letters in the extensive correspondence between Brougham and Roscoe include comment on Anglo-American affairs.

5. Microfilms are at Colonial Williamsburg, and have been made for the Virginia Colonial Records Project.
6. J.M. Hemphill II, 'Virginia and the Parker Family Papers', *Liverpool Libraries, Museums and Arts Committee Bulletin*, vol. vi, pp. 25-7, 1956.
7. See H.A. Taylor, 'David Samwell', *Liverpool Libraries, Museums and Arts Committee Bulletin*, vol. vi, pp. 32-46, 1956, where these letters are quoted.
8. Extracts printed in W.W. Currie, ed., *Memoir of the Life, Writings, and Correspondence of James Currie*, vol. i (London, 1831), pp. 34-8.
9. See H.W. Rickett, 'John Bradbury's Explorations in Missouri Territory', *Proceedings of the American Philosophical Society*, vol. xciv, pp. 59-89, 1950.

Cooper, Thomas. Seven letters from Philadelphia, 1815-9, and one from Columbia, S.C., 1830, include comment on political and scientific affairs.

Daulby, William. Draft letters and copies of letters from 'W.D.', New York, 1817-9. Business matters, mainly concerning importing of steel and hardware, exporting of cotton, with some comment on bankruptcies and other indicators of depressed conditions. Also an 1827 letter from Daulby to W.S. Roscoe, and several relating to the settlement of Daulby's affairs after his death.

Eddowes, Ralph. Twenty-four letters, Philadelphia, 1794-1828, concerning family, political, financial, and business (import of white lead) affairs.

Fraser, John, Jr. London, 1 June 1810, on American plants and seeds.

Heywood, Benjamin A. Manchester, 4 Oct. 1794, on his attitude towards the United States and its prosperity.

Jefferson, Thomas. Washington, D.C., 1 Sept. 1806; and Monticello, 27 Dec. 1820, concerning the proposed university in Virginia.

Tartt, William Macdonald. Two letters, Charleston, S.C., 1810 and 1811, during his visit to the United States, concern politics, Benjamin Rush, etc.

Thornely, Thomas. London, 9 June 1812, concerning the Orders in Council; 12 Dec. 1828 mentioning the conversion to Unitarianism of Philadelphia Quakers and quoting a letter from G.M. Justice of Philadelphia on prison discipline.

Tuffen, T.F. (of Tuffen & Pugh, bankers of Bristol). London, 12 Mar. 1812, to Messrs. Roscoe, Clarke & Roscoe concerning James Slater Hall, who has absconded to America.

William Frederick, 2nd Duke of Gloucester. Correspondence, 1806-25, concerning the slave trade and Anglo-American relations.

Wright, Frances, the feminist, reformer, and freethinker. Two letters, New York and Allenby, Cumberland, 1820, concern her plays.

(*c*) Other American correspondence, 1803-31.
Letters from J.J. Audubon, Benjamin S. Barton, William P.C. Barton, E. Bronson, William Ellery Channing, Joseph Charless, W. Creswell, Joseph Delaplaine, Joseph Gilpin, Maximilian Godefroy, William Gracie, Christopher Hughes, John Lowell, William Maclure, Samuel L. Mitchell, John Richardson, Benjamin Rush, Benjamin Silliman, Mrs. Smallcroft, W.C. Somerville, William B. Sprague, George Ticknor, Aaron B. Tucker, Noah Worcester.

(*d*) A notebook containing manuscript notes about 'the coast of the territory of New Orleans', etc.; and the manuscript journal, 1805-6, of John Williamson, 'who ascended White River in company with his wife, in pursuit of game'. Both of these include extensive descriptions of Indian tribes. The notebook also contains newspaper cuttings on this subject.

AMERICAN CHAMBER OF COMMERCE FOR THE PORT OF LIVERPOOL. Minutes (4 volumes, indexed separately). 1801-1908. (380 AME)

The initial purposes of this British organization were the redress of existing, and the prevention of future, grievances affecting the American trade, and the establishment of regular and settled rules in respect of payments of freights and rates of fees in the customs and at public boards and offices in London. 'The annual survey of the work of the Chamber, the annual financial statement of the Treasurer, meetings of the general committee, of sub-committees and of the financial council, special general meetings and banquets were reported. Important letters received by the Chamber and the replies to them were sometimes recorded in full.'[10]

BROWN, GEORGE ALEXANDER (1803-70). Memoirs and diaries (3 volumes). 1803-63. (920 MD 376)

Merchant and banker. The first of the three volumes describes Brown's boyhood and schooldays in Baltimore; his work in his uncle's firm - Alexander Brown & Sons, linen merchants, Baltimore - including comment on the decline of the linen trade after 1817; his partnership in a merchant firm in Tampico, Mexico, in 1825, and the vicissitudes of this firm; his establishment in Liverpool in 1829.

The diary entries thereafter, including those in the latter two volumes, concern political, family, and business affairs; some of these include notes of the arrival of American ships, and also reactions to two visits from Hawthorne in November 1855.

McIVER, McVICAR & McCORQUODALE. Document (2 folios). 1804. (MD 97)

Accounts for the sale, on behalf of this Liverpool firm, of 197 Negroes, signed by Benjamin Maurice Pickering, Savannah, Ga., 28 Feb. 1804.

JOSEPHS, JOSEPH. Papers (1 vol.). 1805. (380 MD 144)

Silversmith, Liverpool. This volume of privateering papers contains receipts and other papers relating to disposal of prize money; at least one American ship, the *Commerce*, is involved.

HOPE, SAMUEL, & CO. — GEORGE HOLT & CO. 10 ledgers.[11] 1812-66. (MD 230)

Cotton brokers and bankers, Liverpool. The partnership of Samuel Hope and George Holt as cotton brokers and bankers was dissolved in 1821, the cotton side of the business thereafter being known as George Holt & Co. The ledgers contain many entries of sales of sea island and other American cottons; the ledger covering the years 1830-42 includes two pages devoted to 'New Orleans acct.' for the years 1835-40.

HASSAL, JOHN SATTERFIELD. Diaries (3 vols.). 1834-6. (MD 219/9-11)

These diaries provide a fascinating account of Hassal's life in the U.S. from his arrival in New York in 1834 until 1836. He comments on American scenery, the cities which he visits, and his own interests, including phrenology.

BROWN, SHIPLEY & CO. Ledger and letter-book. 1830's -1859. (Acc. 1215)

Merchant bankers, Liverpool.

(*a*) Ledger No. 4 (2 vols.): Accounts concerning business with numerous firms, including many in the U.S., in the 1830's and 1840's. American firms with which Brown, Shipley & Co., had business connexions were located in New York; Boston; Philadelphia; Charleston, S.C.; Columbus, Ohio; Portsmouth, N.H.; Albany, N.Y.; Baltimore, etc.

(*b*) Partner's letter-book. Copy letters, 1851-9, to branch of the firm in New York, dealing with many aspects of the company's business.

10. W.O. Henderson, 'The American Chamber of Commerce for the Port of Liverpool, 1801-1908', *Transactions of the Historic Society of Lancashire and Cheshire*, vol. lxxxv, pp. 1-61, 1933.

11. Mentioned in F.E.Hyde, *Blue Funnel* (Liverpool, 1956).

BROWN, JAMES. Log-book, letter-book. 1843-8. (387 MD, 47-48)

Captain of the Liverpool ship *Gossypium*. The log of the ship covers six voyages from Liverpool to New Orleans and five from New Orleans to Liverpool, 1844-6. The letter copies, 1843-8, include those from Brown in New Orleans, to the owners of the ship - John Croft, and Messrs. Clint and Leftwich - concerning prices, progress, etc., in selling the salt and tin-plate which seem to have been the main cargoes, and in buying cotton and 'Indian corn'.

REPORTS ON THE COTTON MARKET (1 vol.). 1848-63. (380 MD 130)

Weekly summaries of sales, imports, etc., presumably at Liverpool. A brief comment on trade during each week is included, these frequently referring to the United States - e.g, in 1848 there appear such notes as 'American scarce', 'large receipts at NO', 'demand for sea island', and in 1861 'US a/CS more warlike', 'large export to America', 'anxious of U.S., holders determined to sell'.

MANN, WILLIAM THOMPSON. 'Diary of a Trip to America.' 1848-9. (920 MD 377)

Mann went south from New York to Apalachicola, Fla., via Philadelphia, Washington, D.C., Savannah, Ga., etc.: he took a steamer along the coast to New Orleans, and then went north to Kentucky, Ohio, to Montreal and back to New York. Most of the entries relate to sightseeing or social calls paid.

BUCKLEY-MATHEW, GEORGE B. (1807-79). Correspondence (1 vol.). 1831-79. (Acc. 2463)

M.P., Consul at Charleston, S.C., 1850-3, and at Philadelphia 1853-6. The collection includes letters from the following:

Boucicault, Dion. New York, 14 June 1856.

Bulwer, Sir William Henry. Washington, D.C., 3 May 1851, and New York, 2 Aug. 1851, asking for news of the 'Cuban expedition'.

Butler, A.P. Washington, D.C., 15 Feb. 1852, including discussion of the 'kidnapping traffic', i.e. the capture of free West Indian Negro seamen and their sale in the South.

Crampton, John F. Washington, D.C., 18 Dec. 1851 and 20 Feb. 1852, including a discussion of the 'kidnapping traffic'.

Cowper-Temple, W.F. Writing from England, 1855, 'I suppose the American Irish invasion will end in smoke, otherwise we shall have the trouble of sinking them in the Atlantic on their way.'

Gladstone, William. Two letters, 1852, thanking Mathew for information and suggestions; and two, 1856, relating to Mathew's leaving his consular post at the request of the United States government as a result of his attempted recruitment of Americans for service in the Crimean War.

Grey, Sir Charles E. Jamaica, 20 Jan. 1855, referring to the 'kidnapping traffic', and thanking Mathew for his kindness in the United States, especially his introduction to General Ward.

James, G.P.R. Norfolk, Va., 10 June 1855, including discussion of the 'kidnapping traffic'.

Lytton, Edward Robert Bulwer. 29 Feb. 1854, including discussion of reciprocity.

Sumner, Charles. Boston, 10 Sept. 1854.

Thackeray, W.M. [from America]. 7 Jan. [1855].

Letters written to Mathew in America from correspondents in England, containing comment on American affairs, are those from John Bigelow, 1855; the Earl of Ellesmere, 1855; and Miles T. Stapleton (Baron Beaumont), 1854.

The collection also includes a letter from John F. Crampton at the British Legation in Washington, D.C., 9 Sept. 1851, to Daniel Lance, acting Consul at Charleston, S.C., concerning a letter he has had from someone named Randolph which informs him of a plan for releasing Smith O'Brien and other Irish leaders from the penal colony in Tasmania.

BAKER, F.J. and R.L. FREER. 'Account of a Voyage in the *Great Eastern*.' 1862. (H. 387.21 GRE)

Included are details of their stay in New York City - Central Park, the magnificence of the shops, etc. - of their journey up the Hudson River and to Niagara and Buffalo.

WALT WHITMAN MSS. 1880-1. (Acc. 2440)

(*a*) Autograph MS. of Whitman's 'Three young men's deaths', bearing his instructions to the proof reader, with a corrected galley-proof.
(*b*) Four notes, from Whitman to John Fraser, editor of *Cope's Tobacco Plant*, concerning, among other matters, the publication of 'The dalliance of the eagles' in the magazine.
(*c*) Three letters, 1880, from John Ruskin to Herbert J. Bathgate, giving his opinion of Emerson, Lowell, and Whitman.
(*d*) Three autograph postcards, 1880, from Whitman to Bathgate, all addressed from Camden, N.J.

CLEMENS, S.L. ('MARK TWAIN'). Letter, etc. 1907-54. (MD 242)

(*a*) Letter from Mark Twain to Mrs. Edith Draper, Ormskirk, 15 Jan. 1907.
(*b*) Five items, postcard, cutting, etc., of incidental interest, relating to Twain.

MERSEYSIDE CHAMBER OF COMMERCE AND INDUSTRY, No. 1 Old Hall Street, Liverpool L3 9HG

REPORTS (printed). 1850-

The volumes include annual, committee, and special reports of the Chamber, and the proceedings of the annual general meeting. Comment on matters relating to the United States is frequent, since subjects such as the following were dealt with: revision of international maritime law, Atlantic mail and cable services, American tariff policy, problems connected with the *Alabama* case, etc.

MERSEYSIDE COUNTY ARCHIVES, William Brown Street, Liverpool L3 8EN

COBHAM ARCHIVE. Letters and documents. 1861-82.

This important collection consists of fifty-eight letters, along with a will and lawsuit, from and concerning George Cobham of Warren Co., Pennsylvania, and his family. A number of these letters relate to Cobham's emigration to Pennsylvania and to the American Civil War. The material dealing with the Civil War includes Cobham's reflections on slavery, the war experiences of his sons in the Union Army, and the assassination of Abraham Lincoln. Cobham also questions why England should 'show a partiality for the Southern Confederacy' since 'the South has for years shut both her eyes and her ears to the sufferings of the poor negro!'

HAROLD COHEN LIBRARY, UNIVERSITY OF LIVERPOOL, Liverpool L69 3BX

WATERHOUSE & SONS.[1] Ledger. 1799-1800.

Cotton brokers, Liverpool. (Nicholas Waterhouse was probably the most important cotton broker of the time.) The ledger includes entries relating to the sale of Georgia cotton.

CUNARD STEAMSHIP COMPANY ARCHIVES. 1840-*c.* 1945.

The papers are now in the custody of the University Archives (ref. D. 42), but are housed in the Harold Cohen Library due to lack of space in Senate House, where the University Archives office is located. They are mainly the administrative archives of the company, and any American content is diffused throughout the whole series of records. The records consist principally of board minutes, letter-books, passage books, working files on the construction and fitting out of vessels, trading affairs, and publicity department compilations on various vessels and the company's history.

SYDNEY JONES LIBRARY, UNIVERSITY OF LIVERPOOL, P.O. Box 123, Liverpool

RATHBONE COLLECTION.[1] Papers, letters, etc. 1819-97.

The Rathbone family were Liverpool merchants who dealt with the United States as well as with many other countries. The main documents relating to the United States are as follows:
(*a*) Thirty-two packets of correspondence, mainly business (cotton, coffee, tea), from New York, Boston, etc., 1819-73.
(*b*) Two folders of correspondence, mainly personal, between William Rathbone (1819-1902) and his family during his visits to America, 1839-49.
(*c*) One letter-book: William Rathbone (1787-1868) to 'New England Relief Society',[2] 1847, concerned with the relief of distress in Ireland.
(*d*) One packet of personal letters, 1895-7, from J.M. Forbes, of Boston, to William Rathbone (1819-1902).

NORFOLK

PARISH CHURCH, ALBY, Norwich

EMIGRANT RECORDS.

Some documents in the Church safe relate to an emigration loan of £100 at 5 per cent. raised in 1836.

DUKE OF NORFOLK, Arundel Castle[1]

NORFOLK PAPERS. 1633-7 (or 1639?).

(*a*) '1633, 7 Aug. Appointment by Leonard Calvert ... [Governor of Maryland] of Sir Richard Lechford, of Shellwood, Surrey ... as his attorney to receive and dispose of all such merchandizes and commodities as he shall at any time send out of the province of Maryland'.[2]
(*b*) Short letter from London, 6 May 1637 [or 1639?] to Calvert from Sir Richard Lechford, complains that small profits have come from their adventure in Maryland, from which they expected much. He desires that the stock remaining with Calvert may be employed to the best advantage, but will invest no more until better results are seen.[3]
(*c*) Transcript of documents relating to the settlement of Catholics in Maryland in 1634, with a rough sketch of the history of the colonization of Maryland. Two documents, nineteenth century.

LYONS PAPERS.[4]

Correspondence of Richard Bickerton Pemell Lyons, 2nd Baron and 1st Earl Lyons (1817-87), British Minister to the United States 1858-64.

These papers are on temporary deposit with the West Sussex Record Office, County Hall, Chichester, for sorting and listing. They are unlikely to be available to scholars until 1978 at the earliest. See Lyons Papers, West Sussex Record Office, p. 223.

R.Q. GURNEY, Bawdeswell Hall, East Dereham

GURNEY MSS. Letters. 1837-40.[1]

Joseph John Gurney wrote long journal letters to his family while on his ministry for the English Society of Friends to refute the teachings of the 'Hicksites'. He travelled through the Carolinas and New England, visiting Washington and New York. Letters 533, 535, 539-40, 547, and 561 are particularly interesting on slavery and the American Anti-Slavery Society. Visited many institutions, e.g. Sing Sing and a lunatic asylum at Worcester, Mass. Much impressed by the factory system at Lowell (541). Discusses the burning of the Pennsylvania Hall, Philadelphia, following abolitionist meeting in July 1838 (539). Visits Washington and meets Webster, Polk, Clay, and J.Q. Adams (536), and addresses President and Congress (537). A

1. See S. Dumbell, 'The Cotton Market in 1799', *Economic History,* vol. i, pp. 141-8, 1926. F.E. Hyde and others, 'The Cotton Broker and the Rise of the Liverpool Cotton Market', *Economic History Review,* vol. viii, pp. 75-83, 1955.

---

1. *Catalogue of the Rathbone Papers in the University Library, Liverpool. Part i: Family Papers; part ii: Business papers* (Liverpool, 1959-60). See also E.F. Rathbone, *William Rathbone, a Memoir* (London, 1905); E.A. Rathbone, *Records of the Rathbone Family* (Edinburgh, 1913); S.G. Checkland, 'An English Merchant House in China after 1842', *Bulletin of the Business Historical Society,* vol. xxvii, pp. 158-89, 1953; Sheila Marriner, 'Rathbones' Trading Activities in the Middle of the Nineteenth Century', *Transactions of the Historic Society of Lancashire and Cheshire,* vol. cviii, pp. 105-27, 1957, and her *Rathbones of Liverpool* (Liverpool, 1961). S.G. Checkland, 'American versus West Indian traders in Liverpool, 1793-1815', *Journal of Economic History,* vol. xviii, pp. 141-60, 1958.
2. This is the binder's title for the letter-book which relates to various relief committees in towns in New England - there is no single body with the binder's title.

---

1. Access to the archives at Arundel Castle is only by arrangement with the Duke of Norfolk's archivist, Dr. Francis W. Steer.
2. H.M.C. Various Collections, ii [55], p. 343.
3. Synopsis, H.M.C. Various Collections, ii[55], p. 344.
4. Some of the letters in this collection were published in Lord Newton, *Lord Lyons, a Record of British Diplomacy,* 2 vols. (London, 1913).

---

1. Gurney, Joseph John. *A Journey in North America, described in familiar letters to Amelia Opie* (Norwich , priv. print., 1841).

copy of a letter of thanks, 13 June 1839, from President Van Buren (551). Many scattered comments on agriculture, landscape, and manners. (in large box, portfolio C, items numbered 531-61)

PARISH CHURCH, GREAT RYBURGH, Fakenham NR21 OEB

EMIGRANT RECORDS.

Churchwardens' and overseers' accounts of charges on the rates for £400 in 1836 for emigration. Also correspondence with the Poor Law Commissioners. (There are earlier papers for 1809 and 1810 concerning enclosures in the parish).

BRIGADIER H. LONG, O.B.E., M.C., Heydon, Norwich

BULWER, SIR HENRY (1801-72). Papers: 3 dispatch boxes.[1]

William Henry Lytton Earle Bulwer, Baron Dalling and Bulwer (1801-72) (better known as Sir Henry Bulwer); diplomat. The papers mainly relate to his service as Minister at Madrid 1844-9, and then to his time at Constantinople 1857-65. Some papers relate to his earlier travels and residence in Paris, but none directly to his time as Minister in Washington 1849-52. Each of the boxes contains upwards of a thousand letters, including many from, as well as to, Palmerston, Addington, Peel, Aberdeen, etc. There is a rough pencilled list of contents on top of each box.

Box 1: Madrid, 1844-9. Letter, 25 Jan. 1849, from Palmerston offers Bulwer the post of Minister in Washington, which 'would have the advantage of getting you honourably out of the embarrassment as to the question of returning or not returning to Madrid'. A copy of a letter, 10 Nov. 1849, from Bulwer to Palmerston, acknowledges receipt of H.M Government's instructions relating to his American mission and of Palmerston's own instructions.

Box 2: Constantinople, 1857-65.

Box 3: Constantinople, 1858-65. A printed copy, headed 'For use of the Foreign Office, 27 July 1854' of James Buchanan's note from the United States Legation in London, 22 July 1854, entitled *Remarks in Reply to Lord Clarendon's Statement of May 2nd, 1854;* there are marginal notations in Sir Henry Bulwer's hand. Also a copy, n.d., of a letter of Bulwer to Lord Clarendon, urging caution on the above matter - American complaints about British expansion in Central America, particularly on the Mosquito Coast and the island of Roatán, allegedly contrary to the terms of the Clayton-Bulwer Treaty.

PARISH CHURCH, HINDOLVESTON, Dereham

EMIGRANT RECORDS.

A notice of a vestry meeting concerning emigration, *c.* 1836. There may be entries in four volumes of overseers' books.

EARL OF LEICESTER, Holkham, nr. Wells-on-Sea

This is a private library[1] built by successive owners upon the basis of Sir Edward Coke's library (see W.O. Hassall, ed., *A Catalogue of the Library of Sir Edward Coke* (London and New Haven, Conn., 1950) (Yale Law Library Publications Series, no. 12); many papers of Thomas Coke, 'Coke of Norfolk', are also there. As the Librarian is only at Holkham at varying times of the year, it is essential to write well in advance for permission to work in the library.

CHRISTOPHER COLUMBUS. Letter. 1493.

One of seven known contemporary copies of Columbus's own account of his discovery of America, written as Admiral of the Fleet of the Ocean. The original is in Seville. This copy is connected with Planck's first edition - also at Holkham - having the same errors as the title.

BARGRAVE, JOHN. *c.* 1625.

A copy of the petition of John Bargrave, planter in Virginia, to the House of Commons concerning the Virginia Company; it is inserted loose in Sir Edward Coke's own copy of *For the Colony in Virginia Britannia, Lawes Divine, Morall, and Martiall* (London, 1612).

COKE, THOMAS WILLIAM, 1st Earl of Leicester (1754-1842). Letters from Americans. 3 guard-books. 1810-34. Vol. iii contains 47 letters to Coke. Vol. i contains accidentally 2 letters, 1837.

Coke of Norfolk, the agricultural reformer, was a patron of the American cause in Norfolk politics and in the House of Commons during the Revolutionary era. A print of George Washington at Holkham is inscribed: 'Every night during the American War did I drink the health of George Washington as the greatest man on earth.' No letters, however, relating to this earlier period appear to survive: most of the 'Letters from Americans' refer to agricultural reform, though many air strong Whig politics too.

The annual sheep-shearing at Holkham was almost a place of pilgrimage for Americans visiting Europe who were interested in agricultural reform; Coke's methods, and his agricultural shows, were clearly of great influence in America. The letters (arranged chronologically) are from the following:

King, Rufus. 29 July 1810, asking for advice about purchase of cows and discussing the Napoleonic War and American commercial policy.

Logan, George. 'Stenton', Pa., 2 June 1812, concerning his private mission to attempt a reconciliation between the two countries. He discusses the hopes for peace and the common importance of maintaining the agricultural interest over the 'moral and physical evils of the manufacturing system'. Also a letter, 24 Mar. 1817, referring to his stay at Holkham and to a new drilling machine. And a third similar letter, 19 Oct. 1819.

Caton, Richard. Three letters, 20 Mar. 1817, 16 June 1821, 20 May 1833, mostly about exchange of agricultural machinery, animals, products, and information. Caton was a Baltimore merchant, born in England, whose daughters all married into high English society.

Rush, Richard, American statesman and Minister to London. Four letters, 1819-23, concerning agricultural reforms.

1. These papers have now been listed in N.R.A. 6790, and are on loan to the Norfolk Record Office.

1. Virginia material microfilmed by the Virginia Colonial Records Project.

Lyman, Theodore, philanthropist. 6 Aug. 1819, concerning agriculture.

Williams, Charles, Vermont statesman. 6 Aug. 1819, concerning agriculture.

Mease, James, physician and author of Pennsylvania. 14 Sept. 1819, concerning agriculture.

Parish (or Farish), David. Annapolis, N.S., 28 Apr. 1820, announcing that Coke had been made an honorary member of the Montreal Agricultural Society and enclosing a note to that effect from a Mr. Gillespie.

King, Charles. n.d., introducing William Beach Lawrence.

Lowell, John, Boston merchant. 15 Nov. 1821, announcing that Coke had been made an honorary member of the Massachusetts Society for Promoting Agriculture.

Pomeroy, S.W. Brighton, nr. Boston, Mass., n.d., concerning agriculture.

Hughes, Christopher, diplomat. Twenty-two letters, 1823-32, mostly personal and about mutual friends, or rather great acquaintances, though occasional political gossip. He encloses copies of three letters of Lafayette to himself.

Hunter, John Dunn. London, 15 Feb. 1824, flattering Coke. Hunter was the adventurer who falsely claimed to have been raised by the Kickapoo Indians and who was feted by the Royal Society in London.

Harper, Robert Goodloe, United States Senator. 10 Apr. 1824, concerning agriculture.

Weeks, Ezra. 20 Dec. 1824, asking Coke to allow William E. West, American artist, to paint his portrait.

Bainbridge, William. 30 Aug. 1825, introducing James Potter of Savannah, Ga., James Hamilton of Philadelphia, and James Hamilton Couper of Charleston, S.C., to see the improvements and stock at Holkham.

Barbour, James, statesman, Minister to London. 20 Sept. 1829, letter of thanks for a visit to Holkham.

Fisher, John, a New York farmer. Two letters, 10 and 31 Mar. 1831, recalling a visit to Holkham thirty years previously and telling of his delight at now finding Coke's breeds of sheep and cattle all over New York.

D'Evereux, General. Paris, 17 May 1831, introducing a Colonel Thorn of New York.

Jackson, Andrew. 1 Oct. 1834, praising Coke and introducing a Mr. Bradford of Massachusetts.

The first volume of the three guard-books also contains, accidentally, two American letters, both written from London. One from Richard Rush, 22 July 1837, congratulating Coke on his elevation to the peerage, and the other, 21 July 1837, from A. Stevenson on the same subject.

PRINTED MATERIAL: pamphlets, etc.

Several bound volumes of miscellaneous English seventeenth-century pamphlets containing many items of American interest, some rare: e.g. three copies of the English edition of *The Simple Cobler of Aggawam* (London, 1647); a number of religious tracts, e.g., *Severall questions of Serious and necessary Consequence ... unto M. John Cotton of Boston in New-England* (London, 1647); several accounts of the New England and Virginia settlements, including John Underhill's *Newes from America* (London, 1638). One volume is particularly noteworthy for its accounts of Virginia including *Virginia Richly Valued ... translated out of Portuguese by Richard Hakluyt* (London, 1609), *A True Relation of such Occurrences and Accidents of Noate as hath Happened in Virginia ... by Captain Smith* (London, 1608), and several proclamations dated 1610 by the 'Counsell of Virginia', advertising for 'sufficient, honest and good artificers'.

LOCAL STUDIES DEPARTMENT, (NORFOLK COUNTY LIBRARY), Central Library, Bethel Street, Norwich NR2 1NJ

FRED HENDERSON (1867-1957). Press cuttings. 1933-5.

Socialist publicist and Norwich alderman. Henderson toured the United States and Canada in 1933 and again in 1934-5. There are numerous cuttings about these tours, including his address to the Wisconsin State Legislature of 12 Feb. 1935; to the Taylor Society in New York of 8 Dec. 1933; and to the Eighteenth National Convention of the Socialist Party of America, 1934, in Chicago. There are also separate American editions of 1934 of his *Case for Socialism* by the Socialist Party of the United States, Chicago, and the New York State Socialist Party.

NORFOLK RECORD OFFICE, Central Library, Norwich NR2 1NJ

GREAT YARMOUTH ASSEMBLY BOOK. 1598-1625.

The Great Yarmouth assembly book, 1598-1625, (at Yarmouth Town Hall, but viewable by appointment with N.R.O.), contains orders, 1615-6, concerning the town's participation in the Virginia lottery.

NORWICH CITY RECORDS. 1614-7.

Contemporary copies of letters, 1614-7, concerning the Virginia Company Lottery (City Revenues and Letters, fos. 13, 14, 17, 18) and an order, 1617, concerning the same (Mayor's Court Book, no. 15, fo. 164).

FELLOWES COLLECTION. 1743.

List of the inhabitants of Savannah, Ga., with a plan of the town, 1743. (uncatalogued, P151B)

COLMAN COLLECTION.

The autobiography of Samuel Ward of Great Yarmouth (*c.* 1710-1778), who emigrated to Georgia in 1733 and returned to England in 1739. (191, T1303)

GURNEY AND BARCLAY FAMILY PAPERS.

A daughter of David Barclay (1728-1809), banker and merchant, specialist in the American trade, married the father of Hudson Gurney (1775-1864), M.P. and antiquarian, the first of several subsequent alliances between Gurneys and Barclays. Of the surviving papers which pertain to the business and personal interests of these two families, many eighteenth-century documents of American relevance are now deposited in the Norfolk Record Office. A limited inspection revealed the following American items:

(*a*) Commercial letters, 1769-72, to David and John Barclay (in box marked 'Richard Gurney's Executorship', bundle marked '14'). Letters from their agent John Gibson of Philadelphia. General commercial correspondence, mainly on banking, with some references to trade in tea, paper, glass, cottons, and linen. Two letters dated 1770 indicate steps taken in face of American non-importation resolution. Much concern over the debts of one Daniel Wister. (RQG 547)

(*b*) Banking letters, 1790-1800, to and from David and John Barclay (in box marked 'Old Deeds', bundle marked '3'). Letters on various banking subjects from their agent John Ashley of Philadelphia. Letter-book of replies from the Barclays also. Ashley's detailed ac-

counts with the Barclays, and lists of debts outstanding to the bankers. (RQG 549)
(*c*) Banking letters, 1769-70, to David and John Barclay (in large black box, bundle marked '11'). More letters on banking affairs, mainly from the Philadelphia (?) firm of Gibson & Asheton, but also from some others. There are some references to the tea trade. (RQG 546)
(*d*) David Barclay Papers, the other folder of miscellaneous papers in metal box marked 'Mary Gurney's Executorship'.

(i) Copy of letter, 14 Mar. 1764, from Franklin to Dr. J. Fothergill, from Philadelphia, teasing Fothergill for his 'impiety' in saving men by medicine, 'contrary to the plans of Providence', from the just consequences of their excesses; also reporting on the intolerance of the Philadelphia mob to the Quakers - their belief that the Quakers were selling arms to the Indians, and on the ineptness of the new Governor and the general political situation. (No. 3.) (RQG 534)

(ii) Letter, 29 Apr. 1767, from Anthony Benezet of Philadelphia to Barclay, enclosing a treatise on the slave trade and hoping that it may be put in the hands of 'persons of interest and power' to expose the 'corrupt motives and most wicked methods' of the trade. He also alludes to the fear of a slave rebellion, 'a subject of too tender a nature to be exposed to view'. (No. 5.) (RQG 534)

(iii) Certificate of David Barclay's membership in the Pennsylvania Society for Promoting the Abolition of Slavery, 1790, signed by James Pemberton. (RQG 534)

(iv) A printed pamphlet by David Barclay, *An Account of the Emancipation of the Slaves of Unity Valley Pen, in Jamaica* (London, 1801) (20 pages). (RQG 539)

(*e*) Peace negotiations, 1774-7: Dr. Fothergill, David Barclay, and Lord Hyde with Benjamin Franklin. Memoranda and letters (20 items.) These papers relate to the fruitless peace negotiations of 1774-7. The items have been numbered 1-22.[1] (RQG 536)

(i) Memorandum. 'Hints for Conversation Upon the Subject of Terms, that may probably produce a *durable* Union between Great Britain and her Colonies', 4 Dec. 1774. This paper is missing, but something of the same title is in Lettsom's *Works of Fothergill*, vol. iii, p. lxxvii (London, 1784), and a slightly different version in A.H. Smyth's *The Writings of Benjamin Franklin* (New York, 1905-7), included in a letter, 22 Mar. 1775, to his son, vol. vi, pp. 318-99.

(ii) Letter, 13 Dec. 1774, from Lord Hyde to David Barclay, on receipt of a copy of the 'Hints'. (No. 2.)

(iii) Memorandum in Barclay's hand, 'Remarks on Hints'. (No. 3.)

(iv) Memorandum 'Plan for Conciliation', a revision of the 'Hints' showing substantial concessions to the Americans if the 'Dignity of Parliament ... be preserved.' (No. 4.)

(v) Letter, 5 Feb. 1775, from Lord Hyde to Barclay, regretting the receipt of less favourable terms (No. 5.)

(vi) Draft of a letter, 6 Feb. 1775, from Fothergill to Lord Dartmouth, explaining the reasons for the breakdown of the negotiations with Franklin. Partly written in Barclay's hand, partly by another, with numerous emendations. (No. 6.)

(vii) Memorandum in Barclay's hand, 'A *Plan* which it's believed would produce a permanent Union between Great Britain and her Colonies', 16 Feb. 1775. (No. 7.)

(viii) Letters and yet one more 'Plan', 1775-6, between Fothergill, Barclay, and Hyde concerning further efforts made by Barclay and Fothergill, after Franklin had departed, to reach an agreement. (Nos. 8-16.)

(ix) Copy of a letter, 12 Feb. 1781, from Benjamin Franklin to Barclay, praising the work of Dr. Fothergill on hearing of his death. (No. 17.)

(x) Three letters, 1783-6, from Lord Clarendon to Barclay, expressing his doubts about Lettsom's publication of an account of the negotiations in his life of Fothergill.[2] (Nos. 18-20.)

(xi) Letter from the new Lord Clarendon to Barclay, 30 Oct. 1790, acknowledging Barclay's condolences on the death of his father. (No. 21.)

SYLAS NEVILLE PAPERS. 1766-91.

Neville's papers include references to the American Revolution and American affairs among letters from Caleb Fleming, 1769-74 (MC 7/349, 395 x 6), John Wilson, 1777-9 and n.d. (MC 7/549-55, 395 x 7), and John Davidson, 1778 (MC 7/831, 832, 396 x 1). The Record Office also holds Neville's diaries and letter-books, 1766-91.

HOBART COLLECTION.

Bundle of letters and official communiques concerning the Revolution, addressed to the 2nd Earl of Buckinghamshire (1723-93). (N.R.S. 21089, 71 x 2)

WALSINGHAM PAPERS. 1773, 1775.

The papers of the 1st Lord Walsingham, the Attorney General, include a copy letter from Benjamin Franklin to Lord Dartmouth to accompany an address from the House of Representatives, with part of a letter from Mr. Pownall concerning the same, 1773 (WLS LV/69, 428 x 6). Also among the Walsingham Papers is a volume of instructions to governors in North America, mostly on appointments, and including a scheme for the management of Indian affairs, 1775. (WLS LVI/1, 428 x)

WINDHAM, WILLIAM (1750-1810). Paper.[3] 1778.

Draft of a protest, 28 Jan. 1778, drawn up by Windham and Thomas Coke, M.P., opposing the raising of a fund to help carry on the War of Independence.

NORFOLK AND NORWICH COLLECTION. 1824-1917.

(*a*) Norwich Mechanics Union. Minutes, 1824-41. Scattered entries on purchase of books and subjects of lectures, etc., especially 1833-7, show an interest in the allied topics of the Poor Law, emigration, and America.
(*b*) Solomon Lincoln, junior. Manuscript of the *History of Hingham, Mass.* Printed at Hingham, Caleb Gill, junior; and Farmer and Brown 1827. (Rye 136 34 A 6)
(*c*) Letter, 1917, from Mayor of Norwich, Conn., to the Mayor of Norwich, England, concerning the entrance of America into the War. (MS. 20213 38 C 3)

PARISH RECORDS. 1650-1841.

(*a*) Bacton: Records dealing with emigration to the U.S., 1836-41.
(*b*) Bressingham: Agreement concerning emigration to America, 1830. (PD 111/83)
(*c*) Guestwick: Papers relating to an emigration loan of £200 in 1836 to send poor persons to Quebec.
(*d*) North Elmham: An account of collection on brief for the propagation of the gospel in New England, 1653. (PD 209/157)
(*e*) Norwich St. John de Sepulchre: A note in the parish register of emigration to New England, 1650. (PD 90/1(S))
(*f*) Sparham: List of persons wishing to emigrate, 1836. (PD 17/35)

1. Most of these have been printed in R. Hingston Fox, *Dr. John Fothergill and His Friends* (London, 1919), Appendix A, pp. 393-408.
2. J.C. Lettsom, *The Works of John Fothergill: volume 1, Some Account of the late J. Fothergill, M.D.* (London, 1783).
3. Quoted in R.W. Ketton-Cremer, *Early Life and Diaries of William Windham* (London, 1930), p. 188.

SLIPPER , THOMAS. Diary. 19th century.

Diary of journey through the U.S.A. during a visit to William Haddon Slipper, n.d. (notebook dated 1893). (Accn. Wansbrough Jones, 1/9/76, Q 194 D)

OTHER MANUSCRIPTS. 1759-1975.

(*a*) Draft dispatch of George, Marquess Townshend, describing the taking of Quebec, 1759. (MS 21509/49, 368 x 6)
(*b*) Letters to Mr. Salter of Norwich from members of the Mountain family who accompanied the Rev. Jacob Mountain, first Bishop of Quebec, to Canada, including a description of sailing up the St. Lawrence and reasons for disqualification of previous clergymen from Three Rivers, 1792-5. (Accn. Freemen 27/8/62)
(*c*) MS. sermons of the Rev. John Buchan of Charleston, S.C., 1810-21, with brief memoir of him. ((Y) D 39/3)
(*d*) Letter to Elizabeth and Anna Hogarth from David Hogarth, Jr., at Portsmouth, written in course of emigration to Montreal, 1844. (MC17/83, 405 x 7)
(*e*) Letters to Robert Fitch of Norwich from William B. Rogers at Edinburgh, London, Boston, and Lunenburg. Concern geological and antiquarian matters, May Day revels in Boston, etc., 1857-9. ((Y) D27/27-31)
(*f*) Files maintained by the chairman of the Memorial Trust of the 2nd Air Division, U.S. Air Force, 1945-64 (Accn. Copeman, 11/1/72); and 1955-75. (Accn. Eaton 14/7/76, T187E)

PARISH CHURCH, SAXTHORPE, Norwich

EMIGRANT RECORDS.

Overseers' book contains account of sale of cottages belonging to the parish in 1836 to defray part of the cost of the loan for sending poor persons to America. £350 was borrowed in all, from a private individual, Thomas Peaford, who was repaid in yearly installments. The churchwardens' accounts also touch on this transaction which can be followed through, in both sets of books, for the years 1838-40.

NORTHAMPTON

DUKE OF BUCCLEUCH, Boughton House, Kettering

BUCCLEUCH AND QUEENSBERRY MUNIMENTS. 1696-1708 (?).

(*a*) Two letters, both from New York, 20 Sept. 1696, and almost identical, from Colonel Robert Livingston to the Duke of Shrewsbury, and the Earl of Romney respectively, on the activities of Captain Kidd.[1]
(*b*) A long, undated letter, *c.*1700, from J. Nelson to Shrewsbury, especially on the dangers to the colonies from the French. Also a paper by Nelson on 'the methods or ways I propose for the reduction of Canada unto the obedience of the Crown'.[2]
(*c*) A number of papers written by Richard Daniel and others, apparently for the benefit of the Duke of Shrewsbury, on the American colonies, especially recommending the establishment of a Commission responsible for them. There are papers on New England, 'the American Colonies', and New Albion.[3]

1. Transcripts, H.M.C. Buccleuch and Queensberry MSS. ii [45], pp. 405-8.
2. Transcripts, ibid., pp. 723-33.
3. Transcripts, ibid., pp. 733-9.

NORTHAMPTONSHIRE RECORD OFFICE, Delapre Abbey, Northampton NN4 9AW

BRUDENELL PAPERS.[1] 3 agreements. 1582-3.

Agreement, 9 June 1582, between Sir Humphrey Gilbert and two others, in which Gilbert gives them authority to search out and govern lands between the 'Cape of Florida and Cape Britton'. Two further agreements, 1582 and 1583, between the same parties on colonization in America.

GRAFTON PAPERS. Document. 1649.

Letters patent of Charles II, 1649, granting land between the 'Rappahanocke and Potawomeck Rivers and Chesapayocke Bay' to Ralph, Lord Hopton and others.

ISHAM PAPERS. Letter. 1673.

2 Oct. 1673, from Dorothy, Lady Long, to Sir Justinian Isham, mentions that New York, 'a town lying near Verginia' has been 'taken by the Duch'.

WESTMORLAND PAPERS. Letters. 1730-2.

Several from Richard Reynolds, Bishop of Lincoln, to the Earl of Westmorland about obtaining the post of land surveyor of South Carolina for his son Anthony, mentioning also the Lieutenant-Governorship of New Hampshire.

BROOKE PAPERS. 2 documents, etc. 1735.

Grant of a tract of land in South Carolina to Alexander Talley. Seal of province and plan, attached. 1735.

FINCH-HATTON PAPERS. Documents. n.d., 1745.

(*a*) Motion, n.d. [first half of seventeenth century?] against restoring the 'Old Virginia Company'. (3731)
(*b*) Copy of orders by Sir Peter Warren, Vice-Admiral, Commander-in-Chief of British naval forces 'employed in North America to the northward of Carolina', during the operations against Louisbourg, N.S., 1745, with a list of ships engaged in the action. (281. ff. 160*b*-165*b*)

FITZWILLIAM PAPERS. Papers of Edmund Burke: letters, notes and draft speeches on American affairs. 1753-81.[2]

These papers came from Milton, nr. Peterborough, the seat since 1857 of the younger branch of the Fitzwilliam family; and are

1. Printed in D.B. Quinn, ed., *The Voyages and Colonial Enterprises of Sir Humphrey Gilbert* (London, 1940) (Hakluyt Society, 2nd ser., vol. lxxxiv).
2. See T.W.Copeland, L.S. Sutherland, G.H. Guttridge, J.A. Woods, H. Furber, A. Cobban, and R.A. Smith (eds.), *The Correspondence of Edmund Burke, 1744-1797*, 9 vols. (Cambridge and Chicago, Ill., 1958-70).

obviously complementary to the group from the Fitzwilliam (Wentworth Woodhouse) Muniments now in the Sheffield City Library. The papers on American affairs, dealing mainly with the Stamp Act and War of Independence, include:
(*a*)Accounts of quitrents paid from various colonies, 1753-63.
(*b*) Petitions from the American colonies against the Stamp Act, and copy of correspondence about the Act.
(*c*) Statement of distribution of Army in North America, 1765.
(*d*) Account of bullion received from Philadelphia and New York, 1765.
(*e*) Resolution of Pennsylvania Assembly, 1766, about grant of aids to the King.
(*f*) Reports on validity of Acts of New York Assembly, 1773.
(*g*) Accounts of exports and imports of New York, 1774.
(*h*) Report on the American attack on Canada under Col. Arnold, 1775.
(*i*) Resolutions of freeholders of Cork against proceeding to extremities against the colonists, 1776; and many similar petitions, letters of advice, etc., including one from Bristol, 1778.
(*j*) Copies of letters of General Clinton, 1777, about Burgoyne's defeat.
(*k*) 'Letters on the temper of the British Nabobs towards America', 1777.
(*l*) Extracts from letters of Lord George Germain, 1781.
(*m*) Petitions of John Trumbull for release from prison, 1781.

TRYON PAPERS. 1771, 1833.
(*a*) Abstract of a journal kept by Governor William Tryon of an expedition against rebels in North Carolina, 1771.
(*b*) Perth Amboy, N.J., 10 Jan. 1833, from Charles Johnston to Thomas Tryon of Bulwick, Northants. Mentions wages paid for harvesting, the climate, and compares prices with those in England. Asks Tryon to advise his (Johnston's) brother to go over.[3]

SOTHEBY PAPERS. Letter. 1778.
9 April 1778, from John Pilgrim to Ambrose Isted of Ecton, about the effect of the War of Independence on stocks and shares and comments on the War.

FITZWILLIAM CORRESPONDENCE. Letter. 1793.
Halifax, N.S., 23 Mar. 1793, from John Wentworth, Governor of Nova Scotia 1792-1808, to Lord Fitzwilliam, mentions a defeat of the American Army by the Indians, with a loss of six hundred men slain. (And other letters concerning Nova Scotia.)

OVERSTONE PAPERS. Minutes and letters. 1809-52.
(*a*) Minutes of meeting of the Society for the Propagation of the Gospel, New England, 1809.
(*b*) Three letters from E. Chapman, Utica, N.Y., to J.C. Gooch, concerning emigration and life in America, 1849, 1850, 1852. (1036, 1038, 1039)

AMERICAN SOCIETY FOR MELIORATING THE CONDITION OF THE JEWS. Document. 1830.
Instructions issued, 1830, in New York by the Society to the Rev. Judah I. Abraham, 'missionary to the Jews, on the borders of the Mediterranean'.

GOTCH OF KETTERING PAPERS. Letter. 1834.
Letter from Thomas and Rebeccah Hollidge, Philadelphia, to William James, nr. Flower De Lanes, Kettering (their nephew), describing life in Newark, N.J. and Philadelphia, 1834. (998)

MAUNSELL PAPERS. Letters. 1840, n.d.
Several letters written by Mrs. Elizabeth Pery (an emigrant from England) from Philadelphia, describing social life and economic problems there.

ELLESMERE PAPERS. Maps.
Manuscript map of the 'Potowmack and James Rivers showing their several communications with the navigable waters of the New Province on the River Ohio', n.d. Other printed maps of American ports and coast line, 1775-7.

PETERBOROUGH QUARTER SESSIONS RECORDS.
Include royal pardons to certain men sentenced to death, commuting their sentences to transportation to America, 1773.

PARISH RECORDS.
(*a*) Newnham. Notebook of the Rev. Thomas Green, vicar of Badby with Newnham, with particulars of his parishioners at Newnham. Several members of the Shaw family are noted as having gone to America in the 1830's.
(*b*) Sywell. Agreement, 6 Jan. 1830, by five ratepayers to pay a sixpenny rate 'to be applied in conveying paupers or poor persons belonging to the parish to the United States of America'.

NORTHUMBERLAND

DUKE OF NORTHUMBERLAND, Alnwick Castle, Alnwick

NORTHUMBERLAND PAPERS. 1607-1816.[1]
(*a*) Council in Virginia to the Council of Virginia in London, giving an account of what has been accomplished in the first seven weeks of settlement— fortification, building, planting, further exploration, etc.— and a favourable account of the country. 22 June 1607, Jamestown.[2] (Vol. 7)
(*b*) Letter, 29 July 1607, from Captain Christopher Newport to Robert Cecil, Earl of Salisbury, on former's return from Virginia.[3] (Vol. 7)
(*c*) Letter, Jamestown, Va., 17 Aug. 1611, from George Percy, to the Earl of Northumberland, his brother, thanking him for past financial assistance, and asking for more, as his position 'cannot be defrayed with small expense'.[4] (Vol. 9)
(*d*) Account of the raising of money for the building of a free school at Charles City, Va., 1621-2.[5] (Vol. 12)

3. Photostat in the collection of Letters of Emigrants to America in the British Library of Political and Economic Science, London School of Economics.

1. Microfilms of these MSS. are at the British Library.
2. Transcript, H.M.C. iii, pp. 53-54.
3. Transcript, ibid., p.54.
4. Ibid., p.58.
5. Ibid., p. 66.

(*e*) Letter-book of Earl Percy. Various letters and papers, 1774-80, relating to the War of Independence.[6] (Vol. 49)
(*f*) Rebel orderly book (1-13 Sept. 1776), taken at the island of New York, 1776. (This title is in the handwriting of Earl Percy.)[7] (m/S 648)
(*g*) Diary of operations of the Lord Howe's fleet and army in America (Connecticut, Dutch Island, North Goat Island, etc.) 29 July-31 Aug. 1778.[8] (m/S 649)
(*h*) 'Memoir on the commercial intercourse between the United States of America and the British Islands and Colonies in the West Indies, Signed James Leith, Captain General.' n.d. (1814-1816?)[9] (m/S 702)
(*i*) 'Journal of a voyage of a thousand miles down the Ohio (1809-), and an account of the Five Nations, etc., from an early period to the conclusion of the late war between Great Britain and America, by Major John Norton (Teyoninhokokarawen), 1816; dedicated to the Duke of Northumberland. 2 volumes, pp. 967, followed by a vocabulary.'[10] (m/S 716-717)

NORTHUMBERLAND COUNTY RECORD OFFICE, Melton Park, North Gosforth, Newcastle upon Tyne NE3 5QX

CARR ELLISON (HEDGELEY) MSS. Letter- and account books. 18th-early 19th century.

Letter-books and account books of William Cotesworth and Ralph Carr, containing references to American trade, eighteenth-early nineteenth century. Included are letters to Josiah Quincy, Philip Livingston, Samuel Wentworth, and others. (ZCE 10-16)

COOKSON (MALDON) MSS. 1753-1821.

Papers and correspondence concerning the Baltimore estate of Edward Cook, Sr., of Togston, 1753-1821. (ZCK 3)

ALLGOOD OF NUNWICK MSS. Journal. 1759.

Private journal of the siege of Quebec. 1759. (ZAL 87/1)

RIDLEY (BLAGDON) MSS. 1765-1863.

(*a*) Attestation of deed by William Tryon, Chief Justice of North Carolina, 30 Apr. 1765. (ZR1 22/6)
(*b*) Letters, 1777, to Sir Matthew White Ridley from New York, relating to the death of Capt. John Ridley, 28th Foot. (ZR1 30/4a)
(*c*) Letter, 29 Sept. 1787, from Charles Cotesworth Pinckney, New York, to Sir Matthew White Ridley, discussing the passing of the Constitution by Congress. (ZR1 25/13)
(*d*) Reports and notes on building costs of ships, including ships built in America, 1824-6. (ZR1 25/46)
(*e*) Letters, 1862-3, concerning the American Civil War. (ZR1 31/2/34)

DELAVAL (WATERFORD) MSS. 1766-79.

(*a*) Memo, 1766, on foundation of a sugar plantation in East Florida. (ZDE 44/9)
(*b*) Letter, 1771, concerning J.H. Delaval's land holding in East Florida. (ZDE 417)
(*c*) Letters, 1778-9, describing capture of American spy in British Army at Philadelphia, and privateer Paul Jones. (ZDE 12/5)

OTHER MSS. Letters. 1734-1824.

(*a*) Extracts of letters fom George Clinton, Governor of New York 1747; memorandum of complaints against the Governor of North Carolina, 1734; petition of Palatines of North Carolina concerning dispossession of lands, 1747. (NRO/650/C/28)
(*b*) Twenty-nine letters, 1819-23, written from Indiana. (NRO 488/B/15)

NOTTINGHAMSHIRE

NOTTINGHAM CITY ARCHIVES OFFICE, Central Library, South Sherwood Street, Nottingham NG1 4DA

MISCELLANEOUS DOCUMENTS. 1764-1934.

(*a*) Letter, 1871, from Thomas Twells, describing life in Wisconsin. (M2691)
(*b*) Letter, 1859, from J. Hawkins in Wisconsin to his father concerning property, deeds, American life, etc. (M18, 941)
(*c*) Letter, 1814, from Private William Kirke to his father, describing his military activities during the War of 1812, including the British burning of Washington. (MM 43)
(*d*) Letter, 1925, from David McFall (staying at Nottingham) to Authors Syndicate Ltd., London, concerning the forthcoming publication of his work on America. (M23,968)
(*e*) Wragg family papers: MSS. relating to Annie Wragg's visit to America, 1928-34. (WRA/1-4)
(*f*) Quaker collection: The archive's Quaker collection includes several references to America in the 'Minutes of certificates for Nottingham Friends travelling, 1764-86' (Q 305/35-52). There are also some 'Epistles from Women's Yearly Meetings in America to Women's Yearly Meetings in London', 1775-1834. (Q 319a/1-47)

NOTTINGHAMSHIRE RECORD OFFICE, County House, High Pavement, Nottingham NG1 1HR

FOLJAMBE MSS. *c.* 1760-1800.

Includes letters of Sir George Savile and others referring to America. Subjects touched on include British taxation of America, pamphlet war, the constitutional relationship between colony and mother country, observations on American fisheries, and the American War. This collection also contains a letter from Joseph Harrison of New Haven to Sir George Savile, which gives a detailed description of his journey to North America and of his post as a customs collector. (1761)

6. Ibid., p. 108.
7. Ibid., p. 124.
8. Ibid.
9. Ibid., p. 125. Published in 1970 by the Champlain Society in Toronto, Canada.
10. Ibid.

SAVILE COLLECTION. Letters. 1853.

J. Savile-Lumley was in the diplomatic service, and there are occasional letters emanating from Washington, D.C., *c.* 1853. (DDSR)

OTHER RECORDS. 1755-1895.

(*a*) Letters of Matthew Herbert Lancashire at Principio Furnace, Cecil County, U.S.A., contrasting the life of an immigrant settler with that of his family left behind in Nottingham, 1855-95. (DD 419)
(*b*) Letter referring to anti-slavery in America, 1862. (DDWR 31/2)
(*c*) Order for the transportation of John Richardson to the American colonies for stealing a linen shirt valued 10d., 1755. (CP 3/10)
(*d*) Two long, detailed letters about life in Canada, journeying by sea and land, climate, Yankee manners, civil war, prices and wages, crops, etc., 1838-9. (DDH 151/202-203)

THE DEPARTMENT OF MANUSCRIPTS, THE LIBRARY, UNIVERSITY OF NOTTINGHAM, University Park, Nottingham NG7 2RD

MIDDLETON MANUSCRIPTS. 1611-31.[1]

On 2 May [1611] the King had granted letters patent to the Earl of Northampton, Sir Percivall Willoughby, and others to make a plantation and establish a colony in Newfoundland.
(*a*) Bundle of papers, 1611-31, connected with the Newfoundland venture: correspondence, estimates, inventories.
(*b*) 'A journall from the first September [1612] until the last of Aprill 1613 in C[a]pe ... wher the colonie is kept.' This journal gives a day to day report of the weather, the voyages made, and the activities undertaken in Newfoundland.[2]

NEWCASTLE MANUSCRIPTS.[3]

Manuscripts of the 2nd, 3rd, 4th, and 5th Dukes of Newcastle, 1720-1864.
(*a*) Among the forty-four bundles of letters, documents, and copies of documents of the 2nd Duke, Henry Fiennes Clinton (1720-94),[4] are the following:

(i) Clinton, Sir Henry (1738?-95). Over 100 letters and copies of letters and documents, 1775-82.

General, M.P. for Boroughbridge 1772-4 and for Newark 1774-84 (both seats controlled by his cousin, the 2nd Duke of Newcastle). On Howe's return to England after the capture of Burgoyne at Saratoga, Clinton became Commander-in-Chief in North America. The majority of the letters are addressed to the Duke of Newcastle, but the correspondence contains copies of others to Sir William Howe, Lord George Germain, Lieut.-Col. Webster, Vice-Admiral Arbuthnot, and Lord Cornwallis; here also are a number to Clinton's sisters, Richard Reeve, Major-General Edward Harvey, Mr. Carter, and Lord John Pelham Clinton, transmitted by them to the Duke. One paper, presumably the work of Benedict Arnold, is superscribed 'Rules and articles to be observed on this bold and noble attempt to join Sir Henry Clinton'. The correspondence as a whole takes the form of a commentary on the course of the war and on Clinton's feelings, particularly his dissatisfaction with fellow officers and with his own position both before and after his appointment to the senior command in May 1778. Newcastle being his political patron, Clinton poured out to him all his complaints and clearly regarded his letters as confidential. In addition to accounts of military engagements between June 1775 and the attempted relief of Yorktown in Oct. 1781, the correspondence contains vigorous criticism of the government, Howe, Arbuthnot, and Cornwallis. Newcastle is kept informed of Clinton's intentions of resigning, and throughout the war the Duke's replies seem to have urged Clinton to stay at his post. Clinton used the Duke, however, as a channel to the King, requesting release in October 1779 and again in November 1780. The manuscripts include a short and sharp exchange between Lord North and the Duke on 3 and 4 Mar. 1778 (2/25-2/32), showing the latter's concern when he considered that Clinton had a legitimate grievance. The correspondence is chiefly interesting for the light it throws on Clinton's thoughts throughout the war, especially on the virtual military impossibility of subduing the rebellion.

(ii) Phillips, William (1731?-81). 12 letters. 1775-80.

Major-General, M.P. 1775-80 for Boroughbridge, a seat controlled by the Duke of Newcastle, of whom he was an active supporter and political client. The letters cover the period when Phillips served with Carleton and Burgoyne in America, being taken prisoner at Saratoga, N.Y. The letters describe and make vigorous comment on the conduct of the war, particularly on Burgoyne's ill-fated advance from Canada. Some are from prison. The last letter, New York, 14 Oct. 1780, refers to Clinton's secret correspondence with Benedict Arnold and his feelings on the capture and execution of Major André. (These letters are found as: Bundle 1, nos. 37, 41, 42; Bundle 9, nos. 4, 16, 18, 20, 24; Bundle 11, nos. 14, 75, 123, 129.) There are twenty-three other letters from Phillips, 1768-75, in some of which he comments on the American situation.

(iii) Letter, Pay Office, 7 Nov. 1776, from Richard Rigby to the Duke of Newcastle. Has dined with Lord Lincoln; news from America; another campaign needed; meeting between Howe, Adams, and Franklin; fear of warlike preparations in France. (11/33)

(iv) Letter, Cleveland Court, 6 Aug. 1777, from Edward Harvey to the Duke of Newcastle. 'I can't say that I have heard any thing about Howe & Cornwallis that is alarming. Instead of attacking Washington, Howe has embarked his whole Jersey army leaving sufficient posts at N. York, etc., and is proceeding on some expedition. It is to be hoped & credited, (till we hear the contrary) that what he has fix'd on, is the most eligible plan'; expects Ticonderoga to fall without resistance. (35/2)

(*b*) Henry Pelham Fiennes Pelham Clinton, 5th Duke of Newcastle (1811-64), was Colonial Secretary 1852-4 and 1859-64. For both periods there are letter-books and papers relating to North America, including correspondence with Governors-General of the British territories. These papers do, of course, cover relations between Canada and the United States. As Colonial Secretary he accompanied the Prince of Wales on his tour of British North America and the United States in 1860, and the papers include a letter-book containing copies of letters written to the Queen during the visit, and a quantity of newspaper cuttings.

N.R.A. (Catalogue completed.)

1. We thank Lord Middleton for permission to make this report.
2. H.M.C. Middleton MSS. [69], p. 284.
3. We thank the Trustees of the Duke of Newcastle for permission to make this report.
4. Catalogue of the 2nd Duke's Manuscripts compiled as an appendix to his thesis by Clive Priestley, 'The Life and Career of Henry Fiennes Pelham-Clinton, 1720-1794, Ninth Earl of Lincoln and Second Duke of Newcastle-under-Lyme.' Typescript, M.A. thesis, University of Nottingham, 1958.

MELLISH MANUSCRIPTS.[5] 2 bundles of letters; 3 printed sheets; list of pamphlets. 1772-82. (Bundles 171-2.)

Papers belonging to Charles Mellish (*c.* 1737-96), M.P. for Pontefract 1774-80 and for Aldborough 1780-4.
(*a*) Bundle of fifty-four letters, 1772-82, to Charles Mellish from various persons in England and America on North American affairs, including the War of Independence.
(*b*) Nine letters, 1773, 1776-81, from Sir Henry Clinton in America to Charles Mellish, on the War.
(*c*) List of pamphlets (not the actual pamphlets) concerning America, 1776.
(*d*) Proposals made to non-commissioned officers and soldiers of the Pennsylvania line at Princeton, N.J., 7 Jan. 1781. (Printed sheet.)
(*e*) Trenton, N.J.: order of the Board of Committee concerning the discharge and enlistment of soldiers, 10 Jan. 1781. (Printed sheet.)
(*f*) Printed news-sheet published by James Rivington, printer to the King, 17 May 1781, New York (endorsed 'New York Gazette, 1781').
N.R.A. 0893

PORTLAND MANUSCRIPTS.[6]

There is no well-defined group of manuscripts relating to American affairs. On the other hand, reports and comments are embedded within the general political correspondence, especially among the papers of William Henry Cavendish Bentinck, 3rd Duke of Portland (1738-1809), during the period of the War of Independence (e.g., in letters of William Burke and Rockingham).
N.R.A. (Catalogue in preparation.)

DRURY-LOWE MANUSCRIPTS.

Richard Lowe was a wealthy businessman and banker in the banking partnership which later became Williams Deacon's Bank. Among his manuscripts there are papers and deeds relating to an estate in Maryland and/or business activities there.[7] There is an N.R.A. catalogue to these papers.
(*a*) Bundle of correspondence between Richard Lowe and Benjamin Young in Maryland, 1764-8. (Dr C 3 1764-8)
(*b*) Deeds of gift from John Lowe to Stead Lowe of an estate in Maryland, 1748, 1750. (Dr D 121 1748, 1750)
(*c*) Bundle of papers relating to Stead Lowe's plantation, arising out of the estates of the late Vincent Lowe in Maryland, with copies of earlier documents, *c.* 1748-1774. (Dr E 8 *c.* 1748-1774)

OXFORDSHIRE

DUKE OF MARLBOROUGH, Blenheim Palace, Woodstock

SUNDERLAND PAPERS.

Papers of Charles Spencer, 3rd Earl of Sunderland (1674-1722), statesman. (*Letters unless otherwise stated.*)
(*a*) 11 Oct. 1684, from Lord Preston to the Earl of Sunderland on hostilities between French and Bostonians.[1]
(*b*) 1 June 1709, from the Council of Trade to Sunderland about large numbers of German Protestant refugees from the Palatinate arriving in England, some of whom were sent to New York and North Carolina. (Cl-38)[2]
(*c*) 'Papers respecting the relief and settlement of the distressed Protestant Palatines in the colonies of America.' (*c.* 1709?)[3]
(*d*) 'Orders and instructions to Edward Nott, Esq., Lieutenant and Governor General of Virginia, in America.' (32 pages.) (1710.)[4]

BODLEIAN LIBRARY, Oxford OX1 3BG

The following summary of manuscripts is additional to the entries in Andrews & Davenport, pp. 372-421. Since their report, the *Summary Catalogue of Western Manuscripts* has been continued to 1923. Vol. i (historical introduction and conspectus of shelfmarks) and vol. ii (index) were published in 1953. For accessions see *Bodleian Quarterly Record*, vols. i-viii, 1914-38; continued as *Bodleian Library Record* from 1939. Typescript catalogues of accessions are available in the Library.

The material is arranged as follows:
I. Collections Belonging to the Bodleian Library
II. Collections Deposited in the Bodleian Library
III. Miscellaneous Collections Belonging to the Bodleian Library
IV. Miscellaneous Deposits

I. COLLECTIONS BELONGING TO THE BODLEIAN LIBRARY

BANKES PAPERS.

The official papers of Sir John Bankes as Attorney-General 1634-40 purchased by the Library from Lord Bledisloe in 1960; see *Quarterly Review*, Jan. 1951, and *Bodleian Library Record,* iii. 179; iv. 313-23. There is a typescript list of the whole collection compiled by I. Gray, and a detailed calendar and index has been compiled.[1]
5/29. Copies of minutes of the Council of New England, 1635, 1638. Agreements on division, allotment of lands in New England (bundle 23 [uncalendared] also contains extracts of this).
5/30. n.d. [? April 1635]. Agreement setting out lands in New England allotted to Sir Ferdinando Gorges, with careful delimitation of said lands.
7/7. Brief note on the Charter of Massachusetts Bay. n.d. [in or after Trinity Term, 1635].
7/8. Copy of the *quo warranto* exhibited against the Massachusetts Bay Company in King's Bench, 1635.[2]
7/9. Copy of sentence given in King's Bench, 1624, in *quo warranto* proceedings against the Virginia Company.[3]

5. We thank the Mellish Trustees for permission to make this report.
6. We thank the Duke of Portland for permission to make this report.
7. There is a chapter on Richard Lowe in the official history of Williams Deacon's Bank, *Williams Deacon's, 1771-1970* (Manchester, 1971).

---

1. H.M.C. viii (i), p. 30.
2. Ibid., p. 47.
3. Ibid., p. 59.
4. Ibid., p. 47.

---

1. The entries in the calendar relating to Virginia have been duplicated and circulated in a Memorandum from the Alderman Library, Manuscripts Division, University of Virginia, 1953.
2. Printed in translation in T. Hutchinson, *A Collection of Original Papers Relative to the History of Massachusetts Bay,* vol. i (Albany, N.Y., 1865), pp. 114-6.
3. See Alexander Brown, *The First Republic in America* (Boston, 1898), pp. 585-9, 601-3.

7/11. Copy of the sentence concerning Matthew Cradock given in suit in King's Bench of Rex *v.* Massachusetts Bay Company (see 7/8 above), 1635.[4]
7/12. A similar copy concerning John Venn.
7/13. Copy of charter of Massachusetts Bay, 4 Mar. 1629.[5]
8/1. Abstracts of the patent of incorporation of the Council of New England of 3 Nov. 1620; of the royal grants of Avalon to Sir George Calvert, 7 Apr. 1623; and of Maryland to Lord Baltimore, 20 June 1632; and of grants from the Council of New England of Cape Trebizond, Laconia, Piscataqua, and River Bishopscotte, 1622-32; also a note on laws relating to 'plantations in Virginia', and list of legal officers to whom patents for the colonies had apparently been submitted for consideration.[6]
8/2. Copy of representation and petition of the Commissioners for Virginia appointed on 27 June [1631].[7]
8/3. 1635. Lists of charges made by the Virginia Company against Sir John Harvey, the Governor, and against Lord Baltimore's deputies, annotated with page and line references to other papers relating to these disputes.[8]
8/4. ?1635. Petition, apparently of planters of Virginia, then in England, to Privy Council on the alleged infringement of their rights and territories by Sir Robert Heath and Lord Baltimore.
8/6. n.d. 'The names of the chiefest planters that have both ventured their lives and estates for the plantation of Virginia.'
8/7. 1635. Order of the Commissioners for the Plantations that patent for Massachusetts Bay should be questioned by *quo warranto* or *scire facias*. (8/17 is a certified copy of this.)
8/8. 1634. Orders of Commissioners of Plantations for delivery of all patents to Attorney-General [Bankes] for examination.
8/9. Abstracts by Bankes of the letters patent of 20 June 1632, granting Maryland to Lord Baltimore,[9] and of the charter of Massachusetts Bay of 4 Mar. 1629.
8/10. ? 1635. An abstract of the terms of the letters patent by which Charles I granted to Sir William Alexander a proportion of the mainland of New England [with marginal notes and additions by Bankes].[10]
8/12. n.d. Notes by Bankes endorsed 'Desires of the planters of New England'.
8/15. n.d. [after 12 June 1634]. 'Motives and reasons for the petition of the Governor and Company of New Albion' [midway between New England and Virginia]. (See 8/16 below.)
8/16. n.d., after 21 June 1634. Abstract of the [Irish] patent of 21 June 1634 made by advice of Sir Thomas Wentworth, 1st Earl of Strafford, granting to [then follows list] 'all that isle called Isle Plowden or Long Isle, and 40 leagues square of the mainland next adjoining commonly called North Virginia'; this is to be called New Albion.
8/18. n.d. [? 1637]. List of persons against whom a *quo warranto* was exhibited in King's Bench in Trinity Term 1635, for claiming to have certain liberties and franchises as freemen of the Society of Massachusetts Bay; 'with notes of what has been done by any of them and what against them'.[11]
8/19. Copy of 'A breviat of the declaration of the planters in Virginia, dated the 1st of July 1635' a fuller version of 8/3 above in a different order.
8/20. n.d. [? 1636]. Fragments of an abstract of, or notes for, the drafting of an official document relating to Virginia, perhaps renewal of Sir John Harvey's commission as governor, with marginal notes and endorsement by Bankes.
13/27. 1638. Proceedings upon a petition of the defendants in a suit in the Star Chamber of the Attorney-General *vs.* John West, Samuel Mathews, William Tucker and others, protesting against the commissioners nominated by Robert Evelin to examine witnesses in Virginia.

Bundle no. 36 [uncalendared]. 'Memorandum concerning alleged irregular legal proceedings by the Massachusetts Company', undated. [Fragile and defective.]
42/33. Order of the King in Council to prepare a proclamation 'for the restraint of disorderly transporting His Majesties subjects unto any of the plantations within the parts of America'. 23 Apr. 1637. Extract.
50/44. 1638. Warrant for a commission to Sir Francis Wyatt creating him Governor of Virginia in succession to Sir John Harvey.
51/36, 37. Warrants for grants of lands in New England to the Duke of Lennox, and others; the first, 31 May 1635, does not specify the lands; the second, 18 June 1638, adds a grant to the Earl of Stirling, which is defined as 'lands adjoining New Scotland ... with Mattoacks or Long Island . . ., Cole Island, Sandy Point, Hell Gate, Martin's [Martha's] Vineyard, Elizabeth Islands, and Block Island'.
54/23. 1637-8. Warrant for a grant to Robert Evelin of the office of Surveyor-General for the colony of Virginia, void by the death of Gabriel Hawley.
54/33. Petition of Capt. Richard Morrison to be appointed governor of Point Comfort Castle, Virginia, and warrant accordingly, 13 Feb. 1638.

LOCKE PAPERS.[12] 1671-1714. (MSS. Locke)

John Locke (1632-1704), the philosopher, was secretary to the Lords Proprietors for Carolina 1669-72.

MS. Locke.b.5, no. 9. Appointment of Locke as a Landgrave of Carolina, 1671.

c.4, f.8. Letters, 20 Jan. 1698 and 8 Feb. 1699, of James Blair, of Virginia, to Locke.

c.16, f.157. Letters, 30 Mar. 1697, 26 May 1698, 4 Feb. 1699, of Governor Francis Nicholson to Locke.

c.30, f.1. Minutes by Locke of meetings of the Lords Proprietors of Carolina, 1671-5.
f.38. Notes by Locke on trade in Sweden, Denmark, and New England, 1696.
f.40. Notes by Locke on New England [1696].[13]
f.55. Notes by Locke concerning claim of the Duke of Hamilton to lands in Connecticut [1698].

4. Printed in Hutchinson, op. cit., vol. i, p. 117.
5. Printed from original in *Records of the Governor and Company of the Massachusetts Bay*, ed. by N.B. Shurtleff, vol. i (Boston, 1853), pp.3-19.
6. See *Calendar of State Papers, Colonial Series, 1574-1660* (London, 1860), pp.24, 42, 28, 102, 135, 152.
7. See ibid., p. 136.
8. Ibid., p. 211, and 8/19 below.
9. Printed in W. MacDonald, ed., *Select Charters and other Documents Illustrative of American History, 1606-1775* (New York, 1899), pp.53-60.
10. See *Calendar of State Papers, Colonial Series, 1574-1660*, pp. 195, 204 (8/13 is another copy of this).
11. Ibid., p. 251, and also 7/8 and 7/11-12 above.
12. This collection of his papers is that bequeathed by Locke to Peter King. It remained with his descendants until acquired by the Bodleian in 1941. P. Long, *A Summary Catalogue of the Lovelace Collection in the Bodleian Library* (Oxford, 1959) (Oxford Bibliographical Society Publications, N.S. viii).
13. Cf. *Calendar of State Papers, Colonial Series, America and the West Indies, 1696-7* (London, 1904), nos.250, 1120.

f.59. 'Queries to be put to Coll. Henry Hartwell or any other discreet person that knows the constitution of Virginia, August 30 1697.'

f.134. Two copies of a commission of Nicholas Trott as Chief Justice in South Carolina, granted 8 Mar. 1707 and confirmed 8 Sept. 1714 (presumably added to Locke's papers by Peter King).

c.39, f.3. Copy of a note by Locke for the constitution of Carolina.

d.7. 'Of the American plantations', 18 Oct. 1714, a copy of a report by James Stanhope to the Council for Trade and Plantations.[14]

e.9. Papers on Virginia, [1697]. i, 71 leaves.[15]

f.1. 'Some of the chief greivances of the present constitution, of Virginia with an essay towards the remedies thereof.'

f.39. 'Queries' about the land, people, constitution, and revenue of Virginia.

f.43. A paper on public administration in Virginia.

NORTH PAPERS. 1702-78, 1861.

Papers of the North family including a very few of Lord North (1732-92). A catalogue is available in the Library.

a.6, ff.57-68v. Pages 266-89 of a booklet of instructions for the Governors of the Leeward Islands, Maryland, New Jersey, and New York, 1702-14.

f.172. Petition to the King from Glasgow merchants trading in tobacco with the British colonies in America, *c.* 1756. They fear slave risings and attacks by French and Indians, and ask for at least as good a defence system for Virginia and Maryland as is enjoyed by the Northern colonies.[16]

f.187. A comparison of military expenditure in the American plantations and Gibraltar, 1758, 1759.[17]

ff.201-14. Copy of an unsigned letter, London, 15 Jan. 1760 (to the Duke of Newcastle?) suggesting the boundaries necessary for the defence of North America, and other points to be raised in peace negotiations with France.

ff.237-40. Observations of North America made by Captain J. Innis, of the Royal American Regiment, during his residence there, 1756-60. Includes remarks on situation, soil, climates, etc. of Louisiana.[18]

ff.274-80. Copy of a letter, Edinburgh, 15 June 1761, by the writer of the letter in f.201, advocating a policy of exclusion of the French from North America.

a.12. A complete list of ships engaged in American trade, 5 Jan. 1772 - 5 Jan. 1773, with kind, tonnage, and details of voyages, and a list of imports and exports of the colonies (with quantities) for the same period.

b.6, ff.47-50. Letter, 1762, from Peter Collinson to the Earl of Bute, stating that the British should take possession of St. Augustine, Fla., as it is a 'thorn in the side' of the American colonies, a harbour for runaway slaves and criminals, and a base for Spanish depredations.[19]

f.168. Memorial, 3 July 1762, to the Earl of Bute from William Franklin of Pennsylvania, requesting the office of Secretary to South Carolina.

f.178. Petition, Nov. 1762, of Henry Woodward, late Captain of H.M. Provincial Regiment of Virginia, to the King, praying to be appointed 'Commander of Lakes Erie, Huron, etc.' (See also ff. 207, 209, 210: letters of recommendation of Woodward by Governor Francis Fauquier of Virginia.)

f.181. Extract from a letter, Annapolis, Md., 6 Dec. 1762, from Horatio Sharpe, Governor of Maryland, to his brother William, concerning an office in the colony.[20]

ff.186-93. 'Short observations upon North America and the Sugar Islands', 1762. Chiefly comments on what should be done with Canada and Louisiana at the coming peace.[21]

f.219. Note on quit-rents in Georgia.

f.238. Request to the Earl of Bute from Mr. Ware for removal to a better office from that of Comptroller of Customs in New England.

f.241. Memorial to the Earl of Bute from Benjamin Barons, late Collector of Customs at Boston, concerning his suspension from the office.

ff.260-78. Recommendations, 8 June 1763, from the Board of Trade to George III relating to the future administration of newly acquired territories in Canada, Florida, and the West Indies.[22]

ff.297-303. 'Explanation of the several branches of H.M. revenues arising in the plantations at the King's free disposal.' *c.* 1762.[23]

f.327. Petition to the Earl of Bute of Lieutenant Timberlake for expenses incurred in bringing three Cherokee chiefs to London, *c.* 1762-3.

ff.333-4. Statement of account of Lieut.-Col. James Robertson, Deputy Quartermaster-General of H.M. Forces in North America, 1757-65. Includes amounts paid for provisions, etc.[24]

f.339. Extract from a letter, 13 Jan. 1771, from Thomas Bishop of Boston to 'J.T.', stating that the Bostonians desire peace and concord.[25]

ff. 380-2. Extracts from an unsigned letter, New York, 25 Jan. 1778, complaining of Howe's dilatorinesss in carrying on the war. The general tenor is that, with more energy, it could have been won already.[26]

b. 27, ff.96-8, 107-9, 149, 182-6. Papers relating to ships in which Francis North, 2nd Baron Guilford, had an interest; several are about the *Billinghurst* engaged in the slave trade, including (f. 184) a reinsurance policy for a voyage from Jamaica to America and London, 1719.

b.69. 'Copies of all entries of goods and merchandise outwards for North America, which have been made at the port of London, or any other port within . . . England (except such ships as have entered outwards by virtue of licences granted by the Lords Commissioners of the Admiralty for shipping of goods into any ships taken into His Majesty's service bound to North America) since passing an Act to prohibit all trade and intercourse with the colonies ... during the continuance of the present rebellion (from 22 Dec. 1775 to 13 May 1776)...' In every case the ships were bound for Canada or Florida.

b.78, ff.9-17. Rated and unrated East India goods (tea excepted), exported from England between Christmas 1760 and Christmas 1776 to Africa, foreign parts, West India islands, and North American colonies.

14. Cf. *Calendar of State Papers, Colonial Series, America and the West Indies, 1714-1715* (London, 1928), no.236.
15. Cf. *Calendar of State Papers, Colonial Series, America and the West Indies, 1696-7* (London, 1904), nos.1320,1396.
16. Typed transcript at Rhodes House, Oxford, in a bound volume, 'MSS. Brit. Emp. s. 1'.
17. Ibid.
18. Ibid.
19. Ibid.
20. Ibid.
21. Ibid.
22. Ibid.
23. Ibid.
24. Ibid.
25. Ibid.
26. Ibid.

c.83. Alphabetical list of goods imported into North America from Great Britain and Ireland, 5 Jan. 1769 - 5 Jan. 1770.

f.3v. British goods imported into North America, etc.

f.17v. Foreign goods imported into North America, etc.

f.25v. Articles subject to duty.

d.35, ff.56-65. Letter, 9 Nov. 1861, from General Hastings Doyle to (his brother) Colonel S. North,[27] describing the military weakness of New Brunswick, and the possibility of an American attack.[28]

MAYHEW, MATTHEW. 1710.

Mayhew's *A brief narrative of the success which the gospel hath had among the Indians of Martha's Vineyard (and the places adjacent) in New-England* (Boston, 1694) contains an order, 1710, signed by Mayhew as clerk to the Justices of Dukes Co., Mass., to a sheriff of the county to apprehend a fugitive.

WILBERFORCE PAPERS. 1807-71.

(*a*) Letter from James Monroe to William Wilberforce, 1807, about the abolition of the slave trade. (MS. Wilberforce d.14, f.29)

(*b*) Letters, 1853-71, to Samuel Wilberforce, Bishop of Oxford, from various clergymen concerning the Church in North America. Includes comments of American bishops on a proposal for a Revised Version of the Scriptures; also some discussion on Mormonism, Canadian politics in the 1850's, American Indians, and the American Civil War. (MSS. Wilberforce, c.19, ff.114-88)

(*c*) Three letters, 1856, from George Mifflin Dallas to Bishop Samuel Wilberforce about capital punishment. (MSS. Wilberforce, c.11, ff.205, 207-8, 228)

NAPIER PAPERS. Memoirs, letters. 1812, 1838-43. (MS. Eng. lett. c.234; MS. Eng. misc. b.96)

(*a*) Memoirs of a Wiltshire weaver, wounded while fighting against the Americans in the War of 1812.

(*b*) Thirty-seven letters, 1838-43, of G.W. Featherstonhaugh to Henry Stephen Fox (British Minister at Washington); many are concerned with the Maine-New Brunswick boundary dispute.

CLOUGH PAPERS. Letters. (MSS. Eng. lett. c.189-90, d.175-9, e.74-84; Eng. misc. c.359, d.511-5).

The papers of Arthur Hugh Clough, poet, contain correspondence with Emerson, J.R. Lowell, C.E. Norton, and other Americans. See F.L. Mulhauser (ed.), *The Correspondence of Arthur Hugh Clough* (Oxford, 1957), App. III, 'Catalogue of all known letters', pp. 622-49.

PEARSON PAPERS. *c.* 1862-1894.

Papers of C.H. Pearson, British author and statesman.

(*a*) Letter, *c.* 1862, to Pearson from Francis Power Cobbe, enclosing a possible article for the *National Review.* (MS. Eng. lett. d.187, ff.32-3)

(*b*) Letter, 1868, to Pearson from Louis Agassiz about scientific specimens. (MS. Eng. lett. d.186, f.54)

(*c*) Letter to Pearson from Wendell Phillips, *c.* 1868, asking him to attend a reading by R.W. Emerson. (MS. Eng. lett. d.190, ff.105-6)

(*d*) Two letters to Pearson from Charles Eliot Norton, 1868, 1872, concerning personal matters. (MS. Eng. lett. d.189, ff.129-33)

(*e*) Two letters, 1868, 1893, to Pearson from Oliver Wendell Holmes, one of which refers to hospital care in Massachusetts. (MS. Eng. lett. d.188, ff.129-33)

(*f*) Letter, 1873, from Henry Adams to Charles Eliot Norton, offering three dollars a page for publishing rights to an article by Pearson. (MS. Eng. misc. c.386, f.27)

(*g*) Letter to Pearson from Theodore Roosevelt, 1894, commenting on Pearson's *National Life and Character; A Forecast,* and discussing warfare between 'superior' and 'inferior' races and the railroad business as a manly, character-building profession. (MS. Eng. lett. d.190, ff.133-7)

(*h*) Letter, 1894, from Theodore Roosevelt to Mrs. Edith Pearson, expressing his condolences on the loss of her husband. (MS. Eng. lett. d.192, ff.116-8)

BRYCE PAPERS. American papers. 1870-1922.

James Bryce, 1st Viscount Bryce (1838-1922), jurist, historian, and politician; M.P. 1880-1906, and a member of three Cabinets. He first visited the United States in 1871 and last in 1921. Author of *The American Commonwealth* (1888); British Ambassador to the United States 1907-13.

The American papers are arranged as follows:
Bryce-Eliot Correspondence. 2 volumes.
Major American Correspondents. 8 volumes.
Miscellaneous American Correspondents. 11 volumes.
Bryce Letters to Americans. 2 volumes
Letters relating to *The American Commonwealth.* 3 volumes.
Embassy Papers. 7 volumes.
Guardbook.
Bryce U.S.A.: Supplementary Volumes.
Collection of Correspondence, Journals and Ephemera of the Rt. Hon. Viscount Bryce of Dechmont.

Many letters are accompanied by clippings from United States newspapers, pamphlets, etc. It is probable that the volumes of 'English Correspondents' - especially the correspondence of Goldwin Smith and Bryce - and others concerning Bryce's literary and political career will be found to contain some relevant material.

A catalogue of the collection is available in the Library.

(*a*) BRYCE-ELIOT CORRESPONDENCE. 2 volumes. (*Arranged chronologically.*)

Charles William Eliot (1834-1926), President of Harvard University, 1868-1909.

96 letters, 1871-1922, to Bryce, with one photostat copy (1907) and 9 later letters, 1922-6, to Lady Bryce.[29]

136 letters (37 in photostat and 99 in typed copy), 1879-1921, from Bryce to Eliot.[30]

The letters of 1879-1908 from Bryce to Eliot (all in photostat here) are mainly of minor interest, e.g. on lectures to be given by both Bryce and Eliot. Those in typed copy (1909-21) range through all Bryce's American interests, with the notable addition of a considerable amount on labour problems in the United States. Eliot's letters are also noteworthy as expounding the views of one who was convinced that American neutrality in the First World War was the best policy both for the United States and the Allies.

27. Colonel J.S. Doyle, son of Sir C.W. Doyle, took the name of North on his marriage to Susan, Baroness North, in 1835.

28. Typed transcript at Rhodes House, Oxford. See note, (p. 205).

29. Nineteen to Bryce and three to Lady Bryce are printed, in whole or in part, in Henry James, *Charles W. Eliot, President of Harvard University, 1869-1909.* 2 vols. (Boston and New York, 1930; London, 1931).

30. Twenty-one of these are printed in H.A.L. Fisher, *James Bryce, Viscount Bryce of Dechmont,* 2 vols. (London and New York, 1927).

(*b*) MAJOR AND MISCELLANEOUS AMERICAN CORRESPONDENTS. 8 and 11 volumes respectively. (*Arranged alphabetically.*)

Main topics discussed include: various presidential campaigns and elections, 1884-1920; tariff; Negro problem; civil service reform; Canadian-American relations; international copyright legislation; the government of American cities, especially New York; the Armenian question; the Irish question and American opinion; women's suffrage; the Venezuela crisis; the Spanish-American War, Cuba, the Philippines and imperialism generally; repercussions of the Boer War in the United States; Mexico question; the Panama tolls question; the United States and the First World War, notably the organization of support for the Allies, German propaganda activities; division of feeling between the East and West (isolationism being stronger in the West), and maritime disputes with both Britain and Germany; the American League to Enforce Peace; arguments in United States for and against the League of Nations; anti-Wilson sentiment; the struggle over the ratification of the Peace Treaty, 1919-20, and America's retreat from collective security. There is also considerable discussion of academic matters.

Major correspondents are:

Adams, Charles Francis, the younger. 23 letters. 1898-1915.

Barton, J.L., Secretary of the American Board of Commissioners for Foreign Missions (Congregational). 17 letters. 1913-21.

Butler, Nicholas Murray, President of Columbia University. 52 letters (including typed copies). 1891-1921.

Carnegie, Andrew. 39 letters, mostly slight notes. 1891-1917.

Choate, Joseph. 15 letters. 1899-1916.

Garrison, Wendell P., of the *Nation*. 134 letters. 1881-1905.

Godkin, E.L., editor of the *Nation*. 54 letters. 1882-1902, and two from Mrs. Godkin, 1904.

Godkin, Lawrence, son of E.L. Godkin. 11 letters. 1882, 1903-18.

Henry, Bayard, lawyer of Philadelphia. 76 letters. 1915-21.

Jameson, J.F., historian. 19 letters. 1891, 1910-22.[31]

Johnson, Robert Underwood, secretary of the American Copyright League. 40 letters. 1884-1921.

Lodge, Henry Cabot. 34 letters. 1893-1922.

Low, Seth, New York municipal reformer, President of Columbia University. 40 letters. 1887-1916.

Lowell, A. Lawrence, President of Harvard University. 44 letters. 1899-1921.

Macy, Jesse, Professor of Political Science at Grinnell College, Iowa. 18 letters and 3 from Mrs. Macy. 1887-1919.

Marburg, Theodore, member of the executive committee of the American League to Enforce Peace. 31 letters. 1915-20.[32]

Rhodes, James Ford, historian. 31 letters. 1895-1921.

Roosevelt, Theodore. 53 letters.[33] 1886-1918.

Root, Elihu. 11 letters. 1905-20.

Sedgwick, Ellery, editor of the *Atlantic Monthly*. 12 letters. 1914-21.

Storey, Moorfield, businessman. 40 letters. 1906-21.

Taft, William Howard. 19 letters. 1911-21.

Villard, Henry, journalist, railroad promoter, and financier. 16 letters. 1883-1900.

Among the Miscellaneous Correspondents are:

Adams, Herbert B. 4 letters. 1882-96.

Addams, Jane, superintendent of Hull House, Chicago. 1 letter. 1915.

Atkinson, Edward, economist. 1 letter. 1901.

Bancroft, George. 1 letter. 1881.

Beveridge, Albert J., United States Senator. 1 letter. 1915.

Bingham, Hiram, Professor of Latin American History at Yale University. 10 letters. 1911-21.

Bishop, Joseph B., of the New York *Evening Post*. 4 letters. 1895-1921.

Bowker, R.R., publisher and author. 3 letters (one a copy). 1888-1918.

Bradford, Gamaliel, author. 8 letters. 1884-1911.

Burton, Theodore E., United States Senator. 3 letters. 1911-9.

Clemens, Samuel L. ('Mark Twain'). 1 postcard. 1900.

Croly, Herbert. 1 letter. 1917.

Davis, John W., United States Ambassador to Britain 1919-21. 1 letter. 1920.

Edmunds, George F., United States Senator. 1 letter. 1885.

Eggleston, Edward, historian and novelist. 3 letters. 1889-96.

Garrison, Francis J., publisher. 1 letter. 1893.

George, Henry. 1 letter. 1884.

Gilder, Richard W., editor. 17 letters. 1880-1906.

Goodnow, Frank J., political scientist. 2 letters. 1889, 1896.

Gregory, Charles Noble, university dean. 16 letters. 1913-21.

Hart, Albert Bushnell, historian. 1 letter. 1903.

Hay, John. 4 letters. 1887-98.

Higginson, Thomas Wentworth, author. 8 letters. 1881-1904.

Hoar, George Frisbie, United States Senator. 1 letter. 1897.

Holmes, Oliver Wendell, Sr. 2 letters. 1886.

Holmes, Oliver Wendell, Jr. 16 letters. 1871-94, 1914-21; and 5 to Lady Bryce. 1923-6.

Hopkins, Archibald, lawyer. 17 letters. 1916-21.

House, Edward M. 10 letters. 1915-9.

Hughes, Charles Evans. 2 letters. 1910, 1921.

Keen, W.W., surgeon. 3 letters (one printed). 1915-21.

Lansing, Robert. 3 letters. 1915-21.

Laughlin, James L., political economist. 3 letters. 1919.

Lea, Henry C., historian and Philadelphia municipal reformer. 3 letters. 1870-1904.

Longfellow, Henry W. 1 letter. 1871.

Lowell, James Russell. 2 letters. 1884, 1886.

MacVeagh, Wayne, lawyer, diplomat and reformer. 1 letter. 1897.

Marshall, Thomas R., Vice-President of the United States 1913-21. 2 letters. 1917.

Norton, Charles D., banker. 2 letters. 1914, 1921.

Norton, Charles E. 4 letters. 1903-7.

Page, Walter Hines. 7 letters. 1914-7.

Putnam, George Haven, publisher. 6 letters. 1891-1917.

Reed, Thomas B., Speaker of the House of Representatives 1889-91, 1895-9. Letter. 1891.

Schurz, Carl. 2 letters. 1884, 1899.

Shaw, Albert, editor. 6 letters. 1885-1904.

Stimson, Henry L., Secretary of War 1911-3. 6 letters. 1913-20.

Straight, Willard, financier and 'dollar diplomatist' in Far East. 4 letters. 1916-7.

31. Six of these are printed in Elizabeth Donnan and Leo F. Stock, eds., 'An historian's world, selections from the correspondence of John Franklin Jameson', *Memoirs of the American Philosophical Society*, vol. xlii, 1956; and a further five in Leo F. Stock, ed., 'Some Bryce-Jameson Correspondence', *American Historical Review*, vol. 50, pp. 261-98, 1945.

32. Eleven of these are printed in *Development of the League of Nations Idea; Documents and Correspondence of Theodore Marburg*, 2 vols., ed. by John H. Latané (New York, 1932).

33. Only some of these letters have been printed in *Letters of Theodore Roosevelt*, selected and edited by E.E. Morison and others. 8 vols. (Cambridge, Mass., 1951-4).

Thayer, W.R., historian. 14 letters. 1903-20.

Villard, Oswald Garrison, editor of the *Nation*. 3 letters. 1900, 1920.

Washington, Booker T. 2 letters. 1908.

White, Andrew D. 3 letters. 1883-98.

White, Henry, American plenipotentiary to the Peace Conference. 7 letters. 1914, 1919-20.

Wickersham, George, Attorney-General 1909-13. 12 letters. 1914-21.

Wilson, William L., Representative from West Virginia, sponsor of 1893 Tariff. 6 letters. 1892-6.

Wilson, Woodrow. 13 letters. 1888-1918. There is also a draft reply by Bryce on the back of an envelope from Wilson (dated 1919) but Wilson's letter is missing.

(*c*) BRYCE LETTERS TO AMERICANS. 1881-1921. 2 volumes. (*Arranged chronologically.*) Typescript copies - with a few drafts handwritten by Bryce, 1881-1921.

Most of the letters are to the following:

Bingham, Hiram. 34 letters. 1910-21.

Butler, Nicholas Murray. 31 letters. 1893-1919.

House, Edward M. 5 letters. 1915-7.

Low, Seth. 28 letters. 1892-1915.

Lowell, A. Lawrence. 55 letters. 1900-21.

Macy, Jesse. 25 letters, and 1 to Mrs. Macy. 1891-1921.

Rhodes, James Ford. 25 letters. 1900-21.

White, Henry. 8 letters. 1913-9.

Others are to George P. Brett, J.A. Chambliss, R.H. Dana, S. Edelman, Bayard Henry, Thomas W. Higginson, Oliver Wendell Holmes, Jr., Henry Holt, Henry C. Lea, Henry Cabot Lodge, William Loeb, Jr., Denys P. Myers, Charles E. Norton, A.E. Pillsbury, G.H. Putnam, Theodore Roosevelt, Elihu Root, Theodore Stanton, F.J. Stimson, William H. Taft, Everett P. Wheeler, and Sarah Whitman.

Most of the subjects mentioned under 'Major and Miscellaneous American Correspondents (p. 197) are again represented, with - in addition to comments on British politics and matters relating to *The American Commonwealth* - also the following: Cleveland's civil service policy; municipal politics in Philadelphia; immigration; American and British railroad rates; an elective judiciary; the Iowa primary system; the American Labor Party; Wilson's domestic policy. In a letter, 1920, to J.F. Rhodes, Bryce is severely critical of Wilson's handling of the ratification question.

(*d*) *The American Commonwealth*. 3 volumes. (*Arranged alphabetically.*)

Letters to Bryce about the book from many and diverse Americans and Britons; some before the publication of the first edition in 1888 in reply to queries put by him, but most after publication criticizing, or suggesting amendments or further reading. There is a letter from Denis Kearney castigating the chapter on 'Kearneyism in California', and another of the same year setting forth what he (Kearney) claims to be the true position - annotated by Bryce. There are also many replies to questions put by Bryce before revision of the book, 1905-11, e.g. about women's suffrage, boss rule in the cities, the Referendum and Recall, and the Negro problem. Many correspondents enclose printed material which they think will be useful in future editions. There are also a number of letters relating to the libel action brought against Bryce by Oakey Hall, Mayor of New York under Tweed, over Frank J. Goodnow's chapter on the Tweed Ring in the first edition - suppressed in the second edition (1889) - including some from Goodnow himself.

For further material on *The American Commonwealth*, see Bryce Papers, sections (*f*), (*g*), and (*h*) (pp. 198-9).

(*e*) EMBASSY PAPERS. 1907-13. 7 volumes. (*Arranged chronologically.*)

Includes miscellaneous papers - notes, draft letters, aide-memoires by Bryce, copies of telegrams, etc. - and letters from American Cabinet members, notably Root and Knox, Senators and Representatives, other Ambassadors in Washington, and newspaper men. Also letters of thanks for addresses, invitations to lecture, etc.

The collection includes Bryce's commission and credentials as Ambassador; and also letters and papers on: Canadian-American relations (with printed copies of treaties affecting Canada signed during Bryce's tenure of office); Canadian Boundary Waters question; and Passamaquoddy Bay (1908); conservation; proposed transformation of International Prize Court into Arbitration Tribunal (1908); Newfoundland fisheries (1909-12), especially the Hague Award (1910); situation in Central America in 1910; fur seals negotiation (1911) with a draft of the proposed treaty; Canadian Reciprocity Treaty (1911); American armed vessels on the Great Lakes; Panama tolls. There is also a memo (? by George Young) of conversations with Senator Borah on arbitration.

Writers of letters include the following:

Edward VII on Theodore Roosevelt.

Grey, Sir Edward, on the North Atlantic Fisheries Agreement (1912), the faked interview with Bryce on the Oklahoma Constitution (1907), possible action against the British Imperial Tobacco Company under the Anti-Trust Law, a proposed arbitration treaty with the United States, Anglo-American policy in the Far East, Panama tolls, Bryce's retirement and Spring-Rice's appointment - also some short replies by Bryce.

Hardinge, Sir Charles, of the Foreign Office on foreign affairs generally, and American-Canadian and American-Japanese relations in particular.

Howard, Esmé, Chargé while Bryce was on vacation in Britain 1908, on Boundary Waters negotiations, and also copies of dispatches from Howard to Sir Edward Grey.

Innes, A. Mitchell, who was in charge of the embassy while Bryce was in summer quarters in 1909 and 1910, on Boundary Waters, American-German relations, Canadian reciprocity, Far Eastern affairs; and later, 1912, on Panama tolls, the Republican platform and the 'rottenness' of Congress.

Young, George, Attaché at Washington and secretary of the North Atlantic Fisheries Arbitration at The Hague, 1909-1910, chiefly on the latter.

Various members of the embassy staff - notes of minor importance: C.C. Bayley, British Consul at New York - mostly about Irish agitation there; various other Consular letters from Bayley's successors C.W. Bennett and R. Walsh, and from the Consuls in San Francisco and Chicago.

British Ministers in other countries, notably Brazil, Mexico, Guatemala, and Nicaragua, on events in those places.

Johnston, Sir H.H., in Liberia on the Negro problem.

Taft, President. Six letters, 1908-12, with one of which is enclosed a copy of the Senate's resolutions limiting the proposed Arbitration Treaty between Britain and the United States.

Knox, Philander C., Secretary of State, on fisheries (with replies by Bryce).

Laurier, Sir Wilfred, Sir Robert Borden, and various Canadian Cabinet members, officials, etc., as well as Sir William Macgregor and Sir Ralph Williams, Governors of Newfoundland 1908-9 and 1911-2 respectively, and Sir Robert Bond and Sir Edward Morris, Prime Ministers of same, 1909, 1909-12, mostly on Canadian-American relations and fisheries.

(*f*) GUARDBOOK, LETTERS. 1880-1921.

Letters of Bryce to Nicholas Paine Gilman, 1893 (f.1); to Richard

Watson Gilder, 1880 (f.3); to Robert Underwood Johnson (seventeen letters, of which two are joint letters to Johnson and Gilder), 1890-1914 (f.5); to Robert E. Ely about R.U. Johnson, 1913 (f.43); to the Century Company of New York, 1898, with a sheet of corrections (f.49); to Sara Norton, 1915 (f.52).

Also: Eight letters, 1891-1908, to Lloyd Bryce, George Harvey, and others about articles for the *North American Review* (ff.117-32); five letters, 1906-11 and n.d., to William H. Rideing (ff.108-15, 121); postcard, 1907, to James Milne, telling what led him to write *The American Commonwealth* (f.66); twenty-seven letters, 1911-21, to John A. Stewart, New York, about the centenary of Anglo-U.S. peace, Sulgrace Manor, etc. (ff.72-107); letter, 1914, to Robert Underwood Johnson about the Panama tolls question (f.70); unaddressed letter, 1916, about the fraternity system in American universities (f.116); to 'Mr. Putnam' [? G.H.], 1917, praising Choate's performance as U.S. Ambassador to England (f.152); to 'Dr. Anderson', two letters, 1885, on the American university system (ff.153-6); to 'Mr. Donald', 1906, on his reasons for accepting the post of Ambassador (ff.196-7).

(*g*) BRYCE U.S.A.: SUPPLEMENTARY VOLUMES. 1870-1920.

(i) Major American correspondents. (Bryce U.S.A. 34)

Adams, C.F., the younger. 1 letter. 1908.
Barton, J.L. 1 letter. 1918.
Butler, Nicholas Murray. 2 letters. 1905-6.
Carnegie, Andrew. 3 letters. 1911.
Choate, Joseph M. 1 letter. 1912.
Eliot, Charles W. 1 letter. 1919.
Garrison, Wendell P. 4 letters. 1892-1905.
Henry, Bayard. 2 letters. 1917-9.
Lodge, Henry C. 1 letter. 1919.
Low, Seth. 1 letter. 1907.
Lowell, A. Lawrence. 8 letters. 1900-19.
Macy, Jesse. 3 letters. 1910-8.
Rhodes, James Ford. 5 letters. 1904-20.
Roosevelt, Theodore. 8 letters. 1887-1913.
Sedgwick, Ellery. 1 letter. 1919.
Storey, Moorfield. 2 letters. 1920.

(ii) Miscellaneous American correspondents. (Bryce U.S.A. 35-36)
Includes: H.B. Adams, 1884; John Hay, 1897; O.W. Holmes, Jr., 1889, 1892-4, 1915; Francis Parkman, 1881, 1888; Albert Shaw, 1894; Booker T. Washington, 1909; Andrew D. White, 1886, 1892; George Wickersham, 1920.

(iii) Embassy papers. (Bryce U.S.A. 37-38)
Correspondence, Dec. 1906-May 1913, includes: Horace H. Furness, n.d. [?1907]; Thomas E. Holland, 1907; Sir Percy Sanderson, 1907; Marquess of Crewe, 1909; Elihu Root, 1909; Lord Balfour of Burleigh, 1909-10; Rennell Rodd, 1909; George Young, 1911; Sir Edward Grey, 1911-2; Sir R.L. Borden, 1911, 1913; Rollo Ogden, 1912; Henry Watterson, 1912; Sir Cecil A. Spring-Rice, 1913. With draft letters and memoranda, including some by Bryce.

(iv) Papers relating to *The American Commonwealth*. (Bryce U.S.A. 40-46, 49)
Correspondence; travel diary (1870); notebook, containing some jottings; and the original manuscript of *The American Commonwealth* in Bryce's hand, with notes and marginalia. (Some chapters are in several drafts.) There is also a collection of miscellaneous papers relating to *The American Commonwealth*, including incomplete draft chapters, notes on American politics, and suggestions for amendments to the book.

(v) Miscellaneous. (Bryce U.S.A. 50)
Includes a MS., 'de Tocqueville', in Bryce's hand.

(*h*) COLLECTION OF CORRESPONDENCE, JOURNALS AND EPHEMERA OF THE RT. HON. VISCOUNT BRYCE OF DECHMONT.

This massive collection includes approximately 1,000 letters, of which about 400 refer to the United States. Some of the more interesting MSS. are:

(i) Letter from Bryce to his mother, 1874, criticizing the preaching of the American evangelist, D.L. Moody.

(ii) 'Journal of Journey in U.S.A. & Hawaii, 1883-4'. This important MS., besides describing his travels during this visit to America, also contains Bryce's notes for what later became *The American Commonwealth*. His observations on American life are listed under headings such as: 'Constitutional Changes', 'Faults of Democracy', 'Social Phenomena of the U.S.A.', and 'Character of People'.

(iii) Letter to his mother from Bryce, 1890, giving a detailed description of his journeys in Kentucky and South Carolina.

(iv) Several letters, 1901, describing Bryce's impressions of the new U.S. president, Theodore Roosevelt.

(v) Letter, 1908, discussing Tuskegee College in Alabama, where Bryce stayed as the guest of Booker T. Washington.

(vi) Letters, 1909, describing Bryce's impressions of President Taft and other American politicians, his visit to California, and his trip to Ancona, a small Indian village.

(vii) Letter, 4 July 1911, in which Bryce refers to American independence as more of a misfortune than an occasion to celebrate.

(viii) Letter, 1912, concerning President Taft, the Arbitration Treaty, and the diplomacy behind it.

(ix) Thirteen letters, 1921, written to his sister Minnie, describing his last journey to the U.S.

The MISCELLANEOUS ENGLISH CORRESPONDENTS section of the Bryce Papers includes sixteen letters from Henry James to Lord and Lady Bryce.

GILBERT MURRAY PAPERS. Letters. 1906-30. (On restricted access.)

Box 2 of this large and, as yet, uncatalogued collection contains, *inter alia*, bundles labelled: 'Letters about, to and from America, 1906-7' (apparently chiefly about a lecture tour); 'American letters, 1914-15'; 'American letters, 1916-18'; and 'American professors, scholars and friends', *c.* 1919-30.

KENNETH GRAHAME PAPERS. 5 letters. 1907-10.

Five letters, 1907-10, from Theodore Roosevelt to Kenneth Grahame (1859-1932).

H.A.L. FISHER PAPERS. Letters, diaries, etc. 1909-37.

(*a*) Box 6: Letters written from the U.S., 1924, and on voyage to the U.S., 1930.
(*b*) Box 8: Diary for July 1930 in the U.S.
(*c*) Box 9: Packet labelled 'American visit, Summer 1937' and others containing press cuttings and other printed material about the U.S. Also diary of visit, 1909, to the U.S. and Canada.

ASQUITH PAPERS. (On restricted access.)

(*a*) MS. Asquith 17, f.30: Decipher of a dispatch, 1 Aug. 1916, from Sir Cecil Spring-Rice on American reactions to the Casement case and the blockade.
(*b*) MS. Asquith 26, ff.166-193: Two reports, Nov. 1914, by B.P. Blackett on purchase of war supplies in the U.S. (includes a copy of a letter, 27 Nov. 1914, Theodore Roosevelt to Blackett); and a memorandum by Sir George Paish on economic relations with the U.S., n.d. [? late 1914].

(*c*) MS. Asquith 26, ff.245-6: Memorandum, Feb. 1915, by Walter Runciman on American Ship Purchase Bill.
(*d*) MS. Asquith 27, f.252: Decipher of a dispatch, June 1915, from Sir Cecil Spring-Rice about the American government's note to Germany on the *Lusitania* sinking.
(*e*) MS. Asquith 30, ff.70-7: Papers about the U.S. government's protest against seizure of Germans from the American steamer *China*, Apr. 1916.
(*f*) MS. Asquith, ff.101-6: Letters of Balfour and Grey on need to present English view of Irish Easter Rising to the U.S., May 1916.
(*g*) MS. Asquith, ff.166-7: Memorandum by Lloyd George on the financing of American contracts, June 1916.

NATHAN PAPERS. Diary, correspondence. 1926-37.

Sir Matthew Nathan (1862-1939), soldier, civil servant, and colonial administrator. The papers include a diary, 1926, containing details of a visit to the U.S. (MS. Nathan 61); letters, 1926-37, from American friends and English friends in the U.S., and letters about his 1926 visit, including correspondence with the Anglo-American Society, Columbia University, the English-Speaking Union, etc. (MSS. Nathan 211-213)

II. COLLECTIONS DEPOSITED IN THE BODLEIAN LIBRARY

NALSON PAPERS. (The property of the Duke of Portland.)

Vol. xviii, item 90. (Dep. c.171, ff. 233-5.) June 1651. Draft treaty between the United Provinces and England proposed by the Commissioners of the States-General includes provisions 'for settling ... the boundaries of the possessions of either in North America'; and a clause providing that subjects of either power may thereafter trade freely with 'the Caribee Islands and other places of Virginia'.[34]
Vol. xxii, item 157. (Dep. c.175, f.427.) 1651. Petition of Dirck Janson of Middelburgh to the Parliament praying for restoration of the cargo of a ship seized for violating the Act prohibiting trade with Virginia. Had sailed from Europe before passage of the Act, and had left Virginia before news of the prohibition arrived.[35]

ASHURST, HENRY. Letter-book with accounts. 1674-6, 1679-1701. (MS. D.D. Ashurst c.1.)

This letter-book of Henry Ashurst, merchant, contains copies of letters to New England.

SHERARD COLLECTION. Botanical papers. 1679-1784. (Property of Dept. of Botany, Oxford U.)

The collection contains some botanical material relating to America, including lists of names of American plants, copies of drawings of American plants, botanical notes on Virginia. (MSS. Sherard 38; 189-90; 205 f.13; 207 f.40; 237/2 f.278; 453 f.50).

DASHWOOD PAPERS.

See Betty Kemp, 'Some letters of Sir Francis Dashwood, Baron le Despencer, a joint Postmaster General, 1766-81', *Bulletin of the John Rylands Library,* vol. xxxvii. 204-48, 1954.
D.D. Dashwood (Bucks.) b.5.

There is one printed piece, *Narrative of Facts relative to American Affairs* (15 pages). It is a resumé based on official documents and on letters, principally from Governor Francis Bernard of Massachusetts. The latest letters are 1 and 3 Oct. 1768, received on 4 Nov. On the first is the note: 'This paper is given to you in great confidence of your secrecy, with a request that you will not communicate it to any person whatever.'

BLAND BURGES PAPERS.

Sir James Bland Burges (1752-1824) served as Undersecretary of State at the Foreign Office from 1789 to 1795.
(*a*) Nineteen letters to Bland Burges from George Hammond, British Minister in America. (36 ff.8-15, 18-52)

Hammond's letters, ranging in date from 1791 to 1795, discuss various diplomatic issues, including the post-Revolutionary war debt settlement question, the emerging divisions between Federalists and Republicans, rumours of American willingness to support France in any Franco-British conflict, Jay's Treaty, America's frontier controversy with Britain, etc.
(*b*) Twenty-four letters, 1791-5, to Bland Burges from Edward Thornton in Philadelphia and Baltimore. (44 ff.1-55, 58-86)

Thornton (1766-1852) was secretary to George Hammond and British vice-consul in Baltimore from 1793 to 1796. His letters comment on the country and its people, American response to the writings of Thomas Paine, U.S. commercial interests, Indian troubles in the West, his impression of George Washington, U.S. journalism, etc.

MARY SOMERVILLE PAPERS.

Letter from George Washington to Gouverneur Morris, 1793, mentioning Jefferson and Madame Lafayette. (Dep. c.372)

CLARENDON PAPERS (UNITED STATES).[36] 14 volumes manuscripts. 1853-8, 1865-70. 6 volumes papers printed for Cabinet use, etc., 1848-57. 5 boxes letters, papers. 1868-70. (MSS. Clar. Dep.)

George William Frederick Villiers, 4th Earl of Clarendon and 4th Baron Hyde (1800-70), was Foreign Secretary 1853-8, 1865-6, and 1868-70.

I. 1853-8.

MS. Clar. Dep. c.11, 24, 25, 43, 44, 63, 64, 65, 81, 83, are from the series of bound 'in-letters'.
c.11. 'United States: [letters from] Mr. Crampton and miscellaneous, 1853.'

Deal with fisheries; reciprocity; prospects, especially regarding the tariff, for Anglo-American relations during the Pierce administration; filibustering; Honduras; conclusion of international copyright convention; abatement of anti-British sentiment in United States; to Britain's advantage not to intervene in the slavery issue; Cuba; Pierce's inaugural address; isthmian canal; speeches in Congress on the Clayton-Bulwer Treaty; the dispute between the 'Hards' and 'Softs' in New York; division of spoils under Pierce; landing of the Americans at Greytown, Nicaragua; appointment of Pierre Soulé to Madrid; the character of Buchanan; conversations with Marcy about the Clayton-Bulwer Treaty; Central American affairs generally; adverse effects in some quarters of American opinion of Mrs. H.B. Stowe's warm reception in Britain; the Mosquito Coast; the fugitive slave problem; United States attitude on Anglo-Russian relations; navigation of the St. Lawrence; the affair of Koszta, a Hungarian refugee; United States suspicions about British intentions concerning Cuba. (*See also* c.225, p. 201)
c.24. 'United States, January-June 1854.' Mostly from Crampton, with some copy enclosures from American statesmen, and some letters from Consuls, etc.

34. H.M.C. xiii (i), pp. 605-7.
35. Ibid., p. 617.
36. These papers have been deposited by Lord Clarendon on condition that no quotations are made from them without his consent.

Deal with South Carolina's action on coloured seamen; Senator Sumner and arbitration; further discussion of the Clayton-Bulwer Treaty; United States alarm over the Mosquito protectorate; the Nebraska question; alleged fitting out of Russian privateers in United States ports; fisheries; Central America; the belief that the United States was planning the seizure of Cuba; the *Black Warrior* incident.

c.25. 'United States, July-December 1854.' Mostly as c.24 above.

Deal with the Quebec meeting on fisheries; offer of mediation by United States in Crimean War; the Reciprocity Treaty (Crampton says that this is popular in the United States, but there may be delay in its ratification); bombardment of Greytown, Nicaragua; rumours of Hawaiian annexation; Soulé's activities at Madrid; United States' designs on Samaná Bay, Dominican Republic; the 'aggressive' activities of a United States naval officer at the Falkland Islands; the Ostend meeting and manifesto; Nicaragua, the state of which prevents settlement of the Central American question; recruitment in the United States for the Crimean War.

c.43. 'United States, January-August 1855.' Mostly as c.24 above; and including some letters to Clarendon from Buchanan as United States Minister in London.

Mainly about enlistment for the Crimean War, which was finally stopped in this period; steamers for sale in the United States; dropping of treaty with Santo Domingo by the United States; difficulties between the United States and Spain; the United States squadron going to Cuba; hostility towards Britain in the United States; negotiations between Britain and United States over the detention of coloured seamen in Southern ports.

c.44. 'United States, September-December 1855.' Mostly as c.24 above.

Deal with Irish anti-British agitation in United States; indictment of Consuls over Crimean recruiting; unpopularity of the Pierce administration; United States government's desire for Crampton's recall; aversion of mercantile classes to the quarrel with Britain over recruiting; election of Speaker of the House of Representatives.

c.63. 'United States, January-April 1856.' Mostly as c.24 above, with several from Sir Henry Bulwer.

Crampton mentions rumours of his recall; the appointment of Dallas to London; William Walker's activities in Nicaragua; effect of the Peace of Paris in the United States; improvement of feeling towards Britain.

c.64. 'United States, May-July 1856.' Mainly from Crampton until his dismissal in 1856, then from the Chargé and various others, including Bulwer.

Deal with Costa Rica and Walker; Brooks's attack on Sumner; Crampton's dismissal by Pierce; Frémont's nomination for President; aftermath of Crampton's dismissal; the presidential campaign of 1856 (conflicting reports as to the probable outcome from various correspondents).

c.65. 'United States, August-December 1856' (with letters of May and June), from various persons, but notably John S. Lumley, British Chargé.

Deal with dismissal of Consuls; the presidential election; the Kansas question; United States designs on British North America; the transatlantic telegraph; the Oregon Boundary Commission; desire in United States to renew diplomatic relations with Britain; slavery agitation; appointment of Lord Napier as British Minister to the United States; Cass to be the new Secretary of State.

c.81. 'United States 1857.' Principally from Napier.

Chiefly concerned with events in Central America; probable policy of the new administration; negotiations on steamers on the Great Lakes; Cuba; Kansas; the President (Buchanan) on the Clayton-Bulwer Treaty; Stephen A. Douglas; filibustering; Walker's arrest.

c.83. 'Belgium, Netherlands, Denmark, Sweden, Italian States, Greece, United States, 1858.' Letters are from Jan.-Mar. 30 only, mostly from Napier and Sir William Gore Ouseley.

Deal with filibustering; the debate on Kansas; the threatened break-up of the Union; further discussion of the Clayton-Bulwer Treaty.

MS. Clar. dep. c.125-41 are from the series of bound copies of out-letters. All volumes are indexed.

c.125-36 cover the period Feb. 1853-Oct. 1856. They contain a few letters to Crampton and James Buchanan.

c.137-41 cover the period Oct. 1856-Feb. 1858. They contain a few letters to Napier.

MS. Clar. dep. c.224. Register of letters to the U.S., 25 Feb. 1853 - 28 Dec. 1855.

On same subjects as above for same period, and such as frauds practised on British emigrants to Australia passing through the United States; extradition efforts to secure reduction of duties on various British products; Canada.

c.225. 'Register of letters from U.S., 1 Feb. 1853 - 26 Dec. 1853.' (*See* c.11 above.)

Printed Cabinet Papers. c.246-75.

c.246 and c.247. Correspondence relative to the Mosquito territory, 1848-54.

c.260. Correspondence concerning the British North American fisheries, and a commercial convention with the United States, 9 June 1852-28 Apr. 1854.

c.263. Papers concerning recruitment in the United States for the British Army in the Crimea, parts I and II, 1854-5.

c.264. Another copy of c.263 containing also part III, 1855-6, and miscellaneous correspondence.

c.275. Contains correspondence on the boundary between British Guiana and Venezuela, Nov. 1857. Also correspondence, proposals, etc. between British and American governments on maritime law.

II. 1865-6.

c.90. 'America, 1865-1866.' Chiefly from Sir Frederick Bruce, British Minister to the United States 1864-7.

Deal with relations with Seward; Reconstruction; much comment on Fenian activities; reciprocity; Mexico and France; dispute between President Johnson and Congress; fisheries; the Negro problem; arbitration; the tariff; the *Alabama* case.

c.142. Letter-book 'America, 1865-1866', copies of out-letters.

Deal with Maximilian in Mexico; Fenians; neutrality laws; reciprocity; St. Thomas island; Negroes; *Alabama* and *Shenandoah*.

III. 1868-70.

c.476. Box marked 'F.O. Letters to British Embassies III'.

Forty-five letters and one memo, 12 Dec. 1868 - 4 June 1870, chiefly from Clarendon (but two from Edmund Hammond) to Edward Thornton, British Minister to the United States.

For subjects *see* c.480 below.

c.480. Box marked 'F.O. Letters from British Embassies [sic]: Washington, 1868-1869'. Forty-nine letters, 22 Dec. 1868 - 21 Dec. 1869, to Clarendon from Edward Thornton, British Minister to the United States. One from Edmund Hammond, 1 Aug. 1869. Also miscellaneous press cuttings enclosed by Thornton.

Deal with *Alabama* claims - and especially the Johnson-Clarendon Convention; Sumner, and especially his Claims speech; the Cuban insurrection; Congressional legislation, 1868-9; the San Juan boundary; the United States and Santo Domingo; the Tenure of Office Act - especially its partial repeal under Grant in 1869; the characters of Grant and Fish; Motley's appointment to London and Sickles's to

Madrid; Fenians; John Rose's mission to Washington; Canadian public opinion on claims, boundary, etc.

c.481. Box marked as above but for 1870. Thirty-one letters, 4 Jan.-7 June 1870 from Thornton, to Clarendon (also press cuttings).

Deal with desire in some quarters in the United States for annexation of Canada; coolness between Fish and Sumner; visit of Prince Arthur to the United States; rejection of St. Thomas treaty, 1867, with Denmark on the purchase of the island.

c.492. Box marked 'Clarendon Papers F.O. Misc. Papers & Correspondence. U.S.A., *Alabama*, etc.'

Twenty-nine manuscript letters, memos, etc., 4 June 1869- 22 Apr. 1870, to Clarendon from John Laird, William Harcourt, L. Oliphant, Montague Bernard, A. Helps, Edmund Hammond, Lord John Russell, and Edward Thornton - also a copy, 18 June 1870, Clarendon to Bernard - all concerning the *Alabama* claims.

Letter, 3 Nov. 1859, from President James Buchanan to Clarendon on various questions in Anglo-American relations; and one, Paris, 20 May 1868, from Benjamin Rush to Clarendon, on various manifestations of Anglo-American cordiality, e.g. singing patriotic songs in theatres, etc. (*See also* 'Printed Cabinet Papers' below.)

c.493. Box marked 'F.O. Misc. Papers and Correspondence - U.S.A. Embassy, London'. Fifteen letters from Reverdy Johnson, 18 Dec. 1868 - 22 July 1869, and nine from J.L Motley, 8 June 1869 - 13 Jan. 1870.

Several slight notes; also touch upon the Johnson-Clarendon Convention, Sumner's speech on the claims, San Juan, and incidents involving individual Americans.

Printed Cabinet Papers. MS. Clar. dep. c.492 also contains various printed Cabinet memoranda and dispatches, 1869, on the *Alabama* claims, and on possible British and French mediation in the Civil War in 1862.

Also the following: convention on naturalization signed by Clarendon and Motley (n.d. but ? 1869).

Printed *Correspondence ... on the questions of the 'Alabama' and British Claims, Naturalization and San Juan Water Boundary*, 1869.

Printed *Correspondence respecting British and American Claims arising out of the late Civil War in the United States*, 1867.

The above are the major sources of Americana in this collection, but the following volumes will be found to contain scattered items:

1853-65.

MSS. Clar. dep. c.3, c.4, c.14, c.15, c.29, c.30, c.31, c.48, c.49, c.50, c.69, c.70, all of which are volumes of letters to other Cabinet ministers, etc., especially Palmerston, 1853-7. Also c.104, to Russell, 1847, 1854, 1858-65. (All these volumes have indexes.)

1868-70.

MSS. Clar. dep. c.497, 498. Letters from Gladstone, 1868-70. Some allusions to American affairs, notably the *Alabama* claims.

c.501. Letters of Clarendon to Gladstone, 1868-70.

MONK BRETTON PAPERS. (The property of the 3rd Baron Monk Bretton).

The papers of John George Dodson, 1st Baron Monk Bretton (1825-97), politician. The collection includes:

(*a*) Diary of a visit to the U.S. by Dodson, 23 Aug. 1853 - 14 Feb. 1854.

(*b*) American notes by Dodson, 1853-4, consisting of several papers headed respectively 'A birds'-eye view', 'West of the Alleghenies', 'The South', 'Slavery as a system', 'Slavery in practice', and 'Three days at New Orleans'.

(*c*) Notes on the U.S. and Canada at the end (reversed) of Dodson's travel diary for 20 Aug.-30 Oct. 1855.

(*d*) Letter, 2 May 1872, from H.R. Droop to Dodson on reform of private bill legislation in Illinois in 1870.

(*e*) Papers relating to possibility of the Treasury paying to send a barrister to New York to collect evidence for the prosecution in the Tichborne Case, 1873-4.

MAX-MÜLLER PAPERS. 14 letters. 1853-92. (Dep. d.170-1)

Friedrich Max-Müller (1823-1900), philologist. The papers include letters to him from William Dwight Whitney (4 letters, 1853-68), R.W. Emerson (3 letters, 1872-3), Henry George (6 letters, 1883-85), and C.E. Norton (1 letter, 1892).

BENSON PAPERS. 48 letters. 1887-1915.

(*a*) Letter, 1887, from Edward J. Phelps to E.W. Benson. (Dep. Benson 3/6/43)

(*b*) Forty-seven letters, 1892-1915, from Henry James to A.C. Benson. (Dep. Benson 3/53)

III. MISCELLANEOUS COLLECTIONS BELONGING TO THE BODLEIAN LIBRARY

MS. Hatton 51 (S.C. 4099)

Some seventeenth-century notes about methods of making fire, and manufacturing glue in Virginia, written in the margins of an earlier work.

MS. Eng. hist. c.4 (S.C. 29724). f.3.

Copy of a newsletter, 18 Nov. 1610, from George Yardly about affairs in Virginia.

MS. Malone 16 (S.C. 20564).

A common-place book of poems, etc., 1620-30, including a description of a voyage to America.

MS. Add. C. 244 (S.C. 28087). p. 495.

A contemporary copy of the charter granted to the Company of Massachusetts Bay, 4 Mar. 1629.

MS. Add. C. 267 (S.C. 29563).

Copies of letters, invoices, business memoranda, etc., 1655-9, of Thomas Pengelly, cloth and general merchant of London, chiefly relating to his foreign ventures in Virginia, etc. [37]

MS. Add. A. 95 (S.C. 28961).

Diary (29 pages), kept by a Quaker companion of George Fox during his visit to New England, June 1671-Apr. 1673. Endorsed on the flyleaf, 'said to be the autograph of Ellwood, the friend of Milton'.[38]

MS. Aubrey 13 (S.C. 25287). f.98.

Letter, Philadelphia, 13 Apr. 1683, from William Penn to Aubrey, describing the favourable condition of Pennsylvania.

Rawlinson Letters 94 (S.C. 14982). f.188.

Copy of a letter, Boston, 3 Oct. 1683, from Increase Mather to an unnamed friend in Amsterdam, chiefly on affairs in England, and that he expects a large number of believers from there shortly to come to New England.

37. H.M.C. vii, p. 691. (Listed as in possession of the Rev. Thomas William Webb, Hardwick Vicarage, Herefordshire.)

38. Printed in the *Journal of the Friends' Historical Society*, vol. ix, pp. 5-52, 1912.

Rawlinson Letters 108 (S.C. 14996). f.87.

Letter, Boston, 27 Nov. 1683, from Cotton Mather to Richard Chiswell about books.

MS. Aubrey 4 (S.C. 25279). f. 1.

An almost complete draft of an indenture, 1684, between two merchants, William Paggen [place of residence cut away] and John Hardmian, of James River, Va., by which Hardmian agrees to be Paggen's exclusive agent in Virginia.

MS. Carte 81 (S.C. 10527). ff.742-51, 754-65, 779, 803-8.

Papers of Philip Wharton, 4th Baron Wharton (1613-96), and Thomas Wharton, 1st Marquis of Wharton (1648-1716), relating to New England and Virginia, 1689-90. Includes statements of settlers' grievances; patent for the appointment of Sir Edmund Andros as governor of New England; two petitions from Connecticut for fair treatment in the levying of the militia quota; and the 'case' (scarcely legible) of New England in a dispute with New York.

Rawlinson Letters 51 (S.C. 14933). f.329.

Letter, Boston, 11 Sept. 1689, from Increase Mather to Lord Wharton, asking him to speak to the King in order to counteract malicious 'informations' laid against the church in New England.

MS. Eng. th. c.50. f.72.

A letter beginning 'Worthie Mr. Doctor: concerning our plantation in the American world'. The letter is undated, but late seventeenth century, lacking both address and signature, and concerns the conversion of the natives, of which the writer has little hope.

MS. Gough Somersetshire 7 (S.C. 18217).

Copies of papers relating to schemes and calculations addressed to, or connected with, James Brydges, 1st Duke of Chandos (1673-1744). Includes proposals for raising naval stores in Ste.-Croix, Que. 1716 (pp. 122-6). Letter, 14 Aug. 1718, from Col. Alexander Spottiswood [or Spotswood], Lieut.-Governor of Virginia, pointing out the danger from the French in the Lake Erie region, and proposing that the British should occupy the region in strength (pp. 127-35). Paper by Francis Harrison (pp. 231-9), 1724, setting forth the advantages which the Royal African Company may derive by establishing an agency at New York for the supply of Negroes to the Jerseys and New England.

MS. Eng. misc. c.311. ff.4-21.

Register of the patentees for the growth of cochineal and medicinal drugs in the American plantations, including copies of letters patent to George Sinclair, articles of agreement with his partners and minutes of the meetings of the patentees, in the hand of Daniel Campbell, secretary, 1722-8.

MSS. Add. A. 289-300 (S.C. 29404-15).

Letters, notices, and notes of all kinds received by William Henry Turner, who was largely employed in historical and genealogical research at the Bodleian Library by English and American men of letters, *c.* 1860-80. They include a list of papers and an abstract relating to South Carolina in the State Paper Office, London, 1728-40, notes taken from collections of the South Carolina Historical Society, volumes 1 and 2, sent to Turner to check in London by G.B. Chase from Boston, 27 Apr. 1875. (MS. Add. A. 295, f. 162)

MS. Top. Oxon. d.224.

Record of the campaigns of the 52nd (Oxfordshire) Light Infantry, 1755-1822, giving a summary description of its movements, with casualties and promotions, and extracts from dispatches and field orders. The regiment served in Canada, 1765-74, and in America from 1774 to 1778. Its troops were concerned in the skirmish at Lexington, in the battles of Bunker Hill, Brooklyn, Pelham Manor, and Brandywine, in operations on Staten Island and Long Island, and the capture of Forts Montgomery and Clinton.

MS. Montagu d.18 (S.C. 25448). ff.132, 134.

Two letters from George Washington from Mount Vernon. One, 30 Sept. 1762, is presumably to a firm of merchants, and is chiefly about the shipment by him of tobacco; [39] the other, 22 Feb. 1788, is to an unnamed correspondent, asking for red clover seed.[40]

MS. Gough Surrey 8 (S.C. 18247).

Calendars of papers in 'the Lambeth Library', 'Digested by Dr. Ducarel', 1767, including (ff.3-27) papers concerning the American colonies, and the work there of the Society for the Propagation of the Gospel, 1641-1762.

MS. Gough Gen. Top. 40. f.66.

Letter, Enfield, 31 Dec. 1756, from Rev. W. Bush to R. Gough says that reports from America are depressing. Indians have hoisted French colours on a fort built as a bastion against the French. An authoritative source in New England is of the opinion that if the mouth of the St. Lawrence were blockaded the French would surrender within three months.

f. 134. Letter, 5 Jan. 1768, from the same asking Gough's advice about supporting an appeal by Mr. Edwards, a Rhode Island Baptist minister, for funds to enlarge a school there. Gough's reply (f. 135), 11 Jan. 1768, is unfavourable.

MS. Eng. hist, a.5 (S.C. 32934).

Letter, Mount Vernon, 6 Oct. 1773, from George Washington, ordering goods for himself and 'books for Mr. Custis' from Robert Cary & Co., London merchants.[41]

MS. Eng. hist. c.306, f.5. Le Fleming Papers.

Letter, 17 Dec. 1774, from Sir Michael Le Fleming to ____ Moore, on the rebellion in America, and Lord North's attitude thereto.[42]

MSS. Eng. misc. c.132, ff.42-3, 44-5, 53-6.

Letters from Lord Shelburne to Dr. Richard Price, two n.d., third, Bowood Park, 24 Sept. 1777. First says that the American cause is gaining ground in the country, assisted by a recent speech by Lord Mansfield. By next spring, he estimates, the Americans will have thirty frigates and sloops well manned and armed. Second apparently implies that if Britain were to make certain concessions to the colonists they would make faithful subjects. Third contains various comments on military operations in America, the numbers in Washington's army, and the administration's displeasure with General Carleton not employing the Indians sooner.

39. See *Writings of George Washington*, ed. by John C. Fitzpatrick, vol. ii (Washington, D.C., 1931), pp. 383-4.

40. Ibid., vol. xxix, pp. 421-2, quotes a letter from Mount Vernon of the same date to Clement Biddle asking for red clover seed.

41. Ibid., vol. iii, pp. 154-5.

42. Transcript, H.M.C. xii (vii), p. 359. (Listed as in possession of S.H. LeFleming, Esq., of Rydal Hall.)

MS. Eng. lett. b.17, f.149.
Henry Taylor to John Nichols, 1777, suggesting America as a place to sell books.

Curzon b.21, f.99.
Letter from Benjamin Franklin to George Washington, 2 Mar. 1778, recommending M. de Fontevieux, a young man 'willing to serve as a Volunteer' in the American army.

MS. Top. Oxon. c.386.
American account book, 1778-82, relating to the property of the father-in-law of the Rt. Hon. Willoughby, Earl of Abingdon.

Curzon b.21. f.134.
Letter, 1785, from Thomas Jefferson to Stockdale, the London book-seller, mentioning both John Adams and James Madison.

MS. Bor. 48 (S.C. 20689).
'Dissertationem de America ab Islandis ante Columbum detecta ... submittet Geir Vidalinus Hafniae anno MDCCLXXXVII', followed by the dissertation (B.D., 1787).

MS. Fairfax 35 (S.C. 31069). f.283.
An anecdote of Washington's last words (reputed to have been 'I die hard'), also comments on his state of health towards the close of his life (in a letter written from Mount Eagle, near Alexandria, Va., 18 Jan. 1800, by Bryan, Lord Fairfax of Cameron, to an unidentified kinsman).

MS. Eng. lett. b.17. ff.183-7.
Three letters from Isaiah Thomas to John Nichols, 1811-8, illustrating the difficulties of transatlantic postal service.

MS. Maps. misc. a.2 (S.C. 33091). f.8.
'Plan of the operations of the British and American forces before New Orleans between 23 December 1814 and 8 January 1815.'

MS. Eng. misc. d.164. ff.84, 119.
Letters, Boston, 4 June and 10 Sept. 1817, from Rev. Charles Lowell to Mark Noble, concerning the newly-incorporated American Antiquarian Society, with an account of his family history and his own career.

MS. Autogr. c.24. f.142.
Unaddressed letter of Henry Clay, 5 Mar. 1821.

MS. Montagu d.14. f.13.
Letter, 1823, from Thomas Jefferson to John MacLean, Postmaster-General of the U.S., asking for a post office for the University of Virginia.

MS. Eng. misc. c.29 (S.C. 32396).
This is similar to the typescript travel journal of Sir Henry Singer Keating in the Cambridge University Library (p. 15), but the relevant pages are 222-353.

MSS. Lyell empt. 38-9.
Diary of J. Peterham, clerk and member of the City of London Literary and Scientific Institution, with particulars of his social life and opinions on books and sermons. Written in London and New York, 1831-5.

MS. Eng. misc. e.84.
Letters to E. Moore about Dante. Include letters of H.W. Longfellow (to C.E. Norton), 1860; J.R. Lowell, 1881 and 1888; and C.E. Norton, 1894-1907.

MSS. Eng. hist. d.245-7.
Journals of Nassau William Senior, 1860-3. Contain *inter alia* records of conversations with John Slidell, William Lewis Dayton, John Murray Forbes, William Maxwell Evarts, and Henry Hotze. Most of the conversations in these manuscripts are printed in M.C.M. Simpson (ed.), *Conversations with M. Thiers, M. Guizot, and other distinguished persons during the Second Empire,* 2 vols. (London, 1878), and *Conversations with distinguished persons during the Second Empire from 1860 to 1863,* 2 vols. (London, 1880). Those of 1863 with Forbes, Evarts, and Hotze are not, however, included in the above works.

MS. Autogr. d.10 (S.C. 36017). f.23.
Autograph letter, Montgomery, Ala., 18 May 1861, from Jefferson Davis to Professor A.T. Bledsoe, thanking him for his sympathy with 'the great cause' and saying that he cannot leave Montgomery while Congress is in session.

MS. Eng. misc. d.702.
Reminiscences of Major Francis Laurence Gore Little (1841-1914). Vol. III covers the years 1861-4, during which time Little was on military duty in the West Indies. He makes numerous observations about America and Americans during the Civil War, and in particular on the efficacy of the North's naval blockade of the South.

MS. Eng. lett. e.128. ff.165v-170.
Two letters from Richard Cobden to an American, 'Mr. Osborn', 1862-3, discussing free trade, the issue of maritime law during the Civil War, the Morrill Tariff of 1861, and 'greenbacks'.

MS. Autogr. d.19. ff.54.-57.
Two letters, 1868, from Jefferson Davis, former president of the Confederacy, to Mrs. O.L. Blandy about personal matters.

MS. Eng. lett. c.193.
Letter-book of Sir Edward Thornton, British Minister to the U.S., Jan. 1870-Dec. 1872.

MS. Don. e.47. Thomson Papers.
Diary of business done by James Thomson (1834-82), the poet, for the Champion Gold and Silver Company in Colorado, 16 May-31 Dec. 1872 (iii+205 pages, pp. 109-202 blank). Mentions investments in the Company, proposed division of profits, legal proceedings by injunction, visits to Idaho, defects in the mine.

MS. Eng. lett. d.180. ff. 110, 114, 118 and 120, 122, 124.
Letters to Charles Bradlaugh from Robert G. Ingersoll, 1872; Kate Field, 1873; B.F. Underwood (2 letters), 1873; James Freeman Clarke, 1873; Whitelaw Reid, 1874.

MS. Eng. lett. e.86, f.82.
Letter, 1879, from John Bright to J. Wilson about protection in the U.S.

MS. Autogr. e.12.
Letters to the Paget and Thompson families, including one from Henry J. Bigelow, 1881, and five from J.R. Lowell, 1885-8.

MS. Eng. hist. c.48.
Speech by Grover Cleveland to the Democratic Club of the City of New York, 13 Apr. 1891, written, signed and dated by him; with

two letters, 1897, from George F. Parker, presenting this to the Bodleian.

MS. Eng. lett. d.269. f.182.
Letter from O.W. Holmes to Rollo Russell, 1892, thanking him for the gift of a book.

MSS. Eng. hist. d.181-4.
Notes on Columbus's first voyage to America, by Edmund Palmer. Largely a discussion of which islands Columbus discovered first, with charts of islands and anchorages. Two letters, 19 Nov. 1898 and 4 Apr. 1899, enclosed in d.181 about his 'research' on this subject.

MS. Don. d.122.
Forty-seven letters of Henry James to H.G. Wells and four to Mrs. Catherine Wells, 1898-1915.[43]

MS. Eng. hist. c.418.
Correspondence, 1899-1900, of Herbert and Mrs. Hoover with Gustav Detring and others during Hoover's work as chief engineer on the technical staff of the newly-established Chinese Bureau of Mines.

MS. Eng. lett. d.269. ff.204-5.
Letter from Charles Francis Adams to Rollo Russell, 1913, thanking Russell for an opportunity to view the Russell Papers.

MS. Eng. lett. d.269. ff.200-3.
Two letters from Worthington C. Ford to Russell, thanking him for permission to see the Russell Papers.

MS. Autogr. d.15.
Letters, 1916-9, from eminent Americans, including (ff.14, 15) two from Elihu Root, to Professor Walter E. Peck. Personal and academic only.

MS. Don. d.24.
Nine letters from Vachel Lindsay, American poet, to Robert Nichols, 1919-31, discussing, among other matters, his work on *The Golden Book* and his visit to England in 1920.

MS. Eng. lett. e.91. f.6.
Letter, 1927, Theodore Dreiser to Mrs. Martha Feuchtwanger.

MS. Top. Oxon. c.412.
Papers concerning the conferment of the degree of Doctor of Civil Law upon Franklin D. Roosevelt at a Special Convocation of the University of Oxford held at the Harvard Commencement of 19 June 1941.

IV. MISCELLANEOUS DEPOSITS

MS. D.D. Par. Bicester c.1.
Papers, 1830, relating to the emigration of paupers from Bicester Market End to New York.

RHODES HOUSE LIBRARY, Oxford OX1 3RG

NORTH PAPERS. 1756-1861.

Most of the manuscripts in the North Papers in the Bodleian Library relating to the British possessions in North America and the West Indies have been transcribed, and typed copies of them have been bound into a single volume (MSS. Brit. Emp. s. 1) in Rhodes House.

DIARY OF THE SIEGE OF QUEBEC, 1775-6, kept by an English soldier. 1 volume (120 pages). (MSS. Can. r. 2)
'Journal of the most remarkable occurrences in the province of Quebec from the appearance of the rebels [the Americans under Montgomery and Arnold] in September 1775 until their retreat on 6 May 1776.'

CALEF & CHUTER. Letter-book: containing some 1,030 letters. 1783-96. (MSS. Brit. Emp. s. 3)
London merchants and brokers who had a considerable trade with the United States. They dealt in various commodities including tobacco, cordage, firearms, potash, pearls, and timber, and also effected insurances on ships and cargoes. Most of these letters are addressed to American firms.

CLARKSON, THOMAS (1760-1846). Letter (photostat).[1] 1817. (MSS. Brit. Emp. r. 1*)
From Thomas Clarkson to James Monroe, chiefly about colonization of free Negroes in Africa.

ANTI-SLAVERY PAPERS.[2] 1823-1941.
The Anti-Slavery Committee was founded in 1823. The Aborigines Protection Society (1837) and the British and Foreign Anti-Slavery Society (1839) amalgamated in 1909 to form the Anti-Slavery and Aborigines Protection Society (recently its 'working' title was changed to 'Anti-Slavery Society').

The papers of this Society contain considerable American material. There is a convenient handlist and detailed card index of letters in the collection. It is clear from the card index that the known losses which these Papers have suffered - ravages of damp in a cellar over many years - have destroyed correspondence, etc., from American abolitionists such as William Lloyd Garrison, Wendell Phillips, Lucretia Mott, James Gillespie Birney, who should be well represented in this collection, when their epistolary habits are borne in mind. Some such material, which has apparently been destroyed since 1927 by bad storage conditions before the papers were taken over by Rhodes House Library, appears in A.H. Abel and F.J. Klingberg, eds., *A Side-Light on Anglo-American Relations, 1839-58; Furnished by the Correspondence of Lewis Tappan and others with the British and Foreign Anti-Slavery Society* (Lancaster, Pa., 1927). Among particular items of American interest which may be noted are:

MSS. Brit. Emp. s. 18. C 1-121 - main series of nineteenth-century correspondence with the secretaries of the British and Foreign Anti-Slavery Society which contains many American letters from United States abolitionists, particularly from Lewis Tappan of the American Anti-Slavery Society.

MSS. Brit. Emp. s. 19. D. 5/5 - letters and papers relating to the United States lecture tour of Sir John Harris, secretary of the Anti-Slavery and Aborigines Protection Society in 1917.

MSS. Brit. Emp. s. 20. E. 2/11-20 - three volumes of minute-books of the General Anti-Slavery Convention held in London in 1840, at which several American representatives were present.

43. Printed, together with Wells' replies, in *Henry James and H.G. Wells*, ed. L. Edel and G.N. Ray, 1958.

1. Photographed by the New York Public Library. Location of original not known.
2. For microfilms of manuscripts relating to the United States and the suppression of the slave trade see Louis B. Frewer, *Rhodes House Library, its Function and Resources* (1956), p.16. (Reprinted from the *Bodleian Library Record*, vol. v, no. 6, Oct. 1956.)

MSS. Brit. Emp. s. 22 is a section of the papers arranged by territory and it contains substantial American materials. Here, files which may be noted particularly are: G.84-85, correspondence, 1833-97, with various American bodies. G. 86, materials relating to Texas and anti-slavery controversies of the 1840's. G. 87-88, correspondence, 1866-8, with America of the British National Freedman's Aid Association. G. 298, American correspondence, 1930-7, especially the correspondence with Sherwood Eddy on American co-operative experiments. G. 432, materials on the 1921 London Pan-African Congress with letters, etc., from Professor W.E.B. DuBois. G. 492, correspondence on the proposed visit in 1914 of Booker T. Washington to Europe.

The collections also include volumes of press cuttings, newspapers, and photographs for 1906-36 which contain materials on the American Negro and his interest in and influence on Europe and Africa. (MSS. Brit. Emp. s. 24. J 1-49)

In 1961 the records of the present Anti-Slavery Society for 1941-51 were added to Rhodes House Library, and this addition has and will continue at intervals of ten years. As the Society's correspondence is still world-wide and it continues to take an interest in general Negro affairs, it may be expected that this new material will contain fresh items of American interest.

QUINAN, W.R. (1848-1910). Box of papers; and autobiography (1 volume). 1877-99. (MSS. Afr. s. 123-8)

The papers relate to the period 1877-99, during which period Quinan was employed in turn by the Vigorit Powder Works; and the California Powder Works, 1883-99; and consist mainly of business correspondence with mining firms and the military authorities, with a number of references to lawsuits over the manufacture of gunpowder.

DOYLE, JOHN ANDREW (1844-1907). Correspondence: 60 letters. 1882-1904. (MSS. Amer. s. 2)

Sixty letters, 1882-1904, to Doyle about his work *The English in America*, 5 vols. (London, 1882)[3] from American historians, authors, etc., including Justin Winsor, C.F. Adams, Herbert Adams, Moses Coit Tyler, and others.

TREVELYAN, SIR GEORGE OTTO (1838-1928). Manuscript of one volume of *The American Revolution*. 215 leaves. (MSS. Amer. s. 1)

WHITE, MONTAGU (1875-1916). Letter-book and volume of press cuttings. 1899-1900. (MSS. Afr. s. 116,117)

White was sent to the United States in 1899 as a representative of President Kruger of the South African Republic, to arouse sympathy, and if possible gain support, for the Boers against Britain. He mentions interviews with John Hay, and other leading Americans, but gained little more than formal expressions of sympathy, except from the militant anti-British sections of the press and the Irish. Some letters are in Afrikaans.

FORAN MANUSCRIPT.

Major W.R. Foran: unpublished and undated transcript, 'Memories of Theodore Roosevelt'. Foran represented the Associated Press of America on Roosevelt's African safari of 1909-10, and claimed to be the only journalist to cover the whole trip.

HOLT PAPERS. 1937. (MSS. Afr. s. 914)

Holt, W.E.: Memoirs, papers, etc., relating to the Conference on the Education of the American Negroes and the African Natives, University of North Carolina, Yale, and Hampton Institute, 1937. 3 vols.

HAILEY PAPERS. 1942-4. (MSS. Amer. s. 5)

Hailey, Malcolm, 1st Baron: Papers relating to American visits, 1942-4, 1 vol. Also correspondence, etc., relating to Institute of Pacific Relations Conferences, Quebec, Dec. 1942, and Atlantic City, Jan. 1944, and other speaking engagements.

MORRICE MS. Diary. 1957. (MSS. Afr. s. 1457(16))

H.A.W. Morrice, a British official in the Sudan: diary of a trip to the U.S.A. from 17 Apr. to 18 May 1957, to inspect dams and water projects, largely in the western states. 100 pages of typescript.

THE LIBRARY, ALL SOULS COLLEGE, Oxford

VAUGHAN, SIR CHARLES RICHARD (1774-1849). Papers.[1]

Diplomat. Private secretary, 1809-20, to the Earl of Bathurst while Foreign Secretary. British Minister to the United States 1825-35 (on leave of absence 1831-3). Knighted 1833.

A typescript 'Calendar of the Vaughan Papers', prepared by J.A. Doyle, is available in the library,[2] and the following description is taken from it. The papers are arranged in alphabetically labelled packets, and within the packets are arranged either by writer or date, as indicated below. The packets containing most of the American material are A, B, C, and H.

A. 'General Correspondence' (arranged by writer).

The most important American letters, either because of writer or subject, are from the following:

Adams, John Quincy. Two slight notes, 1830 and n.d.

Archer, William Segar. Two letters, 1840. 1840 election and 'financial difficulties'.

Beckett, Henry. Letter, 1836. Philadelphia has chartered new United States Bank; Washington, D.C., news.

Crampton, Sir John F.T. Two letters, 1848. Discussion in the United States of European revolutions of 1848; Cass and Taylor as candidates for the presidency.

Everett, Edward. Three letters, 1833, 1835, 1837. Personal; American foreign relations; Mexico and Texas; abolition.

Grosvenor, Robert, 2nd Earl Grosvenor. Letter, 1828. His estates in Florida.

Hamilton, James Alexander (son of Alexander Hamilton). Three letters, 1830, 1844, 1847. Annexation of Texas and Northern opposition to it; predicts civil war.

Jackson, Andrew. Two slight notes, 1829 and 1832.

Peters, Richard. Letter, 1840. Progress of American affairs since Vaughan left.

Rush, Richard. Several slight notes, 1825-35.

Southard, Samuel Lewis. Three letters, 1829 and 1834. The one of 1834 is on the New Jersey Poor Laws.

3. Reprinted as *English Colonies in America* (New York, 1882-1907).

1. See also Paullin & Paxson, pp. 58-64. Twenty-five of the letters and two memoranda have been printed in 'Papers of Sir Charles R. Vaughan, 1825-1835', ed. by John A. Doyle, *American Historical Review*, vol. vii, pp. 304-29 and pp. 500-33, 1901-2.

2. Microfilm copy also available in Manuscript Division of the Reference Department, Library of Congress, Washington, D.C. The Manuscript Division also possesses microfilms of the bulk of the documents in sections B and H of the Vaughan Papers.

B. 'Dispatches and Official Correspondence in Chronological Order.'

(*a*) Correspondence:

Forty-nine letters (draft or copy), chiefly from Vaughan but some to him, relate to the American period, 1825-35, and deal with such matters as Anglo-American mails, British claims to land in Florida, banking in the United States, the American Navy, state boundaries, cases of individual British subjects in the United States (e.g. of a deserting British seaman), consular fees, slave trade conventions. Some are simply covering letters enclosing official papers.

(*b*) Dispatches (listed from the typescript calendar):

'Vaughan's lists of his Official Correspondence.

Book 1. Précis of Dispatches sent to the Foreign Office, (includes) Washington, 1825-7.

Book 2. Dispatches sent home from America, 1828-35.

Book 3. Inventory of correspondence with Canning and others, 1825-29.

Book 4. (At one end) Correspondence with the Government of the U.S., 1825-34; (at other end) Dispatches from Foreign Office during the same period.

Book 5. (At one end) Dispatches received from the Foreign Office in 1834; (at other end) Correspondence with the American Department of State.'

C. 'Correspondence of Political or General Interest' (arranged by writer).

Addington, Henry Unwin. Thirty-one letters, 1826-30. Chiefly on matters connected with the North-East and North-West boundary controversies. Also four copies, 1826-7, Vaughan to Addington, on the same.

Backhouse, John, Under Secretary of State for Foreign Affairs. Twenty-eight letters, 1829-37. Mainly North-East and North-West boundaries. Also thirty-seven drafts, 1827-38, Vaughan to Backhouse, on the boundaries, tariffs, and individual British subjects in America.

Bankhead, C., and Mrs. Bankhead. Seventeen letters, written chiefly from Washington, D.C., or Mexico, 1831-47. Boundaries, slavery, Mexican affairs (especially the Mexican War).

Bartlett, Dr. John Sherren, editor of the *Albion*, New York. Three letters, 1847-8. Anglo-American hostility, Mexican affairs, trouble over Anglo-American postal rates. Also one copy, 1847, Vaughan to Bartlett, expressing surprise at American ill feeling towards Britain.

Canning, George. Letter, 1826. North-West boundary. Also seven copies, 1825-6, Vaughan to Canning, on legation matters, Rufus King, slave trade.

Clay, Henry. Eight slight notes, 1828-35.

Douglas, Sir Howard, Governor of New Brunswick. Thirty-seven letters, 1825-32. North-East boundary. Also eleven copies, 1825-9, Vaughan to Douglas, on same.

Doyle, Percy W. Three letters, 1843-8. The latter two, 1845-8, are on United States-Mexico affairs, and the settlement of Oregon.

Featherstonhaugh, G.W. Seven letters, 1839-46. Chiefly on North-East and North-West boundaries; in 1846 gives an evaluation of Calhoun.

Hall, Captain Basil and Mrs. Hall. Nineteen letters, 1827-9. Chiefly on their travels in the United States and Hall's book on these. Comments on the incompatibility of slavery and democracy. Also two copies, 1827, Vaughan to Hall, on intercourse of American vessels with British colonies.

Hay, R.W. Four letters, 1829 and 1833, on boundaries and Andrew Jackson; and, 1833, refutation of charges against British officers at New Orleans in 1815.

Kempt, Sir James. Five letters, Quebec, 1829-30. Jackson's Inaugural, boundaries, American trade with the West Indies. Also two copies, 1826-7, Vaughan to Kempt, on the closing of American ports to British vessels.

Ryder, Dudley, 2nd Earl of Harrowby. Three letters, 1824-7. Those of 1826 and 1827 are inquiries about the American banking system. Also one draft, 1824, Vaughan to Harrowby, on banking in America.

Story, Joseph. Thirteen notes, mainly slight, 1828-37, but a letter, 7 Nov. 1837, discusses the effects of currency experiments in the United States, recent elections, and whether Webster would stand for the presidency.

Stuart, Sir Charles, Baron Stuart de Rothesay. Two letters, 1835. His land in Florida. Also one copy, 1835, Vaughan to Lord Stuart de Rothesay on the same, and one letter, 1835, from a Colonel White to Vaughan on the same.

Sumner, Charles. Eight letters, 1839-48. Election campaign of 1840, Harrison, Webster, Everett, Motley (just appointed to St Petersburg), Tyler. Appointments under the Whig administration of 1840; debasing effects of the Mexican War on American politics.

Temple, Henry John, 3rd Viscount Palmerston. Nine letters, 1827-43. Franco-American relations, boundaries, naturalization in the United States. Also eleven drafts, 1831-40, Vaughan to Palmerston, on similar topics.

Van Buren, Martin. Six slight notes, 1830-8. Also one copy, 1830, Vaughan to Van Buren.

Vaughan, Sir Charles Richard. Copy, 1825, to H.T. Kilbee, on British and American Cuban policy, and his (Vaughan's) impressions of America. Nineteen copies, 1827-9, to Joseph Planta of the Foreign Office, mostly slight (enclosing United States State Papers, etc.). Also see copies and drafts of letters from Vaughan to correspondents in this group.

Ward, H.G. Twenty-seven letters, 1825-6, written from Mexico. Deal *inter alia* with Anglo-American relations over Mexico. Also four copies, 1826, Vaughan to Ward, partly on same.

Wellesley, Henry, 1st Baron Cowley. Letter, 1828. Commercial relations of Britain and the United States.

H. 'Papers Relating to America, 1825-37.'

Classified as follows:

(*a*) 'Drafts of Dispatches from Vaughan as British Minister in U.S., 1825-31.'

Contains dispatches successively to Canning, Dudley, Aberdeen, and Palmerston. The numbers of dispatches for each year are as follows: 30-1825, 102-1826, 69-1827, 86-1828, 70-1829, 73-1830, 32-1831.

Subjects dealt with include slavery and the slave trade, fisheries, West Indian trade, Canadian frontier incidents, Latin-American relations with the United States, tariffs (especially that of 1828), Indian affairs, impressment of American sailors, arrest of British subjects in the United States, the Congress of Panama, North-West and North-East boundaries, foundation of a company to cut an isthmian canal, proceedings in Congress, reciprocity, the election of 1828, Jackson's inauguration, efforts of the Southern states to secure repeal of the 1828 Tariff, appointments (especially diplomatic) under Jackson, possible acquisition of Texas by the United States, the Bank of the United States, bills for internal improvements vetoed by Jackson, arrests of free coloured British subjects in the South.

(*b*) 'Drafts of Dispatches from Vaughan as British Minister in U.S., 1833-5 (and Slave Trade, 1833).'

Contains dispatches successively to Palmerston and Wellington: 50-1833, 109-1834, 56-1835, and thirteen to Palmerston on the slave trade, 1833-4.

Subjects include settlement of dissension between the federal government and South Carolina (i.e., over nullification), boundaries, removal of public funds from the Bank of the United States, New York elections of 1834, extradition. The slave-trade dispatches are about the possible accession of the United States to the Anglo-French Slave Trade Convention, and its final refusal to accede.

(*c*) 'America: Dated and Undated Papers.'

Dated, 1824-46. Some sixty or seventy miscellaneous items on suppression of the slave trade, boundaries, interviews with American statesmen, Anglo-American trade, United States tariffs, West Indian trade, probable effects of an Anglo-American war, 1827; invoices of tea shipped at Boston, observations on democracy and vote by ballot in the United States in 1831, the Bank of the United States, the Southern states and the tariff, the Webster-Ashburton Treaty of 1842, Oregon.

Undated. Some thirty miscellaneous items on the American Constitution, political parties in the United States, various treaties - especially that of Ghent, an isthmian canal, trade, fisheries, impressment, tariff, slave labour.

(*d*) 'America: Papers Relating to the Boundary Question.'

Dated, 1824-39. Some fifty miscellaneous items on the North-East boundary, including précis of British and American arguments. Undated. Some thirty miscellaneous items, including an atlas.

I. 'Papers Relating to South America.'

This packet contains a few items relating to Texas and Florida.

K. 'Journals and Commonplace Books.'

The commonplace books do not refer at all to the period of his American sojourn.

(*a*) 'Portsmouth to Annapolis, United States of America, 11 June to 12 August 1825.' Simply a diary of part of his trip out.

(*b*) 'Washington to Niagara... 1826.' Describes an extensive tour through the North East, including a description of the New York navy yard, a visit to Van Buren, descriptions of the locks on the Erie Canal, of the New York State Prison, and of the Philadelphia penitentiary. Lists his expenses.

(*c*) '1829'. A short journal describing a journey into Canada. *En route* he meets Philip Hone and Chancellor Kent in New York.

(*d*) 'From New York to London, 1831' and 'From Liverpool to New York, 24 February 1833.' Both journals are simply accounts of the respective voyages.

THE LIBRARY, MANCHESTER COLLEGE, Oxford OX1 3TD

SHEPHERD MANUSCRIPTS. Papers, letters. 1760-76.

Papers of the Rev. William Shepherd (1768-1847), Unitarian minister.

Vol. V contains an entry in Shepherd's diary for 6 Sept. 1838 (pp. 63-65), where he relates meeting 'an American barrister at law, of the name of Sumner' at the house of Lord Brougham, and showing him one of the stamps, prepared for the administration of the Stamp Act, which had recently been discovered in Somerset House.

Vol. XVIII contains copies of letters,[1] 1760-76, from Henry Hulton to Robert Nicholson, a Liverpool merchant and the father of Mrs. Shepherd. The earlier letters deal with Hulton's experiences as a British official in Germany and in the Treasury in London; but the bulk of the correspondence dates from 1769 to 1776, when he was employed as a revenue officer in Boston. The letters give an eye-witness account of the beginnings of the War of Independence. As early as 1769 Hulton comments on the perils faced by the revenue officers from the colonists. In 1770 he speaks of and suffers from the growth of discontent and mob violence stirred up by demagogues and the press in Boston; he is, however, of the opinion that Boston will find itself unable to manage without British manufactures. He says, in 1774, that since the Tea Party all authority has been in the people's hands, and those who do not 'conform in all things to the will of the people' are persecuted. He describes the battle of Bunker Hill, the flight of many Loyalists to Britain, and the scarcity and high prices of food in Boston in 1776. In Jan. 1776 he says that the aim of the rebels is obviously to establish 'one or more independent republics'. The last letter is written in May 1776 from Halifax, N.S., just before Hulton embarked for Britain.

AMERICAN UNITARIANS. 91 autograph letters (scattered in 2 boxes and 1 volume). 1822-1908.

Writers of these letters, who are mainly Unitarians, include: Elihu Burritt, W.E. and W.H. Channing, James Freeman Clarke, Ralph Waldo Emerson, William Lloyd Garrison, Thomas Wentworth Higginson, Oliver Wendell Holmes, Sr., Julia Ward Howe, A.A. Livermore, James Russell Lowell, Susan Martineau, Samuel J. May, Theodore Parker, and A.P. Putnam. There is also a facsimile of a letter, 2 July 1756, from Benjamin Franklin to George Whitefield, about the possibilities of colonization on the Ohio.[2]

Most of the letters are of personal or theological interest only; however, some include discussion of other matters, as follows:

Burritt, *c.* 1848, comments on the League of Universal Brotherhood and ocean penny post.

Holmes, 1879, on Motley as Minister to Britain, with reasons for his failure in that capacity (including a reference to the Grant-Sumner feud).

Livermore on the success of *Uncle Tom's Cabin*, 1853, the non-smoking aspect of the temperance movement, 1882, and the presidential campaign of 1884.

Martineau, Susan, writes three letters, 1861 and 1864, about a Mrs. Whitaker, who had emigrated to the United States from Britain, and after her husband's death and a period of poverty, had taken a job with the Western Sanitary Commission at St. Louis, Mo., and was working on behalf of the freed Negroes.

And among forty-five letters, 1822-39, to Lant Carpenter, from various correspondents, the slavery question and temperance are touched upon.

OTHER LETTERS. 1851-1907.

(*a*) C.G. Ames to U.D. Davis, Boston, 22 Dec. 1907; E.E. Hale to U.D. Davis, Boston, 12 Nov. 1899. Both letters refer to religious matters in England and America.

(*b*) G.N. Hosmer to R.L. Carpenter (Buffalo?), 4 Jan. 1851. Discusses American slavery, among other subjects.

THE LIBRARY, NEW COLLEGE, Oxford

WASHINGTON, GEORGE. Letter. 1777.

Letter, 1777, from George Washington to ? requesting supplies for his troops.

1. The copies are thought to have been made *c.* 1805; it is not known whether the originals are still in existence.

2. Original in the Autograph Collection, John Rylands University Library, Manchester. Printed in Leonard W. Labaree (ed.), *The Papers of Benjamin Franklin,* vol. 6 (New Haven and London, 1963), pp. 468-9.

THE LIBRARY, NUFFIELD COLLEGE, Oxford OX1 1NF

COBBETT, WILLIAM (1762-1835). Papers. 1794-1835.

(*a*) 6 July 1794, from William Cobbett to Miss Rachel Smithers, describing 'detestable America and Americans'.
(*b*) William Cobbett, Jr. to John Morgan Cobbett, 27 Oct. 1818 about Long Island races, and 10 Nov. 1818 about the New York Forum.
(*c*) Manuscripts of the *Political Register,* vol. xxxiv, nos. 2 and 8, written from North Hampstead, Long Island, 15 May and 28 July 1818. Also part of an article in the *Political Register,* vol. lxix, no. 20, 15 May 1830, to Mr. Haywood... of Sheffield, written from Wolverhampton, 11 May 1830, about emigration to America. The manuscript is not complete.
(*d*) Twenty-one letters, 1819-22, from James Paul Cobbett in America.
(*e*) 30 Sept. 1835, from Susan Cobbett to John Cobbett: recollections of U.S. experiences.
(*f*) 7 Oct. 1835, from John M. Cobbett to Susan Cobbett: memories of Philadelphia.

MILTON AGRICULTURAL LABOURERS UNION (later the Oxford District of the National Agricultural Labourers Union). Minute-book. 1872-9.

Contains resolutions concerning the establishment of, contributions to, and grants from, an emigration fund; also notes of a number of votes to make grants to certain individuals to assist them to emigrate. There is no mention of the destination of the emigrants, although an entry of 2 Sept. 1873 records a proposal that 'in consequence of Mr. Arch (*sic*) visit to America, the emigration fund be left open until further notice'.

G.D.H. COLE COLLECTION. Printed material.

Includes fifty volumes by and about Robert Owen, including material on New Harmony, Ind.; fifty-seven volumes by or about Thomas Paine; eighteen volumes on communitarianism, especially in the United States and particularly about Oneida and Icaria, N.Y.; and over three hundred volumes by or about William Cobbett.

CHERWELL PAPERS.

The college library has the papers of F.A. Lindemann, 1st Lord Cherwell. These include a little wartime material relating to the U.S. Army, a study of the Allied war effort by the U.S. Embassy, information on U.S. pipe-line systems, a study of British requirements from the U.S.A., and some correspondence with scientists living in America.

OXFORDSHIRE COUNTY RECORD OFFICE, County Hall, Oxford OX1 1ND

DILLON COLLECTION. 1872-92.

Bundle of letters, pamphlets, pedigrees, notes, and newspaper clippings, also a volume of pedigrees, 1872-92, relating to a discussion, mainly between C.F. Lee, Jr., of Virginia, and Capt. Harold Dillon, of London, about the descent of the Lees of Virginia, and, in particular, of General Robert E. Lee.

THE PLUNKETT FOUNDATION FOR CO-OPERATIVE STUDIES, 31 St. Giles, Oxford OX1 3LF

PLUNKETT, SIR HORACE CURZON (1854-1932). Papers: correspondence, 1883-1932; diary, 1881-1932.

Advocate of agricultural co-operation, Anglo-Irish statesman. Plunkett actively ranched in the American West in the 1880's (retaining some financial interest long afterwards) before devoting his life to the cause of agricultural co-operatives, first in Ireland and then in Britain and America as well. In this cause he formed intimate friendships in the 1900's with leading American politicians and social reformers, notably Colonel House, Theodore Roosevelt, Gifford Pinchot, and Charles McCarthy of Wisconsin. These friendships led to important unofficial correspondence and conversations by Plunkett in the First World War, concerned both with press information work and with relaying the views of leading British politicians to House and Wilson, particularly on the Irish question as it affected Anglo-American relations - he was the chairman of the abortive Irish Convention of 1917.

Some of Plunkett's papers were destroyed during the troubles of 1923, but most of his public correspondence seems to have survived. In 1972 the papers were indexed by the Historical Manuscripts Commission. They consist mainly of correspondence, not only to but also from Plunkett, who kept typescript carbon copies of all his out-letters. The letters are kept in ten box files, alphabetically arranged under name of correspondent. Miss Margaret Digby makes use of this material in her book *Horace Plunkett: An Anglo-American Irishman* (Oxford, 1949). (Miss Digby also quotes from the fifty-two volumes of his diary, which cover the whole period.) Comment on American affairs can be found throughout Plunkett's war-time letters on the Irish question to British statesmen. The principal correspondents, however, are:

Frewen, Moreton. Chiefly about a dozen letters, 1883-5, concerning the affairs of the Powder River Cattle Company of Wyoming, of which Frewen was the founder and promoter, and Plunkett later a partner. Frewen was an active promoter in the London market of many American ventures, M.P. for North-East Cork 1910-1, author of pamphlets on the silver question, Anglo-American trade, etc.[1] Some of the letters are from Frewen in London to an agent in Cheyenne, and some from Frewen in Wyoming to C.F. Kemp, the London manager (some of these latter include confidential unsigned enclosures about extra-legal tactics to be used against farmers and Texan interlopers). All of the above letters are in a single 'Miscellaneous File'. Also, in the main alphabetical series, are the originals of some letters from Plunkett to Frewen, 1881-6, some from Cheyenne and some from England, on the paper of the Frontier Land and Cattle Company, Cheyenne, Wyo., the letter-head of which gives Plunkett as Treasurer, and John Chaplin as Secretary. Also some twenty letters, 1917-8, between Frewen and Plunkett on the Irish question and English politics.

Roosevelt, Theodore. Six letters to and seven from Roosevelt, 1906-17. Mostly about conservation and rural affairs, with supporting papers including copies of other letters, several from or to Gifford Pinchot. (1 file. In this file there is also a slight note from

1. Frewen's founding of the company is described in long footnotes to Howard B. Lett, 'Diary of Major Wise: Hunting Trip in the Powder River Country in 1880'- *Annals of Wyoming*, vol xii, pp. 85-119, 1940.

Franklin Delano Roosevelt, 10 May 1918, thanking Plunkett for sending him the Proceedings of the Irish Convention.)

Byrne, James. 1908-28. The early letters are mostly about the affairs of the Western Live-Stock and Land Company, in which Plunkett had an interest; the later correspondence turns to international affairs and Byrne's financial support for Plunkett's co-operative organizations in Ireland.

Pinchot, Gifford. Many letters, 1908-18, covering the whole range of his and Pinchot's common interests in agricultural reform. (Large file.)

Grey, Albert Henry George, 4th Earl Grey. 1908-17, on Anglo-American relations, mostly while Grey was Governor-General of Canada. (1 file.)

Lowell, A.L. 1909-28. Interesting on American opinion, 1914-7. (Large file.)

Bryce, James. Over fifty letters, 1909-21, covering many aspects of Anglo-American relations, particularly Ireland and America in 1917; some discuss the work of Charles McCarthy.

Godkin, Lawrence. 1909-18. As well as the whole range of topics covering American opinion and the War, specific letters concern the ambassadorial appointments of Page and Spring-Rice in 1913. (1 file.)

Wallace, Henry. 1909-13, on agricultural reform and politics; Wallace's letters are on the notepaper of *Wallace's Farmer*. (1 file.)

Page, Walter Hines. 1909-14, on Anglo-American relations.

McCarthy, Charles. 1911-9. This would seem to be an extremely interesting source on agriculture and political reform in the Progressive Era. (Large file.)

Hill, James J. Chairman of the Great Northern Railway Company. Three letters, 1911-4.

Chaplin, John. Letter, 13 Apr. 1911, from Plunkett to Chaplin about the affairs of the former Frontier Land and Cattle Company, the successors of which, Plunkett claims, owe him some $60,000.

House, Edward. 1913-32. The most important are the war-time letters in which Plunkett undertook to keep Wilson and House informed on English official and semi-official opinion. Extracts from many, but by no means all, of these have been printed in *The Intimate Papers of Colonel House,* arranged by Charles Seymour, 4 vols. (Boston, 1926; London, 1926-8). House, indeed, writes several letters to Plunkett about the composition and reception of these volumes, reminiscing about himself and Wilson. (2 large files.)

Wilson, Woodrow. 1913-23. Mostly reports by Plunkett to Wilson on English opinion in war-time, similar to those of House, though the earlier letters are on agricultural reform. Wilson's replies are brief and formal. (1 file.)

Walter, Karl. 1916-8. Long reports to and from Plunkett about the work of the Reciprocal News Service in London, which Walter headed, in interpreting British opinion to the Mid-Western press and vice versa - the purpose for which the agency was established. (1 file.)

Spring-Rice, Cecil and Thomas. 1916-7, on Anglo-American relations.

Ladenburg & Thalmann. Some correspondence, 1917, between Plunkett and this New York firm about his Western investments.

Young, Conrad. 1925-7, about the affairs of the Nebraska and Wyoming Investment Company, Omaha, Neb., of which Plunkett was President and Young Manager. (1 file.)

CHARLES EARLY & MARRIOTT (WITNEY) LTD., Witney Mill, Witney OX8 5EB

BUSINESS RECORDS.[1] 1815-24.
Blanket manufacturers.

(*a*) Letter, London, 3 Apr. 1815, from J.H. & C. Lean to Early's requesting a list of articles made by Early's for the United States, with prices, terms of credit, and discounts. Copy of the reply, Witney, 4 Apr. 1815, giving the required information; and a letter of thanks from Lean's, London, 5 Apr. 1815. There are other letters about shipments to the West Indies and Canada.

(*b*) Numerous copies of orders for blankets from the Hudson's Bay Company, and from Wistar, Siter & Price of Philadelphia. An order book for 1823-8 includes an order from the latter firm, 10 Dec. 1824, for 'mock makimaw', a thick blanket at one time distributed to the Indians of the Northwest by the American government; also another from the same firm, 14 Sept. 1824, containing a footnote that 'the new tariff much reduces their profits'.

1. A number of these documents are printed in Alfred Plummer, *The Witney Blanket Industry* (London, 1934), chap.iv, 'Letters and orders', pp. 231-55. Also see Richard E. Early and Alfred Plummer, *The Blanket Makers, 1669-1969: A History of Charles Early & Marriott (Witney) Ltd.* (London, 1969).

SHROPSHIRE

LORD KENYON, Gredington, Whitchurch SY13 3DH

KENYON PAPERS. Letters. 1638-1786.

(*a*) John Wiswall to George Rigby at Peel, 27 Sept. 1638, describing Boston, Mass. and vicinity, its government, its 'plantations' and the neighbouring Indians.[1]

(*b*) Edward Thurlow to Lloyd Kenyon, 15 May 1771, concerning 'the legality of granting a ministerial office in the Court of Justice in America, for more than one life, and I remember two cases upon that head... .'[2]

(*c*) J. Pemberton at Halifax, N.S., to Sir Lloyd Kenyon, Bart., 13 Dec. 1785 and 11 July 1786: two letters describing Halifax and reporting on efforts to settle claims of Loyalists residing in Canada.[3]

(*d*) J. Pemberton at Falmouth to Sir Lloyd Kenyon, 11 Sept. 1785: a letter giving considerable detail about Pemberton's mission to Canada and his administrative arrangements for it.

The Kenyon Papers also include the uncalendared papers of George, 2nd Lord Kenyon and later, relating to the visit to Britain of Philander Chase, first Bishop of Ohio, and to the founding by Chase of a college which later became Kenyon College.

1. Kenyon MSS., H.M.C. xiv (iv), no. 166.
2. H.M.C., no. 1273.
3. H.M.C., nos. 1323, 1329.

CORPORATION OF SHREWSBURY, Guildhall, Shrewsbury SY1 1ER

MUNICIPAL RECORDS. Petition.[1] 1775.

Unanimous petition to the King against the rebellion in America by the Mayor, Aldermen and Burgesses of Shrewsbury, 6 Oct. 1775.

SALOP RECORD OFFICE, Shirehall, Shrewsbury SY2 6ND

SHIREHALL COLLECTION. Papers. 1733-74.

Relating to the Shrewsbury property of Thomas Bowers of Maryland.

SANDFORD HALL COLLECTION.[1] Letters. 1776-7.

Relating to the appointment of Hugh Alexander Kennedy to the forces in America.

MARRINGTON COLLECTION. Papers of Lewis R. Price.[2] *c.* 1833-70.

Lewis R. Price (1818-82) and his brother Daniel spent many years in Mexico engaged in trading ventures. The papers include:

(*a*) Lewis Price's account of his life: his first journey to Mexico in 1833 when he entered the house of Marshall & Manning; his life in Mexico; reference to a journey to New Orleans to buy cotton.

(*b*) Description of a journey to California, 1849, including a description of San Francisco.

(*c*) Letters between Lewis Price and Commodore Dunlop, in which Dunlop asks for advice on the political situation in Mexico during the revolutions of 1860 and 1861. There are references to the effects of the blockade of American ports during the Civil War.

(*d*) Diary of Lewis Price's wife, 1865, describing their life in Mexico City and their return to England via New York.

(*e*) Letters concerning Lewis Price's business, *c.* 1868 onwards, as a director of the North Star Mining Company, which failed, and in connexion with Sierra Buttes Mines. There are also letters from Mr. Coulter, promoter of the London and California Mining Company, in which Price lost money. The account of his life gives a narrative of this incident.

SOMERSET

THE RECORDS OFFICE, C. & J. CLARK LTD., Street

BUSINESS RECORDS.[1] 1825-1900.

Quaker boot and shoe manufacturers, and, up to 1870, makers of sheepskin rugs; a partnership business, 1825-1903.

Extracts from the partners' letter-books, made by the late Mr. L.H. Barber when Archivist to C. & J. Clark Ltd., show that the firm was exporting a few small consignments of sheepskin rugs, wool-lined boots and slippers, and chamois to the United States through a New York agent, Wild & Julian (later Joseph Wild), during the 1850's and 1860's. As Joseph Wild was a personal as well as a business friend, some of the letters contain comments on the political situation, particularly during the Crimean and Civil Wars.

After the 1860's little attempt was made to export footwear to the United States in the face of a growing American manufacture, and the rug business, which had formed the chief contact, was transferred to the firm of Clark, Son & Morland. But C. & J. Clark remained deeply interested in American inventions in shoe-making machinery, from the 1850's onwards, and were informed through friends in the States, usually fellow Quakers, of developments in sewing machines, sole-cutting machines, etc. A letter of 1881 makes it clear that by then they were importing American machinery and that their manager had learned the trade there.

The following are some volumes in this very large collection which are likely to contain American material, though not all of them have yet been examined in detail:

Partners' copy letter-books: 1853-6, 1858-62, 1862-7, 1867-77, 1877-83, 1881-1900, 1892-6, 1896-1900.
Ledgers: 1825-30, 1825-45.
Order book: 1834-6.
Weekly trade account book: 1857-1900.
Stock accounts: 1852-65, 1872-90, 1879-1900.
Summary of stock: 1850-1900.
'Fur' book: 1871-8.

SOMERSET RECORD OFFICE, Obridge Road, Taunton TA2 7PU

PRANKARD AND DICKINSON PAPERS.[1] 1712-93.

Graffin Prankard (d. 1756) was a Quaker merchant of Bristol, mainly in the iron trade. His American and West Indian ventures appear to have been but a small part of his activities, most of which were centered on the Baltic. Caleb Dickinson, the son of a West Indian merchant, was apprenticed to Prankard in 1733 and married his daughter; he was the father of William Dickinson, M.P.

Among Prankard's correspondence, some 'in' and 'out' letters covering every detail of some of his complicated ventures survive, such as the voyage of his ship the *Parham* to South Carolina in December 1730, from whence it took rice and logwood to Hamburg, then to Stockholm in ballast, then to Bristol in Sept. 1731 with iron, deal, and tar.

Dickinson MSS.

(*a*) Caleb Dickinson, 1739-40: mainly business and financial correspondence, principally from London, but including one from Virginia from cousin Thomas Dickinson. (DD/DN/199)

1. H.M.C. xv(x), p. 24. Taken from the original minutes of a meeting of the Council held on 6 Oct. 1775.

---

1. We thank Mrs. H. Sandford for permission to make this report.
2. One of these diaries has been used by W. Turrentine Jackson in 'Mazatlan to the Estanislao; the Narrative of Lewis Price's Journey to California in 1849', *California Historical Society Quarterly*, vol. xxxix, pp. 35-51, 1960; and his article on 'Lewis Richard Price, British Mining Entrepreneur, and Traveler in California', *Pacific Historical Review*, vol. xxix, pp. 331-48, 1960.

---

1. See also the history of the firm, *Clarks of Street 1825-1950* (London, priv. print., 1951).

---

1. See W.E. Minchinton, ed., *The Trade of Bristol in the Eighteenth Century* (Bristol, 1957), pp. 101-22. (Bristol Record Society's Publications, vol. xx).

(*b*) Caleb Dickinson, 1740-1: Includes one letter from Charleston, S.C. (DD/DN/200)

(*c*) Caleb Dickinson, 1744-5: Includes insurance information on ship carrying Negroes from Africa to America. (DD/DN/201)

(*d*) Caleb Dickinson, 1745-7: Two letters, one from Philadelphia and one from Virginia. (DD/DN/202-3)

(*e*) Caleb Dickinson, 1749-51: Five letters from Virginia. (DD/DN/207-8)

(*f*) Caleb Dickinson, 1757: Three letters from Philadelphia and one from Virginia. (DD/DN/214-5)

(*g*) Caleb Dickinson, 1760: One letter from Philadelphia. (DD/DN/218)

(*h*) Caleb Dickinson, 1767: One letter from New Jersey. (DD/DN/223)

(*i*) Caleb Dickinson, 1778: Report on conditions in South Carolina. (DD/DN/228)

Prankard MSS. [2]

(*a*) Prankard letter-books, 1712-8, 1728-56 (8 vols.). (DD/DN/423-9)
Copies of out-going business letters of Graffin Prankard, with frequent bills of lading, instructions to ships' commanders, and promissory notes.

There are in these letter-books references to trade with various places in North America, including Newfoundland, New York, Philadelphia, Maryland, and the Carolinas. Down to 1740 business with America and Europe predominates over local trade, with rice and logwood imported from South Carolina forming an important link in Prankard's trading connexions. Some of his American business correspondents are Jennys and Baker (1728-42) and Watson and McKenzie (1739-46), both of South Carolina.

(*b*) Prankard correspondence, 1735-55. (DD/DN/431-2)
Includes letters addressed to Prankard from Charleston, S.C. and from Philadelphia.

(*c*) Prankard accounts, 1728-40. (DD/DN/433-40)
Journals, ledgers, and waste books, referring to voyages to or from South Carolina and elsewhere in America.

(*d*) Marine insurance, 1740-53. (DD/DN/446)
Policies, generally taken out by Graffin Prankard, on goods in transit between named ports, including Charleston.

(*e*) Trading accounts, 1729-50 (8 vols.). (DD/DN/441-4)
Refer to voyages, including some between South Carolina and the Baltic ports.

(*f*) Jennys of Charleston, 1740. (DD/DN/448)
Trade accounts dealing with shipments to South Carolina of iron, steel, implements, etc.

(*g*) Daniel Goizen of Bristol, 1738-48. (DD/DN/456-7)
Goizen, a business associate of Prankard, has left papers which include some on trade with North America.

Fuller MSS.
Stephen Fuller's daughter married William Dickinson in 1770. Fuller was the family's London-based agent for Jamaica for nearly thirty years.

(*a*) One letter from New York, *c.* 1757, in poor condition. (DD/DN/499)

(*b*) One letter from William H. Lyttelton, Governor of South Carolina, *c.* 1760. (DD/DN/505)

(*c*) Jamaican affairs: includes discussion of relations with America, 1793. (DD/DN/511)

FOX BROS. & CO. LTD., P.O. Box 2, Wellington TA21 OAW

BUSINESS RECORDS. 1783-1807.
This Quaker woollen firm, known as Were & Company until 1796, at which date Thomas Fox became sole partner, possesses Common Letter-books and Foreign Letter-books covering at least the years 1770-1821, and containing extensive references to trade with America, particularly in the years 1783-1807. This trade is mentioned by Hubert Fox in his book *Quaker Homespun* (London, 1958). Chapter 9, headed 'North American Markets', quotes detailed and interesting letters about the difficulties of trade with America during the early years of the Republic. Often, it appears, Thomas Fox had to accept payment in kind for his rough serge and other woollen goods - wheat, indigo, tobacco, turpentine, and rice were all consigned to Were & Company at various times. His cousins, George Croker Fox and Robert Were Fox (G.C. Fox & Co. of Falmouth, Cornwall), acted as agents for these mixed cargoes. There is correspondence to William Anderson, a merchant of Virginia; and relating to the visit in 1787 of Samuel Gardner, a South Carolina merchant, who discussed the requirements of the American market and who subsequently defaulted on his obligations to Thomas Fox.

STAFFORDSHIRE

KEELE UNIVERSITY LIBRARY, Keele ST5 5BG

WEDGWOOD ACCUMULATION. Business and personal papers. 1759- .

(*a*) Letters, 1762-95, of Josiah Wedgwood. Besides the originals there are typescript copies of the letters and a subject index to these. A number of Wedgwood's letters to Thomas Bentley include comment on the obtaining and use of American clay, and on Anglo-American relations; these, and a 1765 letter to Sir William Meredith about possible competition from South Carolina, are printed in K.E. Farrer, ed., *Letters of Josiah Wedgwood, 1762-80* (London, 1903). A draft letter, 1789, to Sir John Dalrymple, including comment on the use of Cherokee clay, is printed in K.E. Farrer, ed., *Correspondence of Josiah Wedgwood, 1781-94* (London, 1906).

(*b*) Thomas Griffith's journal, 1767-8. A photocopy of the original is held by the Wedgwood Museum, Barlaston. The journal describes a journey to Ayoree, in the Cherokee country of South Carolina, in search of clay for Wedgwood. Part of the journal was published in *Ceramic Age* (Nov. 1929).

(*c*) Miscellaneous business papers. An alphabetical index based mainly on personal names is available for the greater part of the accumulation up to about the middle of the nineteenth century. Included are letters about trade with America from James Rivington, New York, 1769; William Knox, Boston, 1784; William Sing of the New York firm of Gailbraith & Sing, 1791; A. Humphrys, Philadelphia, 1801; Richard Shaw, 1809; and Jacob Thomas Waldon, New York, 1810.

2. Available on microfilm from EP Microform.

(*d*) Ledgers, order books, etc.[1] Volumes of business records survive from the late eighteenth century. An experiment book, 'J.W.'s Experiments Nos. 1-4832', begun in 1759, includes records of some experiments using Cherokee clay; an order book for 1849-52 contains orders for ornamental ware from American customers; a letter-book for 1898-1906 contains copies of a few letters to firms in Boston and New York; discussion of the setting up of the firm's American agency occurs in early volumes of the directors' minute-books and shareholders' minute-books, both available from 1895.

RAYMOND RICHARDS COLLECTION.[2] William Davenport & Co. Business papers. 1745-97.

(*a*) Vols. (9), invoices of cargoes, lists of crews, copies of sailing orders (in 2 vols. only, but *see below*), cash accounts— sales of slaves, ivory, etc. ships *Andromache, Badger, Dalrymple, Dobson, Dreadnought, Favourite, Fox, Hawk, Hector, Henry, King of Prussia, Little Britain, Lord Cassils, May, Neptune, Preston, Quixote, Sam, Sisters, Success, Swift, True Blue, Tyrell,* variously owned but mainly by William Davenport & Co., Liverpool, trading with Africa, 'the Winward Coasts of Africa', Benin, Old Calabar, River Cameroons, River Gambia, to Antigua, Barbados, Charleston, Dominica, Granada, Jamaica, St. Croix, St. Kitts, St. Lucia, St. Vincent and back to Liverpool, or Liverpool-Africa-Liverpool, 1761-85, [-88]; waste book, 1745-66; entry book, copies of (890) bills of exchange, etc., some sailing orders and correspondence, 1747-61; ledgers (2), 1763-75, 1788-97; cash book, [1764-], 1768-75; account book, sale of beads and cowries, 1766-70; disbursements, ship *Union,* St. Kitts, 1768 (5 loose sheets only); register, (2,806) bills of exchange, 1769-86.

RAYMOND RICHARDS COLLECTION. Sneyd family papers. 1816.

(*a*) Letters and parts of letters (approx. thirty), Sir Charles and Lady Bagot to their Sneyd relatives, two from New York and Washington, 1816.

RAYMOND RICHARDS COLLECTION. Diary: source unknown. 1881-2.

(*a*) Diary of a traveller in South Africa, Australia, Tasmania, New Zealand and North America, 1881-2. Anonymous.

1. Some of this material was used by R.M. Hower, 'The Wedgwoods: Ten Generations of Potters', *Journal of Economic and Business History,* vol. iv, pp. 281-313, 665-90, 1931-2.
2. Formerly deposited in the John Rylands University Library of Manchester.

STAFFORDSHIRE RECORD OFFICE, County Buildings, Eastgate Street, Stafford ST16 2LZ

WILLIAM SALT LIBRARY EARL OF DARTMOUTH COLLECTION.[1] 1676-1802. (*Letters unless otherwise stated.*) (D(W)1778)

William Legge, 2nd Earl of Dartmouth (1731-1801), was President of the Board of Trade and Foreign Plantations 1765-6; Secretary of State for the American Department and President of the Board of Trade 1772-5; and Lord Privy Seal 1775-82.

H.M.C. xiv (x) is devoted entirely to his American papers. Pp. 1-494 are concerned with what is now the United States; pp. 494-544 with the West Indies; and pp. 545-606 with Canada, Labrador, Newfoundland, Nova Scotia, and the Island of St. John. Pp. iii-xxi give a useful introduction to the collection by B.F. Stevens. The bulk of the manuscripts in this volume falls within Dartmouth's term of office as Secretary of State for the American Department, although the dates actually range from 1676 to 1839. The Canadiana has now gone to Canada, but otherwise, with a few small exceptions, the collection is intact.

The papers are thus of the greatest importance for the study of the beginning of the War of Independence; those for 1765-6 also deal largely with the Stamp Act and its repeal. The collection contains a number of draft schemes for the conciliation of the colonies; correspondence with Franklin and other American agents; papers relating to schemes for settlement in Florida and beyond the Alleghenies; copies of intercepted letters from the American mails; and dispatches from the Colonial Governors 'each with its own tale of the anarchy and strife amongst the people, the acts of the provincial Assemblies, the subversion of the Royal authority, and the final departure of the Royal governors'.[2] There are also some records of the part played by Dartmouth in parliamentary debates on American affairs; and letters in connexion with the foundation of what later became Dartmouth College. *The papers covered by H.M.C. xiv (x), then, are not separately treated here.* However, there are several reports on the other Dartmouth Papers in other H.M.C. reports - principally xi (v) and xv (i), but also ii and xiii (iv), which contain some additional American items;[3] those of some apparent importance being:

18 Mar. 1683, from Thomas, Lord Colepeper, in Virginia, to George Legge, 1st Baron Dartmouth (1648-91), gives favourable account of the progress of the colony.[4]

Boston, 31 Aug. 1687, from Sir Edmund Andros, Governor of New England, to Lord Dartmouth, 'On the fortifications, etc., at Boston....'[5]

New York, 15 Oct. 1688, from Col. Thomas Dongan, Governor of New York, to Lord Dartmouth, stating that the Six Nations of Indians have been annexed to the Crown.[6]

Boston, 17 Feb. and 23 Apr. 1714, from Francis Nicholson to William Legge, 1st Earl of Dartmouth (1672-1750) on seditious propaganda being spread among the people of Boston and other places.[7]

'A long and interesting letter, four folio pages, in 1765, from Wm. Smith of New York, to the Rev. Mr. Whitfield on the discontents of America, specially regarding the Stamp Act.'[8]

Sept. 1765, from the Earl of Hillsborough to Dartmouth, stating that the latter's powers with regard to trade and the colonies should be increased to equal those of the First Lords of the Treasury and Admiralty.[9]

16 Dec. 1765, from Samuel Garbett of Birmingham to Dartmouth on American complaints as to the quality of English nails and prospects of American competition in this field.[10]

24 May 1766, from the Earl of Chesterfield to Dartmouth relative to the latter's appointment as Secretary of State for America and Dartmouth's reply, 25 May.[11]

1. Listed in H.M.C. reports as in possession of the Earl of Dartmouth, Patshull House, Wolverhampton.
2. H.M.C. xiv (x), p. xi.
3. Since the compilation of this report two supplementary N.R.A. reports, both 5197, have been made, which list certain papers not described by the H.M.C. reports.
4. Transcript, H.M.C. xi (v), pp. 80-1.
5. Ibid., p. 134.
6. Synopsis, ibid., p. 162.
7. Synopsis, ibid., p. 320.
8. H.M.C. ii, p. 12. See also H.M.C. xi (v), pp. 331-2, for synopsis of another letter on the same subject from same to same, 6 Dec. 1765.
9. Synopsis, H.M.C. xv (i), p. 179.
10. Transcript, ibid., p. 180.
11. Transcript, ibid., p. 182.

21 Mar. 1767, from Richard Stockton to Samuel Smith on American affairs, contains 'Stockton's scheme for the pacification of Great Britain and her colonies'.[12]

'1771, Oct. 4 - Remarks on some parts of Nova Scotia, New England, and Rhode Island respecting navigation etc. by Commodore Gambier.'[13]

Letters, between 1773 and 1776, chiefly 1774 and 1775, from George III to Dartmouth, on American affairs.[14]

Various letters from George III to Dartmouth in 1774 and 1775, touching upon British determination that the colony of Massachusetts must be reduced to obedience, the measures taken by General Gage, and the skirmish at Concord; that of 28 Feb. 1775 expresses pleasure at 'the very comfortable appearance of temper in the Assembly of New York'.[15]

Several letters from George III to Dartmouth, including one of 28 Jan. 1775, in which he does not approve of Gage as Commander-in-Chief, America; and one, of 10 June 1775, in which he says that America must be a colony or be treated as an enemy.[16]

Letters from Judith Reed, at Philadelphia, 1773-5, some of which touch on the rebellion.[17]

A number of letters from Joseph Reed of Philadelphia to Dartmouth and one from Dartmouth to Reed, 23 July 1773 - 14 Feb. 1775. They discuss the purchase of Indian lands; the history of the American revolt; the non-importation of tea; the bad postal system; the proceedings against Franklin; and the intention of the colonies to hold a General Congress; the prime importance of the question of parliamentary taxation, the actions of the first Congress, and the completeness of non-importation.[18]

A number of letters, 1773-4, from Governor Hutchinson to Dartmouth, describing the deterioration of the political situation in Massachusetts and especially Boston.[19]

Various papers concerning the riots directed against consignees of tea in Boston in 1773.[20]

Letters, 1773, from Mr. Pownall concerning the recall of Governor Hutchinson, and 'the French plot for stealing away our gum trade'.[21]

'Report by the Lords of Trade ... upon a proposed formation of a colony on the banks of the River Mississippi.' 22 Jan. 1773.[22]

19 Apr. 1773, Boston, from Governor Hutchinson to Mr. Pownall on the spread of disaffection from New England to Virginia. Advises that if Parliament is to deal with the situation it must deal with all the colonies together, not singly.[23]

21 Apr. 1773, from John Gray to Dartmouth, enclosing a pamphlet, being a refutation of the answer of the Bostonians to Governor Hutchinson's speech.[24]

5 May and 2 June 1773, from Governor Tryon of New York to Dartmouth; in the former he says that 'His Majesty's instructions and His Majesty's interests are not at all times one and the same thing', and that he (Tryon) has put his own interpretation upon the instructions; in the latter he refers to purchase of lands from the Indians.[25]

(Copy), 7 July 1773, from Franklin, possibly to the Provincial Congress; setting forth the situation in England and advising how the colonists might best obtain redress of their grievances.[26]

23-29 Nov. 1773. Boston. Report of debates in the Council between these dates. Debates show strong opposition to the Governor.[27]

28 Dec. 1773, from Maj.-Gen. Haldimand at New York to Dartmouth, concerning reaction in New York and Philadelphia to the Boston Tea Party.[28]

No date. [1774?] 'Paper, unsigned, as to the advantages and disadvantages of the proposal for a new colony on the banks of the Ohio'.[29]

2 Feb. 1774, from Maj.-Gen. Haldimand to Dartmouth says that New York is quiet, but that 'little matters ... might give new vigour to the spirit of opposition'.[30]

'1774, 25 March. South Carolina. Copy of message from the Commons House of Assembly to the Lieut.-Governor, respecting the rejection of bills passed by them by the Council. Copy of Lieut.-Governor Bull's answer adjourning the House till May. Copy of resolutions of the House of Assembly relative to the distress under which . . . public creditors labour.'[31]

Boston, 30 Mar. 1774, from Governor Hutchinson to Dartmouth enclosing copy of a letter from Mr. Lee, agent of the House of Representatives, of Boston, in England in the absence of Dr. Franklin.[32]

Series of letters[33] from Dartmouth to Governor Gage in 1774, and one from Gage to Dartmouth:

9 Apr. On Gage's appointment. To carry closure of port of Boston into effect; to remove seat of government to Salem; to prosecute at his discretion (i.e., only if impartial verdicts can be obtained) ringleaders in riots; to veto election to Council of persons opposed to the King's Government.

11 Apr. Notifying him of general pardon.

3 June. Requesting him to procure copies of two supposedly treasonable letters from Franklin and Arthur Lee; and two other letters of same date enclosing Acts concerning Massachusetts (including one abolishing elective Council).

6 July. Promising that Boston Port Bill will be rescinded when compensation has been paid to East India Company.

2 Sept. Copy of a long letter from Boston from Governor Gage to Dartmouth about violence offered to members of the Council by colonists and the spread of disaffection to other colonies (especially Connecticut and Rhode Island).

8 Sept. Regrets that colonists have summoned a Congress of Deputies from the several colonies.

17 Oct. On dangerous state of affairs in Massachusetts; more troops being sent.

Extracts from a letter, 9 Aug. 1774, from Major McDonald of the Virginia Militia to Major Connolly at Pittsburgh, describing operations against the Indians.[34]

Extract from a letter, Pittsburgh, 10 Aug. 1774, from Col. George Croghan to Dartmouth on Indian affairs. He has been maintaining the peace with the Six Nations and the Delawares, but cannot do so much longer, unless supplies are sent, and the Virginians stop attacking the Shawnesse Indians.[35]

12. H.M.C. xi (v), p. 332.
13. Ibid., p. 334.
14. Transcripts, H.M.C. xiii (iv), pp. 499-502.
15. Transcripts, H.M.C. xi (v), pp. 439-40.
16. H.M.C. ii, p. 12.
17. Ibid., p. 12.
18. Synopses, ibid., pp. 337, 345, 351, 353, 354, 358, 362-3, 366, 367-8, 371, 372, 373-4.
19. Synopses, H.M.C. xi(v), pp. 338, 339, 341-4, 346-8, 350.
20. Synopses, ibid., pp. 341-2.
21. Synopses, ibid., p. 338.
22. Ibid., p. 334.
23. Synopsis, ibid., pp. 335-6.
24. Ibid., p. 336.
25. Synopsis, ibid., p. 336.
26. Synopsis, ibid., p. 337.
27. Synopsis, ibid., pp. 342-3.
28. Synopsis, ibid., p. 346.
29. Ibid., p. 372.
30. Extract, ibid., p. 348.
31. Ibid., p. 350.
32. Extracts, ibid., p. 350.
33. Synopses, ibid., pp. 351, 352, 353-4, 355, 361-2, 365.
34. Ibid., p. 359.
35. Ibid., p. 360.

Cambridge, Mass., 13 Aug. 1774, from Mr. Brattle to Governor Hutchinson 'mentioning alterations in the constitution of the province which he should rejoice to see effected'.[36]

31 Aug. 1774, from Nathaniel Colver to Dartmouth enclosing a petition from New York Indians complaining of ill usage by New York government, etc.[37]

Various letters to Dartmouth on the unrest in the colonies, including one of 27 Sept. 1774 from Mr. Fraser concerning secret intelligence about America.[38]

Two letters, 13 Oct. 1774, from J. Temple to Mr. Pownall and Dartmouth respectively 'expressive of his mortification at being superseded in the Lieut.-Governorship of New Hampshire'.[39]

27 Oct. 1774, from the Hon. Thomas Walpole to Dartmouth, 'enclosing papers received from America relating to the rupture with the Indians on the River Ohio'.[40]

12 Nov. 1774, 'Viscount Barrington to Dartmouth offering suggestions for the reduction of the rebellion in the colony of Massachusetts'.[41]

22 Nov. 1774, from the Earl of Suffolk to Dartmouth recommending the supersession of Gage.[42]

Minutes of Cabinet meetings on 1 Dec. 1774 and 21 Jan. 1775, to consider what measures shall be taken to restore order in the colonies, especially Massachusetts, and (on the second occasion) agreeing that Britain should desist from taxing colonies (except for commercial purposes) if they could make adequate provision for their defence, etc., and contribute extraordinary supplies in war-time.[43]

20 Dec. 1774. Note endorsed 'Mr. Pownall', about the American petition recently received by Franklin, which is either to be presented to the King by as many Americans as can be persuaded to take part, or delivered to Dartmouth to be presented.[44]

'N.D. (1775). Two drafts of an address from the House of Commons to the King on the subject of the late riots in Massachusetts Bay, Rhode Island and Connecticut'.[45]

N.D. [?1775]. 'Thoughts on the state of the colonies' by the Rev. Mr. Vardill.[46]

Minutes of letters from and to Lord Dartmouth and the Agents for Indian affairs in America of the year 1775.[47]

Bundle of minutes of dispatches from and to Dartmouth, 1775. The majority are from the Governors and Deputy Governors of the various North American colonies. Many of them are undated, but they all deal with the commencement of the war, and are mostly concerned with stating the general temper of the colonies. Included are dispatches from Connecticut, Georgia, Massachusetts Bay, Maryland, New Hampshire, New Jersey, New York, North Carolina, Pennsylvania, Quebec, Rhode Island, South Carolina, and Virginia.[48]

16 Feb. 1775, from James Meyrick to Governor Legge, says that the Ministry and Parliament are determined to force the Americans to submission. Then details the troops ordered to embark for America under Howe, Clinton, and Burgoyne.[49]

17 Feb. 1775, New York, from the Rev. John Rodgers to J.T., Esq., describes loyalty of Americans to the Crown, but also their unanimous intention of opposing the claims of Parliament. The Assembly of New York 'is the only one ... that has met and not approved the measures of the Continental Congress'. This is because they differ from other Assemblies on means not ends.[50]

A long letter, 18 Feb. 1775, unsigned and unaddressed, endorsed 'Thoughts upon American commerce and resistance'.[51]

Two letters, 3 Mar. 1775. Dartmouth to Deputy Governor of Maryland enclosing (enclosure not now with the letter) a resolution of the Commons 'declaratory of the nature of the indulgence they are ready to show to any of the Colonies' that return to their allegiance - this is not to be communicated officially to the Assemblies, but explained by the Governors 'to such persons as may be able by position and connexion to facilitate the measures it points to'.[52]

A series of letters, 23 Apr.-3 Oct. 1775, from General Gage to Governor Legge, chiefly concerning the raising of troops and obtaining of supplies from Nova Scotia; rebel plans to foment trouble there and to attack the province, and counter-plans for its defence by sea; general news of the rebellion (including Washington's assumption of command); and Gage's impending departure for England, and dispositions made before that event.[53]

(Copy), Cambridge, Mass., 13 May 1775, from Dr. Joseph Warren to the select men of Boston, a defence of the colonists' action in taking up arms, and argument against exchanging prisoners with Gage.[54]

London, 11 June 1775. 'Long paper upon the rise and progress of the disputes between Great Britain and America, with suggestions for an accommodation. Unsigned, but marked on the back "Ld. D___d".'[55]

14 June 1775, from John Wesley to Dartmouth, protesting against coercion in America.[56]

Two letters (copies), both 21 June 1775, from British soldiers about the battle of Bunker Hill.[57]

Boston, 25 June 1775, from E. Le Cras to Mr. Le Cras, London. Sends a resolution of the Continental Congress to starve the navy and army.[58]

Two letters, 5 July 1775. One from William Strahan to Franklin urging him to use his influence to settle the dispute; and one from H. Cruger to his brother John Harris Cruger anticipating utter ruin to America.[59]

25, 26 and 27 July 1775, describing the distress of the beleaguered city of Boston.[60]

(Copy), Philadelphia, 4 Aug. 1775, from Thomas Wharton to Samuel Wharton, says that the Canadians and Indians have refused to fight against the colonists. Possibility that General Schuyler will invade Canada.[61]

Paper of 21 Aug. 1775, stated to be by a Mr. Morris, and entitled 'The present state and condition of the colonies with respect to their governors and government'.[62]

36. Synopsis, ibid., p. 360.
37. Synopsis, ibid., p. 361.
38. Synopses, ibid., pp. 363, 364.
39. Ibid., p. 365.
40. Ibid., p. 366.
41. Ibid., p. 368.
42. Transcript, ibid., p. 370.
43. Ibid., pp. 371, 372-3.
44. Transcript, ibid., p. 372.
45. Transcript, ibid., p. 396.
46. Ibid., p. 397.
47. Ibid., p. 396.
48. Synopses, ibid., pp. 390-6.
49. Extract, ibid., p. 374.
50. Transcript, ibid., p. 374.
51. Ibid., p. 374.
52. Synopses, ibid., pp. 374-5.
53. Synopses, ibid., pp. 375-87 *passim*.
54. Synopsis, ibid., pp. 377-8.
55. Ibid., p. 378.
56. Extracts, ibid., p. 378.
57. Transcripts, ibid., pp. 379-81.
58. Ibid., p. 381.
59. Ibid., p. 381.
60. Extracts, ibid., p. 382.
61. Synopsis, ibid., p. 383.
62. Transcript, ibid., p. 384.

A number of letters, written at intervals between Sept. 1775 and Jan. 1778, on military matters and of minor significance, from General Sir William Howe to Governor Legge.[63]

29 Sept. 1775, from Lord Lewisham to his father, the Earl of Dartmouth, about French sympathy for the Americans and shipment of troops to Santo Domingo since the outbreak of the rebellion.[64]

On American plans to attack Nova Scotia. 13 Dec. 1775.[65]

17 Mar. 1776, from General Howe to Governor Legge, informing him that he has evacuated Boston and is proceeding to Halifax.[66]

A long letter, 13 July 1778, from J. Galloway of New York to Ambrose Serle, describing the French blockade of New York and the disposition of the French and British fleets. Says that the British lost more men on the march from Philadelphia than they would have done had they gone out to Valley Forge and there attacked Washington's camp. News of Washington's latest movements, and opinion that even after a junction with Gates he will have only 10,000 men to the British 20,000.[67]

N.D. [?1778]. 'A Squib - "To be sold, the British rights in America. Consisting, among other articles of: The thirteen Provinces in rebellion....The British West Indies will be included in the sale if agreeable. Apply to George Johnston Esquire....To make it easy to the purchasers, a seat in Congress will be taken as part payment, the rest in Continental currency...".'[68]

27 Mar. 1779, from Alexander Macaulay to Lord Lewisham mentions that success in Georgia has elated the friends of Britain [in Holland] and depressed those of France, more than it deserved to do.[69]

23 Sept. 1781, from Granville Sharp to Dartmouth discussing the prospects and desirability of peace with America, regretting that it had not been made earlier, and enclosing an anonymous letter to same effect.[70]

1802. Correspondence between George Legge, 3rd Earl of Dartmouth (1755-1810), and John Wheelock, LL.D., President of Dartmouth College.[71]

AQUALATE HALL COLLECTION. 1 document. Early mid-18th century. (D. 1788/24/6)

Account of the inhabitants, militia, etc., in the several plantations of America (giving the numbers only of the inhabitants and of the militia in the various plantations, in some cases distinguishing between taxables and untaxables, and between whites and Negroes). N.d., but early mid-eighteenth century.

MESSRS. THYNNE AND THYNNE PAPERS. (D 564/12/1/7)

This collection includes correspondence of the 2nd Earl of Dartmouth relating to American affairs, especially notes of a report made verbally by Major Cockran to Lord Dartmouth. This refers to operations on the James River and to movements of a squadron under Admiral Arbuthnot, n.d. [1779].

HATHERTON MANUSCRIPTS. (D 260)

Edward John Littleton, 1st Baron Hatherton (1791-1863), statesman. The forty-eight volumes of his correspondence were indexed by W. Littleton in 1882, in two manuscript volumes under names of correspondents. Among Americans with whom Lord Hatherton corresponded were:

Bassett, F. Five letters, 1849-55, on the state of American politics, American opinion on the Crimean War, agriculture, etc.

Everett, Edward. Letters, 1842-53, include comments on the effects of emigration on Britain, fishery disputes, etc.

Glynn, Captain James, of the United States Navy. Seven letters, 1855-60, with political comments and details of currency problems.

Sumner, Charles. Seven letters, 1855-9, including details of Massachusetts constitutional provisions and the American constitution.

There are also letters from James Buchanan, Henry Colman, William Seward, etc.

Lord Hatherton's journals consist of ninety-one volumes, 1817-62, except for gaps between Mar. 1825-Jan. 1828, Feb. 1828-June 1831, and Aug. 1833-Mar. 1835; they include almost daily entries.[72]

DUKE OF SUTHERLAND'S MANUSCRIPTS. Letters, diary. 1881, 1889. (D 593/P/24/4 and D 593/P/25/3)

This collection includes letters, 1881, and a diary, 1889, relating to U.S. visits of the 3rd Duke of Sutherland.

QUARTER SESSIONS RECORDS. (Q/SB e/9)

One bundle of *c.* fifty bonds, 1720-40, for transporting felons to colonies and plantations in America. One bundle which contains accounts for the transport of prisoners to Liverpool for transportation to America, and a certificate for prisoners consigned to Port York, Va., 1720.

WILLIAM SALT LIBRARY, Eastgate Street, Stafford

SIR THOMAS SALT COLLECTION. Plan. 1683.

Plan of the estate of Thomas, Lord Colepeper, on the James River, Virginia, 1683.

HAND MORGAN MANUSCRIPTS: Drakeford naval papers. 1 document. 1739.

Description of Georgia in 1739: the condition of the plantation and an attempt on the life of Governor Oglethorpe by mutinous soldiers.[1]

WASHINGTON, GEORGE. Will (printed copy); several loose papers.

Printed copy of Washington's will. Observations on the will by the Earl of Buchan, with several other loose papers relating to Washington's bequest to Buchan, etc.

63. Synopses, ibid., pp. 386-9 *passim*, 399, 417.
64. Transcript, H.M.C. xv (i), pp. 221-2.
65. Synopses, H.M.C. xi (v), p. 389.
66. Transcript, ibid., p. 402.
67. Transcript, pp. 417-20.
68. Transcript, ibid., pp. 419-20.
69. Transcript, H.M.C. xv (i), p. 245.
70. Transcript, ibid., pp. 254-6.
71. H.M.C. xi (v), p. 437.
72. See Arthur Aspinall, ed., *Three Early Nineteenth Century Diaries* (London, 1952). One of these is Lord Hatherton's.

1. See S. Burne, *Some Notes on ... Recent Manuscript Additions to the William Salt Library* (Stafford, 1950), p. 7.

HORACE BARKS REFERENCE LIBRARY, Central Library, Bethesda Street, Hanley, Stoke-on-Trent ST1 3RS

POTTERS' EXAMINER AND WORKMAN'S ADVOCATE.[1] 1 volume. 1843-5.

The library holds vol. 1, no. 1, 2 Dec. 1843 - vol. 3, no. 26, 24 May 1845, of this weekly newspaper edited by William Evans for the United Branches of Operative Potters. Much space was taken up by the subject of emigration to the United States. In an early issue Evans urged the formation of an emigration scheme to help solve the problem of surplus pottery labour, and later issues contained articles and letters discussing emigration as a solution, and the particular plan proposed of raising £5,000 to purchase farm land in the United States.

In addition, Evans printed in the *Examiner* a series of forty-two letters from emigrants from 'the Potteries' area to relatives and friends; mainly from Illinois, Ohio, and Wisconsin; these give information about farming and pottery-making methods and prospects, and, urging the correspondents to emigrate, give details of the best routes.

HALL PAPERS. Letters. 1848-52.

Small collection of letters from Charles Hall in America to his mother, 1848-52, and other items.

SUFFOLK

LIEUT. COL. J.F. TODHUNTER, Dunstead, Bures St. Mary CO8 5JT

TODHUNTER FAMILY PAPERS. Letters and diaries. 1819-68.

Lieut. Col. Todhunter possesses a large collection of letters written by Jane Sill to her brother, John Todhunter, between 1825 and 1849. Jane's husband, Joseph Sill, operated a hosiery and haberdashery business in Philadelphia, and John Todhunter acted as the firm's London agent. The letters are largely concerned with family matters, but they also give a remarkable picture of Philadelphia's social life, theatres, and other amusements. Also mentioned are details of the family business, including prices of goods.

Other documents in Lieut. Col. Todhunter's hands relate to another ancestor, Thomas Smith. In 1819 Smith sent his son Thomas to America to investigate the prospects for farming there. The journal of Thomas, junior, gives a good description of his remarkable journey from New York to Pittsburgh, via Niagara, and thence by skiff down the river all the way to Cincinnati, and from Cincinnati on to Kentucky. As a result of his son's investigations, Thomas Smith, senior, went out to America in 1821, and before his death in 1823 he wrote a series of voluminous and detailed letters and diaries on the places he visited, the types of land he saw, the cost of agricultural produce, wages, etc.

Finally there is also among the Todhunter Papers a document which describes at length a journey by Joseph Todhunter from San Francisco to New York in 1868. It contains a vivid account of his adventures *en route*, including a meeting with Brigham Young, and travels by stagecoach, train, and river steamer. Todhunter also offers interesting comments on the mining settlements, the cattle towns, and the violent life of the Old West.

SUFFOLK RECORD OFFICE, BURY ST. EDMUNDS BRANCH, School Hall Street, Bury St. Edmunds IP33 1RX

BARNARDISTON FAMILY PAPERS. 5 letters, documents. 1637-1823.

(*a*) Typed copies of letters from Sir Nathaniel Barnardiston (1588-1653):[1] those of 4 Apr. 1637,[2] 15 Mar. 1640[3] and 19 Mar. 1647[4] to John Winthrop, Governor of Massachusetts; and that of 5 Apr. 1636[5] to his son, John Winthrop, sixth Governor of Connecticut. (613/909)

(*b*) Letter, 15 Mar. 1640, from Sir Nathaniel Barnardiston to John Winthrop, Governor of Massachusetts. (Original of letter of this date in (*a*).) (613/870)

(*c*) Notice, 12 Mar. 1823, to attend a special general court of the Society for the Propagation of the Gospel in New England, with reports on the state of the Society's affairs, sent to Nathaniel Barnardiston (1755-1837). (613/65)

N.R.A. 1015.

THOMAS FAMILY CORRESPONDENCE. 2 letters. 1709, 1743. (E 19/421)

Correspondence between the Thomas family of Lavenham and Carolina include:

London, 10 Nov. 1709, from Edward Brookby to Elizabeth Thomas, concerning the departure of her son Edward, aged 14, to Carolina, and giving a list of all the items purchased for his journey.

South Carolina, 12 May 1743, from Elizabeth Brown, daughter of Edward Thomas, to her uncle Samuel Thomas of Lavenham. Gives some account of the misfortunes which overtook the family. Her father talked of a trip to New York for his health, but she hoped to dissuade him because of the Spanish privateers.

BURWELL, LEWIS. Letter (or copy). 1734. (E 1/29/22)

Letter (or possibly contemporary copy), 8 July 1734, from Lewis Burwell, a student of law in Virginia, to his friend James Burrough of Gonville and Caius College, Cambridge. Concerns his matrimonial prospects, his law studies, and his Cambridge friends.

WATSON, HENRY. Case-book. *c.* 1745-74. (E 2/41/7)

Concerning tithes in estate of Henry Watson of Maryland and London, etc.

1. Used by W.H. Warburton, *The History of Trade Union Organisation in the North Staffordshire Potteries* (London, 1931). See also Harold Owen, *The Staffordshire Potter* (London, 1901); Grant Foreman, 'The Settlement of English Potters in Wisconsin', *Wisconsin Magazine of History*, vol. xxi, pp. 375-96, 1938.

---

1. See 'Letters of Sir Nathaniel Barnardiston' in the 'Winthrop Papers', *Collections of the Massachusetts Historical Society*, 4th ser., vol. vi, pp. 545-50 (Boston, 1863).
2. *Winthrop Papers*, vol. iii (Boston, Massachusetts Historical Society, 1943), p.384.
3. Ibid., vol. iv, pp. 217-8.
4. Ibid., vol. v, pp. 144-5.
5. Ibid., vol. iii, p. 245.

HERVEY FAMILY OF ICKWORTH (Marquises of Bristol). Journals, letters, etc. 1755-1857.

(*a*) Journals of campaigns in North America, 1755-60.[6] (941/53/2)
(*b*) Letter, 1806, from Sir Augustus J. Foster to the 5th Earl of Bristol on conditions in Washington. (941/56/19)
(*c*) Letter, 1832, from Christopher Hughes, American Minister in Sweden, to the 1st Marquis of Bristol. (941/56/23a)
(*d*) MS. 'Journal of a Tour in the United States & Canada in the year 1857'. (941/73/10). Also various certificates, plans of land, etc.[7]

GRAFTON PAPERS.

Papers of Augustus Henry, 3rd Duke of Grafton (1735-1811).

A. Letters from George III, 1767-8.

(*a*) Letter, 17 Feb. 1767, mentioning the conduct of the province of New York. (no. 489)
(*b*) Letter, 10 Mar. 1767, noting an Act of the province of Massachusetts. (no. 494)
(*c*) Letter, 12 Dec. 1767, giving the King's and Lord Shelburne's views on the American branch of the Southern Department. (no. 117)
(*d*) Letter, 18 Feb. 1768, commenting on Lord Hillsborough's attempt to provide a legislature for Canada. (no. 510)
(*e*) Dispatches from Major-General Gage on developments in Boston, Mass., with comment on the behaviour of Governor Bernard. 27 Oct. 1768. (no. 529)

B. Papers on America, 1765-83.

(*a*) Letter, 14 Sept. 1765, from H.S. Conway to Governor Fauquier of Virginia, on resolutions of the colonial Assembly. (Copy.) (no. 788)
(*b*) Letter from the Duke of Grafton to Major-General Gage on events in America, including action on the Stamp Act in New York. 14 Dec. 1765. (Copy.) (no. 787)
(*c*) Letter to Cadwallader Colden, Lt. Governor of New York, on the situation in New York. (Copy.) (no. 820)
(*d*) Note of opinions of speakers in a debate in the House of Lords on repeal of the Stamp Act, n.d. [1766]. (no. 1022b)
(*e*) Draft of an address to the King on employment of German mercenary troops against the American colonies, n.d. [*c.* 1775]. (no. 199)
(*f*) 'Information intended to be given to Ld. W. (Walpole) as Sec. of State by the D. of G. (Grafton) in his way through London.' On preparation of armaments for America in France, 4 Sept. 1776. (no. 202)
(*g*) Note of munitions, etc., required by the American colonists, to be supplied from France, with report of a statement by M. de Vergennes on support for America, n.d. (no. 203)
(*h*) Six letters, 1780-1, from Gen. Charles O'Hara, Commander of the Brigade of Guards in America. O'Hara's letters describe in some detail the final months of the war in America, and reflect the growing disillusionment of British forces fighting an American army which was growing more confident daily. Among the various military battles mentioned are Cornwallis's expedition into North Carolina and Ferguson's defeat at King's Mountain. (nos. 189-92, 195-6)
(*i*) Extract, 2 May 1781, to Sir Henry Clinton from Lord George Germain, on prosecution of the war in America. (no. 767)
(*j*) Letter, 14 Sept. 1782, from Admiral Pigot, Commander-in-Chief, West Indies. Mentions naval movements off America and the evacuation of Charleston.(no. 197)
(*k*) Letter, 17 Jan. 1783, from Pigot, also noting the situation in America. (no. 198)

C. Political correspondence.

The political correspondence of the Duke of Grafton contains some commentary on the incidents leading up to the War of Independence and on the war itself. See especially the letters to Grafton from Thomas Bradshaw, the Earl of Camden, H.S. Conway, Phillips Cosby, the Earl of Northington, the Earl of Radnor, the Earl of Shelburne, Charles Townshend, Thomas Townshend, and Lord Walpole. Walpole's letters to Grafton are especially valuable for their analysis of the war.

D. Miscellaneous correspondence. 1768.

Five letters, 30 July-10 Aug. 1768, from Jeffrey Amherst to the Duke of Grafton, concerning his services in America. (nos. 689, 692-3, 695-6). Also copies of several replies from Grafton to Amherst. (nos. 691, 694)

E. Private correspondence. 1778.

Grafton's private correspondence includes several letters, 1778, from John Hinchcliffe, Bishop of Peterborough from 1769 to 1794, which comment on the war in America.

N.R.A. 2567.

BUNBURY FAMILY RECORDS. Diary (copy). *c.* 1814. (E 18)

Copy of a diary of events to 1814, possibly copy of one kept by Sir Charles James Napier (1782-1853), relating to expeditions against Washington, D.C., and New Orleans.

Napier commanded a brigade which took part in the expedition under General Sir Thomas Sydney Beckwith in operations against the United States, 1813; he commanded an attack on the town of Little Hampton, and was later detached to the coast of Carolina where minor operations took place.

FITZROY PAPERS. (Acc. 2683)

Letters and other documents, including a brief journal, kept by Lieut. Colonel Lord Frederick Fitzroy, who served with the Grenadier Guards in Canada during the winter of 1861-2.

SUFFOLK RECORD OFFICE, IPSWICH BRANCH, County Hall, Ipswich IP4 2JS

IPSWICH CORPORATION GENERAL COURT BOOK, 1572-1636. Document.[1] [1611.]

Order, 4 Mar. [1611], for 'adventuring out of the town treasure one hundred pounds in the name of the bayliffes burgesses and commonaltie of the said towne ... in the voyage to Virginia'; the order being made in compliance with letters from Henry Reynolds.

MIDDLETON PAPERS. 1615-*c.* 1860.

(*a*) Papers of Arthur Middleton (1681-1737), Acting Governor of South Carolina 1725-30, including volume containing copies of documents concerning the Summer Islands and the Company of Adventurers for their Plantations, 1615-73. (HA 93/MI)
(*b*) Correspondence and papers re affairs of William and Henry, sons of Arthur Middleton, 1746-81. (HA 93/M2)
(*c*) Correspondence and papers re affairs of William, Henry and Thomas, sons of William Middleton, chiefly concerning the settlement of Thomas's estates in England and Carolina, 1784-1826. (HA 93/M3)

6. Printed in *Journals of Hon. William Hervey*, ed. S.H.A Hervey (1906), pp. 1-64. Two of the five MS. volumes probably belonged to George Bartman, one possibly to Hervey, and the other two are unidentified.
7. A catalogue of the Hervey family papers is with the N.R.A.

1. H.M.C. ix (i), p.256. (Listed as in possession of the Corporation of Ipswich.) It is possible that the Court Books contain other relevant references, but they have not been checked in detail.

(*d*) Correspondence and papers re affairs of Sir William Fowle Middleton and his son Sir William Fowle Fowle Middleton, chiefly re redemption of a bond held by Sir W.F.M. on security of estate of John Middleton in South Carolina, 1826-40. (HA 93/M4)
(*e*) Correspondence and papers of Sir William F.F. Middleton, chiefly re his remaining property in South Carolina, 1844- *c.*1860. (HA 93/M5)

BERNERS FAMILY ARCHIVES. Deeds. 1622-37. (S1/10/11.1,2)

Title deeds, 1622-37, of the estates of Timothy Dalton, rector of Woolverstone, Suffolk, 1616-36, and of New England.

READ COLLECTION. Will (copy). 1663. (T4/19/3)

Copy of will of Thomas Ives, mercer of Ipswich, including bequests to John Ives, his brother, in Virginia.

TOLLEMACHE COLLECTION. Document. 1705. (In private ownership.) (B1/2 Folder 25a/12)

'Warrant from George, Prince of Denmark, Lord High Admiral of England, to the Earl of Dysart, Vice-Admiral of Suffolk, to lift embargo on ships bound for Virginia and Maryland. 17 March 1704/05.'

NORTH (LITTLE GLEMHAM) FAMILY ARCHIVES. Document. 1706. (331)

Marriage settlement, Dudley North (1684-1729), son and heir of Sir Dudley North, and Katherine Yale, daughter of Elihu Yale, endorsed with account of jewels bought by Yale for his daughter, 1706.

ALBEMARLE PAPERS. Letter-book, documents, letter. 1754-66.

(*a*) Naval letter-book, 1754-61, of Admiral Viscount Keppel. Indexed. Keppel commanded the ships of the North American Station 1754-5. The letter-book covers the command at Virginia and all the coast of North America, Dec. 1754 - Oct. 1755. (461/235)
(*b*) Naval and military documents relating to North America, 1757-58. Two folded sheets ('2nd' and '3rd' recording), being an account of an engagement with the French in which Brig. Wolfe and Col. Hawke were involved, mentioning 'Green Hill', an island. Louisbourg, N.S. 1757-8. (461/12)
(*c*) Letter, 22 Apr. 1766, from General Amherst to Viscount Barrington concerning action to be taken in America. (461/16)

HENNIKER, JOHN (1724-1803), later 1st Baron Henniker. London day-book. 1765-89. (S1/2/102)

Includes business transactions as a merchant for provisioning ships - army and American contracts, adventures to New England, Riga, and the like; purchase and sale of ships and freights.

STANSBURY, GEORGE. Document. 1784. (435) (T108/25)

Testimony, London, 4 Mar. 1784, of Stansbury concerning the activities of Benedict Arnold in supplying information to Sir Henry Clinton. (Stansbury was employed in decoding the correspondence which passed between them.)

BROKE PAPERS. 1809-41.

(*a*) Naval papers of Sir Philip Bowes Vere Broke relating to the War of 1812, including: Journals, logs, letter-books and other papers of H.M.S. *Shannon.* Also documents captured from U.S. frigate *Chesapeake,* including register books, 1809, 1812-3; size roll, 1812-3; inventory of stores, 1813; log book, 1812-3; and letter-book of Captain James Lawrence, 1809-13. (HA 93/6/2)
(*b*) Eighty-seven personal letters by Broke to his wife, from the North American Station, 1811-3, containing many comments on relations between Great Britain and America in the months leading up to the American declaration of war, and on the progress of the war thereafter. (HA 93)
(*c*) Letter of congratulation on the capture of the *Chesapeake,* 1813, from naval officers and others. (HA 93)
(*d*) Accounts of the action by officers and men of *Shannon,* 1813-41. (HA 93)
(*e*) Various papers of an ephemeral nature arising out of the same actions. (HA 93)

HALESWORTH PARISH RECORDS. Log-book. 1825-7. (FC 184/N1/8)

Log-book of the ship *Merope* during a voyage from India to China, thence to the Sandwich Islands and so to California, and back again to India, 1825-7.

FISHER COLLECTION. 16 letters. 1831-62. (2815/1-4)

(*a*) John Fisher. Nine letters,[2] 1831-8, from the United States, to his mother, Mrs. Lydia Fisher of Brooke, Norfolk. They deal with his travels through Canada and New York State, to Michigan Territory; his acquisition of a farm in a new settlement there and its development; his marriage; prices of agricultural produce and wages; a little on farming methods; reflections on the advantages of life in America - no paupers, no poor rates, cheap land for all, an expanding nation, friendship among Methodists, Presbyterians, and Baptists; experiences when caught up in a Methodist revival; advice to a brother contemplating emigration.
(*b*) William Scolten. Letter, Arcade, N.Y., 1837, from Scolten to a friend in England about his purchase of a saw-mill, and about various friends.
(*c*) Robert Fisher Smith. Letter, Franklin, 1848, from Robert Fisher Smith, a carpenter (son of Robert Smith, an emigrant), to Francis Fisher at Brooke, Norfolk, executor of Francis Fisher, deceased, who was apparently Smith's maternal grandfather.
(*d*) Robert Smith. Three letters, Michigan, 1851-60, to Francis Fisher about family matters and sums due to Fisher's children with their receipts.
(*e*) Nathan Pooley. Two letters, Indiana, 1860 and 1862, to Francis Fisher about money due to members of the Pooley family, the history and wanderings of the various members of which, since they moved to America and multiplied there, he outlines.

MACNAB, SIR ALLAN NAPIER (1798-1862). Personal papers.[3] 1837-49. (In private ownership of the Earl of Albemarle.)

Canadian soldier and politician. Bundles 3, 4, and 5 concern the rebellion in Upper Canada, 1837-8 (one of 1849); the *Caroline* affair, 1840-1; and miscellaneous Canadian matters, 1838-40.

WEBBER, CHARLES. Letter. 1847. (50/23/7.6)

Letter from Webber, a ship's surgeon, to George Mingay, Orford, Suffolk; written from Southampton *en route* for the West Indies. Includes description of the American steamer *Washington,* first of the Ocean Steam Navigation Company, New York.

2. Photostats in the collection of Letters of Emigrants to America in the British Library of Political and Economic Science, London School of Economics.
3. Microfilmed by the Public Archives of Canada.

RAVEN, CANON JOHN JAMES (1833-1906). Correspondence and papers. 1888-98. (S2/4/5.13)

Deal with Massachusetts church bells.

EMIGRANT RECORDS.

Information in parish records, government circulars, shipping advertisements, papers, and correspondence about raising the necessary money. Includes Canada and Australia, as well as the United States.

PARISH CHURCH, PEASENHALL, Saxmundham

EMIGRANT RECORDS.

Overseers' Account Book contains an entry for 3 May 1833 giving a detailed account of the cost of a family's migration to America.

SURREY

GUILDFORD MUNIMENT ROOM, Castle Arch, Guildford GU1 3SX

BELLINGHAM FAMILY OF BOSTON. Marriage settlement and deeds. 1695-1707.

Copy of settlement on the marriage of Samuel Bellingham and Elizabeth Savage (details of property in Boston, Wyneysymet and elsewhere in Massachusetts), 30 March 1695. Also subsequent deeds to 1702, submitted for counsel's opinion in 1707. (97/)

ONSLOW COLLECTION. Document. 1718.

Deed, 31 July 1718, bearing the signature of Elihu Yale. (97/16/10)

LOSELEY MSS. Documents. *c.* 1720-60.

Gen. J.E. Oglethorpe, founder of Georgia: one letter, 1752, from him, and ten letters from his wife, to the owner of the Loseley estate. Also deeds, legal case papers, papers relating to Parliamentary elections, *c.* 1720-60. (Loseley MSS. COR/357/113, 358/3, 763/72, 105, 1153, 1158, 1299)[1]

MISCELLANEOUS LETTERS. 1759-1821.

(*a*) Two letters from Edward Bray to his brother William Bray: one from Fort Hunter 'in the midst of the Mohawk Indians', and one from Albany about the hardships of a soldier's life, 1759, 1760. (85/3/2(1) and (2))

(*b*) Letter from George Hogarth, Baltimore, to William Bray, replying to Bray's reference to a Surrey emigrant named Morris Birkbeck, who 'found Paradise in the Illinois free from law, free from religion, no Priests, no Taxes', 1821. (85/3/4(9))

CENTRAL LIBRARY, MUSEUM AND ART GALLERY, Fairfield Road, Kingston-upon-Thames

MUYBRIDGE COLLECTION.

Eadweard Muybridge (1830-1904), the pioneer of animal-motion photography, was born in and died in Kingston: he migrated to the United States and became director of the photographic surveys of the United States government. He left most of his original plates and apparatus, including the zoopraxiscope, to the Kingston Central Library, which preserves them (in the adjacent Museum) together with scrapbooks of press articles about his career kept by Muybridge during his lifetime and subsequently added to - 1860-1930. There is also a microfilm of his notebooks, the originals of which are in the Eastman Museum, Rochester, N.Y.

SURREY RECORD OFFICE, County Hall, Kingston-upon-Thames KT1 2DN

SOMERS PAPERS. Letters, documents. 1693-1709.

John Somers, Baron Somers (1651-1716), was Lord Chancellor of England 1697-1700.

(*a*) Penn, William. Petition, *c.* 1693, and correspondence, 1694-1709.

Petition for the restitution of the province of New York (not in Penn's hand); and letters written by Penn to Lord Somers. Letters, 17 Apr. 1694 (sent with a paper), 23 Nov. 1696 and 22 Nov. 1698, request interviews - that of 1696 about the case of J. Phillips. Letter, 31 Mar. 1709, includes a petition for settling the boundaries between his (Penn's) and Lord Baltimore's territories.

(*b*) Two letters from Richard Coote, 1st Earl of Bellomont (1636-1701), Governor of New York 1697-1701, to Lord Somers:

16 Oct. 1697, requests permission to pardon pirates; refers to Captain Kidd; mentions peculation of troops' allowances at New York, and Blathwayt's patent for collecting revenues.

16 May 1699, discusses proroguing the Assembly and the opposition of Attorney-General Graham and others.

(*c*) Census of population of New York province, 1698. Account, arranged by counties, from Richard Coote, 1st Earl of Bellomont.

(*d*) Abstract of revenue of New York, 8 June - 29 Sept. 1698. Collected and signed by Commissioners and Receivers of the Revenue: Stephanus Van Cortlandt and Ducie Hungerford.

(*e*) Settlement of Palatines (Pfälzer) in North Carolina. Copy of agreement, 10 Oct. 1709 (and copy of bond for execution of agreement, *c.* 1709), between Commissioners of the Palatines and Christopher de Graffenried and Lewis Michel for settling 600 Palatines on their land in North Carolina.

Four letters, all 1709, from Col. Robert Hunter from London to Lord Somers. The first, 19 Oct., discusses the transporting of Palatines to New York, and the proposal that they be armed and enlisted in a regiment for defence of frontiers, etc. The second gives an estimate of the cost of manufacture of tar by Palatines in New York (with copy). The third gives the scheme of an estimate for naval stores if made by Palatines. The fourth contains a statement for sending 3,000 Palatines to New York (unsigned).

N.R.A. 3018.

GOULBURN PAPERS.

Henry Goulburn (1784-1856),[1] statesman, was one of the Peace Commissioners who negotiated with the Americans at Ghent in

1. All of this material relates exclusively to Oglethorpe's Surrey activities.

1. His main American papers are in the William L. Clements Library, Ann Arbor, Mich.

1814. A good handlist revealed no titles of papers likely to be connected with this mission; a brief search merely revealed some personal letters to his wife in 1814 and 1815 that contain some trivial references to the course of the negotiations. Also, among the many letters from Robert Peel, a few in 1817 discuss Irish emigration to America in relation to possible government support of emigration schemes. However, a few pages of a manuscript autobiography deal with the War and the peace negotiations.[2]

A more recent addition to the Goulburn Papers is the California diary of Harvey Tower. On back: 'July 1856 to July 1861. Mexico, California 1858.' On front: 'from July 1858 to July 1861.' (some photographs).

PAUNCEFOTE PAPERS. 18 letters (photostats).[3] 1889-1902.

Sir Julian Pauncefote, 1st Baron Pauncefote (1828-1902), was British Minister, and then first British Ambassador to the United States 1889-1902. Most of his correspondence was destroyed by his widow. The few surviving letters are all of a congratulatory kind; they contain only a few incidental scraps of politics or diplomacy: two letters from the Marquis of Salisbury in 1889 touch briefly on the Bering Sea question; one from the Marquess of Lansdowne in 1900 gives the views of the Cabinet on the Davis Amendment renouncing the Clayton-Bulwer Treaty. John Hay's congratulatory letter, 11 Nov. 1900, when Pauncefote entered the Lords, is some measure of Pauncefote's popularity in Washington.

POOR LAW UNION RECORDS.

The Record Office contains the official minute-books of all the eleven Poor Law Unions in Surrey except Croydon. A search of three of these unions yielded merely a single reference to assisted emigration to the United States: eleven paupers from the Guildford Union in June 1844.

SUSSEX, EAST

UNIVERSITY OF SUSSEX LIBRARY, Brighton BN1 9QL

ROSEY POOL PAPERS. 1945-70. (Sx Ms 19)

Twenty boxes of autograph, typescript and printed papers, photographs and recordings relating to the interests of Dr. Rosey Eva Pool (1905-71) in Negro literature (especially verse and drama) and education in the U.S., 1945-70. Includes catalogues and programmes, correspondence, drafts, periodical issues and press-cuttings, scrapbooks, scripts, etc. Some of the material concerns Owen Dodson, Chester Himes, Langston Hughes, and others, while other documents involve Dr. Pool's connexions with various colleges for Negro students.

MATUSOW PAPERS I. (Sx Ms 8)

Thirty-three boxes of autograph, typescript and printed papers, photographs and ciné-film relating to the career of Harvey Marshall Matusow (1926-) as anti-Communist witness and McCarthyite political aide, 1950-5. Includes much printed material collected by Matusow, especially press-cuttings.

PARISH CHURCH, BURWASH, Etchingham

EMIGRANT RECORDS.[1]

(*a*) Overseers' Account Books, or Disbursements. 6 vols. 1815-36.
(*b*) Poor Law Account Books, or Paupers' Ledgers. 5 vols. 1816-35.
(*c*) Burwash Parish letters. 1 bundle, *c*. 1820-35. Mostly requests for relief.

MUNIMENT ROOM, PUBLIC MUSEUM AND ART GALLERY, John's Place, Hastings

PRIVATEERING. Document. 1779.

Commission for a privateer, the *Roebuck* of Hastings, 1779, to 'cruise against the French and Spanish kings and their subjects and to take any ships, goods, wares or merchandise belonging to them... or to any of the rebellious colonies or any trading with them'.

EAST SUSSEX RECORD OFFICE, Pelham House, Lewes BN7 1UN

RYE MANUSCRIPTS. 2 letters (copies). 1634, 1637.

(*a*) Copy of a letter, 31 Dec. 1634, from the Commissioners of Trade and Plantations to the Lord Warden of the Cinque Ports on restriction of emigration to America.[1]
(*b*) Copy of a circular letter, 7 June 1637, from Sir John Manwood, a gentleman of the King's Privy Council, of Dover Castle, to officials of the Cinque Ports and other places, passing on orders of the Lord Warden to obtain lists of emigrants to America.[2]

SHIFFNER MANUSCRIPTS.[3] American material: 306 documents, 2 miscellaneous bundles, and 1 volume. 1677-1816.

Relates to estates in West Jersey and Pennsylvania which came into the family when Sir John Bridger (knighted 1760) married Rebecca Eliot, heiress of a mercantile family and descendant of Giles Fettiplace of Coln St. Aldwyn, Glos., and John Bellers, through whom the properties came into the family. The properties, passing into the Shiffner family through the marriage of Sir John Bridger's daughter, were disposed of in 1806. The collection includes seventeenth-century leases and releases - to several of which William Penn is a party; correspondence concerning the estates - especially during and after the War of Independence, and in 1794-5 when the owners sent out an agent to report - and their disposal; and Rebecca Eliot's ledger covering 1749-63.

2. See 'A British View of the War of 1812 and the Peace Negotiations', ed. by Wilbur Devereux Jones, *Mississippi Valley Historical Review*, vol. xlv, pp. 481-7, 1958.
3. The originals are in the possession of Lady Bromley.

1. These were used by M.D. Wainwright, 'Agencies for the promotion or facilitation of emigration from England to the U.S.A., 1815-1861', M.A. thesis, University of London, 1951.

1. Transcript, H.M.C. xiii (iv), pp. 195-6. (Listed as in possession of the Corporation of Rye, which deposited them in 1955).
2. Extracts, ibid., p. 203.
3. F.W. Steer, ed., *The Shiffner Archives: a Catalogue* (Lewes, 1959).

SAYER MANUSCRIPT. Letter. 1755.

Letter from Col. James Murray to John Collier concerning the defeat of English forces at Fort Duquesne, 1755. (2099)

BATTLE ABBEY ESTATE MANUSCRIPTS. Documents. 1778-1849.

Extract will of Florentius Vassall concerning estate in New England, 1778, and conveyance of one-third part of this property, 1835; two letters concerning prospecting for gold in California, 1849.

BOUCHER MANUSCRIPTS. (Locker-Lampson). Correspondence.

Correspondence of Rev. Jonathan Boucher, who preached and taught in America and was on friendly terms with George Washington and Robert Eden, Governor of Maryland, 1769-75. The Locker-Lampson MSS. also include three letters from Henry James and one from 'Mark Twain', all of a personal nature.

GILBERT MANUSCRIPTS. Letters and journal. 1838-1908.

Letters concerning world tour, including New York and Philadelphia, 1876-7; letters from Arizona, 1908; letters from the Bowditch family of Boston, Mass., concerning the making of Nathaniel Bowditch's library into a public institution, 1838; journal of a visit to the U.S., 1887. (210, 222, 225, 234)

ASHBURNHAM MANUSCRIPTS. Investment papers. 1884-1910.

Papers concerning investments in American and Australian mining companies, 1884-1910. (632-4, 3071-114)

SUSSEX ARCHAEOLOGICAL SOCIETY, Barbican House, Lewes BN7 1YE

GAGE PAPERS.[1] 1740-1874.

Major-General Henry Gage (1761-1808), the son of General Thomas Gage, inherited through his wife a share in the substantial American estate of Sir Peter Warren (1703-52), Admiral, Governor of Louisbourg, N.S., M.P. for Westminster. This collection is, together with some other papers of Sir Peter Warren's,[2] the record of the administration of these properties, and of other American investments in the nineteenth century, by American agents who were relations of the heirs. The middle and later sections of the collection, then, contain full and candid accounts of the economic and political situation of the time. There is a full calendar (duplicated) of the papers. They are best briefly described under the following heads.

(*a*) Sir Peter Warren's Papers. 1729-51. (G/Am 1-66)

Concerning the administration of his affairs mainly in America - in South Carolina, New England, and New York. They include cash books and account books - the cash book for 1740-7 shows, *inter alia,* a small purchase from Oliver De Lancey, his brother-in-law, of lots in 'Broad Way' for £41. 8s. 7d.

(*b*) Sir Peter Warren's 'Private Letters': letter-book with 37 letters. 1746-7. (G/Am 6)

Written by Warren while Governor of Louisbourg, they concern the war against France in North America, particularly naval affairs; intrigue for the job of Governor of New Jersey - letters to the Duke of Newcastle; instructions to Messrs. Saml. & W. Baker to invest his moneys, and to use their good offices towards the governorship; and a long and far-seeing letter to Lord Sandwich on the military position of the colonies in America.

(*c*) Lady (Susannah) Warren's Papers. 1752-72. (G/Am 67-94)

Many from her brother, Oliver De Lancey, concerning the settlement of her husband's estate. Her bank-books and some household accounts are included.

A more recent accession contains approximately fifty-four letters, 1763-5, from Oliver De Lancey to Susannah Lady Warren, on her financial affairs and estates in America following the death of her husband, Admiral Sir Peter Warren. There are also comments concerning De Lancey's two sons, Oliver and Stephen, and their education in England, the state of the colonies and war with France, personalities, commanders, etc.; also social comparison of England and America. (Accn. 1201)

(*d*) Papers relating to the Settlement of Sir Peter Warren's Estate. 1756-72. (G/Am 95-113)

Detailed accounts of his American holdings (particularly in New York), also of his Irish property. His 'personal estate' amounts to some £31,000 to each of his three daughters (who married Willoughby Bertie, Earl of Abingdon; Charles Fitzroy, Baron Southampton; and Lieut.-General William Skinner. Major-General Henry Gage married the daughter and heiress of the latter.)

(*e*) American Estate Affairs, from Agents and Relatives there. 1768-90. (G/Am 114-203)

Correspondence mainly between Oliver De Lancey in New York and the three above-mentioned heirs, for whom he managed the property. The beginnings of the correspondence between the Kembles and Henry Gage - initially with Peter Kemble, his uncle (Thomas Gage married Margaret Kemble, daughter of Peter Kemble, who was President of the Council of New Jersey and a cousin of De Lancey.)

(*f*) American Estate Affairs, between the Gage and the Kemble Families. 1791-1870. (G/Am 204-338)

These letters (and accounts) between the two generations of the Kemble and Gage families mingle personal affairs with detailed discussions of financial prospects in the American market (and some good letters on contemporary politics throughout the period). Land sales and speculation figure largely in the 1790's, American banking stock and Consols in the 1810's, and by the 1850's, railway investments - with highly informative letters from William Kemble about the standing of various lines (and some letters from his brother, Gouverneur Kemble). In 1870 Henry Hall Gage, 4th Viscount Gage, had American securities valued at $70,000. William Kemble wrote on into his eighty-eighth year and discussed in his letters, *inter alia*, Jackson's election and the Bank of the United States controversy, the Kansas question, the Panic of 1857, American resentment at British attempts to recruit soldiers for the Crimean War, Lincoln's election, the Civil War, war-time finance, and Reconstruction.

(*g*) Wills and Settlements relating to many of the above figures which would reveal actual holdings of American property. (G/Am 1305-16)

(*h*) Miscellaneous: Military Disbursement Accounts. 1763-5. (Accn. 1374)

1. The papers are on loan from the present Lord Gage and were previously at Firle Place, as were the papers of General Gage that were sold to the William Clements Library, Ann Arbor, Mich., in 1930. We are grateful to Lord Gage for permission to examine the papers and make this report.

2. A number of Sir Peter Warren's letters, especially those mentioned in this entry which concern the siege of Louisbourg in 1745 and the proposal to conquer Canada in 1746, have been printed in Julian Gwyn (ed.), *The Royal Navy and North America: the Warren Papers, 1736-52* (Publications of the Navy Records Society, vol. 118) (London, 1973).

(i) Consolidated General Account of disbursements for the army in America amounting to £3980. 19s. 4d., with vouchers, 1763-4. (b)

(ii) Receipted account of James Johnstone of London for salt forwarded to Fort Pitt for use of H.M.'s forces, 1764. (c)

(iii) Memorandum of sundry bills and expenses involving payment in currencies of South Carolina, New York and New England, undated [*c.* 1764]. (d)

(iv) Copies of two letters to Sir Jeffrey Amherst in London from the (?) Quartermaster-General in New York relating to provisions supplied to the troops when under General Amherst's command, and needing his certification before payment for which suppliers are clamouring. Also refers to purchase of army ranks and other matters, 4 May and 20 Sept. 1765. (e)

FULLER PAPERS. Correspondence; business, estate, and political papers. 1754-1811.

The Fullers were iron-masters with an important gun foundry at Brightling mainly engaged on government contracts. Marriage brought them a West Indian fortune and estates, Rose Fuller becoming Chief Justice of Jamaica in 1735 and M.P. for New Romney in 1761. A fairly full list of the papers of Rose and other Fullers reveals no direct business or other connexion with the American mainland, but several references to American affairs; there is likely to be much more in the actual papers.

SUSSEX, WEST

WEST SUSSEX RECORD OFFICE, County Hall, Chichester PO19 1RN

LYONS PAPERS. Correspondence. 1858-64.

Private and official correspondence and papers of Richard Bickerton Pemell Lyons, 2nd Baron and 1st Earl Lyons (1817-87), British Minister to the United States, 1858-64.

Much of the correspondence is with British Consuls in the United States, and Foreign Office officials in London. Many of the letters concern, of course, various aspects of the Civil War and resulting Anglo-American relations; there is also a considerable group of letters concerning the visit to the United States of the Prince of Wales, and another large collection of letters from Lyons to his sister Minna, Duchess of Norfolk, mainly concerning personal and family matters.

JOHN MAX, 2ND BARON EGREMONT, Petworth House, Petworth

NORTHUMBERLAND PAPERS. 1761-*c.* 1838.

(*a*) Letters, 12 Dec. 1761 - 20 July 1762, to and from Sir Jeffrey Amherst, C. Colden, Governor of New York, the Governors of North Carolina, Connecticut, South Carolina, Fort Pitt, Georgia, Maryland, Nova Scotia, New Jersey, New York, New England, New Hampshire, Placentia, Quebec, Virginia, and papers about Montreal and Canada (289 pages). (H.M.C. 163)

(*b*) 1 July 1763, the Earl of Egremont chosen Chancellor of the College of William and Mary in Virginia (choice made on 21 Dec. 1762). (H.M.C. 171)

(*c*) Correspondence about possible purchase of land at Tecumsith, Michigan, and places in Upper Canada, *c.* 1838.

TYNE AND WEAR

GATESHEAD CENTRAL LIBRARY, Prince Consort Road, Gateshead NE8 4LN

ELLISON MSS.,[1] 1754-83.

(*a*) Account of Robert Ellison with Major James Kinnear, for expenditures in Albany, N.Y., 1754. (A/5/11)

(*b*) Letters from Cuthbert Ellison to Henry Ellison, largely concerned with news of the war, 1774-83. (A/24/1-45)

COUNTY ARCHIVES, TYNE AND WEAR DEPARTMENT, 109 Pilgrim Street, Newcastle-upon-Tyne NE1 6QF

NEWCASTLE-UPON-TYNE COMMON COUNCIL BOOK. 1766-85.

Reference, 1775, to fund 'for affording relief to the widows and orphans of such brave men as have fallen or may fall in defending the constitutional government of this country' against the American rebels. (folio 242)

COWEN COLLECTION. Two letters, speech. 1860, 1870.

(*a*) Two letters, July 1860, from Thomas A. Devyr, an emigrant, referring to the American political scene. (C. 1434, C. 1442)

(*b*) Copy of speech, 6 Sept. 1870, made by Joseph Cowen in Newcastle, including references to Anglo-American relations. (A. 910)

ARMSTRONG WHITWORTH COLLECTION. Agreements. 1930's-40's.

Agreements relating to the patent rights of Michael Kadenacy in respect of his inventions connected with the two-stroke cycle internal combustion engine.

OTHER DOCUMENTS.

(*a*) An instruction from George II to the Mayor of Newcastle, Sir Charles Atkinson, John Balker alderman, Hugh Hornby, Edward

1. This collection originally contained the correspondence, diaries, etc., of Colonel Robert Ellison, written while in America, 1733-54. These were presented to Columbia University in November 1933, prior to the bulk of the Ellison MSS. being deposited here.

Collingwood, and John Baker 'to interrogate the respective commanders, masters, officers, mariners and others of the crew of any seized ship belonging to the rebellious colonies'. (20/3/50)
(*b*) A collection of 19th and 20th-century material from the firm of Merz and McLellan, electrical engineers, including reports, contracts, photographs, and designs of the Buenos Aires and Central Argentine Railways from the Philadelphia Electric, American Gas and Electric, Edison Electric, and Chicago Edison Companies.

UNIVERSITY OF NEWCASTLE UPON TYNE, University Library, Queen Victoria Road, Newcastle-upon-Tyne NE1 7RU

TREVELYAN PAPERS. 1836-1912.

(*a*) Papers of Sir Charles Philips Trevelyan Bt. (1870-1958), President of the Board of Education, 1924 and 1929-31, including his letter home from North America in 1898, a letter from Theodore Roosevelt to G.O. Trevelyan about the presidential election, 1908, fourteen short letters from G.O.T. to C.P.T. about America, 1908-12, and other references.
(*b*) Papers of Sir Walter Calverley Trevelyan, Bt. (1797-1879) including seven long letters to Sir Walter from his brother Arthur about A's visit to the U.S. in 1836, and over fifty from William Parker Snow, then a literary hack in New York, 1862-7.

RUNCIMAN PAPERS. 1910-39.

Papers of Walter Runciman, 1st Viscount Runciman of Doxford (1870-1949), President of the Board of Education, 1908-11, and of the Board of Trade, 1914-6 and 1931-7. American references for various dates betweeen 1910 and 1939, but the only major topics are the Arbitration Treaty of 1911, and economic relations around the times of Runciman's visits to the U.S. in 1932 and 1937, there being envelopes containing 43, 61 and 66 items, respectively, for each of these last.[1]

SOUTH TYNESIDE LIBRARIES, Central Library, Catherine Street, South Shields

FOX COLLECTION. American journals (4 volumes). 1831-68.

George Townshend Fox (1810-86), born at Westoe, South Shields, entered the firm of G. Sands & Hodgson, general merchants, Liverpool, in 1830; he was sent to America by Mr. Sands in 1831. Townshend was ordained in 1848 and was Vicar of St. Nicholas, Durham, from 1856 until his retirement in 1882.

The journal covers four separate visits: 1831-2, 1834, 1841, and 1868. The first is through the North-East; the second is down the Southern seaboard to New Orleans; the third is to New York and Ohio; and the fourth is through the North-East to Illinois, containing an account of the oil well at Oil City. The volumes contain comment on religion, social customs, cost of travel, etc.; the comparisons he makes in the fourth journal with New York twenty-four years previously are interesting.

WARWICKSHIRE

SIR ROBERT GEORGE MAXWELL THROCKMORTON, Coughton Court, Alcester

THROCKMORTON PAPERS. 1681, 1882.

(*a*) In a group of papers connected with the Popish Plot there is one of 24 Oct. 1681, which says that Shaftesbury has asked to be allowed to go to Carolina, but has been refused.[1]
(*b*) There are also three letters dated 1882, the first from J.W.F. Throckmorton of New York to the incumbent of Coughton, asking about the Throckmorton estate, the second a letter of advice from Mary Throckmorton, and the third the reply of the Rev. W.H. Thackwell to the American. (Folder 39, nos. 11-13)

REV. CHARLES E. SURMAN, UNITED REFORMED CHURCH (PRES./CONG'L), West Midland Provincial Archives, Spencer Street, Leamington Spa CV31 3NE

CONGREGATIONAL BIOGRAPHY.

Private collection of biographical materials and local church histories relating to the Congregational ministry and churches in Great Britain, *c.* 1640-1972. Among these are various fugitive references to ministers who emigrated to or came from the United States and Canada or received their theological training in one or more of the universities or colleges in the U.S.

The biographical collection is now card-indexed (over 30,000 names) and two copies are available, (*a*) at Dr. Williams's Library, 14 Gordon Square, London WC1H OAG, and (*b*) The Congregational Memorial Hall Trust Ltd., 2 Fleet Lane, London EC4. The compiler retains his original index and many cognate papers.

EARL OF DENBIGH, Pailton House, Rugby

DENBIGH PAPERS. Correspondence and diaries. 1671-1915.

(*a*) Letter from Elias Ashmole referring to Mr. Ogilby's new published account of America, 1671.
(*b*) Correspondence of the 6th Earl of Denbigh referring to American politics in the years prior to the War of Independence. Correspondence sent to the 6th Earl of Denbigh from Major John Bowater and Captain William Feilding while on active service in the Marines in America during the War of Independence.[1]

1. Catalogues of both of these collections have been compiled by A. Elliott and G. Williams and photocopies distributed by the Royal Commission on Historical Manuscripts.

1. H.M.C. x (iv), p. 173.

1. See M. Balderston and D. Syrett, *The Lost War* (Horizon Press, 1975).

(*c*) Correspondence relating to America's part in the French Revolutionary Wars, 1794.
(*d*) Diary of a visit by Gen. William H.A. Feilding to America, 1872.
(*e*) Diary, correspondence and press cuttings regarding the visit of the Honorable Artillery Company to America. Lord Denbigh was colonel of the H.A.C. and his wife accompanied him on this visit, which took place in 1903.
(*f*) Letters from William Jennings Bryan, Democratic presidential candidate, and from Theodore Roosevelt, to Lord Denbigh, 1903-4, 1910.
(*g*) Letters from the American Embassy in London, 1904-15.

PENNANT PAPERS. *c.* 1760-90.
Correspondence, notes, printed plans and engravings relating to the geography, climate, topography, and natural history of America, *c.* 1760-90, with a few papers relating to American politics, especially at the time of the War of Independence.

WARWICK COUNTY RECORD OFFICE, Priory Park, Cape Road, Warwick

HOLBECH OF FARNBOROUGH COLLECTION. Document. 1641. (L1/242)
Bill of lading by Henry Hazard, master of the ship *Sampson* of Bristol for George 'Willys' of Fenny Compton, Warwickshire, of goods for Boston to be delivered to Captain C(oll?)ins, Boston; dated at Bristol, 5 May 1641. (As many of the deeds in this collection are concerned with the Willis family of Fenny Compton, the George Willis mentioned is doubtless the one of that name who settled in Hartford, Conn., where he became governor 1642, and died in 1645.)

WARD-BOUGHTON-LEIGH OF BROWNSOVER COLLECTION. 1742-1813.
(*a*) Extract of will relating to slaves, 1784; four copy grants of land in South Carolina with sketch plans, 1742-63, 1813; appointment of Sir Egerton Leigh as Attorney-General of South Carolina, 1765. (CR 1623/577, 582, 687)
(*b*) Appointments and other papers relating to Sir Egerton Leigh as surveyor and later judge in South Carolina, 1746-81, including part of a journal by George Pawley relating to his mission to the Indians, 1746. (CR840/4)

PHILIPS OF WESTON HOUSE COLLECTION. George Philips and Co.: Business records (9 vols.). 1792-1830. (CR456/vols. 31-36, box 17)
Insurance and general commission business. Founded 1801 as London branch of the Manchester firm. The letter-books, nine volumes, 1801-30, include one for America, 1801-3, which contains correspondence with merchants in Philadelphia, New York, Baltimore, Charleston, S.C., etc., giving details of cargoes, ports of shipment, prices, and conditions of markets. One volume 'Correspondence' 1802, contains day-to-day notes of letters received and written, some of which are from America and from the shipping firm of G.C. Fox & Co., Falmouth, Cornwall. Mr. George Philips's 'Private letter-book 1820-1830' includes letters concerning property in America and difficulties encountered with American agents. The collection also contains some correspondence with Mrs. Rogers in New York, 1792-1802.

SEYMOUR OF RAGLEY COLLECTION. *c.* 1837-68. (CR114A)
(*a*) Pacific, North American, and West Indian naval stations: log-books, journal as commander-in-chief, order books, letter-books, correspondence, etc. of Sir George F. Seymour, *c.* 1837-56; correspondence from E.J. Seymour, 1867-8.
(*b*) Journal of a tour in America and Canada, 1840.
(*c*) Correspondence just before and during the American Civil War, 1859-64.
(*d*) Correspondence from Henry G. Seymour, in North America on active service, 1860.

WEST MIDLANDS

ARCHDIOCESE OF BIRMINGHAM ARCHIVES, Archbishop's House, St. Chad's Ringway, Birmingham, 4

MISCELLANEOUS LETTERS. 1790-1889.
(*a*) Reverend Robert Smelt at Rome to Bishop Thomas Talbot at Wolverhampton - mentions attempts by the Bishop of Baltimore (John Carroll) to get priests in London to go to America; likewise attempts by a Reverend Thayer of Boston. 1790. (A804)
(*b*) Bishop Luke Concannon to Bishop John Milner, 1809, lamenting his appointment as Bishop of New York. (A835)
(*c*) Bishop Concannon to Bishop Milner, 1810, reporting that he is obliged to go to New York. (A837)
(*d*) Letter from Reverend Thaddeus Bryozowski, General of the Jesuits, to one of the Vicars Apostolic, 1815. Regrets that he cannot find any missionaries to send to America. (A1136)
(*e*) Michael Flanagan to his brother, Reverend Thomas Flanagan at Oscott, 1848. Writes from Tacumaya, Mexico, giving a description of life in the U.S. Army, the country and people. (B1143)
(*f*) Reverend Edward McCartney in Illinois to Reverend V. Holcroft, 1889. Describes the prosperity there of priests and people. (B9930)

PUBLIC LIBRARIES, Paradise, Birmingham B3 3HQ

ZACHARY LLOYD PAPERS. Letters. 18th century.
'Among the letters of the 18th century there are several from Thomas Owen, Sarah Middleton, and others, in South Carolina.'[1]

RUSSELL FAMILY PAPERS.[2] 1731, 1735.
(*a*) Copy of the will, 28 Jan. 1731, of William Russell the younger,

1. H.M.C. x (iv), p. 450. (Listed as in possession of S. Zachary Lloyd, Esq., Areley Hall, Stourport, Worcs.)
2. These papers are mentioned in R.A. Pelham, 'The West Midland Iron Industry and the American Market in the Eighteenth Century', *University of Birmingham Historical Journal*, vol. ii, p. 154, 1950.

ironmaster, of Birmingham. Devises all his properties in Britain and America to his father, William Russell. (418824)

See also Russell Diaries below.

(*b*) Indenture between William Russell the elder, ironmaster, of Birmingham, Thomas Russell the elder, his eldest son, and William Russell the younger, another son of the said William Russell the elder, concerning the Principio Works in the province of Maryland, and a furnace called 'Potomack' in the colony of Virginia in America. 19 Aug. 1731 (418822). (And also a similar indenture of 3 Dec. 1735 (418827).)

MATTHEW BOULTON COLLECTION.[3] *c.* 100 boxes of letters, 1750-1810; *c.* 50 letter-books, ledgers, account books and journals of the firms with which Boulton was connected, *c.* 1750-1850.

Matthew Boulton (1728-1809), engineer, corresponded with most of the leading men of the day on topics of considerable scientific and technological interest. The letters are filed alphabetically in boxes, and there is an eleven-volume typescript index under names of correspondents which gives the general contents of each letter. Some names under which letters of American interest can be found are: Dr. J. Baader, Sir F. Baring, S. Bayard, Elias Boudinot, A. Buchanan, T. Cockran, Lord Dartmouth, Benjamin Franklin, J. Gilpin, Peter P. Goelet, Sir G. Jackson, Thomas Jefferson, Rufus King, W. Knox, J. Lacy, Ralph Mather, J.H. Mitchell, S. Moore, I. Ogden, R.N. Patterson, Joseph Priestley, D. Rittenhouse, Nicholas Roosevelt, Turnbull, Forbes & Co., J. Tustin, John Warder, George Watson.

Subjects include supplying copper blanchette to the United States Mint; building a new mint; the state of markets; trade in hardware, buttons, nails, guns, etc.; inventions.

In addition there are boxes containing single subjects, some of which are indexed separately. One labelled 'America' containing a wrapper endorsed 'American disputes 1775' includes notes, drafts of letters, and newspapers concerned with the Birmingham petitions of 1775; one box labelled '(Various) Mints' contains a bundle labelled 'United States Mint, estimates and proposals 1830'; one box containing correspondence of Boulton and Watt with Dr. William Small, physician and natural philosopher, mostly concerning inventions; a manuscript entitled 'An estimate of iron supposed to be manufactured into nails annually, America 1775'.[4]

Letter-books, ledgers, etc., include: Cash books 1752-1814, and letter-books 1757-80, for Boulton & Fothergill. Letter-books 1784, for Boulton & Scale. Boulton's private letter-books *c.* 1760-94. Letter-books 1796-1801, 1815-9, for Boulton Plate Company. Mint and Coinage day book 1834-49, etc.

LYTTELTON PAPERS (Hagley Hall Collection). 2 documents. 1755.

(*a*) Letters patent of George II appointing William Henry Lyttelton Captain-General and Governor-in-Chief of the Province of South Carolina. 1 Mar. [1755]. (390025)

(*b*) Commission from George II to Lyttelton to be Vice-Admiral Commissary and Deputy in the office of Vice-Admiralty in the Province of South Carolina in the room of James Glen. Given at London in the High Court of Admiralty of England, 6 Mar. 1755. (352031)

BOULTON AND WATT COLLECTION. Letters. 1794-1812.

(*a*) 4 Nov. 1794 - 23 Feb. 1805 from Robert Fulton, civil engineer and inventor, concerning the purchase of a suitable steam engine for boat propulsion. Letter, New York, 15 Sept. 1810, mentioning that the engine made for him in 1804 has for four years been used to drive a boat on the Hudson River, and asking for a further engine as he wishes to provide boats on other rivers. Letter, New York, 4 Jan. 1812, dealing with the violation of his patent for steam-boats.[5]

(*b*) Clermont, N.Y., 4 Nov. 1798, from Robert R. Livingston to James Watt, in which he sets forth his ideas on steam-boats.

(*c*) 24 Aug. 1793 - 7 May 1812, from Joseph Priestley, Jr., to James Watt, Jr., the first written just before Priestley left for Northumberland, Pa., four from Northumberland, and four from Philadelphia. Priestley urges Watt to emigrate, and describes his own situation in Northumberland. For the rest the letters cover mainly personal matters. Priestley left for England in Jan. 1812.

RUSSELL DIARIES.[6] 3 journals (and typescript copies), paper. 1794-1801.

Include the journals kept by Misses Martha and Mary Russell, and Thomas Pougher Russell, of their tour to America, 1794-5, travels in America and return voyage, 1796-1801. They were captured by the French during their voyage to America and taken to France. Joseph Bryan secured their release. There is also a manuscript article composed for or by William Russell and addressed to the editor of the *Monthly Magazine*, 1801. (12 pages).

See also the Russell Family Papers, above; and the Russell of Birmingham Papers, Add. MSS. 4499-45022 in the British Library.

EDWARDS, SON, BIGWOOD AND MATHEWS. Deed. 1806.

A solicitor's collection which contains one deed (no. III) relating to land in the county of Franklin, Ga. Parties: Chester Gould, John Startin, Samuel Jackson. 1806.

LADIES' SOCIETY FOR THE RELIEF OF NEGRO SLAVES. Minute-book. 1825-52. (302206)

Chiefly directed towards slaves in British territories, but there are references to talks given to the Society on slavery in the United States and letters read from correspondents in the Southern states.

KING, WILSON (1846-1930). Autograph letters collected by King: 2 volumes. (569342)

United States Consul in Birmingham 1879-85. The letters are very miscellaneous. A brief inspection showed two notes signed by Lincoln on one of which is written 'allow Francis T. King of Baltimore to pass with the English Friends through our lines to North Carolina. Oct. 25, 1864';[7] and two letters, 1880, 1882, from Bret Harte from Glasgow, where he was Consul 1880-5, concerning an invitation to speak in Birmingham and asking for an address, etc.

BIRMINGHAM COLLECTION. Printed pamphlet (4 pages).[8] 1865. (359807)

A copy of the correspondence between the American Secretary of

3. See John Hinckley Mitchell, *The Mitchell-Boulton Correspondence, 1787-1792* (New York, priv. print., 1931); J.P. Muirhead, ed., *The Origin and Progress of the Mechanical Inventions of James Watt, Illustrated by His Correspondence with his Friends and Specifications of his Patents*, 3 vols. (London, 1854); A. and N. Clow, *The Chemical Revolution* (London, 1952); B.D. Bargar, 'Matthew Boulton and the Birmingham Petition of 1775', *William and Mary Quarterly*, vol. xiii, pp. 26-39, 1956; and R.E. Schofield, 'Membership of the Lunar Society of Birmingham', *Annals of Science*, vol. xii, pp. 118-36, 1956.

4. See W.H.B. Court, *The Rise of the Midland Industries, 1600-1838* (London, 1938), p. 196, for use of this manuscript.

5. See H.W. Dickinson, *Robert Fulton:Engineer and Artist, his Life and Works* (London, 1913).

6. See S.H. Jeyes, *The Russells of Birmingham in the French Revolution and in America, 1791-1814* (London, 1911).

7. See *Collected Works of Abraham Lincoln*, ed. by R.P. Basler, vol. viii (New Brunswick, N.J., 1953), p. 76.

8. From City of Birmingham Public Libraries, Reference Department, *A Catalogue of the Birmingham Collection, Supplement, 1918-1931* (Birmingham, 1931).

State, W.H. Seward, and J.M.G. Underhill, concerning the latter's dismissal from the post of United States Consular Agent in Birmingham in favour of Elihu Burritt.

AUTOGRAPH LETTERS.

There are a few letters of American interest, including one, 18 Nov. 1885, from Andrew Carnegie to Joseph Chamberlain, enclosing copy of the *Statistical Atlas of the U.S.*, inscribed 'To Joseph Chamberlain. The leader of the masses and future premier of Britain I send this record of the reign of the people under institutions based upon the only true doctrine "the political equality of the citizen".' (This Atlas became worn out and discarded, but the Library possesses another copy with a similar inscription to the men of Birmingham.) (67419)

JOHN HARDMAN STUDIOS. Business records. 1899-1913.

The firm of John Hardman, which still exists in Birmingham, made monumental brasses and stained-glass windows from 1845 onwards. They had considerable trade with America. References are scattered throughout the collection, but the following are to be particularly noted:
(*a*) Five U.S.A. letter-books, July 1899 - Dec. 1913.
(*b*) One U.S.A. order book, Sept. 1899 - June 1913.

CADDICK, HELEN (1843-1927). Travel diary (typescript with photographs): vol. 6. 1900. (336856)

Miss Caddick visited the principal American cities, often staying with American friends. She describes social customs, scenery, and institutions. (Also visited the Philippines, 1913-4, vol. 12. 336862).

THE MAIN LIBRARY, UNIVERSITY OF BIRMINGHAM, P.O. Box 363, Birmingham B15 2TT

CORBETT COLLECTION. Letter. 1777.

In Autograph Letters, vol. 1, there is a Paris letter, 29 May 1777, from George Chalmers, to George Carlting, London. In code but deciphered. Chalmers was an English spy during the War of Independence. He speaks of an indiscretion by Lord George Germain; he suggests that France and Spain wish to place themselves again where they were before the last war, that France would be glad of the offer of Canada, that Pensacola and both Floridas might be offered to Spain. Negotiations with Baron Schulenburg are mentioned and a visit by Beaumarchais to Dunkirk about artillery. Franklin and Dean are also mentioned.

ALLASON COMMONPLACE BOOK.

Commonplace book of Henry Allason of Virginia (fl. 1784-1802), including mention of a proposal to open a school in Georgetown; also including copies of letters, e.g. two to George Washington.

CHANCE BROS. Account books. 1815-31.

American merchants, Birmingham. The firm of W. & G. Chance was founded in 1815, with William Chance handling the business in Birmingham and his brother George in New York. Besides the account books for W. and G. Chance (1815-26), the Library also has the account book (1821-31) of another brother, Lucas Chance. Lucas Chance's account book contains information about his export business - mainly to America - carried out beginning in 1815 from St. Paul's Wharf, London. He dealt mainly in Crown window glass, and had business relations with his brothers.

FAIRCHILD, LUCIUS. Letter. 1876. (L.Add 1131)

23 Oct. 1876, to Henry A. Bright, giving memories of pioneering days in California, *à propos* of Joaquin Miller's *Life among the Modocs*.

CHAMBERLAIN, JOSEPH (1836-1914). Papers. 1885-1925.

(*a*) A collection of over 700 documents relating to Joseph Chamberlain's part in the Fisheries Conference in Washington in 1887. This includes his private diary and a solid correspondence. (MSS. JC 3/1-14)
(*b*) A smaller collection of miscellaneous Americana from Joseph Chamberlain's collection, of the period 1890-9. (MSS. JC 7/4/2-3)
(*c*) The massive correspondence between Mary, Joseph Chamberlain's third wife, and her mother, Mrs. Endicott of Boston, Mass., over the years 1885-1925. (MSS. AC 4/3/1-2740)
(*d*) A collection of seventy letters relating to Beatrice Chamberlain's visit to the U.S.A., 1897-8. (MSS. BC 1/1-4)
There are also scattered letters to or from the U.S.A. in all the four Chamberlain sequences, but the above are the only significant collections.

OTHER LETTERS.

The Library also holds some miscellaneous letters from Americans in the John Galsworthy and Francis Brett Young collections.

WOODBROOKE COLLEGE, Bristol Road, Birmingham, 29

BEVAN-NAISH COLLECTION. [1]

This collection of Quaker manuscripts, which consists of twenty bound volumes (some of which are indexed) and three boxes, is catalogued. A brief inspection revealed the following items of American interest:
(*a*) Bevan-Naish Library, vol. 4, includes a deed with William Penn's signature; a list of the names of Friends who visited America from Great Britain, 1656-1775; and of Friends who visited Britain from Pennsylvania and New Jersey, 1693-1773.
(*b*) 'Some account of the forepart of the life of Eliz. Ashridge ...', 1713-55. Mainly an account by Elizabeth Ashridge of her life and conversion to the Quaker faith in America, including some account of travels in New England and Rhode Island, her experiences as a bonded servant and as a teacher.
(*c*) 'Letter-book 1770.' Contains a copy of an epistle from some squaw Indians to women Friends, 1797.
(*d*) 'John Pemberton and other letters.' This volume contains extracts from two letters from Philadelphia: one concerns the adventures of Mary Prior, shipwrecked on her way to America, with some details of conditions on board and her fellow passengers, 1798; the other, n.d., gives an account of the conversion of Nicholas Waln, a lawyer of Philadelphia.
(*e*) An envelope inscribed 'Hicksites' contains an extract from a letter, Philadelphia, 11 July 1832, from Samuel Bettle to T. Robson, giving the verdict of a chancery suit in Jersey in favour of the Friends— 'the Hicksites are seceders'.

1. Used by Arnold Lloyd, *Quaker Social History, 1669-1738* (London, 1950).

(*f*) Minutes of the North Warwickshire Monthly Meetings of the Society of Friends, 1862-71. Contains introductions to the Friends Monthly Meetings in Pennsylvania on behalf of Warwickshire Friends settling in Pennsylvania, 1863; a list of Friends who have left Birmingham for America with addresses and circumstances; report of Friends appointed to correspond with members abroad, 1864.

CITY RECORD OFFICE, 9 Hay Lane, Coventry CV1 5RF

CITY ARCHIVES. Letter. 1615.

Covering letter, 22 Mar. 1615, from the Privy Council to the Mayor and Aldermen of Coventry, to a declaration (not found) of the state of the colony in Virginia with a project to help it by a lottery, which the Mayor and Aldermen are asked to support.[1]

TRANSPORTATION RECORDS.

There is a little correspondence, 1741-52, with shipping merchants engaged in the transport of convicts to Maryland and Virginia, together with a few bonds, vouchers, receipts, and copies of orders to 1766.[2]

DOMMETT MSS. Two letters. 1830.

Two letters, 1830, from Benjamin Tilt to James Powney of Coventry, describing his preparations for emigration to America, the hardships of the voyage, and the difficulties which he encountered in trying to establish himself as a ribbon weaver in the United States. (Acc. 373)

MODERN RECORDS CENTRE, UNIVERSITY OF WARWICK LIBRARY, Coventry CV4 7AL

LADY ALLEN OF HURTWOOD (1897-1976). Landscape architect, campaigner for pre-school education and imaginative playground facilities.

The papers of her husband, Clifford Allen, are in the University of South Carolina Library. Her own surviving papers in the Modern Records Centre include correspondence and papers about her visit to the U.S.A. in 1965, organized by the U.S. National Committee of OMEP, and other correspondence with Americans. (MSS. 121)

ROWLAND BARRETT (1877-1950). Socialist, journalist, and campaigner.

File on reformed spelling, including letters from five American spelling reformers, with accompanying ephemera, 1944-8. (MSS. 83/3/RS/1-57)

BIRMINGHAM SMALL ARMS CO. LTD. Company records. 1908-58.

Reports to company *re* trade with U.S. (including business of Burton, Griffiths & Co. Ltd., 1921-2, 1958. File *re* Australian small arms factory contract lost to Pratt & Whitney, 1908-15. (MSS. 19A/1/2/43-4, 47-53; MSS. 19A/3/6; MSS. 19A/7/TE/14)

HOWARD LEAGUE FOR PENAL REFORM. Notebook. 1904.

Notebook recording visit of Secretary of Howard Association, Edward Grubb, to U.S., Jan.-Mar. 1904, describing visits to institutions and interviews. (MSS. 16A/7/7)

MAITLAND-SARA PAPERS. 1935-45.

These include some items relating to the American Trotskyite movement, 1935-45, and to the International Left Opposition in the U.S.A. (MSS. 15)

SIR LESLIE SCOTT (1869-1950). Barrister, Conservative M.P., Solicitor General, Lord Justice of Appeal. Letters.

Approx. thirty letters to Scott from the American jurist, Oliver Wendell Holmes, Jr., 1912-34. Also three letters from Felix Frankfurter. (MSS. 119/3/P/HO; MSS. 119/3/S/LE)

TILLETT/MACKAY PAPERS. 2 letters. 1902-3.

Two letters from Sam Gompers, A.F.L., to Ben Tillett, 1902, 1903. (MSS. 74/3/1/26-7)

UNION OF CONSTRUCTION ALLIED TRADES & TECHNICIANS. Union records. 1895-1920.

Amalgamated Society of Carpenters and Joiners: membership records and reference books, 1895-1920, include details of American branches of the A.S.C. & J. (MSS. 78)

WHELAN COLLECTION. Bulletins. 1939-74.

Includes Socialist Workers' Party (USA) Internal Discussion Bulletins, 1939-73, and Internal Information Bulletins, 1945-74. (MSS. 95)

1. Mentioned in Benjamin Poole, *Coventry: its History and Antiquities* (London, 1870), p.382.
2. Two of the letters are quoted in Frederick Smith, *Coventry. Six Hundred Years of Municipal Life* (Coventry, 1945), pp. 103-4.

VISCOUNT COBHAM, Hagley Hall, Stourbridge

LYTTELTON PAPERS. 1703-1894. (bulk acc. no. 5806)[1]

(*a*) Letter-book of William Henry Lyttelton, Baron Lyttelton of Frankley, while Governor of South Carolina, 1759-60. (parcel no. 2)
(*b*) Letter-book of William Henry Lyttelton, Baron Lyttelton of Frankley, while Governor of South Carolina, containing also some dispatches of Governor Haldane and Lieutenant Governor Moore, 1759-66. (parcel no. 5)
(*c*) Letter-book of William Henry Lyttelton, Baron Lyttelton of Frankley, while Governor of South Carolina, 1757-9. (parcel no. 6)
(*d*) Sixty-nine letters to Lord Lyttelton as Governor of South Carolina and Jamaica, including several from William Pitt, 1757-65. (parcel no. 11)
(*e*) About 130 Acts of Parliament, petitions, accounts, receipts, and other papers mainly concerning William Henry Lyttelton during his term as Governor of South Carolina and Jamaica. 1703-1894. (parcel no. 13)

1. These papers are now on indefinite loan at the Hereford and Worcester County Record Office, Worcester.

OSCOTT COLLEGE, Sutton Coldfield, Birmingham B73 5AA

PAPERS. 2 volumes.

'Noticia de la California, y de su conquista espiritual y temporal hasta el año 1768', 2 vols., *c.* 1768. Relates to the Jesuit missions in California.[1]

1. H.M.C. i, p. 90.

WIGHT, ISLE OF

RUSKIN GALLERIES, Bembridge School, Bembridge, Isle of Wight

WHITEHOUSE, J. HOWARD (1873-1955).[1] Correspondence and papers. 1916-55.

Liberal M.P. 1910-9; Parliamentary Private Secretary to the Chancellor of the Exchequer 1913-5. Whitehouse visited the United States on a number of occasions, including Oct. 1916-Apr. 1917, when he held conversations with Colonel House on the subject of American mediation in the war. Defeated in the general election of 1918, he founded the Bembridge School, putting into practice his own educational theories and devoting much time to trying to establish the teaching of American history as a normal part of English education.

The material includes the following:

(*a*) American mediation, 1916-7.

(i) Original correspondence with Colonel House.

(ii) Reports of conversations and transcripts of letters between Whitehouse and House, 14 Nov. 1916 - 14 Apr. 1917. (During this period they were in almost daily communication.)

(iii) Notes on conversations with House, 18 Apr. 1917.

(iv) Reports of interviews, also on the subject of American mediation, with Secretary of State Robert Lansing, Secretary of the Interior F.K. Lane, and Counsellor Polk; views of Oswald Garrison Villard (with information concerning Henry Morgenthau, Jr.) and Sir Cecil Spring-Rice; reports on the interchange of news and views with America, and on the political situation there (this latter prepared for Whitehouse by M.W. Davis).

(*b*) Miscellaneous correspondence, 1916-55.

(i) Letters, 1916-45, from Oswald Garrison Villard.

(ii) Three files of miscellaneous correspondence and papers, 1916-17, consisting of letters to American universities, newspapers and periodicals, newspaper reports on Whitehouse's lectures in the United States, etc.

(iii) Five files of correspondence, 1923-41, concerning the Sulgrave Institution; among the correspondents are J.A. Stewart, H.S. Perris, and Mrs. Duncan-Whyte. (Further correspondence, up to 1955, is likely.) Correspondence with E.E. Browne concerning Whitehouse's gift to New York University in 1926 of an exhibition illustrating English education. Reports and correspondence of the sub-committee for teaching American history in English schools.

(iv) Correspondence with American bodies in connexion with the American architecture exhibition held at Bembridge in 1928.

(v) Correspondence, 1938-41, between Whitehouse and the headmasters of English schools concerning the teaching of American history in English schools.

(*c*) Articles, pamphlets, lectures, etc., by Whitehouse, from 1916 onwards, on American education and other aspects of American life and culture.

1. See James S. Dearden, 'J. Howard Whitehouse and Anglo-American Understanding', *Bulletin of the British Association for American Studies*, no. vii, pp. 23-27, 1958.

WILTSHIRE

LIBRARY OF THE WILTSHIRE ARCHAEOLOGICAL AND NATURAL HISTORY SOCIETY, 41 Long Street, Devizes SN10 1NS

WYNDHAM, HENRY (1709-88). 25 draft letters to his son. 1765-67.

The Wyndham family had great influence in Salisbury. The son, Henry Penruddocke Wyndham (1736-1819), was a topographer and M.P. for Wiltshire 1795-1812, in the main supporting Pitt's administration. The draft letters from Henry Wyndham were in reply to letters written by the son while on a European tour. They are a complete set, and contain social and political news, including proceedings in Parliament concerning the unrest in America.

MARQUESS OF BATH, Longleat, Warminster

BATH PAPERS. 1607-1778.

(*a*) '... bundle of letters and papers relating to ... Newfoundland ... Carolina ... New York and New England.'[1] n.d. (Coventry Papers, vols. LXXVI, LXXVII)

(*b*) Various papers relating to the plantations during the seventeenth and early eighteenth centuries.[2] (Prior Papers, vols. XVI, XVII)

(*c*) Two parcels labelled 'Virginia and Surinam' and 'Virginia and Barbadoes'. The former contains address, 1674, by Virginians against royal grant of all lands between 'Pottamock and Rapahamock' to Lord Hopton and others in (?) 1652. The latter contains the patent to Sir Thomas Gates, and various letters, charters, and commissions (to Sir Francis Wyatt and Sir W. Berkeley and others) at various times between 1607 and 1663.[3] (Coventry Papers, vols. LXXVI, LXVIII)

(*d*) '(1628, March?) Instructions to shipwrights sent to Virginia to procure masts and ships, timber out of the woods of that country.

1. H.M.C., iv, p. 237.
2. H.M.C., iii, p. 193.
3. H.M.C., iv, pp. 236-7.

Instructions to Captain John Harvey, Governor there; and proposed additions; for him to carry on war against the natives.'[4] (Whitelocke Papers, vol. III)

(*e*) Letters, 1674-7, from Henry Coventry, Secretary of State, to Major Andros, Governor of New York, and Sir William Berkeley, Governor of Virginia. [No indication of contents.][5] (Coventry Papers, LXXVI, LXVIII)

(*f*) 'An interesting account by Edward Randolph of the State of New England, he being sent from England by the King, and letters by him.' (14 pages.) 1676.[6] (Coventry Papers, LXXVII)

(*g*) The correspondence of Matthew Prior while he was engaged in various diplomatic missions in the Low Countries and France includes a number of letters mentioning the American aspect of the negotiations leading up to the Peace of Ryswick, 1697, but nothing of any length or importance.[7] (Prior Papers, XVIII)

(*h*) Among the papers of Thomas Thynne, 3rd Viscount Weymouth and 1st Marquis of Bath, there is an envelope marked 'American affairs, 1777-78. War of Independence', containing twenty-nine letters.

WILTSHIRE COUNTY RECORD OFFICE, County Hall, Trowbridge BA14 8JG

FORMAN FAMILY PAPERS. Accounts, letters, etc. 1681-1767.

Family and estate papers, 1681-1767, relating to the Forman family and others of Chester, Pennsylvania. Included are three letters describing the privations of an individual in the ship *Nicholson*, taken by French privateers off Maryland. (546/253)

SUFFOLK AND BERKSHIRE ARCHIVES. Bundle of papers including letters, maps, copies of deeds, etc. 1773-1808.

Among the papers of the Howard family, Earls of Suffolk and Berkshire, are some relating to the purchase of lands in the province of New York by Colonel Thomas Howard from General Bradstreet. (88/9/18)

WILLES AND LOVELL FAMILIES' PAPERS (of Cole Park, Malmesbury). Letters. 1838.[1]

1838, from J.G. Shawe to his mother, Mrs. Lovell, about travel along the Great Lakes, affairs in Quebec, etc. (161/113)

OTHER RECORDS. 1683-1890.

(*a*) Deed of land in the Nipmug country in Massachusetts, 1683. (516/13)

(*b*) Letter describing events in Boston, 1774. (1300/1952)

(*c*) (i) Papers about the government of Samoa in 1876, and the part played in the unrest there by a U.S. agent, Col. Steinberger.

(ii) Papers relating to the Denver and Rio Grande Western Railway, the Chicago and Rock Island Railway, the Costa Rica Railway, the U.S. Land and Emigration Company, the Minerva iron mine (New York), and lands in New York State, Colorado, and New Mexico. Also letters of the Blackmore family from Santa Fe, New Mexico. (776)[2]

EARL OF PEMBROKE, Wilton House, Salisbury

PEMBROKE PAPERS. Letter. 1780.

New York, 26 Oct. 1780, from Augustus Reebkomp to Lord Herbert, on the fleets of Rodney and Arbuthnot; the impending final defeat of the rebellion; Gates's defeat in Carolina; and Arnold's defection from the American side; the latter has been made a Brigadier-General and appointed 'to raise a regiment of as great scoundrels as himself if he can find them'.[1]

YORKSHIRE, NORTH

NORTH YORKSHIRE COUNTY LIBRARY, Victoria Avenue, Harrogate

GREEVES, CHARLES (1795?-1847). Diary (1 volume). 1842-5.

Land agent and surveyor, Harrogate. His very miscellaneous diary includes reports of visits from friends emigrating to the United States - mainly to the Illinois area; items of news concerning local people living in the United States; and extracts from letters to relatives in Harrogate from T. Ellinsworth, a tailor of Elgin, Ill., from Mr. Brydone of Rock Hall on the Des Plaines River, Ill., and from Mrs. Mary Birch of Kentucky and Missouri. The extracts deal mainly with the quality of the soil, the yield of various crops, etc.

LORD BOLTON, Bolton Hall, Leyburn

BOLTON PAPERS. 1 document. 1782.

Papers of Thomas Orde, afterwards Orde-Powlett, 1st Baron Bolton (1746-1807), Secretary to the Treasury under Shelburne in 1782. Included is a 'List of Americans applying for allowances whose cases have not yet been considered', 3rd June 1782, giving the name, profession, residence, and family of applicants, and names of those persons certifying the application.

C.K.C. ANDREW, ESQ., F.S.A., Hill Brow, Brompton, Northallerton DL6 2TZ

SEVEN YEARS WAR: BRITISH NAVAL AND MILITARY ACTIONS. 1 sheet. 1758.

The manuscript includes a list of the names of French ships burnt, taken, sunk, etc., on various dates in June and July 1758; the numbers of killed and wounded 'the day the troops landed'; the number taken prisoner in the 'garrison of Louisbourgh', etc. The manuscript is thought to be in the hand of, and is endorsed by and found in the family archive of, Philip Rashleigh (1729 - 1811), antiquary and M.P.

4. H.M.C., iii, p. 190.
5. Ibid.
6. H.M.C., iv, p. 237.
7. H.M.C., iii, p. 193.

---

1. Access to these papers is not permitted by the present owner.
2. All of the items in W.R.O. 776 date from *c.* 1870-90, and are at the present time unlisted and only roughly sorted.

---

1. Transcript, H.M.C. ix (ii), p. 383.

NORTH YORKSHIRE COUNTY RECORD OFFICE, County Hall, Northallerton DL7 8SG

BRUCE-DUNDAS MSS. 5 letters. 1778-86.

(*a*) Major A. Dundas, Quebec, to Thomas Dundas, 26 July 1778, discussing reasons for General Burgoyne's defeat at Saratoga, and speculating on the progress of peace negotiations. (ZNK X 2/1/46)
(*b*) Lt. Col. James Bruce, Halifax, to Thomas Dundas, 3 Oct. 1778, commenting on military matters. (ZNK X 2/1/52)
(*c*) Col. James Bruce, Halifax, to Sir Thomas Dundas, 26 Nov. 1781, noting the 'exhorbitantly dear' prices in America. (ZNK X 2/1/238)
(*d*) Charles Morris, Halifax, to Col. James Bruce, 70th Regiment, 20 Nov. 1781, asking Bruce to join with Sir Andrew Hammond in recommending that his appointment as chief surveyor in Halifax be confirmed. (ZNK X 2/L/239)
(*e*) Col. Thomas Dundas, Halifax, to Sir Thomas Dundas, Arlington St., 1 Feb. 1786, mentioning plans for a tour of Nova Scotia and New Brunswick. (ZNK X 2/1/570)

BERESFORD-PEIRSE ARCHIVE. 2 papers. *c*. 1806, 1812. (ZBA)
(*a*) Beresford, Sir John Poo (1766-1844). Memorandum (1 sheet). *c*. 1806.
Admiral; commanded on North American station 1806. The memorandum, believed to be written by Beresford, is dated 13 Dec., no year. It concerns negotiations for an attack on Mexico between Mr. (Aaron) Burr and Mr. M(erry, British Minister to the United States), and news of preparations in New Orleans for 'some expedition'.[1]
(*b*) War of 1812: directions for the taking of Philadelphia (1 sheet). *c*. 1812.

This manuscript was found among the documents of Admiral Sir John Poo Beresford, who was a senior officer on the American coast 1812-4. It is a detailed plan for an attack on Philadelphia.

QUARTER SESSIONS RECORDS.

Bonds, memoranda of contracts, justices' certificates, and orders for payment of fees occasionally relate to the transportation of convicted persons, mainly 1736-73.

OTHER RECORDS. 1775.
(*a*) MS. paper discussing relations of Britain and America, 24 Feb. 1775. (ZNK X 1/16/8)
(*b*) MS. account of battle of Charles Town, Boston, 22 June 1775. (ZNK X 1/16/9)

CENTRAL LIBRARY , Howard Street, Rotherham S65 1JH

PAINE, THOMAS (1737-1809). Letter. 1789.

London, 16 Jan. 1789, from Paine to Thomas Walker of Rotherham, deals with current British political and constitutional issues - '... as a republican I think the British Constitution a hodge-podge'.

SCARBOROUGH BOROUGH COUNCIL, Town Hall, Scarborough YO11 2HG

MUNICIPAL RECORDS. Letter and copy of petition.[1] 1813. (Bundle C4)

22 Apr. 1813, from A.W. Morgan, written from London, to B. Fowler, Trinity House, Scarborough, transmits the (manuscript) form of a petition to Parliament against the admission into the United Kingdom of articles from the United States in neutral shipping, urging that the shipowners of Scarborough consider action on this without delay; Morgan adds that the shipowners and merchants of Liverpool have already petitioned, and those of London are in the course of signing.

BORTHWICK INSTITUTE OF HISTORICAL RESEARCH, St. Anthony's Hall, Peaseholme Green, York YO1 2PW

The Institute houses the archives of the Province and Archdiocese of York.

VIRGINIA TOBACCO TRADE PAPERS.[1] 1675-7.

A number of documents relate to the Virginia tobacco trade in 1675-7, these apparently coming from cases before the Archbishop's Court of Admiralty. The papers consist of evidence, accusations, etc., in the damaged cargo case of Abel Grant *v*. John Bothomley and Andrew Perrott (DRP/Adm.Ct. CP. 1675), and in the breach of charter case of Thomas Cox *v*. George Pattison (DRP/Adm.Ct. CP. 1676). Some are written in Latin and French.

COLLEGE OF WILLIAM AND MARY. Petitions. 1773, 1775.

Appeals to Lord Chancellor from Masters and Professors of the College of William and Mary, Virginia, against the Bishop of London and Mayor and Corporation of the same concerning timber at Brafferton, Yorks. 14 May 1773, 13 June 1775. (CFS. 13)

WRIGHT, JOHN. Letter.[2] 1774.

The letter, which is much damaged, was written, 12 May 1774, from New York to Wright's wife Jane at Paper-mill-beck, near Tadcaster, Yorks. It concerns his plans for buying a well-wooded farm 260 miles from New York and for shipping the wood to Hull.

1. The memorandum appears to add no further details to the story as told in T.P. Abernethy, *The Burr Conspiracy* (London and New York, 1954).

1. Noted in *Catalogue of Ancient Documents Belonging to the Corporation of Scarborough* (Scarborough, 1915), [pages not numbered].

1. The Library of the University of Virginia holds typescripts of much of this material. Also microfilms made by the Virginia Colonial Records Project.
2. A photograph of this letter is held by the Long Island Historical Society, N.Y.

YORKSHIRE, SOUTH

DONCASTER METROPOLITAN BOROUGH COUNCIL, Archives Service, 1 Priory Place, Doncaster

CLARK PAPERS. Diaries. 1837-57. (Books 1-5)

Diaries of the Clark family of Doncaster, Quakers who were involved with liberal causes in the second quarter of the nineteenth century. The diaries include one by William Clark for 1837-8, which has references to the anti-slavery movement. There is also information of American interest in the papers of Richard Ecroyd Clark.

DEPARTMENT OF LOCAL HISTORY AND ARCHIVES, SHEFFIELD CITY LIBRARY, Sheffield S1 1XZ

Most of the following collections are noted or described in *Guide to the Manuscript Collections in the Sheffield City Libraries* (Sheffield, 1956).

WHARNCLIFFE MUNIMENTS. 1749-1893.

This large collection of family papers includes the following:

(*a*) Edward Wortley Montagu (1678-1761), M.P. Montagu was an opponent of the Bill to reduce duty on American iron, and his papers include a bundle containing printed leaflets and pamphlets on the subject, answers in manuscript to some of these, and a few letters and copies of letters about the Bill from Joseph Broadbent of the Wortley Wire Works. 1749-50. (Wh. M. 118)

(*b*) Ainslie and Young Families. (Wh. M. 445)

(i) Letters, 1794-5, from J.A. Stuart, later Stuart-Wortley, when a young naval officer, to Miss C. Ainslie (afterwards Mrs. Young) of Quebec.

(ii) Letters, copies of memorials, etc., from John Young and Mrs. C. Young, 1817-8. John Young was a member of the Executive Council of Lower Canada and was considered entitled to some recompense from the government.

(iii) Several bundles of letters, memorials, etc., from Mrs. C. Young and her son Gilbert, and from Lord Bathurst and others, concerning recompense for the services of John Young, now deceased; 1819-30. The letters are addressed from Quebec and London.

(*c*) Bundle of about a dozen letters, 1805-44, from Col. Thomas Talbot, pioneer colonist in Upper Canada.[1] (Wh. M. 444)

(*d*) A few letters, Quebec, 1820-7, from George Ryland, concerning the office of Receiver-General of Lower Canada. (Wh. M. 447)

(*e*) John Stuart-Wortley, 2nd Baron Wharncliffe (1801-55). The diary kept while he travelled in America in 1824-5 is so faded as to be virtually illegible. (Wh. M. 450-2)

(*f*) Edward Stuart-Wortley-Mackenzie, 1st Earl of Wharncliffe (1827-99):

(i) Three letters, 1840 and 1852, from Charles Sumner, concerning, *inter alia*, Pierce's nomination, Daniel Webster, the Fugitive Slave Bill, and the publication of 'the Cuban correspondence'. A letter, 1846, from W.W. Storey of Boston asks for material to be used in the biography of his father. (Wh. M. 503)

(ii) Printed matter and letters, 1863-5, mostly relating to the Southern Independence Association, of which Wharncliffe was president. The printed material consists of leaflets issued by various organizations urging the necessity of peace, giving details of fund-raising for relief of Southern prisoners, etc. The letters include two from Charles Francis Adams, a number from James Spence in Liverpool, and Alexander Collie in London, and a large group so faded as to be illegible. (Wh. M. 460)

(iii) Over 100 letters, 1864-72, dealing with various aspects of the Civil War; many are very faded. There are a large number of letters from Spence and Collie relating to cotton shipments and other business affairs; letters from Americans now living in Europe, asking for aid, giving first-hand accounts of treatment of prisoners, etc.; letters from correspondents in England concerning disposal of the funds collected for relief, and attitudes towards the war. (Wh. M. 461)

(iv) Powder River Cattle Company. Two bundles contain letters, letter copies, printed reports, and other papers of this British-financed Wyoming cattle ranch. Many of the letters are from or about Moreton Frewen, who was the owner of the land and became manager for the company on its formation in 1882. Most of the material relates to the management and mismanagement of the ranch until the winding-up of the company in the 1890's. (Wh. M. 477)

(v) General correspondence of the 1st Earl of Wharncliffe. (Wh. M. 418)

There is an index of correspondents which covers the years 1856-91. There are numerous letters relating to the Southern Independence Association and the American Civil War, especially from Alexander Collie, Capt. Matthew F. Maury, James Spence, and T. Staley; also from James Murray Mason (3), Hon. Horace Lascelles, R.N., while stationed in Canada 1859-62 (and an unsigned letter from him, 1865, about Gen. Sherman's march through Georgia), Henry Cleveland, a former colonel in the Confederate Army, 1872, and various others.

BAGSHAWE COLLECTION.

(*a*) Barker, John. Letter-book. 1753-60. (493)

Consists of copies of letters from him, John Gardom, and James Crosbie, from Liverpool, Manchester, and various places in Derbyshire, to correspondents in America. Most of the letters deal with the partners' potash business in Philadelphia and elsewhere ('... we have a patent for the sole making of pott:ash or pearl:ashes in all America for fourteen years, which is dated in 1751'). The letters are addressed mainly to the managers in Philadelphia - William Ashe, James Palmer, and Humphrey Robinson - and to the agent in Fredericksburg, Va., Charles Dick; they contain instructions about methods of manufacture and accounting, and about the winding-up of the venture after the death of Crosbie. There are also a few letters to Edward Salter, merchant 'near Bath Town', N.C., concerning the export of deer skins and indigo.

(*b*) B. & W. Wyatt, lead-mine owners, Derbyshire. One folder of their business papers contains documents, 1773 and 1785, relating to the duty on exported lead, including several manuscript copies of an undated three-page article entitled 'Observations on the tax or duty laid upon lead exported by an Act passed the last session of Parliament'; one paragraph of this deals with the possibility of competition from England. (587/66)

(*c*) Frost, John, and Benjamin Bagshawe, Jr. 2 letters. 1871. (776)

Frost's letter, from Tideswell, Derbyshire, 2 Mar. 1871, asks for advice concerning the legality of disposing of his father's estate in

1. Edited by W.H.G. Armytage, 'Thomas Talbot and Lord Wharncliffe: some new letters hitherto unpublished', *Ontario History*, vol. xlv, pp. 177-97, 1953.

order to invest the money in the United States, where he and several members of his family plan to emigrate; his cousin's reply is dated the following day.

FITZWILLIAM (WENTWORTH WOODHOUSE) MUNIMENTS.

(*a*) Rockingham (2nd Marquis) Letters and Papers.[2]
Charles Watson-Wentworth, 2nd Marquis of Rockingham (1730-82), was Prime Minister 1765-6 and 1782, and led the opposition from the House of Lords 1768-81. The collection of his papers is of prime importance for the English side of the War of Independence. There is a mimeographed list in the Library, 'Letters and papers of the 2nd Marquis of Rockingham', to which the reference numbers below refer. Among the more important items are:
R 1: Over 2,000 letters,[3] including letters from America from Thomas Combe, Philadelphia, 14 May and 5 Nov. 1774; James De Lancey, 4 Feb. and 22 Apr. 1769, 26 Oct. 1773, another letter of 1773, and one 22 Oct., no year; Thomas Dowdeswell, Raritan Landing, N.J., 16 Jan. 1777; Benjamin Franklin, 3 Oct. 1776 and 13 Apr. 1782 (both copies); Joseph Harrison, 3 Nov. 1768; James Rivington, New York, 9 May 1782; James Thompson, New York, 12 May 1782; Samuel Wentworth, Boston, 29 July 1759; and anonymous letters. 'A list of persons gone into North America within the last eighteen months or thereabouts [from the Sheffield area]', enclosed in a letter of 16 Jan. 1769. (R 1/1149)

R 19-32: Matters connected with Stamp duties in America, 1763-66. Included in R 24 are letters, 1764-6, of Thomas Hutchinson to W. Bollan, and of Andrew Oliver, John Hughes, and Barlow Trecothick (from New York).

R 33-50: Various matters concerning colonial trade, 1761-6. R 44 contains Major Robert Rogers's proposals, 1765, for finding the Northwest Passage, with a letter, New York, 15 Jan. 1766, to Rockingham. (Another letter from Rogers is in R 75/67.) R 48 contains the papers[4] of Col. George Mercer of the Virginia Regiment, 1763-6, including Virginia committee of correspondence to Edward Montagu, 17 June 1763, and George Mercer to Rockingham, 11 Apr. 1766.

R 51-55: Papers concerning the repeal of the Stamp Act. R 55 contains letters from America about the reception of the news of repeal, including a letter, New York, 6 May 1766, to Barlow Trecothick and the merchants trading to North America; Samuel Carey, Boston, 21 May 1766, to Rockingham; House of Representatives of Massachusetts to Rockingham, 21 June 1766, with a vote of thanks.

R 61: Statistical tables of various aspects of American and British trade, including N. Tucker to Rockingham, 25 Apr. 1779, 'Hints relative to the cultivation of tobacco in Virginia'. (R 61/11/7)

R 62: Quebec papers, 1766-7, including letters from Francis Maseres, 20 Nov. 1766, and William Hey, 31 Jan. 1767.

R 63: Miscellaneous letters from America, 1767-75. Included are letters, 1767-9, from Joseph Harrison, collector of customs at Boston; this is perhaps the most important American correspondence in the whole collection. Also included are letters to Rockingham, 22 Jan. 1768 from Thomas Cushing and 23 Mar. 1770 from James Bowdoin, Samuel Pemberton, and Joseph Warren. (Other Cushing letters are in R 55 and R 152.)

R 64: Case of Governor John Wentworth of New Hampshire, 1772-3: charges brought by Peter Livius about land declared forfeit, with correspondence, briefs, etc.; and R 65. Miscellaneous writings on American problems, including Governor Wentworth's long considerations on American affairs, 1 Sept. 1765. (There is also a separate collection of Wentworth family records within the Fitzwilliam Muniments in the Library.)

R 111: Petitions from American refugees and others, and Sir George Collier's claims for expenses for helping American refugees. *c.* 1782-3.

R 127: A small packet of letters from North America addressed to the Marquis or to Hugh Wentworth, 1767-9, including three letters, 1767-8, from John Clapham from Maryland, and one letter, 1769, from Governor John Wentworth.

R 129: Copies of Captain Keppel's American papers, captured with Henry Laurens in 1780.

R 150: Letters, extracts, copies from America, 1775. Included are letters to Rockingham from Arthur Lee, 2 Sept. 1775, and from James Murray, [1775] and 18 July 1775. There are also copies of two letters of 23 Apr. 1775 from Boston to Dr. Rogers, giving 'truths that the Admiral may rely on' of the expedition to Concord on 18 Apr.

There are also letters from various American governors, including Sir Francis Bernard, Thomas Boone, Thomas Fitch, Stephen Hopkins, Sir Henry Moore, and Samuel Ward; and many copies of official papers.

(*b*) Letters and papers of the 2nd (4th) Earl Fitzwilliam. William Wentworth Fitzwilliam (1748-1833), statesman. No complete examination of these papers was made. They include, however, some correspondence with Governor John Wentworth, and 'Copy of Mr. Champion's account of the state of America', 1785. (F 125)[5]

(*c*) Edmund Burke (1729-97). Letters and papers.[6]
There is a complete list of Burke's correspondence in print,[7] and this includes the letters in the Fitzwilliam Muniments, so an extended report on these well-known papers has not been thought necessary. In addition, the collection includes many drafts of Burke's speeches on American affairs. And in Bk.4 may be found several American letters: 4 Jan. 1775, Oliver De Lancey to Moses Franks; 13 Dec. 1774, John Harris Cruger to Moses Franks; 16 Jan. 1775, Samuel Tufts to Joseph Walds; 19 July 1791, George Washington to Richard Champion.[8]

(*d*) Papers of Charles William Wentworth Fitzwilliam, 5th Earl Fitzwilliam.
Two letters from the Hon. Charles W. Fitzwilliam (the 5th Earl's youngest son) from Fort Atkinson and Fort Laramie, 1852-3. (G77)

(*e*) Papers of William W. Fitzwilliam, Viscount Milton (d. 1877) on Canadian affairs, e.g., concerning publication of 'San Juan Boundary Question', 1869; Red River settlement, 1870; British Columbian affairs, 1860-70, including Nanaimo country, 1860-4. (T 60-65)

(*f*) Twentieth-century estate accounts including California estates of Earl Fitzwilliam: balance sheets and schedules, 1913-8.

2. See *Guide to the Manuscript Collections in the Sheffield City Libraries* (Sheffield, 1956), Appendix II, pp. 87-96, for an index of correspondents. This has been revised and corrected.
3. There is now a full list of these letters in N.R.A. 1083.
4. Printed in J.E. Tyler, 'Colonel George Mercer's Papers', *Virginia Magazine of History and Biography*, vol. lx, pp. 405-20, 1952.
5. There is now a complete handlist and index of correspondents to the 4th Earl Fitzwilliam.
6. A complete microfilm is held by the University of Kentucky.
7. T.W. Copeland and M.S. Smith, *A Check List of the Correspondence of Edmund Burke, Arranged in Chronological Order and Indexed under the Names of 1,200 Correspondents* (Cambridge, printed at the University Press for the Index Society, New York, 1955). Also see T.W. Copeland, L.S. Sutherland, G.H. Guttridge, J.A. Woods, H. Furber, A. Cobban, and R.A. Smith (eds.), *The Correspondence of Edmund Burke, 1744-1797*, 9 vols. (Cambridge and Chicago, Ill., 1958-70).
8. See *Writings of George Washington*, ed. by John C. Fitzpatrick, vol. xxxi (Washington, D.C., 1939), pp. 314-5.

VASSALL, WILLIAM. 2 letter-books. 1769-99. (MD 2047)

Owner of Jamaican sugar plantations, resident of Boston and London. Vassall, born in Jamaica, lived in Boston from childhood until 1775. His business was the export to England of sugar and rum from his Jamaican estates. The letter-books consist of copies of letters from Boston, 1769-75; from Nantucket, Mass., in 1775; and from London, 1775-99, except for a brief period in 1786 when Vassall was in Bristol, R.I. Most of the pre-war letters concern his business, and are addressed to merchants in England and to his agent and others in Jamaica; the letters to England frequently include request for goods to be sent to Boston for his personal use - shoes, the works of Cicero, etc.

After the war there are many letters to Boston and to Bristol, R.I., to a large number of correspondents, concerning the confiscation and sale of Vassall's farm in Bristol, R.I.; he felt this to be a great injustice, since his sympathies had been, if anything, with the Americans, and his removal to Britain had occurred solely because his livelihood depended on the trade between his Jamaican estates and that country.

SPENCER STANHOPE OF CANNON HALL (CANNON HALL MUNIMENTS).

Include:

(*a*) Papers of Benjamin Spencer, a London merchant in a rather small way, consisting of correspondence, bills of lading, seamen's wages, etc., in connexion with his shipping business. A small number relate to the American trade, especially to the port of Charleston, S.C., 1750-9. (60549-52)

(*b*) Fourteen letters, 1774-6, from John and Ashton Shuttleworth, from America, giving accounts of the War of Independence (60542), and five further letters, 1777-81. (60578)[9]

(*c*) Correspondence, accounts, and receipt books of Captain John Shuttleworth, British army officer and apparently paymaster of the 7th Regiment, the Royal Fusileers. Most of the papers concern regimental pay and accounts, the period 1791-4 being at Quebec; three letter-books include copies of a few letters, 1793, dealing with the claim of Isaac Ogden of Quebec for payment for services as counsel for Shuttleworth's late brother in the latter's New York court martial. (60595-8)

(*d*) Prospectus, letters, accounts, etc., concerning the Big Horn Cattle Company, Powder River, Mont. 1883. (60721)

PAYNE LETTERS. 1773-4.

Family letters of Mrs. Eliza Payne of Newhill in Wath, S. Yorks. contains four letters from Mrs. M. Leaver, her sister-in-law, on a Quaker mission to Philadelphia, 1773-4. (MD 5856)

HOLY, NEWBOLD AND SUCKLEY OF SHEFFIELD. Business records. 1793-1826.

Partnership deeds for trading to America, 1793-7; accounts and stock book, 1797; business correspondence from New York; and items relating to the Republic of Colombia, 1820-6. (MD 5734-7)

JAMES MONTGOMERY CORRESPONDENCE. Letters. 1795-1854.

Some 1,500 letters addressed to and from James Montgomery, Sheffield, poet and editor of the newspaper the Sheffield *Iris*, 1795-1854. The correspondents include some Americans, e.g. George Bourne (2 letters), N.C. Brooks (1), Elliott Cresson (2), Joseph and Winifred Gales (4), Charles Pettit McIlvaine (1), James Milner (3), W.B. Sprague (6), and probably others. (SLPS 36) (There is an index of the correspondence.)

BRADBURY, THOMAS, & SONS. Business records.[10] 1805-46.

Silver platers, Sheffield. The earliest references to trade with the United States in the large collection of this firm's records held by the Library appears to be an undated - apparently pre-1806 - order for candlesticks and other goods for John & Lawrence Brickwood of Baltimore, but it was after 1816 that extensive relations developed. From 1817 onwards there are many letters from George H. Newbould, the firm's New York agent; these contain discussion of demand, etc., and give details of orders for particular firms. The correspondence folders also include letters from G.& W. Simmons of Liverpool, who shipped the goods to America, and insurance forms for such goods. Other relevant material includes, e.g., a notebook containing details of shipments in 1844 to particular American firms (Br. Coll. 202), and a 'stock and order book' for 1825-7 showing details of orders (in Apr. 1825, six New York firms are represented). (Br. Coll. 3)

WAINWRIGHT COLLECTION. Letters. 1805-66.

Business and private records of a small yeoman family, the Wainwrights of Thurlstone, including twenty-nine letters from Joseph Wainwright, emigrant to Pittsburgh, Pa., 1805-66.[11]

NOWILL, THOMAS, & CO. Ledger,[12] 1812-25. (LD 196)

Spring-knife cutlers, Sheffield. The ledger for 1812-25 contains entries of transactions with Davis, Brown & Co. of Boston between 1817 and 1821.

JOSEPH RODGERS & SONS. Letters and orders. 1817-53.

Cutlers, Sheffield.

(*a*) Some letters and orders from overseas, including U.S. and Valparaiso, Chile, 1824-53 (mainly photocopies, the originals having been dispersed for postmark interest). (MD 6209)

(*b*) Some letters from customers, 1817-9, relating to shipment of goods and American orders. (MD 6207)

MARSH BROS. & CO. Business records.[13] 1819-76.

Steel, tool, and cutlery manufacturers.

(*a*) The firm maintained agents in the United States from 1817 onwards, but the earliest relevant figures appear to be the £2,600 due from American firms noted for 31 Dec. 1819 in a stock book covering 1810-34.

Much information about the American connexion is available in two letter-books; one of these, labelled 'Extracts of letters from the United States', consists of copies by the Sheffield partners of parts of letters, 1833-42, from James Marsh the younger in Philadelphia, Charles Wreaks in New Orleans, and Joseph Cam and Edward Mullins in New York. As well as the details of orders, these contain information about prices and depositions of competitors, and comment on American financial and political affairs.

The other letter-book was used by John Marsh, Jr., in 1841-2 while he was in Philadelphia dealing with the inefficient organi-

9. Part published in A.M.W. Stirling, *Annals of a Yorkshire House from the Papers of a Macaroni (Walter Spencer-Stanhope) and his Kindred*, vol. i (London, 1911).

10. See P.C. Garlick, 'The Sheffield Cutlery and Allied Trades', M.A. thesis, University of Sheffield, 1951.

11. See *Letters from a Yorkshire Emigrant*, 1967. (Library publication).

12. See Garlick, op. cit.

13. S. Pollard, *Three Centuries of Sheffield Steel: the Story of a Family Business* (Sheffield, priv. print., 1954), is a history of the firm.

zation of the office there; the copies are of letters sent to East Coast firms concerning their accounts with Marshes & Shepherd (as the firm was called then), to the New York agent, Joseph Cam, and to the Sheffield office. It was also used for letters written, 1842-3, by W.N. Woodcock, whom Marsh left in charge of the American branch, now moved to New York.

In addition, a volume containing extracts from and summaries of letters received by the Sheffield firm, 1845-76, includes references to the credit position and general standing of various American firms, including some in Chicago and Indianapolis, as well as in Philadelphia, etc.

(*b*) 212 letters, etc., 1863-7. Most of the letters which deal with details of orders, are from the Sheffield firm to their New York office, addressed to W.N. Woodcock and Theophilus Marsh in 1863-5, and to J.W. Cockayne in 1866-7. There are also a few letters to New York from B. & S.H. Thompson, Birmingham, concerning the sale of their guns and chains. (MD 1485)

ELMHIRST MANUSCRIPTS. Day book. 1827-34.

Day book of Thomas Elmhirst, 1801-37, Quebec merchant. Contains sales, mostly of cutlery, ironmongery, etc., in Canada, to Caldwell and Dupont & McNichol and a number of persons with French names, 1827-34.

J. BAGSHAW LTD. OF SHEFFIELD. Order books. 1841-1910.

Transfer manufacturers for etching on steel surfaces (mainly used for trademarks).

From the orders it can be seen that the various firms exported to Canada, etc.

LEADER COLLECTION. Letter.[14] 1844. (196)

In this large antiquarian collection there is a single emigrant letter, 9 Mar. 1844, from W. C. Beardsall, near Niagara in Upper Canada, to a Mrs. Foster of Sheffield. A lively, very detailed and sensible description of Canadian life; includes a sketch of the farm; some of the letter is written in doggerel verse.

TIBBITTS COLLECTION. Shaw & Fisher: Business records. 1849-54.

Britannia metal and plated wares manufacturers, Sheffield. The business papers of this firm show extensive dealings with the United States, 1850-4, during which period the firm maintained an agent in New York who covered the Eastern seaboard. A bundle of correspondence contains a large number of letters from this agent, Charles Congreve, with discussion of financial arrangements, comment on demand, copies of orders from various American firms, etc.; there are also a few letters in 1849 from Sansom Cariss of Baltimore and Andrew Love of the New Orleans firm of Love, Hogg & Co. Both in this bundle and in another marked 'vouchers' there are records of shipment of goods to particular American firms through the Liverpool house of Cowie, Roxburgh & Co., with financial arrangements being made by Brown, Shipley & Co. of Liverpool. A folder containing bills of exchange includes a few from Charleston, S.C., and from New York. (1056-8)

ROBERTS, JAMES, AND THOMAS J. BRADLEY. 11 letters (photostats).[15] 1849-70. (MD 2027)

James Roberts was a Sheffield cutlery worker who emigrated to the United States in 1849. Five letters fom Waterville, Conn., 1849-50, to his relatives in Sheffield deal with family news, local customs, and working conditions at the Waterville Company. His last letter tells of the company informing its employees that they must start providing their own tools, and the resulting decision of Roberts and fifteen others to set up their own factory - 'we are dermind [*sic*] to have nobody but working men so you can see we are determined to have no capitulists'.

Thomas J. Bradley was the president of this venture (the 'New York Knife Company, of Walden, Orange County, New York and of Wallkill River Works', according to its letter-head) at the time he wrote the letters to Sheffield included in the collection. One of these, 1867, is to his brother and sister; and five, 1869-70, are to James Roberts, who was on a visit to England. The letters mainly concern the obtaining of Sheffield craftsmen for employment by the firm.

BURGON & BALL LTD., LA PLATA WORKS, SHEFFIELD. Papers. 1867-1907.

Makers of sheep shears, tools, and hammers.

The firm had a large overseas trade, mainly with Australia. The following relate to America:

(*a*) Letters from agents abroad, including California, 1867-78. (B & B 68)

(*b*) Some correspondence with San Francisco, 1881, and Salt Lake City, 1901. (B & B 69)

(*c*) Agreements for sales of goods in U.S. and Canada, 1876-1905. (B & B 75)

(*d*) Papers concerning trademarks and patents in Canada and U.S., *c.* 1890-1907. (B & B 59/g and h, 63, 64)

WILSON, HENRY JOSEPH (1833-1914). Correspondence, notebook. 1876-7.

Social reformer, M.P. In 1876 Wilson and the Rev. J.P. Gledstone went to the United States on behalf of the British, Continental, and General Federation for the Abolition of Government Regulation of Prostitution. The collection of Wilson's papers held by the Library includes the following material relating to this journey:

(*a*) Fourteen letters to his family, written from New York, Washington, D.C., etc. Most of these are to his children and contain comment on American customs and attitudes; in a letter to his wife he notes that 'there is no *demand* for us anywhere - people make the best of us when they can't help it'. (MD 2478)

(*b*) Letters to Wilson about his mission - arrangements for meetings, attitudes towards government regulation of prostitution, reasons for American apathy, etc. - from F.A.P. Barnard, James Freeman Clarke, Neal Dow, William Lloyd Garrison, Elizabeth Gay, C.G. Hussey, Enoch Lewis, A.M. Powell, and I.L. Townsend. (MD 2542)

(*c*) A notebook containing names and addresses of possible American contacts, with comment on their positions, outlooks, and probable influence; notes added during the American trip concern help given by some of them. (MD 2543)

SHEFFIELD SMELTING COMPANY. Business records. 1876-1909.

(*a*) H.J. Wilson's notebooks and letters on visits to America concerning visits to refiners in New England, possibility of purchase of

14. Photostat in the collection of Letters of Emigrants to America in the British Library of Political and Economic Science, London School of Economics.

15. Used by J.B. Himsworth, *The Story of Cutlery, from Flint to Stainless Steel* (London, 1953), and C. Erickson, *American Industry and the European Immigrant* (London and Cambridge, Mass., 1957). Photostats also in the collection of Letters of Emigrants to America in the British Library of Political and Economic Science, London School of Economics.

'sweep' from American firms, and American business, 1876, 1886, and 1891-6.
(*b*) Memoranda and correspondence relating to the visit of Cecil Wilson to Canada and U.S., 1909. (SSC 304, 306)

JOHNSON, CHRISTOPHER, & CO. Business records. 1882-90.
Cutlers, Sheffield. The earliest item relating to the United States appears to be a copy of a letter to Jackson & Co., Brooklyn, N.Y., on 14 Mar. 1882, noting that they have no agent in New York but are interested in marketing prospects there (MD 2368). A letter-book for 1888-90 (MD 2369) includes copies of more than twenty letters to Lewis G. Weatherley and to the San Francisco firms with which he was associated, Huntingdon, Hopkins & Co. and Weatherley, Jardine & Co.; these letters deal with orders for razors, knives, scissors, etc. The volume also includes copies of letters written in 1890 to L.A. Jones of Springfield, Mass., and to C.A. Winan of New York.

ALLEN, EDGAR, & CO. LTD. Business records. 1883-1934.
Steel manufacturers, Sheffield.
(*a*) Copies of outgoing letters; a few for 1883-9, but the vast majority for 1890-1900. Included are a few references to the beginning of the firm's interest in the American market (it finally became incorporated in New York in 1909, and in Illinois in 1911); and to the introduction of the Tropenas process of steel-making, of which the company was the British licensee, into the United States. References also to American tariffs, the quality of American steel, and the cheapness of raw material. Letter, 10 Oct. 1899, compares the production per day of United States and British steel firms, and gives the reasons for American superiority as the greater mechanization of the industry in the United States and the American workman's willingness to do an 'honest day's work'.
(*b*) One of the thirty-eight order books held by the Library is for the firm's Chicago and New York agencies; as well as brief notes of orders, it includes occasional extracts from letters referring to orders. A volume marked 'Journal of Accounts' (MD 2336) includes some figures of dealings - steel purchases, freight charges, etc. - with the Chicago agency and American firms.

CARPENTER COLLECTION.[16]
Edward Carpenter (1844-1929), social reformer. The collection of his papers includes:
(*a*) 'Across the Atlantic.' Manuscript notes for a lecture, 1884.
(*b*) A folder containing letters from Carpenter's friends. Included are five long letters, 1894-6, from Robert A. Nicol, Weimar, Calif., about his philosophy and way of life; three letters, 1907, from Edgar Ira Oford, Brooklyn, N.Y., on Carpenter's books and relations between the sexes; and one letter each from Daniel G. Mason, 1902, Anne F. Miller, 1906, and Mrs. L.S.K. Crouse, 1925.
(*c*) A bundle of 142 letters from eight American publishers. These deal mainly with the publication of Carpenter's books in the United States; the letters from A.B. Stockham, Chicago - 100 items, 1900-11 - and John Huschler, San Francisco - nineteen items, 1909-12 - also contain information concerning attitudes towards Carpenter's books, and discussion of some of the subjects raised in these.
(*d*) 'Primitive life in the Maine woods: a modern experiment', [1924]. Manuscript and three typescript copies; also a letter to Curtis Brown, London, asking to arrange for publication.
(*e*) A large number of letters now forming part of the Carpenter collection were received by the Library in 1958. Some of the American correspondents are L.D. Abbott, Ruth Goldby, C.E. Grogan, G.B.M. and J.K. Kinney, Jack London, R.A. Nicol, Annie Riley, Margaret Sanger, H.L. Traubel, and David Thompson.

The collection also includes the original manuscripts, various dates, of Carpenter's articles and books on Walt Whitman.

GEORGE WOSTENHOLM & CO. Business records. 1895-1971.
This firm went into liquidation several years ago. A residue of records was cleared out of the works and brought to the Library. The following relate to America:
(*a*) Letter-book: letters to America, 1895-6. (Wos 3)
(*b*) Correspondence about improper use of Wostenholm's trade name by Empire Knife Co. of Connecticut, 1895-1911. (Wos 4)
(*c*) Papers about agency arrangements in New York, 1926-31. (Wos 12)
(*d*) Frank Colver's notebooks of overseas visits and correspondence with people overseas, 1931-52. (Wos 13, 150)
(*e*) Order forms, credits, files in ledger form, some relating to business abroad, 1950-71. (Wos 28-47)

SPEAR & JACKSON LTD. Business records. 1925, 1934.
Business diaries, notebooks, and letter-books of L.J. Combe during visits to Canada and U.S. A., 1925 and 1934. (SJC 80-9)

BALFOUR DARWINS LTD. Records. 1920's-1950.
Steel manufacturers, Sheffield. Records of the firm of Arthur Balfour & Son, founded 1865, now amalgamated with Darwins.
(*a*) Day books of sales or orders from 1869, but no American trade appears to be recorded until the 1920's. There are day books for the U.S.A. and Canada, 1929-50.
(*b*) Accounts and papers concerning the dissolution of Arthur Balfour (Delaware, U.S.A.), 1921-9.

THE LIBRARY, UNIVERSITY OF SHEFFIELD, Sheffield S10 2TN

MUNDELLA, ANTHONY JOHN (1825-97). Correspondence.[1] 1870-1904.
Statesman. The collection of Mundella's letters to Robert Leader, editor of the *Sheffield Independent,* includes one written from New York during Mundella's visit to the United States in 1870; there are also occasional references to American affairs in other of the letters. In the letters written to Mundella there are thirteen from American correspondents, as follows:
Dana, Richard Henry. Rome, 20 Mar. 1881, concerning Mundella's 1870 New York speech.
Eaton, John. Washington, D.C., 30 Jan. 1871.
Holmes, Oliver Wendell. London, 18 May, no year.
Lowell, James Russell. London, 1880-4, eight letters, including a few concerning Texas fever and trichinosis.
Phelps, T. London, 15 Dec. 1890.
Wells, David A. Norwich, Conn., 13 Jan. (1871).

DESCH, CECIL HENRY, F.R.S. (1874-1958). Papers. 1927, 1931-2, 1947.
Metallurgist and philosopher. These include diaries and notes of his

16. See *A Bibliography of Edward Carpenter* (Sheffield City Libraries, 1949).

1. See W.H.G. Armytage, *A.J. Mundella, 1825-97: The Liberal Background to the Labour Movement* (London, 1951).

visits to America, mostly for professional reasons, 1927, 1931-2 and 1947. (Desch MSS. 1/4-6, 9-11)

YORKSHIRE, WEST [1]

CENTRAL LIBRARY, Prince's Way, Bradford BD1 1NN

SPENCER-STANHOPE COLLECTION. 14 letters.

Fourteen letters written by or to Captain John Shuttleworth, a soldier with the British forces during the American War of Independence. (nos. 1855-9)

CUNLIFFE-LISTER COLLECTION. 14 documents. 1656-1706.

Fourteen documents, including letters about and an account of the Danby estate in Virginia, 1656-1706. (bundle 69, section II)

ARCHIVES DEPARTMENT, BELLE VUE LIBRARY, Halifax

CLAY, J.T., & CO. Business records. 1899-1931.

Woollen manufacturers, Rastrick, Yorkshire. Most of the extensive records held by the Library are volumes of samples; in none of the volumes examined did the occasional correspondence attached to these appear to refer to the United States. However, 'after the year 1868 [woollens] were extensively sold ... through commission houses to customers in the United States', according to the firm's submission before the New York South District Circuit Court in 1899 in its case charging Marks Arnheim with misrepresentation of goods as made by Clay; this document, and several other papers concerning the case, are included in an envelope labelled 'New York Trade Mark'.

Other miscellaneous relevant materials in this collection include a packet of eleven letters, 1905-20, from E.H. Van Ingen of New York and London, on business and personal matters; and a few letters of the 1930's.

LISTER FAMILY. Papers. 1733-75.

The Library's collection includes manuscripts relating to various connexions of the Lister family with America in the eighteenth century - the trading careers in Virginia in the 1730's of several Lister brothers, the service in the War of Independence by one of their sons, and miscellaneous other contacts.

(*a*) Lister letters.

The earliest relevant documents concern the visits to or settlement in Virginia in the 1730's of the brothers Thomas (1708-40), William (1712-43), and Jeremy (1713-88):

(i) Letters to their brother Samuel (1706-66) in Halifax about their reasons for going to Virginia and the trade in tobacco and skins which they hope to carry on there; news in 1735 of their varied activities - purchase of wheat and a share in a ship in which to transport it to Madeira or Lisbon, the pickling of pork to trade for rum and sugar in the West Indies, etc.

(ii) Reports, 1736-40, of Thomas's mismanagement, illness, and death.

(iii) Correspondence, 1743-7, of Samuel with William's widow, Susannah, of New Bern, Neuse River, N.C., and her father, John Lewis of Virginia, concerning difficulties impeding the settlement of William's debts to Samuel.

Also included is a letter of 1769 to Thomas's son William (1734-80) in London from his mother Ann in Virginia, containing news of her marriage to James Sturdivant, since dead.

(*b*) Fawcett letters.

(i) 1744, from William Fawcett (1728-1804), later General Sir William Fawcett, to his uncle, Rev. John Lister (1703-59), concerning his imminent departure for Georgia with Oglethorpe and the hardships to be expected there.[1]

(ii) 1750, from Fawcett to his uncle, Samuel Lister, concerning a proposed woollen business in London and noting that Mr. Caygill of Halifax has just sent £700 worth of Yorkshire goods to New England.

(iii) Correspondence during the War of Independence between Fawcett and the Lister family, concerning the British Army service of his cousin Jeremy Lister (1752-1836) in North America; and a letter to Fawcett from Henry Bassett, Boston, 23 Apr. 1775, giving a brief account of the battle of Lexington.

(*c*) Rev. John Lister papers. Correspondence, 1757, between William Lister (1734-80) and his uncle, Rev. John Lister, concerning the former's intention of returning to Virginia from London, and the latter's objections.

(*d*) Lister manuscripts. Certificate, 1765, respecting the disposal of woollen goods shipped from England by Japhet Lister (1715-82), signed by Thomas Claiborne of Virginia as attorney for William Middleton.

(*e*) Jeremy Lister letters. The papers of Jeremy Lister (1752-1836) include letters written to his family in London and Halifax during his army service in Quebec and Niagara, 1771-4, and while stationed in Boston, 1774-5; although mainly concerned with promotion possibilities, these contain occasional reports of battles, comments on officers, etc. Also included is his journal for 1770-83.[2]

EARL OF HAREWOOD, Harewood House, Leeds

CANNING PAPERS. 5 letters, 1817-23, and dispatch books, 1807-9, 1822-5.

Papers of George Canning (1770-1827), statesman.

(*a*) Washington, D.C., 1 Nov. 1817, 2 and 3 Dec. 1818, from Charles Bagot, British Minister to the United States, to George Canning.

(*b*) Private and confidential, Washington, D.C., 12 Mar. 1823, from Stratford Canning, British Minister to the United States, to George Canning.

(*c*) Précis, Washington, D.C., 10 July 1823, from Stratford Canning to George Canning.

(*d*) Dispatch books of George Canning: U.S.A., 1807-9, 1822-5.

1. Apart from the business records mentioned in the entries for West Yorkshire which follow, the papers of other firms with some smaller American connexions have been located and described in great detail by Patricia Hudson, *The West Riding Wool Textile Industry* (Edington, 1975).

---

1. Printed in full in John Lister, 'John Lister, Master of Bury Grammar School, and his Correspondents', *Transactions of the Lancashire and Cheshire Antiquarian Society*, vol. xxviii, pp. 153-4, 1911.

2. Part of this journal, together with three of the letters written from Boston and a fragment by Lieut.-Col. Val Jones describing the battle at Charlestown, Mass., has been published as Jeremy Lister, *Concord Fight* (Cambridge, Mass., 1931).

BROTHERTON LIBRARY, UNIVERSITY OF LEEDS, Leeds LS2 9JT

BROTHERTON COLLECTION.

(*a*) Alfred Mattison Collection.

The collection includes the following papers relating to John Francis Bray (1809-97), American-born social reformer:

(i) Correspondence, 1802-56, among members of the Bray family. Forty-six letters (of which eleven are transcripts of originals not in the collection) include five from Bray written in 1822-56 - to his mother (2); to his aunt, Mrs. Gauler (1); to his uncle, Joseph Bray (2). Most of the letters, however, are from Boston, from Sarah Bray, mother of John Francis, 1824; from Sarah Barnes ('Barney', a friend of the family), 1827-34; from Charles Frederick Bray, 1828-55; from Edgar W. Bray, 1828-40; and from Edwin Bray Nichols, 1836-40.[1]

(ii) Twentieth-century letters on Bray to John Passmore Edwards, and to Mattison, including letters (copies) from Philip Snowden, 1923, and Ramsay MacDonald, 1925; pamphlets; offprints of articles, etc.

(*b*) Canon Leigh Collection. 3 letters.

Irving, Washington. Ashford, 5 Dec. 1831, to Rev. Reastor Rodes, concerning a prospective tour of England with Van Buren.

James, Henry. Undated portion of a letter.

Longfellow, Henry Wadsworth. Cambridge, Mass., 25 May 1845, to Lady Sitwell, enclosing autographs of Washington and Franklin.

(*c*) Dickens, Charles. 7 letters. 1841-67.

Letters to various correspondents, 11 Dec. 1841 - 10 Nov. 1867, from Britain or on board ship, relating to his visits to America, to George Dolby going there, to his opinion of the American press, and to his *American Notes*.

(*d*) Swinburne, Algernon Charles and Paul Hamilton Hayne. Correspondence (1 volume). 1875-1911.

Letters, 1875-84, between Hayne, of Augusta, Ga. (five letters) and Swinburne (copies of eight letters, mainly from London). They deal with Edgar Allen Poe - his monument and memorial volume - and with American political and literary matters. The volume also contains three letters to W.T. Watts-Dunton, Swinburne's literary executor, concerning possible publication of the correspondence; of these, one, 1910, is from the editor of *Harper's Magazine*, and two 1910 and 1911, from Hayne's son.

(*e*) Gosse, Edmund William. Correspondence. 1873-1923.

Writer. The published catalogue[2] lists the correspondents and the dates of their letters, most of which are to Gosse or members of his family.

Included are letters from Henry Mills Alden, Thomas Bailey Aldrich, George Bancroft, Edwin Booth, John Burroughs, Nicholas Murray Butler (one of the two letters, 27 June 1917, concerns Balfour's reception in the United States), Ralph Waldo Emerson, Edward Everett Hale, Oliver Wendell Holmes, Sr., William Dean Howells, Henry Cabot Lodge, James Russell Lowell, John Singer Sargent, Mrs. Fanny (R.L.) Stevenson, and Owen Wister. There are over 50 letters from Henry James, and a few letters from other members of the James family; letters from many of Gosse's other correspondents include comment on James. There are also photostats of exchanges of letters between Gosse and Walt Whitman in 1873 and 1884.

In addition, there are letters, 1914, on receiving a copy of the White Paper on the European crisis, from Arthur T. Hadley, John G. Hibben, Seth Low, Abbott L. Lowell, and William Howard Taft; letters while on visits to the United States from George Rathbone Benson, 1st Baron Charnwood, Rupert Brooke (including comments on Edwin Arlington Robinson), John Drinkwater, and Alfred Noyes; and various other relevant letters - Marie A. Brown on the difficulty of arranging an American edition of her work, Gosse on his meeting with Mark Twain, George Frederic Watts on the American exhibition of his work.

(*f*) Bram Stoker Correspondence. 20 letters, 3 cards. 1882-1907.

The collection includes letters to Stoker, or to Henry Irving, whose agent he was, from Edwin A. Abbey, Henry Mills Alden, T.B. Aldrich, James Archer, Luigi Arditi, Edwin Booth, William Dean Howells, and Elihu Root.

(*g*) Clement King Shorter Correspondence. 23 letters. 1896-*c*. 1922.

Shorter (1857-1926) was the editor of the London *Sphere* from 1900. The collection includes three letters from William Dean Howells, 1904 and 1910; nineteen letters from Henry James, 1896-1907 - mainly covering letters for work sent for inclusion in the *Sphere*; and a letter [*c*. 1922] from Katherine Osbourne, Monterey, Calif., concerning Robert Louis Stevenson.

(*h*) Edward Clodd Collection. Letter. 1904.

William Dean Howells, London, 5 Apr. 1904, to Clodd: 'It would be adding pleasure if I could meet Hardy at your house.'

(*i*) H.A. Jones Correspondence. 2 letters. 1906, 1912.

William Dean Howells, New York, 1906, concerning the use of stage directions in play-writing, and 1912, both to Jones.

(*j*) Romany Collection. Letter. 1911.

Albert T. Sinclair, Boston, 18 Jan. 1911, to Rev. F.W. Galpin. A covering letter sent with his *Gypsy and Oriental Musical Instruments* (Boston, 1908).

(*k*) Osbourne Manuscripts. 3 letters (2 copies). 1922-3.

Three letters (bound in two volumes) from Katherine Osbourne concerning Robert Louis Stevenson, Fanny Stevenson, and Sir Sidney Colvin. The letters are:

Palo Alto, Calif., 16 Aug. 1922, to Edmund Gosse; 18 pages.
New York, 22 July 1923, to Clement K. Shorter; 9 pages. (Copy.)
New York, 5 Sept. 1923, to an unknown correspondent; 17 pages. (Copy.)

BROTHERTON LIBRARY (MSS. AND SPECIAL COLLECTIONS DEPARTMENT).

I. Business Archives.

The records of a considerable number of West Riding woollen and worsted industry firms - merchants, weavers, spinners, etc. - are deposited in the Brotherton Library. These records include ledgers, letter-books, invoice books, etc.; they refer to periods between the later eighteenth and the early twentieth centuries. The deposit relating most extensively to trade with the United States is that of John Foster & Son Ltd. of Queensbury, Bradford; the profits of this firm's American sales of woollen goods were usually invested in American railroads, etc.[3] Other firms whose records include relevant material are: J. & T. Clay & Sons Ltd., E. Fox & Sons Ltd., James France & Co. Ltd., George Hattersley & Sons Ltd., Isaac Holden & Sons Ltd.,

1. Many of the letters and transcripts are quoted in John Edwards, 'John Francis Bray', *Socialist Review*, vol. xiii, pp. 329-41, 1916; a typescript of the article is in the collection. There are also Bray papers in the British Library of Political and Economic Science, London School of Economics.

2. *A Catalogue of the Gosse Correspondence in the Brotherton Collection* (Leeds, 1950) (University of Leeds, Library Publications No. 3).

3. See E.M. Sigsworth, *Black Dyke Mills* (Liverpool, 1958).

Robert Jowitt & Sons Ltd., William Lupton & Co. Ltd., R.V. Marriner Ltd., and Wormalds and Walker Ltd. These archives are listed with considerable detail in Patricia Hudson, *The West Riding Wool Textile Industry: A Catalogue of Business Records* (1975).

II. Manuscripts.

(*a*) Gott Papers. (MSS. 193 and 194)

Business and family papers, 1797-1867, of Benjamin Gott (1762-1840), woollen manufacturer and merchant of Leeds and of his family. This collection includes documents relating to the firm's extensive American trade, 1770-1860's. The earlier papers are those of Wormald and Fountaine, woollen merchants, the firm to which Benjamin Gott was apprenticed in 1780, of which he became a partner in 1785 and gained control in 1790; in 1792 he began cloth manufacture as an additional activity. Both manufacturing and merchanting were continued by two of his sons who took over the firm when he died; the firm ended with the death of the second of the sons in 1867. For a description of the collection, see P. Hudson, *op. cit.*; for extracts from the papers and studies of them, see 'The Papers of Benjamin Gott in the Library of the University of Leeds', in W.B. Crump, ed., *The Leeds Woollen Industry, 1780-1820* (Leeds, 1931) (Thorsby Society Publications, vol. xxxii), and H. Heaton, 'Benjamin Gott and the Anglo-American Cloth-Trade', *Journal of Economic and Business History*, vol. ii (1929), pp. 146-62.

(*b*) Marshall Papers. (MS. 200)

Leeds was the foremost flax-spinning town in Europe during the early nineteenth century, and these records relate to the principal firm in the trade, Marshalls, from 1788 to 1886. John Marshall made investments in the United States, 1820-40.[4]

(*c*) Richard Offor. (MS. 276)

United States and Canada, [library] buildings; MS. and TS. versions of a report on library buildings made by Dr. Richard Offor (1882-1964) for the Library Association, based on his tour of North America in 1937.[5]

(*d*) Herbert Thompson Papers. (MS. 361)

Thompson (1856-1945) was the music critic of the *Yorkshire Post* from 1886 to 1936, and his correspondence includes:

(i) Two letters from Thomas Tertius Noble (1867-1953), organist at St. Thomas's Church, Fifth Avenue, New York City, from 1912 to 1947. The letters are dated 25 Dec. 1912 and 6 Nov. 1934.

(ii) Five letters from Horatio William Parker (1863-1919), composer, born at Auburndale, Mass. The letters are dated from 12 June 1899 to 12 Aug. 1902.

III. Miscellaneous Letters.

(*a*) Crowther Family. (L. 123/1-6)

Six letters of the Crowther family, 1774-1822, woollen manufacturers and merchants of Gomersal, Churwell, and Leeds, Yorkshire: 1774, from Benjamin Crowther on his departure for North Carolina; and five from David Crowther, Montreal (1811-2) and New York (1813, 1822). In a letter of 12 Jan. 1813, David discusses the war and its effects on Yorkshire trade; his letter of 15 Dec. 1822 includes comment on American concern about piracy in the West Indies, and the case of Lieut. Allen.

(*b*) Charles Thomas Whitmell.

Letters from the United States, 1883-1901, to Charles Thomas Whitmell, inserted in various printed books, from: William A. Bell, James M. Hutchings, Benjamin J. Jeffries, Nathaniel Pitt Langford (2 letters), and Charles A. Young (4 letters). Mainly on literary matters.

(*c*) Arthur Dickson to Paul Barbier. New York, 17 Nov. 1930.

(*d*) Clark S. Northup to Mr. Stokes. Ithaca, N.Y., 4 Oct. 1926.

ARCHIVES DEPARTMENT, PUBLIC LIBRARIES, Leeds LS7 3AP

TEMPLE NEWSAM RECORDS. 2 contracts. 1617. (TN/EA 1/1) (Modern copies in Pawson MSS.)

Two contracts, 1617, between Sir Arthur Ingram and merchant adventurers for Sir Walter Ralegh's voyage to America.[1]

GASCOIGNE COLLECTION. Letters patent. 1635. (GC/F3/1)

Letters patent creating John Gascoigne (1556?-1637) of Parlington a Baron of Nova Scotia, and granting him estates between the rivers Magin, Grand Sohiboyin, and Pargendo for plantation and settlement (never taken up). 1635.

RADCLIFFE OF RUDDING PAPERS. Lease, order books. 1691, 1809-14.

(*a*) Lease, 18 June 1691: John Roach of Leigh in Somerset to William Opie of Bristol and Jedidiah Pickford - 1/16 part of the ship *Joseph* on its voyage from Bristol to Virginia or Maryland and back. (103/100)

(*b*) Order books.

(i) Order book, 1809-13, of Capt. John Talbot while stationed in the Mediterranean, the West Indies, and at Halifax, N.S. This volume actually consists of a log and two order books. The orders issued to Capt. Talbot while in American waters are of particular interest and historical importance. On ff. 100b-101a there is quoted a proclamation, 6 Oct. 1812, warning British subjects that if they were found on U.S. vessels, they would be treated as traitors. (485)

(ii) Order book, 1813-4, including orders received and given by Capt. Talbot commanding H.M.S. *Victorious* while she was engaged on naval operations in North American waters. (486)

NEWBY HALL RECORDS. Orders, correspondence, etc. 1710-1. (NH 2517, 2519)

Papers of Rear Admiral Sir Tancred Robinson: orders and correspondence to Capt. Tancred Robinson, the *Deptford*, including voyage to Virginia 1710; certificates of cargo, bills of lading for ships in convoy from the James River and New York and England.[2]

VYNER/ROBINSON MSS. Journal, letters, notes and memoranda. 1750-69.

(*a*) Journal made by Thomas Robinson, 2nd Lord Grantham, appointed Commissioner of Trade and Plantations in 1766. This journal, 1766-9, contains an abstract of Gen. Gage's dispatches received from New York, 29 Oct. 1768. (5735)

(*b*) The Vyner/Robinson collection also includes the official copies of letters, notes and memoranda which were prepared for the House of Lords in relation to the opening of hostilities between the British and French colonists in Canada, 1750-6. (5711-32)

4. See W.G. Rimmer, *Marshalls of Leeds* (London, 1960), chapter three.
5. Published in Library Association, *A Survey of Libraries* (London, 1938).

1. Microfilmed by the Virginia Colonial Records Project.
2. Ibid.

CATHCART PAPERS. Books, journals, miscellaneous papers. 1759-1853.

The American material is mostly from the papers of Sir George Cathcart (1794-1854), general; and Charles Cathcart, 9th Baron Cathcart (1721-76), soldier and diplomat.

(*a*) Account of an expedition against Quebec under Maj.-General Wolfe, by an engineer, 'P.M.', on that expedition, Apr.-Sept. 1759. (Copied in 1841 from a manuscript lent by Lieut.-General Sir R.D. Jackson, who was Commander of Forces in Canada in 1841.) (45 pages in book form.)

(*b*) 'Journal de l'expedition contre Quebec, 1759', extending from 1 to 10 May.[3]

(*c*) Report on the defence of Canada and Quebec, *c.* 1763.

(*d*) Answer of Francis Bernard, Governor of Massachusetts Bay, to the Lords of Trade, 5 Sept. 1763.

(*e*) Copies of letters, 1766, from Col. Robert Clerk to Lord Shelburne on American affairs.[4]

(*f*) Copy of Lord Chatham's plan for settling America and asserting the sovereignty of Great Britain over her colonies; reduced into a Bill; presented to the House of Lords; read a first time and rejected 1 Feb. 1775.[5]

(*g*) Various papers relating to American affairs, 1778-89, including letters from Andrew Elliot, Collector of Customs at New York and Lieutenant-Governor of New York, of both a political and military nature; and letters, 1780 and 1781, from Sir Henry Clinton.[6]

(*h*) General Wolfe's *Instructions to Young Officers,* etc., 1780 (printed volume).

(*i*) Eight small books relating to North American history, 1838-53. Contain scraps of material useful for the biography of Charles Murray Cathcart, 2nd Earl Cathcart, general.

N.R.A. 3946.

CARR MANUSCRIPTS. 1771-83. (CA)

The copies of deeds and other legal papers in these six volumes appear to have been made for use as precedents in the office of an attorney, probably James Carr of Birstall, Yorkshire. Included in volume 1 are articles of agreement, 2 Sept. 1771, between Wigglesworth, Kent & Co. of Leeds, woollen merchants, and Thomas Gumersall, who is to go to America as their agent. Vol. 4 includes articles of agreement ('special form'), 25 Aug. 1783, between the 'assignees of Ellis' and Cornelius Buck, the agent going on their behalf to the United States to deal with debts owed the estate, etc.

RAMSDEN FAMILY RECORDS. Letters. 1773-1801.

Letters collected by Isabella Ramsden (closely related to the Fitzwilliam Muniments in the Sheffield City Library - see p. 233). Vol. 2, part ii, pp. 35-76: 'Letters relating to Governor Wentworth afterwards Sir John Wentworth; the American War; his two governments Hampshire and Nova Scotia', 1773-1801. These are mostly letters or copies of letters between Wentworth and his wife and Lord and Lady Rockingham.

HOLROYD, JOHN & JOSEPH, *later* JOSEPH HOLROYD & SON. Business records. 1788-1821.

Wool dyers and merchants, Leeds. The firm appears to have carried on a considerable trade with the United States: a book listing bills of exchange, 1788-1807, includes a number shown as due in Savannah, Ga., New York, and other places in America; an account book, covering 1812-21, includes notes of transactions with Marx & Linsley of New York, charges for insurance on woollens sent from Liverpool to New Orleans, details of accounts relating to shipment of cotton from New Orleans by Maunsel White & Co., etc.

CANNING PAPERS. Correspondence, memoranda. 1805-27.

(*a*) U.S.A. 1807-9. Correspondence of George Canning with: William Pinkney and James Monroe, 1808-9; G.H. Rose, 1807-9; F.J. Jackson, 1809; Charles Williamson, 1807; George Clark, 1807; William Armstrong, 1807. Various drafts of dispatches and memoranda. (packet 49)

(*b*) Memoranda: on foreign relations with the United States; on the Canadian fur trade, 1805-6. (packet 58)

(*c*) Large size paper relating to, among other topics, treaties with America. (packet 60)

(*d*) Correspondence of George Canning with Charles Bagot, British Minister to the U.S., 1807-18; also a separate packet, 1811, from Bagot, etc., and endorsed in Canning's hand 'to be burned'. (packet 66a)

(*e*) U.S.A. 1822-7. Correspondence of George Canning with: H.U. Addington (Washington), 1822-7; C.R. Vaughan, 1822-6 (Washington, 1825-6); George Jackson (Washington), 1823. Also correspondence of Canning with Richard Rush, 1822-5; Rufus King, 1825-6; A. Gallatin, 1826-7; Christopher Hughes, 1824-5. (packet 125)

STOWE, HARRIET BEECHER. Address. 1853.

Autograph manuscript of Mrs. Stowe's farewell address to the citizens of Leeds on her return to the U.S. in 1853, giving her experiences in England and mentioning her views on slavery.

PRIESTLEY BROTHERS. Business records. 1890-6. (P 4/1, 2)

L.E. and G.F. Priestley, hardware, etc., manufacturers, Halifax, Yorkshire. Most of the collection relates to their business, which seems to have had no American connexions. However, during the latter part of the 1890's they began investing abroad, and letter-books contain copies of letters from G.F. Priestley to George Murray in London and R. Bridger in New York concerning the Febroline Company; there may also be other American investments involved.

3. H.M.C. ii, p. 30.
4. Ibid.
5. Fuller description, ibid., p. 28.
6. Fuller description, ibid., pp. 29-30.

WALES

CLWYD

CLWYD COUNTY RECORD OFFICE, The Old Rectory, Hawarden, Deeside CH5 3NR

MOSTYN MSS. Instructions. 1740.

Instructions to deputy paymaster of marine detachment for expedition to America, 1740.

GLYNNE-GLADSTONE MSS. Pocket-book. 1789-90.

Pocket-book containing notes by Sir John Gladstone on his journeys to the Low Countries and America, 1789-90.[1]

RHUAL MSS. Journal and correspondence, 1792-3, 1822.

(*a*) Correspondence and accounts concerning payments to F. Philips, an American Loyalist, 1822.
(*b*) MS. copy of the Journal of the Legislative Council of the Province of Lower Canada, 1792-3.

DYFED

NATIONAL LIBRARY OF WALES, Aberystwyth SY23 3BU

The National Library of Wales is rich in Americana, particularly records relating to Welsh emigration to America in the nineteenth century: both emigrant letters and extensive correspondence between Baptist, Congregational, and Methodist ministers in the United States and Wales. There are also voluminous papers relating to the legend of Prince Madoc's discovery of America and the subsequent debate about, and search for, the Padoucas or Welsh Indians. These three types of papers are well listed in the special number of the *National Library of Wales Journal*, vol. ii, nos. 3 and 4, 1942, which was wholly devoted to Wales and the United States of America.[1] It has therefore seemed unnecessary to reproduce fully the manuscript list contained therein. The following list does not purport to be a full list: it omits these papers, covered by the *National Library of Wales Journal*, which chiefly relate to Prince Madoc and the Welsh Indians, and gives details of only a few representative or especially important collections of emigrant letters or ministers' letters. But it includes subsequent accessions under all three heads.

ACCESSIONS TO 1942.

The following report is in archival order, except that the papers relating to Samuel Roberts have been drawn together as one note here at the head.

Papers of and relating to Samuel Roberts. 1834-85. Manuscripts 590C, 3265D, 9522B, 9523A, 9529B, 13195D, 13196D, 13197C, 13199D, 14046-50A, 14091D, 14092C, 14093C.

Samuel Roberts (1800-85), known as 'S.R.', prominent social and political reformer, Welsh poet and journalist. In 1857 he tried to establish a large Welsh settlement called Brynffynon in Scott County, Tenn., together with William Bebb (of Welsh descent), former Governor of Ohio, and others. It failed, largely due to the Civil War and to the vendor having had no clear title. The situation was complicated by Roberts's denunciation of the North for using force to restore the Union. He returned to Wales in 1867, revisiting America in 1870 to dispose of his property.

All his life he kept closely in touch with Welshmen in America, so there is much correspondence describing American life and institutions generally (of which he held exaggerated hopes), Welsh culture and religion in America, as well as letters relating specifically to the conception of the Tennessee venture and its winding up. Among the very many correspondents, there are some letters from William Henry Channing and more from William Bebb. Roberts's letter-books and diaries survive for most of his American sojourn. And, *inter alia,* there is correspondence relating to his claims against the United States government for his losses in Tennessee.

See also Tennessee Papers in Deposited Collections.

474E. Letters of Goronwy Owen (1723-69?), the Welsh poet who emigrated to Virginia in Dec. 1757. Of the last three letters, one, 1757, is addressed to the Cymmrodorion Society in London, soliciting aid to emigrate; and two are to Richard Morris - the first, on board ship, 1757, and the second, Brunswick, Va., 1767, giving his opinion of his neighbours. (*In Welsh.*)

986C. Letters to Jonathan Reynolds ('Nathan Dyfed'). The correspondents include (*in Welsh and English*):

Aneurin Jones, New York, 1884-8, on family news, his life in America, eisteddfodic interests, American politics, his dismissal in 1885 from the post of superintendent of public parks on the defeat of the Democrats, his appointment in 1889 as chief inspector of Brooklyn parks.

J.T. Lewis, New York, 1888, on Stradling inheritance.

987C. Letters of David Howell ('Llawdden'), including a letter addressed to him by Thomas W. Price ('Cuhelyn'), Sacramento, Calif., 1866, on his employment as enrolling clerk to the Senate, the state library, American Grand National Eisteddfod, his proposed biographical dictionary of distinguished Welshmen. (*In English.*)

2163E. Miscellanea relating to Robert Owen, the social reformer, including a typewritten letter, Washington, D.C., 1893, from Henry Hunter to William Beck, Saxondale, on the disappearance of the model of the 'ideal community' and on changes in the furnishings of the Executive Mansion. (*In English.*)

2381B. A 'book of anecdotes or of records' begun by David Stephen Davies when he was a student at the Theological Seminary, Alleghany City, Pa., 1861. (*In English.*)

2600E. Letters sent home by Humphrey and Sarah Roberts, emigrants from the Brymbo district, North Wales. The letters, Madison, Ohio, 1856-64, concern family news, Calvinist emigrants from

1. The County Archivist acts as Hon. Archivist to St. Deiniol's Library. The Glynne-Gladstone MSS., although stored in the Library, are produced for searchers in the Clwyd Record Office, and searchers are requested to give at least two days' notice of intended visits.

1. See also Alan Conway, 'Welsh Emigration to the United States', *Bulletin of the British Association for American Studies*, no. 8, pp. 11-8, 1959, and the bibliography therein.

Llangeitho and Trefecca and their character, Mormons, Catholics, climate and crops, economic depression, American politics, the Kansas question, Civil War news, their three sons in the Northern Army, General Morgan's visit to their settlement, the 'treachery' of Samuel Roberts and his defence of the South. (*In Welsh.*)

2704F. Letter, Marcy, Utica, N.Y., 1848, from Rowland Owen to Morgan Davis ('Clochydd Llanelltud'), giving an account of his own family and of other Merioneth settlers in the United States, and discussing the proposal to start a Welsh church for the benefit of Welsh members of the Established Church in the district. (*In Welsh.*)

2719B. Miscellanea from the collection of Edward Griffith, Dolgelley, including a letter, n.d., from an assembly of Congregational ministers in Monmouthshire to ministers of Welsh denominations in the United States on the Oregon dispute. (*In Welsh.*)

2722D. Transcripts of letters addressed to relatives in Merioneth by the following emigrants (*in Welsh and English*):

Hugh and Catherine Thomas, Trenton, Oneida, N.Y., 1816: description of their holding and neighbourhood near Steuben; religion, wages and prices, success of Welsh settlers, livestock, children.

John Richards, Johnsburgh, N.Y., 1817, encouraging his friends to emigrate; climate, soil, and produce; prices, work on canals, etc; advice to emigrants; all royalists should go to Upper Canada; Welsh preaching at Steuben.

William Thomas, Utica, N.Y., 1818: his work in a canal cut; his disappointment (John Richards's account was misleading) and intention of returning - the district a wilderness, with no market or fair and no dealers buying around Utica; craftsmen no better off than labourers.

David Richard, Utica, N.Y., 1818: his family; his work constructing arches under the canal; prices, rent, taxes and wages; lack of demand for sawyers in Utica; low state of religion.

David Jones, Albany, N.Y., 1817: his voyage; good prospects for all craftsmen except weavers; great demand for joiners; Welsh settlers in Steuben; regrets at not having settled in Canada; relatives in America and Wales; the Indians; arranging to have his two older sons over; the superiority of American ships for emigrants; cautions against slate ships from Caernarvon; labour conditions, etc.; scarcity of homes.

4602. Broomhall MSS. and documents. A record of estate papers which contain a few letters from emigrants to the U.S., concerning their property in Wales. (nos. 63-5, 76, 255, 83, 627-8, 1559) (*In English.*)

4616B. Letters to David Stephen Davies. The correspondents include (*in Welsh and English*):

G. James Jones, Findlay, Ohio, 1888-9, on American degrees and giving autobiographical details.

R. Gwesyn Jones, Utica, N.Y., 1894, on theology, baptism, American politics, the decline of Welsh churches in America.

William S. Jones, Scranton, Pa., 1872, on *Baner America* and *Y Drych* and the Welsh colony in Patagonia, and England's fears lest American Welshmen should emigrate to Patagonia.

R.Roberts, Pittsburgh, Pa., 1875, on D.S. Davies's departure from New York.

David Lodwick, Mystic, Iowa, 1911, on the death of J.J. Davies.

A few papers relate to the Welsh Colonizing and General Trading Co. Ltd., including a list of American subscribers.

4620E. Register of shareholders of the American branch of the Welsh Colonizing and General Trading Company Ltd., 1871. The aim of the American branch was the same as that of the Welsh parent company founded in 1866 to purchase land and buildings and to buy or charter ships to carry on a regular trade with South America, and, more particularly, with the Welsh colony in the Chubut valley, Patagonia. (*In English.*)

5503C. Letters to Henry Richard, M.P., including three from Elihu Burritt, the American internationalist, New Britain, Conn., 1856, 1874, 1876, on the Peace Movement, the Paris conference, the proposed abolition of war on commerce, ill health, Miles and Beckwith, the Geneva Congress, his semi-theological work in an assumed style and name, his simplified grammars of Oriental languages, James Long and the Russian question, his Hebrew handbook, severe haemorrhage, and the secret of his theological work.

6174E. Letters to Griffith Owen, Vaner, Dolgelley, and others, from the following (*in Welsh and English*):

John and Margred Owen, Baraboo, Wis., 1857: regret that they did not emigrate earlier; were the first Welsh family to cross the Wisconsin river; had only a pound left to start life; good land; prices and prospects; no religious meetings; need for missionaries; agriculture and implements.

William and Margaret and William G. Bebb, Van Wert, Ohio, 1850: agriculture; few Welsh settlers (only twelve families); religion.

Edward ___, Miliken's Bend, La., 1863: campaign around Vicksburg.

J.F. Williams, St. Paul, Minn., 1877: seeking information about the family of Howell Roberts.

T.Ll. Williams, Racine, Wis., 1907: a family reunion at Caledonia, Wis.

John Gwylym Owen, Portage, Wis., 1907: the Owen family.

Also two incomplete letters, and photographs of Caledonia Welsh church and Caledonia home-coming, 1907.

7163-6, 7176-7, and 7779E. Correspondence addressed to William Roberts ('Nefydd'), including the following (*in Welsh and English*):

William David, New York, 1843: 'Yankee clocks' and customs duties.

John Gould, Minersville, Pa., 1846: voyage to America; Baptist church at Minersville.

J. Edred Jones, New York, 1871: Utica, N.Y., eisteddfod essay adjudication.

Theophilus Jones, New York, Pughtown, and Philadelphia, 1846-57: the fate of the ship *Virginia*; Welsh Baptist Assembly; economic depression; children's education; family news.

William B. Jones ('ap P.A. Mon'), New York and Kansas, 1858-71: dreams; Wisconsin eisteddfod; Welsh Baptist ministers in America; 'Gohebydd's' impressions of North Missouri; Samuel Roberts's apology for the South; the need for a Welsh Baptist magazine in America; the Neosho and Emporia, Kan., land schemes; the failure of democracy in America; the degree of LL.D. conferred upon 'Nefydd' [William Roberts].

R. Littler, New York, 1848: American Home Mission.

Phillip D. Phillips, Utica, N.Y., 1871: eisteddfod adjudication.

Also an incomplete letter written on notepaper of the office of Aetna Iron and Nail Co., Cleveland, Ohio, containing an inquiry whether William Roberts would accept the pastorate of a church at Newburgh.

8827C. Correspondence relating to a tour of North America made in 1879 by W.J. Parry, mostly letters of introduction. (*In Welsh and English.*)

9108-9D. A photostat facsimile of the 'Ilston Book' made for the

National Library of Wales by permission of the members of the First Baptist Church of Swansea, Mass., at the John Carter Brown Library. The 'Ilston Book', 1649-1855, is a register belonging to the Baptist Church founded in Gower, South Wales, by John Miles, which followed him to Massachusetts in 1662. It contains lists of members of the original church in South Wales and of the First Baptist Church of Swansea, Mass., church decrees and covenants, and transcripts of letters and of the general laws and liberties of New Plymouth. (*In English.*)

9521A. Miscellaneous notes on the United States and on Welsh settlements and settlers there, written by R.D. Thomas ('Iorthryn Gwynedd') during his tours in New York, Ohio, and Pennsylvania, 1851-2. (*In Welsh and English.*)

10297A. An essay by John Robert Pryse ('Golyddan') on the Civil War and its causes. (*In Welsh.*)

10982F. Papers, 1868-9, relating to Harry H. Davis, United States Consul at Cardiff. (*In English.*)

13191D. Letters to Evan Roberts, Dolgadfan Mills, Llanbrynmair, from his children: George Roberts, [Ebensburg, Pa.], 1804-11 - a religious revival originating in Kentucky, news of emigrants from Llanbrynmair, the Louisiana purchase, 1803; and Grace Morgan, 1811 - her family, livestock, and crops. (*In Welsh.*)

13202D. Letters to David Howell, Machynlleth. The correspondents include William Bebb, Hamilton, Ohio, 1848: thanks for gifts of plate by his cousins, Lewis and John Howell in America, the 'unjust war' in Mexico, his 'great faith in the permanency of the American Union'. (*In English.*)

13203D. Letters, mainly to William Bebb, from politicians, lawyers, and members of Congress. The letters relate to public appointments, politics, and public functions during Bebb's governorship of Ohio 1847-9; the correspondents include John W. Allen, ex-Governor M. Bartley, James A. Briggs, Joseph H. Crane, D.T. Disney, N. Evans, T. Ewing, S. Ford, Horace Greeley, J.R. Grindings, J. Mason, John M. Millikin, O.M. Mitchell, J.W. Scott, C.B. Smith, Governor William Smith of Virginia, B. Storer, Charles L. Telford, Governor Philip F. Thomas of Maryland, S.F. Vinton, T. Walker, and John Woods. (*In English.*)

13204D. (*See also* 13189D, 13190D, and 14094E.) Miscellaneous correspondence including letters from (*in Welsh and English*):

George and Jane Roberts, Ebensburg, Pa., 1805-53 - family news, details of husbandry and livestock, offices of constable and assessor, opinion on emigration from Wales, religious life of the community, temperance, transport facilities and their effects on the prosperity of Ebensburg, neighbours and emigrants from the Llanbrynmair district.

Evan R. Bebb, New York, 1835, introducing Dr. Gardiner Spring to Samuel Roberts.

D. Howell, Toledo, Ohio, 1890, on the death of his brother.

Evan R. Morgan, Ebensburg, 1857, giving family news.

13713D. Letters and miscellanea relating to Dr. George Lewis, of Llanuwchllyn, Merioneth, including a letter from the Rev. Jedidiah Morse, Charlestown, Mass., 1793, on a Boston society for the information and advice of foreign settlers, with a list of members, and on vacancies for ministers in the state of Vermont, a very thriving country of good land. (*In English.*)

14110B-14111D. Letters to their relatives in Llanbrynmair from Ann Peat, on board the *France,* 1868; Edward Peat, Liverpool, Ebensburg, Pa., and Gomer, Ohio, 1868-78; Edward Peate, Gomer, 1878-83; and Morris Peat, Ebensburg and Iowa City, Iowa, 1865-87. The letters of Edward Peat are particularly important on account of their detailed descriptions of American customs and the life of the Welsh communities in Ohio.(*In Welsh.*)

14348D. Correspondence and papers of Dr. John Ryland (1753-1825), including the diploma of the degree of Doctor of Theology conferred upon him by Rhode Island College, Providence, 1792, signed by David Howell, Jonathan Mazey, Peres Fobes, Benjamin West, and George Benson (*In Latin.*)

14352C. Typescript copies of correspondence mainly addressed to Robert Owen, from the William Galpin collection. An imperfect letter to William Allen relates to the acquisition of New Harmony, Ind., 1825, and two letters, 1828, from Alexander Campbell and P.O. Skene refer to America, the latter to the Texas scheme. There is also one letter, 1846, by Robert Dale Owen, on Webster's manifesto on the Oregon question, and another fragment by him, 1844, on family accounts in connexion with New Harmony (*In English.*)

20995. Jack Edwards. Letters from America, 1880-7. 2 vols. (*In English.*)

CWRTMAWR MANUSCRIPTS.

818-819E. Letters addressed to Ellis Evans, Baptist minister, Cefnmawr, Denbighshire. The correspondents include (*in Welsh and English*):

William Davies, Deerfield, Utica, N.Y., 1821-2: account of Owen Owens'and his children, his emigration in 1794, the Welsh settlement at Steuben, N.Y.; religion, Baptists in Steuben and Utica, Welsh Baptist ministers, Utica a village of six hundred dwellings, the construction of a canal from Lake Erie to the Hudson River, economic depression, low prices, Welsh people doing very well, the best government in the world.

Jesse Jones, Steuben, N.Y., 1844, on religious disputes, the secession of the Welsh Baptist church at Steuben and its stand for the traditional articles of faith.

Owen Owens, Trenton, Oneida, N.Y., 1821, giving news of members of his family and of Welsh settlers, with a note by his niece Lily Maurice.

1044E. Miscellaneous correspondence including letters by the following (*in Welsh and English*):

Hugh Evans, Utica, N.Y., 1843 - a proposal to revisit Wales, pressing his wife and children to join him on his farm near the Black River in New York State.

John H. Evans, Remsen, 1842, on differing opinions about America, the nature of lands in New York, Pennsylvania, and Ohio, on Wisconsin as the ideal state for Welsh settlers, excellent laws but execution falling short, with slight penalty for murdering a 'Gwyddel' (? Irishman or tramp), scarcity of currency, unsatisfactory state of the banking system, bad roads, good prospects for good craftsmen and for farmers with large families, religious sects (Mormonism a disgrace to humanity).

John Owen Jones, Green Hall, Jackson, Ill., 1848, on his family, his son in the Mexican campaign, his farm and timber, the reasons for his removal from Columbus, Ohio.

DEPOSITED COLLECTIONS.

(*a*) Llanfair and Brynodol Documents.

Among correspondence of the Griffith family in this collection is a letter to Hugh Griffith, Caernarvon, from Evan Thomas, Chester River, Md., 1708: his good and beneficial office with fees settled by Act of Assembly of the province amounting to 30,000 lb. of tobacco; great writing business; inquiring for a clerk assistant; Herbert Griffith's business and death near Annapolis; his building of a house in expectation of his wife's emigration, and to comply with the law that all clerks should reside at the towns where the courts are kept. (*In English.*)

(*b*) Tennessee Papers (Luther Thomas Deposit).

Correspondence and memoranda, 1856-64, relating to the purchase of lands and the Welsh settlement in East Tennessee projected by William Bebb of Illinois, and G. Williams, William and John Roberts Jones, and Samuel and Richard Roberts, all of Llanbrynmair, Montgomeryshire. The correspondents include Edward Bebb, Fountaindale, etc.; James E. Goll, New York; L.D. Howell, Utica, N.Y.; E.B. Jones, Monticello; William Jones and Richard Roberts of Brynffynon; E.D. Saxton and Benjamin J. Timms, of New York; John G. Vaughan, Salem, Ill.; and Mary Vaughan, Paddy's Run. William Bebb's letters relate also to American politics and the Civil War. There are, in addition, a large number of draft letters by Samuel Roberts and memoranda by him on the difficulties which the settlers experienced over the title to their purchases, and on the unsatisfactory arrangements made for them by Saxton, Jones, and Bebb. (*In Welsh and English.*)

(*c*) Dillwyn Diaries and Papers.

The collection includes minutes of William Dillwyn's voyage from Philadelphia to Bristol, 1774; diaries of his tour in Great Britain, his return to America, 1775, and his voyage to England, 1777; and genealogical memoranda of the Dillwyn family. (*In English.*)

(*d*) National Eisteddfod Manuscripts.

Subjects relating to the history and activities of Welshmen abroad have been set for competition from time to time at the National Eisteddfod of Wales. The original manuscripts deposited in the National Library include three entries in a competition for a handbook on emigration for Welsh farmers and workers at the London Eisteddfod, 1887, and the manuscript of 'An enquiry as to the extent to which Welshmen from home retain their peculiar characteristics in the lands of their adoption', submitted to the Mountain Ash Eisteddfod, 1905, by D. Jones, of Scranton, Pa.

ACCESSIONS SINCE 1942.

This list is drawn from the annual *Reports* of the National Library of Wales. Each item below is headed by the year and page number of the *Report* in which it is noted.

1941-2, p. 17. Dr. Erie Evans Deposit.

Manuscripts and printed materials for a biography of Griffith Evans (1835-1935), a pioneer in research into parasitology. Included are a note concerning purchase of land, 3 Jan. 1777 (?), on Lady's Island, Carolina, given to Evans on the battlefield in Virginia in 1864; portions of his Canadian journal, 1864; correspondence, 1921, with John Drinkwater about the latter's play, *Abraham Lincoln.*

1942-3, pp. 25, 34. Luther Thomas Deposit.

Additional material relating to Samuel Roberts and the Roberts family of Llanbrynmair, including letters, 1825-82, from the United States from E.R. Bebb, William Bebb, B. Williams Chidlaw, Ezekiel Hughes, and George Roberts; correspondence, 1859-82, concerning the Welsh settlement in Tennessee founded by Samuel Roberts, and notebooks containing entries relating to the land purchased by Roberts; correspondence and circulars, 1871-83, concerning Roberts's claims against the United States government.

——, p. 34. Sir Charles L. Dillwyn Venables-Llewelyn Deposit.

Passports issued to William Dillwyn to pass through combat areas and to visit England during the War of Independence; and certificates of membership of American institutions, 1777-1802.

1944-5, p. 17. Mrs. John Davies Deposit.

Journal, 1887, kept by Mrs. John Evans during a tour of the United States with her husband.

——, p. 21, Sir Henry Haydn Jones Deposit.

Letters to Richard Jones, including one from James Owen, Remsen, 28 Oct. 1831, and one from Morris and Margred Roberts, Utica, N.Y., 30 Aug. 1832. (*In Welsh.*)

1945-6, p. 20. 16098C. Mr. H.M. Cleaver Deposit.

Letter, St. Louis, Mo., 1867, from George R. Rowland, giving an account of members of the Cleaver family settled in Missouri.

——, p. 28. Luther Thomas Deposit.

Additional material concerning Samuel Roberts's American claims.

1946-7, p. 26. 6710B. Seventeenth-century manuscript containing a critical account of some Congregational churches in New England, said to have been compiled by Richard Sadler, lecturer at Ludlow, Salop.

1947-8, p. 43 (also mentioned 1948-9, p. 61). Mrs. E. Yale Deposit.

Journals of a tour of America by Thomas Lewis, M.P. for Bangor, 1874.

1948-9, p. 31. 15505D. Seven letters, 1799-1834, from Thomas Picton, minister at Woodbury, N.J., and West Point, N.Y.

1949-50. Tredegar Park Muniments.

(*a*) Box 128 - Bradstreet MSS. Letters and papers of Major-General John Bradstreet, who served in the British Army in the North American colonies. 1741-1825.

(*b*) Box 79/24 - Instructions issued to George, Earl of Orkney on his appointment as Governor-General of the colony of Virginia in America. 18th century.

(*c*) Box 79/25-54. Richard Phillips MSS. Phillips was the Governor of Placentia in Newfoundland, and Captain-General and Governor-in-Chief of Nova Scotia. 1719-64.

(*d*) King Gould Papers. MSS. 121, 253-4, 256-62, 272-9, 284-7. 1725-57.

1950-1, p. 23. 15267B. Minutes, 1888-1905, of the Welsh Prairie Presbyterian Church district meetings, United States.

——, p. 28. 17239C. Rev. Gomer M. Roberts Deposit.

J.G. Davies: diary of a voyage to the United States, and letters relating to the voyage, 1893.

1953-4, p. 23. 17537B. Professor T. A. Levi Deposit.

Three manuscript notebooks containing accounts of visits to America by Rev. Thomas Levi, 1867, 1873, and 1874.

1953-4, p. 26. 15532B. Diaries of Rev. David Davies, Oshkosh, Wis., for 1880, 1882-4, 1887-8, 1893, 1895-6, and 1899. Also a bound typescript volume of addresses delivered, 1947, at the centenary celebrations of the Welsh settlement at Oshkosh.

——, p. 28. 15506D. Typewritten copies of letters, 1862-4, written by John G. Jones to his family during the Civil War.

1954-5, p. 49. Admiral Herbert W. Hope Deposit.

Volume containing copies of four letters, 1771-2, from 'J.W.',

Philadelphia, announcing and acknowledging shipments of goods, and accounts of the receipt and payment of bills of exchange, etc.
——, pp. 54-5. Miss F.N. Norman Deposit.

Notes on trade relations with the American colonies, 1769; and a petition, 1778, from merchants, traders, and other inhabitants of New York to the commissioners appointed to quiet the disorders in the American colonies.

1959-60, pp. 42-4. 18334E. Emigrations from Llun to North America between 1785 and 1800. (*In English.*)
——, p. 22. 17613D. Photostat copies of letters from Elias J. Richard, written on active service during the American Civil War, 1863-4.

1960-1, p. 25. 17441E. Two holograph letters, 1846-7, written by John and Isaac Cheshire, Welsh emigrants, from Racine, U.S.A., to Morris Davies, Trefonen.
——, p. 26. Six holograph letters and one typescript copy of a letter, 1870-1925 and n.d., written by Welsh emigrants to the U.S.A., and four letters, 1948-9, to the donor relating to emigration from Wales.
——, p. 23. 17687-8B. Sermons by the Rev. David Davies, Oshkosh, Wis., 1881-1900.
——, p. 36. 17746B. Sermons by the Rev. David Davies, Oshkosh, Wis., 1879-1900.

1961-2, p. 39. 16098C. Typescript copy of a letter from James Davies, Washington, to his parents, 1862.

1963-4, p. 38. 18866E. Letter from David Jones, Aberdare, 1879, afterwards Independent minister at New Quay, Cardiganshire, and Scranton, Pa.
——, p. 24. 18932-6B. Sermons and lectures by Rev. David Davies, D.P., Oshkosh, Wis., 1879-1901.

1964-5, p. 35. 16704D. Letter from Griffith Thomas, Delaware, to Thomas Evans, Spite, Llanfynydd, 1846.
——, p. 38. 16704D. Photographic copy of a letter from John Rees, Bristol, 1853, to his brother, David Rees, Irontown, Ohio.
——, p. 36. 16098C. Two letters from Evan and Rachel Lewis, Bridgend, 1844-5, to their daughter-in-law, Mrs. Jane Lewis, Danbury, Conn.

1966-7, p. 39. Biographies of two Welsh Mormons: John Davis Rees (1816-80) and Zillah Mathias Rees (1839-1923).

1967-8, p. 27. Letter from Jenkin T. Jenkins to his father, Daniel Jenkins.
——, p. 23. The papers of Sir John Cecil Williams, a prominent member of the Honourable Society of Cymmrodorion, relating to his visit to North America in 1957.

1968-9, p. 29. 20017E. Typewritten transcript with English translation of a letter from Robert Davies in service with Company F, 25th Regiment Iowa Volunteer Infantry, Helena, Ark., to his parents at Long Creek Welsh Settlement near Columbus, Ohio, 30 Jan. 1863.
——, p. 35 (also mentioned 1969-70, p. 39). The Elias Papers.

Letters from emigrants to the United States of America, 1872-5.

1969-70, p. 40. 20463C. Lloyd George MSS. Letter from W.C. Williams, Salt Lake City, to Lloyd George, 1919. Also, 20472C, Dame Margaret Lloyd George's speeches and notes for speeches; notes of a visit to Canada and the U.S.A. in 1923.

CYFARTHFA PAPERS.

Letter-books, ledgers and correspondence of the Crawshay family, 1786-1877. The Crawshay ironworks, Cyfarthfa, Merthyr Tydfil, founded by Anthony Bacon, a Maryland settler who returned in 1745,[2] became one of the greatest iron firms of the nineteenth century. The papers were not examined. However, John P. Addis, *The Crawshay Dynasty: a Study in Industrial Organisation and Development, 1765-1867* (Cardiff, 1957), based mainly on these papers, includes references to letters in the 1850's and 1860's concerning the firm's monetary arrangements with American buyers; pricing policies on, for example, rails to the 'Mobile and Ohio pattern'; orders for American rods; the effects of the Civil War; American tariff changes. (*See also* Gwent County Record Office, p. 248).

HARPTON COURT COLLECTION.

Among this large collection are papers of Sir George Cornewall Lewis (1806-63), who was Secretary for War 1861-3.

Some forty letters, 1849-62, from his close personal friend Sir Edmund Head, contain, while Head was Governor-General of Canada 1854-61, discussion of the threat of war with the United States and the defence of Canada. There are also twelve or so letters from Edward Twisleton relating to his visit to the United States, 1850-2, and to the Civil War and British neutrality, 1861. There is also an incomplete draft of a Cabinet memorandum, 1862, on relations with the United States, including the questions of recognition of the Confederacy and possible intervention.

BOB OWEN COLLECTION. Welsh emigrant letters.

The late Mr. Bob Owen, a private scholar and antiquarian, had many emigrant letters from America, mainly in Welsh but some in English, among his large private collection of books and manuscripts. He also had completed in typescript a history of Welsh emigration to America with statistical tables drawn from his own examination of scores of parish registers and possibly hundreds of shipping lists. This material has now been deposited in the National Library of Wales.

DYFED ARCHIVES, CARMARTHENSHIRE RECORD OFFICE, County Hall, Carmarthen SA31 1JP

EMIGRANT LETTERS. 3 letters. 19th century.

Three nineteenth-century letters in Welsh from emigrants to America. (D/CT/3,4,5)

DYFED ARCHIVES, PEMBROKESHIRE RECORD OFFICE, The Castle, Haverfordwest

QUAKER COLLECTION. Documents. 1660-18th century.

Documents produced by families of Quakers involved in the whaling industry, who came to Britain from America in the eighteenth century. The records date from 1660 onwards and are mainly leases, conveyances, etc., of lands in Nantucket, where the Quakers had their original settlement, and wills and other papers from the same period. (D/BT)

2. See L.B. Namier, 'Anthony Bacon, an Eighteenth Century Merchant', *Journal of Economic and Business History*, vol. ii, pp. 20-70, 1929.

TROLLOPE-BELLEW OF CAREW CASTLE COLLECTION. Memoranda, notes, and pamphlets. 1740-2.

Draft memoranda, 'Minutes taken at the Bar of the House of Commons,' notes and two pamphlets on the colony of Georgia, 1740-2.

COURT ESTATE, LLANLLAWER (MORTIMER, GWYNN AND LLOYD FAMILIES). Letters. 1776-88.

Letters to and from Lieut. Daniel Gwynne, 9th Foot, from America and elsewhere, 1776-88. Gwynne's American letters are addressed from, *inter alia*, New York, Frederick Town, (Md.), Charlottesville, (Va.), and Quebec. This collection has not yet been listed in any detail.

GWENT

GWENT COUNTY RECORD OFFICE, County Hall, Cwmbran NP4 2XH

CRAWSHAY, RICHARD (1739-1810). Letter-book. 1789-90.

Ironmaster and merchant. The letter-book contains copies of business and personal letters from Crawshay, in chronological order, 1788-97. Among these are letters of 3 Feb. 1789, regretting the shortage of Baltimore iron; and of 25 May 1790, to H. Charles of Lynn, Mass., arranging to dispatch a shipload of grain to return with a cargo of iron, followed by letters from Crawshay's Cyfarthfa agent James Cockshutt urging the dispatch.

GWYNEDD

THE LIBRARY, UNIVERSITY COLLEGE OF NORTH WALES, Bangor

BANGOR MANUSCRIPTS. 1665-1943.

(*a*) Miscellaneous papers relating to the Welsh settlements, Eisteddfodau, a copy bond of 1665, etc. 1665-1929. (MSS. 26304-26311)
(*b*) Bob Owen on the Welsh emigrants - statistics, etc. Welsh, 1841 onwards. (MSS. 5869, 5876-5879)
(*c*) Letter (Welsh), *c*. 1876. (MS. 2825)
(*d*) Letters of the Rev. Owen Hughes (Llangefni and Amlwch) concerning a visit to the U.S.A. Welsh, 1892. (MS. 549)
(*e*) History of a trip to America as conductor and organiser of the Moelwyn Choir by R. Silyn Roberts, with account book. Welsh, 1911-2. (MSS. 624-5)
(*f*) Miscellany concerning the activities of William Sulzer, Al Smith, etc. 1913-22. (MS. 415)
(*g*) References to the American Fund, alias Chancellor's Fund, alias Lloyd George's Fund, including a letter from Alaska. Welsh, 1915. (MS. 626)
(*h*) Letters. Welsh, 1935. [MS. 2381 (83/114)]
(*i*) Letters of Bob Owen, Croesor, concerning the Welsh emigrants. Welsh, 1942-3. [MS. 4898 (11,13,15,17,18)]
(*j*) 'Europeans in America before Columbus', article by Oswald Mersmüller, OSB. [MS. 413 (xiii)]
(*k*) 'Literature bearing on the Discovery of America by Madog', sixteen items signed P.J.W. [MS. 413 (xiv)]
(*l*) Note-book relating to the Emigrants' Protection Society. Welsh, n.d. (MS. 1732)
(*m*) Dictionary of Welsh-American biography, compiled by Bob Owen (271 pp.). Welsh, n.d. (MS. 14807)

EMIGRANT LETTERS. 1795-1940.

Letters from Welsh emigrants to America, mostly in Ohio - members of Bebb and Howell families, Llanbrynmair, Montgomeryshire, mostly in Welsh.

GWREDOG MANUSCRIPTS. 1832-1913.

(*a*) Material concerning Welsh-American periodicals, 1832-1913. (MS. 699-702)
(*b*) Diaries concerning emigration of the brothers of Elias Jones, Gwredog, 1873-6. (MSS. 53,54,59)

COETMOR MANUSCRIPTS. Article. *c*. 1882.

Article on emigration by W.J. Parry. Welsh, *c*. 1882. (MS. 48)

GABRIEL HUGHES MANUSCRIPTS. 1887-9.

Miscellaneous items on the Welsh settlement, particularly in California. Welsh, 1887-9. (MS. 116)

GWYNEDD AREA RECORD OFFICE, Cae Penarlag, Dolgellau

OWEN, BOB. Biographical material.

Typescript copy of 'Bywgraffiadau Cymry - Americanaidd' (Biographies of Welsh-Americans) by the late Bob Owen, M.A., O.B.E., of Croesor, dealing with those not included in the Welsh Dictionary of National Biography.

EMIGRANT LETTERS. 3 letters. 1861, 1883.

(*a*) From David W. Jones, New York, to a brother in Corris, informing him of family news and commenting on life in America, 1861.
(*b*) Sadorns, Champaign Co., Ill.: Two letters from a Welsh emigrant to his former employer, a carpenter, 1883.

GWYNEDD ARCHIVES SERVICE, Shire Hall, Llangefni LL77 7TW

MISCELLANEOUS DOCUMENTS. 19th century, n.d.

(*a*) Bill for provisions bought of Frye and Bruhn, Port Townsend, Washington, n.d. (Catalogue No. WDC/225)
(*b*) Letters from John Williams, Wisconsin, to his mother at Holyhead, describing farm life, trade, and the Civil War, 1862. Written in Welsh. (Catalogue No. WM115/1-3)
(*c*) Note regarding Thomas Ffraw Evans, born 1819 in Aberffraw, Anglesey, emigrated to North America in 1832, and believed to be the oldest voter in Oneida County, n.d. (Catalogue No. WM/94/2)

POWYS

BRECKNOCK MUSEUM LIBRARY, Glamorgan Street, Brecon

MISCELLANEOUS DOCUMENTS. Bonds. 1727-74.

The Library holds thirty-one bonds, 1727-74, dealing with transportations.

SOUTH GLAMORGAN

CENTRAL LIBRARY, The Hayes, Cardiff CF1 2QU

MS. 3. 173 (*formerly* PHILLIPPS MS. 16056).

(*a*) Manuscript copy in brief of the Dutch records of New York, 1629-45.
(*b*) Memoranda copied from American State Papers, Nov. 1760 - Mar. 1766, under Governor Bernard: Ratification of land grants. Measures against New Orleans smuggling. Colonial policy. Boston customs disputes. Propagation of Christian knowledge among the Indians. Forgery of treasury notes.

BUTE CORRESPONDENCE.

The correspondence, 1752-90, of John Stuart, 3rd Earl of Bute (1713-92), consists mainly of letters written to the Earl, with some written by him. The greatest concentration is in the early 1760's.

A good list revealed the following relevant material:

Amherst, Jeffrey, and Admiral Edward Boscawen. Signed plan of military affairs in North America after the siege of Louisbourg, 8 Aug. 1758.

Anon. Copy of abstracts of resolves of Providence, R.I., Maryland, Essex County, N.J., and Philadelphia, loyally asserting rights of local assemblies to levy taxes, and objecting to the new stamp duties. Sept. 1765.

Boone, Daniel. Letter, 20 Oct. 1760, soliciting a life pension for his wife.

Boscawen, Admiral Edward. Unsigned statement, 1758, of the disposition of his fleet at Louisbourg.

Johnstone, George, Governor of West Florida. Letters, 12 June, 25 July, and 18 Sept. 1765 from Pensacola, Fla. Gossip of Indians, tobacco, plants for Kew. The letter of 12 June contains details of advice on administering the Pensacola area.

Davers, Sir Robert. Memorial, 3 Mar. 1763, requesting a land grant in North America lying in the mouth of the river Detroit.

George III. *c.* 400 personal letters and notes, mostly undated, include sporadic and slight comments on American affairs. Appended to these is his 'Thoughts on the British Constitution', *c.* 1760.

Montagu, Edward Wortley. Letter of 27 June 1763 enclosing a map of the Mississippi mouth from Bayagoulas to the sea.

Philadelphia College, Academy and Charitable Trust. Loyal address of the trustees to Lord Bute, 27 May 1763.

DEPARTMENT OF TRADE, COMPANIES REGISTRATION OFFICE, Companies House, Crown Way, *See* p. 94. Maindy, Cardiff

GLAMORGAN RECORD OFFICE, County Hall, Cathays Park, Cardiff CF1 3NE

DOWLAIS IRON COMPANY. Letters.[1] 1782-1900.

The Dowlais Iron Company was one of the leading iron companies of South Wales in the nineteenth century and, like many of the other great iron companies of that region, concentrated on the production of rolled merchant bars and rails. The letter files which have been deposited include about 563,000 letters, 1782-1900. These are the files of incoming letters formerly kept at the Dowlais works of the Company. Incoming letters to the various sales offices - Cardiff, Liverpool, and London - are not included, nor are copies of any outgoing letters. The incoming records of the London house, and of the Liverpool and Cardiff houses, appear to have been destroyed. The Company now forms part of the Guest Keen and Nettlefolds group of companies, whose head office is in Birmingham.

The letters are divided into two series. The first, 'Dowlais Iron Company', is indexed alphabetically by years, 1782-1900; it covers such topics as labour relations, relations with other iron companies, technical questions concerning the production of iron, transport of iron, purchase of supplies, general financial matters and business of the Merthyr Tydfil Bank. The second series, 'London house', begins in 1837 with the establishment of that house and is arranged chronologically; the letters deal almost exclusively with instructions to the Dowlais works about orders taken by the London house, and are extremely full and informative for certain periods, especially the late 1840's and early 1850's, when every inquiry for iron was discussed in detail. However, for anyone not fully conversant with early American railway history, the usefulness of these letters is impaired by the difficulty of identifying the various orders - even the manager of the works was not always informed for whom he was rolling.

The Company had extensive dealings with American railroad companies, but as the material is so vast, only specimen volumes up to 1854 were examined. American references found in these are as follows:

(*a*) 'D.I.C., 1837, A-Y': Orders for Camden & Amboy Railroad Co. Purchase of New Orleans City Bonds. Preliminary inquiries from Liverpool agent for iron edging for granite paving in New Orleans (catalogued under Ogden). Payment from Grand Junction Railroad, through Glyn, Mills, Hallifax & Co.
(*b*) 'D.I.C., 1838, A-Y': Correspondence on an order of rails through James Maury & Sons for Maury, Latham & Co. of New York and Philadelphia.
(*c*) 'London house, 1841-1842': Transactions with T. & P. George, Philadelphia. Letters from the London agent to Messrs. Baring urging shipment of rails 'to America'. Discussion of rail order from Messrs. Ralston of Philadelphia.
(*d*) 'D.I.C., 1845, E-W': Draft via the Pottsville, Pa., agent from P.R. McMurray, New York. Appeal from Jane Head, Philadelphia, to Sir John Guest to represent her legal interests.

1. Some of the letters are reproduced in *Iron in the Making: Dowlais Iron Company Letters, 1782-1860*, ed. by Madeleine Elsas (Cardiff, 1960).

(*e*) 'London house, 1850-1852': Orders of rails by Boorman, Johnston & Co. of New Orleans, Camden & Amboy Railroad Co. (with difficulties encountered in manufacture and delivery), Michigan Central Railroad Co., and Messrs. Souther of New York. Order of axle iron by T. & P. George, Philadelphia.
(*f*) 'D.I.C., 1854': Importation of timber from Quebec (catalogued under Batchelor).

COPLEY, JR., JOHN SINGLETON, LORD LYNDHURST (1772-1863). Letters. 1795-1863.

The Lyndhurst Papers include three letters, 1795-6, from J.S. Copley, Jr. (later Lord Lyndhurst) to his mother, describing his travels in America. These consist of a brief itinerary of his movements in the U.S., and remarks on American political affairs, e.g. American apprehension of war with France. Copley also comments on American presidential elections and his plans for extended travels in the western States (D/D Ly 1/16-18).

There are other scattered allusions to America in Lord Lyndhurst's correspondence. In 1861, for example, he makes several references to the Civil War in letters to his daughter Sophia. (D/D Ly 2/60, 62) The Civil War and relations between Britain and America are also discussed in six (copy) letters, 1861-3, from Lyndhurst to James S. Amory (D/D Ly 24/1).

Finally, the Lyndhurst Papers contain two letters from the Rev. J.S. Copley Greene, Brookline, Mass., to Mary Copley in London. The first, 3 Apr. 1865, includes news of the American Civil War, while the second, 12 June 1866, mentions an attempted Fenian invasion of Canada (D/D Ly 5/4, 6).

MERTHYR MAWR ESTATE RECORDS.[2] *c*. 60 letters. 1798-1813.

Political correspondence of Sir John Nicholl, British diplomat.
These papers contain information on the effect of British blockades, especially the Orders in Council, on American trade. Topics discussed include United States grievances over operation of trade embargoes, application for restitution of ships and cargoes seized by British vessels, problems of vessels trading under neutral flags, applications to Privy Council for licences to relieve merchants from operation of trade embargo, etc. American correspondents include Rufus King and William Pinkney.

DOCKMASTER'S LETTERS, BUTE DOCK, CARDIFF. 1841-5.

Contains a number of references to American ships being loaded and unloaded at Cardiff while engaged in trade. (D/DXjo)

RHYMNEY IRON COMPANY COLLECTION.

This company had frequent business dealings with America in the mid-nineteenth century, and the invoice books in particular contain information regarding names of American companies, nature and quantity of goods supplied, and the names of the vessels on which goods were carried. (D/DRh)

TENNANT CANAL AND ESTATE RECORDS. Letters. 1891-2.

Correspondence, 1891-2, including about twelve letters from Gertrude and Dorothy Tennant relating to the American tour of Henry Stanley, the explorer. (D/DT 951, 952/1, 2)

EMIGRANT LETTERS. 1822-65.

(*a*) Letter, 27 Oct. 1822, from a Quaker in America to his parents, describing his business and life in America, and encouraging them to emigrate. (Copy.) (D/DX m.g. 8)
(*b*) Letter, 31 May 1846, from Robert and Sarah Morgan, Boston, Mass., to their mother in Newport, Wales, giving news of other Welsh emigrants. (D/DX 16/27)
(*c*) Five letters, 1846-65, from William B. and Rees Thomas, and Mary Thomas, in Philadelphia, to their parents Daniel and Mary Thomas in Caerphilly, relating family news, details of activities in America, etc. (Copies.) (D/DXfq 37/1-5)

SOCIETY OF FRIENDS.

The County Office, which acts as the repository for Society of Friends records in South Wales, has numerous minute-books dating from the late seventeenth to the early twentieth century. Included in these volumes is occasional correspondence from America, e.g. epistles, 1788-93, from the Philadelphia Women's Meeting to the Carmarthenshire and Glamorgan Women's Yearly Meeting. (D/DSF 387)

2. Although these papers are still in private possession, a handlist is available in the County Office, which acts as intermediary between the family and persons wishing to use the documents.

SCOTLAND

DUMFRIES AND GALLOWAY

HORNEL LIBRARY, Broughton House, Kirkcudbright

MISCELLANEOUS LETTERS. 1781-1815.

(*a*) Merchant's letter- and account-book of goods, 1781-9, including shipments of Virginia tobacco to Liverpool or Glasgow.
(*b*) Letters, 1796-1815, from William Muir, Lynchburg and Richmond, Va., to his aunt in Kirkcudbright.

FIFE

MUSEUM AND ART GALLERY, Kirkcaldy

MISCELLANEOUS MSS. 1735-1860.

(*a*) Indenture for service in Carolina, 1735.
(*b*) Two letters, *c.* 1823, from David Chalmers in New York, relating that he has taken a job as a typemaker in a printing firm at seven dollars a week, and giving other personal news.
(*c*) Letters, 1854-60, from members of Galloway family in Savannah, Ga., with personal news.
(*d*) Letter, 1859, from William Hill, New York, telling how he became a Sunday school teacher in New York.

GRAMPIAN

J. & J. CROMBIE LTD., Grandholm Works, Aberdeen

BUSINESS RECORDS.
Woollen manufacturers. Two large entry books record information about business done with customers *c.* 1869-1919. Several American firms are included. In many cases notes are added about the standing, connexions, and prospects of these firms; sometimes these were supplied by the Bradstreet Company and others were from private sources. A few loose items of correspondence are inserted in these volumes.

The Company has other records concerning later trade with America. From 1880 to 1890 it maintained a New York office, but these particular records do not appear to have been preserved.

THE DIOCESAN ARCHIVE OF THE DIOCESE OF ABERDEEN AND ORKNEY, 16 Crown Terrace, Aberdeen

SEABURY CONSECRATION. 23 letters (1 volume). 1784.

These letters, written by Dean John Skinner (1744-1816) of Aberdeen to A. Petrie of Old Meldrum, Aberdeenshire, contain reference to a scheme of Seabury for drawing up a concordat, and other matters. Samuel Seabury (1729-96) was the first bishop of the Episcopal Church in America. After the War of Independence he proceeded to England for consecration, but was refused by the Church of England. He then took himself to the Episcopal Church in Scotland where he was consecrated.

THE LIBRARY, UNIVERSITY OF ABERDEEN, Aberdeen AB9 2UB

ATHOLL PAPERS. 1579-1830.

Calendar of abstracts from the MSS. of the Duke of Atholl housed in the Charter Room at Blair Castle, Blair Atholl, Perthshire, undertaken in Aberdeen University Library between 1953 and 1965, contains numerous references to events in America, especially in the family and estate correspondence from 1579 to 1830. All MSS. have now been returned to Blair Castle, where another copy of the calendar is kept; a third is available for consultation in the National Register of Archives (Scotland). (MS. 2607)

DUFF OF BRACO MUNIMENTS. 2 letters. 1775, 1777.

(*a*) Letter from William Braco Gordon, Charles Town Heights, Mass., on present campaign and possible recall of Gen. Gage, of whose conduct he is highly critical; discusses army dispositions, organization and future movements, 1775. (MS. 2727/1/181)
(*b*) Letter from Lewis Duff, Forres, discussing the American situation and mentioning Burgoyne and military procedures, 1777. (MS. 2727/1/132)

OGILVIE FORBES OF BOYNDLIE MSS. Papers. 1778-1806.

A survey of the National Register of Archives (Scotland) mentions papers relating to the South Carolina settlement of Charles Ogilvie, 1788-92, other papers concerning South Carolina estates and Empire Loyalists, and a collection of American papers, 1778-1806. No further details now available. (MS. 2740)

WASHINGTON, GEORGE. Letter. 1788.

Autograph letter, 10 Apr. 1788, to Richard B. Lee. (MS. 906)

TAYLER, A. AND H., COLLECTIONS. 18th century.

A very extensive collection of letters, etc. to and from members of the Duff family, especially James Duff, 2nd Earl of Fife, and his factor, William Rose, many from persons who had gone to America in the eighteenth century or referring to affairs there; descriptive list now in course of compilation. This material was used by the Taylers for *The Book of the Duffs, Lord Fife and his Factor*, and other works. (MS. 2226)

DAVIDSON AND GARDEN RECORDS, Aberdeen legal firm. Letters and papers. 1802-54.

The survey by the N.R.A. (Scotland) mentions a collection of letters from John Leslie, Norfolk, Va., to Leslie of Berryden, 1808-25. The firm's MSS. also include letters and papers, 1802-54, of James Keith relating to the North West Company and the Hudson's Bay Company. (Keith was in charge of the Columbia District, later Oregon.) (MS. 2769)

LESLIE, JAMES, merchant in Montreal and Canadian political figure. Letters. Early 19th century.

A series of letters of American interest is included in a collection of letters and papers concerning Thomas Reid (1710-96) and his descendants, and the families, including that of Leslie, to whom they were related. These letters of James Leslie (1786-1873) and a relative, Alexander Leslie, employed by the Montreal firm, refer to Canadian affairs and trade in the early nineteenth century. (MS. 2814)

BELL, PATRICK (1799-1869). Journal. 1833-4.

Journal of travels between Great Britain and Upper Canada, 1833-4. The journal contains many references to the northeastern parts of the United States. (MSS. 2137-8)

HAY OF SEATON MSS. Correspondence.

A small bundle of 'American correspondence' is known to be included in this collection, but no further details are now available. (MS. 2254)

ABERDEEN TYPOGRAPHICAL SOCIETY. Minute-books (printed). 1853-twentieth century.

Branch of the Scottish Typographical Association. The minute-books contain occasional references to the emigration of members, and to such public questions as the American copyright controversy.

The Library also holds the *Annual Reports* of the Scottish Typographical Association, Glasgow. From 1890 the accounts of the Association contain a figure for emigration grants paid to members, but no indication is given of the destination of recipients. However, some clues on this subject may be found in the reports from branches, also reprinted in the *Annual Reports*.

ABERDEEN TRADES COUNCIL. Minute-books. 1876-1944, 1952-5.

Minute-books, 1876-1944 and 1952-5, contain occasional references to American emigration. (MS. 2270)

LONGFELLOW, H.W. Letter. 1879.

Letter to W.G. Simpson, 1879. (MS. 2335)

ISABEL DUNCAN PAPERS. Letters. 1884-6.

Letters from Mrs. Isabel Duncan, wife of William Duncan, master of the *Scotia* of Banff, from American and West Indian ports, 1884-6. (MS.2526)

HARTE, FRANCIS BRET. Letter. 1885.

Letter to W.K. Leask, 1885. (MS. 2079)

OPERATIVE MASONS' AND GRAINCUTTERS' JOURNAL. May 1901-Apr. 1909.

This monthly journal dealt with news of interest to members of the Operative Masons' and Granitecutters' Union of Aberdeen. Various, and fairly frequent, references are made to letters received from union members who had left Aberdeen district for the United States, particularly Barre, Vt.

JAMES GODSMAN PAPERS. Diaries. 1918-22.

Diaries covering voyages to America and elsewhere; these contain historical and topographical information and social and political comments, 1918-22. (MS. 2804)

LOTHIAN

HUNTLY HOUSE MUSEUM, Canongate, Edinburgh EH6 8DIS

HOLYROOD FLINT GLASS WORKS. Letters. 1838-48.

Letters from Thomas Leighton, East Cambridge, Boston, commenting briefly on trade in America, 1838-48.

A.W. BUCHAN & CO., POTTERY MANUFACTURERS. Correspondence. 20th century.

Correspondence concerning exports to New York and Minneapolis, [Minn.], twentieth century.

NATIONAL LIBRARY OF SCOTLAND, Edinburgh EH1 1EW

Arranged in alphabetical order by name of collection.

ANDERSON, ROBERT (1750-1830). Correspondence: 26 letters. 1805-29. (Adv. MSS. 22.4.16, vol. vii)

'Original letters' addressed to Robert Anderson, editor of the *Edinburgh Magazine*: six letters, Boston, 1817-26, from Rev. Andrew Bigelow; two letters from Rev. J.W.B. Buckmaster; fourteen letters, Boston, 1805-29, from Rev. Charles Lowell; three letters, Harvard University, 1814-7, from Rev. Dr. Joseph McKean; and one letter, Boston, 1822, from George Ticknor.

ASHBURNER PAPERS. Letters. 1803-67. (Acc. 5724, Boxes 1/1, 2/1)

Letters to or concerning members of the Forrester and Barstow families of Salem, Mass., 1803, 1809, 1822-4, 1839, 1864-7, and genealogical tables of families of Salem.

THOMAS BORTHWICK PAPERS. Correspondence, papers. 1878-85, n.d. (Acc. 4005)

Includes thirty letters of or to Alexander Graham Bell.

SIR GEORGE BROWN PAPERS. Letters. 1850-1, 1861.

Letters, 1850-1, 1861, concerning Canada. (MS. 2847, ff. 424, 483; MS. 2248, ff.54, 89; MS. 2857, f. 218)

BROWN PAPERS. Letters. 1874-1909.

Dr. John Brown, author of 'Rab and his Friends', had among his correspondents several prominent American literary figures, including H.W. Longfellow and O.W. Holmes. (Acc. 6134, Box 2 (1)). There are also seven letters from S.L. Clemens, 1876-1909, and one, 1874, from O.W. Holmes amongst Brown's family correspondence. (Acc. 6289, Box 3)

CADELL OF GRANGE PAPERS. Letters and papers. 1773-1805.

(*a*) Three letters, 1773, concerning a proposed steel mill in New England. (Acc. 5381, Box 31/1)

(*b*) Papers, 1775-1805, concerning overseas trade, including American trade. (Acc. 5381, Box 40)

CAMPBELL JOURNALS. 1874. (Adv. MSS. 50.4.9)

Journal describing a tour made by J.F. Campbell across North America from New York to San Francisco, 1874, illustrated with watercolour sketches and photographs.

CARLYLE, THOMAS (1795-1881). Letter. [1869] (MS. 518, n. 46)

A volume of letters from Carlyle to his family, from 1865, contains an unsigned letter [1869] from Carlyle to Emerson.

CHURCH OF SCOTLAND. Correspondence of the General Assembly. 1826-9.

Correspondence relating to Canada, 1826-9. (MSS. 3436-8, *passim*; 3442, *passim*)

CHURCH OF SCOTLAND. Minute-books. 1836-87. (Acc. 3993)

Sixteen volumes of minutes of Scotland's Assembly Committee on Colonial Churches, 1836-50, the Edinburgh Sub-Committee on Colonial Churches, 1838, and the Acting Committee on Colonial Churches, 1838-87.

COCHRANE PAPERS. (MSS. 2264-505, 2568-608 and 3022)

Correspondence and papers, private and official, 1779-1856, of Admiral Sir Alexander Forrester Inglis Cochrane (1758-1831), who served as Commander-in-Chief of the Leeward Islands 1805-14, and of the North American Station 1814-5; and of his son Admiral Sir Thomas John Cochrane (1789-1872), Governor of Newfoundland 1825-34. The papers contain much information about operations and conditions in these regions.

COCHRANE JOHNSTONE PAPERS. 1804-32. (MS. 9049)

Correspondence and papers, 1804-32, of Andrew Cochrane Johnstone, Governor of Dominica and M.P. for Grampound, mostly concerning his financial and legal affairs. Cochrane Johnstone was involved in various speculative and fraudulent activities, and on his expulsion from Parliament in 1814 he returned to the West Indies. His correspondence includes letters dealing with the shipping of wool and sheep from Spain to North America, 1810-2.

COMBE PAPERS. (MSS. 7201-7515)

George Combe (1788-1858),[1] Writer to the Signet, phrenologist. Besides his phrenological interests Combe was caught up in the general reforming ferment of the first half of the nineteenth century and had some influence on educational reforms. He visited the United States in 1838-40, and met, among others, Van Buren, John Quincy Adams, Nicholas Biddle, H. Mann, L. Mott, W.E. Channing, and W.C. Bryant. He kept a journal of his tour (three volumes) which he later amended and published.[2] His American correspondence is fairly extensive and includes letters from some of the above as well as a good number of others.

COX'S GLUE WORKS LTD. (Acc. 4944)

Analysis book, American and Canadian sales, 1903-16. Vol. 28.

CUNINGHAME, WILLIAM & CO. 3 letter-books.[3] 1767-74. (Microfilm.) (Acc. 2461)

Glasgow merchants with agents in North America. The letter - books - the last is only a fragment - were written by agents in Falmouth and Williamsburg, Va., and are concerned with business matters.

DOWDEN PAPERS. Letters. 1896. (Dep. 171)

Papers of John Dowden, Bishop of Edinburgh, including letters of Dowden to his wife and children, 1896, during a visit to America.

DRUMMOND PAPERS. Letters. 1863-96. (Acc. 5890)

Henry Drummond (1851-97) was Professor of Natural Philosophy at the Free Church College, Glasgow, and a noted evangelist, theologian, and explorer. His letters to his family, 1863-96, include comments on his geological visit to North America, and his work with the American evangelists Moody and Sankey.

DUNLOP PAPERS. 1688-9, 1812-4, 1845.

(*a*) Legal papers concerning William Dunlop's affairs in South Carolina, 1688-9. (Ch. 8456-8)
(*b*) Extracts from a journal kept in Canada, 1812-4. (MS. 9697, ff. 97, 101)
(*c*) Journal, 1845, of a tour in North America of Alexander Graham Dunlop, eldest son of John Dunlop of Gairbraid. (MS. 9267)

ELIBANK PAPERS. 1916-20.

Correspondence, 1918, chiefly drafts and copies of telegrams, of Arthur C. Murray, Viscount Elibank, when Assistant Military Attaché in Washington (MSS. 8806-7); correspondence of Murray with various Americans, including F.D. and Eleanor Roosevelt (MSS. 8808-12); diary, pocket book and miscellaneous papers of Murray, 1916-20. (MSS. 8815-7)

ELLICE PAPERS. (Accs. 1993 and 2072)

Family correspondence.
Letters and journals from Edward Ellice, Sr., to his son Edward, and to Janie, written during his tour of Canada and the U.S.A., 1858. (E66)

Estate and business correspondence.
(*a*) Canada. The seigneury of Anfield or Beauharnois as it was usually called, was purchased by the elder Ellice from the Marquis du Lotbinière. The letters of one of Ellice's agents, Samuel Gerrard, consist of two volumes, 1825-52, and contain numerous comments on local Canadian politics.

There are also several volumes of correspondence with the Canadian partners in whose businesses the Ellices had an interest, namely Forsyth, Richardson and Co., and McGillivray and Thain. E91 contains letters on the elder Ellice's negotiations as trustee for the North West Company when they discussed combining their stock with the Hudson's Bay Company, and the winding-up of the North West Company. There is also a good deal of correspondence on the Hudson's Bay Company, and the difficulties they encountered as the fur trade declined. (E82-E98)
(*b*) U.S.A. The Ellices also owned considerable amount of land in New York State, centering around the town of Little Falls. The correspondence is, again, mostly from agents. (E99-E106)

Journals.
Journal kept by Edward Ellice, Jr., of his tour to Canada as private secretary to Lord Durham, 1838. (E117)

1. A.C. Grant, a postgraduate student of the University of Edinburgh during the compilation of the first edition of this *Guide*, kindly provided this information on the life of Combe.
2. *Notes on the United States of North America, During a Phrenological Visit in 1838-9-40*. 3 vols. (Edinburgh and Philadelphia, 1841).
3. Originals in the possession of the Marchioness of Ailsa.

Financial.
Business account book, with details of Ellice's trading concerns in Britain, Canada, America, and the West Indies, 1797, 1805. (E142)

FETTERCAIRN PAPERS. (Acc. 4796)

Letters to Dr. Myles Cooper from America, 1775-84. (Box 75)

FLEMING OF WIGTOWN PAPERS. (Acc. 3142)

Vol. II of Royal Letters includes a passport signed by, and a letter of, James Monroe, 1811.

FLETCHER OF SALTOUN PAPERS. Letters. 1756-60. (S.C. 18-22)

Twelve letters, 1756-60, of General Sir Henry Fletcher to members of his family concerning the war in North America.

FRASER PAPERS. Letters. 1865-1909. (Dep. 208)

Prof. A. Campbell Fraser was a prominent nineteenth-century philosopher, who also edited the *North British Review* from 1850 to 1857. His papers include a letter from R. W. Emerson, 1873, along with nine from R.G. Hazard, 1865-84, and thirty-two from Prof. James Seth, 1886-1909, two of Fraser's other American correspondents.

GEDDES PAPERS. Correspondence, lectures, notes and other papers of and concerning Sir Patrick Geddes (1854-1932), the prominent sociologist.
(*a*) The letters of Geddes, mostly drafts or copies, include a number dealing with his visit to America in 1900. (MSS. 10508A-20)
(*b*) Geddes also corresponded with Sir Raymond Unwin, the architect, whose letters concern the Cities and Town Planning Exhibition and its possible visit to America. (MS. 10571)

GORDON-CUMMING PAPERS. Diaries and letters. 1781-1910.

(*a*) Six letters, 1878-85, of General Sherman to Sir William Gordon-Cumming, 4th Bart. (Dep. 175, Box 172/2)
(*b*) Diary of Sir W.G.-Cumming, 4th Bart., while in Mexico and the U.S.A. in 1888. (Dep. 175, Box 178)
(*c*) Three letters, 1898-9, 1910, from Theodore Roosevelt to Walter Frederick Gordon-Cumming. (Dep. 175, Box 174/1)
(*d*) Diaries and engagement books of the 3rd Baronet, 1835-65, n.d., including a journal of his travels in the U.S.A. and Canada, 1835-6. (Dep. 175, Box 175/3)
(*e*) Letter, 1781, from L. Grant to A.P.Cumming, commenting on the war in America. (Dep. 175, Inv. No. 3716)

GRAHAM OF GARTMORE AND ARDOCH PAPERS. 1890-1918. (Dep. 205)

The correspondence of Robert Bontine Cunninghame Graham of Gartmore and Ardoch (1852-1936) includes letters from several prominent American literary and political figures, including one from Bret Harte, 1890, four from Henry James, 1901-15, and two from Theodore Roosevelt, 1916-8.

GRIEG PAPERS. Letter. 1743. (Dep. 190, Box 1)

Letter from ? Abercrombie, Boston, Mass., to ? on religious matters, 1743.

HALDANE PAPERS.[4] (MSS. 5901-6108)

Richard Burdon Haldane, Viscount Haldane of Cloan (1856-1928), Secretary of State for War 1905-12. This collection includes letters from Andrew Carnegie, Colonel House, Sir Wilfrid Laurier, and Woodrow Wilson.

HALKETT PAPERS. Correspondence. 1772-95, 1836-7, n.d.

(*a*) Letters, 1772-95, n.d., mostly to Sir John Halkett, Bart. This volume includes twenty letters from Sir William Erskine, 1st Bart., of Torrie, describing the American War of Independence. (MS. 6410)
(*b*) Admiralty correspondence, 1836-7: letters to Admiral Sir Peter Halkett, Bart., when he was Commander-in-Chief of the American and West India Station. A number of these letters concern the slave trade. (MS. 6413)

HOUSTON, ALEXANDER & CO. 3 letter-books, ledgers, rules, and account books, 1729-31, 1776-81, 1792-8, 1777-1807.

Houston & Co. were general merchants and shipowners, Glasgow, trading principally with the West Indies. Most of the letters are to the Company's agents in Great Britain and in the West Indies, and to the captains of the Company's ships, relative to American trade.

JOHNSTONE, JAMES, Chevalier de Johnstone (1719-1800?). 'Memoirs.' (MS. 1028.) (Microfilm; the original with the owner.)

The originals are the manuscripts for two published works by Chevalier de Johnstone, *Memoirs of the Rebellion* (London, 1820), and *Memoirs of the Chevalier de Johnstone,* 3 vols. (Aberdeen, 1870-1), which includes descriptions of the war in Canada in 1758 and 1759.

LISTON, SIR ROBERT (1742-1836). Papers. 1777-1800.

(*a*) Copy of journal, 1777, sent to Robert Liston, concerning the progress of the war in North America. (MS. 5518, f. 11)
(*b*) Papers covering the period of Liston's service as the second British Minister to the United States 1796-1800. They are a file of his personal correspondence, and still more of his wife's (Henrietta Marchant),[5] mainly with her uncle in Glasgow. Comments on social life in Philadelphia; yellow fever; visits to South Carolina, Boston, Albany, N.Y., etc.; personality of Washington and Adams. Correspondence with Coutts, the bankers; George Hammond, Liston's predecessor; Lord Bute, Timothy Pickering, Lord Grenville.

Also, journals of Lady Liston's visits to various places in North America, including Virginia, North and South Carolina, New York, and Lower Canada.

LOCKHART, JOHN GIBSON (1794-1854). Correspondence: 4 letters. 1831-6. (MS. 930, nos. 64-7)

Biographer of Sir Walter Scott. Volume viii of this collection of letters to Lockhart contains four letters, 1831-6, from Washington Irving; one of these is written from New York introducing 'Professor Longfellow'.

MCLEOD OF GEANIES PAPERS. 1773-6. (Acc. 5340)

Letters to Donald McLeod, 3rd of Geanies, from his brother James, from Virginia and St. Vincent, 1773-6. (Box 1, F6)

MACLEOD, JOHN. Letters. 1775-81. (Acc. 6770)

Twelve letters of Lieutenant John MacLeod, Royal Artillery, written while on service in North America, 1775-81.

MATHIESON, WILLIAM LAW (1868-1938). 'Governor Eyre.' *c.* 1938. (MS. 2616)

An account of the Negro rising of 1865 in Jamaica, being the final draft of part of an uncompleted work on Governor Edward John Eyre by William Law Mathieson, *c.* 1938.

4. Permission of the family is necessary for consultation of these papers.
5. These edited by Bradford Perkins, 'A Diplomat's Wife in Philadelphia ... 1796-1800', *William and Mary Quarterly,* 3rd ser., vol. xi, pp. 592-632, 1954.

MAXWELL, MACMURDO AND NEWHALL FAMILY PAPERS. 1747-1803. (Acc. 7199, Boxes 3-4)

Correspondence and papers, 1761-86, between Balling Stark in Virginia and his brother-in-law, George MacMurdo; papers, 1754-1803, relating to business transactions between MacMurdo and Hugh Miller and his son Hugh, merchants in Virginia; letters and papers, 1771-93, of and concerning members of the Ravenscroft family and the Ravenscroft estates; letters, 1770-97, to George MacMurdo from his sons in Virginia and Pennsylvania; and general correspondence and papers, 1747-87, of George MacMurdo.

MELVILLE PAPERS. 1787-1819.

Papers of Henry Dundas, 1st Viscount Melville (1742-1811), and of Robert Saunders Dundas, 2nd Viscount Melville (1771-1851).
(*a*) Memorandum, 1787, on financial affairs in Canada by John Cochrane, Deputy Commissary to Forces in America, addressed to Thomas Harley, Lord Mayor of London, and Henry Drummond, banker. (MS. 3849)
(*b*) Miscellaneous letters, 1787-1815, mostly relating to Canadian affairs. Correspondents include John Graves Simcoe, first Governor of Upper Canada, Sir George Buchan Hepburn, Sir Archibald MacDonald, and Canadian officials. (MS. 3847)
(*c*) Papers on the West Indies, 1791-1819, dealing with estate owners, slaves, and campaigns. Also papers, 1789, 1800-1, n.d., on Russia and the Northern Confederation, with information supplied by Joseph Billings about his voyage to northeast Asia and the American coast. (MS. 1075)
(*d*) Canada and Newfoundland, 1793-1813: papers relating to Canadian convoys, timber, and fishing rights of Newfoundlanders. (MS. 3848)
(*e*) Memorandum, 1800, by General Sir David Dundas, relating to 1762 expedition against Havana. (MS. 3850)
(*f*) Letters, 1815, of General Sir George Murray to the 2nd Viscount Melville, relating to the former's arrival in Canada as Governor, and to Canadian affairs in general. (MS. 3851)
(*g*) Papers of the 2nd Viscount Melville: Correspondence and papers, 1818, concerning fishing by American vessels in Nova Scotian waters. (MS. 9735, ff. 48-119)

MICMAC RELIGIOUS WORK. (MS. 1900)

Catechism, including prayers, doctrinal instructions, the order of the administration of the sacraments, etc., in French and in Micmac, by Antoine Simon Maillard (d. 1768).[6]

MINTO PAPERS (Early family papers). Letters. 1756-73.

(*a*) Letters, 1756-73, of Andrew Elliot, Lieutenant-Governor of New York, relating to affairs in North America. (MS. 11008, chiefly ff. 3, 84, 147-52, 161, 224, 292, 330, 357-62; and MS. 11011, f. 3)
(*b*) Letter, 1764, of Major-General James Grant concerning East Florida. (MS. 11017, ff. 26-7)

MINTO PAPERS. (Papers of the 2nd Earl of Minto). Letters. 1832-44.

(*a*) Letters, 1834, concerning the offer of the Governor-Generalship of Canada to the 2nd Earl of Minto. (MS. 11748, ff. 141-56)
(*b*) Letters, 1841-3, concerning social life in Halifax, N.S. (MS. 11778, ff. 40, 47-51, 59, 156, 177-84, 187; MS. 11779, ff. 58, 65, 116, 132, 167, 178, 190)
(*c*) Letters, 1842, concerning the treaty concluded by Alexander Baring, Lord Ashburton, with the U.S.A. (MS. 11774, ff. 31-3, 36)
(*d*) Letters, 1843-4, of Admiral Sir Charles Elliot, formerly envoy to the Republic of Texas. (MS. 11789, ff. 204-25)
(*e*) Letter, 1832, of Thomas Cooper concerning American politics. (MS. 11793, f. 31)

MINTO PAPERS (Papers of the 3rd Earl of Minto). Letters. 1854-19--.

(*a*) Letters, 1854, 1859-60, of Sir Charles Elliot. (MS. 12258)
(*b*) Letters, 1899-19--, of and to Theodore Roosevelt. (*In* MSS. 12992 *et seq.*)

MINTO PAPERS (Papers of the 4th Earl of Minto). Correspondence and papers. 1883-1905.

Correspondence and papers, *c.* 1883-6, 1898-1905, of the 4th Earl of Minto, chiefly as Governor-General of Canada, and of his wife. (MSS. 12446-587, *passim*)

ERSKINE MURRAY PAPERS. Letters. 1776.

Copies of letters, 1776, from Montreal and South Carolina concerning the war in North America. (MS. 5083, ff. 177-8)

MURRAY PAPERS. 1814-5. (Adv. MSS. 46. 1. 1 to 47. 7. 4)

General Sir George Murray (1772-1846) served in Canada 1814-5, where he commanded the troops and also the civil government of Upper Canada. The papers give information about the conditions of settlement in Canada, relations with the Americans, and operations before New Orleans.

NEWBATTLE COLLECTION. (MSS. from the Library at Newbattle Abbey.)

This collection includes papers relating to historical works by the 8th Marquess of Lothian, among which are notes concerning *The Confederate Secession* (Edinburgh, 1864). (MS. 5763)

NISBET PAPERS. 1756-92.

Papers, 1756-92, of William Molleson, a Comptroller of the Army Accounts and appointed a Commissioner for Auditing the Public Accounts in 1785, containing financial material relating to the British Army and administration in North America. (MSS. 5496-8, 5500-1)

MRS. MARGARET OLIPHANT. Correspondence and literary papers. (Acc. 5793)

Mrs. Oliphant's correspondence includes three letters from Henry James (Box 1, 1). That of her niece and adopted daughter, Janet Mary Oliphant, also includes a letter from James.

PATON COLLECTION. Letter. 1847. (MS. 3218)

Contains a letter, 1847, from Elihu Burritt, and an envelope designed for Ocean Penny Postage, suggested by him, bearing an 1861 postmark.

PITFIRRANE PAPERS. Letters and journal. 1755. (MS. 6506)

Nineteenth-century copies of letters and journal, 1755, concerning the battle of Fort Duquesne. The letters are of Alexander and John Hamilton in Maryland to their brother, Gavin, a bookseller in Edinburgh.

RICHARDS PAPERS. (Acc. 5529, 6 boxes)

Family correspondence and papers, nineteenth century, concerning the family of Richards of Gardiner, Maine.

6. For an account of Maillard see his *Account of the Customs and Manners of the Micmakis and Maricheets Savage Nations, Now Dependent on the Government of Cape-Breton* (London, 1758), (published anonymously).

ROBERTSON-MACDONALD PAPERS. 1765-1805. (MSS. 3942-88)

Family papers of the Robertsons, a branch of the Robertsons of Strowan, and the Macdonalds of Kinlochmoidart. The chief correspondents are William Robertson (1721-93), Principal of Edinburgh University, and his son William, of the College of Justice. Included are the materials collected by Principal Robertson for his work on America; the manuscript, in his hand, of a portion of his *History of America* (London, 1777), published by his son William in 1796; Colonel George Croghan's journal of his journey down the Ohio in 1765.

Also included in the collection are letters on the military experiences of successive Chiefs of the MacDonalds and Robertson-MacDonalds: of Alexander MacDonald in America, 1775-80, and of Donald MacDonald in the West Indies, where he became Governor of Tobago, 1800-5 (both MacDonalds of Kinlochmoidart).

ROSE PAPERS. Letters. 1773-8. (MS. 3523)

Letters, 1773-8, of the 3rd Earl of Marchmont to George Rose containing references to the American problem.

RUSSEL AND AITKEN ARCHIVES. (Dep. 240)

This deposit is a selection made from the archives of Russel and Aitken in Falkirk. It consists of material gathered by the firm while acting as executors, trustees, or liquidators in the course of its normal legal business, and of material brought together by the partners in the firm in connexion with their various mining and industrial undertakings. Among the papers are some relating to William Black, mason in Herbertshire, 1774-6, 1785, including a letter written by him from Williamsburg, Va., 1774.

RUTHERFURD PAPERS. Letters. 1838-9.

(*a*) Letters, 1838, concerning troubles in Canada. (MS. 9697, ff. 97, 101)
(*b*) Letters, 1839, concerning the claims of the Church of Scotland in Canada. (MS. 9711, ff. 39-43)

HUGH SHARP COLLECTION. Letters, document. 1791-1864.

In the collection of first editions there are 230 books and nine newspapers of American and Canadian interest. Also the following manuscripts:
(*a*) Letters of General Philip Schuyler to Stephen van Rensselaer, 1791, and to Alexander Hamilton, 1796; letter, 1814, from Andrew Jackson to David Holmes, Governor of Mississippi Territory; and a note, 1864, to Abraham Lincoln requesting the discharge of a soldier, endorsed with a note of Lincoln's ordering this. (MS. 3310)
(*b*) Deed of sale of a slave woman and child, Edgecombe County, N.C., 1831. (MS. 3316)

STEUART PAPERS. 1751-97.

(*a*) Microfilm[7] of the letter-books, 1751-63, of Charles Steuart, Cashier and Paymaster, American Board of Customs, containing copies of his business correspondence as a merchant in Norfolk, Va. (Acc. 2444)
(*b*) Correspondence and papers of Steuart, 1758-97. The official correspondence is mainly with customs officials, and especially with Nathaniel Coffin, Steuart's deputy in Boston. There are also letters from Loyalists, mainly from Norfolk, Va. Steuart's 'Account books for the years 1776-1796' are also contained in this collection. (MS. 5025-46)

STRACHAN, CHARLES (later Fullarton). Letter-book. 1763-70. (MS. 119)

Trader in Mobile, Ala., 1763-70. The letters are almost exclusively concerned with business affairs. Strachan retired to Scotland in 1770, on the death of his grandfather, to manage the Kinnaber estates.

STUART STEVENSON PAPERS. 1775-9, n.d.

Papers of the family of Stuart of Castlemilk and of Andrew Stuart, W.S., eighteenth century.
(*a*) Memorandum, 1775, of Alexander Speirs of Elderslie concerning America. (MS. 8258, ff. 34-6)
(*b*) Draft of a parliamentary speech, 1777, of Andrew Stuart of Castlemilk concerning America. (MS. 8258, ff. 42-57)
(*c*) Letter, 1779, of Col. Allan MacLean at Montreal concerning the conduct of the Governor of Canada and the British alliance with the Iroquois. (MS. 8250, ff. 34-6)
(*d*) 'Some papers written by Mrs. Gill of Boston, New England', n.d. (MS. 8236)

STUART STEVENSON PAPERS. 1776-88. (MSS. 5320-404)

(*a*) Letters, 1776-7, of Major Hon. Charles Cochrane concerning progress of the war in America.
(*b*) Correspondence of Hon. John Cochrane, Deputy Commissary to Forces in America, mainly concerning a Canadian lawsuit, 1777, 1782-4, 1788.

Also papers relating to the family's West Indian affairs.

STUART OF TORRANCE PAPERS. 1775 and n.d.

(*a*) 'Thoughts on the Present State of America and Lord North's Late Declaration in the House of Commons', Nov. 1775.
(*b*) Copy of a petition to the Treasury by Maj. Gen. Robertson for compensation for losses sustained in the fire in New York soon after British troops took possession of the city, n.d.

WILLIAM SULZER SCRAPBOOK. (Adv. MSS. 81.5.2)

Scrapbook containing correspondence of and related printed items concerning William Sulzer, counsellor-at-law and sometime Governor of New York. The correspondence, which consists mostly of incoming letters, is dated 1920-2, together with a few dated 1916-7, and relates to the aftermath of his political career, which was virtually terminated by his impeachment and removal from office as Governor of New York in Oct. 1913, after less than a year in office; to his investments (mostly in mining shares); and to matters of personal interest. The printed items relate to his political career and to aspects of American internal politics.

TRAILL PAPERS. (Acc. 5744)

Thomas Stewart Traill (1781-1862) was Professor of Medical Jurisprudence at Edinburgh. His correspondence includes letters from J.E. DeKay, an American zoologist; Robert Greenhow, the American physician and historian; and B. Silliman, Professor of Chemistry at Yale. (Box 7, F2) Also J.J. Audubon, the American naturalist. (Box 7, F3)

UNITED PRESBYTERIAN CHURCH. Letters. 1847-79. (*In* MSS. 7638-58)

Copies of letters, 1847-79, to various ministers in Canada.

7. Presented by Colonial Williamsburg, Williamsburg, Va.

WATSON AUTOGRAPHS. (MSS. 577-600)

William Finlay Watson (1831-74), bookseller. The collection covers the period from the sixteenth to the nineteenth century.
(*a*) The volume 'Literary and Scientific' contains a letter, Granada, 9 May 1829, from Washington Irving to his brother Peter at Rouen.
(*b*) The volume 'American and Foreign' contains forty-five items, mainly letters, from various noted Americans to a variety of people. Among the writers are John Quincy Adams, George Bancroft, W.C. Bryant, Elihu Burritt, William Ellery Channing, Benjamin Franklin, Horatio Gates, John Hancock, Oliver Wendell Holmes, Sr., Andrew Jackson, John Jay, Thomas Jefferson, Henry Wadsworth Longfellow, James Monroe, W.H. Prescott, Harriet Beecher Stowe, George Washington, and Daniel Webster.

YESTER PAPERS. 1663-1862.

(*a*) Four papers, including one referring to John Brown's licence for trading in the Caribbee Islands, 1663-4, 1666. (MS. 7033, ff. 29, 49, 59-62; Ch. 7580)
(*b*) Twenty-seven letters and papers, 1695-6, 1698-1702, concerning the Darien scheme. (MSS. 7020-1; 7029-30; 7036)
(*c*) Thirty-one letters, 1757-9, mostly to Lord Charles Hay while on service in Halifax, N.S. Also twenty letters, 1757-81, from John McColme and others; the first seventeen refer to the Seven Years War, the last two to the War of Independence. (MSS. 7083; 7098, ff. 84-7)
(*d*) Journals of Lord Charles Hay, 21 Apr. - 23 June 1758, 3-24 June 1758, and 25 June - 31 July 1758. Major Rodolphe's journal, and his detachment of the militia of Lunenburg, N.S., on the western side of the River Lahave, 1757. Narrative account by Lieutenant Shomberg, of Major General Hopson's regiment, 1756. (MSS. 7084-6; 7092; 7094)
(*e*) Forty-two letters, 1807-15, to George Hay, 8th Marquess of Tweeddale, mainly on military affairs in Canada; also thirty-nine documents of a military nature, mostly monthly returns of regiments in Canada, 1813-4. (MS. 7100)
(*f*) Correspondence of Lord Charles Hay, 1755-60. (Acc. 4862, Box 14)
(*g*) One letter, 1862, about battles near Richmond, Va. (Acc. 4862, Box 30, F3b)

MISCELLANEOUS LETTERS AND DOCUMENTS. 1712-1932.

(*a*) Letters of Cotton Mather to John Stirling, Principal of Glasgow University, 1712-26, and to Robert Wodrow, Minister of Eastwood, 1726; and letters of Benjamin Colman, 1726-9, and Samuel Mather, 1727-9, to Wodrow. The subjects are chiefly theological controversies and the state of religion in New England. At the end are an extract of a letter from Danish missionaries in the East Indies to Cotton Mather, 1725, and 'Some Just Sentiments on the Present Condition of the Protestant Religion. In a letter from a Gentleman beyond Sea, to a Member of the British Parliament', n.d. (Adv. MSS. 27.6.2)
(*b*) List of sailings from Scottish and northern English ports, giving cargoes, destination, and master's name, 1781. (4 folios.) (MS. 1801)
(*c*) Letters of Samuel L. Clemens to F.H. Skrine (making fun of Kipling's 'absent-minded beggar'), 1902; of Oliver Wendell Holmes, Sr., 1883; of James Hourse, 1784; and of Thomas Jefferson to M. Thouin, 1813. (Adv. MS. 7.1.19)
(*d*) Letters relating to Canada, 1787-8, 1793-4, 1804, 1810, 1814-5. (MS. 3847, *passim*; MS. 3848, ff. 1-4, 9-19; MS. 3849; MS. 3851)
(*e*) Letter, 1820, concerning the foundation of the Presbyterian Associate Synod in Canada. (MS. 9814, f. 51)
(*f*) Letter, 1823, of Lord Dalhousie concerning Canada. (MS. 9814, f. 51)
(*g*) Letters of John Bell, settler in Quebec, to his family in Scotland, 1830-2. (MSS. 7198 (vii))
(*h*) Correspondence and press-cuttings (mostly from *The Times*, 1842-4, 1847) concerning the activities of the British-American Association for Emigration and Colonization. (Adv. MSS. 26.2.19)
(*i*) Journal, 1932, of a visit to Canada and the U.S.A. of William Maxwell, Managing Director of R. & R. Clark. (MS. 9759)

NATIONAL REGISTER OF ARCHIVES (SCOTLAND),[1] H.M. General Register House, Edinburgh EH1 3YY

The material listed below has been selected from surveys of muniments, mostly held by private owners, which were carried out by or on behalf of the National Register of Archives (Scotland). Papers subsequently deposited in the Scottish Record Office have been omitted, as they have been described in the Scottish Record Office entry under 'Gifts and Deposits'. (See pp. 272-307). Enquiries about papers still in private hands should be directed to the Secretary of the National Register of Archives (Scotland), H.M. General Register House, Edinburgh, and not to individual owners. Access to such papers is entirely at the discretion of the owners concerned.

The numbers following the titles in the following list are the reference numbers of the surveys. The number shown in brackets after a particular item shows the page on which it appears in the survey.

BALFOUR OF BALBIRNIE. (0011)

Papers, 1865, relating to the American Civil War. (p.6)

EARL OF BALFOUR. (0012)

(*a*) Letter, 1896, from Sen. H. C. Lodge on Venezuela and Anglo-American relations. (p.21)
(*b*) Letter, 1896, from William Everett, an American, about U.S. attitudes to Britain over Venezuelan affair and the threatened war. Enclosed in letter from Henry Sidgwick. (p.46)
(*c*) 'Alice's Diary 1898-99' - notes discussion with American Ambassador, Mr. Hay, about incident of the *Maine* in the Spanish-American War, 27 Apr. 1898. (p.60)
(*d*) Letters, 1904-13, from Sir C. Spring-Rice, including letters from Washington, D.C., to G. W. Balfour covering the period of Spring-Rice's Washington visit. (p.29)
(*e*) Letter from O. Locker Lampson on America, 1910. (p.23)
(*f*) Letter from [Edith Balfour] referring to A. J. Balfour's visit to Washington, 1911. (p.47)
(*g*) Cabinet papers (draft) on President Wilson's peace initiative, 1916. (p.16)
(*h*) Foreign Office minutes, 1916, on Mr. Butler's visit to the U.S.A. (p.23)
(*i*) Letter, 1916, from Colonel House on American opinion; letter from Lord Grey on this. (p.23)
(*j*) Invitation, 1917, from Woodrow Wilson to discussion with Colonel House. (p.23)
(*k*) Letter, 1917, from Alice Balfour, including reference to A. J. Balfour's current visit to the U.S.A. (p. 48)
(*l*) Letters, 1917, from Ian Malcolm and [-] Dormer, on Balfour's mission to the U.S.A. (p.73)

1. This section for the most part consists of a slightly condensed version of the appendix to the Scottish Record Office's *List of American Documents* (Edinburgh, 1976). For the categories of material which have been excluded, see the introduction to the entry for the S.R.O. (p. 272).

(*m*) Letters, 1917, from A. W. Agassiz and other American scientists to F. M. Balfour. (appendix)
(*n*) America, 1920. Correspondence with J. W. Gerrard and Foreign Office. (p.4)
(*o*) Letter, 1921, from A. J. Balfour on his Washington visit. (p.24)
(*p*) Letter, 1921, from Oswald Balfour, Ottawa, referring to A. J. Balfour's arrival in New York and his hopes of seeing him. (p.47)
(*q*) Letter, 1922, from Otto Kahn on Balfour's visit to America. (p.9)
(*r*) Miscellaneous letters, 1922-9, from correspondents in the U.S.A. Correspondents include Sen. H. C. Lodge, ex-President Taft, N. M. Butler, Colonel House, T. W. Lamont, J. D. Rockefeller, Jr., and J. M. Beck. (p.6)
(*s*) Letter, 1925, from Lord Grey of Fallodon about permission to publish memorandum on possible American intervention for peace, 1916. (p.7)
(*t*) Correspondence, 1927, with Sir Maurice Hankey; includes letter on American debt. (p.7)
(*u*) Correspondence, 1927-8, with Colonel House and others on inclusion of letters and papers by A. J. Balfour in *Intimate Papers of Colonel House*. (p.5)
(*v*) Letter, 1928, from Winston Churchill on Anglo-American relations. (p.8)
(*w*) Account (typescript), n.d., of visit to America on News Department work, initialled 'G.G.B.' and addressed to 'Dear Montgomery'. (p.23)

CAMPBELL OF INVERNEILL. (0028)[2]

(*a*) Journal, 1778-9, of the expedition against the rebels in Georgia, by Sir Archibald Campbell. (p. 1)
(*b*) Official correspondence and papers, 1778-9, of Gen. Sir Archibald Campbell. (pp.3, 6, 7)
American items include:
Standing Orders for 71st Regiment, Georgia, June-July 1778. (no. 19)
Papers relating to the Georgia expedition, 1778-9. (no.83)

CHALMERS OF ALDBAR. (0036)

Letter, 1753, from W. Skinner [army officer] at Louisbourg on meeting with Gen. Wolfe, and on his own career. (p. 1)

EARL OF CROMARTIE. (0040)

(*a*) Letter, [1678], from George Scott, London, [? to Lord Tarbat] about the province of Maine 'the most profitable plantation in America' and account of negotiations for its purchase; mentions Sir Simon Andrews [?Edmund Andros], Governor of New York, who had a fort built at Pammagurd to help the inhabitants against the Indians; and that the 'New England Commissioners' thwarted the King's resolution to purchase Maine by purchasing it themselves for £1,200 sterling 'quherat his Ma. exprest a great resentment and hath challenged that government for this bargain'; writer suggests that he purchased it for recipient and lord chancellor. (p. 19)
(*b*) Letter, 1683, from John Werden to [Lord Tarbat] - the Duke has no inclination to leave [?for] New York; ship which is to convey the new lieutenant governor with other officers and supplies is almost ready, 'and we hope from the new priviledges of an assembly etc. and good methods designed for that government, to have a good account of it in tyme'. (p.4)
(*c*) Letter, 1684, from William Blathwayt, Whitehall, to the Lords Proprietors of East Jersey, thanking them for taking notice of his station relating to his Majesty's foreign plantations, and thinking him capable of being useful in prompting their interests in East Jersey. (p.4)
(*d*) Letter, 1712, from Kenneth Mackenzie, Williamsburg, Va., announcing his arrival on the *Severn* man-of-war; has been appointed to St. James, Lawn Creek, one of the best parishes in Virginia, by the governor, Col. Spotswood, and Commissary Blair. (p. 10)

DARROCH OF GOUROCK. (0050)

(*a*) Letter, 4 Apr. 1784, from George Washington, Mount Vernon, to Gen. Dayton, Elizabeth Town, N.J., requesting that all the delegates from New Jersey should attend the meeting at Philadelphia as 'there are powerful reasons for wishing this first meeting may be *full* and *respectable*'. (p. 1)
(*b*) Letters, 1803-4, from Duncan Darroch, schoolmaster, North Carolina, to Duncan Darroch of Gourock, giving news of friends and national affairs. (p. 1)

MACNEAL OF LOSSIT. (0052)

(*a*) Commission, 1757, to Joshua Loring, as commissary, to build suitable boats for H.M. forces in America, to be available at Lake George or Woods Creek. (p. 3)
(*b*) MS. order of battle for troops of Boston, Commander-in-Chief Maj. Gen. Howe, showing regiments under Burgoyne, Cleveland, and Clinton, *c.* 1775. (p. 3)
(*c*) Letter, 1 July 1777, from [-], New York, to Capt. Macneal, giving account of British army moves: 'the march in to the Jerseys was, it is said, to amuse Washington and prevent him from sending any succours to Ticonderoga, which having effected, the General [Howe] is to carry the troops to Providence to join the army under Burgoigne and carry everything before him in New England'. (p. 2)
(*d*) Letter, 1840, from Donald [Mactavish], Kilchrest, to George Macneal of Ugadale, referring to a 'Dr. Macneill', alive in 1799, 'he seems to have been bred a medical man and to have afterwards engaged in trade in Caroline America'. (p. 1)

MAXWELL STUART OF TRAQUAIR. (0054)

(*a*) Business correspondence, 1704-21, addressed to John Brown, merchant, Liverpool, from Virginia, Jamaica, New York, Boston, Philadelphia, and European addresses. (p. 16)
(*b*) Letter, 1753, from Dr. Peter Middleton, New York. (p. 11)

MARQUESS OF ABERDEEN. (0055)

(*a*) Letter of introduction, 1830, by Daniel Webster, Boston, to Samuel Jones, Chief Justice of the Supreme Court, New York, on behalf of Edward B. Emerson, graduate of Harvard. (p. 4)
(*b*) Letters, 1853, from George Shaw-Lefevre in America. (p. 22)
(*c*) Letter, 1892, from James G. Blaine, Secretary of State, Washington, to J.V. Farnell, Chicago, on the initiative of the U.S.A. in urging European nations to adopt the principle of arbitration in international disputes, following adoption of this principle by a majority of American states after the recent American conference. (p. 8)
(*d*) Correspondence with Andrew Carnegie, New York, 1892-1913. (p. 6)
(*e*) Papers, 1893-8, of the 7th Earl of Aberdeen as Governor-General of Canada. (pp. 17-23)
(*f*) Description of a trip to the U.S.A., 1915-7. (p. 12)

2. See Colin Campbell, 'The 71st Highlanders in Massachusetts, 1776-1780', in *New England Historical and Genealogical Register*, cxii (1958).

(*g*) Letter, 28 Mar. 1919, from President Woodrow Wilson, Paris, to Lord Eversley, acknowledging receipt of the latter's book *The Partitions of Poland*. (p. 10)
(*h*) Letters, 1921-4, to Lord Eversley concerning the American debt. (p. 9)
(*i*) Collection of autograph letters, including Oliver Wendell Holmes, Andrew Carnegie, and Samuel L. Clemens [Mark Twain], twentieth century. (p. 34)

NICOL OF BALLOGIE. (0060)

Letters, 1777-1830, some from Washington, D.C., and Baltimore, about personal affairs, with comments on political relations between the U.S.A. and Britain. (p. 2)

FARQUHARSON OF INVERCAULD. (0061)

(*a*) Letters, 1757-62, from Alexander Farquharson in America. (p. 18)
Subjects include:
His determination to join the army to improve his circumstances, 1757.
Account of his military experiences, written from Fort Ontario, Montreal, Staten Island, Albany, and other places, 1760-2.
(*b*) Letter, 30 Apr. 1777, from Aeneas Mackintosh, Perth Amboy, [N.J.], to James Farquharson of Invercauld, giving an account of the 71st Regiment's operations in America from 5 June 1776. (p. 17)

ADAM OF BLAIR-ADAM. (0063)

(*a*) Letters, 1775, from William Adam to his parents, discussing Chatham's motion to withdraw troops from Boston, and other speeches in Commons, and giving a sketch of state of politics regarding America. (p. 1)
(*b*) Letter, 1777, from Lord North stating that reports in French papers of defeats in America are false, 'we have every reason to believe General Burgoyne has taken Ticonderoga', with other news of the war in America. (p. 141)
(*c*) Letters, 1780-1, from Lord Stair, with copies of letters from his son in New York, on defection of Gen. Arnold and death of Major André, French army in America, and affairs in Carolina. (pp. 1-2)
(*d*) Letters, 1781, from G.K. Elphinstone, in American waters and at New York, mainly on naval matters. (p. 132)
(*e*) Letter, 1782, from Lord North on American affairs, including offer of independence. (p. 2)
(*f*) Letter, 1782, from Brook Watson on quartermaster's stores accounts at New York. (p. 7)
(*g*) Letter, 1785, from Sir William Erskine on possible enquiry into accounts for American war. (p. 5)
(*h*) Letter, 1800, from Thomas Erskine about American Minister's kindness to David [Erskine]; encloses two letters from David Erskine in Philadelphia about appointment of commissioner on American side and his own wish to be appointed commissioner on British side. (p. 30)
(*i*) Petition, 1800, of widow of Alexander Learmonth, Edinburgh, tanner and merchant at Charleston, S.C., to be put on H.M. charity roll for Scotland. (p. 31)
(*j*) Letter, 1800, from Thomas Steele about report of the auditors on the American war expenditure. (p. 33)
(*k*) Letters, 1800-02, from Gen. W. Dalrymple on report of enquiry into stores, etc. during American War of Independence. (pp. 29, 35, 42)
(*l*) Letter, n.d., from Col. H. Bruen, about enquiry as to American war supplies. (p. 6)
(*m*) Letters, 1800-02, from P. Bond, Philadelphia. (pp. 29, 34, 41)
Subjects include:
Lord Perth's property; application for David Erskine to have a seat on the Board of Commissioners under 6th article of treaty with the U.S.A., if the Board should resume its functions, 1800. (p. 29)
Appeal of Stephen Girard, Philadelphia, against the capture and condemnation of his ship *Sally* as the property of a Frenchman, 1801. (p. 34)
Introduces D.M. Erskine and his wife, niece of the writer, 1802. (p.41)
(*n*) Letter, 1803, from Gen. W. Dalrymple about help given by Dyckman in American enquiry. (p. 50)
(*o*) Letter, 1810, from John Kemp, Principal and Professor of Philosophy, Columbia College, New York, giving short account of thriving U.S. economy; thinks 'non-intercourse' would be fatal to England. (p. 85)
(*p*) Letter, 1815, from Capt. Edward Codrington about the war in America and New Orleans expedition. (p. 139)
(*q*) Letter, 1842, from Lord Ashburton to Adm. Sir Charles Adam, after signing Treaty of Washington. (p. 132)
(*r*) Letters, n.d., from Capt. C. Elliot, *chargé d'affaires* in Texas. (p. 130)

DUNBAR OF NORTHFIELD. (0065)

Letters, 1778, from Thomas Dunbar (later major general) from camp near Bedford, L.I., and from Philadelphia, mentioning appearance of a French fleet off the coast and the engagement at Brandywine. (p. 6)

DICK-CUNYNGHAM OF PRESTONFIELD. (0068)

Letters and papers, 1766 and n.d., regarding Benjamin Franklin, including verses written by him to Alexander Dick at Coldstream, epitaph on Dr. Franklin written by himself, and letter by Franklin's son about his father. (pp. 1-2)

DICKSON OF MONYBUIE. (0069)

Memorandum, 1813, concerning Robert Dickson, fur trader in Upper Canada, who was sent as an agent to the Indians, to ask their help against America; also on his brothers William and Thomas, taken as hostages by Americans in retaliation. (p. 1)

REV. R.M. MACDONALD. (0091)

Letter, 1871, from Peter Burns, Ontario, to his cousin Robert Burns, giving news of the deaths of recipient's brother, his wife and one of their daughters from yellow fever while staying in 'one of the Southern States, bordering on the Mississippi River'. (p. 3)

GORDON OF CAIRNFIELD. (0095)

Observations on North America, made by an officer in the British service there, 1756-60. (p.3)

GRANT OF MONYMUSK. (0099)

(*a*) Observations on Sir Nathaniel Gould's scheme for preventing frauds in the tobacco trade; also report by Humphrey Brent, commissioner of customs, and replies of merchants, *c.* 1721. (pp. 13, 16)
(*b*) Instructions, 1731, regarding granting of land in South Carolina, with letter from Gen. Abercromby on the subject. (p. 16)
(*c*) Memorandum regarding Carolina, 1742. (p. 17)
(*d*) Memorandum regarding America, sent to Robert Gordon of Halifax, N.S., in London, 1762. (p. 15)
(*e*) Letters, 1767, including correspondence respecting grant to Sir Archibald Grant of 20,000 acres in Florida. (p. 10)

EARL OF HADDINGTON. (0104)

(*a*) Letter, 1724, from W. Keith, Philadelphia, to George Baillie [a

commissioner of the Admiralty], seeking removal of John Moore as collector of the customs, and discussing reform of the city administration, especially that the King should take over the government of the province, and that East Jersey should be added to New York and West Jersey to Philadelphia. (p. 18)
(*b*) Papers, [1841-6], relating to armament on American Lakes. (pp. 40,42,43,46)
(*c*) Letter, 1844, from Adm. Sir Charles Adam, Texas. (p.43)

NOBLE OF ARDMORE. (0159)

Agreement between James Donald, Archibald Lundie and John Mitchell, St. Augustine, Fla., for trading in lumber from Mississippi; with related letters and accounts, 1776-8. (p.3)

ROBERTSON-AIKMAN OF THE ROSS. (0174)

(*a*) Part of a letter, *c.* 1757, from John Forbes on military affairs in North America: the army under his command is on its way to the Ohio River and Fort Duquesne; Indian supports (Cherokees and Catawbas) have gone home, a 'sensible loss'; trouble with 'the governours and assemblyes of all these provinces ... under my direction'. (p.4)
(*b*) Letters, 1781, from A. Strothers and Co., Pensacola, on death of George Aikman and sale of his Florida estate. (pp. 4-5)
(*c*) Letter, 1807, from Lord Torphichen to John Forbes Aikman, stating that war had begun or was certainly expected with America. (p.5)
(*d*) Letter, n.d., from Brig. Gen. James Hamilton to [?the Duke of Hamilton] asking for his help; 'the misfortunes of Saratoga ... hang round me', and his promotion has been denied. (p.9)

SCOTT OF GALA. (0181)

(*a*) Letters, 1766-71, from William Macdougall. (pp. 10,13)
Subjects include:
Details of his partnership with Mr. Southwell, M.P., and Mr. Upton to farm in the province of East Florida; his London agents are to be Messrs. Ross and Mill. London, 1766. (p.13)
Description of his plantation in Florida; mentions his neighbours including Major Moultrie, Lieutenant Governor. 'L'Upton', East Florida, Sept. 1771. (p.10)
Introduces James Penman, the bearer, who will be happy to answer any enquiries about Florida. Charleston, S.C., Dec. 1771. (p.11)
(*b*) Fragment of a letter, 1774, from [-], St. Augustine, Fla., intimating the death of W. Macdougall 'your kinsman' after contracting epilepsy. (p.11)

EARL OF WEMYSS. (0208)

Letters from America, 1861. (p.11)

WARDLAW-RAMSAY OF TILLICOULTRY. (0227)

(*a*) Letters, 1775-6, from R. Balfour, London. (pp.28-30)
Subjects include:
Dispatch of certain regiments to Boston. (no.560)
Capture of the Cameronians at St. John's. (no.563)
Capture of St. John's and other news of the American war. (no. 564)
(*b*) Letters, 1775-6, from James Balfour, St. Vincent's and New York River. (pp.28-30)
Subjects include:
His regiment is ordered to stand by for service in North America in the spring of 1776; requests certain materials for uniform to be sent. (no.555)
Repeats his former request for clothing and equipment; is expecting shortly to sail for America. (no.596)
Awaits the transports to take the regiment to America. (no.597)
The transports are in the bay, ready to take the regiment to New York to join Gen. Howe's army; frequent visits of American vessels to Martinique with grain, and their return with powder and ammunition. (no.598)
News of the voyage from the West Indies to America; arrived about 21 Nov. 1776 after six weeks' voyage; transport attacked by Americans. (no.599)
(*c*) Letters, 1778, from Thomas Roy and Charles Fergusson, London, Philadelphia and New York. (p.31)
Subjects include:
Dispatch of the *Anne and Eliza* with wines for America. (no.621)
News of the voyage of the *Anne and Eliza*; Roy's arrival at Philadelphia and unloading of the cargo; prospects of sales; ship sailing stopped on orders from Lord Howe; trading difficult. (no.625)
Uncertainties of the war situation. (no.627)
Evacuation of Philadelphia. (nos.628-9)
French fleet blocking New York harbour [with details of the types of ships involved]. (no.630)

DUKE OF ATHOLL. (0234)

(*a*) Miscellaneous military papers, 1757-63, relating to Capt. James Murray's Company in North America and including muster rolls of the 2nd Battalion of the Black Watch, 1758, 1760-1. (pp.83, 84)
(*b*) Medical report on illness of 7th Duke of Atholl in Canada, 1864. (p.97)
(*c*) Journal of tour by [7th Duke of Atholl] in Canada and the United States, 1881. (p.131)
(*d*) Correspondence, 1881-3, from 7th Duke to his wife concerning his world tour, including America. (pp.101,105)
(*e*) Letters, 1908-14, to 7th Duke including:
Frederick B. Richards in New York concerning military relics of the American War of Independence. (p.100)
F.E. Wing in Athol, Mass., concerning arrangements for 150th anniversary of the incorporation of the town. (p.100)

STEWART-MEIKLEJOHN OF EDRADYNATE. (0247)

Letter, 1769, from Alexander Robertson, Wicocomico River, Somerset County, Md., to George Robertson with family news. (p.2)

KERR, MACLEOD & MACFARLAN, C.A. (0286)

Report, 1859-80, on history of the City of Glasgow Bank's involvement with Western Union Railroad Co., America, 1880; with appendices on evidence taken in the U.S.A., American railroad reports 1859-79, and statistics of American investments. (pp. 1-2)

J.T. DUNBAR ESQ. (0325)

Papers relating to shipping to Canada and America, 1784-1824. (p.1)

DUKE OF HAMILTON. (0332)

(*a*) Letter, 1700, from Col. Andrew Hamilton, Boston to [the Duke of Hamilton], telling him that Mr. Penn has been well received in America. (p.1030)
(*b*) Letter, 1710, from John Robertson [of Ernock], Boston, to the same, informing him that Col. St. Cailor will bring 'four of the Grand Satchimes out of the five nations of our freindly Indians' to the Duke's lodgings should he wish to see them. (p.1291)
(*c*) Letter, 1710, from Sam Vetch, Boston, to [?the Duke of Hamilton], introducing to him Col. Schuyler and 'the Indian ambassadours', in the belief that their 'aspect as well as painted skins will be not a litle admired through all Europe', and urging him to assert his claim to his American lands. (p.1292)

(*d*) Letters, 1710, from Robert Armstrong, Boston and New Hampshire, to the Duke of Hamilton. (pp. 1297, 1306)

Has agreed with the surveyor 'to survey what lands your grace hath on this continent', but he must keep it private to avoid endangering their lives. Boston, 29 May.

Has 'with a great deale of difficulty surveyd your lands comprehended in your grant in Connecticut and Rhod Island'; has sent the resulting map with Major Robertson. New Hampshire, 8 Dec.

(*e*) Letter, 1711, from Sam Vetch, Boston, to the Duke of Hamilton, enclosing three copies of letters he had written, one to Lord Dartmouth, describing his visit to Annapolis and discussion with the Indians, with an extract from his journal. (p. 1327)

MONCRIEFFE OF TULLIEBOLE. (0333)

(*a*) Letters, 1801-3, from R. Gilmorestone, Baltimore, about John Moncrieff Wellwood. (p. 1)

(*b*) Letters, *c.* 1804-1819, from Jedidiah Morse, Charlestown, [Mass]. (pp. 1-2)

Subjects include:

Moore's Indian school, and establishment of a mission among the Delaware tribe of Indians, 1818.

Theological Institute at Andover, and the addition of a new library, 1818-9.

(*c*) Letter, 1810, from James Blair, secretary to the Presbyterian church, Charlestown, about appointment of a pastor to them. (p.2)

(*d*) Letter, 1816, from David Hyslop, Brookline, [Mass.], about the growth of Bowdoin College, Maine, under the Rev. Jesse Appleton. (p.2)

(*e*) Letters, 1773-99, from Sir Henry Moncrieff Wellwood to his brother Archibald in Baltimore; with one reply and two letters from Robert Moncrieff in St. Vincent's to Archibald. (p.3)

MACLEOD OF MACLEOD. (0361)

Letter, 1771, from Alexander Macleod, Glendale, giving details of mass emigration to North Carolina planned by the tenants of 'Sir Alexander' [? Macdonald]. (p. 12)

MRS. R.S. BARBOUR. (0363)

Accounts of ship *Peggy* on voyages to Virginia, Maryland, etc., 1746-55. (p. 1)

JUTE INDUSTRIES LTD. (0379)

(*a*) New York accounts, 1892-8, of Messrs. J. & A.D. Grimond Ltd. (p. 34)

(*b*) Papers, licenses, etc., 1915-7, relating to export of jute to the U.S.A. by Harry Walker & Sons Ltd. (p. 46)

SMYTHE OF BALHARY. (0387)

(*a*) Letter, 1761, from Henry Smyth, Charleston, S.C., announcing his arrival there. (p. 4)

(*b*) Papers, 1765-7, relating to succession of Dr. James Crockat in South Carolina [to property in Coupar Angus?]. (p.3)

DON BROTHERS, BUIST & CO. LTD., JUTE & FLAX SPINNERS. (0421)

New York and Calcutta letter-book, 1896-7. (p. 1)

J.T. MACKENZIE ESQ. (0427)

Letters, *c.* 1840-1878, from Donald and William Macdonald (and others) to relatives in Skye, written from Mobile, Ala.; New York; Charleston, S.C.; St. Marks, Port Leon, Cedar Keys and Newport, Fla.; and Savannah, Ga. (p.2)

Including:

Letter from William Macdonald giving details of his partnership with Donald in a retail grocery business in Thomasville; describes how he astonished the local young women with his Highland dress and bagpipes. Port Leon, 1841.

Letter from Donald Macdonald telling of the destruction of his warehouse by a severe gale the previous autumn, which left him deeply in debt, but he managed to clear the debt and is now building a new warehouse. Newport, 1844.

EDMONSTON OF BUNESS. (0440)

Letter, *c.* 1846, from Charles Darwin to Edward Forbes, concerning naturalist for 'the Californian Expedition'; assumes it is Thomas Edmonston. (p.2)

HAMILTON OF BARNS. (0560)

Family and legal correspondence, 1740-9, including letters from Robert Hamilton in America. (p.2)

T. & W. WALKER LAIRD, SOLICITORS. (0576)

Correspondence, 1829-80, concerning the Buffalo and Lake Erie Railway Co., etc. (p.4)

LORD STRATHEDEN AND CAMPBELL. (0579)

(*a*) Letter, 1842, from Joseph Story, Cambridge, Mass., thanking [John, 1st Lord] Campbell for copy of his speeches. (p.9)

(*b*) Letters of introduction, 1852, from Daniel Webster, Secretary of State, Washington, and George Bancroft, New York, for George Wood. (p. 11)

(*c*) Letter of introduction, 1852, from Abbott Lawrence, Boston, for Charles G. Loring. (p. 12)

(*d*) Letter, 1853, from Dwight W. Pardee, Hartford, Conn., about rules of evidence and court procedure. (p. 12)

(*e*) Letter, 1857, from Charles Cartlidge [an American], wishing to visit Strangers' Gallery, House of Lords. (p. 12)

(*f*) Letter, 1864, from W.E. Gladstone about report of massacres by Confederate troops, and his desire to have observations of Confederate authorities thereon. (p.3)

CRICHTON-MAITLAND OF ELDERSLIE. (0607)

(*a*) Accounts and business letters, *c.* 1770-1788, of Alexander Spiers, merchant in Glasgow, trading in tobacco and sugar, with details of ventures in Virginia land and export of ironwork to Virginia. Copies of many of these are available in Strathclyde Regional Archives. (pp.2-7)

(*b*) Letter, 1795, from Manchester, Va., describing nail trade of James Cross, Glasgow; and invoice of tobacco shipped by him on board the *Blanford* on behalf of Spiers' estate. (p.4)

(*c*) The American recipe for rheumatism, *c.* 1800. (p.2)

(*d*) Correspondence, 1804-5, concerning 'American Claims' (money owed by American merchants to Alexander Spiers' estate), including letters from James Strange, Petersburg, Va. (p. 10)

BANNATYNE, KIRKWOOD AND FRANCE, SOLICITORS. (0608)

Letter, 1739, from John Haldane, on board the *Leitchfield* at Plymouth, to his parents, describing his travels since 1731, including three trips to Virginia on the second of which he went with 'one Posthoumous Thornton in the ship *Mary* and was taken sick in the country with fever and ague'. (p. 5)

LENNOX OF WOODHEAD. (0616)

Note of trees, seeds, etc. to be commissioned from Carolina, Virginia, Maryland, Pennsylvania, or New England, 1749. (p.3)

DUNLOP OF DOONSIDE. (0620)

(*a*) Letter, 1765, from John Hamilton, Norsemond, Va., about 'our spring cargo this season... the goods in general are quite of a different quality and much cheaper bought than any we ever had since I came to America', and discussing detailed company business. (p.4)

(*b*) Letter, 1781, from William Hamilton, captain in the Royal North Carolina Regiment, acknowledging that he is a prisoner-of-war of the United States of America, and has Gen. Washington's permission to proceed to Charlestown for New York and thence to Europe. (p.5)

(*c*) List of officers, 1782, belonging to the North Carolina Volunteers. (p.4)

(*d*) Roll of detachment, *c.* 1785, of the Royal North Carolina Regiment commanded by Alexander Hamilton, with notes of the day of enlistment, desertion, being taken prisoner-of-war, killed or discharged. (p.4)

(*e*) Account of collected debts of James and Archibald Hamilton & Co. in America, 1791-1816. (p.5)

(*f*) Letter, 1804, from Thomas Hamilton, Norfolk, Va., about business affairs and the blockade of the French frigate *Le Président*, carrying Jerome Bonaparte and his wife, by the British frigate *Le Révolutionnaire*, which was in Hampton Roads to take home the second payment of the British compensation. (p.5)

STEWART OF ARDVORLICH. (0630)

(*a*) Letters, 1820-37, from John Stewart and William Murray Stewart from ports including New York. (p.13)

(*b*) Letters, 1851, from Mr. and Mrs. Stewart, Benares, to W. Roberts, including one concerning communal arrangements for supply of American ice. (p.36)

MARQUESS OF BUTE. (0631)

(*a*) Letter, 1728, from 'P.B.' concerning deputy governorship of Virginia, and rumours that four new deputy governors are to be appointed to supervise construction of four new forts in South Carolina. (p.5)

(*b*) Letter from Charles Boyle, New York, describing his trip to America and the difficulty of getting a commission in American service, as they are considered sinecures for old men; also letter from J. Montgomerie, Governor of New York, complaining of Boyle's direct application to the King for a commission without consulting him, 1729-31. (pp.6-7)

(*c*) Letter, 1736, from Dr. Graeme, asking Earl of Loudoun's support for appointment of a [? provincial] grand master in New England, there being Masons there. (p.8)

(*d*) List of seeds received from Mr. Abercromby in Carolina, 1738. (p.385)

(*e*) Letter, 1749, from Lieut. John Dalrymple, London, about his preparations for settling in North Carolina. (p.390)

(*f*) Letter, 1753, from Admiral Colville concerning his possible election as governor of New England. (p.31)

(*g*) Letter, 1753, from George Fotheringham requesting Earl of Loudoun's support in obtaining the governorship of New York. (p.31)

(*h*) Letters, 1753-4, from John Inglis, Philadelphia, concerning Loudoun's order for seeds and plants; also letter from James Alexander there giving a list of tree seeds sent to Loudoun. (pp.31, 35)

(*i*) List of North American seeds sold by Nathaniel Powell and Co., Holbourne, 1754. (p.34)

(*j*) Draft of a bill for issuing bills of credit [in America], 1755. (p.107)

(*k*) Letter, 1755, from James Leslie quoting letter from Col. Innes to Lord Fairfax with news of reverse at Fort Duquesne. (p. 5)

(*l*) Letters and copies of letters, 1755, with news of Gen. Braddock's death at Fort Duquesne. (p.35)

(*m*) Letters, 1755-6, concerning military and naval preparations for 1756 campaign. (p.75)

(*n*) Two letters, 1755-8, from Lieut. Gen. Anstruther, concerning commissions in the Earl of Loudoun's new regiment, the 60th Royal American Regiment; with other requests for commissions under Loudoun in America, and copies of commissions and warrants. (pp.35-40)

(*o*) Letters, 1756, from John Calcraft, agent for several regiments in the American service. (pp.36-8)

(*p*) Memorial and letter from Master of Lovat concerning his intention of raising a regiment of Highland irregulars for American service, 1756. (p.38)

(*q*) Deposition, 1756, by W. Wilkins of Frederica on relations with Creek Indians and his expedition into their territory the previous year. (p.39)

(*r*) Letter, [?1756], from [?Mr. Moir], mining engineer, asking to accompany Loudoun to America in order 'to look at some mines that are brought there'; proposes to publish a large map of America, giving depths of water along the coast, and 'to try a method of preserving ship's bottoms'. (p. 11)

(*s*) Letters and other papers, 1756-7, concerning stores and fort defences at Fort William Henry and Fort Edward, and discussing Otter Creek route to 'Lake Champion'. (p.39)

(*t*) Letter-book, 1756-8, of John, 4th Earl of Loudoun, from America, mainly to Henry Fox. Contents include account of the state of affairs on his arrival; possible loss of Oswego; relations with Indians; loss of Fort Ontario; arrival of settlers; disposition, pay, supply, and quartering of troops; and recruiting and ship-building. (pp.441-4)

(*u*) Bills for engineers' tools and 4,240 flannel waistcoats for Royal American Regiment, 1757. (p.40)

(*v*) Letters, 1757-8, concerning the affairs of the Royal American Regiment [? and others]. (p.40)

(*w*) Letter, 1758, from Capt. Hugh Arnot on an enclosed manuscript giving an account of Gen. Abercromby's campaign, with detailed description of the army's movements and plans of the battles at Ticonderoga; also copy of Gen. Abercromby's letter to his brother describing the Battle of Ticonderoga. (pp.40-1)

(*x*) Letter, 1758, from Sir Harry Erskine to Lord Bute enclosing letter from Abercrombie [the engineer] from camp at Lake George. (p.138)

(*y*) Letter, [? 1758] from Lieut. Col. Bradstreet, Oswego, telling of his landing near Cadaraqui on 25 August. (p.355)

(*z*) Letter, 1759, from James Abercromby reporting capture of Fort Duquesne. (p.42)

(*aa*) Letter, 1759, from James Abercromby and other papers concerning £50,000 claim by Abercromby and Lord Loudoun, relating to Virginia. (p.42)

(*bb*) Letter, 1759, from Edward Masson about letters on American war, borrowed by Loudoun to make copies. (p.42)

(*cc*) Letter, 1759, from Samuel Martin of the Treasury, concerning condemned American stores, etc. (p.42)

(*dd*) Letter, 1759, from Countess of Moray asking for American seeds. (p.43)

(*ee*) Letters, 1759, from John Calcraft, containing references to American affairs; Amherst and not Loudoun is to be governor of Virginia. (p.44)

(*ff*) Letter, [1759], concerning return of Amherst to Crown Point after unsuccessful campaign at Lake Champlain. (p.374)

(*gg*) Letter, 1760, from the Duke of Devonshire concerning seeds from America. (p.47)

(*hh*) Letter, 1761, from Dr. Richard Huck, New York, giving latest news from America and Canada. (p.48)

(*ii*) Letter, 1761, from James Campbell, Fort Prince George, 310 miles north west of Charles Town, with news of a recent military event there. (p.48)

(*jj*) Letter, 1762, from Nathaniel Ware, Controller of Customs, New England, to Lord Bute. (p.257)
(*kk*) Letter, 1762, from Lord Orford to Lord Bute, recommending secretary of South Carolina. (p.257)
(*ll*) Letters, 1762, from Samuel Chandler, William Smith, and Isaac Jay to Lord Bute, concerning colleges in New York and Philadelphia. (pp.260, 263)
(*mm*) Letter, 1762, from William Franklin expressing his desire to be governor of New Jersey. (p.263)
(*nn*) Letter, 1763, from Scott & Cryer to Lord Bute, concerning American silver mine. (p.311)
(*oo*) Letter, 1764, to Gen. Gage from [-] Rodger, enclosing description and history of Florida with account of the present troop dispositions there. (p.51)
(*pp*) Letters, 1764, from James Campbell, New Orleans, describing the country there and military affairs, including description of voyage from New Orleans to Mobile, during which the boat was attacked by Indians. (p.51)
(*qq*) Letter, 1764, from James MacPherson, secretary for West Florida, to Lord Bute. (p.324)
(*rr*) Letter, 1764, from Lord Eglinton to Lord Bute, enclosing a plan for the southern states of America. (p.326)
(*ss*) Letter, 1764, from J.T. Kempe, New York. (p.329)
(*tt*) Letter, 1765, from James Campbell, Arkansas, describing the countryside and military dispositions. (p.52)
(*uu*) Letter, 1765, from Thomas Hutchinson, member of House of Representatives, describing the destruction of his house at Boston because he opposed a petition to Parliament against stamp duty. (p.52)
(*vv*) Letters, 1766, from George Johnstone and others, Pensacola, [Fla.], to John Pownall and to Lord Bute. (p.331)
(*ww*) Order, 1766, from Lord Halifax concerning command in America. (p.332)
(*xx*) Letter, [1766], from R. Nugent, who had just received a letter from Bristol stating that the Americans have received the repeal of the Stamp Act with great joy. (p.357)
(*yy*) Two letters, 1766-7, from John Campbell, Illinois - intends to sell his commission and settle there; describes the countryside, prospects for his farm, and the settlement in general. (pp.54-5)
(*zz*) Letter, 1767, from John Brown, Niagara, on Indian affairs. (p.55)
(*aaa*) Letters, 1768, from John Calcraft and Dr. Richard Huck commenting on supercession of Amherst. (p.59)
(*bbb*) Letter, 1770, from Thomas Patten, sometime minister at Newport, R.I., requesting subscription for his treatise on the Lord's Supper. (p.64)
(*ccc*) Two letters, 1772-3, from Gen. Lyman on proposed settlement on the Mississippi, based on grants of land to soldiers who have served in the provincial forces; suggests himself as governor. (pp.71-2)
(*ddd*) Papers, 1773-7, relating to the case of Ebenezer Macculloch, manager of British Linen Company, who had taken over the linen side of the bank's business, and was in difficulties as result of 'the American combinations against the sale and ware of British manufacture'. (pp.73, 75, 78)
(*eee*) Letter, 1774, from Lieut. Col. William Dalrymple about possibility of Loudoun's being employed in America. (p.74)
(*fff*) Letter, 12 Dec. 1774, from Capt. Andrew Barclay, H.M.S. *Scarborough,* off Boston - rebellion has begun 'all over New England'; gives news of military preparations on both sides; Worcester is to be the rebel capital. (p.75)
(*ggg*) Two letters, 1774-5, from the Earl of Stair commenting on Lord North's American policy, 'impolitic, not unjust', and justifying his own opposition to American war. (pp.74-5)
(*hhh*) Letters, 1775, concerning Gen. Gage's operations and other news from America; writers include Earl of Loudoun, R. Huck, Archibald Stevenson, and Daniel Leckie. (p.75)
(*iii*) Letters, 1776, from George Ogilvie describing the condition of Loudoun's American regiment on board the transport off Staten Island. (p.76)
(*jjj*) Letter, 1776, from C.W. McKinen, St. Augustine, East Florida, describing events in America and his treatment at the hands of the rebel government, who had detained him and seized his Negroes for not acknowledging the authority of Congress and refusing to pay a fine. (p.76)
(*kkk*) Letters, 1776, from John Gillon, merchant, giving news of American war and its effects on [mainly West Indian] trade and on the island of Dominica. (pp.76-7)
(*lll*) Letter, 25 April 1776, from Colin Lindsay describing the present situation at Boston. (p.77)
(*mmm*) Letter, *c.* 1776-83, from James Gray, describing events in Albany at beginning of American War of Independence, and later episodes including Burgoyne and Carleton's actions at Ticonderoga. (p.11)
(*nnn*) Letters, 1776-80, retailing second-hand news of events in America; writers include Dr. Huck, Thomas Campbell, Nathan Christie (Montreal), Countess of Balcarres, Charles Bembridge, James Mure Campbell, Lieutenant Colonel Gabriel Christie, and R. Saunders. (pp.76-9, 81-2)
(*ooo*) Letter, 1777, from Francis Carr Clerke and general orders from Shunsborough House, with news of the retreat of the Americans from Ticonderoga, 'with the loss of all their cannon and stores'. (p.79)
(*ppp*) List of officers killed and wounded at Still Water, 19 Sept. 1777. (p.79)
(*qqq*) List of ships with ratings that sailed from New York; and lists of those lost at Rhode Island, 1778. (p.80)
(*rrr*) Two letters, 1778, from Lachlan Mackintosh, merchant at Charleston, describing his distressed state, as he has been obliged by the American government to sell his estate and slaves, release his capital in rice or indigo, and go to Holland or France; has been captured by a privateer while on the way to Europe with his son. (p.80)
(*sss*) Letters, 1778, from the Earl of Dumfries seeking a pension for his brother, John McDouall: 'I am informed that there is money granted to give to our merchants who have suffered in this American rebellion. My brother ... resided long in Virginia, and almost his all left in that country'. (p.80)
(*ttt*) Letters, 1778-9, from Capt. Lieut. George Ker [? Keir], describing the condition of Loudoun's regiment in transports off New York bound for St. Augustine, Nov. 1778, and the landing at Savannah, July 1779. (pp.79, 81)
(*uuu*) Letter, n.d., from the Rev. Dr. Smith, provost of the College of Philadelphia, concerning an address. (p.359)
(*vvv*) Letter, n.d., concerning information wanted on exports and imports to North America since 1739. (p.369)
(*www*) Letter, n.d., from J. Fothergill concerning use of watchdogs in America against Indian attacks. (p.380)

MALCOLM OF POLTALLOCH. (0642)

Account of visit to the U.S.A., 1898. (p.2)

ARDTORNISH ESTATE OFFICE. (0656)

Letters, 1917-8, from Owen Hugh Smith describing work with Allied Provision Export Commission in Washington. (pp.24-5)

JOHNSTON OF HOLEHOUSE. (0675)

Family letters, 1849-50, from Thomas Johnston, from Peoria, Ill., and from California; also from other members of the family who had emigrated to America. (p.1)

ALEXANDER PIRIE & CO., PAPER MAKERS. (0732)

(*a*) Certificate of U.S. patent, 1866, with specification and drawings, of an envelope-making machine, in favour of M.G. Puffer of Rockville, Conn., 1858. (p.4)

(*b*) Papers, 1876, relating to International Exhibition at Philadelphia. (p.3)

PAPERS OF JAMES C. WELSH, M.P. (0768)

Letters, 1933, from Ramsay MacDonald. (p.5)

Subjects include:

Ineffectiveness of the American delegation at the Economic Conference, especially in its attitude to social questions, 2 Aug.

His attitude to the forthcoming National Economic Conference, and especially the position of America, 5 Nov.

BRODIE OF BRODIE. (0770)

(*a*) Account of Maryland by John Bracco, 1767. (p.26)

(*b*) Letter, 1778, from Lord North in reply to Brodie's offer to raise a company to fight in America. (p.49)

(*c*) Letter, 1851, from W.C. Grant, Oregon City, describing his travels in America and Canada. (p.10)

MACPHERSON-GRANT OF BALLINDALLOCH. (0771)

I. American Papers of General James Grant, Governor of East Florida, and a military commander during American War of Independence.

(*a*) Papers, 1757-9, relating to military campaigns. Includes extract journal of Cherokee expedition, 1759. Correspondents include Brigadier Bouquet and Col. Montgomery, the Earl of Loudoun, William Pitt, and Brigadier John Forbes. (pp. 76, 110-11, 128, 142-3, 185, 187)

(*b*) Papers, 1760-74, relating to Grant's governorship of East Florida, and his previous campaign against Cherokee Indians, 1760-2. They include letter-books and copies for 1761-2 and 1764-72 (pp.47, 235, 259); correspondence and other papers on civil and military affairs, including dealings with Indians (mainly Cherokee and Creek), with John Stuart, Superintendent of Indian Affairs, Governor Johnstone, and others; on military affairs, (including supplies and building of defences), with Lord Amherst, Gen. Gage, and others; on land grants and settlements, especially Dr. Andrew Turnbull's settlement of Greeks at Smyrnea in East Florida; on economic affairs including crops, trade and roads, with John Pownall, secretary to Commissioners for Trade and Plantations, Governor Morris (on voluntary emigration, and import of Negroes), and others including W.H. Drayton, Lord Adam Gordon, Colonel Henry Laurens, Dr. Richard Huck, Lieut. Col. Cuyler, Richard Oswald of Auchincruive. There are dispatches from the Earl of Hillsborough discussing with approval Grant's conduct of Indian affairs, also land settlement, trade and customs, 1766-71 (pp.91-2, 108, 114); and 'public letters' from the Earl of Shelburne dealing with Indians, the Spanish threat, and other subjects, 1766-7 (pp.97-8). Other correspondents include Lieut. Gov. William Bull, William Knox, agent for East Florida, 1764-70, and Charles Townshend. Other topics include demand for a popular assembly, 1771 (p.96), and appointment of a royal botanist for the Floridas, 1765. (p.136)

(*c*) Papers, 1771-93, concerning James Grant's estates in Florida, and local affairs there, including letters from David Yeats, his manager, F.G. Mulcaster, Lieut. Gov. Moultrie, the Rev. John Forbes, William Knox, John Pownall, and others. Yeats's letters cover estate affairs including indigo crop, mills and Negroes, and the incursions of Spaniards, Indians, and (in 1776), rebels from Georgia. (pp.61, 65-7, 72-5, 78-80, 88, 101-4, 125-7, 130, 133-4, 139, 159, 173-5, 177-80, 186-9, 192-3, 196-7, 221-2, 226, 228-9)

(*d*) Papers concerning American War of Independence, 1775-83. These include letter-books (1775-8) and other correspondence with Lieut. Gov. Moultrie, Sir Henry Clinton, Lord Cornwallis, Gen. Howe, and others. The letters include references to Benjamin Franklin in France, 1776-7; Thomas Digges, Maryland, believed to be an American spy in London; exchange of English and American prisoners, 1779; and Loyalist complaints and claims. There is a letter from George Washington at Morristown, giving a safe-conduct to Hessian baggage as far as Philadelphia, and a surgeon and medicines to Princeton, 8 Jan. 1777 (pp.151-2). Other papers relate to the captured Gen. Charles Lee, and to Indians. (pp.47, 61-4, 72-3, 75, 87, 91-2, 95, 99-104, 111-2, 115, 133, 139, 142, 151-2, 158, 170-1, 174-5, 180, 192, 195, 201, 215, 259)

II. Miscellaneous papers.

(*a*) Letter, 1765, from Edward Mason, secretary to the Duke of Cumberland, about the Duke's intention of making a collection of American plants. (p.197)

(*b*) Letter, 1770, concerning Burke's resolutions on America on 10 May. (p.84)

(*c*) Letter, 1774, from Gen. Alexander Mackay concerning offer of American command to Monckton. (p.250)

(*d*) Papers, 1776-9, relating to Capt. John MacPherson of the 17th Regiment of Foot.

Including:

Letter from MacPherson to his brother, giving a lengthy account of operations in America, 1776. (p.247)

Petition by MacPherson to Sir Henry Clinton for leave to dispose of his company as he was unfit for duty because of a wound received at Princeton in 1777; with copy medical report, 1779. (p.247)

(*e*) Letters, 1779-83, from James Chisholm, an emigrant from Lochbroom at New York, who had served on both sides, about his career in America. (p.246)

(*f*) Letter, 1781, from John MacPherson, Stones Ferry, Johns Island, to his brother in Badenoch about his recent contact with rebel troops. (p.51)

(*g*) Letter, 1788, from Lord Rawdon about claim to East Florida commissioners relating to Earl of Moira's settlement in East Florida. (p.155)

(*h*) Letter, 1794, from Robert Grant of Elchies, London, about American representative's high demands. (pp.63-4)

(*i*) Letter, 1795, mentioning that people go south to Glasgow in summer for employment, then emigrate to America. (p.63)

(*j*) Correspondence, 1803, with Edward Penman and John Mavor concerning agency for Gen. Grant in America. (p.131)

(*k*) Letter, 1885, from secretary of Polled Cattle Society about registration of animals in America. (p.57)

(*l*) Letter, 1887, from C.M. Green, U.S.A., about pedigrees of polled Angus cattle; with reply as to forgery of the same. (p.3)

EARL OF MANSFIELD. (0776)

I. Papers of Viscount Stormont, Ambassador to France, 1772-8, and Secretary of State for the Northern Department, 1779-82.

(*a*) Correspondence, 1756-9, between Viscount Stormont, envoy to Poland, and the Earl of Holdernesse, Secretary of State for the Northern Department.

American subjects include:

Rumours being spread by M. Bellisle of British defeat in North America, 1756. (p.4)

Attempt by Gen. Abercromby on Ticonderoga has failed, but it is hoped to remedy this check with troop reinforcements from Louisbourg, 1758. (p.20)

British victories in North America are such that enemies do not even venture to comment on advantage gained over Gen. Abercromby, 1758. (p.26)

Extract from a letter by Gen. Forbes announcing capture of Fort Duquesne; also news of other British victories in America, 1759. (pp.29, 36)

(*b*) Correspondence, 1763-80, between Stormont and the secretaries of the Northern Department (North, Sandwich, Rochford, and Weymouth), mainly from 1776 to 1778. Topics include operations against the Indians, 1763 (pp. 84-5); American opposition to the Stamp Act and rioting in New York, with copies of letters from Gen. Gage and Lieut. Gov. Colden of New York, 1765 (pp. 105-6); French designs in North America, and their assistance to the rebels in officers, arms, stores, port facilities, and subsidies, 1774-80; activities of American agents, especially Deane and Franklin, in France, Holland, German States, and England, 1776-7; activities of Beaumarchais in support of the American cause, and his connexions with Wilkes and other English sympathizers, 1776-7; operations of American, French, and English privateers, and ships posing as privateers, 1777; activities of British warships, including searching ships to prevent trade in illegal goods or arms with the Americans, 1775-7; rumour of Spanish assistance to the Americans, 1776 (p. 150); alleged Franco-American treaty, 1778 (pp. 179-80); miscellaneous reports from or about America. (pp.58, 85-6, 105-6, 130, 132-3, 139, 142-3, 145-84)

(*c*) Correspondence, 1776-81, between Stormont and various diplomats, and related papers on American affairs, mainly second-hand reports of events in America and their effect on European opinion. Topics include suspicion that John Wilkinson's brother is selling arms to America, 1777 (p. 476); actions of American privateers and French privateers with American captains, and failure of French to prevent this, 1777 (pp.483, 487, 503); rumours of French and Franco-Spanish proposed expedition to North America, 1780 (pp.233, 236); activities of American agents, especially Franklin and Lee, in France, and French aid to the Americans; activities of Lafayette in America (pp.233, 487); seizure of Henry Laurens' papers which give evidence of agreement between America and Holland (pp. 248ff., 386); American agents in Holland and trade with Holland, 1780 (pp.231, 379, 383); provision of German troops for the American war, 1780-1 (pp.250, 265); activities of [John] Paul Jones, 1779 (pp.372-4); impossibility of qualified independence for America, or of mediation by European powers between Britain and America, 1781 (p.216); observations on trade with the U.S.A., by the committee of American merchants, 1783 (p.477); propositions for the employment of H.M. forces in North America for consideration by H.M. confidential servants, by Lord George Germain, n.d. (p.481). (pp.216, 217, 219, 225-6, 228, 231, 233-6, 238-9, 241-2, 247-60, 266, 272, 278, 281, 372-4, 379-80, 382-7, 390, 393, 400, 471, 476-7, 481, 483-8, 496-7, 503-5, 559)

(*d*) Correspondence, 1779-82, between Stormont and George III, containing references to the American War.

Subjects include:

Operations of Count d'Estaing off the American coast, 1779, (p.59)

King's refusal to countenance foreign interference in the terms 'for bringing my rebellious subjects to a sense of their crimes', or to grant them independence, 1781. (pp.66, 72)

Choice of a new commander-in-chief in America, and possibility of a new secretary of state for the American Department, 1781. (p.67)

Instructions to Mr. Wentworth as a result of losses in Virginia and the West Indies, 1782. (p.68)

(*e*) Cabinet minutes, 1779-82, dealing with conduct of the war in North America and the West Indies, and diplomatic endeavours to prevent simultaneous entanglements with Russia and the European powers; movement of troops and ships; command appointments. (pp.39-51)

II. Miscellaneous Papers.

(*a*) Memorial, 1756, on taxation, with a list of taxes proposed to the Duke of Newcastle, n.d. [includes extension of the stamp duties to America]. (p.564)

(*b*) Sixteen letters, 1756-67, from Duke of Newcastle to Lord Mansfield, relating to American policy. (p.564)

(*c*) Speech delivered in the House of Assembly of the province of Pennsylvania by John Dickinson, 24 May 1764. (p.589)

(*d*) Letter, 1770, from William Strachan foreseeing ruin of Britain if doctrine of no taxation in America is established by law. (p.521)

(*e*) Letters, *c.* 1777-8, from William Eden, later Lord Auckland, on Franco-American relations, and British determination not to allow shipments to America; slow progress of British forces there; French sailors captured on an American ship. (p. 184)

(*f*) Miscellaneous correspondence, notes, etc., 1779-91, particularly relating to American war. (pp.569-70)

Including:

Short notes and extracts of the correspondence (particularly of Mr. Fitzherbert) relating to negotiations of the preliminary articles of peace, 1783.

Extracts from Sir Guy Carleton's correspondence as to his opinion of the American situation, 1782-3.

'Important secret list' shown to Lord North of persons in Ireland and England corresponding with Dr. Franklin, 1780.

Account of tobacco revenue, 1784-9; also extract state of the imports from North America to the British sugar colonies, 1771-73.

(*g*) Speech on peace with America delivered to House of Lords, 17 Feb. 1783. (p.399)

(*h*) Minutes of Cabinet meetings relating to appeals in prize causes, especially relating to American ships, 1795. (p.573)

(*i*) Notes on commercial treaty with America, late eighteenth century. (p.550)

(*j*) Plan, n.d., 'for reducing the revolted colonies' and 'establishing a permanent union between Great Britain and America', by 'a native of America'. (p.563)

(*k*) Letters, 1828-9, from David Douglas [botanist], giving probable itinerary of a proposed journey through South America finishing in California. (pp.316, 343)

(*l*) Miscellaneous notes by the Earl of Mansfield on American affairs, 1832-9. (p.432)

(*m*) Letter, [?1847] from Sir George Seymour, referring to American-Mexican war. (p.317)

EARL OF DUNDEE. (0783)

(*a*) Letters from Major Patrick Fergusson [inventor of the Fergusson rifle] in America, 1777-80. (pp.28-9)

Subjects include:

Details of the progress of his military career.

Description of various engagements, including surrender of Charleston, King's Mountain, and Brandywine.

Bursting of one of his cannon, which discredits his unit a little; wishes them to be cast in brass and the balls a tighter fit. Hatts Island, July 1777.

American riflemen, 1777.

(*b*) Letter, 1780, from Major Patrick McArthur, camp on Broad River, South Carolina, giving an account of Patrick Fergusson's death. (p.29)

EARL OF SOUTHESK. (0792)

(*a*) Dispatch from [-], including account of occurrences at a funeral in New York, 1699. (p.69)
(*b*) Letter from [-], London, giving news of arrival at Cowes of ships from America, seventeenth century. (p.64)
(*c*) Two volumes, 1777-83, labelled 'Imports' and 'Exports', listing ships permitted to load or unload cargoes at New York, following Gen. Howe's proclamation of 17 July 1777; gives details of cargoes, destination or last port, masters' names, tonnage, guns, and crew. (p.56)
(*d*) Letters, 1783, to Andrew Elliot, late Lieutenant-Governor of New York, from Elias Boudinot, Gen. Knox, and Gen. Washington; Boudinot and Knox acknowledge the high standard of his conduct during the war; Washington and Boudinot offer him their services in the future, and Washington adds that 'the most perfect regularity and good order prevail in [New York] and that every description of people find themselves under the protection of the laws of the state'. Printed in Sir William Fraser, *History of the Carnegies, Earls of Southesk* (Edinburgh, 1867), i, 229-30. (p.53)

EARL OF DUNMORE. (0796)

(*a*) Papers, 1774-90 (mainly extracts from published official correspondence) concerning Lord Dunmore's service in America [as last British governor of Virginia]. (p.4)
(*b*) 'Log of the Wanderers in the Prairies' - a shooting expedition, 1862. (p.3)
(*c*) Three letters, 1939, concerning deposit of 'Dunmore Papers' at the College of William and Mary. (p.4)

TRUSTEES OF SIR WILLIAM FRASER. (0800)

(*a*) Letter, 1778, from Commodore George Johnston to John Hume, about his unwillingness to take command against the Americans. (p.19)
(*b*) Letter, 1800, from Duke of Roxburgh to John Wauchope, mentioning return of Duke of Orleans from America. (p.17)

J. RICHARDSON & CO., SUGAR REFINERS. (0813)

Letters, 1889, mentioning state of sugar market in America. (p.1)

J. ALLISON & SONS, SAILMAKERS. (0822)

Miscellaneous papers, 1911-2, concerning Seward Peninsular Railway Co., U.S.A. (p.4)

LAUDERDALE MUNIMENTS. (0832)

(*a*) Letter, 1776, acknowledging news of American war. (p.71)
(*b*) Scroll letter, 1778, to town council of Aberdeen, concerning their subscription to raise a regiment 'to assist his majesty to bring his rebellious subjects in America to a proper sense of their duty'. (p.6)
(*c*) 'Impressions of my visit to President Harding at the White House, Washington', 8 Dec. 1922. (p.107)

THE STEWART SOCIETY. (0840)

Letter from Boston, 1772. (p.2)

HUNTER OF HUNTERSTON. (0852)

(*a*) Letters, 1777, from Robert Glasgow, St. Vincent, referring to activities of American privateers, which make it necessary to send duplicates of all letters. (p.57)
(*b*) Letter, 1784, from William Patrick, New York, describing the town since the British evacuation: 'we have been fortunate in having a good governor who hath suppressed the least appearance of tumult or disturbance'. (p.85)
(*c*) Letters, 1832-3, from James Henderson, New York, describing social life there; his preparations to go to Brazil: 'since I declared my intention of giving up my seat in Congress I have been assailed with invitations to dinner'. (p.62)
(*d*) Letter, 1855, from James Henderson, Para, Brazil, describing his sales of religious tracts and bibles for American Bible Society. (p.54)
(*e*) Letter, 1890, from R. Brereton, Forest Grove, Ore., [formerly factor of the Duke of Sutherland] recommending emigration to Oregon, describing the unprofitable wheat-farming of the old settlers, and contrasting it with mixed-farming and fruit growing; encloses a prospectus of his newly established factoring and surveying business in Oregon. (p.27)
(*f*) Letter, 1891, from R.M. Brereton, Forest Grove, Ore., asking to be made British commissioner to 'World's Exposition' in Chicago in 1893. (p.34)

LIEUTENANT COMMANDER H. CAMPBELL-GIBSON. (0853)

(*a*) Journal of a tour in the United States, 1850, by Louisa Campbell of Melfort, describing in detail visits to New York, Philadelphia, Baltimore, Washington, West Point, Albany, and other places in the U.S.A. and Canada. (p.2)
(*b*) Letter, 1857, from F.D. Macdougall, describing life in Maryville, Calif., with special reference to quartz mining; also describes the 'beneficial effects' of the large-scale lynchings in California. (p.6)

DOUGLAS-HOME MUNIMENTS. (0859)

(*a*) Letter, 1758, from John Douglas with military news from Fort Stanwix. (p.70)
(*b*) Letter, 1777, from the Duke of Queensberry to Archibald Douglas - 'There is great reason to believe that Sir William Howe has given Washington's army a thorough drubbing'. (p.69)
(*c*) Letters, 1777-80, from Lord Dunglass to his father. (p.202)
Subjects include:

Details of a skirmish on 1 Dec.; description of the desolated countryside. Philadelphia. Jan. 1777.

Taking of Forts Clinton and Montgomery, and surrender of Burgoyne. Camp near Fort Washington, New York Island, Oct. 1777.

Cornwallis's victory in Carolina. New York, Oct. 1780.

(*d*) Letter, 1828, from Lord Dunglass describing Mr. Barbour 'the new Yanky minister ... a delicious specimen of his cursed country - vain of his country - dirty - free and easy - in short perfectly odious'. (p.206)

MRS. A.V. SWAINSTON. (0876)

Letters, 1784-6, from Capt. Graham containing gossip about the American war. (p.1)

MARQUESS OF LINLITHGOW. (0888)

(*a*) Bill of lading, 1766, for ship *Penn* from Charleston, S.C., to Bristol. (p.66)
(*b*) List of counties, taxable persons, names of sheriffs, clerks, and burgesses elected in northern district of Carolina; list of towns and taxable persons, North Carolina, 1766. (pp.66, 141)
(*c*) Letter, 1771, from William Watson, Boston, relating that the countryside is fine but the inhabitants unfriendly. (p.181)
(*d*) List of regiments intended for America, 1776. (p.274)
(*e*) Letter, 1785, from J. Loudon Macadam concerning vessel impressed by Gen. Prevost during siege of Savannah, and then lost. (p.151)
(*f*) Letter, 1822, from George Canning on appointment of Mr. Reid as vice-consul in Georgia. (p.118)

(*g*) Letter, 1850, concerning emigration of poacher to America. (p.38)
(*h*) Papers, 1932, relating to Lord Linlithgow's visit to the U.S.A.; includes discussion of recession in States, and list of photographs of pictures taken to America. (p.219)

W.S.B. POLLOK-MORRIS ESQ. (0905)

(*a*) Letter-book, 1784-1805, containing copy letters from James Fairlie in Virginia, 1783, and providing very detailed information on the American trade after War of Independence. (p. 1)
(*b*) Journal of Kilmarnock shoemaking firm trading with America, 1785. (p. 1)
(*c*) Correspondence, 1800-7, between Alan and Robert Pollok, Virginia, on tobacco prices and other trade matters. (p.3)
(*d*) Legal papers, 1818-75, concerning recovery of Pollok-Morris estates in Virginia, with plan of Farm-Pollok, by William Robertson, 1842. (p.3)
(*e*) Ledger of Morris Pollok, 1839-62, containing a variety of accounts, memoranda, etc. relating to Scotland and to America, where his interests included tobacco-growing and an experiment in silk-growing. Contents include accounts between Morris Pollok and the Virginia Bank, Danville; letters from Obadiah J. Fountain offering his services as factor of Pollok's American estates and detailing the improvements he would undertake, 1841; and Farm-Pollok [Virginia] general balance book, n.d. (p. 1)

NEWHAILES MUNIMENTS. (0909)

(*a*) Official papers of Gen. St. Clair relating to the American expedition, 1746. (p.75)
(*b*) Letter, 1775, from James Boswell, commenting on Johnson's *Taxation no Tyranny*, in which he 'treats the American rebels with much contemptuous severity'. (p.51)

LORD BALFOUR OF BURLEIGH. (0923)

(*a*) Letters, 1909-10, from James Bryce, British Ambassador in Washington on trade and tariff affairs. (pp. 1, 4)
(*b*) Rough notes [? of 10th Lord Balfour] for speeches on Anglo-American relations, twentieth century. (p.9)

CAMPBELL-PRESTON OF ARDCHATTAN. (0934)

(*a*) Letter, n.d., from John Ferguson, Virginia, explaining tobacco dues. [*ante* 1753]. (p.118)
(*b*) Letter, 1775, from Archibald Campbell on Lord Barrington's opposition to allowing volunteers to serve in America. (p. 130)
(*c*) Letters, 1775-6, from Duncan Campbell, New York, describing in detail the general hostility in America to the British government, and the worsening situation in New York in Nov. 1775. (pp. 102-3)
(*d*) Letters, 1776-80, from Capt. Charles Campbell, serving in America, to his father, Patrick Campbell of Ardchattan. (pp.93-4) Subjects include:

His imprisonment at Dunstable, thirty miles northwest of Boston; is not supposed to use pen, ink and paper, Dec. 1776.

How he was captured by 'an armed banditta, and cast into the common county jail'. New York, Jan. 1778.

Blockade of a British army and fleet. Camp Kingsbridge, July 1778.

Reduction of Charleston by British forces [with many details]. Charleston, 20 May 1780.

(*e*) Letter, 1780, from Major Arthur McArthur of the 71st Regiment, describing the death of Capt. Charles Campbell. (p.94)
(*f*) Letter, 1783, from Isabella Logan complaining that she received no compensation for the losses of her husband, George Logan, in America; encloses a representation of the facts relating to his case, recounting that Logan, late of Princess Anne County, Va., had refused to join the revolution, and as a result 'his elegant mansion house and settlement at Kemps Landing and his rich store-houses there and at Norfolk were ruined'. (p.87)
(*g*) Letter, 1791, from James Campbell, Elizabethtown, [? N.J.], describing his life in America, especially the cheapness of land and the low cost of living. (p.98)
(*h*) Letter, 1811, from Lieut. John Campbell, H.M.S. *Daring*, asking his brother Alexander to use his interest to get him sent to America - 'now is the moment to chastise them, and to put all further disputes down'. (p.88)
(*i*) Letter, 1816, from H. Worsley giving second-hand account of naval action at Machinae, when two American schooners were captured by his son and other officers; quotes a letter of 7 Oct. from Sir George Prevost on the importance of these captures. (p.31)

HOUSTON OF JOHNSTON MUNIMENTS. (0935)

Letter, 1878, from Sir Arthur Gordon, Nasooa [Samoa], with news that an expedition is about to leave San Francisco for Samoa 'which under the guise of helping one of the rival candidates for power among the chiefs is really to re-establish Steinberger by force of arms'. (p.9)

JOHN BOATH, JR., LTD., JUTE MANUFACTURERS. (0949)

Letter-books, 1909-50, relating to foreign, including American, business. (p.3)

AILSA SHIPBUILDING CO. LTD. (0956)

List of ships built by the Ailsa Shipbuilding Company, 1904, including no. 121, T.S.Y. *Warrior*, for S.W. Vanderbilt, New York. (p.17)

CHARLES CONNELL & CO., SHIPBUILDERS. (0965)

List of ships built by Charles Connell & Co., including R.P. *Rithet*, for Welsh & Co., San Francisco, 1891. (p.54)

EDUCATIONAL INSTITUTE OF SCOTLAND. (0969)

(*a*) Report of proceedings of World Federation of Educational Associations at Denver, 1931. (p.43)
(*b*) Files relating to propaganda in the U.S.A., 1939-45. (p. 13)
(*c*) Report (two vols.) of proceedings of World Organization of the Teaching Profession at New York, 1946. (p.44)
(*d*) File relating to National Education Association of the U.S.A., 1946. (p.46)
(*e*) American teachers' gift of books, n.d. (p.50)

PAPERS OF KATHERINE DUCHESS OF ATHOLL. (0980)

Correspondence, 1938, including comments of R. Cavendish, of Industrial Engineers, New York, on Chamberlain's policy on Spain, also Duchess's opinion of what the U.S.A. could do on the 'matter of embargo'. (p. 1)

ROYAL NORTHERN YACHT CLUB. (1005)

(*a*) Log-book of the *Thistle* on voyage from the Clyde to New York for America's Cup, 1887.(p.2)
(*b*) Log-book of *Galatea*, kept by Lieut. Henn, R.N., on his voyage to the U.S.A. for America's Cup race against the *Mayflower*, and on the return trip, 1890. (p.2)
(*c*) Log (4 vols.) kept by the same, of yachting and fishing cruise on the east coast of America; with sketches of other boats and places visited, and photographs, 1891. (p.2)

HOPE OF LUFFNESS. (1021)

(*a*) Letter, 1861, from G.R. Hope, Nassau, describing anti-British feeling in America. (p.66)
(*b*) Letter, 1863, from Philip Smith to H.W. Hope, describing Yankee and Confederate forces. (p.64)
(*c*) Letters, 1874-5, from J. Hepburn, Oregon, describing a tour in western America and his decision to buy land in Oregon. (p.69)
(*d*) Letters, 1881, of H.W. Hope, California, giving a description of the country, with notes on the greater use of farm machinery than in Britain and 'hydraulic mining' in the Brunswick Hills. (p.63)
(*e*) Letter, 1882, from W.L. Brown to H.W. Hope on Capt. G.R. Hope's death at Honolulu. (p.61)

MONRO OF WILLIAMWOOD. (1054)

(*a*) Letter, 1778, from Lord Rawdon, Rhode Island, to Capt. John Brisbane. (p.4)
(*b*) Letter, 3 Sept. 1783, from David Hartley, Jr., to Sir John Stepney, informing him that Hartley had signed the peace treaty with the U.S.A. that day. (p.46)

CAMERON OF ALDOURIE. (1073)

Letter, 1767, from Lord Kames to Elizabeth Montague, recommending Dr. Franklin from Philadelphia, 'a man who makes a figure in the learned world, and who is beloved by all his acquaintances for being a most agreeable companion'. (p.5)

DUKE OF ROXBURGHE. (1100)

(*a*) Bill, n.d., concerning taxation in the North American colonies. (p.2)
(*b*) Letter, 1772, from Robert Innes, then in North America, describing a march of 7-800 miles which took nearly two months 'owing to our being detained at Ticonderoga for want of boats to cross lake Champlain'; comments on the scenery *en route.* (p.8)
(*c*) Letter, 1806, from Major John Cartwright [a radical] deploring the money wasted 'in attempting the destruction of American liberty'. (p.6)

MACNAB OF MACNAB. (1126)

(*a*) Letters, 1881, from Donald Campbell Macnabb describing voyage to San Francisco and travels in the U.S.A. and Canada from San Francisco, via Chicago and Montreal to New York. (p.37)
(*b*) Letters, 1884-5, from same from New York, San Francisco, Santa Barbara, and other places in the U.S.A. (p.38)

GLENTON HOUSE MSS. (1130)

Intelligence report on Irish affairs in the U.S.A., 1916. (p. 1)

HAMILTON OF ROZELLE. (1174)

(*a*) Letter, 1834, from Ralph Rodger, Rotterdam, to Messrs. Hunter & Ballatine, Ayr, concerning the price of tobacco in Holland: 'I wish the scarcity of tobacco in Virginia may have some influence on our mercat here'. (p.32)
(*b*) Letter, 1837, from J. Horsley Palmer to Archibald Hamilton of Rozelle - 'We are all well here and beginning to breathe again after the disaster in the American trade of last year'. (p. 14)
(*c*) Letters, 1843-6, from same, partner in firm of Palmer, Mackillop, Dent & Co., to Archibald Hamilton of Rozelle. (pp. 1-2)
Subjects include:
Description of his visit to the U.S.A., and the current collapse of credit there, Jan. 1843.
Use of electricity in America to grow plants faster, 'putting a pot of garden peas into blossom in 20 days', Sept. 1845.
Spread of potato blight in North America, with prediction that it will appear in Europe, Mar. 1846.

READMAN OF AULDGIRTH. (1219)

(*a*) Letters, 1884-93, from James Readman, Seattle, mainly concerning his financial affairs, but some relate to progress of the Washington Iron Works, Seattle. (p. 1)
(*b*) Incomplete letter, 1885, dated at Corvalla, on business prospects in America. (p.3)

FRANCIS WEBSTER & SONS LTD., SPINNERS & MANUFACTURERS. (1223)

(*a*) Letters, 1908, from Francis Webster, San Francisco, about family and business affairs. (p. 14)
(*b*) Costing notebook, marked 'U.S. of A. - book I had away with me'; contains few entries, 1920-1. (p.8)

J. ROSS ESQ. (1232)

Papers of John Marshall, estate owner, South Carolina, *c.* 1796-1819. (p. 1)
Schedule of the houses, lots, and lands in South Carolina, the property of John Marshall, *c.* 1796.
Account for the purchase of four African slaves, 1804.
Book labelled 'Office of discount and deposit with John Marshall'; includes a memorandum of 1818 on amount of taxes in America on beer, spirits, tea, coffee, cocoa, tobacco, snuff, etc., 1804.
Book containing miscellaneous notes, including journal of a voyage made by Marshall up the east coast of America to Canada and Britain; notes of cargoes, mainly tobacco, purchased; and description of wooden bridge over the Hudson River at Albany, 1808.
Four bills of exchange payable to Marshall signed by David Lamb and James Macadam, 1811-17.
Letter from J. Maverick to Marshall about the ownership of a Negro slave, 1819.

DR. J. C. H. DUNLOP. (1239)

(*a*) Memoirs, *c.* 1800-1850, [typed transcript] of Alexander Dunlop, including stories of American War of Independence, [not personal memories], and account of journey to North America in 1820 and conversation with Carroll [signatory to American Declaration of Independence]. (pp.2-3)
(*b*) Papers relating to James Dunlop's American estate, *c.* 1820. (p.9)
(*c*) Letters, 1820-50, to John Dunlop on various subjects including missions to American Indians; also letters of introduction for American scholars and others. (p. 17)
(*d*) Letters to John Dunlop, 1821-38, from friends in America, including one from Philadelphia Ladies Anti-Slavery Society. (p. 10)
(*e*) Letter, 1831, from John Dunlop in America, containing political reflections. (p.9)
(*f*) 'Travels of John Dunlop of Brockloch, Ayrshire, in the U.S. and Canada', by his sister, Mrs. Cathcart [typescript, four copies] - contains an account of Indians and of American customs; also account of [? John] Dunlop's travels in North America, contained in Mrs. Cathcart's diary, 1831-4. (p.3)
(*g*) Letters, 1831-4, mainly from H. L. Ellsworth to ministers in North America on behalf of John Dunlop; with text of 'The Convention For Making Peace', Fort Leavenworth [Kansas], 1833, and notes on number and location of Indian tribes who signed. (p.4)
(*h*) Letter, *c.* 1835-8, from J.T. Irving, New York, to Edward Ellsworth, Fort Gibson, Ark., on travels in America. (p.7)
(*i*) Draft speeches and other papers, *c.* 1841-7, of John Dunlop relating mainly to anti-slavery movement. Some of these refer to the

allegedly questionable religious activities of [William Lloyd] Garrison. (p.17)
(*j*) Request from editor of American philosophical journal that John Dunlop persuade Sir William Hamilton to write an article for them, 1844. (p.10)
(*k*) Notice of public meeting in Waterloo Rooms [Edinburgh] on education of North American Indians, to be addressed by Kahehewaquonaby [Peter Jones], 1849. (p.10)
(*l*) Letters, 1855-60, to John Dunlop from missionaries in America. (p.10)
(*m*) Letter, 1856, from Elizabeth Jones, a missionary's widow, explaining why she prefers to remain among the Chippewa Indians. (p.7)
(*n*) Letter, 1857, from Connecticut, on the death of Hugh Miller [author and geologist]. (p.7)
(*o*) Family letters, 1880, between members of Brown and Dunlop families, including one describing the town of Jackson, Tenn. (p.4)
(*p*) Ship's accounts of S.S. *Albany*, on a voyage to China and New York, 1884. (p.17)
(*q*) Price list of tools, hardware, and 'notions' of William Lee & Co., importers of American goods to Edinburgh, 1886. (p.11)
(*r*) Directors' reports for companies in Colorado, 1888. (p.11)
(*s*) 'Seaton of Parbroath in Scotland and America', anonymous, New York, 1889. (p.12)
(*t*) Memorandum, 1893, on the Great Falls, Mont., as a subject for investment. (p.16)
(*u*) Notes, n.d., by the secretary of 'The Realization and Debenture Corporation of Scotland Ltd.', on certain American investments [late nineteenth cent.]. (p.5)

SCOTT & ROBERTSON LTD., JUTE MANUFACTURERS. (1241)

(*a*) Agreements between Messrs. James Scott & Sons and (1) John G. Buchan and (2) William J. Horner, as New York agents, 1880-4. (p.4)
(*b*) Family correspondence, *c.* 1890-1895, relating to unsatisfactory state of linen business of Edward Biddle, vice-president, New York branch. (p.5)
(*c*) Correspondence file, 1919-30, relating to George W. Blabon & Co., manufacturers of linoleum, etc., Philadelphia. (p.2)
(*d*) Statement of profits and losses on all accounts including New York, London, and Calcutta, 1920-34. (p.3)
(*e*) Correspondence, agreements, and other papers, 1920-36, between James Scott & Sons Ltd., James Scott & Sons, New York, and Howard Cowing, of Gillespie & Co. of New York Inc., who acted as Scott's agent in New York and later became managing director of James Scott & Sons, New York. (pp.2, 3, 8)
(*f*) Report on a visit to the U.S.A. and Canada by J. Raymond Scott, 1949. (p.1)

MRS. A. W. MILLAR. (1252)

(*a*) Letters [some copies], 1817-26, from David Ireland. (pp.1-3)
Subjects include:

His plans to start out in a lawyer's office or set up a business in Virginia, 1817. (p.2)
Has taken an opportunity to move to Huntsville [Miss.] to manage a concern; gives comments on the American way of bringing up children, and life in the area, 1817. (p.2)
His adventures and observations on settlers' way of life; has now entered the merchant world, 1817. (p.2)
Defeat of the Seminole Indians, 1818. (p.1)
Admission of Alabama to the Union, and accession of the Floridas, 1819. (p.1)
Movements in cotton prices, 1819 and 1822. (pp. 1, 3)
Increase of steamboats on the Tennessee River; lists goods brought by water, 1824. (p.1)
Presidential election of 1824. (p.1)

(*b*) Journals of David Ireland, 1817-32, containing details of his travels in America which covered New York, Mobile, Tuscaloosa, Huntsville (where he was asked to make a fair copy of the constitution of the state of Alabama), Nashville, Louisville, Cincinnati, Sandusky City, Lake Erie, New York, Philadelphia, and Baltimore; also the prairies, the Choctaw, Chickasaw and other Indian areas, with comments on the Indian situation. (pp.1-3)
(*c*) Transcript of notes, 1830, from David Ireland's diary. (p.2)

MRS. ISABEL SCOTT. (1267)

(*a*) Letter, 1822, from William Russell, Philadelphia - because of outbreak of yellow fever in New York, writer took steamboat journey up Hudson River to Albany, then travelled to Philadelphia; gives detailed description of the journey, and account of contemporary Philadelphia. (p.1)
(*b*) Letter, 1823, from James Russell, Augusta, describing his progress in business since he arrived in America, which has been disappointing because of decrease in value of cotton; since 1819 has been in business with a saddler's shop; death of his brother Alexander of the fever in 1821. (p.1)
(*c*) Letter, 1825, from William Russell, Charleston, describing his recent misfortunes including being shipwrecked, losing a boat used for transporting cotton, and making a loss on a load of cotton, which prevent him from sending back money to Scotland; success of the business of his brother James. (pp.1-2)

PAPERS OF PROFESSOR A. A. BOWMAN. (1272)

(*a*) Letters, 1918-55, from C. W. Hendel, former colleague of Professor Bowman at Princeton University, and others on personal, philosophical, and theological matters. (pp.2-3)
(*b*) Correspondence, 1922-37, between Bowman and Dr. M. W. Jacobus, Princeton University, on the teaching of philosophy at Princeton, especially the position of Christianity in the philosophical course; and on Bowman's reasons for returning to Glasgow. (p.2)
(*c*) Papers, 1922-37, concerning Bowman's links with Princeton University and the logic department there, particularly the course on the ethics of Christianity; include a letter from Bowman to the president of the university, refusing the offer of another post there, as need for guidance in moral philosophy in Scotland, particularly the Glasgow area, is greater than in America, mainly because of unemployment, 1930. (pp.6,8)
(*d*) Papers, 1928, concerning Bowman's trip to the U.S.A. and Canada, including statement of expenses and itinerary. (p.5)
(*e*) Letter, 1932, from Eduard Tennesy, of the State Teachers' College, Fresno, California, discussing Bowman's book *The Absurdity of Christianity*. (p.2)

DUKE OF BUCCLEUCH. (1275)

(*a*) Four letters from Ellis or John Huske to Charles Townshend, *c.* 1756. (p.96)
Subjects include:

Report that Fort Duquesne has been surprised cannot be depended on, but the siege of Oswego has been raised.
News from America that Loudoun is to command at siege of Crown Point.
News from America from Sir William Johnson.

(*b*) Letter [unsigned, to Townshend], 1765, on the high regard of American merchants for the latter 'as the best informed person in this country of what mode might be proper to be taken in the present

critical situation of their affairs'; his view that for the present there is an end of the stamp duty, 'as every commissioner is actually intimidated by the whole voice of the people from standing forth in his duty and everyone has voluntarily or by compulsion resigned his post, and certainly no private merchant ship in the river will venture to carry them, and no sloop of war has yet been dispatched'; heads of grievances complained of by the Americans. (p.96)
(*c*) Note, *c.* 1765, in hand of Charles Townshend of heads for a speech on subjects including the New York Bill. (p.96)
(*d*) Letter, 1780, from George, Prince of Wales - wishes to prevent his friend Lake from going with his regiment to America. (p.21)
(*e*) Letter [unsigned, possibly from Benjamin Franklin], 1783, enclosing a memorial on commerce between Great Britain and the American colonies. (p.98)
(*f*) Three letters [unsigned], 1783. (p.98)
Subjects include:
 Encloses copy letter from Dr. Franklin [possibly item listed above].
 Negotiations with American ministers and definitive treaty of commerce, with remarks on the present state of negotiations.
 Natural alliance which ought to subsist between Great Britain and the American states.
(*g*) Letter, 1799, from George Washington, to J.W. Jamieson. (p.16)
(*h*) Letter, 1876, from Robert Spring, Philadelphia, to the Duke of Buccleuch, asking £5 for above letter of 'the immortal Washington'. (p.16)

LORN MACINTYRE ESQ. (1279)

Submission, 1736, between John Cameron, merchant, John McLawchlan, merchant in Fort William, and William Drummond of Balhadies, partners in the ship and cargo of the *Charming Molly* of Fort William for America; with the decreet arbitral. (p.3)

A.R. BROWN MACFARLANE & CO. LTD., ENGINEERS. (1280)

(*a*) Memorandum of agreement, 1886, between the Pacific Mail Steamship Co., of New York, and the Nippon Yusen Kaisha of Tokyo for conveyance of through goods to and from San Francisco and points beyond Shanghai, and such ports in Japan between Yokohama and Shanghai as open to foreign trade. (p.4)
(*b*) Letter, 1906, from W.E. Griffiths, New York, asking for outline of A.R. Brown's career in Japan for a study of foreigners employed by the Japanese government, 1838-1900; with reply. (pp.6, 9)

LORD SALTOUN. (1294)

Letter, 1917, from Lord Aberdeen, explaining his residence in America, 1915-17, with pencilled comment, 'excuse for being in America during the war!!!'. (p.63)

MRS. D. ANDERSON. (1305)

Letter, 1852, from Janet Anderson at Wellanport, Canada, to Alexander Anderson, concerning her recent emigration there. (p.1)

HALCRO-JOHNSTON OF ORPHIR. (1320)

Letters, [1741-1833], to members of the Johnston family in Stromness and in Canada, from correspondents in Canada and the United States, mainly on family matters but including:
 John Moore to John Johnston in Quebec regarding a teaching post which he has been offered in Detroit at £100 per annum, 1781. (p.9)
 John Urquhart in Quebec and in Niagara to Joshua Johnston in Stromness giving an account of his arrival in Quebec, 1781, and a description of American Indians, 1783. (p.8)
 John Purss in Quebec to John Johnston, commenting on mildness of winter and consequent possibility of navigation on the St. Lawrence, and mentioning that he has procured a place for Joshua Halcro in the North West [Trading] Company, 1801. (p.8)

LEWIS C. GRANT & CO. LTD. (1336)

(*a*) Correspondence, 1908-20, relating to rice milling in California and Brazil. (p.5)
(*b*) Letter-book, 1914-5, of Charles E. Douglas on eastern tour, including comments on prospects of market for rice milling machinery in California. (p.3)
(*c*) Memorandum book, 1939, kept by Lewis D. Grant containing technical data relating to setting up and testing of machinery, etc., in Canada, U.S.A., and South America. (p.7)

MRS. M. JESSAMINE. (1343)

Letters, 1842-9, from John McKay at Ashfield by Goderich in Huron District, Upper Canada, to his brother Donald in Beauly, Inverness-shire, describing his voyage to Quebec and his situation in Goderich, advising emigration and how to go about it, and giving local prices for potatoes, grain, and pork. (p.1)

SIR R.L. MACEWEN. (1351)

Letter, 1682, from Charles Charteris to Sir George Campbell of Cessnock concerning proposed transportation of people, cattle, and supplies to Carolina. (p.6)

SCOTTISH RECORD OFFICE, H.M. General Register House, Edinburgh EH1 3YY

The entry for the Scottish Record Office which follows has been compiled almost exclusively from the S.R.O.'s own *List of American Documents* (Edinburgh, 1976). In adapting that excellent volume to the requirements of this *Guide*, we have chosen to retain a considerable amount of detail about most of the collections. Certain materials have been excluded, however; while the S.R.O *List* includes some information about copies, photocopies, microfilms, maps, printed material, and newscuttings in their possession, these in general do not appear here, nor do documents which, though of American interest, seemed of an incidental nature. The researcher who does require information about these areas is encouraged to consult the S.R.O. volume, available from Her Majesty's Stationery Office.

GIFTS AND DEPOSITS

MISCELLANEOUS GIFTS AND DEPOSITS. (GD. 1)

(*a*) Certificate, 1716, dated at Williamsburg, Va., that Robert Stewart, one of the rebel prisoners taken at Preston, is to continue servant to Captain Edward Trafford for seven years. (53/73)
(*b*) Certificate, 1717, dated at York, Va., that Robert Stuart, formerly in Glenbeath, was assigned to William Gordon and had now been sent by him on business to Scotland. (53/74)
(*c*) Letters, 1730-9, from Charles Home, merchant, New York. (384/3; 384/5)
(*d*) Business books, 1731-49, of a merchant in Westmoreland County, Va., possibly William Campbell. (455/1-3)
(*e*) Letter, 1758, from Robert Menzies of Culterallers containing news of friends wounded in America. (337/34/3)
(*f*) Stock in trade and effects of James Hunter of Virginia, 1763. (384/21)

(*g*) Cash book and journal, 1763-7, of George Oswald of Scotstown, merchant in Glasgow, covering the business of Oswald, Dennistoun & Co., trading to Europe and America. (618/1)
(*h*) Letter, 1766, from Hon. Charles Townshend, London, concerning a grant of land in East Florida. (616/168)
(*i*) Indenture, William Logan, Philadelphia, and Hannah, his wife, to Joseph Galloway and other co-partners of the Durham Company, of a tract of land called Logan's Trust, Springfield, County of Bucks, 1773. (384/2)
(*j*) Letters (1 volume) from James Dunlop, merchant in Canada, to his family in Glasgow, concerning trade with the United States and the War of 1812. 1773-1815. (151/1)
(*k*) Letter, 1775, from Adam Hunter, Fredericksburg, Virginia. (384/23)
(*l*) Letter, 1775, from Alexander Robertson [Baron Reid] mentioning the American estates of his son and grand-daughter. (90/8)
(*m*) Account book and papers (26 items) of John Inglis, sutler and merchant, New York, 1777-87. (46/20-1)
(*n*) Letters, 1778-82, from William and James Home serving as officers in Royal Marines on the West Indies station, giving news of the war against the Americans and French. (384/6-7)
(*o*) Account by James Wilson, master, of disbursements for the ship *Lucretia* at Cork, Halifax, New York, Virginia, and in England. 1778-82. (500/69)
(*p*) Papers, 1778-1803, relating to administration of sequestrated estate of James Dunlop of Garnkirk, partner in firm of Colin Dunlop & Sons, Glasgow, and in particular to business in Virginia and Maryland with which the firm had large transactions. (572/33/1-31)
(*q*) Five business letters to William Shedden at Bermuda and New York, 1780-94. (67/1)
(*r*) Charter-party, 1782, between Thomas Bell, owner of the *Lucretia* of London, James Wilson, master, and the Navy Office for use of the ship as a transport to North America or elsewhere. (500/71)
(*s*) Correspondence and papers, 1782-1820, regarding executries of George Craig and his son, Archibald Cumming Craig, of Pennsylvania. (495/35)
(*t*) Papers, 1793-4, concerning claim by Mrs. Mary Didlake, executrix of James Didlake, King and Queen County, Virginia, to a legacy by Griffith Elrington, Liverpool. (26/61)
(*u*) Letter from Patrick Home, Virginia, expressing his hope of selling Rappahannock Forge for £18,000, and MS. copy advertisement for the sale. 1796-1801. (384/10)
(*v*) Letter, 1803, from George Hamilton, Madison County, Virginia, to Hugh Hamilton of Pinmore, describing property near Fredericksburg which he had recently purchased. (581/1)
(*w*) Letter, 1815, from Thomas Carlyle, Annan, 24 May, to Robert Mitchell, Ruthwell Manse, concerning the good prospects of 'the man of music, Andrew' in America. 'He can fiddle, he can dig, and to beg he is not ashamed'. (714/6)
(*x*) Letter, 1822, from Rev. T.R. Malthus to C.W. Le Bas, asking him to calculate the population of America for years 1795 and 1815 and the annual rate of increase. Calculations and reply overleaf. (616/155)
(*y*) Letters, 1834-8, about emigration to Canada of James Aitchison, son of William Aitchison, brewer in Edinburgh, and his escape to the U.S.A. to avoid imprisonment for debt. (92/1-22)
(*z*) Two letters from Thomas Mungo Johnston, Consumnes River, near Sacramento, to his family in Scotland - describes how he works his gold claim; his experiences as a emigrant worker in Salt Lake Valley, comments on Mormons and Indians, arrival in California and life there. 1851. (277/77/3)
(*aa*) Subscribers' agreement, Illinois Investment Company, 1854. (421/94)
(*bb*) General service of Robert Hogg, brass-finisher, New York, as heir to his grandfather, Robert Hogg, seaman in Cromarty, and related documents, 1854-5. (478/5-7)
(*cc*) Letters, 1878-93, from John Bruce, district judge, Middle District of Alabama, to his cousin, James, on family matters. (738/1-2)
(*dd*) Papers, 1889, regarding claim of James Fullarton, Manchester, New Hampshire, to succeed to Kilmichael estate. (19/79)
(*ee*) Letter (incomplete) from Susan Walker, Vienna, Virginia, to her niece, Lilias Campbell, concerning their family history, 1914. (597/9)

BRITISH RECORDS ASSOCIATION.

(*a*) Returns, 1833-6, of the number of emigrants from Liverpool; specified destinations include the United States. (116)
(*b*) Correspondence and papers (12 items), 1876-7, concerning libel action between John Gordon of Cluny and his half-brother, Ashurst Menzies, resident in the U.S.A. (331)

EGLINTON MUNIMENTS. (GD.3)

Letters, 1686-7, from William Dunlop, Carolina, to Sir James Montgomerie of Skelmorlie, discussing various matters including cargoes to and from America and the West Indies, importation of Negro servants, and Spanish attack on Scots colony at Port Royal. (E2/114-20)*

BERTRAM OF NISBET MUNIMENTS. (GD.5)

(*a*) Letter, 1760, from George Bartram at Philadelphia to John Bartram of Carsewell, asking for copy of family coat of arms and other information for himself and his brother in North Carolina, enclosing newspaper and giving information on writer's own birth and career. (593)
(*b*) Extract registered bond, 1785, by William Bertram of Nisbet and another in favour of David Mitchelson, merchant in New York for £460. (416)

BIEL MUNIMENTS. (GD.6)

Summary of patents of Carolina granted to the Earl of Clarendon, n.d. (1019)

BROUGHTON AND CALLY MUNIMENTS. (GD.10)

(*a*) Letters, 1718-36, concerning emigration to America. (1421/46; 1421/489)
(*b*) Letters, 1779-82, concerning naval and military operations during War of American Independence, including defence of Kirkcudbrightshire coast against John Paul Jones. (1421/323; 1421/338; 1421/343-4; 1421/346)

CAMPBELL OF BALLIVEOLAN MUNIMENTS. (GD.13)

Orderly book of [74th] Regiment at New York, 1783. (94)

AIRLIE MUNIMENTS. (GD.16)

Letter, 1813, from Major William Drummond commanding the garrison at St. John: 'I am well - and not yet swallowed up by the Yankees though . . .we have been sometime past expecting to be attacked', 9 Jan. (34/359/11)

CLERK OF PENICUIK MUNIMENTS. (GD.18)

(*a*) Letters, 1716-9, regarding training of James Clerk as a merchant, including a trading voyage to New England. (5288)
(*b*) Invoice of goods shipped on board the *Mayflower* of Boston on account of James Clerk, 1716. (2573)
(*c*) Application, 1720, by James Clerk for appointment as victualler to the fleet at Boston. (5296)

(*d*) Account of sales of merchandise received at Boston from on board the *Swallow* from London on account of Charles Freeman, 1720. (2574)
(*e*) Translation of letter in Hebrew, 1723, from Judah Monis, Harvard College, to Robert Wodrow, minister at Eastwood, Scotland. (4054)
(*f*) Letter, 1733, from Sir John Inglis reporting the intention of Patrick Houston, his cousin, to emigrate to Georgia. (5272/41)
(*g*) Letters, 1736-48, from Patrick Houston, from Savannah and Frederica in Georgia, concerning samples of 'strouds and duffles' he had sent to Scotland; his plantation and plans for planting cotton and indigo; war against Spaniards in Florida; his move to Frederica at request of General Oglethorpe; work of George Whitefield in the colony, including erection of an orphanage; emigrants to the colony; and other matters. (5360/3-9)
(*h*) Letters, 1741-7, from Alexander Gordon, secretary to the governor of South Carolina. (5023)
(*i*) Two letters from Hugh Clerk, merchant in Edinburgh, containing news of a trading voyage to Carolina, 1751. (5321)
(*j*) Letters, 1757-8, from Mathew Clerk in New York regarding the campaign in America. (4201-3)
(*k*) Letter, 1758, from 'J.B.' vindicating the conduct of Mathew Clerk, chief engineer, at the siege of Ticonderoga. (4204)
(*l*) Summary, n.d., of Clinton's 'Narrative' concerning the War of American Independence, and answers of General Cornwallis. (4265)
(*m*) Letter, 1841, from Earl Canning stating that treaties with Bolivia, The Oriental Republic, Mexico, and Texas regarding the slave trade were awaiting exchange and ratification. (3409)
(*n*) Letter, 1841, from William Penson, New York, concerning the trial of Mr. McLeod for his part in the burning of the *Caroline*; rumour that some southern states intended to repudiate their debts; and American attacks on Britain in newspapers and books. (3423)
(*o*) Four letters and papers regarding shipment of barrels of beef from New York for unemployed workers of Paisley, 1842. (3501)
(*p*) Part letter, *c.* 1842-3, from [-] to Sir John Clerk criticizing the American people, politics, and constitution. (3520)
(*q*) Statement of quantities of rolled iron imported into the United States from various countries, 1838-43; and treasury memorandum regarding rates of duty imposed by the U.S.A. on rolled and hammered iron. *c.* 1844. (3653)
(*r*) Statement of quantities of wheat and wheat flour imported from America, 1839-44. *c.* 1845. (3641)
(*s*) Two letters from secretary of G.P.O. on postal arrangements and completion of the treaty with America, 1845. (3699)
(*t*) Letter, 1845, from William Penson, music teacher, New York, on his 'residence of eleven years in this modern pandemonium', visits of musical celebrities to America, and American hostility to Britain. (3746)
(*u*) Letter, 1846, from [-] to Viscount Sandon on reasons for using Chilean ore for the smelting works at Liverpool, and the prospect of being able to use American ore. (3819)
(*v*) Excerpt from statement by Mr. Ellsworth regarding wheat production in the United States, 1846. (3836)

CUNNINGHAM OF THORNTOUN MUNIMENTS. (GD.21)

(*a*) Commission, 1758, by John Blair, president of H.M. Council and Commander-in-Chief of the colony of Virginia, to John Peebles as 1st surgeon's mate in the 2nd Virginia Regiment. (674)
(*b*) Letter, 1763, from I.A. Dalyell, aide-de-camp to Major Lobel, commanding 77th Regiment, New York, informing him that the general had approved application of John Peebles to be allowed to serve as a volunteer. (488)
(*c*) Commissions, 1763-78, by Amherst, Howe, and Clinton, as commanders-in-chief in America, to John Peebles in 42nd Regiment. (676; 678; 681; 683)
(*d*) Bundle of abstracts and accounts of Captain Peebles' company of the 42nd Regiment. 1772-82. (490)
(*e*) Letter, 29 June 1776, from John Peebles, Halifax Harbour, regarding his voyage from Greenock to Boston, and from Boston to Halifax in convoy, and expressing hope that the rebels would soon be defeated. (491/1)
(*f*) Letter, 7 May 1777, from John Peebles, [New] Brunswick, New Jersey, regarding an expedition into New England under General Tryon and Sir William Erskine. (489/2)
(*g*) Letter, 26 Oct. 1778, from John Peebles, Long Island, giving news of the American war. (495)
(*h*) Letter, 30 Aug. 1780, from John Peebles, New York: 'The admiral is still watching the French fleet . . . Mr. Washington is on the other side of the North River within a few miles and has a stronger army in the field than he has had these two years'. (489/3)
(*i*) Letter, 27 Jan. 1781, from John Peebles on sailing of an expedition under Brigadier General Arnold, supposedly for Chesapeake Bay, and of mutinies in the rebel army and British attempts to take advantage of them. (491/2)
(*j*) Note of line of battle of fleet under command of Admiral Thomas Graves, Sandy Hook, 1781. (496)
(*k*) Indenture, 1782, between the superintendents of police of Long Island and Captain John Peebles for the servitude of a Negro boy. (158)
(*l*) Letter, 1802, from T. Kennedy to Captain Peebles declaring that 'according to Sir H. Clinton's narrative no blame can be attached to him for the failure of the expedition to Rhode Island'. (499)
(*m*) Note of census of U.S.A., 1810. (708)
(*n*) Letter, 1816, from Major General David Stewart [of Garth] to John Peebles requesting more details regarding the action of the 42nd Regiment during War of American Independence, and informing him that Graham Stirling of Airth expected to find, among his uncle's, Sir Thomas Stirling's, papers, the journal of his expedition up the Mississippi. (500)
(*o*) Diary, 1876, of hunting trip made by George Wrey in the Rocky Mountains. (482/2)
(*p*) Letters, 1876-83, from George Wrey describing his travels in America, Canada, and elsewhere, hunting trips in the Western U.S.A., his orange groves in Florida, and plans to cultivate vines in California. (482-4)

CUNNINGHAM GRAHAM MUNIMENTS. (GD.22)

Two letters from John Fallowfield, Savannah, and E. Fallowfield, his wife, regarding office of collector of port of Savannah, 1741. (3/314)

BUGHT MUNIMENTS. (GD.23)

(*a*) Five letters from Alexander Macrae, from Edinburgh, London, and Norfolk, Virginia, concerning his journey to Virginia, 1804-5. (6/410)
(*b*) Letter, 1810, from George Ramsay, Albany, New York State, giving a brief account of his career since arriving in New York in 1794, and requesting a favour for Stephen Van Rensselaer who was going to study at Edinburgh College for two years. (6/469)

ABERCAIRNY MUNIMENTS. (GD. 24)

(*a*) Letter, 1685, from D. Toshach, Amboy, to the Earl of Perth, chancellor of Scotland, stating that he had been unable to obtain possession of land in New Jersey sold him by Lord Perth as 'all the campione ground and river sids ar takine up allradie by Quakers, Independents, Presbiterians, Anabaptists, and in a word by all the off scourings of hell'. Printed in *Hist. MSS. Comm.*, x, app. 137. (1/826)
(*b*) Four letters to John Drummond of Quarrell from settlers in North America, 1733. (1/464o)

(*c*) Letter, 1748, from Joshua Crosby, Philadelphia, recommending Charles Moore and Benjamin Morris, physicians, who intended to visit Edinburgh, and discussing possibility of financial help from Philadelphia for Edinburgh Royal Infirmary. (1/833)
(*d*) Twelve letters to Sir William Stirling of Ardoch from his brother, Thomas Stirling, during his career in the Army and relating to the campaigns in America, 1760-97. (1/458)
(*e*) Fifteen letters, 1760-75, from Benjamin Franklin to Lord Kames and his wife, discussing scientific, philosophical, and political subjects. Eight of these letters are printed in *The Life and Works of Benjamin Franklin*, ed. Jared Sparks (Boston, 1836-40). (1/562)
(*f*) Letter, 1778, from Alexander Dundas, Quebec, regarding the American campaign. (1/459)
(*g*) Letter, 1780, to Sir William Stirling from [-], New York, with news that his brother, Brigadier General Stirling, had been wounded. (1/460)

AILSA MUNIMENTS. (GD.25)

(*a*) Two letters from Dr. William Stork and Governor James Grant concerning settlement in East Florida, 1767-9. (sec. 9, box 27)
(*b*) Letter, 1776, from John McColme to the Earl of Cassillis on success of American campaign under General Howe. (sec. 9, box 45)
(*c*) Letters, 1817-8, regarding claim to peerage of Cassillis by Robert Kennedy, Ohio, son of the Rev. Samuel Kennedy of Basking Ridge, New Jersey. (sec. 9, box 46/2)
(*d*) Expenses and doctors' fees of the Earl of Cassillis in New York, 1898. (sec. 9, boxes 11 and 29)
(*e*) Letter, 1909, from Forsyth de Fronsac, U.S.A., concerning a proposed work based on the 'Ragman Roll'. (sec. 9, box 38)

LEVEN AND MELVILLE MUNIMENTS. (GD.26)

(*a*) Petition to King, 1689, by Francis Makemie, minister in Virginia, for restoration of his former liberty and privilege, he having formerly presented an address for six dissenting ministers in Virginia and Maryland with a petition of complaint against Lord Howard of Effingham for imprisoning William Anderson, member of the last Assembly of Virginia. (7/266)
(*b*) Memorial to the King, 1689, regarding 'the hostilities committed in the province of Carolina by the Spainiards', represented by Major William Dunlop, commissioned to that effect. (7/277)
(*c*) Letter, 1751, from Professor Aaron Burr to the Earl of Leven appealing for funds for the College of New Jersey. Printed in W. Fraser, *Melvilles Earls of Melville and Leslies Earls of Leven* (Edinburgh, 1890), ii, 262-3. (1/3/316)
(*d*) Papers, 1764-5, concerning the Rev. George Whitefield's visit to America. (10/103-6)
(*e*) Seven letters between Phillis Wheatley in Boston, Mass., and John Thornton, merchant in London, mainly on religious topics, 1771-5. (13/663)
(*f*) Eighteen letters and other papers regarding Captain William Leslie of 17th Regiment [2nd son of 6th Earl of Leven], with details of actions in the vicinity of Long Island and his death in action, 1771-7. (9/513)
(*g*) Letters, 1773-82, concerning Major General Alexander Leslie's service in America during War of Independence. (9/512/5-21; 9/518)
(*h*) Letter, 21 June 1775, containing 'J. Webster's account of the action at Boston'. (9/514)
(*i*) Letter, 1778, from Dr. Benjamin Rush relating that the funeral expenses of Captain [William] Leslie [killed at battle of Princeton] 'were generously given by General Washington upon hearing that he was my friend'. (13/678)
(*j*) Letter, 1779, from Andrew Hunter, minister at Dumfries, discussing attention paid by Dr. Rush and General Washington to Captain William Leslie, and mentioning Mr. Hepburn's only son with General Burgoyne's army. (13/681)
(*k*) Letter, 1779, from John Donaldson, London, on the war with America. (13/682)
(*l*) Note of journey from Charleston to Petersburg, to join Lord Cornwallis, 1780. (9/521)
(*m*) State of the troops at the battle of Guilford, giving killed, wounded, and missing, 1781. (9/523)
(*n*) Two letters from Robert Skene reporting news of the war in America, 1781. (13/714)
(*o*) Letters, 1783, from Captain Lichenbrodf and General Bose regarding the Hessian Regiment de Bose serving in America. (13/722; 13/728)
(*p*) Part letter, 1784, from'R.J.', describing how Captain Asgill, a prisoner of the Americans who had been condemned to death by General Washington in retaliation for a British crime, was reprieved and set free by the intervention of the French queen. (13/168)
(*q*) Letter, 1794, from Dr. Benjamin Rush to Lord Balgonie introducing Samuel Bayard [American jurist]. (13/763)
(*r*) Letter, 1815, from Lord Torphichen to Lord Leven regarding the signing of treaty with America. (13/175)
(*s*) Two letters, 1818, from Allan Melvill in Boston, Mass. (13/893)

DALQUHARRAN MUNIMENTS. (GD.27)

Instructions, 1715, by surveyor general of customs to the collector at the Lower District of the James River, Virginia. (5/14)

KINROSS HOUSE MUNIMENTS. (GD.29)

(*a*) Papers, 1669-73, concerning proposed voyage by the *Hope* and *James* of Leith to transport Scots settlers to New York, carry on fishing there or trade between Scotland and the American colonies. See P. Gouldesbrough, 'An attempted Scottish voyage to New York in 1669', *Scottish Historical Review*, xl (1961). (106; 1439; 1459)
(*b*) Letters, 1669, from John Kennewie, town clerk of Culross, referring to provision of women to be shipped to America. (1962)

SHAIRP OF HOUSTOUN MUNIMENTS. (GD.30)

Letter, 1739, from James Glen [Governor of South Carolina], London, mentioning his impending journey to America. (1850)

ELIBANK MUNIMENTS. (GD.32)

(*a*) Letter, 1760, from Hon. Mrs. Ferguson of Pitfour to the Governor of Quebec, recommending that Mr. Burnett and his partner, a merchant in Philadelphia, be given orders to supply Quebec garrison. (24/58)
(*b*) Letter, 1766, from the Earl of Eglinton concerning moves to repeal the Stamp Act. (24/19)
(*c*) Note, 1766, by Elias Durnford, of a tract of land in West Florida belonging to Patrick, Lord Elibank, and associates. (25/109)
(*d*) Correspondence, 1934, with Sir John Simon about his attitude to the United States. (25/59)
(*e*) Correspondence, 1938, with Quincy Howe about ideas expressed in his book *England Expects Every American to do his duty*. (25/15)
(*f*) Letter, 1940, from Arthur Glasgow on Anglo-American relations in the war, especially with regard to use of American fleet; with a covering note from Lord Halifax. (25/62)
(*g*) Letter, 1942, from Ormand Lawson Johnston on British War Relief in the United States. (25/16)

HADDO MUNIMENTS. (GD.33)

Catalogue, n.d., of American seeds, etc. for the Earl of Aberdeen. (65/110)

DUNDAS OF OCHTERTYRE MUNIMENTS. (GD.35)

(*a*) Letters, 1773-93, from Dr. David Dundas and his wife. (49/1-55)
Subjects include:

News of American and French landing on Rhode Island and of British naval and military countermeasures leading to its recapture, 1778. (7)

Repulse with heavy losses of attack by General Gates on Lord Cornwallis, 1780. (14)

Surrender of Cornwallis, 1781. (18; 19)

Naval operations by Lord Howe, 1782. (23)

Award of £1,100 by American commissioner to wife of George Dundas, David's brother, for loss of property in America, 1790. (47)

(*b*) Letters, 1780-1, from Ralph Dundas, captain of H.M. sloop *Bonetta*. (57/9-13)
Subjects include:

Hurricane encountered in crossing Atlantic, capture of Charleston, two companies of the Edinburgh Regiment under Colonel Dundas at Charleston, praise of Hessian troops. (9)

Operations on American coast with account of prizes taken, report of capture of large number of Virginia ships by New York privateers, blockade of French fleet at Rhode Island, subjection of the greater part of North Carolina, news of a serious riot at Boston consequent on Washington's requisitioning 3,000 men from the city to augment his army, difficulties and discontent of Washington's troops. (10)

Account of naval and military forces forming at Staten Island for a secret destination reputed to be Virginia to effect a junction with Lord Cornwallis (the troops, under the command of General Arnold with Colonel Dundas of the Edinburgh Regiment second-in-command, included the Edinburgh Regiment, Queen's Rangers, Loyal Americans, and 100 'Yawgers', General Arnold's Corps). (11)

Operations in Virginia and Virginian waters, account of the action at James Island where *Bonetta* covered the boats of Cornwallis's army, with information concerning the losses suffered by the Edinburgh Regiment, the countermanding of projected attack on Philadelphia, news that the Edinburgh Regiment had earned the praise of Cornwallis and had become mounted, some appeared awkward on horseback but there were compensations; 'the lads take care to forage pretty cheap for when they come to a man's that pretends he is a friend to government they tell him he cannot think much of giving them corn etc. for their horses which reasoning always produces it and when they come to a rebel's they help themselves so you see they won't be at a great expence for forage'. (12)

Surrender of Cornwallis (in which the sloop was included); losses of the Edinburgh Regiment had been slight. (13)

(*c*) Letter, 1781, to James Dundas from Hugh and Alexander Wallace, New York, informing him that his brother, Captain Ralph Dundas, was in Virginia and had a share in some tobacco taken by the army and navy on the James River. (64)

(*d*) Letter, 1782, from John Gardiner, London, reporting arrival of Ralph Dundas from America and newspaper attacks on him. (62/5)

(*e*) Letters, 1783-9, from George Dundas giving details of the family of his wife, daughter of late Thomas Thompson, merchant in Norfolk, Virginia, and of her claim before the commissioners for American claims. (66/9, 17)

(*f*) Defences for James Dundas of Manor, residing in Philadelphia, to summons of reduction and declarator raised against him claiming that he was barred by 'alienage' from making any claim to estate of Manor under a deed of entail, *c*. 1835. (174)

(*g*) Letters, 1842, from William Dundas concerning his travels in America, particularly his journey from Washington to St. Louis and projected journeys from Mississippi to Canada, New York, Boston, and the Southern States. (179/15-17)

(*h*) Letter, 1850, from Edward Everett, Cambridge, U.S.A., recommending Rufus Choate 'one of our most eminent lawyers and public men'. (268)

STEUART OF DALGUISE MUNIMENTS. (GD.38)

(*a*) Letter, 1725, from 'G.S.' [Gilbert Stewart] to his father, Thomas Stewart of Kinnaird, mentioning that his brother James, was at sea on his way to Virginia. (2/3*)

(*b*) Letter, 1733, from Gilbert Stewart, Edinburgh, to Thomas Stewart elder of Kinnaird: 'ther is a great maney famalies and persons boath in England and in the country going to settell in this new collony in America called Georgia'; suggests that the latter's idle son might do the same. (2/4/96*)

(*c*) Two letters from James Stewart to his father, John Steuart of Dalguise, referring to his departure from Gravesend for America and arrival at Charleston, South Carolina, where he plans to establish a business, 1749. (2/7/86,96*)

(*d*) Letters, 1751-4, from James Steuart, Charleston, to his father, giving details of his life in South Carolina and of his business as a shipwright. (2/8/24, 33, 60, 64, 84, 107*)

(*e*) Letter, 1755, from Mungo Murray, Deptford, to John Steuart of Dalguise, regarding death of James Steuart in Carolina and execution of his will. (2/9/15*)

(*f*) Letter, 1759, from John Steuart, Edinburgh, to his father John Steuart of Dalguise, regarding efforts to secure what was left to him by his brother, James, in Carolina. (2/9/79*)

(*g*) Letter, 1768, from Captain John Robertson, Edinburgh, to James Robertson of Lude, mentioning news of 'the Devil and all to pay in America, no less than open rebellion . . . I think we are on the eve of a war'. (2/10/98*)

LOTHIAN MUNIMENTS. (GD.40)

(*a*) Letter, 1650, from the Earl of Derby recommending Colonel Whitly and requesting employment for him in Scotland or permission to levy a regiment or to migrate to Virginia. Printed in *Correspondence of the Earl of Ancram and the Earl of Lothian* (Edinburgh, 1875), ii, 309. (portfolio IV, no.49*)

(*b*) Letter, 1665, from Robert Carr at Boston, Massachusetts, to the Earl of Lauderdale concerning the boundaries of various colonies. Printed in *Proceedings of the Massachusetts Historical Society*, 1858-60. (sec. VI, no.41*)

(*c*) Draft letter (unfinished), n.d., from [-] to her brother, who had gone to America from the Highlands. (portfolio XVIII, part 2, no.9*)

PAPERS OF PHILIP KERR, 11TH MARQUESS OF LOTHIAN.[1]

(*a*) Two letters, 1916, from Lionel Curtis to Philip Kerr on proposal to establish Round Table groups in the U.S.A. and necessity for their separate identity; German influence on American thought through the universities. (17/3, pp. 250-65)

(*b*) Notes, 1909, by Philip Kerr during a tour of Canada and the U.S.A., including comments on the colour problem in the U.S.A. (17/5, pp. 1-177)

1. Extensive use was made of these papers in J.R.M. Butler, *Lord Lothian (Philip Kerr) 1882-1940* (London, 1960). A complete list of Lord Lothian's papers is in preparation as a Scottish Record Office publication.

(*c*) Articles, n.d., on foreign policy of the U.S.A. and Monroe Doctrine, part typewritten and part MS. (17/10, pp. 1-26)
(*d*) Letter and article, 1914, on Monroe Doctrine by George M. Smith, Calgary, Canada. Part typewritten and part MS. (17/10, pp. 26a-56)
(*e*) Letter, 1909, from Keith Feiling, British Columbia, to [L.S.] Amery on contacts between Canada and the U.S.A. (17/11, pp. 24-6); and letter from Amery to Lionel Curtis regarding Feiling's letter. (17/11, p. 37)
(*f*) Letters and papers, 1917, on Zionism, including letters from Justice Louis Brandeis, New York. (17/46)
(*g*) Letters and papers, 1917-8, on shipping losses, freight charges, and American ship construction. (17/46)
(*h*) Papers, 1918-9, regarding the drafting of the constitution of the League of Nations, with memorandum on America and the League, reports on American reaction, and letter from Lord Robert Cecil. (17/54)
(*i*) Papers, 1919, regarding negotiations for the Peace Treaty, including memorandum on American reservations. (17/62-3)
(*j*) Papers, 1919-20, on mandates, including American draft of a class 'A' mandate. (17/75)
(*k*) Memoranda, n.d., on constitutional conventions in the Dominions and U.S.A. (17/76)
(*l*) Memoranda and letters, 1919-21, regarding Ireland, including memorandum on American ideas of the Irish problem, and letters from Louis Tracy, New York, on Irish propaganda and support in America. (17/78-80)
(*m*) Letter, 1921, from Felix Frankfurter, Harvard Law School, on Philip Kerr's leaving the government. (17/82, pp. 54-5)
(*n*) Letter, 1922, from Katherine Mayo on Anglo-American relations. (17/82, pp.91-3)
(*o*) Letters and papers, 1928-9, of Royal Institute of International Affairs on Anglo-American relations. (17/97-104)
Subjects include:
Article by Philip Kerr on Anglo-American relations with comments and memoranda on the article, 1928.
Memorandum by Fowke on U.S. debt and foreign investments, 1928.
Memoranda by Professor Pearce Higgins on the Borah resolution, 1928.
Memorandum 'American Public Opinion on the subject of the Peace Pact', 1929.
Memoranda and letters of Admiral Richmond on British and American navies, 1928.
Memorandum by Charles P. Howland on subjects for discussion by Anglo-American group of the Council on Foreign Relations, 1928.
Letters between Professor C.K. Webster, Harvard, and Philip Kerr on the work of the British and American groups and on Professor Webster's conversations with Senator Borah and Sir Esmé Howard on Anglo-American relations, 1929.
Letters and papers from Laura Puffer Morgan, associate secretary of the National Council for Prevention of War, Washington, on Anglo-American naval construction, 1929.
Memorandum from Melbourne Round Table group on naval requirements of British Empire and the U.S.A., 1929.
(*p*) Memoranda and letters, 1929-30, about Oxford University Enquiry Society and their examination of administration of Oxford University, including report by the secretary [H.V. Hodson] on his visit to Canada and the U.S.A. (17/114-6)
(*q*) Memorandum, *c.* 1930, on public works for relief of unemployment in Italy and the U.S.A. (17/138)
(*r*) Letters and papers, 1932-4, relating to American war debts. (17/198-200)
Letter and memoranda from Viscount Astor on war debts and instances of financial troubles in U.S. cities, 1932.
Memorandum by Hon. R.H. Brand on international monetary problems, 1933.
Letters from John Stevenson, *Times* correspondent in Canada, on war debts, tariff barriers and the economic position. Encloses memorandum by Professor W.Y. Elliott of Harvard on 'Debits and Credits', 1933.
Letters between Lord Lothian and Colonel E.M. House on forthcoming Washington Conference, possible debt agreement, and necessity for the U.S.A. and Britain to work together in international and economic affairs both in Europe and Far East, 1933-4.
Correspondence between Lord Lothian, the prime minister and others on American debt negotiations, 1933.
(*s*) General correspondence, 1918-21. (17/206-220)
Writers, recipients, and subjects include:
Frederick Cunliffe-Owen, New York - Medill McCormick, 'the Illinois Senator', a trouble maker and a nuisance; writer's friends including Elihu Root; success of Sir Auckland Geddes as ambassador; U.S. opinion regarding Britain; memorandum of confidential talk with Charles E. Hughes on his regard for Lloyd George; Harding's policy to Britain; and Panama tolls.
Gordon Edwards, New York - Wilson's stubbornness and stupidity the reason for defeat on Peace Treaty in Washington, 23 Nov. [1919].
Moreton Frewen - democracy in America and its 'predatory' taxation, 1920.
Colonel E.M. House, American Commission to Negotiate Peace - 'an extremely delicate situation has been tidied over for the moment', 1919.
C.J.B. Hurst, Foreign Office - views of British government about 'reservations'; private suggestion by Kerr to Polk for a compromise settlement by the American political parties about ratification of the Peace Treaty, 1919.
Lord Northcliffe - American opinion and Ireland, 1917-8.
A.N. Pollen - British propaganda in the U.S.A., 1921.
N.W. Rowell, K.C., Canada - interviews with Root, Hughes, and Colonel House in New York, 1920-1.
John S. Steele, London correspondent of *Chicago Tribune* - Irish affairs, with copies of letters from Colonel Robert R. McCormick, 1919-21.
William H. Taft - to introduce Herbert S. Houston, 1920.
(*t*) General correspondence, 1923-7. (17/221-5)
Writers, recipients, and subjects include:
Viscount Astor - Anglo-American relations; Kellogg's policy for naval disarmament, 1926-7.
Dr. Max Farrand, New York - organization of a research institute at the Huntington Library in California, 1927.
Abraham Flexner, Rockefeller Foundation - discussion with Philip Kerr on the organization of an international research institution for promoting world peace or for examination of other world problems, 1926.
Lloyd George - letters to, from Philip Kerr on the economic life of the U.S.A., 1926.
G.H. Locock, Federation of British Industries - his report of economic and manufacturing conditions in the U.S.A., 1925.
Ramsay Muir - letters to, from Philip Kerr suggesting names of people he should see in the U.S.A., with copies of letters of introduction, 1926.
Round Table - correspondence with John Dove on possible American challenge to preferential system in British Empire tariffs, 1925-6.

E.F. Wise - letters to, with letters of introduction, to persons in the U.S.A., 1925.

(*u*) General correspondence, 1927-8. (17/226-233)

Writers, recipients, and subjects include:

Willis J. Abbot of *Christian Science Monitor* - the Mellon-Churchill debt controversy; problems of international journalism; American presidential campaign; suggestion for exchange of British and American battle trophies including flag of the *Chesapeake*, 1927-8.

Astor, Viscount and Viscountess - letters from Philip Kerr on American Arbitration Crusade and on Astor's article on Anglo-American relations, 1927-8.

Frank Aydelotte, Swarthmore College - selection of American Rhodes scholars, 1927.

E. Beddington Behrens, Hollywood - the film industry, 1927.

Sir Robert L. Borden, Ottawa - the Kellogg proposal, 1928.

W.C. Bridgeman, M.P., Admiralty - American attitude to British Navy; warship ratios, 1927-8.

Hume Cronyn - André Siegfried's book *America Comes of Age*, 1927.

Sir Arthur Currie, McGill University - American naval proposals, 1928.

Lionel Curtis - letters to, from Kerr concerning Round Table conference at Honolulu; Anglo-American Naval Conference, 1927.

Richard Heath Dabney, University of Virginia - articles on alleged indebtedness of European Allies to the U.S.A., and question of whether 18th Amendment was unconstitutional, n.d.

Norman H. Davis, New York - Anglo-American and naval problems; Kellogg-Briand correspondence, 1928.

Geoffrey Dawson, editor of *The Times* - American viewpoint in calling the Geneva Conference; Kellogg proposals, 1927-8.

Raymond L. Buell, research director, Foreign Policy Association, New York - possibility of international conference on maritime law, 1928.

J.C. Maxwell Garnett, secretary of League of Nations Union - hope that the U.S.A. would agree to stoppage of its trade with a nation outlawed by the League, 1928.

Christian Herter, *The Independent*, Boston - responsibility of the U.S.A. in the arms limitation question; role of Canada as interpreter between Britain and the U.S.A.; naval construction, 1928.

Herbert Hoover - acknowledges receipt of reprint of an article by Kerr in March edition of *Round Table*, 1928.

Alanson B. Houghton - implications of the Kellogg treaty, 1927-8.

Thomas Jones, Cabinet Office - Kerr's talks with Hoover in Washington on trade restrictions, 1928.

Frank B. Kellogg, Department of State, Washington - Philip Kerr's article about naval construction problem; Kellogg's proposal for outlawry of war, 1928.

Walter Lippmann, New York - Kerr's article on the naval problem; American presidential election, 1928.

London University - appeal for funds for establishment of a chair of American history, 1927-8.

Vincent Massey, Canadian Legation, Washington - Royal Institute of International Affairs to organize a meeting for Senator Borah; naval problem; outlawry of war movement, 1928.

Observer newspaper - letters between editor, J.L. Garvin, and Philip Kerr about Kerr's articles on U.S. economy, relationships with Britain and Canada, and naval policy, 1928.

Round Table - correspondence on Round Table affairs and regarding Philip Kerr's articles in the *Round Table* magazine on the Anglo-American naval problem and on outlawry of war. Writers include: John Dove (including report on the conference at Geneva, 18 July 1927), D.O. Malcolm, Senator William E. Borah, Norman H. Davis, A. Dulles, Christian Herter, Charles P. Howland, Frank B. Kellogg, S.O. Levinson, and General Smuts, 1927-8.

Whitney Shepardson, New York - proposal for correspondence between Root and Lord Balfour on outlawry of war, with copy letter from James T. Shotwell, 1928.

James T. Shotwell, Carnegie Endowment for International Peace - doctrine of 'freedom of the seas', 1928.

Rennie Smith, secretary of National Council for Prevention of War - memorandum on peace movement in America, 1928.

Philip Noel Baker - limitations of naval construction, 1928.

Cyrus McCormick, Jr. - comments on Ramsay Muir's *America the Golden* and on American industrial methods, 1927.

(*v*) General correspondence, 1929. (17/234-237)

Writers, recipients, and subjects include:

Dr. Frederick Lynch - first meeting in New York of the Anglo-American Committee for International Discussion.

Newton D. Baker, Cleveland, U.S.A. - Philip Kerr's article on naval disarmament.

Raymond L. Buell, Foreign Policy Association, New York - sea law under the Kellogg Pact.

George E.G. Catlin, Cornell University, New York - Kellogg Pact; American tariff policy.

Carrie Chapman Catt, New York - Kellogg Pact.

Norman H. Davis, New York - Anglo-American naval problems; U.S. and the League of Nations.

Allen W. Dulles, New York - naval disarmament; disarmament proposals of the United States.

Abraham Flexner, New York.

Dr. Felix Frankfurter, Harvard Law School - system of seminars of Langdell Hall; praise of Alfred Whitehead; Anglo-American Committee for Outlawry of War.

A.B. Houghton, Dartmouth, U.S.A. - Anglo-American naval problem.

Charles P. Howland, Council on Foreign Relations, New York - Kellogg Pact; Anglo-American relations.

Christian Herter - naval disarmament; Anglo-American relations.

Frank B. Kellogg - Anglo-American naval problems; Kellogg Pact; necessity for disarmament.

S.O. Levinson, chairman of American Committee for Outlawry of War - adjustment of reparations; Peace Pact; League of Nations; his nomination for Nobel Peace Prize.

Ramsay MacDonald - letter to, from Philip Kerr on naval negotiations with America.

Observer newspaper - letters between J.L. Garvin and Kerr on Anglo-American relations; the U.S.A. and the League; naval disarmament.

Charles F. Thwing, Western Reserve University, Cleveland.

H. Wilson Harris - note of comments made by Sir Austen Chamberlain at Geneva on the Kellogg Pact.

(*w*) General correspondence, 1928-30. (17/238-245)

Writers, recipients, and subjects include:

Willis J. Abbot, *Christian Science Monitor* - Kellogg Pact and Anglo-French naval understanding; the press and international misunderstandings, 1928.

Viscountess Astor - Anglo-American relations, 1928; with copies of letters from Walter Lippmann and Oswald Garrison Villard.

Newton D. Baker, Cleveland, Ohio - outlawry of war; possibility of procuring promulgation by the U.S.A. of rejection of right of neutral trade with an aggressor nation; Anglo-American relations; Senator Capper's resolution, 1928-9.

Sir Robert Borden, Ottawa - friction between the U.S.A. and

Britain over naval construction, and need for Canadian mediation (with copies of letters from Professor W.K. Stewart, Dartmouth College); Briand-Kellogg Pact, 1929.
Raymond Buell, Foreign Policy Association, New York - report on the anti-war pact; U.S. anglophobia and Cruiser Bill, 1928-9.
George E.G. Catlin, Cornell University - proposed round table conference of international jurists and opposition to the idea by Sir Cecil Hurst; Anglo-American relations.
Viscount Cecil of Chelwood - ratification of Peace Pact by U.S. Senate; consequences of the Kellogg Pact; his article 'The Freedom of the Seas', 1929.
R.L. Craigie, Foreign Office - American criticism of Chamberlain's 'special interests' reservation to the Peace Pact, 1929.
Lord Cushendun, chancellor of Duchy of Lancaster - implications of the Kellogg Pact; limitation of naval construction; need to avoid raising suspicions of the U.S.A., 1928.
Norman H. Davis, New York - naval construction problems; Coolidge's Armistice Day speech; Anglo-American relations; significance of Kellogg Pact, 1928-9.
Luther H. Evans, Department of Political Science, Dartmouth College, New Hampshire, U.S.A. - part played by Smuts, Philip Kerr, and Round Table in the development of the mandates system at the Peace Conference, 1930.
J.L. Garvin, editor of the *Observer* - implications of the Anglo-French naval compromise and possible American reaction; Coolidge 'was... just as self-centered, irritating and unhelpful as any of our people'; Bridgeman's 'incredible speech', ratification of Peace Pact, 1928-9.
Sir Maurice Hankey, Cabinet Office - Lord Balfour's attitude at the Washington Conference towards the question of cruiser construction, question of belligerent rights against neutral trade; ratification of Peace Pact; Philip Kerr's memorandum on the Anglo-American naval problem, 1928-9.
Harrison Brown, European representative of American Committee for the Outlawry of War - recommendation of Mr. Levinson for the Nobel Peace Prize; Hoover's presidential campaign; American attitude to ratification of Peace Pact; Anglo-American naval construction, 1928-9.
Charles P. Howland, Council on Foreign Relations Inc., New York - Council's publication *Survey of American Foreign Relations*; meeting of Council's Anglo-American group; belligerent rights against neutral trade; implications for America in the Kellogg Pact; origins of the mandate system. 1928-9.
Frank B. Kellogg - Philip Kerr's articles in the *Observer*; ratification of the Pact by U.S. Senate; future of Naval Disarmament Conference.
League of Nations Union - Kerr's article on the outlawry of war; Anglo-American naval negotiations. Writers are John Eppstein and J.C. Maxwell Garnett, 1928-9.
Salmon O. Levinson, chairman of American Committee for Outlawry of War - Philip Kerr's article on the Kellogg Pact and outlawry of war; ratification of Pact by U.S. Senate; Kerr's proposal of a 'police force'; Anglo-American relations and naval construction; British 'reservations' to the Peace Pact; American attitude to 'reservations'; political negotiations in the U.S.A. before ratification of the Pact; conference on naval disarmament, 1928-9.
Sir Ronald Lindsay, Foreign Office - relation between Kellogg Peace Pact and the Convenant of the League; British reply to Coolidge's last naval note, 1928.
Walter Lippmann, the *World*, New York - Philip Kerr's articles in the *Observer*; Anglo-American naval construction, 1928-9.
Lloyd George - letters to, from Philip Kerr, with replies from L.G.'s secretary - debate on Kellogg Pact in Parliament with suggestions; Austen Chamberlain's 'reservation'.
Manchester Guardian - correspondence with C.P. Scott - Kerr's visit to the U.S.A. with Smuts, 1929.
Dr. Charles Clayton Morrison, editor of the *Christian Century*, Chicago - the Peace Pact.
Ramsay MacDonald - Anglo-American relations, 1930.
Royal Institute of International Affairs - Philip Kerr's suggestion of a public conference on the Peace Pact between various institutions in Britain, Canada, and the U.S.A.; Anglo-American relations; American Cruiser Bill. Writers include Whitney Shepardson.
Lionel Curtis, Ivy Lee, and Arnold Toynbee, 1928-9.
General Smuts - his visit to Canada and the U.S.A., 1929-30.

(*x*) General correspondence, 1930-1. (17/246-254)
Writers, recipients, and subjects include:
C.F. Andrews- visit of Tagore to America, 1930.
Sir Robert Borden- Hearst's insistence on a practical alliance between Britain and the U.S.A.; political reasons for rejection of the League Covenant by U.S. Senate, 1930.
Raymond L. Buell, Foreign Policy Association, New York - political aftermath of the London Naval Conference, 1930.
Norman H. Davis - probable nomination of Franklin D. Roosevelt as Democratic presidential candidate, 1930.
Charles Dawes, American ambassador - Professor Coupland's book *The American Revolution and the British Empire*.
Ecuador - invitation to Lord Lothian to serve as joint commissioner under the Treaty between U.S.A. and Ecuador. Writers include Charles Dawes, American ambassador, E. Arroye, Ecuador chargé d'affaires, and H.L. Stimson, U.S. Secretary of State, 1930.
J.L. Garvin - Article 16 of the League Covenant and problem of reconciling views of France and the U.S.A., 1930.
Harrison Brown, European representative of American Committee for the Outlawry of War - attacks on Britain in the American press; Schacht's outburst; postponement of the Nobel Peace Prize for which Levinson had been nominated; visit of Smuts to America; American isolationists.
Salmon O. Levinson, Chicago - visit of General Smuts to U.S.A.; American press and other opposition to the London Treaty, 1929-30.
Philip C. Nash, director of League of Nations Association Inc., New York - amendments to the League Covenant; invitation to Lord Cecil to tour U.S.A., 1930.
Round Table - suggested article on the U.S.A. and Pan America by Whitney Shepardson, 1930.
General Smuts - his visit to America; comparative failure of Naval Conference, 1929-30.

(*y*) General correspondence, 1931. (17/255-260)
Writers, recipients, and subjects include:
Willis J. Abbot - politics in the U.S.A.
James M. Beck, House of Representatives, Washington - power of federal government to enforce Supreme Court judgements against the states; U.S. attitude to League of Nations.
Salmon O. Levinson - American acceptance of the Hoover Proposal; disarmament; proposes preparation of a plan of adjustment of debts and reparations.
Professor Robert McElroy, Oxford - use of force by federal government in the U.S.A. to compel states to conform with its decisions.
Louis Wiley, *New York Times* - British suspension of the gold standard and American reaction.

(*z*) General correspondence, 1932-3. (17/261-270)
Writers, recipients, and subjects include:
Willis J. Abbot of *Christian Science Monitor* - poem by Senator

Ingalls of Kansas; wish for position as American correspondent of the *Observer,* with letter from J.L. Garvin, 1933.
Dr. Nicholas Murray Butler - scheme for international broadcasting, 1933.
Henry Clay - Lausanne Conference and 'moral case' for refusal to pay the American debts, 1932.
Professor R. Coupland - lecture tour in America and Canada, 1933.
Lionel Curtis - letter to, from Sir Malcolm Seton, on American factor in Chinese affairs, 1932.
Abraham Flexner, director of Institute for Advanced Study, New York - subjects to be considered by the Institute in field of government and economics; Roosevelt administration, 1933.
J.L. Garvin - Lord Lothian's article on the war debt situation and American reaction, 1933.
Salmon O. Levinson, Chicago - readjustment of war debts; Senator Borah's support; disarmament, 1932-3.
Round Table - difference between 'mental workings' of the European and American; travels in the U.S.A. and Canada. Writers include F. Clarke, Canada.
James T. Shotwell, director of Social Science Research Council, New York - moral disarmament, 1932.
John Stevenson, *Times* correspondent in Canada - attempt to close the Buffalo - New York outlet for Canadian wheat; American attitude to the Ottawa Conference, n.d.

(*aa*) General correspondence, 1933-4. (17/271-279)
Writers, recipients, and subjects include:
Edgar Abraham - Lord Lothian's and his own part in the preparation of the amendment of Oct. 1918 to President Wilson's 'Fourteen Points' to cover reparations, 1934.
William C. Bullitt, U.S. Ambassador at Moscow, 1934.
Geoffrey Crowther - America's economic recovery and Secretary Wallace's views, 1934.
Patrick Duncan, South Africa - experiments in the U.S.A. to overcome the depression, 1933.
Walter Elliot, Ministry of Agriculture - speech by Wallace, Secretary of Agriculture in U.S.A., 1933.
Salmon O. Levinson, Chicago - developing friction between Britain and the U.S.A.; Disarmament Conference, 1933.
W.O. Payne, Des Moines, Iowa - his plan for Anglo-American union, 1933.
Dr. C.F. Roos, Department of Commerce, Washington - letter from Lord Lothian on the need for international economic planning, 1933.
Dr. Alexander Sachs, New York - international economic planning, 1933.
Charles Seymour, Yale University - Lord Lothian's comments on chapters of his forthcoming book on 'American Diplomacy during the World War', 1933.
Sir Archibald Sinclair - necessity for agreement with Dominions and the U.S.A. on sanctions, and drawbacks to the Kellogg and Locarno Pacts, 1934.

(*bb*) General correspondence, 1934-5. (17/280-288)
Writers, recipients, and subjects include:
Anglo-American naval problems - memorandum, 1934.
Newton D. Baker, Cleveland, U.S.A. - Lord Lothian's article on Japanese-British-American naval problem, 1934.
Robert W. Bingham, U.S. Embassy - criticism of Lord Lothian's article concerning relations between Washington and London, isolationist America and contacts between Washington and Wall Street, 1934.
Nicholas Murray Butler, Carnegie Endowment for International Peace, New York - proposed conference in London, 1934.
Lionel Curtis - determination of the U.S.A. to insist on a 5:3 naval ratio with Japan; American interest in education in India, 1934.
J.W. Dafoe, Winnipeg Free Press Company - Pacific situation: position of the U.S.A., 1934.
C. Delisle Burns - sanctions system and American attitude, 1934.
Stephen Duggan, director of Institute of International Education, New York - education in India and possibility of an American commission to visit India, 1934.
Stanley High - Lord Lothian's proposal regarding America's relationship to the collective system, 1934.
Edward M. House, Austin, Texas - relationships between the U.S.A. and Britain, 1934.
T. Jones, C.H. - letter from Lord Lothian on Anglo-American relations, 1934.
Salmon Levinson, Chicago - Anglo-American relations and handling of the debt situation, 1934.
Round Table - letters regarding articles for *Round Table* magazine, including Lothian's article on naval problems. Writers include Whitney Shepardson and Charles Ross, 1934-5.
Whitney Shepardson, New York - *Round Table* magazine, 1934.
Sir John Simon - Anglo-American co-operation in the Pacific, 1934.
General Smuts - Anglo-American relations, 1934.
Henry L. Stimson, New York, 1934.
Sir William Sutherland - criticism of Roosevelt's policy in the U.S.A., 1934.
R.C. Wyse - economic position and policies of the U.S.A., 1934.

(*cc*) General correspondence, 1935. (17/289-296)
Writers, recipients, and subjects include:
Christian Science Monitor - policy of the paper, including query to Lord Lothian regarding America and the League of Nations.
Norman Davis - letters from Davis, Henry L. Stimson, Sir Archibald Sinclair, and Austen Chamberlain regarding American moves against Japan in the China crisis of 1932; rejection by U.S. Senate of adherence to the World Court, 1934-5.
Salmon O. Levinson, Chicago - his plan for payment of war debts and disarmament.
Whitney Shepardson, New York - possibility of a film based on life of Rhodes; formation of a Round Table group in New York.

(*dd*) General correspondence, 1935. (17/297-305)
Writers, recipients, and subjects include:
Thomas W. Lamont, New York - Supreme Court decisions against National Industrial Recovery Act; temptations of dictatorship in U.S. Constitution - presidents who had given way to temptation: 'it seems to be beginning to be true of F.D.R.'
Henry L. Stimson, New York - divergence of U.S. and British official policies during Manchuria crisis of 1932.

(*ee*) General correspondence, 1935-6. (17/306-316)
Writers, recipients, and subjects include:
Dr. Hamilton Fish Armstrong, editor of *Foreign Affairs* review, New York - article by Lord Lothian for *Foreign Affairs* on American Neutrality Act and the British position, 1936.
Dr. Felix Frankfurter, Harvard Law School - American politics, 1936.
R.C. Leffingwell, New York - collective or isolationist approaches to peace, 1935.
Sir Ronald Lindsay, U.K. Ambassador at Washington - Frank Simonds' book *The Price of Peace,* 1936.
E. Mills, Commissioner for Migration and Statistics, Palestine government - suggests planned emigration of Jews under thirty years old from Germany to Palestine and the U.S.A., 1935.
George L. Shaw, Antung, Manchuria - Japanese policy towards China and necessity for Anglo-American co-operation, 1935-6.

(*ff*) General correspondence, 1936. (17/317-324)
Writers, recipients, and subjects include:
Raymond L. Buell, Foreign Policy Association, New York - opinion that neither Latin America or the U.S.A. for the next few years would take any initiative for the organization of peace.
J.L. Garvin - suggestions that Lord Lothian write articles on his visit to the U.S.A. and the election there.
J.M. Macdonnell, Toronto - impracticability of idea of British-American co-operation.
Anthony Eden - meeting with Felix Morley, editor of the *Washington Post*.
(*gg*) General correspondence, 1936-7. (17/325-333)
Writers, recipients, and subjects include:
William C. Bullitt, U.S. Ambassador at Paris, 1936.
Christian Science Board - correspondence with Charles E. Heitman on Lord Lothian's political and journalistic future, and the future policy of the *Christian Science Monitor*, 1936.
Loring C. Christie, Ottawa - memoranda on U.S. Neutrality Law, 1936.
R.A. Frost - work of Bryce Foundation to help Anglo-American understanding, 1936.
H.A. Garfield, Washington - Anglo-American co-operation for maintenance of peace, 1936.
J.L. Garvin - invitation to speak at annual meeting of American Society of Newspaper Editors, 1936-7.
Charles E. Heitman, Boston, Mass. - policy of *Christian Science Monitor;* criticism of methods of the Roosevelt administration, 1936-7.
Sir Thomas Inskip - American Neutrality Law, 1936.
Dr. Albert Mansbridge - his speech in New York, 1936.
Royal Institute of International Affairs - work of the Institute and application for grant from the Rockefeller Foundation; suggestions for study of Anglo-American relations, 1936-7.
James Brown Scott, secretary of Carnegie Endowment for International Peace; Washington - Lord Lothian's Burge lecture; President Wilson's failure to understand the federal nature of the U.S.A.
General Smuts - letter from Lord Lothian on breakdown of League of Nations as a system of collective security, danger of a system of military alliances, possible basis of agreement with Germany or isolation of Britain and Empire, American participation, 1937.
Henry L. Stimson, New York - letters between Lord Lothian and Stimson on the breakdown of the collective security system; reasons for lack of co-operation between Britain and the U.S.A. during Manchuria crisis; Lord Lothian's suggested remedy of a European federation or an Anglo-American bloc, 1937.
(*hh*) General correspondence, 1937. (17/334-343)
Writers, recipients, and subjects include:
Frank Aydelotte, Swarthmore College - American Neutrality Bill and the 'cash and carry' policy.
Viscount Cecil - Lord Lothian's suggestion of closer co-operation between Britain and the U.S.A. in international affairs.
Geoffrey Dawson, editor of *The Times*-Lord Lothian's speech in the Lords on possible Anglo-American entente.
Anthony Eden - visit of S.O. Levinson from the U.S.A.
H.A.L. Fisher - New College Library appeal in the U.S.A.
Felix Frankfurter, Cambridge, U.S.A.
Lord Halifax - possible co-operation with the U.S.A. in stabilizing the situation in Europe and Far East.
Henry J. Haskell, *Kansas City Star* - possible Anglo-American entente.
S.O. Levinson, U.S.A. - his visit to Britain; refusal of Eden to see him; interviews with Secretary Hull and the President on his return to the U.S.A.
Byron W. Skillin, New York - War Debt scholarship plan, 1937.
(*ii*) General correspondence, 1937. (17/344-351)
Writers, recipients, and subjects include:
Salmon O. Levinson, Chicago - missed opportunity at the coronation for a new Anglo-American entente.
Royal Institute of International Affairs - memorandum on war debts; memorandum on Anglo-American trade agreement.
General Smuts - Roosevelt's Chicago speech.
(*jj*) General correspondence, 1937-8. (17/352-358)
Writers, recipients, and subjects include:
J.M. Macdonnell, Toronto - appointment of Lewis Douglas to McGill University; Douglas's attacks on Roosevelt, 1937.
James M. Witherow, Minnesota, - Anglo-American relations and failure of British diplomacy, 1937-8.
(*kk*) General correspondence, 1938. (17/359-368)
Writers, recipients, and subjects include:
Christian Science - criticism by Lord Lothian of biography of Mary Baker Eddy in the *Dictionary of American Biography*, 1937-8.
Royal Institute of International Affairs - memorandum 'British War Debts: An American View'; memorandum 'An Anglo-American Trade Agreement: A British View'; draft reply by Geoffrey Crowther to American memorandum on war debts.
Whitney Shepardson, New York - his book *The United States in World Affairs,* 1937.
(*ll*) General correspondence, 1938-9. (17/369-378)
Writers, recipients, and subjects include:
Ambassadorship - letters from Lord Halifax and Sir Ronald Lindsay, Ambassador to the U.S.A., on offer to Lord Lothian of position as Ambassador to the U.S.A., 1938.
Clarence Dillon - memorandum and correspondence with Kingsley Wood, Secretary for Air, regarding Dillon's plan to employ the U.S. motor manufacturing industry for production of aircraft parts to be assembled in Canada and transported to Britain and France, 1939.
Ecuador - letters from Cordell Hull, U.S. Dept. of State, and Joseph Kennedy, U.S. Ambassador, regarding Lord Lothian's appointment as joint commissioner on the International Commission under treaty between the U.S.A. and Ecuador, 1938.
J.L. Garvin - articles by Lord Lothian on his visit to America, 1938-9.
Sir Maurice Hankey - memorandum on effect on the U.S.A. of a collapse of the British Empire, 1938.
Malcolm MacDonald, Colonial Office - proposed colonial exhibit at the New York World's Fair, 1938.
Mackenzie King, Ottawa - letter from Lord Lothian enclosing memorandum on possibility of stabilizing the world through the co-operation of the English-speaking democracies, 1939.
Sir John Pratt - refutation of the myth that Britain failed to support the U.S.A. in the Manchuria crisis of 1931; includes letter from Sir John Simon on the subject, 1938.
Gerald Spencer Pryse - proposals for British film propaganda in the U.S.A., 1938-9.
(*mm*) General correspondence, 1939. (17/379-387)
Writers, recipients, and subjects include:
Ambassadorship - letters regarding Lord Lothian's appointment as Ambassador to the U.S.A.
Nicholas Murray Butler, New York - invitation to an international congress on education democracy at Columbia University.
Sherwood Eddy, New York - Lord Lothian's appointment as Ambassador to the U.S.A.
H.A.L. Fisher - U.S. Ambassador's desire for an Oxford degree.

Dr. Abraham Flexner, Princeton - Lord Lothian's appointment as Ambassador; U.S. distrust of British appeasement of Germany.
Professor Felix Frankfurter, U.S. Supreme Court - Lord Lothian's appointment as Ambassador.
T.W. Lamont, New York - U.S. indignation over the Czech coup.
Lord Eustace Percy - Bryce's technique as Ambassador to the U.S.A.
Gerald Spencer Pryse - British propaganda in the U.S.A.
Dr. H.J.A. Tasca - memorandum on U.S. policy of multilateral trade agreements, with letter from Professor J.B. Condliffe, London University, on the subject.
Union Now - correspondence, memoranda, and articles regarding Clarence Streit's book, and the foundation of an organization to support the federal thesis. Correspondents include Clarence Streit, Patrick Ransome, Lionel Curtis, Sir Richard Gregory, D. Caradog Jones, and Gerald Bailey.
William Allen White, editor of the *Emporia Gazette,* Kansas, - meeting the challenge of the bigots in the U.S.A.; new sense of insecurity in the U.S.A.

(*nn*) General correspondence, 1939. (17/388-397)
Writers, recipients, and subjects include:
Professor D.W. Brogan - Streit's *Union Now*, and American Confederation's acquisition of the western lands by 1781.
Dr. Nicholas Murray Butler, Columbia University - Lord Lothian's appointment as Ambassador.
John Dodge - pamphlet on Anglo-American war debt.
Federation of British Industries - memorandum for Lord Lothian to 'meet criticism in America of the attitude of British industry and of the F.B.I. in particular'.
H.A.L. Fisher - study of American history in Britain.
S.O. Levinson, Chicago - American neutrality.
Sir Ronald Lindsay, Ambassador at Washington - urges Lord Lothian not to make any speeches on Anglo-American affairs.
Frank Milner, Oamaru, New Zealand - his lecture tour in the U.S.A., and meeting with Roosevelt.
Robert G. Menzies, Prime Minister of Australia - Lord Lothian's appointment as Ambassador to U.S.A.
Dr. E. Révész, *Cooperation*, Paris - correspondence, including letters from Lord Eustace Percy and Lord Baldwin, regarding a series of broadcasts in the U.S.A. by 'distinguished figures'.
Lord Tweedsmuir, Governor-General of Canada - appointment of Lord Lothian as Ambassador to the U.S.A.
Union Now - letters and other papers regarding the movement in the U.S.A. and Britain for federal union based on Clarence Streit's book. Writers include Clarence Streit, E. Holland-Martin, D. Caradog Jones, A. Eric Baker, Lionel Curtis, J. Burgon Bickersteth (Toronto), Patrick Ransome, Lord Davies, and C.D. Kimer.
William Allen White, editor of the *Emporia Gazette*, Kansas; disillusionment of American Mid-West with Britain.

(*oo*) Correspondence, 1939-40, of Lord Lothian while Ambassador to the U.S.A. (17/398-407)
Writers, recipients and subjects include:
Dean Acheson - his speech at Yale on 'an American Attitude towards Foreign Affairs', 1940.
Lord and Lady Astor - American public opinion against involvement but anti-Hitler; need for supplies of American planes; plan for feeding starving children of Europe from America; question of evacuating children to America, 1939-40.
Frank Aydelotte, president of Swarthmore College and later director of the Institute for Advanced Study, Princeton, American Secretary of Rhodes Scholarship Trust - affairs of the Trust; protests by 'various Rhodes Scholar radicals' at the circulation of Lord Lothian's speech at Swarthmore, 1939-40.
Moritz J. Bonn, Bowdoin College and McGill University - question of whether to return to Britain or help with propaganda in the U.S.A.; American opinion on the war, 1940.
Hon. R.H. Brand, London - dispute between Mexican government and British and American oil companies regarding Mexican oilfields; British propaganda in the U.S.A., 1939-40.
Dr. Nicholas Murray Butler, Columbia University, 1939-40.
Senator Arthur Capper, 1940.
Professor George Catlin, New York and London - his idea of an Anglo-Saxon federation; his journey on the [Wendell] Willkie campaign train; his broadcasts on the foundation of Anglo-Saxony, 1940.
Captain Victor Cazalet, M.P. - European criticism of American attitude to the war, 1939-40.
Christian Science - correspondence with the board of directors, Publishing Society and others, 1939-41.
Professor Karl T. Compton, Massachusetts Institute of Technology - blind landing system developed at the Institute, 1940.
G.G. Coulton, Cambridge - proposed lecture tour in Canada and the U.S.A., 1940.
Geoffrey Dawson, editor of *The Times* - debates in Congress on repeal of arms embargo; British propaganda in the U.S.A., 1939-40.
Clarence Dillon, New York, 1939-40.
John Foster Dulles - his speech at Detroit on 'America's Role in World Affairs'; Lord Lothian's comments on the speech including reference to the 'federal formula'; reply by Dulles to the comments; speech by Dulles on 'The United States and the World of Nations', 1939-40.
Lord Elton, secretary to Rhodes Trustees - 'excessive neutrality' of the U.S.A., 1939-40.
Felix Frankfurter, Justice of the Supreme Court, 1939-40.
Professor A.V. Hill, London, arrangements for exchange of information on service matters between Britain and the U.S.A., 1940.
Joseph Kennedy, U.S. Ambassador to Britain - personal, including letter from John F. Kennedy (17/402/23), 1939-40.
Thomas W. Lamont, New York - British propaganda for the U.S.A.; and personal matters, 1939-40.
Maurice Leon, New York - President Wilson's 'fatal error of using the idea of world peace and the attempted solution by a league of nations as a partisan, a party scheme', 1939-40.
J.M. Macdonnell, Toronto - British lecturers in Canada and the U.S.A., 1939-40.
Professor Robert McElroy - opinion that Hull would be next president of the U.S.A.; suggestion that Canada stay neutral to escape the U.S. Neutrality Bill; suggestion that French vessels be used in any seizures of American cargoes bound for Germany, 1939-40.
Lord Melchett - purchases of planes and other supplies from the U.S.A. for Britain, 1940.
Walton Newbold, Motherwell - his visits to the U.S.A. from 1927 to 1933.
Notes by Lord Lothian of 'possible methods of [U.S.] support', n.d.
Viscount Samuel - British broadcasts and articles for the U.S.A., 1939-40.
Count Sforza - lecture tour in America, 1940.
General Smuts, Pretoria - American neutrality; Lord Lothian's Pilgrims speech, 1939-40.
Speeches, broadcasts and messages by Lord Lothian while Ambassador to the U.S.A.
J.A. Spender, Farnborough, Kent - irritation at some U.S. broadcast comments.

J.A. Spender - attitude of U.S. Ambassador to Britain and of some American newspapers to the war, 1939.

Hugh A. Studdert Kennedy, British Columbia - his biography of Mary Baker Eddy, 1940.

Raymond Gram Swing - folly of sending Sir Nevile Henderson on a lecture tour in the U.S.A., 1940.

Dr. Herbert Bayard Swope - British propaganda in the U.S.A., including Duff Cooper lecture tour, 1939-40.

John Buchan, Lord Tweedsmuir, Governor-General of Canada - advising against propaganda in the U.S.A., 1939.

Percival Witherby, British Columbia - on Clarence Streit's proposals for federal union; attitude of people in British Commonwealth towards the U.S.A.; U.S. neutrality, 1939-40.

James M. Witherow, Minnesota - German propaganda in the U.S.A.; British criticism of the U.S.A.; moral obligations of the U.S.A. towards Belgium and Holland; analysis of existing political situations in the U.S.A.; memorandum on the Monroe Doctrine, 1939-40.

Sir Evelyn Wrench - British-American relations and his visit to the U.S.A., 1940.

(*pp*) Speeches and articles, 1939-40, by Lord Lothian while Ambassador to the U.S.A. (17/408; see also 510/1-22)

(*qq*) Papers, 1936-9, relating to the 1938 trade agreement with the U.S.A. (17/409)

(*rr*) Notes, 1935-9, for Lord Lothian on 'Industrial conditions in the United Kingdom'. Appendices include Anglo-American trade relations and the U.K. - U.S.A. trade agreement. (17/410)

(*ss*) Letters, 1909, from Kerr to his family, mainly describing his travels in Canada and the U.S.A. (17/459/1-14)

Subjects include:

Interview with Bryce, the Ambassador. (12)

State of Negroes in America; visit to Birmingham, Alabama; his wish to write a book about the South of the U.S.A. (13-14)

(*tt*) Letters, 1912, mainly from Kerr to his family, describing his travels in the U.S.A. and elsewhere. (17/462/1-33)

Subjects include:

Christian Science, 1922. (7)

Meeting with Waldorf Astor in New York on 20 May1922 to discuss Round Table. (9; 10; 12)

Lectures given by Kerr at the Institute of Politics, Williamstown, Mass., in Aug. 1922. (14-24)

American Round Table, 1922. (33)

Itinerary and return home; meeting with British debt-funding mission and [Senator] Borah, etc., in Washington, 1923. (37)

Speeches, including one at Harvard, 1923. (39)

(*vv*) Letters, 1923-6, from Kerr to his mother, including some from the U.S.A. (17/468/1-24)

Subjects include:

Article for *Round Table*; request by H.A.L. Fisher for him to write a book on America, 1923. (1)

Regular articles for *Christian Science Monitor*, 1923 (5)

Christian Science, 1923. (7)

Proposed trip to the U.S.A., 1924. (10)

(*ww*) Miscellaneous letters, 1927, mainly from Kerr to his mother, from the U.S.A. and Canada. (17/469/14-28)

(*xx*) Letters, 1938-40, from Lord Lothian to his sisters. (17/470/1-19)

Subjects include:

'The U.S.A. is still strongly isolationist, but also increasingly convinced that if there is a war it will rapidly be dragged in, and that if it does come in it will have to do so on our side', 18 Jan. 1939. (8)

The Welles mission: 'nobody thinks that anything can come of it', 22 Feb. 1940. (10)

The U.S.A. 'has fairly woken up at last. It will only take a direct challenge to America's vital interests by Hitler or Mussolini to bring her in', 12 June 1940. (13)

'America is deeply alarmed now, but very divided as to what to do . . . The trouble is that U.S.A. has done exactly what we did - woken up about 2 years too late', 21 June 1940. (14)

'Public interest here is divided between the election and the war. And they are getting very worried and arming like blazes. Certainly democratic institutions are not good for war', 11 July 1940. (15)

'I've been very busy trying to get destroyers over, and I think it is now settled. The President thought so this morning', 16 Aug. 1940. (18)

(*yy*) Letters, 1956-8, to Professor J.R.M. Butler about his biography. (17/514-6)

Correspondents include:

Elizabeth Long, 1958, enclosing letter from Lothian to her husband, Basil K. Long, 18 Dec. 1939, about the state of American public opinion on the war. (514/42-3)

Sir Alan Lascelles, enclosing three letters to him from Lothian, 1939-40, on American feelings and public opinion about the war, 1958. (514/51-4)

Herman Kahn, director, National Archives and Record Services, Franklin D. Roosevelt Library, New York, explaining that President Roosevelt did not have records made of his conversations with visitors and enclosing list of Lothian material in the library, 1956; with photocopies including letters from Sumner Welles to Roosevelt, enclosing letters and memoranda from Lothian about naval assurances, destroyers, motor torpedo boats, aircraft, etc. and facilities which the British government was prepared to extend to the U.S.A., 8-23 Aug. 1940. (515/1-12)

Joseph Alsop, Washington, and Francis P. Miller, Charlottesville, Virginia; with enclosures about formation and work of the Century Group, statements in Langer and Gleason's *The Challenge of Isolation* and John K. Balderston's newsletter, 1956. (516/1-10)

(*zz*) Papers, 1917-22, relating to economic, labour and industrial matters. (17/691-706)

American items include:

Note on visit of [H.W.] Garrod, Ministry of Munitions, and Joseph [T.] Davies, prime minister's secretariat, to the U.S.A. on invitation of the American Federation of Labor, [1917]. (697)

(*aaa*) Correspondence, 1917-8, between Kerr and R.H. Brand. (17/709-16)

American items include:

Correspondence about the possibility of General Smuts visiting the U.S.A. to explain the concept of empire, and of the publication in American newspapers of 'propaganda' letters by Kerr, Dec. 1917. Writers are R.H. Brand, British War Mission, Washington, D.C., Professor [?G.B.] Adams, Yale University, Dr. Joseph S. Ames, Johns Hopkins University, and F.R. Kent, managing editor, *Baltimore Sun*. (710/1-9)

Letter from R.H. Brand, Washington, to Kerr, enclosing copy of his letter of 6 Feb. to Winston Churchill, Minister of Munitions, on the effect the form of the American Constitution has on its war machine, 1918. (711/1-2)

(*bbb*) General papers, 1919 - 20, relating to Russia. (17/746-820)

American items include:

Correspondence between Dr. Fridjof Nansen, Paris, and the President of the U.S.A. and prime ministers of Great Britain, France and Italy, about organization of a commission to send food and medical supplies to Russia, Apr. 1919. (781/1-6)

Letter from W.H. Buckler, American Commission to Negotiate Peace, to Kerr, enclosing paraphrase of two telegrams from Roland Morris, [U.S.] Ambassador, Tokyo, 17 and 26 July 1919, about domination of the railway from Vladivostok to Irkutsk by the Japanese, and from Irkutsk to Tomsk by the Czechs; and reasons for Koltchak's failure to command confidence in Siberia. (792/1-2)

(*ccc*) Letter, 1917, from Harry Lauder, Hotel Claridge, New York, to Lloyd George, about his propaganda work in the U.S.A., and the need for speakers rather than for pictures and pamphlets, 24 Oct. (17/955/2)

(*ddd*) Letter from Frank L. Polk, American Commission to Negotiate Peace, to Mr. Balfour about the proposed cable to Mr. Wilson, and his delegation's certainty that the president will reject the proposal as it now stands, 5 Sept. 1919. (986/6)

(*eee*) Papers relating to the League of Nations. (17/1381-6)
American items include:

Letter from N.W. Rowell, K.C., Toronto, to Kerr, enclosing copy statement signed by Mr. [C.E.] Hughes and other pro-League Republicans, 14 Oct. 1920, and issued during the presidential campaign, 3 Mar. 1921. (1386/2-3)

DALHOUSIE MUNIMENTS. (GD.45)

(*a*) Declaration, 1714, by certain merchants in Montrose of death in America of Margaret Raitt, daughter of Robert Raitt, shipmaster in Montrose, who several years before had emigrated to Virginia. (17/916)

(*b*) Twelve miscellaneous papers concerning financial transactions of various trading concerns, including the Mississippi Company, 1719-22. (17/957)

(*c*) Letter, 1781, from H. Bruce, Edinburgh, concerning memorandum on preservation of health of Major Hay's and Captain MacMurdoch's companies on a voyage to New York. (14/494)

(*d*) *Papers Relative to the Slave Trade,* including correspondence, 1821, with the U.S.A. Command paper. (24/145)

(*e*) Forty-eight papers, printed and MS., relating to Canadian and U.S. trade, 1841-6, particularly in corn; period covered by statistics is from 1790. (7/3)

(*f*) Papers, 1850-7, of Fox Maule (latterly Lord Panmure) as Secretary at War (1846-52) and Secretary for War (1855-8).
American items include:

Two letters from E. Horsman, Dublin, concerning rumour of an American attack on Ireland, 1855. (8/310)

(*g*) Papers relating to James Glen, Governor of South Carolina, and his family.

(i) Accounts, charge and discharge, between James Glen and late David Bruce of Kinnaird, 1740-6 (made up in 1762), and vouchers of the above (four bundles) including references to goods shipped to Carolina, 1740-62. (19/221-2)

(ii) Letter-book of [James Glen], Governor of South Carolina; at the beginning is a small group of letters and notes concerning a visit to the Catawba, Cherokee, Creek, and Chickasaw Indians. Recipients are: the Commissioners for Trade and Plantations, the Secretary of State, Lord Glenorchy, the Lord President of the Council, Mr. Calvarly, the Duke of Argyll, Thomas Harvey, and Charles Hamilton, 1746-52. (2/1)

(*h*) Papers, 1762-1802, relating to the Drayton family.

(i) Letter from W.H. Drayton of South Carolina, a medical student at Balliol College, to Governor James Glen, concerning his financial affairs and the progress of his studies, 1762. (14/868)

(ii) Two originals of a letter from John Drayton in S. Carolina to [Dr.] Thomas Glen, his brother-in-law, concerning payment of an annuity; with two copies of account, 1767. (14/871)

(iii) Letter from Glen Drayton, Charleston, S. Carolina, to Lady Dalhousie; with draft reply referring to a legacy left to Drayton by Governor Glen, 1793. (14/881)

(*i*) Copies, 1774-5, of the *Edinburgh Almanack* and the *Daily Journal* containing written notes by Governor James Glen and receipts, some referring to S. Carolina. (16/2643)

(*j*) Papers, 1777-8, relating to executry of late Governor Glen.
American items include:

Three accounts of David Erskine, C.S., relating to the affairs of late Governor James Glen, 1778. (16/2653)

Note of eight bonds to James Glen (one by William Drayton, Chief Justice of East Florida, (n.d.), 1778. (16/2654)

(*k*) Papers of Lieutenant Colonel (latterly Brigadier General) John Forbes.

(i) Correspondence, 1757-9, of Brigadier General John Forbes.
Correspondents include:

Captain John Wrightson of the 27th Foot, Elizabethtown and Rimebeck, 1757. (2/14/1-6)

Lieutenant Colonel Charles Rollo of the 22nd Foot, Schenectady, Nov. 1757. (2/19/1-4)

Lieutenant Colonel Arthur Morris of the 17th Foot [Forbes's own regiment]; with copy letter from Morris to Governor Denny of Pennsylvania, 1757-8. (2/21/1-25)

Sir John St. Clair, deputy quartermaster general, Croton Camp, Port Tobacco and Raystown; with five letters to St. Clair from various persons, 1757-8. (2/22/1-9; see also 2/48/1 and 2/83)

Dr. Richard Huck, New York, Hartford and Albany, 1757-8. (2/23/1-5)

Captain John Cosnan of the 45th Foot, on recruiting duty in Boston, 1757-8. (2/24/1-8)

Major A. Murray, Halifax - measures to be taken against Louisbourg, 1757-8. (2/25/1-4)

Lieutenant Colonel John Donaldson of the 55th Foot, New York, Rogers and Albany, 1757-8. (2/26/1-5)

Captain G. West of the 55th Foot, on duty at the frontier, 1757-8. (2/27/1-4)

Lieutenant Colonel Haldimand of the 60th Foot, Philadelphia and Annapolis (in French), 1757-8. (2/28/1-6)

Lieutenant Colonel Simon Fraser of the 78th Foot, Fairfield and Stratford - civil trial of Sergeant Fraser for murder; with copy proceedings of court of enquiry, 1757-8. (2/29/1-5)

Captain William Forbes, Schenectady, 1757-8. (2/30/1-3)

Hugh Wallace, Forbes's agent in New York, 1757-8. (2/31/1-5)

Major General Abercromby, 1757-9. (2/39/1-5)

Francis Halkett, Brigade Major - eleven letters, those dated 1759 written while on his way to England with dispatches; with six letters to Halkett from various persons, 1757-9. (2/42/1-17)

President John Blair of Virginia, 1758. (2/43/1-5)

Governor James Glen, formerly of S. Carolina - Indian affairs and the state of the forts, 1758. (2/44/1-4)

John Robinson - measures taken by Virginia for raising troops, 10 Apr. 1758. (2/47)

C.P. Gist, deputy agent for Indian affairs, Winchester, to Sir John St. Clair and Colonel Washington, 1758. (2/48/1-2)

Governor W.H. Lyttelton of S. Carolina, 1758. (2/49/1-3)

Dr. James Napier, New York - hospital arrangements, 1758. (2/50/1-3)

Sir Allan MacLean of the 77th Foot, Lancaster and Carlisle, 1758. (2/51/1-4)

William Pitt [the elder] - letters to, reporting on conduct of campaign against Fort Duquesne, 1758-9. (2/52/1-7)

Governor William Denny of Pennsylvania - encloses copy of his orders to Captain Nelson, 6 Oct., concerning commandeering transport, 1758. (2/53/1-6; see also 2/21 and 2/95/1)

Major James Grant [of Ballindalloch] of the 77th Foot - progress towards Fort Duquesne; enclosed is a letter from another James Grant, Aug. 1758. (2/61/1-2)

Colonel W. Byrd of the Virginian forces - no. 1 reports on the advance towards Fort Duquesne, 1758-9. (2/62/1-2)

Governor Arthur Dobbs of North Carolina, 1758. (2/65/1-3)

Lord Loudoun - no. 5 is a postscript from Loudoun to a letter from Alexander Wedderburn, 1758. (2/66/1-5)

Colonel (latterly Brigadier General) John Stanwix, Lancaster and New York, 1758. (2/67/1-6)

Colonel John Young, New York, 1758. (2/68/2,4)

Captain Gilbert McAdam, Boston, New York and Greenwich, 1758. (2/68/1, 3, 5-7)

Two French officer deserters - request employment in the British forces (in French), n.d. (2/73)

Lieutenant Colonel John Armstrong of the provincial forces, 1758-9. (2/78/1-7)

Governor Horatio Sharpe of Maryland; with three copies of letters to the Governor from Generals Abercromby and Amherst, 1758-9. (2/79/1-13)

Francis Fauquier, Lieutenant-Governor of Virginia, 1758-9. (2/80/1-4)

Major General Amherst, 1758-9. (2/81/1-7)

Captain Robert Stewart - raising and equipping a troop of horse rangers; with proposals for establishing the troop, establishment of the troop, and account for buying horses, 1758-9. (2/82/1-15)

Richard Peters, secretary to the government at Philadelphia - various news particularly on Indian affairs, 1758-9. (2/84/1-8)

Major John Darby of the 17th Foot; with copy letter from Darby to George Ross in London, 1758-9. (2/85/1-9)

Colonel Henry Bouquet [of the 60th Foot] - letter to, from Brigadier Forbes, concerning Indian affairs, and complaining against Sir John St. Clair, 8 Feb. 1759; letters to Bouquet from various persons, concerning reconnaissances, stores, etc., with copy letter from Bouquet to the Maryland troops at Fort Cumberland, concerning their pay, 1758-9. (2/96; 2/86/1-6)

Colonel Archibald Montgomery of the 77th Foot, 1758-9. (2/87/1-4)

Lord Ligonier - the beginning and result of Forbes's expedition against Fort Duquesne, 1758-9. (2/88/1-3)

Captain A. Bosomworth of the Indian service, 1758-9. (2/89/1-4)

James Robertson, New York - shipping arrangements, 1758-9. (2/92/1-3)

Governor De Lancey of New York - Forbes's health; reverse for General Abercromby's forces, 1758. (2/93/5, 7a, 8b)

Colonel Hugh Mercer to Governor Denny of Pennsylvania; with two copies of minutes of conferences held with the Indians at Pittsburgh, Jan. 1759. (2/95/1-3)

Various persons - military matters and information, 1757-9. (2/32/1-76; 2/90/1-26; 2/93/1-13)

Various persons - personal matters, 1758-9. (2/91/1-9)

(ii) General papers of Brigadier General John Forbes, 1757-9. American items include:

Return of the various regiments on board the transports at Halifax, with a note of ships bound for New York, 3rd Aug. 1757. (2/12/1)

Monthly returns of the forces in North America, Sept. - Oct. 1757. (2/13/1-3)

Memorandum concerning destruction of the lines at Fort Edward, 1 Nov. 1757. (2/17)

Memorials and petitions to Lord Loudoun or Brigadier Forbes, including a petition signed by the officers of a Virginia regiment asking for a Presbyterian chaplain, 1757-8. (2/33/1-6)

Returns and lists of named personnel of regiments in America, including men enlisted, discharged, deserted, and sick, 1757-8. (2/35/1-19)

Numerical returns concerning various regiments in America, 1757-9. (2/36/1-17)

Miscellaneous returns of stores, ordnance, and barrack-room furniture, 1757-9. (2/37/1-9)

Returns, memoranda, etc. concerning strength, equipment, officers, and quarters of the 17th Foot, Forbes's own regiment.

Return of billets for the 63rd Foot in Connecticut, Jan. 1758. (2/41)

Minutes of courts of enquiry at Carlisle and Fort Bedford, 3 June 1758 and 20 Jan. 1759. (2/54/1-2)

Account of Christian Frederic Post's journey from Philadelphia to Wyoming, 20-30 June, 1758. (2/55)

Address to Brigadier Forbes by the Episcopal churches in York and Cumberland Counties, Pennsylvania, complaining of the interruption of their services; signed by churchwardens and vestrymen, 5 July 1758. (2/56)

Memorial of a number of freemen of Pennsylvania to the governor concerning keeping of promises made to the Indians, 12 July 1758. (2/58)

Report by John Rogers on shooting of a deserter from the Maryland forces while resisting arrest, 12 July 1758. (2/59)

Reports by Lieutenant Allen and Ensign Chew of the Virginian forces on reconnaissance towards Fort Duquesne, Aug. 1758. (2/60/1-2)

Statement by Richard Johnson, an escaped prisoner-of-war, on the state of Fort Duquesne, Nov. 1758. (2/63)

Report by H. Basset, engineer, on a reconnaissance of the Ohio, Kishkeminetas, and Conamux Rivers, Dec. 1758. (2/64)

Accounts, personal and official, of Brigadier Forbes, 1758. (2/69/1-7)

Memoranda by Captain Harry Gordon, engineer, on routes to Fort Anne and Fort Duquesne, and a reconnaissance up the Monongahela River, Dec. 1758. (2/70/1-3)

Note of stages and distances on a route from Yorktown to the mouth of Connegogee, n.d. (2/71)

Note of stages and distances on the road from Pittsburgh to New York, 1758. (2/72)

Memoranda (unsigned), one on the proposed campaign on the Ohio, and the other on the campaign in North America generally, 1758. (2/74/1-2)

Medical directions for Brigadier Forbes, [1758]. (2/77)

Note of calculation of most economical method of supplying Pittsburgh, copy of advertisement inviting offers of flour and copy covering letter, 4 Jan. 1759. (2/94)

Note on a proposal to raise 500 rangers, n.d. (2/99)

Proposal by Philip John Schuyler of Albany to supply the troops with spruce and esopus beer, n.d. (2/100)

(iii) Executry papers, 1759-74, of Brigadier General John Forbes, including probate of will appointing his cousin, James Glen, late Governor of Carolina, as his executor, 24 Mar. 1759. (2/97-8)

(*l*) Papers of the 9th Earl of Dalhousie, Lieutenant-Governor of Nova Scotia and Governor-in-Chief of Canada.

(i) General series of letters, memoranda, etc., 1817-28. (3/10-241) American items include:

Correspondence (three items) with G.W. Featherstonhaugh, New York State, 1821-3. (59, 69)

Report on the penitentiary system of the United States, 1822. (94)

Two letters from Commodore Bainbridge, Philadelphia and Boston, arranging to visit Lord Dalhousie, 1823-4. (113)

Letter from Joseph Bouchette, Surveyor-General in Quebec, concerning the U.S. boundary, 1828; with extracts from correspondence dated 1817-8. (119)

Letter from Lord Dalhousie to the Duke of Wellington, concerning

U.S. claim to Rouse's Point, 1824. (136)

Fifteen letters from Sir Howard Douglas, Lieutenant-Governor of New Brunswick, and Earl Howe, concerning problems of that province, particularly the question of the boundary between New Brunswick and Maine; with six copies of letters to Douglas and three copies of correspondence dated 1827 with Enoch Lincoln, Governor of Maine, concerning arrest of an American named John Baker at Madawaska, 1825-8. (159)

Memorandum on the speech by Burke on the conciliation of America in 1775 as applicable to the present government of Canada, 1827. (196)

(ii) Papers, 1819-28, concerning relations with the U.S.A. (3/312-23)

American items include:

Abstract of a report by a joint committee of both Houses of Assembly of Nova Scotia on the convention lately concluded between Britain and America, 1819. (312)

Correspondence (three items) with Thomas Barclay, New York, concerning execution of 4th and 5th articles of the Treaty of Ghent, 1821. (59; 314)

Correspondence (four items) with Stratford Canning, Washington, concerning Congress business and the Canadian frontier, 1821-3. (59; 315)

Two letters from Anthony Barclay, New York, concerning boundary between Canada and the U.S.A., 1822. (316)

Letter from Charles R. Vaughan, British Ambassador in Washington, introducing Baron de Mareuil, French envoy to the U.S.A., and letter from Baron de Mareuil, 1827. (320)

Letter from Charles R. Vaughan, British Minister in Washington, concerning the disputed territory in New Brunswick, Feb. 1828. (321)

Four memoranda relating to the boundary of New Brunswick with Maine, April 1828. (322)

Letter from Andrew Stuart, Quebec, offering his services to assist in establishment of boundary between Lower Canada and New Brunswick and the U.S.A., May 1828. (323)

(iii) Four anecdotes, 1828, of General Wolfe's army, 1758-60, one concerning Captain Montgomery, later a general in the American service; narrated by James Thompson (born 1732), and written by his son. (3/422a)

(iv) Petition, 1826, (in French) by Pawquawkoman *alias* Amable Chevalier, an Ottawa chief, for a pension, explaining that he fought on the British side against the Americans in two wars and that his lands are now American territory. (3/509)

(v) Personal journals, papers and accounts of the Earl of Dalhousie, 1817-31. (3/540-611)

American items include:

Notebook containing miscellaneous anecdotes, information and quotations, mostly North American in subject, 1817-22. (552)

Correspondence (five items) with Solomon Southwick, Albany, N.Y., an editor, who had been 'persecuted by a relentless faction (the Bucktails) for his honest opposition to the declaration of war against England', 1824-7. (572)

Letter from T.W. Charles Moore, New York, concerning the forwarding of a packet, 1827. (586)

Letter from Rupert I. Cochran, New York, concerning likenesses procured from Mr. Hankes [of Reynolds, Hankes & Co., Salem, Mass.]; with two accounts, 1828. (593)

Letter from George Manners, Boston, concerning the forwarding of letters and newspapers, 1830. (598)

Letter from W.S. Skinner, Boston: 'I have enjoyed the pleasure of sending you a file by every opportunity', 1831. (599)

SEAFORTH MUNIMENTS. (GD.46)

(*a*) Letters, 1799-1800, concerning export of sugar from the West Indies in U.S. ships, trade with the U.S.A., etc. (sec. 17, vols. 11 and 14)

(*b*) Letter-books, 1800-6, of William Bishop, President of Council in Barbados, and Lord Seaforth, Governor of Barbados, including letters regarding control of trade with the U.S.A., American-built French privateers, etc. (sec. 7, nos. 1, 7, 11-13)

(*c*) Letter, 1802, from Philadelphia concerning forged bills of exchange. (sec. 17, vol. 21)

(*d*) Letter, 1802, from the comptroller of customs on trade in U.S. ships. (sec. 17, vol. 21)

(*e*) Correspondence, 1802, of Lieutenant General Grinfield on negotiating bills in North America. (sec. 17, vol. 21)

(*f*) Letter, 1805, from president of the Commercial Society [Barbados] on supplies from the U.S.A. (sec. 17, vol. 27)

ROSS ESTATE MUNIMENTS. (GD.47)

Letter, 1799, from James Yuill, Williamsburg, concerning purchase of land. (742)

JOHN MACGREGOR COLLECTION. (GD. 50)

(*a*) Instructions, *c.* 1690, for James Campbell from Lord Neil Campbell and another, to sell to Dr. Coxe or any other merchant three-quarters of the property belonging to them in East New Jersey, with remarks on the property. (186/65)

(*b*) Three letters, 1818-9, from James McCowan, Richmond, Virginia, giving costs of carts, ploughs, etc.; his work and wages; Scottish friends there, etc. (186/125)

MELVILLE CASTLE MUNIMENTS.[2] (GD.51)

(*a*) Documents, 1775-85, concerning the regulations and procedures governing the import and export of tobacco, frauds on the revenue caused thereby and a relative bill to secure duties. (1/354/1-33)

American items include:

Account of tobacco imported from America into Great Britain and of tobacco exported, 1766-75. (2)

Letter from Patrick Colquhoun concerning the state of American commerce, 1785. (29)

(*b*) Correspondence, 1781, between Richard Rigby and Henry Dundas, Lord Advocate, on the question of offering a truce to America, Rigby suggesting that Dundas should displace Lord George [Germain] as Secretary of State for the Colonies. (1/5/1-5)

(*c*) Letter, 1781, from William Adam, M.P., to Henry Dundas, Lord Advocate, commenting on the situation in America. (1/7/3)

(*d*) Letter, 1783, from James Lockhart, envisaging the appointment of consuls when the war with America ends, and requesting the post of consul in Virginia for his brother (unnamed). (6/781)

(*e*) Letters, 1784-5, with enclosures, from [Sir] John Sinclair concerning the China trade. No. 3 relates that the Americans 'are to send 4 ships to Canton this year, one of them the London Packet, that carries Franklin to America. What a pity it is that the old sinner was not taken into Algiers'. (3/192/3-40)

(*f*) Memorandum [by Major General Murray], [1787], on the services of Major General Stirling, mostly in Canada and America. (1/592)

(*g*) Memorandum, 1789, by Patrick Colquhoun of Glasgow about various bills and regulations including the Commissioners of American Claims Bill. (5/174)

2. Most of the items listed are letters written to Henry and Robert Dundas, 1st and 2nd Viscounts Melville, who held various government offices, 1766-1805 and 1807-1830 respectively.

(*h*) Application, *c.* 1790, for patronage made by Major Alan Cameron, stating at length his services in North America from 1774 onwards. (6/5)

(*i*) Letter, 1791, with enclosure, from Thomas Orde regarding the conduct of John Robinson as a member of the committee which directed the distribution of the donation to the Loyalists. (1/477/1-2)

(*j*) Letter, 1792, from R. Beauchamp concerning government tactics in dealing with the reaction to 'Mr. Payne's and similar publications', and mentioning 'the discontents which prevail in America as published in the continental newspapers'. (1/223)

(*k*) Letter, 1794, from Major George Charles Braithwaite relating that he was captured by the French and taken to America while in charge of dispatches from Lord Cornwallis on the surrender of Pondicherry. (3/342/1)

(*l*) Letter, 1794, from John Thomson, Deputy Commissary General, Isle of Wight, requesting return of a certificate of his conduct as an officer during the American war. (1/614)

(*m*) Letters, 1794, from James Ackers, chairman of the merchants and manufacturers in Manchester trading to the U.S.A., requesting explanation of a certain Order in Council relating to the detention for adjudication of ships laden with produce of the French West Indies. (1/371/1-2)

(*n*) Letter, 1795, from John Grieve requesting a passport for his nephew, Thomas Walker, saddler in Dalkeith, and his mother, Ann Walker, who intended emigrating to America. (1/492)

(*o*) Letter, 1795, from Alexander Young, formerly a builder in Edinburgh, requesting a passport to go to America to join his son there. (1/495)

(*p*) Letter, 1795, from John Dawson, enclosing advertisement for sale of cargo of American ship *Henry* from Calcutta. (3/223/1-2)

(*q*) Letter, 1795, from John Dunlop, Lord Provost, Glasgow expressing his willingness to act as one of the American commissioners to meet at Philadelphia. (5/221/1)

(*r*) Requests for patronage, 1795-1800, received directly or indirectly by the Viscounts Melville.

American items include:

Seven letters, with enclosure, from James Shaw, narrating the political and commercial influence of William Douglas of Castle Douglas, the writer's partner in the American trade, and recommending him for a baronetcy, 1795. (1/32/1-8)

Application by A. Mitchell for office; encloses a statement giving details of his services in attempting to secure American mediation to end the war between Britain and France, and relating that when he arrived in New York he found the bulk of the people there so incensed against Great Britain 'that it required all the wisdom, moderation and influence of General Washington to prevent their immediate invasion of Canada', 1795. (6/1033/1-2)

Application by Lord President Ilay Campbell for appointment of P. Colquhoun, a police magistrate in London, as consul in Philadelphia; with a letter from Colquhoun to Campbell, 1795. (6/1098/1-2; for other applications by Colquhoun for public office, see 6/863 and 6/1029/1-3)

Application by John Dunlop for appointment as an American commissioner; also letter from William McDowell [of Garthland, M.P.] stating that Dunlop was no longer seeking this office, 1795. (6/1107/1-3; 1/500)

Two letters from Hercules Ross proposing his father-in-law, John Parish, former U.S. Consul at Hamburg, for some mark of royal favour on account of services rendered to Britain in furnishing transports for the evacuation of British troops from the continent in 1795; enclosed with each letter is a copy letter from Timothy Pickering, U.S. Secretary of State, giving details of accusations that Parish was 'the avowed agent of Great Britain', and informing him that the U.S. president intended to replace him as consul with an American citizen, 1797-8. (1/46/1-2; 6/1226/1-2)

Application by George Leslie, Schenectady, New York, formerly a magistrate of Edinburgh, for a recommendation to the Council of Upper Canada; also supporting letter from John Inglis, mentioning that Leslie had set up as a shopkeeper in New York State, 1797-8. (6/1218, 1257)

Letter from Major [Sir] Henry Sheridan, late New York Volunteers, seeking British rank, and giving details of his service in the Provincial forces, 1798. (6/377)

Letter (incomplete) from the Earl of Cassillis seeking a favour for his son, Robert, who had just arrived from New York, [*ante* 1800]. (6/514)

Application by Lieutenant Colonel W. Dalrymple, late 14th Regiment, and formerly quartermaster general to the forces in North America, seeking command of a regiment, and stating the circumstances in which he had resigned his commission, [*ante* 1800]. (6/525)

(*s*) Letter, 1796, from John Cochrane forwarding a memorial on the subject of Iceland and its importance to Britain: 'I cannot help saying that the moment we are in possession of that island, you may make a present of Newfoundland and all the settlements there to America as soon as you please'. (1/513)

(*t*) Letter, 1796, from F.B. Johnson suggesting that endeavours be made to obtain East Florida or part thereof as being of great value for the defence and supply of the West Indies, and that Creek Indians be employed to serve with the British troops in the West Indies. (1/521)

(*u*) Documents, 1796-1809, dealing with projects for the emancipation of Spanish America and the relative position of the United States; persons involved are [General Miranda], [Colonel A. Cameron], Lord Melville, Lord Chatham, and Lord Castlereagh. (1/520/1-16)

(*v*) Letter, [1798], with enclosure, from the Earl of Kellie offering to raise a corps in America. (1/683/1-2)

(*w*) Letter, 1798, from Donald Cameron stating: 'there was not a Highland regiment in the service except the 42 who did not mutiny after the American War'. (1/898)

(*x*) Draft letter, 1799, from [Henry Dundas] to Rufus King informing him that a passport would be issued to General Miranda to proceed to the U.S.A., but not any of the British colonies or plantations or to any of those taken from the enemy in course of the war. (1/546)

(*y*) Letter, 1800, from the Earl of Elgin to William Pitt dealing with Black Sea commerce, America's intention of making a commercial treaty with Turkey, British commercial and political interests in Turkey, the relative situations of Russia and Turkey, and the conduct of Sir S[idney] Smith and General Kochler.(1/550)

(*z*) Letter, 1800, from Henry Glassford requesting an interview to discuss claims for compensation upon America. (1/974/1)

(*aa*) Letter, 1800, from William Abbott, Charleston, S.C., on cultivation of cotton in India as compared with South Carolina and Georgia. (3/259)

(*bb*) Letter, 1800, from William Huskisson concerning St. Domingo and the conduct of Toussaint and the Americans. (1/529/9)

(*cc*) Letter, 1803, from Charles Williamson offering to perform any services in America and to arrange for certain political influence there to act in the British interest. (1/559)

(*dd*) Letter, 1804, from [Lieutenant Colonel] N. Gordon stating that the French had become acquainted with the nature of the mechanism of the machines used in the late experimental operation at Boulogne through one of them having gone ashore without exploding, and that similar machines used by the Americans against British shipping during the War of Independence had had a device to prevent such an occurrence. (2/255) (*ee*) Letter, *c.* 1806, from Henry Glassford on the case of persons in Glasgow in connexion with American debts. (5/55)

(*ff*) Letter, 1807, from Lord Melville to his son, Robert Dundas, concerning Mr. Bond's pamphlet on North America. (1/195/36)

(*gg*) Letter, 1807, from T[homas] Reid, merchant, stating that he had been apprised in a letter from a Quaker in Philadelphia of the likelihood of a plot in Ireland, 'some of the rankest Irish rebels.... then going to Ireland from America to join in it'. (1/444)

(*hh*) Correspondence, 1807-8, relating to American trade.

Letter from Admiral Sir Alexander Cochrane commenting critically on the extensive American trade with the West Indies, which was prejudicing the mercantile interests in British North America, and acting as an enticement to British seamen to desert. (2/389)

Letter from John Turnbull, enclosing for perusal copy of his letter, 28 August 1807, to Sir Stephen Cottrell, Committee for Trade, recommending establishment of depots for sale of East India goods at Gibraltar and Malta to counter American trade in these goods in the Mediterranean. (3/279)

Letter from George Buchan Hepburn, Baron of Exchequer, regarding extent of American trade with the East Indies and China. (3/280)

Letter from John Innes, enclosing for information extract from letter from Calcutta, 25 July, 3 and 12 August 1807, on several subjects including American trade with India. (3/287)

(*ii*) Requests, 1807-9, for patronage received by the Viscounts Melville.

American items include:

Correspondence concerning application by George Leslie, Schenectady, to succeed to Mr. Russell, Receiver General of Upper Canada, 1807-8. (1/195/63-5)

Application by Sir Alexander Gordon on behalf of his son, David Gordon, merchant, New York, for appointment as consul at Rio de Janeiro, 1807. (6/1571; see also 6/1682 and 6/1691)

Application by William Armstrong, Quebec, to succeed late Colonel MacNeal as consul at New Orleans; also letter from George Canning stating that he had already given the appointment to Mr. Mellish, 1808-9. (6/1657; 1/580)

Letter of introduction from James Gordon on behalf of his brother [David Gordon] formerly merchant at New York; also application by James Gordon for the appointment of his brother as consul at the Azores or at New Orleans. (6/1682, 1691)

(*jj*) Letter, 1808, from [Sir] Alexander Gordon requesting an interview to discuss the state of communication with North America. (9/288)

(*kk*) Letter, 1810, from Alexander Shannan, merchant, Greenock, on the advantages of obtaining East and West Florida. (1/585)

(*ll*) Papers, 1812-4, relating to the War of 1812.

American items include:

Letter from Lord Melville to Lord Chancellor Eldon, forwarding a paper (wanting) as to the expediency of prosecuting an American captain on which an opinion was sought. 30 Aug. 1812. (2/454/2)

Letter, with enclosure, from Captain James R. Dains, late of H.M.S. *Guerrière*, requesting an interview upon an application received from the wives and families of the seamen lately under his command in the *Guerrière*, who were detained at Boston by the American government, wishing to know what was to be the fate of these men, 17 Feb. 1813. (2/473/1-2)

Letters from Sir Rupert George, Transport Office, concerning the question of a reciprocal agreement with the American government about the maintenance of clothing of prisoners of war, April 1813; enclosing list of passengers and crew on board the cartel ship *Fair American* arrived at Liverpool from New York, Feb. 1814. (2/439/10-12)

Letters from Joseph Marryat, chairman of committee at Lloyds, enclosing a statement of the number of British merchant vessels taken by American ships of war and privateers from commencement of hostilities to 30 Apr. 1813, and comparative statement of insurance premiums of Lloyds, 1 May 1812 and 1 May 1813, with the returns for convoy. (2/882/1-4)

Letter from E. Champion to Admiral the Earl of Galloway forwarding a paper (wanting) relating to North America, and hoping that his observations would receive Lord Melville's perusal, 15 June 1813. (2/483)

Letter from Robert Thornton, chairman of the East India Company, enclosing extract of a letter, 31 July 1813, from Sir Evan Nepean, Governor of Bombay, about a report that two American cruisers had taken up station eastward of St. Helena to intercept ships bound for Britain, and about the internment of American trading ships at Canton, Feb. 1814. (2/500/1-2)

Statement sent by the lord president regarding the seizure by the Americans of William and Thomas Dickson, barrister and merchant respectively in Upper Canada, as hostages for their brother, Robert, engaged in gaining the active support of the Indians against the Americans, 7 Aug. 1813. (1/588)

Letter from Rear Admiral David Milne, H.M.S. *Bulwark*, Penobscot River, about the effects of the blockade on the Boston district, 8 Sept. 1814. (2/527)

Letters from Lord Melville to H.R.H. Prince Regent about Sir George Prevost's conduct in the action on Lake Champlain, and a proposed court of enquiry on the conduct of the war, Nov. - Dec. 1814. (1/214/17, 18)

Memorandum from Colonel Barclay, with accompanying sketch, describing a new type of floating battery driven by steam and sails, built by the Americans as an experiment on the recommendation of Mr. Fulton, and known as 'Fulton No. 1', 23 Nov. 1814. (2/530/1-2)

Observations by Captain William King on impropriety of employing hired packets, including an appendix listing packets captured during the American War of 1812, 1827. (2/706)

(*mm*) Letter, 1814, from John Whidbey about procuring naval timber from north-west and central America. (2/492)

(*nn*) Letter, 1814, from Joshua Jepson Oddy, Havana, enclosing a note of the American regulations governing the subsistence and repatriation of their seamen who were, by reason of shipwreck, sickness or captivity, destitute in a foreign port; with note as to Oddy's character marked on the letter. (2/499/1-2)

(*oo*) Memorandum, 1818, from Sir George Cockburn suggesting the employment of a nucleus of reliable, pensioned seamen on board each of H.M. seagoing ships as an example to the crew, and as a means of countering the enticements to desertion practised in America and other foreign countries. (2/581)

(*pp*) Letter, 1819, from Vice Admiral Sir Thomas Freemantle comparing the *Rochfort* with ships of an American squadron at Naples. (2/1086/7)

(*qq*) Correspondence, 1819-20, between Commissioner Robert Barrie and Lord Melville regarding the comparative strengths of the British and American naval establishments on the Lakes; pointing out that Barrie had not received his dormant commission as commodore on the Lakes or any instructions to regulate his conduct in the event of a rupture with America; and describing the rotten condition of the ships on the Lakes. (2/603/1-5; 2/622)

(*rr*) Letter, 1823, from Captain John S. Carden, R.N., about the enticement of British seamen into the American Navy, and suggesting how this might be prevented. (2/650)

(*ss*) Account, 1826, of the United States Navy in Dec. 1825; with accompanying memorandum by Sir Thomas Byam Martin, Comptroller of the Navy. (2/703/1-2)

(*tt*) Memorandum, 1832, by Robert Dundas on the state of the

American Navy and the value of its naval stores; endorsed 'American Navy Estimates of 1832'. (2/733)
(*uu*) Letter, 1842, from the Duke of Buccleuch: 'I suppose you have read President Tyler's message to Congress: the criticism in *The Times* upon it is very fair. What an humiliating confession after the vain boasting that the United States are superior to all the world that no one would lend a sixpence to them, that their credit at home and abroad was gone'. (5/545)

CARRON IRON COMPANY RECORDS. (GD.58)

Letter-books, 1759-1885, contain correspondence with Glasgow merchants concerning iron from America and the supply of iron goods for the American market. (1/1-44; 2/1-6)

BENNAN AND FINNARTS MUNIMENTS. (GD.60)

Letter, 1884, from Roland Fergussone Kennedy, Wild Horse Ranch, Big Springs, Texas, to C.G. Shaw [solicitor in Ayr], requesting an advance of £3,000 to buy cattle in partnership with Lord Aylesford [Heneage, 7th Earl] who 'has about 4,000 acres of land here'. (197)

MURRAY OF LINTROSE MUNIMENTS. (GD.68)

(*a*) Letter, 1758, from Malcolm McPherson, Halifax, giving news of his health and prospects with the army in New England. (2/112)
(*b*) Three letters, 1777, from William Murray to Mungo Murray of Lintrose, his brother, giving news of the campaign in America and of his appointment as lieutenant colonel of the 27th Regiment, with a request to send out his nephew, William, as America 'is the properest place for him to learn his business'. (2/117)
(*c*) Two letters, 1880, from Charles Willing, Philadelphia, to Mrs. Murray [of Lintrose], his sister, on financial matters. (2/60)

BALFOUR OF PILRIG MUNIMENTS. (GD.69)

(*a*) Two letters, 1757-8, from Arthur St. Clair [on service in North America] concerning credit given to him by James Balfour of Pilrig. (171)
(*b*) Letter, 1781, from Lord Cornwallis, Wilkington, to the Rev. Dr. Webster on the death of Webster's son in action. (300)

MONRO OF ALLAN MUNIMENTS. (GD.71)

Four letters, 1875-82, from Frank S. Mackenzie, woollen manufacturer, Woodstock, Vermont, to David Monro his cousin, inviting him to visit America; referring to Frank's adoption of Archie Monro and changing his name to McKenzie; and his wish to import black-faced Highland sheep and cattle to America. (409)

HAY OF BELTON MUNIMENTS. (GD.73)

Letter, 1779, from J. Hay to John Hay of Belton giving an account of his journey from Rhode Island to the island of St. Lucia and of the defence of St. Lucia against the French. (1/76)

HENDERSON COLLECTION. (GD.76)

Volume of letters, 1832-5, from James Henderson of Messrs. Harrop and Henderson, Para, Brazil. (454)
Subjects include:
His poor opinion of the inhabitants of New York, 1832. (10)
His proposed marriage to a New York lady, 1835. (8)

FERGUSSON OF CRAIGDARROCH MUNIMENTS. (GD.77)

(*a*) Letter, 1759, from Philip Morison, Charleston, South Carolina, on the writer's situation, Cherokee Indians, and the expedition against Guadeloupe. (200/6)
(*b*) Mortgage, 1775, by John Bowman, younger of Skiddoway, presently residing in Glasgow, to Alexander Fergusson of Craigdarroch of 500 acres on the island of Skiddoway in parish of Christ Church, Georgia. (168)

MACKAY OF BIGHOUSE MUNIMENTS. (GD.87)[3]

(*a*) Letter, 1727, to [Patrick Campbell of] Barcaldine, asking news of his son, George, in America. (1/3)
(*b*) Letter, 1758, from Captain Allan Campbell [42nd Highlanders], Lake George, to his brother [John Campbell of Barcaldine] informing him of the defeat at Ticonderoga and listing various officers [mainly Campbells] killed and wounded. (1/82)
(*c*) Letter, 1759, from James Moray of Abercairny to Barcaldine informing him that Mr. Pitt had heard from Mr. Dobbs, Governor of North Carolina, that General Forbes had reduced Fort Duqun [Duquesne]. (1/83)
(*d*) Letter, 1759, from Captain Allan Campbell, New York, to same, giving news of Barcaldine's sons, Lieutenant George Campbell in General Gage's Regiment and Major Alexander Campbell at Fort Duquesne, and of the death of Major Duncan Campbell of Inverawe after the retreat from Ticonderoga. (1/84)
(*e*) Letter, 1759, from Major Alexander Campbell, Fort Edward Camp, to same, giving news of their friends serving in America; his regiment was now under the command of General Amherst, 'the conqueror of Loisburg'. (1/85)
(*f*) Letter, 1759, from Major Alexander Campbell, Ticonderoga, to same, informing him that the French had abandoned the fort there on 26 July. (1/87)
(*g*) Letter, 1759, from Major Alexander Campbell, Crown Point, to same, with news that his regiment under General Amherst had taken Crown Point, and that a detachment under General Prideaux had taken Niagara. (1/88)
(*h*) Letter, 1761, from Lieutenant Colonel Alexander Campbell, New York, to same, announcing his appointment as lieutenant colonel to Colonel Burton's regiment in South Carolina, and the departure of regiments under the command of Lord Rollo for an unknown destination. (1/89)
(*i*) Two letters, 1775, from Patrick Campbell of Ardchattan asking John Campbell of Barcaldine and Colonel Alexander Campbell to provide £100 each to enable David Campbell, writer to the Signet, to settle in New York with his family. (1/110-111)
(*j*) Letter, 1786, from [-] to Captain Peter [Patrick ?] Campbell of Barcaldine, informing him that a young lady he had met in Ireland had followed him to London, America, and Scotland and would die if she did not see him. (1/115)

YULE COLLECTION. (GD.90)

(*a*) Post-nuptial marriage contract, 1753, between John Greenlees, merchant in Virginia, and Mary Beveridge, daughter of James Beveridge, merchant in Edinburgh. (2/236)
(*b*) Oath of allegiance to King George III, 1777, by Robert Mercer of the militia of the city of New York, and royal pardon to him, wherein he is designed 'a signer of the late Association, merchant of the city of New York'. (2/245)

S.S.P.C.K. RECORDS. (GD.95)[4]

(*a*) Proposals, *c.* 1712, by George Bell for establishing a colony in Florida in North America. (10, item 38)
(*b*) Commission, 1760, by the committee of directors of the

3. The following letters are printed in *Transactions of the Gaelic Society of Inverness*, vol. xxi (no. 3) and vol. xxiv (nos. 82-5, 87-9, 110, 111).
4. The Society in Scotland for Propagating Christian Knowledge. Apart from the items noted hereunder, there are references to America in the Society's minute-books.

S.S.P.C.K. to the lieutenant governor of the colony of Massachusetts Bay and others as their correspondents in New England. (12/1)
(*c*) Letter, 1760, from Eleazar Wheelock, Lebanon [Connecticut], to William Hyslop about his work in educating Indians. (12/2)
(*d*) Letter-book, 1799-1806, containing the American correspondence of the society. (3/1)
(*e*) Notebook, 1826-39, containing reports and letters regarding Moore's Indian school and the American Indian Fund. (12/9)
(*f*) View of the arguments for and against the application of the Indian Fund to Moore's school, 1839. (12/11)
(*g*) Twenty letters, 1890-8, between the American Board of Commissioners for Foreign Missions and the S.S.P.C.K. regarding the education of Indians at Moore's Indian school and Dartmouth College. (12/16)
(*h*) Notebook, 1901, containing notes by C.C. Nisbet, secretary of the S.S.P.C.K., on his visit to the United States and Canada. With volume entitled 'Moore's Indian Mission Fund' containing notes and transcripts covering period 1767-1901. (12/21)
(*i*) Papers, 1902-10, relating to the application of the American Indian Fund in Canada, including references to the education of Indians at Hampton Industrial Agricultural Normal Institute. (12/22-5)
(*j*) Papers, 1922-3, relating to petition of the S.S.P.C.K. to the court of session to settle a scheme for application of the American Indian Trust Fund. (12/26-30)

HUNTER OF HUNTERSTON MUNIMENTS. (GD.102)

Letter, 1738, to 'Mr. Robert Hunter, mariner in New England, lodging at Henry Sinklars in Boustone, New England', from his mother, informing him of the death of his father, Patrick Hunter of Hunterston, and asking him to return to Scotland. Printed in *Some Family Papers of the Hunters of Hunterston*, ed. M.S. Shaw (Scottish Record Society, 1925). (2/54)

SOCIETY OF ANTIQUARIES OF SCOTLAND COLLECTION. (GD.103)

(*a*) Indenture, 1746, (with signatures of 125 Highlanders concerned in the 1745 rebellion), whereby the signatories are bound for lifetime service to Samuel Smith, merchant, London, who assigns them to John Hanbury for shipment to the American colonies to serve him for seven years, and on discharge to remain in America 'according to the express condition and terms of His Majesty's most gracious pardon'. (2/382-3)
(*b*) Commission, 1761, by Sir Jeffrey Amherst, Commander-in-Chief of H.M. Forces in America, to Lieutenant Alexander Shaw, as adjutant in the 60th Royal American Regiment of Foot. (2/412)
(*c*) Indenture, 1779, between James Lawson, of the city of Glasgow, merchant, on the one part, and John Alston, junior, and Alexander Grindlay, both of the city of Glasgow, merchants, on the other, with reference to sale of lands and forges in Prince William County, Virginia, with Negro slaves. (2/442)

DUFF OF FETTERESSO MUNIMENTS. (GD.105)

(*a*) Legal papers, 1725-30, relating to Helen Cuming, daughter of deceased Sir Alexander Cuming of Culter and spouse of Robert Cuming, merchant, of Concord, Massachusetts. (338-48)
(*b*) Instructions, 1756, to General Abercromby on his appointment as Commander-in-Chief in North America. (396)
(*c*) Commissions, 1757-8, to Edward Whitmore as brigadier general and John Donaldson as colonel in North America. (391 d-e)
(*d*) Letter, n.d., to General Abercromby acknowledging letter to be forwarded to New York. (395)

HAMILTON-DALRYMPLE OF NORTH BERWICK MUNIMENTS. (GD.110)

(*a*) Memorandum, 1736, concerning William and John Kirkwood who went to Boston in New England. (1150)
(*b*) Letters, 1742, from John Rutherford [of Edgerston, advocate] on his impressions of America and tour through the Indian nations. (911/6-7)
(*c*) Letters, 1746-7, from Lieutenant John Suttie, Louisbourg, commenting on the war in North America. (919/8-13)
(*d*) Letter, 1747, from John Dalrymple asking Sir Hew Dalrymple to get the writer made one of the King's council in North Carolina. (988)
(*e*) Letter, 1747, from David Hume of Ninewells asking for Sir Hew Dalrymple's help in getting a Mr. Douglass a chaplainry in one of two Highland regiments to be raised for service in America. (994)
(*f*) Memorial, 1749, for Captain John Rutherfurd, member of council at New York, requesting appointment as lieutenant governor there. (629)
(*g*) Letter, 1754, from Alexander Johnston, London, to Sir Hew Dalrymple, sending American seeds. (1028/1)
(*h*) Letter, 1754, from George Warrander to Sir Hew Dalrymple on hopes of getting a recommendation for John Graham, merchant in Savannah, Ga. [later Deputy Governor of Georgia], to the new governor of that colony. (999/2)
(*i*) Two letters, 1756, from Alexander Pyot, Whitekirk, Dunbar, to Sir Hew Dalrymple, asking for recommendation for his son, going by name of John Graham, merchant at Savannah, Ga., to be appointed a member of the council there. (1046)
(*j*) Letter, *c.* 1776, from Alison Cockburn to Sir Hew Dalrymple, commenting on the American war and mentioning an American friend whose uncle had to pay rent to the rebels for his own house. (1059/2)
(*k*) Letter, 1782, from John Buchan of Letham, mentioning that his son, Hew, had sold his commission in the army in America to pay gambling debts contracted there. (1026/18)

BREADALBANE MUNIMENTS. (GD. 112)

(*a*) State of plantations in America and revenues of the governors, 1739. (61*)
(*b*) Muster rolls and other papers, 1775-85, of the 40th Regiment of Foot while serving in North America. (52/13*; 52/22*)

MURTHLY CASTLE MUNIMENTS. (GD.121)[5]

(*a*) Letter, 1838, to Capt. William Stewart [later Sir William Drummond Stewart] from G. W. Featherstonhaugh, Washington, asking for information about the Rocky Mountains. Printed in W. Fraser, *The Red Book of Grandtully* (Edinburgh, 1868), ii, 375-6. (box 91, no.310*)
(*b*) Correspondence, 1838-9, of Sir William Drummond Stewart. (box 101, bundle 21*)
American writers and subjects include:
John Crawford, British Consul, New Orleans - business ventures; shipment of Sir William's buffaloes to Britain, 1838-9. (82, 105)
News of friends and events in St. Louis, Missouri, 1838-9. (91, 93, 115)
Father F. B. Jamison, St. Louis - [Joseph N.] Nicollet [explorer], 'fears that the government will ask his services for another tour', 1839. (96)

5. See M.R. Porter and O. Davenport, *Scotsman in Buckskin: Sir William Drummond Stewart and the Rocky Mountain Fur Trade* (New York, 1963).

Alfred J. Miller, the artist - description of Stewart's buffaloes and grizzly bear, 1839. (104)

Exhibition of Stewart's paintings at the Apollo Gallery, New York, 1839. (112)

(*c*) Correspondence, 1841-5, of Sir William Drummond Stewart. (box 101, bundle 22*)

American writers and subjects include:

William L. Sublette, St. Louis - shipment of plants and animals to Stewart; preparations for Stewart's expedition to the Rocky Mountains, 1841-4. (4, 31, 33, 37, 52, 65, 77, 91)

J. Watson Webb, New York - shipment of Stewart's paintings. (6)

J.E[ugene] Flandin [formerly assistant to Nicollet], New York - his past connexion with Stewart and present circumstances, 1841. (10, 15)

Alfred J. Miller, the artist, London and Baltimore - his paintings, mainly on biblical subjects, 1841-5. (18, 43, 76, 87, 148)

Robert Campbell, New York - shipment of animals to Stewart, improvements at St. Louis, 1841. (36)

Charles Andrew Geyer, 'cultivator and botanist' - requests permission to join Stewart's next expedition to the Rocky Mountains, as he had accompanied Nicollet on two of his journeys and had been selected as botanical surveyor for the Oregon expedition, 1842. (55)

Hugh Campbell, Philadelphia - crisis affecting American financial institutions, 1842. (56)

Samuel Ward, New York - purchase of articles for 'the professor' [Charles Mersch, botanist], who is joining Stewart's expedition, 1842-3. (68-9)

William Wilson to his mother in Glasgow [to be forwarded by Stewart] - his travels in the Platte country of Missouri, hunting in the mountains, prairie animals, and his plans to settle in the Spanish country, where there are 'no mechanics'; with sketch of 'A Sue Indian'. (73)

Alexander Gordon [Scottish botanist], Mobile and New Orleans - explanation of his conduct on the Rocky Mountains trip. 1843-4. (79, 82)

K[enneth] Mackenzie, St. Louis - asking for loan to improve property near St. Louis, bought from Mr. Astor of New York, 1844. (90)

Rev. Joseph A. Lutz, St. Louis - asking for contribution for a Catholic church he is building, which is to have one very large bell, 'so as to overpower all other bells of the city', 1844. (92)

Leo D. Walker, St. Louis - 'vile slanders' circulating against Stewart, 1844. (93)

Charles E. d'Invilliers, Philadelphia - civil disturbances there, 1844. (106-7)

Washington Hancock, Philadelphia - comments on presidential election, 1844. (126)

Sir William Hooker, Royal Botanic Gardens, Kew - sending published part of Geyer's notes on Missouri and Oregon vegetation. (152)

(*d*) Correspondence, 1846-9, of Sir William Drummond Stewart. (box 102, bundle 23*)

American writers and subjects include:

A. Chauvin, St. Charles [Missouri] - Mexican war, trouble with Indians, Stewart's book *Altowan*, 1846. (124)

Dr. John McLoughlin, Oregon City - effects of discovery of gold in California, influence of Catholic clergy on Indians, Stewart's offer to send him Leicester sheep, 1848. (247)

A. Chauvin, St. Charles - news of friends in St. Louis, trouble among Indians, 1848. (255)

B. M. Power, Baltimore - news of Stewart's American friends; Norwood (chief clerk of the stamp office) hopes to secure election as sheriff of this town, worth $14,000 a year; account of cannibalism among emigrants on the plains and of Indian hostility, 1849. (284)

(*e*) Letter, n.d., from Father F. B. Jamison, St. Louis University, referring to his part in Stewart's reception into the Catholic church. (box 103, bundle 26, no. 169*)

ROSE OF KILRAVOCK MUNIMENTS. (GD. 125)

Letters and papers, 1757-9, of Major James Clephane of Col. Simon Fraser's Highland Regiment. (boxes 22 and 34*)

American items include:

Return of Col. Simon Fraser's Regiment and others embarked with them on board the transports at Halifax Harbour, 17 Oct. 1757. (box 22)

Letter from Charles Farquharson, Charleston, to Major Clephane about the sickness of his men, caused by the excessive heat and bad water, 24 Oct. 1757. (box 22)

Letter from Lieut. Col. Fraser, Connecticut, to Major Clephane at Fairfield, concerning supernumeraries; with other correspondence and papers on the same subject, including returns of various companies in Col. Fraser's Regiment listing supernumeraries, Dec. 1757. (box 22)

Two orderly books of Major Clephane at Fort Stanwix, 1758-9. (box 34)

Return of bedding and stores in the quartermaster general's department, Fort Stanwix, Feb. 1759. (box 22)

Letter from John Clephane, Halifax Harbour, to Major James Clephane at New York, concerning the latter's bad health and his intention to 'sell out', 10 Nov. 1759. (box 22)

STAIR MUNIMENTS. (GD. 135)

Letters, 1712-5, from Robert Hunter, [Governor of] New York, to the Earl of Stair, concerning the writer's financial plight; 'I remaine here loaded with many thousands of pounds of publick debts all contracted by the queen's order and for her service'. (141/1/26, 37, 82*; 141/4/22*)

SINCLAIR OF FRESWICK MUNIMENTS. (GD. 136)

(*a*) Letters, 1772-6, from John Campbell, Maryland and Glasgow, to his cousin William Sinclair. (416/1-4)

Subjects include:

Discouraging prospects for emigrants to Maryland, methods of fighting used by the Indians, and the way of life of settlers in the tobacco colonies, 1772. (1)

American discontent with the British government, and his support for the colonists, 1774. (2)

The difficulties facing British people in America, 'business being entirly at an end', 1775. (3)

His return to Scotland after 'incurring the displeasure of the despotic rulers in America', 1776. (4)

(*b*) Papers, 1807-15, relating to pay due by William Sinclair of Freswick to William Sutherland and other volunteers of Sinclair's company who went to America. (1222; 1225; 1227)

ROBERTSON OF KINDEACE MUNIMENTS. (GD. 146)

Notebook, 1779-81, containing day-by-day account of operations against the Americans in the War of Independence, apparently written by an officer [? Charles Robertson] of the 76th Regiment. (box 18*)

MORTON PAPERS. (GD. 150)

(*a*) Account of the wreck of the *Sarah* of Boston on the shore of Weyland, Orkney, and of the salvaging of her cargo, 1709. (2596)

(*b*) Letter, 1740, from James Wedderburn, South Carolina, to the Earl of Morton about the need to raise troops for defence of the frontier in case of war with the French, and about serious damage occasioned by a recent fire. (3483/11)
(*c*) List of ships cleared out at Kirkwall with foreign goods for the British plantations in America, 1741-64. (2524)
(*d*) Letter, 1743, from James Baird, London, to James Watson of Saughton, concerning vacancy for a surveyor of the customs of Wiccocomoco and Muni in Maryland, a possible lucrative post for James Watson's brother, David. (3526/18)

HAMILTON BRUCE MUNIMENTS. (GD. 152)

Letter (incomplete), 1776, from a prisoner at Concord to his father, describing his captivity in America. (109*)

GILCHRIST OF OSPISDALE MUNIMENTS. (GD. 153)

(*a*) Letter, 10 June 1776, from Alexander Sutherland, Nantasket Road, six miles from Boston, [? to Dugald Gilchrist], describing the activities of armed American schooners off the New England coast, inadequacy of the British naval force there, and scarcity of provisions. (box 1*)
(*b*) Accounts and papers (one volume and five bundles) of the 71st Regiment in America, 1777-85. (box 1*)
Items include:
Roll of the non-commissioned officers, drummers, rank and file of the 71st Regiment taken prisoner at Yorktown, Va., 19 Oct. 1781.
Invoice of clothing sent to the prisoners of the 71st Regiment in Pennsylvania, Mar. 1782.
(*c*) Letter, 17 Jan. 1777, from Capt. William Sutherland, New Brunswick [N.J.], to Dugald Gilchrist, describing expected moves by the British forces in New Jersey; 'We [mu]st determine to burn and utterly destroy this province before we [can] force the miscreants to submit'. (box 1*)
(*d*) Letter, 17 Jan. 1778, from Capt. William Sutherland, aide-de-camp to Sir H. Clinton, New York, to Gilchrist, concerning local opinion about various British generals. (box 1*)

MAXTONE GRAHAM MUNIMENTS. (GD. 155)

(*a*) Four letters, 1776-7, from Charles Cathcart to his sister, Mary, and her husband, Thomas Graham of Balgowan, concerning the campaign in America. (814)
Subjects include:
Writer's intention of going to America as a volunteer with General Howe, 22 Sept. 1776.
Battle of Brandywine and attack on Philadelphia, 15 and 26 Oct. 1777.
(*b*) Letters, 1794-6, from Thomas Maxtone to his sister, Helen, and Thomas Graham of Balgowan, some written while Maxtone was serving on the American station. (855)
Subjects include:
Capture of fourteen American ships 'hired by the French Republic to carry their property', visits to New York and Philadelphia 'at which we were treated more like enemys than the subjects of a nation at peace with them', and possibility of an American war, 23 Aug. 1794.
Arrival of his ship at Norfolk, Va., for water and provisions, 31 Mar. 1795.
(*c*) Letter, 1841, from David MacLaurin, London, to Robert Graham, enclosing a sketch of short North American tour, 'a three months jaunt'. (1015)

POLWARTH MUNIMENTS. (GD. 157)

(*a*) Letter, 1735, from James Scott, Panama, to his sister, describing his departure from England in 1730 in the Honourable South Sea Company's snow *St. Philip* for America. (2810/1)
(*b*) Letter, 1755, from Alexander Hume Campbell, London, to Walter Scott of Harden, giving news of Gen. Johnson's victory over the French at Crown Point. (2247/3)
(*c*) Letter, 1765, from John Pringle of Haining, M.P., to same, about debate on the America Bill in the House of Commons. (2257/13)
(*d*) Memorandum, 3-6 Feb. [1766], on debates in Parliament on American affairs: right to tax America, repeal of the Stamp Act, and compensation for damage suffered in recent rioting by the colonists. (2246/58/2)
(*e*) Letter, 17 May 1766, from James Dickson of Ednam, London, to Walter Scott of Harden: 'it is said that the provance of Boston and Conecdicut has declard for indepency [sic]'. (2265/21)
(*f*) Letter, 18 Nov. 1775, from Andrew Douglas, [Navy Pay Office], to Walter Scott of Harden, concerning Gen. Gage's report on the situation in America, and Lord George Germain's speech on Friday morning explaining his views on this subject. (2246/53)
(*g*) Letter, 21 Nov. 1775, from Gilbert Elliot, London, to same, reporting rather favourable news from America. (2250/39)
(*h*) Letter (in French), 1780, from Baron de Linsingen to Count Bruhl, seeking recommendations for writer's nephew, in service of the king of England in America. (3338)
(*i*) Letter, 1781, from Margaret Johnston, Hilton, to Hugh Scott, regretting that her son George refuses to go to the East Indies, and proposes to go as a volunteer to America. (2301)

HUME OF MARCHMONT MUNIMENTS. (GD. 158)

(*a*) Letter, 1682, to Sir George Campbell of Sesnock, from [-], Edinburgh, about proposed settlement in America. (846)
(*b*) Letter, [1682], from Sir John Cochrane of Ochiltree to [Joseph] Mortone, Governor at Ashley River, about the agreement made by the Lords Proprietors of Carolina. Printed in *Hist. MSS Comm.*, xiv, app. iii, 114. (847)
(*c*) Memorial, *c.* 1682, anent terms proposed by the Scots for their settlement in Carolina. (848)
(*d*) List, *c.* 1730, written by the 2nd Earl of Marchmont, giving population of various parts of America, dividing it into 'souls', 'Negroes', and 'Indians'. (1222)
(*e*) Letter, 1731, from Will Home, Linthill, asking the Earl of Marchmont to speak to Col. Cosbie [Cosby], the new Governor of New York, in favour of the writer's son, who has been there for some time. (1383)
(*f*) Letter, *c.* 1731, from John Abercromby thanking Marchmont for his efforts to get him out of Lee's regiment; has heard that Col. Cosby is going to New York and asks Marchmont to recommend the writer to him. (2221)
(*g*) Letter, 1778, from Samuel Strutt, Parliament Office, to the 3rd Earl of Marchmont, giving details of proceedings in the House of Lords, mainly Rockingham's address to the King disapproving of proclamation of H.M. commission at New York. (2623)

DRUMMOND CASTLE MUNIMENTS. (GD. 160)

(*a*) Papers, 1762-80, relating to an estate in East New Jersey, originally belonging to John, Earl of Melfort. (box 43, bundle 4*)
(*b*) Letters and papers, 1768-80, of Thomas, Lord Drummond. (box 53, bundle 1*)
American subjects include:
Estate in East New Jersey, 1768. (1, 3, 4)

Proceedings for recovery of New Jersey estate, 1770. (9)
Passes from the committee of safety and the general committee of mechanicks in union of New York for Lord Drummond to leave for Bermuda, 1776. (13-14)
Washington's allegation that Drummond broke his parole on leaving New York, 1776-7. (15-19, 24)
Drummond's proposals for carrying on the American war, 1778. (26)
News of French fleet, 1779. (29)

(*c*) Papers, 1775-6, relating to Drummond's proposals for settling the dispute with the American colonists, including minutes of his negotiations at Philadelphia in January-February 1776. See M. M. Klein, 'Failure of a mission: the Drummond peace proposal of 1775', *Huntingdon Library Quarterly*, xxi (1972). (box 53, bundle 2*)

CAMPBELL OF BARCALDINE MUNIMENTS. (GD. 170)[6]

(*a*) Letter, 1734, from Jo[-] Baillie, Savannah, Georgia, to his brother Thomas, asking for servants of various trades, and describing flourishing condition of Georgia, Spanish fort at St. Augustine, and Indian method of fighting. (3558)

(*b*) Indenture of apprenticeship, 1737, between John McLeod, Edinburgh, and William Campbell, son of late Hugh Campbell, tenant in Argyllshire, whereby Campbell agrees to serve McLeod in Carolina for four years. (3339)

(*c*) Letters, 1757-9, from Allan Campbell, brother of Duncan Campbell of Glenure, while serving in the British army in America.
News of his regiment. On board the *Lyon* transport, Sandy Hook, near New York, June 1757. (1465)
Gives news of the taking of Fort Ticonderoga with very little loss; hopes to take Crown Point. Ticonderoga, 27 July 1759. (1067/2)

(*d*) Letter, 1759, from Allan Cameron, Crown Point, announcing the death of his cousin Dungallon of a fever at Quebec. (1045/1)

(*e*) Letter, 1760, from John Campbell of Danna, Inveraray: 'This mail carrys you great and glorious news from N. America which is now all our own without spilling one drop of blood'. (1016/62)

(*f*) Letters, 1774-6, from Major Alexander Campbell, illegitimate son of Duncan Campbell of Glenure.
Is about to sail for New York. Greenock Road, June 1774. (1063/24/1)
Is succeeding beyond expectation in the grocery way; gives particulars of the battle of Bunker Hill, where he was wounded. Boston, 25 June 1775. (1063/25)
Has recovered from his wounds: rebels continue to blockade Boston; New York occupied by 3 to 4,000 rebels under General Lee; expects reinforcements. Hampton Road, Va., 20 Feb. 1776. (1595/13)

(*g*) Letters, 1775-80, from Alexander Campbell, landwaiter, Greenock. (1065/1-6)
Subjects include:
Arrival the previous night of a vessel from Boston 'carrying between 30 and 40 passengers with their families, who have fled from the unhappy troubles in that quarter.... The American orator leader and demigog Doctor Warren was killed in the action', Aug. 1775. (1)
Gives news of Glenure's sons in America, all of whom are doing well especially Sandy, whose success is due to his own merit and spirited behaviour at Bunker Hill, Mar. 1777. (3/1)
Gives news that Gen. Clinton with 10,000 men was to open a battery against Charleston on 18 Mar. [1780]. (5)

(*h*) Letter, 1776, from Ewan Cameron of Fassfern, brother-in-law of Alexander Campbell of Barcaldine, quoting a letter from Charles Cameron, writer's brother, from Staten Island, with an account of their relations fighting in America; also copy of Charles Cameron's letter. (1585/13; 3157)

(*i*) Letter, 1776, from James MacIntyre, Glencoe, asking for news of friends in America, as the 'waff' reports he has been hearing have caused him some uneasiness. (1912/2)

(*j*) Commission, 1776, by Gen. William Howe, Commander-in-Chief of all H.M. forces within colonies on Atlantic Ocean from Nova Scotia to West Florida, to Colin Campbell, as ensign in King's Orange Rangers commanded by Lieut. Col. Commandant John Bayard. (3436)

(*k*) Letters, 1776-82, from Major Patrick Campbell, son of Duncan Campbell of Glenure, while serving in the 71st Regiment in America. (1176/10-15; 1711/12-18)
Subjects include:
Account of a naval engagement between the ship carrying the writer and one with 'Yanky' colours. Halifax, 26 June 1776. (1711/13)
Belief that the [British] army would attack at New York and Long Island. New York Bay, 4 Aug. 1776. (1711/14)
His view of the Americans; 'a scape gallows race, the genuine progeny of their worthy ancestors from Newgate and the Old Baily'; his pity for 'the poor deluded wretches that have emigrated from the Highlands of Scotland' since American trade with the West Indies, their only source of riches, now almost ceased. Perth Amboy, 10 Feb. 1777. (1176/10)
'Mr. Washington is within ten miles of us, his scouting parties and ours meet every day, it is thought we will have a general brush with him in a few days'. Camp near Philadelphia, 28 Nov. 1777. (1176/11)
Intends to sell his farm to pay for a majority; news of detention of Gen. Burgoyne and his troops in breach of the convention entered into between him and the American general. Staten Island, 14 Mar. 1778. (1176/12)
'What does the people of England mean by sending commissioners here, do they think that anything but fire and sword will reclaim these scoundrels?'. Staten Island, 8 July 1778. (1711/17)
Is about to sail on an expedition; gives news of his brothers including Sandy, his half-brother, who intended coming home with his drunken, distracted wife and numerous family, and 'put her into Bedalum, there being in the present situation of affairs no possibility of managing her here'. York Harbour, 9 Nov. 1778. (1176/13)
Has been taken prisoner, and arrived at New York on parole by leave from Mr. Washington. New York, 4 Mar. 1780. (1176/14/1)
Announces his marriage to Miss Sally Pearsall, a Quaker, whose father is worth £20,000 cash. New York, 1 Jan. 1781. (1176/15/1-2)

(*l*) Letter, 31 Mar. 1777, from Col. Mungo Campbell, Staten Island: 'The rebels are coming in with their arms hundreds a day. I believe we will not have another campaign, as I think the rebels will submit about the 1st of June'. (1166)

(*m*) Letter, 7 Feb. 1778, from William MacKenzie, New York, concerning his situation as piper to the battalion and member of Capt. Peter Campbell of Glenure's company; he gets 1s. 6d. per day, and will have 200 acres in America. (3158)

6. Most of the items listed below are letters written to John Campbell of Barcaldine, Duncan Campbell of Glenure (later of Barcaldine), and Alexander Campbell of Barcaldine, advocate. See also GD. 87.

(*n*) Letters, 1778, from Robert Oliphant and Cox and Watson concerning a bill drawn by Duncan Campbell of Glenure's son at New York. (1383; 1199)

(*o*) Letters, 1778-9, from Hugh Campbell, lieutenant in the 35th Regiment, son of Duncan Campbell of Glenure. (1118/7-10)

Subjects include:

Health of various members of the family in America, Jan. 1778. (7)

Blockade of New York by a French fleet 'and my Lord How is inside of them'; the blockade has put an end to fishing, 'which is a very great loss to us, it was the only thing we could buy cheap, that is what we call cheap at a sixpence a pound'. New York, 22 July 1778. (8)

Is on board ship with other sick officers; reports death of 'Charles Fassefern' [? brother of Ewan Cameron of Fassfern] on the expedition to Georgia, Apr. 1779. (10)

(*p*) Letter, 1781, from John McColl, Glasgow, who is going to New York with goods to the amount of £1,600 aboard the *Ruby* of Greenock; hopes to meet Peter, son of Duncan Campbell of Glenure; requests a letter of recommendation to anyone Glenure knows in New York. (1276)

(*q*) Letter, 1782, from David Campbell of Belmont, W.S., from New York, reporting death of Glenure's son, Capt. Peter, at Long Island. (1097/111)

(*r*) Letters, 1782-3, from Thomas Pearsall, merchant, New York, concerning the affairs of late Major Patrick Campbell of the 71st Regiment, son of Duncan Campbell of Glenure, who died at Success in Long Island, 1 Sept. 1782, of Sarah Pearsall, his relict, daughter of said Thomas Pearsall, and of Duncan their son, 'a very diverting child'; with copies of the wills of Major Patrick Campbell and Major Alexander Campbell, late of the 84th Regiment. (1385/1-5)

(*s*) Letter, 1784, from Hugh Crawford, Greenock, relating that he has been unable to trace an emigrant called Patterson, and, as two ships have sailed for America, suggests that he must have changed his name. (1741)

(*t*) Letter, 1784, from Mary Campbell, relict of Major Alexander Campbell, enclosing a petition to the commissioners appointed to enquire into the losses and services of the American Loyalists, showing that her husband was at the battle of Bunker Hill, and she and her children captured in a sloop belonging to her husband on their way from Boston to Halifax. (1705/4/1-2)

(*u*) Letter, 1786, from John Cameron, Nelson County, Va., describing the country, including sugar trees, ploughing, vegetables, and animals. (1059)

(*v*) Letter, 1787, from Colin Campbell, brother of Alexander Campbell of Barcaldine, concerning David Campbell, son of John Campbell of Barcaldine, reported to be in jail in New York for a crime carrying the death penalty: 'What a sad persevering dog he is in villany and bringing disgrace on his family. I wish he was dead without the assistance of the rope'. (1628/40)

(*w*) Letter, 1793, from Daniel Lyman, London, pointing out that he had been ruined by the American war, and has to subsist on half pay. (1833/6)

(*x*) Letter, [1793], from Duncan Pearsall Campbell [son of Major Patrick Campbell and Sally Pearsall Campbell] about his studies at the school in Flat Bush village near New York, where the master is Mr. Peter Wilson, a Scotsman. (1658)

(*y*) Letters, 1793-4, from Thomas Pearsall, brother of Sally [Pearsall] Campbell, relict of Major Patrick Campbell. (2005/1-3)

Subjects include:

Illness of his sister, Mrs. Campbell, who is in New York; progress of her son Duncan's studies; news of a malignant fever in Philadelphia, and precautions taken by New York to keep it off. Limerick, 1793. (1)

(*z*) Letters, 1806-13, from Duncan Pearsall Campbell to Mary Campbell, his aunt by marriage. (2128/1-8)

Subjects include:

His intention of returning to America, postponing a continental tour because of the probability of war between Spain and America. Waterford, Feb. 1806. (2)

Prospect of a speedy adjustment of the differences between England and America; resignation of Jefferson and election of Madison, 'the latter although a democrat is I believe attached to the interests of his country'; Jefferson's attitude towards France. New York, 1809. (4)

Effect of British Orders in Council and French Berlin and Milan Decrees on American trade; quarrel betweeen the President and the Secretary of State. New York, 1811. (7)

Death of his wife, Catherine Bayard, 'the handsomest woman in America'. New York, 1813. (8)

(*aa*) Case, n.d., relating to debt owed since 1731 by late Tweedie Somervell of the province of South Carolina, to Samuel Wragg of London, merchant. (3340/1-2)

(*bb*) Letter, n.d., from Patrick Campbell, nephew of John Campbell of Barcaldine, informing him that 'poor Charles is a prisoner near Boston, however they are well treated, none of their baggage or money taken from them, and allowed to wear their swords'. (1025)

HENDERSON OF FORDELL MUNIMENTS. (GD. 172)[7]

(*a*) American papers (thirty-one items), 1761-86, of Gen. Robertson, including personal accounts and papers concerning lands purchased by Robertson in New York and Philadelphia. (box 48, bundle R.o.*)

Items include:

Order for distributing rebel houses for quartering the troops, providing a fund for the poor and accommodating distressed refugees, n.d. (2)

Account of provisions stored at Springfield and Worcester, 1763. (5)

(*b*) 124 letters, 1761-1811, to Gen. Robertson and his executors, mainly concerning military matters, Robertson's estates and business affairs, applications for patronage, personal matters and Robertson's executry. (box 46, bundle R.d.*)

Subjects include:

Proceedings in Parliament on American affairs. London, 3 Mar. 1775. (20)

Unexpected success at Savannah and the Spanish Main which 'have given a little phillip to our drooping spirits'. London, 6 Jan. 1780. (26)

Petition from William Hartshorne, merchant, New York, for leave to buy wood from Long Island for repairing houses in New York, 1 April 1780. (28)

Contingency plans in case of an enemy invasion of Long Island, 19 July 1780. (31)

Affairs of Congress, then sitting in New York, 8 Feb. 1785. (56)

Measures taken by the people of Boston against British trade 'but it was no legal town meeting'. New York, 2 May 1785. (59)

Distress in America. New York, 7 July 1785. (60)

(*c*) Twenty papers, 1763-86, relating to Gen. Robertson's Florida estate. (box 48, bundle R.r.*)

Items include:

Historical account of Florida written by Gen. Robertson, n.d. (2)

7. The papers listed below all relate to General James Robertson, who served in America from 1756 to 1783, and was Barrackmaster General in America 1765-76, and Governor of New York 1779-83.

(*d*) Fifty-seven accounts and vouchers relating to Gen. Robertson's services in America, 1763-83. (box 49, bundle R.t.*)

(*e*) Seventeen letters from Gen. Robertson, mainly to various military commanders in America, 1766-85. (box 46, bundle R.a.*)

Subjects include:

'It is now absolutely necessary that a magazine of fewel sufficient to supply this garrison be immediately provided'. New York, 6 May 1780. (4)

'For want of forage in this town, it is become necessary to send a number of horses belonging to the king to be grased in the country'. New York, 27 May 1780. (5)

Possible attack by Washington on Staten Island and Paulus Hook. New York, 30 July 1780. (7)

Movements of Gen. Washington. New York, 7 Aug. 1780. (8)

(*f*) Fourteen papers, 1776-91, relating to the claim on Gen. Robertson's estate by Joseph Page, formerly assistant barrack-master to Robertson in America and later employed as his agent. (box 48, bundle R.q.*)

(*g*) Letter-book, 1780-3, of Gen. Robertson as Governor of New York. Indexed. (vol. R.u.*)

(*h*) Order book, 1781-3, of Gen. Robertson as Governor of New York. (vol. R.v.*)

(*i*) Nineteen papers relating to Lord Perth's estate in the Jerseys, over which Gen. Robertson had powers of attorney, 1782-6. (box 48, bundle R.p.*)

Items include:

Letter from Elias Boudinot, Philadelphia, to Robertson: 'I have, tho' with some difficulty, preserved his estate from confiscation, an inquisition having been found against him', 1783. (2)

Account due by Thomas, Lord Drummond, to Dr. Peter Middleton, New York, for medicines and attendance, 1776-8. (8)

Letter from Walter Rutherfurd, Edgerston, to Robertson, noting that the market for land was glutted, 1785. (13)

(*j*) 128 papers, 1783-1817, relating to claim by the Treasury on Gen. Robertson's estate for unsettled accounts contracted during his service in America. (boxes 48-9, bundles R.s.I and II*)

MACLAINE OF LOCHBUIE MUNIMENTS. (GD.174)

I. General

(*a*) Letter of credit, 1756, for James Spalding, who is to carry linen to America; with note concerning Spalding's Indian store at Satilly. (2043)

(*b*) Minute of agreement between James Spalding, merchant in East Florida, and the creditors of the deceased James Spalding of Bonnington Mills [Edinburgh], and related papers. 1770-2. (2068-72)

(*c*) Letter, 1773, from Malcolm McLean, Boston, New England, to John McLean, farmer in parish of Lochbuy, advising on his brother's apprenticeship. (1294)

(*d*) Title deeds and other papers, 1773-95, relating to Bonnington Mills and other lands belonging to James Spalding, merchant in East Florida. (2076; 2082; 2084)

(*e*) Letters of obligation, 1775, by Murdoch McLaine, merchant in Edinburgh, to the trustees for the creditors of James Campbell, saddler in Glasgow, in reference to debt by Messrs. Kelsal and Spalding, merchants in Georgia, to Campbell; and permission by the trustees to McLaine to go to America. (2080)

(*f*) Letter, 1776, from Hector McLaine, New York, describing a shipwreck in which he lost all his family. (1303)

(*g*) Three letters, 1776-9, from Donald McLaine, Edinburgh, to Archibald MacLaine of Lochbuy, in America, advising him on his affairs and military prospects. (1307)

(*h*) Letter, 1778, from Allan Macdougall, Edinburgh, to John McLaine of Lochbuy, giving news of latter's son [Archibald] in America. (1315)

(*i*) Letter, 1778, from Archibald McLaine, Halifax, to Lieut. John McLean of the Royal Highland Emigrants, concerning an account to him. (1317)

(*j*) Four letters, 1778-9, to Archibald Maclaine in America, congratulating him on 'miracoulous eskapes' and giving family news. (1316)

(*k*) Two letters, 1779, from Hector Maclean, Fort Edward [N.Y.], to Capt. Murdoch Maclaine at Halifax, concerning his sister's allowance. (1321)

(*l*) Letter, 1779, from John Ogilvie, London, to Capt. Murdoch McLaine, Edinburgh, advising him to sail to New York. (1323)

(*m*) Twenty-three miscellaneous personal accounts due by Capt. Murdoch Maclaine whilst in North America, 1779-84. (585)

(*n*) Letter, 1780, to Capt. Lieut. John Maclean, Royal Highland Emigrants, Halifax, from John Campbell, his brother-in-law, Edinburgh, who proposes to study English law and then go to Virginia. (1334)

(*o*) Three letters, 1780-1, from Archibald McLaine of Lochbuy, in America, to his brother, concerning his military career. (1339)

(*p*) Two letters, 1781-2, from Capt. Murdoch Maclaine, Charleston, to Donald Maclaine, Edinburgh, mostly giving financial instructions. (1338/2-3)

(*q*) Letter, 1783, from Archibald MacLaine of Lochbuy, N.Y., on financial matters. (1274/4)

(*r*) Two letters (in French), 1783, to Archibald McLaine of Lochbuy from Charlotte Lemaitre, Rivière du Loup [Quebec] and her son, Washington McLaine [evidently Archibald's child]. (1354)

(*s*) Letter, 1783, from William Dickson, Paulus Hook, to Archibald McLean, New York - his men have been ordered to embark and he is too busy to dine. (1355)

(*t*) Letters, 1783-4, from Archibald McLaine of Lochbuy, N.Y., to Capt. Murdoch McLaine, 84th Regiment, concerning the confusion in New York before the British evacuation, and purchase of land in Virginia. (1286/7-8)

(*u*) Letter, 1784, from John McLaine, New York, to Capt. Archibald McLean there, concerning Alan McLean, who robbed his landlady. (1361)

(*v*) Letter, 1784, from William Lowther, New York, to Capt. Archibald McLean, accepting him as a suitor for his daughter. (1363)

(*w*) Deed of sale, 1784, by William Lowther, merchant of the city of New York, to Archibald McLaine, of a Negro wench called Dorcas. (174)

(*x*) Missive of agreement, 1784, between Archibald McLaine and Peter Vanbrooke Livingston, whereby McLaine is to settle 100 families on land in Virginia. (175)

(*y*) Letter, 1784, to Archibald McLaine, at Kingston, Jamaica, from T. Lowther [his brother-in-law] at New York, whither he has had a disagreeable voyage. (1365)

(*z*) Four letters, 1785, from T. Lowther and W. Lowther, New York, to Murdoch McLaine of Lochbuie, concerning the financial position of Archibald McLaine's widow. (1375)

(*aa*) Letter, 1785, from Barbara McLaine [Archibald's widow], Chelsea, to Murdoch McLaine, refusing to return to America. (1377)

(*bb*) Letter, 1834, from Charles Maclean [son of Donald Maclean, writer to the Signet], Edinburgh, to Murdoch Maclaine of Lochbuy, explaining his decision to emigrate to America. (1688/3)

(*cc*) Account settled with the late tenants of Cameron, 'gone to America', 1843. (1180)

II. Papers relating to the Royal Highland Emigrants (84th Foot) serving in North America

(*a*) Letter, 1775, from Major John Small, Charleston, to Hugh

Maclean, writer in Glasgow, concerning regimental clothing. (2092)
(*b*) Obligation, 1775, by passengers on the *Glasgow Packet* to serve in America in the regiment of Royal Highland Emigrants under the command of Lieut. Col. Allan McLean. (2093)
(*c*) Obligation, 1775, by Dugald Campbell, Lagan, to John Gillies, workman there, that his son will serve as piper only upon recruiting service and is not to be enlisted. (2094)
(*d*) Return of clothing and arms, 1775, for the Royal Highland Emigrants. (2095)
(*e*) List of men upon the estate of Lochbuy who engaged to enlist with Archibald McLaine of Lochbuy, 1775. (2096)
(*f*) Statements of account, 1775-6, between Capt. Murdoch Maclaine and the Royal Highland Emigrants. (2097/1-3)
(*g*) Six papers, 1775-9, concerning accounts between the Royal Highland Emigrants and Hugh Maclean, writer in Glasgow. (2098)
(*h*) Stated account, 1776, of the Royal Highland Emigrants with Hugh Fraser and Alexander Chisholm in respect of expenses of the voyage to Boston. (2099)
(*i*) Letter, 1776, from Walter Ross, London, to Col. Allan McLean at Quebec, stating that the account due by the colonel has been settled by Capt. Murdoch McLean. (2101)
(*j*) Invoice of equipment, 1776, for Col. Maclean's corps [Royal Highland Emigrants]. (2102)
(*k*) Seventeen papers, 9 Aug.- 6 Nov. 1776, concerning the voyage of the *Newcastle Jean* from London to Halifax carrying clothing for the Royal Highland Emigrants, and including details of an engagement with an American privateer. (2103)
(*l*) Policy of assurance, 1776, by several subscribers to Donald McLaine, merchant in Edinburgh, on account of Capt. Murdoch McLaine, in respect of equipment on board the *Newcastle Jean* between Spithead and Halifax. (2104)
(*m*) Seventeen papers, 1776-9, concerning visit of Capt. Murdoch McLean to England and Scotland between Feb. and Oct. 1776 to settle business of the regiment of the Royal Highland Emigrants, particularly to procure arms and clothing. (2100)
(*n*) Seven ledger account pay-books, 1776-83, of Capt. Murdoch Maclaine's company in the 84th Regiment in North America. Indexed. (2106/1-7)
(*o*) Letter, 1778, from Gen. Allan MacLean, Quebec, to Major John Small, Royal Highland Emigrants, Halifax, on regimental and personal matters. (2116)
(*p*) Draft letter, 1778, from Murdoch MacLaine, Phila[delphia], to Lieut. Hugh Fraser, Royal Highland Emigrants, instructing him to repair to his regiment. (2119)
(*q*) Lists of men in the 2nd Battalion of the Royal Highland Emigrants, Philadelphia and New York, 1778. (2120/1-4)
(*r*) Five accounts, 1778, of pay, etc., due to soldiers of the 2nd Battalion of the Royal Highland Emigrants. (2121)
(*s*) Instruction, 1778, by Archibald McLaine, New York, to Ensign O'Connell of the 20th Regiment, to pay bearer. (2122)
(*t*) Bond of indemnity (untested), 1778, by Capt. Murdoch Maclean and Capt. Lieut. John Maclean to Capt. Alexander Macdonald, paymaster of the 2nd Battalion of the Royal Highland Regiment, of the balance of his account to Capt. Neil Maclean; with statement of the account and draft discharge. (2124)
(*u*) Five abstract accounts, 1778-83, of Capt. Murdoch Maclaine's company. (2125)
(*v*) Thirty-one miscellaneous papers, 1778-83, concerning the accounts of Capt. Murdoch McLaine in respect of the 2nd Battalion of the 84th Regiment in North America. (2126)
(*w*) Nine letters, 1778-84, from Capt. Alexander McDonald, Fort Edward and Halifax, to Capt. Murdoch McLaine of the 84th Regiment, mostly concerning regimental matters, especially accounts. (2127)
(*x*) Attestation, 1779, by Gen. Eyre Massey of the military service of Capt. Murdoch Maclaine of the 84th Regiment in North America; with copies and covering letter. (2128)
(*y*) Draft of regimental orders, 28 May [1779]. (2129)
(*z*) Letter, [1779], from Allan Maclean, Montreal, to Lieut. Archibald Maclaine of the 84th Regiment, advising him about his new light infantry company. (2133)
(*aa*) List of officers in America sent letters on the *Polly*, 1779. (2134)
(*bb*) Two notes, 1779, of clothes and other merchandise to be obtained for army officers [in Nova Scotia]. (2138)
(*cc*) Stated accounts, 1779-87, between Capt. Alexander McDonald, paymaster of 2nd Battalion, 84th Regiment, and Capt. Murdoch Maclaine, and letters and other papers concerning a dispute arising therefrom. (2140)
(*dd*) Stated accounts, 1779-81, between Capt. Murdoch McLaine and Col. John Small of the 84th Regiment, and related papers. (2141)
(*ee*) Letter, 1780, to [Lieut. Archibald] McLaine, at Niagara, concerning promotion prospects. (2143)
(*ff*) Letter, 1780, from the War Office to Capt. Murdoch Maclaine, permitting him to embark for Canada to rejoin his regiment. (2146)
(*gg*) Letter, 1780, from John McLean, New York, to Capt. Murdoch McLaine of the 84th Regiment, offering pecuniary assistance in purchasing promotion. (2148)
(*hh*) Miscellaneous undated documents, *c*. 1780.
List of residents in Long Island. (2114)
Note from Mr. Livingston to Capt. McLaine, advising British officers not to attend the Assembly. (2149)
Note concerning military clothing to go to New York. (2150)
Prescription for horses of the 84th Regiment at the manor of Edmonston. (2151)
(*ii*) Two letters, 1780-2, from Archibald McLaine of Lochbuy, Quebec, to Capt. Murdoch McLaine of the 84th Regiment in Nova Scotia, giving news of regimental activities including his own court-martial. (2147)
(*jj*) Letters, 1780-4, from Lieut. Hector MacLean in Ireland and North America, to Capt. Murdoch Maclaine of the 84th Regiment, concerning regimental and personal matters. (2154/1-16)
Subjects include:
Protection for the men recruited in Newfoundland for North American regiments but now shipwrecked on the island of Bophin in the west of Ireland. (2)
Battle of Eutaw Springs and its aftermath. (4-7)
(*kk*) Letter, 1781, from W. Hamilton, Quebec, to Lieut. Archibald McLaine, 84th Regiment, gossiping about local and military matters. (2155)
(*ll*) Letter, 14 Feb. 1781, from Lieut. Lachlan McLean, at Camp near Monks Corner, to Capt. Murdoch McLaine, 84th Regiment, at Charleston, concerning the need for horses. (2156)
(*mm*) Letter, 8 Oct. 1781, from Robert Brydon, Charleston, to Capt. Murdoch Maclaine, 84th Regiment, applying to be a non-commissioned officer in the regiment. (2158)
(*nn*) Declaration, 1781, by Duncan McArthur, tailor in the 84th Regiment, concerning regimental clothing in Hector McQuarrie's possession when taken prisoner. (2159)
(*oo*) Three letters, 1781-3, from Capt. Ranald McKinnon, Pocotaligo, North Bluff, and Argyle, to Capt. Murdoch MacLaine, 84th Regiment, requiring money for his company and concerning his family's welfare. (2160)
(*pp*) Letter, 1782, from Lieut. Archibald McLean, New York Volunteers, to Capt. Murdoch McLean, 84th Regiment, concerning his army prospects. (2161)
(*qq*) Twenty-six papers, 1782-3, concerning the court-martial at Quebec of Capt. Archibald Maclaine of Lochbuy, 84th Regiment, on the charge of defaming Brig. Gen. Allan Maclean; includes references

to Maclaine's service in the American war. (2162)
(*rr*) Letter, 1782, from Alexander Grant, Oswego, to Capt. Archibald McLaine, 84th Regiment, at St. Anns, on military matters. (2165)
(*ss*) Letter, *c.* 1782, from R. Houghton, Trois Rivières, to Capt. [Archibald?] McLaine, 84th Regiment, concerning moccasins. (2166)
(*tt*) Statement of account, 1782, of Sir Henry Clinton in respect of the second Battalion of Royal Highland Emigrants. (2169)
(*uu*) Letter, 25 Sept. 1783, from Robert Morse, chief engineer, Annapolis Royal, to Capt. McLean of the 84th Regiment there, requiring a working party to repair fort buildings. (2173)
(*vv*) Letter, 1783, from Donald McKinnon to Capt. Archibald McLean [of Lochbuy], stating that service in the 84th Regiment has been a financial misfortune. (2175)
(*ww*) Provision, fuel and clothing returns, lists and delivery notes, 1783, for the 84th Regiment at Fort Edward [N.Y.]. (2176)
(*xx*) Ten papers, 1783-5, concerning the allocation to officers and men of the 84th Regiment of land in Nova Scotia. (2177)
(*yy*) Letter, 1784, from the War Office to Capt. Murdoch Maclaine, 84th Regiment, concerning a demand for ration money by former prisoners of war. (2179)
(*zz*) List of prisoners taken in 1778, mentioned in an annexed account with Capt. Murdoch Maclaine of the Royal Highlanders, 1784. (2180)
(*aaa*) Letters, 1785-9, from Col. Allan MacLean and Col. John Small, London, to Capt. Murdoch Maclaine of Lochbuy, concerning the settlement of the former accounts of the 84th Regiment. (2187)
(*bbb*) Letter, 1786, from Alexander Chisolm, Glasgow, to Murdoch McLean of Lochbuie, requesting his volunteer's pay retained in 1778 because he was a prisoner with rebels. (2188)
(*ccc*) Two papers, 1790, concerning claim by Capt. Murdoch Maclaine on behalf of his company for prize money won in 1777 which James Park should pay. (2195)
(*ddd*) Memorial, 1790, to the secretary at war from Capt. Murdoch Maclaine, narrating his military services in America and asking to be put on full pay. (2196/1)

COLLINS PAPERS. (GD. 177)

(*a*) Correspondence, 1836-48, of Edward Collins, merchant in Canada, on various topics including threat of war with the United States in 1838, difficulties of banks in Philadelphia, Boston, and New York in 1839, and his travels in Canada and the U.S.A. (box 3*)
(*b*) Diary of a business tour, 1843, by Edward Collins through the country to the north of Lakes Ontario and Erie as far as Detroit. (box 3*)
(*c*) Letters, 1890-3, from Hugh Collins while travelling in Canada and the U.S.A.; includes a letter to his mother, written from Chicago, Jan. 1891, describing recent train journeys: the letterhead is illustrated with a picture of the 'Palmer' hotel, and on the back is 'World's Fair Map, Chicago, 1893' with the route of Collins' journey across Canada and the U.S.A. marked. (box 3*)

CATHCART OF GENOCH MUNIMENTS. (GD. 180)

(*a*) Letters, 1737-42, from William Cathcart to his brother, John Cathcart of Genoch. (604/1-2)
Subjects include:
Gathering together of his cargo of 'goods and medecines' to go to America. London, 1737. (1)
His marriage to 'the governor's d[aughter] in law'; requests wine for the governor and plaid for his wife to be sent. Edenhouse [? North Carolina], 1742. (2)
(*b*) Two letters, 1758-60, from John Rutherfurd of North Carolina, London, [to John Cathcart of Genoch]; with enclosed copy letter from Dr. William Cathcart in North Carolina, brother of Genoch, to Rutherfurd; and copy letter [from John Cathcart] to Rutherfurd. (624/1-4)
Subjects include:
News of Dr. Cathcart: 'by meanes of his vastly extensive business in the phisical way occasioned by the small pox in that country, he has greatly mended his fortunes'. (3)
Education of Dr. Cathcart's son Gabriel, in Scots law. (1, 4)
(*c*) Letters, 1760-9, from Dr. William Cathcart, Virginia and North Carolina, to Robert Cathcart, his nephew. (625/1-4)
Subjects include:
Negro boy named Luck, whom he sends; bill of exchange for the education of his son; and indigo seeds, 1760. (1)
Financial misfortunes of Mr. Palmer, which may defeat Dr. Cathcart's scheme for the education of his son, Gabriel, 1763. (2)
Request for a 'carefull industrious labouring man', 1764. (3)
(*d*) Letters, 1764-5, from Gabriel Cathcart, North Carolina, to Robert Cathcart of Genoch, his cousin. (629/1-2)
Subjects include:
Farming methods; arrangements for a young lad from Ballantrae to come out as an overseer of slaves; request for tea, linen, and boots. (1)
Asks for patronage in order to obtain the post of receiver for North Carolina; repeats his former requests for an overseer, linen, and boots. (2)
(*e*) Letter, 1773, from Samuel Johnston, North Carolina, to Robert Cathcart of Genoch, announcing the death of Dr. William Cathcart, uncle of Robert and father-in-law of Johnston. (644)
(*f*) Letter, 1828, from William Cadell, Edinburgh, to John Cathcart of Genoch, concerning the escape to America of James Stuart of Dunearn, writer to the Signet, who had indulged in many speculations and left many large debts. (685/1)

ABERCROMBY OF FORGLEN MUNIMENTS. (GD. 185)

(*a*) Letter, 1741, from Mary Duff about the death of her son William on a plantation near Georgetown, S.C. (box 6, bundle 28*)
(*b*) Letter, 1757, from Capt. John Abercromby, Halifax, to Sir Robert Abercromby, mentioning Capt. Fesch of the Royal Americans, whom Gen. Montcalm took as hostage for the capitulation of Fort William Henry, and his account of the surrender of the fort. (box 6, bundle 28*)
(*c*) Letter-book, 1788-1806, of Samuel Douglas, of Douglas and Shaw, London, mainly regarding the shipment of goods to New York; most of the letters are written to George Douglas, his brother. (box 38*)
(*d*) Letters, 1852, from the Rev. James Abercrombie, Episcopal clergyman, Cape Vincent, N.Y., regarding his ancestors from Dundee and his family in America. (box 28*)

LEITH ROSS MUNIMENTS. (GD. 186)

(*a*) Papers and correspondence, 1775-90, of John Ross younger of Arnage, relating to his residence in East Florida as plantation factor. (box 4, bundle 10*)
Items include:
Letter from John Ross, St. Augustine, to his father, informing him that he is working for Mr. Gray for £50 a year, supervising the management of several settlements in East Florida, 1776.
Manumission by John Ross of Sophia, aged 9, mulatto child of his Negro slave Bella, 1782.
Letter from John Ross about the evacuation of British troops: 'we have no room to doubt that we are abandoned by our native country', 1782.

(*b*) Ledger of John Ross, 1782-5, East Florida plantations. (box 12, no. 5*)

STEEL-MAITLAND MUNIMENTS. (GD.193)

(*a*) Letters, 1798, from Robert Liston, British Minister in the U.S.A., to Brig. Gen. Thomas Maitland, British commander in Santo Domingo, about French refugees evacuated from Santo Domingo to America, with petitions from them. (box 3, bundle 14*)
(*b*) Letter, 1798, from Liston to Maitland concerning the American attitude to Santo Domingo and complaints of British interference with American trade and shipping. (box 4, bundle 2*)
(*c*) Papers, 1919-21, relating to the world economic crisis after the First World War, including correspondence between Sir Arthur Steel-Maitland and various bankers explaining conditions in America. (box 122, file 3*)
(*d*) Travel diary, 1921, of Sir Arthur Steel-Maitland [typescript], the latter part describing his passage through the Panama Canal and journey across America, including visits to Metro Studios, the Grand Canyon, Chicago, Washington, and New York, and meetings with Hoover, Sen. Lodge, and others; with MS. drafts. (box 84, nos. 1, 3*)
(*e*) Correspondence, 1931, relating to invitation to Steel-Maitland to lecture at the Academy of Political Science, New York. (box 254, bundle 2 'A'*)
(*f*) Correspondence, 1931-3, with L.G. M. Gall, Cheltenham [England], about scheme for hospitality by members of Parliament to visiting American congressmen. (box 254, bundle 2 'G'*)

ROSS OF PITCALNIE MUNIMENTS. (GD.199)

(*a*) Letter, 1748, from Simon Dunbar, Newport, R.I., to John Dunbar of Burgie, his father. Will endeavour to send some money when he reaches Carolina; has been disappointed at Boston of a prize taken by a privateer, 'the accounts of a peace has disconcerted my measures a good deal as I am concerned in privateering'. (99)
(*b*) Letters, 1748-50, from Simon Dunbar to his sister, Mrs. Gordon. (207-8)
Subjects include:
Plans to settle down and perhaps marry. Newport, R.I., 1748. (207)
Robert's imprudent match with his landlady's daughter. Charleston, 1749. (207)
His intention of continuing with his African scheme, but will not stay if the climate disagrees with him. Charleston, 1750. (208)
(*c*) Letter, 1756, from George Seaman, Charleston, S.C., to his cousin, Lady Pitcalny, discussing his reluctance to move to the other side of the water: 'I have even a regard for many of my faithfull slaves that leaves happy been born in my house and dalie fed with soomthing from the table that would probably fall in the hands of those that would use them in ane other manner'. (227)
(*d*) Two letters, 1777-80, from Daniel Ross, Antigua, to Munro Ross of Pitcalny, concerning his departure from Charleston, where he could have made a small fortune, 'but seeing there resolutions in declairing independance obliged me to depart from the seat of rebellion before I woud take up arms against my king and country'. (255; 273)
(*e*) Letter, 1781, from Elizabeth MacKenzie, Inverness, to Lady Pitcalnie, quoting a letter from her sister-in-law in America or perhaps Jamaica, giving an account of distresses and numbers of white people and Negroes dying of want. (119)
(*f*) Letter, [1819], from Edmund Kean [the actor], York to Michael Kelly, informing him that he would quit England for America by the end of September. (181)

CLANRANALD MUNIMENTS. (GD.201)

Letter, 1757, from Roderick Macleod to Clanranald, referring to additional companies for various regiments which are at Greenock, ready to sail for Ireland and thence to America. (4/84)

LINDSAY MUNIMENTS. (GD.203)

(*a*) Letters, 1729-52, from John Lindsay and his wife, Penelope Lindsay, to his family in Scotland. (11/45, bundle 1*)
Subjects include:
His arrival in America: 'this is certainly the finest part of the world and in a few centuries will be much more considerable than Brittain'. Philadelphia, 1729.
Has received a grant of 3,000 acres of land from the governor of New York, 1733.
His marriage to the daughter of Capt. Congreves, an officer in America, 1739.
Proposed settlement of over a hundred families on his land, 1740.
His appointment as lieutenant governor of the fort at Oswego, 1748.
His death of apoplexy, 1751.
(*b*) Letter, 1747, from John Lindsay, Schenectady, [N.Y.], to his brother, the Laird of Wormistone, on the danger from local Indians and his appointment as quartermaster of a fort built about forty miles away by the army raised to go against Canada. (8/2/98*)
(*c*) Letters and papers, 1783-6, relating to the supposed claim of John Bethune of Kilconquhar [formerly Lindsay of Wormistone] to John Lindsay's property in New York State. (11/45, bundle 3*)
(*d*) Letters and papers, 1824-6, relating to the supposed claim of Henry Bethune of Kilconquhar to the above property. (11/45, bundle 4*)
(*e*) Letters and papers, 1887-91, relating to the Earl of Lindsay's supposed claim to the estate of New Wormistone, near Warminster, N.Y. (11/45, bundles 6-8*)
(*f*) Memorials and other papers, 1887-94, relating to the Earl of Lindsay's claim, including biographical sketch of John Lindsay. (11/45, bundle 9*)

OGILVY OF INVERQUHARITY MUNIMENTS. (GD.205)

Royal letter, 1671, instructing Sir John Nisbet, Lord Advocate, to prepare a signature [warrant] for a charter under the great seal of Scotland to certain Scots, of territory lying between 'the river of St. Mathias which bordereth upon the coast of Carolina' and 'the southermost parte of pointe of Cape-Florida... and soe west in a direct line as farre as the South Seas', together with 'the island commonly called Dominica or Domingo, which is one of the Carribee Islands'; with covering letter from the Earl of Lauderdale suggesting that two separate patents should be drawn. See *Calendar of State Papers Domestic*, 1671, 378. (box 40, portfolio 10, nos. 13/3-4*)

HALL OF DUNGLASS MUNIMENTS. (GD.206)

(*a*) Letter, 1752, from Dr. [afterwards Sir] John Pringle to Sir John Hall referring to the weekly meetings between himself, Mr. Smeaton, Dr. Knight, 'the king of magnetism', and [Benjamin] Franklin, 'sovereign of electricity'. (2/554/7)
(*b*) Letters, 1775-6, from Col. James Pringle to William Hall. (2/443)
Subjects include:
'Tedious long days in the House of Commons on American affairs', 1775. (2)
Victory at Long Island, 1776. (7)
(*c*) Letter [unsigned, in French, from a former member of the French

National Assembly], Torniglia, commenting on the writer's exile, the possibility of refuge in America, and his livelihood from painting churches and interiors of houses, 1794. (2/543)

HANNAY PAPERS. (GD.214)

(*a*) Bills of exchange and other papers, 1718, relating to tobacco imported to Glasgow from Maryland. (241/7)
(*b*) Letter, 1762, from Alexander Duncan, Wilmington, N.C., desiring settlement of his partnership accounts with the deceased Michael Ancrum, merchant, Edinburgh, and giving lists of queries about shipments, etc., between 1758 and 1760. (720/1)
(*c*) Letter, 1770, from Patrick Colquhoun, Glasgow, to John Davidson, crown agent, Edinburgh, offering to contract for transporting felons to the colonies. (726/2)
(*d*) Memorial, 1786, for James Drummond of Perth concerning debts affecting his father's estate and the family's property in New Jersey. (436)
(*e*) Letter, 1840, from Capt. Frederick Marryat [the author] to Alexander Young, writer to the Signet, Edinburgh - agrees with Young's opinion of Thomas Jefferson and 'could have stated some facts well known which would prove how very different his practice was from his writings, but the details were too gross for publication'; there is 'more of what the Americans term in their public accounts *Conciliation money* (what we would term Secret Service money) expended in this country than in any other', mainly among the press. (747/20)

SCARTH OF BRECKNESS MUNIMENTS. (GD.217)

Contract, 1668, between Harry Grahame of Breckness and James Grahame his brother on one part and William Foulis, merchant, Edinburgh, bound for Virginia, on the other part, whereby James is to go to Virginia with William Foulis to be indented to a master. (586)

MURRAY OF MURRAYTHWAITE MUNIMENTS. (GD.219)

(*a*) Eight letters, 1747-63, between John Murray of Murraywhat [later Murraythwaite] and his cousin, Dr. John Murray, Charleston, S.C. (284)
Subjects include:
John's prospect of a legal career and purchase of the office of secretary of the province, 1750. (4)
John's brother, William, in medical practice in South Carolina and later in partnership with Dr. Murray, 1753. (5)
The linen trade, 1755. (6)
Comments on governor of South Carolina, 1763. (8)
(*b*) Letter, 1749, from John Fairgreive, London, to his cousin, William Murray, on the latter's departure for South Carolina. (285/1)
(*c*) Twenty letters, 1750-65, from John and William Murray to their mother Elizabeth Dalrymple or Murray, Lady Murraywhat. (287)
Subjects include:
William's medical practice in South Carolina, 1750-3. (1, 4)
John's purchase of the office of secretary of the province and transactions in that office, 1753-4. (2, 3, 7)
John's impressions of Charleston, [1754]. (7)
John's trading ventures, 1755-6. (9-10)
John's expedition with the governor to build a fort among the Cherokees, 1756. (11)
Their plantation near Port Royal, S.C., 1757. (12)
Smallpox epidemic in Charleston, 1763. (16-17)
(*d*) Seventeen letters, 1751-65, between John Murray and William Murray. (288)
Subjects include:
William's medical practice at Georgetown and later at Charleston, 1751-2. (1, 4)
John's purchase of the office of secretary of the province and subsequent dealings with the patentee, John Hammerton, 1753-61. (6, 10-11)
William's actings in the office during John's absence, including arrangement of the records and conversations with the governor, 1754. (7)
Purchase and management of a plantation, 1755-64. (9, 12, 13, 15)
John's efforts to retain office of secretary, 1762. (12, 13)
Effects of the Seven Years War on American trade, 1762. (13)
William's return from South Carolina, 1765. (16-17)
(*e*) Nine letters, 1754-63, relating to John Murray's interest in America. (289)
To John Pownall, secretary to the Board of Trade, about deputation as secretary of South Carolina, 1754. (1)
To Hew Dalrymple, advocate, about visit to South Carolina, 1754. (2)
To James Oswald, Board of Trade, about agreement with Mr. Powell, who had a prior deputation from John Hammerton, that Murray should hold office as 'pro-deputy secretary', 1755. (3)
From John Murray of Philiphaugh about his brother's purchase of a plantation in South Carolina, 1757. (4)
From Dr. William Graham, Westmorland, Jamaica, about trading difficulties arising out of the Seven Years War, 1757. (5)
From Adam Smart, Antigua, on financial matters, 1758. (6)
To Ebenezer McCulloch, manager of the British Linen Company, about company business and linen sent out to Carolina, 1759. (7)
From George Murray, secretary's office, South Carolina, about office business after William Murray's departure, 1761. (8)
From James Murray, Boston, about prospects of obtaining office in North Carolina, 1763. (9)
(*f*) Letter-book, 1756-8, of John Murray, mainly about trading affairs of partnership of John and James Murray, Charleston, and supply of goods from British Linen Company. (290)
Addresses and subjects of letters include:
James Oswald, Board of Trade - arrangements in secretary's office, conditions in South Carolina, negotiations with Cherokees and Creek Indians, proposed forts, 1756. (p.3)
Viscount Stormont - general remarks on America, danger from French, South Carolina's policy of friendship with Indians contrasted with that of other colonies, 1756; account of the last campaign in America, capitulation of Oswego, lack of effect of war on South Carolina, 1757; agreement by congress of governors at Philadelphia to raise troops for mutual defence, 1757. (pp. 13, 33, 44)
James Fea - proposals for shipping route to Orkney rejected by merchants in South Carolina, who prefer to risk loss of cargoes by capture at sea, because they receive full value from the insurers instead of the uncertain price commodities might fetch in the British market, 1756. (p. 18)
Dr. William Graham, Jamaica - trading ventures, Cathcart's ship plundered off Cuba, complaint of 'turbulent disposition' of some American troops, who were responsible for loss of Oswego, 1756. (p.26)
Lord Mansfield - shipment of wines, assistance in retaining office as secretary, [1757]; of ships sailing from Charleston all but two fell into enemy hands, 1757. (pp. 36, 45)
Sir Robert Laurie of Maxweltown - description of late Sir Alexander

Nisbet's estate in South Carolina, 1757. (p.48)
John Murray of Philiphaugh - his brother's plantation on an island near Port Royal, 1757. (p.49)

(*g*) Letter, 1759, from Ann Murray, Charleston, to [Elizabeth Murray, John Murray's mother] with family news. (286/4)

(*h*) Undertaking, 1761, by George Murray to execute the office of secretary [of South Carolina] and to pay 'Mr. Johnston's board and salary for six months or until removal, on payment of £1,000 currency.' (314)

(*i*) Memorandum [by John Murray] on John Hammerton's deputation to him in the office of secretary and register of South Carolina and his willingness to resign for a new joint patent to himself and Murray. [1761] (315)

(*j*) Letter, 1762, from Dr. John Murray, Charleston, to William Murray, about medical practitioners in Charleston. (285/5)

(*k*) Draft memorandum [by John Murray] to Lord Shelburne on the methods of granting lands in the American colonies, with particular reference to Georgia, Florida, and South Carolina, 1763. (317)

(*l*) Six letters, 1771-87, relating to John Murray of Murraythwaite's property and interests in America. (292)

From James Simpson, Charleston, to Robert Wells, about state and value of Murray's property near Saludy River, 1771. (1)

From Robert Wells, Charleston, to Murray about negotiations for sale of part of property to Champneys Terry, as agent for Colonel Taylor of Virginia, and auction of the rest; with postscript reporting sale of the Port Royal tract and the dissolution of the Assembly, no tax bill having been passed since 1769. 1772. (2)

From Elizabeth Alexander, Charleston, to Murray, her cousin referring to her uncle's death and complaining that 'the people here I think are all mad which makes it disagreeable to have anything to do with them', 1774. (3)

From Murray to Lord [-], offering his services as secretary to the commissioners appointed to negotiate with the Americans: 'Your Lordship has been pleased to tell me that my information when last in America was a means of adjusting the southern boundary of our acquisitions on the Missippi [*sic*] at the peace', [draft, *c.* 1778?]. (4)

From Murray to [-], expressing sympathy for 'the situation of you and many other worthy people in Carolina during the usurped authority of the leaders of the rebellion', [draft, *c.* 1781?]. (5)

From Robert Wells, London, to Murray, expressing his fears that Murray's titles were lost at the time of the great fire in Charleston in January 1778, 'when my daughter Susie, to whom I confided them, was driven from the horrid scene and almost from her senses', though a search in the register of mesne conveyances has revealed some entries, 1787. (6)

(*m*) Letter, 1778, from William Murray of Murrayfield to his brother John Murray of Murraythwaite, detailing financial claims against the latter, including sum 'owing me for acting two years in the secretary's office, of which I never received a farthing' and dividend due on their plantation in South Carolina. (294/1)

(*n*) Letter, 1797, to John Murray of Murraythwaite from his nephew, John Murray, about the latter's proposed journey to America. (296/8)

(*o*) Eight letters, 1798-1800, relating to proceedings for ejectment of settlers on John Murray's property in South Carolina, with a view to its sale, and the grant of new titles by James Simpson to replace those which were lost. (298)

(*p*) Draft letter of attorney, 1799, by James Simpson, late of Charleston, S.C., only son, heir at law and executor of William Simpson, clerk to the Council of South Carolina, to Edwyn Gardiner of Charleston, to execute conveyance to John Murray [of Murraythwaite] of 5,000 acres, part of 50,000 acres at or near the Saluda river in the 'district of Ninety-six' in the state of South Carolina, to supply the deficiency of the said John Murray's titles, which had been lost, mislaid, or destroyed. (326)

MONTROSE MUNIMENTS. (GD.220)

Letters, 1710-4, from Robert Hunter, [Governor of New York] to the Duke of Montrose. (sec. 5*) Wishes that Montrose's nominee was in the post he mentions, but [John] Rayner has been commended by the Duke of Newcastle, who bought his estate. Spithead, 19 Mar. 1709/10.

Complains that he has 'suffer'd here past beliefe and have nothing but hopes to live upon, my family increases in proportion that my means decrease'. New York, 10 June 1714.

MACDONALD MUNIMENTS. (GD.221)

(*a*) Letters, 1739, relating to alleged kidnapping of 113 inhabitants of Skye for transportation to the plantations in America. (104*)

(*b*) List, *c.* 1802, of [Lord Macdonald's] tenants intending to emigrate to America. (25*)

BUCCLEUCH MUNIMENTS. (GD.224)[8]

(*a*) Miscellaneous American papers, 1691-1766. (box 37, bundle 22*)

Including:

Report on the government of the colony of Massachusetts Bay, with appended papers, including minutes on a proposal to renew the colony's charter, 1691.

Statement of Great Britain's trade with all the northern colonies (1715, 1738, 1743, 1746); with statements of imports from and exports to New England (1715, 1738), and individual statements for New York, Virginia, and Maryland, and the Carolinas (1715, 1738), and for Pennsylvania and Georgia (1738).

Representation of the case of the province of Massachusetts Bay that fortresses which may be erected for the defence of H.M. territories be garrisoned by regulars rather than by American troops, 1755.

Letters from John Bradstreet, Schenectady and Albany, on feasibility of inland expeditions in America, and on strength of the French forces at 'Tenenderogue' and Crown Point; also extract from a letter from Gen. Shirley to the secretary at war, recommending Bradstreet, of Sir William Pepperell's Regiment, to the King for his services, 1755-6.

Papers relating to the bill to enable recruiting officers in America to enlist servants; including two memorials of consequences of enlisting servants in Pennsylvania for the Cartagena expedition in 1740, and of enlisting servants under Braddock and Dunbar, and extract from American plantation laws relating to servants, *c.* 1756.

Letter from W. Bollan, Leicester Square, to Charles Townshend, First Lord Commissioner for Trade and Plantations, reporting on prospects for supplying masts, yards and bowsprits for the Royal Navy, 1763.

Letter from Peter Hassenclever, New York, to Townshend, reporting on progress of his project to establish iron manufacturers and a hemp plantation in America and on American discontent, 1765; also three papers on cost of ironworks at Ringwood, Long Pond,

8. Most of the items listed form part of the papers of Charles Townshend, M.P., who held various government offices between 1754 and 1767, including Secretary at War 1761, President of the Board of Trade 1763, Paymaster General 1765-6, and Chancellor of the Exchequer 1766-7. Items dated before 1754 are generally later copies.

and Cortland, scheme for a settlement for raising hemp on the Mohawk River, and purchase of the Pequannock land and rivers.

Report by Andrew Symmar for Townshend on American exports and trade, n.d.

Report on agriculture in America, including raising of silk in Carolina (with plan of a silk house), and growing of Indian corn, tobacco, wheat, rice, and indigo, n.d.

Papers concerning distribution of forces in America, n.d.

Proposals relating to drugs imported into North America, n.d.

(*b*) Miscellaneous papers, 1731-64. (box 46, bundle 45*)

American items include:

Minutes on Rhode Island, covering various subjects including constitution, trade, population (white and black), and revenue, 1731. Thoughts concerning Florida, n.d.

(*c*) Volume, 1735-46, recording representations from American and West Indian colonies to members of the British government. (box 50, no. 7*)

(*d*) Miscellaneous papers, 1737-66. (box 39, bundle 24a*)

American items include:

Extracts from papers laid before the House of Commons about victualling the forces in North America, with observations thereon; also papers relating to victualling contracts, 1737-57.

Three papers relating to claim of Samuel Waldo of Boston for compensation for his expenses and losses during his service on the frontier against the French and their Indians, 1744-6.

Letter [from General William Shirley], Boston, defending himself against complaints about his conduct, during the expedition under Johnson, in procuring Indians to go to Oswego, 1757.

Remonstrance of Agent Partridge, on behalf of New Jersey, Connecticut, and Rhode Island, concerning the money intended to be granted by Parliament to colonies which raised forces in the present expeditions under Shirley and Johnson against the French on their frontiers, 1756.

Memorial of Mr. Henderson concerning the merchants of Glasgow, the nature of their commerce with Virginia and Maryland, and the administration of justice in these colonies, 1766.

Plan for preventing frauds in victualling H.M. land and sea forces in North America, n.d.

Reasons against bringing bar iron from America duty-free, n.d.

(*e*) Return of imports and exports, etc., 1739-66. (box 298, bundle 2/1-26*)

American items include:

Account of the value of British and foreign goods annually imported from England to the British colonies in North America, 1739-64. (24)

Accounts of all English goods annually exported to British colonies in America, 1761-2 and 1762-4. (15, 16)

Accounts of all foreign goods annually exported from England to the British colonies in America, 1762-3 and 1763-4. (12, 14)

Account of the duties annually paid on molasses imported into the various northern colonies in America, 1762-5. (22)

Account of all ships arrived in British forts from the British colonies in America, Nov. 1765 - Jan. 1766. (3)

Return from the Commissioners of Trade and Plantations to the House of Commons, relating to annual expense of the establishments of the British colonies in America, 1766. (10)

(*f*) Accounts from the House of Commons and public offices, 1739-67. (box 39, bundle 23*)

American items include:

Account of the annual value of British and foreign goods exported from England to the British colonies in North America, 1739-64.

Account of annual expenses in department of office of ordnance in maintaining H.M. forts and garrisons in America, 1746-65.

Abstract of charge of H.M. forces in North America and the West Indies, with a comparison of expense of each service for 1751 and 1765.

Account of the expenses of the forces in North America and the West Indies, 1756-66, and of monies impressed to contractors for furnishing H.M. forces there with provisions.

Account of the extraordinary services for which the governors and officers in North America and the West Indies have drawn on the Treasury, including presents to the Indians, voyage up the Mississippi, and taking possession of Mobile, *c.* 1759-66.

Amount of bills drawn by above officers for extraordinary services, *c.* 1759-66.

Estimate for victualling the garrison at St. Augustine, 1764-6.

Account of quantity of hemp and flax imported into England from America, 1764-6.

Four papers relating to the duties imposed in 1764 on goods imported into and exported from the British colonies in America, 1764-7.

Account of the quantity of timber imported into England from the British dominions in America, 1765-6.

Account of the quantity of American bar iron exported from England, 1765-6.

Disposition and state of forces in North America, 1766.

Estimates of the charge of H.M. forces in the plantations for 1766 and 1767 compared.

Estimate of the charge of H.M. forces in the plantations and Africa, 1766-7.

Observations on Gen. Gage's estimate of provisions [for North American forces], n.d.

Gen. Gage's estimate of expenses of America for one year, n.d.

(*g*) Papers, 1748-64, relating to the army, navy, customs and excise, and exchequer. (box 40, bundle 26*)

American items include:

Account of extraordinary expenses incurred in Flanders, North Britain, and America, not provided for by Parliament, 1748.

Account of Negroes annually imported from specified parts of Africa to the West Indies and America in Liverpool ships, 1758-64.

(*h*) Miscellaneous Treasury papers, 1753-66. (box 42, bundle 30*)

American items include:

Dr. Franklin's evidence about the American attitude to the taxes levied on them, [1766].

(*i*) Board of Trade Papers, 1754-6. (box 41, bundle 27*)

American items include:

Narrative of the activities of Gen. Shirley, Commander-in-Chief in America, 1754-6.

Letter from six members of the Assembly of Georgia to John Huske in London, stating that the writers had withdrawn from the Assembly to found a new settlement on the Turtle River beyond the boundaries of the province, and that 'at least one half of the people of Georgia will immediately follow us', 18 Jan. 1755.

Resolution of the House of Representatives of Georgia that 'during the secession of so many members as are now absent from their duty', no laws, orders, or resolutions are to be passed except by unanimous consent of the ten remaining members 'which number is an undeniable majority even when the House is full', 15 Jan. 1755.

Draft bill for the better recruiting of H.M. forces in North America, including the recruitment of indented servants, *c.* 1756.

(*j*) Accounts etc. 1755-66, from the House of Commons and public offices. (box 38, bundle 22a*)

American items include:

Account of the produce of half the old subsidy directed by George

III to be detained and not drawn back after May 1764 on the export of foreign goods to the British colonies in America, Christmas 1763-6.

Annual account of the produce of half the above subsidy left on foreign commodities sent to America, 1763-6.

Account of the quantities of East India silks exported from England to the British colonies in America, 1765-6.

(*k*) Miscellaneous papers, *c.* 1757. (box 299, bundle 4*)

American items include:

Reference to the Lords of Trade of the petition of proprietors of East New Jersey about the province's boundary with New York, and Lords of Trade's report thereon; with two related petitions by Robert Charles, agent for the province of New York, 1757. (2-3)

Draft petition of Robert Hunter Morris offering to make salt in North America if given certain security, n.d. (19)

(*l*) Three papers, *c.* 1757, relating to the import of bar iron from America. (box 299, bundle 5*)

(*m*) Papers of Col. Roger Townshend, Deputy Adjutant General in North America, 1757-9. (box 297, bundle 6*)

Items include:

Two commissions to Townshend as Colonel of Foot in America only, and as Deputy Adjutant General in America, 1758.

Letter from James Wall, Stillwater, to Townshend at Saratoga, concerning state of the garrison at Stillwater, 1759.

Letter from David Wooster, at camp at Lake George, to Gen. Amherst, complaining that writer has been wronged respecting his rank, and giving details of his service in America from 1741 onwards, 1759.

Note from Benjamin Mace to Townshend, relating that the soldier of Capt. Cruikshank's independent company who received 'but a part of his punishment some time ago' is now able to receive the remainder, 1759.

Memorial of Aaron Edwards, master of the stage-boat passing between New York and Perth Amboy, and Peter Lot, keeper of a public house and ferry at Perth Amboy, seeking recompence for an attack made on them by officers 'in Hyland dress', 1759.

Weekly return of the Rhode Island Regiment, Babcock Camp at the Falls, 1759.

Monthly return of the independent company of foot commanded by Capt. Cruikshank, Connecticut River, Apr. 1759.

(*n*) Papers, 1760, relating to cases to be heard before the House of Lords and Commissioners of Appeals, and representations to the House of Commons. (box 34, bundle 5*)

American items include:

Case of Major Charles Craven of Sir William Pepperell's Regiment in North America, who had been severely treated in the campaigns of 1756-7.

Petition of the Pennsylvania Land Company concerning their lands.

(*o*) Memorandum, 1761-2, relating to the proceedings at Boston with respect to illicit trade. (box 297, bundle 2*)

(*p*) Minutes, 1762, on Maryland, covering various subjects including constitution, trade, population (white and black), and revenue. (box 44, bundle 35*)

(*q*) Estimate, 1763, of the charge of twenty-one battalions of foot proposed for the service of North America. (box 299, bundle 3*)

(*r*) Miscellaneous papers, 1764-7, relating to America and the West Indies. (box 297, bundle 4*)

American items include:

Estimate of expense of victualling St. Augustine, 1764-7.

Minutes relating to [official] remittances to North America, 1764-6.

Extract from a letter from George Mills, New Haven, Connecticut, on the effects of recent legislation on American trade, 1766.

Report (two copies) of the Board of Trade on establishment of the salaries of governors, judges, etc. in North America, 1767.

Letter from Israel Mauduit asking for a mark of royal favour for Brig. Ruggles, commander-in-chief of the regiments raised by the province of Massachusetts Bay in the late war, 1767.

Proposal by Thomas Mant for furnishing garrisons in America, 1767.

Reasons for impropriety of a duty on tonnage of shipping in America, n.d.

List of grantees of land in East Florida with number of acres granted to each, n.d.

Estimate (two copies) of expences of settling twenty-five Greek families in East Florida, n.d.

Observations on the Free Port Act, n.d.

State of the Crown's title and claim to the islands lying within Delaware Bay and River, n.d.

(*s*) Remarks, *c.* 1765, on the importance of Georgia and suggestions for its improvement. (box 46, bundle 44*)

(*t*) Bill (with marginal amendments), *c.* 1765, for prohibiting the government of the province of New York from passing any Act of Assembly for any other purpose until provision is made by the Assembly for furnishing the King's troops with all their lawful requirements; another copy of the same with amendments approved by the Attorney General. (box 36, nos. 19/63-4*)

(*u*) Papers, 1765-6, mainly relating to American and West Indian trade, mostly undated. (box 44, bundle 34/1-68*)

Including:

Scheme for free ports in America, 1765. (21)

Draft minutes of two meetings of the joint committee of the West India and North America merchants, 1766. (41-2)

Observations on the distressed and declining state of the British Empire in America. (11)

Instructions to commissioners visiting Massachusetts to take note of violations of the Navigation Act. (12)

Examination of Brook Watson, merchant, and others before the Committee for American Affairs on the subject of American trade. (27)

Questions and answers relating to smuggling in North America. (33/1)

Questions and answers on the effect of a duty on rum on the American colonies. (33/2)

Resolutions of the Committee on American Affairs relating to duties on various American imports. (51)

Office paper on Spanish trade to America. (65)

Observations on the American trade by Mr. Kelly. (68)

Two notebooks - the first containing an estimate of the expense and profit of settling 20,000 acres in East Florida, with notes on the amount of work done by Negroes in various states in a year; the second setting out the proper steps to be taken to establish such a settlement. (45-6)

Scheme for a union between Great Britain and her colonies by giving them representation in Parliament. (57)

Memorial of Joseph Sherwood, agent for the colony of Rhode Island, relating to a payment due to the colony for expenses of an expedition against Crown Point. (43)

Advantages of keeping up armed vessels on the Lakes. (48)

(*v*) Papers, 1765-7, about the quartering of troops in North America, estimates of army expenses, and other American papers. (box 41, bundle 28*)

Including:

Accounts of the provisions made by the Assemblies of New Jersey and Connecticut for quartering troops, 1766-7.

Resolutions of the Assembly of Massachusetts Bay concerning their action in passing the bill for compensating sufferers [in the riots over the Stamp Act], 'under a full persuasion that the sufferers had no just claim or demand upon that province', 1766.

Estimates of army and navy expenditure in North America (twenty-two items), including estimate for repairing the church of St. Francis at St. Augustine for soldiers' barracks, list of the officers of the Northern Department of Indian Affairs with their respective salaries, estimate of the expenses of two troops of rangers in Georgia, and estimate of expenses attending a regular post between New York and Albany, 1766.

Observations on the account of the expenses of the government of Massachusetts Bay, n.d.

(*w*) American papers, 1765-7, mainly relating to finance and military matters and mostly undated. (box 42, bundle 31*)

Including:

Account of sundry merchandise shipped from New York for Ireland, 1766-7.

Estimate of cost of services in North America defrayed by aids from Parliament.

Three papers relating to quit-rent bill, with information about quit-rents in various American provinces.

Papers relating to the expense of North America, its revenues, American paper bills, proposed American duties on salt, and proposed duties on wine, oil, and fruit imported into America.

Estimate of the expenses of transporting provisions for one man for one year from Albany to the posts on the Lakes.

Plan for establishment of a board of revenue for managing the duties imposed by Parliament on the American colonies.

Disposition of troops in America.

List of posts in America where troops are quartered, giving the number of troops at each post.

Memorandum on the advantages of keeping armed vessels on the Lakes in North America.

Four papers relating to the cost of provisioning America.

Paper relating to forts in America.

(*x*) Miscellaneous papers, 1765-7, relating to America and the West Indies. (box 296, bundle 5*)

American items include:

Letter from John Bradstreet, New York, offering to raise a regiment of foot in America 'seeing the great loss of troops by sickness in Florida and West India Islands every year', and suggesting that it be officered by sons of the best families in America who would be 'a pledge for the loyalty of their friends and families in America', Dec. 1766.

Extract from a letter from Gov. Franklin, Burlington, N.J. to the Earl of Shelburne [Secretary of State], concerning attitude of Americans to the Act for quartering soldiers in America, 1766.

Estimate of the expense of vessels on the Great Lakes, n.d.

Papers relating to a plan for Indian trade, n.d.

List of books proposed as requisite to be kept under care of secretary to the American Board of Customs, n.d.

Opinion of the merchants of London trading to the continent of America on bills of credit from America, n.d.

Memorial of Mr. Knox relating to reducing the expense of troops in America, n.d.

Catalogue of useful and exotic plants worth cultivating in the American colonies on account of trade, n.d.

(*y*) Draft resolutions, *c.* 1765-7, of a [? Parliamentary] committee that the House of Representatives of New York is disobeying the legislature of Great Britain. (box 46, bundle 46*)

(*z*) War Office papers, 1766. (box 34, bundle 2*)

American items include:

Draft letter proposed to be sent to foreign garrisons including those in North America about regulations governing the incurring of expenses in peace time.

Establishment list of Northern Department of Indian Affairs.

Estimate of the quartermaster general's department at Albany.

(*aa*) American papers, 1766. (box 45, bundle 39/1-5*)

Including:

Report on government policy on land grants in America. (2)

Proposals for establishing paper currency for North America, n.d. (5)

(*bb*) Opinion, 1766, of London merchants trading to North America, recommending 'speedy importation of wheat and flower from the continent of America'. (box 35, bundle 14*)

(*cc*) Memorials, petitions, etc. to the Treasury, 1766-7. (box 46, bundle 41*)

American items include:

Memorial by [William] Bollan, H.M. Advocate for the Province of Massachusetts Bay, about securing a perpetual supply of masts for the Royal Navy and recommending the wood of New Hampshire and Massachusetts.

Request by Mr. Curzon to Charles Townshend, about the petition of Mr. Cuming (and Mr.) Mason, contractors for victualling the troops in East Florida, for increased payments.

(*dd*) Statement, 1767, of the settlement of New Hampshire (1620-1767), giving details of late intrusions on the possessions of the Crown; with list of grantees of certain towns erected in the colony. (box 30, nos. 17/1-2*)

(*ee*) Letter, 1776, from Henry Dundas to the Duke of Buccleuch on various topics including America: 'I find people here in general are in high spirits about [it]'. (box 30, no. 10/2*)

(*ff*) Letter, 17 Aug. 1791, from Hugh Scott [of Gala], Niagara, to Buccleuch: 'I cannot imagine the Americans will presume to quarrel with us for such a place as this'; the latter were now taking the field against the Indians, of whom upwards of 500 had till lately been encamped in the neighbourhood at government expense, 'several of them wore as dress scalps taken from the Americans last autumn'. (box 31, no. 19/2/6*)

(*gg*) Letter, 1793, from Capt. Thomas Scott, at a camp near Valenciennes, to Buccleuch, informing him that they were well supplied with everything, 'very different indeed from an American campaign'. (box 31, no. 19/2/16*)

LEITH HALL MUNIMENTS. (GD.225)

(*a*) Letter, 1775, from William Braco Gordon, Charlestown Heights, giving a lengthy account of the battle of Charlestown, 7 July. (1044, bundle 14*)

(*b*) Statement, 1815, of produce shipped in American and British vessels at Point à Pitre, Guadeloupe. (984*)

TRINITY HOUSE OF LEITH RECORDS. (GD.226)

Account book, 1826-33, of John Smith for voyages in the timber trade, including disbursements at New York and Baltimore. (15/1)

FRASER, STODART AND BALLINGALL COLLECTION. (GD.232)

Missouri Land and Livestock Co. Ltd., cash book no. 1, 1882-8. [Edinburgh office]. (vol. 21*)

DUNDONALD MUNIMENTS. (GD.233)[9]

(*a*) Two letters, 1831, from Francis B. Ogden, American Consul at Liverpool, to Lord Cochrane [later 10th Earl of Dundonald] about obtaining an American patent for his inventions of rotary engines and steam boilers. (box 2, file 31*)

9. The written permission of the present Earl of Dundonald is required for access to these papers.

(*b*) Counsel's opinion and other papers, 1851, relating to American infringements of the Earl of Dundonald's patent for improvements in boilers of steam vessels. (box 5, item 51*)

TODS MURRAY AND JAMIESON COLLECTION. (GD.237)

(*a*) Cash book, 1720-3, of Robert Nisbet, merchant in Charleston, with lists of debts and accounts of cargoes, including goods purchased in Holland. (box 10, bundle 4/1*)

(*b*) Letters, accounts, and other papers, 1721-40, relating to Alexander Nisbet, merchant in Charleston, S.C. (box 10, bundle 1*)

Apprentice indenture of Robert Nisbet, brother of Sir John Nisbet of Dean, as apprentice in South Carolina. Dean [Edinburgh], 15 June 1721.

Partnership agreement between Alexander Kinloch and Nisbet to carry on trade in a store at Red Bank, with list of stock, 4 April 1723.

Marriage contract between John Lloyd of Charles Town and Sarah Collins of Berkly County, 10 Oct. 1724.

(*c*) Day book, 1727-30, of merchants [? Messrs. John Blackwood and Alexander Nisbet] in Charleston, [thereafter in London and Edinburgh]. (box 10, bundle 4/2*)

(*d*) Ledger, 1738-41, of merchants [? Samuel Hyde, Henry Massey and Capt. Michael Covy in Charleston], referring to customers' Negroes, Broad Creek [Broad River, S.C.], voyages to England, pilotage of the *Charles* up the Potomac, Virginia dues, accounts left with Henry Massey, Potomac, and voyage to Maryland. (box 10, bundle 4/3*)

(*e*) Letters, 1745-7, from James Mickie, Charleston, to Sir Alexander Nisbet of Dean on trading matters. (box 10, bundle 2*)

(*f*) Accounts, 1762, of the brig *Harlequin* for a voyage from Philadelphia. (box 88, bundle 4*)

(*g*) Shipping accounts of Messrs. Fairholme: Philadelphia and West Indies to Leith, 1762-4. (box 143, bundle 3*)

(*h*) Crown grant, 1765, to William Hagart, reduced subaltern officer of the 77th Foot, of tract of land in county of Albany, Province of New York. (box 259, bundle 2*)

(*i*) Indenture, 1766, between William Abell of Prince George's County, Md., and Richard Henderson, factor for John Glassford at Bladensburgh in said county, whereby Abell becomes an indented servant to Henderson until sums due to the latter in money and tobacco are fully paid. (box 10, bundle 3*)

(*j*) Letter, 1794, from Thomas Cooper [lawyer, natural philosopher, and politician] stating his intention of returning to America to settle with Dr. [Joseph] Priestley and his friends in Pennsylvania. (box 90, bundle 8*)

BAIRD OF SAUGHTONHALL MUNIMENTS. (GD.238)

(*a*) Account, 1682, of Sir Robert Baird's intromission with the money for the plantation in Carolina. (box 3, bundle 4*)

(*b*) Petition, information, and answers, 1691, in court of session process at instance of Patrick Crawford, seaman, against Sir Robert Baird, as one of the partners of the Carolina Society, for payment of Crawford's wages 'for plying of ane Carrolina voyadge and takeing and bringing home ane map and description of the situatione of that country'. (box 3, bundle 4*)

SHEPHERD AND WEDDERBURN COLLECTION. (GD.242)

(*a*) Letters and papers, 1735-41, regarding claim by [Samuel] Eveleigh, merchant in Carolina, against Sir John Bruce Hope, Governor of Bermuda, in respect of a ship's cargo condemned for illegal trade. (box 34, bundle 10*)

(*b*) 'True account of the late proceedings of the government of the Bahama Islands under John Tinker, the present governor', in relation to a Spanish prize brought in by the privateers *George* and *Joseph and Mary* of Philadelphia, *c.* 1740. (box 34, bundle 10*)

HOPE, TODD, AND KIRK COLLECTION. (GD.246)

Travel journals of Mrs. M.A. Pringle of Whytbank, 1903-4. (box 47, bundle 2*)

Including:

Impressions of San Francisco (1903).(4)

Tour in California and Utah, 1903. (5)

Visits to New York, St. Louis Exposition, and Chicago, 1904. (6)

JOHN C. BRODIE COLLECTION. (GD.247)

(*a*) Business correspondence and papers, 1761-89, of William Cuninghame and Co., tobacco merchants, Glasgow,[10] from agents and customers in America and elsewhere. (box 59, bundle Q*)

Including:

General inventory of slaves and other personal estate belonging to William Cuninghame and Co., merchants in Glasgow, at their different establishments in Virginia in the year 1777, when their factors were expelled from that commonwealth.

(*b*) Certificate of judgement of general court of Virginia and other papers, 1767-8, relative to an action in the court of session at the instance of George Kerr of the city of Williamsburg, Va., merchant, and his factor, against William Cuninghame, late of Falmouth in Virginia, now of Glasgow, merchant, for enforcement of damages and costs awarded to him in Virginia, in suits relative to Kerr's employment as agent for supplying the British forces at Pittsburgh in 1759. (box 140*)

(*c*) Two letter-books, 1767-74, of the agent for William Cuninghame and Co. at Falmouth [Va.] (box 58, bundle O*)

(*d*) Correspondence and business papers, 1770-86, of William Cuninghame and Co. relating to activities in Virginia, Maryland and elsewhere. (box 58, bundle P*)

SEAFIELD MUNIMENTS. (GD.248)

(*a*) Letter, 1726, from John Lang, St. Peters, New Kent, Va., referring to his appointment as minister at St. Peters on Lord [? Findlater's] recommendation, his salary, character of the people, and need for commission of ecclesiastical jurisdiction for suppression of vice and immorality. (box 564, bundle 74*)

(*b*) Letter, 1749, from Alexander Scott, Edinburgh, referring to the preaching of George Whitefield in America. (box 563, bundle 69a, no. 71*)

(*c*) Letter, 30 Oct. 1755, from Lord Dupplin to Lord Deskford referring to failure of efforts against the French by sea and in America. (box 562, bundle 55*)

(*d*) Letters, 1756-8, from Francis Grant, Albany, N.Y. and Fort Edward, mainly on family matters but with occasional references to the campaign. (box 49, bundle 1*)

(*e*) Letter, 1758, from W. Lorimer, Albany, outlining the history of the colony of New York, as it is a violation of the laws of a garrison town to give any news. (box 177, bundle 1, no. 46*)

(*f*) Letters, 1759-63, from Capt. Robert Grant serving in America. (box 507, bundle 3*)

Subjects include:

Capture of Fort Ticonderoga. Ticonderoga, 1759.

Operations on Mohawk River. Albany, 1760.

Setting out on an expedition. New York, 1761.

The new Indian war. New York, 1763.

10. See T.M. Devine, *The Tobacco Lords* (Edinburgh, 1975), chapter v.

(*g*) Notes on British and French colonies in North America, *c.* 1760. (box 471*)
(*h*) Letter[11] from Gavin Corbin, Virginia, concerning his application for the post of receiver general in Virginia, 1762. (box 49, bundle 2*)
(*i*) Letter, 7 Mar. 1764, from Sir Archibald Grant of Monymusk urging purchase of land in America and suggesting places in Canada and the American colonies. (box 49, bundle 2*)
(*j*) Letter, 1764, from James Campbell, Mobile [Ala.], giving a description of Mobile and plan to clear the navigation of Ebervill River to the Mississippi. (box 672, bundle 6*)
(*k*) Letter, 1767, from Sir Alexander Grant, M.P., about debates in Parliament 'till midnight' on the impending American revolt - 'America now setts this country at open defiance'. (box 221, bundle 2*)
(*l*) Notes, *c.* 1767, on legislation passed in the various colonies and plantations in America and on the state of their manufacturing industry and trade. (box 442*)
(*m*) Letter, 29 Oct. 1771, from Capt. Robert Innes, Philadelphia, describing the town. (box 50, bundle 2*)
(*n*) Two letters, 1772, from Capt. Robert Innes, Quebec, describing the country between Albany and Lake George, fortifications at Ticonderoga, settlements between St. Johns and Quebec, and system of landholding in Canada. (box 201, bundle 2*)
(*o*) Letters, 1772-4, from David Duff, Maryland, concerning his voyage to America and situation as a schoolmaster there. (box 349, bundle 3*)
(*p*) Letters and papers, 1772-88, concerning Capt. John Grant (d. 1780), Commissary General and Paymaster of Ordnance in America, and his executry. (box 227, bundle 4*; box 235*; box 244*)
(*q*) Letter, 1775, from James Grant, Inverness, about measures to prevent emigration to America during 'the present disturbances'. (box 52, bundle 1*)
(*r*) Letters, 1775, from Gen. Simon Fraser of Lovat about raising his regiment [for service in America]. Printed in W. Fraser, *Chiefs of Grant* (Edinburgh, 1883), ii, 453-5. (box 3, nos. 531-2*)
(*s*) Letters, 1776, concerning recruiting in Strathspey for regiments going to America. (box 52, bundle 3*)
(*t*) Letter, 29 Dec. 1776, from Sir James Colquhoun of Luss giving news of the war in America during October-November from his son [Capt. William Colquhoun]. (box 53, bundle 4*)
(*u*) Letter, 31 Dec. 1776, from Capt. Duff, Gibraltar, with news of the war in America and the activities of American and French privateers. (box 53, bundle 4*)
(*v*) Letters, 1777, from soldiers serving in America giving news of the war and of friends there.
Including:
- Capt. Robert Grant - effect of Howe's proclamation on rebel army. Camp near Amboy, 5 June. (box 509, bundle 3*)
- Capt. John Grant. New York, 26 June. (box 54, bundle 4*)
- Capt. Robert Innes - mentioning skirmish with rebels and occupation of Ticonderoga. Quebec, 14 July. (ibid.)
- Capt. William Colquhoun - events before his departure from America. London, 22 Aug. (box 54, bundle 5*)
- Duncan Grant, 21st Regiment - news of friends killed in engagements beyond Ticonderoga, 12 Sept. (box 509, bundle 3*)
- Capt. Robert Grant - arrival in Maryland and going in search of Washington. Elk River, Maryland, 31 Oct. (box 55, bundle 1*)
- Same - regiment is going to New York. Camp near Philadelphia, 28 Nov. (ibid.)

(*w*) Letter, 1777, from Henry Mackenzie [the author], commenting on the capture of Ticonderoga. (box 54, bundle 5*)
(*x*) Letter, 1778, from Sir James Colquhoun of Luss, referring to Lewis Grant, a prisoner at Concord in America, and to Col. Archibald Campbell, who was going to Morristown in the Jerseys to be exchanged for Ethan Allen. (box 55, bundle 3*)
(*y*) Letters, 1778-80, from Capt. John Grant, Commissary General and Paymaster of Ordnance, New York, about financial affairs and friends in America. (box 352, bundle 1*)
(*z*) Letter, 1780, from David Duff, Dorset County, Md., about fees charged at his school and his management of the plantation belonging to the school. (box 228, bundle 1*)
(*aa*) Letter, 18 Dec. 1780, from Charles Grant, Winsborough, S.C., about the capture of Charleston. (box 509, bundle 5*)
(*bb*) Letter, 1780, from William Taylor, London, referring to his brother in America, who had been appointed an assistant engineer and had made a plan of Charleston. (box 510, bundle 1*)
(*cc*) Letter, Quebec, 25 Oct. 1780, from William Grant, referring to expeditions by Major Carleton and Sir John Johnston against the Americans. (box 363, bundle 1*)
(*dd*) Letter, 1781, from James Fraser, New York, about the executry of Capt. John Grant, Commissary General at New York. (box 228, bundle 4*)
(*ee*) Letter, 1782, from Archibald Fraser of Lovat, with text of his speech in the House of Commons on Highland questions, including the possibility of renewed emigration to America. Printed in W. Fraser, *Chiefs of Grant,* ii, 478-9. (box 3, no. 478*)
(*ff*) Letter, 1785, from Andrew Murdoch, Philadelphia, about heavy taxes there, immigrants, including many from Ireland who 'will soon fill this country', methods of cultivation, prices of provisions and clothing, and acquaintances from Forres and Elgin he had met. (box 354, bundle 4*)
(*gg*) Letter, 1794, from Dr. Benjamin Rush, Philadelphia, concerning his enquiries about Alexander Grant, said to have died there. (box 687, bundle 3*)
(*hh*) Commonplace book, eighteenth century, compiled (1752-97) by the Rev. John Grant, containing some anecdotes of the American war. (box 614*)
(*ii*) Letter, 1803, from John Grant, Leith, about Highland emigration to America. (box 702, bundle 5*)

LINDSAY OF DOWHILL MUNIMENTS. (GD.254)

(*a*) Letter, 12 Jan. 1777, from George Hutton, Liverpool, to his brother commenting on war news - 'the vast superiority of our troops and their alert behaviour ... the most consummate wisdom, prudence and conduct of our great general and his brother'. (1403*)
(*b*) Letter, 13 Oct. 1778, from John Kirby, on H.M.S. *Unicorn*, to his father - details of prizes taken and an engagement with an enemy ship off Boston Bay. New York. (1411*)

11. Letters listed hereafter are mainly addressed to James Grant, M.P., later Sir James Grant of Grant.

HALDANE, BROWN AND CO. COLLECTION. (GD. 255)

Letter, 1880, from James Duff, president of the Colorado Elevator Warehouse Company etc., Denver, describing prospects for farming in Colorado. (box 6*)

W.E. BOYD COLLECTION. (GD. 257)

Letter, 1898, from Burnham Williams & Co., Baldwin Locomotive Works, Philadelphia, to Clement E. Stretton, Leicester, England, sending diagrams. (2/94)

SCOTT OF ANCRUM MUNIMENTS. (GD. 259)

(*a*) Letters, 1700-1, from John Scott, to Sir John Scott of Ancrum, his father. (box 4, bundle 29*)

Subjects include:

Jamaican sugar is too dear to ship home; proposes instead to return via Pennsylvania and Maryland with cargo of tobacco. Port Royal, Jamaica, 10 May 1700.

His business affairs. New York, 28 Oct. 1700.

Intention of going to Jamaica, where he hears goods markets are now to be had; has a third share in the vessel; hopes for good financial outcome; 'I am sure I deserve it for I venture both person and estates freely for it'. Duckesburg, Staten Island, 'within two leagues of New York', 3 Mar. 1701.

(*b*) Letter, 1709, from Patrick Scott of Ancrum to his son in London, enclosing a packet [wanting] to be sent to John [Scott] by 'first sure ships for New York or Virginia' and apparently referring to John's near financial ruin. (box 4, bundle 2*)

SIR CHARLES A. MURRAY'S PAPERS. (GD.261)

(*a*) Letters, 1835-7, from Sir Charles Vaughan, formerly British Minister at Washington, to Charles Augustus Murray, with comments on news from America. (61*)

Subjects include:

Murray's adventures in America [while travelling with a tribe of Pawnees]; character of Henry Fox, Vaughan's successor at Washington. (2)

Anglophile views of Martin Van Buren and his influence in persuading the President to accept Palmerston's offer of mediation. (3)

(*b*) Letter, 1838, from Martin van Buren to Charles A. Murray, introducing Dr. Macaulay of Baltimore. (57*)

(*c*) Letter, 1843, from Charles Augustus Murray to his brother, commenting on the latter's criticisms of the MS. of his novel *Prairie-bird* [based on Murray's experiences with the Pawnees]. (37*)

(*d*) Letters, 1883, from Charles Augustus Murray to his second wife while he was on a visit to the U.S.A., mainly from 'The Homestead', Geneseo, Livingston County, N.Y. with lengthy descriptions of his activities. (63*)

Including:

Letter describing a meeting with George Bancroft, historian and diplomat - 'he is a very fresh and lively old gentleman of 84, and I doubt not has still considerable conversational powers, but they are marred by his having neglected either to preserve his own teeth or to supply himself with others from a dentist'; encloses Bancroft's autograph. Washington, 28 October.

(*e*) Autobiographical notes, n.d., by Sir Charles A. Murray, including reminiscences of his meeting with Chief Justice Marshall and his own family's connexions with America in the eighteenth century. (14/6*)

(*f*) Memorandum (incomplete) of some peculiarities in the Pawnee language, n.d. (45*)

HEDDLE MANUSCRIPTS. (GD.263)

(*a*) Letter (and typewritten copy), 1836, from Thomas Traill in Canada to Miss Fotheringhame in Kirkwall about family matters and the condition of Texas, which 'though it appears from all accounts to be a fine country is at present in a very unsettled state, in fact the seat of civil wars ... I believe the United States government will find or make a pretext for interfering and will get this fine province ultimately'. (68/1)

(*b*) Letter (and typewritten copy), 1838, from Rev. Thomas Hilliard, Gorham [New England] to Patrick Fotheringhame in Kirkwall, concerning the death of Hilliard's wife [Patrick's sister-in-law]. (64/7)

MISS M.F. MOORE'S PAPERS. (GD.264)

(*a*) Notes, 1952-3, on Capt. John Mason of King's Lynn and his connexions with North America, 1612-59. (box 15, file 15*)

(*b*) Notes, 1955-6, on ships proceeding to America from Scotland, including cargoes of household furniture, 1758-60. (box 19, file 12*)

HOME OF WEDDERBURN MUNIMENTS. (GD.267)

(*a*) Letter, 1733, from John Murray, Kingston in Port Royal Harbour, to Patrick Home, surgeon of H.M.S. *Squirrel*, at Charleston, S.C., concerning sale of green and Bohea tea at Jamaica on account of Patrick and Francis Home. (3/21)

(*b*) Letter from Patrick Home, Rappahannock Forge, Va., to George Home of Branxton, giving news of the murder of the latter's brother [Ninian Home] in a slave rising in Grenada, and offering his services in the West Indies, where 'the knowledge I have acquired in my progress in managing my uncle's estate which was very extensive, and consisted of a good many slaves, will, I trust, enable me to give you ample satisfaction'; explains that his prospects in Virginia are below his original expectations because of lawsuits which are the result of 'the diffused concerns of Uncle James, and the inaccuracy of his books'. 1795. (1/3)

(*c*) Letter, 1801, from James Home, Rappahannock Forge, to George Home of Paxton, with news of his visit to America while his ship was at Halifax; includes details of his journey from New York 'by land in what they call the mail stage, but how unlike the British mail coach! The roads very bad in many places dangerous'; has seen a relation of George Home, a Mr. Francis Hume, 'he is a mild, sedate, placid old gentleman, and very fond of talking about his relations in Scotland'; gives news about the state of American politics: 'the Democratic or French or anti-federal party is gaining ground'. (1/3)

(*d*) Cash book, 1801-36, recording accounts with various people and businesses, including John Craig, Thomas Biddle, and Henry Williams, all Philadelphia merchants. (25/39)

(*e*) Letters, 1862, from George Home of Branxton to Patrick Home of Wedderburn. (1/8)

Subjects include:

Letter which he encloses [wanting] marked with the stamp of Falmouth [New England], 15 July.

'Our American friends know nothing about their father's prior marriage, and it is justifiable in them to believe any story he may have told them about their right of succession to the estate of Wedderburn' but they have no just claim because they are illegitimate, 28 July.

CARNEGIE UNITED KINGDOM TRUST RECORDS. (GD.281)

Files, *c.*1890-1913, relating to grants by Andrew Carnegie for building libraries in Great Britain and Ireland, prior to the formation of the Carnegie United Kingdom Trust. (3/1-356)

CARNEGIE TRUST FOR UNIVERSITIES OF SCOTLAND. (GD.1/464)

(*a*) Press cuttings and letters, 1901, to Andrew Carnegie and the trustees dealing with the inception of the trust, the framing of its terms and initial public reaction thereto. (1/46)

(*b*) Letter, 1901, from Professor Matthew Hay, Aberdeen University, to Andrew Carnegie, suggesting points to be considered in determining the shape which Carnegie's gift should take. (1/34)

(*c*) Miscellaneous original and copy letters, 1902-11, by Andrew Carnegie to the Earl of Elgin and others, relating to the administration of the trust generally, including comments on criticisms made by Principal Sir James Donaldson, St. Andrews University and Sir William Sinclair, *c.* 1906-7. (1/2)

(*d*) Letters from Andrew Carnegie, 1909-10. (1/1)

To the secretary of the trustees: 'If the giving of fees cannot be restricted to proper cases, while I am alive a change could be made in the trust deed which would give more for research'. New York, 18 March 1909.

BERTRAM AND SON LTD. RECORDS. (GD.284)

American patents, 1899-1928, granted to members of firm of James Bertram & Son Ltd., paper-mill engineers, Leith, for improvements in paper making, etc., and licence agreement with an American company for use of one of the patents. (24/4)

CALEDONIAN INSURANCE COMPANY RECORDS. (GD.294)

(*a*) Cash book, 1890-3, including American business. (75)

(*b*) Trustees' ledger (American investments), 1890-1912. (77)

(*c*) General cash book: monthly statements (American business), 1893-6. (78)

(*d*) Correspondence, 1906-9, relating to dissatisfaction among the shareholders at losses incurred by the company over claims arising from the San Francisco disaster. (54)

J. & F. ANDERSON COLLECTION. (GD.297)

'Notes of an excursion to the United States', by Dr. Andrew Combe, physiologist and phrenologist (incomplete, and related only to part of the outward voyage from Liverpool on the *Montezuma*, including description of conditions among Irish emigrants on board), 1847. (34*)

HUNTER, HARVEY, WEBSTER AND WILL COLLECTION. (GD.298)

(*a*) Letter, 26 June 1716, from John Dunbar, Liverpool Castle, to the Laird of Grange - he and twenty gentlemen have agreed with 'those to whome wee are sold by the government'; arrangements for their voyage to America; hopes to settle 'at Sandie Poynt in Vergeinea on James River'; has arranged for future letters to be forwarded through Liverpool. (bundle 379*)

(*b*) Letter, 9 July 1717, from James Dunbar, Rhode Island, to the Laird of Grange - his brother John has arrived from Virginia. (379*)

(*c*) Letter, 23 Feb. 1720, from John Dunbar, Newport, R.I. to his brother, describing events since he left Virginia, including trading voyages along the American coast and a revolt by slaves on board ship. (bundle 376*)

(*d*) Journal, 1765, of a detachment of the 42nd Regiment going from Fort Pitt down the Ohio to the country of the 'Illenoise' to give presents to the Indians and make peace with them in order 'to facilitate the taking possession of that country'; refers to French activity in the area and duplicity of Indian guides, and describes Chief Pontiac, Indian villages, animals, and topography of the region. (196*)

(*e*) Letters, 1779-81, from John Agnew, London, to Vans Hathorn, writer to the Signet, Edinburgh, containing some comments on events during the American war. (bundle 38*)

EAST LOTHIAN ANTIQUARIAN SOCIETY'S PAPERS. (GD.302)

MS. account, n.d., of hunting expedition to Central Prairie by R. Tait Murray, with details of animal and bird life [probably mid-nineteenth century, but with no clear indication of exact dates or places]. (83*)

VARIOUS CLASSES

This section is intended to provide general guidance on possible sources rather than full information about particular classes. Even where detailed lists are offered they should not be regarded as exhaustive but only as an indication of the type of material which may be found.

ADMIRALTY COURT. (AC.)

The Admiralty Court had both civil and criminal jurisdiction in maritime cases and also a customary or common law jurisdiction, concurrently with other civil courts, in mercantile cases even when these did not arise in a maritime context. Its jurisdiction in cases of prize was limited by a decision of 1778 that the English Admiralty Court was also competent to deal with prizes brought into Scottish waters, and was effectively removed by a Treasury order in 1809. The court itself was abolished in 1830, its jurisdiction being transferred to the Court of Session and other courts. Its records contain some references to shipping and trade between Scotland and America but these can be identified only if the names of parties are known.

BOARD OF TRADE, DISSOLVED COMPANIES' FILES. (BT.2)

Among the files of limited companies registered in Scotland are some relating to companies formed for investment in mining, land, livestock, and timber in the U.S.A. They are usually more informative about the capital structure and shareholding of a company than about its American operations, but some do contain reports and papers dealing with the latter. The first date shown is that of registration and the second that of winding-up, though the company may have ceased to be active for some years before its legal extinction. Explanatory notes have been added in a few cases, where the nature of the company is not obvious from its title. For information about companies listed and others, also registered in Scotland, see W. Turrentine Jackson, *The Enterprising Scot* (Edinburgh, 1968), and W.G. Kerr, 'Scottish investment and enterprise in Texas' in *Studies in Scottish Business History,* ed. Peter L. Payne (London, 1967).

(*a*) Glasgow Port Washington Iron and Coal Company Ltd., 1872-88. (399)

(*b*) Utah Cotton Wood Mining and Smelting Company Ltd., 1872-5. (443)

(*c*) Oregon and Washington Trust Investment Company Ltd., 1873-1912. (522)

(*d*) Scottish American Mortgage Company Ltd., 1874-1906. (573)

(*e*) Kirkland Gold and Silver Mining Company of California Ltd., 1875-83. (638)

(*f*) Atchison Mining Company Ltd., 1875-80. (639)
(*g*) Dundee Mortgage and Trust Investment Company Ltd., 1876-1912. (671)
(*h*) Oregon and Washington Mortgage Savings Bank Ltd., 1876-1912. (692)
(*i*) American Mortgage Company of Scotland Ltd., 1877-1919. (770)
(*j*) Dundee Land Investment Company Ltd., 1878-1912. (844)
(*k*) Scottish American Land Company Ltd., 1880-99. (957)
(*l*) Oregonian Railway Company Ltd., 1880-92. (963)
(*m*) Missouri Land Company of Scotland Ltd., 1880-1933. (1001)
(*n*) Prairie Cattle Company Ltd., 1880-1921. (1003)
(*o*) Scottish Pacific Coast Mining Company Ltd., 1881-1899. (1018)
(*p*) American Land and Colonization Company of Scotland Ltd., 1881-1906. (1022)
(*q*) Texas Land and Cattle Company Ltd., 1881-1908. (1075)
(*r*) Missouri Land and Livestock Company Ltd., 1882-1911. (1101)
(*s*) Dundee Investment Company Ltd., 1882-1912. (1115)
(*t*) American Lumber Company Ltd., 1882-8. (1117)
(*u*) California Pastoral and Agricultural Company Ltd., 1882-1916. (1129)
(*v*) Arizona Copper Company Ltd., 1882-1930. [New company registered 1884]. (1114; 1375)
(*w*) Wyoming Cattle Ranche Company Ltd., 1882-97. (1151)
(*x*) Dundee American Real Property Company Ltd., 1882-1900. (1154)
(*y*) Scottish Mortgage and Land Investment Company of New Mexico Ltd., 1882-1944. (1161)
(*z*) Matador Land and Cattle Company Ltd.,[12] 1882-1957. (1181)
(*aa*) Hansford Land and Cattle Company Ltd., 1882-1914. (1182)
(*bb*) Western Ranches Ltd., 1883-1911. (1203)
(*cc*) Texas and New Mexico Land Syndicate Ltd., 1883-5. (1221)
(*dd*) Swan Land and Cattle Company Ltd., 1883-1927. (1225)
(*ee*) Oregon Mortgage Company Ltd., 1883-1961. (1234)
(*ff*) Arizona Trust and Mortgage Company Ltd., 1883-95. (1304)
(*gg*) American Trust and Agency Company Ltd., 1884-1921. (1328)
(*hh*) Montana Sheep and Cattle Company Ltd., 1884-1900. (1369)
(*ii*) Scottish Californian Orange and Vineyard Company Ltd., 1884-1906. (1388)
(*jj*) Florida Mortgage and Investment Company Ltd., 1884-1910. (1412)
(*kk*) Cresswell Ranche and Cattle Company Ltd., 1885-1902. (1443)
(*ll*) Humboldt Redwood Company Ltd., 1885-1909. (1477)
(*mm*) Edinburgh and San Francisco Redwood Company Ltd., 1885-1906. (1495)
(*nn*) Oregon Trust and Agency Company Ltd., 1890-1904. (2059)
(*oo*) Mining Development Syndicate (of Colorado) Ltd., 1892-1905. (2371)
(*pp*) Alaska Glasgow Gold Mine Ltd., 1895-1901. (2916)
Mining in California; no apparent connexion with Alaska.
(*qq*) California Consols Ltd., 1896-1923. (3341)
Mining in California.
(*rr*) Californian Mines Financiers Ltd., 1898-1905. (3760)
(*ss*) California Copper Syndicate Ltd., 1901-6. (4791)
(*tt*) Idaho Alamo Consolidated Mines Ltd., 1903-12. (5300)
(*uu*) Espuela Syndicate Ltd., 1903-8. (5358)
(*vv*) Western Ranches and Investment Company Ltd., 1910-21. (7485)
(*ww*) Scottish American Development Corporation Ltd., 1914-5. (9007)
(*xx*) Glasgow America Trust Company Ltd., 1914-61. (9161)

CHANCERY PATENT SPECIFICATIONS. (C.20)

The Scottish Chancery was an administrative department only and did not develop into a court of law. Its records are almost entirely concerned with the tenure of lands and offices within Scotland,[13] though the charters creating Nova Scotia baronetcies between 1625 and 1637 did include tracts of land in the province for colonization. Until 1852 it was necessary to obtain separate patents to protect inventions in Scotland, the grantee being required to lodge a detailed specification, or description, in chancery. Specifications for patents granted to Americans include the following:
(*a*) Joseph Chessborough Dyer, of Boston, for machinery for cutting and heading nails; and for machinery to be used in manufacturing cards for carding wool etc., 1812. (12/10, 13)
(*b*) Joseph Chessborough Dyer, of Boston, for improvements in carding machines, 1815. (15/16)
(*c*) Jeptha Avery Wilkinson, formerly of New York, for improvements in manufacturing weavers' reeds, 1818. (18/29)
(*d*) George Clymer, late of Pennsylvania, for improvements in printing presses, 1818. (18/37)
(*e*) James Neild, machinist, Taunton, Mass., for improvements in looms, 1814. (44/42)
(*f*) Erastus B. Bigelow, of Boston, for improvements in looms for carpets, 1846. (46/91)
(*g*) Henry Mandeville Mead, of New York, for improvements in distilling; and for improvements in manufacturing bread, 1846. (46/116-7)
(*h*) Samuel Colt, for improvements in firearms, 1850. (50/91)
(*i*) Ethan Baldwin, of Philadelphia; for method of generating steam applicable to propelling vessels, locomotives, etc., 1850. (50/118)
(*j*) Ethan Campbell, practical and experimental engineer, New York, for generating motive power, 1850. (50/155)
(*k*) John Flack Winslow, ironmaster, Troy, [N.Y.], for machinery for blooming iron, 1852. (52/145)

CUSTOMS AND EXCISE RECORDS. (CE.)

The minutes of the Scottish Board of Customs, 1723-1828 (CE.1), contain occasional references to American trade, and information about individual ships is sometimes found in the outport records (CE.51-87), which begin at various dates from 1708 onwards. These records, are, however, purely administrative and the sole surviving financial records, containing details of ships and cargoes, are those which were lodged in the Exchequer for auditing (see EXCHEQUER RECORDS). The Scottish Record Office holds copies of the Public Record Office series Customs 14, ledgers of imports and exports, Scotland, 1755-1827, made up partly of duplicate volumes (RH.20/1-28) and partly of photocopies (RH.2/4/10-54). The Library of H.M. Customs and Excise, London, has retained a few Scottish records, including some referring to John Paul Jones. The registers of shipping, which are still held at the various ports, include one of the few surviving registers of ships allowed to trade with the plantations, for Campbeltown, 1763-80.

CHURCH OF SCOTLAND, GENERAL ASSEMBLY PAPERS. (CH.1/2)

In its early years the Presbyterian Church in America maintained close relations with its parent body in Scotland, which are illustrated by the items listed below. Further material can be found in the uncatalogued papers from 1731 onwards and also in the registers of Acts of the

12. See W.M. Pearce, *The Matador Land and Cattle Company* (University of Oklahoma Press, 1964).
13. There is a gift and provision to John Gordon, D.D., H.M. Chaplain at New York, as Bishop of Galloway, 4 Feb. 1688 (C3/12, no. 426). The Latin warrant for this is printed in George Dallas, *System of Stiles as now practicable within the kingdom of Scotland* (Edinburgh, 1697), pp. 700-1.

General Assembly (CH. 1/1) and the records of the synods of Clydesdale (formerly Glasgow and Ayr, CH.2/464), and Lothian and Tweeddale (CH.2/252), and the presbytery of Edinburgh (CH.2/121). A few of the more modern papers and records refer to the Presbyterian churches in other countries.

(*a*) Letter, 1704, from Johnson Lynch and others, Wando River, S.C., to Robert Sandilands, minister at Edinburgh, complaining that they are without a minister unless a supply can be sent from Scotland; with scroll reply. (24/1, fos. 110-12)

(*b*) Two letters, 1705, from Archibald Stobo, Charleston, to the moderator of the presbytery of Edinburgh, lamenting that dissensions in Carolina make his return to Scotland imminent. (24/2, fos. 224-7)

(*c*) Petitions, 1709, signed by Presbyterian inhabitants of Newcastle, Pa., asking for a minister to preserve them from superstitions and heresies; with covering letter from James Coutts giving further details about the church. (28, fos. 388-91)

(*d*) Letters, 1712, from South Carolina to the moderator of the presbytery of Edinburgh, including one from Archibald Stobo asking for a serious, sober young man to be sent as a Presbyterian minister, with a call signed by the inhabitants in and about James Island. (32, fos. 531-40)

(*e*) Letters, 1715, from New England to the presbytery of Edinburgh, including three from John Squyre, Charleston and Boston, and one from Archibald Stobo, Boston; the letters give a very unfavourable picture of the state of Carolina in religious affairs and of the Indians and their methods of torture. (35, fos. 189-94)

(*f*) Case of the Presbyterian congregation at New York, 1724, including petition of John Nicoll and address of the presbytery of Long Island; these give details of the origin, history, and present state of the congregation. (49, fos. 43-58)

(*g*) Reasons of John Squyre for leaving James Island [Carolina] offered to and accepted by the presbytery of Edinburgh, 1725. (51, fo. 99)

COURT OF SESSION PRODUCTIONS. (CS.96)

The records of the Court of Session, the supreme civil court of Scotland, form one of the largest Scottish archive groups. Cases involving America came before the court from the seventeenth century onwards but these are not readily identifiable from the existing indexes and finding-aids, which are based on the names of parties only. The items listed below have been removed from the original processes (files of papers in particular cases) to form a separate series. They include a number of business books produced as exhibits, as well as reports and sederunt books (minutes) relating to sequestrations (bankruptcies). Notes have been added to show the particular connexion of each entry with America.

(*a*) William Fraser, merchant, London: journal, 1699-1711. (524)
Trading with North America, particularly Boston and Virginia.

(*b*) James Watson, merchant, Greenock: business books, 1740-50. (1919-22)
Trading with Virginia.

(*c*) James & Thomas Corbet, merchants and shipowners, Dumfries: business books, 1745-53. (2156-62)
Trading with Virginia.

(*d*) Kerr, Pollock & Co., cloth manufacturers, Paisley: business books, 1751-61. (2009, 2020-2)
Goods consigned to Philadelphia.

(*e*) Jamieson, Semple & Lawson, merchants, Glasgow and Maryland: business books, 1751-79. (1176-1202)
Trading in tobacco from Maryland and Virginia; ledgers, etc. for Maryland and Virginia concerns. 1750-74.

(*f*) Roger Hog of Newliston, merchant, London: business books, 1754-74. (1833-5)
Financial dealing in Boston, South Carolina, and New York.

(*g*) William Lang, shipmaster, Glasgow: journal and cargo account, 1756-65. (652-3)
Insurance of ships to America; trading from Antigua to Philadelphia and Maryland.

(*h*) Buchanan & Simpson, tobacco merchants, Glasgow: business books, 1758-73. (502-9)
Imports from Virginia and Maryland; reference to duty on slaves imported into Virginia and Maryland.

(*i*) A. Ferguson, shipping agent: invoice ledger, 1763-75. (2248)
Consignments to Boston and Philadelphia.

(*j*) [Unidentified] agent, Edinburgh: letter-books, 1772-5. (2250, 2260)
Consignments to Charleston.

(*k*) Alexander Bain & Co., merchants, Greenock: business books, 1772-83. (71-80)
Trading with New York and Charleston, S.C.

(*l*) Sinclair, Brebner & Co., shipowners, Greenock: business books, 1778-82. (1413-15)
Trading with New York.

(*m*) William Mitchell, merchant, London: cash book, 1780-1. (600)
Invested in trading with New York and Charleston.

(*n*) Lyle and Mitchell, merchants, Richmond, Va.: business books, 1784-1800. (1750-64)

(*o*) Findlay, Hopkirks & Co., merchants, Glasgow and Maryland: list of debts, 1788-99. (2232)

(*p*) Hugh Miller, merchant, Virginia, thereafter in London: report, 1793. (2026)
Business activities, 1761-93.

(*q*) James Lawson & Co., merchants, Glasgow: report, 1793. (1531)
Trading in tobacco from Maryland, 1765-93.

(*r*) John Burnside, Alexander Burnside, Burnside & Waddell, shipping agents, Glasgow and Montreal: business books, 1795-1833. (2582-9, 2624-44)
Client in New York.

(*s*) McKnight & McIlwraith, merchants and shipowners, Ayr: ledger, 1798-1802. (1233)
Trading with New York and Savannah.

(*t*) [Unidentified], merchants, Greenock: journal, 1799. (1293)
Trading with New York, Charleston, and Virginia.

(*u*) Sharp & Mackenzie, merchants, Glasgow: sederunt book, 1799-1800. (1257)
Trading with North America.

(*v*) David Kessock, calico printer, Glasgow: sederunt book, 1801-2. (763)
Creditor in New York.

(*w*) Log-book of brig *Peggy*, 1802. (1533)
Voyaging to Virginia and Maryland.

(*x*) James Duncan, grain and linen merchant, Dundee: business books, 1802-20. (18-36)
Trading with North America.

(*y*) [Unidentified], merchants, [? Glasgow]: letter-book, 1807-10. (1494)
Trading in American goods.

(*z*) George Yuille, merchant and cotton miller, Glasgow: business books, 1807-19. (2224-31, 2234-8, 2240-1)
Trading with Virginia and Charleston.

(*aa*) George Austen, manufacturer, Glasgow: sederunt book, 1809-10. (736)
Creditors in Boston and Charleston.

(*bb*) James Coats, manufacturer, Glasgow: sederunt book, 1810-4. (888)
Goods consigned to New York.

(*cc*) James Stewart, merchant, New York: receipt book, 1812-13. (1570)

(*dd*) James Stewart, cloth merchant, New York: business books, 1812-14. (1007-17)
Trading with Charleston, New Haven, Philadelphia, and Providence.

(*ee*) James Boyd, merchant, Edinburgh: sederunt book, 1814-7. (830)
Army debtors in America.

(*ff*) Shannon, Stewart & Co., merchants, Greenock; Shannon, Livingston & Co., merchants, Newfoundland: sederunt book, 1816-30. (905)
Invested in trading with New York; creditors in the U.S.A.

(*gg*) James McAlpine, wood merchant and trader, Corpach: sederunt book, 1817-21. (162)
Accounts for voyages to New Orleans.

(*hh*) Saunders & Mellis, merchants, Aberdeen: sederunt books, 1819-29. (417/1-5)
Trading with North America.

(*ii*) Borthwick & Goudie, weavers, Belhaven, etc.: sederunt books, 1822-36. (326-32)
Partner absconded to America.

(*jj*) John Caldwell & Co., cloth manufacturers, Paisley: sederunt book, 1825-6. (136)
Partner absconded to New York.

(*kk*) Inglis & Robb, cotton merchants, Glasgow: sederunt book, 1825-6. (378)
Trading with New York.

(*ll*) Henry Gray, merchant and cotton manufacturer, Glasgow: sederunt book, 1826-33. (361)
Goods consigned to New York and Charleston.

(*mm*) Alexander G. Thomson, cloth manufacturer, Glasgow: report, 1827. (232)
Trading with New Orleans, 1815-27.

(*nn*) Cameron, Thomson & Co., cotton yarn manufacturers, Glasgow: report, 1827. (1940)
Goods consigned to New Orleans, 1816-27.

(*oo*) David Miller & Sons, manufacturers, Glasgow: sederunt book, 1827-31. (715)
Goods consigned to New Orleans and New York.

(*pp*) James & William Whyte, merchants, Leith: sederunt book, 1828. (443)
Creditors in Virginia and New York.

(*qq*) William Louden, cloth manufacturer, Dundee: sederunt book, 1829-33. (152)
Trading with New York.

(*rr*) Matthew Wotherspoon, merchant, Glasgow: sederunt book, 1829-33. (446-7)
Trading with New York and Philadelphia.

(*ss*) Lancaster, Duncan & Co., merchants, Glasgow: sederunt book, 1830-1. (912)
Trading with New York.

(*tt*) George & William Aitken, cloth manufacturers, Glasgow: sederunt book, 1830-3. (314)
Goods consigned to New York.

(*uu*) Morrison & Ewing, yarn merchants, Greenock: sederunt book, 1832-3. (259)
Trading with New York.

(*vv*) William Black & Co., cloth manufacturers, Glasgow: sederunt book, 1832-3 (463)
Goods consigned to New York.

(*ww*) Hoome, Wilson & Co., manufacturers, Glasgow: sederunt book, 1832-3. (751)
Goods consigned to New York, New Orleans, and Philadelphia.

(*xx*) McDonald, Son & Co., dyers, printers, and merchants, Glasgow: sederunt book, 1832-4. (171)
Goods consigned to Baltimore, Boston, New Orleans, New York, and Philadelphia.

(*yy*) David Maxwell, clothier and merchant, Dundee: sederunt book, 1833-4. (173)
Trading with New York.

(*zz*) J.W. & T. Deans, carpet manufacturers, Stewarton: sederunt book, 1834-5. (353)
Goods consigned to New York.

(*aaa*) Archibald McIndoe & Co., merchants and calico printers, Glasgow: sederunt book, 1836-42. (2074)
Creditors in New Orleans and New York.

(*bbb*) Thomas C. Walker, commission agent and merchant, Edinburgh: sederunt book, 1838. (2361)
Debtors in Savannah.

(*ccc*) John Boath junior, cloth manufacturer, Forfar: sederunt book, 1843-8. (556)
Goods consigned to New York.

(*ddd*) Australian Company of Edinburgh: report, 1845. (103)
Vessels voyaged to America, 1822-43.

(*eee*) William & Thomas Jeffs, railway contractors, Dumfries: cargo book, 1851. (1173)
Goods consigned to New York.

(*fff*) Walter Henderson & Co., cloth and yarn merchants, Glasgow: letter-book, 1853. (285)
Business trip to New York and San Francisco.

(*ggg*) Log-books of ship *Catharine*, 1863-4. (2969-70)
Voyaging to Boston, New York, and Philadelphia.

(*hhh*) Jaffe Brothers & Co., Dundee and Manchester: accounts, 1910-11. (2474-8)

EXCHEQUER RECORDS. (E.)

The Exchequer exercised a general supervision over the Crown's revenues, particularly in the auditing of accounts. Most of these relate to internal revenue, but the customs accounts, both before and after the Union of 1707, provide the major source of information about Scotland's trade. Though there are references to the importation of tobacco from the 1620's onwards, most of the pre-Union trade with the American colonies appears to have been indirect and the few references to direct trade are mainly confined to Port Glasgow in the 1680's, though it must be noted that the records for all ports are very imperfect. The post-Union period saw a great expansion of direct trade, but unfortunately detailed records prior to 1742 have not survived. Thereafter the records for all ports are virtually complete until 1796. There are gaps between Oct. 1796 and Oct. 1805 and between Oct. 1807 and Oct. 1810, after which the series continues until its conclusion on 5 Jan. 1830, when the auditing of the accounts was transferred to London. Apart from the gaps, the accounts for 1742-1830 provide full details of all goods imported and exported and particulars of the ships on which they were carried. The American trade was concentrated on Port Glasgow and Greenock, though almost every other port had some share in it. No similar records exist for the period after 1830.

The Exchequer was also a court dealing with revenue cases, including smuggling, and the enforcement of debts due to the Crown, but its records tend to be very formal and provide little background information about the cases.

(*a*) Customs books, Aberdeen, Leith, Port Glasgow, etc., 1663-91. (E.72)

(*b*) Papers relating to an estate in New Jersey, alleged to belong to John Cameron of Lochiel, attainted for participation in the 1715 Rebellion, 1713-25. (E.663, box 205*)

(*c*) Collectors' quarterly accounts (customs), all ports, 1742-1830. (gaps: 1796-1805, 1807-10) (E.504)
(*d*) Letters and papers, 1780-92, relating to the activities of Major George Hay as commissary for captures and agent for captured property, in procuring provisions for the forces and dealing with rebel property captured by the fleet and army during the siege of Charleston, S.C. The papers relate mainly to his dealings with Lieut. Col. James Moncrieff and James Fraser, his fellow commissaries, and the auditing of their accounts, and were transmitted to the barons of the Scottish Exchequer by order of the Treasury in 1790, with a view to recovering the balances in Hay's hands. (E.381, box 15*)
(*e*) Exemplification of account of Lieut. Gen. James Robertson, Barrackmaster General in North America, 1765-76, 1796. (E.350, box 1*)

SCOTTISH HOME AND HEALTH DEPARTMENT. (HH.)

The Scottish Office, which was set up in 1885,[14] and its constituent departments are exclusively concerned with internal affairs. The files listed below are concerned with Americans in Scotland or Scotswomen married to Americans.[15]
(*a*) Sinking of S.S. *Athenia*: police report on previous activities of an American passenger; welfare of survivors, including Americans, 1939. (HH.50/6)
(*b*) Armed forces maintained by Allied governments in the United Kingdom, 1941-2. (HH.1/2787)
(*c*) Military deserters, etc. among Allied forces in the United Kingdom; circulars, police action, correspondence, 1941-56. (HH.55/572; closed until 1986)
(*d*) Marriage laws: requirements of Allied [including United States] and Dominion forces, proposals, representations, etc., 1942-4. (HH.1/1277)
(*e*) Marriage laws: difficulties of G.I. brides, scheme for providing legal assistance, 1946-52. (HH.1/1283; closed until 1983)

PRIVY COUNCIL. (PC.)

The records of the Privy Council of Scotland have been printed up to 1691 (*Register of the Privy Council of Scotland*, 1st, 2nd, and 3rd series, Edinburgh, 1877-1970) and continue in manuscript until its abolition in 1708. Apart from a proposal to deport malefactors on the Borders to Virginia in 1618 (1st series, xi) and references to the Nova Scotia colonization scheme from 1621 onwards (1st series, xii-xiii), there is little or no American material prior to 1666. From 1666 onwards (3rd series, ii-xvi) the records contain frequent references to the banishment or deportation of offenders to the American plantations, including Virginia, especially during the religious persecutions of the 1680's. There are also occasional references to trade and shipping and to the proposed Scottish settlements in Carolina and New Jersey. Similar material will probably be found in the unprinted records from 1692 onwards.

UPPER CLYDE SHIPBUILDERS' RECORDS. (UCS.)

The records contain very few references to ships built on the Upper Clyde for American owners. Alexander Stephen and Sons Ltd. of Linthouse built three paddle steamers for New York owners in 1871 and two other steamships between 1879 and 1896. Fairfields Shipbuilding and Engineering Company Ltd. of Govan constructed two survey vessels for the U.S. Navy in 1970-1. Some ships subsequently came into American ownership, for instance the *Sea King* built by Stephen's, which became the Confederate ship *Shenandoah*, but these can be traced in the records only if the original name is known.

MISCELLANEOUS PAPERS. (RH.9)[16]

(*a*) Cash book (fragment) of general merchant at Albany and New York, 1726. (1/221)
(*b*) Indenture, 1741, between John McLeod, merchant in Edinburgh, and John Eason, gardener in the parish of Blairgowrie, whereby Eason binds himself as apprentice and servant to McLeod until arrival in Maryland or any other of H.M. Plantations, and for five years thereafter; with declaration [endorsed] by McLeod that he was twenty-four years of age. (17/308)

MISCELLANEOUS BUNDLES. (RH.15)

(*a*) Titles to lands in East New Jersey, 1683-5, in favour of John Hancock of Wallyford, East Lothian, Johanna Sonmans, eldest daughter of Stron Sonmans of Rotterdam, and Francisca Hancock, relict of Arent Sonmans of Rotterdam. (131/1-3)
(*b*) Letter, 1689, from Francis Scott, London, to Alexander Campbell, merchant in Edinburgh, asking 'whether ther be any servands to be gott for transportation. If ther were 2 or 3 hundrett of them, I should find a way to gett them sent to Virginia ... When I get your answear then I will send yow word wher the profeit lyes and how I bring it about. I have allreddy spoke with a master of a ship in the north bound for Virginia'. (14/46)
(*c*) Letters and papers, 1689-97, of Andrew Russell, Scots merchant in Rotterdam, relating to business transactions with John Borland, merchant in Boston, and consignments of furs, indigo, and other goods. (106, box 20*)
Including:
Letter from Borland to Russell - 'We have not yett any ships directly from England but by way of Virginia and West Indies we have accountt of strange revolutiones in England. [I] hear nothing concerning Scotland. Pray favour me with a particular accountt of affaires in Scotland, which will much oblidge me being the needfull att present'. Boston, 8 April 1689.
(*d*) List, 1696, of twenty-eight men and women delivered at Newhaven [near Edinburgh] to be transported by Thomas Emmes. (14/58)
(*e*) Letter, 1714, from Thomas Campbell, Amsterdam, to his brother-in-law, describing how he had suffered from frostbite on the voyage from Boston. (14/139/2)
(*f*) Letter, 1716, from Dugald Campbell, Killberry, to his cousin, referring to a servant who had deserted from one of H.M. ships [*c*. 1708] and later died in Virginia. (14/157/1)
(*g*) Papers, 1725-45, relating to Dr. Roderick Gordon, mainly comprising letters written by him to his brother, Arthur Gordon of Carnousie, whilst serving as a ship's surgeon on voyages to Maryland and Virginia, 1727-8, and whilst resident in King and Queen County, Va., 1729-44. (1/95)
Subjects include:
List of goods for which there is a market in Virginia, 1730. (25)
Description of trade of Virginia; 'pity it is that thousands of my country people should stay starving att home, when they may live here in peace and plenty, as a great many who have been transported for a punishment have found pleasure, profit and ease and would rather undergo any hardship than be forced back to their

14. The Scottish Record Office holds photocopies of the main state paper, Treasury and Home Office series relating to Scotland, 1707-1885, in the Public Record Office. These, too, relate mainly to internal affairs.
15. Scottish Education Department records include a file on the adoption of Scottish children by citizens of the U.S.A., but this is closed for 100 years. (ED. 11/32)
16. The following classes form part of the Register House series, which comprises material of mixed or uncertain provenance.

own country'; list of goods, clothing, etc. to be shipped out from Scotland for sale, 1734. (31)

His estate is worth £200 yearly 'but our estates are precarious because they depend chiefly on slaves, who are very mortal in this country', 1736. (32)

'Virginia declin's and so do's most countries under our present government and trade declin's every day'; list of goods, including tartan, to be sent from Scotland, 1737. (34)

(*h*) Three letters, 1744, from James Gordon, King and Queen County, Va., to his father, Arthur Gordon of Carnousie, on family and business matters. (1/220)

(*i*) Ten letters, 1757-9, from George Ross [London] to Hugh Forbes, advocate, Edinburgh, giving news of the latter's brother, Brig. John Forbes, in America, including his capture of Fort Duquesne and death. (38/120)

(*j*) Letter, 1759, from Alexander Wedderburn, St. Germains, to Hugh Forbes, with news of sickness of Brig. Forbes at Philadelphia. (38/140)

(*k*) Two letters, 1759, from William Scrogie, London, late servant of Brig. Gen. Forbes, to Hugh Forbes, giving details of the general's possessions in his house in Pennsylvania and quoting his last words. (38/145)

(*l*) Memorials, *c.* 1759, for Brig. Gen. Forbes and his brothers, relative to his services and expenses on his expedition to the Ohio and Fort Duquesne. (38/81-3)

(*m*) Ten letters and papers, 1759, relating to Mr. Secretary Pitt's approval of Hugh Forbes's memorial asking for £1,000 in consideration of Brig. Forbes's services. (38/146)

(*n*) Letter, 1781, from Lieut. John Ross, 71st Regiment Grenadiers, New York, to Lord Ankerville, giving news of his release after eighteen months' imprisonment by the rebels, and of the defeat of the King's forces about 200 miles from Charleston. (44/103)

THE LIBRARY, UNIVERSITY OF EDINBURGH, Edinburgh EH8 9LJ

LAING MANUSCRIPTS. 1635-1877.

These are part of the collection formed by David Laing (1793-1878), antiquary and librarian to the Signet Library. Since these have been covered by an H.M.C. report only the more important items are noted (*Letters unless otherwise stated.*)

(*a*) Edward Gorges, Baron Gorges, President of the Council of New England. Copy of a petition to the King on behalf of the members of the Council for the drawing of the patents to their lands in terms of an arrangement made, 1 May 1635. Officially certified copy used in the Chancery suit between John Penn and Lord Baltimore, signed by Sir Edward Northey.[1] (La. II. 637/14)

(*b*) 8 Nov. 1676, from Edward Sherburne to George Wharton, treasurer and paymaster of H.M. Ordnance, desiring him to pay certain sums to some gunners 'appointed to attend the expedition to Virginia'.[2] (La. II. 639/19)

(*c*) 'Coppie of a letter from ... Carolina, Charleston, 18 May 1680', from N. Matthew, giving a description of Charleston (4 pages).[3] (La. II. 718/1)

(*d*) Diary, 1661-1722, of the Rev. Francis Borland, clergyman at Glassford, Lanarkshire. He spent some time at Boston, 1682-5, 1690-1, 1700-1.[4] (La. III. 262)

(*e*) Brief memorandum, 8 Oct. 1700, sent by R. Wodrow to R. Birnie. Queries about Virginia.[5] (La. III. 355, f.81)

(*f*) Letter, 1717, of G. Stewart about Patrick McLauren and David Durham, who are in South Carolina. (La. Add. 13/6)

(*g*) Treasury order, 8 July 1719, for payment to Jonathan Forward, a London merchant, for the transportation of malefactors to Maryland.[6] (La. II. 640/26)

(*h*) 28 May 1735, from Samuel Mather, Boston, to an unknown correspondent, touching on the state of education and religion in New England.[7] (La. II. 184)

(*i*) Letter of Alexander Malcolm to C. Mackie. New York, 3 July 1738. He is teaching classics and says that learning is the worst cargo that can be brought to America. (La. II. 91)

(*j*) 'Poems on several occasions by Archibald Home, Esq.', late Secretary and one of His Majesty's Council for the Province of New Jersey, North America, 1738-9. (La. III. 452)

(*k*) List, 25 Aug. 1740, of military stores sent to General James Oglethorpe for the defence of South Carolina and Georgia.[8] (La. II. 640/30)

(*l*) 22 July 1741, from Rev. Alexander Malcolm, Marblehead, Mass., to Prof. Charles Mackie, about Rev. Hooper and Rev. Charles Chauncy of Boston, opponents of George Whitefield.[9] (La. II. 91)

(*m*) 13 Aug. and 1 Sept. 1742, from Arthur Robertson, Glasgow, to Thomas Crawford of Cartsburn about George Whitefield.[10] (La. II. 479)

(*n*) Letters, 3 Dec. 1743, from Governor Gabriel Johnston, Edenton, N.C., to the Bishop of ... and to Adair, about Lord Carteret's 'prodigious bargain' in the Carolinas and elsewhere, and a statement of Johnston's financial condition.[11] (La. II. 647/225-228)

(*o*) Suggestions by Duncan Forbes of Culloden after the Rebellion of 1745 include the possibility of transporting some of the Highlanders to America, *c.* 1746-7.[12] (La. II. 123)

(*p*) Report on Arthur Dobbs's petition to the Privy Council on the subject of the Northwest Passage. 10 Aug. 1748.[13] (La. II. 641^2/24)

(*q*) 'Statement of the relative numbers belonging to the Church of England and to the Dissenters in the province of Nova Scotia'. *c.* 1762.[14] (La. II. 678)

(*r*) Instructions, 7 Dec. 1763, from George III to George Johnstone, Governor of West Florida.[15] (La. II. 76)

(*s*) Two letters from P. Sim to J. Cumming. New York, 11 Oct. 1765, 29 Dec. 1766. (La. II. 82)

(*t*) A bundle of correspondence, 1775-6, about General Simon Fraser's raising of the 71st Regiment to engage in the war in America.[16] (La. II. 506)

(*u*) 2 Aug. 1775, from William H. Zuylestein, 4th Earl of Rochford, to the Lords Commissioners of the Treasury, about Major Roche's plan for raising recruits in Ireland to serve in America.[17] (La. II. 640/40)

(*v*) 10 June 1776, from George Warrington, collector of customs, Whitehaven, to Sir James Johnstone (?) about the arrival of the ship *Kings Fisher* from Cape Ann, Mass.[18] (La. II. 73/128)

1. H.M.C. Laing MSS. i[72], p. 194.
2. Ibid., p. 410.
3. Printed in *South Carolina Historical Magazine*, LV (1954), 153-9.
4. H.M.C. Laing MSS. i[72], p. 331.
5. Printed in *Early Letters of Robert Wodrow, 1698-1709*, ed. by L.W. Sharp (Edinburgh, 1937), p. 115.
6. H.M.C. Laing MSS. i[72], p. 204.
7. Extract, ibid., pp. 240-1.
8. Ibid., p. 324.
9. Extract, ibid., pp. 327-8.
10. Extracts, ibid., pp. 329-30 and 335.
11. Extracts, ibid., pp. 336-40.
12. Transcript, ibid., p. 382.
13. Transcript, ibid., pp. 395-9.
14. Transcript, ibid., pp. 434-7.
15. Ibid., p. 440.
16. Brief extracts, ibid., pp. 486-7.
17. Ibid., pp. 470-1.
18. Extract, ibid., pp. 488-9.

(*w*) 14 July 1776, from N. Ferguson, Ayr, to Archibald Crawford, Cartsburn, giving 'an account of the state of Pennsylvania and the other provinces at the time of my leaving it'.[19] (La. II. 480/9)
(*x*) Three letters, 1777-8, from Lieut.-Col. Patrick Ferguson, about the beginning of the War of Independence.[20] Also a copy of a letter from T. Butler to Captain Douglas describing the naval battle on Lake Champlain, 1777. (La. II. 456)
(*y*) 8 Jan. and 24 Feb. 1777, from Alexander Cochrane, Rhode Island, to his brother Archibald, Lord Cochrane, about the engagement with the Americans at White Plains, N.Y.[21] (La. Writs (Dundonald))
(*z*) 'Address to His Excellency the President and other members of Congress etc.' Apparently drawn up by Professor Adam Ferguson (2 pages, incomplete). *c.* 1778. On peace between Britain and America. (La. II. 73)
(*aa*) Headquarters, 9 June 1778, from George Washington to Dr. Adam Ferguson of Edinburgh University, regretting that the passport requested cannot be issued to Sir Henry Clinton 'without the previous direction of Congress'. Signed by Washington, but in the hand of his secretary, Robert Hanson Harrison.[22] (La. II. 163)
(*bb*) 'Remarks on the present state of affairs between Great Britain and America', relating to the effects of the War of Independence on Britain's trade, etc. 18th cent. [1780?] (La. II. 679)
(*cc*) 19 Dec. 1780 and 23 Apr. 1781, from Francis Dundas to his brother Robert, from Charleston, S.C., and from Wilmington, N.C., about various campaigns.[23] (La. II. 500)
(*dd*) Letter of R. Mackinlay to J. Cumming. Woodside, 2 Oct. 1781. Sends his journal 'written on the bark of the Birch tree, which I was often under the necessity of doing while in the woods of America'. (La. II. 82)
(*ee*) Philadelphia, 11 Sept. 1786, from Dr. Walter Minto to David Steuart Erskine, 11th Earl of Buchan, about the probability of his accepting the chair of mathematics at Washington College in Maryland, and other matters.[24] (La. II. 588)
(*ff*) New York, 28 Oct. 1787, from W. Minto to the Earl of Buchan about New Jersey College, the American constitution, etc. (La. II. 588)
(*gg*) Letter of Dr. A. Carlyle about Canada, 1792. (La. III. 352)
(*hh*) 26 Apr. 1793, from James Fraser, Edinburgh, to Sir Henry Moncreiff about his problems as a Loyalist.[25] (La. II. 500)
(*ii*) 25 May 1794, from Washington's secretary, Tobias Lear, to the Earl of Buchan, on opportunities for emigrants from Great Britain to America. (La. II. 588)
(*jj*) Philadelphia, 20 Feb. 1796, from George Washington to the Earl of Buchan, about his preference for farmers from Britain rather than 'the slovenly farmers of this country'.[26] (La. II. 588)
(*kk*) Letter on scientific matters from B.S. Barton to C. Stewart, 1804. (La. III. 353)
(*ll*) Paris, 28 Feb. 1806, from James Bowdoin, American Minister to Spain, to Sir Robert Barclay about Anglo-American political and economic relations; and a covering letter from Barclay to C.J. Fox.[27] (La. II. 504)
(*mm*) St. Marys, Ga., 20 July 1807, from George Ker to General Walter Ker about his loyalty to Great Britain and about American anger over the *Chesapeake* affair.[28] (La. II. 118/4, no.2)
(*nn*) A collection of forty-four letters, 1811-9, to and from Thomas Douglas, 5th Earl of Selkirk: chiefly correspondence with Alexander Macdonald, Writer to the Signet, on the obtaining of settlers from the Scottish Highlands for Hudson Bay, Assiniboia, the Red River area, etc.[29] (La. II. 202)
(*oo*) Letters written from Toronto by Sir D. Wilson, to D. Laing, 1855-77, including mention of the American Civil War. (La. IV. 17)
(*pp*) Letter of George Gilfillan, 1864, giving his views on the American Civil War. (La. II. 354)
(*qq*) In addition to the above, the Laing Manuscripts are also noted as containing letters from: William Ellery Channing to R. Ainslie, 9 November 1832.[30] (La. II. 369); George Johnstone[31] (La. II. 73); Walter Minto[32] (La. II. 588); John and Charles Wesley[33] (La. II. 125); and George Whitefield[34] (La. II. 125 and La. II. 283). The Lear and Minto letters are to David Steuart Erskine, 11th Earl of Buchan.

COLDEN, CADWALLADER (1688-1776). Papers.

Lieutenant-Governor of New York 1761-76. Early American scientist.
(*a*) Notebook of 'Notes from the lectures of Wm. Law, Regent at Edinburgh, 1705'. (Gen. 71D)
(*b*) Materials for a new edition of Colden's *The Principles of Action in Matter* (London, 1751). Printed, with manuscript notes and corrections. (Dc. 1. 25-26)
(*c*) Supplement to *The Principles of Action in Matter,* 1757, by Cadwallader's son David. Printed, with manuscript notes and corrections. (*In* Dc. 1. 26)

BRAINERD, DAVID (1718-47). Journal. 1745-6. (Dc. 7. 68)

Missionary. From 1742 until his death Brainerd, commissioned by the correspondents of the Society in Scotland for Propagating Christian Knowledge, was a missionary among the American Indians. The journal appears to be the same as that printed in Jonathan Edwards, *Life ... of David Brainerd* (Edinburgh, 1765), pp. 375-437, and covers the Crossweeksung, New Jersey, Indians.

BLACK, JOSEPH. 3 letters. *c.* 1770-1784.

(*a*) Letter from A. J. Alexander to Joseph Black, Professor of Medicine and Chemistry at Edinburgh University, including a reference to Dr. Franklin, *c.* 1770. (Gen. 875/I/149-156F)
(*b*) Letter from Dr. John Morgan, Philadelphia, introducing John Rodgers, a prospective student of chemistry, 1784. (Gen. 873/II/169-170)
(*c*) Letter from Dr. John Shore, Petersburg, Va., introducing Dr. Gibbons of Philadelphia, a medical student, and also concerning a species of plantain as an antidote to spider venom, 1784. (Gen. 874/IV/9-10)

BROWN, ANDREW (1763-1834). 'History of North America during the War of Independence and afterwards.' (Gen. 154-159)

Scottish Presbyterian minster. Ordained in 1787 to pastoral charge of the Scottish church, Halifax, N.S. Returned to Scotland in 1795. In 1801 he was appointed Professor of Rhetoric and Belles Lettres in Edinburgh University, and in 1813 elected moderator of the General Assembly of the Church of Scotland. He left an unfinished history of

19. Extract, ibid., pp. 491-3.
20. Ibid., p. 494.
21. Extract and transcript, ibid., pp. 495-7.
22. See *Writings of George Washington*, ed. by John C. Fitzpatrick, vol. xii (Washington, D.C., 1934), p. 39.
23. Transcript, H.M.C. Laing MSS. ii[72], pp. 503 and 509-11.
24. Transcript, ibid., p. 524.
25. Extract, ibid., pp. 558-9.
26. Transcript, ibid., pp. 587-8. See *Writings of George Washington*, ed. by John C. Fitzpatrick, vol. xxxiv (Washington, D.C., 1940), pp. 471-2.
27. Transcript, ibid., pp. 697-8.
28. Extract, ibid., pp. 710-2.
29. Selection, ibid., pp. 716-56.
30. Ibid., p. 801.
31. Ibid., p. 144.
32. Ibid., p. 530.
33. Ibid., i, p. 379.
34. Ibid., i, p. 379 and ii, p. 804.

America, interesting for the accounts of the curious conferences and harangues of the Indian chiefs in good classical style.

JARDINE, SIR WILLIAM (1800-74). Correspondence: 6 letters. 1830-40. (Dk. 6. 20)

Naturalist. Six letters to Jardine from: R. Parnell, New Orleans, 30 Jan. 1840, with his impressions of that town; R. MacDowall, New York, 23 Apr. 1840, about the ornithology of West Africa; W. MacMillan, Librarian and Collector of Natural History to the University of Alabama (four letters), 1830-1, mostly about ornithology.

HALLIWELL-PHILLIPPS, JAMES ORCHARD (1820-89). Correspondence: 158 letters. 1851-85. (H.-P. Coll. L.O.A.)

Shakespearian scholar. One hundred and fifty-seven letters to Halliwell-Phillipps mainly on literary and personal topics, six on Shakespeare. Correspondents include: Hiram Corson of Cornell University (11); Joseph Crosby of Zanesville, Ohio (6); Horace H. Furness (55); W.G.Medlicott of Massachusetts (6); Henry Stevens, bookseller, of Vermont and London (70); Genevieve Ward, actress (3); Justin Winsor, librarian of Harvard University (6). There is one letter from Halliwell-Phillipps to Horace H. Furness.

AGASSIZ, ALEXANDER (1835-1910). 288 letters. 1867-1910.

Seventy-one letters to Sir C. Wyville Thomson and 217 to Sir J. Murray. Mainly about coral reefs. (Dk. 6. 13)

MUIRHEAD, ROLAND EUGENE (1868-). Papers.[35] 1900. (Gen. 715/2)

In 1900 Mr. Muirhead visited the Co-operative Brotherhood Colony of Burley, Washington (one of the last communitarian attempts of the Social Democracy of America), and the Mutual Home Association, an anarchist colony at Home, Henderson Bay, Washington. The papers relating to this visit are:
(*a*) His diary for 1900, which also contains material on his visit to British Columbia.
(*b*) A few letters between Muirhead and the anarchists Jay Fox and Oliver Verity, leading members of the Mutual Home Association.
(*c*) Copies of the anarchist journals *Agitator* and *Discontent*.
(*d*) Fifteen photographs of the two colonies.

The collection is a small but interesting record of this recently revitalized form of American social experiment.

MISCELLANEOUS AMERICAN MATERIALS.

(*a*) Letter, Charleston, S.C., 17 (rest of date torn off), for Lionel Chalmers to Robert Whytt, Professor of the Theory of Medicine, Edinburgh University 1747-66, mentioning an outbreak of smallpox. (Dc. 44. 98/1)
(*b*) 'Copy of an account laid before the Rt. Hon. Lewis Lord Sondes, Auditor of the Imprests', for the Province of Georgia, 1765-70, by John Campbell, Agent, 30 Nov. 1770. Mentions Benjamin Franklin. (Dc. 1.67, ff. 677-705)
(*c*) Enquiries about Florida in a letter of J. Bowman, Jr., to R. Oswald, 1768. Letter of J. Bowman about his son's visit to America, 1770. (Dk. 1. 30, ff. 94, 113)
(*d*) Letter, 1769, to Capt. John Campbell from J. Ogilvie, with copy of letter from Col. A. Campbell about a decision taken against the Crown in an American court. (Gen. 886*/10, no. 2)
(*e*) A clergyman and a Philadelphia professor 'come over upon a begging embassy', mentioned in a letter of A. Dalzel, 1774. (Dk. 7. 52/42)
(*f*) References to the War of Independence in letters of Alexander Oswald, 1776-7. (Dk. 1. 30, ff. 144*, 145, 147)
(*g*) Letter, 11 Dec. 1777, from David Murray, 7th Viscount Stormont, from Paris, to William Eden, Baron Auckland, on the War of Independence. (Dc. 4. 101-3)
(*h*) Mention of an American privateer in a letter of Mrs. E. Lindsay, [1778]. (Dk. 7. 52/64)
(*i*) 'Memorial of the late inhabitants of North Carolina'. New York, 16 Oct. 1778. (Andrew Brown Papers) (Gen. 155)
(*j*) 'Proceedings of H.M. Commissioners ... to treat, consult and agree upon the means of quieting the disorders in ... North America'. 1778-9. 365 pp. Partly in the hand of Adam Ferguson, the Secretary. (Dc. 1. 6)
(*k*) War with America mentioned in a letter of P. Campbell, 1782. (Dk. 7. 53/20)
(*l*) List of American students in Professor John Walker's class in natural history and mineralogy at Edinburgh University, 1783-1800. (From the original records in Walker's own hand.) (Dc. 1. 18/9)
(*m*) Petition to the King by the settlers in W. Florida, mentioned in a letter of A. Dalzel, 1783. (Dk. 7. 52/103)
(*n*) 'Account of some curiosities presented to the Edinburgh Royal Society, by Andrew Graham', 1787. Concerns North American Indians. (*In* Dc. 1. 57)
(*o*) Nova Scotia: defence in the event of war with America. 49 letters. 1791-1813.

Forty-nine letters, the authors of which include Henry Dundas, Sir John Wentworth, and others concerned with North American defence. (Dc. 1. 15)

(*p*) American Physical Society. Dissertations, 1794-7. (Da.)

This was a society of American medical students at Edinburgh University.

(*q*) Two letters, 1795, from J. Renton about a projected trip to Charleston, S.C. (Gen. 863/5, ff. 1, 3)
(*r*) A collection of manuscripts relating to the Quakers in Great Britain and America, 4 vols. 18th cent. (selected and copied by James Cruickshank.) (Gen. 545-8D)
(*s*) Letter, 1803, from Capt. J.J. Stuart to his brother Sir C. Stuart, mentioning the high wages offered by American ships to seamen, thereby inducing many British seamen 'to quit their country'. (Dk. 6. 25³)
(*t*) Jefferson, Thomas. Letter (copy). 1803. (Dc. 6. 111, ff. 83-84)

Copy of a letter, Washington, D.C., 10 July 1803, to the Earl of Buchan. The copy is in the Earl's hand, and was sent by him as a gift to Dugald Stewart on 21 Dec. 1803. Jefferson thanks the Earl 'for a volume on the life and writings of Fletcher of Saltoun'; praises his states-rights sentiments; and discusses the war between Britain and France.

(*u*) 'Universities of France MSS.' 1 volume. The volume relates to l'Université Imperiale, and contains documents dated 1808-13. (Dc. 6. 82)

An undated six-page memorandum in the volume is entitled 'Idées sur l'établissement d'une maison d'éducation française et d'une maison de commerce aux États Unis d'Amérique'. There is no indication of the author.

(*v*) Letter, 1815, from A. Bruce in New York, to Prof. R. Jameson. (Ja. 9)
(*w*) Letter of John Donaldson to W. Legget of Barlockhart, Stranraer, chiefly about business of T. Hutchinson with America, 1 Nov. 1815. (Dk. 7. 61/17)

35. See 'Private papers: an unexpected Scottish Nationalist source', *Bulletin of the British Association for American Studies*, no. 5, p. 32, 1957.

(*x*) Letter of Henry William Ducachet, New York physician, to J.A. Albers about Ducachet's inaugural essay on the action of poisons and his translations from Hippocrates, and to Hosack's *System of Practical Nosology*. New York, 15 June 1819. (Dc. 10. 48/14)
(*y*) Letter of ? Dupuy, secretary of the Medical Society of New Orleans, to J.A. Albers, acknowledging the receipt of books and promising to send some natural history specimens. New Orleans, 20 May 1820. (Dc. 10. 48/16)
(*z*) Letter of George Frick, oculist at the General Dispensary in Baltimore, to J.A. Albers. Refers to new medical publications and to an outbreak of yellow fever in Philadelphia. 1 Sept. 1820. (Dc. 10. 48/18)
(*aa*) Letter of Edward J. Coales, the Baltimore bookseller, to J.A. Albers. Contains references to Dr. Potter's 'valuable work on contagion', to Prof. Hall of the University of Maryland and to a reputed cure for hydrophobia. 1 Sept. 1820. (Dc. 10. 48/11)
(*bb*) Correspondence of various Glasgow cloth merchants about trade with Mexico, New Orleans, Valparaiso, etc. 1831-8. (Dk. 7. 47/73-4, 76-7, 79-81, 85)
(*cc*) Two letters of John and Robert Dick, 1835-6, containing their impressions of New York as immigrants. (Gen. 717/14[1-2])
(*dd*) Letter of John Ainslie, 1836, proposing to write a book on America. (Gen. 1429/18/1)
(*ee*) Letter, 1837, of Adams and Anderson about the Illinois Investment Company. (Dk. 7. 47/8)
(*ff*) Letter of Sir C. Lyell from Albany, N.Y., 1841, about the 'rapid progress of things' in America. (AAF)
(*gg*) Letter, 1842, from Sir C. Lyell about a lecture tour in America. (Dc. 4. 101-3)
(*hh*) Letter, 1844, of P.T. Mounsey to T.J. Torrie, asking him for money to enable him to emigrate to America. (Gen. 1996/1/24)
(*ii*) Letter to an American psychologist from Rev. James Hamilton, 1865, containing documents on Anglo-American relations. (Gen. 1981/143)
(*jj*) Letters of administration issued to Janet and John McCallum by H.G. Basset, Judge of the Probate Court, Fillmore County, Minn. 3 Feb. 1875. (Gen. 748*)
(*kk*) Reminiscences of the Swan Land and Cattle Co., Wyoming, 1883-1947. (Gen. 717)
(*ll*) Journal by H.G. Stewart, 1885, about a tour in Canada and the U.S.A. (Dk. 7. 43-44)
(*mm*) Letter [1888?] of J.A. Froude about the possibility of Canada's union with America. (AAF)
(*nn*) Letter, 1908, of J.W.W. Spenser about the Niagara Falls. (Dc. 4. 101-3)
(*oo*) Letter, 1919, from J.E. Creighton to Prof. N. Kemp Smith, about American reaction to the peace treaty of 1919. (Gen. 1416)
(*pp*) 'Impressions of America', written by Col. James Dick of Durban, 1920. (56 pp.) (Gen. 1957/7)
(*qq*) Two diaries, 1924, 1930, by Prof. J.H. Ashworth, describing his visits to America. (Gen. 856-8)
(*rr*) Letter, 1939, about public opinion in America towards the Second World War, from Christian Gauss to Prof. N. Kemp Smith. (Gen. 1416)
(*ss*) Letter about America, 1940, from Mary Hamilton to Prof. D'Arcy W. Thompson. (*In* JA 3479)
(*tt*) Letter from Freya Stark to Reginald Davies, 1944, describing San Francisco. (Gen. 1899/263)

ORKNEY ISLANDS

ORKNEY ISLANDS AREA ARCHIVES, Laing Street, Kirkwall

WATT OF BRECKNESS MSS. 5 letters. 1753-79.

(*a*) Letter from William Gilchrist at Boston *en route* to Jamaica, describing his prospects there, 1753.
(*b*) Letter from Hugh Mouat, Stromness, hoping for good news of the oppressed Bostonians and the other colonies, and for repeal of the cruel acts against the Americans, 1774.
(*c*) Letter from Baikia Harvey, Snowhill, near Augusta, Ga., describing his life in America; gives an account of the armed skill of the Liberty Boys, 1775.
(*d*) Letter from Capt. Magnus Laughton, at Burntisland, describing his encounter with an American privateer, 1777.
(*e*) Letter from Lord Caithness, Ratter, mentioning that his son is on the way to America with his regiment, 1779.

SUTHERLAND-GRAEME OF GRAEMESHALL. Papers. 1763, 1799.

(*a*) Papers, 1763, relating to the estate of George Todd, surgeon, Caroline County, Va., son of Charles Todd, Westshore, Holm, Orkney.
(*b*) Letter, 1799, from David Petrie, factor to Alexander Graeme of Graemeshall, referring to the packet *Edinburgh* of New York, wrecked on South Ronaldsay.

BALFOUR OF BALFOUR AND TRENABIE. Papers. 1764-1813.

(*a*) Account book of voyages to New England and South Carolina, 1764-7.
(*b*) Letters, 1773-6, from Capt. William Manson to his parents. Includes reference to Revolutionary troubles.
(*c*) Papers, 1775-89, relating to American Loyalist claims by William and John Chapman and Capt. William Manson, formerly in Georgia.
(*d*) Letters, 1776-83, from Gen. Ligonier, containing references to American wars, including illness of Washington and military capacity of Mr. Gates, proposed as his successor.
(*e*) Letter, 1777, from Thomas Taylor, Philadelphia, about Capt. Manson's move to Augusta, Ga., because of Indian attacks.
(*f*) Agreement between William Manson, merchant, Augusta, Ga., and William Roche, Augusta, formerly in Savannah, Ga., as to land in Savannah, 1780.
(*g*) Accounts, 1798-1813, with Warder and Sons, Philadelphia.

TRAILL-DENNISON MUNIMENTS. *c.* 1849.

Papers relating to the wreck of the *Washington* of Portsmouth, N.H., Capt. Burleigh, wrecked on the Ruff Dyke, North Ronaldsay, *c.* 1849.

MISCELLANEOUS DEPOSITS. 1771-82.

Papers, 1771-82, relating to the American estate of William Manson, merchant, late of Augusta, Ga., a Loyalist, and co-partner with William and John Chapman, merchants, Newcastle-upon-Tyne; includes a list of his debts, and two plans of his lands in Georgia, surveyed by James McFarland in 1776.

STRATHCLYDE

THE MITCHELL LIBRARY, North Street, Glasgow G3 7DN

DUNLOPS OF GARNKIRK AND TOLLCROSS. Papers. 1682-1701.

Of the 480 items in the collection, sixteen refer to America, fifteen being in the period 1682-4, when John Dunlop, a younger son of the 2nd Laird, planned and undertook a trading voyage to New York and to the West Indies, dying at Curacao. In 1701 his brother Archibald also wrote home a letter describing his activities in America.

SHAWFIELD PAPERS. 1691-1714.

Daniel Campbell (1671?-1753) of Shawfield was a Glasgow merchant, much of whose trading was done with America, which he visited more than once in the 1690's. There are many items of American interest in this collection of *c.* 600 items dealing with his affairs between 1691 and 1714. An index is being compiled.

BOGLE PAPERS.[1] Letter-book, *c.* 100 letters. 1725-80.

Merchants of the firm of Bogle & Scott. The Bogle family lived at Daldowie, Lanarkshire. The letter-book, 1725, of George Bogle contains many references to the tobacco trade; most of the letters are written from Leyden or Rotterdam. (Throughout the period 1730 to 1780 there are many references in the papers to the tobacco trade, mainly with America). Also commercial letters, some of 1729-31 and some of 1759-61, from agents and members of the family, from the Rappahannock River, Va., Glasgow, and London. By the later period the firm had a London office and was freighting in London ships outward bound to America.

JOHNSTON, JAMES, OF BISHOPBRIGGS, sea captain. Log and receipt. 1766, 1779.

This small collection includes the log of the *Betsy* from Glasgow to Virginia, 1766, and a receipt for three slaves bought at Savannah, 1779.

BARCLAY, JEAN. Letter. 1774.

ALS., Aberdeen, 8th October 1774, to Thomas Fuller, London, referring to the financial arrangements of her son 'now making the Tour of North America'.

MACKAY, DANIEL. Journal.

'Struggles through Life' (autobiographical journal).

Mackay (1758-1839) spent forty years in the West Indies, but his original destination when he left Scotland was New York. His journal gives an account of the capture of the ship in which he sailed in 1779 by an American privateer, of his time as a prisoner of war in New York before his repatriation to Halifax, and of his second attempt to reach New York, wherein he was disappointed when bad weather drove the vessel to the West Indies.

HENDERSON, ROBERT, merchant of Glasgow and Philadelphia. Correspondence and papers. 1781-9.

Forty-one items, mostly letters from family and friends in Glasgow, and from business associates, including Peter McDougall and Thomas Maule of New York, and Richard Wells of Philadelphia.

WILLIAM SMEAL COLLECTION.[2] Manuscripts and printed material. *c.* 1833-76.

William Smeal (1792?-1877) was a Glasgow Quaker grocer who took a leading part in reform - especially anti-slavery movements in nineteenth-century Glasgow. He was secretary of the Glasgow Emancipation Society throughout its history, 1833-75, and was a leading supporter of the William Lloyd Garrison wing of the Scottish anti-slavery movement.

Includes the following important anti-slavery materials:

(*a*) Glasgow Emancipation Society minute-books, 1833-76: 4 volumes, bound in one. There is a great deal of correspondence with George Thompson on his anti-slavery campaign in the United States in 1834. An entry for 1861 refers to the memorial to Palmerston calling on the British government not to recognize the Confederacy; another for 1863 deplores the aid given by some M.P.s and British capitalists to the Confederacy.

(*b*) Glasgow Emancipation Society cash book, 1833-76.

(*c*) Over a hundred volumes of anti-slavery pamphlets, tracts, and books, which include annual reports of the Glasgow Emancipation Society, and a wide range of American anti-slavery writings. 1833-61.

(*d*) Glasgow Emancipation Society subscription book, 1833.

(*e*) Sundry papers relating to the anti-slavery movement in Glasgow. Included are various broadsides on American slavery, press cuttings, and two letters from George Thompson. 1834-5.

(*f*) Miscellaneous collection of letters, posters and papers on the anti-slavery activities of the Glasgow Emancipation Society. 1841-76.

(*g*) Glasgow Freedmen's Aid Society minute-book, 1864-7. (William Smeal was its secretary.)

GLASGOW FEMALE ANTI-SLAVERY SOCIETY. 4 annual reports (printed pamphlets). 1843-51.

Second, fourth, fifth, and sixth reports for 1843, 1845, 1846, and 1851 respectively. Contain extracts from letters of Mrs. Maria Weston Chapman, secretary of the Boston Female Anti-Slavery Society, to this Glasgow society. The fourth report contains a copy of a letter from William Lloyd Garrison concerning his attitude towards Christianity.

MORTON, ALFRED (1854-1941?). Diaries: volume 48. (Autobiography covering 1854-82.)

Birmingham bricklayer. Morton went to the United States in 1871 and returned to England in 1882. The first forty-seven volumes of his diaries contain little of American interest; the last, Morton's autobiography, describes his American experiences. He travelled quite extensively in the United States - New York, Pittsburgh, Pa., Cleveland, Ohio, and through the Southwest - mainly in search of employment. On his return to England he continued to correspond with various people in the United States, mainly in the Pittsburgh area.

CLYDE SCREW STEAM PACKET CO. 1850's.

Of the 150 items in this collection, about thirty are concerned with the Glasgow-New York runs made by the *Clyde* in 1854 and 1857, and by the *Prince Arthur* in 1856.

1. Microfilms made by the Virginia Colonial Records Project.

2. This collection has been used in Robert Botsford, 'Scotland and the American Civil War', Ph.D. thesis, University of Edinburgh, 1955. See also George Shepperson, 'Harriet Beecher Stowe and Scotland, 1852-53', *Scottish Historical Review*, vol. xxxii, pp. 40-46, 1953.

AMERICAN LIBRARY PARTY PAPERS. 1897.

Papers and correspondence relating to a visit to Glasgow, 11th August 1897, by a party of American librarians touring Britain after the Second International Library Conference. 1 vol.

STRATHCLYDE REGIONAL ARCHIVES, City Chambers, Glasgow G2 1DU

CAMPBELL OF SUCCOTH. Letters. 1755-6.

Letters from James Campbell, from 'Camp at Osweygo', concerning war in America, 1755-6. (TD 219/3/40,41)

MITCHELLS, JOHNSTON, HILL & HOGGAN, SOLICITORS. Papers. 1761-1816.

(*a*) Papers relating to the creditors of McCall, Smellie & Co., Virginia merchants, 1781-3. (T-MJ 416)
(*b*) Invoices of goods sent out by Norman McLeod, merchant in Boston, 1761-5. (T-MJ 377 (c))
(*c*) Journal of a co-partnership between James Baird, John Hay, Ninian Menzies, and Peter Hay, to be under the direction of James Baird in Glasgow and the firm of Baird, Hay & Co., commencing in Virginia, 1772-1816. (T-MJ 79)
(*d*) Papers in lawsuit: James Ritchie & Co. *v*. Alexander Houston & Co., concerning quality of Virginia tobacco, 1779. (T-MJ 405)
(*e*) Miscellaneous documents relating to Virginia, 1780-1802. (T-MJ 422)
(*f*) Ledger of John Leitch, containing accounts with Virginia companies and some payments for tobacco, 1798-1805. (T-MJ 80)
(*g*) Letters from Thomas Boyd, Virginia, concerning affairs of family and estate of Penkill, in Virginia and Ayrshire, late eighteenth century. (T-MJ 304)

COLHOUN, WILLIAM. Letters. 1770.

Letters from William Colhoun, seaman, concerning the slave trade. One is written from Senegal, July 1770, and relates that he is mate on a fine vessel, bound for the Potochan River, Virginia, with 150 slaves; another is written from Oxford, Maryland, Oct. 1770. (TD 301/6)

STIRLING OF KEIR. Papers. 1777 - *c*. 1876.

(*a*) Letter from Archibald Erskine to Archibald Stirling of Keir, 6th June 1777, including references to the War of Independence and a mention of General Washington. (T-SK 11/3/109)
(*b*) Letters to Sir William Stirling Maxwell, M.P., historian and art collector, from J.L. Motley, *c*. 1860 - *c*. 1876, and from other American correspondents during the Civil War. The letters from Motley are mainly personal and social, but include comments on contemporary events in America, including the Civil War. (T-SK 29)
(*c*) There are also letters from and relating to Motley in a related collection, the papers of Maxwell of Pollok. These are addressed to Sir William's wife, Lady Anna Stirling Maxwell, and are entirely social and personal. They cover the period *c*. 1865 - *c*. 1874. (T-PM 119)

MISCELLANEOUS DEPOSITS. 1753-1949.

(*a*) Records of George Kippen, John Glassford & Co., merchants, including letters concerning freight to and from New York, Maryland, Virginia, and elsewhere, 1753-64. (TD 132)
(*b*) Indenture of apprenticeship of Neill Campbell to Archibald Ingram, John Glassford & Co., to serve five years in Virginia under the company's managers, 1758. (TD 200/53)
(*c*) Two letters relating to the Fergusson family of Goose Creek and Carthage, Tenn., 1815, 1829. (TD 375)
(*d*) Sederunt books relating to a trust of lands at Almaden, Santa Clara County, Calif., owned by Robert Walkinshaw of Helensburgh, formerly of San Francisco, 1858-1949. (T-MR 10/1-4)
(*e*) Letter from Henry Ashworth to Dr. Strang, City Chamberlain of Glasgow, asking him to accept a copy of his 'Tour in the United States, Cuba and Canada', 1861. (TD 68/5/101)

UNIVERSITY OF GLASGOW LIBRARY, Hillhead Street, Glasgow G12 8QE

DOCUMENTS RELATING TO EXPORTS AND IMPORTS. 1770-1836.

(*a*) Account of all goods exported from Scotland to Newfoundland between 1770 and 1785. (MS. Gen. 1057/8)
(*b*) Charges on vessels trading between Scotland and America (Customhouse, Edinburgh), 1790. (MS. Gen. 1057/18-19)
(*c*) Eight letters, 1836, from Stewart & Wilson, export merchants, of Glasgow, to Frederick Huth & Co., exporters, London. Although South American interests figure prominently in this correspondence there is also mention of the effect of a fire in New York upon export trade from Glasgow. (MS. Gen. 531/14)

BANNERMAN MSS. 3 letters. 1775-85.

(*a*) Letter from Capt. W.S. Laurie, 1775, concerning the Battle of Bunker Hill and Boston patriots. (MS. Gen. 1035/152)
(*b*) Letter from Alexander Wedderburn to Adam Smith, 1776, mentioning the American Revolution. (MS. Gen. 1035/153)
(*c*) Letter from Robert Reid to Adam Smith describing his travels in Canada, 1785. (MS. Gen. 1035/167)

HUNTER MSS. 1741-75.

(*a*) Arthur Dobbs' account of his attempt to find a Northwest Passage. (Hunter 434)
Dobbs, colonial governor of North Carolina, induced the Admiralty in 1741 to send an expedition to search for the Northwest Passage.
(*b*) Contemporary copy of a journal kept by Captain Durben, an officer who travelled with Benedict Arnold during his march on Quebec in 1775. (Hunter 608)

MISCELLANEOUS MSS. 1698-1919.

(*a*) Nineteen letters and documents (some copies), 1698-1701, relating to the Darien scheme, an attempt to transport Scotsmen to settlements on the Isthmus of Darien. (BH 19-y, 16-17, 19-20)
(*b*) Letter from Francis Hutcheson to Thomas Drennan, *c*. 1740, containing references to the state of religion in Pennsylvania. (MS. Gen. 1018)
(*c*) Letter, 1765, from William Shippen to William Hunter relating to the founding of a medical school at Philadelphia. (Douglas Papers IV (lb))
(*d*) Letter from Benjamin Franklin to Richard Price, 1784, asking for Price's opinion regarding the decision of the King of France to establish a Sinking Fund. (MS. Gen. 510/14)
(*e*) Covering letter, 1789, from George Washington to John Marshall, mentioning an enclosed letter (not present) concerning the Wilkinson conspiracy in Kentucky. (MS. Gen. 502 (15))
(*f*) Newspaper cuttings, bills, pamphlets, and some letters, 1908-19, relating to William Sulzer, Governor of New York. Most of these relate to the period after he had been removed from office, when he was connected with the American Party and the Liberty League. (MS. Gen. 643)

(*g*) Letter, 1917, from Woodrow Wilson to Albert Venn Dicey. (MS. Gen. 508 (46))
(*h*) Letter from Woodrow Wilson to Sir Donald MacAlister, 1919, regretting his inability to accept an invitation to visit Glasgow. (MS. Gen. 510 (12))

DEPARTMENT OF ECONOMIC HISTORY, UNIVERSITY OF GLASGOW, Glasgow G12 8QQ

COLQUHOUN COLLECTION OF BUSINESS RECORDS.

(All enquiries should be directed to the Archivist, University Archives, Glasgow)

(*a*) Alexander Sharp & Co., merchants: Cash book, 1754-7. (UGD/19/1/1)
(*b*) Blackie & Sons, publishers: New York ledger, 1857-9. (UGD/61/7)
(*c*) James Finlay & Co. Ltd., merchants: Correspondence concerning Wyoming Ranch Purchase, 1904, including copy of Article of Partnership between John Walsh and J.B. Muir, both of Sheridan, Wyoming. (UGD/91/232)
(*d*) William Beardmore & Co., steelmakers: Report on a visit to the U.S.A. by P.A. Thomas and T.O. Thomson, 1959. (UGD/100/1/13/27)
(*e*) Burt Papers: Peter Burt and his son Thomas were the designers of the first Burt Single Sleeve Valve Engine. This collection of papers consists mainly of material relating to licence agreements for the engine, including some letters from American representatives of the Burts, 1924-8. (UGD/103)

Other firms dealing with America include William Denny & Bros., Dunbarton (shipbuilders), 1844-1952, and Alexander Stephen & Sons, Linthouse (shipbuilders), 1848-1968. Companies with occasional American business interests are Glenfield & Kennedy Ltd., Kilmarnock (hydraulic engineers), 1870-1944; Dubs & Co., Glasgow (locomotive builders), 1864-1902; Neilson & Co., Glasgow (locomotive builders), 1850-1902; and North British Locomotive Co., Glasgow (locomotive builders), 1903-48.

RENFREW DISTRICT LIBRARY SERVICE, Marchfield Avenue, Paisley PA3 2RJ

CAIRN OF LOCHWYNYOCH COLLECTION.

The Cairn of Lochwynyoch collection consists of a number of volumes compiled by Andro Crawfurd. Most of the material refers to Scottish affairs, although some of the printed and MS. items, including those listed below, concern Americans and American affairs.
(*a*) Nova Scotia Baronetcies (Subtitle of 'Baron Renfrew and Baron Coulston'), vol. 31, sec. 4. 1847/8 newspaper correspondence (cuttings) and some original letters, between R. Broun, Bart., and 'J.R.' P. 7 discusses the British American Association.
(*b*) Weaving. Many references, e.g., vol. 10, p. 233ff. Many major U.S. textile plants, e.g. at Pawtucket, R.I., are offshoots of the Paisley works. There is much description of working conditions, wages, and technical details throughout the 'Cairn'.
(*c*) Wilson, Alexander, poet and ornithologist. Vol. 6, p. 19ff and vol. 7, p. 144ff. Very useful and detailed articles, treating of the life and letters of Alexander Wilson, and also quoting selected poems, often in the various early/unpublished forms.
(*d*) Witherspoon, Rev. John, D.D., L.L.D. Vol. 30, sec. 2, pp. 91-2. Sidelights on his early days in Beith and Paisley. In *Paisley Pamphlets*, 1737-1893, there is the text of many of J. Witherspoon's works (sermons and letters to students at Princeton, etc.) *See the index*.
(*e*) 'The folly and falsehood of the Book of Mormon', 1839. 3½ pages quoted from the *Lunenburg Colonial Churchman*. Vol. 24, no. 20.

PAISLEY PAMPHLETS. 19th century.

This large collection includes much material of American interest, especially regarding slavery and the anti-slavery crusade in America, and emigration to the United States.

TAYSIDE

ALLIANCE TRUST CO. LTD., Meadow House, 64 Reform Street, Dundee

BUSINESS RECORDS.[1]

Records consisting of minute-books, balance sheets, scrapbooks, company reports, etc., concerning investment in the United States, especially farm mortgages, land speculation, and railroads, 1873-1914. The operations of the various trusts which have now amalgamated to form the Alliance Trust Co. Ltd. covered a wide area, including Oregon, Washington, New Mexico, Wisconsin, and Hawaii.

NORTHERN AMERICAN TRUST CO., LTD., Friarfield House, Dundee

BUSINESS RECORDS.[1] *c*. 350 volumes. 1873-current.

Group of investment trust companies since 1970 comprising the First Scottish American Trust Co. Ltd. and the North American Trust Co. Ltd. Prior to this date five companies were included in the group. The records consist primarily of minute-books, journals, ledgers, balance sheets, lists and valuation of investments and registers of members. The trusts' extensive interests in the United States, including investments in railroads, are portrayed in considerable detail.

UNIVERSITY LIBRARY, Dundee DD1 4HN

RUGGLES BEQUEST. 2 certificates. 1864.
(*a*) Certificate of Commission appointing F.R. McReady as 1st Lieu-

1. See J.C. Gilbert, *A History of Investment Trusts in Dundee, 1873-1938* (London, 1939), *passim*; W. Turrentine Jackson, 'The Chavez Land Grant: A Scottish Investment in New Mexico, 1881-1940', *Pacific Historical Review*, vol. xxi, pp. 349-66, 1952. See also *When Grass was King* (Boulder, Colo., University of Colorado Press, 1956), particularly a monograph on 'British Interests in the Range Cattle Industry'. Professor Jackson was able to examine certain records of other investment trusts which we were not able to; some of them figure in the above works, others in his *The Enterprising Scot* (Edinburgh, 1968).

1. See J.C. Gilbert, *A History of Investment Trusts in Dundee, 1873-1938* (London, 1939).

tenant in the 51st Regiment of Infantry, New York State Volunteers, to become effective from 19th Mar. 1864. 14th Apr. 1864. (MS. 29/2/9)
(*b*) Certificate of Commission appointing F.R. McReady as Captain in said regiment, effective from 12th Oct. 1864. 7th Dec. 1864. (MS. 29/2/10)

GLASSITE CHURCH. Letter. 1765

Letter, 7th Apr. 1765. Oliver Deming, Wethersfield, Connecticut, to Robert Sandeman, Portsmouth, New Plymouth. Mentions particular doctrinal matters arising out of *Letters of Theron* by Sandeman; expresses regret that Sandeman's other writings 'are not spread into this Part of America'. (MS. 9/4/2 (6))

ABERDEEN-ANGUS CATTLE SOCIETY, Pedigree House, 6 Kings Place, Perth

PEDIGREE EXPORTATION CERTIFICATES (manuscript).[1] 7 volumes. 1887-to date.

These volumes contain a complete record of all exports of pedigreed Aberdeen-Angus cattle from Great Britain, Northern Ireland, and Eire, and include many references to American buyers. Exports prior to 1887 can be found in the first ten volumes of the Society's *Herd Book*, dating back to *c*. 1840.

PERTH MUSEUM AND ART GALLERY, George Street, Perth

LITERARY AND ANTIQUARIAN SOCIETY OF PERTH. Correspondence and address. 1741-75.

(*a*) Letters and other papers relating to James Freeman, tobacco planter and merchant, Maryland, 1741-3.
(*b*) Correspondence from William Wallace, planter, Potomac River, concerning American tobacco crop and Spanish depredations on shipping, 1741-3.
(*c*) Address from county of Perth to George III, condemning sedition in American colonies, 1775.

1. See Alvin H. Sanders, *History of Aberdeen-Angus Cattle, with Particular Reference to... North America* (Chicago, 1928).

NORTHERN IRELAND

ANTRIM

PUBLIC RECORD OFFICE OF NORTHERN IRELAND, 66 Balmoral Avenue, Belfast BT9 6NY

There is no county archive system in Ulster, but the Public Record Office acts as a repository of private papers as well as of public documents. Indeed, the Office is extremely energetic in searching out materials relevant to the six counties of Northern Ireland and, when it cannot obtain the originals, in making photographic reproductions, or occasionally typescripts.

Public documents have only been deposited in Belfast since the establishment of the separate government of Northern Ireland in 1921, although some papers of the period prior to partition have been transferred from Dublin.

There is a card index of names mentioned in the records; otherwise the researcher must rely on the lists of accessions and the descriptions of the principal collections to be found in the series of Deputy Keeper's *Reports*.

The references to the materials examined were all located with the help of the Deputy Keeper and his staff. 'D' refers to deposited original documents, 'T' and 'Mic' indicate copies.

DOBBS PAPERS. 1683-1775. (D. 162)

Arthur Dobbs (1689-1765),[1] Irish author and statesman, Governor of North Carolina 1754-65. Even before he was appointed governor, he was greatly interested in North American affairs, particularly Canada; and he became a vigorous critic of the activities of the Hudson's Bay Company. So the collection includes important manuscripts relating to Canada that he collected, as well as his own papers. Among the latter there are a few official papers of his governorship, but more concerning his efforts to stimulate American trade; including the journal of the ship *California* (N. 44) which he dispatched in 1746 to Hudson Bay to find a Northwest Passage. Of particular interest are the following:

(*a*) Journal of Henry Kelsey, 1683-1722.[2] It covers the life of a Hudson's Bay Company official, and gives an account of Kelsey's explorations, north of Churchill, in 1689 and two years later among the Indians, actually reaching the Prairies.

(*b*) Twelve or more letters or copies of letters, 1749-52, from Dobbs, or sponsored by Dobbs, concerning conditions and prospects for settlement in North Carolina; also some references to the Ohio region. (Nos. 45-48, 52, 57, 60-61, 69.)

(*c*) Letter, London, 10 Mar. 1750, from P. Collinson to Dobbs concerning trees and fruits imported from America.

(*d*) Statement of reasons for high price and scarcity of beaver fur in London. n.d. (*c.* 1751).

(*e*) Paper attacking the management of the affairs of the Hudson's Bay Company. n.d. (*c.* 1752).

(*f*) Letter, 17 Mar. 1755, from Dobbs to Alex McAulay, on his work in North Carolina and his efforts for direct trade with Ireland.

(*g*) Anonymous diary, 27 June to 19 Sept. 1759 (about 8,000 words), apparently kept by an officer of Wolfe's staff and relating to the Quebec campaign.

(*h*) Letters and legal documents relating to the disposal of Dobbs's estates in North Carolina, 1764-75.

FLOYD PAPERS. (T. 1095)

Journal of Capt. Alexander Chesney (1755-1815).[3] The 'journal' is really an autobiography, written at various times and with some additions, concerning previous and subsequent family history, probably by his son, Charles Francis. Alexander Chesney's parents settled in South Carolina about 1768 and prospered; he served under Cornwallis and Hastings, raising companies of Loyalists. The descriptions of Loyalist sentiment and action are detailed and interesting. He then returned to press claims for compensation in London, and became a customs officer in County Down.

SEVEN YEARS' WAR. Diary. 1759-60. (D. 678)

Diary of the British campaign in Canada, July-Sept. 1760, including copies of correspondence, July-Aug. 1759, between Generals Wolfe and Murray; the writer may have been an officer on the staff of Murray, perhaps a secretary, and he gives a vivid day-to-day account of the campaign.

PERCEVAL PAPERS. Letters. 1759-60, 1768. (D. 906)

(*a*) The correspondence of William Perceval, Dublin barrister, includes a group of letters, 1759-60, which report on the activities of Alexander and Joshua Cathcart, serving in Canada.

(*b*) The correspondence of Rev. Dr. Kane Perceval, Dublin, includes a request, 1768, for advice about settling in East Florida, with references to the purchase of stock, Negroes, implements, etc.

POMEROY PAPERS. 1760's-70's. (T. 2954)

Letters and papers of the Rt. Hon. General John Pomeroy, younger brother of the 1st Viscount Harberton.

(*a*) About twenty letters and papers to General John Pomeroy, several of which are of some importance. One letter from J. Stuart to Pomeroy, 6 July 1775, contains an account of the Battle of Bunker Hill and tells of the attempts of the British to gain reinforcements from the Canadians and Indians. A second account of the battle, dated 26 June 1775, is sent to Pomeroy from William [Hatton?]. A third letter from Arthur James Pomeroy to his uncle, Gen. John Pomeroy, comments on the state of hostilities in North America in July 1776.

(*b*) Col. (later Gen.) Pomeroy's diary of his voyage with the 64th Regiment of Foot to North America, Sept. 1768.

MACARTNEY PAPERS. 1770-89. (D. 572)

George Macartney (1737-1806), 1st Earl Macartney; statesman, Secretary for Ireland 1769-72. Many of the letters come from Thomas Allan, an M.P. in the Irish Parliament, who appears to have acted as a kind of agent for the Irish government in London.[4] Macartney was not

1. See Desmond Clarke, *Arthur Dobbs Esquire, 1689-1765* (London, 1957).
2. Published as *The Kelsey Papers*, with an introduction by A.G. Doughty and Chester Martin (Ottawa, 1929).
3. Published as *The Journal of Alexander Chesney, a South Carolina Loyalist in the Revolution and After*, ed. by E. Alfred Jones and others (Columbus, 1921). (Ohio State University Studies. Contributions in history and political science, no. 7.)
4. See Edith M. Johnston, 'The Career and Correspondence of Thomas Allan, *c.* 1725-1798', *Irish Historical Studies*, vol. x , pp. 298-324, 1957.

directly involved in American affairs. A typed calendar has the following American entries:
(*a*) Discussion of Burke's motion on America. 1770. (Vol. 3, no. 67.)
(*b*) Lord North and the repeal of the American Acts. 1770. (Vol. 3, no. 40.)
(*c*) Commons debate on American taxes. 1770. (Vol. 3, no. 43.)
(*d*) Repeal of American duties. 1770. (Vol. 3, no. 39.)
(*e*) A justification of the War of Independence. 1789. (Vol. 9, no. 49.)

PERCEVAL-MAXWELL PAPERS. 1774-8. (Transcripts and photostats.) (T. 1023)

The American section of these papers mainly concern Richard Montgomery (1736-75), a distinguished general in the Continental Army, who was born in Donegal (his father was M.P. for Lifford), and served at the taking of Quebec in 1759. In 1772 he settled in America, at Rhinebeck, N.Y., and in 1775 was appointed brigadier general by Congress, and the attack on Canada fell into his hands; he was killed in the assault on Quebec. Some of the later documents may have passed through the hands of Hugh Maxwell, born in Ireland, emigrated to New England, also a distinguished American officer. There is a typed calendar.
(*a*) Loyal address, Sept. 1774, of Canadian citizens of Quebec to George III dissociating themselves from *'murmures du très petit nombre'*. (No. 112)
(*b*) Letter, 21 Feb. 1775, of Samuel Adams, W. Mackay, and Joseph Warren on behalf of the Boston Committee of Correspondence to certain 'friends of liberty' at Quebec (Zachary McCawley, John Aitkin, John Lee, John Patterson, John Wells, and Randal Meredith) arguing the American cause. (No. 113)
(*c*) Draft of a reply, 12 April 1775, to the above, criticizing 'the mode the Congress at Philadelphia thought proper to pursue'. Ignorance and the power of the priests make any concurrence with the rebels unlikely in Quebec, and besides they expect speedy redress of grievances from the next Parliament. (No. 114)
(*d*) Letter, 18 May 1775 (endorsed 'a true and *exact* copy') from Ethan Allen to James Morrison and 'the merchants that are friendly to the cause of liberty in Montreal', demanding provisions for the Continental Army. (No. 115)
(*e*) 'Resolutions of His Majesty's loyal subjects and inhabitants of the city of Quebec' to secure property, peace, and order (the leading signatures are all of English officers!), 20 July 1775. (No. 116)
(*f*) Various letters, 22 Oct. 1775 - 19 Jan. 1776, from Richard Montgomery to Governor Carleton and others demanding the surrender of Montreal and then Quebec, and concerning treatment of prisoners of war. The letter, 19 Jan. 1776, is from Donald Campbell to Clinton, thanking him for General Montgomery's watch, and referring to treatment of prisoners, etc. (Nos. 117-21)
(*g*) Monthly return, 1 April 1776, of H.M. forces in the garrison at Quebec. (No. 22)
(*h*) General Schuyler at Saratoga to Col. John Paterson giving detailed orders for his regiment to go to Quebec, 29 April 1776. (No. 123A)
(*i*) Contemporary copy of a letter, 24 May 1776, from Moses Hazen, La Prairie, Que., to the Commissioners of Congress at Montreal describing a visit to Benedict Arnold's camp and discussing policy towards the Indians. (No. 124)
(*j*) Printed circular (in French), 31 Jan. 1778, from H.T. Cramahé to the officers of the militia asking for continued vigilance, and announcing the rates of compensation for those who took part in the campaigns of 1776 and 1777. (No. 125)
(*k*) Letter (in French), 18 Sept. 1778 [or 1779?] from Jas. Livingston, to the officers of the militia, asking them to bring their men to La Pointe Olivie, Que., and conveying the thanks of General 'Bastonay'. (No. 126)

FERGUSON, ANDREW. Letter-books. 1775-87. (D. 1130)

Out-letter books (2 vols.) of Andrew Ferguson, a general merchant in Londonderry, 1775-80 and 1783-7. His correspondence is with various firms, giving and confirming orders for general goods, and settling accounts. There is some reference to trade with Philadelphia.

DOWNSHIRE PAPERS (HILLSBOROUGH COLLECTION). Letters and sketches. 1778-80. (D. 607, D. 671)

The large collection of papers relating to Wills Hill, 1st Earl of Hillsborough, and 1st Marquis of Downshire (1718-93) is, from an inspection of a typescript calendar in the Record Office, mainly estate papers having almost no reference to his service as Lord North's Secretary of State for the Northern Department of Europe during the later part of the War of Independence, 1779-82. However, it includes the following:
(*a*) Belfast, 28 Nov. 1778, from Thomas Greg to Lord Downshire expressing anxiety for his property at New York and Dominica. He has sent his son to New York and asks for letters of recommendation for him.
(*b*) 6 May 1779, from Haddon Smith, formerly rector of Savannah, Ga., to Downshire, thanking him for the vicarage of Kilmud (or Kilmood), County Down, but asks for a compensation or pension as well.
(*c*) Memoranda, 21 June 1779, from Robert Hodgson setting out a plan for the military and economic domination of North and South America by the utilization of the British West Indies and Nicaragua as military and naval bases.
(*d*) Sketches, 1780, of the British siege operations before Charleston, S.C. (D. 671)

PILLAR, WILLIAM. Correspondence, accounts (4 documents). 1785-9. (T. 1334)

Correspondence and accounts, 1785-9, some relating to William Pillar of Baltimore.

DUNLAP, JOHN (1747-1812). Letters. 1780's. (T. 1136)

Immigrant to Philadelphia from Strabane, County Tyrone, printer of the *Pennsylvania Packet*, printer to the Convention of 1774, to the First Continental Congress, and of the Declaration of Independence. An incomplete examination showed about a dozen letters, mostly in the 1780's, mostly on family affairs, but some account of his role as a captain of the militia in putting down the rebellion of 1794 in Western Pennsylvania.

EARL OF GOSFORD PAPERS. Letter. 1780's. (D. 1606)

Among this extremely large collection are a notable concentration of letters between Lord Gosford and his son, Arthur Acheson. Dated 1785 to 1789, the letters touch upon a number of subjects, and include one which discusses unrest in the American colonies in 1775.

MASSEREENE-FOSTER PAPERS. (D. 562)

Among this huge collection, 1625-1845, a basic source for Irish eighteenth-century history, the papers of John Foster, Baron Oriel (1740-1828) and of his father Antony, contain many important references to trade with America. John Foster was Chief Baron of the Exchequer 1766-77; both John and Antony were closely connected with the Linen Board. For further details of the general nature of the collection see Deputy Keeper's *Report* for 1949-50, pp. 13-7. Time allowed only a quick inspection of the following papers in which the

typescript calendar specifically mentions America, but obviously many general headings under 'Linen' would also refer to such exports.
(*a*) Bundle of about two dozen long letters and highly detailed statistical reports, 1763-97, on Irish-American trade, some on London's exports to America, American Loyalists, abstracts of American laws, including that setting up a bank of the United States. (No. cviii)
(*b*) Six manuscript and annotated printed drafts of different states of a Bill on American trade, 1783-5. (No. cl)
(*c*) Bundle of miscellaneous papers: two land sale circulars from New Hampshire, 1785. Printed pamphlet, *Facts and calculations respecting the population and territory of the United States of America*, *c.* 1797. Some notes on a Bill or Act headed 'Alterations for American Trade Bill, n.d. Copy of His Majesty's Advocate's opinions given to cases referred to him from the Treasury on various problems arising from the Peace Treaty concerning American trade, 1785'. (No. ci)
(*d*) Bundle of papers concerning the Irish Linen Board and exports, and petition to Parliament in 1804 for the removal of export duties; includes a table giving the quantity and type of linen exported to twenty-three different markets in America, Canada, and the West Indies, 1795-1805; also a table of the total quantities and value of all linen exports to America, 1798-1807. (No. ccxcviii)

YOUNG FAMILY. Correspondence. 1786-94. (D. 729)

Correspondence, 1786-94, relating to the business interests of the Young family, general merchants in New York and Belfast.

PRENDERGAST, JAMES. Typescript account. 1789-1834. (T. 2410)

Typescript account of Lieut. Prendergast, Co. Monaghan, describing his military career and his settling in Canada.

DUFFIN, ADAM. Correspondence. 1794, 1814-34. (T. 1252)

Correspondence relating to the linen business of Adam Duffin in Charleston, S.C., including a letter, 1794, from J. Davison in Baltimore about the shipment of linen to Charleston; and others, 1814-34, about the linen business and family affairs in Belfast and South Carolina.

FORBES, JOHN. Documents, letter. 1797-9, 1801. (T. 1372)

Two documents, 1797-9, containing an account of the debts due by John Forbes to 'Messrs. Snodgrass & Coy., late of Glasgow', and a letter, 1801, from Forbes in Columbia, Va., to Messrs. Moody & May relating to his debt.

GREER FAMILY. Correspondence. 18th century. (D. 1044)

Correspondence of the Greer family of Co. Tyrone, including some relating to their linen trade with America, carried on through Samuel and John Morton of Philadelphia.

BRYSON, ANDREW. Document. 1801. (T. 1373)

Long account written in 1801 by Andrew Bryson of New York, describing his transportation to the West Indies as a United Irishman and his enforced military service there.

L'ESTRANGE AND BRETT (solicitors, Belfast). Documents. 1802-*c.* 1850. (D. 1905)

c. 100,000 documents, including letter-books, 1802 and 1834-41, of James Stevenson of Belfast, trading in wine and linen with New York, and correspondence, etc., relating to shares in an emigrant ship to New York and Quebec, *c.* 1850.

HOLMES, SAMUEL. Journal. 1814-5. (T. 1970)

This journal, kept probably by an army surgeon named Samuel Holmes in 1814 and 1815, runs to over 200 pages, and is detailed, well informed, and self-consciously literary. He begins by describing the voyage from Cork to Quebec, and from the point where he lands in Canada he becomes absorbed with questions of Canadian history, politics, society, emigration, etc.

DAWSON, LIEUT. A.C. Diary. 1818-21. (D. 618)

This diary of a voyage to the West Indies contains a rather slight account (pp. 168-9) of a short visit to New York. He visits a penitentiary, the dockyards, and generalizes rapidly and tritely about the relative beauty of English and American women and American national expansion.

GREER, HAMILTON AND GAILEY, SOLICITORS. Documents. 1821-*c.* 1865.

(*a*) Correspondence between Robert Given in Alabama and New Orleans, and his father, John Given, in Dervock, Co. Antrim, 1821-2. (D. 1141)
(*b*) Diary kept by J.B. Hamilton, 1859-60, in which he records a journey from Belfast to New York and then to Augusta, Ga., and comments on slavery and on cotton processing (D. 1518)
(*c*) Correspondence, etc., of the Stavely family of Ballyboyland, Co. Antrim, including emigrant letters from Georgia in 1823. (D. 1835)
(*d*) Letter from John Hamilton in New York, commenting on the state of trade there, *c.* 1865. (T. 2201)

R. AND J. WORKMAN OF BELFAST. Ledgers. 1825-45. (Mic. 142)

Ledgers (3 vols.) of R. and J. Workman, muslin manufacturers in Belfast, with details of voyages to various ports, including Quebec, 1825-45.

TYLER PAPERS.[5] 1828-67.

(*a*) Long letter, New York, 22 Apr. 1828, from William Sampson (the exiled revolutionary of 1798) to Dr. Henry H. Tyler, concerning Tyler's claim for a legacy in America.
(*b*) 'Journal of a Voyage to America',[6] 1836, by Thomas Cather. Cather and Henry Tyler, son of the above Dr. Tyler, made a ten-week tour of the United States, covering most of the inhabited country, meeting many celebrities, including President Jackson, Martin Van Buren, and Henry Clay.
(*c*) Six letters, from Liverpool, New York, Baltimore, Charleston, S.C., Havana, and New Orleans, 2 Feb. - 7 July 1836, from Henry Tyler while on the above tour to relatives at home. Mainly descriptive; one of 7 May quite interesting on Southern habits of violence.
(*d*) Seven letters, 19 Mar. - 3 Aug. 1836, from Thomas Cather. These are fuller letters than Tyler's; they include references to visits to meet President Jackson, and then Senators Clay and Crittenden in Kentucky; the widow of Wolfe Tone; to a Shaker settlement at Pleasant Hill; and some ordinary but spontaneous comments on the fine prospects for the emigrant from Ireland.
(*e*) Two letters, 1 Aug. 1853 and 17 Mar. 1867 (?), from one D.S.

5. These papers, formerly in the possession of the late Sir Henry MacDonald-Tyler, The Umbra, Magilligan, were placed in the Public Record Office of Northern Ireland in late 1976.
6. Published in part as Thomas Cather's *Journal of a Voyage to America in 1836* (London and Emmaus, Pa.: [Rodale Press], 1955).

Cooper, a family friend, to Henry H. Tyler, describing briefly his investments on the New York stock exchange; and, very fully, his fishing trips in Maine and New Brunswick. Some inevitable and salty comments on American character.

MONTGOMERY, HENRY RIDDELL. Diary. 1830's. (T. 1491)

Diary kept by Henry Riddell Montgomery of Co. Antrim, including description of voyage to the West Indies and New York.

GLASGOW. Journal of a voyage on board from Liverpool to New York, Oct. to Dec. 1833. (D. 280)

Journal [a fifth of which is missing] addressed by an unknown writer to his mother, giving full and detailed account of the voyage - usual brutality of crew and apparent fecklessness of passengers in not bringing enough food with them.

DAWSON, LIEUT. ROBERT PEEL. Extracts of letters from the United States. 1838-9. (T. 850)

Dawson, a nephew of Robert Peel, was a young officer with the 2nd Grenadier Guards. He was involved in the operations to crush the rebellion of 1838 in Canada, and the following year toured in the United States, through the north-east to Maryland and Virginia. He was much impressed by both New York and Virginian society. All this he describes in rather simple letters home to his parents.

D. CAMPBELL & SON. Letter. 1841. (T. 1270)

Letter, 1841, from D. Campbell & Son, Liverpool, to William Fulton, Ballycastle, Co. Antrim, about payment for cotton received from Robert Fulton in New Orleans.

MITCHELL FAMILY. Documents. 1842-93. (D. 1665)

Includes letters from Capt. William Mitchell to his family and to his employers, J. and J. Cooke, shipowners, in Londonderry, 1842-55; among other places, he writes from Quebec, New Orleans, and Philadelphia, and gives details of voyages, cargoes, emigrant passengers, etc. Also the log-book of William Mitchell's barque *Barbara*, 1852-5, and the log-book of Charles Mitchell's voyage from Swansea to San Francisco via Cape Horn, 1892-3.

SWINEY, DANIEL (1826-1915). Autobiography. 19th century. (T. 3193)

Typescript copy of Daniel Swiney's autobiography entitled 'The Rockingstone'. Born in 1826 at Moyagh, Co. Donegal, he describes his childhood in Ireland and his adventures as a sailor in the early 1840's. He emigrated to the U.S. in 1846, settling in Iowa but making regular journeys back to Ireland where he worked for lengthy periods. The autobiography was written *c.* 1912, three years before his death.

McCLOY, DAVID. Diary. 19th century. (T. 2515)

Diary of David McCloy from Ballymena, Co. Antrim, giving details of his family, and especially emigration to Canada in 1847.

ROTHWELL FAMILY. Letters. *c.* 1850-1866. (T. 2621)

A few letters concerning Richard Rothwell, the painter, after his move to the U.S. in the 1850's. There are also what are in effect emigrant letters from Richard Rothwell, Jr., in Montreal, written to his mother between 1863 and 1866.

SMILEY, SAMUEL. Documents and correspondence. 1852-6. (D. 2723)

(*a*) Letters of Samuel Smiley, a sea captain in Liverpool, to his brother in Islandmagee, Co. Antrim, relating to the shipping business between Liverpool and the U.S.
(*b*) Smiley's log-book of the ship *Lady Russell* during her voyage from Liverpool to Mobile, Ala., 1853-4.

MITCHEL, JOHN (1815-75). 15 letters. 1850's - 60's. (T. 413 and D. 1078)

Irish journalist and Fenian leader who was transported to Van Diemen's Land in 1848, then in 1853 escaped to the United States where he edited the *Citizen* in New York, then the *Southern Citizen* at Knoxville, Tenn., and the *Richmond Enquirer* during the Civil War - he consistently supported the slave power; two of his sons were killed in the Confederate Army. Three letters (*a*, *b*, and *c*) are addressed to a Miss Thompson, while twelve, including some from America, are to Mitchel's sister, Matilda Dixon, in Co. Down.
(*a*) New York, 24 Apr. 1854, upholding his defence of slavery against charges of being inconsistent with his work for Irish emancipation.
(*b*) Stonington, Conn., 26 Aug. 1854, describing the puritanical 'dreariness' of Connecticut, professing to prefer Virginia, and arguing that justice can never by expected from England 'until the whole structure of society... shall have been destroyed by a revolution'.
(*c*) Tucaleechee Cove, Tenn., 1 Nov. 1855, vividly describing the primitiveness of the mountain people, the beauty of the landscape, the prospects of Tennessee, also criticizing the attitude of the Catholic clergy in Ireland to nationalism and hoping for a war between England and America as the best possible thing for Ireland.
(*d*) Twelve letters, 1848-74, from Mitchel to his sister, Matilda Dixon, in Co. Down, written during his exile in Bermuda, Tennessee, Washington, D.C., and Paris. The American letters in this group reflect his sympathy with the South and with Southern institutions during the pre-Civil War period.

WILLIAM McCORKELL AND COY., LONDONDERRY. Account book. 1855-60. (T. 2511)

274 pages of detailed accounts regarding all phases of the shipping business. Much information on disbursements from each voyage, insurance on shipping, and some emigrant passenger lists, 1855-60.

STEPHENS, JAMES (1825-1901). American diary, 13 Oct. 1858 to 25 Mar. 1860. (About 22,000 words.) (D. 518)

Stephens, the well-known Fenian leader, wrote an account of his trip to secure control of the funds in the hands of the 'Directory' formed in 1848 when revolution seemed imminent in Ireland. He apparently intended to deposit the diary with John O'Mahony as a defence of his own actions. He visits John Mitchel himself at Knoxville, Tenn., who gives him letters to the leaders of the Directory asking them to accede to his wishes as regards available funds. The five recipients were: T.F. Meagher, Judge Robert Emmet, Judge O'Connor, Richard O'Gorman, and Horace Greeley. The diary is a vivid and detailed account of Ireland-in-exile, and of the very beginnings of the Fenian movement.

WHIGHAM, WILLIAM. Business papers. *c.* 1860 - *c.* 1900. (D. 953)

Correspondence, etc., *c.* 1860 - *c.* 1900, relating to the business activities of William Whigham of Co. Armagh in San Francisco and Tahiti.

THOMPSON, JOHN. 2 letters. 1861. (T. 1585)

Two letters, 1861, from Private John Thompson, 1st U.S. Artillery, to his father Robert Thompson, Co. Londonderry, containing an eye-witness account of the siege of Fort Sumter.

McFARLAND, WILLIAM. Letter. 1864. (D. 732)

Letter, 1864, from William McFarland, Portsmouth, Va., to John McFarland in Philadelphia, describing his service as a Federal soldier at the siege of Richmond, Va.

REID, MAYNE. Documents and correspondence. 1865-83. (D. 2802)

300 documents. These consist mainly of letters written by Mayne Reid, novelist and adventurer, from New York and London to Charles Ollivant. Reid was born in Ballyroney, Co. Down, in 1818. In the U.S. during the 1840's and 1850's he fought in the Mexican War, started a newspaper, and wrote novels of romance and adventure.

JAMES CALDWELL AND SON. Passenger account book. 1868-1934. (Mic. 203)

Passenger account book (2 vols.) providing details of money paid by prospective emigrants to North America.

WORKMAN, THOMAS. Journals. 1869-91. (D. 2778)

Journals (with photographs) of journeys to the United States and the East Indies by Thomas Workman of Belfast.

SHAW, ROBERT. Diary and letter. 1872-4. (T. 1913)

Diary kept by Robert Shaw from 1872 to 1874. Shaw was born in Indianapolis in 1852 and in 1867 left for Newry where he worked as an assistant in William Galbraith's grocery shop. He was then employed as a purser clerk on the S.S. *City of London*, travelling between Liverpool and New York. In 1873 he returned to the U.S. and finally settled in Earlham [New Mexico?] as a herdsman. There is also a letter from Shaw whilst in Jacksonville, Ill., in 1874.

GAFFIKIN AND COY., BELFAST. Letter-book. *c.* 1874 - *c.* 1926. (D. 1796)

Out-letter book (2 vols.) of Gaffikin & Coy., linen manufacturers, including some correspondence with firms in the United States.

WILLIAM MITCHELL LTD. Business records. 1879, 1889-1907. (D. 864)

A telegraphic code book, 1879, Messrs. Gill & Fisher, Baltimore; and correspondence and accounts, 1889-1907, relating to flour shipments from the United States.

FULLERTON, ROBERT (1845-1945). Autobiography. 19th-20th centuries. (T. 3186)

Typed notes on the life of Robert Fullerton, born in 1845 in Ballyrichard, near Larne, Co. Antrim. He emigrated to the U.S. in 1867 and managed a lumber business in Des Moines, Iowa. He died in Pasadena, Calif., 1945. (Compiled by Ora D. Fullerton.)

BROADWAY DAMASK COY. LTD. Business records. 1882-*c.* 1950. (D. 1193)

Accounts, correspondence, order books, including details of sales to the United States.

GRIBBON & SON. Sales books. 1902-13. (D. 1191)

The business records, 1847-1936, of Gribbon & Son, linen manufacturers, Coleraine, include sales books for New York, 1902-13.

ANNESLEY PAPERS. (D. 1225)

This large collection has little direct relevance to American affairs, although there are occasional letters of interest, e.g. a letter from William B. Cochran in New York, 1904, which describes 'the rather stormy debates which marked the late Congressional Session'.

BALLYGARVEY SPINNING AND WEAVING COY. Accounts, etc. 1908-31. (D. 1933)

Accounts, etc., of the Ballygarvey Spinning & Weaving Coy., Co. Antrim, 1901-31, with details of sales to the U.S., Canada, etc. from 1908.

CARSON PAPERS. Letter, 1916. (D. 1507)

These surviving papers of Lord Carson of Duncairn are an incomplete archive and consist of the material not destroyed in his London house during the Blitz. Among the Admiralty Papers (1916-7) is a letter from Noel Buxton, M.P., describing American attitudes towards the War in 1916.

DUFF, WALTER. Documents and correspondence. 1916-44. (D. 2481)

Letters from Walter Duff to his aunt, Rosanna Duff, Coagh, Co. Tyrone, mainly relating to his activities as an evangelistic preacher in Oregon.

HENDERSON AND EADIE OF LISBELLAW. Business records. 1937-62. (D. 1938)

In-letters from the agents of Henderson & Eadie, woollen manufacturers. Letters originate from places like New York and California and include, for example, comments on the poor market for tweeds in New York in 1938.

EMIGRANT LETTERS AND RECORDS. 18th-20th centuries. (In various collections.)

The Public Record Office of Northern Ireland possesses one of the largest collections of emigrant letters and records available anywhere in the British Isles or Ireland. Because of the size of these holdings, these MSS. are listed below according to the state of the Union to which they relate. Those collections which refer to more than one state are listed separately.

ALABAMA

Letter from Miss Nancy Wightman, a teacher near Florence, Ala., to John Arnold in Belfast, 1845. (D. 1771)

CALIFORNIA

(*a*) Two letters, from San Francisco, [1851?], and Marysville, Calif., 1851, from Thomas Vogan, who had originally emigrated to Australia, but had left there for California in 1849. (D. 268, nos. 7,8)
(*b*) Emigrant letters from members of the Williamson family in California, 1853-68. (Mic. 66)
(*c*) Letters, 1875-89, from members of the Breeze family in San Francisco and San Miguel, Calif., to relatives in Co. Down. (T. 1381)

COLORADO

Letter, 1902, from Bert Spotten, Sanford, Colorado, to his uncle in Ireland, describing conditions in a mining camp. (D. 693)

FLORIDA

(*a*) Emigrant letter from William Holmes in Pensacola, Fla., to his father in Tullygoney, Co. Tyrone, 1777. (D. 1782)
(*b*) Emigrant letter from Annie McKeown, Miami, Fla., to Nan Trimingham, Belfast, *c*. 1925. (T. 1777)

GEORGIA

(*a*) Correspondence, 1762-99, including letters from members of the Wylly family in Savannah, Ga., with some comment on climate, dress, and rice and deer skins as local products. (D. 955)
(*b*) Campbell-Allen family papers. Includes diaries kept by William J. Campbell-Allen of Greenisland, Co. Antrim, during visits to the U.S. in 1831 and 1838. Also more than 200 letters relating to family business and property connexions in Savannah, Ga., *c*. 1820-*c*. 1850. (D. 1558)

ILLINOIS

(*a*) Two letters, 1842-3, from James Sloan in Nauvoo, Ill., to his cousin, Andrew McReynolds, in Detroit. Sloan was a Dungannon solicitor who emigrated in 1834. After working for three years in a store he became a Mormon clerk, and he describes the tenets and practices of his church in some detail. (T. 2304)
(*b*) Thirty emigrant letters from members of the Porter family in Chebanese, Ill., to the Browne family of Mullaghglass, 1844-1928. (D. 1152)
(*c*) Legal papers, 1889-1903, relating to the eviction of Bernard McGroggan, Antrim, and his emigration to Illinois. (D. 741)

INDIANA

Emigrant letter from John Gorman in Indiana to his brother, Philip, in which he discusses farming conditions, 1866. (T. 1743)

IOWA

Emigrant letter, 1856, from Henry Allen in Iowa to his cousin, Rev. Robert Allen, of Dublin. (T. 3084)

KENTUCKY

Emigrant letter from Henry Neill in Louisville, Kentucky, to Samuel Neill, Banbridge, Co. Down, 1839: "tis as customary here to set up and sell Negroes at auction as it is horses in Ireland....' (T. 1796)

LOUISIANA

(*a*) Four letters, 1818-20, from Thomas Clark in New Orleans to his family in Limavady, on his voyage to, and his first impressions of life in, America. (D. 3127)
(*b*) Caldwell & Robinson, Solicitors, Londonderry. This collection of *c*. 100 documents includes a few emigrant letters from the Campbell family in Vermilion, La., 1844-50, which comment on the election of President Polk and on the Oregon Question. (D. 1781)
(*c*) Emigrant letter, 1866, from Hugh McCloskey, New Orleans, to his nephew, advising him to obtain a good education before considering emigrating. (T. 1767)
(*d*) Letters, 1917-8, from George Langtry in New Orleans, with some comment on the course of the First World War. (D. 1177)

MARYLAND

(*a*) Several letters, 1817-8, from four families living in Baltimore to families in various towns in Co. Londonderry, describing life in America. (D. 2547)
(*b*) Letter from Mary Galbraith in Baltimore, 1832. (D. 2095)

MASSACHUSETTS

(*a*) Letter from David Bailey in Boston to his brother, John Bailey, Co. Tyrone. (T. 2332)
(*b*) Four emigrant letters from James Fleming in Boston, 1861-5. (Mic. 162)
(*c*) Letter from Hugh McSherry in Boston to Patrick Gillfedere, Lough Hill, Co. Fermanagh. (D. 2235)
(*d*) Emigrant letter from Boston mentioning the visit of Bishop Alexander of Derry, 1892. (D. 1712)
(*e*) Letter from Mrs. P. McNally in Massachusetts to her brother, John McNally, 1933. (D. 2721)

MICHIGAN

Emigrant letter from John McKay, Campbell's Corner Post Office, Mich., to Robert McConaghy, Ballintoy. (D. 2007)

MISSISSIPPI

Letter, *c*. 1862, from John Knight near Corinth, Miss., to his brother and sister, with references to the Civil War and the battle of Pittsburgh.

MONTANA

Letter, 1889, from Hannah Smith, Dillon, Montana, to her cousin in Co. Down. (T. 1441)

NEW JERSEY

(*a*) Emigrant letter from John and Jane Chambers in Monmouth County, N.J., 1796, to their relatives at Moneyglass, Co. Armagh. The letter discusses the economics of farming and the provisions essential for an emigrant voyage, including '3 gallons of porter'. (T. 2299)
(*b*) Letter from William McKibbin in Uniontown, N.J., 1882. (D. 2235)
(*c*) Letters, 1894-6, from N.K. Harshaw, Paterson, N.J., to relatives in Co. Down. (T. 1505)

NEW YORK

(*a*) Letter from H. Pringle in Fort Carillon, Lake George [N.Y.], to Col. Havilland in Fort Edward, Mar. 1758, describing some of his activities during the French and Indian War. (T. 2095)
(*b*) Letters, 1774-96, written by members of the Blair family in New York and later as merchants in the East Indies to relatives in Newry, Co. Down. (Blair Family Papers) (D. 717)
(*c*) Correspondence of the Hilton family, Garvagh, Co. Londonderry, including three emigrant letters from New York in 1812. (D. 1226)
(*d*) Two letters, *c*. 1812, from Charles Martin in New York to his family in Ballooly, Co. Down. Refers to war between the U.S. and Canada. (D. 2722)
(*e*) Letters, 1820's, from Andrew Robb, New York, to relatives in Co. Down. (T. 1454 or T. 1469)
(*f*) Four letters to and from members of the Park family in New York and Ireland. Subjects discussed include wages in America, prices of

land and livestock, and agriculture in general. 1821-38. (Park Family Papers) (T. 3172)

(*g*) Six letters, 1828-33, from John and Catherine McLees, New York, to their family in Co. Londonderry. (D. 904)

(*h*) Letter, 1829, from Thomas M. Grey in New York to Mrs. McCleery, Portaferry, Co. Down, giving family news.

(*i*) Letter, 1840, from James Knox, New York, to John Knox, Co. Antrim. (T. 1483)

(*j*) Collection of *c.* seventy documents, including a number of emigrant letters from members of the Weir family in New York, 1840-60, with some details about the selling of linen goods there in 1860. (D. 1948)

(*k*) Letter, 1842, from George Moore, Buffalo, N.Y., to his father in Co. Down; letter, 1861, from William Moore, New York, to his brother in Co. Down. (D. 877)

(*l*) Letter, 1845, from James and Mary Toal, New York, to Edward Toal in Belfast. (T. 1543)

(*m*) Letter, 1850, from William Young in New York to Robert Taylor in Coleraine, Co. Londonderry. (T. 1823)

(*n*) Letter, 1851, from Edward McNally, Middletown, [N.Y.?], to Captain William McNally, Co. Down. (T. 1448)

(*o*) Letter, 1852, from Walter Daly, Chatham, N.Y., to Michael Daly, Co. West Meath; also a letter, 1852, from Michael Daly to his sister in which he refers to his children, Walter and Mary, in the United States. (T. 1573 or T. 1577)

(*p*) Two letters, *c.* 1860, from James Ferris, New York, to his family in Co. Antrim. (T. 1458)

(*q*) Two letters of appreciation, 1871, from emigrants reaching New York: from agents of the Latter Day Saints to the captain, etc., of the S.S. *Minnesota*, and from passengers on the S.S. *Idaho* to the editor of the Liverpool *Mercury*. (T. 1370)

(*r*) Letter, 1871, from Elizabeth Dornan, New York, to relatives in Co. Down, commenting on the 'robbing and murdering in the city'; and two letters, 1871 and 1873, from John Ard, New York, to his relatives in Co. Down. (T. 1597)

(*s*) Forty-three documents, including letters from various members of the Sample family in New York, to Mrs. Ellen McIntyre and Mrs. Catherine Throne, Strabane, Co. Tyrone. 1876-1902. (T. 2722)

(*t*) *c.* fifty emigrant letters from the Wilson family in New York, 1883-1909, with comments on the Irish 'dynamiters' in New York in 1885, and on the Cuban War in 1898. (D. 1921)

(*u*) Two emigrant letters from C. Hobson in New York to his niece in Richhill, Co. Armagh, 1893, in which he describes in detail a visit to Ontario and Niagara Falls. (T. 1795)

(*v*) Several letters from New York, 1898; *c.* eighty letters from Rev. Charles McCready, Holy Cross Church, New York, to Miss Mary Maguire in Strabane, *c.* 1898-1914. (D. 1420)

(*w*) Several letters from Hugh and George Taylor in New York to their brother Alexander in Belfast, 1898-1903. (T. 2296)

(*x*) Emigrant letter from New York to Charles Connor in Belfast, 1907, commenting on the building trade in the city. (T. 2085)

(*y*) McCormick family correspondence, 1918-25. Includes two emigrant letters from New York to Ballycastle, Co. Antrim. (D. 2083)

NORTH CAROLINA

(*a*) Some notes on emigration from Ulster to North Carolina, 1736-7. (T. 342)

(*b*) Two letters from A. and J. de Bernière, 1799, to Edward Jones, North Carolina, requesting information on a suitable place in the U.S. to settle. (T. 2625)

OHIO

(*a*) Letter, 1836, from Moses Dawson, Cincinnati, to James Stuart, Pittsburgh, relating to the trusteeship of the Lancasterian School, Belfast. (D. 926)

(*b*) Emigrant letter, 1848, from John Orr in Ohio to his sister, Rebecca Orr, in Omagh, Co. Tyrone, discussing work for women in America. (T. 2027)

(*c*) Emigrant letter from Cincinnati, Ohio, 1853. (D. 2168)

(*d*) Six emigrant letters from the Crawford family in Ohio to relatives in Ballymena, Co. Antrim, 1860-87. (T. 2338)

PENNSYLVANIA

(*a*) *C.* seventy documents. These include an exceptionally good group of emigrant letters sent to the Weir family in Stewartstown, Co. Tyrone, from Philadelphia. Subjects discussed include American religion and politics in the 1770's. The remaining letters, 1780-*c.*1850, are concerned with the business activities, mostly in linen and woollens, of friends and relatives of the Weirs in various places, e.g. Philadelphia. (D. 1140)

(*b*) Emigrant letter from Andrew Martin in Philadelphia to John Martin in Downpatrick, 1785. (T. 1752)

(*c*) Emigrant letter from John Denison in Pennsylvania to Samuel Denison in Dromore, Co. Down, 1789: 'Land can be purchased hear for twenty shillings a acer....' (T. 2294)

(*d*) Three letters, 1794-6, between William Wade and Joseph Bralston, a prominent Freemason, of Philadelphia. (T. 1269, nos. 1-3)

(*e*) Three letters, 1795-1830, to relatives in Co. Donegal: 1795, from John Colhoun in Chambersburg, Pa.; 1807, from Alexander Reed in Washington, Pa.; and 1830, from William Colhoun in Washington, Pa. (T. 1466)

(*f*) Letters, 1810 and 1814, from William Heazleton, Pittsburgh, to John Greeves, Co. Tyrone, describing conditions in America. (Heazleton had opened a store in Pittsburgh); and correspondence settling Heazleton's estate, post-1815. (D. 592, nos. 10, 13, 16, 17, 18, 26, 29, 30, 32)

(*g*) Letter, *c.* 1814, from Samuel Simmeral, Kittaning, Pa., to Thomas Sprott, relating to the Sprott family of Co. Down. Also a 'Chronological index of remarkable events in the French Revolution', compiled in 1811 by Simmeral. (T. 1445)

(*h*) Two letters, 1821 and 1835, from John McClelland, Philadelphia, to his relatives in Co. Antrim. (D. 1005)

(*i*) Letter from James Dalzell in Ballywatticock, Co. Down, to his brothers, Matthew and John, in Pittsburgh, 1824, giving details of his proposed emigration and the cost involved. (T. 2298)

(*j*) Thirty-two emigrant letters from members of the Smith family in Philadelphia, to relatives in Moycraig, Co. Antrim, 1832-48. (D. 1828)

(*k*) Six emigrant letters from Alexander, Robert, and Thomas McCoy in Pennsylvania, 1839-42, to relatives in Liverpool, telling them not to emigrate to the United States. (D. 1444)

(*l*) Two letters, 1846, from John Milliken, Philadelphia, to his brother James Milliken in Co. Antrim; letter, 1894, from Elizabeth Gillespie, Philadelphia, to her nephew James Milliken in Co. Antrim. (D. 985)

(*m*) Letters, 1847-*c.*1857, from John Capper, John Macoun, and Robert Moore, written from Philadelphia, regarding the sale of linen sent from Ulster, with comments on the state of the linen trade. (D. 2794)

(*n*) Eight emigrant letters from Matthew Brooks, Philadelphia, to his relatives in Urney, Co. Tyrone, *c.* 1849-*c.* 1872. (T. 2700)

(*o*) Emigrant letter, 1854, from James Mack in Pennsylvania. (D. 2244)

(*p*) Emigrant letters from Alexander Lowry in Pittsburgh, 1856, referring to his having worked as a blacksmith in New Orleans. (T. 2018)

(*q*) Two emigrant letters from James and Margaret Carson in Philadelphia, 1857, commenting on 'these periodic panics in our monetary system in this country'. (D. 1520); also four emigrant letters from Archibald and James Carson in Philadelphia, 1854-7 and 1885. (T. 2077)

(*r*) Letter from William Richey in Pennsylvania in 1865 to Mrs. J. Heron in Killyleagh, commenting on the course of the American Civil War. (T. 1766)

(*s*) Emigrant letter from John Barr in Erie, Pa., 1872. (T. 2229)

(*t*) Emigrant letter from James Caughey in McKeesport, Pa., 1888, commenting on the growing importance of natural gas in his area. (T. 2040)

(*u*) Emigrant letter from Hugh Graham in Pittsburgh, to Walter Smith [in Belfast?], describing his employment in the liquor trade, 1892. (T. 2186)

SOUTH CAROLINA

(*a*) Nine letters to and from members of the Rose family in South Carolina, 1732-54, mostly concerning family matters and inheritances, but with some reference to planting [indigo?]. (T. 2717)

(*b*) McDowell Family Correspondence. James McDowell emigrated from Newry, Co. Down, to South Carolina, *c.* 1786, and the main section of the correspondence is concerned with the management of the family rice plantation until 1838. There are also two letters from William Hill in Abbeville, S.C., dated 1859 and 1865. (T.2305)

(*c*) Letter from Charles Lewis in Kilkeel, Co. Down, to Davison McDowell in Georgetown, S.C., 1816. He refers to mutual friends and events around Kilkeel, but is obviously very much interested in conditions in America. (T. 2030)

(*d*) Three emigrant letters from Abbeville and Charleston, S.C., to the Hill family in Ballynure, Co. Antrim; the Abbeville letter of 1847 comments on the Mexican War and on the poor cotton crop, and the Charleston letters of 1854 and 1855 refer to the cholera epidemic, the execution of three Negroes on a murder charge, and the value of the writer's house and 'negro property'. (T. 1830)

(*e*) Emigrant letter from Robert Fullerton in South Carolina to his cousin in Armoy, Co. Antrim, 1879; he describes the United States government as 'one of the most corrupt on the inhabited globe' and asks for news from Armoy. (D. 1951)

VIRGINIA

(*a*) Twenty letters, 1811-5, from Mary Cuming, Petersburg, Va., to her father and sister in Co. Antrim, describing her voyage, domestic routine in her new home, and commenting on the outbreak of the War of 1812. (T. 1475)

(*b*) Letter, 1840, from Moses Paul in Petersburg, Va., to John Graham, Co. Londonderry, describing his gay social life and giving details of the market in slaves. (T. 1568)

(*c*) McElderry Family Papers. Nineteen documents, including emigrant letters from William McElderry in Virginia to relatives in Ballymoney, Co. Antrim, containing some references to slavery in Virginia. 1850-4. (T. 2414)

(*d*) Five letters, 1856-69, from Mary Parke in Monaghan to her husband, William, in Petersburg, Va. (D. 1648)

(*e*) Letter, 1861, from Robert and Eleanor McKelvey, Williamsburg, Va., to Mrs. Lawers in Belfast, including comment on the Civil War. (D. 893)

(*f*) Letter, 1886, from Lazewell Thompson, Norfolk, Va., including much detail about the emigration of the Thompson family to Norfolk and their business activities, *c.* 1800, in the West Indies (typescript copy). (D. 898)

CANADA

(*a*) Letter, 1832, from Dr. William Campbell, Peterborough, Upper Canada, to Rev. Robert Campbell, Templepatrick, describing the hardships of the voyage and giving some account of Co. Antrim emigrants to Canada. (D. 693)

(*b*) Two emigrant letters from Nathaniel and Joseph Carrothers in London and Westminster, Ont., to their brother William in Lisbellaw, Co. Fermanagh, in 1839 and 1855. Comment on food prices, farming methods, the economics of emigration, etc. (T. 1886)

(*c*) Letter, 1843, from Charlotte Bacon, Montreal, to her parents in Co. Londonderry. (T. 1639)

(*d*) Emigrant letter from Mark Duggan in Kingston, Ont., to his sister in Dungiven, Co. Londonderry. (T. 2946)

(*e*) Two emigrant letters from Joseph and Nathaniel Carrothers in Westminster, Ont., to their brother William in Lisbellaw, Co. Fermanagh in 1848 and 1853; both letters deal with farming and the price of land, food, etc. (T. 1888)

(*f*) Eleven emigrant letters from William Hutton in Montreal, St. Catherine's, and Toronto, 1848-56. (D. 2298)

(*g*) Letter, 1849, from Richard Breathwait, Ontario, to his parents in Co. Antrim, about farming conditions and prices. (T. 1362)

(*h*) Emigrant letter from A. Tyrell in Weston, Ont., 1850. (D. 2068)

(*i*) Two emigrant letters from members of the Topley family in Port Hope, Ont., to relatives in Tandergee, Co. Armagh, 1850, 1852. (T. 2149)

(*j*) Emigrant letter from Robert Byron in Trenton, Canada, 1857, describing his life as a farmer and the opportunities for teachers. (T. 2227)

COLLECTIONS OF EMIGRANT MSS. FROM MORE THAN ONE STATE

(*a*) Five documents, 1706-12, relating to Beck family property in Virginia (T. 1215); and letter, 1845, from James Beck, Dinsmore, Ohio, to James A. Beck in Co. Down, commenting on state of political parties in the U.S., the economy of the country, and the possibility of war against England and Mexico. (T. 1468)

(*b*) Some notes on emigration from Newry and district, 1783. (Drennan-Bruce letters) (D. 553, no. 14)

(*c*) Letters, 1787-1837, from the McClorg family in the U.S. and Canada to relatives in Ireland, including letters, 1787-94, from David Pollock, Chambersburg and Greenburg, Pa.; letters, 1819-26, from Robert McClorg in Philadelphia, including description of the voyage out and his search for work, and letters, 1822-3, from McClorg to Robert Hunter in New York; letters, 1820-37, from John McClorg, St. John's, N.B., and other members of the family in Philadelphia. (T. 1227)

(*d*) Four emigrant letters from members of the McElderry family in Baltimore to their relatives in Leitrim, Co. Antrim, 1795-8; letter of 1856 from Robert McElderry in Philadelphia describing his activities as a general merchant or agent; letter, 1859, from William McElderry in Lynchburg, Va., in which he describes his success in the 'draying' business; further letter, 1860, from W. McElderry commenting on the increasing interest in membership of local militia regiments since the 'John Brown Affair'; two letters, 1864, relating to the service of Robert McElderry in the Confederate Army and the difficulty of getting letters to him; two emigrant letters from William McElderry in New Orleans in 1867 and from John McElderry in Morrisville [N.Y.?], *c.* 1870. (Mic. 57)

(*e*) Some occasional references to emigration in 1796. (Rentals of the McCartney Estate, e.g. D. 572/21/98/13)

(*f*) Typescript copy of 'The Anecdotal Recollections of Morgan Jellett' (*c.* 1830). Includes mention of his emigration to the U.S. in 1799, and six years' residence in Baltimore. (T. 2777)

(*g*) Fourteen letters, 1801-10, from James Horner in Philadelphia, Georgetown, Del., and Chestertown, Md., to the Horner family in Londonderry. (T. 1592)

(*h*) Twenty-five emigrant letters to Robert Simms, a Belfast merchant, from George Cuming, John Caldwell, T.A. Emmet, and John Chambers in New York, and from John Campbell White in Baltimore, 1802-25. The letters are written by professional or business men, and they discuss, in an informed way, the prospects of employment in the U.S., the political state of both Ireland and the U.S., trade between Great Britain and the U.S., etc. (T. 1815)

(*i*) Emigrant letter from B. Boyd in Charleston to his brother, John, in Strabane, Co. Tyrone, with some reference to the slave trade in Savannah, 1808; also an emigrant letter from William Weir in Philadelphia to William Boyd in Strabane, describing the voyage out, 1840. (T. 1873)

(*j*) Documents from Augustus John Foster, Minister Plenipotentiary to the U.S. from 1811, including letters to his mother, Lady Elizabeth Foster, telling about the U.S. and especially about prospects for European emigrants. (Mic. 183)

(*k*) Stavely Family Papers. This collection includes *c.* twenty letters of the Stavely family, Ballymoney, with detailed information on the Presbyterian Church in America, including three letters from Alexander McLeod, New York, 1811-25, and nine letters of Alexander McLeod Stavely from Augusta, Ga., and St. John's, N.B. (D. 1792)

(*l*) Several emigrant letters from members of the Wray family in New York, etc., 1817-22. (T. 1727)

(*m*) Emigrant letters from David Robinson, Lexington, Kentucky, to his mother, Mary Robinson in Londonderry, 1817, and from Jane Agnew, New York, to her uncle, Rev. William Stavely, Kellswater, Co. Antrim, 1821. (D. 2013)

(*n*) Journal kept by Hugh Quin from the time of his departure from Portaferry, Co. Down, to his arrival at New Orleans, 1817; also two emigrant letters from another Hugh Quin in Mississippi to Strangford, Co. Down, 1854. (T. 2874)

(*o*) Letter, 1819, from John Phillips, Fairfield, S.C., to James Phillips in Co. Antrim; and a memorandum, 1825, by John Phillips relating to property in the Detroit area. (T. 1449)

(*p*) Two emigrant letters from J. Mulligan in Flatbush, N.Y., 1819, and in New Brunswick, N.J., 1829, to his relatives in Banbridge. Writing in 1819 he comments shrewdly on the value to an intending emigrant of a good education and on the increased status of the clergy in the States as compared with Ireland; his letter of 1829 discusses American politics. Also an emigrant letter from William Martin in Canoe, U.S., describing the Independence Day celebrations there in 1866. (D. 1757)

(*q*) McBride Family Papers. Sixteen documents. Emigrant letters received by the McBride family of Derriaghy, Co. Antrim, mostly from John McBride in Quebec, Canada, and Watertown, N.Y., 1819-27, but also some from Robert Craig, Birmingham, Alabama, 1820-2, and Mrs. Charlotte Graham, Watertown, N.Y., 1848-9. (T. 2613)

(*r*) Graham Family Letters. Twenty-five emigrant letters received by the Graham family of New Park from relatives in Cambridge, Mass., in 1821, Pittsburgh in 1843-6, New York in 1847, Cincinnati in 1848, New Orleans in 1849-50, Louisville in 1850, Pittsburgh in 1851, Van Buren, Ark., in 1852, Wellington, Miss., in 1852, and Cedarville, Ohio, in 1853, etc.; the letters are extraordinarily full and detailed on the process and equipment needed for emigration, the finding of jobs in various parts of the U.S., rates of pay, standards and costs of living, education, farming, etc. (Mic. 144)

(*s*) Five letters, 1826-61, to correspondents in Ireland: 1826, from David Armstrong, Paddytown, Va., referring to the resemblance between Paddytown and Crossgar, Co. Down; 1840, from Thomas Davison in East Liberty, [Va.?]; 1843, from Jane Armstrong, Romney, Va., sending news of relatives and friends; 1852, from William Porter in Pittsburgh, about financial arrangements and his carpet-weaving business; 1861, from Alexander Gamble in Pittsburgh, with details of 'how provisions rate about Pittsburgh'. (D. 682)

(*t*) Redmond Family Papers. A number of letters from the Redmond family in Charleston and New York, 1827-81, with a good deal of alert comment on the linen trade, investments, the American Civil War, the New Jersey Zinc Co., and the sale of a cotton plantation in Florida. (D. 1364)

(*u*) Anderson Family Papers. Twenty-four letters from members of the Anderson family in Pennsylvania, Ohio, and Indiana, to their relatives near Coleraine, Co. Londonderry, 1832-79; there are unusually detailed comments on farming conditions and on the opportunities available to emigrants. (D. 1859)

(*v*) Three emigrant letters from Baltimore in 1833 and 1849, and from Philadelphia in 1846. (Mic. 138)

(*w*) Eight letters, 1833-84, from members of the Anderson family, Cincinnati and Pittsburgh, to relatives in Ballymaguire. (T. 1664)

(*x*) Houston Family Papers. Three letters from John Houston to his family in Larne, Co. Antrim, 1836; three letters from Jane Park Houston, Cincinnati, 1850-3; journal of a voyage from Belfast to New Orleans, 1843-4. (T. 2581)

(*y*) Hunter Family Letters. Six emigrant letters from North Missouri in 1841 and *c.* 1890, from Ohio in 1852, and from Barrie, Ont., 1882-9. (D. 1441)

(*z*) Wallace Family Papers. *c.* forty very articulate emigrant letters from Augusta, Maine, 1841-60, from Goderich, Ont., 1849-67, and from New York in 1893. (D. 1195)

(*aa*) Letters, 1842-84, from St. Louis, New York, and Florence, Ala. (T. 1475)

(*bb*) *C.* forty letters, 1843-1932, from the Hanlon family in New York, Nebraska, Pittsburgh, Chicago, etc., to their relatives in Co. Down. (D. 885)

(*cc*) Bruce Family Papers. Nine letters, 1845-63, mostly from Samuel Bruce in Canada. The letters are quite descriptive, and primarily concern the wilderness experiences of Bruce in Manitoba and Quebec. (T. 2919)

(*dd*) Twenty emigrant letters from John Donnan to his parents in Co. Down. Comments on rates of pay, farming, and freedom of the U.S., 1848-9. (D. 2795)

(*ee*) Letters, *c.* 1850-1872, from Joseph and Margaret Cleland, Royalton, Pa., and East Guillensburg, Ont., to Margaret's parents in Co. Down. (Mic. 33)

(*ff*) Carlisle Family Papers. Twenty-five documents. Emigrant letters from James Carlisle and his wife Kate in New York and Washington to relatives in Ballycastle, 1851-92; they include a number of Civil War letters. James Carlisle emigrated *c.* 1850 and worked as a teacher, shop assistant, and salesman. He was advised by friends to train as a lawyer and qualified *c.* 1856. He enlisted in the Federal Army as a private in 1861 and became 1st Lieutenant in 1864. After the war he set up a law practice in Washington. (Mic. 143)

(*gg*) Twenty-five emigrant letters from Andrew Greenlees in the U.S.

to his relatives, probably in Magheramorne, Co. Antrim, 1852-1907. Greenlees worked as a moulder and then as a farmer, but it is interesting to see how mobile he is, since he writes, intelligently and vividly, from New York State, Michigan, Ohio, Kansas and Oklahoma. There is also an emigrant letter from William Colhoun in Washington, Pa., to his father in Leck, Co. Donegal, 1830. (T. 2046)

(*hh*) Three letters, 1853-8, to various correspondents in Ireland: 1853, from Mrs. Jane Fleming, commenting 'the people in this country all works for their living'; 1856, from Margaret Johnston in Pittsburgh, discussing the problems of living and working there; 1858, from Francis Johnston, Mansfield, Ohio, mainly on family matters. Also an account of the emigration of the Johnston family from Co. Fermanagh to New York and Pennsylvania in the early nineteenth century. (D. 1047)

(*ii*) Two emigrant letters, one of 1853 from Missouri, and the other, 1865, from Pennsylvania. (D. 556, nos. 517, 621)

(*jj*) McClure Family Papers. Eight letters, 1857-1906?, to and from members of the McClure family. The letters are written from New York, Pennsylvania, North Dakota [?], and Michigan, and discuss, among other subjects, agriculture, economic depression in the U.S., and wages. (T. 3102)

(*kk*) Emigrant letters, 1858-85, from several correspondents in various American states to their relatives in Ireland. (T. 2345)

(*ll*) Several emigrant letters from John and James Gallier in New York, etc., 1861-8, to Elizabeth Carlisle of Forkill, Co. Armagh. (T. 1790)

(*mm*) Emigrant letter, 1863, from Robert Orr in Providence, R.I.; also *c.* thirty emigrant letters from John, Margaret, and Mary Ann Sinclair in Healdsburg and San Francisco, Calif., 1879-89. (D. 1497)

(*nn*) Adams Family Papers. *c.* twenty letters, etc., from the Adams family in New York and Nashville, Tenn., concerning the settlement of the estates of James and David Adams in Strabane, Co. Tyrone, *c.* 1867-82. (Mic. 26/1-2)

(*oo*) Letters, 1867-89, from John Henry, Clay Centre, Kansas, and Eden, Ill., to his family in Co. Antrim. (T. 1480)

(*pp*) Thompson Family Papers. Twenty-two documents. These consist almost entirely of emigrant letters from members of the Thompson family in Cincinnati and Philadelphia to their relatives in Articlave, Co. Londonderry, 1868-c. 1930. (T. 1866)

(*qq*) Buchanan Family Papers. *c.* fifty documents. Correspondence between emigrant members of the Buchanan family in Philadelphia and New York and their relatives in Milford, Co. Donegal, *c.* 1870-1894. (D. 1473)

(*rr*) *C.* forty emigrant letters to Ireland from Philadelphia, New York, etc., mostly late nineteenth century. (Mic. 80/1)[7]

(*ss*) Collection of sixteen letters, 1872-1915, from the Gass family in Indiana and California to the family at home in Co. Armagh. (T. 1396)

(*tt*) Over 100 nineteenth-century letters of the O'Hanlon family in various states in America and at home near Downpatrick, Co. Down. (D. 882)

(*uu*) Eleven emigrant letters from members of the Quin family in New York, and the Park family in Illinois, to relatives in Stewartstown, *c.* 1873-1885. (D. 1819)

(*vv*) Five letters, 1883-8, to Mrs. Mary McKeown in Belfast: two, 1883 and 1884, from Thomas McCann in New York and Minneapolis; two, 1884 and 1885, from Maggie McCann in Madison [Wisc.?]; and one, 1888, from Lizzie Clarke, Minneapolis. (T. 1456)

(*ww*) Letter, 1884, from [Thomas?] McCullough to Robert [Kennedy?] from aboard the ship *Otago,* telling of his adventures while bound for America; also one letter from William Kennedy to his brother in Ireland, 1910. (T. 3152)

(*xx*) Two anonymous letters from New York, 1885 and 1891, and containing mostly family news, but with some comment on the recent harvest in America. (T. 3033)

(*yy*) About fifty emigrant letters to the Hall family of Armagh, from John Hall in Washington and Lytle Black in Chicago, 1889-91. (D. 2041)

(*zz*) Emigrant letters from New York in 1893 and from Richmond, Va., in 1909. (D. 1791)

(*aaa*) Several emigrant letters from Philadelphia in 1897 and from California in 1917. (T. 2278)

EMIGRANT PASSENGER LISTS.

The Office contains various transcripts and originals of lists of emigrants sailing to America, culled from newspapers and other sources: e.g., of 1792 (T.711), of 1802-4 and 1833-5 (T. 1011), of 1804-5 (T. 521), of 1836 (T. 671), of 1850-7 (D. 2892), and of 1860-70 (T. 1428). There is also some related material, like the out-letter book, 1826-34, of Messrs. William McCorkell & Coy., shipowners, which gives details of cargoes and the emigrant trade. (Mic. 13)

MISCELLANEOUS DOCUMENTS. 1707/8-1886.

(*a*) Conveyance of property in Garden Alley, Philadelphia, 1707/8, with a recital of conveyances from 1696. (D. 827)

(*b*) Typescript account of the emigration in 1748 of 200 Presbyterian families from Monaghan and Ballyboy to Salem, Mass. (T. 1791)

(*c*) Reminiscences of Sir Arthur Brooke regarding his military career, including the Anglo-American War of 1812. (D. 3004- unlisted)

(*d*) Twenty-four documents, including correspondence of Moses Staunton of Belfast, with details of his being shipwrecked off Newfoundland whilst emigrating to Canada in 1854. Also legal correspondence, 1822-5, relating to the death in Augusta, Ga., of Dr. Robert Means, and various emigrant letters written from Jersey City [N.J.], 1877, Minnesota, 1855, and New York, 1895. (T. 2284)

(*e*) A detailed description of a journey from Quebec to Toronto and Kingston, Ont., made by emigrant Friends, *c.* 1823. (D. 1762)

(*f*) Report of cholera in Quebec, 1834. (D. 1604)

(*g*) Diary, 1837-44, of an agent for cotton and provisions in Charleston, dealing with Glasgow, Belfast, and Liverpool; after a fire in Apr. 1838 he returns to Belfast. (D. 1725)

(*h*) Bundle of papers relating to Joseph Rea, born in Ripley Co., Indiana, on 13 Nov. 1837. Rea was a farmer who volunteered to serve in the Union Army during the American Civil War. The papers include: a printed statement, sworn by Philip Cook, J.P., that he married Joseph Rea to Sally Ann Muse in 1862; printed form, completed by Rea, by which he voluntarily enlisted as a soldier; and various papers relating to Rea's army service, including an honourable discharge. (T. 2699)

(*i*) Short, anonymous MS., written in 1868, which records incidents occurring on an emigrant voyage from Liverpool to New York. (T. 2620)

(*j*) Series of diaries which include Fred Crawford's visit to New York in 1886. (D. 1700)

7. See Arnold Schrier, *Ireland and the American Emigration, 1850-1900* (Minneapolis, 1958).

ISLE OF MAN

ISLE OF MAN

THE MANX MUSEUM, Douglas

BRIDGE HOUSE PAPERS. Correspondence. 18th century.

Correspondence, eighteenth century, relating to the purchase of a land grant in Florida and to trading activities in the West Indies and Nova Scotia.

KELLY FAMILY. Journal. 1827-8. (M.M. Mss. 5200C)

Photostats of journal, 1827-8, of Kelly family on journey from Doolough, Jurby, Isle of Man, to Painsville, Ohio.[1]

1. From Miss A.S. Heffner, 301 W. Buckeye, Clyde, Ohio, who presumably has the original.

CHANNEL ISLANDS

CHANNEL ISLANDS

GREFFE, Royal Court, Guernsey

DE SAUSMAREZ DEPOSIT.[1] Miscellaneous volumes. 1777-82.

Volume twenty-one of this large collection includes a list of privateers fitted out from the islands of Guernsey and Alderney during the War of Independence, 1777-82, and a list of prizes taken from the enemy, 1777-82.

PRIAULX LIBRARY, Candie Road, St. Peter Port, Guernsey

CARTERET PRIAULX & CO. Letters. 18th and 19th centuries.

The shipping firm of Carteret Priaulx & Co. did an extensive trade ranging world-wide from the middle of the eighteenth to the middle of the nineteenth century. Much of this material concerns trading contacts with America, particularly Newfoundland.[1]

SOCIÉTÉ JERSIAISE, The Museum, 9 Pier Road, St. Hélier, Jersey

CHEVALIER, JEAN. Diary. 1643-51.

This diary contains frequent references to Sir George Carteret and his enterprises, including his interests in North America.[1]

ROBIN, CHARLES (1743-1824). Diary and papers. 18th century.

The Société holds the diary, commencing in 1776, of Charles Robin, along with other Robin papers relating to the family's Gaspé trade.

LE COUTEUR PAPERS. Diaries. 19th century.

The diaries of Sir John Le Couteur (1794-1875) contain a description of the march of the British 104th Regiment from Fredericton to Kingston in Feb.-Apr. 1813, during the War of 1812.

OTHER DOCUMENTS.

There is also in the Société a number of depositions referring to American vessels captured by Channel Island privateers.

1. The de Sausmarez deposit undoubtedly includes other documents relating to American trade and to privateering in the eighteenth century. These will be listed in detail in a forthcoming volume of the List and Index Society, edited by Professor John Le Patourel, which will be devoted exclusively to this important collection. Also see the Special Series of the List and Index Society, *List of Records in the Greffe*, vol. 1 (1969).

1. See C.R. Fay, *Channel Islands and Newfoundland* (Cambridge, 1961), especially pp. 36-45.

1. See J.A. Messervy, ed., *Journal de Jean Chevalier* (St. Hélier, 1914 [1906-14]).

REPUBLIC OF IRELAND

CARLOW

MISS M.B. BAYLISS, Wykeham House, Bagenalstown

FITZGERALD, FORBES AND THORNTON FAMILIES. Letters and other documents. 1774-1877.

About 120 letters and associated items, 1774-1877, of or connected with the families of Fitzgerald, Forbes and Thornton, in Kentucky and Virginia.[1]

DUBLIN

GENEALOGICAL OFFICE, The Castle, Dublin

Since there has been so much emigration from Ireland to America it is but to be expected that the records of the Genealogical Office would have some relevance to American history. While there is no corpus of material relating exclusively to America, the series of Registered Pedigrees would naturally contain references to families or individuals who had settled in the New World. Again, in the Registers of Grants and Confirmations of Arms occasional entries relating to Americans may be found. To these major series must be added the many other collections - will abstracts, unofficial pedigrees, funeral entries, etc. - which might prove to be of assistance in any effort to ascertain the ancestry or immediate background of people of Irish descent who achieved prominence in American history.

IRISH MANUSCRIPTS COMMISSION, 73 Merrion Square, Dublin 2

The Commission, unlike its English equivalent, does not itself keep lists and indexes of material in archives and private possession throughout the country. But there is little need to do this in the Republic of Ireland, since, apart from Cork, there are virtually no local archives and the National Library of Ireland collects vigorously and microfilms whatever records are still in private hands. (The actual work of inspecting such records, has, indeed, been temporarily transferred from the Manuscripts Commission to the National Library.)

The Commission, rather, sponsors the publication of manuscripts relating to Ireland, more than a hundred volumes having already been issued. It publishes also the *Analecta Hibernica*, which calendars or prints manuscripts and includes the reports of the Commission:

No. 4, pp. 139-286, Oct. 1932, reprints many documents concerning the Irish in the West Indies in the seventeenth and eighteenth centuries. Some of these documents also relate to Virginia, and include extracts on Irish prisoners transported to Virginia, *c.* 1620. Daniel Gookin (1612?-1687), writer on American Indians, in Virginia, *c.* 1621-3. Edmund and Simon Tuchin in Virginia, *c.* 1623-4, two brothers expelled from Ireland for adherence to the Catholic religion who went to Virginia as adventurers in 1623. Two specimens of indentures of Irish servants, *c.* 1677-9, one of which was to serve in Maryland 'or any part within the Cape of Virginia'.

No. 15, pp. 126-7, Nov. 1944 (from the Longford Papers, property of the Earl of Longford, Pakenham Hall, Castlepollard, Co. Westmeath) reprints calendar entries including twenty-one letters, 1776-78, from Richard Pakenham, an officer in the British Army, to his brother Thomas Pakenham, from various places in America during the War of Independence, dealing with current affairs, chiefly the progress of the campaign. Copy of a report dated Port aux Basques, Newf., 20 Sept. [17]86, by Edward Pakenham to a correspondent unknown, on Labrador and other parts of the North American continent, dealing with fishing, native customs, French officers, etc. Description, 1815 (with five diagrams), of musket alleged to have been used by the Americans, 1814-5, at Plattsburg, N.Y., and elsewhere, showing a primitive machine gun.

No. 22, pp. 329-94, June 1960, contains papers from the Quit Rent Office in the Public Record Office of Ireland relating to a state-aided emigration scheme in the 1850's (see p. 349).

The Commission has also published:

The Correspondence of Emily, Duchess of Leinster, 1731-1814, ed. by Brian Fitzgerald. Vol. ii (Dublin, 1953), pp. 36-8, 57-60, contains letters from Lord Edward Fitzgerald written from America in 1782 and 1788.

The Inchiquin Manuscripts, ed. by John Ainsworth (Dublin, 1961). Pp. 197, 218-21 contain summaries of several letters, 1766-78, to and from the barrister-politician Sir Lucius O'Brien (1735-95), which make slight reference to American trade and to the War of Independence.

NATIONAL LIBRARY OF IRELAND, Kildare Street, Dublin

The National Library of Ireland contains probably the largest collection of historical manuscripts in Ireland, and is pursuing a vigorous policy of acquisition, both by microfilming and by the searches throughout the Republic of Ireland by an Inspector of Manuscripts, attached to the Irish Manuscripts Commission.

There is a card index of names of principal families in the collection, and also a card index to a special Autograph Collection. The manuscripts have been indexed as a part of a huge undertaking aimed at indexing all materials, printed and manuscript, relating to Irish history. See *Manuscript Sources for the History of Irish Civilisation,* 11 vols. (Dublin, 1965).

It will be seen that the principal American relevance is in the American side of the records relating to the nineteenth and early twentieth-century nationalist movements. Since they are so interrelated they have been grouped together, and are placed first; the other papers follow in chronological order. There may be some other letters of less obvious importance in other collections of post-1848 nationalists.

HICKEY COLLECTION. (MSS. 3225-6)

(*a*) 'Young Ireland', Volume 1: Typescript copies of two manuscript biographies, each of about 10,000 words, by Michael Cavanagh, of:

(i) Joseph Brenan (1828-57), the poet and Irish Nationalist who fled to America in 1849; describes his life there, first in New York and then in New Orleans.

1. This collection is larger than indicated; other letters and papers are not yet examined, having only come to light in 1976.

(ii) John Mitchel (1834-64), the son of John Mitchel (1815-75); joined his father in America in 1853; killed in action while commanding Fort Sumter for the Confederates.

(*b*) 'Young Ireland', Volume 2: 6 letters (typescript copies). 1854-67. Collection illustrating the 'Young Ireland' movement. Items of American interest are:

(i) Letters from John Mitchel. New York, 18 Feb. 1854, to one Reid, a friend in Tasmania. Describes life in New York and the hostility to his new journal, the *Citizen*. Three letters to Mrs. Williams, a friend in Tasmania. Tucaleechee Cove, Tenn., 24 July 1855, describing at length his rustication and the primitive habits of his neighbours who, he asserts, still believe that they are voting for General Jackson. Knoxville, Tenn., 16 Feb. 1858, announcing his founding of a newspaper 'intended to advocate ... a revival of the slave-trade from Africa'. Washington, D.C., 1 May 1859, mostly describing the success of O'Brien's American tour, and more praise for the Southern cause.

(ii) Two letters from Thomas Francis Meagher to his father. New York, 17 July 1865, mentions that he is joining an emigrant train to Indian Territory, with letter of introduction from the Rev. Father Provincial of the Province of Missouri; Virginia City, Mont., 15 June 1867, mentions that he had been in charge in Governor Smith's absence, and has been inspecting defences against the Indians.

O'BRIEN, WILLIAM SMITH (1803-64). Letters and papers. (MSS. 426-62)

William Smith O'Brien, M.P., 1828-31 and 1835-49, was transported to Tasmania for his part in the rising of 1848. He returned to Ireland in 1856. He visited the United States in 1859. His letters show that he kept in touch with the prominent Irishmen of his time and provide a commentary on the political scene.

There are 3,434 letters, covering O'Brien's lifetime. They are bound into twenty-four volumes and there is a name index with hundreds of entries. In addition there are thirteen unindexed books containing speeches and notes on many subjects. Among the correspondents in America are John Mitchel, Thomas Francis Meagher, Richard O'Gorman, James Gibbons of Philadelphia, Lucius O'Brien of Toronto, the Albany Repeal Association, the Repealers of Newfoundland, Halifax, N.S. Repeal Association, and the Emmett Club of New Orleans.

MEAGHER, THOMAS FRANCIS (1823-67). 2 letters. 1858, 1866. (Autograph Collection.)

Young Irelander and American soldier. Two letters to James Roche: 5 Mar. 1858, announces his departure to Central America, and asks Roche to take over the editorship of the *Irish News* in his absence. 28 Mar. 1866, from the Executive Office of the Territory of Montana, urging Roche to come to Montana and to bring John Duffy with him to found an Irish newspaper.

LARCOM, SIR THOMAS AISKEW (1801-79). Papers. 1851. (MSS. 7453-7792)

Papers as Under Secretary of Ireland 1853-68. The handlist to the 191 volumes of these papers showed these obvious items of American interest:

(*a*) List of the total emigration from Ireland for each year 1851-9; and some press cuttings on Irish and Scottish emigration from Liverpool, 1860. (MS. 7603)

(*b*) Letters on American Fenianism. 1855-67. (MS. 7517)

(i) Copies of letters, 1855-67, to Larcom giving reports on Fenianism and the Nationalist movement in America, including a short history of Fenianism.

(ii) Copies of letters, 1867, from Pierrepont Edwards, Acting Consul in New York, reporting on Fenianism.

(*c*) Letter, 1863, on recruitment in Ireland for the Federal Army in the Civil War (MS. 7585), and another, 1864, on recruitment for American ships. (MS. 7587)

(*d*) Volume of newspaper cuttings of 1865 on Canadian Confederation and the reunion of the United States. (MS. 7470)

(*e*) References to the Fenian raid on Canada and the Canadian trials; to President Johnson's message and to General Meade's report on the raid into Canada, 1866. (MS. 7680)

(*f*) Six volumes of newspaper cuttings, 12 Aug. 1871 - 23 Sept. 1872, mainly concerned with the *Alabama* incident. (MSS. 7464-7469)

FENIAN ORGANIZATION IN AMERICA. Paper. *c*. 1860. (MS. 5771)

Undated, anonymous - signed 'Cato' - manuscript, *c*. 1860, of about 1,200 words describing the Fenian organization in the United States and comparing it with the Irish Fenians, rather to the discredit of the latter; speculates on the possibility of war between Britain and America, but thinks, even then, an American invasion of Ireland unlikely.

'AN ACCOUNT OF FENIANISM FROM APRIL 1865 TILL APRIL 1866 BY ONE OF THE HEAD CENTRES FOR IRELAND. NEW YORK 1866.' (143 folios). 1866. (MS. 5963)

This anonymous manuscript contains considerable information on the activities and membership of the Fenian Brotherhood of America, as well as in Ireland. O'Mahony and Stephens figure prominently; there are some pages on the Fenian raids in Canada.

KEARNEY, FREDERICK. 'Memoir of Major-General Thomas Francis Meagher' (400 pages). 1869. (In Hickey Papers.)

This memoir is a manuscript for a book - never published - by Frederick Kearney, written in New York. Meagher was transported to Tasmania after the unsuccessful rebellion of 1848, but escaped to America in 1852. He served with distinction in the Irish Brigade of the Federal Army, becoming a brigadier-general and commanding the Brigade in their famous stand at Fredericksburg, Va. In 1865 he was appointed Secretary (or Acting Governor) of the Territory of Montana. Over half of the 400-page manuscript is concerned with Meagher's career in America.

DEVOY PAPERS. Letters and documents. 1871-1914.

John Devoy (1842-1928), Fenian leader. Devoy joined the Irish Revolutionary Brotherhood in 1860, was imprisoned in 1866 and released on condition that he left Ireland, and thereafter spent most of his life in America. This collection is a fundamental source for the study of the American aspects of the Fenian movement.

The papers include:

(*a*) Letters and telegrams of Dr. William Carroll, Philadelphia, to John Devoy, mainly regarding Clan-na-Gael activities. 296 items. 1875-1914. (MS. 18,002)

(*b*) Letters, telegrams, and addresses to released Fenian prisoners arriving in the U.S., mainly from political organizations and Irish societies. *c*. 60 items. 1871. (MS. 18,030)

(*c*) Letters, telegrams, and memoranda concerning Charles Stewart Parnell and his family, mainly dealing with his American visit, 1879-80, and efforts to obtain support in the U.S. after the Split, including letters of Anna and Delia Parnell and William Redmond. 45 items. 1879-99. (MS. 18,041)

(*d*) Copy of letter of Howard M. Jenkins to Louis T. Michener regarding the views of Devoy and Irish-Americans on the Harrison administration, 2 Feb. 1889. Also three short letters of E. Halford, private secretary to President Harrison, to John Devoy, Mar.-May 1889. (MS. 18,053)
(*e*) Letters, telegrams, statements, and Pinkerton reports concerning the murder of Dr. P.P.H. Cronin at Chicago, May 1889. *c.* 100 items. (MS. 18,058)
(*f*) Irish Political Prisoners Fund Association correspondence and memoranda, including many letters of members of Congress, mostly to Gen. James R. O'Beirne. *c.* 100 items. 1896-8. (MS. 18,065)
(*g*) Memoranda from Irish-American societies and labour organizations protesting against the Arbitration Treaty between the U.S. and Britain. (Some printed.) 1911. (MS. 18,079)
(*h*) Rough draft of unsigned letter from London to Colonel House, proposing American involvement in a League of Nations. 22 Sept. 1915. (MS. 18,092)
The Library also holds a variety of printed and unprinted material relating to Devoy and his activities in the U.S., but the above items are among the most significant in this large collection.

IRISH NATIONAL LAND LEAGUE. American correspondence: 121 letters. 1880-1. (MS. 8291)

Among the records of the Irish National Land League is this file of letters, 1880-1, enclosing donations for relief from individuals and Irish organizations in America, e.g. from Irish famine relief funds in California, Boston, New York, Milwaukee, Wis., New Orleans, Georgia, etc.; the Shoemakers Union of New York City contributes; the editor of the *Irish World*, New York, organized appeals, as did J.J.W. Donoghue of the *Chronicle* - among the moneys he forwards is $4,000 from the Democratic Committee of Tammany Hall. Several of the letters are addressed personally to Parnell. A list of such American donations shows about £13,000 contributed between 9 Jan. and 6 Mar. 1880.

IRISH NATIONAL LEAGUE OF AMERICA. 7 letters. 1890. (MS. 8582/2)

From the Rev. Dr. Charles O'Reilley, of Detroit, treasurer of the Irish National League of America, to Dr. Joseph E. Kenney, of Dublin, treasurer of the National League of Ireland. The letters discuss fund-raising in America, the abuse coming from the 'Chicago press', and American-Irish sentiment generally.

HARRINGTON, TIMOTHY CHARLES (1851-1910). American travel diary. 1890. (MS. 2195)

M.P., Hon. Secretary of the Irish National League, prominent in the Land League movement. Harrington was on tour in America with his colleagues Dillon and O'Brien in 1890, raising funds for the Home Rule agitation, when the Parnell-O'Shea scandal broke. The first part of the diary concerns the well-attended fund-raising meetings, but the main part concerns Harrington's disputes with his colleagues over Parnell's leadership of the Irish Parliamentary Party. However, the diary throws some light on the reaction of American Catholics to Parnell's disgrace, both before and after the Irish bishops denounced him.

LUBY, THOMAS CLARKE (1821-1901). 'Brief synopsis of early Fenian events in Ireland and America.' (346 pages.) 1890-1. (MS. 331)

Written as a series of letters by Thomas Luby at Newark, N.J., beginning 27 July 1890, to John O'Leary. Much of the American interest of the diary appears, on partial inspection, to centre on James Stephens's fund-raising visit to America in 1863; but there are constant references throughout to the American Fenian Brotherhood - detailed and very lively. O'Leary drew on these letters for his *Recollections of Fenians and Fenianism*, 2 vols. (London, 1896).

REDMOND, JOHN (1856-1918), Irish political leader. Correspondence. 1890-1917.
(*a*) Letters from John O'Callaghan, Secretary of the United Irish League of America, 1893-1911, mainly 1904-7, with many enclosures. *c.* 300 items. (MS. 15,213)
(*b*) Overseas Series. Letters to John Redmond from persons and bodies in the U.S. concerning the United Irish League, Parnell memorial, Redmond's visits, etc., in America, 1890-1917, with associated documents. Correspondents include Richard Croker, W. Bourke Cochran, P. Egan, J. Finerty, P. Ford, T. St. J. Gaffney, M. Jordan, M. Keogh, Shane Leslie, E. O'Flaherty, Theodore Roosevelt, M.J. Ryan. *c.* 500 items. (MS. 15,236)
(*c*) Correspondence between John Redmond, M.J. Jordan, and other Americans and officers of the United Irish League of America, Sept. 1914-April 1915. Twenty-three letters and telegrams (two incomplete). (MS. 15,524)

McGARRITY, JOSEPH (1874-1940). Correspondence. 1901-39.
(*a*) Thirty-five letters of Major Michael H. Enright to McGarrity and five replies from McGarrity, mainly relating to activities of Clan-na-Gael in Chicago, 1923-39. (MS. 17,450)
(*b*) Fifteen letters from McGarrity to John T. Ryan, an agent of Clan-na-Gael, primarily dealing with the De Valera campaign in the United States, 1919-20. (MS. 17,486)
(*c*) About 700 letters. Includes information regarding a British agent briefing of an Irish informer in Philadelphia, particularly about the American activities of John Devoy, Luke Dillon, Joseph McGarrity, and Liam Pedlar, 1901-12. (MS. 17,495)
(*d*) Sixteen page typescript copy of correspondence between McGarrity and the American Secretary of State [Cordell Hull] regarding the status of the Free State government, 1938-9. (MS. 17,545)
(*e*) Six letters of Rev. Michael Collins, Phoenixville, Pa., to McGarrity, with references to Clan-na-Gael activities, *c.* 1912-21, 1938. (MS. 17,437)

ANCIENT ORDER OF HIBERNIANS IN AMERICA. Membership ledger. 1911. (MS. 3278)

Gives members' names, dues paid, occasional comments, and subscriptions to *Irish News*. The names include most, if not all, of the prominent Irish-American politicians of the day.

CASEMENT, SIR ROGER (1864-1916). Letters. 1915-6. (MS. 8605)

Fourteen letters, 1 Apr. 1915 - 13 Mar. 1916, to St. John Gaffney. Gaffney was United States Consul in Munich in 1915 until he was dismissed, allegedly for his friendship to Casement. Casement, from Berlin and then Munich, discusses Gaffney's dismissal in a ten-page letter, 1 Nov. 1915; and comments on the American attitude to the British 'fabrications' about himself. Other letters allude slightly to Casement's contacts with Irish nationalist groups in the United States.

J.J. HEARN PAPERS. Letters. 1917-24.
(*a*) Ten autograph letters of Liam Mellows to Mrs. John J. Hearn of Westfield, Mass., and four letters of Mellows to John J. Hearn containing accounts of Mellows' life in the U.S., and references to the Irish Convention, 1917, John Devoy, Eamon De Valera and the Irish movement in America, and Terence MacSwiney, 1917-20. (MS. 15,986)

(*b*) Letter from Maire Comerford to Mrs. Eileen Hearn regarding the Irish in New York, 22 July 1924. (MS. 15,994)

McCARTAN PAPERS. Letters. 1918-20.

(*a*) Ten letters from Ellen Leahy in Washington, D.C., to Dr. Patrick McCartan; mainly relating to the imprisonment of Larry de Lacy in the U.S. and to Irish political affairs in the U.S., 1919-20.
(*b*) Four letters to McCartan from Mrs. Mary McWhorter, president of the Ladies' Auxiliary, Ancient Order of Hibernians of America. Concerning affairs of Irish political organizations in the U.S., 1918-19. (MS. 17,670)

FRANK GALLAGHER PAPERS. Letters and documents. 1929-30.

(*a*) Letters to Gallagher from Sean Moynihan in the U.S., relating to the visit of Eamon De Valera to the U.S., references to his itinerary and to Irish personalities in America. Seven items. Nov. 1929-April 1930. (MS. 18,345)
(*b*) Documents relating to a tour of the U.S. by Gallagher as secretary to Eamon De Valera; include pages from diary, expenses notebook, addresses of Irish sympathizers in the U.S., etc. Fifty items. Nov. 1927-March 1928. (MS. 18,359). Also documents relating to a visit by Gallagher to the U.S. in connexion with De Valera's 1938 tour of America. (MS. 18,357)

ORMONDE PAPERS. 1678-1710.

(*a*) 'The importation of tobacco', four papers:[1] (In MS. 2382)

(i) Deposition by Col. John Custis of Virginia that he has satisfied the King's Collector in Virginia about duty.

(ii) An invoice for the amount of tobacco shipped for Custis on board the *Providence*.

(iii) Affidavit of one of the crew of the ship that Custis had paid the duty.

(iv) Statement concerning the case, especially on the state of the tobacco when it arrived in England.

All the papers are dated 1678; the shipment took place in Nov. 1678.

(*b*) In a 'catalogue of letters and papers from 1665 to 1679 inclusive' is mentioned one, 16 Sept. 1678, from James Butler of Boston to Ormonde.[2] (In MS. 2377)
(*c*) Letter, Dublin, 26 Nov. 1684, from Israel Feilding to the Earl of Arran, mentions the King's 'rebellious subjects in New England'; and that of 2 Dec. 1684 says that military service there is likely 'to be hot'.[3] (In MSS. 2440 and 2441)
(*d*) Letter, Dublin, 5 June 1686, from Primate Boyle to Ormonde speaks of French Protestants, driven from France, desiring to leave England and Ireland for Pennsylvania.[4] (In MS. 2449)
(*e*) Brigadier John Corbet petitions the Earl of Oxford and Mortimer, Lord High Treasurer, 'for a moiety of the matters in the hands of the President and Council of Maryland to be paid to him'.[5] n.d., *c*. 1710. (In MS. 2495)

PARKER-HUTCHINSON PAPERS. Letters. 1726-*c*.1780. (MS. 11,418)

Sixty-three letters, mostly addressed to Anthony Parker and dated 1726-*c*.1780. Includes some from America, and a few of these dated 1776.

KING, GILBERT. Notebook. 1761-8. (MS. 3240)

Notebook of an Irish ensign, Gilbert King, serving with the British forces in Canada and containing personal accounts, copies of letters, and two songs, 1761-8.

O'HARA MSS. Letters. 1761-84. (MSS. 16,886-7)

A collection of 115 letters, 1761-84, mostly written by Edmund Burke, but including a few of William Burke, Richard Burke, and Dr. John Nugent, primarily addressed to Charles O'Hara, the elder. A number of these letters discuss the troubles in America during the agitation there for independence.

BALFOUR PAPERS. 3 letters. 1764-5.

These letters were written by James Pillson of New York to Harry Brabazon of Drogheda, County Louth, merchant, about the marketing of flax-seed and butter.

ISLE ST. JOHN (Prince Edward Island). Account. *c*. 1770. (MS. 246)

A table of the proprietors, giving the size and quality of their holdings, extracts from a report of the Board of Trade, and a copy of the 'Articles of agreement between proprietor and settlers'.

MANSFIELD PAPERS. Letters. 1782, 1874-85.

(*a*) 13 May and 18 June 1782, written by William Snow to his brother Robert of Waterford city, Ireland. He describes his plight as a prisoner in New York, though he was offered the post of aide-de-camp to General O'Hara when he would be exchanged. New York is an 'extravagant place' where a dollar has only as much value as a sixpence in Waterford.
(*b*) Six letters, 1874-85, to George Patrick Lattin Mansfield (1820-89), of Morristown Lattin, County Kildare, by his first cousin, Owen Mansfield, appealing for aid when the crops of maize failed for two successive seasons in Iroquois County, Ill. The first letter was written after a silence of twenty-five years and a cheque for £20 was dispatched immediately. Money gifts were sent on at least four occasions on the strength of 'hard-times' in Illinois.

FILGATE FAMILY. Account book. 1783-1823. (MS. 11,942)

Account book of the family of Filgate, of Ardee, Co. Louth, containing domestic, estate, and business accounts, with many references to textiles and trade with Philadelphia, 1783-1823.

PARNELL, JOHN. Journal. 1834. (MS. 2036)

Journal of a tour in the United States and Canada, 1834.

OSBORNE, RICHARD BOYSE (1808-*c*.1897). Diary. (MSS. 7888-95)

Railway engineer. Volume 1 of his seven-volume diary is an account of the life of his grandfather, Richard Boyse of Graige, of his own early life in Ireland, and the financial overthrow of his eccentric father. Volumes 2 and 3 concern life in Upper Canada, whence they emigrated, and then in 1835 a journey to Reading, Pa., stopping at Centerville, Mich., Chicago, St. Louis, Mo., and Baltimore. By 1842 Osborne was chief engineer to the Philadelphia and Reading Railroad, and was first to make use of the 'iron Howe bridge'. He resigned in 1845 and worked in Ireland for Vignoles on the Waterford and Limerick Railway; met Robert Stephenson, and then worked a short while in Darien as an engineer for Graves & Sons of Liverpool.

1. H.M.C. Ormonde MSS. N.S. iv [36], pp. 304-5. (Listed as in possession of the Marquis of Ormonde, Kilkenny Castle.)
2. H.M.C. vi, p. 763.
3. H.M.C. Ormonde MSS. N.S. vii [36], pp. 289, 291.
4. Ibid., pp. 423-4.
5. H.M.C. vii, p. 828.

Returning to America he was, successively, 1851-61, chief engineer to the following railroads: the Catawissa, the Camden and Atlantic, the Dauphin and Susquehanna, the Cornwall, and the Lebanon Valley Railroad.

MONTEAGLE PAPERS.

Time did not allow examination of the 105 volumes and the several thousand loose documents that are the papers of Thomas Spring-Rice, 1st Baron Monteagle of Brandon (1790-1866), Secretary to the Treasury in Grey's administration 1830-4, Chancellor of the Exchequer in Melbourne's second ministry 1835-9. These papers are largely unexplored and there is no list of them, but there are certainly documents relating to Irish emigration, colonial affairs (including Canadian dispatches), and the slave trade.

ALL HALLOWS COLLEGE, DUBLIN. Letters (microfilms). 1843-77. (P. 2782 and P. 3849-51)

This is a collection of letters the originals of which are in All Hallows College, Drumcondra, Dublin, a college founded in 1842 for the education of missionary priests for foreign countries, especially the countries of Irish emigration. By 1843, bishops from American dioceses were seeking Irish priests. On P. 2782 is a selection of letters from over twenty of the American bishops. Accounts are given of conditions and diocesan organization, with references to contemporary events. At least fourteen are in French.

P.3849 consists of part of a thesis submitted by Patrick F. Murray for an M.A. degree, University College, Dublin, Autumn 1956. This is 'A Calendar of the Overseas Missionary Correspondence of All Hallows College, Dublin, 1842-1877', which has an introduction and index, a chronological list of documents and a calendar of correspondence from the United States and elsewhere. Only 1,583 letters of the calendar are as yet microfilmed; of these, 1,196 are from the United States, 251 from Canada and Newfoundland, and 136 from the West Indies and Central America. P. 3849-50 give those American and Canadian letters not included on P. 2782.

LALOR CORRESPONDENCE. 1843-84. (MS. 8567)

About thirty family letters, with a few exceptions written to Richard Lalor (1823-93), Tenakill, Mountrath, King's County (Leix); brother of the Irish nationalist James Finton Lalor, M.P. 1880-92. Nine were written by his brother William, a farmer in Wisconsin, who describes the ups and downs of farming. Three were written from the Convent of the Visitation, St. Louis, Mo. - two by a cousin, Mary Anne Murphy - seeking information about Alice Lalor, founder of the Visitation Order in the United States, who emigrated from Ireland in 1784. Other cousins who wrote, mostly about family affairs, were A.M. Darcy, Mary Darcy, Maria Dillon (*née* O'Brien), George Dillon; and H.T. Lalor from New Orleans, seeking some hard-working emigrants.

PAKENHAM-MAHON PAPERS. Letters. 1846-7.

These estate papers contain letters written mainly by Major Denis Mahon (1787-1847) to his agent in Ireland arranging for the emigration of his tenants in County Roscommon to Canada and the United States in May-June 1847. The names and sailing dates of the emigrant ships are given, but no lists of names were found nor is it possible to say from the letters how many emigrated, though an estimate of 1,600 families is mentioned at an early date. Major Mahon was shot, it was alleged, by some of his tenants for his insistence on the emigration scheme.

COOLATTIN EMIGRATION RECORD. List. 1847. (MS. 4974)

A list of the members of three hundred and twelve families from Coolattin, with their ages, who were emigrating to America in 1847, evidently due to distress and evictions on the FitzWilliam estates, County Wicklow.

SMITH, PHILIP. Diary. 1852-3. (P. 3235)

Diary of Philip Smith, an emigrant to America, 1852-3. With some letters, poems and a biographical note. (Photostat.)

H.M.S. *PLOVER*. Journal of the voyage (21 volumes). 1852-4. (MSS. 267-8)

Journal of the *Plover*'s Arctic explorations, touching on Alaska and Bering Strait.

LOCKE FAMILY PAPERS. 12 letters, 1858-63; and *c*. 25, 1880-90.

The earlier letters were written by Charles H. Locke to his brother John, an official of the Incumbered Estates Court, Dublin, and a writer on Irish economic problems. They describe his wanderings and his efforts to get work from Canada to New Orleans; his adventures in the Confederate Army, his subsequent desertion and surrender. He used money sent to him by John to buy clothes to replace his 'rebel' uniform. He had two married daughters living in Detroit who had given him up for dead. The remainder were written by Richard, son of John Locke, his wife Lelia and children, to Miss Jeannette Locke, Dublin. Richard Locke kept a store in Bonafacio, Fla.; the letters deal mainly with family affairs, and refer to his economic prospects.

SHIELS LETTERS. 1858, 1873-5. (P. 5329)

Letters by Maj.-Gen. James Shiels, U.S.A., 1858, 1873-5. With a note on his family background in Ireland. (Photostats.)

KEOGH, MYLES WALTER (1840-76). 32 letters. 1861-9. (MS. 3885)

Letters from or concerning Keogh to his brother Thomas of Carlow. Myles Keogh fought in the Army of the Potomac as a captain of cavalry, later as a colonel. He served in the Mississippi campaign, where he was taken prisoner but soon exchanged; joined General Sheridan's staff and was in the Tennessee campaign. The letters contain graphic descriptions of the fighting and of the Army's morale. (Keogh served in the United States Cavalry in the Indian Wars after the Civil War, and died with Custer at Little Bighorn, Mont.; no papers from this period survive, but there are several mementoes in the National Museum of Ireland.)

CAIRNES PAPERS. Letters. 1862-74.

(*a*) Letters to John E. Cairnes from G.W. Curtis, dealing with American political questions, together with letters from the Emancipation Society, 1862-74. (MSS. 8948-9)

(*b*) Letters to John E. Cairnes from Frank G. Shaw, Annie Shaw, and Sarah B. Shaw in relation to the National Freedman's Relief Association and to anti-slavery in America, 1862-8. (MSS. 8964-5)

CAIRNES, JOHN E. Letter-book. 1862-8. (MS. 4493)

A letter-book containing copies of letters from John E. Cairnes to Mrs. F.G. Shaw, mainly dealing with slavery and the American Civil War. Also two letters from Cairnes to George Walker of New York. 1862-8.

TOWNLEY HALL PAPERS. Letter. n.d. (MS. 10,351)

Portion of a letter describing a tour through America, n.d.

WOULFE LETTERS. 1863-81. (P. 3887)

Letters written from America by Maurice Woulfe [or Wolfe] of Cratice, Co. Limerick, 1863-81. (Photostats.)

O'CAHILL, JOHN M. (1840-1928). Irish verse (3 volumes). *c.* 1863-1926. (MSS. G. 510, G. 529, and G. 543)

Accounts in prose and verse in the Irish language by John M. Cahill of Peatwater, Mich., of his experiences in America, notably the Indian Wars, including his captivity. He was born in Templeglantine, County Limerick, and emigrated in 1863.

BUCHANAN, SAMUEL (1837-post 1905). 32 letters (typed copies). 1870-1903. (Buchanan Papers.)

Letters written by Samuel Buchanan to various relatives in Dublin, from Cincinnati, Ohio; Haysville, Ala.; Nashville, Tenn.; and Branchville, Summerton, Silver, and St. Pauls, S.C. They describe the life of a 'rolling stone' who worked as a train collector from Toronto to Niagara Falls; a cotton plantation overseer; cotton grower and mechanical engineer. He describes the changed economic conditions on the plantations since the Civil War.

FITZPATRICK OF OSSORY PAPERS. Letter. 1878. (In Autograph Collection.)

Charles E. Starr, of the United States Army, was stationed at Fort Lincoln, Dakota Territory; the letter, 1 Apr. 1878, is written to Bernard Fitzpatrick, Granston Manor, Abbeyleix, Ireland, in reply to a query on hunting trips in the Mid-Western states. Among the guides he suggests are Frank Gruard, Chief of Scouts for General Crook, 'Texas Jack', and 'Buffalo Bill' (W.F. Cody). The letter also records his vicissitudes in the Civil War. Some autobiographical details follow. Starr left Ireland, from Roscrea, County Tipperary, at the age of ten with an uncle who was returning to near Gainesville, Fla., and whose name he adopted.

CLARKE, WAD. *c.* 120 letters. 1880-95. (MS. 8746)

Emigrated to Canada. Letters written to his mother at Liverpool describing his life in Manitoba.

McCALL PAPERS. Letters. Late 19th century. (MS. 13,852)

Four letters to M.F. Hughes, including two from his brother John in San Francisco, with one to Miss Hughes.

J.S. STARKEY PAPERS. Letters. 1934-5. (MS. 15,592)

Seven letters from 'A.E.' to Seumas O'Sullivan on literary and personal matters, including his American visit. Feb. 1934-Aug. 1935.

MISCELLANEOUS EMIGRANT LETTERS. 1811-97.

(*a*) Six letters from Co. Tyrone emigrants in the U.S., describing conditions there to friends and relatives at home. Three letters are from Bernard McKenna in New York to Rev. Henry Conwell, Dungannon, two are from E. Toner in Pennsylvania to his brother Peter at Cookstown and to P. Donnelly of Pomeroy, and the last is to John Campbell of Coalisland from his brother in Youngstown, Ohio. 1811-9. (MS. 2300)
(*b*) O'Hara Papers. Emigrant's letters to Charles King O'Hara from Thomas Gunning in New York, with descriptions of a journey to Texas. Five items, 1831-8. (MS. 20,328)
(*c*) Studdert Papers. Three letters to Michael Studdert of Rehy Park, Kilrush, Co. Clare, from John Browne, writing from New Brunswick in Canada. Mainly concerning economic conditions in Canada, the U.S., and Ireland. 1845-9. (MS. 20,628). Also some letters from members of the Studdert family in the U.S., nineteenth century. (MS. 20,629)
(*d*) Sixteen letters to John M. Kelly, Dublin, 1846-8, from John Brady, Liverpool, and Thomas Reilly, Saratoga, N.Y., on personal affairs, with some comment on matters of public interest. (MS. 10,511)
(*e*) Letter of George Crosley, [? Boston] Navy Yard, U.S.A., to his mother at Craughwell, Co. Galway, 28 Mar. 1847. (MS. 13,549)
(*f*) Twenty-one letters from Irish emigrants to the offices of C. Grimshaw, a shipping firm in Liverpool, in connexion with the booking of passages to America, 1864-6. (MS. 15,784)
(*g*) Rowan Papers. Accounts of Col. William Rowan of Tralee, with J. Kershaw of Queenstown, Co. Cork, for the provision of board and lodging for emigrants to the U.S. (with lists of names). Ten items, May-June 1884. (MS. 20,616)
(*h*) Incomplete letter from an Irish emigrant rancher in Park Co., Montana, to a schoolmaster in Ireland, 10 Apr. 1897. (MS. 15,647)
(*i*) Copies and some originals of letters from emigrants to the U.S., collected in 1961 by Dr. E.R.R. Green. (MS. 11,428)

OTHER RECORDS. *c.* 1793-1912.

(*a*) Collection of correspondence of members of the Edgeworth family of Co. Longford, including letters from relatives in Georgia and North Carolina, with references to cotton farming. *c.* 1793-1879. (MS. 18,780)
(*b*) Autobiography of Arthur I.C. Mitchell from 1859 to 1912, with an extensive account of his work as manager of Oelrich's Cattle Station, Fall River Co., S. Dakota, in the late 1880's and 1890's. (Copies.) (N. 6205; P. 6942)
(*c*) An account by Margaret E. Mitchell of her life at Oelrich's Cattle Station, S. Dakota, in the 1890's. (Copies.) (N. 6205; P. 6942)
(*d*) Letters and memoranda regarding the American lecture tour of W.B. Yeats, mainly letters to Yeats and John Quinn, with some letters of Quinn to Yeats. Fifteen items, Dec. 1903-July 1904. (MS. 18,564)

PUBLIC RECORD OFFICE OF IRELAND, Four Courts, Dublin 7

This Office receives records from government departments and offices (including embassy and consular records in America), from the courts (Circuit to Supreme), from probate registries and from other sources through purchase or donation of non-governmental or private records.

At present total holdings extend to about 24,000 linear feet of shelving, covering in the main records from the nineteenth and twentieth centuries. For a description of the records held, see Deputy Keeper Reports nos. 55-9 and *A Short Guide to the Public Record Office of Ireland,* available in photocopy form from the Office. For material held in this Office until 1922, when the repository was destroyed in military operations, see Deputy Keeper Reports nos. 1-54 and *A Guide to the Records deposited in the Public Record Office of Ireland* (Dublin, 1919).

This Office has an active accessioning programme, bringing in records now in government departments and offices. Some of the accessioned material will refer to America, and research students should consult the office from time to time so that they may be informed of additional accessions both in the Public Record Office of Ireland and in the State Paper Office, Dublin Castle, which at present form one single administrative unit.

Applications to inspect public records to which there is, with a small number of exceptions, open access, should be addressed to the Deputy Keeper of Public Records.

Documents of American interest may be found in individual cases in the records received from all the sources outlined above. Some examples are:

ABSTRACTS OF EXPORTS AND IMPORTS OF IRELAND. 4 volumes. 1764-73; 1784-8; years ending 25 Mar. 1790 and 25 Mar. 1800. (M 2482-3, 2489-90)

These would appear to be complete returns of the trade of Ireland for the years mentioned. There are tabulated entries giving the names of the ports, countries of consignment, names of the goods, amount and value. Among the goods exported were 'aqua vita', beef, pork, books, bread, butter, candles, drapery, glass, glue, linen, tallow, tongues, fish, salmon, etc. Imports included apples, juniper berries, cider, corn, dyestuffs, furs, nuts, pitch, tobacco, whalebone, etc. Goods were sent to Carolina, New England, New Providence, Pennsylvania, Quebec, Virginia, and the West Indies.

PROCLAMATIONS.

Among the proclamations, printed and engrossed, 1701-1875, the following are of American interest:
(*a*) 3 Mar. 1795: The embargo was removed on ships sailing for Newfoundland.
(*b*) 10 Apr. 1795: One ordinary seaman was allowed on ships bound for Newfoundland.
(*c*) 31 Oct. 1817: Ships from Charleston, S.C., were to be quarantined due to the prevalence of a 'malignant fever' there.
(*d*) 7 Nov. 1817: Similar. Ships from Savannah, Ga.

CUSTOMS AND EXCISE RECORDS. 1778-1837.

These include records relating to American ships, goods imported from America, etc., indexed under America, American, New York, and Quebec.

JOSEPH McDONNELL LETTERS. 1812-37. (999/49)

McDonnell took part in the Rebellion of 1798. The Public Record Office of Ireland has photocopies of twenty-one letters written by him as an exile in the U.S.A.

CENSUS RETURNS. 1821-51, 1901, 1911.

Frequently used for genealogical and emigration studies. The earliest complete census returns for the entire country are for 1901 and 1911. There are also some surviving returns for Cos. Cavan, Fermanagh, Galway, Meath, and Offaly (King's Co.) for 1821, for Co. Derry for 1831, for Co. Cavan for 1841, and for Co. Antrim for 1851.

TITHE APPLOTMENT BOOKS. 1824-37.

These books are of considerable use in genealogical studies. Originally compiled to record the amount of tithe payable for individual holdings, they give under parishes and townlands the names of resident families and the amount of land held. A surnames index for each county is available in the Office.

QUIT RENT OFFICE. Crown estates records. *c.* 1850.

This office was absorbed in the Land Commission in 1943; it had dealt with the quit rents and other land revenues of the Crown, the management of Crown property, and related matters from the seventeenth century onwards. There are lists of emigrants from Crown lands to the United States and Canada under a State-subsidized emigration scheme in the 1850's, and also miscellaneous letters and documents relating to the whole scheme. The estates were those at Kingwilliamstown, Co. Cork; Ballykilcline, Co. Roscommon; Boughill and Irvilloughter, Co. Galway; and Kilconcouse, Offaly.[1]

VALUATION OFFICE COLLECTION.

Of possible interest as sources of emigration studies are:
Reports on the General Valuation of Rateable Property in Ireland (printed), in the 1850's, together with some of the manuscript note-books or 'house-books' used by the inspectors in compiling these reports - these latter will occasionally note that a householder has emigrated.

RECORDS OF THE REGISTRAR GENERAL OF SHIPPING AND SEAMEN. 1863-1913.

These records formed part of a record group relating to the whole of the United Kingdom and Ireland. Samples were taken by the P.R.O. (London) and by the British National Maritime Institute. The remaining records relating to ships registered in Irish ports were accessioned by the Public Record Offices of Ireland and of Northern Ireland. They consist mainly of crew agreements, with some official logs of voyages to and from American ports.

CHURCH OF IRELAND PAROCHIAL RECORDS.

These are also a possible source for emigration studies. Church of Ireland parish records were made public records in 1875, following the disestablishment of 1869. But a further Act, in 1876, allowed local retention where suitable storage existed. Many registers transferred to the Record Office in Dublin were lost in the destruction of 1922; those surviving in the Record Office came in after that date. However, the Office can supply information as to which registers survive and whether copies exist of those that have perished.

RELIGIOUS SOCIETY OF FRIENDS IN IRELAND, 6 Eustace Street, Dublin 2

AMERICAN REVOLUTION. Letters and documents. 1776-82.

(*a*) Letter from James Pemberton to ?, describing the position of American Friends during the War of Independence. 16 June 1776. (Grubb Collection Commonplace Book I, p. 77)
(*b*) Extract of letter from Samuel Emlen, Jr., *et al.* to John Fothergill *et al.*, 16 Dec. 1777, reporting on the distress in Philadelphia and asking for assistance. (Shelf L.D., Port. 4.51)
(*c*) Irish Friends' relief to American Friends, and their reply, 1777-94. (Shelf L.D., Port. 5B/45)
(*d*) Letter from London Friends, 1778, recommending relief to Friends in America. (Port. 19, no. 87)
(*e*) Appeal by English Friends for relief to Friends in Philadelphia, 6 Mar. 1778. (Shelf L.D., Port. 10.77)
(*f*) Letter from Friends in Philadelphia, acknowledging aid, 1779. (Port. 19, no. 87)
(*g*) Letter from Philadelphia and New Jersey Meeting for Sufferings, 10 Feb. 1779, signed 'Nicholas Waln'. Concerns relief from Ireland to America. (Grubb Collection, Book III, p. 165)
(*h*) List of Dublin subscribers for the relief of Friends suffering in America, 1782. (Port. 19, 95abcd)

AMERICAN CIVIL WAR. Diary and minutes. 1861-8.

(*a*) There are occasional references to the American Civil War and its aftermath in the minutes of both the Ireland Yearly Meeting (A.7) and the Dublin Monthly Meeting (D.30). In the Yearly Meeting proceedings, see minutes 37 (1861), 16 and 48 (1864), 22 and 24

1. *Analecta Hibernica*, no. 22, pp. 329-94, June 1960, prints many of these documents, including the lists of names; the accounts for the voyage; interdepartmental correspondence between the Commissioners of Woods, the Quit Rent Office, and the Treasury; letters and memorials from tenants, local landlords, and agents; and four letters from emigrants shortly after their arrival in the United States.

(1865), and 23, 27, 33, and 38 (1866). The Dublin Monthly Meeting includes references in minute 7 (6th month, 1864), minute 7 (1st month, 1866), and minute 10 (5th month, 1868).
(*b*) The correspondence of Jonathan Pim contains some letters on the American Civil War. These letters, which are all endorsed by Frederic Pim (see his diary, below), discuss among other subjects the position England should take in the conflict. (Pim Correspondence, Room 4)
(*c*) Diary of a visit to America in 1864 by Frederic W. Pim. Pim travelled to the U.S. as a representative of his father, a linen merchant, and his diary entries emphasize the effect of the Civil War on the North's economy. (Shelf 0.30, 31)

MISCELLANEOUS LETTERS, JOURNALS AND DOCUMENTS. 1705-*c*. 1930.

(*a*) Letter, 1705, from Benjamin Chandlee in Philadelphia to his brother, offering advice on the journey to America, describing what goods to take, etc. (Shelf L.D., Port. 4.43)
(*b*) Account of money distributed since 1788 by Philadelphia Friends from the donation sent by Friends in Ireland. (Shelf L.D., Port. 11.12)
(*c*) Letters from members of the Wright family, 1801-43. These letters, nearly all written by James Wright (1788-?) and of a domestic character, include a few which describe Wright's activities as a settler in Ohio. (Wright Papers)
(*d*) Letter, 1809, from Jonathan Pim to his brother Thomas, mentioning that war between England and America seemed 'likely'. (Pim MSS. a.21, 2 lower)
(*e*) Letter, 1841, from Joseph Sturge to members of the Religious Society of Friends in America, describing his work for the anti-slavery movement. (Shelf L.D., Port. 5B.22)
(*f*) Comments on a visit to the U.S. in 1850 by James Hill in his journal for 1847-68. Hill describes his trip in great detail, and mentions stops in New York, Philadelphia, and Albany, N.Y. He expresses much interest in American machinery and the buildings in Philadelphia, but complains that 'the state of morals cast a stigma on its inhabitants. There was more wickedness committed in Philadelphia in one year than in all Ireland.' (Shelf 0.1)
(*g*) Notes by S.R. Barcroft on the history of American Friends, *c*. 1930. (Shelf L.D., Port. 12/66)

ROYAL IRISH ACADEMY, 19 Dawson Street, Dublin 2

CHARLEMONT MANUSCRIPTS. 1776-96.

Papers of James Caulfeild, 4th Viscount and 1st Earl of Charlemont (1728-99), Irish statesman. There are nineteen bound volumes of correspondence with a calendar of contents at the beginning of each volume. (*Letters unless otherwise stated.*)
(*a*) Memoirs by the Earl of Charlemont briefly mentioning the war in America, and chiefly its effect upon Ireland. 1776-82.[1]
(*b*) New York, 15 Dec. 1777, from C. Lee at New York to Charlemont on personal affairs.[2]
(*c*) London, 20 Apr. 1782, from Annesley Shee to Charlemont, suggesting that Ireland might mediate between Britain and America.[3]
(*d*) 2 June 1782, from Alexander Henry Haliday, a Belfast physician, to Charlemont, describing the conduct and misfortunes of his brother, formerly collector of Charleston, S.C. - the only collector, he says, 'who had the firmness to get the obnoxious teas stored, instead of being sent back or destroyed'.[4]
(*e*) St. Petersburg, 10 Sept. 1784, from Lord Carysfort to Charlemont mentions America as an example for Ireland.[5]
(*f*) Bandon, County Cork, 16 Nov. 1784, from George Wood to Charlemont, commends the non-establishment of any church in the United States.[6]
(*g*) 31 Dec. 1789, from Sir Edward Newenham, M.P., to Charlemont, in which he quotes extensively from a letter he has just received from Benjamin Franklin, in which the latter describes the formation of the Union, the reluctance of Carolina and Rhode Island to accede, the greatness of George Washington as a statesman, and the desirability of a commercial treaty between the United States and Ireland.[7]
(*h*) Dublin, 15 Dec. 1791, from Charlemont to A.H. Haliday, in which he states that the American constitution will last only until 'that immense region ... shall be divided into various states, republics, and kingdoms'.[8]
(*i*) Belfast, 13 and 20 Nov. 1793, from A.H. Haliday to Charlemont; the former advising quarantine for all ships from Philadelphia, where a plague is raging, the latter expressing satisfaction that this has been imposed.[9]
(*j*) 19 and 23 June 1794, between Charlemont and A.H. Haliday refer to the 'wisdom and firmness' of George Washington, especially over non-importation.[10]
(*k*) 29 Oct. 1794, from Charlemont to Edmund Malone deprecating the advisability of war with America; and Malone's reply, 7 Nov., that no such war is contemplated in England.[11]
(*l*) 26 June 1796, from A.H. Haliday to Charlemont, mentions emigration of thousands of Irish Catholics to America, under pressure of Orange persecution.[12]

ORDNANCE SURVEY OF IRELAND, MANUSCRIPT MEMOIRS. 52 boxes. 1833-9.

Arranged under counties, subdivided into parishes. The Survey, made during the 1830's, provides historical, archaeological, social, and other information for most of the counties of Ireland, as well as maps, sketches, and statistics, the last mentioned including 'lists of emigrants, 1833-1839'. These lists are very detailed for Antrim and Londonderry. Short notes on emigration, of a very general nature, occur for counties of Armagh, Cavan, Donegal, Down, Fermanagh, Leitrim, Longford, Mayo, Sligo, Tyrone. There is a typed calendar.

STATE PAPER OFFICE, Dublin Castle, Dublin 1

The State Paper Office was established as a paper office in 1702 for the purpose of taking copies of the Chief Governor's book of entries, warrants, orders, petitions, and other papers dating from 1697. Papers relating to the administration of Ireland before that year must be sought amongst the records in the custody of the Public Record Office, London, and in particular among the record classes given in the 'Guide to the Contents' under the title 'State Papers, Ireland' (S.P. 60-S.P. 67). These state papers are described in the *Calendar of State Papers Relating to Ireland, 1509-1670*, and after that date in the *Calendar of State Papers, Domestic.*

1. H.M.C. xii (x), pp. 32,42,45,49,50,59.
2. Transcript, ibid., p. 173.
3. Transcript, ibid., p. 401.
4. Transcript, ibid., pp. 404-5.
5. Transcript, H.M.C. xiii (viii), p. 6.
6. Transcript, ibid., pp. 8-9.
7. Transcript, ibid., p. 113.
8. Transcript, ibid., pp. 181-3.
9. Transcripts, ibid., pp. 220, 223.
10. Transcript, ibid., pp. 242-3.
11. Transcripts, ibid., pp. 251-2.
12. Transcript, ibid., pp. 274-5.

State papers kept in the State Paper Office were transferred from time to time to the Public Record Office of Ireland, and by 1922 practically all state papers down to 1790 had been deposited there. With the destruction of the repository of the Public Record Office in 1922, the transferred state papers perished, so that the present holdings of the State Paper Office, which extend to about 7,500 linear feet of shelving, cover only the years 1790 to 1944. The state papers for these years are open to all persons who have permission to inspect them. Applications for permission to use these papers and other queries should be addressed to the Keeper of State Papers, who is also Deputy Keeper in the Public Record Office of Ireland.

From its original restricted purposes, the State Paper Office grew in time to become the record repository for the office of the Chief Secretary to the Lord Lieutenant (i.e., head of British administration in Ireland). The main record groups and classes containing or likely to contain material of American interest are set out below. The latest additions (1976) to the papers received are the records relating to the cabinet work of the Irish government from 1922 to 1944; it is possible that further deposits of such cabinet records will be received in the future.

REBELLION AND OTHER PAPERS. 1790-1831.

The Rebellion Papers are concerned with the state of the country as it was at the time of the rebellions of 1798 and 1803. They cover the years 1796-1809, and are contained in sixty-six cartons. A calendar in four volumes and an index to it are available in the Office. Items of American interest include:

(*a*) 'The transported felon's sorrowful account of 14 years transportation at Virginia in America' by James Ruel, 'the unhappy sufferer', n.d. (8 pages).

(*b*) Colonel Durham of the Fife Fencibles to Rev. C. Soden, 29 May 1796: 'Powder comes from America in flax seed casks.'

(*c*) Capt. Alexander Chesney, Prospect, Kilkeel, Co. Down, 3 June 1797, to Thomas Pelham, Chief Secretary for Ireland, describing the behaviour of the people of Charleston, S.C., during the War of Independence.[1]

(*d*) Portion of a letter, 1 Aug. 1797, written from New York to George Ivie, Dublin, describing a voyage from Europe, the boarding of a vessel by French privateers, scenes on board ship, suspected vessels, boarding houses, and wages.

(*e*) Papers of Thomas Russell (1767-1803), United Irishman. Among these is a letter from Wolfe Tone describing his life in Philadelphia and Washington's aristocratic leanings in politics, n.d.

Further information about the Rebellion Papers may be found in the printed Deputy Keeper's reports, nos. 8 (p. 23), 9 (p. 17), 13 (p. 14), 15 (p. 182), 16 (p. 14) and 22 (p. 34). Other contemporary papers of a similar nature for which there are MS. calendars in two volumes are the State of the Country Papers, 1790-1831, which in turn are continued in Outrage Reports, CSO R.P., from 1832-52, and thereafter in constabulary and police reports in CSO R.P. Also concerned with the internal state of the country and some external affairs are the Westmorland Papers, sometimes referred to as the Fane Collection. These papers, contained in two cartons, are the correspondence of John Fane, 10th Earl Westmorland (1759-1841), while he was Lord Lieutenant of Ireland, Jan. 1790-Jan. 1795; they are described in Deputy Keeper's report no. 16 (pp. 13-4). A calendar with index is available. Among the American items are five printed documents on the American and West Indian Intercourse Bill, 1806, giving the case for the petitioners against the bill, the proceedings of the committee of the port of London, and the position regarding the remaining British colonies in America.

OFFICIAL PAPERS, CHIEF SECRETARY'S OFFICE.

As well as the CSO R.P. (1818-1924), there were also official papers which were received in the Chief Secretary's Office or in ancillary offices but which do not appear to have passed through the central registry. They are arranged in chronological order, and the following separate classes exist at present:

Official Papers, 1790-1831. There is a MS. calendar in two volumes and a card index available to these papers.

Official Papers, 1832-82. A subject index in alphabetical order is available in MS.

Official Papers, MA, 1832-82. A calendar with an index is available in MS.

Items of American interest include: permission to sail being sought by an American vessel in Cork harbour, 1811; the *Angus,* American brig of war, at the Pigeon House, Dublin Bay, 1813; distress on British ships due to regulations on taking passengers to American ports, 1816-9.

Special reference should be made to passenger lists of immigrants to the United Kingdom, 1858-67, which were sent to the Lord Lieutenant by order of the Commissioners of Customs, 1858, mostly from Liverpool and Glasgow but also from London, Southampton, Greenock, Cork, Galway, and Derry. The details supplied by the ship's master included ship's name, the name, age, nationality, and profession or occupation of the passengers, the ports of departure and arrival, and the ports at which passengers had contracted to land. Ports of embarkation in America were Montreal; Quebec; St. John's, Newfoundland; Portland, Me.; Dorchester, Mass.; Boston; New York; Philadelphia; and New Orleans.

CONVICT DEPARTMENT, CHIEF SECRETARY'S OFFICE.

The main class of records consists of convict papers, including petition files of convicted persons, 1836-1924. There are also corresponding reference books in which the cases are entered in alphabetical order. For the period 1778-1836 the prisoners' petitions and cases (20 cartons) should be consulted; a MS. calendar is available. In some cases applications to remove to America were approved.

POLICE AND CRIME RECORDS, INCLUDING FENIAN PAPERS.

Among the police and crime records, the Fenian Papers, 1857-83, contain many references to America, due to the shared ambition of the organization at home and the Fenian Brotherhood in the United States of America to achieve an Irish Republic. The contents of the Fenian Papers are described in *Irish Historical Studies*, vol. xvi, no. 63 (March 1969). Those of most interest for American research include:

(*a*) Reports from New York by police sub-inspector Doyle on the Phoenix movement in the U.S., 1859-61.

(*b*) A Files, 1864-8 and 1877-83, from sub-inspector Doyle and consular officials in the United States on Fenian activities.

(*c*) Abstracts of cases under Habeas Corpus Suspension Acts, 3 vols., 1866-8. The abstracts give a synopsis of grounds for suspicion and arrest, the details of arrest and custody, and the records of the prisoner's health while in custody and other documents leading to discharge. Many of those arrested had come to Ireland from America and claimed U.S. citizenship and protection to secure or speed up their release; many others were released on condition of going to America.

(*d*) F Papers, 1866-74, 14 cartons. These papers were assembled for a rudimentary special branch for political crime by the brothers Anderson - Samuel Lee, in Dublin, and his brother Robert, in London, who together watched Fenian activities in Ireland, Britain, and America.

1. See the Floyd Papers in the Public Record Office of Northern Ireland (p. 323).

REGISTERED PAPERS, CHIEF SECRETARY'S OFFICE.

This is the largest single record group in the State Paper Office; in it are to be found papers for each year from 1818 to 1924. They fill some 3,770 cartons (1,800 cu. ft. in volume) and consist of incoming correspondence to which subsequent papers are attached to form a file on the particular person, place, incident, or act of administration. The subject matter of registered papers can be divided roughly into two broad categories: (i) executive and administrative work of the Chief Secretary to the Lord Lieutenant and (ii) law and order work, being in the main reports from police sources. These papers were received in a central registry and entered daily in registers, 1818-1922; contemporary index volumes showing names of correspondents and subjects are available for 1818-1924 (296 vols.).

Among the registered papers (abbreviated to CSO R.P.) are many items of American interest; the following may be cited as examples:

(*a*) American agents appointed at the principal Irish ports, 1861-2. (CSO R.P. nos. 2090, 2128, 2147, 3023, 6847, 10926)

(*b*) Discussion at length of the problems of extradition from the United States which arose in the case of Michael Hayes, suspected of having shot a landlord's agent. (CSO R.P. 1861-2, no. 14992)

(*c*) Reports that both sides in the American Civil War were enlisting men for their armies. (CSO R.P. 1863-4, no. 4372 [from Mitchelstown, Co. Cork]; no. 4608 [from Cahir, Co. Tipperary]; and no. 4704 [from Charleville, Co. Cork])

(*d*) Recruitment in Dublin of group of about 100 men to work on American railways but forced on arrival to enlist. (CSO R.P. 1864, no. 5606 [1,278 enlisted men sail from Cork]; no. 14056 [letter of John to his brother Thomas Carroll in Dublin describing his forced enlistment]; and no. 16765 [on the forced enlistment])

(*e*) Correspondence (printed, 84 pp.) respecting the recent Fenian aggression upon Canada, presented to both Houses of Parliament, Feb. 1867. (CSO R.P. 1870/13772)

Where a matter of American interest is found in the registered papers, the letter-books known as Government Correspondence Books (99 vols.) should also be consulted; in general, they were indexed contemporaneously. Also to be found among the registered papers are Situation and Relief Papers from 1791 which include petitions from persons seeking assistance to go to America, 1818, and Michael O'Kelly to go to Canada.

DÁIL ÉIREANN SECRETARIAT. Files. 1919-22.

529 files covering the administration of the early Dáil (or Irish Parliament) until the treaty with Great Britain in 1922. Some items of interest are:

(*a*) Dáil loan, resolution of thanks to American subscribers. 17 Aug. 1921. (DE 2/280)

(*b*) American Committee for Relief in Ireland: correspondence about a meeting with the President, 1921. (DE 2/298)

(*c*) American Federation of Labor: telegrams from President De Valera to the Federation, 1921. (DE 2/395)

CABINET MINUTES AND RELATED FILES.

(*a*) Cabinet minutes: forty-one volumes covering the period 1922-44, deposited in Feb. 1976 by authority of the Taoiseach (Prime Minister).

(*b*) 'S' files, which are files of the Department of the Taoiseach connected with the business before the Cabinet and which are referred to in the minutes. Items of American interest include:

(i) James Larkin: release from U.S.A., 1922-4. (S 2009)

(ii) Text of broadcast by President Cosgrave to the American people, 1931. (S 5111/7)

(iii) Congratulatory messages from people in the U.S.A. on President Cosgrave's broadcast, 1931. (S 5111/8)

(iv) Development of tourist traffic with U.S.A., 1924-9. (S 5472)

THE LIBRARY, TRINITY COLLEGE,[1] Dublin 2

SPANISH AMERICA. 603 folios (*c.* 100 are now missing). First half of 17th century. (MS. 959)

Papers relating to proceedings - ecclesiastical, civil, and military - in Spanish America in the first half of the seventeenth century. At the beginning of the collection it is stated that they are 'originals'. Spanish (and some Portuguese) is used, and there is a table of contents.

CARIBBEES AND BARBADOS. Papers. (187 pages). Mid-17th century. (MS. 736)

Consists of copies of grants, inquiries, etc., in connexion with the grant of the Caribbee islands and Barbados to the Earl of Carlisle; reports of the connexion of the 2nd Earl with the islands, and an account of the island of Barbados. There is also a copy of the charter of the Company of Massachusetts, 1628.[2]

NEW ENGLAND LAWS.[3] 15 folios [n.d. but before 1670]. (MS. 861, ff. 118-32)

KING PAPERS. (MSS. 1998-2008)

Correspondence of William King, Archbishop of Dublin, contains items in 1704-5 touching upon the Protestant Church in South Carolina and the plantations.[4] (Listed and indexed.)

CONOLLY PAPERS. (MSS. 3974-84, nos. 448-50, 452, 463, 477, 479, 1797-1800)

A small archive detailing Major Apollos Morris's attempt to play the peacemaker between Washington and Sir William Howe, Jan.-June 1777, is included among the papers of the Conolly family of Castletown, Co. Kildare. (Listed and indexed.)

TONE, THEOBALD WOLFE (1763-98). Notes. 1795-6. (MS. 2046/7/0)

Autobiographical notes include an account of his visit to America, 1796.

NEW MEXICO AND CALIFORNIA VOYAGES. Bound volume (33 leaves). [late 18th century]. (MS. 1453)

Written in Spanish, giving an account of missionary voyages and discoveries in New Mexico and California. There is also a diary, pp. 47-63, written by a Jesuit, Father Fernando Consag. (The paper and binding suggest that the manuscript was written in the Philippines.)

1. T.K. Abbott, *Catalogue of the Manuscripts in the Library of Trinity College, Dublin* (Dublin, 1900).
2. H.M.C. viii (i), p.585.
3. Ibid.
4. H.M.C. ii, p. 234.

CORBET LETTERS. (MS. 5966)

Many of the letters of William Corbet, the United Irishman, are addressed to his brother in New York, 1804-14. (Listed and indexed.)

HARVEY FAMILY LETTERS. 1816-48. (MS. 3641)

236 letters written to Jacob Harvey, a Quaker merchant from Limerick who emigrated to New York. Although the letters are written from Ireland, there is much reference to business affairs in New York. (Calendared.)

CRAMPTON CORRESPONDENCE. (MSS. 4176-80)

Sir Philip Crampton's correspondence contains material of interest about his son, Sir John F.T. Crampton, the British Minister in Washington, 1845-56. (Listed and indexed.)

WEBB AUTOGRAPHS. (MS. 4787)

The autographs, mostly from correspondence of Richard Davis Webb, include single letters from R.W. Emerson, 1847, W.L. Garrison, 1872, I.T. Hopper (2), 1842, George Kennan, 1889, J.G. Whittier, 1869, and W. Whitman, 1872. (Listed.)

HART PAPERS. (MSS. 6464-5)

American travel journal of Charles H. Hart, 1848-9, and a commonplace book he kept while there.

DILLON PAPERS. (MSS. 6455-7)

The papers of John Blake Dillon, the Young Irelander, mostly date from his exile in New York, 1849-56.

PURDON PAPERS. (MSS. 4824-32)

Letters from Marian Fetherston to her sister-in-law Sarah Purdon, 1856-71.

DE VERE PAPERS. (MS. 5055b)

Among the Aubrey de Vere materials are copies of his letters to Prof. C. Eliot Norton, 1857-1900.

R.R. MADDEN PAPERS.

A collection of the papers of R.R. Madden, the historian of the United Irishmen, contains correspondence about exiles in America. (These are entered in Abbott's *Catalogue* under nos. 873, 1469, 1470, and 1472.) (Listed and indexed.)

LECKY, WILLIAM EDWARD HARTPOLE (1838-1903). Letters. (MSS. 1827-36)

A few letters from the U.S. are included in the correspondence of Lecky, historian and M.P. (Listed and indexed.)

DILLON PAPERS. (MSS. 6458-6909)

The papers of John Dillon, the last leader of the Irish Parliamentary Party, contain much of American interest, particularly the memoranda books kept during his tour with Charles Stewart Parnell in 1880 (MSS. 6536-7). Other American material include his correspondence, 1881-1927, with his brother William, who, after a spell in ranching at Little Rock, Colorado, practiced as a lawyer in Chicago (MSS. 6869-71); John Dillon's own stay at Little Rock, 1883-5, recorded in letters to his cousin, Mrs. Anne Deane (MS. 6885); letters to Mrs. Deane from Irish emigrants (MS. 6893); letter from John Devoy, 1891 (MS. 6837); regular briefing on American affairs from Shane Leslie, 1916-9 (MS. 6840) and from T.P. O'Connor (MSS. 6741-2) and Richard Hazleton (MS. 6755) during 1917-8; general letters from American correspondents, 1871-1927 (MSS. 6844-6).

YEATS, JOHN BUTLER. Letters. (MS. 3459)

Portrait painter. Sixty-six letters, 1899-1921, from Yeats to Miss Clare Marsh, painter. Yeats lived in New York from 1908 until his death.

DOWDEN, EDWARD (1842-1913). Letters. (MSS. 3147-54)

Professor of English Literature. His correspondence, for which an index is available, contains a few letters from the United States. (Listed and indexed.)

SYNGE CORRESPONDENCE. (MSS. 4424-6)

John Millington Synge's correspondence includes letters from John Quinn, 1907-8. (Listed and indexed.)

O'SULLIVAN PAPERS. (MSS. 4461-7)

The papers of Seumas O'Sullivan (pseudonym of James Sullivan Starkey), poet and editor of the *Dublin Magazine* (1922-58) contain letters from some American literary figures like Vincent O'Sullivan and Jesse Stuart. (Listed and indexed).

IRISH RACE CONVENTION (NEW YORK). 1932.

The papers of the chairman, Thomas J. Ford, including the minutes of the arrangements committee and correspondence.

DEPARTMENT OF IRISH FOLKLORE, UNIVERSITY COLLEGE, Belfield, Dublin 4

EMIGRATION TO AMERICA. Questionnaires: 5 volumes. 1955. (Vols. 1407-1411)

In 1955 Dr. Arnold Schrier, in conjunction with the Irish Folklore Commission, prepared a questionnaire to collect oral tradition relating to emigration to America in particular, and former attitudes to America in general. Twenty-one interviewers of the commission returned twenty-six notebooks of about 100 pages each from all over Ireland. The material was used by Dr. Schrier for his doctoral dissertation submitted to Northwestern University in 1956, 'Ireland and the American Emigration, 1850-1900',[1] of which a microfilm is in the Department of Irish Folklore.

1. See Arnold Schrier, *Ireland and the American Emigration, 1850-1900* (Minneapolis, 1958).

LONGFORD

EARL OF GRANARD, Castle Forbes, Newtownforbes

GRANARD PAPERS. Letters. 1776-81.

Letters of Francis, Lord Rawdon, including details connected with civil and military affairs in America, 1776-81.[1]

TIPPERARY

EARL OF DONOUGHMORE, Knocklofty, Clonmel

DONOUGHMORE PAPERS. 3 letters. 1774-6.

16 Mar. 1774, from Lord Townshend to John Hely Hutchinson, on the blockade of Boston and the pending alteration of the Boston Charter. Criticisms of Chatham and 'Rockingham's faction' for alleged support of American independence.[1] Also two letters, 25 Oct. 1775 and 6 Mar. 1776, from Charles Jenkinson to John Hely Hutchinson concerning the rebellion, and debates in Parliament thereon.[2]

1. H.M.C. iii, pp. 430-1. An extract from one of the letters is given - a description of the battle of Camden, dated 19 Sept. 1780.

---

1. Transcript, H.M.C. xii (ix), p. 279.
2. Transcripts, ibid., pp. 284-5.

INDEX

INDEX

ALL SUBJECTS, unless otherwise qualified, relate to the United States, e.g. Agriculture is agriculture in the U.S.
NOBLEMEN appear under their family names, with references from their titles. Owners of manuscripts are entered under their titles only.
Life dates of persons have been given only when readily available.
ALPHABETICAL arrangement is 'word by word'.
CITIES and towns are listed under states.
UNDER STATES (U.S.), provinces (Canada), islands (West Indies), the arrangement is:
(i) History (divided by periods).
(ii) Subject subdivisions. (Please note that DESCRIPTION includes travel; MERCHANTS includes individual merchants and groups of merchants, whilst TRADE covers trade and commodities; SETTLEMENT covers also exploration.)
(iii) Geographical subdivisions.

A

Abbe, Cleveland (1838-1916), 148
Abbey, Edwin Austin (1852-1911), 238
Abbot, Benjamin, 94
Abbot, Charles, 2nd Baron Colchester (1798-1867), 139
Abbot, Willis J., 278, 279
Abbott, Andrew (1743-1819), 28
Abbott, Charles Stuart Aubrey, 3rd Baron Tenterden (1834-82), 68, 71, 72, 133, 140
Abbott, John, 28
Abbott, Sir John Joseph Caldwell (1821-93), 38
Abbott, L. D., 236
Abbott, T. K., *Catalogue of the MSS. in the Library of Trinity College, Dublin*, 352 fn.
Abbott, William, 287
Abbott Collection, 28
Abduction, 131
Abdy, Nicholas, 31
Abdy Papers, 31
Abel, A. H., and F. J. Klingberg, eds., *A Side-Light on Anglo-American Relations* (1927), 205
Abell, William, 304
Abercairny Muniments, 274
Abercrombie, ______ (*fl.* 1743), 256
Abercrombie, ______ (*fl.* 1758), 264
Abercrombie, James, 297
Abercromby, Gen. (*fl.* 1731), 261
Abercromby, Mr., 264
Abercromby, James (1706-81), 45, 64, 264, 266, 267, 284, 285, 290
Abercromby, John (*fl. c.* 1731), 292
Abercromby, John (*fl.* 1757), 297
Abercromby, Sir Robert, 297
Abercromby of Forglen Muniments, 297
Aberdeen and Orkney, Diocese of (Diocesan Archive), 253
Aberdeen-Angus Cattle Society, 319
Aberdeen, Earl of, 275
Aberdeen, 4th Earl of, *see* Gordon, George Hamilton (1784-1860); 7th Earl of, *see* Gordon, John Campbell (1847-1934)
Aberdeen, Marquess of, Mss., 260
Aberdeen, Scotland, 253-4; Customs records, 310; Merchants, 310
Aberdeen Papers, 66-7
Aberdeen Trades Council, 254
Aberdeen Typographical Society, 254
Aberdeen University, 307; Library, 253-4
Abergavenny, Marquess of, 44
Abergavenny Papers, 44
Abernethy, T. P., *The Burr Conspiracy*, 231 fn.
Aberystwyth, Dyfed, 243-7; Customs records, 93
Abingdon, 4th Earl of, *see* Bertie, Willoughby (1740-99)
Abolition of slavery, *see* Slavery: Anti-slavery movements
Aborigines Friend and Colonial Intelligencer, 51
Aborigines Protection Society, 51, 205
Abraham, Edgar, 280
Abraham, Judah I., 190
Académie des Sciences, 170
Academy of Natural Sciences, Philadelphia, 6
Academy of Political Science, New York, 298
Acadia (Settlement), 79, 83
Acheson, Archibald, 1st Viscount Gosford (1717-90), 323
Acheson, Arthur, 324
Acheson, David, 181
Acheson, Dean (1893-1971), 282
Acheson, Edward Goodrich (1856-1931), 163
Ackers, James, 287
Acland, C. T. D., 24
Acland, Thomas Dyke, 10th Baronet (1787-1871), 24
Acland Papers, 24
Acteon (ship), 142
Acton, Sir John Emerich Edward Dalberg, 1st Baron (1834-1902), 15, 72
Adair, James (*c.* 1709- *c.* 1783), 312
Adair, W. A., 124
Adam, Sir Charles (1780-1853), 261, 262
Adam, William (*fl.* 1775-81), 261, 286
Adam, William (*fl.* 1821-49), 96
Adam of Blair–Adam Mss., 261
Adams, Charles Fox Frederick (1852-1913), 38
Adams, Charles Francis (1807-86), 60, 61, 68, 71, 129, 170, 232
Adams, Charles Francis (1835-1915), 58, 163, 197, 199, 205, 206
Adams, David, 332
Adams, Edward Dean (d. 1931), 162
Adams, [?G. B.], 283
Adams, Henry Brooks (1838-1918), 68, 69, 170, 196
Adams, Herbert Baxter (1850-1901), 177, 197, 199, 206
Adams, James, 332
Adams, John (1735-1826), 32, 62, 82, 95, 148, 151, 161, 171, 192, 204, 256
Adams, John Quincy (1767-1848), 25, 57, 61, 62, 67, 76, 148, 167, 168, 185, 206, 255, 259
Adams, Samuel (1722-1803), 40, 44, 324
Adams, Mrs. Samuel, 40

Adams, W., 94
Adams, William (1807-80), 71
Adams and Anderson, 315
Adams family, 332
Adams Family Papers, 332
Adamson, John, 41
Addams, Jane (1860-1935), 164, 197
Addington, Henry, 1st Viscount Sidmouth (1757-1844), 12, 25, 27
Addington, Henry Unwin (1790-1870), 25, 186, 207, 240
Addis, J. P., *The Crawshay Dynasty*, 247
Adirondack Museum, New York, 20 fn.
Admiralty, 43, 119-22, 262, 278, 317; Records, 119-20, 122, 123
Admiralty, Archbishop's Court of, 231
Admiralty, Court of, 10, 307; *see also* Vice-Admiralty Courts
Admiralty, High Court of, 122, 136, 226
Admiralty, Lords Commissioners of the, 120, 195
Adoption, 311 fn.
Advocate, 96
Aetna Iron and Nail Co., 244
Africa: Colonization by Negroes, 165, 205; Slave trade, 344; *see also* Congo; Liberia; Sierra Leone; West Africa.
African Company, *see* Royal African Company
African Institution of London, 51
African Squadron, 169
Agassiz, A. W., 260
Agassiz, Alexander (1835-1910), 15, 147, 162, 314
Agassiz, Elizabeth (1822-1907), 162
Agassiz, Jean Louis Rodolphe (1807-73), 15, 196
Agitator, 314
Aglionby, Ch., 166
Agnew, Jane, 331
Agnew, John, 307
Agricultural colonies, 151
Agricultural machinery, 11, 149, 150, 270
Agricultural workers: Immigrants, 209; Statistics, 63, 64
Agriculture: Colonial period, 10, 137, 148-51 *passim*, 266, 301; 1776-1800, 11, 32-3, 42, 137, 313; 19th century, 11, 20, 50, 52, 63, 64, 103, 137, 156, 166, 186-7, 216, 217, 230, 328, 331, 332; 20th century, 137, 209, 210, 332
See also BUTTER; Cattle; Cheese; Grain; Horticulture; Maize; Olives; Orange growing; Patrons of Husbandry; Peas; Potash; Potatoes; Rapeseed; Rhubarb; Wheat; *see also subdivision* Agriculture *under countries, states, etc.*
Agriculture and Fisheries, Ministry of, Records, 122, 137
Agriculture, Board of (1793-1822), 11
Agriculture, Co-operative, 209, 210
Aikman, George, 262
Aikman, John Forbes, 262
Ailsa, Marchioness of, 255 fn.
Ailsa Muniments, 275
Ailsa Shipbuilding Co. Mss., 269
Ainslie, Miss C. (*later* Mrs. Young), 232
Ainslie, John, 315
Ainslie, Robert (1766-1838), 313
Ainsworth, John, ed., *The Inchiquin Manuscripts*, 343
Air Ministry, 122, 123-4
Air War College, 165
Aircraft: Navigation, 282; Parts, 281
Airlie Muniments, 273
Aitchison, James, 273
Aitchison, William (*fl.* 1774), 182
Aitchison, William (*fl.* early 19th cent.), 273
Aitken, George & William, 310
Aitken, John, 324
Aitken, William Maxwell, 1st Baron Beaverbrook (1879-1964), 112, 128
Akers, Charles Edmond (1861-1915), 38
Alabama, 1800-60, 325; Civil War, 1861-5, 60
CONSTITUTION, 271; Education, 199, 327; Finance, 100; Immigrants, 331; Law, 273; Politics, 271; Senators, 165
BIRMINGHAM, 283, 331; Florence, 331; Huntsville, Description, 271 (*see also* Mississippi); Middle District, 273; Mobile, 265, 301, 326, Consular reports (British), 130, Customs administration, 87, Description, 271, 305; Tuscaloosa, Description, 271
Alabama (ship), Building, 59, 60, 121, 130, 177; Claims, 13, 52, 58, 59, 60, 68, 70-3 *passim*, 90, 121, 130, 132, 133, 136, 139, 140, 179, 184, 201, 202, 344; Voyages, 121
Alabama, University of, 314
Alaska, 130 fn.; Boundaries, 38, 39, 111, 130; Cession by Russia, 130; Description, 15, 347; Gold, 165; Mining, 36
Alaska Glasgow–Gold Mine Ltd., 308
Albany (ship), 271
Albany Repeal Association, 344
Albemarle, Earl of, 219
Albemarle, 2nd Earl of, *see* Keppel, William Anne (1702-54); Albemarle, 3rd Earl of, *see* Keppel, George (1724-72)
Albemarle Papers, 219
Albers, J. A., 315
Albert, *Prince Consort* (1819-61), 40, 71
Albery, Thomas, 10
Albion, New York, 207
Alby, Parish church, 185
Aldborough, Customs records, 89
Aldborough (ship), 120
Aldeburgh, Customs records, 93
Alden, Henry Mills (1836-1919), 238
Alderman Library, 193 fn.
Alderney, Channel Islands, 339
Aldrich, Thomas Bailey (1836-1907), 238
Aldworth, Neville and, Papers, 141
Aldworth, Richard Neville, *see* Neville, Richard Neville Aldworth
Alexander VIII, *Pope*, 54
Alexander, A. J., 313
A[lexander], A[nn], 41
Alexander, Ed., Jr., 69
Alexander, Elizabeth, 300
Alexander, Harold, 1st Earl of Tunis (1891-1969), 145
Alexander, Henry, 4th Earl of Stirling (1639?-1691), 10
Alexander, Henry, 5th Earl of Stirling, (1664-1739), 10
Alexander, James, 264
Alexander, Sir William, 1st Earl of Stirling (1576-1640), 10, 194
Alexander, William, *claimed to be* 6th Earl of Stirling (1726-83), 149
Alexander, William (1824-1911), 328
Alexandra (Confederate ship), 17, 59
Alien and Sedition Laws, 95
Aliens, 131, 207; *see also* Americans in G. B., Legal status of; Naturalization; Suffrage
All Hallows College, Dublin, 347
All Souls College, Oxford, 206-8
Allan, D. G. C., "Colonel William Tatham," *Journal of the Royal Society of Arts* (1960), 151 fn.; "The Origin and Growth of the Society's Archives, 1754-1847," *ibid.* (1958), 148 fn.

Allan, Thomas (*c.* 1725-98), 323
Allason, Henry (*fl.* 1784-1802), 227; Commonplace Book, 227
Allegheny Mountains, 202
Allegheny River, 19
Allen, Lieut., 46, 285
Allen, Archibald, 28
Allen, Clifford, 228
Allen, Edgar, & Co., Ltd., 236
Allen, Elizabeth, 28
Allen, Ethan (1738-89), 305, 324
Allen, Henry, 328
Allen, John W., 245
Allen, Joseph Henry (1820-98), 176
Allen, Rev. Robert, 328
Allen, W. O. B., and E. McClure, *Two Hundred Years: The History of the Society for Promoting Christian Knowledge*, 152 fn.
Allen, William (1770-1843), 51, 245
Allen, William (1793-1864), 239
Allen & Hanburys Ltd., 50-1
Allen, Lady, of Hurtwood (1897-1976), 228
Allgood of Nunwick Mss., 191
Alliance Trust Co. Ltd., 318
Allied Provision Export Commission, 265
Allison, J., & Sons Mss., 268
Alnwick Castle, Northumberland, 190-1
Alsop, Joseph, 283
Alston, John, Jr., 290
Alston, Willis (1769-1837), 9
Alston, Cumbria, 21
Altgeld, John Peter (1847-1902), 164
Amalgamated Society of Carpenters and Joiners, 163, 228
Amalgamated Society of Engineers, 163
Amalgamated Textile Workers' Union, 179
Amalgamated Weavers' Association, Northern Counties, 179
Ambassadors, 27; *see also* names of individuals
Amcotts Deposit, 50
Amendments to the Constitution, *see* Constitution, Amendments
America's Cup, 269
American Air Force Daily, 158
American and West Indian Intercourse Bill (1806), 351
American Anti-Slavery Society, 51, 95, 96, 169, 185, 205
American Antiquarian Society, 204; *Proceedings*, 147 fn.
American Association for the Advancement of Physical Science, 170
American Aviation Mission Report (1919), 111
American Baptist Missionary Union, 165
American Bible Society, 268
American Board of Commissioners for Foreign Missions (Congregational), 197, 290
American Breeders' Association, 170
American Chamber of Commerce for the Port of Liverpool, 183
American Coal and Iron Co., 28
American Committee for Relief in Ireland, 352
American Committee for the Outlawry of War, 278, 279
American Committee on Africa, 113
American Co-operative Union, 174
American Copyright League, 197
American Debt Settlement, 16
American Ethnological Society, 171
American Expeditionary Force, 144
American Federation of Labor, 283, 352
American Fund (*alias* Chancellor's Fund, *alias* Lloyd George's Fund), 248
American Gas and Electric Co., 224
American Geographical and Statistical Society, 146, 147
American Guild of St. Barnabas for Trained Nurses, 75
American Hereford Association, 36
American Historical Association, Committee for the Study of War Documents, 136
American Home Mission, 244
American Hospitality Committee, 27
American Independence Week (1943), 27
American Indian [Trust] Fund, 290
American Land and Colonization Co. of Scotland Ltd., 308
American League to Enforce Peace, 116, 197
American Loyalist Claims Commission, 97
American Lumber Co. Ltd., 308
American Mortgage Co. of Scotland Ltd., 308
American Museum in Britain, 5
American Naturalist, 66
American Party, 317
American Philosophical Society, 6, 19 fn., 149 fn., 156 fn.
American Physical Society, 314
(American) Pioneer Regiment (4th), 102
American Recovery Programme, 165, 166
American Revolution, *see* War of Independence
American Ship Purchase Bill, 200
American Social Science Association, 170
American Society for Meliorating the Condition of the Jews, 190
American Society for the Diffusion of Useful Knowledge, 169
American Society of Newspaper Editors, 281
American Steam Navigation Bill (1826), 108
American Trust and Agency Co. Ltd, 308
American War Relief Trust (1941-59), 27
American West, 179
Americanisms, 62
Americans in Great Britain, Legal status of, 137, 232-3
Americans in House of Commons, Colonial period, 65
Americans in Scotland, 314
Amery, Leopold S., 277
Ames, C. G., 208
Ames, Joseph S., 283
Amherst, Jeffrey (1677-1750), 45
Amherst, Jeffrey, Baron (1717-97), 44, 45, 119, 143, 145, 218, 219, 223, 249, 264, 265, 266, 274, 285, 289, 290, 302
Amherst, William, 45
Amherst College, 96
Amherst Mss., 45
Amherst Papers, 142, 143
Amity (ship), 21
Amory, James S., 250
Amphitrite (ship), 44
Anabaptists, 274; *see also* Baptists
Analecta Hibernica, 343, 349 fn.
Anarchism, 137, 314
Ancaster, Earl of, 49
Ancaster Deposit, 50
Ancaster Papers, 49
Anchors, 15
Ancient and Honorable Artillery Company of Massachusetts, 143
Ancient Order of Hibernians in America, 345; Ladies Auxiliary, 346
Ancona (Indian village), 199
Ancrum, Michael, 299
Anderson, ——, 136
Anderson, Dr., 199
Anderson, Alexander, 272

Anderson, Sir Allan Garrett (1877-1952), 141
Anderson, Mrs. D., Mss., 272
Anderson, Sir Henry Percy (1831-96), 72
Anderson, J. & F., Collection, 307
Anderson, Janet, 272
Anderson, Robert (1750-1830), 254
Anderson, Sir Robert (1841-1918), 352
Anderson, Samuel Lee (1837-86), 352
Anderson, William (*fl.* 1689), 275
Anderson, William (*fl.* late 18th cent.), 212
Anderson family, 331
Anderson Family Papers, 331
Anderson Papers, 141
André, John (1751-80), 102, 148, 192, 261
"Andrew," 273
Andrew, C. K. C., Esq., 230
Andrews, C. F., 279
Andrews, Charles M., *Guide to the Materials for American History, to 1783, in the Public Record Office*, 122, 126, 139, 140, 141
Andrews, Charles M., and Frances G. Davenport, *Guide to the Manuscript Materials for the History of the United States to 1783, in the British Museum, in Minor London Archives . . .*, 16, 17, 85, 86, 94, 96, 97, 99 fn., 106, 106 fn., 115, 118 fn., 122, 137, 143, 147, 152, 154, 157, 158, 159, 171
Andrews, J., 34
Andrews?, Sir Simon, *see* Andros, Sir Edmund (1637-1714)
Andros, Sir Edmund (1637-1714), 31, 54, 203, 213, 230, 260
Anglo-American Brush Electric Light Corp., 111
Anglo-American Committee for International Discussion, 278
Anglo-American Committee for Outlawry of War, 278
Anglo-American Relief Fund, 27
Anglo-American Society, 200
Anglo-American Trade Agreement, 112
Anglo-Californian Bank Ltd., 125
Anglo-Californian Gold Mining and Dredging Co., 125
Angus (ship), 351
Anina, Antonio de, 169
Ankerville, Lord, 312
Anne (ship), 32
Anne and Eliza (ship), 262
Annesley Papers, 327
Anson, William, 104
Anstruther, Philip, 264
Anthill, Edward, 148
Anthony de la Conception, Fry [i.e. Fray], 57
Anti-Communism, 221
Anti-Federalist Party, 95
Anti-slavery, *see* Slavery, Anti-slavery movements; *and names of anti-slavery societies*
Anti-Slavery and Aborigines Protection Society, 51, 205
Anti-Slavery Committee, 51, 205
Anti-slavery conventions, 51
Anti-Slavery Examiner, 51
Anti-Slavery Magazine, 51
Anti-Slavery Record, 51
Anti-Slavery Reporter, 51
Anti-Slavery Society, 51, 205, 206
Anti-trust law, 198
Antigua, 15, 65; Trade, 31, 309
Antwerp Club, London, 180
Apollo Gallery, New York, 291
Appleby, George, 50
Appleton, Jesse, 263
Appleton, Nathaniel (1693-1784), 148
Apprehension of Offenders (America) Bill, 110
Apprentices, 5, 6, 27, 34, 46, 97, 295; *see also* Indentured servants; Transportation of criminals
Aqualate Hall Collection, 216
Arabia, Piracy, 10
Arago, Dominique François Jean (1786-1853), 170
Arbitration, International, 38, 63, 70, 71, 72, 131, 132, 138, 140, 142, 157, 198, 201, 260, 278, 345; *see also* Arbitration Treaty, 1911; Permanent Court of [International] Arbitration at The Hague
Arbitration Treaty (1911), 199, 224, 345
Arbuthnot, John (1667-1735), 83
Arbuthnot, Marriott (1711?-1794), 62, 192, 216, 230
Arch, Joseph (1826-1919), 209
Archbishops' Papers, 115; 18th century, 115
Archdale, John (*c.* 1642-*c.* 1717), 154
Archdiocese of Birmingham Archives, 225
Archer, James (1823-1904), 238
Archer, William (1856-1924), 74; Correspondence, 74
Archer, William Segar (1789-1855), 206
Archevesque, ______, 41
Archibald, Sir Edward Mortimer (1810-84), 58
Architecture, 97, 116, 229
Arctic exploration, 146-7, 347; *see also* Northwest Passage
Ard, John, 329
Arden, Miss, 179
Arditi, Luigi (1822-1903), 238
Ardtornish Estate Office Mss., 265
Argentina, Trade with U.S., *see* Trade with Argentina
Argyll, 3rd Duke of, *see* Campbell, Archibald (1682-1761); 8th Duke of, *see* Campbell, George Douglas (1823-1900)
Arizona: Agriculture, 166; Description, 222; Finance, 308; Immigrants, 166; Mining, 308
GRAND CANYON, 298; Phoenix, 166
Arizona Copper Co. Ltd., 308
Arizona Trust and Mortgage Co. Ltd., 308
Arkansas: Description, 265; Finance, 100; Immigrants, 331
VAN BUREN, 331
Arlington, Earl of, *see* Bennet, Henry (d. 1685)
Armenian question, 197
Armistice Day, 279
Armstrong, David, 331
Armstrong, Edward, 68
Armstrong, Edward Frankland (1878-1945), 163
Armstrong, Hamilton Fish, 280
Armstrong, Henry Edward (1848-1937), 163
Armstrong, Jane, 331
Armstrong, John, 285
Armstrong, Robert, 263
Armstrong, William, 240, 288
Armstrong Papers, 163
Armstrong Whitworth Collection, 223
Army, 15, 77, 143, 144, 206, 225, 347, 348; Medical service, 162; *see also* Deserters; *and subdivision* Army *under wars*
Army, British, 257, 275, 287, 305, 310; *see also* Canada: Army (British); *and subdivision* Army, British *under* Seven Years War, 1756-63, War of 1812, War of Independence, World War I, *and* World War II, *and under states, etc.*
COLONIAL PERIOD, 15, 21, 28, 48, 50, 55, 64, 65-6, 75, 76, 82, 103, 160, 190, 195, 203, 220, 222, 243, 257, 264, 266, 275, 301, 302, 303, Supplies, 301, 303; *see also* Regiments, British; Regiments of Foot

Armytage, W. H. G., *A. J. Mundella*, 236 fn.; ed., "Thomas Talbot and Lord Wharncliffe," *Ontario History* (1953), 232 fn.
Arnold, Benedict (1741-1801), 48, 57, 141, 190, 192, 205, 219, 230, 261, 274, 276, 317, 324
Arnold, John, 327
Arnold Arboretum, 146
Arnot, Hugh, 264
Arnot, Raymond H., 75, 164
Arpin, Edward, 9
Arrigrande, Sieur Gratian d', 41
Arroye, E., 279
Art: 19th century, 26, 66, 116, 176; *see also* Architecture; Cameos; Painting
Arthur William Patrick Albert, Duke of Connaught and Strathearn (1850-1942), 202
Artisans: Immigrants, 28, 244, 245; *see also* Apprentices; Blacksmiths; Building trades workers; Cabinet workers; Carpenters; Engineers; Iron and steel workers; Miners; Printers; Textile workers
Arundel, Customs records, 89, 93
Arundel Castle, West Sussex, 185
Asbury, Francis (1745-1816), 95, 117
Asgill, Captain, 275
Ashbee, Charles Robert (1863-1942), 116; *The American League to Enforce Peace*, 116
Ashburner Papers, 254
Ashburnham Mss., 222
Ashburton, 1st Baron, *see* Baring, Alexander (1774-1848); *also* Webster–Ashburton Treaty (1842)
Ashcombe Autograph Collection, 16
Ashe, William, 232
Ashley, Evelyn, 104, 105
Ashley, John, 187
Ashley, Sir William (d. 1927), 66; Papers, 66
Ashmole, Elias, 224
Ashridge, Elizabeth, 227
Ashridge II Mss., 39
Ashton, Elizabeth, 179
Ashton, Elizabeth Marion, 179
Ashton, Margaret, 179
Ashton, T. S., *An Eighteenth Century Industrialist: Peter Stubs of Warrington, 1756-1806*, 178 fn.
Ashton Papers, 179
Ashurst, Sir Henry, 83
Ashurst, Henry (*fl.* 1674-1701), 200
Ashworth, Henry, 317
Ashworth, J. H., 315
Askham Hall, Cumbria, 21
Aspinall, A., ed., *Three Early Nineteenth Century Diaries*, 216 fn.
Asquith Papers, 199-200
Assassination, 111
Assiento, 160; *see also* Slave trade
Assiniboia, Settlement, 313; *see also* Red River Settlement
Associated Press of America, 206
Association of British Chambers of Commerce, 100
Astley Papers, 102
Astor, John Jacob (1763-1848), 291
Astor, Nancy, Viscountess (1879-1964), 11, 27, 278, 282
Astor, Waldorf, 2nd Viscount (1879-1952), 11, 27, 277, 278, 282, 283
Astor Library, New York, 64
Astor Papers, 11, 27
Astronomy, 148, 163
Aswarby Muniments, 50
Atchison Mining Co. Ltd., 308
Atchison, Topeka and Santa Fe Railroad, 96
Athenaeum, Liverpool, 180-1
Athenia (ship), 311
Atherton, Agnes Mary (Hall), Lady, 176
Atherton, Gertrude (1857-1948), 78; *American Wives*, 78
Atholl, Duchess of, *see* Murray, Katherine (Marjory) (d. 1960)
Atholl, 7th Duke of, *see* Murray, John (1840-1917)
Atholl, Duke of, Mss., 262
Atholl Papers, 253
Atkins, Edmund, 55
Atkinson, Aaron (1665?-1740), 153
Atkinson, Sir Charles, 223
Atkinson, Edward (1827-1905), 197
Atlantic and Great Western Railroad, 26, 52
Atlantic cables, *see* Cables, Atlantic
Atlantic crossing, *see* Voyages to America
Atlantic Mail Steam Navigation Co., 111
Atlantic Monthly, 113, 164, 197
Atlantic Telegraph Co. Bill, 110, 111
Atomic bomb, 166
Atomic energy, 128, 139; *see also* Atomic bomb; Thorium; World War II: Atomic bomb
Attlee, Clement, Viscount Prestwood (1883-1967), 166
Attwood, Thomas, 161
Attwood–Hadley Papers, 161
Aubrey, ______, 202
Aubrey, Letitia (Penn), 97
Aubrey, William, 97
Aubrey Mss., 202, 203
Auckland, 1st Baron, *see* Eden, William (1744-1814)
Auckland Papers, 74-5, 75-6
Audley End Papers, 31
Audubon, John James (1785-1851), 174, 183, 258
Aufrère, Israel Antoine (1667-1758), 113
Aufrère Papers, 113
Austen, George, 309
Austen, John J., 97
Austin, Benjamin W., 74
Austin, R., comp., *Catalogue of the Gloucestershire Collection*, 33 fn.
Australia, Immigrants, 14, 201, 327; *see also* Trade with Australia
Australian Co. of Edinburgh, 310
Austria, Emigrants, *see* Immigrants from Austria
Authors Syndicate Ltd., London, 191
Autograph collections, 16, 62, 66, 75, 77, 161, 170-1, 174, 178, 182, 227, 259, 261, 343, 353
Aviation, 111, 127, 139; *see also* Balloons
Avon, 1st Earl of, *see* Eden, Anthony (1897-1977)
Avon, England, 5-8
Aydelotte, Frank, 278, 281, 282
Aylesbury, Buckinghamshire, 11-3
Aylesford, 7th Earl of, *see* Finch, Heneage (1849-85)
Ayr, Scotland, Merchants, 309

B

"B., G. G.," 260
"B., J.," 274
"B., P.," 264
Baader, J., 226
Babb, ______, 24

Bache, Alexander Dallas (1806-67), 148
Backhouse, Edward, 30
Backhouse, Hannah Chapman (1787-1850), 30
Backhouse, John (*fl.* 1774), 29
Backhouse, John (*fl.* 1827-38), 207
Backhouse, Jonathan, 30
Backhouse, William, 29
Backhouse Collection, 29
Backhouse Papers, 29-30
Bacon, Anthony (*c.* 1717-*c.* 1785), 247
Bacon, Charlotte, 330
Bacon's Rebellion (1675-6), 11, 48
Badeau, Adam (1831-95), 62
Baden–Powell, Sir George Smyth (1847-98), 38
Badgery Accumulation, 47
Bagenalstown, Carlow, 343
Bagot, Sir Charles (1781-1843), 63, 102, 129, 213, 237, 240
Bagot, Mary Charlotte Anne (Wellesley–Pole), Lady (d. 1845), 213
Bagot Papers, 102
Bagshaw, J., Ltd. of Sheffield, 235
Bagshawe, Benjamin, Jr., 232
Bagshawe Collection, 232-3
Bagshawe of Ford Hall Muniments, 175
Bahamas: Agriculture, 149; Governors, 304; Loyalists from America, 120, 138; Shipping, 124; Trade with U.S., 130
NASSAU, 124
Bailey, David, 328
Bailey, Gerald, 282
Bailey, Henry, 94
Bailey, John (1643-97), 94
Bailey, John (*fl.* 19th cent. ?), 328
Bailey, Joseph Weldon (1863-1929), 164
Bailey Committee, 123
Baillie, George, 261
Baillie, Jo[–], 293
Baillie, Thomas, 293
Baily, H. R., 16
Bain, Alexander, & Co., 309
Bainbridge, William (1774-1833), 187, 285
Baines, Henry, 43
Baines of Bell Hall, 43
Baird, James (*fl.* 1743), 292
Baird, James (*fl.* late 18th cent.), 317
Baird, John, 166
Baird, Sir Robert, 304
Baird, Hay & Co., 317
Baird of Saughtonhall Muniments, 304
Baker, A. Eric, 282
Baker, Benjamin, 150
Baker, Donald S., "Charles Wesley and the American War of Independence," *Proceedings of the Wesley Historical Society* (1964), 178 fn.; "Charles Wesley and the American Loyalists," *Proceedings of the Wesley Historical Society* (1965), 178 fn.
Baker, F. J., 184
Baker, Frank, *Charles Wesley as Revealed by His Letters*, 117 fn.
Baker, George, 26
Baker, Henry (1698-1774), 148, 174-5
Baker, John (*fl.* 18th cent.), 224
Baker, John (*fl.* 1827), 286
Baker, Newton D. (1871-1937), 278, 280
Baker, Philip Noel, 278
Baker, Samuel & W., 222
Baker, Sophia, 39
Baker, Sir W., 149
Baker, William (1743-1824), 39
Baker Mss., 39
Baker Wilbraham Collection, 18
Balcarres, Countess of, *see* Lindsay, Anne
Balderston, John K., 283
Balderston, M., and D. Syrett, *The Lost War*, 224 fn.
Baldwin, Ethan, 308
Baldwin, Stanley, 1st Earl Baldwin of Bewdley (1867-1947), 16, 135, 282
Baldwin, William (1677?-1720), 153
Balfour, Earl of, Mss., 259
Balfour, Alice, 259
Balfour, Arthur James, 1st Earl of (1848-1930), 77, 135, 141, 200, 238, 259, 260, 278, 279, 284
Balfour, Arthur, & Son, 236
Balfour, Edith, 259
Balfour, F. M., 260
Balfour, Gerald William, 2nd Earl of Balfour (1853-1945), 259
Balfour, Harold, 112
Balfour, James, of Pilrig, (*fl.* 1757-8), 289
Balfour, James (*fl.* 1775-6), 262
Balfour, Nisbet (1743-1823), 8, 139
Balfour, Oswald, 260
Balfour, R., 262
Balfour Darwins Ltd., 236
Balfour of Balbirnie Mss., 259
Balfour of Balfour and Trenabie Mss., 315
Balfour of Burleigh, 10th (or 6th) Baron, *see* Bruce, Alexander Hugh (1849-1921)
Balfour of Burleigh, Lord, Mss., 269
Balfour of Pilrig Muniments, 289
Balfour Papers, 77, 346
Balgonie, Lord, *see* Leslie, David, 6th Earl of Leven (1722-1802)
Balker, John, 223
Ballantine, James, 112
Balliol College, Oxford, 284
Balloons, 147
Ballygarvey Spinning and Weaving Coy., 327
Balsams, 150
Baltimore, 1st Baron, *see* Calvert, George (1580?-1632); 3rd Baron, *see* Calvert, Charles (1637-1715); 5th Baron, *see* Calvert, Charles (1699-1751); 6th Baron, *see* Calvert, Frederick (1731-71)
Baltimore and Ohio Railroad Co., 28, 180
Baltimore *Sun*, 178, 283
Bamburgh, W. C., 164
Bancroft, George (1800-91), 68, 69, 148, 197, 238, 259, 263, 306
Bancroft Library (of Western American History), *see* California, University of, Bancroft Library
Baner America, 244
Bangor, Gwynedd, 248
Bangor & Aroostock Railroad, 96
Bangor Mss., 248
Bank of Charleston, 181
Bank of England, 46, 51-2, 63, 104, 108
Bank of Liverpool, 181
Bank of the United States, 51, 52, 63, 172, 206, 207, 208, 222, 325
Bank records (British), 29, 96, 105, 115-6, 117-8, 169, 181; *see also* Banking
Bankes, Sir John (1589-1644), 193, 194

Bankes Papers, 193-4
Bankhead, Charles (d. 1870), 77, 104, 207
Banking: 18th century, 187-8; 19th century, 51-2, 57, 63, 69, 117-8, 130, 163, 181, 207, 245; 20th century, 117-8; *see also* Investments; *subdivision* Banking *under states, etc.; also names of individual banks*
Bankruptcy, 131, 172; Court of, 122, 124
Banks, Sir Joseph (1743-1820), 147, 150
Bannatyne, Kirkwood and France Mss., 263
Bannerman Mss., 317
Baptists, 203, 244, 245; Missions, 96, 165
Barbados, 15, 20; Council, 286; Governors, 31, 286; Immigrants, 34; Land grants, 352
BRIDGETOWN, Customs collectors, 87
See also TRADE WITH BARBADOS
Barbara (barque), 326
Barber, John, 27
Barber, Melanie, *Index to the Letters and Papers of Frederick Temple, Archbishop of Canterbury, 1896-1902, in Lambeth Palace Library*, 115
Barbier, Paul, 239
Barbour, Sir David Miller (1841-1928), 163
Barbour, James (1775-1842), 187, 268
Barbour, Mrs. R. S., Mss., 263
Barbour, Thomas Seymour (1853-1915), 165
Barclay, Col., 288
Barclay, Abram Rawlinson, 154; Mss., 154
Barclay, Alex., 60
Barclay, Andrew, 265
Barclay, Anthony, 286
Barclay, Charles, 154
Barclay, David (1728-1809), 154, 156, 187, 188; *An Account of the Emancipation of the Slaves of Unity Valley Pen, in Jamaica* (1801), 188
Barclay, George, 9
Barclay, Jean (*fl.* 1774), 316
Barclay, John, 187, 188
Barclay, Sir Robert, 313
Barclay, Robert, of Bury Hill (1751-1830), 154
Barclay, Robert, of Urie (*fl.* 1760-86), 154
Barclay, Thomas (1753-1830), 43, 286
Barclay of Bury Hill Mss., 154
Barclays Bank Ltd., Durham, 29; Barclays Bank Ltd., Liverpool, 181; Barclays Bank Ltd., London, 52
Barcroft, Lieut., 46
Barcroft, Ambrose, 46
Barcroft, S. R., 350
Barcroft, Thomas, 46
Barcroft, William, 46
Barcroft Papers, 46
Bargar, B. D., "Matthew Boulton and the Birmingham Petition of 1775," *William and Mary Quarterly* (1956), 226 fn.
Bargrave, John, 186
Barham, 1st Baron, *see* Middleton, Charles (1726-1813)
Barham Papers, 101
Barilla, 150
Baring, Alexander, 1st Baron Ashburton (1774-1848), 63, 67, 104, 141 fn., 168, 257, 261; *see also* Webster–Ashburton Treaty, 1842
Baring, Sir Francis (1740-1810), 226
Baring Bros.& Co., 52, 169, 249
Barker, John, 232
Barlaston, Baron of, *see* Wedgwood, J. C.
Barlier, H., 180
Barlier, W. (?), 180
Barnabee, John, 10
Barnard, Frederick Augustus Porter (1809-89), 235
Barnard, Henry (1811-1900), 58
Barnardiston, Sir Nathaniel (1588-1653), 217
Barnardiston, Nathaniel (1755-1837), 217
Barnardiston Family Papers, 217
Barnes, Albert (1798-1870), 85
Barnes, E. R., and J. H. Owen, eds., *The Private Papers of John, Earl of Sandwich*, 102 fn.
Barnes, H., 148
Barnes, James J., *Authors, Publishers amd Politicians: The Quest for an Anglo-American Copyright, 1815-1854*, 41 fn.; "Edward Lytton Bulwer [*sic*] and the Publishing Firm of Harper & Brothers," *American Literature* (1966), 41 fn.
Barnes, Sarah, 238
Barnetts, Hoares, Hanbury & Lloyd, 115
Barnstaple, Devonshire, 26, 27; Customs records, 89, 91, 93
Barnum, E. E., 173
Barnum, Phineas Taylor (1810-91), 75, 114, 182
Barons, Benjamin, 195
Barr, John, 330
Barraclough, William, 175
Barrett, Ann (Crowther), 117
Barrett, George, 117
Barrett, Mary, 117
Barrett, Rowland (1877-1950), 228
Barrie, Robert, 288
Barrington, Sir Eric (1847-1918), 38, 39
Barrington, William Wildman, 2nd Viscount (1717-93), 45, 64, 215, 219, 269
Barrington–Ward Papers, 157
Barrow, John (*fl.* 1775), 29
Barrow, John (*fl.* 1839-63), 47, 155
Barrow, Customs records, 93
Barstow family, 254
Bartlett, John, 10
Bartlett, John Russell (1805-86), 171
Bartlett, John Sherren (1790-1863), 207
Bartley, Mordecai (1783-1870), 245
Bartman, George, 218 fn.
Bartol, Cyrus Augustus (1813-1900), 176
Barton, Benjamin Smith (1776-1815), 170, 183, 313
Barton, James Levi (1855-1936), 197, 199
Barton, Seth, 161
Barton, William Paul Crillon (1786-1856), 183
Bartram, George, 273
Bartram, John (1699-1777), 180
Bartram, John, of Carsewell (*fl.* 1760), 273
Bass, James, 33
Basset, H., 285
Basset, H. G., 315
Bassett, F., 216
Bassett, Henry, 237
Bate family, 20
Bates, Joshua (1788-1864), 52
Bath, Marquess of, 229-30
Bath, 1st Marquess of, *see* Thynne, Thomas
Bath, Avon, 5
Bath Papers, 229-30
Bathgate, Herbert J., 184
Bathurst, Henry, 3rd Earl (1762-1834), 83-4, 101, 206, 232

Bathurst Papers, 83-4
Battle Abbey Estate Mss., 222
Battles, *see subdivision* Campaigns *under wars*
Bavaria, Emigrants, *see* Immigrants from Bavaria; Palatines
Bavin, Thomas, 58
Bawdeswell Hall, Norfolk, 185-6
Bax-Ironside, Sir Henry George Outram (d. 1930), 38
Baxter, Alexander, 147
Baxter, Richard (1615-91), 94
Bayard, Catherine, *see* Campbell, Catherine (Bayard)
Bayard, James Asheton (1799-1880), 169
Bayard, John, 293
Bayard, Samuel (1767-1840), 226, 275
Bayard, Thomas F. (1828-98), 85
Bayley, Charles Clive, 198
Bayley, James Roosevelt (1814-77), 71
Baylie, R., 151
Bayliss, Miss M. B., 343
Baynes, John (1758-87), 161
Baynes, John W., 177
Baynton, W., 144
Bazley, Sir Thomas (1797-1885), 64
Beaconsfield, 1st Earl of, *see* Disraeli, Benjamin (1804-81)
Beadie, H. W., & Co., 180
Beale, John, 42
Beard, John Relly (1800-76), 176
Beardmore, William, & Co., 318
Beardsall, W. C., 235
Beatty, ———, 180
Beauchamp, 6th Earl, *see* Lygon, Frederick (1830-91)
Beauchamp, R., 287
Beaulieu, Jean, 10
Beaumarchais, Pierre Augustin Caron de (1732-99), 227, 267
Beaumaris, Customs records, 89, 93
Beaumont, 8th Baron, *see* Stapleton, Miles Thomas (1805-54)
Beaverbrook, Lord, *see* Aitken, William Maxwell (1879-1964)
Beaverbrook Library, 112
Beaverbrook Mss., 112-3
Beaverbrook Papers, 112
Beavers, *see* Fur trade
Bebb, Edward, 246
Bebb, Evans R., 245, 246
Bebb, William (1802-73), 245, 246
Bebb family, 244, 248
Beck, James (*fl.* 1845), 330
Beck, James A., 330
Beck, James M. (1861-1936), 113, 260, 279
Beck, William, 243
Beck, William, and T. Frederick Ball, *The London Friends' Meetings*, 154
Beck family, 330
Beckett, Henry, 206
Beckett, J., 27
Beckett & Davies, 175
Beckwith, George C. (1800-70), 244
Beckwith, Sir Thomas Sydney (1772-1831), 218
Beddoe, Henry Robert, 36
Bedford, 4th Duke of, *see* Russell, John (1710-71)
Bedford, 4th Earl of, *see* Russell, Francis (1593-1641)
Bedford, England, 8-9
Bedford (ship), 25
Bedford Estates, Trustees of the, 52
Bedford Papers, 52
Bedfordshire County Record Office, 8-9
Beef, *see* Cattle trade
Beer, 285
Bees, 149
Begbie & Manson, 120
Behrens, E. Beddington, 278
Belcher, Jonathan (1682-1757), 31, 141
Belfast, Antrim, 323-32
Belgium, Relations with U.S., *see* Relations with Belgium
Belhaven, Scotland, Manufacturers, 310
Bell, Alexander Graham (1847-1922), 162, 254
Bell, E. Seymour (b. 1857), 133
Bell, George, 289
Bell, H. C., D. W. Parker, *et al.*, *Guide to British West Indian Archive Materials*, 171
Bell, John (*fl.* 1830), 168
Bell, John (*fl.* 1830-2), 259
Bell, Mary, 19
Bell, Patrick (1799-1869), 254
Bell, Thomas, 273
Bell, Whitfield J., Jr., 50 fn.
Bell, William A., 239
Bella (slave), 297
Bellers, John (1654-1725), 221
Bellingham, Elizabeth (Savage), Mrs. Samuel Bellingham, 220
Bellingham, Samuel, 220
Bellingham family of Boston, 220
Bellisle, M., 266
Bellomont, 1st Earl of, *see* Coote, Richard (1636-1701)
Bellows, Henry Whitney (1814-82), 176
Belsham, Thomas (1750-1829), 95
Belson Papers, 11
Belvoir Castle, Leicestershire, 48
Belwood, ———, 83
Bembridge, Charles, 265
Bembridge, Isle of Wight, 229
Bembridge School, 229
Bend, W. B., 22
Benezet, Anthony (1713-84), 103, 154, 156, 188
Benn, Anthony Wedgwood (1925), 113
Benn, Margaret Eadie (Holmes), 113
Benn, William Wedgwood, 1st Viscount Stansgate (1877-1960), 113
Bennan and Finnarts Muniments, 289
Bennet, Henry, Earl of Arlington (d. 1685), 49
Bennet, John, 150
Bennett (or Bennet), Andrew, 103
Bennett, Courtenay Walter, 198
Bennett, Lincoln, 180
Bennett St. Sunday School Mutual Improvement Class, *see* St. Paul's Literary and Educational Society
Benson, Arthur Christopher (1862-1925), 202
Benson, Edward White (1829-96), 202
Benson, George (1699-1762), 174
Benson, George (*fl.* 1792), 245
Benson, George Rathbone, 1st Baron Charnwood (1864-1945), 238
Benson, John, 175
Benson, Martin (1689-1752), 61
Benson and Mordaff Records [Solicitors, Cockermouth], 21
Benson Papers, 202
Bensusan, S. L., 33
Bensusan Papers, 26

Bentham, George (1800-84), 146
Bentham, Jeremy (1748-1832), 167-8; *Anti-Senatica*, ed. by C. W. Everett, 168 fn.; *Manual of Political Economy*, 167; *A System of Penal Law for the State of Louisiana*, 167 fn.
Bentham, Sir Samuel (1757-1831), 16
Bentinck, William Henry Cavendish, 3rd Duke of Portland (1738-1809), 80, 193
Bentley, Thomas (1731-80), 212
Benyon, R., 10
Benyon Papers, 10
Beresford, Sir John Poo (1766-1844), 231
Beresford Papers, 23
Beresford–Peirse Archive, 231
Bering Sea Controversy, 30, 38, 130, 132, 133, 198, 221; *see also* Fur trade
Bering Strait, 347
Berkeley, E., and D. Smith, *Dr. Alexander Garden of Charleston*, 149 fn., 175 fn.
Berkeley, George (1685-1753), 61, 62, 76; *Works*, 61 fn.
Berkeley, George (*fl.* 1764), 61
Berkeley, George Cranfield, 17th Baron (1753-1818), 83
Berkeley, John, 1st Baron (d. 1678), 10, 17
Berkeley, Sir William (1606-77), 11, 82, 229, 230
Berkeley family, 33
Berkshire, England, 10-1
Berkshire Record Office, 10-1
Berlin and Milan Decrees, 77, 294
Bermuda, 36, 293; British Army, 143, 144; Customs collectors, 87; Education, 76; Governors, 304; Merchants, 273; Tobacco, 81
Bernard, Sir Francis (1712-79), 66, 103, 120 fn., 148, 200, 218, 233, 240, 249
Bernard, Montague (1820-82), 68, 69, 202
Bernard Family Papers, 102-3
Bernard–Morland, Scrope (1758-1830), 102, 150
Berners Family Archives, 219
Berry, Sir John (1635-90), 17; Journal, 17
Bertie, Francis Leveson, 1st Viscount Bertie of Thame (1844-1919), 135
Bertie, Peregrine, 12th Baron Willoughby de Eresby (1555-1601), 49
Bertie, Willoughby, 4th Earl of Abingdon (1740-99), 204
Bertie Family Papers, 50
Bertram, James, & Son Ltd., 307; Records, 307
Bertram, William, 273
Bertram of Nisbet Muniments, 273
Berwick, Customs records, 89, 93
Berwicke & Co., 50
Bethell, Richard, 1st Baron Westbury (1800-73), 139
Bethune, Henry, 298
Bethune, John, 298
Betsy (ship), 316
Bettle, Samuel, 227
Bevan, Joseph Gurney (1753-1814), 50-1
Bevan, Silvanus I. (1691-1765), 50, 51
Bevan–Naish Collection, 227-8
Beveridge, Albert Jeremiah (1862-1927), 197
Beveridge, James, 289
Beveridge, William Henry, 1st Baron (1879-1963), 165-6
Beveridge Plan, 165, 166
Beverley, Humberside, 42, 43
Bible, Revised Version, 196; Translations into Indian language, 53, 147, 151
Bible societies, 53
Bibliotheca Pepysiana, 16-7; *A Descriptive Catalogue*, 16
Bicameralism, 168
Bickersteth, J. Burgon, 282
Bicknell Family Papers, 98
Biddle, Clement, 203 fn.
Biddle, Edward, 271
Biddle, Nicholas (1786-1844), 52, 255
Biddle, Thomas, 306
Bideford, Customs records, 89, 93
Biel Muniments, 273
Bien Aimé (ship), 120
Big Horn Cattle Co., 234
Bigelow, Andrew, 254
Bigelow, Erastus B., 308
Bigelow, Henry J., 204
Bigelow, John (1817-1911), 67, 69, 184
Bill, E. G. W., *A Catalogue of Manuscripts in Lambeth Palace Library*, 115; *A Catalogue of Manuscripts in Lambeth Palace Library. MSS. 1907-2340*, 115
Billinghurst (ship), 195
Billings, John Shaw (1838-1913), 170
Billings, Joseph (b. 1758?), 257
Bimetallism, 34, 52, 161, 162, 163, 172; *see also* Silver Question
Bingham, Hiram (b. 1875), 197, 198
Bingham, Robert W., 280
Birch, Mrs. Mary, 230
Birchfield, Maurice, 160
Bird–Quin, 171
Birds, 42, 147, 148, 314
Birkbeck, Morris, 220
Birket, John, 47
Birket(t) Family Papers, 47
Birmingham, West Midlands, 225-8; Merchants, 73, 235; Petition of 1775, 226, 226 fn.; Trade with America, 41; *see also* Business records: Birmingham
Birmingham and Midland Freedmen's Aid Association, 176, 177
Birmingham Collection, 226-7
Birmingham Public Libraries, 115 fn., 225-7
Birmingham Small Arms Co. Ltd., 228
Birmingham University, 66; Main Library, 227
Birney, James Gillespie (1792-1857), 205
Birnie, Clatworthy, 78
Birnie, R., 312
Birth–control movement, 79, 118
Biscoe, Joseph, 35
Bishop, Joseph Bucklin (1847-1928), 197
Bishop, Thomas, 195
Bishop, William, 286
Bishopscotte River, 194
Bishopsgate Institute, 52-3
Bison, 290, 291
Bispham, David Scull (1857-1921), 178
Bizonal Fusion Agreement, 112
Blabon, George W., & Co., 271
Black, Joseph, 313
Black, Lytle, 332
Black, William (*fl.* 1774-85), 258
Black, William, & Co., 310
Black Warrior (ship), 201
Black Watch, 262
Blackett, Sir Basil Phillott (1882-1935), 199
Blackie & Sons, 318

Blackmore family, 230
Blacksmiths, 330; Wages, 47
"Blackwell, Mr.," 8
Blackwood, John (*fl.* 1727-30), 304
Blackwood, John (1818-79), 40
Blackwood, William (1776-1834), 40
Blagden, Sir Charles (1748-1820), 147-8
Blaine, James Gillespie (1830-93), 38, 72, 177, 260
Blair, James (1656-1743), 194, 260
Blair, James (*fl.* 1810), 263
Blair, John (1687-1771), 274, 284
Blair, John Insley (1802-99), 131
Blair family, 328
Blair Family Papers, 328
Blakeney, Customs records, 89
Blakney [or Blakeney], William, 50
"Blanche, Lady," 161
Blanche (ship), 121
Bland Burges Papers, 200
Blandy, Mrs. O. L., 204
Blanford (ship), 263
Blankets, Trade, 22, 210
Blatchford, Robert [Peel Glanville] (1851-1943), 172
Blathwayt, William (1649?-1717), 34, 220, 260
Blavatsky, Mme. H. P., 74
Bleaymire, Rev., 166
Bleaymire, Messrs. W. E., 166
Blechynden Papers, 74
Bledisloe, Lord, 193
Bledisloe, Albert Taylor (1809-77), 204
Blenheim Palace, Oxfordshire, 193
Blewett, Harvey & Vivian & Co., 20
Blickling Hall, Norfolk, 24 fn.
Bliss, George, 94
Blockade, 77, 140, 250, 264; *see also* Embargo; Smuggling; *and subdivision* Blockade *under wars*
Blodget, Samuel (1724-1807), 148, 150
Blodgett, Rebecca, 49
Blount, William (1749-1800), 81
Blumenfeld, Ralph David (b. 1864), 112
Blumenfeld Papers, 112
Blunt, Lady Anne, 78
Blunt, Wilfrid Scawen (1840-1922), 78
Blyth, Customs records, 93
Board of Trade, Companies Registration Office, 125
Boath, John, Jr., 310; Mss., 269
Bodleian Library, 193-205; 15 fn., 99, 115 fn.; Carnegie refuses aid, 72
Bodley Library Record, 193
Bodley Quarterly Record, 193
Boer War, 1899-1902, American interest, 129, 144, 197, 206
Bogle, George, 316
Bogle & Scott, 316
Bogle Papers, 316
Bolden, William, 182
Bolitho, *firm*, 20
Bollan, William, 233, 300, 303
Bolton, Lord, 230
Bolton, 1st Baron, *see* Orde, *afterwards* Orde–Powlett, Thomas (1746-1807)
Bolton, Greater Manchester, 172; *see also* Business records: Bolton, Greater Manchester
Bolton Metropolitan Borough Archives, 172
Bolton Papers, 230
Bolton Public Library, 172
Bolton Whitman Fellowship, 172, 177
Bonaparte, Jerome (1784-1860), 264
Bonaparte, Mme. Jerome, 101, 264
Bonar, Horatius (1808-89), 85
Bond, Mr., 288
Bond, George Phillips (1825-65), 148
Bond, Kate (Catherine), 47
Bond, M. F., *Guide to the Records of Parliament*, 106
Bond, P., 261
Bond, Phineas (1749-1815), 81, 101, 154
Bond, Sir Robert (1857-1927), 198
Bond Family Papers, 47
Bonds, *see* Investments
Bonetta (sloop), 276
Bonn, Moritz J., 282
Bonnor, Thomas, 119
Bonsell, Charles, 155
Bonsell, E. H., 155
Bookselling, 22, 50, 204
Boone, Daniel (1734-1820), 249
Boone, Thomas, 233
Boorman, Johnston & Co., 250
Booth, Charles, 161
Booth, Edwin Thomas (1833-93), 238
Booth, Evangeline (1865-1950), 151
Booth, William (1829-1912), 151
Booth, William Bramwell (1856-1929), 151
Booth Papers, 161
Boots and shoes, Trade, 211
Borah, William Edgar (1865-1940), 165, 198, 277, 278, 280, 283
Borden, Sir Robert Laird (1854-1937), 198, 199, 278, 279
Borden, Spencer, 78
Borland, Francis, 312
Borland, John, 311
Borthwick, Thomas, Papers, 254
Borthwick & Goudie, 310
Borthwick Institute of Historical Research, 231
Bosahan Mss., 20
Boscawen, Edward (1711-61), 45, 249
Bose, General, 275
Bosomworth, A., 285
Boss rule, *see* Corruption (in politics)
Boston, Lincolnshire, Customs records, 89, 92, 93
Boston anti-slavery bazaars, 6
Boston Borough Records, 50
Boston Committee of Correspondence, 324
Boston District Council, 50 fn.
Boston Female Anti-Slavery Society, 316
Boston Gazette and Country Journal, 28
Boston Port Act (1774), 12, 214, 315
Boston Tea-Party (1773), 99, 143, 182, 208, 214
Boston, *see also* Massachusetts: Boston
Boswell, James (1740-95), 269
Botany and botanists, 36, 145-6, 147, 148, 182, 183, 200, 249, 266, 267, 291, 297; *see also* Horticulture; Live oak; *and subdivision* Botany *under individual states*
Bothomley, John, 231
Botsford, Robert, "Scotland and the American Civil War" (Thesis), 316 fn.
Boucher, Jonathan, 222
Boucher Mss., 222

Bouchette, Joseph, 285
Boucicault, Dion (1820?-1890), 184
Boudinot, Elias (1740-1821), 226, 268, 295
Boughton House, Northampton, 189
Boulton, Matthew (1728-1809), 226
Boulton & Fothergill, 226
Boulton & Scale, 226
Boulton and Watt Collection, 226
Boulton Plate Co., 226
Boundaries, 276, 300; Canada, 25, 30, 31, 34, 49, 56, 57, 63, 66, 70, 72, 77, 84, 103-4, 110, 111, 120, 123, 132, 139, 143, 144, 148, 168, 169, 198, 202, 285, 286; *see also* Alaska, Boundaries; Juan de Fuca Strait; North American Boundary Commission; North-East Boundary; North-West Boundary; Oregon Question
FRENCH COLONIES, 200
NETHERLANDS, 22, 31, 195
STATE, 138, 207
See also subdivision BOUNDARIES *under countries, states, etc.*
Bouquet, Henry (1719-65), 266, 285
Bourchier, Lady, ed., *A Memoir of the Life of Admiral Sir Edward Codrington*, 121 fn.
Bourke, Robert, 1st Baron Connemara (1827-1902), 133
Bourne, George, 234
Bourne, Robert, 13, 50
Bouton, J. W., 74
Bouverie, William Pleydell, 1st Earl of Radnor (1725-76), 218
Bowater, John, 224
Bowditch, Nathaniel (1773-1838), 148, 222
Bowditch family, 222
Bowdoin, James (1726-90), 233
Bowdoin, James (1752-1811), 313
Bowdoin College, 263, 282
Bowe & Bushby, 22
Bowen, Samuel, 150
Bowers, Thomas, 211
Bowker, John (b. 1770), 121
Bowker, Richard Rogers (1848-1933), 197
Bowman, A. A., *The Absurdity of Christianity*, 271; Papers, 271
Bowman, Isaiah, 147
Bowman, J. (*fl.* 1770), 314
Bowman, J., Jr., 314
Bowman, John, 289
Bowring, Sir John (1792-1872), 167
Box, George, 150
Boyd, B., 331
Boyd, Baptiste, 166
Boyd, James, 310
Boyd, John, 331
Boyd, Thomas, 317
Boyd, W. E., Collection, 306
Boyd, William, 331
Boyle, Charles, 264
Boyle, Michael (1609?-1702), 346
Boyle, Hon. Robert (1627-91), 99, 115, 147
Boyle's Charity, *see* Christian Faith Society
Boys, William, *Collections for a History of Sandwich*, 44 fn.
Boyse, Richard (b. 1726), 346
Brabazon, Harry, 346
Bracco, John, 266
Brace, H. W., ed., *The First Minute Book of the Gainsborough Monthly Meeting of the Society of Friends, 1669-1719*, 154
Brace Deposit, 50
Bradbury, Sir John (1872-1950), 142
Bradbury, John (*fl.* 1806-11), 182
Bradbury, Thomas, & Sons, 234
Bradbury Papers, 142
Braddock, Edward (1695-1755), 29, 79, 102, 118, 120, 264, 300
Bradford, Alden (1765-1843), 182, 187
Bradford, Gamaliel (d. 1839), 182
Bradford, Gamaliel (1863-1932), 197
Bradford, West Yorkshire, 237
Bradford Central Library, 237
Bradlaugh, Charles (1833-91), 204
Bradley, Thomas J., 235
Bradshaw, Thomas, 218
Bradstreet, John (*c.* 1711-74), 230, 246, 264, 300, 303
Brady, John, 348
Bragg, John, 22-3
Brainerd, David (1718-47), 313
Brainerd, John, 103
Braithwaite, Anna (1788-1859), 155; Mss., 155
Braithwaite, Catherine L., 156; Collection, 156
Braithwaite, George Charles, 287
Braithwaite, William Charles (1862-1922), 154; Mss., 154; *Beginnings of Quakerism*, 154, 154 fn.
Bralston, Joseph, 329
Bramble (ship), 40
Bramwell, Thomas, 172
Bramwell Correspondence, 172
Brand, E., 173
Brand, R. H., 277, 282, 283
Brandeis, Louis D., (1856-1941), 116, 277
Brass–finishers, 273
Brattle, Mr., 215
Braund, Samuel, 32
Braund, William (1695-1774), 32
Bray, Mrs. Anna, 163
Bray, Charles Frederick (1816-83), 163, 238
Bray, Edgar W., 238
Bray, Edward, 220
Bray, John Francis (1809-97), 163, 238; *Labour's Wrongs and Labour's Remedy*, 163; *A Voyage from Utopia*, ed., by F.M. Lloyd–Pritchard, 163 fn.
Bray, Joseph, 238
Bray, Sarah, 238
Bray, Thomas (1656-1730), 105
Bray, William, 220
Bray Collection, 163
Braybrooke, 1st Baron, *see* Griffin, Sir John Griffin (1719-97)
Braye Mss., 106
Brazen (ship), 43
Brazil, Rio de Janeiro, 288; *see also* Relations with Brazil; Trade with Brazil
Bread making, 308
Breadalbane Muniments, 290
Breathwait, Richard, 330
Brecknock Museum Library, 249
Brecon, Powys, 249
Breeze family, 327
Brenan, Joseph (1828-57), 343
Brent, Humphrey, 261
Brereton, R., 268
Brett, George Platt (1858-1936), 198
Brett, John, 27
Brett, Thomas (1667-1744), 45
Brewster, William (1567-1644), 37, 177

Brewster Islands, 12
Bribery, *see* Corruption (in politics)
Brickmaking machinery, 114
Brickwood, John & Lawrence, 234
Bridge House Papers, 335
Bridgeman, W. C., 278, 279
Brigden, Edward, 148
Bridger, Sir John, 221
Bridger, R., 240
Bridges, Sir Edward (1892-1969), 128
Bridges, 270; Construction, 150, 162, 346
Bridgewater, Dukes of, *see* Egerton family
Bridgewater, 8th Earl of, *see* Egerton, Francis Henry (1756-1829)
Bridgwater, Customs records, 89, 93
Briggs, James A., 245
Briggs, R. B., 98
Bright, Henry Arthur (1830-84), 17, 176, 182, 227
Bright, John (1811-89), 67-8, 70, 168, 169, 170, 179, 204; Papers, 67-8
Bright, Margaret Elizabeth (Leatham), Mrs. John Bright (d. 1878), 168
Brighton, East Sussex, 221
Brisbane, John, 270
Bristol, 1st Earl of, *see* Digby, Sir John (1580-1653)
Bristol, Marquises of, *see* Hervey family of Ickworth
Bristol, 5-8, 49, 183; Customs records, 89, 91, 93; Merchants, 56, 115, 124; Petition of 1778, 190; Trade, Colonial period, 5-8 *passim*, 34, 122, 225; *see also* Business records: Bristol
Bristol and Clifton Auxiliary Ladies Anti-Slavery Society, 95
Bristol and Frenchay Monthly Meeting of the Society of Friends, 5, 6
Bristol Archives Office, 5-6
Bristol Central Library, 7; Reference Library, *Early Bristol Newspapers: A Detailed Catalogue*, 7
Bristol Corporation Records, 34
Bristol Custom House, 7
Bristol University, Library, 8
"Britain Today," 135
"Britannicus," *pseud.*, 9
British American Association, 318
British-American Association for Emigration and Colonization, 259
British American Land Co., 110
British American Nickel Corp., 142
British-American Peace Centenary Committee, 97
British and Canadian Telegraph Co. Bill, 110
British and Foreign Anti-Slavery Society, 51, 169, 205-6
British and Foreign Bible Society, 53
British Broadcasting Co., 82
British Columbia, 128; 19th century, 40, 110, 111, 128, 233
CONFEDERATION, 40; Defence, 142, 143; Description, 314; Governors, 110
CHALM BAY, 21; Esquimalt, 142, 143; Nanaimo country, 233
British Columbia Boundaries Bill, 111
British, Continental, and General Federation for the Abolition of Government Regulation of Prostitution, 235
British German Legion, 143
British Guiana, Boundaries with Venezuela, 38, 39, 72, 162, 197, 201
British Imperial Tobacco Co., 198
British King (ship), 140
British Library, 53-84; 115 fn., 190 fn., 226; Additional Charters, 53, 82; Additional Mss., 54-81; Egerton Mss., 53, 81-2; Loans, 82-4; Macvey Napier Papers, 14 fn.
British Museum Quarterly, 53
Catalogue of Additions to the MSS., 53, 57 fn.; *Catalogue of the Gladstone Papers*, 53, 70; "Rough registers," 53
British Library of Political and Economic Science, *see* London University, London School of Economics
British Linen Co., 265, 299
British Museum (Library), Natural History Department, 62, 66
British National Freedman's Aid Association, 206
British National Maritime Institute, 349
British North America Act [Bill], 111, 162
British Records Association, 273
British War Relief, 275
Britton, Elizabeth Gertrude Knight (d. 1934), 146
Brixham, Customs records, 93
Broadbank, Thomas (1752-1808), 156
Broadbent, Joseph, 232
Broadcasting, 179, 280
Broadfield, E., 149
Broadway Damask Coy. Ltd., 327
Brock, Sir Isaac (1769-1812), 83
Brockman, William (d. 1742), 66; Papers, 66
Brodie, James, 266
Brodie, John C., Collection, 304
Brodie of Brodie Mss., 266
Brodrick, William St. John Fremantle, 1st Earl of Midleton (1856-1942), 38, 141
Brogan, D. W., 282
Broke, Sir Philip Bowes Vere (1776-1841), 219
Broke Papers, 219
Bromborough, Cheshire, 17
Bromley, Lady, 221 fn.
Bromley, Mr., 103
Bromwich & Co., 150
Bronner, Edwin B., *"The Other Branch": London Yearly Meeting and the Hicksites, 1827-1912*, 152
Bronson, E., 183
Brookby, Edward, 217
Brooke, Dr., 148
Brooke, Sir Arthur (1772-1843), 332
Brooke, Richard, 174
Brooke, Rupert (1887-1915), 238
Brooks, Matthew, 330
Brooks, N. C., 234
Brooks, Phillips (1835-93), 176
Brooks, Preston Smith (1819-57), 69, 201
Brooks, William Keith (1848-1908), 162
Broomhall Mss., 244
Brotherton Collection, 238
Brotherton Library, 238-9
Brougham, Henry Peter, 1st Baron Brougham and Vaux (1778-1868), 168-9, 182, 208
Broughton and Cally Muniments, 273
Broun, R., Bart., 318
Brown, A., & Sons, 22, 183
Brown, A. R., 272
Brown, Alexander, *The First Republic in America*, 193 fn.; *Genesis of the United States*, 44 fn.
Brown, Andrew (1763-1834), 313-4; Papers, 314
Brown, Curtis (1866-1945), 236
Brown, David, 18
Brown, David, Sr., 18
Brown, Elizabeth, 217

Brown, Sir George, Papers, 254
Brown, George Alexander (1803-70), 183
Brown, Harrison, 279
Brown, J., 9
Brown, Col. J., 119
Brown, James, 184
Brown, John (*fl.* 1663-6), 259
Brown, John (*fl.* 1704-21), 260
Brown, John (*fl.* 1767), 265
Brown, John (1800-59), 331
Brown, John (1810-82), 254
Brown, John A., 22
Brown, John L., 85
Brown, Jonathan (d. 1784), 21
Brown, Marie A., 238
Brown, W. & J., & Co., 52
Brown, W. L., 270
Brown, William, 104
Brown MacFarlane, A. R., & Co., Mss., 272
Brown, Shipley & Co., 46, 104, 169, 183, 235
Brown Bros., 46
Brown family, 271
Brown Papers, 254
Brown University, John Carter Brown Library, 245; *see also* Rhode Island College
Browne, Edward Everts (1868-1945), 229
Browne, John, 348
Browne, Sir William, 44
Browne family, 328
Brownjohn, William, 51
Bruce, A., 314
Bruce, Alexander Hugh, 10th (or 6th) Baron Balfour of Burleigh (1849-1921), 199, 269
Bruce, David, 284
Bruce, Sir Frederick William Adolphus (1814-67), 129, 201
Bruce, H., 284
Bruce, James (*fl.* 1778-81), 231
Bruce, James (*fl.* 1878-93), 273
Bruce, John, 273
Bruce, Sir John Hope (1684?-1766), 304
Bruce, Samuel, 331
Bruce, Thomas, 7th Earl of Elgin (1766-1841), 287
Bruce, Victor Alexander, 9th Earl of Elgin (1849-1917), 307
Bruce Family Papers, 331
Bruce–Dundas Mss., 231
Brudenell, George Bridges, 102
Brudenell Papers, 189
Bruen, H., 261
Bruhl, Count, 292
Brunner, Andrew, 181
Bruyeres, Ralph H., 143
Bruz, ———, 48
Bryan, Joseph, 226
Bryan, William Jennings (1860-1925), 116, 164, 225
Bryant, George, 174
Bryant, William Cullen (1794-1878), 174, 176, 255, 259
Bryce, Mrs., 199
Bryce, Elizabeth Marion, Lady (d. 1939), 196, 197, 199
Bryce, James, Viscount (1838-1922), 30, 65, 68, 72, 179, 196-9, 210, 269, 282, 283; *The American Commonwealth*, 196, 198, 199; "De Tocqueville," 199
Bryce, Lloyd, 199
Bryce, Minnie, 199
Bryce Foundation, 281
"Bryce Group," 116
Bryce Papers, 196-9
Brydges, James, 1st Duke of Chandos (1673-1744), 203
Brydon, Robert, 296
Brydone, Mr., 230
Bryn Mawr College, 177
Bryner, M., 78
Brynmor Jones Library (Hull University), 42-3
Bryozowski, Thaddeus, 225
Bryson, Andrew, 325
Buccleuch, Duke of, 189; *see also* Scott, Henry, 3rd Duke of (1746-1812); Scott, Walter Francis, 5th Duke of (1806-84)
Buccleuch, Duke of, Mss., 271-2
Buccleuch and Queensbury Muniments, 189
Buccleuch Muniments, 300-3
Buchan, 11th Earl of, *see* Erskine, David Steuart (1742-1829)
Buchan, A. W., & Co., 254
Buchan, Hew, 290
Buchan, John, of Letham (*fl.* 1782), 290
Buchan, John, 1st Baron Tweedsmuir (1875-1940), 138, 282, 283
Buchan, Rev. John, 189
Buchan, John G., 271
Buchanan, ———, 137
Buchanan, A., 226
Buchanan, James (1791-1868), 25, 64, 67, 77, 104, 176, 186, 200, 201, 202, 216
Buchanan, James (*fl.* 1838), 63
Buchanan, Samuel (1837-*post* 1905), 348
Buchanan & Simpson, 309
Buchanan family, 332
Buchanan Family Papers, 332
Buchanan Hastie & Co., 116
Buchanan Papers, 345
Buck, Cornelius, 240
Bucke, Richard Maurice (1868-99), 172
Buckingham, 1st Marquis of, *see* Grenville, George Nugent–Temple– (1753-1813)
Buckingham and Chandos, 1st Duke of, *see* Grenville, Richard Temple Nugent Brydges Chandos (1776-1839); 3rd Duke of, *see* Grenville, Richard Plantagenet Campbell Temple Nugent Brydges Chandos (1823-89)
Buckinghamshire, Earl of, 11, 12
Buckinghamshire, 2nd Earl of, *see* Hobart, John (1723-93); 4th Earl of, *see* Hobart, Robert (1760-1815)
Buckinghamshire, England, 11-3; *see also*, Immigrants from Buckinghamshire
Buckinghamshire Papers, 24 fn.
Buckinghamshire Record Office, 11-3
Buckle, George Earle (1854-1935), 38, 162
Buckler, W. H., 283
Buckley, Abraham, 173
Buckley, G. E., Esq., 173
Buckley, Henry, 173
Buckley, Hugh, 173
Buckley, John, 173
Buckley, John, & Sons, 173
Buckley family, 173
Buckley–Mathew, George B. (1807-79), 184
Buckmaster, J. W. B., 254
Buckmaster, John, 39
Buckminster, W., 95
Bucks & Oxon Union Bank, 116

Buell, Raymond L., 278, 279, 281
Buffalo, State University of New York at, Lockwood Library, 85 fn.
Buffalo and Lake Erie Railway Co., 263
Buffalo Bill, *see* Cody, William Frederick (1846-1917)
Buffaloes, *see* Bison
Bught Muniments, 274
Building trades, 99, 228, 294; Workers, 228
Bull, John, 41
Bull, William (1710-91), 149, 214, 266
Buller, J. W., 25
Buller, T. W., 25
Buller Family Papers, 47
Buller Papers, 25
Bullion, Exports, 12, 190
Bullitt, William C., 280, 281
Bullock, Henry, 33
Bullock Papers, 33
Bulwark (ship), 288
Bulwer, William Henry Lytton Earle, Baron Dalling and Bulwer (*better known as* Sir Henry Bulwer) (1801-72), 77, 124, 135, 184, 186, 201; *see also* Clayton–Bulwer Treaty
Bunbury Family Records, 218
Bunch [?], Robert, 58
Bunghurst, Joseph, 51
Burch, William, 105
Bures St. Mary, Suffolk, 217
Burge lecture, 281
Burges, Sir James Bland (1752-1824), 80, 200
Burgess, Eliseus, 40
Burgess, Walter H. (1867-1943), 177
Burghley, 1st Baron, *see* Cecil, William (1520-98)
Burgon & Ball Ltd., 235
Burgoyne, John (1722-92), 26, 39, 44, 48, 92, 144, 190, 192, 215, 231, 253, 260, 261, 265, 268, 275, 293
Burgoyne, Sir John Fox (1782-1871), 104, 143
Burke, Edmund (1729-97), 39, 189, 233, 266, 286, 346; *Correspondence* . . ., ed. by T. W. Copeland, 189 fn., 233 fn.
Burke, Richard, 346
Burke, William (d. 1798), 193, 346
Burleigh, Capt., 315
Burley, Bennet G., 130
Burne, S., *Some Notes on . . . Recent Manuscript Additions to the William Salt Library*, 216 fn.
Burnet, William (1688-1729), 40, 54
Burnett, Mr., 275
Burnham Williams & Co., 306
Burnley, Joseph Hume, 61
Burns, Mr., 130
Burns, C. Delisle, 280
Burns, Peter, 261
Burns, Robert, 261
Burnside, Alexander, 309
Burnside, Ambrose Everett (1824-81), 59
Burnside, John, 309
Burnside & Waddell, 309
Burr, Aaron (1716-57), 103, 275
Burr, Aaron (1756-1836), 16, 167, 168, 231
Burridge family, 27
Burritt, Elihu (1810-79), 71, 155, 157, 178, 208, 227, 244, 257, 259
Burrough, Sir James (1691-1764), 217
Burroughs, John (1837-1921), 172, 238
Burrow & Co., Cullompton, 24
Burt, Peter, 318
Burt, Thomas, 318
Burt Single Sleeve Valve Engine, 318
Burton, Ralph, 289
Burton, Theodore Elijah (1851-1929), 197
Burton, Griffiths & Co. Ltd., 228
Burwash Parish Church, 221
Burwell, Lewis, 217
Bury, Customs records, 89
Bury St. Edmunds, Suffolk, 217-8
Busby, C. A., 182
Bush, W., 203
Bushby, W. P., 22
Bushby, Son & Foster, 22
Business Archives, 157
Business records, Aberdeen, 253; Belfast, 325, 327; Birmingham, 73, 226, 227; Bolton, Greater Manchester, 172; Bristol, 6, 8, 211-2; Bromborough, Cheshire, 17; Cardiff, 94, 249; Carlisle, 21-2; Churwell, Yorkshire, 116-7; Coleraine, 327; Cornwall, 20; Derbyshire, 232; Dundee, 318; Falkirk, 258; Glasgow, 255, 256, 318; Gomersal, W. Yorkshire, 116-7; Halifax, W. Yorkshire, 240; Keswick, 22; Kingston-upon-Hull, Humberside, 43; Lancashire, 117-8; Leeds, 116-7, 175, 239, 240; Lisbellaw, 327; Liverpool, Merseyside, 46, 117-8, 175, 180-1, 182, 183, 185, 213; London, 28, 31, 32, 46, 50-1, 94, 96, 99, 102, 117-8, 126, 145, 169, 202, 205, 219, 225, 227, 234; Londonderry, 326; Manchester, 175; Merthyr Tydfil, 247, 249; Newcastle-upon-Tyne, 191, 224; Poole, Dorset, 28; Rastrick, W. Yorkshire, 237; Saddleworth, Yorkshire, 173; Sheffield, 234, 235, 236; Staffordshire, 212-3; Stockport, Greater Manchester, 180; Street, Somerset, 211; Styal, Cheshire, 19; Warrington, Cheshire, 178; Wellington, 212; Witney, Oxfordshire, 210; Yorkshire, 238-9
Busk, Edward, 103
Butcher, Marianne, 6
Butcher, W., 6
Butcher family, 6
Bute, 3rd Earl of, *see* Stuart, John (1713-92); 4th Earl and 1st Marquess of, *see* Stuart, John (1744-1814)
Bute, Marquess of, Mss., 264-5
Bute Correspondence, 249
Butler, Mr., 259
Butler, Andrew Pickens (1796-1857), 184
Butler, Benjamin Franklin (1818-93), 58, 65
Butler, Frank D., 75
Butler, J. R. M., 283; *Lord Lothian (Philip Kerr) 1882-1940*, 276 fn.
Butler, James, 12th Earl and 1st Duke of Ormonde (1610-88), 346
Butler, James (*fl.* 1678), 346
Butler, Nicholas Murray (1862-1947), 78, 113, 197, 198, 199, 238, 260, 280, 281, 282
Butler, Richard, Earl of Arran (1639-86), 346
Butler, Samuel, 178
Butler, T., 313
Butter, Trade, 346
Buttons, Trade, 226
Butts, Henry, 98
Buxton, Noel Edward Noel–, 1st Baron (1869-1948), 327
Buxton, Sir Thomas Fowell (1786-1845), 169
Buxton family, 155
Byrd, W., 285
Byrne, James (1857-1942), 210
Byrnes, James F. (1879-1972), 139

Byron, John (1723-86), 120
Byron, Robert, 330

C

C., F. C., 149
Cabinet (British), 71, 139, 140, 267; Papers, 202, 259
Cabinet Office, 122, 126-8
Cabinet workers, Immigrants, 114
Cables, 111; Atlantic, 70, 184; Pacific, 38, 143
Cadbury, Caroline, 156
Caddick, Helen (1843-1927), 227
Cadell, William, 297
Cadell of Grange Papers, 254
Cadwallader, Thomas, 154
Caernarvon, Customs records, 89, 91-2, 93, 94
Caiger, E., 149
Caillouel, Abigail, 28
Caird, Sir James (1816-92), 60
Cairn of Lochwynyoch Collection, 318
Cairnes, John E. (1823-75), 347
Cairnes Papers, 347
Caithness, William, 10th Earl of, 315
Calcraft, John (1726-72), 29, 264, 265
Caldecote, 1st Viscount, *see* Inskip, Thomas Walker Hobart (1876-1947)
Caldwell, 235
Caldwell, James, and Son, 327
Caldwell, Sir John, 175
Caldwell, John (*fl.* early 19th cent.), 331
Caldwell, John, & Co., 310
Caldwell & Robinson, 328
Caledonian Insurance Co., Records, 307
Calef & Chuter, 205
Calhoun, John C. (1782-1850), 207
Calico, *see* Cotton goods
California: 19th century, 20, 63, 77, 227
AGRICULTURE, 100, 151, 270, 274, 308; Climate, 148; Communications, 100; Consular reports (British), 131; Description, 15, 146, 148, 156, 199, 211, 221, 270, 273, 304; Earthquake, 1906, 98, 307; Education, 271; Finance, 163, 308; Flora, 148; Gold discoveries, 64, 105, 117, 211, 222, 273, 291; Immigrants, 100, 243, 248, 265, 327, 332; Industry, 272; Land, 233, 317; Libraries, 165, 243; Lynchings, 268; Mining, 100, 268, 270, 307, 308; Natural history, 263, 267; Politics, 198; Postal service, 96; Relations with G.B., 77; Relief for Irish famine, 345; Religious history, 152, 229, 352; Settlement, 75, 352; Suffrage, 84; Trade, 35, 121, 206, 219, 235, 272, 327
BRUNSWICK HILLS, 270; Bunning, 19; Ensenada, 100; Fresno, 271; Healdsburg, 332; Los Angeles, Consular reports (British), 135; Marysville, 268, 327; Monterey, 67; Pasadena, 327; San Francisco, 121, 137, 198, 272, 310, 326, 327, 332, Consular reports (British), 130, 134, Description, 81, 211, 217, 255, 270, 304, 315, Merchants, 236; San Miguel, 327; Santa Barbara, 270
California (ship), 323
California, University of, 135, 139; Bancroft Library, 125 fn., 131 fn., 132 fn.; Henry E. Huntingdon Library, 85 fn., 277; Research Library, 85 fn.
California Consols Ltd., 308
California Copper Syndicate Ltd., 308
California Pastoral and Agricultural Co. Ltd., 308
California Powder Works, 206
Californian Mines Financiers Ltd., 308
Call, Annie Payson, 74
Calmady Hamlyn Muniments, 24
Calvarly, Mr., 284
Calvert, Charles, 3rd Baron Baltimore (1637-1715), 220
Calvert, Charles, 5th Baron Baltimore (1699-1751), 118
Calvert, George, 1st Baron Baltimore (1580?-1632), 24, 194, 312
Calvert, Leonard (1606-47), 185
Calvert, Samuel, 10
Calvert family, Lords Baltimore (1629), 35
Cam, Joseph, 235
Camachie Emigration Society, 108
Cambridge, Cambridgeshire, 13-7
Cambridge Modern History, 15
Cambridge Union, 14
Cambridge University, American lectureship, 16; Senate, 16
Cambridge University, Library, 14-6
Cambridgeshire, England, 13-7
Cambridgeshire County Record Office, Cambridge, 13-4
Cambridgeshire County Record Office, Huntingdon, 17
Camden, 1st Earl, *see* Pratt, Charles (1714-94)
Camden & Amboy Railroad Co., 249, 250
Camden & Atlantic Railroad Co., 347
Cameos, 175
Cameron, A., 287
Cameron, Alan, 287
Cameron, Allan, 293
Cameron, Charles, 293, 294
Cameron, Donald, 287
Cameron, Ewan, 293
Cameron, John, of Lochiel (*fl.* 1715), 310
Cameron, John (*fl.* 1736), 272
Cameron, John (*fl.* 1786), 294
Cameron, Thomson & Co., 310
Cameron of Aldourie Mss., 270
Camm, John, 115
Campbell, A., 314
Campbell, Alexander, 2nd Earl of Marchmont (1675-1740), 292
Campbell, Alexander (*fl.* 1689), 311
Campbell, Alexander (*fl.* 1759-61), 289
Campbell, Alexander, Major (*fl.* 1774-6), 293, 294
Campbell, Alexander (landwaiter) (*fl.* 1775-80), 293
Campbell, Alexander, of Barcaldine, 293, 293 fn., 294
Campbell, Alexander (1788-1866), 245
Campbell, Alexander (*fl.* 1811), 269
Campbell, Alexander Hume, 292
Campbell, Allan, 289, 293
Campbell, Archibald, 3rd Duke of Argyll (1682-1761), 149, 284
Campbell, Sir Archibald (1739-91), 260
Campbell, Archibald (*fl.* 1775), 269
Campbell, Archibald, Col. (*fl.* 1778), 305
Campbell, C. S., *Anglo-American Understanding, 1898-1903*, 131 fn.
Campbell, Catherine (Bayard), 294
Campbell, Charles, 269
Campbell, Colin, Ensign (*fl.* 1776), 293
Campbell, Colin (*fl.* 1787), 294
Campbell, D., and Son, 326
Campbell, Daniel (1671?-1753), 203, 316
Campbell, David (*fl.* 1775-82), 289, 294
Campbell, David (*fl.* 1787), 294
Campbell, Donald (*fl.* 1776), 324

Campbell, Dugald (*fl.* 1716), 311
Campbell, Dugald (*fl.* 1775), 296
Campbell, Duncan (d. 1759), 289
Campbell, Duncan (*fl.* 1775), 269
Campbell, Duncan (merchant, *fl.* 1776), 56
Campbell, Duncan, of Glenure (later of Barcaldine), 293, 293 fn., 294
Campbell, Duncan Pearsall (b. *c.* 1781), 294
Campbell, Ethan, 308
Campbell, Sir George (*fl.* 1682), 272, 292
Campbell, George (*fl.* 1727), 289
Campbell, George (*fl.* 1759), 289
Campbell, George Douglas, 8th Duke of Argyll (1823-1900), 71, 72
Campbell, Hugh (*fl.* early 18th cent.), 293
Campbell, Hugh (*fl.* 1778-9), 294
Campbell, Hugh (*fl.* 1842), 291
Campbell, Sir Ilay (1734-1823), 287
Campbell, J. F., 255
Campbell, James (*fl. c.* 1690), 286
Campbell, James (*fl.* 1755-6), 317
Campbell, James (*fl.* 1761-5), 264, 265
Campbell, James (*fl.* 1764), 305
Campbell, James (saddler, *fl.* 1770's?), 295
Campbell, James (*fl.* 1791), 269
Campbell, James Daniels (1839-1925), 38
Campbell, James Mure, 265
Campbell, John, 2nd Earl of Breadalbane (1662-1752), 284
Campbell, John, 4th Earl of Loudoun (1705-82), 31, 36, 64, 264, 265, 266, 271, 285
Campbell, John (1708-75), 55, 314
Campbell, John, of Barcaldine (*fl.* 1758), 289, 293 fn., 294
Campbell, John, of Danna (*fl.* 1760), 293
Campbell, John (*fl.* 1766-7), 265
Campbell, John (*fl.* 1772-6), 291
Campbell, John, 1st Baron (1779-1861), 263
Campbell, John, of Edinburgh (*fl.* 1780), 295
Campbell, John, of Coalisland (*fl.* 1810's), 348
Campbell, John, Lieut (*fl.* 1811), 269
Campbell, Lilias, 273
Campbell, Louisa, 268
Campbell, Mary, 294
Campbell, Mungo, 293
Campbell, Lord Neil (d. 1693), 286
Campbell, Neill, 317
Campbell, P., 314
Campbell, Patrick, of Ardchattan, 269, 289
Campbell, Patrick, of Barcaldine, 289
Campbell, Patrick, Major (d. 1782), 293, 294
Campbell, Peter [?Patrick], of Barcaldine, 289
Campbell, Peter, of Glenure, 293, 294
Campbell, Robert (*fl.* 1832), 330
Campbell, Robert (*fl.* 1841), 291
Campbell, Sally (Pearsall), 293, 294
Campbell, Sandy, 293
Campbell, Thomas (*fl.* 1714), 311
Campbell, Thomas (*fl.* 1770's), 265
Campbell, William (*fl.* 1731-49), 272
Campbell, William (*fl.* 1737), 293
Campbell, Lord William (d. 1778), 76
Campbell, William (*fl.* 1832), 330
Campbell & McIlvain, 22
Campbell family, 328
Campbell Journals, 255
Campbell of Balliveolan Muniments, 273
Campbell of Barcaldine Muniments, 293-4
Campbell of Inverneill Mss., 260
Campbell–Allen, William J., 328
Campbell–Allen Family Papers, 328
Campbell–Bannerman, Sir Henry (1836-1908), 65
Campbell–Bannerman Papers, 65
Campbell–Gibson, Lt. Commander H., Mss., 268
Campbell–Preston of Ardchattan Mss., 269
Canada, 128, 134; to 1756, 10, 83, 189, 298; 1756-64, 45, 74, 79, 140, 195, 223; 1775-83, 12, 20, 120, 143, 145, 190, 205, 215, 313, 317, 323, 324; 1783-1811, 15, 57, 210, 223, 243, 257, 259, 313; War of 1812, 83, 102, 142, 143, 255, 257, 259; 1815-39, 23, 57, 67, 102, 144, 192, 223, 255-6, 257, 259, 286, 346; Rebellion 1837-8, 34, 102, 104, 109, 219, 258, 326, 346; 1840-66, 13, 23, 40, 70, 77, 102, 104, 110, 111, 121, 123, 129, 143-4 *passim*, 247, 254, 255-6, 276; Fenian invasions 1866-70, 68, 69, 111, 250, 344, 352; Confederation, 13, 40, 111, 141, 344; 1867- , 134, 139, 142, 143, 144
AGRICULTURE, 150, 151, 166, 192; Army (British), 102, 104, 110, 140, 141, 142, 218, 260, 346; Birds, 148
BOUNDARIES, *see* Alaska: Boundaries; Boundaries: Canada; Juan de Fuca Strait; North-East Boundary; North-West Boundary; Oregon Question; San Juan Islands
CANALS, 121; Coinage, 40; Customs administration, 21, 125; Description, 15, 20, 30, 33, 34, 36, 39, 45, 95, 102, 113, 146, 150, 187, 192, 208, 218, 219, 235, 246, 254, 255, 256, 270, 271, 276, 277, 283, 290, 297, 305, 317, 346; Economic conditions, 348; Education, 110; Emigrants, 351; Finance, 102, 110, 142, 257; Fur trade, 83, 146, 240, 261; Governors, 30, 38, 45, 69, 102, 104, 110, 124, 129, 144, 210, 223, 247, 257, 258, 260, 285; Immigrants, 14, 21, 23, 34, 36, 42, 46, 63, 97, 109, 114, 137, 166, 235, 244, 259, 272, 313, 325, 326, 330, 332, 346, 347, 348, 349, 352; Indians, 141, 261; Industry, 150; Judicial system, 23; Land, 34, 36, 110, 111, 138, 223, 255-6; Land tenure, 305; Liquor trade, 160; Merchants, 273, 297; Pauperism, 23; Politics, 110, 138, 140, 162, 195, 218, 232, 287, 288, 325; Possible invasion by U.S., 287; Railways, 110, 111; Relations with Great Britain, 112, 278; Religious history, 14, 53, 96, 110, 138, 159, 171, 255, 258, 259, 347; Settlement, 146, 257; Timber trade, 250; Trade with Great Britain, 108, 110, 128, 210, 235, 236, 254, 255-6, 284; Trade with Ireland, 325, 327; Trade with West Indies, 161; Union with U.S., 315; *see also* Fisheries; Reciprocity; Relations with Canada; Trade with Canada; *also under individual provinces*: British Columbia; Manitoba; New Brunswick; Newfoundland; Nova Scotia; Ontario; Prince Edward Island; Quebec; Saskatchewan
Canada and New Brunswick Boundary Bill Amendment, 110
Canada Company, 34; Bill, 110
Canada Indemnity Bill, 110
Canada, etc., Railroad Co., 110
Canada Union Act Amendment Bill, 110
Canals, Workers, 244; *see also* names of canals, *e.g.* Erie Canal; Panama Canal
Candler, John (1787-1869), 156
Caner, Henry (?1700-92), 8
Canfield, Louisa, 50
Cannibalism, 291
Canning, Charles John, Earl Canning (1812-62), 274
Canning, George (1770-1827), 25, 54, 57, 83, 107, 133, 207, 237, 240, 268, 288
Canning, Stratford, 1st Viscount Stratford de Redcliffe (1786-

1880), 49, 84, 237, 286
Canning Papers, 237, 240
Canterbury, Kent, 44
Canterbury Cathedral Library, 44
Capital punishment, 157, 196, 330
Capoulade, Mons., 113
Capper, Arthur, 278, 282
Capper, John, 329
Capuchins, 171
Carbery, 6th Baron, *see* Evans–Freke, John (1765-1845)
Carden, John S., 288
Cardiff, South Glamorgan, 94, 249-50; Bute Dock, 250; Customs records, 89, 91, 93
Cardiff Central Library, 249
Cardigan, Customs records, 89, 93
Cardwell, Edward, Viscount (1813-86), 141
Cardwell Papers, 141
Carew family, 11
Carey, Mathew (1760-1839), 176
Carey, Samuel, 223
Carhart, Henry Smith (1844-1920), 162
Caribbean, Relations with U.S., *see* Relations with Caribbean
Caribees: Land grants, 352; Trade with Netherlands, 200; *see also* Leeward Islands
Cariss, Sansom, 235
Carleton, Major, 305
Carleton, Sir Dudley, 1st Viscount Dorchester (1573-1632), 29, 37
Carleton, Sir Guy, 1st Baron Dorchester (1724-1808), 15, 30, 57, 107, 119, 141, 143, 192, 203, 265, 267, 324
Carleton Papers, 66, 141
Carlile, Christopher, 18
Carlisle, 2nd Earl of, *see* Hay, James (*c.* 1580-1636); 4th Earl of, *see* Howard, Henry (1694-1758); 5th Earl of, *see* Howard, Frederick (1748-1825)
Carlisle, Elizabeth, 332
Carlisle, James, 331
Carlisle, Kate, 331
Carlisle Family Papers, 331
Carlisle, Cumbria, 21-2; Customs records, 89, 93
Carlisle Peace Commission, 1778, 121
Carlow, Republic of Ireland, 343
Carlting, George, 227
Carlyle, A., 313
Carlyle, Thomas (1795-1881), 255
Carlyle, Thomas (*fl.* 1815), 273
Carmarthen, Marquis of, *see* Osborne, Sir Thomas, *successively* 1st Earl of Danby, Marquis of Carmarthen and 1st Duke of Leeds (1631-1712)
Carmarthen, Marquis of (*styled*, 1761-89), *see* Osborne, Francis, 5th Duke of Leeds (1751-99)
Carmarthen, Dyfed, 247; Customs records, 89, 93
Carmarthenshire Record Office, 247
Carnarvon, 4th Earl of, *see* Herbert, Henry Howard Molyneux (1831-90)
Carnarvon Papers, 139
Carnegie, Andrew (1835-1919), 68, 71, 72, 73, 78, 197, 199, 227, 256, 260, 261, 306, 307
Carnegie Endowment for International Peace, 78, 278, 280, 281
Carnegie Institution of Washington, xxiii
Carnegie Trust for Universities of Scotland, 307
Carnegie United Kingdom Trust, 307; Records, 306-7
Carolina: 17th century, 10, 36, 194, 195, 229, 275, 298; 1700-60, 18, 31, 34, 112, 253, 261, 263, 264, 298
AGRICULTURE, 149, 150, 151, 301; Boundaries, 102; Constitution, 195; Governors, 292; Immigrants, 22, 224, 272, 292, 293; Land, 36, 246, 312; Land grants, 273; Lords Proprietors, 292; Maps, 27, 304; Merchants, 304; Religious history, 174; Settlement, 36, 45, 304, 311; Trade, 8, 18, 55, 91, 260, 274, 284, 349
ASHLEY RIVER, 292; St. Giles plantation, 36
See also for later periods NORTH CAROLINA; South Carolina
Carolina Clinchfield Railroad, 96
Carolina Society, 304
Caroline (ship), 77, 129, 219, 274; *see also* McLeod, Alexander (*fl.* 1840's)
Carpenter, Edward (1844-1929), 172, 236; *Bibliography of Edward Carpenter*, 236 fn.
Carpenter, Lant (1780-1840), 208
Carpenter, Mary (1807-77), 6
Carpenter, R. L., 208
Carpenter Collection, 236
Carpenters, Immigrants, 25, 97, 163, 228
Carpet–weavers, Immigrants, 331
Carpets, Trade, 310
Carr, H. J., "John Francis Bray," *Economica* (1940), 163 fn.
Carr, James, 240
Carr, Ralph, 191
Carr, Robert, 276
Carr, T., 179
Carr Mss., 240
Carr–Ellison (Hedgeley) Mss., 191
Carroll, C., 30
Carroll, John (1735-1815), 171, 225, 270
Carroll, John (*fl.* 1864), 352
Carroll, Thomas, 352
Carroll, William, 344
Carron Iron Co. Records, 289
Carrothers, Joseph, 330
Carrothers, Nathaniel, 330
Carrothers, William, 330
Carson, Archibald, 330
Carson, Edward, *The Ancient and Rightful Customs*, 93 fn.; "The Customs Records of Portsmouth," *Journal of the Society of Architects* (1977), 90 fn.
Carson, Edward Henry, Baron Carson (1854-1935), 327
Carson, James, 330
Carson, Margaret, 330
Carson Papers, 327
Carte Mss., 203
Carter, Charles (1707-64), 149
Carter, [John, 1737-81?], 192
Carter, William, 149
Carteret, Sir George (d. 1680), 8, 339
Carteret, John, 1st Earl Granville (1690-1763), 312
Carteret Papers, 8
Carteret Priaulx & Co., 339
Cartier, Sir George Etienne (1814-73), 40
Cartlidge, Charles, 263
Cartwright, Sir George, 82
Cartwright, John (1740-1824), 270
Carvells of New York, 169
Cary, Eugene, 164
Cary, Robert, & Co., 28, 203
Cary, Samuel, 95
Carysfort, 1st Earl of, *see* Proby, Sir John Joshua (1751-1828)
Case & Southworth, 181-2

Case Papers, 115
Casement, Sir Roger [David] (1864-1916), 199, 345
Cass, Lewis (1782-1866), 201, 206
Cassell, John (1817-65), 168
Cassillis, Earl of (*fl.* 1898), *see* Kennedy, Archibald (1847-1938)
Cassillis, 10th Earl of, *see* Kennedy, David (*c.* 1727-92); 12th Earl of, *see* Kennedy, Archibald (1770-1846)
Cassillis, Peerage of, 275
Cassini, Count, 38
Castle Forbes, Longford, 353
Castlereagh, Viscount (*better known as*), *see* Stewart, Robert, 2nd Marquis of Londonderry (1769-1822)
Cataract Construction Co., 162
Catawissa Railroad, 347
Catesby, Mark (1679?-1749), 147
Catharine (ship), 310
Cathcart, ——, 299
Cathcart, Mrs., 270
Cathcart, Alexander, 323
Cathcart, Charles, 9th Baron (1721-76), 240
Cathcart, Charles (*fl.* 1776-7), 292
Cathcart, Charles Murray, 2nd Earl (1783-1859), 240
Cathcart, Gabriel, 297
Cathcart, Sir George (1794-1854), 240
Cathcart, John, 297
Cathcart, Joshua, 323
Cathcart, Robert, 297
Cathcart, William, 297
Cathcart of Genoch Muniments, 297
Cathcart Papers, 240
Cather, Thomas, 325; *Journal of a Voyage to America in 1836*, 325 fn.
Catholic Church, 30, 37, 54, 71, 95, 126, 157, 171-2, 225, 244, 291, 345, 347, 350; Missions, 85; Modernist movement, 75; *see also* Converts; Jesuits; Monasteries
Catlin, George E. G., 278, 279, 282
Catlyn, Hugh, 18
"Cato," *pseud.*, 344
Caton, Richard (1763-1845), 186
Catt, Carrie Chapman, 84, 179, 278
Catt, Henry, 69
Cattermole, Richard, 26
Cattle: Pedigrees (Angus), 266; Ranching, 209, 210, 289, 308, 318 fn.; Registration, 266; Towns, 217
"Cattle range idiom," 62
Cattle trade, 36, 64, 137, 180, 274, 289, 319; *see also* Feeding stuffs; Livestock; Pigs; Sheep
Catton Collection, 23
Caughey, James, 330
Caulfeild, James, 4th Viscount and 1st Earl of Charlemont (1728-99), 350
Cavanagh, Michael, 343
Cavendish, R., 269
Cavendish, William, 4th Duke of Devonshire (1720-64), 264
Cawley, Elizabeth H., ed., *The American Diaries of Richard Cobden*, 70 fn.
Cay Sal, Sovereignty, 131
Caygill, ——, 237
Cazalet, Victor, 282
Cecil, Lord Edgar Algernon Robert, Viscount Cecil of Chelwood, 78, 135, 279, 281; "The Freedom of the Seas," 279
Cecil, Robert, 1st Earl of Salisbury (1563?-1612), 37, 190
Cecil, Robert Arthur Talbot Gascoyne–, 3rd Marquess of Salisbury (1830-1903), 13, 37-8, 221
Cecil, Lord Robert (*fl.* 1918-9), 277
Cecil, William, 1st Baron Burghley (1520-98), 37
Cecil of Chelwood, Viscount, *see* Cecil, Lord Edgar Algernon Robert
Cecil of Chelwood Papers, 78
Cecil Papers, 37
Census, 64, 274; *see also* Vital statistics
Central America, Relations with Great Britain, 77, 186; *see also* Mosquito Coast; Relations with Central America
Central City (Colorado) Mining Co. Ltd., 125
Century, 74
Century Company, New York, 199
Century Group, 283
Ceramic Age, 212
Chadwick, Sir Edwin (1800-90), 170
Chains, Trade, 235
Chalkley, Thomas (1675-1741), 153
Chalmers, David, 253
Chalmers, George (1742-1825), 160
Chalmers, George (*fl.* 1777), 227
Chalmers, Lionel, 314
Chalmers of Aldbar Mss., 260
Chaloner, W. H., 178; ed. with B. M. Ratcliffe, "A Philadelphia Textile Merchant's Trip to Europe . . . ," *Trade and Transport: Essays in Honour of T. S. Willan* (1977); "Dr. Joseph Priestley, John Wilkinson and the French Revolution, 1789-1802," *Trans. of the Royal Historical Soc.* (1958), 19
Chamberlain, (Arthur) Neville (1869-1940), 269
Chamberlain, Beatrice, 227
Chamberlain, Joseph (1836-1914), 38, 227
Chamberlain, Sir (Joseph) Austen, 278, 279, 280
Chamberlain, Mary (Endicott), Mrs. Joseph Chamberlain, 227
Chambers, Jane, 328
Chambers, John (*fl.* 1796), 328
Chambers, John (*fl.* early 19th cent.), 331
Chambliss, John Alexander (1887-1951), 198
Chamerovzow, Louis Alexis, 169
Champernowne family, 26
Champernowne Papers, 26
Champion, E., 288
Champion, Richard (1743-91), 122, 233
Champion Gold and Silver Co., 204
Champlain Society, 191 fn.
Champlin, John F., 182
Chance, George (1790-1861), 227
Chance, R. Lucas (1782-1865), 227
Chance, Wade, 141
Chance, William (1788-1856), 227
Chance, W. & G., 227
Chancery, Court of, 122, 126; Scottish, 308
Chandlee, Benjamin, 350
Chandler, George, *Liverpool Under Charles I* (1965), 181 fn.; *Liverpool Under James I* (1960), 181 fn.
Chandler, Samuel, 265
Chandos, 1st Duke of, *see* Brydges, James (1673-1744)
Channel Islands, 339; Arming of Confederate ships, 136; Illicit trade, 90, 91; *see also* Trade with Channel Islands
Channing, E., "The American Board of Commissioners for the Customs," *Proceedings of the Massachusetts Historical Society* (1909-10), 87 fn.
Channing, William Ellery (1780-1842), 94, 176, 183, 208, 255, 259, 313
Channing, William Francis (1820-1901), 162

Channing, William Henry (1810-64), 176, 208, 243
Chaplin, John, 210
Chaplin, Mrs. Thomas, 50
Chapman, Mr., 176
Chapman, E., 190
Chapman, John, 315
Chapman, Maria (Weston), Mrs. Henry Grafton Chapman (1806-95), 95, 316
Chapman, William, 315
Chapman–Huston, D., and E. C. Cripps, *Through a City Archway*, 50 fn.
Chapone, Mrs. Sally Kirkham, 117
Charities, 103
Charlemont, 4th Viscount and 1st Earl of, *see* Caulfeild, James (1728-99)
Charlemont Mss., 350
Charles I (1600-49), 19, 27, 194
Charles II (1630-85), 17, 54, 98, 99, 189, 230, 260
Charles, H., 248
Charles, Robert, 302
Charles (ship), 304
Charless, Joseph, 183
Charming Molly (ship), 272
Charnwood, 1st Baron, *see* Benson, George Rathbone (1864-1945)
Charteris, Charles, 272
Charters, Colonial, 83, 126, 129, 298; *see also* Massachusetts Bay Company; New England Company; Virginia Company of London; *and subdivision* Charters *under states*
Chartists, 68
Chase, G. B., 203
Chase, Philander (1775-1852), 210
Chase, Salmon Portland (1808-73), 68
Chatard, Francis Silas (1834-1918), 162
Chatham, 1st Earl of, *see* Pitt, William (1708-78); 2nd Earl of, *see* Pitt, John (1756-1835)
Chatsworth, Derbyshire, 23
Chatto, Andrew, 84
Chatto, Andrew, Esq., 33, 84
Chatto, Andrew, Jr., 33
Chatto & Windus Ltd., 33, 81, 84
Chauncy, Charles, 312
Chauvin, A., 291
Chaworth, Lady, 48
Checkland, S. J., "American versus West Indian Traders in Liverpool, 1793-1815," *Journal of Economic History* (1958), 185 fn.; "An English Merchant House in China after 1842," *Bulletin of the Business Historical Society* (1953), 185 fn.
Checkley, John (1680-1754), 85
Cheese, Trade, 47
Cheffins, Richard, 150
Chelmsford, Essex, 31-3
Chepstow, Customs records, 89, 93
Cheriton Bishop Parish, Devon, 25 fn.
Cherwell, Viscount, *see* Lindemann, F. A. (1886-1957)
Cherwell Papers, 209
Chesapeake (ship), 81, 104, 144, 219, 278, 313
Chesapeake Bay, 274
Cheshire, Isaac, 247
Cheshire, John, 247
Cheshire, England, 17-9; *see also* Cotton famine; Immigrants from Cheshire
Cheshire Libraries and Museums, 19
Cheshire Record Office, 18
Chesney, Alexander (1755-1815), 323, 351; *Journal*, 323 fn.
Chesney, Charles Francis, 323
Chester, Cheshire, 18-9; Customs records, 89, 93
Chester City Record Office, 18-9
Chesterfield, 4th Earl of, *see* Stanhope, Philip Dormer (1694-1773)
Chesterfield, Derbyshire, 23
Chevalier, Amable, *alias*, *see* Pawquawkoman
Chevalier, Jean, 339
Chevallier, Mrs. A. O., 101
Cheveley Parish, Cambridgeshire, 14
Chew, Ensign, 285
Chicago (ship), 137
Chicago and Rock Island Railway, 230
Chicago Edison Co., 224
Chicago Great Western Railway Syndicate, 96
Chicago, Milwaukee, and St. Paul Railway, 105
Chicago Silver Mining Co. Ltd., 125
Chicago Tribune, 277
Chicago, *see also* Illinois: Chicago
Chichely, Sir Thomas (1618-99), 11
Chichester, 2nd Earl of, *see* Pelham, Thomas (1756-1826)
Chichester, Lady, 43
Chichester, Sir Charles, 43
Chichester, West Sussex, 185, 223; Customs records, 89, 93
Chichester–Constable of Burton Constable, 42
Chidlaw, Benjamin Williams (d. 1892), 246
Children, Immigrants, 31, 86, 97
Chile, Relations with U.S., *see* Relations with Chile
China: 20th century, 144, 280
  MISSIONS, 144
  CANTON, 288; *see also* Immigrants from China; Relations with China; Trade with China
China (ship), 200
Chinaware, *see* Pottery
Chinese Bureau of Mines, 205
Chinese vetch, *see* Feeding stuffs
Chinnery, G. A., *A Handlist of the Cholmondeley (Houghton) MSS.*, 15 fn.
Chisholm, Alexander, 296, 297
Chisholm, James, 266
Chiswell, Richard (1639-1711), 203
Chiswick Press, Further Records of, 70
Choat, Mr., 33
Choate, Joseph Hodges (1832-1917), 39, 75, 77, 129, 164, 176, 197, 199
Choate, Rufus, 276
Cholera, 18, 137, 155, 170, 330, 332
Cholmondeley, Marquess of, 14-5
Cholmondeley (Houghton) Mss., 14-5
Chorlton Union (Poor Law Guardians), 179
Christian Century, 279
Christian Faith Society, 115; Papers, 115
Christian Science Monitor, 278, 279, 280, 281, 283
Christian Science Movement, 11, 281, 282, 283
Christianity, 95, 271
Christie, Gabriel, 265
Christie, Loring C., 281
Christie, Nathan, 265
Christopher, J., 144
Christophers, John, 168
Christy, Stephen, 180
Christy & Co., 180
Christy Collection, 180

Chronicle, 345
Church history, 18; *see also subdivision* Religious history *under states, etc.; also names of denominations, sects, churches, etc.*
Church of England, 41-2, 83, 85, 94, 105, 110, 131, 132, 151, 158-9 *passim*, 196, 285, 312; Missions, 85, 94, 116, 151, 158-9 *passim*; *see also* Puritans
Church of Ireland, 349
Church of Jesus Christ of Latter–Day Saints, *see* Mormons and Mormonism
Church of Scotland, 255, 258; Committees on colonial churches, 255; General Assembly, 255, 308-9, 313-4
Church schools, 158
Churchill, Armistead, 140
Churchill, Sir Winston (1874-1965), 112, 260, 278, 283
Churchill College, Cambridge, 16
Churchill Papers, 139
Churwell, Yorkshire, Business records, *see* Business records: Churwell, Yorkshire
Cinchona, 151
Cinque Ports, Lord Warden of, 221
Cities: 19th century, 15, 179, 183; 20th century, 179, 277; *see also* Municipal government
Cities and Town Planning Exhibition, 256
Citizen, New York, 326, 344
City of Glasgow Bank, 262
City of London (ship), 327
City of London Literary and Scientific Institution, 204
City of London Polytechnic, 84
Civil service, 177, 197, 198
Civil War (1861-5), 13, 29, 42, 72, 123, 132, 148, 179, 181, 191, 222, 225, 259, 313, 317, 330, 331, 349-50; Aftermath, 29, 156; Army, Federal, 36, 58, 59, 60, 104, 130, 138, 166, 184, 270, 318-9, 326, 327, 331, 332, Deserters, 144, Negro troops, 69, Irish recruits, 104, 344, 352; Blockade, 58, 59, 60, 69, 70, 72, 89, 104, 111, 121, 123, 130, 131, 204, 211
CAMPAIGNS, 61, 65, 143; Battle of Cedar Mountain, 1864, 76; Battle of Chancellorsville, 1863, 76; Battle of Chattanooga, 1863, 59; Battle of Fredericksburg, 1862, 60, 76, 344; Battle of Gettysburg, 1863, 5, 59, 76; Battle of Malvern Hill, 76; Battle of New Orleans, 1862, 58; Battle of Pittsburgh, 328; Battle of Vicksburg, 1863, 168, 244; Battle of Winchester, 76; Fort Sumter, 327; Georgia, 61, 130, 169, 232; Great Lakes, 59, 68, 121, 123, 130; Louisiana, 76; Maryland, 59; Massachusetts, 68; Mississippi, 60, 328; Pennsylvania, 59; Tennessee, 59; Vermont, 130; Virginia, 59, 76, 246, 259, 327
CAUSES, 68, 71, 155, 168, 169, 245, 331, *see also* Slavery; Economic effects, 13, 60, 68, 118, 130, 130 fn., 136, 247, 348, 350; Finance, 222
FOREIGN OPINION, British, 13, 25, 42, 52, 58, 59, 67, 68, 69, 71, 104, 121, 139, 141, 168, 169, 170, 184, 196, 204, 223, 247, 250, 350; French, 67; Irish, 347; Scottish, 316 fn.
NAVAL OPERATIONS, 68, 70, 130; Pacifists, 157; Peace, 13, 58, 59, 60, 69, 71, 73, 104, 143, 202; Personal narratives, 25, 65, 76, 157, 211, 225, 244, 246, 247, 248, 326, 347, 348; Prizes, 121, 144; Religious aspects, 226
See also CONFEDERATE STATES
Claiborne, Thomas, 237
Claims against Great Britain, 56, 130, 130 fn., 131, 142; *see also* *Alabama* (ship), Claims; Johnson–Clarendon Convention, 1869
Claims of British subjects, 9, 54, 56, 121, 130, 286, 287, 288, 295, 298; *see also* Debts to British merchants; Loyalists: Claims
Clan na Gael, 344, 345
Clanranald, 298
Clanranald Muniments, 298
Clap, Thomas (1703-67), 149
Clapboards, Trade, 24
Clapham, John, 233
Clapham, Sir John, *The Bank of England*, 51
Clarendon, 1st Earl of, *see* Hyde, Edward (1609-74)
Clarendon, 1st Earl of the 2nd creation, *see* Villiers, Thomas (*known as* Lord Hyde, 1756-76) (1709-86); 3rd Earl of the 2nd creation, *see* Villiers, John Charles (1757-1838); 4th Earl of the 2nd creation, *see* Villiers, George William Frederick (1800-70)
Clarendon, Lord, 200 fn.
Clarendon Papers (United States), 200-2
Clarges, Sir Thomas (d. 1695), 82
Clarina, 1st Baron, *see* Massey, Eyre (1719-1804)
Clark, Alvan (1804-87), 148
Clark, C. & J., Ltd., 211
Clark, D. M., "The American Board of Customs, 1767-1783," *American Historical Review* (1939-40), 87 fn.
Clark, E. A. G., "The Estuarine Ports of the Exe and Feign . . . 1660-1860" (Thesis), 25 fn.
Clark, G. N., *Guide to English Commercial Statistics, 1696-1782*, 88 fn., 89 fn.
Clark, George, 148, 240
Clark, R. & R., 259
Clark, Richard Ecroyd, 232
Clark, Thomas, 328
Clark, William (*fl.* 1770's), 105
Clark, William (*fl.* 1837-8), 232
Clark, Son & Morland, 211
Clark Papers, 232
Clarke, Sir Alured (1745?-1832), 139
Clarke, D., *Arthur Dobbs Esquire, 1689-1765*, 323 fn.
Clarke, F., 280
Clarke, George (1676-1760), 54
Clarke, George Sydenham, Baron Sydenham of Combe (1848-1933), 143
Clarke, Isaac W., 150
Clarke, James Freeman (1810-88), 176, 204, 208, 235
Clarke, Lizzie, 332
Clarke, Richard, 39
Clarke, Wad, 348
Clarke, William (d. 1852), 146
Clarke, Oglethorpe Accumulation, 47
Clarkson, Thomas (1760-1846), 51, 151, 169, 205
Clavering–Cowper, George Nassau, 3rd Earl Cowper (1738-89), 40
Clay, 212, 213
Clay, Henry (1777-1852), 171, 185, 204, 207, 325
Clay, Henry (*fl.* 1932), 280
Clay, J. & T., & Sons Ltd., 238
Clay, J. T., & Co., 237
Clayburne, William, 17
Clayton–Bulwer Treaty (1850), 39, 69, 77, 131, 186, 200, 201, 221
Cleaveland, Samuel, 145
Cleaver, Mr. H. M., Deposit, 246
Cleland, Joseph, 331
Cleland, Margaret, 331
Clemens, Clara, 33
Clemens, Jean, 33
Clemens, Samuel Langhorne (1835-1910), 33, 81, 84, 184, 197, 222, 238, 254, 259, 261; *Adventures of Huckleberry Finn*, 81; *Adventures of Tom Sawyer*, 84; *A Connecticut Yankee in King Arthur's*

Court, 81; *The Prince and the Pauper*, 81
Clephane, James, 291
Clephane, John, 291
Clergy Reserves (Canada) Bill, 110
Clerk, Hugh, 274
Clerk, James, 273
Clerk, Sir John, 274
Clerk, Mathew, 274
Clerk, Robert, 240
Clerk of Penicuik Muniments, 273
Clerke, Sir Francis Carr, 8, 265
Cleveland, General, 260
Cleveland, Henry, 232
Cleveland, Stephen Grover (1837-1908), 161, 164, 177, 198, 204
Clifford, Henry William, 32
Clifton Muniments, 47
Climate, 15, 62, 148, 149, 150, 225, 328
Clint & Leftwich, 184
Clinton, De Witt (1769-1828), 9, 94
Clinton, George (*c.* 1686-1761), 31, 191
Clinton, George (1739-1812), 64
Clinton, Sir Henry (1738?-95), 24, 65, 139, 141, 145, 190, 192, 193, 215, 218, 219, 240, 260, 266, 274, 292, 293, 297, 313
Clinton, Henry Fiennes, 2nd Duke of Newcastle-under-Lyme (1720-94), 192
Clinton, Henry Pelham Fiennes Pelham, 5th Duke of Newcastle–under–Lyme (1811-64), 104, 105, 192
Clinton, Lord John Pelham, 192
Clive, Robert, Baron (1725-74), 175
Clodd, Edward (1840-1930), 238
Clodius, 136
Cloth, *see* Textile industry
Cloture, 72
Clough, Arthur Hugh (1819-61), 196
Clough Papers, 196
Clover, 203
Clow, A. and N., *The Chemical Revolution*, 226 fn.
Clwyd, Wales, 243
Clwyd County Record Office, 243
Clyde (ship), 316
Clyde Screw Steam Packet Co., 316
Clymer, George, 308
Coal: Mining, 164, 307; Trade, 28, 91, 92, 109, 124
Coal Mining Papers, 180
Coales, Edward J., 315
Coast: Surveys, 57, 62, 120, 140, 148; Northwest, 133, 138
Coates, T., 169
Coats, James, 309
Cobb, H. S., *The Political Papers of Herbert, First Viscount Samuel*, 113 fn.
Cobb Collection, 36
Cobbe, Francis Power, 196
Cobbett, James Paul, 209
Cobbett, John, 209
Cobbett, John Morgan, 209
Cobbett, Susan, 209
Cobbett, William (1762-1835), 174, 209
Cobbett, William, Jr., 209
Cobbett's Weekly Political Register, 174, 209
Cobden, Frederick, 179
Cobden, Richard (1804-65), 69, 70, 170, 179, 204; *American Diaries*, 70 fn.
Cobden Papers, 69, 70
Cobham, Viscount, 228
Cobham, George, 184
Cobham Archive, 184
Cochineal, 203
Cochran, Rupert I., 286
Cochran, William Bourke, 327, 345
Cochrane, Sir Alexander Forrester Inglis (1758-1832), 43, 255, 288, 313
Cochrane, Archibald, 9th Earl of Dundonald, *styled* Lord Cochrane (1748-1831), 313
Cochrane, Charles (d. 1781), 258
Cochrane, Sir John (d. 1695?), 292
Cochrane, John (*fl.* 1777-96), 257, 258, 287
Cochrane, Thomas, 10th Earl of Dundonald (1775-1860), 303, 304
Cochrane, Sir Thomas John (1789-1872), 255
Cochrane Papers, 255
Cochrane Johnstone Papers, 255
Cockayne, J. W., 235
Cockburn, Sir Alexander James Edmund (1802-80), 70
Cockburn, Alison, 290
Cockburn, Sir George (1772-1853), 288
Cockerell, H. A. L., and Edwin Green, *The British Insurance Business, 1547-1970*, 118 fn.
Cockerell, Sir Sydney Carlyle (1867-1962), 78
Cockerell Papers, 78
Cockfield, Zachariah, 156
Cockington Papers, 25
Cockran, Major, 216
Cockran, T., 226
Cockshutt, James, 248
Coddington, Mr., 47
Codman, Charles A., 164
Codrington, Edward (*fl.* 1764-1812?), 34
Codrington, Sir Edward (1770-1851), 121, 121 fn., 261
Codwise, Edward, 50
Cody, William Frederick (1846-1917), 137, 348
Coetmor Mss., 248
Coffee: Cultivation, 93; Trade, 89, 91, 185
Coffin, Joshua, 95
Coffin, Nathaniel, 258
Coghlan, John, 6
Cogswell, Joseph Green (1786-1871), 64
Coigny, Louise-Marthe de Conflans d'Armentières, Marquise de (d. 1832), 98
Coinage, 52, 107, 108, 226; Colonial period, 10, 31; *see also* Bimetallism; Currency; Dollars; Gold; Mints; Silver Question
Coit, Stanton (1857-1944), 96
Coke, Sir Edward (1552-1634), 186
Coke, Edward Thomas, 102; *A Subaltern's Furlough* (1833), 102
Coke, Sir John (1563-1644), 23, 24
Coke, S. T., 102
Coke, Thomas (1747-1814), 95, 117
Coke, Thomas William, 1st Earl of Leicester of Holkham (1754-1842), 41, 186-7, 188
Coke Mss., 102
Coke Papers (Sir John Coke, 1563-1644), 23-4
Coke Papers (Thomas Coke, 1747-1814), 117
Colborne, Sir John, 1st Baron Seaton (1778-1863), 102
Colchester, 2nd Baron, *see* Abbot, Charles (1798-1867)
Colchester, Customs records, 89, 93
Colchester Papers, 139
Colden, Cadwallader (1688-1776), 55, 149, 218, 223, 267, 313;

The Principles of Action in Matter, 313
Colden, David, 313
Cole, G. D. H., Collection, 209
Cole, George, 27
Colebrooke, Sir George, 10
Colebrooke, Sir James, 10
Colepeper, Thomas, 2nd Baron (1635-89), 49, 82, 213, 216
Coles, John, 102
Colfax, Schuyler (1823-85), 68
Colfox, Hannah Abbott, 28
Colfox, T. C., 28
Colfox Papers, 28
Colhoun, John, 329
Colhoun, William (*fl.* 1770), 317
Colhoun, William (*fl.* 1830), 329, 332
Collective security, 20th cent., 280, 281; *see also* Peace movement
College of Arms Library, 84
Collet, Sir Mark Wilks (1816-1905), 46
Collet Mss., 46
Collie, A., 131
Collie, Alexander, 232
Collier, Sir George (1738-95), 120-1, 233
Collier, John, 222
Collier, Sir Robert Porrett, 1st Baron Monkswell (1817-86), 60
Collingwood, Edward, 223-4
Collins, Captain, 225
Collins, Edward, 297
Collins, Hugh, 297
Collins, Michael, 345
Collins, Sarah, 304
Collins Papers, 297
Collinson, Peter (1694-1768), 149, 195, 323
Collinson, Sir Richard (1811-83), 100
Collyer, Robert (1823-1912), 176
Colman, Benjamin, 259
Colman, Henry (1785-1849), 216
Colman Collection, 187
Colombia, Republic of, 1820-6, 234; *see also* Relations with Colombia
Colonial Land and Emigration Commissioners, 137
Colonial Office, 15, 40, 122, 125, 141, 151; Papers, 128-9
Colonial records, 162
Colonies: pre-1700, 7-8, 10, 16-7, 21, 25, 26, 27, 37, 52, 57-8, 82, 97, 114, 140, 161, 189, 213, 229, 248, 260, 292, 339; 1700-66, 8, 10, 15, 31, 32, 40, 50, 52, 54, 79, 83, 119, 138, 140, 189, 193, 195, 203, 213, 216, 222, 224, 225, 229, 240, 249, 257, 262, 264, 267, 290, 292, 300-3 *passim*, 305, 317; 1766-76, 10, 24, 40, 44, 57, 79, 126, 182, 200, 213-6 *passim*, 218, 229, 231, 233, 240, 257, 261, 265, 266, 267, 276, 286, 291, 292, 294, 298, 301-3 *passim*, 305, 314, 319, 323-4, 329, 346, 354; *see also subdivision* Colonial period *under subjects, e.g.* Trade, Colonial period, *and under states*; *also* France: Colonies; Spain: Colonies
Colonization by Negroes, *see* Negroes, Colonization
Colorado: Agricultural colonies, 151; Agriculture, 306; Cowboys, 44; Finance, 98; Industry, 271; Land, 98, 230; Mining, 204, 308, 327; Ranching, 353
BLACK CANYON, 20; Burlington, 20; Denver, 20; Estes Park, 20; Little Rock, 353; Longmont, 20; Sanford, 327
Colorado Elevator Warehouse Co., 306
Colorado, University of, 177
Colpitts, Thomas, 150
Colquhoun, Sir James, 305
Colquhoun, Patrick (1745-1820), 80, 286, 287, 299
Colquhoun, William, 305
Colquhoun Collection of Business Records, 318
Colt, Samuel (1814-62), 308
Colton, Samuel H., 155
Columbia River, 125, 146, 148
Columbia University, 5, 78, 113, 177, 197, 200, 223 fn., 261, 281, 282; *see also* King's College, New York
Columbus, Christopher (1446 or 1451-1506), 186, 205
Colver, Frank, 236
Colver, Nathaniel, 215
Colville, Admiral, 264
Colvin, Sir Sidney (1845-1927), 238
Combe, Andrew (1797-1847), 307
Combe, George (1788-1858), 255; *Notes on the United States of North America*, 255 fn.
Combe, L. J., 236
Combe, Thomas, 233
Combe Papers, 255
Comegys, C., 175
Comerford, Maire, 346
Cometti, Elizabeth, *The American Journals of Lt. John Enys*, 20 fn.
Commerce (American ship), 183
Commerce, *see* Trade
Commercial Society [Barbados], 286
Committee for Promoting Arts, Williamsburg, Va., 149
Communications, 288; *see also* Postal service; Telegraph; Telephone
Communist Club, New York, 53
Communitarianism, 209, 314; *see also* Shakers
Compagnie de la Baye du Nord du Canada, 14
Compagnie des Indes, *see* Mississippi Company
Compagnie Royale Américaine, 15
Companies Registration Office, Board of Trade, 125
Companies Registration Office, Department of Trade: London, 94; Cardiff, 249
Compromise of 1850, 77, 156
Compton, Karl T., 282
Compton, William, 10th Earl of Northampton (1568?-1630), 192
Conamux (Conemaugh) River, 285
Conant, J. B. (b. 1893), 165
Concannon, Luke, Bishop, 225
Condliffe, J. B., 282
Confederate Cotton Loan, 67, 68, 72
Confederate Sequestration Act, 130
Confederate States, 49, 72, 104, 111, 166, 326; Agents, 18; Army, 104, 166, 263, 270, 331, Irish troops, 326, 344, 352, Prisoners, 232, Recruiting in Britain, 130, 136; British support and aid, 13, 58-61 *passim*, 71, 72, 73, 104, 136, 204, 232, 244, 247, 316, 326; Cotton trade, 124, 130, 232; European support, 69; French recognition, 60; Navy, 13, 17, 58-61 *passim*, 67, 68, 69, 71, 73, 130, 136, 141; *see also Alabama* (ship); Civil War; Cotton famine; *Nashville* (ship); *Shenandoah* (ship); Southern Independence Association; *Tuscarora* (ship)
Conference on the Education of the American Negroes and the African Natives (1937), 206
Congo, Colonization by Negroes, 165
Congo Free State, 165
Congo Reform Association, 165
Congregational Churches, 40, 74, 84-5, 103, 197, 224, 244, 246; Missions, 103
Congregational Memorial Hall Trust Ltd., 84-5, 224
Congregational Union of England and Wales, 103
Congress, 25, 57, 67, 68, 71, 77, 78, 95, 104, 173, 185, 191,

198, 201, 268, 282, 286, 289, 298, 327, 345; *see also* House of Representatives; Senate
Congress, Continental, 10, 12, 39, 44, 145, 214, 215, 260, 265, 294, 313, 324
Congreve, Charles, 235
Congreve, R., 74
Congreve, Mrs. R., 74
Congreves, Capt., 298
Conkey Family Papers, 5
Conkling, Roscoe (1829-88), 177
Connah's Quay, Customs records, 93
Connecticut, 1765-75, 10, 214, 215, 292
AGENTS, 301; Army, 203; Assembly, 12, 302; Boundaries with New York, 65, with Pennsylvania, 8; Courts, 82; Description, 326; Governors, 10, 12, 82, 83, 217, 223, 225; Immigrants, 47, 225, 235, 247; Industry, 98, 149, 235, 236; Land, 5, 194; Land grants, 263; Religious history, 8, 83, 105, 158, 159, 319; Trade, 310
FAIRFIELD, 8; Hartford, 225; New Bristol, 42; New Haven, 82, 310, Customs collectors, 87; New London, 5, Customs collectors, 87; Stonington, 20; Waterville, 235
See also NEW ENGLAND
Connegogee (Conococheague) Creek, 285
Connell, Charles, & Co., Mss., 269
Connemara, 1st Baron, *see* Bourke, Robert (1827-1902)
Connolly, John (*c.* 1743-1813), 214
Connor, Charles, 329
Conolly, John (1750-1825), 171
Conolly Papers, 352
Conover (?), Mrs., 75
Consag, Fernando, 352
Conservation of natural resources, *see* Natural resources
Conservative Party (Great Britain), 13
Conservator, 177
Constable, Robert, Vicount Dunbar (1651-1714), 42
Constable, Thomas, 42
Constable, Walter, 42
Constitution, 32, 95, 161, 168, 191, 199, 208, 216, 274, 280, 283, 313, 350; Amendments, 69, 167, 168, 278
Constitutions, State, 10, 32, 167, 277; *see also subdivision* Constitution *under states*
Consuls: in G.B., 6, 9, 19, 61, 62, 64, 131, 132, 226, 227, 245, 303; in Hamburg, 287
Consuls (British) and Consular reports, 33, 58, 60, 61, 63, 67, 81, 98, 102, 121, 124, 125, 129, 130, 131, 132, 184, 198, 200, 201, 223, 268, 286, 287, 288, 290, 351
Consuls, French, 57
Consumer affairs, 66
Consumer's Council, 66
Contracts for supplies, 10
Convents, 131
Conway, Mrs., 179
Conway, Alan, "Welsh Emigration to the U.S.," *Bulletin of the British Association for American Studies* (1959), 243
Conway, Henry Seymour (1721-95), 39, 218
Conway, Katrina (Lambard), 16
Conway, Lady (Martin), 161 fn.
Conway, Moncure Daniel (1832-1907), 33, 74, 75, 84, 176
Conway, William Martin, Baron Conway of Allington, 16
Conway, Customs records, 89
Conwell, Henry (*c.* 1745-1842), 171, 348
Conybeare, J. C., *et al.*, 110, 111
Coode, Peter, 10
Cook, A. M., *Lincolnshire Links with the U.S.A.*, 49 fn.
Cook, C., *Sources in British Political History, 1900-1951*, 157
Cook, Edward, 191
Cook, John, 117
Cook, Philip, 332
Cooke, Alfred Alastair (b. 1908), 178
Cooke, J. and J., 326
Cooke, Relph & Barnardeston, Messrs., 47
Cookson (Maldon) Mss., 191
Coolidge, Calvin (1872-1933), 75, 279
Cooper, Anthony Ashley, 1st Earl of Shaftesbury (1621-83), 36, 224
Cooper, Antony Ashley, 7th Earl of Shaftesbury (1801-85), 105
Cooper, D. S., 325-6
Cooper, Duff, 283
Cooper, James, 40
Cooper, James Fenimore (1789-1851), 98, 174, 182
Cooper, Myles, 256
Cooper, Theodore (1839-1919), 162
Cooper, Thomas (1759-1840), 167, 170, 183, 257, 304
Co-operation, 52, 53, 174, 206; *see also* Agriculture, Co-operative
Cooperation (Paris), 282
Co-operative Brotherhood Colony, 314
Co-operative News, 174
Co-operative Union Congress, 174
Co-operative Union Ltd., 173-4
Coote, Sir Eyre (1762-1823), 119
Coote, Richard, 1st Earl of Bellomont (1636-1701), 83, 119-20, 220
Coote Papers, 119
Cope, E. D., 66
Cope, Edmond Reilly, 36
Cope, Thomas Pym (1768-1854), 182
Cope, Sir Walter (d. 1614), 37
Cope's Tobacco Plant, 184
Copeland, T. W., ed., *The Correspondence of Edmund Burke*, 189 fn., 233 fn.; and M. S. Smith, *A Check List of the Correspondence of Edmund Burke*, 233 fn.
Copland Papers, 33
Copley, John Singleton (1737-1815), 17
Copley, John Singleton, 1st Baron Lyndhurst (1772-1863), 17, 168, 250
Copley, Mary, 250
Copley, Sophia, 250
Copper, 160, 226; Mining, 10, 20, 82, 124, 308
Coppinger, J. P., 105
Copyright, International, 14, 38, 40, 116, 118, 131, 169, 197, 200, 254; *see also* Patents; Trade marks
Copyright, U.S., 79
Copyright Office, 122, 137
Coram, Thomas (1668-1751), 83, 119
Corbet, James & Thomas, 309
Corbet, John, 346
Corbet, William, 353
Corbet Letters, 353
Corbett Collection, 227
Corbin, Gavin, 305
Cordage, 205
Cork trees, 151
Corn, *see* Grain
Corn, Indian, *see* Maize
Corn laws, 108
Cornbury, Viscount (*styled*, 1711-4), *see* Hyde, Edward, 3d Earl of

Clarendon (1661-1723)
Cornell, Peter, 5
Cornell University, 52, 278, 279, 314
Cornish, Hugh, 18
Cornubian, 20
Cornwall, England, 19-20; *see also* Immigrants from Cornwall
Cornwall County Record Office, 19-20
Cornwall Railroad, 347
Cornwallis, Charles, 1st Marquis and 2nd Earl (1738-1805), 24, 25, 48, 81, 120, 139, 143, 192, 218, 266, 268, 274, 275, 276, 287, 289, 323
Cornwallis, Sir William (1744-1819), 120
Cornwallis Papers, 120, 139
Cornwallis West Collection, 120
Corpach, Scotland, Merchants, 310
Corporation of Foreign Bondholders, Council of, 100
Corporation of London Records Office, 85-6
Correspondence of the Earl of Ancram and the Earl of Lothian, 276
Corrie & Co., 180
Corrie, Gladstone & Bradshaw, 180
Corruption (in politics), 164, 177, 198, 200, 207, 299; *see also* Lobbying
Corson, Hiram (1828-1911), 314
Cosby, Phillips, 218
Cosby, William (*c.* 1690-1736), 292
Cosgrave, William Thomas (1880-1965), 352
Cosnan, John, 284
Cost of living, 36, 111; *see also* Prices; Wages
Costa Rica, Relations with U.S., *see* Relations with Costa Rica
Costa Rica Railway, 230
Cotesworth, William, 191
Cottenham Common, Cambridgeshire, 13
Cottington, Francis, Baron (1578?-1652), 10
Cotton, John (1584-1652), 98, 187
Cotton, William, 27
Cotton famine (1861-4), 6, 13, 58, 59, 60, 69, 73, 130, 136, 141, 180
Cotton, Growing, 64, 150, 169, 274, 287, 330, 331; Processing, 125, 325; Trade, 13, 18, 19, 21, 46, 48, 52, 57, 71, 91, 108, 116, 117-8, 138, 160, 169, 173, 175, 181-5 *passim*, 187, 211, 232, 240, 271, 326, 332; *see also* Confederate States, Cotton trade
Cotton goods, Trade, 56, 63, 64, 108, 109, 175, 178, 179, 309, 310
Cotton wool, Trade, 107
Cottrell, Sir Stephen, 54, 288
Coues, Elliott, 74, 162
Coughton Court, Warwickshire, 224
Coulson, Thomas, 79
Coulter, Mr., 211
Coulton, G. G., 282
Council on Foreign Relations, 277, 278, 279; *Survey of American Foreign Relations*, 279
Couper, James Hamilton (1794-1866), 187
Coupland, R., 280; *The American Revolution and the British Empire*, 279
Court, W. H. B., *The Rise of the Midland Industries, 1600-1838*, 226 fn.
Court Estate, Llanllawer, 248
Courtney, Catherine (Potter), Lady, 164
Courts martial, 144, 144 fn.; Naval, 43, 108, 123
Coutts, Angela Georgina Burdett, 40
Coutts, James 309
Coutts, Thomas, 83
Coutts & Co., 86, 256
Covent Garden, 82
Coventry, Henry (1619-86), 230
Coventry, Thomas, 1st Baron (1578-1640), 19
Coventry, West Midlands, 228
Coventry City Record Office, 228; City Archives, 228
Covy, Michael, 304
Cowell, John W., 52, 104
Cowen, Joseph, 223
Cowen Collection, 223
Cowes, Isle of Wight, 90, 93
Cowie, L. W., *Henry Newman*, 152 fn.
Cowie, Roxburgh & Co., 235
Cowing, Howard, 271
Cowley, 1st Baron, *see* Wellesley, Henry (1773-1847)
Cowley, 1st Earl , *see* Wellesley, Henry Richard Charles (1804-84)
Cowley Papers, 134
Cowper, 1st Earl of, *see* Cowper, William (1665-1723); 3rd Earl of, *see* Clavering–Cowper, George Nassau (1738-89)
Cowper, William, 1st Earl Cowper (1665-1723), 40
Cowper, William (1731-1800), 51
Cox, John, 30
Cox, Thomas, 231
Cox and Watson, 294
Cox's Glue Works Ltd., 255
Coxe, Daniel, 286
Cracroft, Francis, 50
Cracroft, Robert Weston, 50
Cradock, Matthew (d. 1641), 194
Crafer, T., 124
Craig, Archibald Cumming, 273
Craig, George, 273
Craig, John, 306
Craig, Robert, 331
Craigie, R. L., 279
Cramahé, Hector Theophilus, 324
Crampton, Sir John Fiennes Twisleton (1805-86), 40, 77, 81, 105, 118, 125, 134, 184, 200, 201, 206, 353
Crampton, Sir Philip, 353
Crampton Correspondence, 353
Crane, Professor, 162
Crane, Edward Nicholas, 37
Crane, Joseph H., 245
Crane, Robert Newton (1848-1927), 39
Cranfield Papers, 45
Craven, Charles, 302
Crawford, Archibald, 313
Crawford, Fred, 332
Crawford, Hugh, 294
Crawford, John, 290
Crawford, Patrick, 304
Crawford, Thomas, 312
Crawford, William, 29; "In Steerage," 29
Crawford family, 329
Crawfurd, Andro, 318
Crawley, George, 179
Crawshaw, Titus, 166
Crawshaw, William, 166
Crawshay, Richard (1739-1810), 248
Crawshay family, 247
Creighton, J. E., 315
Creighton, Robert, 178

Creole (ship), 63, 67
Cresson, Caleb, 182
Cresson, Elliott, 234
Cresswell Ranche and Cattle Co. Ltd., 308
Creswell, W., 183
Crevet, John, 149
Crewdson, Thomas, 22
Crewe, Marquess of, *see* Crewe–Milnes, Robert Offley Ashburton, 2nd Baron Houghton (1858-1945)
Crewe–Milnes, Robert Offley Ashburton, 2nd Baron Houghton (1858-1945), 199
Crichton, A. W., 36
Crichton, Patrick, 6th Earl of Dumfries (1726-1803), 265
Crichton–Maitland of Elderslie Mss., 263
Crick, B., and M. Alman, *Guide to Manuscripts Relating to America in Great Britain and Ireland*, xxi-xxv
Crick, W. F., and J. E. Wadsworth, *A Hundred Years of Joint Stock Banking* (1936), 117 fn.
Cricket, 117
Crime, 131, 196, 295, Colonial period, 284; *see also* Capital punishment; Prisons; Probation system; Transportation of criminals; *and subdivision* Crime *under states*
Crimean War, 1853-6, American opinion, 201, 211, 216, 222, 244; Recruiting in U.S., 65, 73, 81, 184, 201
Cripps, Sir Stafford (1889-1952), 128
Cripps Papers, 45
Critical Quarterly, 178
Crittenden, John Jordan (1787-1863), 325
Crockat, James, 263
Croft, John, 184
Croghan, George (d. 1782), 116, 214, 258
Croker, Richard, 345
Croly, Herbert David (1869-1930), 197
Croly, Jennie Cunningham, 74
Cromartie, Earl of, Mss., 260
Crombie, J. & J., Ltd., 253
Crombleholme Accumulation, 47
Cronin, P. P. H., 345
Cronyn, Hume, 278
Crook, George, 348
Crosbie, James, 232
Crosby, Joseph, 314
Crosby, Joshua, 275
Crosby Ravensworth Mss., 22
Crosfield, J. D., "Richard Smith and his Journal," *J. F. H. S.* (1916 and 1917), 156 fn.
Crosfield, Joseph (1821-79), 156
Crosfield Mss., 154
Crosley, George, 348
Cross, James, 263
Crouse, Mrs. L. S. K., 236
Crowther, Benjamin, 116, 117, 239
Crowther, David, 116, 117, 239
Crowther, Geoffrey, 280, 281
Crowther, George (brother of Mrs. Ann Barrett), 117
Crowther, George (son of Mrs. Ann Barrett), 117
Crowther, George, & Co., 116
Crowther, Thomas, 117
Crowther & Porrit, 117
Crowther family, 116-7, 239
Croydon Parish, Cambridgeshire, 14
Cruden, John, 139
Cruger, Henry (1739-1827), 215
Cruger, John Harris (1738-1807), 215, 233
Cruickshank, James, 314
Cruikshank, Capt., 302
Crumbleholme, George, 117
Crump, W. B., ed., *The Leeds Woollen Industry, 1780-1820*, 239
Cuba: 1810-99, 62, 131, 173, 201; Insurrection, 1849-51, 77, 184; Insurrection, 1868-78, 59, 60, 70, 131; Revolution, 1895-8, 38, 85, 131, 142; *see also* Spanish-American War, 1898
CUSTOMS ADMINISTRATION, 60; Relations with G.B., 200, 207, 257; Slavery, 60; Sugar, 38; *see also* Relations with Cuba; Trade with Cuba
HAVANA, 60, 62, 257, Consular reports (British), 130, Description, 32, 325; Santiago de Cuba, Consular reports (British), 130
Cubah, 50
Cuffe, Paul (1759-1817), 51
Culling, E. B., 164
Culpeper or Culpepper, *see* Colepeper
Culpeper family, 45
Culpin, Edw., 9
Cumberland, Duke of, *see* Henry Frederick (1745-90)
Cumberland (ship), 130
Cumbria, England, 21-3
Cumbria County Library, 22-3
Cumbria Record Office, Carlisle, 21
Cumbria Record Office, Kendal, 22
Cuming, Mr., 303
Cuming, Sir Alexander (d. early 18th cent.), 290
Cuming, Sir Alexander (1690?-1775), 61, 62
Cuming, George, 331
Cuming, Helen, 290
Cuming, Mary, 330
Cuming, Robert, 290
Cummersdale Print Works, 21-2
Cumming, A. P., 255
Cumming, J., 312, 313
Cumming, Thomas, 42
Cummington Press, 177
Cunard, Sir Samuel (1787-1865), 124
Cunard Steam-Ship Co. Ltd., 96; Archives, 185
Cuninghame, William, 304
Cuninghame, William, & Co., 255, 304
Cunliffe, John, 47
Cunliffe, M. F., "Notes on the Dorsey–Stanley Correspondence (1871-1873)," *Bulletin of the John Rylands Library* (1954), 177 fn.
Cunliffe–Lister Collection, 237
Cunliffe–Owen, Charles (d. 1841), 39
Cunliffe–Owen, Frederick, 277
Cunningham, W., "Common Rights at Cottenham and Stretham in Cambridgeshire," in Royal Historical Society, *Camden Miscellany*, vol. xii, 13 fn.
Cunningham Graham Muniments, 274
Cunningham of Thorntoun Muniments, 274
Currell, Kilshaw & Co., 22
Currency, 62, 63, 68, 112, 139, 142, 207, 216; Colonial period, 7, 141, 222-3, 249, 303; *see also* Bimetallism; Bullion; Coinage; Gold; "Greenbacks"; Silver Question
Currie, Sir Arthur William (1875-1933), 278
Currie, Bertram Wodehouse (1827-96), 172
Currie, James (1756-1805), 170, 181, 182
Currie, W. W., ed., *Memoir of . . . James Currie*, 182 fn.
Currie & Co., 172
Currie Papers, 182

Curry, Louis Simon, 36
Curtis, George William, 173, 347
Curtis, Lionel, 276, 277, 278, 279, 280, 282
Curtis, Timothy Abraham, 104
Curtis Family Papers, 5
Curwen of Workington Hall Records, 21
Curwin family, 22
Curzon, Mr., 303
Curzon, George Nathaniel, 1st Marquess (1859-1925), 38, 135
Curzon Mss., 204
Cushenden, Baron, *see* McNeill, Ronald John (1861-1934)
Cushing, Luther Stearns (1803-56), 72; *Manual of Parliamentary Practice*, 72
Cushing, Thomas (1725-88), 149, 233
Cussans, James Edwin, 42
Custer, George Armstrong (1839-76), 347
Custis, John, 346
Custis, John Parke, 203
Custom House, Library Services, Museum and Records Unit, 86-94; 308
Customs administration, Colonial period, 55-6 *passim*, 86-94 *passim*, 160, 191, 195, 196, 258, 266, 310, 311; *see also as subdivision under states, cities, etc.*
Customs, Board of, 109, 303; Scottish, 308
Customs duties, 35, 56, 63, 106-9 *passim*, 111, 125, 131, 138, 183, 244, 317, 325; Colonial period, 45, 55, 159-60, 232, 301, 302; *see also* Tariff; Tobacco duties
Customs officers in Wales, 21
Cutler, John, 27, 28
Cutler, Timothy (1684-1765), 85, 151
Cutler–Rackett–Caillouel Papers, 27-8
Cutlery, Trade, 161, 234, 235, 236
Cutting, John Brown, 80
Cuyler, Lt. Col., 266
Cuyler, Theodore Ledyard (1822-1909), 174
Cwmbran, Gwent, 248
Cwrtmawr Mss., 245
Cyfartha Papers, 247
Cymmrodorion Society, London, 243, 247
Czechoslovakia, Relations with U.S., *see* Relations with Czechoslovakia

D

Dabney, Richard Heath, 278
Daccarette, Mme. Françoise, 41
Dafoe, J. W., 280
Daily Express, 112
Daily Journal (Edinburgh?), 284
Daily News, 72
Dains, James R., 288
Dakota Territory, Tin mining, 20
FORT LINCOLN, 348
Dakota, North, *see* North Dakota
Dalcho, Frederick (1770-1836), 159
Dale, G. E., 113
Dale, Sir Thomas (d. 1619), 48
Dalhousie, 9th Earl of, *see* Ramsay, George (1770-1838); 11th Earl of, *see* Maule, Fox (1801-74)
Dalhousie, Lady, *see* Ramsay, Elizabeth (Glen) (d. 1807)
Dalhousie Muniments, 284-6
Dallas, G., *System of Stiles as now Practicable within the Kingdom of Scotland*, 308 fn.
Dallas, George Mifflin (1792-1864), 129, 146, 196, 201
Dalling and Bulwer, Baron, *see* Bulwer, William Henry Lytton Earle, *better known as* Sir Henry Bulwer (1801-72)
Dalquharran Muniments, 275
Dalrymple (or Murray), Elizabeth, Lady Murraywhat (*fl.* 1750-65), 299, 300
Dalrymple, Sir Hew (1690-1755), 290, 299
Dalrymple, John, 2nd Earl of Stair (1673-1747), 291
Dalrymple, John, 5th Earl of Stair (1720-89), 261, 265
Dalrymple, Sir John (1726-1810), 212
Dalrymple, John (*fl.* 1747-9), 264, 290
Dalrymple, William, 261, 265, 287
Dalton, Hugh (1887-1962), 166
Dalton, Timothy, 219
Daly, Mary, 329
Daly, Michael, 329
Daly, Walter, 329
Daly, Walter, Jr., 329
Dalyell, I. A., 274
Dalzel, A., 314
Dalzell, James, 329
Dalzell, John, 329
Dalzell, Matthew, 329
Damask, Trade, 327
Dampier, John, 28
Dampier, T[homas] (*fl.* 1776), 39
Dampier, Thomas (*fl.* 1785-6), 28
Dampier Papers, 28
Dana, James Dwight (1813-95), 66, 147
Dana, Richard Henry (1815-82), 170, 198, 236
Danby, 1st Earl of, *see* Osborne, Sir Thomas (1631-1712)
Danby, Christopher, 42
Danby, Sir Thomas, 42
Danford, J., 76
Daniel, Richard, 189
Daniels, G. W., "The Early Records of a Great Manchester Cotton-Spinning Firm," *Economic Journal* (1915), 175 fn.; "American Cotton Trade with Liverpool under the Embargo and Non-Intercourse Acts," *American Historical Review* (1916)," 175 fn.
Dante, 204
Darby, John, 285
Darcy, A.M., 347
Darcy, Mary, 347
D'Arcy, Peter, 82
D'Arcy, Robert, 4th Earl of Holderness (1718-78), 61, 82, 266
Darien Scheme, 160, 259, 317; Company, 160
Daring (ship), 269
Darlington, Durham, 29
Darnell family, 32
Darroch, Duncan (of Gourock, Scotland), 260
Darroch, Duncan (of North Carolina), 260
Darroch of Gourock Mss., 260
Dartmoor Prison, 27
Dartmouth, Earl of, 213 fn.
Dartmouth, 1st Earl of, *see* Legge, William (1672-1750); 2nd Earl of, *see* Legge, William (1731-1801); 3rd Earl of, *see* Legge, George (1755-1810)
Dartmouth, 1st Baron, *see* Legge, George (1648-91)
Dartmouth, Devonshire: Customs records, 89, 91, 93; Newfoundland fishing trade, 27
Dartmouth (ship), 99

Dartmouth College, 213, 216, 278, 279, 290
Darwin, Charles Robert (1809-82), 15, 162, 263
Darwin Papers: Handlist, 15 fn.
Dashwood, Sir Francis, Baron Le Despencer (1708-81), 200
Dashwood (Bucks.) Mss., 200
Dashwood Papers, 200
Daulby, William, 183
Dauphin and Susquehanna Railroad, 347
Daux, J.A., 149
Davenant, Sir William (1606-68), 17
Davenport, James (1716-57), 85
Davenport, William, & Co., 213
Davers, Sir Robert, 249
Davey, Thomas, 20
David, Major, 131
David, William, 244
David Lee Willis, 39
Davids, James, *alias* John Dixwell (d. 1690), 82
Davidson, Hugh, 141
Davidson, John (*fl.* 1770), 299
Davidson, John (*fl.* 1778), 188
Davidson, Randall Thomas, Archbishop of Canterbury (1848-1930), 115
Davidson, William Lee (1746-81), 139
Davidson and Garden Records, 253-4
Davies, Lt.-Col., 150
Davies, David (*fl.* 1879-1901), 246, 247
Davies, David, 1st Baron (1880-1944), 282
Davies, David Stephen (1841-98), 243, 244
Davies, J. Conway, ed., *Catalogue of MSS in the Library . . . . of the Inner Temple*, 114 fn.
Davies, J. J., 244
Davies, J. S., 246
Davies, James, 247
Davies, Mrs. John, Deposit, 246
Davies, Joseph T., 283
Davies, K. G., ed., *Documents of the American Revolution, 1770-1783*, 128
Davies, Morris, 247
Davies, Reginald, 315
Davies, Robert (*fl.* 1863), 247
Davies, William, 245
Davis, Mr., 103
Davis, Harry H., 245
Davis, Jefferson (1808-89), 64, 68, 71, 204
Davis, John W., 197
Davis, M. W., 229
Davis, Morgan, 244
Davis, Norman H., 278, 279, 280
Davis, P. W., *Education of Females*, 84
Davis, U. D., 208
Davis, W. M., 147
Davis, Brown & Co., 234
Davison, J., 325
Davison, Thomas, 331
Davison, Newman & Co., 99
Davy Family Correspondence, 22
Dawes, Charles G. (1865-1951), 279
Dawson, A. C., 325
Dawson, George, 119
Dawson, (George) Geoffrey (1874-1944), 278, 281, 282
Dawson, John, 287
Dawson, Moses, 329
Dawson, Robert Peel, 325
Dawson, W. R., *The Huxley Papers* (1946), 162
Dawson Papers, 157
Dayton, Elias, 260
Dayton, William Lewis, 204
De Berdt, D., & Co., 175
de Bernière, A., 329
de Bernière, J., 329
De Forest Radio Co., 170
de Fronsac, Forsyth, 275
de Grey, Earl (*known as*), *see* Robinson, George Frederick Samuel, 1st Marquess of Ripon (1827-1909)
de Grey, Thomas, 41
De Kay, J. E., 258
de La Penja, Joseph, 146
De La Ramée, Marie Louise (1839-1908), 65
De La Warr, 3rd Baron, *see* West, Thomas (1577-1618)
De La Warr Papers, 45
de Lacy, Larry, 346
De Lancey, James (1703-60), 50, 285
De Lancey, James (1732-1800), 233
De Lancey, Oliver (1749-1822), 222, 233
De Lancey, Oliver, Jr., 222
De Lancey, Stephen, 222
de Lotbinière, C., 45
de Morgan, Augustus (1806-71), 161
de Rigaud, Pierre François, Marquis de Vaudreuil, 45
De Sausmarez Deposit, 339
De Valera, Eamon (1882-1975), 345, 346, 352
de Vere, Aubrey, 353; Papers, 353
De Wesselow, *see* Simpkinson, Francis Guillemard, 15
Deal: Customs records, 89, 93; Borough records, 45
Dean, ——, [Deane, Silas?], 227
Deane, Anne, 353
Deane, Silas (1737-89), 267
Deans, J. W. & T., 310
Dearsen, J. S., "J. Howard Whitehouse and Anglo-American Understanding," *Bulletin of the B. A. A. S.* (1958), 229
Deaville, John (1779-1857), 23
Deaville, Robert (1785-1858), 23
Deaville Papers, 23, 23 fn.
Debts, Public, 95; *see also* American Debt Settlement; Confederate Cotton Loan; Southern states: Debts; *and relevant categories under* World War I
Debts to British merchants, 9, 51, 52, 56, 80, 81, 82, 86, 99, 106, 107, 172, 182, 200, 263, 264, 294, 310, 325; *see also* Claims of British subjects; Jay's Treaty, 1794
Declaration of Independence, 270, 324
Deer skins, *see* Hides and skins
Defence, 112, Colonial period, 10, 11, 292, 299-303 *passim*; *see also* Army
Defoe, Daniel (1661?-1731), 83
Delane, John Thadeus (1817-79), 59
Delane Papers, 157
Delany, Daniel, 98
Delany, Lloyd, 98
Delaplaine, Joseph, 183
Delaval, J. H., 191
Delaval (Waterford) Mss., 191
Delaware: 17th century, 10; 18th century, 55
BOUNDARY WITH NEW JERSEY, 40; Immigrants, 97, 331; Land, 175; Merchants, 236; Religious history, 117
GEORGETOWN, 331

Delaware Bay, 62, 302
Delaware River, 302
Delbridge, John, 26
Delemare, J., 149
Delph, Greater Manchester, 173
Demerara, Guiana, Trade, 161
Deming, Oliver, 319
Democracy, 105, 198, 199, 208, 244, 277, 281, 283, 294
Democratic Club, New York, 204
Democratic Party, 59, 61, 62, 161, 164, 279; *see also* Elections
Democratic–Republican Party, 95, 306; Bucktail faction, 286
Denbigh, Earl of, 224-5
Denbigh, 6th Earl of, *see* Feilding, Basil (1719-1800)
Denbigh Papers, 224-5
Denham, J. D., 9
Denison, George Taylor (1839-1925), 37
Denison, John, 329
Denison, Samuel, 329
Denison, William, 70
Denman, Thomas, 1st Baron (1779-1854), 169
Denmark, Relations with U.S., *see* Relations with Denmark
Dennett, Mrs. Mary Ware, 79
Denny, William (1709-65), 160, 284, 285
Denny, William, & Bros., 318
Dent, Abraham, 22
Dent, Robert, 175
Denton, William (1605-91), 11
Denver and Rio Grande Railway, 230
Department of Trade, Companies Registration Office: London, 94; Cardiff, 249
Deptford (ship), 239
Derby, 7th Earl of, *see* Stanley, James (1607-51); 14th Earl of, *see* Stanley, Edward George Geoffrey Smith (1799-1869); 15th Earl of, *see* Stanley, Edward Henry (1826-93) *styled* Lord Stanley 1851-69; 16th Earl of, *see* Stanley, Frederick Arthur (1841-1908)
Derby, Derbyshire, 23
Derby Central Library, 23
Derbyshire, England, 23-4; *see also* Business records: Derbyshire
Derbyshire County Record Office, 23
Desch, Cecil Henry (1874-1958), 236-7
Description (and travel), *see* Travel diaries; *and subdivision* Description *under place names*
Deserters, Military and naval, 35, 38, 131, 144, 145, 288
Deskford, Lord, 304
Despatch (ship), 93
Detring, Gustav, 205
D'Evereux, Gen., 187
Devine, T. M., *The Tobacco Lords*, 304 fn.
Devizes, Wiltshire, 229
Devon Record Office, 24-5
Devonshire, Duke of, 23; 4th Duke of, *see* Cavendish, William (1720-64)
Devonshire, England, 24-7; *see also* Immigrants from Devonshire
Devonshire Association, 26
Devonshire Papers, 23
Devoy, John (1842-1928), 344, 345, 353
Devoy Papers, 344-5
Devyr, Thomas A., 223
Dewey, Davis Rich (1858-1942), 164
Dewey, Orville, 176
Diaries, *see* Travel diaries
Dicey, Albert Venn, 318
Dick, Alexander, 261
Dick, Charles, 149, 232
Dick, James (*fl.* 1920), 315
Dick, John (*fl.* 1835-6), 315
Dick, Robert (*fl.* 1835-6), 315
Dick–Cunyngham of Prestonfield Mss., 261
Dickens, Charles (1812-70), 14, 40, 118, 238; *American Notes*, 14, 238
Dickenson, Capt., 122
Dickins, Asbury, 9
Dickinson, Anna Elizabeth (1842-1932), 96
Dickinson, Caleb, 7, 211, 212
Dickinson, H. W., *Robert Fulton*, 226 fn.
Dickinson, John (1732-1808), 267
Dickinson, Thomas, 211
Dickinson, William (1771-1837), 211, 212
Dickinson, Prankard and, Papers, 211-2
Dickson, Arthur, 239
Dickson, James, 292
Dickson, Robert, 261, 288
Dickson, Thomas, 261, 288
Dickson, William (*fl.* 1783), 295
Dickson, William (*fl.* 1813), 261, 288
Dickson of Monybuie Mss., 261
Dictionary of American Biography, 281
"Dictionary of Welsh-American Biography," 248
Didlake, James, 273
Didlake, Mary, 273
Digby, Henry, 7th Baron and 1st Earl (1731-93), 29
Digby, Sir John, 1st Earl of Bristol (1580-1653), 10, 29
Digby, M., *Horace Plunkett*, 209
Digby, S. Wingfield, Esq., 29
Digby, W., 37
Digby Papers, 29
Digges, Thomas, 266
Diligence (ship), 12
Dilke, Sir Charles Wentworth (1843-1911), 70
Dilke Papers, 53, 70
Dillon, Clarence, 281, 282
Dillon, George, 347
Dillon, Harold, 209
Dillon, John (1851-1927), 345, 353; Papers, 353
Dillon, John Blake, 353; Papers, 353
Dillon, Luke, 345
Dillon, Maria (*née* O'Brien), 347
Dillon, William, 353
Dillon Collection, 209
Dillwyn, William (1743-1824), 51, 246
Dillwyn Diaries and Papers, 246
Dimsdale Mss., 155
Diplomacy, *see* Relations with (*country*) *and names of individual ministers and ambassadors*
Diplomatic service, 207-8; Immunities, 64; *see also* Consuls; *and names of individual ambassadors, ministers and consuls*
Direct United States Cable Co., Ltd., 111, 125
Disarmament, Great Lakes, 67, 130, 198, 201
Disarmament, Moral, 280
Disarmament, Naval, 127, 277, 278, 279, 280; *see also* London Naval Conferences, 1930, 1935-6; Naval Disarmament Conference; Washington Armament Conference, 1921-2
Discharged Prisoners Aid Society, 61
Discontent, 314
Disney, D. T., 245
Disney Papers, 32

Disputed Territory Fund, 67
Disraeli, Benjamin, 1st Earl of Beaconsfield (1804-81), 13
Dissenters, 99, 312; *see also* Anabaptists; Baptists; Congregational Churches; Friends; Methodist Church; Presbyterian Church
Distilling, 308
Dixon, C. H., 113
Dixon, Jonathan, 166
Dixon, Thos., & Co., 22
Dixwell, John, *alias, see* Davids, James (d. 1690)
Dobbs, Arthur (1689-1765), 285, 289, 312, 317, 323
Dobbs Papers, 323
Dobrée, Bonamy, 52
Dobrée Mss., 51
Docton Accumulation, 47
Dr. Bray's Associates, 159
Dr. Williams's Library, 94-6; 103
Doddridge, Philip (1702-51), 103
Dodds, Thomas, 169
Dodge, John, 282
Dodge, Robert, 168
Dodson, Capt., 97
Dodson, John Charles, 3rd Baron Monk Bretton (b. 1924), 202
Dodson, John George, 1st Baron Monk Bretton (1825-97), 202
Dodson, Owen, 221
Dolby, George (d. 1900), 238
Dolgellau, Gwynedd, 248
Dollars, 107, 108, 142
Dolly (American frigate), 9
Dominica: Governors, 255; Land, 324; Trade, 265
ROSEAU, Customs collectors, 87
Dominican Republic, 24, 216, 287, 298; Relations with Haiti, 77; Sugar, 109; *see also* Immigrants from Santo Domingo; Relations with Dominican Republic; Relations with Santo Domingo
SAMANÁ BAY, 201
Dommett Mss., 228
Don Brothers, Buist & Co., 263
Donaghue, T. J., 171
Donald, Mr., 199
Donald, James, 262
Donaldson, Mr., 95
Donaldson, Sir James (1831-1915), 307
Donaldson, John (*fl.* 1757-8), 284, 290
Donaldson, John (*fl.* 1779), 275
Donaldson, John (*fl.* 1815), 314
Donaldson & Stotts, 181
Doncaster, South Yorkshire, 232
Doncaster Metropolitan Borough Council Archives Service, 232
Dongan, Thomas (1634-1715), 213
Donnan, E., and L. F. Stock, eds., "An historian's world . . . from the correspondence of John Franklin Jameson," *Memoirs of the American Philosophical Society* (1956), 197 fn.
Donnan, John, 331
Donnelly, P., 348
Donoghue, J. J. W., 345
Donoughmore, Earl of, 354
Donoughmore Papers, 354
Dorcas (slave), 295
Dorchester, 1st Viscount, *see* Carleton, Sir Dudley (1573-1632)
Dorchester, 1st Baron, *see* Carleton, Sir Guy (1724-1808)
Dorchester, Dorset, 27-9
Dorchester Borough Records, 27
Doremus family, 5
Dormer, _____, 259
Dornan, Elizabeth, 329
Dorset, 3rd Duke of, *see* Sackville, John Frederick (1745-99)
Dorset, England, 27-9
Dorset Record Office, 27-9
Dorsey, Sarah Anne (Ellis), Mrs. Samuel W. Dorsey (1829-79), 177
Dossie, Robert, 150
Douch, H. L., 20
Douglas, Andrew, 292
Douglas, Archibald, 268
Douglas, Charles, 3rd Duke of Queensberry (1698-1778), 268
Douglas, Sir Charles (d. 1789), 313
Douglas, Charles E., 272
Douglas, David (1798-1834), 145, 147, 148, 267; *Journal*, 147 fn.
Douglas, George, 297
Douglas, Sir Howard (1776-1861), 25, 84, 207, 286
Douglas, James, 4th Duke of Hamilton (1658-1712), 194, 262, 263
Douglas, James, 14th Earl of Morton (1703-68), 292
Douglas, John, 268
Douglas, Lewis, 281
Douglas, Samuel, 297
Douglas, Stephen Arnold (1813-61), 201
Douglas, Thomas, 5th Earl of Selkirk (1771-1820), 313
Douglas, William, 287
Douglas, Isle of Man, 335
Douglas and Shaw, 297
Douglas–Home Muniments, 268
Douglass, Mr., 290
Douglass, Frederick (1817?-1895), 176
Dove, John, 277, 278
Dover, Younghusband & Co., 22
Dover, Kent, Customs records, 89, 90, 93, 94
Dow, Neal (1804-97), 68, 176, 235
Dowden, Edward (1842-1913), 353
Dowden, John (1840-1910), 255
Dowden Papers, 255
Dowdeswell, Thomas, 233
Dowlais Iron Co., 249-50
Downing, Emanuel, 24
Downs, William, 43
Downshire, Marquess of, 10 fn.
Downshire, 1st Marquis of, *see* Hill, Wills, 1st Earl of Hillsborough (1718-93)
Downshire Papers, 10
Downshire Papers (Hillsborough Collection), 324
Downton, James, 98
Downton, John (d. 1841), 98
Downton, William, 98
Downton Family Papers, 98
Doyle, Sub-Inspector, 351
Doyle, Sir Charles Hastings (1805-83), 196
Doyle (*later* North), John, 196 fn.
Doyle, John Andrew (1844-1907), 206; "Calendar of Vaughan Papers," 206; *English Colonies in America*, 206 fn.; *The English in America*, 206; ed., "Papers of Sir Charles R. Vaughan," *American Historical Review* (1901-2), 206 fn.
Doyle, P., 81
Doyle, Percy William (1806-88), 207
Drake, Sir Francis (1540?-1596), 37
Drake, Francis, 80
Drake, Thomas E., *Patterns of Influence in Anglo-American Quakerism*, 152

Drake, William, 13
Drakeford Naval Papers, 216
Draper, Edith, 184
Draper, John William (1811-82), 148
Draper, William, 57
Drayton, Glen, 284
Drayton, John, 284
Drayton, William Henry (1742-79), 266, 284
Drayton family, 284
Dreiser, Theodore (1871-1945), 205
Drennan, Thomas, 317
Drennan–Bruce Letters, 330
Drinkwater, John (1882-1937), 238; *Abraham Lincoln*, 246
Droop, H. R., 202
Dropmore Papers, 79-81
Drought, 41
Drugs, 203; Trade, 50-1, 301; *see also* Sarsaparilla
Drummond, Edward (1792-1843), 63
Drummond, Henry (d. 1794), 257
Drummond, Henry (1851-97), 255
Drummond, James, 4th Earl of Perth (1648-1716), 274
Drummond, James, *de jure* 10th Earl of Perth (1707-81), 261, 295, 299
Drummond, James, 11th Earl of Perth (1744-1800), 261
Drummond, John, 1st Earl and titular Duke of Melfort (1649-1714), 292
Drummond, John, 274
Drummond, Lord Thomas (*fl.* 1768-80), 292-3, 295
Drummond, Thomas (?1790-1835), 145
Drummond, William (*fl.* 1736), 272
Drummond, William (*fl.* 1813), 273
Drummond Castle Muniments, 292-3
Drummond Papers, 255
Drury–Lowe Mss., 193
Drych, Y, 244
du Cane, Peter, 32
du Cane Papers, 32
Du Ponceau, Pierre Étienne (1760-1844), 113, 161; *An Historical Review of the . . . Silk Culture . . .*, 161
Du Pré, Josias, 25
Duane, James (1733-97), 149
Dublin, 343-53; Merchants, 62
Dublin Magazine, 353
Dubois, John (1764-1842), 171
DuBois, William Edward Burghardt (1868-1963), 206
Dubose, Robert, *see* Le Brette, Robert
Dubs & Co., 318
Ducachet, Henry William, 315
Ducarel, Andrew Coltee (1713-85), 203
Dudley, 1st Earl of, *see* Ward, John William (1781-1833)
Dudley, Joseph (1647-1720), 40
Dudley, Sir Matthew, 83
Dudley, Robert, 1st Earl of Leicester (1532?-1588), 16
Duer, William (1747-99), 119
Duff, Capt., 305
Duff, David, 305
Duff, James, 2nd Earl of Fife (1729-1809), 253
Duff, James (*fl.* 1880), 306
Duff, Lewis, 253
Duff, Mary, 297
Duff, Rosanna, 327
Duff, Walter, 327
Duff, William, 297
Duff family, 253
Duff of Braco Muniments, 253
Duff of Fetteresso Muniments, 290
Duffin, Adam, 325
Duffy, John, 344
Duggan, Mark, 330
Duggan, Stephen, 280
Dulles, Allen W., 278
Dulles, John Foster (1888-1959), 282
Dumbell, S., "The Cotton Market in 1799," *Economic History* (1926), 185 fn.
Dumfries, 6th Earl of, *see* Crichton, Patrick (1726-1803)
Dumfries and Galloway, Scotland, 253; Merchants, 309, 310
Dunbar, General?, 300
Dunbar, Viscount, *see* Constable, Robert (1651-1714)
Dunbar, David, 120
Dunbar, J. T., Esq., Mss., 262
Dunbar, James, 307
Dunbar, John (*fl.* 1716-20), 307
Dunbar, John (*fl.* 1748), 298
[Dunbar?], Robert, 298
Dunbar, Simon, 298
Dunbar, Thomas, 261
Dunbar of Northfield Mss., 261
Dunbarton Oaks Conference, 1944, 165
Duncan, Commissioner, 119
Duncan, Alexander, 299
Duncan, Henry, 122
Duncan, Mrs. Isabel, 254; Papers, 254
Duncan, James, 309
Duncan, Patrick, 280
Duncan, William, 254
Duncan–Whyte, Mrs., 229
Dundas, A., 231
Dundas, Alexander, 275
Dundas, Sir David (1735-1820), 257
Dundas, David, 276
Dundas, David, wife of, 276
Dundas, Francis (d. 1824), 313
Dundas, George (*fl.* 1783-9), 276
Dundas, George (*fl.* 1858-9), 40
Dundas, George, wife of, 276
Dundas, Henry, 1st Viscount Melville (1742-1811), 80, 81, 101, 257, 286, 286 fn., 287, 288, 303, 314
Dundas, James, 276
Dundas, Ralph, 276
Dundas, Robert (1758-1819), 313
Dundas, Robert Saunders, 2nd Viscount Melville (1771-1851), 83, 121, 257, 286 fn., 288
Dundas, Sir Thomas, 231
Dundas, Thomas, 231
Dundas, William, 276
Dundas of Ochtertyre Muniments, 276
Dundee, Earl of, Mss., 267
Dundee, Tayside, 318-9; Manufacturers, 310; Merchants, 309, 310
Dundee American Real Property Co. Ltd., 308
Dundee Investment Co. Ltd., 308
Dundee Land Investment Co. Ltd., 308
Dundee Mortgage and Trust Investment Co. Ltd., 308
Dundee University Library, 318-9
Dundonald, Earl of, 303 fn.
Dundonald, 9th Earl of, *see* Cochrane, Archibald, *styled* Lord

Cochrane (1749-1831); 10th Earl of, *see* Cochrane, Thomas (1775-1860)
Dundonald Muniments, 303-4
Dungallon, ——, 293
Dunglass, Lord Cospatric, 268
Dunk, George Montagu, 2nd Earl of Halifax (1716-71), 31, 265
Dunlap, John (1747-1812), 324
Dunlop, Commodore, 211
Dunlop, Judge, 72
Dunlop, Alexander, 270
Dunlop, Alexander Graham (d. 1892), 60, 255
Dunlop, Archibald, 316
Dunlop, Colin, & Sons, 273
Dunlop, Dr. J. C. H., Mss., 270
Dunlop, James (*fl.* late 18th cent.), 273
Dunlop, James (*fl.* 1773-1815), 273
Dunlop, James (*fl.* early 19th cent.), 270
Dunlop, John (d. 1684), 316
Dunlop, John (1755-1820), 287
Dunlop, John (*fl.* 1820-60), 270, 271
Dunlop, John (*fl.* 19th cent.), 255
Dunlop, William (*fl.* 1686-9), 255, 273, 275
Dunlop family, 271
Dunlop of Doonside Mss., 264
Dunlop Papers, 255
Dunlops of Garnkirk and Tollcross, 316
Dunmore, 4th Earl of, *see* Murray, John (1732-1809)
Dunmore, Earl of, Mss., 268
Dunmore Papers, 268
Dunwich, Customs records, 89
Dupont & McNichol, 235
Dupplin, Lord, *see* Hay, Thomas, Viscount Dupplin and 9th Earl of Kinnoull (1710-87)
Dupuy, ——, 315
Durand, Sir Henry Mortimer (1850-1924), 30, 129, 167; Papers, 167
Durben, Captain, 317
Durham, 1st Earl of, *see* Lambton, John George (1792-1840)
Durham, Col., 351
Durham, David, 312
Durham, England, 29-30; City of, 29-30
Durham Company, 273
Durham County Library, 29
Durham County Record Office, 29
Durham Miners' Association, 29
Durham University, Department of Palaeography and Diplomatic, 29-30
Durham University Library, 29
Durivall, M., 16
Durnford, Elias, 275
Duscomb, J. W., 125
Dwight, Louis, 182
Dyckman, ——, 261
Dyer, ——, 83
Dyer, Joseph Chessborough, 308
Dyes, 150, 310; *see also* Cochineal; Indigo; Logwood; Madder
Dyfed, Wales, 243-8
Dysart, 3rd Earl of, *see* Tollemache, Lionel (1649-1727)

E

"E., A.," 348
E., J., 112
EP Microform Ltd., xxv
Eagle (ship), 42, 122
Eagle Street College, 172
Earl Grey Papers, 30
Earle, Ralph [Anstruther] (1835-79), 13
Early, Charles, & Marriott (Witney) Ltd., 210
Early, R. E., and A. Plummer, *The Blanket Makers, 1669-1969: A History of Charles Early & Marriott (Witney) Ltd.*, 210 fn.
Eason, John, 311
East Devon Record Office, 25-6
East Florida, *see* Florida, East
East India Company, 32, 214
East Indies, 302; Merchants, 328; *see also* Trade with East Indies
East Jersey, *see* New Jersey, East
East Lothian Antiquarian Society, Papers, 307
East Sussex Record Office, 221-2
Eastman Museum, Rochester, N.Y., 220
Eaton, Daniel Cady (1834-95), 145
Eaton, Dorman Bridgman (1823-99), 68
Eaton, John (1829-1906), 75, 170, 236
Ebervill River, Navigation, 305
Eccles (Lancashire) Public Library, 114
Eccleston, Chester, Cheshire, 19
Economic conditions: 1783-1800, 49, 183, 294; 19th century, 49, 68, 148, 163, 183, 186, 261, 270, 289, 330, 331, 332, 348; 20th century, 112, 128, 266, 269, 277, 278, 280, 298, 332; *see also* Agriculture; Industry; Natural resources; Panic of 1837; Panic of 1857; Prices; Raw materials; Wages
Economists, 165
Ecuador, Relations with U.S., *see* Relations with Ecuador
Eddowes, Ralph, 183
Eddowes, Sarah, 18
Eddy, Mary Baker (1821-1910), 281, 283
Eddy, Sherwood (1871-1963), 206, 281
Eddy, Thomas, 182
Edelman, S., 198
Eden, Anthony, 1st Earl of Avon (1897-1977), 281
Eden, Robert, 222
Eden, William, 1st Baron Auckland (1744-1814), 44, 74-5, 75-6, 80, 81, 267, 314
Edgar, W. B., "A Letter from South Carolina," *Journal of the Royal Society of Arts* (1974), 150 fn.
Edgeworth family, 348
Edinburgh, Lothian, 254-315; Merchants, 289, 295, 296, 299, 304, 310, 311
Edinburgh (ship), 315
Edinburgh Almanack, 284
Edinburgh and San Francisco Redwood Co. Ltd., 308
Edinburgh College, 274
Edinburgh Magazine, 254
Edinburgh Royal Infirmary, 275
Edinburgh Royal Society, 314
Edinburgh University, 162, 313, 314
Edinburgh University Library, 312-5
Edison Electric Co., 224
Edmondes, Sir Thomas (1563?-1639), 10, 29
Edmonston, Thomas, 263
Edmonston of Buness Mss., 263
Edmunds, George Franklin (1828-1919), 68, 197

Education: Pre-1800, 49, 58, 222, 305; 19th century, 156, 164, 170, 173, 179, 255, 314, 331; 20th century, 97, 112, 179, 229, 269, 278; *see also* Church schools; Indians, Education; Negroes, Education; Rhodes Scholars; Teachers; Universities; *and subdivision* Education *under states, etc.*
Education, Technical, 131, 150
Education of women, 84, 96
Educational Institute of Scotland Mss., 269
Edward III, *King* (d. 1377), 85
Edward VII, *King* (1841-1910) [*was* Prince of Wales, 1869], 105, 192, 198, 223
Edward, Duke of Kent (1747-1820), 101
Edwardes, Henry George, 38, 129
Edwardes, Thomas, 41
Edwards, A. C., ed., *English History from Essex Sources, 1550-1750*, 31 fn.
Edwards, Aaron, 302
Edwards, Frederick George (1853-1909), 81; Papers, 81
Edwards, Gordon, 277
Edwards, Henry, 66
Edwards, Jack (*fl.* 1880-7), 245
Edwards, John (*fl.* 1752), 85, 112
Edwards, John, "John Francis Bray," *Socialist Review* (1916), 238 fn.
Edwards, John Passmore (1823-1911), 238
Edwards, Jonathan, 151; *Life . . . of David Brainerd*, 313
Edwards, Morgan (1722-95), 203
Edwards, Pierrepont, 344
Edwards, Son, Bigwood and Mathews, 226
Edwards Partnership Papers, 112
Effingham, Earl of, *see* Howard, Francis, 5th Baron Howard of Effingham (1643-95)
Egan, P., 345
Egerton, Archdeacon, of Derby, 39
Egerton, Francis, 1st Earl of Ellesmere (1800-57), 184
Egerton, Francis Henry, 8th Earl of Bridgewater (1756-1829), 39
Egerton family, 39
Egerton Mss., 53, 81-2
Eggleston, Edward (1837-1902), 197
Eglinton, 10th Earl of, *see* Montgomerie, Alexander (1723-69)
Eglinton Muniments, 273
Egmont, 1st Earl of, *see* Perceval, Sir John (1683-1748)
Egmont Papers, 76
Egremont, 2nd Earl of, *see* Wyndham, Sir Charles (1710-63)
Egremont, 2nd Baron, *see* Max, John
Egremont Papers, 140
Egypt, Relations with U.S., *see* Relations with Egypt
Eisenhower, Dwight David (1890-1969), 77, 166
Eisteddfod, 243, 244, 246, 248
Eldon, 1st Earl of, *see* Scott, John (1751-1838)
Eleanor (ship), 21
Elections, 58, 59, 78, 197, 207, 250; Primaries, 198; States, 38, 208; *see also* Presidents: Elections; Voting
Electricity, 111, 162, 163, 170, 270; Research, 175
Elgin, 7th Earl of, *see* Bruce, Thomas (1766-1841); 9th Earl of, *see* Bruce, Victor Alexander (1849-1917)
Elias Papers, 247
Elibank, 5th Baron, *see* Murray, Patrick (1703-78)
Elibank, 3rd Viscount, *see* Murray, Arthur C. (1879-1962)
Elibank Muniments, 275
Elibank Papers, 255
Eliot, Charles William (1834-1926), 74, 164, 196, 199
Eliot, Edward, 1st Baron (1727-1804), 19
Eliot, Jared (1685-1763), 149, 150
Eliot, John (1604-90), 98, 99, 147
Eliot, John (*fl.* 1735-52), 155
Eliot, John (*fl.* 1814-25), 28
Eliot, Rebecca, 221
Eliot, Thomas Stearns (1888-1965), 96
Eliot Papers, 19
Elizabeth I, *Queen* (1533-1603), 17, 37, 85
Elizabeth II, *Queen* (1926-), 141 fn.
Elizabeth (ship), 47
Ellenborough, 1st Earl of, *see* Law, Edward (1790-1871)
Ellesmere, 1st Earl of, *see* Egerton, Francis (1800-57)
Ellesmere Papers, 190
Ellice, Alexander, 42
Ellice, Edward (1781-1863), 255, 256
Ellice, Edward, Jr. (1810-80), 255
Ellice, Janie, 255
Ellice Papers, 255-6
Ellinsworth, T., 230
Elliot, Andrew (1728-97), 80, 240, 257, 267
Elliot, C., 261
Elliot, Sir Charles (1801-75), 67, 257
Elliot, Gilbert (*fl.* 1775), 292
Elliot, Gilbert, 2nd Earl of Minto (1782-1859), 257
Elliot, Gilbert J. M., 4th Earl of Minto (1845-1914), 257
Elliot, Hugh (1752-1830), 76
Elliot, Thomas Read, 176
Elliot, Walter, 280
Elliot, William Hugh, 3rd Earl of Minto (1814-91), 257
Elliott, W. Y., 277
Ellis, ———, 240
Ellis, George James Welbore Agar, 1st Baron Dover (1797-1833), 161
Ellis, Henry (1721-1806), 114, 140, 149
Ellis, John (1710?-76), 149
Ellis, John (*fl.* 1794), 175
Ellis, John Tracy, "Three American Letters from the Wiseman Papers," *Catholic Historical Review* (1958), 30 fn.
Ellis, Mary, 175
Ellis, Welbore, 1st Baron Mendip (1713-1802), 45
Ellison, Cuthbert, 223
Ellison, Henry, 223
Ellison, Robert, 223
Ellison, S. K., *Handlist of the Papers of William Wedgwood Benn, M. P., First Viscount Stansgate*, 113 fn.
Ellison, T., *The Cotton Trade of Great Britain*, 180 fn.
Ellison Papers, 223
Ellsworth, Edward, 270
Ellsworth, H. L., 270, 274
Ellwood, Thomas (1639-1713), 202
Elmhirst, Thomas (1801-37), 235
Elmhirst Mss., 235
Elmstead, Essex, 33
Elphinstone, George Keith, Admiral Viscount Keith (1746-1823), 121, 261
Elrington, Griffith, 273
Elsas, M., ed., *Iron in the Making*, 249 fn.
Elton, Godfrey, 1st Baron (b. 1892), 282
Elwin, Whitwell (1816-1900), 59
Ely, Robert E., 199
Emancipation Proclamations (1862, 1863), 58, 72, 130, 157
Emancipation Society, 347
Embargo, 219, 269, 349; *see also* Blockade, *and subdivision* Blockade

under wars; Non-intercourse
Embassies (in London), 225
Emerson, Annie L., 179
Emerson, Edward B., 260
Emerson, Ralph Waldo (1803-82), 33, 66, 174, 176, 178, 179, 184, 196, 202, 208, 238, 255, 256, 353
Emery, Charles Edward (1838-98), 170
Emigrant letters, 14, 20, 22, 25, 26, 27-8, 32-3, 34, 35, 46-8, 70, 94, 97, 98, 166, 231, 232, 243-8 *passim*, 250, 263, 265, 266, 273-4 *passim*, 276, 327-32, 347, 348, 350, 353; *see also* Immigrants; Trade unions (British), Emigration schemes
Emigrants' Protection Society, 248
Emlen, Samuel, Jr., 349
Emmens, S. H., 75
Emmes, Thomas, 311
Emmet, Robert, 326
Emmet, T. A., 331
Emmett Club of New Orleans, 344
Emmison, F. G., ed., *Guide to the Essex Record Office*, 31 fn., 32 fn.
Emory, William Hemsley (1811-87), 148
Empire Knife Co., 236
Employment, 331
Emporia Gazette, 282
Endicott, Mrs., 227
Engineers, Immigrants, 20
Engelmann, George (1809-84), 145
English, J., 149
English–Speaking Union of the Commonwealth, 81, 200
Enola C. (ship), 132
Enright, Michael H., 345
Enys, John, 20
Epidemics, 80, 137, 138, 314; *see also* Cholera; Smallpox; Yellow Fever; *and subdivision* Epidemics *under individual states and* Southern states
Episcopal Church, *see* Church of England; Church of Ireland; Protestant Episcopal Church in U.S.
Eppstein, John, 279
Equalitarianism, 22
Erickson, Dr. Charlotte, *American Industry and the European Immigrant, 1860-1885*, 29 fn., 163 fn., 235 fn.
Erie Canal, 208, 245
Erie, Lake, 297; Description, 271
Erie, Philadelphia & Reading Railroad, 52
Erith, E. J., ed., *Essex Parish Records*, 33 fn.
Erskine, Archibald, 317
Erskine, Charles, 8th Earl of Kellie (d. 1799), 287
Erskine, D. M., 261
Erskine, David (*fl.* 1778), 284
Erskine, David (*fl.* 1800), 261
Erskine, David Steuart, 11th Earl of Buchan (1742-1829), 216, 313, 314
Erskine, Sir Harry [or Henry] (d. 1765), 264
Erskine, James, Laird of Grange (1679-1754), 307
Erskine, Thomas, 261
Erskine, Sir William (1728-95), 256, 261, 274
Erskine Agreement, 1809, 95
Erskine Murray Papers, 257
Eskimoes, Missions, 118
Espuela Syndicate Ltd., 308
Essex, England, 31-3
Essex Record Office, 31-3
Essex Review, 32 fn.
Estaing, Charles Hector, Comte d' (1729-94), 76, 267
Estcourt, J. B. R., 34
Estlin, John Bishop (1785-1855), 6, 95
Estlin, Mary, 95, 96
Estlin Papers, 6, 95-6
Ethical Movement, 96
Eure, Ralph, 3rd Baron (1558-1617), 82
Eureka (ship), 124
Europe, Relations with U.S., *see* Relations with Europe
Europe and American Steam Shipping Co., Ltd., 124
European and American Printing Telegraph Co., 110
Eustis, William (1753-1825), 182
Evangelical Magazine, 174 fn.
Evans, Ellis (1786-1864), 245
Evans, Dr. Erie, Deposit, 246
Evans, Griffith (1835-1935), 246
Evans, Hugh, 245
Evans, Mrs. John, 246
Evans, John H., 245
Evans, Jno., 145
Evans, Lewis (*c.* 1700-56), 149
Evans, Luther H., 279
Evans, N., 245
Evans, Thomas (*fl.* 1846), 247
Evans, Thomas Ffraw, 248
Evans, William, 217
Evans and Harvey–George Families' Papers, 32
Evans–Freke, John, 6th Baron Carbery (1765-1845), 84
Evarts, William Maxwell (1818-1901), 68, 69, 204
Eveleigh, Samuel, 304
Evelin, Robert, 194
Evening Post, New York, 197
Everett, Edward (1794-1865), 17, 63, 64, 67, 75, 144, 148, 168, 206, 207, 216, 276
Everett, William, 259
Eversley, Baron, *see* Shaw–Lefevre, George John (1831-1928)
Everyman's Library, 81
Evory, Mr., 180
Ewing, Thomas (1789-1871), 245
Exchequer, Chancellors of the, 142, 160
Exchequer, King's (or Queen's) Remembrancer, Records, 129
Exchequer, Lord Treasurer's Remembrancer, Records, 129
Exchequer and Audit Records, 122, 124
Exchequer Records, 122, 129; Scottish, 310-1
Exemption (Law), 131
Exeter, Devon, 24-6; Customs records, 89, 91, 93
Exeter Central Library, 26
Exeter University Library, 26
Exploration, 111, 146-7, 152, 204, 290, 291, 323; *see also* Arctic exploration; Northwest Passage; *and subdivision* Settlement *under states*
Exports, *see* Trade
Exquemelin, Alexander Oliver, *De Americaensche Zee-Rovers*, 99
Extradition, 38, 125, 128, 130, 130 fn., 133, 136, 137, 176, 201, 208, 352
Eyre, Edward John, 256
Eyre, Sir William (1805-59), 140
Eyre Papers, 140

F

Fair American (ship), 288
Fairbank, J. K. (b. 1907), 165
Fairchild, Lucius, 227
Fairfax, Lord, 264
Fairfax, Bryan, Lord Fairfax of Cameron (1737-1802), 204
Fairfax family, 45
Fairfax Mss., 204
Fairfields Shipbuilding and Engineering Co. Ltd., 311
Fairgreive, John, 299
Fairholme, Messrs., 304
Fairlie, James, 269
Falabia (ship), 127
Falconer, Thomas (1738-92), 31
Falconer, Thomas (1805-82), 168
Falkland Islands, Relations with U.S., *see* Relations with Falkland Islands
Falkland Islands Co., 132
Fallowfield, E., 274
Fallowfield, John, 274
Falmouth, Cornwall, 19; Customs records, 91, 93
Fame (ship), 138
Fane, Francis, 50
Fane, John, 10th Earl of Westmorland (1759-1841), 351
Fane, Thomas, 6th Earl of Westmorland (1680-1736), 189
Fane Collection, 351
Fane of Fulbeck Deposit, 50
Fanny (brig), 181
Far East: American investment, 197; *see also* Relations with Far East
Faribauer, Pierre, 41
Farm–Pollok [Virginia], 269
Farmborough, Thomas, 8
Farnell, J. V., 260
Farquharson, Alexander, 261
Farquharson, Charles, 291
Farquharson, James, 261
Farquharson of Invercauld Mss., 261
Farrand, Max, 277
Farrar, Thomas P., 177
Farrer, K. E., ed., *Correspondence of Josiah Wedgwood*, 212; *Letters of Josiah Wedgwood*, 212
Farrer, Sir Thomas Henry, 1st Baron Farrer (1819-99), 163
Farrer Collection on Banking and Currency, 163
Faulkner, T. W., 79
Fauquier, Francis (1704?-68), 24, 149, 195, 218, 285
Faversham, Customs records, 89, 93
Fawcett, Millicent Garrett (1847-1929), 179
Fawcett, Sir William (1728-1804), 143, 237
Fawcett Engineering Ltd., 17
Fawkener, W., 150
Fay, C. R., *Channel Islands and Newfoundland*, 339 fn.
Fea, James, 299
Fearon, Benson, 149
Featherstonhaugh, George William (1780-1866), 196, 207, 285, 290
Febroline Co., 240
Federal Army, *see* Civil War, Army, Federal
Federal Convention (1787), 49
Federalism, 198, 279, 281, 282, 283
Federalist Party, 95, 200
Federation of British Industries, 277, 282
Feeding stuffs: Production, 64, 149; Trade, 108, 109, 118; *see also* Clover
Feilding, Basil, 6th Earl of Denbigh (1719-1800), 224
Feilding, Israel, 346
Feilding, William, 224
Feilding, William H. A., 225
Feiling, Keith, 277
Fell, Margaret (1614-1702), 154
Fell family, 154
Fellowes Collection, 187
Felons, Transportation, *see* Quarter sessions records; Transportation of criminals
Fels, Joseph (1854-1914), 116
Feltmakers and Haberdashers, 6
Female Medical College of Pennsylvania, 96
Fendell family, 86
Fenian Papers, 351-2
Fenians, 38, 59, 68, 69, 71, 72, 130, 130 fn., 132, 140, 184, 198, 201, 202, 326, 343-5 *passim*, 351-2; *see also* Canada, Fenian invasions, 1866-70; Ireland, Home rule
Fenwick, Edward Dominic (1768-1832), 171
Ferguson, Mrs., 275
Ferguson, A., 309
Ferguson, Adam (1723-1816), 313, 314
Ferguson, Andrew (*fl.* 1775-87), 324
Ferguson, James, 149
Ferguson, John, 269
Ferguson, N., 313
Ferguson, Patrick (1744-80), 218, 313
Fergusson, Alexander, 289
Fergusson, Charles, 262
Fergusson, Sir James (1832-1907), 37, 104
Fergusson, Patrick, 267
Fergusson family, 317
Fergusson of Craigdarroch Muniments, 289
"Fergusson rifle," 267
Ferrar, John, 17
Ferrar, Nicholas (1592-1637), 17
Ferrar Papers, 17
Ferris, James, 329
Ferriss, Benjamin, 22
Fesch, Capt., 297
Fetherston, Marion, 353
Fettercairn Papers, 256
Fettiplace, Giles, 221
Feuchtwanger, Mrs. Martha, 205
Fewins, George, 25
Field, Cyrus West (1819-92), 68, 69, 71
Field, Rev. H. M., 75
Field, Kate, 204
Field Museum of Natural History, Chicago, Ill., 146
Fife, 2nd Earl of, *see* Duff, James (1729-1809)
Fife, Scotland, 253
Fiji, Land claims by Americans, 128, 131; *see also* Relations with Fiji
Filgate family, 346
Filibustering, 77, 200, 201
Fillmore, Millard (1800-74), 77
Film industry, 278
Filmer, Henry, 45
Filmer Papers, 45
Finance, 46, 99, 112, 142, 167-8, 172, 264, 277, 280, 286, 291, 299, 307, 308; *see also* Banking; Debts, Public; Investments; Panic of 1837; Panic of 1857; *and subdivision* Finance *under states, etc.*
Finch, Heneage, 7th Earl of Aylesford (1849-85), 289

Finch–Hatton Papers, 189
Findlater, 4th Earl of, *see* Ogilvy, James (1664-1730)
Findlay, Hopkirks & Co., 309
Fine arts: 18th century, 151; 19th century, 66; *see also* Architecture; Cameos; Painting
Finer, Herman (1898-1969), 164
Finerty, J., 345
Finlay, James, & Co. Ltd., 318
Finney, John (*c.* 1671-1728), 18
Finney, Samuel (*fl.* 1701), 18
Finney, Samuel (d. post 1764), 18
Finney, Samuel, III, 18
Finney of Fulshaw Mss., 18
Finnie, Elihu, 163
Fire prevention, 99
Fire-making, 202
Firearms, 144, 223, 308; Trade, 15, 81, 143, 205, 226, 228, 235; *see also* Gunpowder
First Scottish American Trust Co. Ltd., 318
Firth, Sir Charles Harding (1857-1936), 162
Fish, Hamilton (1808-93), 68, 71, 72, 201, 202
Fish, Trade, 24; *see also* Sturgeons; Torpedo fish
Fisher, ———, (*fl.* 1697), 83
Fisher, ———, (*fl.* 1796), 155
Fisher, Francis, 219
Fisher, H. A. L., 281, 282, 283; *James Bryce*, 196 fn.; Papers, 199
Fisher, J., 24
Fisher, James, 112
Fisher, John (*fl.* 1831), 187
Fisher, John (*fl.* 1831-8), 219
Fisher, Mrs. Lydia, 219
Fisher, Miers, 102
Fisher, Roger, 120; *Heart of Oak*, 120
Fisher, T., 24
Fisher Collection, 219
Fisheries, 128; 1776-1818, 62, 83, 102, 124, 140; 1819-54, 81, 140, 200, 201, 207, 208, 216; 1855-71, 67, 68, 71, 72, 77, 128, 130, 130 fn., 132, 140; 1872-84, 38, 128, 130, 130 fn., 132, 133, 140; 1885-1911, 38, 130, 130 fn., 132, 133, 142, 198, 227
GREENLAND, 91; Newfoundland, 21, 26, 27, 30, 35, 38, 40, 56, 88, 91, 101, 111, 121, 130, 140, 161, 198, 257; Nova Scotia, 121, 130, 257; Prince Edward Island, 124, *see also* Washington, Treaty of, 1871; Whaling
Fishguard, Customs records, 93
Fishing, 326, 343
Fiske, John (1842-1901), 162
Fitch, Robert, 189
Fitch, Thomas (*c.* 1700-74), 233
Fitzgerald, B., ed., *The Correspondence of Emily, Duchess of Leinster*, 343
Fitzgerald, Lord Edward (1763-98), 343
Fitzgerald family, 343
Fitzherbert, Alleyne (1753-1839), 267
Fitzherbert, Sir Robert, 23
Fitzherbert, William, 23
Fitzherbert of Tissington Papers, 23
Fitzpatrick, Bernard, 348
Fitzpatrick of Ossory Papers, 348
Fitzroy, Augustus Henry, 3rd Duke of Grafton (1735-1811), 218
Fitzroy, Lord Frederick, 218
Fitzroy Papers, 218
Fitzwilliam, Charles William Wentworth, 3rd Earl Fitzwilliam (*styled* Viscount Milton *until* 1833) (1786-1857), 9
Fitzwilliam, Charles William Wentworth, 5th Earl Fitzwilliam (1786-1830), 233
Fitzwilliam, Hon. Charles W., 233
Fitzwilliam, William Charles de Meuron, 7th Earl Fitzwilliam (1872-1943), 233
Fitzwilliam, William W., Viscount Milton (d. 1877), 233
Fitzwilliam, William Wentworth, 2nd (4th) Earl Fitzwilliam (1748-1833), 190, 233, 233 fn.
Fitzwilliam Correspondence, 190
Fitzwilliam Muniments, 233, 240
Fitzwilliam Museum, 16, 78
Fitzwilliam Papers, 189-90
Fitzwilliam (Wentworth Woodhouse) Muniments, 233
Flaget, Benedict Joseph (1763-1850), 171
Flanagan, Michael (*fl.* 1848), 225
Flanagan, Thomas, 225
Flandin, J. Eugene, 291
Flax: Cultivation, 10; Trade, 24, 138, 160, 239, 301, 346; *see also* Linen
Fleetwood, Customs records, 93
Fleming, Sir Alexander (d. 1955), 78; Papers, 78
Fleming, Caleb, 188
Fleming, Henry, 21, 22
Fleming, James, 328
Fleming, Jane, 332
Fleming, Sir (John) Ambrose (1849-1945), 170
Fleming, Robert, & Co., Ltd., 96
Fleming of Wigtown Papers, 256
Flemming, Lady Virginia, 96
Fletcher, Andrew (1655-1716), 314
Fletcher, Benjamin (*c.* 1640-1703), 83
Fletcher, Sir Henry, 256
Fletcher, John Gould, 74
Fletcher of Saltoun Papers, 256
Flexner, Abraham, 277, 278, 280, 282
Flindall, Murray, 150
Florida: To 1763, 16-7, 37, 55, 140, 298, 301; 1763-84, 10, 19, 55, 98, 126, 140, 181, 195, 227, 249, 314; 1784-1821, 43, 56, 66, 102, 138, 140; 1821-61, 32, 97, 208; Civil War, 1861-5, 60
AGRICULTURE, 50, 262, 266, 274; Army, 265, 303; Assembly, 266; Boundaries, 102; Coast, 148; Customs administration, 55; Description, 55, 265; Education, 96; Finance, 100, 308; Forts, 293, 301, 302; Governors, 249, 266, 312; History, 294; Immigrants, 35, 266, 328, 347; Indians, 249; Land, 46, 76, 97, 206, 207, 262, 266, 275, 294, 295, 331; Land grants, 261, 273, 300, 302, 335; Loyalists, 138; Merchants, 169, 263, 295; Politics, 271; Relations with France, 56; Relations with Spain, 97; Settlement, 16-7, 37, 55, 140, 213, 266, 274, 275, 289, 297, 302; Slavery, 50, 67, 77, 266, 297, 323; Trade, 140, 181, 347
BONAFACIO, 347; Gainesville, 348; Katesbourne, 50; Key West, 67, Consular reports (British), 134; Mandarin, 96; Miami, 328, Consular reports (British), 134, Description, 81; Pensacola, 66, 131, 181, 227, 328, Consular reports (British), 130, 135, Customs collectors, 87; St. Augustine, 55, 140, 195, 265, 293, 301, 302, Church of St. Francis, 303; Smyrnea, 266; Tallahassee, 169; Thomasville, 263
Florida (Confederate ship), 17, 59, 61
Florida, East, 19, 80, 98, 126, 138, 191, 257, 262, 266, 273, 275, 284, 287, 288, 295, 297, 298, 302, 303, 323
Florida, West, 10, 34, 48, 56, 102, 138, 149, 249, 265, 275, 288, 312, 314
Florida Land and Colonization Co. Ltd., 166

Florida Mortgage and Investment Co. Ltd., 308
Floridablanca, José Moñino y Redondo, Conde de (1728-1808), 44
Flory, F. D., 69
Floud family, 26
Floud Papers, 26
Faber and Faber Ltd., 96
Factory system, 185
Fagg, John Edwin, "Sir Charles Webster" in S. W. Halperin, ed., *Some Twentieth-Century Historians* (1961), 165 fn.
Flour, 108, 109, 169, 173, 175, 182, 285, 303, 327; Prices, 64; *see also* Grain; Maize; Wheat
Flour-milling machinery, Trade, 140
Flower, Eliza Julia, 94
Flower, George, 94
Floyd Papers, 323, 351 fn.
Fludyer Maitland & Co., 102
Fobes, Peres, 245
Foljambe Mss., 191
Folkestone, Customs records, 89, 93
Follen, Mrs. E. L., 96
Folliott, George, 180
Fontevieux, M. de, 204
Food processing, Machinery, 43
Foran, W. R., 206; MS., 206
Forbes, Duncan (1685-1747), 312
Forbes, Edward, 263
Forbes, Hugh, 312
Forbes, John (1710-59), 262, 266, 267, 284, 285, 289, 312
Forbes, John (*fl.* 1797-1801), 325
Forbes, Rev. John (*fl.* late 18th cent.), 266
Forbes, John Murray (1813-98), 185, 204
Forbes, William, 284
Forbes family, 343
Ford, Bessie, 172
Ford, Sir Francis Clare (1828-99), 133
Ford, Isabella, 172
Ford, J. W., ed., *Some Correspondence between the Governor and Treasurers of the New England Company in London and the Commissioners of the United Colonies in America*, 99 fn.
Ford, P., 345
Ford, P. and G., *A Guide to Parliamentary Papers*, 106
Ford, S., 245
Ford, Thomas J., 353
Ford, Worthington Chauncey (1858-1941), 164, 205
Forde & Co., 166
Foreign Affairs, 280
Foreign Enlistment Act (British) 1819, 73
Foreign Office, 122, 129-35; Correspondence, etc., 15, 104, 105, 125, 136, 140, 141, 207, 259, 260
Foreign Policy Association, 278, 279, 280
Foreign relations, *see* Relations with (*country*)
Foreman, G., "The Settlement of English Potters in Wisconsin," *Wisconsin Magazine of History* (1938), 217 fn.
Forerunner, 84
Forfar, Scotland, Manufacturers, 310
Forman Family Papers, 230
Forrester, Lady, 41
Forrester family, 254
Forset (or Fawcet), Mr., 103
Forster, John (1812-76), 14, 40; Collection, 14
Forster, Josiah, 51, 156
Forster, Nathaniel (1726?-90), 32
Forsyth, Richardson & Co., 255
Fort Atkinson, 233
Fort Delaware, 18
Fort Hunter, 220
Fort Laramie, 233
Fort Riley, 5
Fortescue, G. G., 80
Fortescue (Dropmore) Mss., 80-1
Forward, Jonathan, 312
Forward, Walter (1786-1852), 63
Foster, Mrs., 235
Foster, Abby Kelley (1810-87), 84
Foster, Antony, 324
Foster, Sir Augustus John (1780-1848), 218, 331
Foster, Lady Elizabeth, 331
Foster, James, 47
Foster, John, Baron Oriel (1740-1828), 324
Foster, John, & Son Ltd., 238
Foster, W. & J., Records, 47
Foster, Massereene–, Papers, 324-5
Fothergill, Anthony (1732?-1813), 5
Fothergill, Eliza, 51
Fothergill, J., 265
Fothergill, John (1712-80), 156, 188, 349; *Works . . .*, ed. by J. C. Lettsom, 188, 188 fn.
Fothergill, John Milner (1841-88), 170
Fothergill, Samuel (1715-72), 154
Fotheringham, George, 264
Fotheringhame, Miss, 306
Fotheringhame, Patrick, 306
Foulis, William, 299
Foundling Hospital, London, 97
Fountain, Obadiah J., 269
"Fourteen Points," 77, 280
Fourth Army Papers, *see* Rawlinson Collection
Fourth of July celebrations, 47, 199, 331
Fowey, Customs records, 89, 93
Fowke, ———, 277
Fowler, B., 231
Fox, Mr., 176
Fox, Charles James (1749-1806), 76, 313; Papers, 76
Fox, E., & Sons Ltd., 238
Fox, G. C., & Co., 19, 212, 225
Fox, George (1624-91), 5, 6, 30, 154, 202; *Journal*, ed. by J. L. Nickalls, 6
Fox, George Croker, 212
Fox, George Townshend (1810-86), 224
Fox, Henry, 1st Baron Holland (1705-74), 28, 64, 264
Fox, Henry Edward (1755-1811), 119
Fox, Henry Richard Vassall, 3rd Baron Holland (1773-1840), 81
Fox, Henry Stephen (1791-1846), 63, 67, 77, 103, 196, 306
Fox, Hubert, *Quaker Homespun*, 212
Fox, Jane Gurney, 41
Fox, Jay, 314
Fox, R. H., *Dr. John Fothergill*, 188 fn.
Fox, Robert Were (1754-1818), 212
Fox, Thomas (1747-1821), 212
Fox (ship), 5
Fox Bros. & Co., Ltd., 212
Fox Collection, 224
France, James, & Co. Ltd., 238
France, R. S., *Guide to the Lancashire Record Office*, 46 fn.
France: Colonies, 12, 16-7, 22, 31, 41, 45, 159, 195, 305; Sinking fund, 317; *see also* Huguenots; Immigrants from France; Rela-

tions with France; Trade with France
France (ship), 245
Franchise, *see* Voting
Francis, Henry M., 167
Francis, Philip (1708?-73), 64
Francis, Sir Philip (1740-1818), 64
Francis, Robert, 131
Francis Papers, 64
Frankfurter, Felix (1882-1965), 116, 166, 228, 277, 278, 280, 281, 282
Frankland, Henry (d. 1739), 153
Franklin, Benjamin (1706-90), 10, 16, 21, 32, 44, 51, 61, 76, 94, 120, 147, 149, 151, 156, 168, 174, 175, 180, 182, 188, 192, 204, 208, 213, 214, 215, 226, 227, 233, 238, 259, 261, 266, 267, 270, 272, 275, 286, 298, 301, 313, 314, 317, 350; *Papers* . . ., ed. by L. W. Labaree, 149 fn.; *Writings* . . ., ed. by A. H. Smyth, 188
Franklin, John, 352
Franklin, William (1731-1813), 195, 265, 303
Franklin Institute, Pennsylvania, 79
Franks, Moses, 233
Fraser, Mr., 215
Fraser, Sergeant, 284
Fraser, A. Campbell, 256; ed., *The Works of George Berkeley*, 61 fn.
Fraser, Archibald, 305
Fraser, Hugh, 296
Fraser, James (*fl.* 1781), 305, 311
Fraser, James (*fl.* 1793), 313
Fraser, John (1750-1811), 150
Fraser, John (*fl.* 1880), 184
Fraser, John, Jr. (*fl.* 1810), 183
Fraser, Simon (d. 1777), 312
Fraser, Simon, Master of Lovat (1726-82), 264, 284, 291, 305
Fraser, William (*fl.* 1699-1711), 309
Fraser, William (*fl.* 1774), 61
Fraser, Sir William (1816-98), *Chiefs of Grant*, 305; *History of the Carnegies, Earls of Southesk*, 268; *Melvilles, Earls of Melville and Leslies, Earls of Leven*, 275; *Red Book of Grandtully*, 290
Fraser, Sir William, Trustees of, 268
Fraser Papers, 256
Fraser, Stodart and Ballingall Collection, 303
Fray, John, 172
Freame, John, 42
Frederick Jenning, Jr. (ship), 130
Free Society of Traders in Pennsylvania, 82
Free trade, 36, 161, 181, 204
Freeman, Charles, 274
Freeman, Edward Augustus (1823-92), 177
Freeman, James (*fl.* 1741-3), 319
Freeman, James (1759-1835), 94
Freemantle, Sir Thomas Francis (1765-1819), 288
Freemantle Collection, 13
Freemasons, 68, 264, 329; *see also* Patrons of Husbandry
Freer, R. L., 184
Frémont, John Charles (1813-90), 146, 201
French and Indian War, 1756-63, *see* Seven Years War, 1756-63
French Hospital, Rochester, Kent, 113
French National Assembly, 298-9
French Protestants, *see* Huguenots
French Reformed Church, London, 113
French Revolutionary Wars, 33, 225, 329; *see also* Napoleonic Wars
Frewen, Moreton (1853-1924), 209, 232, 277
Frewer, L. B., *Rhodes House Library*, 205 fn.
Frick, George, 315
Fridge, Alexander, 166
Fridge family, 166
Friendly Society of Freetown, Sierra Leone, 51
Friends, Darlington Society of, 29
Friends, Religious Society of, 5-6, 8, 11, 13, 15, 19-20, 22, 27, 29-30, 31, 32, 34, 37, 40-1, 42, 47, 51, 85, 152-7 *passim*, 160, 183, 185-6, 188, 191, 202, 211-2, 226, 227-8, 232, 247, 250, 274, 288, 293, 314, 332, 349-50, 353; Missions, 234
Friends Association for Abolishing the State Regulation of Vice, 156
Friends Historical Association, *Bulletin*, 152, 154 fn.
Friends Historical Society, *Journal*, 152, 202 fn.
Friends Historical Society of Philadelphia, *Bulletin*, 152
Friends, Library of the Society of, 152-7
Friendship (ship), 27
Fries, John Jacob, 174
Frizington, Cumbria, 22
Frobisher, William, 148, 149
Frontier Land and Cattle Co., 209, 210
Frost, John, 232
Frost, R. A., 281
Frost, Robert (1874-1963), 166
Frothingham, Frederick, 95
Froude, Miss, 62
Froude, James Anthony (1818-94), 62, 315
Fruit: Cultivation, 268, 308; Duties, 303; Trade, 323
Fry, Elizabeth (Gurney), Mrs. Joseph Fry (1780-1845), 155, 182
Frye & Bruhn, 248
Fugitive slaves, *see* Slavery: Fugitive slaves
Fulford, Francis, 14
Fulham Palace, 115
Fulham Papers, 115, 159
Fullarton, James, 273
Fuller, Rose, 223
Fuller, Stephen, 212
Fuller, Thomas, 316
Fuller Papers, 223
Fullerton, Ora D., 327
Fullerton, Robert (1845-1945), 327
Fullerton, Robert (*fl.* 1879), 330
Fulton, Robert (1765-1815), 226, 288
Fulton, Robert (*fl.* 1841), 326
Fulton, William, 326
Fur trade, 15, 31, 55, 83, 88, 146, 180, 256, 311, 323; *see also* Bering Sea controversy; Hudson's Bay Company
Furness, Horace Howard (1833-1912), 199, 314
Furness, William Henry (1802-96), 176

G

G., C., 112
Gaelic Society of Inverness, *Transactions*, 289 fn.
Gaffikin and Coy., 327
Gaffney, T. St. John, 345
Gage, Lord, 222 fn.
Gage, Henry (1761-1808), 222
Gage, Henry Hall, 4th Viscount (1791-1877), 222
Gage, Matilda (Joslyn), Mrs. Henry H. Gage (1826-98), 84
Gage, Thomas (1721-87), 12, 45, 48, 65, 75, 79, 105, 120 fn., 141, 214, 215, 218, 222, 239, 253, 265, 266, 267, 289, 292, 301

Gage Papers, 222-3
Galatea (ship), 269
Galbraith, Mary, 328
Galbraith, V. H., *An Introduction to the Use of Public Records*, 122
Galbraith, William, 327
Galbraith & Sing, 212
Gale, Benjamin (1715-90), 149
Gale, E. Morant, 26
Gale, Thomas, 114
Gale family, 26
Gale–Morant Papers, 26
Gales, Joseph, 234
Gales, Winifred, 234
Gall, L. G. M., 298
Gallagher, Frank, Papers, 346
Gallagher, Thomas, 38
Gallatin, Albert (1761-1849), 25, 76, 240
Gallier, James, 332
Gallier, John, 332
Galloway, 8th Earl of, *see* Stewart, George (1768-1834)
Galloway, Joseph (1730-1803), 55, 216, 273
Galloway family, 86, 253
Galpin, Francis William (b. 1858), 238; *Gypsy and Oriental Musical Instruments*, 238
Galpin, William, Collection, 245
Galsworthy, John (1867-1933), 227
Galton, Sir Francis (1822-1911), 170
Gambier, James (1723-89), 214
Gambier, James, 1st Baron (1756-1833), 46
Gambier Papers, 46
Gamble, Alexander, 331
Gane, D. M., "The Early Records of Tristan da Cunha," *United Empire* (1933), 70
Gangreben, Lieut., 143
Gannett, William Channing (1840-1923), 176
Garbett, Samuel, 213
Garden, Alexander (1730?-91), 149, 150, 151, 174, 175
Gardening, *see* Horticulture
Gardiner, Edwyn, 300
Gardiner, John, 276
Gardner, H., 40
Gardner, Samuel, 212
Gardom, John, 232
Garfield, H. A., 281
Garland, G. and J. B., 28
Garland, George (*fl.* 1794-1826), 28
Garlick, P. C., "The Sheffield Cutlery and Allied Trades" (Thesis), 234 fn.
Garnett, J. C. Maxwell, 278, 279
Garnett Muniments, 47
Garratt, Catherine, 18
Garrett Papers, 46
Garrison, Francis Jackson (1848-1916), 96, 197
Garrison, Wendell P., 197, 199
Garrison, William Lloyd (1805-79), 95, 96, 177, 205, 208, 235, 270, 316, 353
Garrod, H. W., 283
Garth, Charles (*c.* 1734-84), 149
Garvin, James Louis (1868-1947), 278, 279, 280, 281
Gas, Natural, 330
Gascoigne, J., 120
Gascoigne, John (1556?-1637), 239
Gascoigne Collection, 239
Gaskell, Elizabeth Cleghorn (Stevenson), Mrs. William Gaskell (1810-65), 176, 178
Gaskell, William (1805-84), 176
Gaskell Collection, 176, 178
Gaspé trade, 339
Gass family, 332
Gates, Horatio (1728-1806), 216, 230, 259, 276, 315
Gates, Sir Thomas (*fl.* 1596-1621), 10, 44, 229
Gateshead, Tyne & Wear, 223
Gateshead Central Library, 223
Gauler, Mrs., 238
Gauss, Christian, 315
Gay, Elizabeth, 235
Gazette, Quebec, 63
Geddes, Sir Auckland, 277
Geddes, Sir Patrick (1854-1932), 256
Geddes Papers, 256
Gee, Joshua (d. 1730), 160; *The Trade and Navigation of Great Britain Considered*, 160
Genealogical material, 84
Genealogical Office, Dublin, 343
Genealogists' Magazine, 48 fn.
Genealogy, 273; Irish, 343, 349
General Anti-Slavery Convention, London (1840), 205
General Armstrong (American privateer), 77
General Post Office, 96-7
Geneva Arbitration (1872), *see* *Alabama* (ship), Claims
Genoa Conferences (1922), 127; (1927), 278
Geneva Convention, Red Cross, 142
Geology, 162, 189, 255
George II, *King* (1683-1760), 35, 62, 195, 223, 226
George III, *King* (1738-1820), 18, 19, 62, 64, 85, 101, 150, 167, 195, 211, 214, 215, 218, 249, 267, 289, 292, 301-2, 312, 319, 324
George IV, *King* (1762-1830), 108, 272, 288
George, Prince of Denmark (1653-1708), 219
George, Prince of Wales, *see* George IV
George, Henry (1839-97), 100, 161, 177, 197, 202; *The Condition of Labor*, 161
George, Sir Rupert, 288
George, T & P., 249, 250
George (ship), 304
Georgia: Colonial period, 10, 15, 32, 52, 55, 64, 98, 140, 215, 248, 302, 303, 312, 315; 1776-83, 98, 260, 265, 266, 268, 294; War of 1812, 138; Civil War, 1861-5, 60, 61, 130, 169
AGRICULTURE, 148-51 *passim*, 274, 287, 348; Assembly, 301; Boundaries, 103; Charters, 32; Cotton, 118, 130, 175, 185, 348; Council, 290; Description, 216, 293, 328; Epidemics, 349; Finance, 100; Governors, 10, 98, 114, 216, 223, 290; Immigrants, 32, 36, 47, 152, 181, 187, 274, 276, 325, 328, 331; Indians, 32, 52; Land, 6, 33, 103, 226, 289, 315, 328; Land grants, 300; Land tenure, 55, 195; Law, 301; Loyalists, 324; Merchants, 271, 295; Petitions, 32; Provincial Congress, 98; Relations with South Carolina, 15; Relief for Irish famine, 345; Religious history, 34, 49, 85, 103, 117, 118, 159, 274, 324; Settlement, 15, 52, 76, 118, 140, 152, 237; Slavery, 6, 103, 183, 331; Trade, 56, 114, 173, 175, 240, 300, 309, 310; Transportation, 174
ALTAMAHA RIVER, 32; Atlanta, 61, 169, Consular reports (British), 134; Augusta, 118, 315, 325, 331, 332; Bethesda, 103; Franklin County, 226; Frederica, 274; Okefinokee, 174; St. Andrew's Fort, 32; St. Mary's River, 174; Savannah, 61, 85, 98, 130, 173, 183, 187, 240, 253, 265, 268, 274, 294, 309, 310,

315, 324, 328, 331, 349, Consular reports (British), 130, 134, Customs collectors, 87, 274, Description, 159, 184, Merchants, 118, 175, 290, 328; Skiddoway, 289; Susquehannah, 103; Tybee Island, 62, 98; Ware County, 47
Georgia (ship), 59, 130
Geraldine, Mons., 52
Germain, George Sackville, 1st Viscount Sackville (1716-85), 8, 103, 139, 143, 145, 190, 192, 218, 227, 267, 286, 292
German Foreign Legion, 143
German Foreign Ministry Records, Captured Enemy Documents, 122, 135-6
German-Americans: Attitude to World War I, 116
Germany, Influence in U.S., 276; *see also* Immigrants from Germany; Relations with Germany; Trade with Germany
Gerrard, J. W., 260
Gerrard, Samuel, 255
Geyer, Charles Andrew, 291
Ghent, Treaty of (1814), 25, 59, 67, 73, 83, 102, 208, 275, 286
Ghies, Hassuna D', 168
Ghirelli, M., *A List of Emigrants from England to America, 1682-1692*, 86 fn.
Gibbon, Edward (1737-94), 19; *Letters* . . ., ed. by J. E. Norton, 19 fn.
Gibbons, Dr., 313
Gibbons, James Sloan (1810-92), 344
Gibbs, Josiah Willard (1839-1903), 147
Gibert, Jean Louis, 149, 150
Gibson, Edmund (1669-1748), 151
Gibson, John, 187
Gibson & Asheton, 188
Gibson Mss., 154
Gilbert, Sir Humphrey (1539?-83), 189
Gilbert, J. C., *A History of Investment Trusts in Dundee*, 318 fn.
Gilbert, W. S., 77; *Engaged*, 77; *H.M.S. Pinafore*, 77; *The Pirates of Penzance*, 77; Papers, 77
Gilbert Mss., 222
Gilchrist, Dugald, 292
Gilchrist, William, 315
Gilchrist of Ospisdale Muniments, 292
Gilder, Richard Watson (1844-1909), 197, 198-9
Giles, Daniel (1760-1831), 39
Giles–Puller, Arthur, 39
Giles–Puller, Charles, 39
Giles–Puller, Ellen, 39
Giles–Puller Mss., 39
Gilfillan, George, 313
Gill, Mrs., 258
Gill, E. G., 78
Gill, Henry, 21
Gill, Joseph, 156
Gill & Fisher, Messrs., 327
Gillespie, Mr., 187
Gillespie, Elizabeth, 329
Gillespie & Co. of New York, 271
Gillfedere, Patrick, 328
Gillies, John, 296
Gilliss, James Melville (1811-65), 148
Gillman, Henry (1833-1915), 15
Gillmore, A., 174
Gillmore, Reginald E., 113
Gillon, John, 265
Gilman, Charlotte (Perkins), Mrs. George Houghton Gilman (1860-1935), 74, 84
Gilman, Daniel Coit (1831-1908), 162
Gilman, Nicholas Paine, 198
Gilmorestone, R., 263
Gilpin, F., 149
Gilpin, J., 226
Gilpin, Joseph, 183
Ginger, Trade, 18, 91
Girard, Stephen, 261
Girtin, Thomas Calvert (d. 1874), 114
Gist, C. P., 284
Gittins, L., "Premiums for Vegetable Alkali," *Journal of the Royal Society of Arts* (1963), 151 fn.
Given, John, 325
Given, Robert, 325
Gladstone, H. N., 75
Gladstone, Herbert John, Viscount Gladstone (1854-1930), 75; Papers, 75
Gladstone, James Paterson, 156
Gladstone, Sir John (1764-1851), 180, 243
Gladstone, Robertson (1805-75), 180
Gladstone, William Ewart (1809-98), 58, 64, 67, 68, 70-3 *passim*, 104, 169, 184, 202, 263
Gladstone & Co., 180
Gladstone Collection, 180
Gladstone Papers, 53, 70-3
Glamorgan Record Office, 249-50
Glasgow, Arthur, 275
Glasgow, George, 144
Glasgow, Robert, 268
Glasgow, Strathclyde, 316-8; Customs records, 310; Manufacturers, 309, 310; Merchants, 80, 195, 263, 289, 290, 301, 304, 309-10 *passim*, 315, 316, 317, 325; Trade with America, 31, 253, 289, 309, 310, 317; *see also* Business records: Glasgow
Glasgow-American Trust Co. Ltd., 308
Glasgow Emancipation Society, 316
Glasgow Emigration Society, 108
Glasgow Female Anti-Slavery Society, 316
Glasgow Freedmen's Aid Society, 316
Glasgow (ship), 326
Glasgow Packet (ship), 296
Glasgow Port Washington Iron and Coal Co. Ltd., 307
Glasgow University, Department of Economic History, 318
Glasgow University Library, 317-8
Glass, Trade, 187, 227
Glasscock, John Laybank, "Stortford Emigrants to New England, 1630-1640," 42
Glassford, Henry, 287, 288
Glassford, John, 304
Glassite Church, 319
Gledstone, J. P., 235
Glen, James (1701-77), 160, 226, 275, 284, 285
Glen, Thomas, 284
Glenfield & Kennedy Ltd., 318
Glenny, James, 150
Glenorchy, Lord, *see* Campbell, John, 2nd Earl of Breadalbane (1662-1752)
Glenton House Mss., 270
Glenwood Hot Springs Co., 46
Gloucester, 2nd Duke of the 5th creation, *see* William Frederick (1776-1834)
Gloucester, Gloucestershire, 33-5; Customs records, 89, 93
Gloucester Corporation Records, 34
Gloucestershire, England, 33-5

Gloucestershire and Wiltshire Quarterly Meeting of the Society of Friends, 34
Gloucestershire Banking Co., 116
Gloucestershire County Libraries, 33-4
Gloucestershire Records Office, 34-5
Glue: Manufacture, 202; Trade, 255
Glyn Mills & Co., 169 fn., 172
Glyn, Mills, Hallifax & Co., 249
Glynn, James (1801-71), 216
Glynn, William, 10
Glynne–Gladstone Mss., 243, 243 fn.
Goad, T. W., 146
Goddard, James Stanley, 149
Godefroy, Maximilian (*fl.* 1806-24), 183
Godkin, Edwin Lawrence (1831-1902), 72, 163, 164, 173, 197
Godkin, Lawrence (b. 1860), 197, 210
Godsman, James, 254; Papers, 254
Godwin, William (1756-1836), 176
Goelet, Peter P., 226
Goizen, Daniel, 212
Gold: Imports, 52; Mining, 64, 125, 211, 273, 307, 308; Prices, 105; *see also* Bimetallism; Silver Question
Gold Rush, 1849, 18, 222
Gold standard, 279
Gold Standard Defence Association, 163, 172
Goldby, Ruth, 236
Goldsmiths' Library of Economic Literature, 160, 161-2
Goll, James E., 246
Gollop, Maximilian, 27
Gomersal, Yorkshire, Business records, *see* Business records: Gomersal, Yorkshire
Gompers, Samuel, 228
Gooch, G. P., ed., *The Later Correspondence of Lord John Russell*, 139 fn.; and H. Temperley, eds., *British Documents on the Origins of the War*, 131 fn.
Gooch, J. C., 190
Gooch, Richard, 15
Gooch, Sir William (1681-1751), 114
Goodman & Martin, Messrs., 10
Goodnow, Frank Johnson (1859-1939), 197, 198
Goodwin, Charles, 112
Gookin, Daniel (1612?-87), 343
Goole, Customs records, 93
Gordon, Mrs., 298
Gordon, Lord Adam (1726?-1801), 266
Gordon, Alexander (*fl.* 1741-7), 274
Gordon, Sir Alexander (1786-1815), 288
Gordon, Alexander (*fl.* 1843-4), 291
Gordon, Arthur, 311, 312
Gordon, Arthur Charles Hamilton–, 1st Baron Stanmore (1829-1912), 269
Gordon, Cosmo, 98, 144
Gordon, D. A., 119
Gordon, David, 288
Gordon, George Hamilton, 4th Earl of Aberdeen (1784-1860), 25, 63, 64, 66, 67, 169, 173, 186, 207
Gordon, Harry, 285
Gordon, Hunter, 169
Gordon, James (*fl.* 1744), 312
Gordon, James (*fl.* early 19th cent.), 288
Gordon, John (1644-1726), 308 fn.
Gordon, John (*fl.* 1807), 16
Gordon, John (1807-80), 176
Gordon, John (*fl.* 1876-7), 273
Gordon, John Campbell, 7th Earl of Aberdeen and 1st Marquess of Aberdeen and Temair (1847-1934), 260, 272
Gordon, N., 287
Gordon, Robert, 261
Gordon, Roderick, 311
Gordon, William (*fl.* 1717), 272
Gordon, William (1728-1807), 32, 94
Gordon, William Augustus, 119
Gordon, William Braco, 253, 303
Gordon of Cairnfield Mss., 261
Gordon–Cumming, Sir Alexander Penrose, 3rd Baronet (1816-66), 256
Gordon–Cumming, Walter Frederick (1859-1913), 256
Gordon–Cumming, Sir William Gordon, 4th Baronet (1848-1930), 256
Gordon–Cumming Papers, 256
Gore, Charles, 40
Gorges, Edward, Baron (1583-*c.* 1650), 312
Gorges, Sir Ferdinando (1566?-1647), 26, 37, 193
Gorges, Thomas (1618-71), 25
Gorhambury, Hertford, 37
Gorhambury Mss., 41
Gorman, John, 328
Gorman, Philip, 328
Gosford, Earl of, Papers, 324
Gosford, 1st Viscount, see Acheson, Archibald (1717-90)
Goss, C. W. F., *A Descriptive Bibliography of George Jacob Holyoake*, 53 fn.
Gosse, Sir Edmund William (1849-1928), 238
Gossypium (ship), 184
Gotch of Kettering Papers, 190
Gott, Benjamin (1762-1840), 239
Gott Papers, 239
Gouger, Robert, 173
Gough, Hugh, 3rd Viscount (1849-1919), 38, 39
Gough, R., 203
Gough Somersetshire Mss., 203
Gough Surrey Mss., 203
Goulburn, Henry (1784-1856), 54, 83, 84, 220, 221
Goulburn Papers, 220-1
Gould, Benjamin Apthorp (1824-66), 147
Gould, Chester, 226
Gould, John, 244
Gould, Sir Nathaniel, 261
Gould, Robert Howe, 67
Gouldesbrough, P., "An Attempted Scottish Voyage to New York in 1669," *Scottish Historical Review*, xl (1961), 275
Gourlie, Mr., 174
Government publications, Exchange, 131
"Governor and Company of Copper Miners in England," 82
Governors, Colonial, 10, 49, 65, 87, 126, 138, 143, 158, 188, 195, 213, 215, 216, 223, 233, 246, 265, 290, 299, 301, 302, 317; State, 167; *see also subdivision* Governors *under states; and names of individual governors*
Gracie, William, 183
Gradwell, Robert (1777-1833), 171
Graeme, Dr., 264
Graeme, Alexander, 315
Graffenried, Christopher, Baron de (1661-1743), 220
Grafton, 3rd Duke of, *see* Fitzroy, Augustus Henry (1735-1811)
Grafton Papers, 189, 218
Graham, Capt., 268

Graham, Andrew, 314
Graham, Mrs. Catherine (Macaulay) (1731-91), 49
Graham, Charlotte, 331
Graham, David (1808-52), 168
Graham, Sir Fergus, 22
Graham, Sir Frederick Ulric, 41
Graham, Hugh, 330
Graham, James (d. 1701), 220
Graham, James, 4th Marquis and 1st Duke of Montrose (d. 1742), 300
Graham, James Duncan (1799-1865), 148
Graham, John (*fl.* 1754-6), 290
Graham, John (*fl.* 1840), 330
Graham, Mary, 292
Graham, Richard, 1st Viscount Preston (1648-95), 22, 193
Graham, Robert, 292
Graham, Robert Bontine Cunninghame (1852-1936), 256
Graham, Thomas, 292
Graham, William, 299
Graham family, 331
Graham Family Letters, 331
Graham of Gartmore and Ardoch Papers, 256
Graham Papers, 22
Grahame, Harry, 299
Grahame, James (*fl.* 1668), 299
Grahame, James (1790-1842), 148; *History of the United States*, 148
Grahame, Kenneth (1859-1932), 199; Papers, 199
Grain: Prices, 64, 272; Trade, 8, 15, 91, 107-9 *passim*, 138, 169, 248, 262, 284, 309; *see also* Wheat
Grampian, Scotland, 253-4
Granard, Earl of, 354
Granard Papers, 354
Granby, Marquess of (*from 1770 to 1779*), *see* Manners, Charles, 4th Duke of Rutland (1754-87)
Granby, Marquess of, *see* Manners, John (1721-70)
Grand Junction Railroad, 249
Grand Trunk Railroad, 52
Grange, Laird of, *see* Erskine, James (1679-1754)
Grant, A. C., 255
Grant, Abel, 231
Grant, Sir Alexander (*fl.* 1767), 305
Grant, Alexander (*fl.* 1782), 297
Grant, Alexander (d. 1794?), 305
Grant, Sir Archibald, 261, 305
Grant, Charles, 305
Grant, Duncan, 305
Grant, Francis, 304
Grant, James (1720-1806), 257, 266, 275, 284
Grant, Sir James (1738-1811), 305 fn.
Grant, James (*fl.* 1758), 284
Grant, James (*fl.* 1775), 305
Grant, John (*fl.* 1752-97), 305
Grant, John (d. 1780), 305
Grant, John (*fl.* 1803), 305
Grant, Julia Dent (Mrs. Ulysses S. Grant), 68
Grant, L., 255
Grant, Lewis, 305
Grant, Lewis C., & Co., Mss., 272
Grant, Lewis D., 272
Grant, Robert (*fl.* 1759-77), 304, 305
Grant, Robert (*fl.* 1794), 266
Grant, Ulysses Simpson (1822-85), 59, 62, 68, 71, 96, 137, 201, 208
Grant, W. C., 266
Grant, William, 305
Grant of Monymusk Mss., 261
Grantham, 2nd Baron, *see* Robinson, Thomas (1738-86)
Granville, 1st Earl, *see* Carteret, John (1690-1763); 2nd Earl, *see* Leveson–Gower, Granville George (1815-91)
Granville family, 139
Granville Papers, 133, 139-40
Grasses, 149, 150, 151
Grattan, Thomas Colley (1792-1864), 67
Graves, Thomas, 1st Baron (1725?-1802), 101, 120, 274
Graves & Sons, 346
Gray, Mr., 297
Gray, Asa (1810-88), 15, 145, 146, 147, 148
Gray, Charles (*c.* 1695-1782), 31
Gray, Harrison, 94
Gray, Henry, 310
Gray, I., 193
Gray, James, 265
Gray, John, 214
Graybell, Mr., 16
Great Britain, *see* Immigrants from Great Britain; Parish records; Quarter sessions records; Relations with Great Britain; Trade with Great Britain; Trade, Colonial period; Transportation of criminals; West Indies, Trade with Great Britain
Great Eastern (ship), 184
Great Exhibition (1851), American exhibits, 35
Great Lakes, 32, 63, 70, 120, 144, 230, 262, 288, 302, 303; War of 1812, 39, 40, 144; Civil War, 1861-5, 59, 68, 121, 123, 130 DISARMAMENT, 67, 131, 198, 201; Navigation, 131
Great Northern Railway Co., 210
Great Ryburgh, Parish church, 186
Great War (1914-8), *see* World War I (1914-8)
Great Western Canal, 44
Great Yarmouth, Norfolk, Customs records, 89, 92-3
Great Yarmouth Assembly Book, 187
Greater London, England, 50-172
Greater London Record Office (London Section), 97
Greater London Record Office (Middlesex Section), 97-8
Greater Manchester, England, 172-80
Gredington, Shropshire, 210
Greeley, Horace (1811-72), 53, 68, 69, 245, 326
Green, C. M., 266
Green, Duff (1791-1875), 63
Green, E. R. R., 348
Green, James, 173
Green, John, 181
Green, Priscilla (1802-77), 156
Green, Richard T., 132
Green, Thomas, 190
"Greenbacks," 204
Greene, Benjamin D., 145
Greene, Elizabeth Gair, 179
Greene, J. S. Copley, 250
Greenhow, Robert, 258
Greenland: Birds, 148; *see also* Fisheries: Greenland
Greenlees, Andrew, 331, 332
Greenlees, John, 289
Greenlees, Mary (Beveridge), 289
Greenlees, R. D., 180
Greenock, Scotland: Merchants, 309, 310; Trade with America, 310
Greenwich Hospital, 57

Greenwood, Robert (d. *c.* 1814), 31
Greer, Hamilton and Gailey, Solicitors, 325
Greer family, 325
Greeves, Charles (1795?-1847), 230
Greeves, John, 329
Greffe, 339
Greg, Samuel, 19
Greg, Thomas, 324
Greg Family Papers, 19
Gregory, Mr., 105
Gregory, Charles Noble (1851-1932), 197
Gregory, Sir Richard, 282
Gregory, Robert, 48
Gregson, Matthew (1749-1824), 182
Gregson, Holt and, Papers, 182
Grenada, Slave insurrection, 306
GRENVILLE BAY, Customs collectors, 87
Grenfell, Col., 131
Grenville, George (1712-70), 65, 66
Grenville, George Nugent–Temple–, 1st Marquis of Buckingham (1753-1813), 62, 80
Grenville, Sir Richard (1541?-91), 49
Grenville, Richard Plantagenet Campbell Temple Nugent Brydges Chandos, 3rd Duke of Buckingham and Chandos (1823-89), 69
Grenville, Richard Temple Nugent Brydges Chandos, 1st Duke of Buckingham and Chandos (1776-1839), 97
Grenville, *afterwards* Grenville–Temple, Richard Temple, Earl Temple (1711-99), 65, 66, 79, 80
Grenville, Thomas (1755-1846), 76, 97
Grenville, William Wyndham, Baron (1759-1834), 54, 57, 79, 80, 81, 101, 107, 256
Grenville family, 65
Grenville Papers, 65-6, 79
Greville, Charles Cavendish Fulke (1794-1865), 65
Greville, Francis Evelyn (Maynard), Countess of Warwick (d. 1938), 33
Greville, George, Earl of Warwick (1746-1816), 101
Greville Letters, 65
Grew, Mary, 95
Grey, Albert Henry George, 4th Earl (1851-1917), 30, 210
Grey, Charles, 1st Earl (1729-1807), 30
Grey, Charles, 2nd Earl (1764-1845), 30, 169
Grey, Charles (1804-70), 30
Grey, Sir Charles Edward (1785-1865), 184
Grey, Sir Edward, Viscount Grey of Fallodon (1862-1933), 135, 198, 199, 200, 259, 260
Grey, Sir Frederick, 121
Grey, Henry (*fl.* 1738), 31
Grey, Henry George, Viscount Howick, *and afterwards* 3rd Earl Grey (1802-94), 30, 161
Grey, Ralph, 4th Baron Grey of Warke (d. 1706), 31
Grey, Thomas M., 329
Grey, Sir William de, 1st Baron Walsingham (1719-81), 188
Grey, Zachary (1688-1766), 85
Gribbon & Son, 327
Grieg Papers, 256
Grieve, John, 287
Griffin, Sir John Griffin, 1st Baron Braybrooke (1719-97), 31
Griffin, William Hall (d. 1907), 74; *Life of Robert Browning*, 74
Griffith, Edward, 244
Griffith, Goldsborough Sappington (1814-1904), 6
Griffith, Herbert, 246
Griffith, Hugh, 246
[Griffith, Margaret], *A Short Guide to the Public Record Office of Ireland*, 348
Griffith, Mattie, 96
Griffith, Thomas, 212
Griffiths, J., 85
Griffiths, W. E., 272
Grimond, Messrs. J. & A. D., 263
Grimsby, Customs records, 89, 93
Grimshaw, C., 348
Grimsthorpe, Lincoln, 49
Grimston, Harriot (Walter), Viscount (d. 1786), 41
Grimston, James Bucknall, 3rd Viscount Grimston, 1st Baron Verulam of Gorhambury (1747-1809), 41
Grimston family, 41
Grimston Papers, 42
Grindings, J. R., 245
Grindlay, Alexander, 290
Grinfield, William, 286
Grinnell, Henry (1799-1874), 75
Grinnell College, Iowa, 197
Griscom, J. W., 51
Griscom, John (1774-1852), 182
Griswold, Rufus Wilmot (1815-57), 69, 74
Grizzly bear, 291
Grogan, C. E., 236
Grosvenor, Richard, 1st Earl (1731-1802), 19
Grosvenor, Robert, 2nd Earl (1767-1845), 206
Grover, Smith & Grover, 39
Gruard, Frank, 348
Grubb, Edward, 228
Grubb, J., 9
Grubb Collection, 349
Grundy Family Papers, 47
Grynsell, John, 41
Guadeloupe, 10; *see also* Seven Years War; Trade with Guadeloupe
Guardian, 279; Archives, 178
Guardian Assurance Co., 99
Guatemala, Anglo-American education in, 135; *see also* Relations with Guatemala
Guerard, John, 31
Guernsey, Channel Islands, 339
Guerrière (ship), 288
Guest, Sir Josiah John (1758-1852), 249
Guest, Keen & Nettlefolds Ltd., 249
Guide to Microforms in Print, xxv
Guide to Reports of the Royal Commission on Historical Manuscripts (1914-74), 100 fn.
Guide to the Bedfordshire Record Office, 8 fn.
Guide to the Berkshire Record Office, 10 fn.
Guide to the Contents of the Public Record Office, 122
Guide to the Huntingdonshire Record Office, 17 fn.
Guide to the Kent County Archives Office, 44 fn.
Guide to the MS. Collections in the Sheffield City Libraries, 232, 233 fn.
Guide to the Public Records, 122
Guild of Handicraft, 116
Guildford, Surrey, 220
Guildford Muniment Room, 220
Guildhall Library, 98-100; 86
Guilds, London, 99
Guilford, 2nd Baron, *see* North, Francis (1673-1729)
Guilford, 2nd Earl of, *see* North, Frederick, *better known as* Lord North (1732-92)
Gumersall, Thomas, 240

Gums and resins, 214
Gunnersbury Park Museum, 100
Gunning, Thomas, 348
Gunpowder: Manufacture, 206; Trade, 31, 138, 351
Guns, *see* Firearms
Gurney, Anna (1795-1857), 155
Gurney, Hudson (1775-1864), 30, 187
Gurney, Jane, 30
Gurney, Joseph John (1788-1847), 30, 155, 185; *A Journey in North America*, 185 fn.
Gurney, Mary, 188
Gurney, R. Q., 185-6
Gurney, Richard, 187
Gurney and Barclay Family Papers, 187-8
Gurney Mss., 155, 185-6
Gwent, Wales, 248
Gwent County Record Office, 248
Gwredog Mss., 248
Gwyn, Julian, ed., *The Royal Navy and North America: The Warren Papers, 1736-52*, 222 fn.
Gwynedd, Wales, 248
Gwynedd Archives Service, 248
Gwynedd Area Record Office, 248
Gwynn family, 248
Gwynne, Daniel (*fl.* 1776-88), 248
Gypsum, 11

H

Habeas Corpus Suspension Acts, 351
Haberdashery and hosiery, 217
Habersham, James (1712-75), 149, 150, 174
Haddington, Earl of, Mss., 261-2
Haddo Muniments, 275
Hadley, Arthur Twining (1856-1930), 238
Hadwen, Dorcas, 22
Hadwen, Elizabeth, 22
Hadwen, John, 22
Hafnia, Geir Vidalinus, 204
Hagart, William, 304
Haggard, Sir Henry Rider (1856-1925), 151
Hagley Hall, West Midlands, 228
The Hague Conference (1929-30), 127
The Hague Peace Conference, 1st (1899), 39
The Hague Permanent Court of Arbitration, Fisheries award (1910), 142, 198
Hailey, Malcolm, 1st Baron (1872-1969), 206
Hailey Papers, 206
Haines, Daniel (1801-77), 6
Haiti, 38; Relations with Dominican Republic, 77; Trade with Great Britain, 109
Hakluyt, R., trans., *Virginia Richly Valued* (1609), 187
Halcro, Joshua, 272
Halcro–Johnston of Orphir Mss., 272
Haldane, George (d. 1759), 228
Haldane, John, 263
Haldane, Richard Burdon, Viscount Haldane of Cloan (1856-1928), 256
Haldane, Brown and Co., Collection, 306
Haldane Papers, 256
Haldimand, Sir Frederick (1718-91), 15, 214, 284
Hale, Edward Everett (1822-1909), 176, 208, 238
Halford, E., 345
Halford, Sir Henry, I (1766-1844), 49
Halford, Sir Henry, II (1797-1868), 49
Haliday, Alexander Henry (1728?-1802), 350
Halifax, 2nd Earl of, *see* Dunk, George Montagu (1716-71)
Halifax, 1st Viscount, *see* Wood, Charles (1800-85); 3rd Viscount, *see* Lindley, Edward Frederick (1881-1959)
Halifax, West Yorkshire, 237; *see also* Business records, Halifax, W. Yorkshire
Halifax Archives Department, 237
Halifax Fisheries Commission (1877), 38, 130, 133; *see also* Washington, Treaty of (1871)
Halkett, Francis, 284
Halkett, Sir John, 256
Halkett, Sir Peter, 256
Halkett Papers, 256
Hall, Prof., 315
Hall, [Abraham] Oakey (1826-98), 198
Hall, Basil (1788-1844), 169, 207
Hall, Charles, 217
Hall, Foster, 113
Hall, James Slater, 183
Hall, John (*c.* 1631-1709), 74; Notebooks, 74
Hall, Sir John (*fl.* 1752), 298
Hall, John (*fl.* 1889-91), 332
Hall, William, 298
Hall family, 332
Hall Griffin Papers, 74
Hall of Dunglass Muniments, 298-9
Hall Papers, 217
Hallé, Sir Charles (1819-95), 178
Halleck, Fitz–Greene (1790-1867), 69
Halliwell–Phillipps, James Orchard (1820-89), 314
Halsey, Francis W., 164
Halsey, Thomas, 39
Halsey family, 39
Halsey Mss., 39
Hamer, H., *A Catalogue of Works by and Relating to Walt Whitman*, 172 fn.
Hamilton, ——, 101
Hamilton, 4th Duke of, *see* Douglas, James (1658-1712)
Hamilton, Duke of, Mss., 262
Hamilton, Lieut., 119
Hamilton, Alexander (*fl.* 1755), 257
Hamilton, Alexander (*fl.* 1785), 264
Hamilton, Alexander (1757-1804), 258
Hamilton, Andrew (d. 1703), 262
Hamilton, Archibald (d. 1795), 139
Hamilton, Archibald (*fl.* 1837), 270
Hamilton, Charles (1691-1754), 284
Hamilton, Douglas, 8th Duke of Hamilton (1756-99), 262
Hamilton, Gavin, 257
Hamilton, George, 1st Earl of Orkney (d. 1737), 246
Hamilton, George (*fl.* 1803), 273
Hamilton, Hugh, 273
Hamilton, J. B., 325
Hamilton, James (*fl.* 1777), 262
Hamilton, James (1786-1857), 67, 104
Hamilton, James (*fl.* 1825), 187
Hamilton, James (*fl.* 1865), 315
Hamilton, James Alexander (1788-1878), 168, 206
Hamilton, James and Archibald, & Co., 264
Hamilton, John (*fl.* 1755), 257

Hamilton, John (*fl.* 1765), 264
Hamilton, John (*fl.* 1865), 325
Hamilton, Mary, 315
Hamilton, Robert, 263
Hamilton, Thomas, 264
Hamilton, W., 296
Hamilton, William (*fl.* 1781), 264
Hamilton, Sir William (1788-1856), 271
Hamilton, William Richard (1777-1859), 101
Hamilton Bruce Muniments, 292
Hamilton of Barns Mss., 263
Hamilton of Rozelle Mss., 270
Hamilton–Dalrymple of North Berwick Muniments, 290
Hamlyn, ———, 24
Hammerstein, Oscar (1895-1960), 166
Hammerton, John, 299, 300
Hammond, Sir Andrew, 231
Hammond, Edmund, Baron (1802-90), 58, 59, 70, 201, 202
Hammond, George (1763-1853), 80, 101, 200, 256
Hammond, Jabez Delano (1778-1885), 174
Hammond, John Hays (1855-1936), 38
Hammond, Margaret (Allen), Mrs. George Hammond, 101
Hammond, William, 101
Hammond Papers, 101
Hampden, 1st Viscount, *see* Trevor, Robert Hampden– (1706-83)
Hampshire, England, 35-6; *see also* Immigrants from Hampshire; Quarter sessions records, Hampshire
Hampshire Record Office, 36
Hampton, Samuel, 150
Hampton Industrial Agricultural Normal Institute, 290
Hanbury, John, 290
Hanbury, Taylor, Lloyd & Bowman, 115, 116
Hancock, Francisca, 311
Hancock, John (*fl.* 1683-5), 311
Hancock, John (1737-93), 259
Hancock, N. J., ed., *Handlist of Hardinge Papers at the University Library, Cambridge*, 16 fn.
Hancock, Washington, 291
Hand Morgan Mss., 216
Hankes, Mr., 286
Hankey, Sir Maurice, 260, 279, 281
Hanlon family, 331
Hannah (ship), 21
Hannay Papers, 299
Hannon, Sir Patrick Joseph Henry (1874-1963), 112
Hannon Papers, 112
Hansford, Charles, 115
Hansford Land and Cattle Co. Ltd., 308
Harberton, 1st Viscount, *see* Pomeroy, Arthur (d. 1798)
Harbours, 10, 124, 325
Harcourt, Sir William George Granville Venables Vernon (1827-1904), 202
Hardcastle, J., 130
Hardie, [James] Keir (1856-1915), 172
Harding, Sir J., 60
Harding, Warren Gamaliel (1865-1923), 268, 277
Hardinge, Charles, 1st Baron Hardinge of Penshurst (1858-1944), 16, 198
Hardinge Papers, 16
Hardman, Agnes, 47
Hardman, John, Studios, 227
Hardmian, John, 203
Hardware, Trade, 183, 226, 271; *see also* Cutlery; Nails; Tools
Hardwicke, 1st Earl of, *see* Yorke, Philip (1690-1764); 2nd Earl of, *see* Yorke, Philip (1720-90)
Hardy, Edward, 179
Hardy, K., 34
Hardy, Thomas (1840-1928), 238
Hardy & Page, 40
Hardy & Reckitt, 40
Harewood, Earl of, 237
Harewood House, West Yorkshire, 237
Hargreaves family, 47
Hargreaves–Mawdsley, R., ed., *Bristol and America*, 5
Harlé, Mons. de, 12
Harlequin (ship), 304
Harley, Sir Edward (1624-1700), 82
Harley, Sir Robert (1579-1656), 82
Harley, Sir Robert (1626-73), 82
Harley, Robert, 1st Earl of Oxford and Mortimer (1661-1724), 82, 83, 346
Harley, Thomas (1730-1804), 257
Harley family, 82
Harmsworth, Alfred Charles William, Viscount Northcliffe (1865-1922), 277
Harned, Thomas B. (1850-1920), 172
Harney, Julian (1817-97), 68
Harold, W. V., 171
Harper, Kenneth, 131
Harper, Robert Goodloe (1765-1825), 187
Harper & Bros., 40
Harper's Magazine, 238
Harpers Ferry, W. Va., John Brown's raid (1859), 176
Harpton Court Collection, 247
Harriman, W. Averell (b. 1891), 112
Harrington, Timothy Charles (1851-1910), 345
Harris, H. Wilson, 278
Harris, James Howard, 3rd Earl of Malmesbury (1807-89), 13, 36, 40, 83
Harris, Sir John H. (1874-1940), 205
Harris, William Torrey (1835-1909), 179
Harrison, Benjamin (1833-1901), 38, 157, 345
Harrison, Ethelberta, 164
Harrison, Francis, 203
Harrison, Frederic (1831-1923), 164
Harrison, G., 149
Harrison, Henry, 181
Harrison, Joseph (*fl.* 1767-9), 191, 233
Harrison, Richard, 28
Harrison, Robert Hanson (1745-90), 313
Harrison, Thomas, 47
Harrison, W. H. (*fl.* 1829-33), 28
Harrison, William Henry (1773-1841), 62, 207
Harrison & Watson, 22
Harrison Papers, 28
Harrod, R. F., 166
Harrogate, North Yorkshire, 230
Harrop and Henderson, Messrs., 289
Harrowby, 1st Earl of, *see* Ryder, Dudley (1762-1847); 2nd Earl of, *see* Ryder, Dudley (1798-1882)
Harrowby Papers, 101-2
Harshaw, N. K., 328
Hart, Albert Bushnell (1854-1943), 197
Hart, Charles H., 353
Hart, William, 42
Hart Jackson Accumulation, 47

Hart Papers, 353
Harte, Mrs. Eleanor, 6
Harte, [Francis] Bret (1836-1902), 62, 226, 254, 256
Hartlepool, Customs records, 93
Hartlepool, West, Customs records, 93
Hartley, David (1732-1813), 10, 120, 270
Hartley Russell Papers, 10
Hartshorn, William, 30
Hartshorne, William, 294
Hartwell, Henry, 195
Harvard College, 32, 99, 174, 260, 274
Harvard University, 64, 147, 164, 165, 177, 196, 197, 205, 254, 277, 283, 314; Arnold Arboretum, 146; Botanical Garden, 146; Divinity School, 177; Gray Herbarium, 146; Houghton Library, 19 fn.; Law School, 49, 278, 280; Cambridge University American lectureship, 16
Harvey, Baikia, 315
Harvey, Edward, 192
Harvey, George, 199
Harvey, Jacob, 353
Harvey, James, 104
Harvey, Joel, 149
Harvey, Sir John (d. 1646), 24, 194, 230
Harvey, Thomas, 284
Harvey Family Letters, 353
Harvey–George Families' Papers, Evans and, 32
Harwich, Essex, Customs records, 93
Haskell, Henry J., 281
Haslewood, Edward, 170
Hassal, John Satterfield, 183
Hassall, W. O., ed., *A Catalogue of the Library of Sir Edward Coke*, 186
Hassenclever, Peter, 300
Hastings, Francis Rawdon–, 1st Marquis of Hastings and 2nd Earl of Moira (1754-1826), 139, 266, 270, 323, 354
Hastings, East Sussex, 221; Customs records, 89
Hastings Muniment Room, Public Museum and Art Gallery, 221
Hasyard, T., 138
Hat Corporation of America, 180
Hatchett, Charles (1765?-1847), 147
Hatfield House, Hertford, 37-9
Hatherton, 1st Baron, *see* Littleton, Edward John (1791-1863)
Hatherton Mss., 216
Hathorn, Vans, 307
Hats: Manufacture, 180; Trade, 6, 88, 175, 180
Hattersley, George, & Sons Ltd., 238
[Hatton?], William, 323
Hatton Mss., 202
Hauel, Jules, 98
Haverford College, Quaker Collection, 152
Haverfordwest, Dyfed, 247-8
Haviland [or Havilland], William (1718-84), 328
Hawaii: Description, 164, 199; Finance, 318; *see also* Relations with Hawaii
HONOLULU, 278, Consular reports (British), 130, 133
Hawarden, Clwyd, 243
Hawke, Col., 219
Hawkesbury, Lord (*known as* 1803-8), *see* Jenkinson, Robert Banks, 2nd Earl of Liverpool (1770-1828)
Hawkins, J., 191
Hawkins, Sir John (1532-95), 17
Hawks, Francis Lister (1798-1866), 182
Hawley, Gabriel, 194
Hawthorne, Julian (1846-1934), 17, 78
Hawthorne, Nathaniel (1804-64), 17, 64, 176, 182, 183; *The Marble Faun* (also published as *Transformation*), 73
Hawthorne, Sophia, 17
Hawthorne, Una, 17
Hawthorne family, 17
Hawxhurst, Martha, 30
Hay, Major, 284
Hay, Lord Charles (d. 1760), 144, 259
Hay, George (*fl.* 1780-90), 311
Hay, George, 8th Marquis of Tweeddale (1787-1876), 259
Hay, J., 289
Hay, James, 2nd Earl of Carlisle (*c.* 1580-1636), 352
Hay, John (*fl.* 1772-1816), 317
Hay, John (*fl.* 1779), 289
Hay, John Milton (1838-1905), 38, 129, 165, 197, 199, 206, 221, 259
Hay, Matthew, 307
Hay, Peter, 317
Hay, R. W., 207
Hay, Thomas, Viscount Dupplin and 9th Earl of Kinnoull (1710-87), 304
Hay of Belton Muniments, 289
Hay of Seaton Mss., 254
Hayes, Edward, 14
Hayes, Howard W., 40
Hayes, John (1775-1838), 43
Hayes, Michael, 352
Hayes, Rutherford Birchard (1822-93), 58, 62, 173
Haymarket Massacre (1886), 137
Hayne, Paul Hamilton (1830-86), 69, 238
Haynes, Miss E. J., 50
Hayward, Jacob Scott, 102
Haywood, Mr., 209
Hazard, Henry, 225
Hazard, R. G., 256
Hazen, Moses (1733-1803), 324
Hazleton, Richard, 353
Hazlitt, Margaret, 58
Hazlitt, William, the younger, 58
Hazlitt, William Carew (1834-1913), 58
Hazlitt Papers, 58
Head, C. F., 104
Head, Sir Edmund Walker (1805-68), 40, 247
Head, Jane, 249
Health, General Board of, 137
Health, Ministry of, 122, 137
Health, National Board of, 131
Hearn, Eileen, 346
Hearn, J. J., 345; Papers, 345-6
Hearn, Mrs. John J., 345
Hearst, William Randolph (1863-1951), 279
Heath, Sir Robert (1575-1649), 23, 45, 194
Heath and Verney Papers, 81
Heathcote, Caleb (1666-1721), 40, 50, 83
Heathcote, Samuel, 36
Heathcote, Sir William (*fl.* 1876-7), 18
Heathcote, William (*fl.* early 18th cent.), 50
Heating, Domestic, 150
Heaton, H., "Benjamin Gott and the Anglo-American Cloth-Trade," *Journal of Economic and Business History* (1929), 239; "Yorkshire Cloth Traders in the United States, 1770-1840," *Thoresby Miscellany* (1945), 116 fn.

Heazleton, William, 329
Hebrew language, 274
Heddle Mss., 306
Heffner, A. S., 335 fn.
Heitman, Charles E., 281
Helps, Sir Arthur (1813-75), 202
Helston, Customs records, 89
Hely Hutchinson, John (1724-94), 354
Hemingway, Ernest (1899-1961), 114
Hemp: Cultivation, 10, 11, 55, 300, 301; Trade, 24, 88, 148-51 *passim*, 160, 301; *see also* Cordage
Hemphill, J. M., II, "Virginia and the Parker Family Papers," *Liverpool Libraries, Museums and Arts Committee Bulletin* (1956), 182 fn.
Hendel, C. W., 271
Henderson, Mr., 301
Henderson, Fred [James Frederick] (1867-1957), 187; *Case for Socialism*, 187
Henderson, James, 268, 289
Henderson, Sir Nevile Meyrick (1882-1942), 283
Henderson, Richard, 304
Henderson, Robert (*fl.* 1781-9), 316
Henderson, W. O., "The American Chamber of Commerce for the Port of Liverpool," *Trans. of the Historic Soc. of Lancashire and Cheshire* (1933), 183 fn.
Henderson, Walter, & Co., 310
Henderson & Eadie, 327
Henderson Autograph Collection, 16
Henderson Collection, 289
Henderson of Fordell Muniments, 294-5
Hendrick, Burton J., 75
Hendrick, Ellwood (1861-1930), 163
Henley, Robert, 2nd Earl of Northington (1747-86), 218
Henn, Lieut., 269
Henniker, John, 1st Baron (1724-1803), 219
Hennikers, Messrs., 119
Henry Frederick, Duke of Cumberland and Strathfarn (1745-90), 266
Henry, Bayard, 198, 199
Henry, John, 332
Henry, John V., 16
Henry, Joseph (1797-1878), 148
"Henry, O." (*pseud.*), *see* Porter, William Sydney (1862-1910)
Henry, Patrick (1736-99), 156
Henry (ship), 287
Henry George Foundation, 100
Hepburn, Mr., 275
Hepburn, Sir George Buchan (1739-1819), 257, 288
Hepburn, J., 270
Herbert, George Augustus, 11th Earl of Pembroke (1750-1827), 230
Herbert, George Henry, 65
Herbert, Henry Howard Molyneux, 4th Earl of Carnarvon (1831-90), 40, 111, 139
Herbert, Sir Michael Henry (1857-1903), 38, 129
Hereford and Worcester, England, 36-7; Hereford, 36; Worcester, 37
Hereford and Worcester County Record Office, 37, 228 fn.
Hereford Herd Book Society, 36
Hereford Record Office, 36
Herford, Brooke (1830-1903), 177
Hering, Rudolph (1847-1923), 170
Heron, Mrs. J., 330
Herrick, Edward Claudius (1811-62), 148
Herschel, Sir John Frederick William (1792-1871), 148
Herschell, Farrer, 1st Baron (1837-99), 38, 39
Herter, Christian (1895-1967), 278
Hertford, England, 37-43
Hertfordshire Record Office, 37, 39-42
Hervey, Frederick William, 5th Earl and 1st Marquess of Bristol (1769-1859), 218
Hervey, Isaac, 156
Hervey, S. H. A., *Journals of Hon. William Hervey*, 218 fn.
Hervey Family of Ickworth (Marquises of Bristol), 218
Hesse Cassel, Landgrave of, *see* Maurice (1572-1632)
Hessian mercenaries, *see* War of Independence, German mercenaries
Hewitt, Abram Stevens (1822-1903), 170
Hey, William (1733-97), 233
Heydon, Norfolk, 186
Heysham (Lancaster), Customs records, 92, 93
Heywood, Arthur, Sons & Co., 181
Heywood, Benjamin A., 183
Heywood, Eli, 102
Heywood, Messrs. John, & Son, 172
Heywood, Richard, 181
Heywood, Robert (1786-1868), 95; *A Journey to America in 1834*, 95 fn.
Heywood, Robert (*fl.* 1810's), 172
Heywood, T., ed., *The Norris Papers*, 181 fn.
Heywood Correspondence, 172
Hibben, John Grier (1861-1933), 238
Hichborn, Mr., 16
Hickey Collection, 343-4
Hickey Papers, 344
Hicks, Elias (1748-1830), 30
Hicks family, 98
Hicks *v.* Ellison, 21
Hicks–Beach, Sir Michael Edward, 1st Earl St. Aldwyn (1837-1916), 34
Hicks–Beach, Michael John, 2nd Earl St. Aldwyn, 34
Hicks–Beach Mss., 34
Hides and skins, Trade, 7, 122, 175, 232, 328
Higgins, Pearce, 277
Higginson, Thomas Wentworth (1823-1911), 197, 198, 208
High, Stanley, 280
High Wycombe, Buckinghamshire, 13
Hill, A. V., 282
Hill, Arthur W. (1875-1941), 146
Hill, James, 350
Hill, James Jerome (1838-1916), 210
Hill, John, 103
Hill, William (*fl.* 1859), 253
Hill, William (*fl.* 1859-65), 330
Hill, Wills, 1st Earl of Hillsborough and 1st Marquis of Downshire (1718-93), 213, 218, 266, 324
Hill family, 330
Hill Hall Papers, 31
Hilldrup, R. H., "A Campaign to Promote the Prosperity of Colonial Virginia," *Virginia Magazine of History and Biography* (1959), 149 fn.
Hilliard, Thomas, 306
Hillsborough, 1st Earl of, *see* Hill, Wills, *later* 1st Marquis of Downshire (1718-93)
Hillsborough Collection, 324
Hilton family, 328
Himes, Chester, 221

Himsworth, J. B., *The Story of Cutlery*, 235 fn.
Hinchcliffe, John, 218
Hincks, John, 18
Hindle, B., *The Pursuit of Science in Revolutionary America, 1735-1789*, 148 fn.
Hindley, Thomas H., 175
Hindolveston, Parish church, 186
Hinton, R. W. K., *The Port Books of Boston: 1601-1640*, 89
Hiort, Henry, 168
Hippocrates (460?-377 B.C.), 315
Hiss, Alger (b. 1904), 165
Historical Manuscripts Commission and National Register of Archives, 100-5; 77, 82, 83, 209
History, American, Teaching in Great Britain, 16, 229, 278, 282
History of the Times (1935-1952), 157
Hitchcock, T., 174
Hitler, Adolf (1889-1945), 282, 283
Hoar, George Frisbie (1826-1904), 85, 197
Hoare, C., & Co., 105
Hoare (Pitt) Mss., 141
Hobart, John, 2nd Earl of Buckinghamshire (1723-93), 24, 188
Hobart, Robert, 1st Baron Hobart, 4th Earl of Buckinghamshire (1760-1816), 12
Hobart Collection, 188
Hobart Papers, 12-3
Hobbs, Henry, 27
Hobhouse, Edmund (1817-1904), 159
Hobhouse, H., *Memoirs of the Hobhouse Family*, 6 fn.
Hobhouse, Isaac (1685-1763), 7
Hobhouse Papers, 6
Hobson, C., 329
Hobson, J. S. & G., 175
Hobson, S. T., 22
Hoby, Sir Edward (1560-1617), 57-8
Hodgkin, John, 29
Hodgson, Robert, 324
Hodson, H. V., 277
Hoe, J. H., 167
Hoffman, Charles Fenno (1806-84), 69
Hoffman, G. B., & Brother, 22
Hog, Roger, of Newliston, 309
Hogan, William, 171
Hogarth, Anna, 189
Hogarth, David, Jr., 189
Hogarth, Elizabeth, 189
Hogarth, George, 220
Hogg, Robert (grandfather of Robert Hogg), 273
Hogg, Robert (grandson of Robert Hogg), 273
Hogs, *see* Pigs
Holbech of Farnborough Collection, 225
Holcroft, V., 225
Holden, Isaac, & Sons Ltd., 238
Holderness, 4th Earl of, *see* D'Arcy, Robert (1718-78)
Holkham, Norfolk, 186-7
Holland, 1st Baron, *see* Fox, Henry (1705-74); 3rd Baron, *see* Fox, Henry Richard Vassall (1773-1840)
Holland, F. H., 70
Holland, Thomas, 37
Holland, Thomas E., 199
Holland Deposit, 50
Holland–Martin, E., 282
Holles, John, 1st Duke of Newcastle (of the second creation) (1662-1711), 300
Hollidge, Rebeccah, 190
Hollidge, Thomas, 190
Hollis, Thomas, 32
Hollis, Thomas Brand, 32
Hollowell, Benjamin, 120
Holman, Mrs. M., 22
Holman family, 126
Holme, Benjamin (1682/3-1749), 153
Holmes, ______, 83
Holmes, David (1770-1832), 258
Holmes, Oliver Wendell (1809-94), 69, 75, 162, 170, 178, 196, 197, 205, 208, 236, 238, 254, 259
Holmes, Oliver Wendell (1841-1935), 197, 198, 199, 228, 261
Holmes, Peter, 24
Holmes, Samuel, 325
Holmes, William, 328
Holroyd, John & Joseph, *later* Holroyd, Joseph, & Son, 240
Holroyd, John Baker, 1st Earl of Sheffield (1735-1821), 75, 160; *Observation of the Commerce of the American States* (1783), 160, 167
Holst, Hermann Edouard von (1841-1908), 164
Holt, George, & Co., 183
Holt, Henry (1840-1926), 198
Holt, Jane, 179
Holt, Jessie, 179
Holt, John (1743-1801), 182
Holt, Joseph, 155
Holt, Rowena, 179
Holt, Thomas, 179
Holt, W. E., 206
Holt and Gregson Papers, 182
Holt Papers, 206
Holworthy, W. T., 46
Holworthy Papers, 46
Holy, Newbold and Suckley of Sheffield, 234
Holyoake, George Jacob (1817-1906), 53, 173; *Travels in Search of a Settler's Guide - Book of America and Canada*, 53 fn.
Holyoake Collection, 53
Holyrood Flint Glass Works, 254
Homage to the War Dead, 158
Home, Archibald, 312
Home, Charles, 272
Home, Francis, 306
Home, George, of Branxton (*fl.* 1795), 306
Home, George, of Paxton (*fl.* 1801), 306
Home, Henry, Lord Kames (1696-1782), 270, 275
Home, James (*fl.* 1778-82), 273
Home, James (*fl.* 1801), 306
Home, Ninian, 306
Home, Patrick (*fl.* 1733), 306
Home, Patrick (*fl.* 1796-1801), 273, 306
Home, Patrick, of Wedderburn (*fl.* 1862), 306
Home, Will, 292
Home, William, 273
Home of Wedderburn Muniments, 306
Home Office, 122, 136-7, 311 fn.
Home rule (Ireland), *see* Ireland, Home rule
Homes, William, 149
Homestead law, 131
Honduras, Relations with U.S., *see* Relations with Honduras
Hone, Philip (1780-1851), 208
Hone Papers, 62
Honorable Artillery Company, 225

Hood, Samuel, 1st Viscount (1724-1816), 18, 65, 66, 101, 120; Letters, 120 fn.
Hooke, Robert, Papers, 99
Hooker, Sir Joseph Dalton (1817-1911), 146
Hooker, Sir William Jackson (1785-1865), 145, 291
Hooker Correspondence, 145
Hoome, Wilson & Co., 310
Hoon, E. E., *The Organization of the English Customs System, 1696-1786*, 87 fn., 89 fn.
Hooper, Richard, 27
Hooper, Rev. [William], 312
Hooten [or Hooton], Elizabeth (d. 1672), 156
Hoover, Herbert Clark (1874-1964), 66, 205, 278, 279, 298
Hoover, Mrs. Herbert, 205
Hoover, J. Edgar (1895-1972), 79
Hoover moratorium, 138
Hope, G. R., 270
Hope, H. W., 270
Hope, Admiral Herbert W., Deposit, 246-7
Hope, Sir James (1808-81), 13, 123
Hope, Sir John Bruce, *see* Bruce, Sir John Hope (1684?-1766)
Hope, Richard, 140
Hope, Samuel, & Co., 183
Hope, Victor A. J., 2nd Marquess of Linlithgow (1887-1952), 269
Hope (ship), 275
Hope, Todd, and Kirk Collection, 304
Hope of Luffness Mss., 270
Hopkins, Archibald, 197
Hopkins, Harry Lloyd (1890-1946), 112
Hopkins, S. M., 182
Hopkins, Stephen (1707-85), 233
Hopkins, Thomas, 10
Hopper, I. T., 353
Hopson, Peregrine Thomas (d. 1759), 259
Hopton, Ralph, 1st Baron (1598-1652), 189, 229
Hopwood, Samuel (1674-1760), 153
Horace Barks Reference Library, Stoke-on-Trent, 217
Hornby, Hugh, 223
Hornby Castle, Yorkshire, 82
Hornby Library Autograph Letters, 182
Horne, David, 11
Hornel Library, 253
Horner, James, 331
Horner, William, 8, 9
Horner, William J., 271
Horner family, 331
Hornet (U.S.S.), 43
Horrabin, Winifred, 43
Horses: Breeding, 78, 170; Exports, 143
Horsman, E., 284
Horticulture, 13, 42, 149, 180, 263, 264, 270, 275, 290, 303
Hosack, ———, *System of Practical Nosology*, 315
Hosmer, Frederick Lucian (1840-1929), 176
Hosmer, G. N., 208
Hotham, Charles, 48
Hotham, Sir Henry (1777-1833), 43
Hotham, William, 1st Baron Hotham (1736-1813), 42
Hotham Collection, 42-3
Hotten, John Camden (1832-73), 33, 84; *The Original Lists of . . . [persons emigrating] to the American Plantations, 1600-1700*, 129
Hotze, Henry, 204
Houghton, 1st Baron, *see* Milnes, Richard Monckton (1809-85)
Houghton, Mrs., 47
Houghton, Alanson B., 278
Houghton, D., 47
Houghton, R., 297
Houghton Mss., *see* Cholmondeley (Houghton) Mss.
Houghton Muniments, 47
Hourse, James, 259
House, Edward Mandell (1858-1938), 197, 198, 209, 210, 229, 256, 259, 260, 277, 280, 345; *Intimate Papers*, 210, 260
House of Commons, 18, 26, 107, 108, 109, 110, 186, 248, 292, 298, 301, 302, 305; Members from the Colonies, 65
House of Commons Library, 105
House of Lords, 32, 65, 160, 218, 239, 240, 263, 267, 281, 292, 302
House of Lords Record Office, 106-13
House of Representatives, 62, 164, 188; Speaker, 197, 201
Housing, 111
Houston, Alexander, & Co., 256, 317
Houston, Herbert S., 277
Houston, Jane Park, 331
Houston, John, 331
Houston, Patrick, 274
Houston Family Papers, 331
Houston of Johnston Muniments, 269
How Papers, 8
Howard, Bronson, 74
Howard, Charles P., 165
Howard, Esmé William, Baron Howard of Penrith (1863-1939), 198, 277
Howard, Francis, 5th Baron Howard of Effingham (1643-95), 82, 275
Howard, Frederick, 5th Earl of Carlisle (1748-1825), 44, 76
Howard, Sir George (1720?-96), 12
Howard, Henry, 22nd Earl of Suffolk (1739-79), 65, 76, 215
Howard, M. S., *Jonathan Cape, Publisher*, 114
Howard, Samuel Lloyd, 98
Howard, Thomas, 230
Howard Association, 58, 228
Howard family, Earls of Suffolk and Berkshire, 230
Howard League for Penal Reform, 228
Howard de Walden Papers, 133
Howard–Vyse Deposit, 12
Howe, Frederick Webster (1822-91), 144
Howe, J. M., 28
Howe, Joseph (1804-73), 81
Howe, Julia (Ward), Mrs. Samuel Gridley Howe (1819-1910), 176, 208
Howe, Quincy, *England Expects Every American to Do His Duty*, 275
Howe, Richard, Earl (1726-99), 42, 76, 120, 276, 294
Howe, Samuel Gridley (1801-76), 95
Howe, Sir William, 5th Viscount (1729-1814), 12, 43, 44, 76, 141, 145, 192, 195, 215, 216, 260, 262, 266, 268, 274, 275, 292, 293, 305, 352
Howell, D. (*fl.* 1890), 245
Howell, David (1747-1824), 245
Howell, David (1831-1903), 243
Howell, David, of Machynlleth (*fl.* 1848), 245
Howell, George (1833-1910), 52
Howell, L. D., 246
Howell family, 248
Howells, William Dean (1837-1920), 74, 75, 238
Hower, R. M., "The Wedgwoods," *Journal of Economic and Business History* (1931-2), 213 fn.
Howick, Viscount (*styled* 1807-45), *see* Grey, Sir Henry George,

afterwards 3rd Earl Grey (1802-94)
Howick, Henry, 98
Howis, Charlotte, 98
Howland, Arthur, 72
Howland, Charles P., 277, 278, 279
Howland, Elizabeth, 72
Huck, Richard, 264, 265, 266, 284
Huddleston, Ferdinand, 13
Huddleston family, 13
Hudson, D., and K. W. Luckhurst, *The Royal Society of Arts*, 148 fn.
Hudson, Henry (d. 1611), 37
Hudson, Patricia, *The West Riding Wool Textile Industry*, 237 fn., 239
Hudson, Mrs. Sara, 18
Hudson, Stephen (*pseud.*), *see* Schiff, Sydney
Hudson Bay, 14, 22, 146
Hudson River, 22, 162, 270, 271
Hudson's Bay Company, 15, 19, 110, 111, 124, 130, 130 fn., 138, 146, 146 fn., 160, 210, 254, 255, 323; *see also* North West Company
Huggins, Robert, 16
Hughenden Manor, Buckinghamshire, 13
Hughes, Miss, 348
Hughes, Charles Evans (1862-1948), 197, 277, 284
Hughes, Christopher (1786-1849), 183, 187, 218, 240
Hughes, Ezekiel (1767-1849), 246
Hughes, Gabriel, Mss., 248
Hughes, (James) Langston (1902-67), 221
Hughes, John (*fl.* 1760's), 233
Hughes, John (*fl.* late 19th cent.), 348
Hughes, M. F., 348
Hughes, Owen (*fl.* 1892), 248
Hughes, R. T., 32, 33
Hughes, Thomas (1822-96), 68, 163
Hughes Families' Papers, Sandford and, 32-3
Huguenot Library, 113
Huguenot Society of London, 113
Huguenots, 12, 86, 113, 346
Hulbert, George Redmond (1774-1825), 121
Hull, Cordell (1871-1955), 281, 282, 345
Hull, F., ed., "The Tufton Mss. and the Virginia Connection," *Virginia Magazine of History and Biography* (1957), 45 fn.
Hull & Bowne, 51
Hull, Humberside, 42-3; Customs records, 89, 92, 93; Merchants, 107
Hull House, Chicago, 197
Hulls, Mrs. E. M. C., 28
Hulton, Henry (*c.* 1731-91), 175, 208
Humberside, England, 42-3
Humberside County Record Office, 42
Humberston, Francis Mackenzie, 1st Baron Seaforth and Mackenzie (1754-1815), 286
Humboldt Redwood Co. Ltd., 308
Hume, ———, 173
Hume, David, 290
Hume, Francis, 306
Hume, Hugh, 3rd Earl of Marchmont and Baron Polwarth (1708-94), 258, 292
Hume, James Deacon (1774-1842), 63
Hume, John, 268
Hume, Joseph (1777-1855), 161
Hume of Marchmont Muniments, 292
Humphrey, Herbert Alfred (1868-1951), 163
Humphrey Papers, 163
Humphries, Francis Richmond, 16
Humphrys, A., 212
Humphrys, Richard, 74
Hungerford, Ducie, 220
Hunt, John, 154
Hunt, Joseph, 101
Hunt, Nathan (1758-1853), 51
Hunt, William, 31
Hunter, ———, 167
Hunter, Adam, 273
Hunter, Andrew, 275
Hunter, Henry, 243
Hunter, James, 272
Hunter, John Dunn, 187
Hunter, Patrick (d. 1738?), 290
Hunter, Robert (d. 1734), 220, 291, 300
Hunter, Robert (*fl.* 1738), 290
Hunter, Robert (*fl.* 1822-3), 330
Hunter, William (1718-83), 317
Hunter, Harvey, Webster and Will Collection, 307
Hunter & Ballatine, Messrs., 270
Hunter Family Letters, 331
Hunter Mss., 317
Hunter of Hunterston Mss., 268
Hunter of Hunterston Muniments, 290
Hunting, 20, 41, 274, 291, 307, 348
Huntingdon, Collis P. (1821-1900), 166
Huntingdon, Randolph, 78
Huntingdon, Selina, Countess of (1707-91), 103; American Papers, 103
Huntingdon, Cambridgeshire, 17
Huntingdon, Hopkins & Co., 236
Huntly House Museum, 254
Hurst, C. J. B., 277
Hurst, Sir Cecil, 279
Hurst, Joseph, 179
Hurst Mills, Greater Manchester, 180
Huschler, John, 236
Huske, Ellis (1700-55), 271
Huske, John (1692?-1761), 271, 301
Huskisson, William (1770-1830), 57, 84, 287
Huskisson Papers, 57
Hussey, Curtis Grubb (1802-93), 235
Hustler, Christiana, 41
Hutcheson, David, 164
Hutcheson, Francis, 317
Hutchings, James M., 239
Hutchinson, Elizabeth, 82
Hutchinson, John Hely, *see* Hely Hutchinson, John (1724-94)
Hutchinson, Peter Orlando, 26
Hutchinson, T., 314
Hutchinson, Thomas (1711-80), 61, 214, 215, 233, 265; *A Collection of Original Papers Relative to the History of Massachusetts Bay*, 193 fn.
Huth, Frederick, & Co. Ltd., 169, 317
Hutton, Sir Edward Thomas Henry, 78
Hutton, George, 305
Hutton, Hugh, 95
Hutton, William, 330
Hutton Papers, 78
Huxley, Thomas Henry (1825-95), 162

Huxley Papers, 162
Hyam, Thomas, 51, 149, 151
Hyde, 1st Baron (*from* 1756-76), *see* Villiers, Thomas, 1st Earl of Clarendon (1709-86); 4th Baron, *see* Villiers, George William Frederick, 4th Earl of Clarendon (1800-70)
Hyde, Edward, 1st Earl of Clarendon (1609-74), 273
Hyde, Edward, 3rd Earl of Clarendon (1661-1723) (*styled* Viscount Cornbury, 1711-14), 10
Hyde, F. E., *Blue Funnel*, 183 fn.; and others, "The Cotton Broker and the Rise of the Liverpool Cotton Market," *Economic History Review* (1955), 185 fn.
Hyde, Samuel, 304
Hydrographic surveying, 144, 264, 311
Hydrophobia, 315
Hyrne, Edward, 50
Hyrne, Elizabeth, 50
Hyslop, David, 263
Hyslop, William, 290
Hythe, Customs records, 89

I

Ice, Trade, 264
Ickes, Harold L. (1874-1952), 163
Idaho: Description, 204; Mining, 308
Idaho (ship), 329
Idaho Alamo Consolidated Mines Ltd., 308
Iddesleigh, 1st Earl of, *see* Northcote, Sir Stafford Henry (1818-87)
Ilchester Collection, 27
Île St. Jean, *see* Prince Edward Island
Ilfracombe, Customs records, 89, 93
Illinois: Agriculture, 22, 245, 346; Description, 24, 156, 224, 346; Education, 47; Governors, 164; Immigrants, 22, 28, 35, 47, 217, 220, 230, 245, 248, 265, 328, 331, 332, 346; Industry, 236; Land, 28; Law, 202; Politics, 62; Religious history, 28, 47, 96, 225; Senators, 277; Settlement, 155, 265, 307; Trade, 46, 63, 133, 236; Wages, 28
CHEBANESE, 328; Chicago, 72, 96, 281, 331, 332, 345, 353, Consular reports (British), 130, 133, 135, 137, 198, Description, 20, 32, 148, 164, 270, 298, 304, Merchants, 235, 236, Palmer hotel, 297, World's Columbian Exposition (1893), 268, 297; Eden, 332; Edwards County, 155; Elgin, 230; Iroquois County, 346; Jacksonville, 327; Mount Pleasant, 47; Nauvoo, 328; Peoria, 47, 265; Prasau Creek, 28; Robins Nest, 24
Illinois Central Railway, 105
Illinois Investment Co., 273, 315
Illinois, University of, Illinois Historical Survey, 140 fn.
"Ilston Book," 244, 245
Immigrants from Austria, 152; Bavaria, 124, 220; China, 38, 96, 131; France, 15, 53, 86, 113, 346; Germany, 143, 280
GREAT BRITAIN, Colonial period, 55, 129, 202, 305, 350; 1776-1800, 80, 138, 170, 313; 19th century, 22, 36, 39, 42, 47, 52, 61, 79, 108-10 *passim*, 129, 131, 136, 137, 138, 152, 169, 172, 190, 198, 201, 208, 209, 216; 20th century, 111, 125; *see also* Emigrant letters; Parish records; Quarter sessions records; Trade unions (British), Emigration schemes; Transportation of criminals.
GREECE, 266, 302; Ireland, 46, 61, 63, 84, 108, 111, 117, 124, 137, 221, 305, 307, 323-32 *passim*, 343-4 *passim*, 346-53 *passim*; Netherlands, 90; Prussia, 157; Santo Domingo, 298
SCOTLAND, 22, 108, 173, 182, 253-4 *passim*, 263, 265, 266, 269, 273-6 *passim*, 287, 291-5 *passim*, 299, 300, 305, 310, 313, 315, 316, 318, 344; Wales, 243-8 *passim*, 250
BEDFORDSHIRE, 9; Berkshire, 11; Buckinghamshire, 154; Cambridgeshire, 14; Cheshire, 179; Cornwall, 20, 50; Devonshire, 25, 26, 98; Dorset, 28, 29; Durham, 29; Essex, 32-3; Gloucestershire, 5, 34, 35; Hampshire, 36; Hertford, 42; Kent, 44, 46; Lancashire, 9, 46-8 *passim*, 179; Leicestershire, 49; London, 31; Manchester, Greater, 179; Merseyside, 273, 307, 344; Middlesex, 98; Norfolk, 129, 185, 186, 188, 189; Northamptonshire, 190; Nottinghamshire, 192; Oxfordshire, 205; Staffordshire, 217; Suffolk, 217, 219, 220; Surrey, 220, 221; Sussex, 221; Warwickshire, 228; Wiltshire, 114; Yorkshire, 230, 233, 234, 235, 237
See also subdivision Immigrants *under states, etc.*
Immigrants to the United Kingdom, 351
Imperial College of Science and Technology, *see* London University. Imperial College of Science and Technology
Imperial War Museum, 113-4
Imperialism, 165, 197
Imports, *see* Trade
Impressment of seamen, 30, 80, 81, 131, 137, 207, 208; *see also* *Chesapeake* (ship); *Trent* (ship)
Imprisonment, Illegal, 125
Indentured servants, 27, 35, 45, 47, 48, 84-5, 253, 272, 293, 299, 300, 301, 304, 311, 343; *see also* Transportation of criminals
The Independent, 278
Independents, 274; *see also* Congregational churches
Index to the Letters and Papers of Edward White Benson, Archbishop of Canterbury, 1882-1896, in Lambeth Palace Library, 115
India, 96, 280, 287; Pondicherry, 287; *see also* Relations with India; Trade with India
Indian Affairs, Commissioners for, 99
Indian corn, *see* Maize
Indiana: Agriculture, 328, 331; Description, 30, 156; Finance, 100, 181; Immigrants, 20, 47, 191, 219, 328, 331, 332; Merchants, 235; Religious history, 41, 156; Settlement, 173, 245
INDIANAPOLIS, 235, 327; New Harmony, 173, 209, 245; Ripley County, 332
Indians, 78; Colonial period, 10, 22, 28, 35, 40, 41, 45, 55, 66, 94, 101, 138, 141, 156, 174, 195, 214, 215, 262, 263, 265, 266, 285, 290, 292, 293, 301, 303, 309, 323, 324; 1775-83, 12, 188, 203, 266, 272, 315, 324; 1783-1800, 56, 80, 101, 107, 155, 200, 314; 19th century, 38, 56, 83, 101, 109, 156, 196, 207, 270, 271, 273, 291; 20th century, 199
WARS, 1750-1815, 9, 12, 45, 47, 48, 50, 102, 142, 156, 174, 190, 203, 258, 262, 264, 266, 267, 291, 303, 304, 323; 1816-95, 5, 20, 271, 291, 347
CATAWBA, 262, 284; Cayuga, 131; Cherokee, 61, 62, 195, 262, 266, 284, 289, 299; Chickasaw, 66, 271, 284; Chippewa, 45, 271; Choctaw, 271; Creek, 264, 266, 284, 287, 299; Delaware, 79, 214, 263; Five Nations, 191, 262; Flat Bow, 146; Iroquois, 258; Kickapoo, 187; Kootenai, 146; Maricheets, 257 fn.; Micmac, 257; Mohawk, 220; Ochese, 66; Ottawa, 45, 286; Pawnee, 306; Seminole, 271; Seneca, 19; Shawnee, 79, 116, 214; Sioux, 291; Six Nations, 12, 213, 214; Talapoosa, 66; Welsh, 243
EDUCATION, 103, 158, 263, 271, 290; Guides, 307; Land, 214; Languages, 53, 147, 151, 306; Missions, 19, 31, 83, 85, 94, 98, 99, 116, 118, 147, 152, 155, 158, 160, 174, 188, 203, 225, 227, 249, 270, 313; Origin, 19; Petitions, 158; Presents, 301, 307; Religion and mythology, 115, 147, 151, 257, 291; Social

life and customs, 146, 147, 183, 307, 343; Trade, 7, 210, 295, 303; Treaties, 45, 270
FLORIDA, 249; Georgia, 32, 52; Indian Territory, 344; Massachusetts, 19, 99, 210; Montana, 344; New England, 10, 94; New Jersey, 103, 313; New York, 19, 31, 131, 215, 244, 298; Ohio, 156, 215; Pennsylvania, 31, 156; Quebec, 114; South Carolina, 50, 66, 160, 284, 299; South Dakota, 5; Virginia, 10, 214, 230
Indigo: Cultivation, 266, 274, 301, 330; Seeds, 97; Trade, 212, 232, 311
Indirect claims, *see Alabama* (ship), Claims
Industry, 54, 56, 64, 125, 143, 166, 277, 278; Colonial period, 10, 149, 226; Labour, 63; *see also* Factory system; Foundries; Machinery; Sawmills; Shipbuilding; *and subdivision* Industry *under states*
Industry (ship), 102
Ingalls, John James (1833-1900), 280
Ingersoll, Charles Jared (1782-1862), 167
Ingersoll, J. R., 75
Ingersoll, Jared (1722-81), 149
Ingersoll, Robert Green (1833-99), 173, 204
Ingham, Benjamin, 49
Inglis, Agnes, 163
Inglis, Charles (1734-1816), 86
Inglis, Sir John (*fl.* 1733), 274
Inglis, John (*fl.* 1753-4), 264
Inglis, John (*fl.* 1777-87), 273
Inglis, John (*fl.* 1797-8), 287
Inglis & Robb, 310
Ingram, Archibald, 317
Ingram, Sir Arthur (d. 1642), 239
Inheritance of land, *see* Land tenure
Inner Temple Library, 114
Innes, Lt.-Col., 145
Innes, Col., 264
Innes, Alfred Mitchell, 198
Innes, John, 288
Innes, Robert, 270, 305
Innis, John, 195
Inskip, Thomas Walker Hobart, 1st Viscount Caldecote (1876-1947), 281
Inspector-General of Imports and Exports, 8, 88
Institute for Advanced Study, New York and Princeton, 280, 282
Institute of Agricultural History, 11
Institute of Bankers Library, London, 115 fn.
Institute of International Education, New York, 280
Institute of Pacific Relations, Conferences, Quebec (1942); Atlantic City (1944), 206
Institute of Politics (Williamstown, Mass.), 283
Institution of Mechanical Engineers, 114
Insurance, 99, 100, 111, 307, Marine, 32, 99, 161, 173, 205, 212, 288, 309, 326
Internal combustion engine, 223
International Co. of Mexico, 100
International Conferences of American States, 131, 157
International Left Opposition, 228
International Library Conference (1897), 317
International Marine Conference, Washington (1889), 38, 131
International Monetary Conference, Brussels (1892), 172
International Penal and Prison Congress, 1st, London (1872), 6
International Postal Congress, 5th, Washington (1897), and 6th, Rome (1906), 132
International Prize Court, 198
International Woman Suffrage Alliance, 84, 179
International Workingmen's Association, 1st, 52-3
Inventions, 34, 47, 131, 137, 226, 266, 303, 304, 308
Investments, 165, 175, 258, 277, 331; Far East, 197; British, 20, 22, 28, 46, 51-2, 96, 98, 100, 102, 103, 105, 111, 115-6, 117, 118, 125, 142, 155, 166, 169, 170, 172, 181, 204, 209-10, 211, 222, 232-3, 239, 262, 271, 273, 289, 290, 307, 308, 318; Irish, 326; *see also* Banking; Land speculation; Mining industry and finance; Railways, Finance
Invilliers, Charles E. d', 291
Iowa, Elections, 198; Immigrants, 172, 244, 245, 326, 327, 328; Religious history, 152
DES MOINES, 327
Iowa, University Libraries, 85 fn.
Ipswich, Suffolk, 218-20; Customs records, 89, 93, 94
Ireland, Alexander (1810-94), 179; Collection, 178-9
Ireland, David, 271
Ireland, J. N., 74
Ireland: Rebellion of 1798, 349, 351; Rebellion of 1803, 351; Rebellion of 1867, 351-2; Easter Rising of 1916, 200
CENSUS RETURNS, 349; Famines, 185, 345
HOME RULE: Support in America, 71, 72, 77, 112, 126, 197, 209, 210, 270, 277, 288, 344, 345, 346; *see also* Genealogy, Irish; Immigrants from Ireland; Investments, Irish; Parish records: Ireland; Relations with Ireland; Trade with Ireland
Ireland, Cabinet Minutes, 352
Ireland: Chief Secretary's Office, Official Papers, 351; Convict Department, 351; Registered Papers, 352
Ireland, Dáil Éireann Secretariat, Files, 352
Ireland, Department of the Taoiseach (Prime Minister), Files, 352
Ireland, Outrage Reports, 351
Ireland, State of the Country Papers, 351
Iris, Sheffield, 234
Irish-Americans, 77, 343-6 *passim*; *see also* Fenians
Irish [Constitutional] Convention (1917), 209, 210, 345
Irish Folklore Commission, 353
Irish Historical Studies, 351
Irish in the Civil War, *see* Civil War: Federal Army, Irish recruits; Confederate States: Army, Irish troops
Irish Linen Board, 325
Irish Manuscripts Commission, 343
Irish National Land League, 345
Irish National League, 345
Irish National League of America, 345
Irish nationalist movement, 329, 343-6 *passim*, 351-2; *see also* Fenians
Irish News, 344, 345
Irish Parliamentary Party, 353
Irish Political Prisoners Fund Association, 345
Irish Race Convention, New York, 353
Irish Revolutionary Brotherhood, *see* Fenians
Irish World, New York, 345
Iron, 144; Duties, 125, 232, 274, 301; Manufacture, 308; Mining, 230, 307; Trade, 24, 125, 126, 150, 160, 211, 212, 234, 247, 248, 249, 250, 263, 274, 289, 301, 302
Iron and steel industry, 6, 28, 112, 125, 183, 226, 234-5, 236, 270, 274, 300, 318
Iron and steel workers, Trade unions, 164
Iron Molders' Union, 53
Irvine, George W., 16
Irving, David (1778-1860), 161
Irving, Sir Henry (1838-1905), 238
Irving, J. T., 270

Irving, Peter (1771-1838), 259
Irving, Thomas, 161
Irving, Washington (1783-1859), 26, 64, 174, 182, 238, 256, 259
Isaac Hicks (ship), 122
Isaacs, Rufus Daniel, 1st Marquess of Reading (1860-1935), 77, 135
Iselin, J., 35
Isham, Sir Justinian (1610-74), 189
Isham Papers, 189
Isinglass, 149, 150
Isis (British ship), 120
Island Mutual Development Company, 29
Isle of Man, 335; *see also* Trade with Isle of Man
Isle of Wight, 229
Isle St. John, *see* Prince Edward Island
Islington Libraries, 114
Islington Literary and Scientific Society, 114
Ismay, Sir George (b. 1891), 128
Isolationism, 279, 280, 283
Isthmian canal, *see* Nicaraguan canal controversy; Panama Canal
Italy, Naples, 288; *see also* Relations with Italy
Ives, John, 219
Ives, Thomas, 219
Ivie, George, 351
Ivory, Trade, 213

J

"J., R.," 275
Jackson, Andrew (1767-1845), 66, 95, 167, 187, 206, 207, 222, 258, 259, 306, 325, 344
Jackson, Arthur, 6
Jackson, F. J., 240
Jackson, Sir George (1785-1861), 226, 240
Jackson, Sir Richard Downes (1777-1845), 240
Jackson, Samuel, 226
Jackson, T. M., 75
Jackson, Thomas Jonathan ["Stonewall"] (1824-63), 76
Jackson, W. Turrentine, "The Chavez Land Grant," *Pacific Historical Review* (1952), 318 fn.; "Lewis Richard Price," *Pacific Historical Review* (1960), 211 fn.; "Mazatlan to the Estanislao . . .," *California Historical Society Quarterly* (1960), 211 fn.; *The Enterprising Scot*, 307, 318 fn.
Jackson, William (1759-1828), 31
Jackson, William, *The Records of the Court of the Stationers' Company*, 157
Jackson & Co., 236
Jacobus, M. W., 271
Jacobus family, 5
Jacomb-Hood, Mrs. Rita, 79
Jaffe Bros. & Co., 310
Jaffray, John, 79
Jamaica, 15, 315; Insurrection (1865), 256
BRITISH ARMY, 50; Chief Justices, 223; Governors, 228; Merchants, 212; Trade with Great Britain, 26, 212, 260, 306; *see also* Relations with Jamaica; Trade with Jamaica
KINGSTON, Customs collectors, 87; Montego Bay, 172, Customs collectors, 87
James I, *King* (1566-1625), 26, 37, 192
James II, *King* (1633-1701), 54, 82, 260
James, Duke of York and Albany *see (later)*, James II, *King* (1633-1701)
James, George Payne Rainsford (1799-1860), 98, 184
James, Henry (1843-1916), 65, 78, 79, 84, 161, 162, 164, 199, 202, 205, 222, 238, 256, 257; *Confidence*, 84
James, Henry (1879-1947), *Charles W. Eliot*, 196 fn.
James, John, 51
James, Thomas Potts (1803-82), 145
James, William (*fl.* 1834), 190
James (ship), 275
James and Peggy (transport), 91
Jameson, John Franklin (1859-1937), 165, 197
Jameson, R., 314
Jamieson, J. W., 272
Jamieson, Semple & Lawson, 309
Jamison, F. B., 290, 291
Janson, Dirck, 200
Japan, *see* Relations with Japan; Trade with Japan
Jardine, Sir William (1800-74), 314
Jarvis, Edward (1803-84), 170
Jarvis, R. C., ed., *Customs Letter Books of the Port of Liverpool, 1711-1813*, 92
Jarvis, Thomas, 27
Java (ship), 108
Jay, Isaac, 265
Jay, John (1745-1829), 11, 80, 94, 259
Jay, Mary, 36
Jay's Treaty (1794), 54, 56, 80, 81, 95, 107, 200
Jeaffrison, J. C., ed., *Middlesex County Records . . . 1549-1687*, 97 fn.
Jeannette (ship), 146
Jee, John, Jr. (d. 1808), 32
Jeffers, J. R., 74
Jefferson, Thomas (1743-1826), 6, 11, 12, 16, 19, 57, 68, 80, 95, 168, 171, 172, 182, 183, 200, 204, 226, 259, 294, 299, 314; *Notes on the State of Virginia*, 178; *Papers . . .*, ed. by J. P. Boyd and others, 57 fn.; *Writings*, ed. by P. L. Ford, 95 fn.
Jeffries, Benjamin Joy (1833-1915), 239
Jeffries Collection, 6, 7
Jeffs, William & Thomas, 310
Jellett, Morgan, "Anecdotal Recollections," 331
Jenckes, Joseph (1656-1740), 62
Jendwine, J. W., 166
Jenifer family, 86
Jenkins, Daniel, 247
Jenkins, Howard M., 345
Jenkins, Sir Leoline (1623-85), 22
Jenkins, Jenkin T., 247
Jenkinson, Charles, 1st Earl of Liverpool (1727-1808), 54, 55, 354
Jenkinson, H., *Guide to the Public Records*, 122
Jenkinson, Robert Banks, 2nd Earl of Liverpool (*known as* Lord Hawkesbury, 1803-8) (1770-1828), 54, 57, 83, 84, 107, 161, 168
Jenks, Jeremiah Whipple (1856-1929), 164
Jennings, George Bryan, 64
Jenny (ship), 54
Jennys & Baker, 212
Jersey, Lady Sarah Sophia, (1785-1867), 98
Jersey, *see* New Jersey
Jersey, Channel Islands, 339
Jervois, Sir William Francis Drummond (1821-97), 104
Jessamine, Mrs. M., Mss., 272
Jesuits, 37, 171, 225; Missions, 157, 229, 352; in Canada, 45, 138

Jewson, C. B., *Transcript of Three Registers of Passengers*, 129
Jeyes, S. H., *The Russells of Birmingham*, 73 fn., 226 fn.
John (brig), 181
John Carter Brown Library, 245
John Randolph (American ship), 17
John Rylands University Library, University of Manchester, 174-8; 208 fn., 213 fn.
Johns family, 86
Johns Hopkins University, 162, 177, 283
Johnson, Andrew (1808-75), 62, 68, 201, 344
Johnson, Christopher, & Co., 236
Johnson, Edmunds, 180
Johnson, F. B., 287
Johnson, H. N., 176
Johnson, Sir John (1742-1830), 101
Johnson, John Ormsby, 101
Johnson, Josiah, 50
Johnson, Lady Mary (d. 1815), 101
Johnson, Oliver (1809-89), 95, 96
Johnson, Reverdy (1796-1876), 68, 70, 72, 129, 201, 202
Johnson, Richard, 285
Johnson, Robert Underwood (1853-1937), 70, 74, 197, 199
Johnson, Samuel (1696-1772), 61
Johnson, Samuel (1709-84), 269; *Taxation no Tyranny*, 269
Johnson, Thomas, 181
Johnson, Sir William (1715-74), 64, 101, 174, 271, 292, 301
Johnson–Clarendon Convention, 1869, 69, 70, 201, 202
Johnson Family History, 101
Johnston, Mr., 300
Johnston, A., 50
Johnston, Alexander, 290
Johnston, Charles, 190
Johnston, E. M., "The Career and Correspondence of Thomas Allan," *Irish Historical Studies* (1957), 323 fn.
Johnston, Francis, 332
Johnston, Gabriel (1699-1752), 312
Johnston, George (*fl.* 1778), 216, 268
Johnston, George (*fl.* 1781), 292
Johnston, Sir Harry Hamilton (1858-1927), 198
Johnston, James, of Bishopbriggs (*fl.* 1766-79), 316
Johnston, James (*fl.* 1770), 149
Johnston, James (*fl.* 1774), 39
Johnston, James Finlay Weir, 29; *Report on the Agricultural Capabilities of the Province of New Brunswick* (1850), 29; *Notes on North America, Agricultural, Economical and Social* (1851), 29
Johnston, Jane, 39
Johnston, Sir John (*fl.* 1780), 305
Johnston, John (*fl.* 1801), 272
Johnston, John Frederick (1793-1816), 39-40
Johnston, Joshua, 272
Johnston, Margaret (*fl.* 1781), 292
Johnston, Margaret (*fl.* 1856), 332
Johnston, Ormand Lawson, 275
Johnston, Samuel (1733-1816), 297
Johnston, Thomas, 265
Johnston, Thomas Mungo, 273
Johnston family, 39, 272, 332
Johnston of Holehouse Mss., 265
Johnstone, Andrew Cochrane (*fl.* 1814), 255
Johnstone, George (1730-87), 249, 265, 266, 312, 313
Johnstone, James, Chevalier de Johnstone (1719-1800?), 256; *Memoirs*, 256
Johnstone, James (*fl.* 1764), 223
Johnstone, Sir James (*fl.* 1776), 312
Joliffe, M. F., "John Francis Bray," *International Review of Social History* (1939), 163 fn.
Jollie Papers, 94
Jonathan Cape Ltd., 114
Jones, Alexander, 144
Jones, Alfred, 166
Jones, Allen (1739-1807), 145
Jones, Aneurin, 243
Jones, Ann, 166
Jones, Corris, 248
Jones, D., 246
Jones, D. Caradog, 282
Jones, Davey, 36
Jones, David (*fl.* 1817), 244
Jones, David (*fl.* 1879), 247
Jones, David W. (*fl.* 1861), 248
Jones, E. (*fl.* 1737), 30
Jones, E., *Index to Records . . . on the Lord Treasurer's Remembrancer's Side of the Exchequer*, 129 fn.
Jones, E. B., 246
Jones, Edward, 329
Jones, Elias (*fl.* 1873-6), 248
Jones, Elizabeth, 271
Jones, G. James, 244
Jones, George, 66
Jones, Henry, 169
Jones, Henry Arthur (1851-1929), 238
Jones, Sir Henry Haydn, Deposit, 246
Jones, J. Edred, 244
Jones, Jesse, 245
Jones, John G. (*fl.* 1862-4), 246
Jones, John Gale (1769-1838), 161; *An Oration on the late General Washington*, 161
Jones, John Owen, 245
Jones, John Paul (1747-92), 23, 43, 44, 76, 92, 181, 191, 267, 273, 308
Jones, John Roberts, 246
Jones, Katherine (1850-1929), 157
Jones, L. A., 236
Jones, P. E., and R. Smith, *A Guide to the Records in the Corporation of London Records Office and the Guildhall Library Muniment Room*, 85 fn., 98 fn.
Jones, Peter, *see* Kahehewaquonaby
Jones, R. Gwesyn, 244
Jones, Rebecca, 20, 40
Jones, Richard, 246
Jones, Rufus M., and others, *The Quakers in the American Colonies*, 154
Jones, Samuel, 260
Jones, Theophilus (1810-96), 244
Jones, Thomas, 278, 280
Jones, Val, 237 fn.
Jones, Wilbur D., "The British Conservatives and the American Civil War," *American Historical Review* (1952-3), 13 fn.; ed., "A British View of the War of 1812 and the Peace Negotiations," *Mississippi Valley Historical Review* (1958), 221 fn.
Jones, William (1826-99), 157
Jones, William B., 244
Jones, William Roberts (*fl.* 1854-64), 246
Jones, William S., 244
Jordan, M. J., 345
Jorgensen, Jorgen, 9

Joseph (ship), 239
Joseph and Mary (ship), 304
Josephs, Joseph, 183
Journalism, International, 278; *see also* Newspapers; Press
Jowitt, Robert, & Sons Ltd., 239
Joy, G., 169
Juan de Fuca Strait, 71, 77, 133, 233; *see also* San Juan Islands; Washington, Treaty of (1871)
Jucker, N. S., *The Jenkinson Papers*, 54 fn.
Judge Advocate General's Records, 144
Judges: Colonial period, 210, 302
ELECTION, 198; Supreme Court, 279
Judith (ship), 26
Jurist, 167, 169
Justice, G. M., 183
Justice, Walter, 42
Jute, Trade, 263, 269, 271
Jute Industries Ltd., Mss., 263

K

Kadenacy, Michael, 223
Kahehewaquonaby [Peter Jones], 271
Kahn, Herman, 283
Kahn, Otto, 260
Kames, Lord, *see* Home, Henry (1696-1782)
Kaminkow, J. and M., *A List of Emigrants from England to America, 1718-1759*, 86 fn.
Kane, J. K., 75
Kane Monument Association of New York, 75
Kansas: 1854-61, 201, 222, 244
FINANCE, 98; Immigrants, 47, 332; Land, 98, 244; Religious history, 152; Slavery, 201, 222, 244
CLAY CENTER, 332; Emporia, 244; Fort Leavenworth, 270; Neosho, 244
Kansas City, Fort Scott and Memphis Railroad, 96
Kansas City Star, 281
Kansas City Street Railway, 96
Kansas–Nebraska Act (1854), 201
Kaye, Brig. J. W., 22
Kean, Edmund (1787-1833), 298
Kearney, Lieut.-Col., 144
Kearney, Denis (1847-1907), 198
Kearney, Frederick, 344
Keath, James, 14
Keating, H. S., 15
Keating, Sir Henry Singer (1804-88), 15, 204
Keele University Library, 212-3
Keeler, Oscar, 69
Keen, ——, 24
Keen, Robert, 103
Keen, Rosemary, *A Survey of the Archives of Selected Missionary Societies*, 117 fn.
Keen, William Williams (1837-1932), 197
Keep, John (1781-1870), 95
Kegan Paul, Trench, Trübner & Henry S. King, 170
Keith, Admiral Viscount, *see* Elphinstone, George Keith (1746-1823)
Keith, James, 253
Keith, Sir William (1680-1749), 261
Kellaway, W., "The Archives of the New England Company," *Archives* (1954), 98 fn.; *New England Company, 1649-1776*, 98 fn., 99 fn.
Keller, C. M., 180
Kellie, 8th Earl of, *see* Erskine, Charles (d. 1799)
Kellogg, Frank B. (1856-1937), 277, 278, 279
Kellogg, Miner K. (1814-89), 66
Kellogg–Briand Peace Pact (1927), 277-80 *passim*
Kelly, Mr., 302
Kelly, John M., 348
Kelly, Michael, 298
Kelly family, 335
Kelsal and Spalding, Messrs., 295
Kelsey, Henry (*c*. 1670- *c*. 1724), 323; *The Kelsey Papers*, 323 fn.
Kemble, Gouverneur (1786-1875), 222
Kemble, Peter, 222
Kemble, William, 222
Kemble family, 222
Kemp, Mr., 24
Kemp., B., "Some Letters of Sir Francis Dashwood," *Bulletin of the John Rylands Library* (1954), 200
Kemp, C. F., 209
Kemp, John, 261
Kempe, J. T., 265
Kempt, Sir James (1764-1854), 144, 207
Kendal, Cumbria, 22
Kennan, George, 353
Kennaway Papers, 26
Kennedy, ——, 180
Kennedy, Archibald, 12th Earl of Cassillis and 1st Marquess of Ailsa (1770-1846), 287
Kennedy, Archibald, [14?] Earl of Cassillis and 3rd Marquess of Ailsa (1847-1938), 275
Kennedy, David, 10th Earl of Cassillis (*c*. 1727-1792), 275
Kennedy, Hugh A. Studdert, 75, 283
Kennedy, Hugh Alexander, 211
Kennedy, John F. (1917-63), 282
Kennedy, Joseph P. (1888-1969), 112, 281, 282
Kennedy, Robert (*fl. ante* 1800), 287
Kennedy, Robert (*fl*. 1817-8), 275
[Kennedy?], Robert (*fl*. 1884), 332
Kennedy, Roland Fergussone, 289
Kennedy, Samuel, 275
Kennedy, T., 274
Kennedy, W. P. M., 162
Kennedy, William (1799-1871), 67
Kennedy, William (*fl*. 1910), 332
Kennett, Margaret, 45
Kennewie, John, 275
Kenney, Joseph E., 345
Kenrick, Francis Patrick (1796-1863), 171
Kenrick, George, 176
Kenrick, Peter Richard (1806-96), 30
Kenrick, Samuel (1728-1811), 94
Kenrick Papers, 95
Kent, F. I., 98
Kent, F. R., 283
Kent, James (1763-1847), 208
Kent, England, 44-6
Kent County Archives Office, 44-6
Kentucky: Description, 95, 156, 184, 199, 217, 325; Immigrants, 230, 328, 331, 343; Land, 112; Religious history, 116, 171, 245; Settlement, 101; Trade, 47; Wilkinson Conspiracy, 317

BARDSTOWN, 171; Fayette County, 112; Lexington, 331; Louisville, 328, 331, Description, 271; Mammoth Cave, 177; Mason County, 112
Kentucky, University of, 233 fn.
Kenyon, Lord, 210
Kenyon, George, 2nd Baron (1776-1855), 210
Kenyon, Lloyd, 1st Baron (1732-1802), 210
Kenyon, Roger, Sr., 47
Kenyon, Roger, Jr., 47
Kenyon College, 210
Kenyon Muniments, 47
Kenyon Papers, 210
Keogh, M., 345
Keogh, Myles Walter (1840-76), 347
Keogh, Thomas, 347
Keppel, Augustus, 1st Viscount (1725-86), 120, 219, 233
Keppel, George, 3rd Earl of Albemarle (1724-72), 75
Keppel, William Anne, 2nd Earl of Albemarle (1702-54), 75
Keppel Papers, 75
Ker, George, 313
Ker [Keir?], George, 265
Ker, John, 3rd Duke of Roxburgh (1740-1804), 268
Ker, Walter, 313
Kerr, George, 304
Kerr, Philip Henry, 11th Marquess of Lothian (1882-1940), 135, 276-84 *passim*; Papers, 276-84
Kerr, W. G., "Scottish Investment and Enterprise in Texas," in P. L. Payne, ed., *Studies in Scottish Business History*, 307
Kerr, W. S. R. (1832-70), 8th Marquess of Lothian, 257
Kerr, MacLeod & MacFarlan Mss., 262
Kerr, Pollock & Co., 309
Kershaw, J., 348
Kessock, David, 309
Keston Copper Mine, Arizona, 20
Keswick, Cumbria, 22
Ketton–Cremer, R. W., *Early Life and Diaries of William Windham*, 188 fn.
Key, Francis Scott (1779-1843), 78
Keynes, John Maynard (1883-1946), 128, 139
Keyserlike Adelair (ship), 5
Kidd, William (d. 1701), 83, 189, 220
Kidnapping, 131, 184, 300
Kilbee, H. T., 207
Kimber, Abby, 95
Kimer, C. D., 282
King, Benjamin [Giles], 39
King, Charles (1789-1867), 27, 187
King, Edward, 164
King, Francis T., 226
King, Gilbert, 346
King, John (d. 1734), 6
King, Mackenzie, 281
King, Martin Luther, Jr. (1929-68), 113
King, Mary, 39
King, Peter, 7th Baron (1776-1833), 194 fn., 195
King, Rufus (1755-1827), 66, 80, 81, 142, 148, 186, 207, 226, 240, 250, 287
King, Samuel, 6
King, William (1650-1729), 352
King, William (*fl.* late 18th cent.), 142
King, William (*fl.* 1827), 288
King, William Poole, 6
King, Wilson (1846-1930), 226
King, Brown & Co., 111
King George's War (1744-8), 222, 290, 298, 301
King Gould Papers, 246
King Papers, 352
King's Advocate, 56
King's Chapel, Boston, 8, 94
King's College, New York, 54; *see also* Columbia University
King's College Library, Cambridge, 116 fn.
King's Lynn, Norfolk, Customs records, 92, 93, 94
Kings Fisher (ship), 312
Kingsbury, S. M., *The Records of the Virginia Company of London*, 17 fn.
Kingsley, Charles (1819-75), 16, 73
Kingston–upon–Hull, Humberside, 43
Kingston–upon–Hull City Record Office, 43
Kingston–upon–Thames, Surrey, 220-1
Kingston–upon–Thames Central Library, Museum and Art Gallery, 220
Kinloch, Alexander, 304
Kinnear, James, 223
Kinney, G. B. M., 236
Kinney, J. K., 236
Kinross House Muniments, 275
Kipling, Rudyard (1865-1936), 259
Kippen, George, 317
Kirby, John, 305
Kirkbude, K., 19
Kirkcaldy, Fife, 253
Kirkcaldy Museum and Art Gallery, 253
Kirkcudbright, Dumfries and Galloway, 253
Kirke, William, 191
Kirkland Gold and Silver Mining Co. of California Ltd., 307
Kirkwall, Orkney Islands, 315
Kirkwood, John, 290
Kirkwood, William, 290
Kishkeminetas River, 285
Kizell, John, 51
Klein, M. M., "Failure of a Mission: The Drummond Peace Proposal of 1775," *Huntingdon Library Quarterly* (1972), 293
Knaplund, Paul, 75; and C. M. Clewes, eds., "Private Letters from the British Embassy in Washington . . .," *Annual Report of the American Historical Association* (1941), 140 fn.
Knight, Gowin (1713-72), 298
Knight, Henry, 28
Knight, John (*fl.* 1720-6), 31
Knight, John (*fl.* 1724-9), 97
Knight, John (*fl.* 1862), 328
Knight Papers, 31
Knill, Henry, 168
Knitters' Circular and Monthly Record, 47
Knives, *see* Cutlery
Knocklofty, Tipperary, 354
Knowling, Andrew, 41
Knox, Alexander, 95
Knox, Henry (1750-1806), 268
Knox, James, 329
Knox, John, 329
Knox, K. M., *The Sharples*, 7 fn.
Knox, Philander Chase (1853-1921), 198
Knox, William (1732-1810), 65, 66, 212, 226, 266, 303
Kochler, General, 287
Kodak Ltd., 111
Koltchak, Alexander, 284

Kopman, Sidney, 75
Korea, Relations with U.S., *see* Relations with Korea
Kosyta, Martin, 200
Kraus Reprint Co., xxv
Kruger, Stephanus Johannes Paulus (1825-1904), 206
Kuhn, Loeb & Co., 96

L

La Cépède, Bernard Germain Etienne de la Ville sur Ilon, Comte de (1756-1825), 170
Labaree, L. W., *The Papers of Benjamin Franklin*, 174 fn., 208 fn.
Labor Party, 198
Labour, 33, 53, 63, 64, 196, 297; *see also* Apprentices; Artisans; Guilds; Indentured servants; Negroes: Employment; Slavery; Trade unions; Wages; Women: Employment
Labour movement, 52, 187, 198, 345; *see also* Haymarket Massacre, 1886; Trade unions; Working classes
Labour relations, 38
Labrador, Sovereignty, 146
Lachlan, J. M., 166
Lacy, J., 226
Ladenburg and Thalmann, 210
Ladies' Society for the Relief of Negro Slaves, 226
Lady Hobart (packet), 172
Lady Russell (ship), 326
Lafayette, Mme. de, 200
Lafayette, Marie Joseph, Marquis de (1757-1834), 98, 113, 182, 187, 267
Laing, David (1793-1878), 312, 313
Laing Mss., 312-3
Laird, John (1805-74), 13, 202
Lake, ——, 272
Lalor, Alice, *known as* Mother Teresa (*c.* 1766-1846), 347
Lalor, H. T., 347
Lalor, James Finton (d. 1849), 347
Lalor, Richard (1823-93), 347
Lalor, William, 347
Lalor Correspondence, 347
Lamb, David, 170
Lamb, Frederick James, 3rd Viscount Melbourne (1782-1853), 104
Lamb, Isaac W., 47
Lambeth Conferences, 115; Papers, 115
"Lambeth Library," 203
Lambeth Palace Library, 114-5; 158
Lambton, John George, 1st Earl of Durham (1792-1840), 256
Lamont, Thomas W., 78, 260, 280, 282
Lampson, O. Locker, 259
Lancashire, Matthew Herbert, 192
Lancashire, England, 46-8; *see also* Cotton famine; Immigrants from Lancashire
Lancashire Independent College Mss., 177
Lancashire "Plan," 179, 329
Lancashire Public School Association, *see* National Public School Association
Lancashire Record Office, 46-8
Lancaster, Customs records, 89, 93
Lancaster, Duncan & Co., 310
Lance, Daniel, 184
Land: Clearing, 149, 266; Grants, 55, 97, 138, 265, 303; Speculation, 222, 305, 307, 308, 318; Taxation, 100; Tenure, 13, 52, 55, 131, 158, 170, 190, 195, 261, 262, 273, 282, 303; Valuation, 166, 204, 328; *see also subdivision* Land *under* Indians *and under states, etc.*; Pre-emption rights
Land and Liberty, 100
Land Commission, 349
Land Values, 100
Lane, Franklin Knight (1864-1921), 229
Lane & Booth, 150
Lang, John, 304
Lang, William, 309
Langdale, Josiah (d. 1723), 153
Langdon, Walter, 174
Langer, William L. (b. 1896), 165; and S. E. Gleason, *The Challenge of Isolation*, 283
Langford, Nathaniel Pitt (1832-1911), 239
Langham, Jeremiah, 82
Langley, Samuel Pierpont (1834-1906), 147
Langton family, 50
Langton Mss., 50
Langtry, George, 328
Lanier, Sidney (1842-81), 69
Lansdowne, 1st Marquess of, *see* Petty, William (1737-1805); 5th Marquess of, *see* Petty–Fitzmaurice, Henry Charles Keith (1845-1927)
Lansdowne Papers, 66
Lansing, Robert (1864-1928), 77, 197, 229
Lanyon, John, 26
Larcom, Sir Thomas Aiskew (1801-79), 344
Lardner, Dionysius (1793-1859), 178
Larish, J., 169
Larkin, James, 352
Larkin, John (1801-58), 30
Larpent, Francis Seymour (1776-1845), 27
Lascelles, Sir Alan, 283
Lascelles, Hon. Horace, 232
Lashley, Thomas, 41
Laski, Harold, 166
Latchworth, T. E., 156; Mss., 156
Latimer, J., *The History of the Society of Merchant Venturers*, 8
Latin America, Relations with U.S., *see* Relations with Latin America
Laud, William (1573-1645), 19, 114
Lauder, Harry, 284
Lauderdale, 2nd Earl of, *see* Maitland, John (1616-82)
Lauderdale Muniments, 268
Laughlin, James Laurence (1850-1933), 197
Laughton, Magnus, 315
Laurence, Anne, 41
Laurens, Henry (1724-92), 103, 233, 266, 267
Laurie, Sir Robert (*fl.* 1757), 299
Laurie, W. S. (*fl.* 1775), 317
Laurier, Sir Wilfrid (1841-1919), 256
Lausanne Conference (1932), 280
Lauterbach, Edmund, 67
Law, Edward, 1st Earl of Ellenborough (1790-1871), 169
Law, William, 313
Law, 115, 168, 245, 263, 275, 276; Colonial period, 10, 19, 138, 305; Codification, 167, 168; Digests, 325; *see also subdivision* Law *under states, etc.*; Judges; Libel (Law); Negroes: Law
Law, International, 66
Law, Maritime, 66, 69, 138, 184, 201, 204, 278; *see also* Admiralty, Court of
Law officers, Reports, 132
Lawers, Mrs., 330

Lawley, Francis, 158
Lawrence, Mr. or Miss, 166
Lawrence, Abbott (1792-1855), 30, 36, 263
Lawrence, E. P., *Henry George in the British Isles*, 100 fn.
Lawrence, Henry (1600-64), 34
Lawrence, James, 219
Lawrence, John, & Co., 182
Lawrence, Robert, 150
Lawrence, William Beach (1800-81), 187
Lawson, James, & Co., 290, 309
Layard, Sir Austen Henry (1817-94), 58, 59-61 *passim*, 66
Layard Papers, 58-61, 66
Laycock, John Charles, 168
Laye, Francis, 119
Le Bas, Charles Webb (1779-1861), 273
Le Brette, Robert, Lord Dubose, 159
Le Couteur, Sir John (1794-1875), 339
Le Couteur Papers, 339
Le Cras, Mr., 215
Le Cras, E., 215
Le Despencer, Baron, *see* Dashwood, Sir Francis (1708-81)
Le Fleming, Sir Michael, 203
Le Fleming Papers, 203
Le Hardy, W., ed., *Middlesex County Records . . . 1612-1618*, 97 fn.
Le Hardy Mss., 40
Le Marchant, Sir John Gaspard (1803-74), 81
Le Patourel, John, 339 fn.
Le Président (frigate), 264
Le Revolutionaire (frigate), 264
Lea, Miss E., 65
Lea, Henry Charles (1825-1909), 197, 198
Lead: Mining, 124; Trade, 181, 232
Leader, Robert, 236
Leader Collection, 235
Leadly, John, 149
League of Nations, 77, 112, 113, 277, 278, 279, 281, 282, 345; Mandates, 277, 279; U.S. attitude, 197, 197 fn., 277-80 *passim*, 284
League of Nations Association, 279
League of Nations Union, 278, 279
League of Universal Brotherhood, 208
Leahy, Ellen, 346
Leake, Francis Martin, 40
Leake, Isabel Martin, 40
Leamington Spa, Warwickshire, 224
Lean, J. H. & C., 210
Lear, Tobias (1762-1816), 313
Learmonth, Alexander, 261
Leask, W. K., 254
Leather goods, Trade, 109
Leaver, Mrs. M., 234
Lebanon Valley Railroad, 347
Lechford, Sir Richard, 185
Leckie, Daniel, 265
Lecky, William Edward Hartpole (1838-1903), 353
Ledgard, Gosse and Chancey, Messrs., 28
Ledue, W., 173
Lee, Archibald, 148
Lee, Arthur (1740-92), 44, 76, 214, 233, 267
Lee, C., 350
Lee, C. F., Jr., 209
Lee, Charles (1731-82), 48, 119, 266, 293
Lee, Ivy, 279
Lee, John (*fl.* 1775), 324
Lee, John (*fl.* late 18th cent.), 112
Lee, Richard B., 253
Lee, Richard Henry (1732-94), 86
Lee, Robert Edward (1807-70), 59, 209
Lee, Thomas Sim (1745-1819), 86
Lee, William, 42
Lee, William, & Co., 271
Lee Family Papers, 112
Leech, John, 49
Leeds, 1st Duke of, *see* Osborne, Sir Thomas (1631-1712); 5th Duke of, *see* Osborne, Francis (1751-99)
Leeds, West Yorkshire, 237-40; Merchants, 239; *see also* Business records, Leeds
Leeds Papers, 82, 140
Leeds Public Libraries, 239-40
Leeds Times, 163
Leeds University, Brotherton Library, 238-9
Leek taw, *see* Feeding stuffs
Leeward Islands: Customs officers, 87; Governors, 195
See also Antigua; Montserrat; Nevis; St. Christopher; St. Martin; Sombrero
Leffingwell, R. C., 280
Legaré, Hugh Swinton (1797-1843), 64
Legge, Francis (1719-83), 215, 216
Legge, George, 1st Baron Dartmouth (1648-91), 213
Legge, George, 3rd Earl of Dartmouth (*held title of* Viscount Lewisham *till succession in* 1801) (1755-1810), 216
Legge, William, 1st Earl of Dartmouth (1672-1750), 213, 263
Legge, William, 2nd Earl of Dartmouth (1731-1801), 10, 57, 188, 213-6 *passim*, 226
Legget, W., 314
Leicester, Earl of, 186-7
Leicester, 1st Earl of the 4th creation, *see* Dudley, Robert (1532?-88); 1st Earl of the 5th creation, *see* Sidney, Robert (1563-1626)
Leicester of Holkham, 1st Earl of, *see* Coke, Thomas William (1752-1842)
Leicester, Leicestershire, 48-9
Leicestershire, England, 48-9
Leicestershire Record Office, 48-9
Leigh, Canon, Collection, 238
Leigh, Sir Egerton (d. 1781), 225
Leighton, Thomas, 254
Leisler, Jacob (1640-91), 66
Leitch, John, 317
Leitchfield (ship), 263
Leiter, L. Z., 75
Leiter, Mrs. Mary T., 75
Leith, Sir James (1763-1816), 191
Leith, Lothian: Customs records, 310; Merchants, 310
Leith Hall Muniments, 303
Leith Ross Muniments, 297-8
Leland, C. G., Collection, 62
Leland, C. S., 75
Lemaitre, Charlotte, 295
Lemonius & Co., 118
Lend-Lease, 112, 125, 127, 128, 135, 137, 139
Lennard, Sir Samuel (*c.* 1553-1618), 45
Lennox, 4th Duke of, *see* Stuart, James (1612-55)
Lennox, Charles, 4th Duke of Richmond (1764-1819), 84
Lennox, Lord Henry Charles George Gordon– (1821-86), 13
Lennox of Woodhead Mss., 263
Lenthall Papers, 11

Leon, Maurice, 282
Leonard, Daniel (1740-1829), 73; *Letters to the Inhabitants of the Province of Massachusetts Bay*, 73
LeRoy, Bayard & M'Evers, 172
Lesley, Peter (1819-1903), 148
Leslie, Alexander, 5th Earl of Leven (*c.* 1699-1754), 275
Leslie, Alexander, 7th Earl of Leven (1749-1820), 275
Leslie, Alexander, Maj-Gen. (*fl.* 1777), 139, 275
Leslie, Alexander (*fl.* early 19th cent.), 254
Leslie, David, 6th Earl of Leven (1722-1802), 275
Leslie, George, 287, 288
Leslie, James (*fl.* 1755), 264
Leslie, James (1786-1873), 254
Leslie, John, 253
Leslie, Shane, 345, 353
Leslie, William, 275
Leslie of Berryden, 253
Lester, Benjamin (*fl.* 1761-96), 28
Lester, Isaac (*fl.* 1765-78), 28
L'Estrange and Brett, 325
Letchworth, John, 19
Lethbridge, Sir Roper, 26
Lethbridge Joint Services Mission, 123
Lett, H. B., "Diary of Major Wise," *Annals of Wyoming* (1940), 209 fn.
Letters and Papers of Charles, Lord Barham . . . 101 fn.
Letters of Charles Dickens, Pilgrim Edition, 14
Lettsom, John Coakley (1744-1815), 170, 188; ed., *The Works of Dr. John Fothergill*, 188, 188 fn.
Leven, 5th Earl of, *see* Leslie, Alexander (*c.* 1699-1754); 6th Earl of, *see* Leslie, David (1722-1802); 7th Earl of, *see* Leslie, Alexander (1749-1820)
Leven and Melville Muniments, 275
Leventhal, F. M., *Respectable Radical*, 52 fn.
Leveson–Gower, George Granville William Sutherland, 3rd Duke of Sutherland (1828-92), 216, 268
Leveson–Gower, Granville George, 2nd Earl Granville (1815-91), 70, 72, 111, 133, 139-40
Levett, Christopher, 23, 24
Levi, Prof. T. A., Deposit, 246
Levi, Thomas, 246
Levinson, Salmon O., 278-82 *passim*
Lewes, Sussex, East, 221-3; Customs records, 89
Lewis, Charles, 330
Lewis, E. A., *Welsh Port Books: 1550-1603*, 89
Lewis, Enoch, 235
Lewis, Evan, 247
Lewis, George (1763-1822), 245
Lewis, Sir George Cornewall (1806-63), 72, 104, 247
Lewis, J. T., 243
Lewis, Jane, 247
Lewis, John, 237
Lewis, L. R., 82
Lewis, N. B., "The Abolitionist Movement in Sheffield, 1823-1833," *Bulletin of the John Rylands Library* (1934), 176 fn.
Lewis, Rachel, 247
Lewis, Sinclair (1885-1951), 114
Lewis, Thomas (1742-95), 121
Lewis, Thomas (*fl.* 1830), 103
Lewis, Thomas (*fl.* 1874), 246
Lewis, William (1714-81), 149
Lewis, Sir Willmott, 158
Lewisham, Viscount (*till* 1801), *see* Legge, George, 3rd Earl of Dartmouth (1755-1810)
Leyburn, North Yorkshire, 230
Leyland, Bullins & Co., 117, 118
Leyland, F., & Co., 181
Libel (Law), 167
Libel action, 273
Liberal Party (Great Britain), 72
Liberal Republican Party, 69
Liberia: Colonization by Negroes, 153, 198; Religious history, 117
Liberty League, 317
Libraries and librarians, 64, 161, 239, 317
Library Association, 239
Library of Congress, 19 fn., 22 fn., 50 fn., 66, 116 fn., 123 fn., 129 fn., 130 fn., 132 fn., 139 fn., 140 fn., 141 fn., 143 fn., 144 fn., 145 fn., 158 fn., 159 fn., 172, 206 fn.; *Information Bulletin* (1953), 19 fn.
Lichenbrodf, Capt., 275
Lieven, Prince Christopher (1774-1839), 76
Lieven Papers, 76
Life (magazine), 112
Lighthouses, 107
Ligonier, Edward, 1st Earl (d. 1782), 315
Ligonier, John, *otherwise* Jean Louis, 1st Earl (1680-1770), 45, 285
Lilcot, Capt., 83
Lincoln, Earl of, *see* Pelham–Clinton, Henry Fiennes (1750-78)
Lincoln, Abraham (1809-65), 58, 59, 60, 61, 62, 68, 69, 111, 155, 168, 169, 174, 179, 184, 222, 226, 258; *Collected Works* . . ., ed. by R. P. Basler, 226 fn.
Lincoln, C. H., ed., *Correspondence of William Shirley*, 64 fn.
Lincoln, Enoch (1788-1829), 286
Lincoln, Francis H., 58
Lincoln, Robert Todd (1843-1926), 38, 129, 164
Lincoln, Solomon, Jr., *History of Hingham, Mass.* (1827), 188
Lincoln, Lincolnshire, 49-50
Lincoln Cathedral Library, 49
Lincolnshire, England, 49-50
Lincolnshire Archives Office, 49-50
Lindemann, F. A., Viscount Cherwell (1886-1957), 209
Lindley, Edward Frederick, 3rd Viscount Halifax (1881-1959), 275, 281
Lindsay, 10th Earl of, *see* Lindsay–Bethune, John Trotter (1827-94)
Lindsay, Anne, Countess of Balcarres, 265
Lindsay, Colin, 265
Lindsay, Mrs. E., 314
Lindsay, George, Laird of Wormistone (d. 1764), 298
Lindsay, John, 298
Lindsay, Penelope, 298
Lindsay, Sir Ronald Charles (1877-1945), 135, 279, 280, 281, 282
Lindsay, Vachel (1879-1931), 205; *The Golden Book*, 205
Lindsay, William Schaw (1816-77), 60
Lindsay Muniments, 298
Lindsay of Dowhill Muniments, 305
Lindsay–Bethune, John Trotter, 10th Earl of Lindsay (1827-94), 298
Lindsey, Robert (1801-63), 156, 156 fn.
Lindsey, Sarah (1805-76), 156, 156 fn.
Lindsey, Theophilus (1723-1808), 94, 95
Linen: Manufacture, 12; Trade, 31, 79, 109, 175, 178, 182, 183, 187, 265, 271, 295, 299, 309, 324, 325, 327, 329, 330, 331
Linlithgow, 2nd Marquess of, *see* Hope, Victor A. J. (1887-1952)
Linnaeus, Carl von (1707-78), 180
Linoleum, Trade, 271
Linsingen, Baron de, 292
Lippmann, Walter (1889-1974), 278, 279
Liquor traffic, 111, 131, 330; *see also* Prohibition

Lisbon Collection, 30
Lisgar, 1st Baron, *see* Young, Sir John (1807-76)
Lisle, Viscount, and 1st Earl of Leicester, *see* Sidney, Robert (1563-1626)
Lissner, Will, 177
List and Index Society, 141; *List of Records in the Greffe*, 339 fn.
List of Backhouse Papers, 30 fn.
Lister (*later* Sturdivant), Mrs. Ann, 237
Lister, Japhet (1715-82), 237
Lister, Jeremy (1713-88), 237
Lister, Jeremy (1752-1836), 237; *Concord Flight*, 237 fn.
Lister, John (1703-59), 237; "John Lister," *Transactions of the Lancashire and Cheshire Antiquarian Society* (1911), 237 fn.
Lister, Samuel (1706-66), 237
Lister, Susannah (Lewis), Mrs. William Lister, 237
Lister, Thomas (1708-40), 237
Lister, William (1712-43), 237
Lister, William (1734-80), 237
Lister family, 237
Liston, Henrietta (Marchant), Lady (d. 1828), 256
Liston, Sir Robert (1742-1836), 81, 256, 298
Liston, Thomas, 6
Literary and Antiquarian Society of Perth, 319
Little, Francis Laurence Gore (1841-1914), 204
Little Abington Parish, Cambridgeshire, 14
Littlehampton, Customs records, 89, 93
Littler, R., 244
Littleton, Edward John, 1st Baron Hatherton (1791-1863), 216
Littleton, W., 216
Live oak, 120
Livermore, Abiel Abbot (1811-92), 208
Liverpool, 1st Earl of, *see* Jenkinson, Charles (1727-1808); 2nd Earl of, *see* Jenkinson, Robert Banks (1770-1828)
Liverpool, Merseyside, 64, 176, 180-5; Banking, 183; Customs records, 89, 92, 93; Merchants, 7, 34, 46, 52, 56, 58, 70, 118, 155, 173, 175, 180, 181, 182, 183, 185, 208, 213, 224, 234, 235, 326; Shipping, 35, 60, 61, 108, 124, 141, 156, 172, 175, 180, 181, 182, 183, 326; Slave trade, 70, 213, 301; Trade with America, 18, 41, 181, 182, 183, 240, 253; *see also* Business records: Liverpool; Immigrants from Merseyside
Liverpool Central Libraries, 102, 181-4
Liverpool Commercial Banking Co., 181
Liverpool Cotton Brokers' Association, 180 fn.
Liverpool Papers, 54-7
Liverpool Register of Shipping, 180
Liverpool Steamship Owners' Association, 181
Liverpool Union Bank, 116
Liverpool University, 165
Liverpool University, Harold Cohen Library, 185
Liverpool University, Sydney Jones Library, 185
Livestock: Investment, 307, 308; Prices, 328
Livingston, Edward (1764-1836), 167, 182
Livingston, James (1747-1832), 324
Livingston, John, 168
Livingston, Peter Vanbrooke, 295, 296
Livingston, Philip (1716-78), 149, 150, 191
Livingston, Robert (1654-1728), 189
Livingston, Robert R. (1746-1813), 226
Livius, Peter (1727?-95), 233
Lizardi, F. de, & Co., 52
Llanelly, Customs records, 93
Llanfair and Brynodol Documents, 245-6
Llangefni, Gwynedd, 248
Lloyd, Arnold, *Quaker Social History, 1669-1738*, 227 fn.
Lloyd, Charles, 155
Lloyd, Francis, 116
Lloyd, Henry, 99
Lloyd, John (*fl.* 1724), 304
Lloyd, John (*fl.* 1781-1805), 34
Lloyd, Richard (*fl.* 1842), 33
Lloyd, William (1627-1717), 40
Lloyd, Yarburgh George, 43
Lloyd, Zachary, Papers, 225
Lloyd (ship), 122
Lloyd family, 248
Lloyd George, David (1863-1945), 112, 113, 200, 247, 277, 279, 284
Lloyd George, Dame Margaret (d. 1941), 247
Lloyd George Mss., 247
Lloyd George Papers, 112-3
Lloyd Greame of Sewerby, 43
Lloyd Papers, 33
Lloyd's, 99, 180, 288
Lloyd's Register of British and Foreign Shipping, 121
Lloyds Bank Ltd., 115-6
Lobbying, 39
Lobel, Major, 274
Local government officers: Exchange visits, 97; *see also* Municipal government
Local Studies Library, 180
Locarno Peace Pact, 280
Lock, James, 169
Locke, Charles H., 347
Locke, Jeannette, 347
Locke, John (1632-1704), 55, 194, 195
Locke, John (*c.* 1805-88), 347
Locke, Lelia, 347
Locke, Richard, 347
Locke Family Papers, 347
Locke Papers, 194-5
Locker–Lampson Mss., 222
Lockhart, James, 286
Lockhart, John Gibson (1794-1854), 256
Locock, G. H., 277
Locomotive works, 306; *see also* Railways *and names of individual railway companies*
Lodge, Henry Cabot (1850-1924), 78, 164, 197, 198, 199, 238, 259, 260, 298
Lodwick, David, 244
Loeb, William (1866-1937), 198
Logan, George (1753-1821), 11, 186
Logan, George (*fl.* 1770's), 269
Logan, Hannah, 273
Logan, Isabella, 269
Logan, James (1674-1751), 154
Logan, Walter, 102
Logan, William, 154, 156, 273
Logan's Trust, 273
Logwood, Trade, 15, 211, 212
London, Jack, 236
London, England, 50-172; Bishops, 115, 151, 159, 160, 171; Customs records, 93; Merchants, 31, 32, 33, 55, 56, 86, 97, 99, 102, 154, 160, 161, 203, 240, 290, 294, 303, 304, 309, 312; Shipping, 56, 106, 107, 108, 124; Trade, 88, 211, 303; *see also* Business records: London; Immigrants from London; Parish records: London; Quarter sessions records: London
London and California Mining Co., 211
London and Provincial Bank, 52

London and South Western Bank, 52
London & South Western Railway Co., 35
London & Virginia Gold and Copper Mining Co., 124
The London Assurance, 99
London Bookbinders' Papers, 79
London Conference (1931), 127
London Economic Conference (1933), 266
London Library, 116
London, Liverpool & North American Screw Steam Ship Co., 124
London Missionary Society, 116
London Naval Conferences (1930, 1935-6), 127, 279
London Packet (ship), 161, 286
London Provincial and South Western Bank, 52
London Reparations Conference (1924), 127
London School of Economics, *see* London University, London School of Economics
London Stock Exchange, 100
London Trades Council, 52
London University, 278, 282
London University, Imperial College of Science and Technology, 162-3
London University, Institute of Historical Research, 161 fn.
London University Library, 159-62; *Catalogue of the Collections of Proclamations and Broadsides*, 162; *Catalogue of the Manuscripts*, 159; Palaeography Room, 161 fn.
London University, London School of Economics, 163-6; 25 fn., 28 fn., 47 fn., 115 fn., 190 fn., 219 fn., 235 fn., 238 fn.
London University, New College, 103
London University, School of Oriental and African Studies, 166-7; 116 fn.
London University, University College, 167-70; 113
Londonderry, 1st Marquis of, *see* Stewart, Robert (1739-1821); 2nd Marquis of, *see* Stewart, Robert, *better known as* Viscount Castlereagh (1769-1822)
Long, Basil K., 283
Long, Borden, 150
Long, Lady Dorothy (Leech) (d. 1710), 189
Long, Elizabeth, 283
Long, George (1800-79), 169
Long, Brigadier H., 186
Long, James, 244
Long, P., *A Summary Catalogue of the Lovelace Collection in the Bodleian Library*, 194 fn.
Long Island Historical Society, N.Y., 231 fn.
Longfellow, Henry Wadsworth (1807-82), 170, 174, 176, 197, 204, 238, 254, 256, 259; *Aftermath*, 170; *New England Tragedies*, 170
Longford, Earl of, 343
Longford, Republic of Ireland, 354
Longford Papers, 343
Longleat, Wiltshire, 229-30
Longley, Charles Thomas, Archbishop of Canterbury, 115
Longsdon, J. & W., 175
Lonsdale, Earl of, 21
Lonsdale, 1st Earl of, *see* Lowther, James (1736-1802)
Lonsdale Papers, 21
Looe, Customs records, 89
Loomis, Elias (1811-89), 148
Lorimer, W., 304
Loring, Charles G., 263
Loring, Joshua, 260
Loseley Mss., 220
Lotbinière, Marquis de, 255
Lothian, Marquess of, 23-4
Lothian, 8th Marquess of, *see* Kerr, W. S. R. (1832-70); 11th Marquess of, *see* Kerr, Philip Henry (1882-1940)
Lothian, Scotland, 254-315
Lothian Mss., 24 fn.
Lothian Muniments, 276
Lottery, *see* Virginia: Lottery
Louden, William, 310
Loudoun, 4th Earl of, *see* Campbell, John (1705-82)
Loughborough, Baron, *see* Wedderburn, Alexander (1733-1805)
Loughlin, Samuel H., 62
Louisiana: Colonial period, 21, 45, 48, 195; 1803-65, 12, 76; War of 1812, 121, 172, 204, 207, 257; Civil War, 1861-5, 58, 76
BANKING, 52, 181; Coast, 140, 183; Description, 265; Finance, 100, 166, 249; Health, 131; Immigrants, 326, 328, 330, 331, 347, 351; Law, 167, 169; Settlement, 48; Slavery, 63, 67, 70, 344; Social life, 177; Sugar, 63; Trade, 118, 140, 175, 184, 211, 234, 235, 240, 249, 310, 315, 326
NEW ORLEANS, 25, 32, 39, 46, 58, 67, 70, 77, 118, 121, 124, 140, 172, 175, 184, 204, 207, 211, 249, 257, 265, 310, 325, 326, 328, 330, 331, 343, 344, 345, 347, 351, Consular reports (British), 130, 134, Description, 32, 183, 202, 224, 314, 325, 343, Merchants, 22, 118, 130, 169, 234, 235, 240, 249, 326; Vermilion, 328
Louisiana Purchase (1803), 95, 101, 245
Louisville and Nashville Railroad, 20
Lovat, Master of, *see* Fraser, Simon (1726-82)
Love, Andrew, 235
Love, Hogg & Co., 235
Lovell, Mrs., 230
Low, Robert, & Son, 98
Low, Seth (1850-1916), 164, 197, 198, 199, 238
Lowe, Capt., 102
Lowe, John, 193
Lowe, Richard, 193
Lowe, Stead, 193
Lowe, Vincent, 193
Lowell, Abbott Lawrence (1856-1943), 197, 198, 199, 210, 238
Lowell, Charles, 204, 254
Lowell, James Russell (1819-91), 52, 58, 62, 70, 74, 75, 81, 129, 162, 178, 184, 196, 197, 204, 208, 236, 238
Lowell, John (1769-1840), 183, 187
Lowell, Robert (1917-77), 96
Lowestoft, Customs records, 93
Lowry, Alexander, 330
Lowther, A. B., 43
Lowther, James, 1st Earl of Lonsdale (1736-1802), 21
Lowther, Sir John (d. 1706), 21
Lowther, T., 295
Lowther, William, 295
Loyalists, 10, 12-3, 39, 41, 86, 230, 258, 289, 291, 313, 315, 325; Claims, 17, 45, 54, 56, 124, 138, 139, 174, 210, 233, 234, 266, 269, 276, 287, 294, 315, 323; Emigration, 6, 8-9, 22-3, 80, 120, 138, 148, 159, 208, 293, 298
FLORIDA, 138, 265; Georgia, 324; Massachusetts, 73; New York, 56; Nova Scotia, 120, 148; Pennsylvania, 55; Rhode Island, 234; South Carolina, 6, 17, 253, 265, 323; Virginia, 12-3, 22-3, 258, 269
Luby, Thomas Clarke (1821-1901), 345
Lucas, John, 13
Lucas Mss., 8-9
Lucas Papers, 9
Luce, Henry R. (1898-1967), 112

Lucerne, *see* Feeding stuffs
Luck (slave), 297
Luckhurst, K. W., "The Society's Early Days," *Journal of the Royal Society of Arts* (1954), 149 fn.
Lucretia (ship), 273
Ludlow Collection, 162
Ludwell, Philip, 149
Lumber, *see* Timber
Lumley, John Saville, 201
Lundie, Archibald, 262
Lunenburg Colonial Churchman, 318
Lupton, William, & Co. Ltd., 239
Lusitania (ship), 127, 200
Luther, Thomas, Deposit, 246
Lutwidge, Walter, 21
Lutz, Joseph A., 291
Lyall, D., 145, 146
Lyell, Sir C., 315
Lyell Mss., 204
Lygon, Frederick, 6th Earl Beauchamp (1830-91), 13
Lyle and Mitchell, 309
Lyman, Daniel (d. 1809), 12, 294
Lyman, Phineas, 265
Lyman, Theodore (1792-1849), 187
Lyme, Customs records, 89
Lyme Regis Borough Archives, 27; Customs records, 93
Lynch, Frederick, 278
Lynch, Johnson, 309
Lyndhurst, 1st Baron, *see* Copley, John Singleton (1772-1863)
Lyndhurst Papers, 17, 250
Lynn, Customs records, 89
Lyon (ship), 293
Lyons, Richard Bickerton Pemell, 2nd Baron and 1st Earl (1817-87), 58, 68, 71, 72, 121, 129, 139, 185, 223
Lyons Papers, 185, 223
Lyttelton, William H., 1st Baron (1724-1808), 212, 226, 228, 284
Lyttelton Papers, 226, 228
Lytton, Edward George Earle Lytton Bulwer, 1st Baron (1803-73), 40, 118
Lytton, Edward Robert Bulwer, 1st Earl of (1831-91), 13, 179, 184
Lytton (Knebworth) Mss., 40

M

M., J., 9
Mabery, Professor, 163
McAdam, Gilbert, 285
Macadam, J. Loudon, 268
Macadam, James, 270
McAdam, John, & Co., 173
MacAlister, Sir Donald, 318
McAlpin, Alex. B., 22
McAlpine, James, 310
McArthur, Arthur, 269
MacArthur, Douglas (1880-1964), 139
McArthur, Duncan, 296
McArthur, Patrick, 267
Macartney, George, 1st Earl (1737-1806), 323
Macartney Papers, 323-4
Macaulay, Dr., 306
McAulay, Alex, 323
Macaulay, Alexander, 216
Macaulay, Thomas Babington, 1st Baron (1800-59), 161
Macaulay, Zachary (1768-1838), 169
Macbean, Forbes (1725-1800), 145
McBride, John, 331
McBride family, 331
McBride Family Papers, 331
McCabe, Joseph, *Life and Letters of George Jacob Holyoake*, 53 fn., 173 fn.
McCall, Smellie & Co., 317
McCall Papers, 348
McCallum, Janet (*fl.* 1875), 315
McCallum, John (*fl.* 1875), 315
McCann, Maggie, 332
McCann, Thomas, 332
McCartan, Patrick, 346
McCartan Papers, 346
McCarter, Robert H., 40
McCarthy, Charles (1873-1921), 209, 210
McCarthy, Gerald, 74
McCarthyism, 221
McCartney, Edward, 225
McCartney Estate, Rentals, 331
McCausland, Robert, 147
McCawley, Zachary, 324
McCleery, Mrs., 329
McClellan, George Brinton (1826-85), 59, 68
McClelland, John, 329
McClintock, Emory, 74
McClintock, Walter, 78; *The Old North Trail*, 78
McClorg, John, 330
McClorg, Robert, 330
McClorg family, 330
McCloskey, Hugh, 328
McCloy, David, 326
McClure family, 332
McClure Family Papers, 332
McColl, John, 294
MacColl, N., 70
McColme, John, 259, 275
McConaghy, Robert, 328
McConnel & Kennedy, 175
McCorkell, William, and Coy., 326, 332
McCormick, Cyrus, Jr., 278
McCormick, Joseph Medill (1877-1925), 277
McCormick, R. P., "The Society, the Grape and New Jersey," *Journal of the Royal Society of Arts* (1962), 148 fn.
McCormick, Robert R., 277
McCormick, Robert Sanderson (1849-1919), 129
McCormick Family Correspondence, 329
McCowan, James, 286
McCoy, Alexander, 329
McCoy, John (d. 1831), 51
McCoy, Robert, 329
McCoy, Thomas, 329
McCready, Charles, 329
Macculloch, Ebenezer, 265, 299
McCulloch, Hugh (1808-95), 68
MacCulloch, John Ramsay, 161
McCullough, [Thomas?], 332
Macdonald, Lord (*fl.* 1802), 300
McDonald, Major, 214

[Macdonald?], Sir Alexander, 263
MacDonald, Alexander (*fl.* 1775-84), 258, 296
Macdonald, Alexander (1791?-1850), 313
MacDonald, Sir Archibald (1747-1826), 257
Macdonald, Arthur, 150
MacDonald, Donald (*fl.* 1800-05), 258
Macdonald, Donald (*fl.* 1840-78), 263
MacDonald, [James] Ramsay (1866-1937), 135, 141, 172, 238, 266, 277, 278, 279; Papers, 141
MacDonald, Sir John Alexander (1815-91), 68
MacDonald, Malcolm, 281
Macdonald, R. M., Mss., 261
Macdonald, Thomas, 9, 81
Macdonald, W., ed., *Select Charters...illustrative of American History*, 194 fn.
Macdonald, William, 263
MacDonald, Robertson–, Papers, 258
McDonald, Son & Co., 310
Macdonald Muniments, 300
MacDonald–Tyler, Sir Henry, 325 fn.
Macdonnell, J. M., 281, 282
McDonnell, Joseph, 349; Letters, 349
McDouall, John, 265
Macdougall, Allan, 295
Macdougall, F. D., 268
McDougall, Peter, 316
Macdougall, W., 262
Macdougall, William, 262
MacDowall, R., 314
McDowell, Davison, 330
MacDowell, E. A., 81
McDowell, James, 330
McDowell, William, 287
McDowell Family Correspondence, 330
Mace, Benjamin, 302
Macedonia (ship), 43
McElderry, John, 331
McElderry, Robert, 330, 331
McElderry, William, 330, 331
McElderry family, 330
McElderry Family Papers, 330
McElroy, Robert, 279, 282
M'Euen, Thomas, & Co., 172
MacEwen, Sir R. L., Mss., 272
McFall, David, 191
McFarland, James, 315
McFarland, John, 327
McFarland, William, 327
McGarrity, Joseph (1874-1940), 345
McGill University, 278, 281, 282
M'Gillivray, Duncan (d. 1808), 146; *Journal*, 146 fn.
M'Gillivray, William, 146; ed., *On the Origin and Progress of the North West Company*, 146 fn.
McGillivray & Thain, 255
McGrane, R. C., *Foreign Bondholders and American State Debts*, 169 fn.
McGrath, P., ed., *Merchants and Merchandise in Seventeenth Century Bristol*, 5 fn., 7; *Records Relating to the Society of Merchant Venturers*, 7; *The Merchant Venturers of Bristol*, 8
Macgregor, John (1797-1857), 63
MacGregor, John, Collection, 286
Macgregor, Sir William (1846-1919), 198
McGroggan, Bernard, 328
Machada, John A., 132
McHenry, George, 169
McHenry, James, 104
Machinery: Trade, 125, 150; *see also* Agricultural machinery; Aircraft parts; Brickmaking machinery; Chains; Flour-milling machinery; Food processing machinery; Mining machinery; Printing machinery; Pumping machinery; Shoe machinery; Sugar, machinery; Tools
McIlvaine, Charles Pettit, 234
McIndoe, Archibald, & Co., 310
Macintosh, Lachlan, 265
McIntyre, Ellen, 329
MacIntyre, James, 293
MacIntyre, Lorn, Esq., 272
McIver, McVicar & McCorquodale, 183
Mack, James, 330
Mackay, Alexander, 266
Mackay, Daniel (1758-1839), 316
McKay, Donald, 272
McKay, John (*fl.* 1842-9), 272
McKay, John (*fl.* 19th cent.?), 328
Mackay, T. M., 60
Mackay, W., 324
Mackay of Bighouse Muniments, 289
McKean, Joseph, 254
Mackeleaneane, Sir Robert, 10
McKelvey, Eleanor, 330
McKelvey, Robert, 330
McKenna, Bernard, 348
McKenzie, Alexander, 166
McKenzie, Archie (Monro), 289
MacKenzie, Elizabeth, 298
Mackenzie, Frank S., 289
MacKenzie, George, Viscount Tarbat (1630-1714), 260
Mackenzie, Henry, 305
Mackenzie, J. T., Esq., Mss., 263
McKenzie, James, 166
Mackenzie, John (*fl.* 1774-5), 61
McKenzie, John (*fl.* 1840-7), 166
Mackenzie, Kenneth (*fl.* 1712), 260
Mackenzie, Kenneth (*fl.* 1844), 291
Mackenzie, Robert Shelton (1809-80), 168
MacKenzie, William, 293
Mackenzie Papers, 61
Mackenzie River, 146
McKeown, Annie, 328
McKeown, Mary, 332
Mackeson, John, 46
McKibbin, William, 328
Mackie, Charles, 312
Mackie, George, & Co., 22
Mackillar, P., 119
McKinen, C. W., 265
Mackinlay, R., 313
McKinley, William (1843-1901), 38
McKinley Tariff, 20, 34, 42
McKinnon, Donald, 297
McKinnon, Ranald, 296
Mackinnon, Sir William (1823-93), 166
Mackintosh, Aeneas, 261
McKnight & McIlwraith, 309
McLaine (McLean), Archibald, of Lochbuie, 295-7 *passim*
McLaine, Barbara, 295

McLaine, Donald, 295, 296
McLaine, Hector, 295
McLaine (McLean), John (of New York, *fl.* 1780-4), 295, 296
McLaine, Murdoch (merchant, *fl.* 1775), 295
McLaine (Maclaine, McLean), Murdoch (*fl.* 1775-1834), 295-7 *passim*
McLaine, Washington, 295
MacLaine of Lochbuie Muniments, 295-7
McLane, Louis (1786-1857), 63, 67
McLauren, Patrick, 312
MacLaurin, David, 292
McLawchlan, John, 272
McLean, Alan, 295
MacLean, Allan (1725-84), 258, 284, 296, 297
McLean, Archibald (officer in New York Volunteers), 296
Maclean, Charles, 295
McLean, Donald (*fl.* 1777), 51
Maclean, Donald (*fl.* early 19th cent.?), 295
McLean (Maclean), Hector, 295, 296
Maclean, Hugh, 295-6
McLean, John (*fl.* 1773), 295
McLean (Maclean), John (*fl.* 1778-80), 295
MacLean, John (1785-1861), 204
McLean, Lachlan, 296
McLean, Malcolm, 295
Maclean, Neil, 296
McLees, Catherine, 329
McLees, John, 329
Macleod, Alexander (*fl.* 1771), 263
McLeod, Alexander (*fl.* 1811-25), 331
McLeod, Alexander (*fl.* 1840's), 67, 170, 274
McLeod, Donald, 3rd of Geanies (*fl.* 1773-6), 256
McLeod, James, 256
McLeod, John (*fl.* 1737-41), 293, 311
MacLeod, John (*fl.* 1775-81), 256
McLeod, Norman, 317
MacLeod, Roderick, 298
McLeod of Geanies Papers, 256
Macleod of Macleod Mss., 263
McLoughlin, John, 291
Maclure, William (1763-1840), 183
McMahon, Dr., 178
MacMillan, W., 314
Macmillan Archive, 78
Macmillan Co., New York, 78
MacMurdoch, Capt., 284
McMurray, P. R., 249
Macnab, Sir Alan Napier (1798-1862), 219
Macnab of Macnab Mss., 270
Macnabb, Donald Campbell, 270
McNair, A. D., *Law of Treaties*, 132 fn.; ed., *International Law Opinions*, 132 fn.
McNally, Edward, 329
McNally, John, 328
McNally, Mrs. P., 328
McNally, William, 329
Macneal, Capt., 260
MacNeal, Col., 288
Macneal, George, 260
Macneal of Lossit Mss., 260
Macneill, Dr., 260
McNeill, Ronald John, Baron Cushendun (1861-1934), 279
Macoun, John, 329
MacPherson, James, 265
MacPherson, John, 266
McPherson, Malcolm, 289
MacPherson–Grant of Ballindalloch Mss., 266
McQuarrie, Hector, 296
Macrae, Alexander, 274
McReady, F. R., 318, 319
McReynolds, Andrew, 328
McSherry, Hugh, 328
MacSwiney, Terence, 345
[Mactavish], Donald, 260
MacVeagh, [Isaac] Wayne (1833-1917), 197
Macvey Napier Papers, 14 fn.
McVickar, John (1787-1868), 5
McWhorter, Mary, 346
Macy, Jesse (1842-1919), 197, 198, 199
Macy, Mary Maud (Little), Mrs. Jesse Macy, 198
Madden, Richard Robert (1798-1886), 353; Papers, 353
Madder, 149
Madeira, 36
Madison, Dolly (Payne), Mrs. James Madison (1768-1849), 101
Madison, James (1751-1836), 9, 16, 62, 107, 140, 148, 167, 168, 204, 294
Madog ab Owain Gwynedd [Prince Madoc?] (1150?-80?), 243, 248
Magdalene College, Cambridge, 16-7
Magilligan, Londonderry, 325 fn.
Maguire, Mary, 329
Mahon, Viscount (*styled* 1816-55), *see* Stanhope, Philip Henry (1805-75)
Mahon, Denis (1787-1847), 347
Maidstone, Kent, 44-6
Mail service, *see* Postal service
Maillard, Antoine Simon (d. 1768), 257; *Account of the Customs and Manners of the Micmakis and Maricheets Savage Nations*, 257 fn.
Maine, David, 149
Maine: Banking, 130; Boundaries with Canada, *see* North-East Boundary; Webster–Ashburton Treaty, 1842; Claims of British subjects, 130; Climate, 148; Coast, 148; Description, 236; Education, 130, 263; Fishing, 326; Governors, 130, 286; Immigrants, 331, 351; Indians, 260; Industry, 300; Land, 5, 68, 260; Land grants, 54; Religious history, 158
AUGUSTA, 331; Gardiner, 148, 257; Long Pond, 300; Pammagurd, 260; Portland, 351, Consular reports (British), 130
Maine (ship), 259
Maitland, Frederic William (1850-1906), 16
Maitland, John, 2nd Earl of Lauderdale (1616-82), 276, 298
Maitland, John (*fl.* 1801), 102
Maitland, Sir Thomas (1759?-1824), 298
Maitland Papers, 33
Maitland–Sara Papers, 228
Maize, 64, 149, 184, 301, 346
Makemie, Francis (1658-1708), 275
Malby, Thomas, 10
Malcolm, Alexander, 312
Malcolm, D. O., 278
Malcolm, Ian, 259
Malcolm of Poltalloch Mss., 265
Maldon (Malden), Customs records, 89, 93
Mallett, John William (1832-1912), 163
Malmesbury, 1st Earl of, *see* Harris, James (1746-1820); 3rd Earl of, *see* Harris, James Howard (1807-89)
Malmesbury Papers, 36
Malone, Edmund (1741-1812), 350

Malone Mss., 202
Malthus, Thomas Robert (1766-1834), 273
Manchester, 4th Duke of, *see* Montagu, George (1737-88)
Manchester, Greater Manchester, 173-9; Customs records, 93; Merchants, 107, 175, 310
Manchester Association of Importers and Exporters, 178
Manchester Chamber of Commerce, 178
Manchester Collection, 17
Manchester College, Oxford, 208
Manchester Guardian, *see Guardian*
Manchester Public Libraries, 178-9
Manchester Society for Women's Suffrage, 179
Manchester University, Department of Economic History, 178
Manchuria, Relations with U.S., *see* Relations with Manchuria
Mander–Jones, Phyllis, ed., *Manuscripts in the British Isles Relating to Australia, New Zealand, and the Pacific*, xxv
Manesty, Joseph, 18
Mangowit, Michel–Ange–Bernard, 57
Manitoba: Immigrants, 331, 348
CHURCHILL, 323; Fort Garry, 140, 142
See also Red River Settlement
Mann, Ab., 9
Mann, Horace (1796-1859), 255
Mann, William Thompson, 184
Manners, Charles, Marquess of Granby (*styled* 1770-9), 4th Duke of Rutland (1754-87), 48
Manners, Charlotte (Mrs. George Manners), 98
Manners, George, 98, 286
Manners, John, 1st Duke of Rutland (*styled* Lord Roos *till* 1679) (1638-1711), 48
Manners, John, Marquess of Granby (1721-70), 48
Manners, John Henry, 5th Duke of Rutland (1778-1857), 14
Manners, Lord Robert (1758-82), 48
Manners, Roger, 5th Earl of Rutland (1576-1612), 48
Manners and customs, 15, 41, 46, 168, 179, 186, 270; *see also* Indians: Social life and customs; *and subdivision* Description *under states*
Manning, Henry Edward (1808-92), 71, 172
Manross, W. W., *The Fulham Papers in the Lambeth Palace Library . . .*, 115; *S. P. G. Papers in the Lambeth Palace Library . . .*, 115, 158 fn.
Mansbridge, Albert, 281
Mansell Publishing, xxv
Mansfield, 1st Earl of, *see* Murray, William (1705-93)
Mansfield, Earl of, Mss., 266-7
Mansfield, George Patrick Lattin (1820-89), 346
Mansfield, John, 9
Mansfield, Owen (1818-88), 346
Mansfield, Richard, 78
Mansfield Papers, 346
Manson, William, 315
Mant, Thomas, 302
Manufactures, *see* Industry
Manuscript Sources for the History of Irish Civilisation, 343
Manvers, Prof., 169
Manwaring, Asa, 5
Manwood, Sir John, 221
Manx Museum, 335
Maps, Early, 8, 27, 129, 135, 190, 263
Marble, Abigail, 16
Marble, Manton Malone (1835-1917), 16, 161; Collection, 161
Marburg, Theodore (b. 1862), 197; *Development of the League of Nations Idea . . .*, ed. by John H. Latané, 197 fn.
Marchet, G. L., 49
Marchmont, 2nd Earl of, *see* Campbell, Alexander (1675-1740); 3rd Earl of, *see* Hume, Hugh (1708-94) & Baron Polwarth
Marconi Company of America, 170
Marcy, William Learned (1786-1857), 16, 125, 200
Maréchal, Ambrose (1764-1828), 30, 171
Mareuil, Baron de, 286
Marion, Kitty (1873-1944), 84, 118
Maritime law, *see* Law, Maritime
Mark, Jacob, 61
Markham, Sir Clement, *Markham Memorials*, 11
Markham, William (1686-1771), 11
Markham Note Books, 11
Marks Arnheim, 237
Marlborough, Duke of, 193
Marquess of Linlithgow Mss., 268
Marriner, R. V., Ltd., 239
Marriner, S., *Rathbones of Liverpool*, 185 fn.; "Rathbones' Trading Activities in the Middle of the Nineteenth Century," *Trans. of the Historic Society of Lancashire and Cheshire* (1957), 185 fn.
Marrington Collection, 211
Marris, C. S., Esq., 116-7
Marryat, Frederick (1792-1848), 299
Marryat, Joseph, 288
Marsden, Joshua, 117
Marsden, R. G., 89 fn.
Marsh, Clare, 353
Marsh, James, Jr., 234
Marsh, John, Jr., 234, 235
Marsh, Theophilus, 235
Marsh Bros. & Co., 234-5
Marshall, John (1755-1835), 81, 306, 317
Marshall, John, of South Carolina (*fl.* 1796-1819), 270
Marshall, John (*fl.* 1820-40), 239
Marshall, Thomas Riley (1854-1925), 197
Marshall Aid, 112
Marshall & Manning, 198
Marshall Collection, 26
Marshall Library of Economics, Cambridge, 115 fn.
Marshall Papers, 239
Marshalls (firm), 239
Marshes & Shepherd, 235
Martin, Alexander (1740-1807), 16
Martin, Andrew, 329
Martin, Bryan (1731-98), 45
Martin, Charles, 328
Martin, George (*fl.* 1779-1800), 23
Martin, George F. (d. 1852), 46
Martin, Henry (d. 1721), 8
Martin, James, 97
Martin, John (d. 1761), 23
Martin, John (*fl.* 1785), 329
Martin, Josiah, the elder (*fl.* 1729-40), 65
Martin, Josiah (1737-86), 65
Martin, Lewis, 23
Martin, Samuel (*fl.* 1768), 48, 264
Martin, Samuel, Jr. (*fl.* 1759-85), 65
Martin, Samuel (d. 1800), 23
Martin, Sella, 176
Martin, Sir Theodore, *Life of Lord Lyndhurst*, 17 fn.
Martin, Thomas, 169
Martin, Sir Thomas Byam (1773-1854), 288
Martin, Thomas Commerford (1856-1924), 162

Martin, William, 331
Martin, Wise & Fitzhugh, 181
Martin family, 45
Martin Leake Mss., 40
Martin Papers, 65
Martineau, Harriet (1802-76), 168, 169; *Autobiography*, 168; *Society in America*, 168
Martineau, James (1805-1900), 95
Martineau, Susan, 208
Martinique, Relations with U.S., *see* Relations with Martinique
Martins Bank Ltd., 181
Martyn, Benjamin (1699-1763), 52
Martyn [or Martin], Richard (d. 1663), 25
Marx, Karl (1818-83), 53
Marx & Linsley, 240
Mary (of Modena), Queen of England (1658-1718), 82, 83
Mary (ship), 263
Mary Lowell (ship), 131
Mary of Maldon (ship), 33
Maryland: to 1700, 10, 34; 1700-64, 263, 306, 311; 1765-75, 215, 249; 1776-1800, 324; Civil War, 1861-5, 59
AGRICULTURE, 148, 305; Army, 285; Assembly, 73, 246; Boundaries with Pennsylvania, 8, 39, with Virginia, 194; Constitution, 302; Customs administration, 87, 92; Defence, 195; Description, 116, 266, 326; Education, 305, 313; Governors, 64, 86, 185, 194, 195, 215, 222, 223, 245, 285; Immigrants, 5, 46, 49, 70, 86, 129, 166, 211, 228, 246, 291, 312, 328, 330, 331, 343; Industry, 28, 112, 226; Land, 10, 32, 48, 57, 191, 193, 217, 346; Land grants, 39, 118, 194; Law, 73, 301; Maps, 8; Merchants, 73, 83, 86, 309; Population, 302; Religious history, 28, 30, 37, 48, 105, 117, 118, 154, 155, 157, 159, 171, 185, 225, 275; Settlement, 185; Shipping, 121; Slavery, 30, 175, 309; Tobacco, 7, 21, 299, 309, 313; Trade, 7, 8, 21, 31, 56, 88, 89, 91, 169, 185, 212, 248, 273, 299-304 *passim*, 309, 310, 317
ANN ARUNDEL COUNTY, 48; Annapolis, 30, 73, 208, 263
BALTIMORE, 62, 121, 161, 171, 248, 303, 310, 324, 330, 331, Consular reports (British), 130, 134, Description, 30, 43, 95, 98, 156, 159, 183, 268, 271, 325, 328, 346, General Dispensary, 315, Merchants, 22, 166, 169, 175, 183, 186, 225, 234, 235, 319, 327, Politics, 177, 291
CAROLINE COUNTY, 57; Cecil County, 97; Chestertown, 331; Dorchester County, 57; Fort Cumberland, 285; Frederick County, 97; Patapsco, Customs collectors, 87; Patuxent, Customs collectors, 87; Pocomoke, Customs collectors, 87; Queen Tree Patuxent, 13; St. Inigoe's 13; Wiccocomoco [Wicomico] River, Surveyor of customs, 292
Maryland and New York Iron and Coal Co., 28
Maryland Coal Loan, 1840, 28
Maryland, University of, 315
Marylebone Cricket Club, 117
Maryport, Customs records, 93
Mascarene, J., 149
Maseres, Francis (1731-1824), 233
Maseres Mss., 114
Mason, Mr., 303
Mason, A., 149
Mason, Daniel G., 236
Mason, Edward, 266
Mason, James Murray (1798-1871), 59, 69, 232
Mason, Jeremiah (1768-1848), 245
Mason, John (1586-1635), 10, 306
Mason–Slidell affair, *see Trent* (ship)
Masot, José, 66
"Massachusettensis" (*pseud.*), *see* Leonard, Daniel (1740-1829)
Massachusetts: Colonial period, 10, 22, 36, 40, 65, 66, 82, 138, 193, 194, 213, 300, 303; 1765-75, 10, 24, 54, 55, 65, 66, 79, 138, 195, 214-5 *passim*, 218, 233, 261, 268, 292, 302, 317, 354; Civil War, 1861-5, 68; 1865- , 68
AGENTS, 303; Agriculture, 148, 187; Army, 143, 302; Banking, 297; Charters, 300, 352; Climate, 148; Commonwealth of, 5; Constitution, 216; Customs administration, 105, 195, 233, 249; Finance, 309; Governors, 10, 32, 40, 42, 61, 64, 66, 86, 102, 103, 105, 164, 200, 214, 215, 217, 218, 240, 249, 290; Hospitals, 196; House of Representatives (or Assembly), 54, 214, 233, 265, 302; Immigrants, 9, 26, 27-8, 245, 290, 328, 331, 351; Indians, 19, 99, 210; Industry, 7, 185; Land, 13, 220, 230, 247; Land grants, 94, 249; Law, 54, 55, 57, 105; Loyalists, 73; Lunatic asylum, 185; Merchants, 169, 236, 290; Politics, 54, 233; Riots, 302; Relations with French, 193; Relief for Irish famine, 345; Religious history, 8, 25, 35, 84, 94, 95, 99, 105, 151, 158, 177, 220, 225, 245, 256, 263, 312, 328; Shipping, 273; Slave trade, 57; Theatres, 178; Trade, 32, 55, 56, 82, 99, 185, 225, 260, 274, 303, 309, 310
BOSTON, 9, 12, 26, 35, 42, 55, 65, 66, 67, 79, 82, 120, 151, 179, 185, 189, 195, 208, 213, 214, 218, 230, 233, 249, 254, 260, 261, 265, 268, 269, 273, 274, 276, 284, 288, 290, 292, 293, 294, 296, 297, 298, 302, 309, 310, 311, 312, 315, 328, 345, 351, 354, Arlington Street Church, 177, Consular reports (British), 67, 130, 134, Customs collectors, 87, Description, 30, 32, 36, 95, 98, 117, 179, 210, 256, Government, 210, Merchants, 22, 99, 183, 187, 213, 234, 311, 317, Tremont Theatre, 178; *see also* Boston Committee of Correspondence; Boston Port Act; Boston Tea-Party
ANDOVER, 263; Athol, 262; Brockton, 6; Bunker Hill, 12, 317; Cambridge, 331; Cambridge Bay, 12; Cape Ann, 312; Charlestown, 121, 231, 237 fn., 263; Chelsea, 13; Concord, 233, 290, 292, 305; Dedham, 105; Deer Island, 94; Dorchester, 351; Duke's County, 196; Dunstable, 269; East Cambridge, 254; Elizabeth's Island, 194; Fox Island, 94; George's Bank, 62; Hingham, History, 188; Lexington, 12, 13; Lowell, 185; Malden, 13; Marblehead, 12, Customs collectors, 87; Martha's Vineyard, 99, 194; Nantucket, 43, 62, 247, Customs collectors, 87; Natick, 99; New Bedford, 169; Noddle's Island, 5; Pelham, 5; Plymouth, 245, Customs collectors, 87; Roxbury, 12; Salem, 30, 176, 214, 254, Customs collectors, 87; Springfield, 236, 294; Stoughton, 105; Swansea, 245; Watertown, 12; Worcester, 155, 185, 265, 294; Wrentham, 5
See also New England
Massachusetts Bay Company, Charters, 193, 194, 202
"Massachusetts Bible," 151
Massachusetts Commission for International Justice, 165
Massachusetts Gazette and the Boston Weekly News-Letter, 12, 140
Massachusetts Historical Society, 58, 94; *Collections*, 217 fn.; Library, 99; *Proceedings*, 276
Massachusetts Institute of Technology, 164, 282
Massachusetts Society for Promoting Agriculture, 187
Massereene–Foster Papers, 324-5
Massey, Eyre, 1st Baron Clarina (1719-1804), 296
Massey, Henry, 304
Massey, Vincent, 278
Massingberd, Burrell, 50
Massingberd and Massingberd–Mundy Deposits, 50
Massingberd of Gunby Mss., 49
Masson, Edward, 264
Master, Joseph, 28

Master, William (*fl.* 1762), 27
Master, William (*fl.* 1832), 28
Matador Land and Cattle Co. Ltd., 308
Matching (Meeching, *now* Newhaven), Customs records, 89
Mather, Cotton (1663-1728), 99, 174, 203, 259
Mather, Increase (1639-1723), 82, 99, 151, 174, 202, 203
Mather, Ralph, 226
Mather, Richard (1596-1669), 174
Mather, Samuel (1706-85), 259, 312
Mathewe, Walter, 37
Mathews, Samuel (*c.* 1600-60), 24, 194
Mathieson, William Law (1868-1938), 256
Matlock, Derbyshire, 23
Matthew, John, 42
Matthew, N., 312
Matthew, Thomas, 42
Matthews, J. B., 74
Matthews, N., and M. D. Wainwright, *Guide to Manuscripts and Documents in the British Isles Relating to Africa*, xxv
Matthiesson, F. C., 64
Mattison, Alfred, Collection, 238
Matusow, Harvey Marshall (b. 1926), 221
Matusow Papers, 221
Mauduit, Israel, 302
Maule, Fox, 2nd Baron Panmure and 11th Earl of Dalhousie (1801-74), 284
Maule, Thomas, 316
Maunsel White & Co., 240
Maunsell Papers, 190
Maurice, Landgrave of Hesse Cassel (1572-1632), 10
Maurice, Lily, 245
Maury, James, & Sons, 249
Maury, Matthew Fontaine (1806-73), 148, 232
Maury, Latham & Co., 249
Maverick, J., 270
Mavor, John, 266
Max, John, 2nd Baron Egremont, 223
Max–Müller, Friedrich (1823-1900), 202
Max–Müller Papers, 202
Maximilian, Emperor of Mexico (1832-67), 201
Maxted, Frederick, 44
Maxted, William Bullock, 44
Maxted Papers, 44
Maxtone, Helen, 292
Maxtone, Thomas, 292
Maxtone Graham Muniments, 292
Maxwell, Lady Anna Stirling, 317
Maxwell, David, 310
Maxwell, Edward, 48
Maxwell, Hugh (1733-99), 324
Maxwell, William (1784-1857), 182
Maxwell, William (*fl.* 1932), 259
Maxwell, Sir William Stirling, 317
Maxwell of Pollok, Papers, 317
Maxwell, Perceval–, Papers, 324
Maxwell Stuart of Traquair Mss., 260
Maxwell–Constable, M. F., 42
Maxwell–Constable of Everingham, 42
May, Samuel, Jr., 6, 96
May, Samuel Joseph (1797-1871), 208; *Rights and Condition of Women*, 84
Maybrick, Mrs., 39
Mayer, Max, 178
Mayer Collection, 178
Mayflower (ship, 17th cent.), 89 fn.
Mayflower (ship, 18th cent.), 273
Mayflower (ship, 1890), 269
Mayhew, Experience (1673-1758), 98, 99
Mayhew, Jonathan (1720-66), 94, 149, 174
Mayhew, Matthew, 196; *A Brief Narrative of the Success which the Gospel hath had among the Indians of Martha's Vineyard*, 196
Mayhew, Thomas, 98
Maynard family, 14
Mayo, Katherine, 277
Mazey, Jonathan, 245
Mead, Henry Mandeville, 308
Mead, Gabriel, & Co., 22
Meade, George Gordon (1815-72), 59, 344
Meade–Waldo, E. R., 113
Meagher, Thomas Francis (1823-67), 326, 344
Means, Robert, 332
Meares, John (1756?-1809), 138
Mease, James (1771-1846), 150, 187
Meat, 111
Meatyard, Mary, 28
Meatyard, Robert (*fl.* 1836-8), 28
Mechanician (ship), 129
Mechanics, 16; *see also* Perpetual motion
Mechanics' institutes, 169
Mediation, American, 287; *see also* Arbitration, International
Medical Society, New Orleans, 315
Medicine, 18th century, 295, 297, 299, 300; 19th century, 263; 20th century, 78-9
Medlicott, W. G., 314
Mees, ———, 83
Melbourne, 3rd Viscount, *see* Lamb, Frederick James (1782-1853)
Melbourne Hall, Derbyshire, 23-4
Melchett, 2nd Baron, *see* Mond, Henry Ludwig (1898-1945)
Melfort, 1st Earl and titular Duke of, *see* Drummond, John (1649-1714)
Mellish, Mr., 288
Mellish, Charles (*c.* 1737-96), 193
Mellish Mss., 193
Mellon, Andrew W. (1855-1937), 278
Mellows, Liam, 345
Melvill, Allan, 275
Melville, 1st Viscount, *see* Dundas, Henry (1742-1811); 2nd Viscount, *see* Dundas, Robert Saunders (1771-1851)
Melville, Herman (1819-91), 74
Melville Castle Muniments, 286-9
Melville Papers, 257
Mendip, 1st Baron, *see* Ellis, Welbore (1713-1802)
Mentor (ship), 138
Menzies, Ashurst, 273
Menzies, Ninian, 317
Menzies, Robert G., 272, 282
Mercer, George, 233
Mercer, Hugh, 285
Mercer, Robert, 289
Mercers' Company Records, 117
Merchant Venturers, Society of, 7-8
Merchants, 22, 80; Colonial period, 8-9, 21, 26, 27, 54, 56, 293, 302; *see also* Trade; Trade, Colonial period; *and subdivision* Merchants *under states and cities*
Mercury, Liverpool, 329
Meredith, Randal, 324

Meredith, Sir William (d. 1790), 212
Merivale, Herman (1806-74), 40
Merope (ship), 219
Merry, Anthony, 101, 140, 231
Merryworthy, Thomas, 155
Mersch, Charles, 291
Merseyside, England, 180-5; *see also* Immigrants from Merseyside
Merseyside Chamber of Commerce and Industry, 184
Merseyside County Archives, 184
Mersmüller, Oswald, 248
Merthyr Mawr Estate Records, 250
Merthyr Tydfil, Business records, *see* Business records: Merthyr Tydfil
Merz and McLellan, 224
Meserve, Nathaniel (*c.* 1705-58), 120
Mesmerism, 114
Messervy, J. A., ed., *Journal de Jean Chevalier*, 339 fn.
Metallurgy, 236-7
Metals, 147
Metcalfe, Sir Charles Theophilus, 1st Baron (1785-1846), 129
Meteorology, *see* Climate
Meteyard, E., *Life of Josiah Wedgwood*, 175
Metford, Joseph (1776-1863), 156; "Transatlantic Travels," 156
Methodist Archives, 178
Methodist Archives and Research Centre, 178
Methodist Church, 34, 65, 85, 95, 219, 243; Missions, 117
Methodist Episcopal Church, 117
Methodist Missionary Society, 117
Meux, Thomas, 49
Mexican Land and Colonisation Co., 100
Mexico: 1800-45, 66, 211, 231; War with U.S., 1845-8, *see* War with Mexico, 1845-8; European intervention, 1861-7, 131, 201, 211, British, 58, 59, French, 68
DESCRIPTION, 225, 256; Merchants, 183; Mining, 111; Petroleum, 111; Relations with Texas, 206; Trade with Scotland, 315; *see also* Relations with Mexico; Trade with Mexico
MATAMOROS, 130, 131; Mexico City, Description, 211; Tacumaya, 225; Tampico, 183; Yucatan, 66
Mexico, Gulf of, 174
Meyrick, James, 215
Michel, Lewis, 220
Michelmore, Loveys & Carter, Totnes, 25
Michener, Louis T., 345
Michigan: Agriculture, 219; Education, 272; Immigrants, 219, 328, 332; Land, 223, 331; Religious history, 75, 177
CAMPBELL'S CORNER, 328; Centerville, Description, 346; Detroit, 45, 75, 272, 282, 297, 328, 331, Consular reports (British), 134, Description, 20, 32, Forts, 80, 144; Michilimackinac, 144; Tecumsith, 223
Michigan Central Railroad, 250
Michigan, University of, William L. Clements Library, 66 fn.
Mickie, James, 304
Micklethwaite, John, 175
Microform Review, xxv
Middlesborough, Customs records, 93
Middlesex, *see* Immigrants from Middlesex
Middleton, Lord, 192 fn.
Middleton, Arthur (1681-1737), 218
Middleton, Charles, 1st Baron Barham (1726-1813), 101; *Letters and Papers . . .*, 101 fn.
Middleton, Henry (*fl.* 1746-81), 218
Middleton, Henry (*fl.* 1784-1826), 218
Middleton, John, 219
Middleton, Peter, 260, 295
Middleton, Sarah, 225
Middleton, Thomas (*fl.* 1784-1826), 218
Middleton, William (*fl.* 1746-81), 218
Middleton, William (*fl.* 1765), 237
Middleton, William (*fl.* 1784-1826), 218
Middleton, Sir William Fowle, 219
Middleton, Sir William Fowle Fowle, 219
Middleton Mss., 192
Middleton Papers, 218-9
Midland Bank Ltd., 117-8
Midleton, 1st Earl of, *see* Brodrick, William St. John Fremantle (1856-1942)
Midleton Papers, 141
Mifflin, Ann, 19, 156
Mildmay Papers, 32
Miles, James Browning (1822-75), 244
Miles [or Myles], John (1621-84), 245
Miles, Samuel, 5
Miles, W. Porcher, 104
Miles Collection, 5
Milford, Customs records, 89, 93
Mill, James (1776-1836), 169
Millar, Mrs. A. W., Mss., 271
Miller, Aaron, 149
Miller, Alfred J., 291
Miller, Anne F., 236
Miller, David, & Sons, 310
Miller, Francis P., 283
Miller, Hugh (*fl.* 1793), 309
Miller, Hugh (1802-56), 271
Miller, J. R., 21
Miller, James, 45
Miller, Joaquin, 70; *Life among the Modocs*, 227; "Songs of the Sierras," 70
Milliken, James, 329
Milliken, John, 329
Millikin, John M., 245
Mills, E., 280
Mills, George, 302
Mills, Cave, Baillie & Co., 115
Milne, A. Taylor, *A Catalogue of the MSS of Jeremy Bentham*, 167
Milne, Sir Alexander (1806-96), 13, 121, 123
Milne, Sir David (1763-1845), 288
Milne, James, 199
Milne, Richard, 173
Milne Papers, 121
Milner, Frank, 282
Milner, James, 234
Milner, John (1752-1826), 171, 225
Milnes, Richard Monckton, 1st Baron Houghton (1809-85), 17, 105
Milton, Viscount (*styled till* 1833), *see* Fitzwilliam, Charles William Wentworth, 3rd Earl Fitzwilliam (1766-1857)
Milton, Viscount, *see* Fitzwilliam, William W. (d. 1877)
Milton, Customs records, 89
Milton Agricultural Labourers Union, 209
Milward, Isabel (*née* Zonche), 23
Milward, Robert, 23
Minard, Duane E., 40
Minchinton, W. E., ed., *The Trade of Bristol in the Eighteenth Century*, 6 fn., 7 fn., 8 fn., 124, 211 fn.; "The Virginia Letters of Isaac Hobhouse," *Virginia Magazine of History and Biography* (1958), 7 fn.

Minehead, Customs records, 89
Minerals, 111
Miners, Immigrants, 20, 29
Mines, Submarine, 143, 264
Mingay, George, 219
Mining Development Syndicate (of Colorado) Ltd., 308
Mining industry and finance, 10, 29, 204, 206, 211, 222, 258, 270, 307, 308; Settlements, 217; *see also* Coal mining; Copper mining; Gold mining; Lead mining; Tin mining
Mining Journal, 20
Mining machinery, Trade, 19, 20
Ministry of Aviation, 122, 124
Ministry of Production, 125, 126
Minnesota, Immigrants, 332; Trade, 254
MINNEAPOLIS, 254, 332; St. Paul, Consular reports (British), 134
Minnesota (ship), 329
Minto, 2nd Earl of, *see* Elliot, Gilbert (1782-1859); 3rd Earl of, *see* Elliot, William Hugh (1814-91); 4th Earl of, *see* Elliot, Gilbert J. M. (1845-1914)
Minto, Lady Mary Caroline Elliot (1858-1940), 257
Minto, Walter (1753-96), 313
Minto Papers, 257
Mints, 172, 226
Miranda, Francisco de (*c.* 1750-1816), 287
Missions, 116, 118, 144, 152, 155, 156, 157, 158, 174, 177, 197, 347, 352; *see also subdivision* Missions *under* Eskimoes; Indians; *and also under religious sects*
Mississippi: 1776-83, 13; 1783-1860, 276; Civil War, 1861-5, 60, 328
DESCRIPTION, 271; Finance, 170; Governors, 258; Immigrants, 271, 331; Merchants, 271; Trade, 262
HUNTSVILLE, 271 (*see also* Alabama); Natchez, 21; Ocean Spring, 39; Vicksburg, 168, 244; Wellington, 331
Mississippi Company, 284
Mississippi River, 12, 13, 45, 140, 214, 249, 274, 300, 301, 305
Mississippi Valley Trading Co., 174
Missouri: Description, 182 fn., 244, 346; Flora, 291; Immigrants, 25, 166, 230, 246, 331, 332; Land, 98, 291, 308; Livestock, 308; Religious history, 157, 171, 291, 344
CORINTH, 58; Jackson County, 25; Kansas City, Consular reports (British), 134; St. Louis, 172, 291, 331, 346, Botanical Garden, 146, Consular reports (British), 130, 134, Description, 276, 290, 291, Exposition (1904), 131, 304
Missouri Land and Livestock Co. Ltd., 303, 308
Missouri Land Co. of Scotland Ltd., 308
Mitchel, John (1815-75), 326, 344
Mitchel, John (1838-64), 344
Mitchell, A., 287
Mitchell, Sir Andrew (1708-71), 79
Mitchell, Arthur I. C., 348
Mitchell, Charles, 326
Mitchell, J., 75
Mitchell, John (*fl.* 1776-8), 262
Mitchell, John Hinckley (1767-1832), 226; *The Mitchell–Boulton Correspondence*, 226 fn.
Mitchell, Margaret E., 348
Mitchell, O. M., 245
Mitchell, Robert (1778-1848), 16
Mitchell, Robert (*fl.* 1815), 273
Mitchell, Samuel L., 183
Mitchell, William (*fl.* 1780-1), 309
Mitchell, William (*fl.* 1852-5), 326
Mitchell, William, Ltd., 327
Mitchell & Anderson, 62
Mitchell family, 326
Mitchell Library, Glasgow, 316-7
Mitchell Papers, 79
Mitchells, Johnston, Hill & Hoggan, 317
Mitchelson, David, 273
Mobile and Ohio Railroad, 247
Modern Poetry Collection, 178
Moelwyn Choir, 248
Moffat, Thomas, 149
Moir(?), Mr., 264
Moira, Earl of, *see* Hastings, Francis Rawdon–, 2nd Earl (1754-1826)
Molasses: Duties, 301; Trade, 55, 301
Molesworth, Sir William, 104
Molleson, William, 257
Molyneux, Mrs., 131
Molyneux, A. L., 175
Molyneux, Richard, 48
Monasteries, 131
Monck, Sir Charles Stanley, 4th Viscount (1819-94), 69, 104
Monckton, Robert (1726-82), 266
Moncrieff, Archibald, 263
Moncrieff, Sir Henry, *afterwards* Sir Henry Moncrieff Wellwood (1750-1827), 263, 313
Moncrieff, James, 311
Moncrieff, Robert, 263
Moncrieffe of Tulliebole Mss., 263
Mond, Henry Ludwig, 2nd Baron Melchett (1898-1945), 282
Mongovo George (ship), 70
Monis, Judah, 274
Monk Bretton, 1st Baron, *see* Dodson, John George (1825-97); 3rd Baron *see* Dodson, John Charles (b. 1924)
Monk Bretton Papers, 202
Monkswell, 1st Baron, *see* Collier, Sir Robert Porrett (1817-86)
Monongahela River, 285
Monro, Alida (d. 1969), 79
Monro, David, 289
Monro, Harold E., 79; and Poetry Bookshop Papers, 79
Monro of Allan Muniments, 289
Monro of Williamwood Mss., 270
Monroe, James (1758-1831), 13, 16, 30, 61, 66, 148, 196, 205, 240, 256, 259
Monroe Doctrine, 25, 61, 162, 277, 283
Monson, Charles, 50
Monson, John, 1st Baron (1693-1748), 50
Monson, John, 2nd Baron (1727-74), 50
Monson Family Papers, 50
Montagu, Lord Charles Greville (1741-84), 17
Montagu, Edward (1692-1775), 233
Montagu, Edward Wortley (1678-1761), 232
Montagu, Edward Wortley (1713-76), 249
Montagu, George, 4th Duke of Manchester (1737-88), 76
Montagu, John, 4th Earl of Sandwich (1718-92), 102, 120, 222, 267; *Private Papers*, 102 fn.
Montagu Mss., 203, 204
Montague, Elizabeth, 270
Montana: Agriculture, 234; Governors, 344; Immigrants, 328, 344; Indians, 344; Investments, 271; Ranching, 308, 348
DILLON, 328; Great Falls, 271; Little Big Horn, 347; Park County, 348; Powder River, 234
Montana Sheep and Cattle Co. Ltd., 308

Montcalm, Louis Joseph, Marquis de (1712-59), 119, 297
Monteagle of Brandon, 1st Baron, *see* Spring–Rice, Thomas (1790-1866)
Monteagle Papers, 347
Montezuma (ship), 307
Montgomerie, Alexander, 10th Earl of Eglinton (1723-69), 265, 275
Montgomerie, Sir James, 273
Montgomerie, John (d. 1731), 264
"Montgomery," 260
Montgomery, Archibald, 266, 285
Montgomery, Henry Riddell, 326
Montgomery, James (*fl.* 1795-1854), 234
Montgomery, Richard (1736-75), 57, 205, 286, 324
Monthly Magazine, 226
Montmorenci, Henri, Duc de (1534-1614), 159
Montreal, *see* Quebec: Montreal
Montreal Agricultural Society, 187
Montresor, John (1736-88?), 45
Montrose, 4th Marquis and 1st Duke of, *see* Graham, James (d. 1742)
Montrose Muniments, 300
Montserrat: Customs collectors, 87; Trade with Great Britain, 15
Monumental brasses, Trade, 227
Monypenny, W. F., *The Life of Benjamin Disraeli, Earl of Beaconsfield*, 13 fn.
Moodie, Mr., 33
Moody, Dwight Lyman (1837-99), 199, 255
Moody, Richard Clement (1813-87), 40
Moody & May, Messrs., 325
Moore, ———, 203
Moore, Charles, 275
Moore, Edward (1835-1916), 204
Moore, George, 329
Moore, Sir Henry (1713-69), 228, 233
Moore, John (*fl.* 1724), 262
Moore, John, Archbishop of Canterbury (1730-1805), 115
Moore, John (*fl.* 1781), 272
Moore, Miss M. F., Papers, 306
Moore, Rebecca, 96
Moore, Robert, 329
Moore, S., 226
Moore, T. W. Charles, 286
Moore, William, 329
Moore's Indian school, 290
Moran, Benjamin, 69
Morant family, 26
Moravian Church, 118, 174
Moravian Church in Great Britain and Ireland, 118
Moray, Countess of, *see* Stuart, Margaret (d. 1779)
Moray, James, 289
Mordecai, Sam, 175
More, John, 10
More, Samuel, 149, 151
Morel, Edmund Dene (1873-1924), 165
Morewood, George, 105
Morgan, A. W., 231
Morgan, Evan R., 245
Morgan, James Dada (1810-96), 244
Morgan, John (*fl.* 1784), 313
Morgan, John Pierpont (1837-1913), 78, 118
Morgan, John Tyler (1824-1907), 165
Morgan, Junius Spencer (1813-90), 69, 118
Morgan, Laura Puffer, 277
Morgan, Robert, 250
Morgan, Sarah, 250
Morgan, Thomas, 104
Morgan Grenfell & Co. Ltd., 118
Morgenthau, Henry, Jr., 229
Morison [Moryson], Francis, 17
Morison, Philip, 289
Morland, Richard, 103
Morley, Felix, 281
Mormons and Mormonism, 70, 137, 164, 196, 244, 245, 247, 273, 318, 328, 329
Morning Chronicle, 42
Morocco, Relations with U.S., *see* Relations with Morocco
Morrice, H. A. W., 206; Ms., 206
Morrill Tariff, 204
Morris, Governor, 266
Morris, Apollos, 352
Morris, Arthur, 284
Morris, Benjamin, 275
Morris, Charles, 231
Morris, Corbyn (1710-79), 31, 141
Morris, Edward Patrick, 1st Baron (1859-1935), 198
Morris, Gouverneur (1752-1816), 80, 200
Morris, J. P., & Co., 114
Morris, Luke, 102
Morris, May, 74
Morris, Richard (*c.* 1705-79), 243
Morris, [Richard (1730-1810)?], 215
Morris, Robert (1734-1806), 80, 180, 182
Morris, Robert Hunter (*c.* 1700-64), 302
Morris, Roland, 283
Morris, William (*fl.* 1790), 102
Morris, William (1834-96), 74; Correspondence and Papers, 74
Morris family, 47
Morrison, Charles Clayton, 279
Morrison, James, 324
Morrison, Richard (*fl.* 1638), 194
Morrison, Robert (1782-1834), 116
Morrison, Cryder & Co., 52, 99
Morrison, Sons & Co., 99
Morrison & Ewing, 310
Morrow, D. W., 75
Morrow, J. J., 75
Morse, Jedidiah (1761-1826), 245, 263
Morse, Robert, 297
Morse, Samuel Finley Breese (1791-1872), 124, 138, 170
Morshead, Paschow, 20
Mortimer, Benjamin (1767-1834), 174
Mortimer, R. S., "Bristol Quakerism, 1654-1700" (Thesis), 5 fn.
Mortimer family (England), 174
Mortimer family (Wales), 248
Morton, 14th Earl of, *see* Douglas, James (1703-68)
Morton, A. S., *A History of the Canadian West to 1870-71*, 146 fn.; ed., *The Journal of Duncan M'Gillivray*, 146 fn.
Morton, Alfred (1854-1941?), 316
Morton, John, 325
Morton [Mortone], Joseph, 292
Morton, Samuel, 325
Morton Papers, 291-2
Mosquito Coast, 77, 80, 186, 201
Moss, Henry, 155
Moss, William, 115

Mostyn Mss., 243
Mothe, Charles Groteste de la, 113
Mother's Clinic for Constructive Birth Control, London, 79
Motley, John Lothrop (1814-77), 59, 62, 68, 71, 72, 96, 129, 174, 201, 202, 207, 208, 317
Mott, Lucretia (Coffin), Mrs. James Mott (1793-1880), 205, 255
Motz, Henry, 150
Mouat, Hugh, 315
Moultrie, John (1729-98), 262, 266
Mounsey, P. T., 315
Mount Holyoke College, Massachusetts, 177
Mount Savage Ironworks, 28
Mount Savage Railroad, 28
Mount's Bay, Customs records, 89
Mountain, Jacob (1749-1825), 189
Mountain family, 189
Mountford, William, 105
Movement for the Taxation of Land Values, 100
Moynihan, Sean, 346
Muir, J. B., 318
Muir, Ramsay, 277; *America the Golden*, 278
Muir, William, 253
Muirhead, J. P., ed., *The Origin and Progress of the Mechanical Inventions of James Watt*, 226 fn.
Muirhead, Roland Eugene (1868- ?), 314
Mulcaster, F. G., 266
Mulhauser, F. L., ed., *The Correspondence of Arthur Hugh Clough*, 196
Mullett, Thomas, 9
Mulligan, J., 331
Mullings and Ellett Papers, 34
Mullins, E. L. C., *Texts and Calendars: An Analytical Guide to Serial Publications* (1958), 100 fn.
Mullins, Edward, 234
Mundell, Alexander, 169
Mundella, Anthony John (1825-97), 236
Municipal government, 164, 197, 198, 200; *see also* Local government officers
Municipal ownership, 164
Munitions supplies, 13
Munro, James, *Acts of the Privy Council*, 137
Murchison, Charles F., *see* "Murchison letter"
Murchison, Sir Roderick Impey (1792-1871), 75, 146; Papers, 75
"Murchison letter," 38
Murdoch, Andrew, 305
Murdock, Kenneth B. (b. 1895), 165
Murdock family, 166
Murphy, Mary Anne, 347
Murray, Mrs., 289
Murray, A., 284
Murray, Ann, 300
Murray, Arthur C., 3rd Viscount Elibank (1879-1962), 255
Murray, Sir Charles Augustus (1806-95), 306; Papers, 306; *Prairiebird*, 306
Murray, Charles Fairfax, 176
Murray, David, 7th Viscount Stormont and 2nd Earl of Mansfield (1727-96), 266, 267, 299, 314
Murray, George (*fl.* 1761), 299, 300
Murray, Sir George (1772-1846), 144, 257
Murray, George (*fl.* 1890-6), 240
Murray, Gilbert, 199; Papers, 199
Murray, Sir J., 314
Murray, James (1719?-94), 114, 275, 286, 323
Murray, Sir James (1751?-1811), 233
Murray, Col. James (*fl.* 1755), 222
Murray, Capt. James (*fl.* 1757-63), 262
Murray, James (*fl.* 1763), 299
Murray, James (*fl.* 1767), 166
Murray, John, 4th Earl of Dunmore (1732-1809), 12, 124, 268
Murray, John (*fl.* 1733), 306
Murray, John (1737-1808), 51
Murray, Dr. John (*fl.* 1747-63), 299, 300
Murray, John, of Murraythwaite (*fl.* 1747-97), 299-300 *passim*
Murray, John, of Philiphaugh (*fl.* 1757), 299, 300
Murray, John (*fl.* 1797), 300
Murray, John (*fl.* 1803), 12
Murray, John, 7th Duke of Atholl (1840-1917), 262
Murray, John, Ltd. (Publishers), 118
Murray, John and James (trading firm), 299
Murray, Katherine (Marjory), Duchess of Atholl (d. 1960), 269
Murray, Mungo (*fl.* 1755), 276
Murray, Mungo (*fl.* 1777), 289
Murray, P. F., "A Calendar of the Overseas Missionary Correspondence of All Hallows College, Dublin, 1842-1877" (Thesis), 347
Murray, Patrick, 5th Baron Elibank (1703-78), 275
Murray, R. Tait, 307
Murray, William, 1st Earl of Mansfield (1705-93), 203, 267
Murray, William, of Murrayfield (*fl.* 1750-78), 299-300 *passim*
Murray, William (*fl.* 1777, uncle of William Murray), 289
Murray, William (*fl.* 1777, nephew of William Murray), 289
Murray of Lintrose Muniments, 289
Murray of Murraythwaite Muniments, 299-300
Murray Papers, 144, 257
Murraywhat, Lady, *see* Dalrymple (or Murray), Elizabeth (*fl.* 1750-65)
Murthly Castle Muniments, 290-1
Muscovy, *see* Russia
Muse, Sally Ann (*later* Mrs. Joseph Rea), 332
Museum of London, 118
Musgrave, Sir William (*fl.* 1735-86), 89
Music, 81, 82, 274, 275
Musical Times, 81
Muslin, Manufacture, 325
Mussolini, Benito (1883-1945), 283
Musson, A. E., *The Typographical Association*, 9
Mutual Home Association, 314
Mutual Security Act, 112
Muybridge, Eadweard (1830-1904), 26, 220
Muybridge Collection, 220
Myers, Albert Cook, *Quaker Arrivals at Philadelphia, 1682-1750 . . .*, 153
Myers, Denys P., 198
Myers, Myer, 46
Myles, *see* Miles

N

Nails: Manufacture, 213, 308; Trade, 15, 182, 226, 263
Nairne, Thomas, 66; "Accounts," 66
Nalson Papers, 200
Namier, Sir Lewis, "Anthony Bacon," *Journal of Economic and Business History* (1929), 247 fn.
Nansen, Fridjof, 283
Napier, Sir Charles James (1782-1853), 78, 218
Napier, Sir Francis, 9th Baron (1819-98), 201
Napier, James, 284

Napier, Sir William Francis Patrick (1785-1860), 104
Napier Papers, 78, 196
Napoleon I (1769-1821), 56
Napoleon III (1808-73), 60
Napoleonic Wars, 9, 140, 186; *see also* Berlin and Milan Decrees; French Revolutionary Wars
Nash, Mrs. A. van B., 174
Nash, Philip C., 279
Nashville (ship), 13, 58, 59
Nasmyth, James (1808-90), 114
Nassa, Gustus, 29
Nathalie (ship), 131
Nathan, Sir Matthew (1862-1939), 200; Papers, 200
Nathanael, Brother, 174
Nation, 197, 198
National Agricultural Labourers Union, Oxford district, 209
National American Woman's Suffrage Association, 84
National Army Museum, London, 118-9
National Calendar, 167
National Council for Prevention of War, 277, 278
National Economic Conference, 266
National Education Association, 269
National Freedman's Relief Association, 347
National Gazette, 167
National Graphical Association, 9
National Industrial Recovery Act, 280
National Institute for the Promotion of Science, Washington, D.C., 150
National Intelligencer, 62, 167
National Labour Congress Report, 53
National Library of Ireland, 343-8
National Library of Scotland, 254-9
National Library of Wales, 243-7; *Journal*, 243
National Maritime Museum, 119-22
National Museum of Ireland, 347
National Public School Association (*formerly* Lancashire Public School Association), 179
National Register of Archives (London), *see* Historical Manuscripts Commission and National Register of Archives
National Register of Archives (Scotland), 259-72; 253
National Review, 196
National Trust (Great Britain), 24 fn., 116
National Union of Mineworkers (Durham area), 29
National Union of Women's Suffrage Societies, 179
National Woman's Party (U.S.), 118
Natural history, 66, 225
Natural resources, 63, 198, 209; *see also* Agriculture; Fisheries
Naturalization, 131, 202, 207
Naval Disarmament Conference, 279
Naval stores: Trade, 40, 83, 88, 107, 119, 160, 203, 289, 300; *see also* Pine; Pitch; Tar; Turpentine
Navigation, 12, 15, 146, 214; Great Lakes, 131; St. Lawrence, 84, 124, 144, 200; Schuylkill River, 174; *see also* Harbours; Hydrographic surveying; Lighthouses; Shipping
Navigation Acts, 87, 90, 91, 92, 103, 302
Navy, 27, 35, 57, 65, 70, 105, 123, 128, 138, 207, 277, 280, 288, 289, 311, 314, 351; Colonial period, 15, 66, 123, 302, 303; *see also* Royal Navy, *and subdivision* Naval operations *under names of wars*
Navy, French, 105
Navy Board, 119
Navy Office, 273
Neal, John (1793-1876), 168
Neale, Edward Vansittart (1810-92), 174
Neale, Leonard (1746-1817), 171
Neath, Customs records, 89
Neave, Messrs. E., 149
Nebraska: 1854, 201
  FINANCE, 210; Immigrants, 22, 331; Religious history, 158
  OMAHA, 20, 210, Consular reports (British), 134
Nebraska and Wyoming Investment Co., 210
Negroes, 12, 29, 69, 77, 95, 124, 155, 156, 184, 197, 198, 200, 201, 265, 283, 292, 298, 302
  COLONIZATION, 130, Africa, 205, Congo, 165, Liberia, 153, Sierra Leone, 43, 51
  EDUCATION, 95-6, 156, 206, 221; Employment, 208; Law, 105; Literature, 221; Missions, 51, 117, 155, 158; Suffrage, 96; *see also* Slavery, *and subdivision* Negroes *under states*
Neild, James, 308
Neill, Henry, 328
Neill, Samuel, 328
Neilson, Mr., 174
Neilson, Francis (1867-1961), 177
Neilson, James, 149
Neilson & Co., 318
Nelson, Captain, 284
Nelson, Jeremiah, 174
Nelson, John (1660-1721), 189
Nelson, Nellie, 177
Nepean, Sir Evan (1751-1822), 288
Neptune (ship), 43
Nesselrode, Karl Robert, Count (1780-1862), 76
Netherby, Cumbria, 22
Netherlands, *see* Immigrants from the Netherlands; Relations with the Netherlands; Trade with the Netherlands
Neutrality, 73, 81, 116, 131, 137, 140, 141, 157, 196, 201, 280, 281, 282, 283; *see also* Blockade; Isolationism; Search, Right of
Nevell [Nevill], John (d. 1697), 83
Nevell, Robert, 97
Neville, Richard Neville Aldworth (1717-93), 141
Neville and Aldworth Papers, 141
Nevins, Pim, 19
Nevis, Trade with Great Britain, 15
New Albion, 189; Petitions, 194
New Brunswick: 18th century, 231; 19th century, 36, 110, 196, 286, 348
  BOUNDARIES, 110, 144, 286; Defence, 196; Education, 290; Fishing, 326; Governors, 25, 36, 124, 207, 286; Immigrants, 14, 330, 331; Land, 110; Land grants, 138; Railways, 110; Timber duties, 108
  EDMONSTON, 296; Fredericton, 36, Description, 36; Passamaquoddy Bay, 198; St. John's, 305, 330, 331
  See also Acadia; Nova Scotia
New Brunswick and Canada Railway and Land Co., 110, 111; Bill, 110, 111
New College (London), Archives, 103
New College, Oxford, 208, 281
New England: Colonial period, 5, 10, 20, 40, 42, 49, 189, 194, 203, 229, 230, 263, 264, 265, 289
  ARMY, 346; Boundaries, 104; Climate, 149; Council, 193, 194; Customs officers, 21; Defence, 23; Description, 15, 58, 154, 202, 227; Disputes with Canada, 15, with New York, 203; Education, 32, 179, 312; Finance, 55; Fishing rights, 26; Governors, 25, 119, 203, 213, 223, 264; Immigrants, 27, 31, 42, 49, 129, 188, 202; Indians, 10, 94; Industry, 235, 254; Land, 5, 10, 13, 142, 219, 222; Land grants, 39, 194, 312; Law,

49, 52, 352; Merchants, 15, 45, 141; Mining, 10, 82; Navigation, 214; Religious history, 8, 34, 40, 72, 74, 82, 85, 98-9, 105, 151, 152, 153, 159, 174, 188, 190, 203, 217, 246, 259, 290, 312; Settlement, 10, 17, 24, 25, 27, 83, 187; Shipbuilding, 120; Shipping, 315; Slavery, 203; Trade, 5, 7, 8, 23-4, 31, 34, 35, 45, 49, 89, 91, 119, 194, 237, 273, 300, 349
See also Connecticut; Massachusetts; New Hampshire; Rhode Island
"New England Commissioners," 260
New England Company, 98-9, 147, 151
New England Relief Society, 185
New Hampshire: Colonial period, 10, 34; 1765-75, 10, 215
FINANCE, 57; Governors, 10, 167, 215, 223, 233, 240; Land, 233; Politics, 167; Religious history, 158, 159; Settlement, 303; Shipping, 315; Trade, 303
MANCHESTER, 273; Piscataqua, Customs collectors, 87; Portsmouth, 57, 315, Merchants, 183
See also New England
New Jersey: Colonial period, 5, 10, 34; 1765-75, 10, 215, 249; 19th century, 5; Civil War, 1861-5, 58
AGENTS, 301; Agriculture, 31, 33, 70, 148, 149, 190, 328; Assembly, 302; Boundary with Delaware, 40; Description, 50, 179; Education, 271; Epidemics, 70; Governors, 6, 10, 31, 50, 102, 103, 141, 195, 222, 223, 265, 303; Immigrants, 28, 65, 166, 190, 269, 328, 331, 332; Indians, 103, 313; Industry, 300; Labour, 33; Land, 8, 142, 154, 269, 274, 293, 295, 299, 301, 310; Law, 206; Religious history, 27, 37, 71, 85, 103, 154, 155, 158, 159, 227, 274; Settlement, 311; Slavery, 203
BETHEL, 103; Camden, 184; Cohansey, Customs collectors, 87; Elizabethtown, 269; Jersey City, 332; Monmouth County, 328; Morristown, 305; New Brunswick, 331; Newark, 190; Paterson, 328; Pequannock, 301; Perth Amboy, 302; Princeton, 31, 271; Ringwood, 300; Salem, Customs collectors, 87; Uniontown, 328
New Jersey, College of, 275, 313; *see also* Princeton University
New Jersey, East, 262; Boundary with New York, 302; Land, 45, 58, 286, 292; Land grants, 311; Lords proprietors, 260, 302; Politics, 260
New Jersey, West, 262; Finance, 172; Land, 221
New Jersey Training School for Nurses, 75
New Jersey Zinc Co., 331
New Mexico: Finance, 308, 318, 318 fn.; Land, 230, 308; Relations with Great Britain, 131; Religious history, 352; Settlement, 146, 352
EARLHAM, 327; Santa Fe, 230
New Orleans City Bonds, 249
New Providence, Trade with Ireland, 349
New Scotland, 194
New Shoreham, Customs records, 89
New Spain, 140
New York: Before 1700, 10, 21, 34, 54, 66, 189, 203, 229, 249; 1700-65, 5, 34, 40, 45, 55, 285, 302, 306; 1765-75, 5, 10, 12, 56, 65, 213, 214, 215, 218, 239, 293, 303; 1776-83, 5, 24, 64, 76, 144, 145, 192, 216, 247, 258, 284, 292-6 *passim*, 313, 346; 1783-1861, 5, 34, 46, 179, 276, 294, 295, 306, 325; Civil War, 1861-5, 58, 59; 1862-1900, 50, 198, 347; 20th century, 132, 143
AGENTS, 302; Agriculture, 179, 187, 244, 245, 301; Army, 40, 220, 274, 289; Banking, 183, 297; Boundary with Connecticut, 65, with East New Jersey, 302; Census, 220; Constitution, 167; Council, 290; Crime, 294, 329; Customs administration, 240; Description, 7, 15, 32, 34, 40, 95, 116, 158, 179, 217, 224, 255, 256, 267, 268, 270, 271, 274, 289, 292, 298, 305, 325, 326, 344; Disputes with New England, 203; Education, 54, 96, 265, 294, 312; Epidemics, 138, 271; Finance, 31, 46, 55, 142, 190, 220, 309; Fine arts, 149; Governors, 10, 31, 40, 50, 54, 55, 57, 64, 65, 66, 75, 80, 165, 191, 195, 213, 214, 218, 220, 223, 230, 240, 257, 258, 260, 264, 268, 285, 291, 292, 294, 295, 298, 300, 313, 317; History, 304; House of Representatives (or Assembly), 40, 55, 215, 220, 260, 296, 302, 303; Immigrants, 11, 14, 34, 35, 46, 47, 61, 97, 137, 166, 190, 193, 205, 243, 244, 245, 246, 248, 253, 266, 275, 289, 315, 324, 325, 328-32 *passim*, 346, 348, 351; Indians, 31, 131, 215, 244, 298; Industry, 28, 31, 40, 235, 301, 329; Iron mines, 230; Labour, 345; Land, 10, 19, 27, 31, 42, 54, 55, 175, 194, 222, 230, 256, 294, 324; Land grants, 298, 304; Law, 55, 190, 202, 260; Loyalists, 56; Merchants, 22, 51, 118, 126, 161, 169, 172, 173, 175, 178, 180, 181, 183, 225, 227, 234, 235, 236, 237, 240, 249, 250, 272, 273, 287, 288, 289, 294, 295, 310, 311, 325, 353; Police, 274; Politics, 58, 84, 161, 164, 262; Population, 296; Prisons, 208, 325; Railways, 46; Relief for Irish famine, 345; Religious history, 42, 84-5, 103, 117, 152, 156, 158, 159, 171, 174, 177, 225, 244, 245, 253, 308 fn., 309; Riots, 267; Settlement, 83, 298; Shipbuilding, 119; Shipping, 47, 124, 132, 309, 315, 316; Slavery, 32, 274, 295; Trade, 8, 20, 21, 31, 40, 46, 91, 92, 116, 117, 119, 132, 133, 138, 150, 181, 185, 190, 212, 234, 235, 239, 240, 253, 254, 260, 263, 271, 273, 294, 297, 300, 303, 309, 310, 317, 325, 327, 329, 346, 349
ALBANY, 14, 34, 95, 144, 180, 256, 270, 271, 303, 304, 305, 350, Consular reports (British), 130, Description, 268, Merchants, 183, 311; Argyle, 5; Buffalo, 43, 280, 329, Consular reports (British), 130, Description, 95, 180, 184; Chatham, 329; Cortland, 301; Crown Point, 264, 271, 289, 292, 293, 300, 302; Ellis Island, 111; Flatbush, 5, 294, 331; Fort Carillon, 328; Fort Clinton, 268; Fort Edward, 264, 285, 297, 328; Fort Montgomery, 268; Fort Niagara, 143, 289; Fort Ontario, 264; Fort Stanwix, 174, 268, 291; Fort William Henry, 264, 297; Icaria, 209; Lake Champlain, 20, 264, 270, 288; Lake George, 260, 305; Little Falls, 255; Lockport, 179; Long Island, 12, 29, 65, 156, 194, 209, 274, 293, 294, 296, 298, 309; Manhattan Island, 50; Middletown, 329; Mohawk River, 301, 304; Morrisville, 331; New Lebanon, 22; New Wormistone, 298
NEW YORK CITY, 23, 30, 176, 310, Botanical Gardens, 146, British Library of Information, 165, Consular reports (British), 63, 130, 132, 198, Customs collectors, 87, Description, 22, 30, 36, 43, 44, 98, 156, 180, 185, 222, 304, 350, Dockyards, 208, 325, Edison Electric Light Station, 170, Forum, 209, Government, 197, 198, 200, Holy Cross Church, 329, Libraries, 64, Parks, 243, Rockefeller Foundation, 165, St. Thomas's Church, 239, Tammany Hall, 164, 198, 345; World's Fair, 1939, 281
NIAGARA, 32, 40, 43, 95, 184, 208; Oneida, 209; Oswego, 39, 114, 264, 271, 298, 299, 301; Paulus Hook, 295; Rhinebeck, 324; Rochester, 46; Rouse's Point, 286; Saratoga, 5, 8, 192, 231; Skenesborough (Shunsborough) House, 265; Staten Island, 114, 276, 295; Stillwater, 265, 302; Syracuse, 44; Ticonderoga, 20, 31, 82, 95, 192, 264, 265, 266, 270, 274, 289, 293, 300, 304, 305; Troy, 14; Utica, 190, 245; Watertown, 331; West Point, 15, 268; White Plains, 313; Yates County, Italy Hill, 50
New York Central Railroad, 52, 105
New York City Guard, 105
New York Coffee House, London, 180
New York Draft Riots (1863), 59, 61, 96
New York Emigrant Society, 34
New York General Congregational Association, 103

New York Herald, 81, 134, 146
New York Herald Tribune, 178
New York Knife Co., 235
New York Life Insurance Co., 111
New York, Pennsylvania and Ohio Railroad Co., 180
New York Public Library, 33, 141 fn., 205 fn.; *Bulletin*, 33
New York State Socialist Party, 187
New York State Volunteers, 319
New York Times, 178, 279
New York University, 229
New York *World*, 16, 161
New Zealand: Cables, 143; *see also* Relations with New Zealand
Newbattle Abbey Library, 257
Newbattle Collection, 257
Newbold, Walton, 282
Newbould, George H., 234
Newby Hall Records, 239
Newcastle Jean (ship), 296
Newcastle Mss., 192
Newcastle–on–Tyne, Duke of, *see* Holles, John, 1st Duke of the 2nd creation (1662-1711)
Newcastle–under–Lyme, 1st Duke of, *see* Pelham–Holles, Thomas (1693-1768); 2nd Duke of, *see* Clinton, Henry Fiennes (1720-94); 5th Duke of, *see* Clinton, Henry Pelham Fiennes Pelham (1811-64)
Newcastle-upon-Tyne, Tyne and Wear, 191, 223-4; Customs records, 89, 92, 93; Gladstone's speech, 1862, 58, 71; Merchants, 191, 315; *see also* Business records: Newcastle-upon-Tyne
Newcastle-upon-Tyne, University of, Library, 224
Newcomb, Simon (1835-1909), 147
Newdigate, B. H., 74
Newel, Samuel, 82
Newenham, Sir Edward (1732-1814), 350
Newfoundland: 17th century, 18, 26, 27, 35, 229; 18th century, 21, 45, 75, 79, 101, 138, 143, 257, 296; 19th century, 49, 138, 255, 257, 332
ADMINISTRATION, 26, 27; Customs collectors, 87; Defence, 143; Fires, 110; Governors, 36, 109, 138, 198, 246, 255; Immigrants, 28, 351; Land, 24, 26, 36, 42, 45; Land grants, 138, 193, 194; Merchants, 26, 28, 310; Mining, 124; Petitions, 26, 27, 138; Politics, 109; Relief for Irish famine, 110; Settlement, 192; Slavery (Anti-slavery movements), 344; Trade, 21, 27, 28, 32, 34, 35, 88, 91, 161, 212, 317, 339, 349; *see also* Fisheries, Newfoundland
BELLE ISLE, 85; Fort Townsend, 143; Placentia, 223, 246; St. John's, 21, 26, 36, 42, 110, 119, 273, 351; Trinity, 36
Newhailes Muniments, 269
Newhaven, Customs records, 89, 93
Newman, George, 155
Newman, Henry (1670-1743), 152; *Salzburger Letterbooks*, ed. by George Fenwick Jones, 152 fn.
Newman, Henry (*c.* 1775-1835), 155
Newman family, 155
Newman Letters, 152
Newport, Christopher (1565?-1617), 82, 190
Newport, Customs records, 93
Newspapers, 112, 258; Welsh-American periodicals, 248; *see also* Journalism, International; Press; *also names of individual newspapers*
Newton, Lord, *Lord Lyons*, 185 fn.
Newton, Hubert Anson (1830-96), 147
Niagara Falls, 147, 315, 329; Niagara electric scheme, 162
Nicaragua: *see* Relations with Nicaragua; *see also* Mosquito Coast
GREYTOWN, 105, 200, 201
Nicaraguan Canal Controversy, 38, 39, 77, 124, 131, 200, 201; *see also* Clayton–Bulwer Treaty, 1850; Panama Canal
Nicholas, R. B., 40
Nicholl, Sir John (1759-1838), 140, 250
Nicholl Papers, 140
Nichols, Mrs. Clarina Irene Howard, *Responsibilities of Women*, 84
Nichols, Edwin Bray, 238
Nichols, Henry, 146
Nichols, John (1745-1826), 204
Nichols, Robert Malise Bowyer (1893-1944), 205
Nicholson, Abigail, 30
Nicholson, Alfred Osborne Pope (1808-76), 62
Nicholson, Francis (1665-1728), 158, 159, 194, 213
Nicholson, James and Thomas, 175
Nicholson, Robert (1727-79), 175, 208
Nicholson Papers, 175
Nicholson (ship), 230
Nicol, Robert A., 236
Nicol of Ballogie Mss., 261
Nicoll, John, 309
Nicollet, Joseph N., 290, 291
Nightingale, Florence (1820-1910), 75
Nightingale Papers, 2nd series, 75
Niles' Register, 167
Nimms, J., 182
Nineteenth Century, 73
Nipher, Francis Eugene (1847-1927), 162
Nippon Yusen Kaisha, 272
Nisbet, Sir Alexander, 299-300, 304
Nisbet, C. C., 290
Nisbet, Claud, 42
Nisbet, Sir John (1609?-87), 298
Nisbet, Sir John, of Dean (*fl.* 1720's?), 304
Nisbet, Robert (merchant, *fl.* 1720-3), 304
Nisbet, Robert (apprentice, *fl.* 1721), 304
Nisbet Papers, 257
Nobel Peace Prize, 278, 279
Noble, Mark (1754-1827), 204
Noble, Thomas Tertius (1867-1953), 239
Noble of Ardmore Mss., 262
Noblet Ruddock & Co., 6
Nogarei, F., 182
Nonconformists, *see* Dissenters
Non-importation agreements, 66, 79, 187, 195, 214, 265
Non-intercourse, 83, 116, 261, 350
Nooth, John Mervin (d. 1828), 41, 150
Nootka Sound Dispute, 80
Norfolk, Minna (Lyons), Duchess of (1821-86), 223
Norfolk, Duke of, 185
Norfolk, England, 185-9; *see also* Immigrants from Norfolk; Parish records, Norfolk
Norfolk and Norwich Collection, 188
Norfolk County Library, Local Studies Department, 187
Norfolk Papers, 185
Norfolk Record Office, 187-9; 186 fn.
Norman, Miss F. N., Deposit, 247
Norman, John (d. 1854), 166
Norman Papers, 46
Norris, Richard (1670-1731), 181
Norris Papers, 181
North, Christopher (*pseud.*), *see* Wilson, John (1785-1854)
North, Sir Dudley (1641-91), 219

North, Dudley (1684-1729), 18, 219
North, Francis, 2nd Baron Guilford (1673-1729), 195
North, Frederick, 2nd Earl of Guilford, *better known as* Lord North (1732-92), 44, 45, 62, 75, 76, 143, 192, 195, 203, 258, 261, 265, 266, 267, 324
North (*formerly* Doyle), John Sydney, 196
North, Katherine (Yale), Mrs. Dudley North, 219
North, Mary, 23
North, William, 23
North Papers, 195-6, 205
North American Boundary Commission, 34, 132, 145, 146
North American Colonial Association of Ireland Bill, 109
North American Indian Institution, 103
North American Review, 61, 70, 71, 199
North American Supplies Council, 112
North American Trust & Banking Co., 181
North and South Wales Bank, 117, 118
North British Locomotive Co., 318
North British Review, 256
North Carolina: Colonial period, 65, 190; 1765-75, 215, 268; 1776-83, 313, 314; Civil War, 1861-5, 60, 65
AGRICULTURE, 166, 297, 348; Cotton, 150, 348; Council, 290; Description, 154, 156, 256; Education, 158; Finance, 100; Governors, 65, 190, 191, 223, 285, 289, 297, 312, 317, 323; Immigrants, 39, 50, 166, 193, 220, 263, 329; Land, 47, 55, 191, 323; Politics, 268, 297, 299; Religious history, 42, 155, 156, 159, 174; Settlement, 264, 323, 329; Slavery, 297; Trade, 56, 212, 300, 323
ALBEMARLE SOUND, 47; Bartie County, 47; Beaufort, Customs collectors, 87; Bethabara, 174; Brunswick, Customs collectors, 87; Cape Fear River, 65; Fort Hatteras, 65; New Bern, 158; Nixonton, 182; Ocracoke Bay, 138; Warren County, Ridgeway, 50; Wilmington, 159
North Dakota, Immigrants, 332
North-East Boundary, 25, 57, 63, 66, 67, 78, 103, 196, 207, 208, 286; *see also* Jay's Treaty, 1794; Ghent, Treaty of, 1814; Webster–Ashburton Treaty, 1842
North (Little Glemham) Family Archives, 219
North Star Mining Co., 211
North-West Boundary, 25, 63, 64, 66, 67, 80, 130, 130 fn., 133, 140, 207, 208; *see also* Jay's Treaty, 1794; Juan de Fuca Strait; Oregon Question; Oregon Treaty of 1846; San Juan Islands; Washington, Treaty of, 1871
North West Coast, 133; Exploration, 138
North West Company, 146, 254, 255, 256; *see also* Hudson's Bay Company
North-Western Territories (British America) Bill, 110
North Yorkshire County Library, 230
North Yorkshire County Record Office, 231
Northallerton, North Yorkshire, 230-1
Northampton, 10th Earl of, *see* Compton, William (1568?-1630)
Northampton, England, 189-90
Northamptonshire Record Office, 189-90
Northcliffe, Viscount, *see* Harmsworth, Alfred Charles William (1865-1922)
Northcliffe Papers, 157
Northcote, Henry Stafford, Baron (1846-1911), 69
Northcote, Sir Stafford Henry, 1st Earl of Iddesleigh (1818-87), 68, 71, 72
Northern American Trust Co., Ltd., 318
Northern [Baltic] Confederation, 257
Northey, Sir Edward (1652-1723), 312
Northington, 2nd Earl of, *see* Henley, Robert (1747-86)
Northumberland, Duke of, 190-1
Northumberland, 2nd Duke of, *see* Percy, Sir Hugh (1742-1817)
Northumberland, 9th Earl of, *see* Percy, Sir Henry (1564-1632)
Northumberland, England, 190-1
Northumberland County Record Office, 191
Northumberland Papers, 190-1, 223
Northup, Clark S., 239
Northwest Passage, 150, 233, 312, 317, 323
Norton, Charles D., 197
Norton, Charles Eliot (1827-1908), 68, 164, 196, 197, 198, 202, 204, 353
Norton, J. E., ed., *The Letters of Edward Gibbon*, 19 fn.
Norton, John, 191
Norton, Sara, 164, 199
Norumbega, 58
Norwich, Norfolk, 187-9
Norwich Mechanics Union, 188
Norwood, ——, 291
Notestein, W., F. H. Relf, and H. Simpson, eds., *Commons Debates, 1621*, 33 fn.
Nott, Edward, 193
Nott, H. E., ed., *Deposition Books of Bristol*, 5 fn.
Nottingham, Nottinghamshire, 191-3
Nottingham City Archives Office, 191
Nottingham University Library, 192-3
Nottinghamshire, England, 191-3
Nottinghamshire Record Office, 191-2
Nova Scotia: to 1763, 41, 85, 259; 1775-83, 39, 138, 215, 216, 296; 1791-1813, 231, 314; 1849-51, 32
ARMY, 101; Assembly, 286; Baronetcies, 318; Campaigns, 26; Education, 103; Forts, 297; Governors, 81, 190, 223, 240, 246, 285; Land, 76; Land grants, 41, 49, 138, 239, 297, 308; Loyalists, 120, 148; Navigation, 214; Navy, British, 239; Relief for Irish famine, 110; Religious history, 312, 313; Settlement, 45, 311; Slavery (Anti-slavery movements), 344; Trade, 36, 88, 90, 119, 335; *see also* Fisheries, Nova Scotia
ANNAPOLIS ROYAL, 297; Cape Breton Island, 85, 138; Halifax, 36, 39, 41, 43, 104, 119, 120, 138, 142, 143, 231, 239, 257, 274, 285, 291, 294, 296, Customs collectors, 87, Description, 210, Repeal Association, 344; Louisbourg, 35, 41, 45, 74, 119, 145, 189, 219, 222, 230, 249, 260, 266, 284, 289
Nowill, Thomas, & Co., 234
Noyes, Alfred (1880-1958), 238
Nuffield College, Oxford, 209
Nugent, John, 346
Nugent, R., 265
Nullification, 78
Nussey, Sarah, 117
Nuttall, Thomas (1786-1859), 145

O

Oake, William, 149
Oakeys & Robinson, 175
Oakington Parish, Cambridgeshire, 14
Oats, *see* Feeding stuffs
O'Beirne, James R., 345
Oberlin College, 95
O'Brien, Sir Lucius (1735-95), 343
O'Brien, Lucius (*fl.* 19th cent.), 344
O'Brien, William (1852-1928), 345
O'Brien, William Smith (1803-64), 184, 344

Observer, 278, 279, 280
O'Cahill, John M. (1840-1928), 348
O'Callaghan, John, 345
Ocean Steam Navigation Company, 219
Oceanic (ship), 73
O'Connell, Ensign, 296
O'Connor, Judge, 326
O'Connor, T. P., 353
"Odds and Ends," 179
Oddy, Joshua Jepson, 288
Oelrich's Cattle Station, 348
Official Report of Parliamentary Debates, House of Commons (Hansard), 105
Offor, Richard (1882-1964), 239; *A Survey of Libraries*, 239 fn.
O'Flaherty, E., 345
Oford, Edgar Ira, 236
Ogden, Francis B., 303
Ogden, Isaac (1739-1824), 226, 234
Ogden, Rollo, 199
Ogden, T. L., 166
Ogden Manuscripts Collection, 168
Ogg, F. A., 75
Ogilby, Mr. [John (1600-76)?], 224
Ogilby, William (d. 1864), 67
Ogilvie, Charles, 253
Ogilvie, George, 265
Ogilvie, J., 314
Ogilvie, John, 295
Ogilvie Forbes of Boyndlie Mss., 253
Ogilvy, James, 4th Earl of Findlater and 1st Earl of Seafield (1664-1730), 304
Ogilvy of Inverquharity Muniments, 298
Ogle, Sir Chaloner, 31
Oglethorpe, James Edward (1696-1785), 15, 32, 64, 144, 216, 220, 237, 274, 312
O'Gorman, Richard (1820-95), 326, 344
O'Hanlon family, 332
O'Hara, Charles (1740?-1802), 218, 346
O'Hara, Charles King, 348
O'Hara Mss., 346
O'Hara Papers, 348
Ohio: Seven Years War, 1756-63, 82, 92
AGRICULTURE, 150, 151, 244, 331; Climate, 148, 244; Description, 156, 184, 224; Education, 210; Governors, 245; Immigrants, 47, 97, 217, 243-4, 245, 247, 248, 329, 331, 332, 348, 350; Indians, 156; Industry, 244; Land, 23, 46; Religious history, 152, 171, 210, 244; Settlement, 208, 323
CEDARVILLE, 331; Cincinnati, 62, 148, 171, 173, 329, 331, 332, Consular reports (British), 132, 134, Description, 95, 155, 217, 271; Cleveland, 244, 316, Consular reports (British), 134; Columbus, 95, 245, Merchants, 183; Dinsmore, 330; Hudson, 148; Mansfield, 332; Painsville, 335; Sandusky City, Description, 271; Smithfield, 156; Wapakoneta, 156; Wilmington, 152
Ohio River, 82, 92, 262, 285, 307, 312; Description, 190, 191, 258, 285; Indians, 215; Settlement, 174, 214
Oil, *see* Petroleum industry
O'Kelly, Michael, 352
Oklahoma: Constitution, 198; Immigrants, 332; Oil, 165
Olcott, J.W., 69
Oldham, Greater Manchester, 179
Oldham Local Interest Centre, 179
Oldham Operative Cotton Spinners, 179
O'Leary, John (1830-1907), 345; *Recollections of Fenians and Fenianism*, 345
Oliphant, Janet Mary, 257
Oliphant, Laurence (1829-88), 202
Oliphant, Mrs. Margaret, 257
Oliphant, Robert, 294
Oliver, Andrew (1706-74), 233
Oliver, Peter (1713-91), 105
Oliver, Thomas (1734-1815), 61
Oliver (ship), 126
Olives, 149
Ollivant, Charles, 327
Olney, Richard (1835-1917), 38
O'Mahony, John (1816-77), 326, 344
O'Malley, Thadeus (1796-1877), 171
Omohundron, John B. (d. 1880), 348
O'Neill, John (1834-78), 130
Onley, Charles, 32
Onslow Collection, 220
Ontario, 14; Agriculture, 330; Education, 330; Immigrants, 272, 330, 331, 332; Land, 330
BARRIE, 331; East Guillensburg, 331; Goderich, 272, 331; Kingston, 330, 332; London, 330; Peterborough, 330; Port Hope, 330; St. Catherine's, 330; Toronto, 14, 96, 330, 332, Description, 36, 329; Trenton, 330; Westminster, 330; Weston, 330; Windsor, Description, 36; York, 14
Ontario, Lake, 39, 297
Ontario Boundary Commission, 38
Operative Masons' and Granitecutters' Journal, 254
Operative Masons' and Granitecutters' Union of Aberdeen, 254
Opie, Mrs. Amelia (Alderson) (1769-1853), 155
Opie, John, 6
Opie, Susannah, 6
Opie, William, 239
Opie Papers, 6
Opium trade, 148
Oppenheimer, Robert (1904-67), 165
Orange growing, 274
Orde, *afterwards* Orde-Powlett, Thomas, 1st Baron Bolton (1746-1807), 230, 287
Orders in Council (1794), 287; (1807), 77, 81, 83, 107, 108, 183, 250, 294, *see also* Erskine Agreement (1809)
Ordnance, Board of, 15, 144, 145
Ordnance Survey of Ireland, 350
Oregon: 19th century, 57, 254
AGRICULTURE, 268; Banking, 308; Description, 156, 270; Finance, 46, 307, 308, 318; Flora, 291; Immigrants, 268; Land, 270; Religious history, 152, 327; Settlement, 291; Surveying, 268
PORTLAND, 121, Consular reports (British), 130, 134
Oregon and Washington Mortgage Savings Bank Ltd., 308
Oregon and Washington Trust Investment Co. Ltd., 307
Oregon Historical Society, Quarterly, 146 fn.
Oregon Mortgage Co. Ltd., 308
Oregon Question, 63, 64, 67, 77, 110, 168, 173, 201, 207, 208, 244, 245, 328; *see also* Juan de Fuca Strait; Nootka Sound Dispute, 1790; North-West Boundary; Oregon Treaty of 1846; Russia: Territorial convention with U.S., 1824
Oregon Treaty of 1846, 66
Oregon Trust and Agency Co. Ltd., 308
Oregonian Railway Co. Ltd., 308
O'Reilley, Charles, 345
O'Reilly, A., 105

O'Reilly, Thomas, 75
Orford, 1st Earl of, *see* Walpole, Sir Robert (1676-1745); 3rd Earl of, *see* Walpole, George (1730-91)
Organisation Mondiale Pour L'Education Préscolaire, 228
Oriel, Baron, *see* Foster, John (1740-1828)
Orkney, 1st Earl of, *see* Hamilton, George (d. 1737)
Orkney Islands, 315
Orkney Islands Area Archives, 315
Orleans, Duke of, Louis-Philippe, 268
Ormonde, Marquis of, 346 fn.
Ormonde, 12th Earl and 1st Duke of, *see* Butler, James (1610-88)
Ormonde Papers, 346
Ormsby, W., *Crisis in the Canadas 1838-9,* 30 fn.
Ormston, Joseph, 58
Orr, John, 329
Orr, Rebecca, 329
Orr, Robert, 332
Orsini, [Cesare (1835-98)?], 53
"Osborn, Mr.," 204
Osborne, Charles S., 75
Osborne, Francis, 5th Duke of Leeds (*known till 1789 as* Marquis of Carmarthen) (1751-99), 82
Osborne, Richard Boyse (1808-*c.* 1897), 346, 347
Osborne, Sir Thomas, *successively* 1st Earl of Danby, Marquis of Carmarthen, and 1st Duke of Leeds (1631-1712), 140
Osborne family, Dukes of Leeds, 82
Osbourne, Katherine, 238
Osbourne Mss., 238
Oscott College, 229
O'Shea, William Henry (1840-1905), 345
Ostend Manifesto (1854), 201
O'Sullivan, Seumas (*pseud.*), *see* Starkie, James Sullivan
O'Sullivan, Vincent, 353
O'Sullivan Papers, 353
Oswald, Alexander, 314
Oswald, George, 273
Oswald, James (1715-69), 299
Oswald, R., 314
Oswald, Richard (1705-84), 266
Oswald, Dennistoun & Co., 273
Otago (ship), 332
Otolonghe, Joseph, 149, 150
Ottawa Conference, 280
Ottoboni, Pietro, Pope Alexander VIII (1610-91), 54
Ouida (*pseud.*), *see* De La Ramée, Marie Louise (1839-1908)
Ouseley, Sir William Gore (1797-1866), 201
Over-Seas Club, 81
Overstone Papers, 190
Owen, A.E.B., ed., *Handlist of the Political Papers of Stanley Baldwin* (1973), 16 fn.
Owen, Bob, 248; Collection, 247
Owen, Goronwy (1723-69?), 243
Owen, Griffith, 244
Owen, H., *The Staffordshire Potter*, 217 fn.
Owen, James, 246
Owen, John, 244
Owen, John Gwylym, 244
Owen, Margred, 244
Owen, Sir Richard (1804-92), 62
Owen, Robert (1771-1858), 64, 173, 209, 243, 245
Owen, Robert Dale (1801-77), 173, 245
Owen, Rosamund Dale, 173
Owen, Rowland, 244
Owen, Thomas (*fl.* 18th cent.), 225
Owen, Thomas (fl. 1821-6), 175
Owens, Owen, 245
Owens, Owen & John, 175
Oxford, 1st Earl of, *see* Harley, Robert (1661-1724)
Oxford, Oxfordshire, 193-210
Oxford University, 205, 277, 281; Department of Botany, 200
Oxford University Enquiry Society, 277
Oxfordshire, England, 193-210
Oxfordshire County Record Office, 209
Oxfordshire Light Infantry, 52nd, 203
Oxley, William, 168

P

"P.M.," 240
Pacific cables, *see* Cables, Pacific
Pacific Mail Steamship Co., 272
Pacific Ocean, 111
Pacifism, 157; Pacifists, 157
Packet ships, 91, 93, 140, 288, 316
Padoucas, *see* Indians, Welsh
Padstow, Customs records, 89, 93
Page, Joseph, 295
Page, Walter Hines (1855-1918), 197, 210
Page and Moody Collection, 35
Paget family, 204
Paggen, William, 203
Paine, D., 148
Paine, Joseph, 142
Paine, Thomas (1737-1809), 101, 150, 182, 200, 209, 231, 287
Painting, 16, 49, 58, 151, 187, 291, 326, 353
Paish, Sir George, 199
Paisley, Strathclyde, 318; Manufacturers, 310; Merchants, 309
Paisley Emigrant Society, 108
Paisley Pamphlets, 318
Pakenham, Edward, 343
Pakenham, Richard (*fl.* 1776-8), 343
Pakenham, Sir Richard (1797-1868), 64, 67, 77
Pakenham, Thomas, 343
Pakenham–Mahon Papers, 347
Pakington, Sir John Somerset (1799-1880), 40
Palatines, 193, 220
Palestine, U.S. rights, 112; *see also* Relations with Palestine
Palfrey, John Gorham (1796-1881), 176
Palgrave, Francis Turner (d. 1897), 75; *Golden Treasury*, 75; Papers, 75
Palk, Sir Robert (1717-98), 25
Palk Papers, 25-6
Palliser, John (1807-87), 111
Palmer, Mr., 297
Palmer, Charles Ray, 85
Palmer, Edmund, 205
Palmer, James, 232
Palmer, John Horsley (1779-1858), 63, 270
Palmer, R.S., 28
Palmer, Ray (1808-87), 85
Palmer, Sir Roundell, 1st Earl of Selborne (1812-95), 60, 139
Palmer, Thomas, 9
Palmer, Mackillop, Dent & Co., 270
Palmerston, 3rd Viscount, *see* Temple, Henry John (1784-1865)
Palmerston Papers, 77, 78, 103-5

Pamphlets: 16th century, 161-2; 17th century, 17, 49, 113, 152, 161-2, 187; 18th century, 10, 17, 152, 160, 161-2, 181; 19th century, 9, 52, 84, 152, 160, 161-2, 177, 181, 288; 20th century, 181
Pan-African Congress, London (1921), 206
Pan-American Conferences, *see* International Conferences of American States
Panama Canal, 38, 39, 131, 207, 208, 298; Tolls, 197, 198, 199, 277; *see also* Clayton-Bulwer Treaty, 1850; Nicaraguan Canal Controversy
Panama Congress (1826), 84, 207
Panic of 1837, 52, 99, 173; 1857, 22, 52, 222, 330
Panmure, 2nd Baron, *see* Maule, Fox (1801-74)
Panshanger Mss., 40
Paper, Trade, 187
Paper-making, 307
Papworth, James, 14
Pardee, Dwight W., 263
Pares, R., *A West India Fortune*, 8 fn.
Parham (ship), 211
Paris, Treaty of, 1763, 52; 1783, 76; 1856, 201
Paris Resolutions, 1918, 126
Parish (or Farish), David, 187
Parish, John, 287
Parish records: Bedfordshire, 9; Berkshire, 11; Cambridgeshire, 14; Dorset, 28-9; England, 137; Essex, 33; Gloucestershire, 34, 35; Hampshire, 36; Hertford, 42; Ireland, 349; Kent, 46; Lancashire, 47; Leicestershire, 49; London, 97; Norfolk, 137, 185, 186, 188, 189; Northamptonshire, 190; Suffolk, 219, 220; Sussex, East, 221; Wales, 137
Park, Alice, 84
Park, James, 297
Park, Robert Ezra (1864-1944), 165
Park family, 328, 332
Park Family Papers, 328-9
Parke, Mary, 330
Parke, William, 330
Parker, Anthony, 346
Parker, George, 117
Parker, George F., 205
Parker, H.A., 82
Parker, Sir (Horatio) Gilbert (George) (1862-1932), 75
Parker, Horatio William (1863-1919), 81, 239
Parker, Sir Hyde (1714-82), 101
Parker, James (1729-1815), 182
Parker, John G., 169
Parker, Joseph (1714-93), 94
Parker, Joseph (1744-1834), 94
Parker, Patrick, 182
Parker, Sir Peter (1721-1811), 90
Parker, Robert, 25
Parker, Theodore (1810-60), 208
Parker, William (*fl.* 1663), 27
Parker, William (*fl.* 1840), 172
Parker family, 94
Parker Family Papers, 182
Parker of Alkincoats and Browsholme Muniments, 46
Parker–Hutchinson Papers, 346
Parkes, Joseph (1796-1865), 69, 169, 170
Parkes, Mrs. Joseph, 170
Parkman, Francis (*fl.* 1816), 95
Parkman, Francis (1823-93), 199
Parks, 184, 243
Parliament for America, 65, 302
Parnell, Anna, 344
Parnell, Charles Stewart (1846-91), 38, 344, 345, 353
Parnell, Delia, 344
Parnell, John, 346
Parnell, R. , 314
Parrott, Anne, 26
Parrott, John, 26
Parrott, Margaret ("Peggy"), 26
Parry, W.J., 244, 248
Parson & Prior, Messrs., 47
Partridge, Richard, 301
Parvin, Robert J., 176
Passenger ships, 137, 156, 288, 351; *see also* Voyages to America
Passfield, 1st Baron, *see* Webb, Sidney [James] (1859-1947)
Passfield Papers, 164
Passport Office Records, 134
Passports, 112, 287
Patagonia, Immigrants, 244
Patent Rolls, 126
Patents, 65, 82, 131, 138, 180, 223, 235, 266, 298, 300, 303, 304, 307, 308
Paterson, Col. John (1744-1808), 324
Patey, Captain, 13
Paton Collection, 257
Patrick, William, 268
Patriote (ship), 44
Patrons of Husbandry, 174
Patry, Henry, & Co., 46
Patten, Thomas, 265
Patterson, ———, 294
Patterson, R.N., 226
Patterson, Robert (1743-1824), 148
Patterson, Walker (d. 1798), 138
Pattison, George, 231
Pattison, James (1724?-1805), 145
Pattison, Nathaniel, 150
Paul, Alice, 118
Paul, Moses, 330
Paull, Samuel, 105
Paullin, C.O., and F.L. Paxson, *Guide to the Materials in London Archives for the History of the U.S. since 1783*, 96, 97, 106, 111, 122, 137, 138, 206 fn.
Pauncefote, Sir Julian, 1st Baron (1828-1902), 37, 38, 39, 129, 221
Pauncefote Papers, 221
Pawley, George, 225
Pawquawkoman, *alias* Chevalier, Amable, 286
Pawson Mss., 239
Payne, Mrs. Eliza (*fl.* 1773-4), 234
Payne, Hugh, 78
Payne, Sir Peter (1763-1843), 9
Payne, W.O., 280
Peabody, George (1795-1869), 68, 75, 99, 118, 170
Peabody Memorial Committee, 99
Peace movement, 78, 112, 127, 138, 176, 244, 277, 278, 279, 281, 282, 345; *see also* American League to Enforce Peace; Kellogg–Briand Pact; Locarno Peace Pact; Washington Conference, 1921
Peacock (H.M.S.), 43
Peaford, Thomas, 189
Peake, Snow, and Jeudwine Deposit, 50
Pearce, W.M., *The Matador Land and Cattle Company*, 308 fn.

Pearl (schooner), 161
Pearl–ash, *see* Potash
Pearls, Trade, 205
Pearsall, Sally (or Sarah), *see* Campbell, Sally (Pearsall)
Pearsall, Thomas (brother of Sally Pearsall Campbell), 294
Pearsall, Thomas (father of Sally Pearsall Campbell), 294
Pearson, Charles Henry (1830-94), 196; *National Life and Character; A Forecast*, 196
Pearson, Edith Lucille (Butler), Mrs. Charles Henry Pearson, 196
Pearson, E[liphalet (1752-1826)?], 148
Pearson, Sir Richard (1731-1806), 44
Pearson Papers, 196
Peary, Robert Edwin (1856-1920), 147
Peas, 11, 47
Pease, John, 29
Pease, Joseph, 29, 30
Peasenhall Parish Church, 220
Peat, Ann, 245
Peat, Edward, 245
Peat, Morris, 245
Peate, Edward, 245
Peck, Walter E., 205
Peckover, Edmund (1695/6-1767), 153
Pedlar, Liam, 345
Pedro Cays, 131, 132
Peebles, John, 274
Peel, Sir Robert (1788-1850), 63-4 *passim*, 173, 186, 221
Peel Papers, 63-4
Peggy (brig), 309
Peggy (ship), 263
Pegran, Lieutenant, 13
Peirce, Benjamin (1809-80), 147, 148
Peirce, Harold, 74
Pelham, Henry (1696-1754), 50
Pelham, R.A., "The West Midland Iron Industry and the American Market in the 18th Century," *University of Birmingham Historical Journal* (1950), 225 fn.
Pelham, Thomas, 2nd Earl of Chichester (1756-1826), 351
Pelham–Clinton, Henry Fiennes, Earl of Lincoln (1750-78), 192
Pelham–Holles, Sir Thomas, 1st Duke of Newcastle (1693-1768), 195, 222, 267
Pellerin, Jean, 161
Pelling, H., *America and the British Left,* 52 fn.
Pemberton, Israel, 154, 156
Pemberton, J. (*fl.* 1785-6), 210
Pemberton, James (1723-1809), 155, 156, 188, 349
Pemberton, John (1727-95), 154, 155, 227
Pemberton, Mary, 154
Pemberton, Samuel (1723-79), 233
Pembroke, Earl of, 230
Pembroke, 11th Earl of, *see* Herbert, George Augustus (1759-1827)
Pembroke Papers, 230
Pembrokeshire Record Office, 247-8
Penfold, P.A., ed., *Maps and Plans in the Public Record Office*, vol. 2, *America and West Indies*, 129, 135
Pengelly, Thomas, 202
Penman, Edward, 266
Penman, James, 262
Penn, John (*fl.* 1635), 312
Penn, John (1729-95), 39, 82, 174
Penn, Richard (d. 1771), 82
Penn, Thomas (1702-75), 174
Penn, William (1644-1718), 6, 8, 10, 18, 21, 30, 31, 37, 82, 83, 86, 97, 154, 160, 174, 202, 220, 221, 227, 262
Penn (ship), 268
Penn Mss., 154
Pennant Papers, 225
Pennell, Joseph (1860-1926), 74
Penney, Norman, 156
Pennington of Warter, 43
Pennsylvania: Colonial period, 10, 18, 21, 34, 160, 202, 263, 300, 306; 1765-75, 10, 214, 215, 249; 1776-83, 76, 313; Whiskey Rebellion, 1794, 170, 324; Civil War, 1861-5, 59
AGRICULTURE, 174, 245, 305, 331; Assembly, 8, 267; Banking, 181, 187, 188, 297; Boundaries with Connecticut, 8, with Maryland, 8, 39; Charters, 8, 31; Council, 18; Customs administration, 262; Description, 116; Education, 40, 96, 265; Epidemics, 80, 138, 155, 170, 294, 315; Finance, 190; Governors, 10, 83, 116, 156, 160, 167, 188, 284, 285; Immigrants, 9, 28, 46, 47, 90, 97, 166, 184, 190, 226, 234, 244, 245, 304, 305, 324, 326, 329-30, 331, 332, 346, 348, 351; Indians, 31, 156; Industry, 7, 149, 330; Land, 6, 8, 24, 39, 42, 46, 82, 97, 102, 142, 158, 221, 294, 302, 329, 332; Land grants, 37, 39, 273; Law, 8, 56; Loyalists, 55; Miners, 29; Petitions, 138; Prices, 48; Religious history, 8, 13, 15, 20, 27, 28, 32, 34, 37, 42, 53, 117, 118, 152-5 *passim*, 158, 159, 171, 174, 183, 188, 227, 234, 243, 244, 245, 247, 250, 285, 309, 317; Shipping, 121, 132; Trade, 7, 8, 21, 28, 46, 55, 82, 166, 181, 182, 212, 260, 271, 300, 304, 309, 310, 315, 324, 326, 330, 346, 349; Trade with Virginia, 8
ALLEGHANY CITY, 243; Bucks County, 273; Carlisle, 285; Chambersburg, 329, 330; Chester, 230, Customs collectors, 87; Cumberland County, 285; Erie, 330; Fort Anne, 285; Fort Bedford, 285; Fort Duquesne, 222, 257, 262, 264, 267, 271, 284, 285, 289, 312; Fort Pitt, 223, 307; Gettysburg, 59; Greenburg, 330; Kittaning, 329; Luzerne County, 102, 154; McKeesport, 330; Monongahela River, 29; Nazareth Hall, 174; Newcastle, 309; Northumberland, 95; Northumberland County, 154; Old Chester, 19
PHILADELPHIA, 5, 8, 18, 21, 24, 29, 30, 34, 40, 42, 55, 59, 80, 90, 132, 157, 166, 171, 177, 181, 182, 184, 217, 265, 276, 285, 287, 288, 293, 297, 299, 304, 310, 315, 324, 326, 329, 330, 331, 332, 345, 349, 350, 351, Centennial Exposition, 1876, 131, 266, Consular reports (British), 67, 130, 135, Customs collectors, 87, Description, 15, 28, 30, 36, 43, 95, 98, 116, 156, 159, 180, 184, 190, 222, 256, 268, 271, 292, 305, 350, 351, Garden Alley, 332, Government, 197, 198, 262, Medical School, 317, Medicine, 275, Merchants, 9, 15, 22, 31, 54, 102, 118, 126, 154, 161, 169, 172, 175, 178, 181, 182, 183, 225, 232, 234, 235, 246-7, 249, 250, 275, 306, 316, 325, 329, 330, Pennsylvania Hall, 185, Politics, 166, 177, Prison, 208, Riots, 291, Stanton Hill, 42
PITTSBURGH, 285, 304, 329, 330, 331, 332, Consular reports (British), 134, Description, 32, 95, 155, 217, 316, Government, 164, Merchants, 329, 331; Pottsville, 249; Reading, 346; Royalton, 331; Solebury, 46; Springfield, 273; Sunbury, Customs collectors, 87; Valley Forge, 216; Washington, 181, 329, 332; West Town, 40; Wyoming, 285; York County, 285
Pennsylvania Historical Association, 73 fn.
Pennsylvania, Historical Society of, 156 fn.
Pennsylvania Hospital, 51, 170
Pennsylvania Land Co., 24, 157, 302
Pennsylvania Packet, 324
Pennsylvania Railroad, 96, 105
Pennsylvania Society for Promoting the Abolition of Slavery, 188

Pennsylvania, University of, 19 fn.
Pennsylvania Volunteers, 5
Penryn, Customs records, 89
Pensions, Military (British), payable in U.S., 142
Penson, William, 274
Pentland, William, 168
Penzance, Cornwall, Customs records, 91, 93
Pepperell, Sir William (1696-1759), 300, 302
Perceval, Sir John, Viscount Perceval and 1st Earl of Egmont (1683-1748), 76
Perceval, Kane, 323
Perceval, Spencer (1762-1812), 77; Papers, 77
Perceval, William, 323
Perceval family, 76
Perceval Papers, 323
Perceval–Maxwell Papers, 324
Percival, Andrew, 36
Percy, Capt., 88
Percy, Lord Eustace, 282
Percy, George (1580-1632), 190
Percy, Sir Henry, 9th Earl of Northumberland (1564-1632), 190
Percy, Sir Hugh, 2nd Duke of Northumberland (1742-1817), 150, 191
Perin, William Philip, 23
Perkins, B., "A Diplomat's Wife in Philadelphia," *William and Mary Quarterly* (1954), 256 fn.; "George Canning, Great Britain and the United States," *American Historical Review* (1957), 101 fn.; 102 fn.
Perlman, Selig (1888-1959), 164
Permanent Court of [International] Arbitration at The Hague, 135
Perowne, Edward Henry (1826-1906), 16
Perpetual motion, 150
Perrie, J., 150
Perris, H.S., 229
Perrot, Andrew, 231
Perseus (ship), 121
Pershing, John Joseph (1860-1948), 75
Persia, Relations with U.S., *see* Relations with Persia
Perth, 4th Earl of, *see* Drummond, James (1648-1716); 10th Earl of, *see* Drummond, James (1707-81); 11th Earl of, *see* Drummond, James (1744-1800)
Perth, Tayside, 319
Perth Museum and Art Gallery, 319
Peru, Relations with U.S., *see* Relations with Peru
Pery, Elizabeth, 190
Peter, William (1788-1853), 24, 67, 104
Peterham, J., 204
Peterhoff (ship), 130
Peters, M., 150
Peters, M.W., 113
Peters, Richard (*fl.* 1758-9), 285
Peters, Richard (1810-89), 206
Peters, W.S., 173
Petitions, 55, 56, 107, 138, 194, 195
Petre, Maude Dominica Mary, 75
Petre Papers, 32
Petrie, A., 253
Petrie, David, 315
Petroleum industry, 111, 165, 282; Duties, 303
Pettibone, Daniel, 150
Petty, William, 1st Marquess of Lansdowne and 2nd Earl of Shelburne (*better known as* Lord Shelburne) (1737-1805), 203, 218, 230, 240, 266, 300, 303
Petty–Fitzmaurice, Henry Charles Keith, 5th Marquess of Lansdowne (1845-1927), 37, 135, 221
Petworth House, West Sussex, 223
Pevensey, Customs records, 89
Peyre family, 35
Pharmaceutical products, *see* Drugs
Phelps, Edward John (1822-1900), 38, 129, 202
Phelps, T., 236
Phelps, W.L., 74
Philadelphia and Reading Railroad, 346
Philadelphia College, 265; Academy and Charitable Trust, 249
Philadelphia Electric Co., 224
Philadelphia Ladies Anti-Slavery Society, 270
Philadelphia "Union" Convention (1866), 68
Philadelphia, *see also* Pennsylvania: Philadelphia
Philanthropy, 68, 71, 173, 306-7
Philippa (ship), 98
Philippine Islands, 146; Insurrection, 1896-8, 38, 123, 132, 197; 1899-1901, 39, 40, 123, 131
DESCRIPTION, 40, 227
MANILA, 40, 132, 144, Consular reports (British), 130
Philips, F., 243
Philips, George (*fl.* 1820-30), 225
Philips, George (*fl.* late 19th cent.), 164
Philips, George, & Co., 225
Philips of Weston House Collection, 225
Phillips, Mr., 167
Phillips, J., 220
Phillips, James, 331
Phillips, John, 331
Phillips, Phillip D., 244
Phillips, Richard, 246
Phillips, Wendell (1811-84), 53, 84, 196, 205
Phillips, William (1731?-81), 139, 192
Phillipps Ms., 249
Philosophical Transactions [of the Royal Society], 147 fn.
Philosophy, 271, 275
Philpot, John, 166
Phipps, Sir Charles Beaumont (1801-66), 40
Phipps, Thomas, 35
Phips, Sir William (1651-95), 42
Phoebe (H.M.S.), 36
Phoenix Movement, 351
Photography, 26, 98, 111, 162, 220, 269
Phrenology, 183
"Phylopatria" (*pseud.*), 150
Pickering, Benjamin Maurice, 183
Pickering, Timothy (1745-1829), 256, 287
Pickford, Jedidiah, 239
Picton, Thomas, 246
Pierce, Edward Lillie (1829-97), 67
Pierce, Franklin (1804-69), 67, 200, 201, 232
Piercy, William, 103
Pierrepont, Edwards (1817-92), 38, 129
Piggott, Sir Francis Taylor (d. 1925), 66; "Relations between the Belligerents and the United States," 66
Piggott Papers, 66
Pigot, Hugh, 218
Pigs, 47, 64, 137; *see also* Pork
Pike, James A. (1913-69), 113
Pike, Richard, 22
Pilgrim, John, 190
Pilgrim Fathers, 177

Pilgrim Fathers' Church, Southwark, 85
Pillar, William, 324
Pillsbury, Albert Enoch (1849-1930), 198
Pillsbury, Parker (1809-98), 95
Pillson, James, 346
Pilmere, J., 34
Pim, Frederic W., 350
Pim, Jonathan, 350
Pim, Thomas, 350
Pim Correspondence, 350
Pim Mss., 350
Pinchot, Gifford (1865-1946), 209, 210
Pinckney, Charles Cotesworth (1746-1825), 11, 191
Pinckney, Thomas (1750-1828), 80
Pinckney, Thomas (*fl.* 1755), 150
Pine, Robert Edge (1730-88), 49
Pine, 120, 148, 149
Pine Ridge Agency, 5
Pinkerton detectives, 345
Pinkney, William (1764-1822), 9, 77, 102, 107, 240, 250
"Pinkney's Gazette," 182
Pinney, John, 8
Pinney & Tobin, 8
Pinney Papers, 8
Pioneers, 155, 227
Pipe-line systems, 209
Pipestaves, Trade, 24
Piracy, 10, 18, 31, 83, 180, 220, 239; Turkish, 26; *see also* Privateering; Smuggling
Pirie, Alexander, & Co. Mss., 266
Piscataqua River, 194
Pitcairn, John (1722-75), 61
Pitcalny, Lady, 298
Pitch, 24, 120
Pitfirrane Papers, 257
Pitt, John, 2nd Earl of Chatham (1756-1835), 141, 287
Pitt, Percy (d. 1932), 82; Papers, 82
Pitt, William, 1st Earl of Chatham (1708-78), 17, 45, 66, 141, 168, 228, 240, 261, 266, 284, 289, 312, 354
Pitt, William (1759-1806), 66, 80, 82, 101, 161, 229, 287
Place, Francis (1771-1854), 167
Plant-collecting, *see* Botany and botanists
Planta, Joseph (1787-1847), 207
Plantation Books, 138
Plantations, *see* Colonies; Trade and Plantations
Plate-metal work, Trade, 235
Plater, George (1735-92), 86
Plath, Sylvia (1932-63), 96
Platt, William, 98
Playfair, Lyon, 1st Baron Playfair of St. Andrews (1818-98), 162
Playfair Papers, 162
Playne, Mary, 164
Plover (H.M.S.), 347
Plumer, William (1759-1850), 167
Plummer, Alfred, *The Witney Blanket Industry*, 210 fn.
Plumsted, Robert, 15
Plunkett, Sir Francis Richard (1835-1907), 133
Plunkett, Sir Horace Curzon (1854-1932), 209-10
Plunkett Foundation for Co-operative Studies, 209-10
Plymouth, Devonshire, 18, 26-7, 35, 37, 49, 120; American wives living in, 1949-51, 27; City records, 26-7; Customs records, 89, 91, 93; Merchants, 27; Ship owners and masters, 27
Pocock, Nicholas (1741?-1821), 122
Poe, Edgar Allan (1809-49), 238
Poetry, 74, 178
Poland, Relations with U.S., *see* Relations with Poland
Poletica, Pierre de, 76
Polhill, Charles, 45
Polhill–Drabble Papers, 45
Political parties, 95, 197, 198, 208, 277, 330; *see also names of parties, e.g.* Democratic Party
Political rights, 174
Politics, 1783-1865, 22, 33, 39, 41, 51, 77, 78, 81, 95, 148, 167-8, 183, 200, 216, 222, 223, 229, 257, 260, 270, 274, 294, 306, 331, 347; 1865-1900, 33, 133, 164, 177, 330, 347; 20th century, 33, 77, 113, 126, 158, 164, 165, 209, 210, 221, 258, 279, 280, 281, 283; *see also* Elections *and subdivision* Politics, *under states, etc.*
Polk, Frank Lyon (1871-1943), 229, 277, 284
Polk, James Knox (1795-1849), 16, 62, 67, 185, 328
Pollard, S., *Three Centuries of Sheffield Steel*, 234 fn.
Polled Cattle Society, 266
Pollen, A.N., 277
Pollock, David, 330
Pollok, Alan, 269
Pollok, Morris, 269
Pollok, Robert, 269
Pollok–Morris Esq., W.S.B., Mss., 269
Pollok–Morris estates, 269
Polly (ship), 47, 296
Polwarth Muniments, 292
Polygamy, 137; *see also* Mormons and Mormonism
Pomeroy, Arthur, 1st Viscount Harberton (d. 1798), 323
Pomeroy, Arthur James, 323
Pomeroy, John, 323
Pomeroy, S.W., 187
Pomeroy Papers, 323
Ponsonby, George (1755-1817), 9
Pontiac (*c.* 1720-69), 307
Pontiac's Rebellion, 45
Pool, Rosey Eva (1905-71), 221
Pool Papers, 221
Poole, Benjamin, *Coventry: Its History and Antiquities*, 228 fn.
Poole, Dorset, 161; Customs records, 89, 90-1, 93
Pooley, Nathan, 219
Poor Law Commissioners for England and Wales, 46, 137
Poor Law Guardians, *see* Chorlton Union
Pope Leo XIII (1810-1903), *see* Leo XIII, *Pope*, 161
Pope Alexander VIII (1610-91), *see* Alexander VIII, *Pope*, 54
Popham, Sir John (1531?-1607), 37
Popish Plot, 1678, 224
Population: Colonial period, 292, 325; 19th century, 64, 99, 273; *see also* Census; Vital statistics
Pork, Prices, 272
Port Eliot, Cornwall, 19
Port of Bristol Authority, 7
Port Talbot, Customs records, 93
Porter, Sir James (1710-86), 79
Porter, M. R., and O. Davenport, *Scotsman in Buckskin: Sir William Drummond Stewart and the Rocky Mountain Fur Trade*, 290
Porter, Robert Percival, 158
Porter, William, 331
Porter, William Sydney, *alias* "O. Henry" (1862-1910), 74; "The Missing Child," 74
Porter family, 328
Porteus, Beilby (1731-1809), 160

Porteus Library, 160
Portland, Duke of, 193 fn., 200
Portland, 3rd Duke of, *see* Bentinck, William Henry Cavendish (1738-1809)
Portland Mss., 193
Portland Papers, 82-3
Portsmouth, Hampshire, Customs records, 89, 90, 93
Portugal, *see* Relations with Portugal; Trade with Portugal
Positivism, 74, 164
Positivist Papers, 74
Post, Christian Frederic, 160, 285
Postal service, 35, 96-7, 111, 124, 132, 156, 161, 184, 204, 207, 257, 274; Colonial period, 140, 214
CENSORSHIP, 112; Rates, 53, 77, 208; *see also* Communications; Telegraph; Telephone
Postlethwayt, Malachy, 160
Potash, 24, 148-50 *passim*, 205, 232
Potato blight, 270
Potatoes, 64; Prices, 272
Potomac River, 120, 304, 319; Customs collectors, 87
Potter, Dr., 315
Potter, Alonzo (1800-65), 169
Potter, James, 187
Potters' Emigration Society, London District Committee, 163
Potters' Examiner and Workman's Advocate, 217
Pottery: Manufacture, 217, 254; Trade, 161; *see also* Clay
Potts, Thomas (1778-1842), 9
Poulton, Mr., 166
Poulton, George, 166
Poulton, Mary, 166
Pound, Ezra (1885-1972), 81
Powder River Cattle Co., 209, 232
Powell, Mr., 299
Powell, A.M., 235
Powell, Henry Watson, 119
Powell, J.F., 28
Powell, Nathaniel, and Co., 264
Power, B.M., 291
Power, Charles, 66
Pownall, John, 265, 266, 299
Pownall, Thomas (1722-1805), 50, 65, 86, 119, 188, 214, 215
Powney, James, 228
Powys, Wales, 249
Prairie Cattle Co. Ltd., 308
Prankard, Graffin (d. 1756), 212
Prankard and Dickinson Papers, 7, 211-2; Dickinson Mss., 211-2; Prankard Mss., 212; Fuller Mss., 212
Pratt, Charles, 1st Earl Camden (1714-94), 45, 218
Pratt, John (*fl.* 1779-1805), 102
Pratt, Sir John (1876-1970) 166, 281
Pratt & Whitney, 228
Pratt Papers, 45
Pray, Capt., 180
Pre-emption rights, 131
Pre-Raphaelite movement, 176
Preble, William Pitt (1783-1857), 25
Premiums, Colonial period, 148-51 *passim*
Prendergast, James, 325
Presbyterian Associate Synod, 259
Presbyterian Church, 40, 103, 158, 263, 274, 275, 285, 308, 309, 313-4, 331, 332
Presbyterian Historical Society, 158
Presbyterian Historical Society, *Journal* (Philadelphia), 158
Presbyterians, Immigrants, 246
Prescott, Robert (1725-1816), 101
Prescott, William Hickling (1796-1859), 64, 259
Presidents, 49, 68, 167; Election, 1808, 294; 1824, 25, 271; 1828, 207; 1840, 206, 207; 1844, 64, 291, 328; 1848, 77, 206; 1856, 201; 1864, 58, 59, 61, 68; 1872, 69; 1876, 18, 161; 1880, 38; 1884, 161, 177, 208; 1884-1920, 197; 1888, 164; 1892, 38; 1896, 38; 1900, 39; 1904, 65; 1908, 224; 1920, 284; 1928, 278, 279; 1936, 281; 1940, 282, 283; Letters, 62, 77, 132; Messages to Congress, 77, 107
Press, 81, 169, 200, 238, 278, 279, 299, 327; Middle West, 210; *see also* Journalism, International; Newspapers; *also names of individual newspapers*
Press cuttings, 9, 20, 116, 161, 163, 178-9
Press-gangs, *see* Impressment of seamen
Preston, 1st Viscount, *see* Graham, Sir Richard (1648-95)
Preston, Mr. and Mrs. A.E., 11
Preston, Ann (1813-72), 96
Preston, George, 49
Preston, John W., 81
Preston, Thomas, 143
Preston, Lancashire, 46-8; Customs records, 93
Preston Banking Company, 117
Preston Family Papers, 49
Preston Papers, 11
Prestwood, Viscount, *see* Attlee, Clement (1883-1967)
Pretor, Simon, 8
Pretter, Stephen, 51
Prevost, Augustine (1723-86), 116, 268
Prevost, Sir George (1767-1816), 269, 288
Priaulx Library, 339
Price, Daniel, 211
Price, Henry Edward (1824-1908?), 114
Price, Lewis Richard (1818-82), 211
Price, Mrs. Lewis R., 211
Price, Richard (1723-91), 203, 317
Price, Thomas W., 243
Prices: 18th century, 56, 305; 19th century, 64, 169, 172, 286, 330; 20th century, 111
Prichard, James Cowles, 6
Prideaux, John (1718-59), 289
Priestley, C., "The Life and Career of Henry Fiennes Pelham-Clinton, 1720-94 ... 2nd Duke of Newcastle-under-Lyme" (Thesis), 192 fn.
Priestley, G.F., 240
Priestley, Joseph (1733-1804), 19, 73, 95, 170, 226, 304
Priestley, Joseph, Jr. (1768-1833), 226
Priestley, L.E., 240
Priestley Bros., 240
Priestley Letters, 95
Primaries, *see* Elections: Primaries
Prime Minister's Office, 122, 123, 138-9
Prince Consort of England, *see* Albert, *Prince Consort* (1819-61)
Prince, Thomas (1687-1758), 174
Prince Arthur (ship), 316
Prince Edward Island: 18th century, 138
FINANCE, 110; Governors, 138; Land, 21, 42, 50, 346; *see also* Fisheries: Prince Edward Island
Princeton University, 271; Institute for Advanced Study, 165; Library, 85 fn.
Pringle, H., 328
Pringle, James, 298
Pringle, Sir John (1707-82), 298

Pringle, John (*fl.* 1765), 292
Pringle, Mrs. M.A., 304
Pringle, Robert, 150
Printers: Immigrants, 9, 253; Wages, 164
Printing, 151, 310
Printing machinery, 308; Trade, 9
Prior, Mary, 227
Prior, Matthew (1664-1721), 230
Prisoners, Political, 345, 346
Prisoners Aid Society, Discharged, 61
Prisoners of war, *see subdivision* Prisoners *under wars*
Prisons, 58, 156, 182, 183, 285, 325; Reform, 155
Pritchard Mss., 155
Privateering, 6, 77, 78, 89-93 *passim*, 160, 181, 182, 183, 221, 298, 299, 315; *see also* Piracy; Search, Right of
Privateers, 265, 286, 304, 305, 314, 316; Channel Islands, 339; French, 18, 182, 230, 305, 351; Russian, 201; Spanish, 217
Privy Council, 10, 26, 27, 49, 58, 61, 97, 112, 122, 137-8, 140, 150, 194, 221, 312; Papers, 159; Committee for Trade and Plantations, 56, 160, 194; Scottish, 311; *Register*, 311
Prize courts, 80, 111, 121, 136, 198, 267
Prizes, 78, 89, 90, 120, 121, 138, 142, 143, 144, 182, 183, 261, 292, 297, 298, 307; *see also subdivision* Prizes *under wars*
Probate records, Carlisle, 21
Probation system, 111
Proby, Sir John Joshua, 1st Earl of Carysfort (1751-1828), 350
Prohibition, 111; *see also* Liquor traffic; Temperance
Prompte (frigate), 108
Prostitution, 235
Protectionism, 204
Protestant churches, 352; Attitude to Catholic Church, 30
Protestant Episcopal Church in U.S., 47, 63, 95, 115, 158, 159, 253, 297; Colonial period, 115
Protestant succession, Colonial attitude, 40
Protestants: Education, 171; Immigrants, 152, 193
Protestants in France, *see* Huguenots
Proud, Ann, 156
Proud, Robert, 156
Proud, Thomas, 156
Providence (ship), 346
Providence of Mostyn (ship), 18
Provincial Typographical Association, 9
Prudence Hannah (brigantine), 31
Pruson, Thomas, 112
Prussia, *see* Immigrants from Prussia; Relations with Prussia; Trade with Prussia
Pryse, Gerald Spencer, 281, 282
Pryse, John Robert (1840-62), 245
Psyche (frigate), 108
Public Archives of Canada, 146 fn., 219 fn.
Public health, 90, 131, 138, 170; *see also* Epidemics, *and subdivision* Epidemics *under states*
Public opinion, 73, 200, 270, 274, 287
Public Record Office (Chancery Lane and Kew), 122-45; 15, 53, 66, 66 fn., 89 fn., 90 fn., 103, 308, 311 fn., 349, 350; *Annual Report*, 122; *Calendar of State Papers, Colonial Series*, 14 fn., 128, 194 fn., 195 fn.; *Calendar of State Papers, Domestic*, 298, 350; *Calendar of State Papers Relating to Ireland, 1509-1670*, 350; Customs records, 88-9; *Guide*, 122
Public Record Office of Ireland, 348-9; 351; *Guide*, 348; Quit Rent Office, 343, 349; *Report of the Deputy Keeper*, 348, 351; Valuation Office, 349
Public Record Office of Northern Ireland, 323-32; 349, 351 fn.
Public Records Act (1967), 122
Publishing, 33, 50, 74, 78, 84, 169, 191, 196; *see also* Copyright, International
Puerto Rico, Consular reports (British), 130
Puffer, M. G., 266
Puget Sound, 77
Pugh, R. B., "Privy Council Minutes . . .," *Bulletin of the Institute of Historical Research* (1949), 138; *Records of the Colonial and Dominions Offices*, 128
Pugh, Sarah, 95
Puller, Sir Christopher (1774-1824), 39
Puller, Louisa [King], 39
Pumping machinery, 20, 149
Purdie & Dixon almanac (1771), 182
Purdon, Sarah, 353
Purdon Papers, 353
Puritans, 17
Purss, John, 272
Purton Parker & Co., 46
Purvis, Mr., 131
Putnam, General, 43
Putnam, A. P., 208
Putnam, E., "Two early passenger lists 1635-7," *New England Historical and Genealogical Register* (1921), 44 fn.
Putnam, George Haven (1844-1930), 74, 197, 198, 199
Putnam, George Palmer (1814-72), 68
Putnam, Ruth, 164
Pwllheli, Customs records, 93
Pyot, Alexander, 290
Pyrites Company Inc., 145

Q

Quadrupeds, Oviparous, 170
Quaker History, 152
Quakers, *see* Friends, Religious Society of
Quarry Bank Mill, 19
Quarter sessions records: Bedfordshire, 9; Chester, 18; Cumberland (Cumbria), 21; Derbyshire, 23; Essex, 33; Gloucestershire, 35; Hampshire (and Southampton), 35; Hertford, 41; Humberside, 43; Kent, 46; Lancashire, 47-8; Leicestershire, 49; London, 85-6; Middlesex, 97; Northamptonshire, 190; Staffordshire, 216; Yorkshire, 231
Quartering of troops, 302, 303
Quarterly Review, 193
Quartz mining, 268
Quashebald, 50
Quebec, 36, 40, 305, 331, 332; Attack by New Englanders, 1690, 15; Seven Years War, 1756-63, 45, 74, 119, 189, 191, 240, 275, 293, 323; 1765-75, 141, 205, 215, 317, 324; 1776-83, 57, 76, 146, 205, 257, 296, 324; 1783-1800, 102; 1800-61, 21; Civil War, 1861-5, 104
AGRICULTURE, 114; British administration, 45; British Army, 60, 114, 234; Description, 32, 36, 40, 230, 272, 325; Epidemics, 332; Finance, 114; Fires, 110; French administration, 45, 114; Governors, 39, 114, 223, 275; Immigrants, 188, 189, 259, 325, 326, 330, 331, 332, 351; Indians, 114; Industry, 150; Land, 45; Land grants, 138; Merchants, 235, 324; Population, 114; Religious history, 45, 109, 114, 189; Shipping, 309; Trade, 55, 114, 160, 250, 325, 326, 349

La Pointe Olivie, 324; Montreal, 14, 45, 102, 109, 223, 254, 309, 326, 330, 351, Description, 32, 36, 40, 184, 270; St. Croix, 203; St. Sulpice, 109
Quebec Act (1774), 31
Queensberry, Duke of, *see* Douglas, Charles, 3rd Duke of (1698-1778)
Quicke Papers, 26
Quin, Hugh (*fl.* 1817), 331
Quin, Hugh (*fl.* 1854), 331
Quin family, 332
Quinan, W. R. (1848-1910), 206
Quincy, Edward, 150
Quincy, Eliza Susan, 148
Quincy, Josiah (*fl.* 1743-75), 191
Quincy, Josiah (1772-1864), 17, 148, 182
Quincy, Josiah (*fl.* 1898), 164, 173
Quinn, D. B., "Edward Hayes, Liverpool Colonial Pioneer," *Trans. Hist. Soc. of Lancs. and Cheshire* (1959), 14 fn.; ed., *The Voyage and Colonial Enterprises of Sir Humphrey Gilbert*, 189 fn.
Quinn, John, 348, 353
Quintard, Mrs. L. W., 75
Quit-rent, *see* Land, Tenure
Quit Rent Office, 343, 349
Quo warranto, 193, 194

R

R., J., 318
Race problems, 114, 276; *see also* Immigrants; Negroes
Rackett, Mr. and Mrs. Thomas, 27
Radcliffe, John (1738-83), 40
Radcliffe, Sir Thomas, 3rd Earl of Sussex (1526?-83), 37
Radcliffe family, 40
Radcliffe Mss., 40
Radcliffe of Rudding Papers, 239
Radicals in Great Britain, 67, 169
Radnor, 1st Earl of, *see* Bouverie, William Pleydell (1725-76)
Raffles, Thomas (1788-1863), 174
Railton, John, 21
Railways, 297; Construction, 148, 224, 249-50, 346-7, 352; Finance, 20, 46, 52, 96, 100, 115, 118, 197, 228, 238, 308, 318; Management, 69, 196; Rates, 198; *see also* Locomotive works; *also names of individual railway companies*
Rainbow (ship), 120
Rainier, G.S., 121
Raitt, Margaret, 284
Raitt, Robert, 284
Ralegh, Sir Walter (1552?-1618), 14, 31, 239
Raleigh (N.C.) *Times*, 178
Ralston, Messrs., 249
Ramm, A., ed., *The Political Correspondence of Mr. Gladstone and Lord Granville, 1868-1876*, 70 fn.
Ramsay, Sir Andrew Crombie (1841-91), 162
Ramsay, Elizabeth (Glen), Lady Dalhousie (d. 1807), 284
Ramsay, George, 9th Earl of Dalhousie (1770-1838), 49, 285, 286
Ramsay, George (*fl.* 1810), 274
Ramsay Papers, 162
Ramsden, Isabella, 240
Ramsden Family Records, 240
Ramsgate, Customs records, 93
Ranching, 308, 348
Rand, B., *Berkeley and Percival*, 76 fn.
Randall, L., 34
Randolph, ——, 184
Randolph, Edmund (1753-1813), 23, 80, 182
Randolph, Edward (*c.* 1632-1703), 82, 230
Ranelagh, Katherine (Boyle), Viscountess (1614-91), 147
Rankin, Henry, 98
Ransome, Patrick, 282
Ranstead, Joseph, 37
Rapeseed, 10
Rappahannock Forge, 273
Raquet, Condy, 169
Rashleigh, Philip (1729-1811), 230
Rastrick, West Yorkshire, Business records, *see* Business records: Rastrick, W. Yorkshire
Rathbone, E.A., *Records of the Rathbone Family*, 185 fn.
Rathbone, E.F., *William Rathbone*, 185 fn.
Rathbone, William (1787-1868), 185
Rathbone, William (1819-1902), 61, 185
Rathbone, William, & Co., 116
Rathbone Collection, 185
Rathbone family, 185
Rauthmell, Robert, 22
Raven, John James (1833-1906), 220
Raverdiere, Lord, 159
Raw materials, 55; *see also* Agriculture; Natural resources; *and individual products*
Rawdon, Francis (*until 1790, then after 1793 known as* Rawdon–Hastings), *see* Hastings, Francis Rawdon–, 1st Baron Rawdon and 1st Marquis of Hastings (1754-1826)
Rawlinson Collection (4th Army Papers), 113
Rawlinson Letters, 202, 203
Rawlinson Mss., 99
Rawson, William, & Co., 105
Rawson Collection, 176
Raymond, R.S., 113
Rayner, John, 300
Rea, Joseph, 332
Read, Thomas, 97
Read Collection, 219
Reade, Charles (1814-84), 116; "The Rights and Wrongs of Authors," 116
Reade & Bogardus, 181
Reading, 1st Marquess of, see Isaacs, Rufus Daniel (1860-1935)
Reading, Berkshire, 10-1
Reading, University of, Institute of Agricultural History and Museum of English Rural Life, 11; Library, 11
Reading and Witney Monthly Meetings of the Society of Friends, 11
Readman, James, 270
Readman of Auldgirth Mss., 270
Realization and Debenture Corp. of Scotland, 271
Rebecca (ship), 33
Recall, 198
Reciprocal News Service, 210
Reciprocity, 34, 38, 57, 59, 71, 77, 81, 128, 130, 184, 198, 200, 201, 207; *see also* Tariff; Trade with (particular country)
Reconstruction, 1865-98, 156, 201, 222
Red Cross, 142
Red River expedition (1869), 143, 144
Red River settlement, 140, 233
Redditch Public Library, 20

Redfield, William C. (1789-1857), 148
Redford, A., *Manchester Merchants and Foreign Trade*, 178 fn.
Redmond, John (1856-1918), 345
Redmond, William H.K. (1861-1917), 344
Redmond family, 331
Redmond Family Papers, 331
Reebkomp, Augustus, 230
Reed, Alexander, 329
Reed, Joseph (1741-85), 214
Reed, Judith, 214
Reed, Thomas Brackett (1839-1902), 164, 197
Rees, David, 247
Rees, John (*fl.* 1853), 247
Rees, John Davis (1816-80), 247
Rees, Zillah Mathias (1839-1923), 247
Reeve, Richard, 12, 192
Reeves, John, 101
Referendum, 198
Reform League, 52
Regiments, British: Royal Marines, 273; 35th, 294; 42nd Royal Highlanders, 274, 287, 289, 307; 74th Highlanders, 273; 84th Highlanders (Royal Highland Emigrants), 294, 295, 296, 297
Regiments, Hessian: de Bose, 275
Regiments of Foot (British): 14th, 287; 17th (Richbell's), 266, 275, 284, 285; 20th, 296; 21st, 305; 22nd, 284; 26th (Cameronians), 262; 27th, 284, 289; 29th, 20; 40th, 290; 45th, 284; 51st (Pepperell's), 300, 302; 52nd, 140; 55th, 284; 60th (Loudoun's Royal Americans), 264, 265, 284, 285, 290, 297; 63rd, 285; 64th, 323; 71st Highlanders (Fraser's), 260, 261, 269, 292, 293, 294, 305, 312; 76th, 291; 77th, 274, 284, 285, 304; 78th Highlanders (Fraser's), 284, 291; 80th (Edinburgh) (Gage's), 276, 289; 95th (Burton's), 289
Regiments, Tory: Arnold's Corps, 276; King's Orange Rangers, 293; Loyal Americans, 276; New York Volunteers, 296; Queen's Rangers, 276; Royal North Carolina Regiment, 264
Reid, ______, 344
Reid, Mr., 268
Reid, Alexander, *see* Robertson, Alexander
Reid, Mayne (1818-83), 327
Reid, Robert, 317
Reid, Thomas (1710-96), 254
Reid, Thomas (*fl.* 1807), 288
Reid, Whitelaw (1837-1912), 75, 204
Reilly, Thomas, 348
Relations with Belgium, 283; Brazil, 132, 198; Canada: to 1867, 24, 63, 83, 84, 111, 129, 130, 139, 192, 201, 286, 297, 324; 1867-1900, 38, 39, 68, 72, 131, 133, 197, 202; 20th century, 30, 112, 138, 139, 197, 198, 277, 278, 280, 282; *see also* Bering Sea Controversy; Boundaries: Canada; Fisheries; Reciprocity; World War I; World War II
CARIBBEAN, 143; Central America, 198, 200, 201; Chile, 38, 132; China, 34, 38, 39, 144, 280; Colombia, 131; Costa Rica, 201; Cuba, 38, 59, 60, 70, 105, 131, 134, 200, 201, 207, 232; Czechoslovakia, 282; Denmark, 202; Dominican Republic (*also* Santo Domingo), 81, 201, 216, 298; Ecuador, 131, 279, 281; Egypt, 135; Europe, 41, 281; Falkland Islands, 77, 201; Far East, 198, 281; Fiji, 128, 131; France, 12, 32, 49, 56, 57, 59, 66, 67, 69, 71, 73, 77, 81, 91, 101, 104, 112, 142, 169, 200, 207, 250, 279, 286, 292, 294, Colonial period, 14, 15, 40, 82, 143, 152, 195, 203, 292, 299, 301, 307; *see also* France: Colonies; King George's War, 1744-8; Seven Years War, 1756-63; War of Independence: French participation and opinion; World War II
GERMANY, 133, 135-6, 140, 198, 200, 282, Colonial period, 93; Germany (West), 112; *see also* War of Independence: German participation; World War I; World War II
GREAT BRITAIN, 157-8; 1783-1811, 25, 49, 56, 66, 80-3 *passim*, 95, 101, 107-8 *passim*, 117, 140, 173, 175, 182, 200, 218, 219, 240, 250, 261, 266, 267, 270, 272, 287, 292, 294, 298, 303, 313, 350, 351; *see also* Colonies *for relations to 1775*; War of Independence; 1812-14, *see* War of 1812; 1815-65, 13, 25, 43, 59-60 *passim*, 63, 64, 66, 67, 69, 77, 78, 102, 103-5 *passim*, 109, 110, 124, 131, 132, 139, 140, 155, 168, 169, 173, 175, 182, 186, 200-2 *passim*, 206-8 *passim*, 223, 240, 250, 261, 268, 269, 274, 286, 288, 306, 330, 344, 353; *see also* Civil War: Foreign opinion, British; Confederate States: British support and aid; Crimean War: Recruiting in U.S.; 1865-1900, 13, 34, 38, 39, 59, 68, 71, 72, 128, 129-33 *passim*, 137, 139-40, 177, 179, 197, 201-2 *passim*, 208, 223, 259, 315; 20th Century, 16, 77, 111-3 *passim*, 125, 126, 127, 129, 131, 135, 138-44 *passim*, 165, 166, 196, 197, 199, 200, 209-10 *passim*, 224, 259, 260, 269, 276-83 *passim*, 345; *see also* World War I; World War II
GUATEMALA, 198; Hawaii, 38, 67, 131, 133, 201; Honduras, 200; India, 112, 280; Ireland, 31, 111, 136, 284, 344-5 *passim*, 349, 350, 352; *see also* War of Independence: Irish participation and opinion
ITALY, 138; Jamaica, 212; Japan, 38, 198, 280; *see also* World War II: Atomic bomb
KOREA, 139; Latin America, 197, 207; Manchuria, 166, 280, 281; Mexico, 38, 131, 133, 134, 197, 198, 282, 330; *see also* War with Mexico, 1845-8
MOROCCO, 131; Netherlands, 25, 283, Colonial period, 200; *see also* War of Independence: Netherlands participation and opinion
NEW ZEALAND, 132; Nicaragua, 77, 105, 131, 198, 200, 201; Palestine, 139; Persia, 135; Peru, 124; Poland, 143; Portugal, 57, 77; Prussia, 76, 131; Russia, 38, 71, 73, 76, 78, 112, 125, 133, 169, 200, 201, 280, 283, 284; Samoa, 38, 230, 269; Saudi Arabia, 135; South Africa, 38, 129, 206; South America, 54, 84
SPAIN, 25, 54, 59, 60, 62, 66, 76, 84, 101, 131, 132, 133, 200, 201, 202, 287, 294, 319, Colonial period, 140, 141, 160, 195, 266, 273, 274, 275; *see also* *Black Warrior* (ship); Spain: Colonies; War of Independence: Spanish participation and opinion; War of Jenkin's Ear, 1739-42
TONGA, 38; Tripoli, 168; Turkey, 132; Vatican, 77
See also Isolationism
Religion, 15, 24, 103, 117, 199, 224, 268, 271, 275, 304, 329, 331; *see also names of denominations, sects, churches, etc.; subdivision* Religious history *under names of states, etc.; subdivision* Religious aspects *under wars*; Indians: Religion and mythology; Slavery and the churches
Religious liberty, 72, 95, 167, 174, 346, 350; *see also* Dissenters; Huguenots
Religious Society of Friends in Ireland, 349-50
Remington Typewriter Co., 42
Remsen, Peter, 149, 150
Remson, Peter, & Co., 175
Renfrew District Library Service, 318
Rent, 111
Renton, J., 314
Renwick, M.A., 148
Reparations, 112, 138, 260, 278, 279, 280; *see also* Lausanne Conference (1932); London Reparations Conference (1924)
Repealers of Newfoundland, 344
Republican Party, 96, 198, 200, 284
Republicanism in Great Britain, 16, 52, 231

Resolution (ship), 21
Retz, Francis, 171
Reuben, Karl, 163
Revenue, Colonial period, 65, 159-60, 195, 208; *see also subdivision* Finance *under states, etc.*
Revenue, H. M., Commissioners of, 62
Révész, E., 282
Revivals, 151
Revolution, American, *see* War of Independence
Revolutions of 1848, American opinion, 206
Reynolds, Anthony, 189
Reynolds, Edward (1599-1676), 151
Reynolds, Henry, 218
Reynolds, Jonathan (1814-91), 243
Reynolds, Richard (1674-1743), 189
Reynolds, Richard (1735-1816), 154
Reynolds family, 154
Reynolds, Hankes & Co., 286
Reynolds Mss., 154
Rhett, Robert Barnwell (1800-76), 67
Rhinelander Papers, 5
Rhoads, Samuel, Jr., 154
Rhode Island: 17th century, 115; 1765-75, 12, 214, 215, 249; 1776-89, 48, 76, 289
AGENTS, 301, 302; Army, 302; Assembly, 57; Banking, 57; Constitution, 301; Customs collectors, 87; Description, 227; Education, 203; Governors, 62, 68, 115; Immigrants, 332; Land, 76, 194; Land grants, 263; Merchants, 162; Navigation, 214; Population, 301; Religious history, 30, 42, 61, 117, 154, 158, 203, 265; Slavery, 62; Trade, 91, 301, 310
BLOCK ISLAND, 194; Newport, 61, 76, 91, 95; Providence, 310, 332, Consular reports (British), 134; *see also* New England
Rhode Island College, 245; *see also* Brown University
Rhodes, Cecil John (1853-1902), 280
Rhodes, James Ford (1848-1927), 197, 198, 199
Rhodes House Library, 205-6
Rhodes scholars, 278
Rhodes Scholarship Trust, 282
Rhual Mss., 243
Rhubarb, 149
Rhymney Iron Co. Collection, 250
Rhys, Ernest, 81; Papers, 81
Ricardo, John Lewis (1812-62), 161
Rice: Cultivation, 103, 301, 328, 330; Milling, 272; Trade, 8, 55, 56, 73, 88, 91, 122, 138, 169, 173, 211, 212
Richard, David, 244
Richard, Elias J., 247
Richard, Henry (1812-88), 69, 157, 244
Richard, Linda A., 75
Richard Penn (ship), 44
Richards, Frederick B., 262
Richards, John, 244
Richards, Raymond, Collection, 213
Richards family, 257
Richards Papers, 257
Richardson, Major J., 104
Richardson, J., & Co. Mss., 268
Richardson, John (*fl.* 1755), 192
Richardson, John (*fl.* early 19th cent.), 183
Richey, William, 330
Richmond, 1st Duke of, *see* Stuart, James (1612-55); 4th Duke of, *see* Lennox, Charles (1764-1819)
Richmond, Sir Herbert William (1871-1946), 277
Richmond, James Cook, 94
Richmond Enquirer, 326
Rickards Family Papers, 98
Rickett, H.W., "John Bradbury's Explorations in Missouri Territory," *Proc. of the American Philosophical Society* (1950), 182 fn.
Rideing, William Henry (1853-1918), 70, 71, 75, 199
Ridley, John, 191
Ridley, Sir Matthew White, 191
Ridley (Blagdon) Mss., 191
Rigby, George, 210
Rigby, Henry, 47
Rigby, Richard (1722-88), 32, 192, 286
Rigby, William, 47
Rigby Papers, 32
Right of search, *see* Search, Right of
Riley, Annie, 236
Riley, D.W., 178
Rimmer, W.G., *Marshalls of Leeds*, 239 fn.
Ring, John, 11
Rio Grande Irrigation & Land Co., 131
Rio Tinto-Zinc Corporation Ltd., 145
Ripon, 1st Marquess of, *see* Robinson, George Frederick Samuel (1827-1909)
Ripon Papers, 68-9
Rising States (American privateer), 90
Ritchie, James, & Co., 317
Rithet (ship), 269
Rittenhouse, David (1732-96), 226
Ritter zu Groenestyn, Lothair (b. 1868), 136
Rivers, Navigation, 12, 84, 124, 144, 146, 174, 200
Rivington, James (1724-1803), 193, 212, 233
Rix, Joseph, comp., "Some Account of the Nonconformist Churches at Hail Weston and St. Neots...Huntingdon," 94
Rix, Samuel Wilton, 94
Rix family, 94
Rix Papers, 94
Roach, John, 239
Roads, 170
Roatán Island, 186
Robb, Andrew, 328
Robert Burton (ship), 179
Robert Samuel (ship), 97
Roberts, Benjamin, 12
Roberts, Evan, 245
Roberts, George (1769-1853), 245, 246
Roberts, Rev. Gomer M., Deposit, 246
Roberts, Humphrey, 243
Roberts, James, 235
Roberts, Jane (Mrs. George Roberts), 245
Roberts, Margred, 246
Roberts, Morris, 246
Roberts, R., 244
Roberts, R. Silyn, 248
Roberts, Richard (1810-83), 246
Roberts, Samuel (1800-85), 244, 245, 246
Roberts, Sarah, 243
Roberts, W., 264
Roberts, William (1813-72), 244
Robertson, Alexander, 262
Robertson, Alexander (*alias* Reid), 273
Robertson, Arthur, 312
Robertson, Charles, 291

Robertson, George, 262
Robertson, James (1720?-88), 45, 195, 258, 294, 295, 311
Robertson, James (*fl.* 1758-9), 285
Robertson, James (*fl.* 1768), 276
Robertson, John (*fl.* 1710), 262, 263
Robertson, John (*fl.* 1768), 276
Robertson, William (1721-93), 258; *History of America*, 258
Robertson, William, Jr. (*fl.* 1796), 258
Robertson, William (*fl.* 1842), 269
Robertson of Kindeace Muniments, 291
Robertson–Aikman of the Ross Mss., 262
Robertson–Macdonald Papers, 258
Robin, Charles (1743-1824), 339
Robin family, 339
Robinson, Messrs., 170
Robinson, David, 331
Robinson, Edwin Arlington (1869-1935), 238
Robinson, Frederick (*fl.* 1778-86), 9
Robinson, Sir Frederick Philipse (1763-1852), 83
Robinson, George Frederick Samuel, 1st Marquess of Ripon (*known as* Earl de Grey) (1827-1909), 68, 71, 72
Robinson, Henry Crabb (1775-1867), 94; Correspondence, 94
Robinson, Humphrey, 232
Robinson, John (1576?-1625), 177
Robinson, John (1727-1802), 44, 287
Robinson, John (*fl.* 1758), 284
Robinson, Mary, 331
Robinson, Richard, 13
Robinson, Robert, 26
Robinson, Sir Tancred (d. 1748), 239
Robinson, Thomas, 2nd Baron Grantham (1738-86), 8, 239
Robinson & Bros., 34
Robinson & Sons Ltd., 23
Robson, Elizabeth (1771-1843), 155, 155 fn.
Robson, Henry, 155
Robson, Robert (b. 1754), 172
Robson, T., 227
Rochdale, Greater Manchester, 179
Roche, Alfred (1819-76), 146
Roche, Sir Boyle (1743-1807), 312
Roche, James, 344
Roche, William, 315
Rochester, Customs records, 89, 94
Rochester, University of, Library, 85 fn.
Rochford, 4th Earl of, *see* Zuylestein, William Henry (1717-81)
Rochfort (ship), 288
Rockefeller, David (b. 1915), 166
Rockefeller, John D. (1839-1937), 166
Rockefeller, John D., Jr. (1874-1960), 260
Rockefeller Foundation, 277, 281
Rockingham, 2nd Marquis of, *see* Watson-Wentworth, Charles (1730-82)
Rocky Mountains, 274, 290, 291
Rodd, James Rennell, 1st Baron Rennell (1858-1941), 199
Rodes, Reastor, 238
Rodger, ______, 265
Rodger, Ralph, 270
Rodgers, A. Robertson, 176
Rodgers, John (1727-1811), 215
Rodgers, John (*fl.* 1784), 313
Rodgers, Joseph, & Sons, 234
Rodney, Caesar Augustus (1772-1824), 16
Rodney, George Brydges, 1st Baron (1719-92), 18, 101, 230
Rodolphe, Major, 259
Roe, Humphrey Verdon, 79
Roebuck, John Arthur (1801-79), 60, 104
Roebuck (privateer), 221
Rogers, Dr., 233
Rogers, Mrs., 225
Rogers, John, 285
Rogers, Robert (1727-1800), 45, 233
Rogers, Stephen, 97
Rogers, T.D., and H.M. Young, "A Handlist of the Personal Correspondence of Charles Booth and Mary Catherine Booth," 161 fn.
Rogers, William, 174
Rogers, William B., 189
Rolfe, James, 41
Rollo, Andrew, 5th Baron (1700-65), 75, 289
Rollo, Charles, 284
Rollo Papers, 75
Rolls House, 88
Rolph, John, 34
Rolph, Thomas, 34
Rolph family, 34
Romaine, W.G., 13
Roman Catholic Church, *see* Catholic Church
Romanoff Land and Mining Co., 36
Romany Collection, 238
Romilly, Sir Samuel (1757-1818), 161
Romney, Earl of, *see* Sidney [or Sydney], Henry (1641-1704)
Romney, Customs records, 89
Ronquillo, Don Pedro, 10
Rooke, W.F.H., 34
Rookes, George, 10
Roos, Lord (*styled thus, though erroneously, till 1679*), *see* Manners, John, 1st Duke of Rutland (1638-1711)
Roos, C.F., 280
Roosevelt, Edith Kermit (Carew), Mrs. Theodore Roosevelt (1861-1948), 16
Roosevelt, Eleanor (1884-1962), 113, 178, 255
Roosevelt, Franklin Delano (1882-1945), 112, 113, 138, 139, 166, 205, 210, 255, 279, 280, 281, 282, 283
Roosevelt, Franklin D., Library, 283
Roosevelt, James R., 39
Roosevelt, Nicholas (1767-1854), 226
Roosevelt, Theodore (1858-1919), 16, 30, 65, 74, 78, 113, 116, 143, 146, 147, 164-5 *passim*, 196-9 *passim*, 206, 209, 224, 225, 256, 257, 345
Root, Elihu (1845-1937), 30, 197, 198, 199, 205, 238, 277, 278
Roper–Curzon, Henry Francis, 14th Baron Teynham (1767-1842), 104
Rosati, Joseph (1789-1843), 171
Roscoe, W.S., 183
Roscoe, William (1753-1831), 9, 182
Roscoe, Clarke & Roscoe, 183
Roscoe Papers, 182-3
Rose, Alexander, 50
Rose, George (1744-1818), 66, 83, 258
Rose, Sir George Henry (1771-1855), 240
Rose, Hugh Henry, Baron Strathnairn (1801-85), 66
Rose, Sir John (1820-88), 202
Rose, Lewis, 151
Rose, Philip, 40
Rose, William, 253
Rose Downs and Thompson Ltd., 43

Rose family, 330
Rose of Kilravock Muniments, 291
Rose Papers, 66, 258
Ross, Archibald, 146
Ross, Charles, 280
Ross, Daniel, 298
Ross, David, & Co., 8
Ross, George, 285, 312
Ross, Hercules, 287
Ross, J., Esq., Mss., 270
Ross, John (*fl.* 1775-90), 297, 298
Ross, John (*fl.* 1781), 312
Ross, Munro, 298
Ross, Walter, 296
Ross, William, 131
Ross and Mill, Messrs., 262
Ross Estate Muniments, 286
Ross of Pitcalnie Muniments, 298
Rosslyn, 1st Earl of, *see* Wedderburn, Alexander (1733-1805)
Rotch, Francis, 99
Rotherham, North Yorkshire, 231
Rotherham Central Library, 231
Rothery, Henry Cadogan (1817-88), 133, 136
Rothwell, Richard (1800-68), 326
Rothwell, Richard, Jr., 326
Rothwell family, 326
Round Papers, 31
Round Table, 278, 280, 283
Round Table groups, 276-80 *passim*, 283
Routledge, George, & Co., 170
Routledge and Kegan Paul Ltd., 170
Rowan, William, 348
Rowan Papers, 348
Rowell, N.W., 277, 284
Rowland, George R., 246
Rowland, Henry Augustus (1848-1901), 147, 162
Rowley, Sir Joshua (1730?-90), 101
Roxburgh, Duke of, *see* Ker, John, 3rd Duke of (1740-1804)
Roxburghe, Duke of, Mss., 270
Roy, Rammohun, 96
Roy, Thomas, 262
Royal African Company, 21, 25, 160, 203
Royal Agricultural Society, 11
Royal Air Force, 113, 124
Royal American Regiment (60th), 195
Royal Archives, Windsor, 126, 127
Royal Artillery Institution, 145
Royal Atlantic Steam Navigation Co., 111
Royal Botanic Gardens Library, Kew, 145-6
Royal Commission on Historical Mss., 224 fn.
Royal Commonwealth Society, 146
Royal Cornwall Gazette, 20
Royal Empire Society (*now* Royal Commonwealth Society), *Subject Catalogue of the Library*, 146 fn.
Royal Geographical Society, 146-7
Royal Geological Society, 20
Royal Horticultural Society, 147, 148
Royal Institute of International Affairs, American Section, 165, 277, 278, 279, 281
Royal Institution of Cornwall, 20
Royal Institution of Great Britain, 147; 141 fn.
Royal Irish Academy, 350
Royal Navy, 15, 105, 120, 122, 123, 143, 225, 269, 277, 278, 288, 300, 303, 311; *see also* Admiralty; Navy
Royal Northern Yacht Club Mss., 269
Royal School of Mines, 162
Royal Society, 147-8; 170, 187
Royal Society of Arts, 148-51
Royal Society of Literature, 26
Royal William (American ship), 17
Ruberg, Alfred, 68
Ruby (ship), 294
Ruel, James, 351
Rugby, Warwickshire, 224-5
Rugeley Papers, 9
Ruggles, Brig. Gen., 302
Ruggles, Thomas (1737?-1813), 149, 150
Ruggles Bequest, 318-9
Rugs, Trade, 211
Rum: Duties, 302; Trade, 18, 89, 234, 237
Rumford, Count von, *see* Thompson, Sir Benjamin (1753-1814)
Rumford Letters, 147
Runciman, Walter, 1st Viscount Runciman of Doxford (1870-1949), 200, 224
Runciman Papers, 224
Runcorn, Customs records, 94
Runkle, John Daniel (1822-1902), 148
Rush, Benjamin (1745-1813), 170, 183, 275, 305
Rush, Benjamin (1811-77), 69, 202
Rush, Richard (1780-1859), 25, 54, 57, 76, 167, 168, 186, 187, 206, 240
Ruskin, John (1819-1900), 176, 184
Russell, Mr., 288
Russell, Alexander, 271
Russell, Andrew, 311
Russell, Mrs. Ann, 86
Russell, Champion, 32
Russell, Edith (Lady Playfair), 162
Russell, Francis, 4th Earl of Bedford (1593-1641), 25
Russell, George, 73
Russell, James (*fl.* 1764-1804), 112
Russell, James (*fl.* 1770's), 86
Russell, James (*fl.* 1823), 271
Russell, John, 4th Duke of Bedford (1710-71), 65
Russell, Lord John, 1st Earl (1792-1878), 58, 59, 60, 71, 72, 104, 105, 111, 139, 202; *The Later Correspondence*, 139 fn.
Russell, Martha (1766-1807), 226
Russell, Mary (1768-1839), 226
Russell, Rollo, 205
Russell, Thomas, Sr. (*fl.* 1731), 226
Russell, Thomas (1767-1803), 351
Russell, Thomas Pougher (1775-1851), 73, 226
Russell, William, Sr. (*fl.* 1731), 226
Russell, William, Jr. (*fl.* 1731), 225, 226
Russell, William (1740-1818), 73, 226
Russell, William (*fl.* 1822), 271
Russell, William Howard, 158
Russell and Aitken Archives, 258
Russell Diaries, 226
Russell Family Papers, 225-6
Russell of Birmingham Papers, 73
Russell Papers, 32, 86, 139, 205
Russia: Cession of Alaska, 130; Relations with Great Britain, 200; Settlement in California, 75; Territorial convention with U.S., 1824, 25; *see also* Relations with Russia; Trade with Russia
Rutherford, John (*fl.* 1742), 290

Rutherford, William, 150
Rutherfurd, John (*fl.* 1749), 290
Rutherfurd, John (*fl.* 1758-60), 297
Rutherfurd, Walter, 295
Rutherfurd Papers, 258
Rutland, Duke of, 48
Rutland, 1st Duke of, *see* Manners, John (1638-1711); 4th Duke of, *see* Manners, Charles (1754-87); 5th Duke of, *see* Manners, John Henry (1778-1857)
Rutland, 5th Earl of, *see* Manners, Roger (1576-1612)
Rutland Papers, 48
Rutter, Thomas, 166
Ryan, John T., 345
Ryan, M.J., 345
Ryder, Dudley, Viscount Sandon and 1st Earl of Harrowby (1762-1847), 101, 274
Ryder, Dudley, 2nd Earl of Harrowby (1798-1882), 207
Ryder, Richard (1766-1832), 101, 102
Ryder Collection, 28
Rye, Customs records, 89, 94
Rye Mss., 221
Ryland, George H., 40, 232
Ryland, John (1753-1825), 245
Ryswick, Peace of (1697), 230

S

S.E.A.C., 139
Sabine, Sir Edward (1788-1883), 148
Sachs, Alexander, 280
Sackville, 1st Viscount, *see* Germain, George Sackville (1716-85)
Sackville of Knole, 2nd Baron, *see* Sackville–West, Sir Lionel Sackville (1827-1908)
Sackville, John Frederick, 3rd Duke of Dorset (1745-99), 32
Sackville–West, Sir Lionel Sackville, 2nd Baron Sackville of Knole (1827-1908), 37, 38, 129
Sackville Papers, 45
Saddleworth, Yorkshire, Business records, *see* Business records: Saddleworth, Yorkshire
Sadler, Richard, 246
Saffin, John, 42
Saffin, Rebecca, 42
St. Aldwyn, 1st Earl, *see* Hicks–Beach, Sir Michael Edward (1837-1916); 2nd Earl, *see* Hicks–Beach, Michael John (b. 1912)
St. Andrews University, 307
St. Cailor, Col., 262
St. Christopher, 14, 15; Trade, Colonial period, 34
  SANDY POINT, Customs collectors, 87
St. Clair, Arthur, 289
St. Clair [Sinclair], James (d. 1762), 269
St. Clair, Sir John, 284, 285
St. Deiniol's Library, 243 fn.
St. Germans, Earl of, 19
St. Helena, 288
St. Ives, Customs records, 89, 94
St. John's United Copper and Lead Mining Co., Newfoundland, Ltd., 124
St. Kitts, *see* St. Christopher
St. Lawrence River, 40, 119, 189; Island ceded to U.S., 84; Navigation, 84, 124, 144, 200, 272; Settlement, 166
St. Lucia, Attacks on, 102, 289
St. Luke's Hospital, New York, 75
St. Martin, 182
St. Mary Extra Parish Register, 36
St. Mary's Seminary, Baltimore, 30
St. Mathias River, 298
St. Paul-Minneapolis [and Manitoba] Railway, 105
St. Paul's Literary and Educational Society (*formerly* Bennett St. Sunday School Mutual Improvement Class), 179
St. Philip (snow), 292
St. Thomas, 130, 201, 202
Salcombe, Customs records, 94
Salem witchcraft trials, 176
Salesky, Bernard L., 180
Salford, Greater Manchester, 180; Customs records, 93
Salford Central Library, 180
Salisbury, Marquess of, 37-9; 37 fn.
Salisbury, 3rd Marquess of, *see* Cecil, Robert Arthur Talbot Gascoyne (1830-1903)
Salisbury, 3rd Marquess of, Papers, 37-9
Salisbury, 1st Earl of, *see* Cecil, Robert (1563?-1612)
Sally (American ship), 91
Sally (ship), 261
Salop Record Office, 211
Salt, Sir Thomas, Collection, 216
Salt: Duties, 303; Manufacture, 302; Trade, 35, 181, 182
Salter, Mr., 189
Salter, D.M., 39
Salter, Edward, 232
Saltonstall, Gurdon (1666-1724), 82, 83
Saltonstall, Richard (1586-1658), 24
Saltoun, Lord, Mss., 272
Saltpetre, 138, 149
Salvation Army, 151
Samoa, 230; *see also* Relations with Samoa; Trade with Samoa
Sample family, 329
Sampson, William (1764-1836), 325
Sampson (ship), 225
Sampson Low & Co., 40
Samuel, Herbert, 1st Viscount (1870-1963), 113, 282
Samuel Papers, 113
Samwell, David (1751-98), 182
San Juan Islands, 71, 72, 130, 201, 202
Sanctions, 20th century, 280
Sand, Black, 149
Sandeman, Robert, 319; *Letters of Theron*, 319
Sanders, A.H., *History of Aberdeen-Angus Cattle*, 319 fn.
Sanders, Thomas, 171
Sanderson, Sir Percy, 199
Sandford, Sheppard, 33
Sandford and Hughes Families' Papers, 32-3
Sandford Hall Collection, 211
Sandidge, J. M., 177
Sandilands, James, 9th Baron Torphichen (1759-1815), 262, 275
Sandilands, Robert, 309
Sandom, William, 139
Sandon, Viscount, *see* Ryder, Dudley, 1st Earl of Harrowby (1762-1847)
Sands, David, 31
Sands, G. & Hodgson, 224
Sandwich, 4th Earl of, *see* Montagu, John (1718-92)
Sandwich: Borough records, 44; Customs records, 89, 94
Sandwich Islands, *see* Hawaii
Sandwich Papers, 102
Sandys, Sir Edwin (1561-1629), 17, 44

Sandys, Ellin, 47
Sanford, Henry Shelton (1823-91), 69
Sanford (ship), 82
Sanger, Margaret, 79, 236
Sanitarian, 170
Sanitation, 170
Sankey, Ira D. (1840-1908), 255
Sanskrit literature, 71
Santa Magritta (ship), 62
Santo Domingo, *see* Dominican Republic; *see also* Immigrants from Santo Domingo
Sarah (ship), 291
Sargent, Charles Sprague (1841-1927), 146
Sargent, John Singer (1856-1925), 79, 178, 238
Sargent, Joseph, 95
Sarsaparilla, 148, 150
Saskatchewan, Description, 146
Saudi Arabia, Relations with U.S., *see* Relations with Saudi Arabia
Saunders, Lieut., 44
Saunders, R., 265
Saunders & Mellis, 310
Savage, H. W., 82
Savage, William (1770-1843), 147
Savery, Robert, 166
Savile, Sir George, 191
Savile Collection, 192
Savile–Lumley, J., 192
Savoy Church, London, 113
Sawmills, 40, 149, 150, 219
Saws, *see* Tools
Saxthorpe Parish Church, 189
Saxton, E.D., 246
Sayer Ms., 222
Sayers, J. E., and E. G. W. Bill, *Calendar of the Papers of Charles Thomas Longley, Archbishop of Canterbury, 1862-1868, in Lambeth Palace Library*, 115
Sayers, R. S., *Lloyds Bank*, 115
Scales, William, 179
Scarborough, North Yorkshire, 231; Customs records, 89, 94
Scarborough (ship), 265
Scarborough Borough Council, 231
Scarlett, Richard, 166
Scarth of Breckness Muniments, 299
Schacht, Hjalmar, 279
Scheiffelin, W. H., & Co., 51
Schenck, Robert Cumming (1809-90), 70, 71, 129
Schiff, Sydney, 78
Schiff, Mrs. Sydney, 78
Schiff Papers, 78
Schlesinger, Arthur (1888-1965), 165
Schofield, H., & Co., 173
Schofield, R. E., "Membership of the Lunar Society of Birmingham," *Annals of Science* (1956), 226 fn.
School of Oriental and African Studies, *see* London University, School of Oriental and African Studies
Schoolcraft, Henry Rowe (1793-1864), 146
Schrier, A., *Ireland and the American Emigration, 1850-1900*, 332 fn., 353 fn.
Schulenburg–Wolfsburg, Gebhard Gerhard, Freiherr von (1722-88), 227
Schurz, Carl (1829-1906), 68, 197
Schuyler, Eugene, 70
Schuyler, Peter (1657-1724), 40, 83, 262
Schuyler, Philip John (1733-1804), 150, 215, 258, 285, 324
Schuylkill River, Navigation, 174
Schwabe, Mrs. Salis, 178
Schwatka, Lieut., 146
Science: 18th century, 147, 174-5, 226, 275; 19th century, 15, 36, 147, 162-3 *passim*, 183, 196, 313; 20th century, 209; *see also* Botany and botanists; Birds; Mathematical instruments; Mechanics; Minerals; Quadrupeds, Oviparous; Serpents; Zoopraxiscope
Scientific cooperation, 123
Scientific instruments, Trade, 51
Scilly, Customs records, 94
Scolten, William, 219
Scorpion (ship), 144
Scotia (ship), 254
Scotland, *see* Immigrants from Scotland; Trade with Scotland
Scott, Mr., 132
Scott, Alexander, 304
Scott, Buchanan, 100
Scott, Charles Prestwich (1846-1932), 279
Scott, Eliza (Huxley), 162
Scott, Francis, 311
Scott, George (*fl.* 1678), 260
Scott, George (*fl.* 1851), 114
Scott, Henry, 3rd Duke of Buccleuch (1746-1812), 303
Scott, Hugh (*fl.* 1781), 292
Scott, Hugh, of Gala (*fl.* 1791), 303
Scott, Mrs. Isabel, Mss., 271
Scott, J. Raymond, 271
Scott, J. W., 245
Scott, James, 292
Scott, Messrs. James, & Sons, 271
Scott, James Brown, 281
Scott, John (*fl.* 1700-1), 306
Scott, Sir John, of Ancrum (*fl.* 1700-1), 306
Scott, John, 1st Earl of Eldon (1751-1838), 288
Scott, Sir Leslie (1869-1950), 228
Scott, Patrick, 306
Scott, Thomas, 303
Scott, Walter, of Harden (*fl.* 1755), 292
Scott, Sir Walter (1771-1832), 69
Scott, Walter Francis, 5th Duke of Buccleuch (1806-84), 272, 289
Scott, Wm., 22
Scott, Winfield (1786-1866), 77
Scott & Cryer, 265
Scott & Robertson Ltd., Mss., 271
Scott of Ancrum Muniments, 306
Scott of Gala Mss., 262
Scottish American Development Corp. Ltd., 308
Scottish American Land Co. Ltd., 308
Scottish American Mortgage Co. Ltd., 307
Scottish Californian Orange and Vineyard Co. Ltd., 308
Scottish Education Department, 311 fn.
Scottish Home and Health Department, 311
Scottish Land Restoration Union, 100
Scottish Mortgage and Land Investment Co. of New Mexico Ltd., 308
Scottish Pacific Coast Mining Co. Ltd., 308
Scottish Record Office, 272-312; 90 fn., 259; *List of American Documents*, 79, 259 fn., 272
Scottish Typographical Association, 9, 254
Scotts, Job, 31
Scripture, Edward Wheeler, 74

Scrogie, William, 312
Sea Island cotton, 183
Sea King (ship), *see Shenandoah*
Seabury, Samuel (1729-96), 253
Seabury consecration, 253
Seafield, 1st Earl of, *see* Ogilvy, James (1664-1730)
Seafield Muniments, 304-5
Seaforth, Lord, *see* Humberston, Francis Mackenzie (1754-1815)
Seaforth Muniments, 286
Sealing, *see* Bering Sea Controversy
Seaman, George, 298
Seamen, 77, 90, 105, 124, 131, 137, 201, 288; *see also* Impressment of seamen
Seamen, British, 57, 78, 125, 201, 288
Search, Right of, 59, 69, 77, 101, 121, 168
Seaton, 1st Baron, *see* Colborne, Sir John (1778-1863)
Seaton of Parbroath, 271
Seaton Papers, 102
Second chambers, *see* Bicameralism
Securities, *see* Investments
Sedgwick, Catharine Maria (1789-1867), 176
Sedgwick, Edward, 79
Sedgwick, Ellery (b. 1872), 197, 199
Seebohm, Benjamin (1798-1871), 40, 41, 156
Seebohm, Esther, 41
Seebohm Mss., 40-1
Seeley, Miss A. E., 15
Seeley, Sir John Robert (1834-95), 15
Selborne, 1st Earl of, *see* Palmer, Sir Roundell (1812-95)
Selden, Cary, 150
Self, Mr., 166
Selkirk, 5th Earl of, *see* Douglas, Thomas (1771-1820)
Sellers, Coleman (1827-1907), 162
Selwyn, William, 49
Senate, 16, 38, 70, 72, 156, 164, 197, 279, 280; Foreign Relations Committee, 68
Senhouse, Humphrey, 21
Senhouse of Netherhall Maryport Records, 21
Serapis (H.M.S.), 43, 92
Serjeant, W., 105
Serjeant, W. R., "The Tarleton Papers," *Liverpool Libraries . . . Bulletin* (1956), 181 fn.
Serle, Ambrose (1742-1812), 216
Serpents, 170
Session, Court of, 307; Productions, 309-10
Seth, James, 256
Seton, Sir Malcolm, 280
Seven Years War (1756-63), 12, 28, 31, 42, 45, 47, 79, 102, 119, 140, 152, 203, 222, 240, 256, 264, 266, 271, 272, 274, 285, 289, 292, 297, 299, 301, 304, 312, 328; British Army, 36, 55, 74, 101, 119, 140, 143, 195, 222, 230, 260, 261, 262, 264, 285, 286, 289, 290, 291, 293, 298, 302, Supplies, 222, 264, 275, 284, 285, 291, 304
CAMPAIGNS: Canada, 74, 85, 119, 218, 259, 323, Guadeloupe, 289, Halifax, 119, Lake Champlain, 264, Lake George, 260, Louisbourg, 45, 74, 119, 145, 230, 249, 266, 284, 289, Montreal, 45, Newfoundland, 45, Nova Scotia, 259, Ohio River, 82, 92, 262, 285, 312, Quebec, 45, 74, 119, 189, 191, 240, 275, 293, 323, St. John's, 119, St. Lawrence River, 119, Ticonderoga, 31, 82, 264, 274, 289, 293, 300, 304, West Indies, 74, 266, Woods Creek, 260
CAUSES, 239; Courts martial, 144, 144 fn.; Deserters, 285; Economic effects, 50, 299; Indian troops, 262, 301; Medical services, 284, 285; Naval operations, 219, 230, 260; Peace, 52, 140 fn., 141, 195; Personal narratives, 45, 74, 261, 293, 323, 346; Prisoners, 285; Reconnaissance, 285; Recruiting, 284, 285, 300, 301
Seventh Cavalry, 5
Severn (man-of-war), 260
Sewall, Jonathan (1728-96), 55
Sewall, Samuel (1652-1730), 99 fn.
Seward, Anna (1747-1809), 102; *Monody on Major André*, 102
Seward, William Henry (1801-72), 18, 58, 60, 61, 68, 111, 169, 201, 216, 227
Seward Peninsular Railway Co., 268
Seymour, Charles, 280
Seymour, Edward Adolphus Seymour, 12th Duke of Somerset (1804-85), 13, 121
Seymour, E. J., 225
Seymour, Sir George Francis (1787-1870), 225, 267
Seymour, Henry G., 225
Seymour of Ragley Collection, 225
Sforza, Count Carlo, 282
Shaftesbury, 1st Earl of, *see* Cooper, Anthony Ashley (1621-83)
Shairp of Houstoun Muniments, 275
Shakers, 15, 22, 39, 325; *see also* Communitarianism
Shakespear, John, 150
Shakespeare, William (1564-1616), 314
Shannan, Alexander, 288
Shannon (H.M.S.), 219
Shannon, Livingston & Co., 310
Shannon, Stewart & Co., 310
Shardeloes Papers (Amersham), 13
Shares, *see* Investments
Sharp, Alexander, & Co., 318
Sharp, Granville (1735-1813), 216
Sharp, Hugh, Collection, 258
Sharp, J.F., 113
Sharp, John, Jr., 178
Sharp & Mackenzie, 309
Sharpe, Horatio (1718-90), 64, 195, 285
Sharpe, Sutton, 169
Sharpe, William, 195
Sharples, Ellen (Wallace), Mrs. James Sharples (1769-1849), 6, 7
Sharples, James (1750?-1811), 6, 7, 16
Shaver, Mr., 111, 131
Shaw, Albert, 164, 197, 199
Shaw, Alexander, 290
Shaw, Annie, 347
Shaw, B., 28
Shaw, C. G., 289
Shaw, Frank G., 347
Shaw, Mrs. Frank G., 347
Shaw, George Bernard (1856-1950), 78, 164; Papers, 78
Shaw, George L., 280
Shaw, James, 287
Shaw, M. S., *Some Family Papers of the Hunters of Hunterston*, 290
Shaw, Richard, 212
Shaw, Robert, 327
Shaw, S., 28
Shaw, Sarah B., 347
Shaw, W. B., Library, 158
Shaw & Fisher, 235
Shaw family, 190
Shaw–Lefevre, George John, Baron Eversley (1831-1928), 260, 261; *The Partitions of Poland*, 261

Shaw–LeFevre, Sir John George (1797-1879), 106
Shawe, J.G., 230
Shawfield Papers, 316
Shea, John Dawson Gilmary (1824-92), 61
Shearman, Robert, 21
Shedden, Robert, & Sons, 161
Shedden, William, 161, 273
Shedden Papers, 161
Shee, Annesley, 350
Sheep, 137, 150, 255, 289, 291, 308
Sheffield, 1st Earl of, *see* Holroyd, John Baker (1735-1821)
Sheffield, 4th Baron, *see* Stanley, Edward Lyulph (1839-1925)
Sheffield, South Yorkshire, 232-7
Sheffield City Library, Department of Local History and Archives, 232-6; 240
Sheffield Female Anti-Slavery Society, 176
Sheffield Independent, 236
Sheffield Smelting Co., 235-6
Sheffield University, Library, 236-7
Shelburne, 2nd Earl of, *see* Petty, William, 1st Marquis of Lansdowne (1737-1805)
Sheldon, Alfred, 131
Shenandoah (Confederate ship), 201, 311
Shepardson, Whitney, 278, 279, 280, 281; *The United States in World Affairs*, 281
Shepherd, Frances (Nicholson), Mrs. William Shepherd (d. 1829), 208
Shepherd, Thomas, 74
Shepherd, William (1768-1847), 208
Shepherd and Wedderburn Collection, 304
Shepherd Mss., 208
Shepperson, G., "Harriet Beecher Stowe and Scotland, 1852-53," *Scottish Historical Review* (1953), 316 fn.
Shepperson, W.S., *British Emigration to North America* (1957), 163 fn.
Sherard, William (1659-1728), 147
Sherard Collection, 200
Sherb, Christopher, 149
Sherborn, Charles Davies (d. 1942), 66
Sherborn Autographs, 66
Sherborn Bequest, 75
Sherborne Castle, Dorset, 29
Sherburne, Sir Edward (1618-1702), 312
Sheridan, Sir Henry, 287
Sheridan, Philip Henry (1831-88), 347
Sherman, John (1823-1900), 71
Sherman, T., 178
Sherman, William Tecumseh (1820-91), 61, 232, 256
Sherwen, William, 18; Mss., 18
Sherwin, Capt., 130
Sherwood, Joseph, 302
Shields, North, Customs records, 94
Shields, South, Customs records, 94
Shiels, James, 347
Shiels Letters, 347
Shiffner family, 221
Shiffner Mss., 221
Shillitoe, Thomas, 47
Shipbuilding, 7, 56, 68, 89, 90, 92, 119, 120, 149, 150, 191, 269, 276-9 *passim*, 286, 311; *see also* Timber
Shipley, Mr., 175
Shipley, William (1714-1803), 150
Shippen, William, 317
Shipping, 38, 42, 43, 56, 57, 99, 123, 124, 128, 131, 137, 138, 161, 286, 298, 302, 303; Rates, 131, 161, 183, 277
BRITISH, 34, 55, 56, 75, 86-94 *passim*, 99, 124, 126, 132, 140, 160, 161, 180, 181, 182, 183, 185, 195, 250, 262, 301, 306-11 *passim*, 315, 319, 326, 332; *see also subdivision* Shipping *under* Liverpool *and* London
See also Blockade; Embargo; Privateering; Prizes; Seamen; Search, Right of; Trade; *and subdivision* Shipping *under states*
Ships, 30, 130, 130 fn.; Log books, 15, 120, 122, 123, 184, 219, 225, 239, 269, 310, 316, 326, 349; Passenger, 125, 137, 156, 325, 326, 331, 351; Quarantine, 90, 349, 350; Registration, 56, 93-4, 349; *see also* Packet ships; Steamships; *and names of individual ships*
Shipwrecks, 291, 295, 296, 311
Shireburn, Charles, 171
Shirehall Collection, 211
Shirley, William (1694-1771), 32, 64, 101, 300, 301; Correspondence, 64 fn.
Shoe machinery, 211
Shoemakers Union of New York City, 345
Shoes, Trade, 269
Shomberg, Henry, 259
Shoolbred, James, 33
Shoolbred, John, 33
Shore, John (*fl.* 1784), 313
Shoreham, Customs records, 94
Short, Algernon L. H., 50
Short, Charles Wilkins (1794-1863), 145
Shorter, Clement King (1857-1926), 238
Shotwell, James T., 278, 280
Shrewsbury, Duke of, *see* Talbot, Charles (1660-1718)
Shrewsbury, Shropshire, 211
Shrewsbury Corporation, 211
Shropshire, England, 210-1
Shropshire Record Office, *see* Salop Record Office
Shubrick, Thomas, 150
Shurtleff, N. B., ed., *Records of the Governor and Company of the Massachusetts Bay*, 194 fn.
Shuttleworth, Mr., 176
Shuttleworth, Ashton, 234
Shuttleworth, John, 234, 237
Sickles, Daniel Edgar (1825-1914), 59, 60, 201
Sidgwick, Henry, 259
Sidmouth, Viscount, 25 fn.
Sidmouth, 1st Viscount, *see* Addington, Henry (1757-1844)
Sidmouth Papers, 25
Sidney (or Sydney), Henry, Earl of Romney (1641-1704), 189
Sidney, Robert, Viscount Lisle and 1st Earl of Leicester (1563-1626), 44
Sidney Papers, 44
Siegfried, André, *America Comes of Age*, 278
Sierra Buttes Mines, 211
Sierra Leone: Colonization by Negroes, 43, 51; Vice-Admiralty Court, 33
Signet Office, 136
Sigsworth, E. M., *Black Dyke Mills*, 238 fn.
Silas Greenman (ship), 137
Silk manufacture and trade, 148-51 *passim*, 161, 269, 301, 302
Sill, Jane (Todhunter), Mrs. Joseph Sill, 217
Sill, Joseph, 217
Silliman, Benjamin (1779-1864), 51, 183, 258
Silloth, Customs records, 93
Silver mining, 265, 307

Silver party, 85
Silver Question, 52, 85, 161, 163, 172, 209; *see also* Bimetallism; Gold
Silver-plated ware, Trade, 234
Sim, P., 312
Simcoe, John Graves (1752-1806), 24, 25, 257
Simcoe Papers, 24
Simmeral, Samuel, 329
Simmons, G. & W., 234
Simms, Robert, 331
Simms, William Gilmore (1806-70), 74
Simon, E. D., Lord Simon of Wythenshawe (1879-1960), 179
Simon, Sir John, 1st Viscount (1873-1954), 166, 275, 280, 281
Simon Papers, 179
Simonds, Frank, *The Price of Peace*, 280
Simpkinson, Francis Guillemard (*later* De Wesselow), 15
Simpson, James (*fl.* 1771-99), 300
Simpson, James (*fl.* 1795-6), 28
Simpson, Juliana, 97
Simpson, Louis (b. 1923), 178
Simpson, M. C. M., ed., *Conversations with M. Thiers...*, 204; *Conversations with Distinguished Persons...*, 204
Simpson, W. G., 254
Simpson, William, 300
Simson, Nathan, 126
Sinclair, Albert T., 238
Sinclair, Sir Archibald, 280
Sinclair, George, 203
Sinclair, James, *see* St. Clair, James (d. 1762)
Sinclair, Sir John (1754-1835), 286
Sinclair, John (*fl.* late 19th cent.), 332
Sinclair, Margaret, 332
Sinclair, Mrs. Mary, 78
Sinclair, Mary Ann, 332
Sinclair, Upton (1878-1968), 78
Sinclair, William (*fl.* 1772-1815), 291
Sinclair, Sir William (*fl.* 1906-7), 307
Sinclair, Brebner & Co., 309
Sinclair of Freswick Muniments, 291
Sinclar, David, 47
Sing, William, 212
Sing Sing, New York, 185
Single tax, 100, 177
Single Tax, 100
Sinnett, Alfred Percy, Mahatma Papers, 74
Sion College, 151-2
Sitwell, Lady, 238
Sivilla Merchant (ship), 129
Sixsmith, Charles F., 177
Size of U.S., 68
Skeene, P., 150
Skene, P. O., 245
Skene, Robert, 275
Skillin, Byron W., 281
Skinner, John (1744-1816), 253
Skinner, W., 260
Skinner, W. S., 286
Skrine, F. H., 259
Slagg, John, 69
Slave trade, 6, 7, 18, 21, 25, 33, 47, 57, 63, 64, 67, 70, 80, 92, 105, 106, 123, 129, 132-3 *passim*, 136, 138, 153, 155, 157, 160, 168, 169, 175, 181-4 *passim*, 188, 195, 196, 203, 207-8 *passim*, 212, 213, 256, 266, 273, 274, 284, 301, 309, 316, 317, 330, 331, 344, 347; *see also* Search, Right of
Slavery, 23, 24, 26, 29, 32, 41, 46, 52, 77, 105, 106, 158, 159, 162, 184, 185, 202, 207, 208, 225, 226, 240, 318, 325, 326, 347, and the churches, 103, 155-7 *passim*, 176
ANTI-SLAVERY MOVEMENTS, 6, 29-30, 51, 59, 62, 95, 96, 153, 157, 168, 169, 176, 177, 185, 192, 200, 201, 204-6 *passim*, 232, 270, 316, 318, 344, 347, 350
EMANCIPATION, 32, 50, 61, 68, 69, 70, 95, 132, 155, 156, 188, 297, 347, *see also* Emancipation Proclamation, 1862; Emancipation Society; Harpers Ferry, John Brown's raid, 1859
FUGITIVE SLAVES, 95, 132, 136, 139, 176, 200, 232, *see also* Compromise of 1850; Insurrections, 188, 195, 306, 307
CUBA, 60; Florida, 50, 67, 77, 266, 297, 323; Georgia, 6, 103, 183, 331; Kansas, 201, 222, 244; Kentucky, 328; Louisiana, 63, 67, 70, 344; Maryland, 30, 175, 309; New England, 203; New Jersey, 203; New York, 32, 274, 295; North Carolina, 297; Rhode Island, 62; South Carolina, 6, 50, 175, 270, 298, 304, 330; Texas, 67, 206, 274; Virginia, 63, 304, 312, 330
Slidell, John (1793-1871), 59, 69, 204
Slipper, Thomas, 189
Slipper, William Haddon, 189
Sloan, James, 328
Small, John, 295, 296, 297
Small, William, 226
Smallcroft, Mrs., 183
Smalley, George, 158
Smallpox, 155, 297, 299, 314
Smart, Adam, 299
Smeal, William (1792-1877), 316; Collection, 316
Smeaton, John (1724-92), 298
Smedes, Mrs. S. D., *Memorials of a Southern Planter*, 73
Smelt, Robert, 225
Smiley, Samuel, 326
Smith, Miss A., 75
Smith, Adam (1723-90), 317
Smith, Al (1873-1944), 248
Smith, Caleb Blood (1808-64), 245
Smith, Frederick, *Coventry, 600 Years of Municipal Life*, 228 fn.
Smith, George M., 277
Smith, Gerrit (1797-1874), 96
Smith, Goldwin (1823-1910), 37, 52, 71, 196
Smith, Green C. (1832-95), 344
Smith, H.W., and J. Fiske, *The Presidents of America*, 62
Smith, Haddon, 324
Smith, Hannah, 328
Smith, J., 95
Smith, James Youngs (1809-76), 68
Smith, John (1580-1631), 52; *The Seaman's Grammar*, 49; *A True Reflection of such Occurrences...as hath Happened in Virginia*, 187
Smith, John (*fl.* 1826-33), 303
Smith, John Abel (1801-71), 104
Smith, John Adams, 167
Smith, John Benjamin (1794-1879), 179
Smith, Joseph, 174
Smith, Mary, 166
Smith, N. Kemp, 315
Smith, Nathan (1762-1829), 170
Smith, Mrs. Oakes, *Sanctity of Marriage*, 84
Smith, Owen Hugh, 265
Smith, Philip (*fl.* 1852-3), 347
Smith, Philip (*fl.* 1863), 270
Smith, Rennie, 278
Smith, Richard (1784-1824), 156, 156 fn.
Smith, Richard (*fl.* 1794), 161
Smith, Robert (1757-1842), 77

Smith, Robert (*fl.* 1851-60), 219
Smith, Robert Fisher, 219
Smith, Roland, "Manchester as a Centre for the Manufacture and Merchanting of Cotton Goods, 1820-1830," *Birmingham University Historical Journal* (1953), 175 fn.
Smith, Samuel (*fl.* 1746), 290
Smith, Samuel (*fl.* 1767), 214
Smith, Sir Sidney, *see* Smith, Sir William Sidney (1764-1840)
Smith, Southwood, 167
Smith, Bishop Thomas (*fl.* 1812), 171
Smith, Thomas, Sr. (d. 1823), 217
Smith, Thomas, Jr. (*fl.* 1819), 217
Smith, Thomas (*fl.* 1830), 174
Smith, W.J., ed., *The Grenville Papers*, 65
Smith, Walter, 330
Smith, William (1727-1803), 150
Smith, William (1728-93), 213, 265
Smith, William (1797-1887), 245
Smith, William L., *Comparative View of the Constitutions of the Several States*, 167
Smith, Sir William Sidney, *known as* Sir Sidney Smith (1764-1840), 287
Smith, William Stephens (1755-1816), 80
Smith, William Tasker, 61
Smith family, 329
Smith–Masters Papers, 45
Smithers, Rachel, 209
Smithsonian Institution, 146, 148
Smoking, 208
Smuggling, 7, 10, 90-2 *passim*, 249, 302, 304, 310
Smuts, Jan Christian (1870-1950), 278, 279, 280, 281, 282, 283
Smyth, A. H., ed., *The Writings of Benjamin Franklin*, 188
Smyth, F., 148
Smyth, George Stacey, 36
Smyth, Henry, 263
Smyth, John (1567-1641), 33
Smyth, Sir Robert (1744-1802), 32
Smyth of Nibley Papers, 33
Smyth Papers, 32
Smythe of Balhary Mss., 263
Sneyd Family Papers, 213
Snodgrass & Coy., 325
Snow, Robert (*fl.* 1770), 39
Snow, Robert (*fl.* 1782), 346
Snow, Thomas, 33
Snow, William, 346
Snow, William Parker, 224
Snowden, Philip, Viscount (1864-1937), 238
Snowe, W., 83
Snyder, John (b. 1895), 166
Social Democracy of America, 314
Social Science Research Council, New York, 280
Social sciences, 168
Socialism, 78, 113, 163, 165, 173, 228; *see also* Anarchism; Labour movement
Socialist Party of America, 187
Socialist Workers' Party (USA), 228
Socianism, 16
Société Jersiaise, 339
Society for Constructive Birth Control and Racial Progress, 79
Society for Promoting Christian Knowledge, 152
Society for the Diffusion of Useful Knowledge, 169
Society for the Encouragement of Arts, Manufactures, and Commerce, 148
Society for the Propagation of the Gospel in Foreign Parts, 158-9; 8, 105, 113, 115, 203
Society for the Propagation of the Gospel in New England, 98-9, 151, 190, 217
Society in Scotland for Propagating Christian Knowledge, 313; Records, 289-90
Society of Antiquaries of Scotland Collection, 290
Society of Authors Archive, 79
Society of Jesus, English Province, Department of Historiography and Archives, 157
Society of the Sons of St. George, 101
Soden, E., 351
Solly, Mr., 176
Solly, R.M., 151
Sombrero, 130
Somers, John, Baron (1651-1716), 220
Somers Islands, *see* Bermuda
Somers Islands Co., 23
Somers Papers, 220
Somerset, 12th Duke of, *see* Seymour, Edward Adolphus Seymour (1804-85)
Somerset, England, 211-2
Somerset (ship), 22
Somerset Papers, 13
Somerset Record Office, 211-2
Somervell, John, *Isaac and Rachel Wilson, Quakers of Kendal, 1714-1785*, 155 fn.
Somervell, Tweedie, 294
Somerville, Mary, Papers, 200
Somerville, W.C., 183
Sondes, Lord Lewis, 314
Sonmans, Arent, 311
Sonmans, Johanna, 311
Sonmans, Peter, 58
Sonmans, Stron, 311
Sons of Liberty, 48, 143, 315
Sophia (mulatto child), 297
Soroptimist clubs: Bunning, California, 19; Old Chester, Pennsylvania, 19
Sotheby Papers, 190
Soulé, Pierre (1801-70), 200, 201
South Africa, 113; *see also* Relations with South Africa
South African War, 1899-1902, *see* Boer War (1899-1902)
South America: Relations with Europe, 54; *see also* Relations with South America
South Carolina: Colonial period, 36, 140, 141, 160, 195, 203, 255, 265, 289, 294, 299, 312; 1765-75, 65, 214, 215; 1776-83, 9, 48, 65, 90, 139, 212, 257, 293, 298, 300, 305, 313, 350, 351; 1783-1861, 9, 34, 35, 78, 207; Civil War, 1861-5, 60, 326
AGRICULTURE, 149, 160, 287, 299, 300, 330; Army, 64; Assembly, 214, 300; Banking, 117, 181; Boundaries, 102, with Georgia, 15; Clay, 212; Climate, 32, 62, 160; Currency, 7, 62, 139; Customs administration, 350; Description, 62, 199, 256, 299; Epidemics, 32, 138, 314, 330, 349; Finance, 100, 270, 309; Fires, 292, 300; Forts, 264, 284, 299; Governors, 17, 76, 160, 212, 214, 218, 223, 226, 228, 266, 274, 275, 284, 285, 299; Immigrants, 32, 50, 217, 276, 299, 304, 323, 330, 331; Indians, 50, 66, 160, 284, 299; Land, 6, 9, 24, 50, 55, 218, 219, 222, 225, 253, 261, 270, 300; Land grants, 112, 189, 300; Land tenure, 300; Law, 225, 299; Loyalists, 6, 17, 323; Merchants, 212, 271, 299, 304; Negroes, 201, 330; Plants, 147; Politics, 299, 300; Religious history, 28, 85, 117, 143, 144, 154, 155, 159, 309, 352; Settlement, 9, 140; Shipping,

268, 299, 315; Silk production, 149, 150; Slavery, 6, 50, 175, 270, 298, 304, 330; Timber, 150; Trade, 31, 50, 56, 62, 99, 122, 160, 173, 175, 211, 212, 234, 235, 299, 300, 304, 309, 310, 325, 332
ABBEVILLE, 330; Broad River, 304; Charleston, 32, 36, 49, 50, 57, 67, 74, 77, 80, 90, 125, 138, 184, 212, 267, 268, 269, 275, 276, 293, 298, 299, 300, 305, 309, 310, 311, 312, 314, 330, 331, 332, 349, 351, Consular reports (British), 130, Customs collectors, 87, 350, Description, 34, 45, 159, 299, 312, 325, Merchants, 99, 112, 175, 183, 225, 261, 265, 304, 325; Cherokee Country, Ayoree, 212; Fairfield, 331; Georgetown, 50, 297, 299, 330; James Island, 309; Ninety-Six District, 300; Port Royal, 273, 299, 300; Purisburgh, 151; Red Bank, 304; Saludy River, 300; Wando River, 309; Winyah Bay, 62
South Carolina Historical Magazine, 312 fn.
South Carolina Historical Society, 203
South Dakota: Indians, 5; Ranching, 348
ABERDEEN, CONSULAR REPORTS (BRITISH), 134; Fall River County, 348; Wounded Knee, 5
South Glamorgan, Wales, 249-50
South Sea Company, 292
South Shields, Tyne and Wear, 224
South Tyneside Libraries, 224
South West Kansas Land and Irrigation Co., 98
Southall, Anna Mary, 155
Southampton, 3rd Earl of, *see* Wriothesley, Henry (1573-1624)
Southampton, Hampshire, 35-6; Customs records, 89, 90, 94; Shipping, 35
Southampton City Record Office, 35-6
Southampton Dock Co., 35
Southampton Record Society, 35
Southard, Samuel Lewis (1787-1842), 206
Souther, Messrs., 250
Southern Citizen, 326
Southern colonies, 265; Description, 291; Religious history, 158
Southern Independence Association, 67, 232
Southern states, 72, 202, 276, 283; Debts, 274; Education, 96; Epidemics, 261; Land tenure, 68; Manners and customs, 39, 325; Scenery, 39; Trade, 46; *see also* Confederate States
Southesk, Earl of, Mss., 268
Southey, Robert (1774-1843), 182
Southwark Diocesan Curia, 157
Southwark Mss., 154
Southwell, Edward (1671-1730), Papers, 57
Southwell, Edward (*fl.* 1766), 262
Southwell Papers, 7
Southwick, Solomon, 286
Southwold, Customs records, 89
Spafford, Horatio Gates, 94
Spain, T. D., 75
Spain: Colonies, 16-7, 25, 54, 57, 97, 140, 352; Relations with France, 16; Relations with Great Britain, 80; *see also* Relations with Spain; Trade with Spain
Spalding, James (of East Florida), 295
Spalding, James (of Edinburgh), 295
Spalding, Lyman (1775-1821), 170
Spanish-American War (1898), 38, 132, 142, 164, 197, 329; Causes, 85, 259; Claims, 131; Effect on trade, 118; Naval operations, 123, 142; Neutrality, British, 131, 137; Peace, 39, 131; Red Cross, 142; *see also* Cuba: Revolution (1895-8); Philippine Islands: Insurrection (1896-8)
Sparks, Jared (1789-1866), 75, 95; *Life and Works of Benjamin Franklin*, 275
Sparling, John, 182
Sparling & Bolden, 182
Sparrow, Jackson, 98
Speakman, J., & Co., 175
Spear & Jackson Ltd., 236
Spectator, 113
Spedding, John, 21
Speedwell (ship), 44
Speirs, Alexander, 258, 263
Spelling reform, 228
Spence, James, 232
Spence Mss., 154
Spencer, Benjamin, 234
Spencer, Charles, 3rd Earl of Sunderland (1674-1722), 193
Spencer, John Poyntz, 5th Earl (1835-1910), 140
Spencer, Nicholas, 42
Spencer, Nicholas Cole, 42
Spencer, William, 42
Spencer Stanhope of Cannon Hall (Cannon Hall Muniments), 234
Spencer–Stanhope Collection, 237
Spender, J. A., 282, 283
Spenser, J. W. W., 315
Sperling, Henry, 31
Sperling, John, 31
Sperling Papers, 31
Sperry Gyroscope Corp., 113
Sphere, London, 238
Spices, 148
Spiritualism, 173
Spoils system, *see* Corruption (in politics)
Spotten, Bert, 327
Spottiswood [or Spotswood], Alexander (1676-1740), 203, 260
Sprague, William Buell (1795-1876), 84, 85, 94, 103, 183, 234; *Annals of the American Pulpit*, 84
Sprague Papers, 84-5
Spring, Gardiner (1785-1873), 245
Spring, Robert, 272
Spring–Rice, Sir Cecil Arthur (1859-1918), 16, 77, 135, 163, 198, 199, 200, 210, 229, 259
Spring–Rice, Stephen, 163
Spring–Rice, Thomas, 1st Baron Monteagle of Brandon (1790-1866), 347
Spring–Rice, Sir Thomas Aubrey (*fl.* 1916-7), 135, 210
Sprott, Thomas, 329
Sprott family, 329
Spry, Thomas, 101
Squirrel (ship), 306
Squyre, John, 309
Stabb, Ewen, 33
Stacey, George, 155
Stacey Mss., 155
Stafford, William (b. 1914), 178
Stafford, Staffordshire, 213-6
Staffordshire, England, 212-7
Staffordshire Record Office, 213-6
Stained-glass windows, Trade, 227
Stair, 2nd Earl of, *see* Dalrymple, John (1673-1747); 5th Earl of, *see* Dalrymple, John (1720-89)
Stair Muniments, 291
Staley, T., 232
Stalybridge, Greater Manchester, 180
Stamp Act, 1765: 10, 24, 65, 208, 213; Opposition, 54, 190, 213, 218, 249, 265, 267, 272, 302-3; Repeal, 55, 90, 218, 233, 265, 275, 292
Standard Oil Co., 131

Stanford Papers, 113
Stanhope, James, 1st Earl (1673-1721), 195
Stanhope, L., 167
Stanhope, Philip Dormer, 4th Earl of Chesterfield (1694-1773), 213
Stanhope, Philip Henry, 5th Earl (*styled* Viscount Mahon 1816-55), (1805-75), 118
Stanley, Mrs. Ann, 34
Stanley, C. H., 81
Stanley, Edward George Geoffrey Smith, 14th Earl of Derby (1799-1869), 13, 40, 63, 104
Stanley, Edward Henry, 15th Earl of Derby (*styled* Lord Stanley 1851-69), (1826-93), 13, 40, 133, 179
Stanley, Edward John, 2nd Baron Stanley of Alderley (1802-69), 169
Stanley, Edward Lyulph, 4th Baron Sheffield and 4th Baron Stanley of Alderley (1839-1925), 177
Stanley, Frederick Arthur, 16th Earl of Derby (1841-1908), 37, 38
Stanley, Sir Henry Morton (1841-1904), 250
Stanley, James, 7th Earl of Derby (1607-51), 276
Stanley, William, 34
Stanley, William Sloane, 36
Stanley Correspondence, 177
Stanmore, 1st Baron, *see* Gordon, Arthur Charles Hamilton–(1829-1912)
Stanmore Papers, 53
Stansbury, George, 219
Stansfield, Mr., 150
Stansgate Mss., 113
Stanton, Mrs. Elizabeth Cady (1815-1902), 84
Stanton, Theodore (1851-1925), 198
Stanwix, John (1690?-1766), 285
Stapleton, Miles Thomas, 8th Baron Beaumont (1805-54), 184
"Star-Spangled Banner," 78
Stark, Freya, 315
Starke, John, 120
Starke, Thomas, 42
Starkey, J. S., Papers, 348
Starkie, James Sullivan, 348, 353
Starr, Charles E., 348
Stars and Stripes, 158
Startin, John, 226
State Paper Office, Dublin, 348, 350-2
State Paper Office, London, 203
State Papers, Access to American students, 63
State Teachers' College, Fresno, 271
Stationers' Company, *Records*, 157
Stationers' Hall Registry, 157
Statistical Atlas of the U.S., 227
Statter, Thomas, 47
Staunton, Sir George Leonard (1737-1801), 150
Staunton, Moses, 332
Stave trade, 182
Stavely, Alexander McLeod, 331
Stavely, William, 331
Stavely family, 325, 331
Stavely Family Papers, 331
Staysmore Manor, Bedford, 9
Stead, McAlpin & Co. Ltd., 21-2
Steam navigation, 308
Steamships, 219, 226, 271, 311, 316
Stebbing, J. R., 35
Stebbing, Robert, 31
Stebbing, Thomas, & Son, 31
Stedman, Alex, 31
Stedman, Charles, 31
Steed Papers, 157
Steel industry, *see* Iron and steel industry
Steel–Maitland, Sir Arthur (1876-1935), 298
Steel–Maitland Muniments, 298
Steele, John S., 277
Steele, Thomas, 261
Steer, F. W., ed., *The Shiffner Archives*, 221 fn.
Steinberger, Col. A. B., 230, 269
Steinthal, Samuel Alfred, 95, 176
Stenerson, Douglas C., "An Anglican Critique of the Early Phase of the Great Awakening in New England: A Letter by Timothy Cutler," *William and Mary Quarterly* (1973), 151 fn.
Stephen, Alexander, & Sons, 311, 318
Stephen, James (1758-1832), 77
Stephens, James (1825-1901), 326, 344, 345
Stephens, Morse, 164
Stephens, Sir Philip (1725-1809), 44
Stephenson, Isaac, 155
Stephenson, Robert (1803-59), 346
Stepney, Sir John, 270
Stern, B. H., 79
Steuart, Charles, 258
Steuart, John (*fl.* 1749-59), 276
Steuart, John (*fl.* 1759), 276
Steuart of Dalguise Muniments, 276
Steuart Papers, 258
Steuben, Friedrich Wilhelm Ludolf Gerhard Augustin, Baron von (1730-94), 64
Stevens, Benjamin Franklin (1833-1902), 66, 213
Stevens, Edmund, 48
Stevens, Henry (1819-96), 314
Stevens, Wallace (1879-1955), 177, 178; *Esthétique du Mal*, 177; *Notes toward a Supreme Fiction*, 177; *Three Academic Pieces*, 177
Stevens & Brown, 74
Stevens family, 178
Stevens Papers, 177-8
Stevens Transcripts, 66
Stevenson, Adlai (1900-65), 165
Stevenson, Andrew (1784-1857), 67, 75, 104, 168, 187
Stevenson, Archibald, 265
Stevenson, Fanny (van de Grift, *later* Mrs. Osbourne), Mrs. Robert Louis Stevenson, 238
Stevenson, James, 325
Stevenson, John, 277, 280
Stevenson, Ralph, 9
Stevenson, Robert Louis (1850-94), 238
Stewardson, Thomas, 155
Stewart, Mr., 264
Stewart, Mrs., 264
Stewart, Alexander Turney (1803-76), 131
Stewart, C. (*fl.* 1804), 313
Stewart, David (1772-1829), 274
Stewart, Dugald (1753-1828), 314
Stewart, G., 312
Stewart, George, 8th Earl of Galloway (1768-1834), 288
Stewart, Gilbert, 276
Stewart, H. G., 315
Stewart, Sir Houston (1791-1875), 123 fn.
Stewart, James (*fl.* 1725), 276
Stewart (or Steuart), James (*fl.* 1749-54), 276
Stewart, James (*fl.* 1774), 151
Stewart, James (*fl.* 1812-4), 310

Stewart, John (*fl.* 1757), 42
Stewart, John (*fl.* 1820-37), 264
Stewart, John Aikman (1822-1926), 199, 229
Stewart, Robert (*fl.* 1716), 272
Stewart, Robert, 1st Marquis of Londonderry (1739-1821)
Stewart, Robert (*fl.* 1758-9), 285
Stewart, Robert, 2nd Marquis of Londonderry, *better known as* Viscount Castlereagh (1769-1822), 54, 83, 84, 287
Stewart, Thomas, 276
Stewart, W. K., 279
Stewart, William, 51
Stewart, Sir William Drummond, 290, 291; *Altowan*, 291
Stewart, Sir William Houston (1822-1901), 121
Stewart, William Murray, 264
Stewart & Wilson, 317
Stewart of Ardvorlich Mss., 264
Stewart Society Mss., 268
Stewart–Meiklejohn of Edradynate, 262
Stewarton, Scotland, Manufacturers, 310
Stiles, Ezra (1727-95), 94
Stillman, Mrs. Marie, 176
Stillman, W. J. (1828-1901), 176
Stillman Correspondence, 176
Stilwell, Silas Moore (1800-81), 168
Stimson, Frederic Jesup (1855-1943), 198
Stimson, Henry Lewis (1867-1950), 197, 279, 280, 281
Stirling, 1st Earl of, *see* Alexander, Sir William (1576-1640); 4th Earl of, *see* Alexander, Henry (1639?-91); 5th Earl of, *see* Alexander, Henry (1664-1739); 6th Earl of (*claimed to be*) *see* Alexander, William (1726-83)
Stirling, A. M. W., *Annals of a Yorkshire House*, 234 fn.
Stirling, Archibald, 317
Stirling, Graham, 274
Stirling, Sir James (1791-1865), 43
Stirling, James Hutchinson (1820-1909), 179
Stirling, John, 259
Stirling, Sir Thomas (1733-1808), 274, 275, 286
Stirling, Sir William, 275
Stobo, Archibald, 309
Stock, L. F., ed., "Some Bryce–Jameson Correspondence," *American Historical Review* (1945), 197 fn.
Stockdale, James, 47
Stockdale, John (1749?-1814), 204
Stockham, A. B., 236
Stockport, Greater Manchester, 180
Stockport Central Library, 180
Stocks and shares, *see* Investments
Stockton, Richard (1730-81), 214
Stockton-on-Tees, Cleveland, Customs records, 92, 94
Stork, William, 275
Stoke-on-Trent, Staffordshire, 217
Stoker, Bram, 238
Stoker, V., 150
Stokes, Mr., 239
Stokes, Gilbert, 35
Stonard, Joseph, 103
Stone, Mrs. Sarah, 50
Stonor, Christopher (d. 1795), 157
Stonyhurst College Papers, 48
Stopes, Marie Charlotte Carmichael (1880-1958), 79; Papers, 79
Storer, B., 245
Storey, Moorfield (1845-1929), 197, 199
Storey, W. W., 232
Stormont, 7th Viscount, *see* Murray, David (1727-96)
Story, Joseph (1779-1845), 207, 263
Story, Thomas (1670?-1742), 154, 157
Stourport-on-Severn, Hereford & Worcester, 37
Stourton, Lady Catherine, 32
Stout, William (1665-1752), 179
Stowe, Harriet (Beecher) (1811-96), 9, 96, 176, 178, 200, 240, 259; *Uncle Tom's Cabin*, 9, 114, 208
Strachan (*later* Fullarton), Charles, 258
Strachan, William, 267
Strachey, John St. Loe (1860-1927), 113
Strachey Papers, 113
Stradling inheritance, 243
Strafford, 1st Earl of, *see* Wentworth, Sir Thomas (1593-1641)
Strahan, William (1715-85), 215
Straight, Willard Dickerman (1880-1918), 197
Strang, Dr., 317
Strange, James, 263
Stratford de Redcliffe, 1st Viscount, *see* Canning, Stratford (1786-1880)
Strathclyde, Scotland, 316-8
Strathclyde Regional Archives, 317; 263
Stratheden, Lord, and Campbell Mss., 263
Straton, John, 41
Street, Christopher J., 176
Street, James C., 176
Street, Somerset, 211
Streit, Clarence, 283, *Union Now*, 282
Stretton, Clement E., 306
Strothers, A., and Co., 262
Strutt, Samuel, 292
Strutt, William (1756-1830), 16
Stuart, Andrew (*fl.* 1777), 258
Stuart, Andrew (*fl.* 1828), 286
Stuart, Sir C., 314
Stuart, Sir Charles, Baron Stuart de Rothesay (1779-1845), 207
Stuart, Ferdinand Smyth, 143
Stuart, J., 323
Stuart (*later* Stuart–Wortley), J. A., 232
Stuart, J. J., 314
Stuart, James, 4th Duke of Lennox and 1st Duke of Richmond (1612-55), 194
Stuart, James (1775-1849), 297
Stuart, James (*fl.* 1836), 329
Stuart, Jesse, 353
Stuart, John (1700?-79), 266
Stuart, John, 3rd Earl of Bute (1713-92), 21, 61, 195, 249, 264, 265
Stuart, John, 4th Earl and 1st Marquess of Bute (1744-1814), 256
Stuart, Margaret, Countess of Moray (d. 1779), 264
Stuart, Robert, 272
Stuart, Sir William (d. 1896), 60, 61, 140
Stuart of Torrance Papers, 258
Stuart Papers, 8, 140
Stuart Stevenson Papers, 258
Stuart–Wortley, J. A., *see* Stuart, J. A.
Stuart–Wortley, John, 2nd Baron Wharncliffe (1801-55), 232
Stuart–Wortley–Mackenzie, Edward, 1st Earl of Wharncliffe (1827-99), 232
Stubbs [or Stubbe], John (1543?-91), 49
Stubs, Peter, 178
Stubs, Peter, Ltd., 178
Stubs, Wood & Co., 178

Stucley [Stuckly], Thomas (1525?-78), 37
Studdert, Michael, 348
Studdert family, 348
Studdert Papers, 348
Studley, ———, 83
Sturdivant, James, 237
Sturge, Joseph (1793-1859), 69, 96, 155, 169, 350
Sturge Collection, 28
Sturge Papers, 69
Sturgeon, 149, 151
Styal, Cheshire, 19
Styles, ———, 111
Sublette, William Lewis (1799?-1845), 291
Suffolk, 22nd Earl of, *see* Howard, Henry (1739-79)
Suffolk, England, 217-20
Suffolk and Berkshire Archives, 230
Suffolk Record Office, Bury St. Edmunds branch, 217-8
Suffolk Record Office, Ipswich branch, 218-20
Suffrage, 62; *see also* Negroes: Suffrage; Voting; Women: Suffrage
Suffragette Fellowship Collection, 118
Sugar: Machinery, 17; Plantations, 26, 191; Prices, 63; Trade, 8, 55, 91, 107, 109, 181, 195, 234, 237, 268, 286, 306
Sugar Act (1764), 55, 180
Sugar Islands, *see* West Indies
Sulgrace Manor, 199
Sulgrave Institution, 229
Sulphur (H.M.S.), 15, 100
Sulzer, William (1863-1941), 165, 248, 258, 317
Summer [Somer] Islands, 218; *see also* Bermuda
Summersett, Thomas, 31
Sumner, Charles (1811-74), 53, 68-9 *passim*, 71, 72, 105, 168, 170, 184, 201-2 *passim*, 207, 208, 216, 232
Sun Fire Office, 32
Sunderland, 3rd Earl of, *see* Spencer, Charles (1674-1722)
Sunderland Papers, 193
Sunderland, Tyne and Wear, Customs records, 92, 94
Superior, Lake, 111
Supreme Court, Decisions, 280; *see also* Judges
Surman, Rev. Charles E., 224
Surprise (privateer), 5
Surrey, England, 220-1
Surrey Record Office, 220-1
Surveying, 263; *see also* Hydrographic surveying
Sussex, 3rd Earl of, *see* Radcliffe, Sir Thomas (1526?-83)
Sussex, East, England, 221-3
Sussex, West, England, 223
Sussex Archaeological Society, 222-3
Sutcliffe, E. G., "Charles Reade's Notebooks," *Studies in Philology* (1930), 116 fn.
Sutherland, 3rd Duke of, *see* Leveson–Gower, George Granville William Sutherland (1828-92)
Sutherland, Alexander, 292
Sutherland, Duke of, Mss., 216
Sutherland, L. S., *A London Merchant, 1695-1774*, 32 fn.
Sutherland, William (*fl.* 1777-8), 292
Sutherland, William (*fl.* 1807-15), 291
Sutherland, Sir William (*fl.* 1934), 280
Sutherland–Graeme of Graemeshall Mss., 315
Suttie, John, 290
Sutton Coldfield, West Midlands, 229
Swain Collection, 178
Swainston, Mrs. A. V., Mss., 268
Swallow (ship), 274
Swan Land and Cattle Co., 308, 315
Swan Sonnenschein & Co., 161
Swanley, Robert, 36
Swann, B., and M. Turnbull, "Treasury Board Papers," unpub. list of documents (duplicated), 141
Swansea, 1st Baron, *see* Vivian, Sir Henry Hussey (1821-94)
Swansea, West Glamorgan, Customs records, 89, 91, 94
Swarthmore College, Pennsylvania, 278, 281, 282
Swarthmore Mss., 154
Swinburne, Algernon Charles (1837-1909), 238
Swiney, Daniel (1826-1915), 326; "The Rockingstone," 326
Swing, Raymond Gram, 283
Swinton, John, 74
Swope, Herbert Bayard, 283
Sydenham of Combe, Baron, *see* Clarke, George Sydenham (1848-1933)
Sydney, *see* Sidney
Sykes, William Henry (1790-1872), 40
Sylas Neville Papers, 188
Sylvis, William H. (1828-69), 53
Symmar, Andrew, 301
Symmes, John Cleves (1742-1814), 62
Syndicate Lands and Irrigating Corporation, Colorado, 98
Synge, John Millington (1871-1909), 353; Correspondence, 353

T

T., J., 195, 215
Tabor, Samuel (*fl.* 1773-88), 32
Tabor Papers, 32
Tackle, Thomas, 83
Taft, William Howard (1857-1930), 75, 197, 198, 199, 238, 260, 277
Tagore, Sir Rabindranath (1861-1941), 279
Tait, William (1793-1864), 168
Tait's Edinburgh Magazine, 168
Talbot, Charles, Duke of Shrewsbury (1660-1718), 189
Talbot, James (1726-90), 171
Talbot, Sir John (1769?-1851), 239
Talbot, Thomas (1771-1853), 232
Talbot, Bishop Thomas (*fl.* 1790), 225
Tallack, William (1831-1908), 58
Talley, Alexander, 189
Tammany Hall, New York, 164, 198, 345
Tangye, N., 113
Tankyns, John, 56
Tanner, J. R., ed., *A Descriptive Catalogue of the Naval MSS. in the Pepysian Library at Magdalene College, Cambridge*, 16
Tappan, Lewis (1788-1873), 68, 157, 168, 205
Tar, Trade, 24, 182
Tarbat, Viscount, *see* MacKenzie, George (1630-1714)
Tariff: 1816-30, 25, 57, 67, 78, 160, 207, 208, 210; 1831-60, 63, 64, 69, 77, 78, 110, 124, 125, 184, 200, 207, 208, 247; 1861-99, 38, 69, 73, 125, 177, 197, 198, 201, 204; 1900- , 30, 111, 197, 269, 277, 278; *see also* Customs duties; Protectionism; Reciprocity
Tarleton, Sir Banastre (1754-1833), 102, 181
Tarleton, John (1719-73), 102, 181
Tarleton & Backhouse, 181
Tarleton Papers, 102, 181
Tartan, Trade, *see* Woollen goods

Tartt, William Macdonald, 183
Tasca, H. J. A., 282
Tasmania, Irish prisoners in, 184
Tate Hodgson & Co., Messrs., of Whitehaven, 21
Tatham, William (1752-1819), 151
Taunton, Somerset, 211-2
Taussig, Frank William (1859-1940), 172
Tavernier (ship), 136
Taws, Lewis, 114
Taxation, 69, 112, 270, 277, 305; *see also* Land taxation; Revenue; Single tax
COLONIAL PERIOD, 55, 79, 191, 214, 215, 267, 292, 300, 301, 324; *see also* Stamp Act, 1765; Sugar Act, 1764; Townshend duties
Tayler, A. & H., 253; *The Book of the Duffs*, 253; *Lord Fife and his Factor*, 253
Taylor, Col., 300
Taylor, Alexander, 329
Taylor, Edward (*fl.* 1855-9), 22
Taylor, Edward (*fl.* 1872), 177
Taylor, George, 329
Taylor, H. A., "David Samwell," *Liverpool Libraries . . . Bulletin* (1956), 182 fn.
Taylor, H. G., 75
Taylor, Henry, 204
Taylor, Hugh, 329
Taylor, James, 95
Taylor, John, *Scripture Doctrine of Atonement*, 174
Taylor, Robert, 329
Taylor, Robert Arthur (1886-1934), 43
Taylor, Sedley, 16
Taylor, Thomas, 315
Taylor, William, 305
Taylor, Zachary (1784-1850), 77, 156, 206
Taylor Family Correspondence, 22
Taylorism, 187
Tayside, Scotland, 318-9
Tea: Cultivation, 148; Trade, 55, 185, 187, 188, 208, 306, 350
Teachers, 199, 227; Exchange visits, Great Britain, 97; Immigrants, 166, 331
Technical education, *see* Education, Technical
Technology, 148-50; *see also* Industry; Machinery; Science; *and names of specific industries*
Teignmouth, Customs records, 94
Telegraph, 110, 114, 124, 125, 131, 138, 158, 201; *see also* Communications; Postal service; Telephone
Telephone, 162; *see also* Communications; Postal service; Telegraph
Telford, Charles L., 245
Temperance, 208, 245
Temple, Earl, *see* Grenville (*afterwards* Grenville–Temple), Richard Temple (1711-99)
Temple, Henry John, 3rd Viscount Palmerston (1784-1865), 60, 69, 71, 77, 103-5 *passim*, 168, 186, 202, 207, 306, 316; Diaries, 105
Temple, J., 215
Temple, Sir John (1730-98), 65, 66, 80
Temple, William, 6
Temple Newsam Records, 239
Templeman, Peter (1711-69), 151
Tenagra, Bishop of, 171
Tennant, Dorothy, 250
Tennant, Gertrude, 250
Tennant Canal and Estate Records, 250
Tennessee: Civil War (1861-5), 59, 60
DESCRIPTION, 156, 326, 344; Finance, 100; Immigrants, 243, 332; Settlement, 163, 246; Trade, 47
CARTHAGE, 317; Chattanooga, 59; Goose Creek, 317; Jackson, Description, 271; Knoxville, 326; Memphis, 169; Nashville, Description, 271; Rugby, 68, 163
Tennessee Papers, 246
Tennessee River, 271
Tennessee Valley Authority, 164
Tennesy, Eduard, 271
Tenterden, 3rd Baron, *see* Abbott, Charles Stuart Aubrey (1834-82)
Tenterden Papers, 133
Tenure of Office Act (1867), 201
Teresa, Mother, *see* Lalor, Alice (*c.* 1766-1846)
Terrell, George W., 67
Territorial waters, 130; *see also* Bering Sea Controversy
Terry, Champneys, 300
Texas: Republic (1836-46), 62, 67, 104, 168, 206, 207, 208, 257, 306
CATTLE, 209; Description, 348; Immigrants, 173; Land, 308; Merchants, 66, 118, 181; Relations with Great Britain, 67, 261, 262, 272, with Mexico, 206; Settlement, 173, 245; Slavery, 67, 206, 274
DALLAS, CONSULAR REPORTS (BRITISH), 134; El Paso, Consular reports (British), 134; Galveston, 66, 118, Consular reports (British), 130, 134; Houston, 118, Consular reports (British), 134; Paris, 181; Port Arthur, Consular reports (British), 134
Texas and New Mexico Land Syndicate Ltd., 308
Texas fever, 236
"Texas Jack," *see* Omohundron, John B. (d. 1880)
Texas Land and Cattle Co. Ltd., 308
Textile industry and fabrics, 310, 318; Machinery, 161, 308; Trade, 21-2, 47, 161, 309, 310, 315, 346; *see also* Blankets; Carpets; Cotton goods; Dry goods; Dyes; Hemp; Linen; Rugs; Silk; Woollen goods
Textile workers, Immigrants, 47
Teynham, 14th Baron, *see* Roper–Curzon, Henry Francis
Teyoninhokokarawen, *see* Norton, John
Thacher, Peter (1651-1727), 174
Thackeray, William Makepeace (1811-63), 184
Thackwell, W. H., 224
Thatcher, Benjamin Bussey (1809-40), 168
Thayer, Rev., 225
Thayer, William Roscoe (1859-1923), 198
Theatre: Careers, 50; Productions, 77, 78
Theosophy, 74
Thistle (ship), 269
Thomas, Miss, 164
Thomas, Abel C., 176
Thomas, Catherine, 244
Thomas, Daniel, 250
Thomas, Edward, 217
Thomas, Elizabeth, 217
Thomas, Evan, 246
Thomas, Frederick, 98
Thomas, Griffith (*fl.* 1846), 247
Thomas, Hugh, 244
Thomas, Isaiah (1750-1831), 204
Thomas, John, 48
Thomas, Mary (mother), 250
Thomas, Mary (daughter), 250
Thomas, P. A., 318
Thomas, Philip Francis (1810-90), 245

Thomas, R. D., 245
Thomas, Rees, 250
Thomas, Richard Symmes, Jr., 62
Thomas, Samuel, 217
Thomas, Walter, 112
Thomas, William, 244
Thomas, William B., 250
Thomas Family Correspondence, 217
Thomas Gilcrease Institute of American History and Art, 32 fn.
Thomas Koulikan (ship), 90
Thomlinson, Thomas, 158
Thompson, Miss, 326
Thompson, Professor, 130
Thompson, B. & S. H., 235
Thompson, Sir Benjamin, Count von Rumford (1753-1814), 147
Thompson, Charles (1740?-99), 101
Thompson, Sir Charles Hotham (1738-92), 42
Thompson, D'Arcy W., 315
Thompson, David (1770-1857), 146; "The Discovery of the Source of the Columbia River," *Quarterly of the Oregon Historical Society* (1925), 146 fn.
Thompson, David (*fl.* 19th cent.), 236
Thompson, Francis, 175
Thompson, George (1804-78), 95, 176, 316
Thompson, Henry Yates (1838-1928), 16
Thompson, Herbert (1856-1945), 239
Thompson, James (b. 1732), 286
Thompson, James (*fl.* 1782), 233
Thompson, James Charles, 48
Thompson, John, 327
Thompson, Lazewell, 330
Thompson, Pishey, 50
Thompson, Robert, 327
Thompson, Silvanus Phillips (1851-1916), 162
Thompson, Thomas (1673-1727), 153
Thompson, Thomas (d. late 18th cent.?), 276
Thompson, Thomas (1775-1861), 154
Thompson, Thomas Perronet (1783-1869), 43
Thompson family, 154, 156, 204, 330, 332
Thompson Family Papers, 154, 332
Thompson Papers, 162
Thomson, Alexander G., 310
Thomson, Sir Charles Wyville (1830-82), 314
Thomson, Elihu (1853-1957), 162
Thomson, George Augustus, 166
Thomson, James (1834-82), 204
Thomson, John, 287
Thomson, T. O., 318
Thomson Papers, 204
Thorium, 139
Thorn, Col., 187
Thornely, Thomas, 9, 169, 183
Thornton, Sir Edward (1766-1852), 200
Thornton, Sir Edward (1817-1906), 37, 38, 59, 60, 68, 69, 70, 129, 133, 201, 202
Thornton, John, 275
Thornton, Posthoumous, 263
Thornton, Robert, 288
Thornton family, 343
Thorold, George, 48
Thoroton, Thomas (1723-84), 48 fn.
Thouin, André (1747-1824), 259
Threlkeld, J., 24
Throckmorton, J. W. F. (*fl.* 1882), 224
Throckmorton, Mary, 224
Throckmorton, Sir Robert George Maxwell, 224
Throckmorton Papers, 224
Throne, Catherine, 329
Thurlow, Edward, 1st Baron (1731-1806), 80, 210
Thurston, Mrs. Jane P., 68
Thwing, Charles F., 278
Thynne, Thomas, 3rd Viscount Weymouth and 1st Marquess of Bath (1734-96), 230, 267
Thynne and Thynne, Messrs., Papers, 216
Tibbitts Collection, 235
Tichborne Case, 1873-4, 202
Tichenor, Isaac (1754-1838), 16
Ticknor, George (1791-1871), 183, 254
Tigress (American ship), 144
Tilden, Samuel Jones (1814-86), 161
Tillett, Ben, 228
Tillett/Mackay Papers, 228
Tilt, Benjamin, 228
Timber, 33, 150, 229, 231, 294, 327; Investment, 307, 308; Trade, 20, 24, 92, 107, 108, 119-20, 160, 171, 205, 257, 262, 288, 301, 303, 310, 323; *see also* Live oak; Pipe-staves; Saw-mills; Stave trade
Timberlake, Henry (*fl.* 1765), 195
Time (magazine), 112
The Times, 59, 69, 157-8, 277, 278, 280, 281, 282, 289; *Index*, 157
Times Newspapers Ltd., 157-8
Timms, Benjamin J., 246
Timrod, Henry (1828-67), 69
Tin mining, 20
Tinker, John, 304
Tinplate, Trade, 184
Tipperary, Republic of Ireland, 354
Tippet, Alice O., 75
Toal, Edward, 329
Toal, James, 329
Toal, Mary, 329
Tobacco, 23; Cultivation, 10, 64, 249, 269, 301; Duties, 7, 55, 106, 107, 233, 267, 269, 286
TRADE, 6, 21, 55, 86, 106, 107, 109, 152, 182, 205, 212, 231, 253, 269, 270, 276, 304, 316, 317; Colonial period, 5, 6, 8, 18, 21, 23, 27, 34, 36, 49, 79, 81, 83, 85, 90-2 *passim*, 158, 181, 195, 203, 261, 286, 299, 304, 306, 309, 310, 319, 346
See also Smoking
Tobago, Governors, 258
Todd, Charles, 315
Todd, George, 315
Todd, Henry J., *A Catalogue of the Archepiscopal Manuscripts in the Library of Lambeth Palace*, 115
Todd, Michael, 57
Todd family, 57
Todhunter, Lieut. Col. J. F., 217
Todhunter, John, 217
Todhunter, Joseph, 217
Todhunter Family Papers, 217
Tods, Mr., 103
Tods Murray and Jamieson Collection, 304
Tollemache, Lionel, 3rd Earl of Dysart (1649-1727), 219
Tollemache Collection, 219
Tolles, F. B., *The Atlantic Community of the Early Friends*, 152
Tompkins, Daniel D. (1774-1825), 16

Tone, Theobald Wolfe (1763-98), 351, 352
Tone, Mrs. William Theobald Wolfe, 325
Toner, E., 348
Toner, Peter, 348
Tonga, Relations with U.S., *see* Relations with Tonga
Tonnant (ship), 121
Tools, 150, 178, 234; Trade, 161, 271
Tootal, Edward, 64
Topley family, 330
Topography, 225, 307
Torbek, Ann, 97
Torpedo fish, 175
Torphichen, 9th Baron, *see* Sandilands, James (1759-1815)
Torrey, John (1796-1873), 15, 145
Torrie, T. J., 315
Toshach, D., 274
Totnes, Devonshire, 27
Toussaint L'Ouverture, Pierre Dominique (1743-1803), 287
Tout, Thomas Frederick (1855-1929), 177
Tower, Henry, 221
Tower, Sir Reginald (1860-1939), 38, 39
Tower, Thomas (d. 1778), 32
Tower Papers, 32
Townley Hall Papers, 347
Townsend, I. L., 235
Townshend, Charles (1725-67), 45, 119, 218, 266, 271, 272, 273, 300, 300 fn., 301, 303
Townshend, George, 4th Viscount and 1st Marquis (1724-1807), 24, 119, 145, 189, 354
Townshend, Roger (1708-60), 302
Townshend, Thomas, 218
Townshend duties (1767), 55, 65, 66
Townshend Papers, 118-9
Toynbee, Arnold (1889-1975), 279
Tracy, Louis, 277
Trade, 47, 99, 100, 103, 125, 126, 130, 269, 274, 278, 279, 282, 286, 294, 298
COLONIAL PERIOD, 5-8 *passim*, 10, 12, 15, 22-4 *passim*, 27, 29, 31, 35, 45, 49-50, 54, 55-6 *passim*, 62, 63, 82-3 *passim*, 85-94 *passim*, 99, 103, 114, 119, 122, 124, 129, 140, 148-51 *passim*, 160, 179, 181-2 *passim*, 191, 194-6 *passim*, 200, 202, 211-5 *passim*, 232-4 *passim*, 237, 247, 259, 264, 265, 266, 267, 271-3 *passim*, 284, 297, 299-305 *passim*, 307, 309, 316, 317, 323, 324, 325, 339 fn., 343, 346; Illicit, *see* Smuggling; Statistics, 57; *see also subdivision* Trade *under individual commodities and under states; also subdivision* Merchants *under states*
TRADE WITH ARGENTINA, 112; Australia, 112; Bahamas, 130; Barbados, 286, Colonial period, 34; Brazil, 34; Canada, 32, 56, 77, 112, 125, 128, 131, 140, 198, 200, 201, 273, 280; *see also* Reciprocity
CHANNEL ISLANDS, 339; China, 109, 272, 286, 288; Cuba, 34; East Indies, 80, 195, 288; France, 12, 99, Colonial period, 10, 23, 214; Germany, 131, 211, 282
GREAT BRITAIN, 7, 10, 19-22 *passim*, 25, 31, 35, 36, 41, 46, 47, 51, 52, 54, 56-7 *passim*, 59, 63, 64, 73, 80, 81, 86, 89, 90, 99, 106-9 *passim*, 112, 117, 124, 125, 126, 128, 129, 131, 132, 133, 137-42 *passim*, 160-2 *passim*, 169, 175, 178, 179, 180, 182, 183, 191, 200, 201, 205, 207, 208, 209, 212-3, 225-8 *passim*, 234-9 *passim*, 263, 267-70 *passim*, 272, 274, 281, 283, 284, 286, 287, 294, 309, 310, 325, 331, 332, 351; *see also* Business records; Debts to British merchants
GUADELOUPE, 303; India, 26, 140, 264, 288; Ireland, 107-8 *passim*, 324, 325, 327, 332, 346, 349, 350, Colonial period, 24, 34, 62, 196, 303, 323, 325, 346, 349; Isle of Man, 92; Jamaica, 56, 124, 181-2; Japan, 272; Madeira, 237; Martinique, 262; Mexico, 124, 211; Netherlands, 135, 139, 267, Colonial period, 24, 200, 304, 311; Portugal, 173, 237; Prussia, 56; Russia, 57, 76, 135, Colonial period, 83; Samoa, 39
SCOTLAND, 108, 253-6 *passim*, 269-74 *passim*, 307-11 *passim*, 315, 332, Colonial period, 79, 195, 273, 275, 292, 299, 304, 308, 309; Spain, 76, 132, 140, 255, Colonial period, 15, 160, 302; Turkey, 287; Wales, 247, 249-50; West Africa, 7; West Indies, 25, 41, 56, 81, 84, 124, 130, 138, 181, 191, 207, 208, 286, 288, 293, 330, Colonial period, 8, 55, 160, 181, 237, 309
Trade and Plantations, Commissioners for, 56, 160, 194, 221, 239, 266, 284, 300, 301; Committee of, 21, 27
Trade and Plantations, Council for, 57, 161, 195
Trade, Board of, 56, 83, 87, 88, 102, 109, 114, 122, 124-6, 132, 138, 140, 160, 195, 301, 302, 307-8; Companies Registration Office, 94, 125, 249; Marine Department, 137
Trade, Council of, 27, 193
Trade, Lords of, 54, 55, 214, 240, 302
Trade marks, 131, 180, 235, 237
Trade unions, 29, 53, 228, 345; Iron and steel workers, 164; Women's, 163; *see also* Guilds; *and names of individual unions*
Trade unions (British), Emigration schemes, 9, 29, 52, 162, 163, 179, 209, 217, 254
Trades Union Congress, 139
Trademarks Protection Society, 180
Trafford, Captain Edward, 272
Traill, Thomas (*fl.* 1836), 306
Traill, Thomas Stewart (1781-1862), 258
Traill Papers, 258
Traill–Dennison Muniments, 315
Train and Bayne, 79
Tramways, 97
Transatlantic voyages, *see* Voyages to America
Transport, Ministry of, 122, 137
Transportation, 47, 103, 141, 266, 306; *see also* Canals; Harbours; Postal service; Railways; Shipping; Tramways
Transportation of Americans to New South Wales, 169
Transportation of criminals, 9, 18, 21, 23, 25, 33, 35, 41, 42, 43, 44, 49, 70, 85-6 *passim*, 97, 181, 192, 194, 228, 231, 249, 290, 299, 307, 311, 312, 325, 343, 351; *see also* Quarter sessions records
Trapping, *see* Fur trade
Trask, Katrina [Mrs. Spencer], 164
Traubel, Anne (Montgomerie), Mrs. Horace L. Traubel, 172, 177
Traubel, Horace L. (1858-1919), 172, 177, 236
Travel diaries and letters, 347; pre-1700, 156, 202; 1700-76, 40, 45, 155, 156, 182, 212, 274, 285, 290; 1783-1820, 7, 20, 20 fn., 34, 39, 40, 117, 156, 191, 217, 226, 243, 250, 256, 270, 271, 306, 331, 352; 1820-66, 15, 20, 22, 29, 30, 32, 36, 43, 44, 50, 70, 72, 95, 98, 102, 146, 155, 156, 159, 161, 171-2 *passim*, 180, 183-6 *passim*, 202, 204, 208, 211, 218, 224, 225, 232, 254-6 *passim*, 266, 268, 270, 271, 292, 297, 306, 325, 328, 332, 335, 346-7, 350, 353; 1866-1900, 20, 24, 34, 39, 50, 53, 116, 143, 146-7, 161, 164, 172, 179, 180, 189, 199, 213, 216, 217, 222, 225, 246, 250, 255, 262, 265, 274, 297, 316, 327, 332, 345, 348, 353; 1900- , 11, 34, 43, 46, 79, 81, 113, 115, 116, 141, 146, 147, 156, 161, 162, 165, 177, 180, 187, 199, 200, 206, 227, 228, 236-7, 254, 259, 260, 271, 276, 277, 279-83 *passim*, 290, 298, 304, 314, 315, 346, 348; *see also* Voyages to America; *and subdivision* Description *under states, etc.*
Treasury (British), 51-2, 55, 87, 88, 90, 96, 119, 123, 136, 140-2 *passim*, 264, 301, 303, 311, 311 fn.
Treasury, Lords Commissioners of the, 42, 120, 161, 312
Treasury Solicitor, 122, 123, 142

Treaties: Collections, 102, 106, 208; *see also* Relations with (*particular country*)
Trecothick, Barlow (1728-78), 8, 233
Tredegar Park Muniments, 246
Tregagle, Nathaniel, 50
Tremont Theatre, Boston, 178
Trent (ship), 58, 59, 60, 68, 69, 70, 71, 72, 121
Tretwell, Ralph, 174
Trevelyan, Arthur, 224
Trevelyan, Sir Charles Philips (1870-1958), 164, 224
Trevelyan, Sir George Otto (1838-1928), 206, 224; *The American Revolution*, 206
Trevelyan, Sir Walter Calverley (1797-1879), 224
Trevelyan Papers, 224
Trevor, Mr., 104
Trevor, Robert Hampden–, 1st Viscount Hampden and 4th Baron Trevor (1706-83), 11, 12
Trevor Papers, 11-2
Trichinosis, 236
Trimingham, Nan, 328
Trinitarians, 167
Trinity College, Cambridge, 17
Trinity College, Dublin, 352-3
Trinity College, Toronto, 14
Trinity House, 158
Trinity House of Leith Records, 303
Tripoli, Relations with U.S., *see* Relations with Tripoli
Tristan de Cunha, Raiding base in War of 1812, 70
Trollope–Bellew of Carew Castle Collection, 248
Trotskyite movement, 228
Trott, Nicholas (1663-1740), 195
Trowbridge, Wiltshire, 230
Truman, Harry S. (1884-1972), 139, 166
Trumbull, John (1756-1843), 190
Trumbull, Jonathan (1710-85), 12
Trumbull, William (d. 1635), 10, 29
Trumbull, Sir William (1639-1716), 10
Truro, Cornwall, 19-20; Customs records, 89, 94
Tryon, Thomas, 190
Tryon, William (1725-88), 57, 65, 75, 150, 190, 191, 214, 274
Tryon Papers, 190
Tuchin, Edmund, 343
Tuchin, Simon, 343
Tucker, Aaron B., 183
Tucker, George (1775-1861), 169
Tucker, N., 233
Tucker, William (1589?-1640?), 194
Tuckerman, Joseph (1778-1840), 176
Tudor, William (1779-1830), 182
Tuffen, T. F., 183
Tuffen & Pugh, 183
Tufton, Sir Nicholas, 45
Tufton Papers, 45
Tufts, Samuel, 233
Tufts College, Massachusetts, 82
Tuke, Esther (1727-94), 40
Tuke, William (1732-1822), 40
Tunbridge Wells, Kent, 44
Tunis, 1st Earl of, *see* Alexander, Harold (1891-1969)
Tunstall, J. H., 131
Turkey, Piracy, 26; *see also* Relations with Turkey; Trade with Turkey
Turnbull, Andrew, 266
Turnbull, John, 288
Turnbull, Forbes & Co., 226
Turner, Paul, 79
Turner, William Henry, 203
Turner, Winifred, ed., *The Aufrère Papers*, 113 fn.
Turpentine, Trade, 119, 122, 182, 212
Turtle River, 301
Tuscaloosa (ship), 61
Tuscany (ship), 24
Tuscarora (ship), 13
Tuskegee College, 199
Tustin, J., 226
Tuttle, C., 26
Tuttle, Charles Wesley (1829-81), 148
Twain, Mark, *pseud.*, *see* Clemens, Samuel Langhorne (1835-1910)
Tweed, William Marcy (1823-78), 198
Tweeddale, 8th Marquis of, *see* Hay, George (1787-1876)
Tweedsmuir, 1st Baron, *see* Buchan, John (1875-1940)
Twells, Thomas, 191
Twemlow, J. A., ed., *Liverpool Town Books*, 181 fn.
Twine, Trade, 182
Twining & Co., 116
Twisden, Sir William, 46
Twisden Family Papers, 46
Twisleton, Edward Turner Boyd (1809-74), 247
Tyler, Henry, 325
Tyler, Henry H., 325, 326
Tyler, J. E., "Colonel George Mercer's Papers," *Virginia Magazine of History and Biography* (1952), 233 fn.
Tyler, John (*fl.* 1776), 105
Tyler, John (1790-1862), 62, 67, 207, 289
Tyler, Moses Coit (1835-1900), 206
Tyler, Samuel (1809-77), 148
Tyler Papers, 325-6
Tyne and Wear, England, 223-4
Tyne & Wear Department, County Archives, 223-4
Typewriters and typewriter equipment, 42
Typographers, *see* Printers
Typographical Protection Circular, 9
Typographical Societies' Monthly Circular, 9
Tyrell, A., 330
Tyrell, George, 75

U

Udall, William, 37
Uley Baptist Church, 34
Umbrellas, Trade, 175
Underhill, J. M. G., 227
Underhill, John, *Newes from America*, 187
Underwood, B. F., 204
Underwood, E. A., "Edward Jenner, Benjamin Waterhouse, and the Introduction of Vaccination into the United States," *Nature* (1949), 171 fn.
Underwood, John T., 42
Underwood's Inks, 42
Unemployment, 277
Unicorn (ship), 305
Union Bank of Louisiana, 181
Union Gold Mines, Virginia, 20
Union of Construction Allied Trades & Technicians, 228
Union of Democratic Control, 165

Union Pacific Railroad, 96
Union with Canada, 72
Union with Great Britain, Colonial period, 55, 188, 267; 20th century, 282, 283
Unitarian Churches, 94, 95, 96, 167, 174, 176, 177, 183, 208
United Branches of Operative Potters, 217
United Colonies, Commissioners of the, 99
United Committee for the Taxation of Land Values Ltd., 100
United Irish League of America, 345
United Irish Society, 325, 353
United Irishman, New York, 140
United Kingdom Atomic Energy Authority, 122, 123
United Nations Conference on International Organisation, San Francisco (1945), 165
United Nations Organisation, 165
United Presbyterian Church, 258
United Reformed Church History Society, 158
United Society for the Propagation of the Gospel, 158-9
United States Air Force, Memorial Trust of the 2nd Air Division, 189
United States and Brazil Steamship Company, 166
United States and South American Investment Trust Co., 111
United States Bank of Pennsylvania, 52
United States Brewery Co., 105
United States, Department of Agriculture: Bureau of Plant Industry, 146
United States, Department of Education, 75
United States, Naval Observatory, 148
United States, Register's Office, 172
United States, State Department, 61
United States, Supreme Court, 40
United States Land and Emigration Co., 230
United States Land Co., 125
United States Strategic Air Forces in Europe, 113
Universal Peace Conference, Boston (1904), 165
Universities, 54, 183, 197, 199, 276; *see also* names of individual universities
Universities' Mission to Central Africa, 158
Universities of France Mss., 314
University College, Dublin, Department of Irish Folklore, 353
University College, London, *see* London University, University College
University College of North Wales, 248
University College of Wales, Aberystwyth, 165
University of California, Berkeley, 146
University of South Carolina, Library, 228
University of Sussex, Library, 221
Unwin, Sir Raymond, 256
Unwin, William Cawthorne (1838-1933), 162
Unwin Papers, 162
Upper Clyde Shipbuilders' Records, 311
Upton, Mr., 262
Urquhart, John, 272
Ury, John (d. 1741), 171
Ushaw College, 30
Utah: Description, 304; Immigrants, 273; Mining, 307
SALT LAKE CITY, 164, 179, 235; Salt Lake Valley, 273; *see also* Mormons and Mormonism
Utah Cotton Wood Mining and Smelting Co. Ltd., 307

V

Vail, Aaron (1796-1878), 76, 104
Van Buren, Martin (1782-1862), 16, 30, 104, 186, 207, 208, 238, 255, 306, 325
Van Cortlandt, Stephanus (1643-1700), 220
Van Ingen, E. H., 237
Van Rensselaer, Stephen (1764-1829), 258
Van Rensselaer, Stephen (*fl.* 1810), 274
Van Wyck, Robert Anderson (1849-1918), 164
Vancouver, Charles (*fl.* 1785-1813), 101
Vancouver, George (1758-98), 92
Vancouver Island, 124, 128
Vancouver Island Steam Sawing Mill & Agricultural Co., 124
Vanderbilt, S. W., 269
Vanderhorst, Elias, 6
Vanderhorst and Duncombe Collection, 6
Vansittart, A. C., 129
Vardill, John (1749-1811), 215
Vasey, Thomas, 65
Vassall, Florentius, 222
Vassall, William, 234
Vassar College, New York, 177
Vatican, Relations with U.S., *see* Relations with Vatican
Vaudreuil, Marquis de, *see* de Rigaud, Pierre François
Vaughan, Sir Charles Richard (1774-1849), 49, 66, 67, 77, 104, 133, 206-8, 240, 286, 306
Vaughan, Daniel (*c.* 1818-79), 148
Vaughan, Herbert Alfred (1832-1903), 172
Vaughan, J., 161
Vaughan, John G., 246
Vaughan, Mary, 246
Vaughan, W., 167
Venables–Llewelyn, Sir Charles L. Dillwyn, Deposit, 246
Venezuela, Boundaries with British Guiana, 38, 39, 72, 162, 197, 201, 259
Venn, John (1586-1650), 194
Vere Hodge Mss., 119
Vergennes, Charles Gravier, Comte de (1717-87), 218
Verity, Oliver, 314
Vermont: Civil War (1861-5), 130
CLIMATE, 148; Description, 30; Immigrants, 47; Religious history, 158, 159, 245; Trade, 54
BARRE, 254; Burlington, 148; Green Mountains, 39; St. Albans, 130
Verney, John, 1st Baron (1640-1717), 11
Verney, Sir Ralph (1613-96), 11
Verney Papers, 11
Verplanck, Gulian Crommelin (1786-1870), 182
Verulam, Earl of, 37
Verulam Mss., 37, 41
Verulam of Gorhambury, 1st Baron, *see* Grimston, James Bucknall (1747-1809)
Vetch, Sam, 262, 263
Vice: Anti-vice campaigns, 95; *see also* Prostitution
Vice-admiralty courts, 136, 138
Victoria, *Queen* (1819-1901), 38, 40, 68, 71, 110, 111, 131, 192
Victoria Library, City of Westminster Archives Department, 171
Victorious (ship), 239
Vienna, University of, 74
Vignoles, Charles Blacker (1793-1875), 346
Vigorit Powder Works, 206
Villard, Henry (1835-1900), 197

Villard, Oswald Garrison (1872-1949), 197, 229, 278
Villiers, Sir Francis Hyde (1852-1925), 38
Villiers, George William Frederick, 4th Earl of Clarendon and 4th Baron Hyde (1800-70), 58, 64, 70, 72, 105, 186, 200-2
Villiers, John Charles, 3rd Earl of Clarendon (1757-1838), 188
Villiers, Thomas, 1st Earl of Clarendon, (*1756-76 known as* Lord Hyde) (1709-86), 188
Vinton, Samuel Finley (1792-1862), 245
Virginia: 17th century, 10, 11, 17, 20, 24, 26, 29, 34, 37, 45, 48, 49, 81, 82, 83, 99, 117, 186, 187, 190, 194-5 *passim*, 202, 203, 213, 228, 237, 311, 312; 1700-65, 21, 115, 140, 263, 264, 284, 306, 311; 1765-75, 10, 21, 24, 65, 182, 215; 1776-83, 57, 286, 317; 1783-1802, 317; Civil War, 1861-5, 59, 60, 65, 246, 259
AGRICULTURE, 10, 11, 149, 269, 294; Army, 50, 233, 274, 284, 285, 330-1; Assembly, 21, 23, 82, 90, 218, 275; Banking, 269; Botany, 200; Boundaries with Maryland, 194; Constitution, 195; Council, 10, 24, 37, 274; Counties, 21; Customs administration, 87, 181; Defence, 10, 17, 195; Description, 116, 154, 156, 256, 294, 304, 326; Education, 41-2, 50, 95, 183, 190, 217, 223, 227; Epidemics, 182; Finance, 7, 100; Fine arts, 149; Firemaking, 202; Fishing, 26
GOVERNORS, 10, 11, 24, 44, 49, 57, 82, 124, 193, 194, 195, 203, 218, 223, 230, 245, 246, 260, 264, 268, 285; Immigrants, 5, 11, 31, 33, 34, 37, 45, 46-7 *passim*, 49, 70, 85, 86, 129, 166, 182, 228, 237, 243, 271, 276, 284, 286, 295, 299, 307, 311, 330, 331, 332, 343, 351; Indians, 10, 214, 230; Industry, 6, 12, 202, 226, 273, 290; Land, 6, 12, 23, 33, 34, 36, 42, 45, 47, 102, 112, 158, 237, 263, 269, 273, 286, 290, 295, 317, 330; Land grants, 194, 229; Land tenure, 15, 55; Law, 301, 306; Lottery, 10, 18, 25, 48, 61, 157, 187, 228; Loyalists, 12, 22-3, 45, 258, 269; Merchants, 83, 86, 124, 169, 175, 181-2 *passim*, 203, 212, 255, 258, 264, 265, 272, 276, 289, 304, 309, 317; Mining, 20, 29, 180
PETITIONS, 10; Politics, 305; Religious history, 10, 37, 41-2, 103, 115, 117, 154, 155, 158, 159, 260, 275, 304, 343; Settlement, 10, 26, 31, 33, 42, 44, 48, 82, 187, 190, 218, 295; Shipping, 21, 49, 120, 330; Slavery, 33, 41, 63, 290, 304, 309, 312, 317, 330; Tobacco, 5, 6, 7, 10, 18, 21, 23, 27, 34, 36, 49, 55, 81, 83, 181, 231, 233, 253, 263, 269, 270, 276, 304, 309, 316, 317, 346; Trade, 7, 8, 15, 21, 31, 34, 35, 49, 55, 56, 88, 89, 91, 92, 116, 129, 200, 202, 229, 239, 253, 260, 263, 269, 273, 300, 301, 304, 309, 310, 311, 312, 317, 349
ACCOMAC, CUSTOMS COLLECTORS, 87; Alexandria, 102; Caroline County, 315; Charles City, 190; Chesterfield, 180; College of William and Mary, 50, 115, 223, 231, 268; Columbia, 325; Danville, 269; East Liberty, 331; Falmouth, 304; Fredericksburg, 60, 65, 232, 273, 344; Georgetown, 227; Hampton Roads, 120; James Island, 276; James River, 149, 203, 216, 239, 276, 307, Customs collectors, 87, 275; Jamestown, 11, 24, 37; Kanawha County, 112; Kemps Landing, 269; Kerry Point, 42; King and Queen County, 311; King Capscoe, 42
LYNCHBURG, 253, 330; Mulberry Island, 45; Nelson County, 294; Nominy, 42; Norfolk, 21, 46, 98, 159, 182, 253, 276, 292, 330; Northumberland County, 42; Paddytown, 331; Peninsula, 59; Petersburg, 275, 330; Popes Creek, 42; Port York, 216; Portsmouth, 8; Potomac River, 6; Prince William County, 290
RAPPAHANNOCK DISTRICT, 49, Customs collectors, 87; Richmond, 29, 46, 61, 102, 253, 309, 332, Consular reports (British), 130; Romney, 331; St. James, Lawn Creek, 260; St. Peters, New Kent, 304; Sandy Point, 307; Skin Bottom, 102; Vienna, 273; Westmoreland County, 42, 272; Wheeling, 95; Williamsburg, 12, 21, 182, 258 fn., 304, 330; York River, 182, Customs collectors, 87; Yorktown, 285, 292
See also West Virginia
Virginia (ship), 130, 244
Virginia Association of 1771, 182
Virginia Bank, 269
Virginia Colonial Records Project, 10 fn., 46 fn., 86 fn., 147 fn., 148 fn., 151 fn., 152 fn., 158 fn., 174 fn., 181 fn., 186 fn., 231 fn., 239 fn., 316 fn.; *The British Public Records Office*, 122
Virginia Company of London, 17, 17 fn., 23, 33, 36, 44, 48, 81, 186, 187, 189, 193, 194
Virginia Gazette, 182
Virginia State Library, 86 fn., 122
Virginia, University of, 204, 278; Library, 231 fn.; Alderman Library, 193 fn.
Virginius (ship), 60, 133
Viry, Joseph–Marie–François–Justin, Comte de (1737-1813), 140
Visitation Order in the United States, 347
Vital statistics, 170
Viticulture, 148, 149, 150, 274; *see also* Wine, Trade
Vivian, Sir Arthur Pendarves (1834-1926), 20; *Wanderings in the Western Land*, 20
Vivian, Sir Henry Hussey, 1st Baron Swansea (1821-94), 20; *Notes of a Tour in America*, 20
Vivian, J. H., 20
Vogan, Thomas, 327
Voting, 105, 167, 170, 208; *see also* Elections; Suffrage
Voyages to America, 14, 18, 27, 31, 32, 39, 41, 46, 47, 49, 57-8, 73, 114, 122, 137, 159, 166, 179, 184, 195, 202, 208, 218, 226, 227, 239, 244, 246, 262, 263, 264, 269, 270, 271, 272, 274, 275, 276, 284, 292, 293, 295, 296, 298, 300, 304, 305, 306, 307, 309, 310, 311, 315, 316, 323, 325, 326, 328, 330, 331, 332, 348, 349, 351
Vrelinghuyson, Fortin, 32
Vyner/Robinson Mss., 239

W

"W. J. A.," 41
"W. R. C." Letter (1890-1), 5
Wace, C. R., 166
Wade, William, 329
Waddington, John (1810-80), 59, 85
Wages, 28, 111, 164, 166, 246, 286, 328, 331, 332
Wainwright, Joseph, 234; *Letters from a Yorkshire Emigrant*, 234 fn.
Wainwright, M. D., "Agencies for the Promotion or Facilitation of Emigration from England to the U.S.A., 1815-61" (Thesis), 33 fn., 221 fn.
Wainwright, M. D., and N. Matthews, *Guide to Western Manuscripts and Documents in the British Isles Relating to South and South East Asia*, xxv
Wainwright, Nicholas B., "Turmoil at Pittsburgh: Diary of Augustine Prevost, 1774," *Pennsylvania Magazine of History and Biography* (1961), 116 fn.
Wainwright Collection, 234
Wakefield, West Yorkshire, 96
Walberswick, Customs records, 89
Waldo, Samuel, 301
Waldon, Richard Thomas, 212
Walds, Joseph, 233
Wales, *see* Immigrants from Wales; Trade with Wales

Walker, Amasa (1799-1875), 68
Walker, Ann, 287
Walker, Benjamin, 64
Walker, E., 74
Walker, George, 347
Walker, Harry, & Sons, 263
Walker, John (*fl.* before 1709), 23
Walker, John (1731-1803), 314
Walker, Leo D., 291
Walker, Mary (Zonche), 23
Walker, Robert John (1801-69), 64
Walker, Susan, 273
Walker, Thomas (*fl.* 1789), 231
Walker, Thomas (*fl.* 1795), 287
Walker, Thomas C., 310
Walker, Timothy (1802-96), 245
Walker, William (*fl.* 1709), 23
Walker, William (1824-60), 201
Walker Laird, T. & W., Mss., 263
Walkinshaw, Robert, 317
Wall, James, 302
Wall, W. Sawyer, 51
Wallace, Alexander, 276
Wallace, Henry (1836-1916), 210
Wallace, Henry Agard (1888-1965), 280
Wallace, Hugh, 276, 284
Wallace, J. W. (1856-1926), 172, 177
Wallace, William, 319
Wallace Family Papers, 331
Wallace Papers, 33
Wallace's Farmer, 210
Wallas, Graham (1858-1932), 164
Waller, Gerald, 166
Waller, John, 22
Waller, R. D., ed., "Letters Addressed to Mrs. Gaskell by Celebrated Contemporaries," *Bulletin of the John Rylands Library* (1935), 176 fn.
Walmsley Accumulation, 47
Waln, Nicholas (1742-1813), 227, 349
Walne, P., "The Collections for Henrico College 1616-1618," *Virginia Magazine of History and Biography* (1972), 41 fn.; "The English Ancestry of George Washington: Some New Evidence," *New England Historical and Genealogical Register* (1975), 41 fn.; *Guide to Manuscript Sources for the History of Latin America and the Caribbean in the British Isles*, xxv
Walpole, George, 3rd Earl of Orford (1730-91), 265
Walpole, Horatio, 1st Baron Walpole of Wolterton (1678-1757), 12
Walpole, Sir Robert, 1st Earl of Orford (1676-1745), 32; Archive, 14-5
Walpole, Thomas (1727-1803), 215, 218
Walsh, John (1725?-95), 175
Walsh, John (*fl.* 1904), 318
Walsh, Reginald (b. 1868), 198
Walsh, Robert (1784-1859), 148
Walsingham, 1st Baron, *see* Grey, Sir William de (1719-81)
Walsingham Papers, 188
Walter, John (1739-1812), 151
Walter, Karl (b. 1880), 210
Walter, Thomas (*c.* 1740-89), 151
Walter, William, 112
Walter family, 35
Walter Papers, 157
Walton, William V., 76
Walton of Alston Family Papers, 21
War debts, *see* Reparations *and relevant categories under* World War I
War of 1812, 9, 24, 43, 49, 54, 57, 81, 108, 116, 169, 179, 182, 219, 261, 273, 286, 328, 330; Army, American, 62; Army, British, 35, 83, 148, 339; Blockade, 43, 91, 121, 136, 138, 288
CAMPAIGNS, 54, 138, 218, Alexandria, 121, Canada, 83, 142, 143, 144, 169, 257, 259, 261, 273, Fredericton, 339, Georgia, 138, Great Lakes, 39, 40, Kingston, 339, Michilimackinac, 144, New Orleans, 25, 172, 204, 207, 218, 257, 261, Oswego, 39, Plattsburg, 83, 343, Sackett's Harbour, 40, St. John's, 273, Washington, D.C., 121, 191, 218
CAUSES, 81, 83, 107, 162, 183, 262, 269; Effect on British trade, 9, 90, 121, 172, 231, 239; Indian troops, 286, 288; Naval operations, 9, 39, 40, 43, 70, 108, 121, 144, 172, 219, 231, 239, 288; Peace, 54, 57, 83, 101, 102, 108, 186, 220-1, *see also* Ghent, Treaty of, 1814
PERSONAL NARRATIVES, 28, 39, 46, 83, 191, 196, 218, 332, 339; Portuguese attitude, 57; Prisoners, 27, 35, 43, 121, 261, 288; Privateers, 288; Prizes, 91, 121, 288
War of 1898, *see* Spanish-American War, 1898
War of Independence, 8, 10, 12, 19, 20, 22, 24, 29, 30, 34, 35, 39, 42-6 *passim*, 47, 55, 75-6, 93, 101, 102, 119, 143, 152, 160, 179, 188, 191, 193, 218, 225, 230, 232, 240, 255, 258, 266, 268, 269, 270, 274, 275, 276, 287, 289, 305, 307, 314, 315, 317, 323, 324, 343
ARMY, AMERICAN, 24, 46, 48, 102, 145, 218, 274, 276, 305, 315, 324, Mutiny, 193, 274, Supplies, 91, 93, 262, 267, 324
ARMY, BRITISH, 5, 8, 12, 15, 20, 35, 40, 44, 46, 48, 90, 101, 102, 119, 139, 141, 143, 145, 175, 179, 203, 211, 218, 224, 237, 253, 260, 261, 262, 264, 265, 266, 267, 268, 269, 276, 284, 287, 292, 293, 295, 296, 312, 315, 324, Deserters, 264, Recruiting, 296, 305, Supplies, 20, 32, 34, 55, 91, 101, 122, 145, 261, 262, 267, 273, 276, 292, 294, 295, 296, 297, 311, *see also* Regiments, British; Regiments of Foot (British)
BLOCKADE, 267, 269, 276, 293, 294; British public opinion, 14, 35, 39, 41, 43, 83, 85, 94, 178, 188, 190, 203, 211, 212, 265, 267, 269, 286, 290, 292, 293, 305, 324, 346
CAMPAIGNS, 20, 48, 120, 192, 203, 260, 275, 354, Battle of Brandywine Creek, 1777, 261, 267, 292, Battle of Bunker Hill, 1775, 8, 12, 26, 48, 208, 215, 275, 293, 294, 317, 323, Battle of Camden, 1780, 181, 354, Battle of Charles Town, 1775, 231, 303, Battle of Concord, 1775, 214, Battle of Eutaw Springs, 1781, 296, Battle of Guilford Courthouse, 275, Battle of King's Mountain, 218, 267, Battle of Lexington, 1775, 12, 237, Battle of Long Island, 1776, 48, 298, Battle of Princeton, 1777, 266, 275, Battle of Saratoga, 1777, 192, 231, 258, 262, Battle of White Plains, 1776, 313, Canada, 12, 40, 57, 143, 145, 190, 205, 262, 296, 313, 317, 324, Florida, 34, 98, 297, Georgia, 98, 260, 265, 266, 268, 294, Maryland, 305, Massachusetts, 12, 253, 265, 276, Mississippi, 13, New England, 260, 274, New Jersey, 260, 292, New York, 29, 64, 76, 144-5 *passim*, 191, 192, 258, 260, 261, 262, 265, 268, 269, 275, 276, 293, 294, 295, 305, North Carolina, 218, 261, 268, 276, 313, Pennsylvania, 24, 42, 76, 262, 276, 292, Rhode Island, 12, 76, 260, 265, 274, 276, South Carolina, 48, 65, 80, 90, 218, 261, 267, 268, 269, 276, 293, 305, 311, 313, 351, Virginia, 57, 267, 276, 292, West Indies, 267, 273
CANADIAN ATTITUDE, 215, 324; Causes, 24, 25-6, 31, 57, 65, 66, 79, 86, 143, 162, 182, 191, 195, 208, 213-6 *passim*, 218, 261, 265, 272, 292, 302, 303, *see also* Stamp Act, 1765; Non-importation agreements
COURTS MARTIAL, 119, 144, 234, 296; Economic effects, 26,

91, 171, 190, 208, 261, 265, 267, 291, 292, 294, 298, 313
FRENCH PARTICIPATION AND OPINION, 24, 44, 48, 62, 76, 192, 204, 216, 218, 221, 227, 261, 262, 267, 273, 274, 275, 276, 289, 293, 294; German mercenaries, 120, 143, 218, 266, 267, 275, 276; German participation, 93, 267; History, 262; Indian troops, 203, 215, 286, 323; Invasion of Britain, Possibility of, 138, 273; Irish participation and opinion, 31, 218, 267, 346, 350; Medical services, 140, 147, 266; Naval operations, 12, 18, 42-3, 48, 62, 76, 101, 102, 120-1 *passim*, 191, 216, 218, 261, 262, 265, 267, 268, 269, 273, 274, 276, 287, 289, 292, 293, 305, 313; Negro troops, 12; Netherlands participation and opinion, 216, 267
PAMPHLETS, 193; Peace, 10, 56, 74, 76, 121, 148, 188, 213, 216, 231, 261, 267, 270, 286, 293, 300, 313, 314, 325, 352; Personal narratives, 13, 20, 22-3, 24, 45, 62, 76, 120, 140, 175, 181, 182, 223, 234, 237, 248, 256, 258, 260, 274, 289, 291, 292, 305, 312, 313, 317, 343; Prisoners, 10, 39, 46, 102, 120, 139, 143, 182, 223-4, 264, 266, 269, 275, 292, 293, 294, 296, 297, 305, 312, 316, 324, 346; Privateers, 6, 90, 267, 268, 276, 296, 339; Prizes, 276, 305, 339; Protection of British shipping, 43; Prussian attitude, 76; Relief for British widows and orphans, 223, 261; Religious aspects, 158, 159, 349; Spanish participation and opinion, 44, 62, 76, 221, 227, 267; Spies, 44, 191, 227, 266
War of Jenkins' Ear, 1739-42: Prizes, 304; Recruiting for Cartagena expedition, 300
War of the Rebellion, *see* Civil War, 1861-5
War Office, 123, 141, 142-4, 296, 297, 303; Library, 143
War with Mexico, 1845-8, 46, 63, 64, 67, 77, 173, 207, 245, 267, 291, 327, 330
Warburton, W. H., *The History of Trade Union Organisation in the North Staffordshire Potteries*, 217 fn.
Ward, Genevieve (1838-1922), 314
Ward, George Cabot, 176
Ward, Sir Henry George (1797-1860), 207
Ward, John, 99
Ward, John Henry Hobart (1823-1903), 184
Ward, John William, 1st Earl of Dudley (1781-1833), 207
Ward, Lester Frank (1841-1913), 164
Ward, Samuel (*c.* 1710-78), 187
Ward, Samuel (1725-76), 233
Ward, Samuel (*fl.* 1842-3), 291
Ward–Boughton–Leigh of Brownsover Collection, 225
Warden, Captain, 123
Warder, Anna A., 75
Warder, John, 226
Warder & Sons, 315
Wardlaw–Ramsay of Tillicoultry Mss., 262
Ware, Nathaniel, 195, 265
Warfare, Racial, 196
Warfield family, 86
Waring, George Edwin (1833-98), 170
Waring, J. I., "Correspondence between Alexander Garden, M.D. and the Royal Society of Arts," *South Carolina Historical and Genealogical Magazine* (1963), 149 fn.
Warner, Brig. Gen., 119
Warrander, George, 290
Warren, Henry, 51
Warren, James, 40
Warren, Sir John Borlase (1753-1822), 121
Warren, Joseph (1741-75), 215, 233, 293, 324
Warren, Sir Peter (1703-52), 189, 222
Warren, Susannah (De Lancey), Lady, 222
Warrin, F. C., 113
Warrington, George, 312
Warrington, Cheshire, 19; *see also* Business records: Warrington
Warrior (ship), 269
Warwick, Earl of, *see* Greville, George (1746-1816)
Warwick, Frances Evelyn Greville, Countess of (1861-1938), 33
Warwick (ship), 121
Warwick, Warwickshire, 225
Warwick County Record Office, 225
Warwick University Library, Modern Records Centre, 228
Warwickshire, England, 224-5
Washington, Capt., 11
Washington, Lieut., 15
Washington, Booker Taliaferro (1856-1915), 198, 199
Washington, George (1732-99), 6, 7, 8, 11, 12, 17, 34, 45, 49, 62, 64, 73, 77, 80, 95, 102, 103, 114, 119, 139, 174, 180, 186, 200, 203, 204, 208, 215, 216, 222, 227, 233, 238, 253, 256, 259, 260, 264, 266, 268, 272, 274, 275, 276, 284, 287, 293, 295, 305, 313, 315, 317, 350, 351, 352; *Writings*, ed. by John C. Fitzpatrick, 11 fn., 17 fn., 49 fn., 64 fn., 73 fn., 170 fn., 233 fn., 313 fn.
Washington, George Augustine (d. 1793), 174
Washington, John (*fl.* 17th cent.), 41
Washington, John (1800-63), 40
Washington, Lawrence (*fl.* 17th cent.), 41
Washington, Lawrence (*fl.* 1702), 42
Washington, Mildred, 41
Washington family, 41, 86
Washington, D.C., War of 1812, 121, 191, 218
CONSULAR REPORTS (BRITISH), 134; Description, 6, 15, 25, 30, 36, 43, 60, 81, 95, 131, 156, 157, 164, 184, 185, 208, 259, 268, 276, 298; Immigrants, 331; Law, 331; Merchants, 50; Religious history, 117, 159, 171
GEORGETOWN, 24
Washington (State): Banking, 308; Boundaries, *see* Juan de Fuca Strait; San Juan Islands; Coast, 148; Education, 46; Finance, 307, 318; Immigrants, 332; Industry, 270; Merchants, 46, 248; Mining, 307
BURLEY, 314; Henderson Bay, 314; Seattle, Consular reports (British), 134; Tacoma, Consular reports (British), 134
Washington (emigrant ship), 110
Washington (ship, of New Hampshire), 315
Washington (ship, of New York), 219
Washington Armament Conference (1921-2), 127, 279
Washington Conference (1921), 112
Washington Conference (1930's), 277
Washington Iron Works, 270
Washington National Museum, 146
Washington Post, 281
Washington, Treaty of (1840's), 104
Washington, Treaty of (1871), 59, 68, 70, 71, 72, 73, 111, 130, 133
Waterbury Watch (Sales) Co. Ltd., 98
Waterford and Limerick Railway, 346
Waterhouse, Benjamin (1754-1846), 170, 171
Waterhouse, Nicholas, 181, 185
Waterhouse & Sons, 185
Waters, Henry F., "An Examination of the English Ancestry of George Washington," *New England Historical and Genealogical Register* (1899), 41
Waterston, Anne, 96
Waterville Co., 235
Watkin, Edward William, 40

Watson, Sir Brook (1735-1807), 261, 302
Watson, David, 292
Watson, George, 226
Watson, Henry, 217
Watson, James (*fl.* 1740-50), 309
Watson, James (*fl.* 1743), 292
Watson, John, 151
Watson, William, 268
Watson, William Finlay (1831-74), 259
Watson & McKenzie, 212
Watson Autographs, 259
Watson–Wentworth, Charles, 2nd Marquis of Rockingham (1730-82), 31, 48, 180, 193, 233, 240, 292, 354
Watson–Wentworth, Mary (Bright) (1752-1804), 240
Watt, James (1736-1819), 226
Watt, James (1769-1848), 226
Watt of Breckness Mss., 315
Watterson, Henry (1840-1921), 199
Watts, George Frederic (1817-1904), 238
Watts, Isaac (1674-1748), 94
Watts–Dunton, Walter Theodore (1832-1914), 238
Wauchope, John, 268
Wayne, James Moore (*c.* 1790-1867), 174
Weapons, 143
Weather, *see* Climate
Weatherley, Lewis G., 236
Weatherley, Jardine & Co., 236
Weaving, *see* Textiles
Webb, Beatrice (Potter) (1858-1943), 163, 164; *Diaries, 1912-1924*, 164 fn.; *Diaries, 1924-1932*, 164 fn.; *My Apprenticeship*, 164 fn.; *Our Partnership*, 164, 164 fn.; *see also* Webb, Sidney
Webb, J. Watson, 291
Webb, Mrs. Mary E., 114, 176
Webb, R. K., *Harriet Martineau*, 169 fn.
Webb, Richard David, 96, 353
Webb, Sidney [James], 1st Baron Passfield (1859-1947), 163, 164; and B. Webb: *History of Trade Unionism*, 163, *Industrial Democracy*, 163
Webb, Thomas H., 161
Webb, Thomas William, 202 fn.
Webb Autographs, 353
Webb Trade Union Collection, 163
Webber, Charles, 219
Webster, Lt.-Col., 192
Webster, Rev. Dr., 289
Webster, Sir Charles Kingsley (1886-1961), 165, 277; *Foreign Policy of Palmerston, 1830-1841*, 103 fn.
Webster, Daniel (1782-1852), 49, 63, 64, 94, 99, 174, 176, 185, 207, 232, 245, 259, 260, 263
Webster, Francis, 270
Webster, Francis, & Sons, Mss., 270
Webster, J., 275
Webster, William, 132
Webster–Ashburton Treaty (1842), 63, 67, 144, 168, 208, 257, 261
Wedderburn, Alexander, 1st Baron Loughborough and 1st Earl of Rosslyn (1733-1805), 44, 76, 285, 312, 317
Wedderburn, James, 292
Wedgwood, J. C., Baron of Barlaston, 114
Wedgwood, Josiah (1730-95), 175, 212
Wedgwood Accumulation, 212-3
Wedgwood family, 175
Wedgwood Museum, 212
Weeks, Ezra, 187
Weights and measures, 150
Weir, Joseph, 132
Weir, William, 331
Weir family, 329
Weiss Geophysical Corporation of Canada & the U.S.A. (*later known as the* Barbican Corporations of Canada & the U.S.A.), 145
Weld, Angelina Grimké, 84
Weld, Charles, 28
Weld, Edward (*fl.* 1760), 28
Weld, Edward, Jr., 28
Weld, Henry, 28
Weld, Henry T., 28
Weld, Humphrey, 28
Weld, James, 28
Weld, Joseph (1777-1863), 28
Weld, Joseph, Jr. (*fl.* 1852-89), 28
Weld of Chideock Papers, 28
Weld of Lulworth Papers, 28
Welland, Dennis, "John Camden Hotten and Emerson's Uncollected Essays," *Yearbook of English Studies* (1976), 33 fn.; *Mark Twain and England*, 33 fn., 84 fn.
Wellcome Institute for the History of Medicine, 170-1
Welles, Sumner (1892-1961), 283
Wellesley, Arthur, 1st Duke of Wellington (1769-1852), 83, 84, 104, 207, 285; *Supplementary Despatches*, 83
Wellesley, Henry, 1st Baron Cowley (1773-1847), 207
Wellesley, Henry Richard Charles, 1st Earl Cowley (1804-84), 49, 134
Wellesley, Richard Colley, Marquis (1760-1842), 98
Wellington, 1st Duke of, *see* Wellesley, Arthur (1769-1852)
Wellington, Somerset, 212
Wells, Mrs. Catherine, 205
Wells, David Ames (1828-98), 163, 236
Wells, Herbert George (1866-1946), 205
Wells, Ida B., 176
Wells, John, 324
Wells, Richard, 316
Wells, Robert, 300
Wells, Susie, 300
Wells & Cley, Customs records, 94
Wellwood, Sir Henry Moncrieff, *see* Moncrieff, Sir Henry (1750-1827)
Wellwood, John Moncrieff, 263
Welsh, James C., Papers, 266
Welsh, John (1805-86), 38, 129
Welsh & Co., 269
Welsh Colonizing and General Trading Co., 244
Wemyss, Earl of, Mss., 262
Wendell, Jacob, 32
Wendell, John, 32
Wentworth, Mr., 267
Wentworth, Frances (Wentworth Atkinson, Jr.), 240
Wentworth, Hugh, 233
Wentworth, Sir John (1737-1820), 8, 150, 190, 233, 240, 314
Wentworth, John (*fl.* 1874), 70
Wentworth, Samuel, 191, 233
Wentworth, Sir Thomas, 1st Earl of Strafford (1593-1641), 194
Wentworth Bequest, 78
Wentzel, Willard Ferdinand, 146
Wenvoe Hematite Iron Ore Co., 28
Werden (or Worden), Sir John (1640-1716), 260
Were & Co., 212

Wesley, Charles (1707-88), 117, 178, 313
Wesley, John (1703-91), 65, 117, 215, 313
Wesleyan Methodist Missionary Society, 117
West, Benjamin (1730-1813), 245
West, Benjamin (1738-1820), 151
West, G., 284
West, James (1704?-72), 102
West, John, 24, 194
West, Thomas, 3rd Baron De La Warr (1577-1618), 44
West, William Edward (1788-1857), 187
West Africa: Slave trade, 70; *see also* Trade with West Africa
West Briton, 20
West Devon Record Office, 26-7
West Florida, *see* Florida, West
West Germany, *see* Relations with West Germany
West India Committee, 171
West India Company, 52
West Indian Produce Association, 99
West Indies: 1756-63, 74; 1791-1819, 257
ADMINISTRATION, 195; British Army, 41, 257, 273, 303; Confederate agents, 18; Customs administration, 21, 86, 87; Description, 46, 156; Governors, 138; Immigrants, 31, 223, 325, 343; Land, 181, 257; Merchants, 302; Navy, British, 218, 239; Negroes, 184; Piracy, 99; Prize courts, 80; Religious history, 158; Settlement, 82; Shipping, 56, 58; Slave trade, 160, 184, 301; Slavery, 257, 306; Slaves, Fugitive, 43
TRADE WITH CANADA, 161, Great Britain, 6, 18, 49, 86, 87, 88, 89, 99, 107, 108, 181, 265, 302, 316, 335, Ireland, 349, Scotland, 256, 273, 304; *see also* Trade with West Indies
See also Bahamas; Barbados; Cuba; Dominican Republic; Haiti; Jamaica; Leeward Islands; St. Thomas; Tobago; Windward Islands
West Jersey, *see* New Jersey, West
West Midlands, England, 225-9
West New Jersey Society, 97, 142
West Point, U.S. Military Academy at, 143
West Sussex Record Office, 223; 185
West Virginia: Immigrants, 47; U.S. congressmen, 198; *see also* Virginia
Westbury, 1st Baron, *see* Bethell, Richard (1800-73)
Western Bank of Philadelphia, 181
Western Live-Stock and Land Co., 210
Western Pacific Railroad, 96
Western ports, England, and Newfoundland fishing trade, 27
Western Quarterly Meeting of the Society of Friends, 37
Western Ranches and Investment Co. Ltd., 308
Western Ranches Ltd., 308
Western Reserve University, 177, 278
Western Sanitary Commission, St. Louis, Mo., 208
Western Union Railroad Co., 262
Westminster, Trustees of the late 2nd Duke of, 19
Westminster City Council Archives, 171
Westminster Diocesan Archives, 171-2
Westminster Papers, 19
Westmorland, 6th Earl of, *see* Fane, Thomas (1680-1736)
Westmorland, Lady, 21
Westmorland Papers, 189
Weston, Edward (1703-70), 79
Weston, Mary (1712-66), 155, 155 fn.
Weston Papers, 79
Westwood, Nicholas, 14
Wetter, Axel, 177
Weyler y Nicolau, Valeriano, Marquis of Teneriffe, Duque de Rubi y Grande de España (1838-1930), 38
Weyman, Arnold, 75
Weymouth, 3rd Viscount, *see* Thynne, Thomas
Weymouth, Dorset, Customs records, 89, 91, 94
Whaling, 55, 56, 91, 92, 106, 107, 124, 247
Whalley, Lancashire, 48
Wharncliffe, 2nd Baron, *see* Stuart–Wortley, John (1801-55)
Wharncliffe, 1st Earl of, *see* Stuart–Wortley–Mackenzie, Edward (1827-99)
Wharncliffe Muniments, 232
Wharton, Edith (1862-1937), 78
Wharton, Sir George (1617-81), 312
Wharton, Philip, 4th Baron (1613-96), 203
Wharton, Samuel, 215
Wharton, Thomas, 1st Marquis of (1648-1716), 203
Wharton, Thomas (1735-78), 215
Wharton, Thomas Isaac (1791-1856), 182
Whatcoat, Richard (1736-1806), 65, 117
Whately, Thomas (d. 1772), 65, 66
Wheat: Prices, 64; Production, 63, 64, 80, 268, 274, 301; Trade, 41, 55, 56, 63, 86, 107, 108, 109, 110, 112, 141, 212, 237, 274, 280, 303
Wheatley, Phillis (*c.* 1753-84), 103, 169, 275
Wheeler, Elizabeth, 40
Wheeler, Everett Pepperrell (1840-1925), 198
Wheeler, Katharine V., *A Guide to the Political Papers, 1874-1970, Deposited by the First Beaverbrook Foundation*, 113 fn.
Wheelock, Eleazar (1711-79), 290
Wheelock, John (1754-1817), 216
Whelan Collection, 228
Whewell, William (1794-1866), 17
Whichcote, Sir Paul (1643-1721), 50
Whichcote, T., 50
Whichcote Family Papers, 50
Whidbey, John, 288
Whigham, William, 326
Whiskey Rebellion (1794), 324
Whistler, James Abbott McNeill (1834-1903), 174
Whitaker, Mrs., 208
Whitaker, George, 14
Whitaker family, 28
Whitbread, James, 61
Whitbread, Samuel (1764-1815), 9, 161
Whitbread Papers, 9
Whitby, North Yorkshire, Customs records, 92, 94
White, Col., 207
White, Andrew Dickson (1832-1918), 198, 199
White, Campbell P. (1787-1859), 9
White, Henry (1850-1927), 38, 39, 129, 198
White, Horace (1834-1916), 163; *Answers to Questions of the Gold and Silver Commission*, 163
White, Horace, *"Fossets:" A Record of Two Centuries of Engineering*, 17 fn.
White, John Campbell, 331
White, Montagu (1875-1916), 206
White, William Allen (1868-1944), 282
White lead, Trade, 183
Whitefield, George (1714-70), 34, 85, 118, 151, 174, 208, 213, 274, 275, 304, 312, 313
Whitefield, Mrs. George, 85
Whitehaven, Cumbria, 21-3 *passim*; Customs records, 89, 92, 94; Merchants, 56; Trade, 116
Whitehaven News, 23 fn.

Whitehead, Alfred North (1861-1947), 278
Whitehouse, J. Howard (1873-1955), 229
Whiteside, Mrs. M., 172
Whitfield, James (d. 1834), 171
Whiting, W. E., 95
Whitlock, John, 181; Papers, 181
Whitly, Col., 276
Whitman, Sarah Helen (Power), Mrs. John Winslow Whitman (1803-78), 198
Whitman, Walt (1819-92), 61, 81, 172, 177, 179, 184, 236, 238, 353; Mss., 184; "The Dalliance of the Eagles," 184; "Three Young Men's Deaths," 184
Whitman Collection, 172
Whitmell, Charles Thomas, 239
Whitmore, Edward, 290
Whitney, William Dwight, 202
Whitstable, Customs records, 93
Whittaker, John, 180
Whittelsey, Chauncey, 182
Whittier, John Greenleaf (1807-92), 68, 155, 156, 157, 353
Whittingham, Charles, I, 70
Whittingham, Charles, II, 70
Whitworth, Sir Charles (1714?-78), 150
Whyte, James & William, 310
Whytt, Robert (1714-66), 314
Wickersham, George Woodward (1858-1936), 198, 199
Wiehl, Emil Karl (b. 1886), 136
Wier, Daniel (d. 1781), 32
Wiffen, Mr., 52
Wigan, Greater Manchester, 180
Wigan Record Office, 180
Wiggin, Timothy, & Co., 52
Wigglesworth, Kent & Co., 240
Wigham, Miss, 96
Wightman, Nancy, 327
Wilberforce, Samuel (1805-73), 196
Wilberforce, William (1759-1833), 9, 155, 169, 196
Wilberforce Papers, 196
Wilbraham, Sir Richard (1811-1900), 18
Wild, Joseph, 211
Wild, W., 180
Wild & Julian, 211
Wilder, Thornton (1897-1975), 78
Wildes, George, & Co., 52
Wiles, John, 166
Wiley, Louis, 279
Wilkes, John (1727-97), 267
Wilkins, Lewis Morris (1801-85), 81
Wilkins, W., 264
Wilkinson, Elizabeth, 22
Wilkinson, James (1757-1825), 16
Wilkinson, Jeptha Avery, 308
Wilkinson, John (1728-1808), 19
Wilkinson, John, his brother (*fl.* 1777), 267
Wilkinson, Thomas (1751-1836), 155
Wilkinson Mss., 155
Willard, Mr., 148, 149
Willard, James F., 177
Willcox, William B., *The Papers of Benjamin Franklin*, 175 fn.
Willert, Sir Arthur, 158
Willes and Lovell Families' Papers, 230
William III, *King*, 82, 203
William Frederick, 2nd Duke of Gloucester of the 5th creation (1776-1834), 183
William, Nassau, Sr., 204
William and Mary College, 50, 115, 223, 231, 268
William L. Clements Library, Ann Arbor, Mich., 66 fn., 220 fn., 222 fn.
William Salt Library, 216; Earl of Dartmouth Collection, 213-6
Williams, Mrs., 344
Williams, Abby D., 75
Williams, Charles, 187
Williams, Charles Richard (1853-1927), 38
Williams, G., 246
Williams, Henry, 306
Williams, J. F., 244
Williams, John (*fl.* 1862), 248
Williams, Sir John Cecil, 247
Williams, John Fletcher (1834-95), 244
Williams, N. J., 89; "England's Tobacco Trade in the Reign of Charles I," *Virginia Magazine of History and Biography* (1957), 89 fn.; "Francis Shaxton and the Elizabethan Port-Books," *English Historical Review* (1951), 89; "The London Port-Books," *Trans. of the London & Middlesex Archaeological Soc.* (1955), 89, 89 fn.
Williams, Nathaniel F., 62
Williams, Sir Ralph, 198
Williams, Roger (*c.* 1603-83), 151
Williams, Samuel (*fl.* 1790), 147
Williams, Samuel (*fl.* 1817), 166
Williams, T. Ll., 244
Williams, W. C., 247
Williams, Sir William Fenwick (1800-83), 59, 61
Williams & Glyn Bank Ltd., 172
Williams & Lyon, 36
Williams Deacon's Bank, 193; *Williams Deacon's, 1771-1970*, 193 fn.
Williamson, Andrew (*c.* 1730-86), 48
Williamson, Charles, 240, 287
Williamson, John, 183
Williamson family, 327
Dr. Williams's Library, 94-6; 224
Willing, Charles, 289
Willis (or Wyllys), George (d. 1645), 225
Willis, Nathaniel Parker (1806-67), 174
Willis, Thomas, 150
Willkie, Wendell (1892-1944), 282
Willoughby, Major, 38
Willoughby, Sir Percivall, 192
Willoughby de Eresby, 12th Baron, *see* Bertie, Peregrine (1555-1601)
Wilmot Proviso (1846), 77, 173
Wilmot–Horton, Sir Robert John (1784-1841), 23
Wilson, Alexander, 51, 318
Wilson, Mrs. Amelia, 18
Wilson, Cecil, 236
Wilson, Sir D., 313
Wilson, Henry Joseph (1833-1914), 156, 235
Wilson, J., 204
Wilson, James (*fl.* 1778-82), 273
Wilson, James (1805-60), 64
Wilson, John (*fl.* 1777-9), 188
Wilson, John (*fl.* 1786), 166
Wilson, John (1785-1854), 179
Wilson, John (1837-1915), 29
Wilson, Joshua (1795-1874), 85
Wilson, Peter, 294
Wilson, Rachel (1720-75), 155
Wilson, S. S., *The Cabinet Office to 1945*, 126, 127

Wilson, Thomas, 103
Wilson, Thomas, & Co., 46, 52
Wilson, W. S., 22
Wilson, William, 291
Wilson, William Lyne (1843-1900), 198
Wilson, Woodrow (1856-1924), 62, 77, 97, 113, 127, 164, 197, 198, 210, 256, 259, 261, 277, 280, 281, 282, 284, 318
Wilson family, 329
Wilton, Samuel (1744-78), 94
Wilton family, 94
Wilton House, Wiltshire, 230
Wiltshire, England, 229-30; *see also* Immigrants from Wiltshire
Wiltshire Archaeological and Natural History Society, 229
Wiltshire County Record Office, 230
Winan, C. A., 236
Winchelsea, Customs records, 89
Winchester, Hampshire, 36
Windham, Sir Charles Ash (1810-70), 65
Windham, William (1750-1810), 39, 41, 188
Windmills, 149
Windward Islands, *see* Dominica; St. Lucia
Wine: Duties, 303; Trade, 56, 62, 262, 299, 325
Wing, F. E., 262
Wingfield, Edward Maria (*fl.* 1586-1613), 82
Winnipeg Free Press Co., 280
Winscales and Dean, Cumbria, 21
Winscom, ______, 117
Winslow, John Flack, 308
Winsor, Justin (1831-97), 206, 314
Winthrop, Adam, 99 fn.
Winthrop, John (1588-1649), 217
Winthrop, John (1606-76), 217
Winthrop, Robert Charles (1809-94), 148
Winthrop, Waite, 83
Winthrop Papers, 217 fn.
Wisbech, Customs records, 94
Wisconsin, 19th century, 191
AGRICULTURE, 244, 248, 347; Finance, 318; Immigrants, 157, 217, 244, 245, 248, 332, 347; Relief for Irish famine, 345; Religious history, 244, 246, 247; State Legislature, 187; Trade, 248
CALEDONIA, 244; Madison, 332; Milwaukee, 157, 345; Watertown, 112
Wisconsin Central Railroad, 96
Wisconsin University, Memorial Library, 85 fn.
Wise, E. F., 278
Wiseman, Nicholas [Patrick Stephen] (1802-65), 30, 171, 172
Wiseman, Sir W., 77
Wister, Daniel, 187
Wister, Owen (1860-1938), 238
Wister, Siter & Price, 210
Wiswall, John, 210
Witchcraft, 176
Witham Monthly Meeting of the Society of Friends, 32
Wither, John, 10
Witherby, Percival, 283
Witherow, James M., 281, 283
Withers, Stanley, 178
Withers Collection, 178
Witherspoon, John (1723-94), 318
Witney, Oxfordshire, 210
Witz, T. L., 9
Woad, 10
Wodehouse Papers, 61
Wodrow, James (1730-1810), 94
Wodrow, Robert (1679-1734), 259, 274, 312; *Early Letters . . .*, ed. by L. W. Sharp, 312 fn.
Wodrow–Kenrick Correspondence, 94
Woertendyck Family Papers, 5
Wogan, (Sir) Charles, *known as the* Chevalier Wogan (1698?-1752?), 15
Wolcott, Edward Oliver (1848-1905), 38, 163
Wolcott, Roger (1847-1901), 164
Wolcott, Oliver (1760-1833), 116
Wolfe, James (1727-59), 45, 119, 219, 240, 260, 286, 323; *Instructions to Young Officers*, 240
Wolfe (ship), 39
Woman's International Peace Association, 176
Woman's Rights Conventions, 84
Women: Birth-control, 84; Education, 84; Employment, 163, 164, 329; Rights of women, 95, 179, 183, 325; Suffrage, 84, 96, 118, 179, 197, 198
Women's Centennial Committee for Ohio, 75
Women's Suffrage Collection, 179
Wood, Charles, 1st Viscount Halifax (1800-85), 104
Wood, George (*fl.* 1784), 350
Wood, George (*fl.* 1852), 263
[Wood, H. H.], *A Guide to the Records Deposited in the Public Record Office of Ireland*, 348
Wood, Juliana (Westray), Mrs. William Burke Wood, 98
Wood, Kingsley, 281
Wood, William Burke (1779-1861), 97, 98
Wood Gibson, 175
Woodall, John, 10
Woodbridge, Customs records, 89, 94
Woodbrooke College, 227-8
Woodcock, W. N., 235
Woodcock Accumulation, 47
Woodgate, Harvey, 46
Woodgate Papers, 46
Woodin, Thomas, 150
Woodmason, Charles, 150
Woodridge, Major, 29
Woods, John, 245
Woodward, Henry, 195
Woodward, Sir Llewellyn, *British Foreign Policy in the Second World War*, 133
Wool: Production , 149; Trade, 109, 173, 237, 255
Woollen goods: Manufacture, 63, 64, 173; Trade, 22, 109, 116, 117, 173, 175, 212, 237-40 *passim*, 253, 312, 327, 329
Woolman, Elizabeth, 94
Woolman, John (1720-72), 27, 94
Woolwich (ship), 39
Wooster, David, 302
Worcester, Noah (1758-1837), 183
Worcester, Hereford and Worcester, 37
Worcester Cathedral Library, 37
Workers, *see* Artisans; Unemployment
Working classes, 111, 131; *see also* Labour movement
Workington, Customs records, 94
Workman, R. and J., 325
Workman, Thomas, 327
World (New York), 279
World Court, 280
World Federation of Educational Associations, 269
World Organization of the Teaching Profession, 269
World War I, 1914-18, 66, 272; Allies, 127, 139, 144, 265, Post-war debt to U.S., 278, 280, 281; Army, American, 126;

Army, British, 143-5 *passim*; Blockade, 199; British post-war debt to U.S., 112, 127, 260, 277, 278, 281, 282, 283; Canadian participation , 112, 144; Causes, 127, 199, 200, 238; Diaries, 144; Entry of U.S., 1917, 77, 111, 112, 126, 188, 259; History, 123, 127; Naval operations, 277; Neutrality of U.S., 157, 196; Peace, 77, 112, 126, 127, 134, 135, 197, 198, 229, 259, 260, 277, 279, 283, 284, 315; Propaganda, British, 283, 284, German, 197; Public opinion, American, 78, 126, 179, 209, 210, 259, 327, 328, British, 210; Supplies, 112, 126, 135, 199, 200, 265; U.S.-British cooperation, 112, 113, 114, 126, 143; *see also* Paris Resolutions, 1918
World War II, 1939-45, 126, 144, 145; Allies, 123, 128, 145, 209, 311, Deserters, 311; Army, American, 113, 128, 143, 145, 209; Army, British, 113, 143-5 *passim*; Army Air Force, U.S., 113, 123, 124; Atomic bomb, 124; Blockade, 135; Canadian participation, 145; Censorship, 135, 177; D-Day landings, 113; Diaries, 113, 144; Entry of U.S., 177; Evacuation from Great Britain, 27; History, 123, 128; Naval operations, 123, 128, 275; Neutrality of U.S., 282, 283; Personal narratives, 113; Post-war aid, 137, 139, 166; Propaganda, 135, 269, 281, 282, 283; Public opinion, American, 165, 282, 283, 315; Recruitment, 143; Royal Air Force, 113; Supplies, 112, 124, 125, 127-8 *passim*, 135, 143, 282, 283; U.S.-British cooperation, 113-4, 123, 124, 125, 127-8 *passim*, 134, 135, 139, 143, 275, 281, 282, 283; U.S.-Canadian cooperation, 124; U.S.-French cooperation, 135, 281; U.S. role and influence, 113, 123, 127-8 *passim*, 135, 143, 144, 145, 282; Wartime oil interests of U.S., 135; *see also* British War Relief; Lend-Lease
Wormald & Fountaine, 239
Wormalds and Walker Ltd., 239
Wormeley, James, 101
Wormeley, Ralph, 12
Wormistone, Laird of, *see* Lindsay, George (d. 1764)
Worrall, Dr., 174
Worrall, Samuel, 7
Worsley, H., 269
Worth, R. N., *Calendar of the Plymouth Municipal Records*, 26 fn., 27 fn.
Wortley Wire Works, 232
Wostenholm, George, & Co., 236
Wotherspoon, Matthew, 310
Woulfe [or Wolfe], Maurice, 347
Woulfe Letters, 347
Wragg, Annie, 191
Wragg, George, & Co., 175
Wragg, Job, 179
Wragg, Samuel, 294
Wragg Family Papers, 191
Wray family, 331
Wreaks, Charles, 234
Wrench, Sir John Evelyn Leslie (1882-1966), 81, 283; Papers, 81
Wrey, George, 274
Wright, Carroll Davidson (1840-1909), 164
Wright, Charles, 150
Wright, Frances (1795-1852), 183
Wright, Sir James (*c.* 1716-85), 103
Wright, James (b. 1788), 350
Wright, Jane, 231
Wright, Jermyn, 150
Wright, John (*fl.* 1774), 231
Wright, Susanna, 156
Wright, Taylor & Co., 178
Wright family, 350
Wrightson, John, 284
Wriothesley, Henry, 3rd Earl of Southampton (1573-1624), 36
Wriothesley Deeds, 36
Wuliger, Robert, "The Idea of Economic Imperialism, with Special Reference to the Life and Works of E. D. Morel" (Ph. D. thesis), 165 fn.
Wyatt, B. & W., 232
Wyatt, Sir Francis (1575?-1644), 24, 194, 229
Wyett, Thomas, 32
Wykeham–Martin, Major R. F., 120 fn.
Wykeham–Martin Papers, 45
Wyld, James (1812-87), 40
Wylly family, 328
Wyman, J., 15
Wyndham, Sir Charles, 2nd Earl of Egremont (1710-63), 45, 114, 140, 223
Wyndham, Henry (1709-88), 36, 229
Wyndham, Henry Penruddocke (1736-1819), 229
Wynkoop, Cornelis C. (b. 1732), 32
Wynn, Charles Watkin Williams (1775-1850), 57
Wyoming: Cattle, 209, 232, 308, 315; Finance, 210; Land, 315, 318
CHEYENNE, 20, 209
Wyoming Cattle Ranche Co. Ltd., 308
Wyse, Francis, 104
Wyse, R. C., 280

Y

Yale, Mrs. E., Deposit, 246
Yale, Elihu (1648-1721), 18, 219, 220
Yale College, 8, 151
Yale University, 74, 197, 280, 282, 283
Yalta Conference (1945), 139
"Yankees," 15
Yardly [or Yeardley], Sir George (1580?-1627), 202
Yarmouth, Customs records, 94
Yarnall, Charles, 30
Yates, A. V. S., 113
Yates, Edward, 105
Yates, James (1789-1871), 176
Yates, John, 166
Yearley, Clifton K., *Britons in American Labor*, 174 fn.
Yeats, David, 266
Yeats, John Butler, 353
Yeats, William Butler (1865-1939), 348
Yellow fever, 70, 170, 182, 256, 271, 315
Yellowstone Park, 179
Yeo, Sir James Lucas (1782-1818), 39, 40, 83
Yeomans, Edward Livingstone (1821-87), 162
Yester Papers, 259
York and Albany, Duke of, *see* (*later*) James II, *King* (1633-1701)
York, North Yorkshire, 231
York River Tea Party (1774), 182
Yorke, Philip, 1st Earl of Hardwicke (1690-1764), 54
Yorke, Philip, 2nd Earl of Hardwicke (1720-90), 54
Yorkshire, North, England, 230-1
Yorkshire, South, England, 232-7
Yorkshire, West, England, 237-40
Yorkshire Post, 239
Young, Mr., 131

Young, Alexander (*fl.* 1795), 287
Young, Alexander (*fl.* 1840), 299
Young, Benjamin, 193
Young, Brigham (1801-77), 70, 217
Young, Charles Augustus (1834-1908), 239
Young, Conrad, 210
Young, Francis Brett (1884-1954), 227
Young, Sir George, 3rd Baronet of Formosa Place (1837-1930), 199
Young, George (b. 1872), 198
Young, Gilbert, 232
Young, Henry, 150
Young, John (*fl.* 1758), 285
Young, John (*fl.* 1817-29), 232
Young, John (*fl.* 1818), 175
Young, Sir John, 1st Baron Lisgar (1807-76), 68, 71, 72
Young, William, 329
Young family, 325
Young Ireland Movement, 344, 353
Young Men's Anti-Slavery Society, 169
Youth's Companion, 73
Yuill, James, 286
Yuille, George, 309
Yule Collection, 289

Z

Zacharie, Mr., 130
Zealous (ship), 39
Zionism, 116, 277
Zonche, Sir John, 23
Zoology, *see* Quadrupeds, Oviparous; Serpents
Zoopraxiscope, 220
Zuylestein, William Henry, 4th Earl of Rochford (1717-81), 267, 312